# Yearbook on
# International
# Communist Affairs
# 1987

# Yearbook on International Communist Affairs

# 1987

*Parties and Revolutionary Movements*

| | |
|---|---|
| EDITOR: | Richard F. Staar |
| ASSISTANT EDITOR: | Margit N. Grigory |

AREA EDITORS

| | | |
|---|---|---|
| Thomas H. Henriksen | • | Africa |
| William Ratliff | • | The Americas |
| Ramon H. Myers | • | Asia and the Pacific |
| Richard F. Staar | • | Eastern Europe and the |
| Robert Conquest | | Soviet Union |
| James H. Noyes | • | The Middle East |
| Dennis L. Bark | • | Western Europe |

HOOVER INSTITUTION PRESS
Stanford University, Stanford, California

The text of this work is set in Times Roman;
display headings are in Melior. Typeset by
Harrison Typesetting, Inc., Portland, Oregon.
Printed and bound by Braun-Brumfield, Inc.,
Ann Arbor, Michigan.

Hoover Press Publication 365

International Standard Book Number 0-8179-8651-0
International Standard Serial Number 0084-4101
Library of Congress Catalog Number 67-31024

# Contents

## ASIA AND THE PACIFIC

## EASTERN EUROPE AND THE SOVIET UNION

## THE MIDDLE EAST

## WESTERN EUROPE

# Preface

This edition of the *Yearbook*, the twenty-first consecutive one, includes profiles by 77 contributors, covering 107 parties and revolutionary movements as well as ten international communist fronts and two regional organizations (the Council for Mutual Economic Assistance and the Warsaw Pact). In addition, eleven biographic sketches of prominent communist leaders follow individual profiles. The names and affiliations of contributors are given at the end of each essay.

This *Yearbook* offers data on the organization, policies, activities, and international contacts during all of calendar 1986 of communist parties and Marxist-Leninist movements throughout the world. Information has been derived primarily from published sources, including official newspapers and journals, as well as from radio transmissions monitored by the U.S. Foreign Broadcast Information Service. Dates cited in the text without indicating a year are for 1986.

Whether to include a party or a group that espouses a quasi-Marxist-Leninist ideology, yet may not be recognized by Moscow as "communist," always remains a problem. It applies specifically to certain among the so-called national liberation movements and, more significantly, even to some ruling parties. In making our decisions, the following criteria have been considered: rhetoric, the organizational model, participation in international communist meetings and fronts, and adherence to the USSR's foreign policy line. It seems realistic to consider the regime of Nicaragua, for example, in the same category as that of Cuba. The ruling parties in the so-called "vanguard revolutionary democracies" appear to be clearly affiliated with the world communist movement. They also are discussed in the Introduction.

Our thanks go to the librarians and staff at the Hoover Institution for checking information and contributing to the bibliography. The latter was compiled by the *Yearbook* assistant editor, Mrs. Margit N. Grigory, who also provided liaison with contributors.

Richard F. Staar
*Hoover Institution*

\*   \*   \*

The following abbreviations are used for frequently cited publications and news agencies:

| | |
|---|---|
| CSM | *Christian Science Monitor* |
| FBIS | *Foreign Broadcast Information Service* |
| FEER | *Far Eastern Economic Review* |
| IB | *Information Bulletin* (of the *WMR*) |
| JPRS | *Joint Publications Research Service* |
| LAT | *Los Angeles Times* |
| NYT | *New York Times* |
| WMR | *World Marxist Review* |
| WP | *Washington Post* |

| | |
|---|---|
| *WSJ* | *Wall Street Journal* |
| *YICA* | *Yearbook on International Communist Affairs* |
| ACAN | Agencia Central Americano Noticias |
| ADN | Allgemeiner Deutscher Nachrichtendienst |
| AFP | Agence France-Presse |
| ANSA | Agenzia Nazionale Stampa Associata |
| AP | Associated Press |
| BBC | British Broadcasting Corporation |
| BTA | Bulgarska Telegrafna Agentsiya |
| ČETEKA | Československá Tisková Kancelář |
| DPA | Deutsche Presse Agentur |
| EFE | Spanish News Agency |
| KPL | Khaosan Pathet Lao |
| MENA | Middle East News Agency |
| MTI | Magyar Tavirati Iroda |
| NCNA | New China News Agency |
| PAP | Polska Agencja Prasowa |
| RFE | Radio Free Europe |
| RL | Radio Liberty |
| TASS | Telegrafnoe Agentstvo Sovetskogo Soiuza |
| UPI | United Press International |
| VNA | Vietnam News Agency |

# Party Congresses

| Country | Congress | Date (1986) |
|---------|----------|-------------|
| Burma | 3d | 9 September–2 October 1985 |
| Iraq | 4th | 10–15 November 1985 |
| Honduras | 4th (clandestine) | January |
| Panama (PPP) | 8th | 24–26 January |
| San Marino | 11th | 27 January |
| Ireland | 19th | 31 January–2 February |
| Portugal | 11th (Extraordinary) | 2–6 February |
| Cuba | 3d | 4–7 February; 30 November–2 December |
| USSR | 27th | 25 February–6 March |
| India (CPI) | 13th | 10–18 March |
| Czechoslovakia | 17th | 24–28 March |
| Bulgaria | 13th | 2–5 April |
| Italy | 17th | 9–13 April |
| East Germany | 11th | 17–21 April |
| Belgium | 25th | 18–20 April |
| New Zealand (CPNZ) | 23d | 22 April |
| Bolivia | Extraordinary | 26–29 April |
| Greece (KKE–I) | 4th | May |
| West Germany | 8th | 2–4 May |
| Austria | Nat'l conference | 23 May |
| Mongolia (MPRP) | 19th | 28–31 May |
| Yugoslavia (SKJ) | 13th | 25–28 June |
| Poland (PZPR) | 10th | 29 June–3 July |
| Syria | 6th | July |
| United States | Nat'l conference | 6–8 August |
| Albania (PPS) | 9th | 3–8 November |
| Argentina | 16th | 4–7 November |
| Sweden (APK) | 28th | 7 November |
| Laos (LPRP) | 4th | 12–14 November |
| Cyprus (AKEL) | 16th | 26–30 November |
| Netherlands | 30th | 29 November–2 December |
| Iran | Nat'l conference | 1986 (in exile) |

# Register of Communist Parties

**Status:** * ruling    # unrecognized
             + legal      0 proscribed

| Country: Party(ies)/Date Founded | Mid-1986 Population (est.) (World Factbook) | Communist Party Membership (claim or est.) | Party Leader (sec'y general) | Status | Last Congress | Last Election (percentage of vote; seats in legislature) |
|---|---|---|---|---|---|---|
| **AFRICA (12)** | | | | | | |
| Angola<br>Popular Movement for the Liberation of Angola (MPLA), 1956 (MPLA-PT, 1977) | 8,164,000 | 35,000 cl. | José Eduardo dos Santos | * | Second<br>2–9 Dec. 1985 | (1980); all 203 MPLA approved |
| Benin<br>People's Revolutionary Party of Benin (PRPB), 1975 | 4,141,000 | less than 2,000 | Mathieu Kerekou (chairman, CC) | * | Second<br>18–24 Nov. 1985 | (1984); all 196 PRPB approved |
| Congo<br>Congolese Labor Party (PCT), 1969 | 1,853,000 | 9,000 est. | Denis Sassou-Ngouesso (chairman) | * | Third<br>23–30 July 1984 | 95.0 (1984); all 153 PCT approved |
| Ethiopia<br>Workers' Party of Ethiopia (WPE), 1984 | 35,210,000 | 50,000 est. | Mengistu Haile Mariam | * | First (Const.)<br>6–10 Sept. 1984 | n/a |
| Lesotho<br>Communist Party of Lesotho (CPL), 1962 | 1,552,000 | no data | Jacob M. Kena | 0 (tolerated) | Seventh<br>Nov. 1984 | (1985) |

| Country / Party (year founded) | Population | | Party leader | Communist party membership | Last party congress | Last election (% vote); seats |
|---|---|---|---|---|---|---|
| Mozambique<br>Front for the Liberation of Mozambique (FRELIMO), 1962 | 14,022,000 | * | Samora Moisés Machel (died 10/19/86; Joaquim Albert Chissano (elected 11/3/86) | 110,323 cl. (*African Communist* 4th quarter, 1983) | Fourth 26–29 Apr. 1983 | (1986); incomplete |
| Nigeria<br>Socialist Working People's Party (SWPP), 1978 (Socialist Workers and Farmers Party, 1963) | 94,181,000 | 0 | Dapo Fatogun | no data | First Nov. 1978 | (1983) |
| Réunion<br>Réunion Communist Party (PCR), 1959 | 552,500 | + | Paul Vergès | 2,000 est. | Fifth 12–14 July 1980 | 29.2 (1986); 13 of 45 left coal., 7 for PCR (local assembly); 2 in Paris |
| Senegal<br>Independence and Labor Party (PIT), 1981 (Parti de l'Indépendence du travail, 1957) | 6,980,000 | + | Amath Dansoko | no data | Second 28 Sept.–2 Oct. 1984 | 0.5 (1983); none |
| South Africa<br>South African Communist Party (SACP), 1921 | 33,241,000 | 0 | Moses Mabhida (died 3/86); Joe Slovo, chairman | no data | Sixth Dec. 1984 or early 1985, in London | n/a |
| Sudan<br>Sudanese Communist Party (SCP), 1946 | 22,932,000 | + | Muhammad Ibrahim Nugud Mansur | 9,000 est. | Fourth (legal) 31 Oct. 1967 | (1986) 2 in geogr., 3 in grad. constituencies, of 301 |
| Zimbabwe<br>Zimbabwe African National Union (ZANU-PF), 1963 | 8,984,000 | * | Robert G. Mugabe | no data | Fifth 8–12 Aug. 1984 | 76.0 (1985); 64 of 100 (64 of 80 reserved for blacks) |
| TOTAL | 231,812,500 | | | 217,323 | | |

## THE AMERICAS (29)

| Country: Party(ies)/Date Founded | Mid-1986 Population (est.) (World Factbook) | Communist Party Membership (claim or est.) | Party Leader (sec'y general) | Status | Last Congress | Last Election (percentage of vote; seats in legislature) |
|---|---|---|---|---|---|---|
| **Argentina** Communist Party of Argentina (PCA), 1918 | 31,186,000 | 70,000 est. | Athos Fava | + | Sixteenth 4–7 Nov. 1986 | 2.0 (1985); none FREPU coalition |
| **Bolivia** Communist Party of Bolivia (PCB), 1950 (split 1985) | 6,638,000 | 500 cl. | Simón Reyes Rivera (majority faction); Carlos Soria Galvarro (minority faction) | + | Fifth 9–13 Feb. 1985 Extraord. 26–29 April 1986 | 2.21 (1985); 4 of 130 FPU coalition |
| **Brazil** Brazilian Communist Party (PCB), 1960 (Communist Party of Brazil, 1922) | 143,277,000 | 20,000 cl. | Giocondo Dias | + | Seventh (called National Meeting of Communists) Jan. 1984 | (1986); 2 of 487 |
| **Canada** Communist Party of Canada (CPC), 1921 | 25,644,000 | 2,500 est. | William Kashtan | + | Twenty-sixth 5–8 Apr. 1985 | 0.05 (1984); none |
| **Chile** Communist Party of Chile (CPC), 1922 | 12,261,000 | 20,000 est. | Luís Corvalán Lepe | 0 | Sixteenth June 1984 (clandestine) | n/a |
| **Colombia** Communist Party of Colombia (PCC), 1930 | 29,956,000 | 16,000 est. | Gilberto Vieira | + | Fourteenth 7–11 Nov. 1984 | 1.4 (1986); 9 of 199 Patriotic Union |
| **Costa Rica** Popular Vanguard Party (PVP), 1931 | 2,714,000 | 3,500 est. (prior to split) | Humberto Vargas Carbonell | + | Fifteenth 15–16 Sept. 1984 | 0.8 (1986); 1 of 57 Popular Alliance Coalition |

| Country / Party (founded) | Population | Party membership | Party leader | | Last congress | Electoral / parliamentary strength |
|---|---|---|---|---|---|---|
| Costa Rica<br>Costa Rican People's Party (PPC), split from PVP, 1984 | | no data | Manuel Mora Valverde | + | Fourteenth<br>10–11 Mar. 1984 | 0.8 (1986); 1 of 57 United People's Coalition |
| Cuba<br>Cuban Communist Party (PCC), 1965 | 10,221,000 | 523,639 cl. | Fidel Castro Ruz | * | Third<br>4–7 Feb. and 30 Nov.–2 Dec. 1986 | (1986); all 499 PCC approved |
| Dominican Republic<br>Dominican Communist Party (PCD), 1944 | 6,785,000 | 750 est. | Narciso Isa Conde | + | Third<br>15–17 Mar. 1984 | 0.28 (1986); none |
| Ecuador<br>Communist Party of Ecuador (PCE), 1928 | 9,647,000 | 500 est. | René Mauge Mosquera (member of parliament) | + | Tenth<br>27–29 Nov. 1981 | 3.6 (1986); 3 of 71 Broad Leftist Front, FADI 4.0 (1984) in pres. elec. |
| El Salvador<br>Communist Party of El Salvador (PCES), 1930 (one of five in FMLN) | 5,105,000 | 1,000 est. | Shafik Jorge Handal | 0 | Seventh<br>Apr. 1979 | n/a (1985) |
| Grenada<br>Maurice Bishop Patriotic Movement (MBPM), 1984 | 92,000 | no data | Kenrick Radix (chairman) | + | First<br>Oct. 1985 | 5.0 (1984); none |
| Guadeloupe<br>Communist Party of Guadeloupe (PCG), 1958 | 334,000 | 3,000 est. | Guy Daninthe | + | Eighth<br>27–29 Apr. 1984 | no data (1986); 22 of 41 left coal., local (PCG: 10 of 22) also 1 of 3 in Paris |
| Guatemala<br>Guatemalan Party of Labor (PGT), 1952 | 8,600,000 | 500 est. | Carlos González ("Camarilla" faction); Daniel Rios (National Leadership Nucleus Faction) | 0 | Fourth<br>Dec. 1969 | n/a (1985) |

| Country:<br>Party(ies)/Date Founded | Mid-1986<br>Population (est.)<br>(World Factbook) | Communist Party<br>Membership<br>(claim or est.) | Party Leader<br>(sec'y general) | Status | Last<br>Congress | Last Election<br>(percentage of vote;<br>seats in legislature) |
|---|---|---|---|---|---|---|
| Guyana<br>People's Progressive Party<br>(PPP), 1950 | 771,000 | 200 est.<br>(100 leadership) | Cheddi Jagan | + | Twenty-second<br>3–5 Aug. 1985 | 16.8 (1985); 8 of 53<br>elected members |
| Haiti<br>Unified Party of Haitian<br>Communists (PUCH), 1968 | 5,870,000 | 350 est. | René Théodore | + | First<br>1979 | n/a (1984) |
| Honduras<br>Honduran Communist Party<br>(PCH), 1954 (one of six in the<br>Honduran Revolutionary Move-<br>ment, MHR, 1982) | 4,648,000 | 200 est. | Rigoberto Padilla<br>Rush (in exile);<br>Mario Sosa<br>Navarro (in<br>Honduras) | 0 | Fourth<br>Jan. 1986<br>(cland.) | n/a (1985) |
| Jamaica<br>Workers' Party of Jamaica<br>(WPJ), 1978 | 2,288,000 | 75 est. | Trevor Munroe | + | Third<br>14–21 Dec. 1984 | (1983) |
| Martinique<br>Martinique Communist Party<br>(PCM), 1957 | 328,000 | 1,000 est. | Armand Nicolas | + | Eighth<br>12–13 Nov.<br>1983 | no data (1986); 3 of<br>41 (local assembly);<br>none in Paris |
| Mexico<br>United Socialist Party of Mexico<br>(PSUM), 1981 | 81,709,000 | 40,800 cl. | Pablo Gómez<br>Alvarez | + | Second<br>9–14 Aug. 1983 | 3.24 (1985); 12 of 400 |
| Nicaragua<br>Nicaraguan Socialist Party<br>(PSN), 1937 | 3,342,000 | no data | Gustavo Tablada | + | Tenth<br>Oct. 1973 | 1.3 (1984); 2 of 96 |
| Sandinista Front of National Libera-<br>tion (FSLN), 1960 | | 4,000 cl. | Daniel Ortega<br>(coord. of Execu-<br>tive Commission) | * | | 63.0 (1984); 61 of 96 |

| Country Party (founded) | Population | Party membership | Party leader | Status | Last congress | Last election |
|---|---|---|---|---|---|---|
| **Panama** People's Party of Panama (PdP), 1943 | 2,227,000 | 750 est. 35,000 cl. (500–1,000 militants) | Rubén Darío Souza | + | Eighth 24–26 Jan. 1986 | (1984); none |
| **Paraguay** Paraguayan Communist Party (PCP), 1928 | 4,119,000 | 4,000 est. | Julio Rojas (acting); Antonio Maidana (arrested in 1980) | 0 | Third 10 Apr. 1971 | (1973) |
| **Peru** Peruvian Communist Party (PCP), 1930 | 20,207,000 | 2,000 est. | Jorge del Prado Chavez | + | Eighth Extraord. 27–31 Jan. 1982 | 26.0 (1984); 48 of 180 United Left coal. (6 PCP repr. of 48) |
| **Puerto Rico** Puerto Rican Communist Party (PCP), 1934 | 3,300,520 | 125 est. | Frank Irrizarry | + | unknown | 0.3 (1984); none |
| **Suriname** Revolutionary People's Party (RVP), 1981 (quasi-independent within 25 FM) | 381,000 | 100 est. | Edward Naarendorp | + | unknown | n/a |
| **United States of America** Communist Party USA (CPUSA), 1919 | 240,856,000 | 17,500 cl. | Gus Hall | + | Twenty-third 10–13 Nov. 1983 | 0.01 (1984); none |
| **Uruguay** Communist Party of Uruguay (PCU), 1920 | 2,947,000 | 7,500 est. | Rodney Arismendi | + | Twentieth Dec. 1970 | 6.0 (1984); none Frente Amplio coal. |
| **Venezuela** Communist Party of Venezuela (PCV), 1931 | 17,791,000 | 4,000 est. | Alonso Ojeda Olaechea | + | Seventh 24–27 Oct. 1985 | 2.0 (1983); 3 of 195 |
| TOTAL | 683,244,520 | 744,489 | | | | |

## ASIA AND THE PACIFIC (20)

| Country: Party(ies)/Date Founded | Mid-1986 Population (est.) (World Factbook) | Communist Party Membership (claim or est.) | Party Leader (sec'y general) | Status | Last Congress | Last Election (percentage of vote; seats in legislature) |
|---|---|---|---|---|---|---|
| **Australia** | 15,793,000 | | | | | |
| Communist Party of Australia (CPA), 1920 | | 1,000 est. | Judy Mundey | + | Twenty-eighth 4 Nov. 1984 | negl. (1984); none |
| Socialist Party of Australia (SPA), 1971 | | 500 est. | Peter Dudley Symon | + | Fifth 28 Sept.–1 Oct. 1984 | negl. (1984); none |
| **Bangladesh** | 104,205,000 | | | | | |
| Communist Party of Bangladesh (CPB), 1948 | | 3,000 est. | Muhammed Farhad | + | Third Feb. 1980 | (1986); 5 of 300 |
| **Burma** | 37,651,000 | | | | | |
| Burmese Communist Party (BCP), 1939 | | 3,000 cl. | Thakin Ba Thein Tin (chairman) | 0 | Third 9 Sept.–2 Oct. 1985 | n/a |
| **Cambodia** | 6,388,000 | | | | | |
| Kampuchean People's Revolutionary Party (KPRP), 1951 | | 7,500 est. | Heng Samrin | * | Fifth 13–16 Oct. 1985 | 99.0 (1981); all 117 |
| Party of Democratic Kampuchea (PDK), or Kampuchean Communist Party (KCP), 1951 | | no data | Pol Pot | 0 | Third 14 Dec. 1975 | n/a |
| **China** | 1,045,537,000 (1,060,000,000 China State Bureau) | over 44,000,000 cl. | Hu Yaobang (resigned 1/18/87; Zhao Ziyang (acting) | * | Twelfth 1–11 Sept. 1982 | (1981); all 3,202 CCP approved |

| Country / Party (founded) | Population | Party Membership | | Secretary / Leader | Last Congress | Last Election |
|---|---|---|---|---|---|---|
| **India** | | | | | | |
| Communist Party of India (CPI), 1928 | 783,940,000 | 479,000 cl. | + | C. Rajeswara Rao | Thirteenth 12–17 Mar. 1986 | 2.71 (1984); 6 of 544 |
| Communist Party Marxist (CPM), 1964 | | 361,500 cl. | + | E. M. S. Namboodiripad | Twelfth 25–30 Dec. 1985 | 5.96 (1984); 22 of 544 |
| **Indonesia** | | | | | | |
| Indonesian Communist Party (PKI), 1920 (split) | 176,764,000 | 2,200 est. (incl. exiles) | 0 | Jusuf Adjitorop (pro-Beijing faction) Satiadjaya Sudiman (pro-Moscow faction) | Seventh Extraord. Apr. 1962 | n/a |
| **Japan** | | | | | | |
| Japan Communist Party (JCP), 1922 | 121,402,000 (121,048,923 *Japan Times*, 11 Nov. 1986) | 470,000 est. | + | Tetsuzo Fuwa (Presidium chairman) Kenji Miyamoto (CC chairman) | Seventeenth 19–25 Nov. 1985 | 9.47 (1986); 27 of 512 |
| **Korea (North)** | | | | | | |
| Korean Workers' Party (KWP), 1946 (as united party, 1949) | 20,543,000 | 2,500,000 est. | * | Kim Il-song | Sixth 10–15 Oct. 1980 | 100 (1986); all 706 KWP approved |
| **Laos** | | | | | | |
| Lao People's Revolutionary Party (LPRP), 1955 | 3,679,000 | 47,000 cl. (WMR) (44,000 cl. Radio Vientiane) | * | Kaysone Phomvihane | Fourth 13–15 Nov. 1986 | (Dec. 1975); Supreme People's Assembly (all 46 appointed by LPRP) |
| **Malaysia** | | | | | | |
| Communist Party of Malaya (CPM), 1930 | 15,820,000 | 2,200 est. | 0 | Chin Peng | 1965 (last known) | (1984) |
| Communist Party of Malaysia (MCP), 1983 | | 800 est. | 0 | Ah Leng | unknown | (1984) |
| **Mongolia** | | | | | | |
| Mongolian People's Revolutionary Party (MPRP), 1921 | 1,942,000 | 88,150 cl. | * | Jambyn Batmonh (Dzambiin Batmunkh) | Nineteenth 28–31 May 1986 | 93.5 (1986); 346 of 370 MPRP approved |

| Country: Party(ies)/Date Founded | Mid-1986 Population (est.) (World Factbook) | Communist Party Membership (claim or est.) | Party Leader (sec'y general) | Status | Last Congress | Last Election (percentage of vote; seats in legislature) |
|---|---|---|---|---|---|---|
| Nepal<br>Nepal Communist Party (NCP), 1949 (factions) | 17,422,000 | 5,000 est. (75% pro-Beijing and neutral) | Man Mohan Adhikary | 0 | Third 1961 (before split; right wing held its own third in 1968) | n/a |
| New Zealand<br>Communist Party of New Zealand (CPNZ), 1921 | 3,266,200 | 50 est. | Richard C. Wolfe | + | Twenty-third 22 Apr. 1984 | (1984); none |
| Socialist Unity Party (SUP), 1966 | | 300 est. | George H. Jackson | + | Seventh 26–27 Oct. 1985 | 0.5 (1984); none |
| Pakistan<br>Communist Party of Pakistan (CPP), 1948 | 101,855,000 | under 200 est. | Ali Nazish | 0 (since 1954) | First 1976 (cland.) | n/a |
| Philippines<br>Philippine Communist Party (PKP), 1930 | 58,091,000 | 200 est. | Felicismo Macapagal | + | Eighth 1980 | (1986) |
| Communist Party of the Philippines (CPP), 1968 | | 20,000 est. | Rafael Baylosis | 0 | Re-establishment 26 Dec. 1968 | (1986) |
| Singapore<br>Communist Party of Malaya, Branch (CPM), 1930 | 2,584,000 | 350 est. | Chin Peng | 0 | unknown | (1984) |
| Sri Lanka<br>Communist Party of Sri Lanka (CPSL), 1943 | 16,638,000 | 5,000 est. | Kattorge P. Silva | + | Twelfth 27–29 Jan. 1984 | 1.9 (1977); 1 of 168 |
| Thailand<br>Communist Party of Thailand (CPT), 1942 | 52,438,000 | 600 est. | Pracha Tanyapaiboon | 0 | Fourth Mar.–Apr. 1984 (cland.) | n/a |

| Country / Party | Population | Party membership | Leader | | Congress | Election |
|---|---|---|---|---|---|---|
| Vietnam<br>Vietnamese Communist Party (VCP), 1930 | 61,994,000 | 1,700,000 cl. | Le Duan (died July 1986) Truong Chinh (14 July–17 Dec.) Nguyen Van Linh (since 18 Dec.) | * | Sixth 15–19 Dec. 1986 | 97.9 (1981); 496 of 614 all VCP endorsed |
| TOTAL | 2,647,952,200 | 53,697,150 | | | | |

## EASTERN EUROPE AND USSR (9)

| Country / Party | Population | Party membership | Leader | | Congress | Election |
|---|---|---|---|---|---|---|
| Albania<br>Albanian Party of Labor (APL), 1941 | 3,020,000 | 147,000 cl. | Ramiz Alia | * | Ninth 3–8 Nov. 1986 | 99.9 (1982); all 250 Democratic Front |
| Bulgaria<br>Bulgarian Communist Party (BCP), 1903 | 8,990,000 | 932,055 cl. | Todor Zhivkov | * | Thirteenth 2–5 Apr. 1986 | 99.9 (1986); all 400 Fatherland Front |
| Czechoslovakia<br>Communist Party of Czechoslovakia (KSC), 1921 | 15,542,000 | 1,675,000 cl. | Gustáv Husák | * | Seventeenth 24–28 Mar. 1986 | 99.0 (1986); all 350 National Front |
| Germany: German Democratic Republic<br>Socialist Unity Party (SED), 1946 | 16,692,000 | 2,304,121 cl. | Erich Honecker | * | Eleventh 17–21 Apr. 1986 | 99.94 (1986); all 500 National Front |
| Hungary<br>Hungarian Socialist Worker's Party (HSWP), 1956 | 10,624,000 | 870,992 cl. | János Kádár | * | Thirteenth 25–28 Mar. 1985 | 93.9 (1985); all 352 Patriotic People's Front |
| Poland<br>Polish United Workers' Party (PUWP), 1948 | 37,546,000 | 2,125,762 cl. (Polityka, July 1986) | Wojciech Jaruzelski | * | Tenth 29 June–3 July 1986 | 78.8 (1985); all 460 Fatherland Front |

| Country: Party(ies)/Date Founded | Mid-1986 Population (est.) (World Factbook) | Communist Party Membership (claim or est.) | Party Leader (sec'y general) | Status | Last Congress | Last Election (percentage of vote; seats in legislature) |
|---|---|---|---|---|---|---|
| Romania Romanian Communist Party (RPC), 1921 | 22,830,000 | 3,557,205 cl. | Nicolae Ceaușescu | * | Thirteenth 19–22 Nov. 1984 | 97.8 (1985); all 369 Socialist Democracy and Unity Front |
| USSR Communist Party of the Soviet Union (CPSU), 1898 | 279,904,000 | 18,500,000 cl. | Mikhail S. Gorbachev (Mar. 1985) | * | Twenty-seventh 25 Feb.–6 Mar. 1986 | 99.9 (1984); all 1,500 CPSU approved (71.4% are CPSU members) |
| Yugoslavia League of Communists of Yugoslavia (LCY), 1920 | 23,284,000 | 2,168,000 cl. | Milanko Renovica (president of Presidium) | * | Thirteenth 25–28 June 1986 | (1986); all 308 Socialist Alliance (all LCY approved) |
| TOTAL | 418,432,000 | 32,280,135 | | | | |

## MIDDLE EAST (15)

| Country: Party(ies)/Date Founded | Mid-1986 Population (est.) (World Factbook) | Communist Party Membership (claim or est.) | Party Leader (sec'y general) | Status | Last Congress | Last Election (percentage of vote; seats in legislature) |
|---|---|---|---|---|---|---|
| Afghanistan People's Democratic Party of Afghanistan (PDPA), 1965 | 11,000,000 est. | 40,000 est. (170,000 cl.) | Dr. Najib (since 4 May; Babrak Karmal resigned) | * | First 1 Jan. 1965 | (1985) (local council) |
| Algeria Socialist Vanguard Party (PAGS), 1920 | 22,817,000 | 450 est. | Sadiq Hadjeres (first secretary) | 0 | Sixth Feb. 1952 | (1982) |
| Bahrain Bahrain National Liberation Front (NLF/B), 1955 | 422,000 | negligible | Yusuf al-Hassan al-Ajajai | 0 | unknown | n/a |

| Country / Party, year founded | Population | Party membership | Party leader | Status | Last congress | Electoral / representation |
|---|---|---|---|---|---|---|
| Egypt<br>Egyptian Communist Party (ECP), 1921 | 50,525,000 | 500 est. | Farid Mujahid (apparently) | 0 | Second 1984 or early 1985 | n/a |
| Iran<br>Communist Party of Iran (Tudeh Party), 1941 (banned May 1983) | 46,604,000 | 1,500 est. | Ali Khavari (first sec'y of CC; party leader in exile) | 0 | National Conf. 1986 | n/a |
| Iraq<br>Iraqi Communist Party (ICP), 1934 | 16,019,000 | no data | Aziz Muhammad (first secretary) | 0 | Fourth 10–15 Nov. 1985 | (1984) |
| Israel<br>Communist Party of Israel (CPI, "RAKAH"), 1948 (Palestine Communist Party, 1922) | 4,208,000 (excl. E. Jerusalem and the West Bank) | 2,000 est. | Meir Vilner | + | Twentieth 4–7 Dec. 1985 | 3.4 (1984); 4 of 120 |
| Jordan<br>Communist Party of Jordan (CPJ), 1951 | 2,794,000 | no data | Fa'iq Warrad | 0 | Second Dec. 1983 | n/a |
| Lebanon<br>Lebanese Communist Party (LCP), 1924 | 2,675,000 | 2,500 est. | George Hawi | + | Fourth 1979 | (1972) |
| Morocco<br>Party of Progress and Socialism (PPS), 1974 (Moroccan Communist Party, 1943) | 23,667,000 | 2,000 est. (30,000 cl.) | 'Ali Yata | + | Third 25–27 Mar. 1983 | 2.30 (1984); 2 of 306 |
| Palestine<br>Palestine Communist Party (PCP), 1982 | 4,500,000 Palestinians | 200 est. | Bashir al-Barghuti (presumed) | 0 (tolerated) | First presumably in 1984 | n/a |
| Saudi Arabia<br>Communist Party of Saudi Arabia (CPSA), 1975 | 11,519,000 | negligible | Mahdi Habib | 0 | Second Aug. 1984 | n/a |
| Syria<br>Syrian Communist Party (SCP), 1944 | 10,931,000 | 5,000 est. | Khalid Bakhdash | + | Sixth July 1986 | (1986); 8 of 195 |

| Country: Party(ies)/Date Founded | Mid-1986 Population (est.) (World Factbook) | Communist Party Membership (claim or est.) | Party Leader (sec'y general) | Status | Last Congress | Last Election (percentage of vote; seats in legislature) |
|---|---|---|---|---|---|---|
| **Tunisia** Tunisian Communist Party (PCT), 1934 | 7,424,000 | 2,000 est. (4,000 cl.) | Muhammad Harmel (first secretary) | + | Eighth Feb. 1981 | (1986); none (PCT boycotted elections) |
| **Yemen (PDRY)** Yemen Socialist Party (YSP), 1978 | 2,275,000 | 26,000 cl. | 'Ali Salim al-Bayd | * | Third 11–16 Oct. 1985 | (1978); all 111 YSP approved |
| TOTAL | 217,380,000 | 82,150 | | | | |

## WESTERN EUROPE (23)

| Country: Party(ies)/Date Founded | Mid-1986 Population (est.) (World Factbook) | Communist Party Membership (claim or est.) | Party Leader (sec'y general) | Status | Last Congress | Last Election (percentage of vote; seats in legislature) |
|---|---|---|---|---|---|---|
| **Austria** Communist Party of Austria (KPO), 1918 | 7,546,000 | 15,000 est. | Franz Muhri (chairman) | + | Twenty-fifth 13–15 Jan. 1984 National Conference, 23 May 1986 | 0.72 (1986); none |
| **Belgium** Belgian Communist Party (PCB-KPB), 1921 | 9,868,000 | 5,000 est. | Louis van Geyt (president) | + | Twenty-fifth 18–20 Apr. 1986 | 1.2 (1985); none |
| **Cyprus** Progressive Party of the Working People (AKEL), 1941 (Communist Party of Cyprus, 1922) | 673,000 | 12,000 cl. | Ezekias Papaioannou | + | Sixteenth 26–30 Nov. 1986 | 27.4 (1985); 15 of 56 |

| Country / Party (founded) | Population | Party leader | | Membership | Congress (date) | Last election |
|---|---|---|---|---|---|---|
| **Denmark** | | | | | | |
| Communist Party of Denmark (DKP), 1919 | 5,097,000 | Poul Emanuel (secretary) Jørgen Jensen (chairman) | + | 10,000 est. | Twenty-seventh 12–15 May 1983 | 0.7 (1984); none |
| **Finland** | | | | | | |
| Finnish Communist Party (SKP), 1918 | 4,931,000 | Esko Vainionpää | + | 20,000 cl. | Twentieth 24–26 May 1984 Extraord. 23 Mar. 1985 | 14.0 (1983); 27 of 200 |
| SKP "Shadow," 1986 | | Jouko Kajanoja | + | 16,663 cl. | (First planned for 1987) | |
| **France** | | | | | | |
| French Communist Party (PCF), 1920 | 55,239,000 | Georges Marchais | + | 610,000 cl. | Twenty-fifth 6–10 Feb. 1985 | 9.8 (1986); 35 of 577 |
| **Germany: Federal Republic of Germany** | 60,190,000 (excl. W. Berlin) | | | | | |
| German Communist Party (DKP), 1968 | | Herbert Mies (chairman) | + | 40,000 est. | Eighth 2–4 May 1986 | 0.2 (1983); none |
| **Great Britain** | | | | | | |
| Communist Party of Great Britain (CPGB), 1920 | 56,458,000 | Gordon McLennan | + | 11,000 est. | Thirty-eighth 12–15 Nov. 1983 Special 18–20 May 1985 | 0.03 (1983); none |
| New Communist Party of Britain (NCPB) (New Kabul Times, 12/24/85) | | Eric Trevett | + | no data | Fifth 23–24 Nov. 1985 | no data |
| **Greece** | 9,954,000 | | | | | |
| Communist Party of Greece (KKE), 1921 | | Kharilaos Florakis | + | 42,000 est. | Eleventh 15–18 Dec. 1982 | 9.9 (1985); 13 of 300 |
| Communist Party of Greece–Interior (KKE-I), 1968 | | Leonidas Kyrkos | + | 12,000 est. | Fourth May 1986 | 1.8 (1985); none |

| Country / Party | Membership | Leader | Front | Party congress | Last election | Population |
|---|---|---|---|---|---|---|
| **Portugal** Portuguese Communist Party (PCP), 1921 | over 200,000 cl. | Álvaro Cunhal | + | Eleventh Extraord. 2–6 Feb. 1986 | 15.49 (1985); 38 of 250 United People's Alliance Coalition | 10,095,000 |
| **San Marino** Communist Party of San Marino (PCS), 1921 | 300 est. | Gilberto Ghiotti | + | Eleventh 27 Jan. 1986 | 24.3 (1983); 15 of 60 | 23,000 |
| **Spain** Spanish Communist Party (PCE), 1920 | 60,000 est. | Gerardo Iglesias | + | Eleventh 14–18 Dec. 1983 | 4.6 (1986); 7 of 350 United Left Coalition | 39,075,000 |
| Communist Party of the Peoples of Spain (PCPE), 1984 | 35,000 cl. | Ignacio Gallego | + | First 13–15 Jan. 1984 | n/a | |
| **Sweden** Left Party Communists (VPK), 1921 | 17,500 cl. | Lars Werner (chairman) | + | Twenty-seventh 3–6 Jan. 1985 | 5.4 (1985); 19 of 349 | 8,357,000 |
| Communist Workers' Party (APK), 1977 | 5,000 cl. | Rolf Hagel (chairman) | + | Twenty-eighth 7 Nov. 1986 | 0.1 (1982); none | |
| **Switzerland** Swiss Labor Party (PdAS), 1921 | 3,000 est. | Armand Magnin | + | Twelfth 21–22 May 1983 | 0.9 (1983); 1 of 200 | 6,466,000 |
| **Turkey** Communist Party of Turkey (TCP), 1920 | negligible | Haydar Kutlu | 0 | Fifth Oct. or Nov. 1983 | (1983) | 51,819,000 |
| **West Berlin** Socialist Unity Party of West Berlin (SEW), 1949 | 4,500 est. | Horst Schmitt (chairman) | + | Seventh 25–27 May 1984 | 0.6 (1985); none | 1,861,000 |
| TOTAL | 2,746,601 | | | | | 408,119,179 |
| GRAND TOTAL | 89,767,648 | | | | | 4,606,940,399 |

# MAJOR INTERNATIONAL FRONT ORGANIZATIONS*

| Organization (12) | Year Founded | Headquarters | Claimed Membership | Affiliates | Countries |
|---|---|---|---|---|---|
| Afro-Asian Peoples' Solidarity Organization (AAPSO) | 1957 | Cairo | unknown | 87 | – |
| Christian Peace Conference (CPC) | 1958 | Prague | unknown | – | ca. 80 |
| International Association of Democratic Lawyers (IADL) | 1946 | Brussels | 25,000 | – | ca. 80 |
| International Federation of Resistance Movements (FIR)[a] | 1951 | Vienna | 5,000,000 | 68 | 29 |
| International Organization of Journalists (IOJ) | 1946 | Prague | ca. 200,000+[b] | – | 120 plus |
| International Union of Students (IUS) | 1946 | Prague | 10,000,000 | 120 | 112 |
| Women's International Democratic Federation (WIDF) | 1945 | East Berlin | 200,000,000 | 136 | 118 |
| World Federation of Democratic Youth (WFDY) | 1945 | Budapest | 150,000,000 | ca. 270 | 123 |
| World Federation of Scientific Workers (WFSW) | 1946 | London | 740,000[c] | ca. 46 | 70 plus |
| World Federation of Teachers' Unions (FISE)[d] | 1946 | E. Berlin | 25,000,000 | – | – |
| World Federation of Trade Unions (WFTU) | 1945 | Prague | ca. 206,000,000[e] | 92 | 81 |
| World Peace Council (WPC) | 1950 | Helsinki | unknown | – | 142 plus |

*All known or presumed participants in meetings of "closely coordinating" international nongovernmental organizations during 1981–1985.

a. Union of International Organizations, *Yearbook of International Organizations, 1985–1986.* (Munich: K. G. Saur, 1986), entry D1996; and Warsaw, PAP, 12 September; *FBIS*, 18 September.

b. Sofia, *Rabotnichesko delo*, 20 October.

c. *Moscow News*, 24–25 July.

d. Union of International Organizations, op. cit., entry B3535.

e. 296,000,000 claimed by East Berlin Radio, 21 September.

# Introduction
# The Communist World, 1986

The world communist movement has been fragmented for more than a quarter century, although Moscow continues to maintain the myth of leadership over a nonexistent organization. All of this may be changing, with the retirement of veteran Comintern functionary Boris Ponomarev, who had been a candidate Politburo member and directed the International Department in the Communist Party of the Soviet Union (CPSU) Central apparatus until 1986. His successor, Anatoly Dobrynin, certainly gives the impression of a pragmatic style and seems to have more of a voice in the foreign-policy decisionmaking process than the nominal head of the government's ministry, Eduard Shevardnadze.

The extent of CPSU influence over other communist parties and revolutionary movements could be gauged by the 152 delegations, from 113 foreign countries, that attended the Twenty-seventh CPSU Congress during 25 February–6 March.[1] Neither the Albanians nor the Chinese, among ruling parties, were there. All of the bloc countries in Eastern Europe sent their communist leaders, as did Afghanistan, Cuba, Ethiopia, and Vietnam. Only deputy general secretaries came from France, Italy, Japan, and North Korea. Represented among the foreign delegations were sixteen socialist, social-democratic, and labor parties.

All members of the CPSU Politburo, except for Geidar Aliiev, made speeches heard by approximately 5,000 Soviet and other uncounted delegates. CPSU leader Mikhail Gorbachev engaged in an abusive ideological harangue, attacking world capitalism for its alleged policy of hegemonism and for starting the arms race. He claimed that the liberation struggle in the Third World had been triggered by the 1917 revolution and that the course of history, based on the laws of Marxism-Leninism, could not be stopped. Gorbachev asserted that capitalism and imperialism were pursuing aggressive, adventuristic policies that had resulted in neocolonialist exploitation of the lesser developed countries. Poverty, backwardness, and indebtedness would be overcome through an irreversible process of socioeconomic transformation with the assistance of the so-called socialist (that is, communist-ruled) states.[2]

With regard to world communism, Gorbachev took a conciliatory approach. He stressed comradely consultations, acknowledging that the movement included differences and disagreements and that unity supposedly had nothing to do with uniformity. However, the newly adopted CPSU program states that the advance of world communism depends on fraternal relations based upon "socialist internationalism"— loyalty to Moscow—and upon adherence to Marxist-Leninist precepts by all ruling communist parties.[3]

It is interesting to note that General Wojciech Jaruzelski stated at his ruling party's congress in June that Polish communists thought a world conference of fraternal movements on the topic of defending peace should be held in the near future. Early in December, a ranking Czechoslovak party member (Vasil Bilak) told a meeting of his comrades that, although 80 communist parties allegedly supported the proposal, Gorbachev had informed bloc leaders at the Council for Mutual Economic Assistance (CMEA) summit in June that a conference should not weaken the world movement but strengthen it.[4] This meant, of course, an indefinite postponement.

The Register of Communist Parties in this volume names 96 or so geographic entities with communist parties. Thirteen of the countries have at least two (in Spain, three) movements each, identified on the chart: Australia, Cambodia, Costa Rica, Finland, Great Britain, Greece, India, Morocco, New Zealand, Norway, the Philippines, Spain, and Sweden. In certain cases, the CPSU recognizes two factions. Nonsovereign territories with communist parties include Guadeloupe, Martinique, Palestine, Puerto Rico, Réunion, and West Berlin.

Also included on the Register are the following most radical among the 24 political movements designated as "revolutionary democratic" by Moscow: those in Afghanistan, Angola, Bahrain, Benin, Cambodia, Congo, Ethiopia, Grenada, Mozambique, Nicaragua, South Yemen, and Zimbabwe.[5] Only the ones in Bahrain and Grenada are not in power. Some of the more important communist parties unrecognized by Moscow are pro-Chinese, such as Burma, New Zealand (CPNZ), Philippines (CPP), Thailand (CPT), and large factions in Indonesia, Malaysia, and Nepal.

For those movements without the designation "Communist Party of. . .," the acronym and full name appear in the Register. All population estimates are for July.[6] Party membership figures, either officially recorded claims or estimates as of 31 December, are provided by the author of each profile in the *Yearbook*. The Register also includes the names of party leaders (general secretary or chairman), dates for the latest congress or national conference, legal status of the movement, and, if applicable, the percentage of votes won in the most recent elections.

Increased membership in the ruling parties was claimed by Afghanistan (20,000); Albania (25,000); Bulgaria (20,000); China (4 million); Cuba (90,000); Czechoslovakia (25,000); East Germany (11,000); Laos (5,000); Mongolia (8,000); Poland (13,000); Romania (57,000); and the Soviet Union (600,000). The Alliance of Yugoslav Communists lost almost 11,000 members. Estimates for the parties in Austria, Brazil, Colombia, Finland, India (both factions), Israel, Italy, Malta, the Netherlands, New Zealand (SUP), the Philippines (CPP), Sudan, and Tunisia have been increased. Those for Belgium, France, Malaysia, New Zealand (CPNZ), and West Germany have declined.

Notable changes of top leaders in 1986 included Ali Nasir (South Yemen), ousted in February; Seydou Sissoko (Senegal), died in Moscow at the CPSU congress; Moses Mabhid (South Africa), died in March; Babrak Karmal (Afghanistan), removed in May; Le Duan (Vietnam), died in July; Samora Machel (Mozambique), killed in an airplane crash in October; and the jailed Nureddin Kiamuri (Iran), succeeded in exile sometime during the year.

The Table of Party Congresses in this volume lists 29 party congresses and three national conferences held during 1986; this is nine more congresses than were listed in 1985. Two of the movements—those in Haiti and the Philippines—achieved legal status. Gatherings already scheduled for 1987 will be convened in Denmark, Finland, Lebanon, Norway (NKP), The Philippines, Portugal, Spain, and Sweden (VPK).

Voters went to the polls in 23 countries during the past year, five of them under communist or Marxist-Leninist rule: Bulgaria, Czechoslovakia, East Germany, Mozambique, and North Korea. The latter results were predictable in that one candidate ran for each seat in the so-called National Parliament. Otherwise, the communists, frequently running as part of a coalition, did not make appreciable gains in most other elections. A discussion of major developments in various regions of the world follows:

**Sub-Saharan Africa.** Mozambique's FRELIMO (Front for the Liberation of Mozambique), a Marxist-Leninist vanguard party, suffered a setback in 1986 with the death of its leader, Samora Machel, in an airplane crash on 19 October. The former foreign minister, Joaquim Alberto Chissano, succeeded him as head of state and commander of the armed forces. Like his predecessor, Chissano had been born in Gaza province and came from the Shangana subgroup of the Tsonga, the second largest among Mozambique's ten major ethnic groups. Chissano is regarded as a moderate and pragmatic politician who is likely to continue fighting the rebels and looking to the West for aid while remaining in the Soviet orbit. Machel's death caused a temporary interruption in the country's elections for local, provincial and national assemblies, which were announced as completed in mid-December. Mozambique signed a cooperation agreement with the CMEA, the first of its kind with a southern African country.[7]

In nearby Zimbabwe, the ruling Zimbabwe African National Union (ZANU) expanded its parliamentary majority of 64 seats by two because of defections. ZANU president and prime minister Robert Mugabe has begun to move toward a one-party state and a powerful executive. The economy remains divided between private enterprise and government ownership; the latter controls major businesses and newspapers. However, ZANU continues to face deep ethnic rivalries within its ranks and the country itself. Zimbabwe is being drawn deeper into the fighting over the Beira Corridor in Mozambique, alongside

FRELIMO. The eighth summit of the Nonaligned Movement nations, during which Mugabe was elected to serve as chairman until 1989, met in Harare.[8]

Angolan leadership changes took place among the ruling Marxist-Leninists in their Movement for the Liberation of Angola–Labor Party (MPLA-PT). President José Eduardo dos Santos removed his second in command and ideological chief, Lucio Lara, along with former director of security and intelligence Ludy Kissassunda and minister of agriculture, Evaristo Domingos.[9] They were veteran revolutionaries on the Politburo, and their purge suggests a dismissal of those who doubt dos Santos's economic policies and the war with UNITA (National Union for the Total Independence of Angola). Antonio dos Santos Neto, who was dismissed from his position as head of the Central Committee's Department for Defense and Security, was succeeded by José Pereira Teixeira.[10] Later in the year, corruption was cited as the reason for further dismissals and for the posting of influential party members as ambassadors abroad.[11]

The Workers' Party of Ethiopia (WPE) completed drafting a constitution for a regime that is to become known as a people's democratic republic. The draft also calls for the WPE to be the vanguard and only party that "is the guiding force of the state and the entire society."[12] Ethiopia continued its forced resettlement from the north to the southwest region, with three million people already relocated or about 10 percent of those possibly involved.[13]

The South African Communist Party (SACP) also underwent a leadership change after the death of Moses Mabhida, the 62-year-old general secretary living in Mozambique. A party member since 1942, he had been an active trade unionist, served as SACP head since 1978, and was an executive committee member of the African National Congress. The SACP anounced that Joe Slovo, a 60-year-old Lithuanian-born white lawyer who had also been active in the party since the 1940s, had been elected chairman, a position vacant since Yusef Dadoo's death in 1983. For the SACP, this selection was viewed as symbolizing "the new era in which our party lives and fights—the era of revolutionary struggle for the final liberation of the South African people." The SACP continued its longtime affinity for the Soviet Union but, in a break with the past, a SACP delegation led by Slovo made a ten-day visit to Mainland China after decades of hostility toward the communist party there.[14]

The Congolese Party of Labor (PCT) engaged in a continuous purge directed at "alien elements."[15] In August, a death sentence was passed on Claude Ndalla, a prominent leftist critic of the regime. Five-year suspended sentences were meted out to Jean-Pierre Thystere Tchikaya, who until 1985 had been the second most powerful man in the country, and army colonel Blaise Nzalakanda, indicating problems for the regime with the army. In fact, President and PCT general secretary Dennis Sassou-Ngouesso addressed the army on its twentieth anniversary, stressing the importance of indoctrination and increased party control.[16]

The Revolutionary Party of the People of Benin (PRPB) continued its main preoccupation of the previous year, consolidating the party at the grass-roots level. To implement this goal, the PRPB placed greater emphasis on party-building activities by the twelve Politburo members, set up regular party publications, and moved to establish a party school.[17]

Among several Marxist and left-leaning parties in Senegal, the one recognized by Moscow is the Party of Independence and Labor (PIT). Its chairman, Seydou Cissoko, died at age 57 while attending the CPSU congress in Moscow. He had been a founder of the PIT and served as its general secretary from 1967 to 1984, when he was elected chairman. Since the post of chairman had been specifically established for Cissoko when he stepped down from the general secretaryship, no successor was immediately named.[18]

**The Americas.** Nicaragua remained the focus of international attention in Latin America. During 1986 the Sandinista government greatly reduced the already limited freedoms in the country, most obviously at mid-year by closing down *La Prensa*, the only opposition paper, for "stepping up its level of provocation and disinformation." One opposition leader in the country was quoted in the Paris daily *Le Monde* of 24 June as saying that Nicaragua's legislative assembly was "designed for export purposes . . . In practice it has no power and is a mere sham." Nonetheless, five political parties decided to run as a coalition in the 1987 local elections. The government also escalated its attack on the popular Miguel Cardinal Obando y Bravo and the Roman Catholic Church.

Daniel Ortega, Nicaraguan president and member of the Sandinista Front of National Liberation (FSLN) National Directorate, admitted to a West German magazine that the government holds about 2,700 political prisoners; however, a paper published in Costa Rica by former *La Prensa* editor Pedro Joaquin Chamorro put the figure at more than 9,000. In October, the Interior Ministry even admitted that torture has been used on prisoners.[19]

The economy continued to deteriorate, with inflation of at least 300 percent. By year's end, total USSR aid was estimated at about $1 million daily. Military ties to the Soviet bloc expanded, not least with the arrival in Nicaragua of fifteen more MI-17 helicopters. Political relations deteriorated between the Sandinistas and governments/groups in Western Europe and elsewhere.

Anti-Sandinista forces operated abroad under the political umbrella of the United Nicaraguan Opposition (UNO), headed by three prominent Nicaraguans, including two who had served for some time in top positions of the Sandinista government. UNO's military arm is widely known as the *contras*. Although efforts to develop a fully unified stance against the Sandinistas repeatedly ran into difficulties, the U.S. Congress, after much debate, finally voted $100 million to support UNO and the guerrillas. Shortly after the congressional vote at mid-year, however, news broke of a Reagan administration arms deal with Iran, which reportedly diverted money to the *contras*, and at year's end the resulting scandal threatened renewed support for the guerrillas in 1987.

In El Salvador, the military forces of the Duarte government maintained the upper hand in their war against the Farabundo Martí National Liberation Front (FMLN) guerrillas. The military penetrated what had previously been insurgent strongholds. Open splits occurred in the political umbrella organization of the guerrillas, the Revolutionary Democratic Front, with some of the more moderate members returning to El Salvador to participate openly in political and labor activities. The guerrillas discussed forming a united, vanguard, Marxist-Leninist party, and three of the five members of the FMLN—including the communist party—attended the Twenty-seventh Congress of the CPSU together and evidently were treated as the same organization politically, militarily, and ideologically.[20]

In Honduras, the military was evidently successful in putting down an uprising in the northern part of the country by the Cinchoneros group. The insurgents had apparently been trained and armed in and by Cuba and Nicaragua.[21] In Guatemala, the democratically elected government of Vinicio Cerezo, which took power in January, offered an amnesty to that country's guerrillas, and as many as 2,000 accepted it; there were mixed signals from other insurgents regarding peace overtures, however, and conflict increased during the second half of the year.

The Cuban Communist Party held its Third Congress in two sessions: the first in February and the second in December. Speakers noted that economic production had suffered from work stoppages, absenteeism, discontent, incompetence, and unemployment. Fidel Castro said that convertible currency income available for buying products from Western nations would drop from $1.2 billion in 1986 to $600 million in 1987; he also announced a wide-ranging austerity program that included drastic cuts in energy available to government and private consumers.[22]

A "strategic revolutionary counteroffensive" is intended to concentrate more power in the hands of Castro, who emphasized moral over material incentives for workers. He continued to speak of diversifying the economy, whereas the Soviet Union promotes integration with the CMEA and would like to see Cuba as a provider of raw materials and agricultural products for the Soviet and East European economies. In 1986, international policies took second place to domestic. Support for revolutions in Latin America continued, however, ranging from a strong Cuban presence in Nicaragua to supplying arms for insurgents in Chile. Castro attended the Nonaligned Movement summit in Harare, Zimbabwe, and promised to maintain troops in Angola until apartheid has been eliminated from South Africa.

The pro-Soviet Communist Party of Colombia (PCC) is the leading member of a leftist coalition, the Patriotic Union, which substantially increased its representation in both Senate and House after the 1986 elections. The front's level of national support can be measured by the 4.5 percent of the vote received by its presidential candidate. The Columbian government's continuing effort to keep a truce with its insurgents worked only with the PCC's Revolutionary Armed Forces of Colombia (FARC). Otherwise, there was an escalation of guerrilla conflict—in which one of the main groups involved was the M-19—often with a connection to drug dealers. The new president, Virgilo Barco, adopted an increasingly hard line toward the violence.

Leftists in Peru were divided as to whether they should form a loyal opposition to the government of Alan García or expand the level of violence against it. The pro-Soviet Peruvian Communist Party and most other leftist groups participated in the United Left (IU) electoral front, which was the second major political force in the country and the leading parliamentary opposition to the ruling APRA party. The IU often was not united, but its overall orientation was to pressure García to live up to his promises of an "anti-imperialist state."

Toward the end of the year, García spoke increasingly often of the "need to combat international terrorism with the power of national security forces." He criticized military excesses, stressed that the main terrorist group, the Sendero Luminoso, struck out at innocents, and asked citizens to become "soldiers of the antiterrorist cause."[23] The Maoist-oriented Sendero Luminoso selects major targets in cities, such as state offices and especially local APRA meeting halls. More than 100 municipal officials have been killed in five years, 30 of them between January and September 1986. Other major targets were police and military officers and the national infrastructure. In all, nearly 10,000 lives have been lost.

In Chile, most of the violence can be traced directly or indirectly to the Communist Party of Chile (PCC), which fifteen years ago was the continent's main advocate of the nonviolent road to power. In 1986, the PCC argued that all forms of struggle should be pursued, though its support for violence alienated it from most of the other groups that oppose the continuation of the Pinochet government. Massive amounts of arms and ammunition were discovered during the year, and a clear Cuban link was found. This suggested that the party and its terrorist group, the Manuel Rodriguez Patriotic Front, plan a civil war or violent national uprising. Five hundred bombings occurred between January and August, and the most publicized terrorist action of the year was the attempted assassination of President Pinochet in September.

In Ecuador, guerrilla activities increased, as did deaths among guerrilla leaders. There was continuing evidence of ties between the Alfaro Vive! guerrillas of Ecuador and the Colombian M-19. The Argentine Communist Party, at its congress in November, seemed to be contemplating a more violence-oriented strategy, with considerble admiration expressed for the Nicaraguan experience.

Among the parties stressing the electoral road were those in Brazil, where in November three Marxist-Leninist groups won a total of 22 seats in the 487-member National Congress; they would have undoubtedly won more had it not been for alliance complications in São Paulo. The main winner was the Workers' Party, with strong Trotskyist and radical Christian tendencies. Leftist parties in Venezuela began looking toward a coalition for the 1988 elections, even as the Venezuelan Communist Party, a possible holdout, was on the verge of its fifth split. The left in Mexico also began seeking unified participation in that country's 1988 national elections.

In Guyana, the pro-Soviet People's Progressive Party (PPP) continued to be the main opposition to the People's National Congress (PNC). In 1986, the PNC elevated former PPP theoretician Ranji Chandisingh to deputy leader of the party. The second significant opposition group remained the Working People's Alliance (WPA), which has maintained a more moderate line since the overthrow of the New Jewel Movement of Grenada in 1983 because, as one WPA leader stated, it feared the Reagan Doctrine would lead to U.S. intervention if a violent revolution occurred in Guyana.[24]

In Grenada, the big event of the year for the left was the conviction and death sentences given to fourteen members of the former People's Revolutionary Government who overthrew and killed Prime Minister Maurice Bishop and more than 100 others. Among those sentenced were Bernard Coard and Hudson Austin. Haitian communists rushed back home after President-for-Life Jean-Claude Duvalier fled the country in February, but they tried to restrain worker demonstrations, which they feared might provoke a violent reaction from the military.

In the United States, the communist party concentrated on defeating congressional candidates who supported the "hypocritical racist" Ronald Reagan.[25] The party was pleased with the outcome of the congressional elections.

**Asia and the Pacific.** In the Philippines, the New People's Army (NPA) forces, estimated to range in size from 16,500 to 32,000, had been operating on as many as 60 fronts around the country, sometimes in company-size (200–300 men) operations. Their shadow regime controlled 10–15 percent of the country's villages. The Corazon Aquino government released more than 500 political prisoners, including a founder of the communist party, Jose Maria Sison, and a former head of the NPA, Bernabe Buscayno. On 5 August, negotiations opened and, after three months, both sides agreed to a 60-day cease-fire. Both sides continued to maneuver for political advantages, before violence resumed.[26]

The three communist-ruled states of North Korea, China, and Vietnam experienced challenges and difficulties that in two cases led to change at the top. Kim Il-song and his son Kim Chong-il toured North Korea, while the father sought to guarantee a smooth transfer of power to his offspring. The defection of a film director and his actress wife to the U.S. embassy in Vienna probably dealt a severe blow to Kim Chong-il's succession hopes, lending credence to rumors about his privileged life style. The sudden, unannounced visit in late October of Kim Il-song to Moscow also seemed linked with difficulties to ensure transfer of power to his son.[27]

Throughout 1986, newspapers and journals in the People's Republic of China published articles discussing the ideas of major Western thinkers and writers. In December, massive student demonstrations erupted in cities such as Wuhan, Nanjing, Shanghai, and Beijing, challenging the Chinese Communist Party (CCP) to initiate political reforms as a complement to recent economic reforms. The marches were peaceful and well organized; security personnel and police refrained from stopping them, although some arrests were made and students later released. The state-controlled press went on the offensive with editorials, castigating those who had challenged the party's authority and calling for adherence to the four cardinal principles: maintain the socialist road, uphold the proletarian dictatorship, hold fast to Marxism-Leninism and Mao Zedong thought, and retain the supremacy of the communist party. The press and party have attacked and condemned "bourgeois liberalism" and "complete Westernization." According to the *Organization and Personnel Information Newspaper*, a leader of the CCP Central Committee commented on political reform by saying: "We may give play to their respective functions in our propaganda, but not to the division of power between the party and the government."[28]

Similarly, in Vietnam the regime continued to be plagued by serious economic troubles and declining morale. Of the Politburo's inner circle of five, only Pham Hung remained on that body by the end of 1986. In mid-December, the Sixth Party Congress took place. Significant changes in the Politburo were announced, with greater emphasis on selecting people of a more pragmatic orientation for solving economic problems. This new group on the Politburo, led by Nguyen Van Linh, who succeeded the deceased Le Duan, will govern as a collective leadership. The congress also called for a massive self-criticism emulation movement and urged that younger party members be recruited. The Political Report frankly admitted the party's inability to achieve goals set over the past decade, blaming much of the trouble on economic problems.[29]

Throughout the rest of Asia, communist parties (legal and illegal), continued to operate and perform as in the past with only slight differences. The Japanese Communist Party (JCP) activities and stature remained unchanged. Secret talks in 1985–1986 with the Chinese communists failed to resolve differences.[30] In Bangladesh, voters elected five communist party members to the newly revived National Assembly. The party had aligned itself with other "bourgeois" groups to mobilize votes for its candidates. In Burma, the clandestine communist radio reached the outside world in February to announce that the party's third congress in 47 years had been held between 9 September and 2 October, with 170 delegates attending.[31] They elected a new Central Committee of 29 members and pledged to rely on Marxism, Leninism, and Mao Zedong's thought to formulate a new party line.

In India, the communists, like other opposition parties, stepped up their criticism of Prime Minister Rajiv Gandhi.[32] In Indonesia, the communist party's top leaders remained in exile with no sign of any organized activity in the country throughout the year. Little reliable information surfaced about the communist party in Thailand.

**Eastern Europe and the USSR.** During the first half of the year, communist party congresses were convened in the Soviet Union, Czechoslovakia, Bulgaria, East Germany, and Poland. Basic continuity has been maintained in Moscow's relations with its client states, as evidenced by the Twenty-seventh CPSU Congress proceedings. In general, these gatherings rubber stamp policies agreed upon in advance by the respective political bureaus of each party.

The four East European congresses devoted much time to discussion of economic problems, with their Soviet mentors pressing for greater integration through the CMEA. All member states recognize the need for increased efficiency and the benefits from shared technology. The USSR has apparently decided not to interfere with domestic approaches to the economy, such as the New Economic Mechanism reform in Hungary or private agriculture in Poland.

Albania, outside the bloc since 1961, held its Ninth Party Congress in November, at which time Ramiz Alia was confirmed as successor to the late Enver Hoxha. Three candidates were elevated to full membership on the Politburo, which now numbers thirteen. Soviet overtures to re-establish normal relations have been ignored, and an Albanian party journal called the Kremlin leadership a "Khrushchevian clique" pursuing neocolonial policies toward Eastern Europe.[33]

The first bloc congress to follow the one in Moscow was held in Czechoslovakia. It took stock of the preceding fifteen years and attempted to assess the economic future. A new constitution will be drafted to replace the 1960 one, which has been amended several times. The only change in leadership involved the addition of three candidate members to the party Presidium (called the Politburo elsewhere). General Secretary Gustáv Husák pointed out that every seventh citizen belongs to the communist party.[34]

The party congress in Bulgaria also discussed technology, cadres, and discipline as well as reorganization of economic management. No changes in the leadeship occurred, although two Politburo members had been dropped earlier in the year. General Secretary Todor Zhivkov, 75, has been in power longer than anyone else in the bloc, and no heir apparent can be identified. Parliamentary elections were held for the National Assembly in June. "Practically all" of the 99.9 percent of eligible voters supported the official list.[35]

Soviet leader Mikhail Gorbachev attended the East German party congress, where his counterpart Erich Honecker brought three regional secretaries into the Politburo as full members, two of whom had been candidates for membership. It would seem that Egon Krenz is the heir apparent to 74-year-old Honecker, who had reportedly been the target of an unsuccessful coup in 1985.[36] East Germany also had elections to its Parliament, with only 7,512 votes cast against the National Front ticket.

The party congress in Poland supposedly marked attainment of "normalization" and re-establishment of communist control over the country. Gorbachev's presence, as in East Berlin, provided endorsement for General Wojciech Jaruzelski's military junta. Unlike the other congresses, the one in Warsaw made major changes: the thirteen-member Politburo expanded to fifteen, with seven persons dropped and nine newcomers added.[37] This policymaking body is more homogeneous, the previous one having had opposing groups among its membership.

The Yugoslav congress, its second since the death of Tito, devoted considerable time to self-criticism. Debates revealed disagreement and frustration, with blame cast on previous communist administrations. According to Milovan Djilas, the meeting was a "meaningless repetition of similar past events."[38] Elections for the two-chamber parliament also took place last year, under a complicated system of delegates. Relations with the USSR remained cordial and correct, with the president of Yugoslavia visiting Moscow during December.

Only the Hungarian and Romanian ruling parties did not hold congresses in 1986, having convened theirs in 1985 and 1984, respectively. However, the regime in Budapest did host the CMEA in early November. That deliberative body heard complaints about shortages of electricity, due to the nuclear accident at Chernobyl. At the beginning of the year, the Soviet-Hungarian Committee on Economic, Technical, and Scientific Cooperation signed 28 agreements on specialization.[39]

Finally, the Romanians are undergoing an economic and political crisis. Nicolae Ceauşescu is basking in a "cult of personality" that includes his wife, who is now in charge of key party appointments. Their son Nicu is an alternate member of the Political Executive Committee (Politburo) and heads the communist youth movement. Relatives of the leader, by birth or marriage, all benefit from institutionalized nepotism. Others in the party hierarchy can never be assured of their positions, unless they ingratiate themselves with the Ceauşescu family.[40]

**The Middle East.** The civil war that broke out in the People's Democratic Republic of Yemen in January devastated the Marxist ruling Yemeni Socialist Party (YSP) and set the already indigent country's development programs back many years.[41] The region's other ruling Marxist movement, the People's Democratic Party of Afghanistan (PDPA), also fared poorly in efforts to widen its political base and to achieve any substantial degree of military control over the countryside, independent of direct Soviet military force. In neither country have the USSR's many years of effort and investment produced reliable and deeply rooted Marxist parties. There seems little doubt that the PDPA would collapse amid slaughter if Soviet occupation troops were to be withdrawn. The YSP's fratricidal struggle resulted in the loss by death or exile of almost all the movement's founders, leaving opportunists and "unreliable" bureaucrats to lead the country. Followers of deposed president Ali Nasir Muhammad in many cases still remain in exile with him. His successor, Haydar Abu Bakr al-Attas, lacks popularity and confronts exacerbated tensions with tribes and with neighboring states that are a legacy of the civil war.

The Tudeh Party of Iran managed to hold a national conference (location unknown) attended by more than 100 cadres "from all over the world, including the party's clandestine organization in Iran."[42] Newly elected Central Committee secretary Ali Khavari criticized the party's early cooperation with the Khomeini regime, whose subsequent repression brought down the Tudeh as well as the Fedayeen-el Khalq and other progressive Iranian groups.[43]

A subsequent revelation that the CIA had given the Teheran regime a list of KGB agents and Tudeh collaborators in 1983—which had precipitated the execution of over 200 suspects, banned the party, and caused the expulsion of eighteen Soviet diplomats—evoked a torrent of abuse at this "disgraceful revelation" that "proved" the continuing link between CIA and Iranian intelligence services.[44] Presumably the broadcasters, operating with Soviet assistance, were aware that the late 1982 defection of Vladimir Kuzichkin, senior KGB officer in Teheran, to the British provided the data later conveyed to Khomeini by the CIA.

News of U.S. arms shipments to Iran provoked angry responses from the USSR, despite heavily publicized plans for renewed Iranian-Soviet economic cooperation announced on 11 December. Iran was attacked by the official USSR government newspaper for helping the United States with its undeclared war against Afghanstan and its "unbridled, hostile campaign" against the Soviet Union over the latter's support for the Kabul government, noting especially Vice Admiral John Poindexter's assertion that some of the weapons sent to Iran were for Afghan guerrillas.[45]

February elections gave the Syrian communists eight seats in the 195-member parliament, with 129 going to the ruling Ba'th party. With two of its members in the cabinet, the communist party exercises the appearance but not the reality of genuine influence. Veteran leader Khalid Bakdash deviates from Ba'th dictates with extreme caution, a recent example being his endorsement for the Palestine Liberation Organization (PLO) to act as sole representative of the Palestinians at a proposed international peace conference on the Middle East.[46] This suggestion came at the time of President Hafez Assad's conflict with PLO leader Yassir Arafat.

The Communist Party of Jordan, which has enjoyed somewhat increased freedom (despite a formal ban) since the sale of weapons were denied to Amman by the U.S. Congress, suffered a setback after violent demonstrations at al-Yarmouk University in April. The party's entire leadership was arrested and not released until September.[47]

Egyptian authorities cracked down late in the year on a communist organization called Revolutionary Current, whose aim, according to the Interior Ministry, is to "impose communism on the country by force." A group of 23 persons was arrested while holding a general congress and, shortly thereafter, an additional 21 members were detained in other districts. Ministry officials trace the group to 1977 arrests of individuals who resumed revolutionary activity following their release from prison. Among the leaders of the group, according to the ministry, are prominent professors, journalists, and attorneys.[48]

**Western Europe.** Only twelve of the region's 23 communist parties are represented in the parliaments of Cyprus, Finland, France, Greece, Iceland, Italy, Luxembourg, Portugal, San Marino, Spain, Sweden, and Switzerland. Party members held no cabinet posts for the third consecutive year, except for San Marino. Four national elections were held during 1986 (compared with seven in 1985). They took place in Austria, France, the Netherlands, and Spain. The Italian Communist Party remains the strongest (29.9 percent of the vote and 198 of 630 seats). Cyprus holds the next highest percentage (27.4), followed by San Marino (24.3), Iceland (17.3), Portugal (15.5), Finland (14), Greece (9.9), France (9.7), and Sweden (5.4).

The leaders of the French Communist Party (PCF) spent virtually the entire year dealing with the domestic and international ramifications of the movement's continuing decline. Unprecedented electoral losses in March[49] prompted reformist demands for an extraordinary party congress (the 26th is scheduled for 1990), while new changes in the electoral system threatened to erode even further the PCF's electoral support. General Secretary Georges Marchais's decision not to stand as a candidate in the 1988 presidential elections is, therefore, not a surprise.

The Communist Party of Italy (PCI) did not experience the same internal strife and concentrated on an effort to cultivate the so-called Euroleft. PCI parliamentary leader Giorgio Napolitano emphasized that "the communist parties can only go forward in the context of a European left." This analysis provided the background for the first PCI extraordinary congress held in Florence in April. At that meeting, the most significant achievements were said to have been made by "members who have participated, and still participate, in the movements characteristic of our time—movements for women's liberation, movements for the emancipation of oppressed peoples, and pacifist and environmental movements."[50] The party continued to talk about the goal of "overcoming the capitalist system," but no longer referred to the teachings of Lenin.

The communists in Spain are the most deeply divided among all movements in Western Europe and are fragmented into three main groups: the official PCE remains Eurocommunist; the secessionist Communist Party of the Peoples of Spain (PCPE) is pro-Soviet; and the Committee for Communist Unity (MUC) is the smallest in size. In preparation for the June elections, the PCE formed a coalition of leftist parties, including the PCPE. This United Left ticket won only seven seats, four by communists. The MUC received 1.1 percent of the vote and no seats.[51]

The Portuguese Communist Party (PCP) is controlled by one of the most Stalinist, pro-Soviet leaderships in the region. Support given by the PCP to socialist Mario Soares contributed to his re-election as president in February. This endorsement came at an extraordinary party congress, convened earlier that same month. PCP backing for Soares was mocked by the press as a decision to "swallow the live toad."[52] For the remainder of the year, the party concentrated its energies on trying unsuccessfully to negotiate a "democratic convergence" in the National Assembly.

In Cyprus, Greece, Malta, San Marino, and Turkey, the weakness of the communist parties did not allow any of them to exert significant influence on the conduct of domestic or foreign affairs. In San Marino, the movement (CPSM) is an extension of the Italian party. The communists, who had received 24.3 percent in the most recent elections, and the Christian Democrats (42.1 percent) formed a coalition for the first time. Of the country's three executive secretaryships, the CPSM received internal affairs.[53]

The Communist Party of Malta (CPM) exerts little impact on Maltese political life but plans to participate in national elections scheduled for April 1987. The CPM continued to maintain substantial contacts with communist parties throughout both parts of Europe. The Maltese labor government, which has extensive economic relations with the USSR, significantly increased the number of economic and cultural agreements with the countries of Eastern Europe.[54]

The Communist Party of Cyprus (AKEL) draws its primary support from the Greek majority that composes approximately 80 percent of the island's population. It is proscribed in the region of the island known as the Turkish Republic of Northern Cyprus. AKEL general secretary Ezekias Papioannou is 78 years old, and the average age of other senior leaders is well over 65. Although these issues were not on the agenda at the party's Sixteenth Congress in November, they pose a major problem for the future.[55] Change may take place after the presidential elections in February 1988.

In Greece, the party remains split into pro-Soviet and Eurocommunist factions. The latter, known as KKE-Interior, has adopted an increasingly independent position and retains little of its Marxist-Leninist heritage. It is represented with one seat in the Greek Parliament, but announced at its Fourth Congress in May that it would dissolve itself in the spring of 1987 and re-emerge as a major component of the noncommunist left, to be known as the New Greek Left (NEA).[56] The pro-Soviet KKE refused to support the ruling socialist PASOK candidates in the second round of October municipal elections, which led to the PASOK loss of Athens, Piraeus, and Saloniki among twenty mayoralties.

The Communist Party of Great Britain (CPGB) continued to experience its lowest membership level since World War II; it has not been represented in parliament since 1950, yet retains one member in the upper house, Lord Milford. The Eurocommunist leadership did not succeed in regaining control over the party newspaper, *Morning Star*, which was seized by a pro-Soviet faction.[57]

The role played by the Communist Party of Denmark (DKP) during the year continued to be insignificant. A former Central Committee member has described the leadership as a clique that prohibits open debate and rejects efforts by the rank and file to participate in policymaking.[58] With the next congress scheduled for April 1987, discussion at the end of the year focused on possible successors to the party chairman, who may resign at age 65 with a meager record during his ten years of leadership. In an effort at renewal, the Belgian movement modified its structure and leadership at the Twenty-fifth Congress in April 1986. Louis Van Geyt retained his position as president, although both vice presidents for Wallonia and Flanders resigned.[59] The party has moved in the direction of a federalized structure.

The internal affairs of the Finnish Communist Party (SKP) were characterized by factional strife throughout the year. The draft of a new program appeared that will be presented at the next congress, scheduled for June 1987. The purpose is to "examine Finland and the world in terms of the future" and to develop the SKP into a popular movement.[60] The most striking feature is the absence of doctrinal phrases and professed allegiance to Marxism-Leninism. The response of the hard-line minority came when it elected a duplicate set of officials from among those expelled from the SKP. The split, therefore, seems final.

Richard F. Staar
*Hoover Institution*

## NOTES

1. *Pravda* (Moscow), 26 February 1986, p. 1.
2. Ibid., pp. 2–10, carries the full text.
3. Ibid., 7 March 1986, pp. 3–8.
4. Kevin Devlin, "The World Communist Movement," RFE/RL, *RAD Background Report*, no. 1 (3 January 1987): 57.
5. See Table 1.3 in Richard F. Staar, *USSR Foreign Policies After Détente*, rev. ed. (Stanford, Calif.: Hoover Institution Press, 1987), p. 14, for all 24 revolutionary democratic movements.
6. U.S. Central Intelligence Agency, *World Factbook: Nineteen Hundred and Eighty-Six*, CR WF 86-001 (Washington, D.C.: U.S. Government Printing Office, 1986).
7. Radio Maputo, 22 May 1986; *FBIS*, 28 May 1986.
8. *New York Times*, 12 September 1986.
9. Radio Luanda, 6 February 1986; *FBIS*, 7 February 1986.
10. Ibid., 29 August 1986; *FBIS*, 29 August 1986.
11. Ibid., 19 November 1986; *FBIS*, 20 November 1986.
12. Radio Addis Ababa, 12 September 1986; *FBIS*, 15 September 1986.
13. *NYT*, 28 October 1986. See also "Power and Famine in Ethiopia," *Wall Street Journal*, 12 January 1987.
14. *African Communist* (London), no. 106 (1986): 26; NCNA (Beijing), 18 September 1986.
15. *World Marxist Review* (Toronto) 29, no. 1 (January 1986): 44.
16. *Krasnaia zvezda* (Moscow), 20 June 1986, p. 3.
17. *WMR* 29, no. 8 (August 1986): 39–40.
18. Ibid., no. 5 (May 1986): 118.
19. *Der Spiegel* (Hamburg), 28 April 1986; *Barricada* (Managua), 3 October 1986; *Nicaragua Hoy*, supplement to *La Nacion* (San Jose, Costa Rica), 31 January 1987.
20. *Pravda*, 3, 6 March 1986; *Izvestiia* (Moscow), 8 March 1986.
21. *Los Angeles Times*, 6 November 1986.
22. *Granma*, 27 December 1986.
23. *Resumen Semanal* (Lima), 24–30 October 1986.
24. *Intercontinental Press* (New York), 28 July 1986.
25. *WMR* 29, no. 5 (May 1986): 5–9.
26. *Christian Science Monitor*, 6 January 1987; *WSJ*, 12 January 1987.

27. *WSJ*, 19 January 1987, p. 21.
28. *Zuzhi renshi xinxi bao* (Beijing), 8 January 1987; *FBIS*, 8 January 1987.
29. *Nhan Dan* (Hanoi), 16 December 1986.
30. Devlin, "World Communist Movement."
31. Voice of the People of Burma (clandestine), 7 February 1986; *FBIS*, 12 February 1986.
32. *Times of India* (Delhi), 30 June 1986.
33. *Rruga e partise* (Tirana), no. 11 (November 1986): 86.
34. *Rude pravo* (Prague), 25 March 1986.
35. *Rabotnichesko delo* (Sofia), 9 June 1986.
36. *Bild* (Hamburg), 24 July 1986, pp. 1, 5.
37. *Trybuna ludu* (Warsaw), 4 July 1986.
38. *Daily Telegraph* (London), 27 June 1986.
39. *Nepszava* (Budapest), 31 December 1986.
40. RFE, *Situation Report*, 24 February 1986.
41. *Pravda*, 19 December 1986, p. 4.
42. *Morning Star* (London), 23 July 1986.
43. *Pravda*, 4 March 1986; *FBIS*, 19 March 1986.
44. Radio of Iran Toilers (clandestine from USSR), 26 November 1986; *FBIS*, 28 November 1986.
45. *Izvestiia*, 1 December 1986.
46. *Pravda*, 6 March 1986; *FBIS*, 25 March 1986; *The Soviet Union in the Middle East* 11, nos. 3–4 (1986): 18–20.
47. *Jordan Times* (Amman), 5 September 1986.
48. Radio Cairo, 16 December 1986; *FBIS*, 17 December 1986.
49. *Le Monde*, 17 March 1986.
50. *NYT*, 3 February 1986; *L'Unita* (Rome), 10 April 1986.
51. *Diario 16* (Madrid), 3 July 1986; *JPRS*, 19 August 1986.
52. *NYT*, 19 February 1986. See also *Pravda*, 31 December 1987, p. 4, which mentions PCP leader Alvaro Cunhal's visit to Moscow.
53. *La Repubblica* (Rome), 16 July 1986.
54. *The Times* (Malta), 7 Decembr 1986.
55. *The Economist* (London), 16 November 1986.
56. Devlin, "World Communist Movement," p. 57.
57. Ibid., p. 56.
58. *Socialistisk Weekend* (Copenhagen), 15 August 1986.
59. *Drapeau Rouge* (Brussels), 17 June 1986.
60. *Kansan Uutiset* (Helsinki), 24 January 1986.

# AFRICA

# Introduction

Many of the problems that plagued Marxist ruling parties and communist movements in past years persisted in 1986. The year was also marked by leadership changes through death, defections, or reorganizations. Replacements at the top took place in Mozambique, Angola, Zimbabwe, Ethiopia, and the Congo as well as within the South African Communist Party and Senegal's Party of Independence and Labor.

Mozambique's Front for the Liberation of Mozambique (FRELIMO), a "Marxist-Leninist vanguard party," suffered a loss in 1986 with the death of President Samora Machel in an airplane crash on 19 October. Foreign Minister Joaquim Alberto Chissano then became FRELIMO president as well as head of state and commander of the armed forces. Chissano is regarded as a moderate and pragmatic politician who is likely to continue his predecessor's policies of simultaneously fighting the rebels, looking to the West for aid, and keeping the People's Republic of Mozambique within the Soviet orbit (*NYT*, 21 October). Machel's death caused a temporary interruption in the country's elections for local, provincial, and national assemblies, which were completed in December. Mozambique signed a cooperation agreement with the Council of Mutual Economic Assistance (CMEA), the first of its kind with a southern African country (Maputo Domestic Service, 22 May; *FBIS*, 28 May). The military success of the Mozambique National Resistance (RENAMO), which is fighting in much of the countryside, has placed the FRELIMO government in an ever more precarious position.

In Angola, leadership changes also marked the year for the ruling Marxist-Leninist party, the Popular Movement for the Liberation of Angola–Labor Party (MPLA-PT). President José Eduardo dos Santos carried out a number of reorganizations. In February, he removed his second in command and head of ideology, Lucio Lara, from the Politburo, in addition to the former director of security and intelligence operations, Ludy Kissassunda, and the minister of agriculture, Evaristo Domingos (Radio Luanda, 6 February; *FBIS*, 7 February). They were veteran revolutionaries on the Politburo, and their removal implied the dismissal of doubters about dos Santos's policies on the economy and war with the National Union for the Total Independence of Angola (UNITA). In August, Antonio dos Santos Neto was dismissed from the post of director of the Central Committee Department of Defense and Security and was replaced by José Pereira Teixeira (Radio Luanda, 29 August; *FBIS*, 29 August). Later in the year, corruption was cited as the reason for further dismissals or for the posting of party members as ambassadors abroad (Radio Luanda, 19 November; *FBIS*, 20 November).

Much of the MPLA-PT's attention was directed toward the lingering guerrilla war with Dr. Jonas Savimbi's UNITA, which remains the dominant force in the southeastern region. In spite of the presence of some 30,000 Cuban troops and advisers, UNITA remains unconquered. Savimbi's visit to Washington, D.C., in January brought UNITA greater recognition and U.S. shipments of arms to counter the Soviet and Cuban military assistance to the MPLA-PT.

In nearby Zimbabwe, the ruling party, the Zimbabwe African National Union (ZANU), expanded its parliamentary majority of 62 seats by two additional seats through defections. ZANU president and prime minister of the country Robert Mugabe has thus begun to move toward a one-party state and a powerful executive presidency. While ZANU professes to be Marxist in orientation, the economy has remained politically mixed; the government owns major businesses and newspapers. Mugabe's moves over the past year have strengthened his position in the party and created a more centralized party structure. But ZANU continued to face deep ethnic rivalries within its ranks and the country itself.

ZANU is a party dominated by the Shona ethnic community, which makes up some 80 percent of the country's population. The Ndebele, who constitute much of the remaining population, continued in large measure not only outside ZANU but also within the Zimbabwe African People's Union (ZAPU)—a rival party formed during the independence struggle. Bitter fighting between ZANU and ZAPU has characterized their past dealings, despite merger talks during the year. Within ZANU, the party was riven by clashes between rival clans of the Shona people in 1986. Mugabe defused the conflicts, which stemmed from charges of malfeasance and ethnic antagonism, by expelling Herbert Ushewokunze from the Politburo and by relieving Byron Hove from his position as ZANU secretary in the Midland province. Mugabe is being drawn deeper into fighting in the Beira Corridor in Mozambique alongside its hard-pressed ally, FRELIMO. In September, Zimbabwe hosted the eighth summit of the Movement of Non-aligned Nations, during which Mugabe was elected to serve as the movement's chairman until 1989 (*NYT*, 12 September).

The Workers' Party of Ethiopia (WPE), headed by General Secretary Mengistu Haile Mariam, completed the drafting of a constitution for what is to become the People's Democratic Republic of Ethiopia. The draft constitution also calls for the WPE to be the vanguard party and the "guiding force of the state and the entire society" (Addis Ababa Domestic Service, 12 September; *FBIS*, 15 September). The draft constitution in the main sets up a legislative structure and government bureaucracy to carry out the directives of the WPE. Ethiopia continued its forcible resettlement of the population from the north to the southwest region. Three million people were relocated in the villagization program, which could encompass as many as 30 million (*NYT*, 28 October). Foreign Minister Goshu Wolde fled Ethiopia and sought political asylum in the West. He stated that "doctrinaire policies are leading the country and the people into misery and destruction" (ibid.). His replacement is one of the most powerful figures in the Politburo of the WPE, Berhanu Bayih.

The South African Communist Party (SACP) also underwent leadership losses with the death in Mozambique of Moses Mabhida, the 62-year-old African general secretary. A party member since 1942, Mabhida had been an active trade unionist, served as general secretary since 1978, and was a member of the Executive Committee of the African National Congress (ANC) until his death. Shortly thereafter, the SACP announced that Joe Slovo, a 60-year-old, Lithuanian-born white barrister who had also been active in the party since the 1940s, had been elected party chairman. For the SACP, Slovo's election was viewed as symbolizing "the new era in which our party lives and fights—the era of revolutionary struggle for the final liberation of the South African people. . ." (*African Communist*, no. 106).

The SACP continued its close collaboration with the ANC amid charges that communists control the latter. ANC president Oliver Tambo asserted: "We cooperate a lot, but the ANC is accepted by the SACP as leading the struggle" (*Cape Times*, 4 November 1985). The SACP optimistically viewed the widespread violence in South Africa as confirmation that "the idea of a people's war has taken root" (*African Communist*, no. 107).

The SACP also continued its longtime affinity with the Soviet Union but, in a break with the past, an SACP delegation led by Slovo also made a ten-day visit to China after decades of hostility to the Chinese Communist Party (NCNA, 18 September). Earlier in the year, Slovo received the Order of the Friendship of the Peoples of the USSR on the occasion of his 60th birthday.

In the People's Republic of Congo, the Congolese Party of Labor (PCT) engaged in a continuous purge of "alien elements" (*WMR*, January). In August, a death sentence was passed against Claude Ndalla, a prominent leftist critic of the regime. Five-year suspended sentences were meted out to Jean-Pierre Thystere Tchikaya, who until 1985 had been the second most powerful man in the country, and army colonel Blaise Nzalakanda; these sentences indicated that intraparty rivalries have spilled into the military.

President and General Secretary Denis Sassou-Ngouesso addressed the army on its twentieth anniversary and stressed the importance of indoctrination and increased party control (*Krasnaya Zvesda*, 20 June).

In the west African country of the People's Republic of Benin, the Revolutionary Party of the People of Benin (PRPB) continued its main preoccupation of the previous year: consolidating the party at the grassroots level. To implement this goal, the PRPB placed greater emphasis on party-building activities by the twelve Politburo members instead of administrative duties, set up regular party publications, and moved to establish a party school (*WMR*, August). At the fourth ordinary session of the Central Committee, the members conceded to requirements from the International Monetary Fund (IMF) in order to receive assistance to revive the economy and address the growing debt.

Among Senegal's numerous Marxist and left-leaning parties, the one recognized by Moscow, the Party of Independence and Labor (PIT), lost its chairman when Seydou Cissoko died at the age of 57. Cissoko had been a founder of the PIT and served as its general secretary from 1967 to 1984, when he was elected chairman at the party's Second Congress. He died while attending the twenty-seventh Congress of the Communist Party of the Soviet Union (CPSU) in Moscow. Since the post of chairman had been created specifically for Cissoko when he stepped down from the general secretaryship, no successor was immediately named (*WMR*, May).

The PIT's most active point in the year came with its hosting a conference, in conjunction with the *World Marxist Review*, on the "Socio-Economic Development of Black Africa and Problems of Democracy." Representatives came from all the main Senegalese political parties, including the ruling Socialist Party (PS), as well as intellectuals, trade union leaders, and delegates from Nigeria, the French Communist Party, and the *African Communist*. However, Senegal refused visas to representatives from the *World Marxist Review*, the Soviet Union, and East Germany; delegates from Ethiopia and the Sudanese Communist Party were refused entry at the airport (*African Communist*, no. 106).

The Sudanese Communist Party's (SCP) election platform, dated 6 March, called for the adoption of a democratic constitution during the election of a Constituent Assembly, which was held in April. The SCP took only two of the 301 seats in the assembly, but the party stood to benefit within Sudan as Khartoum and Moscow moved during the year to improve their bilateral relationship. Each country exchanged delegate visits and entered into joint communiqués.

On the island of Réunion, which is a French overseas department and hence an integral part of the French Republic, the Réunion Communist Party (PCR) captured only 29.2 percent of the vote in the 16 March legislative election and 28 percent in the regional election. Thus, it lost the presidency of the Regional Assembly to a conservative member. By use of a proportional representation voting system, the PCR did get two of the five seats in the National Assembly, which met in Paris; this is the first time in 30 years that the PCR has been represented in that body.

In both Nigeria and Lesotho, the parties displayed only limited activities. The military government in Lesotho has prohibited all political activity, but General Secretary Jacob M. Kena of the Communist Party of Lesotho (CPL) attended the congress of the World Federation of Trade Unions in East Berlin in his capacity as the leader of the Mine Workers' Union. Other members of the CPL attended communist meetings, some anonymously, others openly. In Nigeria, the Socialist Working People's Party (SWPP) appeared on the surface to be the least active of the movements in this region. General Secretary Dapo Fatogun did attend the Marxist conference in Senegal noted above, but the extent that the SWPP played any role in the political life of Nigeria is difficult to assess.

In neighboring Somalia, a country not covered in the following profiles, the Somali People's Vanguard Party (SPVP) is worthy of a brief mention in this introduction. The SPVP grew out of a "Unity Conference" of the Communist Party of Somalia and the Somali Working People's Party in February 1985. The long-term aim of the SPVP is the "creation of a socialist society in which there would be no exploitation of man by man" (*African Communist*, no. 104). Many of the leaders of the new party are known activists in Somalia, and the general secretary is Omer Salad Elmi (ibid.).

Thomas H. Henriksen
*Hoover Institution*

# Angola

**Population.** 8,164,000
**Party.** Popular Movement for the Liberation of Angola–Labor Party (Movimento Popular de Libertação de Angola–Partido do Trabalho; MPLA-PT)
**Founded.** 1956 (renamed, 1977)
**Membership.** 35,000 (*African Communist*, no. 105 [Second Quarter 1986]: 58)
**General Secretary.** José Eduardo dos Santos
**Politburo.** 11 members
**Central Committee.** 90 members
**Status.** Ruling party
**Last Congress.** Second, 9–11 December 1985
**Last Election.** 1980; all 203 candidates MPLA-PT approved
**Auxiliary Organizations.** MPLA Youth (JMPLA), Organization of Angolan Women (OMA), Angolan Teachers' Association, National Union of Angolan Workers (UNTA)
**Publications.** No data

In 1986 Angola continued to suffer from the civil war that has decimated the country since independence in 1975. The attempts of the MPLA-PT to consolidate its rule suffered setbacks as often as it moved forward. The position of the armed opposition, the National Union for the Total Independence of Angola (UNITA), continued to improve, particularly with the barnstorming trip by UNITA leader Dr. Jonas Savimbi to the United States in January and to Western Europe in the spring. News reports indicated shortly thereafter that the United States had begun shipments of arms, including antiaircraft Stingers, to UNITA, thereby reducing its dependence on South Africa. The MPLA-PT continued to rely on Cuban troops and Soviet arms while the Angolan economy quietly deteriorated.

**Party Leadership.** The leadership of the party remained in the hands of President dos Santos. In the course of the year, however, he carried out a number of reorganizations that severely shook the structure of the MPLA-PT. In February, he removed his second in command and head of ideology, Lucio Lara, from the Politburo, along with Ludy Kissassunda, formerly director of the security and intel-

ligence operation (DISA), Evaristo Domingos, minister of agriculture, and João Luis Neto (Radio Luanda, 6 February; *FBIS*, 7 February). They were veteran revolutionaries in the Politburo, and their removal implied excision of the remaining doubters about dos Santos' policies on the economy and the war with UNITA.

With that shift, dos Santos largely settled his leadership problems for the year. An exception came in August, when Antonio dos Santos Neto was dismissed from the post of director of the Central Committee Department of Defense and Security. He was replaced by José Pereira Teixeira. (Radio Luanda, 29 August; *FBIS*, 29 August.) Some problems of corruption also appeared later in the year whereby the minister of construction was replaced and some leading party members were dispatched as ambassadors abroad, but generally the position of dos Santos as party leader was secure. (Radio Luanda, 19 November; *FBIS*, 20 November.)

**Party Affairs.** The top organs of the MPLA-PT held their usual meetings in the course of 1986. The Central Committee met on 16–17 January, where emphasis was placed on the need for increased agricultural output and the role of front organizations in the life of Angola. The number of Central Committee departments was expanded to include those two areas, with Santana Andre Pitra appointed to the job of heading Agrarian Policy and Paulo Miguel appointed to head the Department of Youth and Mass and Social Organizations. (Radio Luanda, 18 January; *FBIS*, 21 January.) Immediately thereafter, the eleventh ordinary session of the People's Assembly opened on 23 January and engaged in its usual formalistic activities on the budget.

The party was reported to have about 35,000 members, comprising industrial workers (26.4 percent), peasants (23 percent), intellectuals (6 percent), government officials (21.9 percent), and others (*African Communist*, no. 105 [Second Quarter, 1986]).

As oil prices continued to fall, the party preached increasing austerity for the Angolan people. In March, the Politburo enacted a number of specific measures, entailing even greater sacrifice "for the revolution," that were ratified by the Central Committee in June (Radio Luanda, 25 June; *FBIS*, 26 June). The People's Assembly held on 11–13 August confirmed the trend. By the time of dos Santos' year-end address, he was able to recognize the problems caused by the economy. The first paragraph of his speech dealt with the oil revenue crisis: "The entire country has felt its effect, and the first months of 1986 were in fact marked by a certain uneasiness among cadres and officials who, taken aback by the sudden fall in the price of oil on the world market, had no ready answers in confronting this serious situation" (Radio Luanda, 1 January 1987; *FBIS*, 2 January 1987). His speech clarified the change of emphasis in the party that had been made possible by the departure of Lucio Lara; dos Santos spoke extensively of budgetary and military problems, but little was said of ideology.

**International Relations.** There was little change in the pattern of Angolan foreign relations during 1986, except for enhanced hostility toward the United States. The willingness of the United States to receive UNITA president Savimbi in Washington, and the subsequent leak to the media of the increased flow of U.S. military assistance to UNITA, created tension between Washington and Luanda. In concrete terms, however, little changed, since the MPLA-PT has long accused UNITA of being dependent on outside forces.

The MPLA-PT continued to form ties with the communist world and Third World socialists. The year opened with diplomatic relations being established with Iran and the visit of Iran's president to Luanda (Radio Luanda, 14, 19 January; *FBIS*, 15, 23 January). The new economic agreement signed on 30 January by Lopo do Nascimento during his Moscow visit called for Soviet assistance in building up a meat-processing complex and farm machine/tractor stations. Little was done to correct the chronic trade imbalance between the two countries; in 1984, Soviet exports to Angola were $183 million whereas Angolan exports to the Soviet Union were only $4 million. (Xinhua, 31 January; *FBIS*, 5 February.)

Dos Santos attended the twenty-seventh Congress of the Communist Party of the Soviet Union (CPSU) and gave a rousing condemnation of "imperialist forces" undermining the MPLA-PT (*Pravda*, 1 March; *FBIS*, 17 March). He returned for a bilateral visit in May. Concrete assistance—described as from Soviet sources—included reconstruction of numerous railway bridges, a new hospital in Lubango, and $86 million for the purchase of equipment (Radio Luanda, 6 May; *FBIS*, 6 May). Aside from the usual discussions, dos Santos met with Gorbachev for extended talks and for the signing of the CPSU-MPLA-PT party cooperation document for 1986–1988 (TASS, 6 May; *FBIS*, 7 May). Emphasis was said to be placed on "consultations on current international problems, interparty cooperation, training of cadres, and assistance to MPLA–Labor Party schools" (Radio Luanda, 9 May; *FBIS*, 9 May). The final communiqué for the visit stressed both sides' satisfaction with the ten years of the USSR-Angola Friendship and Cooperation Treaty of October 1976 (*Pravda*, 11 May; *FBIS*, 20 May).

A variety of cooperation agreements were signed with communist countries during the course of the year. The German Democratic Republic signed an agreement on the training of youth cadres that focused on Angolan youth attending the East German science institute during the following five years (Radio Luanda, 19 March; *FBIS*, 25 March). In April, the Angolan-Cuban Commission for Bilateral Cooperation confirmed prior agreements and extended the scope of their defense ties (Radio Luanda, 9 April; *FBIS*, 10 April). In August, Soviet delegates signed the technical cooperation protocol for 1986–1990, including the establishment of an Angolan state corporation in the construction area (*Izvestiia*, 4 August; *FBIS*, 7 August). In November, the Hungarians agreed to increase their cooperation in economic and technical areas, with priority given to agriculture (seed production) and automobile assembly training (Radio Luanda, 5 November; *FBIS*, 6 November).

There was much international activity in Luanda both before and after the Harare (Zimbabwe) Non-aligned Summit of early September; for example, Fidel Castro spent several days in Angola after the meeting (Radio Luanda, 10 September; *FBIS*, 11 September). Dos Santos attended the summit in order to generate Third World support for the MPLA-PT in opposition to UNITA. Regional affairs took priority as dos Santos attempted to work out an arrangement with Zambia for Angolan army forces to operate from Zambian territory. After Savimbi made that demarche public, however, Zambia pulled back from whatever tentative commitment it had made (Radio Johannesburg, 22 August; clandestine KUP, 21 September; *FBIS*, 22 August, 23 September).

Richard E. Bissell
*Georgetown University*

# Benin

**Population.** 4,141,000
**Party.** Revolutionary Party of the People of Benin (Parti Révolutionnaire du Peuple du Bénin; PRPB)
**Founded.** 1975
**Membership.** Less than 2,000
**Chairman.** Mathieu Kerekou
**Politburo.** 11 members, elected November 1985: Mathieu Kerekou, Martin Dohou Azonhiho, Joseph Deguela, Gado Girigissou, Roger Imorou Garba, Justin Gnidehou, Sanni Mama Gomina, Romain Vilon Guezo, Vincent Guezodje, Idi Abdoulaye Malam, Simon Ifede Ogouma
**Central Committee.** 45 members
**Status.** Sole and ruling party
**Last Congress.** Second, November 1985
**Last Election.** 1984, all 196 National Assembly members approved by and on the PRPB list.
**Auxiliary Organizations.** Organization of the Revolutionary Youth of Benin (PJRB); Organization of the Revolutionary Women of Benin (OFRB); National Federal of Workers' Unions of Benin (UNSTB); Committees for the Defense of the Revolution (CDR)
**Publications.** *Handoria* (PRPB publication); *Ehuzu* (government-controlled daily)

The main preoccupation of the ruling PRPB remained the same as in previous years: the expansion and strengthening of the party itself. In a revealing article in the *World Marxist Review* (August), Politburo member Azonhiho clearly made the recruiting of new party members a priority, and he admitted that, after more than ten years of existence, the PRPB formation "has been consummated mainly at the higher and medium levels. There are no primary organizations at industrial facilities, in the services industry, in garrisons, at schools and institutions of higher learning, [or] in residential neighborhoods" (ibid.). In other words, there has been no real link between the party and the population, and control of the latter by the former has been shaky, even in the vital case of the military. The main instrument selected to improve this situation was an attempt to strengthen the separation line between state and party positions. Thus, the twelve Politburo members were encouraged to stress their party-building activity rather than continuing to spend most of their time on administrative and governmental activities. In practical terms, this resulted in the reduction of Central Committee departments from twelve to seven (ibid.). To improve the ideological training of existing members, both *Handoria* and the party's theoretical journal were to become regular publications, and a party school was to be established.

**Domestic Affairs.** On the domestic scene, the largest problem confronting the regime was still the state of the economy, which continued to deteriorate at a rapid pace. The Central Committee's fourth ordinary session in August concluded with a decision to accept a structural readjustment program suggested by the International Monetary Fund (IMF). The main reasons for this humiliating concession were given as the international economic crisis and the "lack of performance of the public and semipublic enterprises, because most of them did not fulfill their missions well" (*FBIS*, 14 August). Another reason given was the growing debt, which had accumulated as a result of heavy investments in industrial projects that were not matched by growing exports (ibid.).

The dramatic economic situation that forced the regime to accept IMF conditions came on the heels of growing domestic difficulties, such as plots by junior army officers, vocal opposition from radical intellectuals, and indications of unreliability on the part of the police forces (*Africa Now*, April). All this resulted in a general toughening of the regime, including open hostility to external critics and denial of entry visas.

**Foreign Affairs.** Despite the fact that Benin's ideological friends, such as Libya and the Soviet bloc, did not provide any significant help with the economy, the regime's foreign policy remained closely linked to them.

So far as relations with Libya were concerned, the highpoint came after the U.S. bombing of that country in April. A PRPB statement the day of the raid qualified the attack as "ignoble and barbaric aggression" and a result of "the warlike maneuvers of American imperialism" (*FBIS*, 16 April).

Regarding contacts with communist states, Benin continued its policy of good relations with both the USSR and China. Thus, although Kerekou's visit to Moscow in November were his first, he carefully balanced it with a trip to China the same month; although Bulgaria was included in the itinerary, so were North Korea and Yugoslavia. Speaking before his departure, Kerekou made it clear that his main objective was economic: "For us, essentially it will be more a question of exchanging our experiences . . . and jointly finding ways and means to fight the nefarious effects of the world economic crisis, drought, desertification, and other natural calamities with which our country is so harshly confronted" (*FBIS*, 24 November). It is significant that the announcement of Kerekou's trip to the USSR, Bulgaria, Yugoslavia, North Korea, and China came the same day as a new aid agreement with France was signed. The aid package included an amount of 275 million francs to be used for the National University, road maintenance, and water management (ibid. 13 November).

Michael Radu
*Foreign Policy Research Institute, Philadelphia*

# Congo

**Population.** 1,853,000
**Party.** Congolese Party of Labor (Parti Congolaise du Travail; PCT)
**Founded.** 1969
**Membership.** 9,000 (estimated)
**Chairman.** Denis Sassou-Ngouesso
**Politburo.** No data
**Status.** Ruling and sole official party
**Last Congress.** Third, July 1984, in Brazzaville
**Last Election.** 1984, 95 percent, all 153 members PCT approved
**Auxiliary Organizations.** Congolese Trade Union Confederation (CSC); Revolutionary Union of Congolese Women (URFC); Union of Congolese Socialist Youth (UJSC)
**Publications.** *Mweti* (daily, under government control); *Etumba* (weekly, organ of the PCT Central Committee); *Elikia* (quarterly, under PCT control)

The People's Republic of Congo is the oldest self-proclaimed Marxist-Leninist state in Africa. It gained independence from France in 1960 and was known as Congo-Brazzaville; in 1968 the country witnessed a radical military coup, and in 1969 it was proclaimed a People's Republic. Since then the regime has claimed allegiance to "scientific socialism" and has moved increasingly closer to the Soviet bloc in ideological, political, and military terms; however, the Congo has remained dependent on trade with the West and has received significant amounts of French foreign aid.

**Party and Domestic Affairs.** From an ideological viewpoint, 1986 started with an almost formal Soviet recognition of the Leninist, "vanguard" nature of the PCT, together with the ruling parties in Benin and Ethiopia (*WMR*, January). PCT Central Committee member Kouka-Kampo was quoted as saying that the party had the same number of members as it did a few years ago, about 9,000, because it was engaged in continuous purges directed at "alien elements" (ibid.).

The *WMR* article also observed that of the three parties under discussion, the PCT was the most deeply implanted at the grass-roots level—a fact

that, if true, may be explained by the relatively large number of members in proportion to the total population. Kouka-Kampo also implied that the purges were related to a process of ideological purification, which had been accelerated since the beginning of a series of early "theoretical colloquia" between the PCT and the Communist Party of the Soviet Union (CPSU); the sixth (and most recent) of the colloquia took place in 1985 in Brazzaville.

During the year purges and demotions did occur, in some cases involving formerly prominent leaders. In August, a death sentence was passed against Claude Ndalla, who was accused of plotting the 1982 bombings in the capital. Ndalla had been one of the most prominent radicals in the country since the mid-1960s and a consistent critic of the regime from a leftist position. At the same trial, a suspended five-year sentence was imposed on Jean-Pierre Thystere Tchikaya, who until 1985 had been the second most powerful man in the country (*FBIS*, 18 August). The fact that Tchikaya received a suspended sentence may indicate that he has retained enough support, domestically or internationally (from the Soviets), not only to have his life spared but perhaps also to come back in the future. Equally interesting is the similar sentence given to army colonel Blaise Nzalakanda, since it indicated that intraparty rivalries have spilled into the military and that the present leadership cannot be completely sure of the loyalty of even prominent military officers. The seriousness of the problem was underscored by President and General Secretary Sassou-Ngouesso himself during his address to the servicemen on the twentieth anniversary of the National People's Army (Armee Nationale Populaire; ANP). He stressed the importance of indoctrination of the military and the need for increased party control over it. The speech was considered important enough to be printed by the Soviet Army's own journal (see *Krasnaya Zvesda*, 20 June).

On 30 November, the Central committee of the PCT was convened unexpectedly and decided to reduce the size of the Politburo from thirteen to ten. This amounted to a purge; the three victims were Pierre Nze, formerly in charge of external affairs for the Secretariat and one of the few prominent civilians left in the decisionmaking apparatus; Foreign Minister Antoine N'Dinga Oba, who retained his cabinet post; and Health Minister Combo Matsiona. (*Afrique-Asie*, 12–25 January 1987.) Despite the apparent importance of the purge, by the end of the year it was still unclear what implications it might have for the position of the president and the direction of PCT affairs in general.

**Economic Affairs.** The primary preoccupation of the regime during 1986 was the economy, which worsened steadily as the result of years of mismanagement and collapsing oil prices. The severity of the situation was demonstrated by a decision to cut the state budget in half (*FBIS*, 24 March). Although the salaries of the overgrown number of state employees were not touched, the regime finally had to ask its Western creditors to reschedule its debt. Following negotiations with the major creditors (France, the United States, Brazil, England, and Switzerland), a ten-year repayment schedule was agreed upon in July. The agreement was the result of previous Congolese acceptance of International Monetary Fund (IMF) demands for restructuring the state sector, giving a larger share of the economy to the private sector, and taking more responsible approaches to the size and structure of the government budget.

In large part as a result of this forced reassessment of economic realities, the regime also proclaimed its intention of shifting emphasis from the urban industrial/service sector to agriculture, with the proclaimed goal of improving rural life, eliminating "backwardness," and stopping the continuous exodus toward the cities (*FBIS*, 29 April). As part of the Structural Adjustment Program adopted by the government and linked directly to the twenty-year agreement signed with the IMF, a politically risky measure was adopted: the imposition of a highly unpopular tax on city dwellers that was intended to enhance food production. Finally, what in different circumstances would have been very promising news, the discovery of the rich Tchiboula oil field had little impact in an era of cheap oil and scarce investment capital in that industry.

**Foreign Affairs.** The most important, and problematic, development of 1986 was Sassou-Ngouesso's election as chairman of the Organization of African Unity (OAU). Despite his relatively skillfull handling of the position, he had no choice but to alienate certain African countries, as well as some Western states, while making little headway in solving perennial African conflicts such as those in Chad and Western Sahara. Thus, by receiving the "president" of the so-called Sahrawi Democratic Arab Republic in June, Sassou-Ngouesso reinforced existing differences over the issue; meetings with the leaders of Benin and Sao Tome encouraged further accusations of leftist bias; and a meeting with the Libyan protégé in Chad, Goukouni Weddei, was seen as an insult by the recognized government in N'Djamena—despite Sassou-Ngouesso's attempts to play a balanced role and the sincere admission that the OAU had again failed to solve the military and legitimacy crisis in Chad (see *FBIS*, 29 April). As a counter to accusations of leftist bias, the Congo greatly improved relations with Egypt, which offered economic aid, and with such moderate francophone states as Senegal and Togo. Despite a small but violent border incident in June, the Congo has also maintained good relations with neighboring Zaire.

Relations with the West continued to remain stable, as did the flow of aid. The latter was the main topic of discussion during a meeting in Brazzaville between French cooperation minister Michel Aurillac and Prime Minister Poungui in May. Despite the official PCT condemnation of the U.S. raid on Libya, and the even stronger language used in a joint communiqué with the Palestine Liberation Organization during Yassir Arafat's visit in May, relations with the United States improved. The most significant development in this respect was Sassou-Ngouesso's visit to Washington, D.C., in September, where he met President Reagan. The meeting dispelled some of the clouds in bilateral relations following clearly antisemitic remarks made at the United Nations by Congolese foreign minister Oba. Following strong U.S. protests, Sassou-Ngouesso himself offered a formal apology.

Brazzaville's relations with the communist world continued as usual with closer party and government ties to the Soviet bloc and fairly good relations with China. Both Moscow and Brazzaville celebrated the fifth anniversary of the signing of the Congo-USSR treaty of friendship and cooperation; the Soviets took the opportunity to point out the results of their aid, including the PCT party school, a coal mine, the Cosmos Hotel, and the training of hundreds of cadres (*Izvestiia*, 13 May). Such ties were further strengthened when a new accord was signed between the two ruling parties, providing for joint colloquia and Soviet training of Congolese cadres (*Pravda*, 8 April). More details were discussed at the August meeting in Brazzaville between the deputy chairman of the CPSU control

commission, Voropayev, and high-level PCT leaders (ibid., 19 August). That same month, a PCT control-commission delegation met its Mozambican counterpart in Inhambane for an exchange of views and experience (*WMR*, August). Additional contacts with the Soviet bloc and its close allies included a visit by Nicaraguan Daniel Ortega to the Congo in August, PCT member Pierre Nze's trip to Romania in October, and the signing of agreements with Bulgaria and Poland. In contrast, a PCT Politburo delegation headed by ideology chief Goma Foutou visited China in March and met with the Chinese party counterparts (*FBIS-China*, 18 March). In July, a Chinese delegation led by the deputy minister for information visited the Congo and signed an agreement of cooperation between the two countries' information agencies.

Michael Radu
*Foreign Policy Research Institute*
*Philadelphia*

# Ethiopia

**Population.** 35,210,000 (*Political Handbook of the World, 1986–87*)
**Party.** Workers' Party of Ethiopia (WPE)
**Founded.** September 1984
**Membership.** 50,000
**General Secretary.** Mengistu Haile Mariam
**Politburo.** 11 full members: Mengistu Haile Mariam, Fikre-Selassie Wogderess, Fisseha Desta, Tesfaye Gebre Kidan, Berhanu Bayih, Legesse Asfaw, Addis Tedlay, Hailu Yimenu, Amanuel Amde Michael, Alenu Abebe, Shimelis Mazengia; 6 alternate members
**Secretariat.** 8 members: Fisseha Desta, Legesse Asfaw, Shimelis Mazengia, Fasika Sidelil, Shewandagn Belete, Wubeset Desie, Ashagre Yigletu, Embibel Ayele
**Central Committee.** 136 full members, 64 alternate members
**Status.** Ruling party
**Last Congress.** First, 6–10 September 1984, in Addis Ababa
**Last Election.** None
**Auxiliary Organizations.** All-Ethiopian Peasants' Association; Kebelles; All-Ethiopia Trade Union; Revolutionary Ethiopia's Women's Association; Revolutionary Ethiopia's Youth Association
**Publications.** *Serto Ader, Meskerem, Yekatit, Addis Zemen, Ethiopian Herald, Negarit Gazeta*

The most important development in 1986 was the drafting of the constitution of the People's Democratic Republic of Ethiopia (PDRE) by a commission set up by the WPE. In addition, the WPE continued its resettlement and villagization programs and expanded its relationship with other socialist countries.

**Leadership and Party Organization.** In June the draft constitution, which had been in preparation since 1985, was published. According to WPE general secretary Mengistu, after "the entire people . . . discuss and take a stand," the constitution and the PDRE would be established (Addis Ababa Domestic Service[AADS], 12 September).

The draft constitution is divided into four parts: social order; citizenship, freedoms, rights, and duties; structure and functions of the state; and general provisions. Based on the principle of democratic centralism, the WPE would be, according to Article 6, the vanguard political party; it "determines the perspective for the development of the country and is the guiding force of the state and the entire society."

Although the WPE would be set up as the most powerful entity in society, the administration of state power would lie in the hands of a National Shengo (or parliament), a president, a prime minister, and a council of ministers. The one-house legislature would share the power of initiating legislation with the president and other organs of government, but it would hold the power to approve all legislation. Its deputies would be nominated for election by the WPE, and all legislation must adhere to the guidelines set up by the party. The National Shengo would also elect the president, the prime minister, and the cabinet. The president would be head of state and commander in chief of the armed forces and ensure the implementation of domestic and foreign policy. The prime minister and council of ministers would direct and coordinate the activities of ministries and supervise regional shengos. According to the constitution, the prime minister and the council would be inferior to the president. The National Shengo, president, and prime minister would serve terms of office of five years. A Supreme Court and lower judiciary would also be established. Although civil and individual rights would be guaranteed, virtually every right—according to Article 59—would be "limited by law in order to protect the interests of the state and society as well as the freedoms and rights of others." Finally, Article 8 states the underlying framework of the constitution: "to accelerate the process of laying the foundation for the construction of the socialist system."

Overall, the constitution in draft form indicates that the WPE would be at the pinnacle of the power structure. Although the National Shengo would be the supreme organ of state power, at least officially, it would appear that the president would easily be able to direct the parliament through his own office and through that of the prime minister. Clearly, nothing would occur without the approval of the WPE and its general secretary. Although civil rights are articulated, they would be limited by reasons of state. The draft constitution thus establishes a government bureaucracy to carry out the directives of the WPE. If the draft were promulgated, it would be Ethiopia's third constitution; the first two were established in 1931 and 1955, although the country has been without a constitution since 1974.

**International and Political Activities.** A number of agreements were signed during 1986. Since the population "at risk" from starvation declined from nearly 11 million to 6.5 million, an aid agreement for Soviet transportation and medical equipment was extended for one year. Ethiopia and Yugoslavia agreed on an economic, scientific, and technical protocol to carry out joint construction projects, and a two-year protocol was signed with the German Democratic Republic (GDR) to expand economic and technical cooperation. Czechoslovakia agreed to build a new textile factory and to import coffee and leather for footwear. Over the course of the year, Mengistu traveled to the USSR and the GDR. Food aid from the West declined sharply, due in large part to the lessening of publicity regarding the famine.

It was revealed early in the year that, in 1985, Dawit Wolde Giorgis, Ethiopia's commissioner for relief and rehabilitation, and Berhane Deressa, the deputy commissioner, sought and received political asylum in the United States. Both had criticized the socialist direction taken by Ethiopia. Ethiopia's foreign minister, Goshu Wolde, also resigned and sought asylum in the West. He claimed that "doctrinaire policies are leading the country and the people into misery and destruction" (*NYT*, 28 October). He was promptly replaced by Berhanu Bayih, one of the more powerful figures in the WPE Politburo.

The resettlement of famine victims from the north to the southwest continued in 1986. Ethiopia pushed hard to move ahead with its villagization program, to which the Italian government contributed $220 million. Three million peasants were relocated from the interior to centralized villages, and plans called for the eventual relocation of thirty million people. The project's primary goal has been to centralize the population to a greater degree so as to limit the negative effects of nature and to give the government more control over social and political life.

Although the wars in Eritrea and Tigre provinces had virtually come to a halt, a major government offensive took place in May to eliminate remnants of the rebels. It was reported that 5,000 Soviet pilots

and technicians helped prepare for the offensive (AFP, 15 April).

The 8,000 Ethiopian Jews who were secretly flown from the Sudan to Israel in 1985 were placed in 74 absorption centers in 53 towns, cities, and settlements throughout Israel. Although Israel had planned to spend upwards of $300 million to absorb the Ethiopians into Israeli culture, numerous racial and cultural problems exist that have inhibited successful integration (*Jerusalem Post*, 19 April).

Peter Schwab
*State University of New York
College at Purchase*

# Lesotho

**Population.** 1,552,000
**Party.** Communist Party of Lesotho (CPL)
**Founded.** 1962
**Membership.** No data
**Chairman.** R. Mataji
**Secretariat.** Jacob M. Kena (general secretary), John Motloheloa, Khotso Molekane
**Status.** Illegal (but tolerated)
**Last Congress.** Seventh, November 1984
**Last Election.** September 1985
**Auxiliary Organization.** Mine Workers' Union
**Publication.** *Mozhammokho* (Communist)

The coup that ousted Prime Minister Leabua Jonathan and brought the military regime of Major General Justin Metsing Lekhanya to power on 20 January appeared not to have been particularly disastrous for the CPL. The party seems to have been under no greater restriction than the conservative ones that had actively opposed the Jonathan regime; it was lucky, in retrospect, that its approaches toward cooperation with the latter had been rebuffed (see *YICA*, 1986). All political party activity has been prohibited by the new regime, but CPL general secretary Kena attended the Eleventh Congress of the World Federation of Trade Unions (WFTU) in East Berlin in September (WFTU, Eleventh Congress, *List of Participants*). Kena did this in his legal capacity as general secretary of the Mine Workers' Union, just as he had done at the 1982 WFTU Tenth Congress; at the Eleventh Congress, however, he was also listed as representing the Lesotho Congress of Free Trade Unions (neither union is a WFTU affiliate). CPL delegates to the March congresses of the Indian and Czechoslovak communist parties remained anonymous, but the party's representative on Prague's *World Marxist Review*, Sam Moeto, seemed perfectly open about his activities (New Delhi, *New Age*; 23 March; Prague, *Rudé právo*, 24 March; *WMR*, July).

Consistent with the Lesotho government's apparent tolerance of this rather muted CPL activity was the failure of the new regime to break off relations with the Soviet Union. This was in spite of the fact that the South African economic blockade, which contributed to the overthrow of Jonathan, had been undertaken because of Lesotho's alleged harboring of African National Congress (ANC) guerrillas who were raiding South African territory. The ANC did receive open propaganda support from the Soviets (and many others), but the South African media had gone so far as to claim that the eight additional Soviets sent to Lesotho in late 1985 were "sabotage experts in contact with the ANC military" (Radio Johannesburg, 21 January; *FBIS*, 21 January). Moreover, two of Lesotho's new cabinet members appeared to have pro-Soviet and pro-ANC backgrounds, respectively: Minister of Planning and Economic Affairs Michael M. Sefali, a violently anti–South African leftist with a doctorate from Moscow University; and Minister of Law, Public Service, Constitutional, and Parliamentary Affairs Halaki Sello, who had been jailed in South Africa for ANC activities (*Africa Now*, March; Johannesburg, *The Star*, 14 March). Sefali and Sello were confidants of King Moshoeshoe II, which helps explain their positions, since the king has regained much of his political power after the coup (ibid.).

The elements of the pro-Soviet left that were repressed during 1986 were those that had been part of Jonathan's governing mechanism. Ex-information minister Desmond Sixishe and ex-foreign minister Vincent Makhele died under mysterious circumstances in November. Sixishe was deemed to have been the leader of the left wing of Jonathan's Basotho National Party (BNP), and Makhele, as chairman of the Lesotho Peace and Solidarity Council and a member of the World Peace Council (WPC) to which it was affiliated, had been the country's most prominent communist-front personality (*Africa Now*, January; *YICA*, 1985).

The most dramatic action taken by the new government against any foreign communist power was against North Korea, whose personnel were alleged to have given military training to the BNP Youth League (*Africa Now*, March). Armed elements of this group had become Jonathan's virtual private political army and had clashed with Lekhanya's Lesotho Paramilitary Force during the January coup. It was not surprising, then, that twenty North Korean technicians were sent home in February with the excuse that the Lesotho government could no longer afford to pay them, nor that three North Korean diplomats were expelled in late August for having become "involved in internal politics" (Radio Maseru, 6 February; *FBIS*, 6 February; *NYT*, 23 August).

Two authoritative communist articles published in late 1986 appear to have been designed to curry favor with the new regime. One of the South African Communist Party's publications carried a favorable article on King Moshoeshoe I, presumed ancestor of the current king, on the 200th anniversary of his birth (*African Communist*, 4th quarter).

More puzzling was Prague's Peace and Socialism Publishers' *Information Bulletin* (no. 23) in its coverage of an alleged "special conference on the Communist Party of Lesotho." According to this account, the meeting criticized a minority CPL faction for having gone too far in support of the Jonathan regime and reorganized the Central Committee so as to rid it of that group. One unusual aspect of this report was that it claimed the special conference had been held on 2–3 March *1985*, whereas the *Information Bulletin* is normally devoted to relatively current materials—for example, the other dated items in that issue ranged from 11 August to 12 October *1986*. The second unusual aspect of the article was that it ignored completely what the *African Communist* (3d Quarter, 1985) had described as the CPL's November 1984 "Seventh *Special* Congress" (emphasis added), which was alleged to have called for a united front in support of the Jonathan regime against the South African threat. In fact, by stating that "our last Congress [was] in 1982," the *Information Bulletin* strongly implies that the November 1984 congress had never taken place.

Wallace H. Spaulding
*McLean, Virginia*

# Mozambique

**Population.** 14,022,000
**Party.** Front for the Liberation of Mozambique (Frente de Libertação de Moçambique; FRELIMO)
**Founded.** 1962
**Membership.** 110,323 (*African Communist*, 4th Quarter, 1983)
**President.** Joaquim Alberto Chissano
**Politburo.** 10 members: Marcelino dos Santos, Joaquim Alberto Chissano, Alberto Chipande, Armando
  Emilio Guebuza, Jorge Rebelo, Mariano de Araújo Matsinhe, Sebastião Marcos Mabote, Jacinto
  Soares Veloso, Mário de Graça Machungo, José Óscar Monteiro
**Secretariat.** Marcelino dos Santos, Joaquim Alberto Chissano, Jorge Rebelo, Armando Panquene, José
  Luís Cabaço
**Central Committee.** 130 members
**Status.** Ruling party
**Last Congress.** Fourth, 26–29 April 1983, in Maputo
**Last Election.** 1986
**Auxiliary Organizations.** Organization of Mozambican Women (Organização da Mulher Moçambicana;
  OMM); Mozambique Youth Organization (OJM); Mozambique Workers' Organization (OTM)
**Publications.** *Notícias* (daily); *O Tempo* (weekly); *Diário de Moçambique* (daily); *Domingo* (Sunday
  paper); *Voz de Revolução* (Central Committee organ)

The People's Republic of Mozambique underwent an extremely tumultuous period in 1986. A continuing guerrilla war and ongoing economic problems plagued FRELIMO. Crippled by civil war, widespread hunger, drought, and failed socialist policies, the southeast African country appeared to have experienced all possible disasters. But another devastating blow to its fortunes came with the death of the president, Samora Moisés Machel, on 19 October in a plane crash. Foreign Minister Joaquim Alberto Chissano was elected by the Central Committee to become FRELIMO president as well as head of state and commander of the armed forces. The death of Machel brought no respite to the internal problems of Mozambique. Rural insurgency and sabotage laid waste to the country's resources, and, to avoid the fighting, large numbers of Mozambicans fled across the border to Malawi. International support for FRELIMO increased from communist and neighboring states. The Republic of South Africa, however, announced the gradual expulsion of some 52,000 Mozambican mine and farm workers in retaliation for a landmine blast, which it blamed on guerrillas of the African National Congress (ANC) based in Mozambique. Money sent home by the Mozambicans accounted for some 30 percent of the country's foreign-exchange income (*The Economist*, 24 October). FRELIMO's current problems reflect its history.

FRELIMO came to power in 1975 after a ten-year guerrilla war for independence and a Marxist-inspired revolution. Formed from three small parties, it held its first congress in 1962 as a front for national liberation. Two years later it launched a rural insurgency against Portugal. During the war, FRELIMO shifted to the political left. With the collapse of Portuguese colonial rule, FRELIMO—the only legal political party—proclaimed an independent people's republic on 25 June 1975. (For additional background, see *YICA*, 1982). FRELIMO's domestic policies to create a Marxist state, and its foreign policy of supporting African rule in what was then Rhodesia (now Zimbabwe), led to internal opposition. By the second decade of independence, Mozambique's economy was failing and its countryside was engulfed in warfare and turbulence.

**Organization and Leadership.** Machel's death represented the single most significant event of 1986. A charismatic leader, Machel had been the most dominant personality in the FRELIMO hierarchy since his coming to the presidency in 1969 when the party's first president, Eduardo Mondlane, was assassinated. As head of the guerrilla army, Machel had a secure power base in the party. He presided over the initial sweeping changes that marked FRELIMO's first years in power, but he also adopted more pragmatic policies of aid and trade contacts with the West when previous Marxist programs produced sharp economic decline.

Chissano is expected to carry on the policies of his predecessor. Like Machel, he was born in southern Mozambique, in the town of Chibuto in Gaza province in 1939. Chissano was among the first African students to study at the main high school in Lourenço Marques (now Maputo). With a scholarship to study medicine, he went to Lisbon, from which he left to engage in politics with Marcelino Dos Santos in Paris. During the independence war, Chissano headed FRELIMO's security department. He became the party's chief representative in Tanzania, which provided rear bases for FRELIMO forces in their guerrilla offensive. He served as prime minister during the nine-month transition government that led to independence. Afterward, he became the foreign minister and also held a less-publicized role as chief of security, which reportedly won him support of the country's military commanders. He was given the rank of major general for his role during the independence war. Like Machel, Chissano has also been a member of the Shangana subgroup of the Tonga.

Outside observers have regarded Chissano as a moderate and pragmatic politician. Sources have contended, however, that he did not take part in the negotiations that led to the Nkomati Accord with South Africa (South Africa, *Sunday Tribune*, 26 October). He was reputed to be against accommodation with South Africa but said to favor continuing the policy of cooperation with the United States while keeping Mozambique within the socialist orbit.

The Third Congress in 1977 approved the Central Committee's recommendation to transform FRELIMO into a "Marxist-Leninist vanguard party." Well before the congress, however, FRELIMO had operated along communist party lines. According to the constitution, the politburo shapes policy and its members also hold ministerial portfolios entitling them to seats on the Council of Ministers, or cabinet. The Central Committee, like other such communist organs, is to seek approval of the congress for major policy and to carry out those policies. The president of FRELIMO is also head of the party. The constitution empowers the president to appoint provincial governors and ministers of the Council of Ministers, among others. He also holds the power to annul decisions of provincial assemblies. On occasion, ministerial officials have been dismissed from their posts and dispatched to provincial or even district positions.

The People's Assembly is the highest legislative body. The party has also set up local, district (112), and provincial (10) assemblies, but the rural insurgency has called into question the claim of how many are genuinely functioning. Elections for the National People's Assembly were to take place every five years, but at the thirteenth session in June 1985 the assembly unanimously postponed the elaborate, countrywide election process until 1986.

The elections began on 15 August with direct voting at mass meetings for local assemblies. The elections were to have finished on 15 November, but they were extended to 15 December due to the death of Machel. After the first phase of elections for local assemblies, the second phase involved district and city assemblies. Rules called for votes to be secret in the cities, and there were supposed to have been 20 percent more candidates than seats available. One reported surprise in the second phase was the voters' rejection in the Beira city assembly of Lourenço Marra, who has been a FRELIMO first secretary in the city and a member of the Central Committee. He was reputedly the highest ranking person rejected by the voters (*Dakar Pana*, 22 November; *FBIS*, 22 November). The final phase called for elections to the provincial assemblies and then to the National People's Assembly.

Due to the insurgency, it was reported that elections could not take place in five districts, including Zumbo and Mutarara (Maputo in English, 3 December; *FBIS*, 4 December). The virtual civil war in the countryside made it unlikely that elections were carried out as smoothly as in 1977.

**Mass Organizations.** In the course of the war against Portugal, FRELIMO had attempted to organize various sectors of the population, especially women and youths. FRELIMO built on these specific appeals in an effort to rally the population and then to replicate communist mass organizations. Thus, it established in 1973 the OMM, which has announced goals of liberating women from traditional low standing and of improving women's economic and political position in the country. It has, for example, taken stands against child marriage, polygamy, and the bride-price. The OMM also helps publicize and implement the party line among women. It held its forth major gathering in November 1984.

FRELIMO also organized the youth into the OJM after the party's Third Congress. The OJM's charter seeks to mobilize Mozambicans between the ages of 18 and 35. In the past, the OJM has conducted campaigns against what it determined were "bourgeois habits," which included materialism, fashionable dress, and other incorrect political behavior. The generalized instability in Mozambique made it uncertain as to the effectiveness of the OJM as a prop to FRELIMO in 1986.

The same unstable conditions have also reduced the effectiveness of other FRELIMO efforts to mobilize and control segments of the population. For example, in 1976 FRELIMO set up production councils to engage workers in factories, mills, and foundries. It was reported that the councils were to mobilize these workers "in active, collective, and conscious ways in the discussion and resolution of their problems, especially in relation to production and productivity" (*Notícias*, 12 November 1976). In May 1986, OTM general secretary Augusto Macamo met with a delegation of the Soviet All-Union Central Council of Trade Unions. The OTM signed a cooperation protocol that called for the exchange of information, training, and trade union education (Maputo Domestic Service, 22 May; *FBIS*, 23 May). Efforts to organize other groups, such as artists and journalists, did not move much beyond the blueprint stage due to economic and military preoccupations of the FRELIMO leadership.

*The People's Forces for the Liberation of Mozambique (FPLM).* FRELIMO's ragtag guerrilla force won an unconventional war against Portugal. After independence, FRELIMO began converting its insurgent force into a conventional army (known as the FPLM) of some 15,000 with the help of Soviet advisers and equipment. A national draft was implemented to bring recruits to the military ranks of an army estimated in 1986 at 51,000, which includes regular troops of the brigades and local militia forces (*Jane's Defence Weekly* 6, no. 1 (12 July): 22). Soon afterward, however, the FPLM faced its own insurgency, and draft evasion became widespread.

What started as a small-scale rural insurgency in the late 1970s had become by 1986 a virtual civil war in Mozambique and the central preoccupation of the FRELIMO government. The insurgency developed out of opposition to FRELIMO's domestic and foreign policies. Its agricultural collectivization, re-education camps, security police, and disruptive religious and social policies created instability and discontent among the population. Former FRELIMO fighters, ethnic communities left out of the power sharing, and disgruntled elements staged various forms of protest.

That this inchoate opposition developed into an organized movement was helped by the government's foreign policy toward the white settler state of then-Rhodesia. FRELIMO first closed Mozambique's borders for Rhodesian traffic to and from the Indian Ocean port of Beira as a means to deprive the white settlers of foreign trade. Next FRELIMO granted sanctuary camps to Robert Mugabe's Zimbabwe African National Union for its guerrillas to stage raids into Rhodesia. In retaliation, Rhodesia relentlessly pounded Mozambique's economic infrastructure and helped to organize and train the internal Mozambican opposition. The opponents to FRELIMO coalesced into the Mozambique National Resistance (*Resistência Nacional Moçambicana*; RENAMO, formerly MNR) and posed a serious challenge to the Maputo regime by the mid-1980s. When the Rhodesian government collapsed, assistance to RENAMO flowed from the Republic of South Africa. Pretoria supported RENAMO as a counterforce against raids from the guerrillas of the ANC, which launched attacks from Mozambican bases. The RENAMO radio station, *Voz da Africa* (Voice of Free Africa), which played an important role in the formation of the movement, moved from Rhodesia to Phalaborwa in the northern Transvaal.

Early in 1986, RENAMO captured Casa Banana, its principal headquarters located in Gorongosa National Park of central Mozambique. The camp had been seized in August 1985 by a combined Mozambican-Zimbabwean force, and some 1,000 Mozambican troops were left to hold the base. However, after RENAMO routed the FPLM forces, the latter reportedly abandoned armored vehicles, antiaircraft guns, and munitions. It was stated that the recapture angered the Zimbabweans, who questioned their mission in Mozambique since the FPLM proved unable to regain the initiative. Costs to Zimbabwe for its expeditionary force have been estimated at $325,000 a day (*WP*, 2 March).

By the end of 1986, RENAMO's military successes were viewed as a credible threat to the life of the FRELIMO regime. RENAMO guerrillas operated in all ten of the country's provinces. Desertion plagued the FPLM, and the rural population in the northwest no longer relied on FRELIMO for safety. Mozambique's news agency reported that 200,000 people fled across the border into Malawi during the fall, which offered safety to the refugees and sanctuary to RENAMO forces poised for forays into Mozambique (*NYT*, 20 November). RENAMO forces have been estimated at 23,000 guerrillas (*Washington Times*, 3 September). The rebels were also accused of planting car bombs in the capital, of placing antipersonnel landmines on the Costa do Sol beach outside Maputo, and of setting up booby-trapped radios (Maputo Domestic Service, 10 February; *FBIS*, 12 February). Although RENAMO denied these activities, it did take responsibility for causing electrical power outages in the capital from time to time.

RENAMO's president Afonso Dhlakama, like many of his followers, served first in FRELIMO ranks during the independence war. Dhlakama succeeded to the head of the movement after its founder, Andre Matadi Matsangaisse, was killed leading an assault and after the white general secretary Orlando Cristina, a former big game hunter for the wealthy industrialist Jorge Jardim, died under mysterious circumstances in South Africa. RENAMO's conditions for cease-fire talks have remained unchanged—free elections and the withdrawal of all foreign troops from Mozambique—although its military success has grown (*CSM*, 24 September). This success was also a reflection of its diplomatic activity. In late October, Dhlakama declared war on the Zimbabwean government. The declaration came after Zimbabwean prime minister Robert Mugabe pledged to prevent RENAMO from taking power (*NYT*, 20 October).

In order to maintain its position, FRELIMO has had to rely increasingly on some 20,000 foreign military and police forces from the Soviet Union, Cuba, North Korea, Vietnam, and the German Democratic Republic as well as Zimbabwe and Tanzania. East German advisers, for example, have been responsible for training FRELIMO's secret police, the National Service for the People's Security (*Serviço Nacional de Segurança Popular*; SNASP). Along with its security duties, the SNASP operates the prisons and re-education camps where a reported 200,000–300,000 people have been imprisoned and an estimated 75,000 have died (*Reason*, 15 December).

**Domestic Affairs.** Observers predicted that President Chissano would continue his predecessor's pragmatic economic policy, which represented some departures from "scientific socialism." In May 1985, for example, as part of its plans to encourage private enterprise and foreign investments, the Machel government had eliminated price controls on a variety of food products. Farmers close to Maputo have thus been encouraged to offer their produce at higher prices, which resulted in greater surplus in markets in 1986. But prices on foodstuffs remained beyond the reach of the ordinary worker living on regular pay. As in other socialist countries, the Mozambican population has turned to black-market means to circumvent governmental control (*CSM*, 31 October).

Since the Fourth Congress in 1983, Mozambique has moved toward a mixed economy. The FRELIMO leadership acknowledged that socialist economic policies of collectivization, nationalized industry, price controls, and inflexible central planning had resulted in disaster for output and for the population (*WP*, 31 October).

During his May Day speech in Maputo, Machel had reiterated a long-standing policy against vagrancy in the capital, where there were a reputed 200,000 unemployed men and women. He said they "roam the streets and thus become parasites. This could corrupt our society." He added that the unemployed would be evacuated to grow food and cotton in the main river valleys of southern Mozambique and "to rid the city of migrants who engage in petty and illegal trade" (Maputo Domestic Service, 1 May; *FBIS*, 5 May; United Kingdom, *Mozambique News Review*, 21 May). Forced evacuations from the urban centers first took place in 1983, when the unemployed were flown to "re-education" camps mainly in the northern province of Niassa.

The shift to a market Marxism in hopes of restoring the economy did not arrest the general decline. According to figures from the Bank of Mozambique, only cotton production among agricultural figures increased in output to 6,000 tons in 1984 and 10,300 in 1985, and yet it remained far below the

1985 level of 157,000. Tea, sugar, and sisal continued to fall in output from previous years. Cement production also fell in 1985 more than 25 percent as compared to 1984 and declined three and a half times what it had been in 1975 (*Marchés Tropicaux*, 28 September).

Food production was not evenly spread throughout the country. At the end of 1986, the governor of Sofala in the central zone stated that more than 100,000 people faced starvation because of the war. He called on the international community for assistance (Maputo in English, 1 December; *FBIS*, 2 December).

**International Affairs.** Mozambique's insurgency dominated foreign policy as much as it did domestic issues. A cornerstone of FRELIMO's foreign relations remained the 1984 Nkomati Accord with South Africa. That nonaggression pact forbade the signatories to support insurgent groups opposed to the respective governments. In other words, FRELIMO is required to deny support for the ANC and South African Communist Party, and the Pretoria regime is proscribed from aiding RENAMO. Both sides charge the other with specific violations. Late in the year, in his first news conference, Chissano accused South Africa of breaking the pact: "We have information which indicates that the terrorists [RENAMO] who are arriving from Malawi are doing it because the South Africans are working with them, organizing them, supplying them" (*NYT*, 5 December).

The concern over Malawi's alleged participation in RENAMO's struggle moved FRELIMO to concoct a destabilization scheme, according to documents purporting to be minutes of a meeting in Maputo on 16 October between Machel and a Zimbabwean delegation. Machel reportedly considered using Mozambicans living in Malawi as a "fifth column" to help undermine that government. Pretoria claimed to have found the minutes of the meeting among the wreckage of the aircraft that crashed in South Africa, killing Machel and 33 other passengers (London, *The Times*, 11 November). Mozambique and Zimbabwe charged that the documents were false and were simply a South African method of deflecting its role in causing the crash of the plane. Zimbabwe and Tanzania have deployed some 15,000 troops to fight alongside FRELIMO soldiers in northern and central Mozambique. Almost one-third of Zimbabwe's army is fielded in central Mozambique in a desperate effort to keep the Beira Corridor open. (*CSM*, 1 April).

Mozambique's closer relations with Washington continued to result in aid from the United States. Since 1983, Washington has been Maputo's biggest food donor, having furnished $73 million in grain and other foodstuffs and designating $36 million more for 1987. However, because Washington has not provided all the aid desired by Maputo, in part due to congressional opposition, FRELIMO's foreign minister expressed disenchantment in May with conciliation policies toward the United States. Chissano also noted dissatisfaction with Washington for its lack of success in restraining South Africa's support of RENAMO (*WP*, 15 May). Nonetheless, Chissano is expected to continue the policy of seeking U.S. assistance and private investment, and it appeared that Washington would also continue its policy of rapprochement with FRELIMO. President Reagan sent his daughter, Maureen Reagan, as his representative to Machel's funeral.

Despite closer relations with the United States and the West, FRELIMO maintained its ties to the Soviet Union. Mozambique continued to rely on the Soviet bloc for military arms and advisers. There were an estimated 2,000 Cubans, 1,000 Soviets, 500 East Germans, and thousands of other Soviet-bloc personnel in Mozambique. FRELIMO was said to have received $1 billion from Moscow in military equipment, including assault helicopters and jets. (*Insight*, 10 November.)

As in past years, the two countries exchanged delegations and visitors. In late March, for example, Machel made a working visit to Moscow, where he met with Mikhail Gorbachev, general secretary of the Communist Party of the Soviet Union (CPSU) Central Committee, as well as other high Soviet officials. The communiqué reporting their talks declared that Machel had conveyed "deep gratitude to the CPSU and the Soviet people for their combat solidarity and fraternal selfless assistance" (*Izvestiia*, 4 April; *FBIS-USSR International Affairs*, 4 April). Other exchanges involved Mariano Matsinhe traveling to the USSR in April and May (Moscow Domestic Service, 2 May; *FBIS-USSR International Affairs*, 6 May) and Jacinto Veloso to Moscow (TASS, 14 June; *FBIS-USSR International Affairs*, 16 June).

More significant, the year marked the signing of a cooperation agreement in May following the first session of the Mozambique Council for Mutual Economic Assistance (CMEA) joint commission, which detailed plans to assist the development of Mozambique. The agreement was the first between

CMEA and a southern African country (Maputo Domestic Service, 22 May; *FBIS*, 28 May). In June, the Mozambique-USSR Friendship Committee was established to carry out concrete actions within the context of already existing relations of friendship and cooperation. The committee developed out of previous initiatives by the Soviet societies for friendship and cultural relations with foreign countries (Maputo Domestic Service, 11 June; *FBIS*, 12 June). Late in the year, Chissano welcomed the new Soviet ambassador, Nikolay Kirillovich Dybenko, to Mozambique by expressing "friendship and cooperative relations with the USSR" (Maputo Domestic Service, 9 December; *FBIS*, 11 December).

FRELIMO continued to enter into exchanges with China. The OTM signed a protocol for cooperation with the All-China Federation of Trade Unions. The protocol established areas of cooperation, such as training OTM cadres and the exchange of delegations (Maputo Domestic Service, 10 October; *FBIS*, 16 October). Following an agreement to supply Mozambique with oil on preferential terms in August 1985, Iranian president Ali Khamene'i visited Maputo in January and expressed "pleasure at the increased bilaterial relations" between Iran and Mozambique (Maputo in English, 19 January; *FBIS*, 23 January).

**Publications.** Since independence, FRELIMO has controlled the country's print and broadcast media. The party depends on two publications to carry its written message: the daily paper *Notícias* and the weekly magazine *O Tempo*. In 1981 the government launched two more national circulation newspapers: *Diário de Moçambique* in Beira, the country's second largest city, and a Sunday paper, *Domingo*. (For additional background, see *YICA*, 1982.) Another publication, *Voz da Revolução*, deals with Marxist theory and FRELIMO policies.

Thomas H. Henriksen
*Hoover Institution*

# Nigeria

**Population.** 94,181,000 (*Political Handbook of the World, 1986–87*)
**Party.** Socialist Working People's Party (SWPP)
**Founded.** 1963 (SWPP: 1978)
**Membership.** No data
**General Secretary.** Dapo Fatogun
**Politburo.** 4 members: Chaika Anozie (chairman), Wahab Goodluck (deputy chairman), Hassan Sunmonu, Lasisi A. Osunde
**Central Committee.** No data
**Status.** Proscribed
**Last Congress.** First, November 1978
**Last Election.** August–September 1983, SWPP ineligible
**Auxiliary Organizations.** No data
**Publications.** *New Horizon*

With the ban on political parties still in effect from the 1983 military coup, Marxist political activity and organization remained faint in Nigeria during 1986. However, the liberalization of the political climate under military president Ibrahim Babangida did give more scope for leftist and populist political forces to attempt to organize popular support. This opportunity was increased further by the continued depression in the Nigerian economy, which, coupled with the imposition of International Monetary Fund (IMF)-style austerity measures (including an effective devaluation of the currency by two-thirds, and cuts in consumer subsidies), further eroded standards of living for the Nigerian poor and middle classes, especially in the cities.

This was the political and economic background for the first visible stirrings of Nigerian Marxist activity since the December 1983 coup. While it is not clear to what extent the SWPP continued to exist, even as an underground organization, the Marxist journal, *New Horizon*, was revived in 1985 under the editorship of SWPP general secretary Fatogun. In an interview in the December 1985 issue of *World Marxist Review*, Fatogun said his journal was revived "in response to the crying need to puncture the ongoing political debates in Nigeria with Marxist-Leninist ideas and presentations. Our journal is very well received in trade union circles, by students among whom radical sentiment is strong, and by a large body of progressive national intellectuals." He claimed that the August 1985 issue, which carried Fidel Castro's statement on the Latin American debt, sold out in three days.

In February 1986, Fatogun attended the Marxist conference in Senegal on the "Socioeconomic Development of Black Africa and Problems of Democracy." There he also emphasized that, with political parties still banned, trade unions and youth organizations, were "in the forefront of the fight against reaction, the imperialist monopolies and their local agents" (*WMR*, August). In fact, he was not incorrect in noting the central role of trade unions and other popular organizations in mobilizing overwhelming popular opposition to the Babangida government's proposal for an IMF loan in 1985. Because of this popular opposition, the government has felt itself politically unable to reach a formal accord with the IMF, although it did proceed to implement most of the standard IMF austerity program in 1986.

Although it is unclear and perhaps doubtful to what extent Marxists have been connected with and responsive to the international communist movement, they do have a significant presence in many Nigerian trade unions and universities, and some Nigerian university students think of themselves as Marxists, although they vary considerably in their knowledge of Marxist theory and practice and their degree of commitment. Marxist intellectuals have been especially prominent in the social sciences; some of them are nationally known and have a certain following.

The presence of a significant number of Marxists in the trade unions and universities, and the uncertainty as to their precise degree of strength and organization, may have accounted for some of the nervousness of the regime and its security apparatus with respect to student and labor political activity. The most serious crisis for the Babangida regime began on 23 May, when police went on a rampage at Ahmadu Bello University (ABU) in Zaria, killing several students and injuring many more. Police put the death toll at four, but independent reports placed the number of fatalities at between ten and thirty-two. ABU has long been a center of student and intellectual militance, with Marxist and Islamic fundamentalist tendencies both prominent. The police had been summoned to the campus following student protests the previous day commemorating the killing of eight ABU students by police in 1978. Reports said the student demonstrations were sparked in part by disciplinary measures recently imposed against two leaders of the 10,000-member ABU student union.

The news of the killings provoked outrage and sympathy demonstrations on a number of other university campuses around the country, leading to further confrontation and violence. Two students were injured by police gunfire at Lagos University in the capital, and two students were reported shot dead and seven others wounded in demonstrations at Kaduna Polytechnic, near ABU. In the majority of Nigerian universities, students boycotted lectures to support ABU student demands for the dismissal of the minister of education and the vice-chancellor of ABU. Most of the major universities were ordered closed temporarily in the highly charged atmosphere. On 27 May, Nigerian police prevented Lagos University students from marching on the seat of the military government. That same day, rampaging students burned down a police station in Lagos, closed another police station and a major expressway, and attacked the Lagos office of an eastern state newspaper, smashing windows and destroying equipment. These actions were roundly condemned by the press. The rioting continued the next day with attacks on vehicles and government officials in Lagos. In Ife, rioting university students set free 218 inmates from a nearby prison. The government stated that its intelligence service believed "some disgruntled elements" who were not students had taken advantage of the disorder to foment trouble.

Although the Babangida government immediately appointed a commission of inquiry to investigate the disturbances at ABU, its liberal reputation was further damaged when it quashed a planned sympathy demonstration by the Nigerian Labor Congress (NLC) on 4 June. Seven NLC leaders were arrested, including its president, Alhaji Ali Chiroma. (A few days earlier, the chairman of the ABU chapter of the Academic Staff Union of Universities had been briefly detained by police.) The government accused the trade unionists of "subversive activities," and the semi-official *New Nigerian* reported that a government search of trade union offices revealed evidence of intent in some quarters to draw together trade unionists, teachers, and students into a "common front against the government" (*FBIS*, 13 June).

In fact, leftists have long been prominent in the NLC, which has been the country's sole national labor federation, composed of 42 recognized trade unions representing some three and a half million wage earners. After the December 1983 coup, the NLC called for a new governmental structure based on an alliance of workers, soldiers, youth, intellectuals, and peasants that would pursue socialist policies. Still, for the most part the NLC has been reluctant to confront the government, just as the government has been reluctant to alienate the unions. In what the government claimed was "an act of magnanimity" on its part and a demonstration of its commitment to individual rights, the NLC leaders were released unconditionally after eleven days of detention, and the congress implied it would continue its collaboration with "other mass organizations on specified issues" (*West Africa*, 23 June).

Government fear of combined labor, student, and intellectual mobilization against it may have also played a role in the most sensational event in Nigeria during 1986: the assassination by parcel bomb of the country's most creative and respected journalist and editor in chief of the influential *Newswatch* magazine, Dele Giwa, on 19 October. Two days before his murder, Giwa had been summoned to the headquarters of the State Security Service (SSS; which is responsible for domestic intelligence). There the deputy director of the SSS accused him of holding discussions with the NLC, the Academic Staff Union of Universities, and students with a view to destabilizing the country and bringing about the birth of a socialist revolution. Among other things, Giwa was also accused of holding talks with some people to import arms into the country for the above purpose. The charges against Giwa, a liberal committed to democracy and nonviolence, were both shocking and absurd. Although Giwa was informed (minutes before his assassination) that the allegations were being dropped, some analysts have interpreted the entire incident both as a sign of government unease over the potential for broad-based popular mobilization against it and as a possible warning to its opposition.

In its foreign relations, Nigeria maintained its general nonaligned orientation, which has been sympathetic to the West but has also sought to cultivate friendly relations with communist-bloc countries. On 15 December, Nigeria signed a cultural and educational program agreement with the Soviet Union aimed at enhancing the cooperation in these areas dating back to the basic agreement between the two countries signed in 1970. Under previous agreements, a number of Nigerian undergraduate and postgraduate students have studied in the USSR. During the year, Nigeria also held discussions with officials from Cuba, Hungary, Bulgaria, and Romania regarding existing and possible future economic, technical, and cultural cooperation agreements. Further demonstrating its independence, Nigeria continued to pursue a vigorous, if largely rhetorical, policy of opposition to apartheid and of support for tough economic sanctions against South Africa, while also condemning the U.S. bombing raid on Libya in "unequivocal terms."

Larry Diamond
*Hoover Institution*

# Réunion

**Population.** 552,500
**Party.** Réunion Communist Party (Parti communiste réunionnais; PCR)
**Founded.** 1959
**Membership.** 7,000 claimed; 2,000 estimated
**General Secretary.** Paul Vergès
**Politburo.** 12 members: Julien Ramin; remaining members unknown
**Secretariat.** 6 Members: Paul Vergès, Elie Hoarau, Jean-Baptiste Ponama, Lucet Langenier; remaining members unknown
**Central Committee.** 32 members: Bruny Payet, Roger Hoarau, Daniel Lallemand, Hippolite Piot, Ary Yee Chong Tchi-Kan, Laurent Vergès; remaining members unknown
**Status.** Legal
**Last Congress.** Fifth, 12–14 July 1980, in Le Port
**Last Election.** Legislative election, 16 March 1986, 29.2 percent; regional election, 16 March 1986, 28 percent; 7 of 45 in local assembly; 2 in Paris
**Auxiliary Organizations.** Anticolonialist Front for Réunion Autonomy; Réunion Front of Autonomous Youth; Réunion Peace Committee; Réunion General Confederation of Workers (CGTR); Committee for the Rally of Réunionese Unemployed (CORC); Committee for the Rally of Réunionese Youth (CORJ); Réunion Union of Women (UFR); Réunion General Union of Workers in France (UGTRF); Réunion General Confederation of Planters and Cattlemen (CGPER)
**Publications.** *Témoignages* (daily), Elie Hoarau, chief editor; *Travailleur Réunionnais* (semimonthly), published by CGTR; *Combat Réunionnais*, published by UGTRF

The island of Réunion is a French overseas department and as such is an integral part of the French Republic. It is governed by a Paris-appointed commissioner (who is the senior local official), a 36-member General Council, and a 45-member Regional Assembly. It is represented in the French parliament by five deputies and three senators. The PCR, a small party that gathers most of its support from sugarcane cutters and workers in the Le Port area, was founded in Le Port in 1959, when the Réunion Federation of the French Communist party became autonomous. The PCR advocates increased autonomy without complete independence from France.

The PCR earned 29.2 percent of the vote in the 16 March legislative election and 28 percent in the regional election. The use of a proportional representation voting system in the election, which had been introduced by the Socialists, gave the PCR two of the five seats in the National Assembly, the first time in 30 years that the PCR has been represented in that body. Paul Vergès and Elie Hoarau serve as deputies in Paris (*Témoignages*, 18 March). The conservatives' razor-thin majority in France brought Jacques Chirac in as prime minister to serve under Socialist president François Mitterrand in a delicate power-sharing situation dubbed "cohabitation." Uncertainty at the outset of the stability of cohabitation caused the PCR at its 22 March Central Committee meeting to keep its members mobilized in case new elections were called (ibid., 24 March). The PCR received thirteen of the forty-five regional counselor seats, and four of the fifteen bureau members came from the party's ranks. The presidency of the Regional Assembly, however, passed from PCR member Mario Hoarau to conservative Pierre Lagourgue (ibid., 18, 22–23 March).

The party, which was virtually assured of the two National Assembly seats, undertook a public information campaign to ensure that voters knew the mechanics of the new electoral system. Almost daily coverage was given to the fact that there would only be one round of voting and that voters would be required to vote for both a legislative and a regional list. A major effort was made by the party daily, *Témoignages*, to inform its readers of the PCR electoral list symbol—a "V" for victory sign—and locations of voting offices (ibid., 18–19 January).

The PCR made development on the island its top priority; Paul Vergès told Réunionese employers that the island's society was "upside down" because its base was in the service sector (ibid., 13 February). He urged PCR members to vote to prevent a conservative victory that would increase the incidents of racism and unemployment and would undo social gains—particularly the 39-hour work week, five weeks of paid vacation, and retirement at age 60—that the Socialist government had achieved during the previous five years (ibid., 1–2 February, 3 March). The party platform was thin on specifics; Vergès announced that he refused to "promise anything just to get elected" and maintained that a well-defined political will was all that was necessary (ibid., 13 March).

Once in the National Assembly, Vergès and Hoarau presented their four priorities for Réunion: 1) to defend Réunion's interests by fighting for the government to increase the price of sugarcane and to get Economic Community (EC) authorities to authorize that increase; 2) to ask the government to raise the credits for the unemployed; 3) to relaunch construction on the island to help employment; and 4) to guarantee rights to Réunionese to social security benefits (ibid., 1 April). Not surprisingly, the PCR mounted strong opposition throughout the year to the conservative government's policies, which the party decried as racist, socially inequal, and unjust. The PCR strongly condemned the return to the two-round majority voting system (ibid., 4 July) and electoral redistricting, which hurt communist and extreme right parties. Modifying an antiracist slogan in metropolitan France, the PCR headlined its daily newspaper with "Don't touch our two deputies" because the electoral system and districting changes would be likely to prevent the PCR from regaining its two seats in the National Assembly during the next election, scheduled for 1991.

The party also hotly criticized the Chirac government's use of Article 49.3 of the Constitution, which allowed the majority to preclude debate on bills presented to parliament, because it resulted in a loss of representation (ibid., 10–11 May).

Government policies for the overseas departments and territories (DOM-TOM) received particularly harsh opposition from the PCR deputies, who claimed that they would reduce the gains of decentralization of powers to the Regional Assembly and give them to the General Council (ibid., 14 April). On 16 May, the party charged that Chirac and Minister of Overseas Departments and Territories Bernard Pons had not yet adequately explained their policy for the DOM-TOM and that the government was using the racist logic of not giving all the DOM-TOM aid to the inhabitants because they were said to be incapable of using it correctly (ibid., 16 May). The PCR proposed dividing Réunion into two departments to help resolve the institutional quarrels between the Regional Assembly and the General Council. At the same time, Vergès denied that the proposal had anything to do with a further integration of the island into metropolitan France (ibid., 5–6 July).

Promising to fight for equal justice for all on Réunion, the PCR accused the right of injustice and singled out conservative Jean-Paul Virapoullé again for their attacks. Several trials of Virapoullé's alleged henchmen accused of attacking PCR members during the election campaign resulted in nonconvictions. The PCR publicized several of the attacks, notably the apparent assassination attempt against Pierre Vergès (ibid., 8–9 March).

The 1986 elections shed some light on internal party dissension. In composing the legislative list prior to 16 March, the respected French daily *Le Monde* reported on 21 May that a strong minority in the party opposed placing Laurent Vergès in the number three slot instead of Claude Hoarau. After the PCR agreed to the "one man, one mandate" rule to improve their elected officials' performance and increase party involvement in elected office (*Témoignages*, 7 February), three members elected to the Regional Assembly resigned to give the next three on the list a seat (ibid., 19–20 April). However, Paul Vergès and Elie Hoarau did not submit to the rule. The resignations allowed Vergès's son, Pierre, to accede to the Regional Assembly and to raise again the question of "Vergès dynasty" in the PCR (*Le Monde*, 21 May).

There was an apparent fluctuation in party policy on autonomy for Réunion, although there was officially no dissidence on the subject (ibid.). At the Fifth Party Congress in 1980, the PCR oriented its strategy to fight for democratic and popular autonomy; the Socialist victory in 1981 had put that strategy on hold. Since then, however, the policy has undergone some modification. On 19 March, for example, the PCR organized a large celebration of the 40th anniversary of the law that gave Réunion department status. Party founder Raymond Vergès (Paul Vergès's father) pushed that law as the best way to achieve social benefits and protection for all classes (*Témoignages*, 11 February). Paul Vergès carefully explained that the celebration was not for departmentalization as such but for the struggle for social justice (ibid., 20 March). He defended his father's fight for the island's status in the mid-1940s by saying that it was appropriate at that time but that a succession of conservative governments in France had been incapable of foreseeing the future needs of Réunion to assure its development (ibid., 14 February). Although Vergès has appeared moderate in his demands for autonomy, many conservatives on the island continued to believe that he harbors thoughts of independence (*Le Monde*, 21 May).

There have been some indications that all is not well within the PCR on party policy. At an 18 May Central Committee meeting, Paul Vergès evoked the "impatient members" who wanted to talk about the island's status (*Le Monde*, 21 May). An advocate of departmentalization, Mario Hoarau relinquished his functions as president of the Regional Assembly in March and turned his energies to his duties as mayor of Saint-Leu. There he usurped the dominance of Vergès confidant Ary Yee Chong Tchi-Kan and questioned Saint-Leu's membership in the SIVOMAR, a collection of PCR communes (except Sainte-Rose) established in 1983 that is presided over by Paul Vergès and administered by his son Pierre (ibid.).

The PCR, through the CGPER, continued the fight to help sugarcane cutters in Réunion. Throughout most of the year the PCR and CGPER lobbied to increase the price of a ton of sugarcane, saying that cutters could not survive with less than a 6 percent price increase (*Témoignages*, 13 May). The EC had authorized an increase of 1.4 percent, and the cutters went on strike to force the government to come up with additional funds. The government delayed its decision until mid-June, when it agreed to a 4.3 percent raise (ibid., 13 June). Although the CGPER continued to clamor for the 6 percent, it presented the 4.3 percent increase as a "victory" for the workers (ibid., 16 June). Immedi-

ately following that victory, the Bourbon Sugar Industry announced that it was closing two processing plants, and cutters—feeling that their jobs and industry were seriously threatened—continued their labor actions to try to prevent the closures.

Unemployment remained a serious problem on Réunion, with official figures citing the number of jobless at 72,000, or about 13 percent (ibid., 29 September). Problems in the sugarcane industry dominated much of the concern about unemployment. The PCR urged the government to increase the number of two-week work periods available to the unemployed (ibid., 12 May). The party also noted the injustice of expecting Réunionese to emigrate to France to find jobs, the awarding of public service jobs to metropolitan Frenchmen instead of Réunionese (ibid., 23 May), and the inequality of minimum wage standards between the metropole and the island. According to figures cited in *Témoignages* (5–6 July), metropolitan workers received a 1.4 percent increase in minimum wages, while Réunionese workers received nothing. There was a 22 percent difference between metropolitan and island minimum wages, with metropolitan workers receiving over 1,000 francs more per month (ibid., 9 July).

The party daily highlighted what it saw as increased U.S. intelligence activities in Réunion. It reported on 2 January that PCR nemesis Virapoullé and several other island rightists attended the World Anti-Communist League (WACL) congress in Dallas, Texas. The PCR went on to claim that Virapoullé and the WACL had ties to the U.S. Central Intelligence Agency (CIA), which the PCR claims prevents economic liberation of people, sows terror, arms and trains mercenaries, and kills innocent people (ibid., 6 January). An article in the French weekly *Le Point* of 16 December 1985 said that Mormons, who had allegedly worked for the CIA, were going door-to-door in New Caledonia and Tahiti (ibid., 11 March).

**Party Organization and Leadership.** Paul Vergès has been PCR general secretary since 1959, a deputy in the National Assembly and to the European parliament, and mayor of Le Port. He also headed the SIVOMAR. *Le Monde* reported in 1984 that Vergès's popularity has waned because he has adopted the image of a "notable" and a charismatic revolutionary, and because fellow PCR members have charged him with nepotism. *Le Monde* of 21 May 1986 noted further problems with Vergès's image after his two sons won elective office.

Secretariat member (and number two in the party) Elie Hoarau also won a seat in the National Assembly in March. He served concurrently as member of the Regional Assembly Bureau, secretary of the Réunion Peace Committee, general secretary of the CGTR, and a member of the World Peace Council (WPC). He was also mayor of Saint-Pierre and chief editor of *Témoignages*. Bruny Payet, a member of the party's Central Committee, served concurrently as president of the Réunion Peace Committee, head of the CGTR, and first deputy mayor of Sainte-Marie. Payet was also a member of the WPC and the General Council of the World Federation of Trade Unions (WFTU). Ary Yee Chong Tchi-Kan, a member of the Central Committee, headed the youth sector of the party. Other PCR members holding elected office were Mario Hoarau (mayor of Saint-Leu), Lucet Langenier (Secretariat member, mayor of Sainte-Suzanne, and regional counselor), Central Committee member Roger Hoarau (regional counselor), and Laurent and Pierre Vergès (regional counselors). Other noteworthy PCR members were Julien Ramin, Daniel Lallemand, Hippolite Piot, Roland Robert (mayor of La Possession), Claude Hoarau (mayor of Saint-Louis), and Patrick Boîtard (youth leader).

Prominent leaders within the PCR auxiliary organizations were Angelo Lauret, president of the CGPER; Georges-Marie Lépinay, deputy general secretary of the CGPER (*Témoignages*, 1 January); Isnelle Amelin, president of the UFR; and Huguette Bello, UFR leader.

**Domestic Policies and Activities.** The major goals of the PCR in 1986 were to achieve increased autonomy for Réunion from France, a more balanced economy, redress of inequalities between social benefits in France and on the island, and development of Réunionese industry. The party has emphasized an increased number of development projects, including self-construction projects, on the island, and it wants to produce more products on Réunion, although it realizes some of the difficulties in placing new industries on the island. The PCR continued to favor projects to develop the island's tourism industry and to favor independence for New Caledonia, a French territory.

PCR deputies met with other communist deputies from French overseas departments to discuss opposition to the government's proposed law for the DOM-TOM and the budget. The PCR dedicated 1986 to fighting for the municipal employees' rights to job security, career continuity, and an end to clientelism of mayors with regard to those workers (ibid., 6 January). The party's domestic policies continued to fight against the racism and injustice of government policies toward Réunionese on the island and in metropolitan France. The party continued to condemn apartheid in South Africa; for example, the PCR strongly opposed holding a meeting of the Indian Ocean Commission in a hotel owned by South African businessmen (ibid., 7 January). The party also favored imposing trade sanctions on South Africa (ibid., 9 January); Réunion imported peppers and other agricultural goods from South Africa that were grown on the island (ibid., 30 July). Paul Vergès said in 1985 that the Réunionese needed to take up their responsibility for developing the island and not rely on more aid from metropolitan France to solve Réunion's problems (*Le Monde*, 8 November 1985). He stated that the other parties on the island need to work with the PCR to reach a development policy (*Témoignages*, 10 January). In Sainte-Marie, the PCR signed a protocol with the Socialists and other leftist parties to bar the right from retaking the commune (ibid., 5–6 July).

**International Affairs.** The PCR has had a strong interest in regional development in the Indian Ocean and kept in close contact with neighboring communist parties as well as communist parties in France and other French departments. After a PCR delegation led by Paul Vergès traveled to China in November 1985 to resume relations between the parties, *Témoignages* ran a lengthy series of articles on political and cultural relations with China. Vergès led a European Parliament delegation to India in April to discuss relations and development (ibid., 26–27 April). Upon his return, he asked the government to favor economic and cultural exchanges, specifically Air India flights to the island, between India and Réunion (ibid., 23 May). The PCR also wanted increased trade with Madagascar. The situation in South Africa dominated newspaper coverage, and the PCR continued to oppose apartheid. It supported the liberation struggles of the Namibian people and the African National Congress and endorsed the actions of the Palestine Liberation Organization. It favored the creation of a zone of peace in the Indian Ocean and has repeatedly called for the removal of military, particularly nuclear, forces from the region. The PCR decried what it perceived as the U.S. rejection of Soviet proposals for an arms control agreement at the Reykjavik summit and the

U.S. Strategic Defense Initiative, which it called a diabolic invention that risks relaunching the arms race and carrying war into space (ibid., 3 January). More so than in recent years, the PCR denounced American "imperialism" as being at the source of most conflicts; examples cited were Thailand, Angola, Iran and Iraq, Lebanon, Afghanistan, Nicaragua, El Salvador, and Libya (ibid., 16 April, 4 November).

**Biography.** *Camille Dieudonné.* Camille Dieudonné grew up in the 1950s in a communist family of modest means. After receiving her baccalauréat (high school diploma), she earned a law degree and studied in Paris to become an inspector of the Posts and Telecommunications Ministry (PTT). She worked for four years as a PTT inspector in Thionville (northeastern France). While there, she became active in cultural action and Mahgrebian aid societies. In 1978 she was posted to Réunion, where she soon joined the PCR and the UFR. In 1973 she was elected a deputy mayor of Sainte-Suzanne, and she has also been a member of the UFR Executive Bureau (ibid., 25 February, 4 March). Dieudonné was an alternate candidate on the party's list for the legislative election (ibid., 24 February). She has been a particularly strong advocate of children's and family rights (ibid., 4 March).

Hilarie Slason
*Arlington, Virginia*

---

# Senegal

---

**Population.** 6,980,000
**Party.** Independence and Labor Party (Parti de l'indépendance du travail; PIT)
**Founded.** 1957
**Membership.** No data
**General Secretary.** Amath Dansoko
**Politburo.** 14 members: Amath Dansoko, Samba Dioulde Thiam, Maguette Thiam, Mady Danfaka, Sadio Camara, Seydou Ndongo, Semou Pathe Gueye, Makhtar Mbaye, Bouma Gaye, Mohamed Laye (names of other four not known)
**Secretariat.** 7 members: Amath Dansoko, Semou Pathe Gueye, Maguette Thiam, Samba Dioulde Thiam, Mady Danfaka, Makhtar Mbaye (replacement of Seydou Cissoko not yet named)
**Central Committee.** 55 members (secretary: Semou Pathe Gueye)
**Status.** Legal
**Last Congress.** Second, 28 September–2 October 1984, in Dakar
**Last Election.** 1983, 0.5 percent, no seats
**Auxiliary Organization.** Women's Democratic Union
**Publications.** *Daan Doole*, *Gestu*

Senegal's numerous Marxist and leftist parties continued to struggle on the margin of political life in 1986. It was reflective of their weakness and disarray that the only significant news from their quarter was the death on 10 March of Seydou Cissoko, chairman of the PIT, at age 57. Of some eight Marxist or quasi-Marxist parties, the PIT is the one that is officially recognized by Moscow and is the most prominent in the international communist movement (for background on this and other parties, see *YICA*, 1986). Cissoko was a founder of the PIT—which his obituary in the *World Marxist Review* (May) described as the first Marxist-Leninist party in tropical Africa—and served as its general secretary from 1967 to 1984, when he was elected chairman at the party's Second Congress. Cissoko died in Moscow, where he had gone to attend the Twenty-seventh Congress of the Communist Party of the Soviet Union (CPSU). His funeral in Senegal was attended by representatives of numerous other political parties, including the ruling Socialist Party (PS). The post of chairman had been specially created for Cissoko when he stepped down as general secretary in 1984, and a successor was not immediately named.

A highlight of PIT activity in 1986 was the conference it sponsored on 1–2 February, in conjunction with the *WMR*, on the "Socio-Economic Development of Black Africa and Problems of Democracy." The conference was attended by representatives from all the main Senegalese political parties, including the PS, as well as intellectuals, trade union leaders, and delegates from Nigeria, the French Communist Party, and the *African Communist*. (Representatives from the *WMR*, the Soviet Union, and East Germany were refused visas by Senegal, and those from Ethiopia and the Communist Party of Sudan were refused entry at the airport and deported.) In his remarks at the conference, Cissoko blamed imperialism for most of the problems facing the people of Africa, denounced multinational corporations for evading taxes, and asked whether the time had not come for African countries to renounce their external debt. PIT general secretary Dansoko urged that Senegal take the initiative to improve trade and other relations with the Soviet Union.

The *African Communist* (no. 106) described the "historic seminar" as "a sign, however tiny, that many forces in Africa now recognize that they have to work together with communists." However, in his remarks to the conference, Babikar Sine, who represented Senegal's president, Abdou Diouf, criticized Marxists and questioned their commitment to democracy. Asking whether the PIT would continue to support the idea of pluralism if it took power, he argued that history showed that once the communists take power they dominate all political life, and one party, the communist party, directs and dominates everything; he said that he therefore prefers bourgeois democracy (ibid.).

PIT leaders continued to be active in international communist forums. In an article in the *WMR* (February), Dansoko paid homage to the leading role of the Soviet Union in the international communist movement and termed the new edition of the CPSU program the "Communist Manifesto of the close of the twentieth century." Politburo member Semou Pathe Gueye, a frequent contributor to the *WMR*, participated in an international research group the journal commissioned on "general problems of theory," and in a *WMR* conference in Prague on the Soviet program for peace, disarmament, and world security. Pathe also coauthored—with representatives of the communist parties of India and the Sudan—an article in the *WMR* (August) on the nonaligned movement (which held its eighth conference in Zimbabwe at the close of August, marking its 25th year). While noting the vulnerabilities of the nonaligned movement—including the efforts of "imperialism and reactionary forces" to undercut its unity and "divert it from its anti-imperialist positions"—the article praised the movement for its stands on decolonization, the new international economic order, and the nuclear arms race, which "not only have the understanding but coincide directly with the aspirations of the communists" (ibid.).

Although the left was generally quiescent in terms of public demonstrations during the year, there was a brief stir in April over the U.S. bombing of Libya. The People's Liberation Party, which was the only left-wing party with representation (one seat) in the 120-member National Assembly, denounced the bombardment as a "use of brutal force" that "constitutes an overall threat to all Third World countries"; the party also called on Diouf, who was then chairman of the Organization of African Unity, "to clearly condemn the attack" (*FBIS*, 18 April). Four days later, Senegalese authorities deployed police to prevent University of Dakar students from carrying out a protest march they had organized against the American bombing raid. However, the students were able to meet at the call of the Dakar Students' Union (which is close to Marxist and leftist parties) on the university campus to denounce the American raid and the "passive attitude" of President Diouf (ibid., 23 April).

The PS enjoyed near-monolithic control of the National Assembly—particularly with the defection to the PS of three parliamentarians from the moderate Senegalese Democratic Party (PDS), the largest opposition party—and the opposition parties were already beginning to focus on the next general elections, due in early 1988. In particular, both the Marxist and non-Marxist parties were beginning to maneuver to demand provisions that would ensure the fairness of those elections. (In 1984, twelve of the fourteen opposition parties boycotted the local elections in protest against electoral irregularities.) The PDS announced it would boycott the 1988 presidential and legislative elections unless the election laws were amended to permit opposition members at the polling stations, to ensure fair distribution of electoral cards, and to require presentation of an identity card at the time of voting. In an interview on the British Broadcasting Corporation, General Secretary Abdoulaye Bathily of the Democratic League of Senegal (LD) denounced the provision banning parties from forming coalitions to compete in the elections, which he claimed guarantees a PS victory. Bathily, whose party is a Marxist-Leninist competitor to the PIT, also criticized the lack of any means for identifying voters and the corruption of the ruling party.

With the economy sagging under the heavy weight of statism and widespread corruption, and with living standards declining further under International Monetary Fund–sponsored austerity measures, the opposition parties (both Marxist and non-Marxist) saw potential for mobilizing popular discontent against the ruling party. But none of the opposition parties showed any indication of being able to mobilize significant popular support. The popular bases of the Marxist parties—including not only the PIT and the LD but also the African Independence Party and the (Trotskyist) Socialist Workers' Organization—have been manifestly slim, and they appeared more preoccupied with arguing doctrine and the "correct line" than with organizing opposition to the government.

With unemployment reaching record levels and real wages plummeting, political opposition could come from the relatively well organized trade union movement. But the movement has been plagued with divisions, some of which were encouraged by the government as it attempted to limit the unions' strength and autonomy.

The most serious threat to the political hold of the ruling party stemmed not from any of the other parties, moderate or left, but from the rapidly growing Islamic fundamentalist movement. Islamic fundamentalist literature has proliferated, along with calls for making Senegal an Islamic state. Two pro-Iranian publications have been prominent in criticizing immorality, corruption, nepotism, and mismanagement in government. Intellectuals have been attracted in increasing numbers, and Islamic fundamentalism appeared to have taken a particular hold at the University of Dakar main campus. Marxist intellectuals in Senegal were particularly frustrated by this development. Dr. Raphael Sarr, a member of the PIT Central Committee and lecturer at Dakar University, stated, "Our party believes that one of the fundamental lines of its activity is to win over an ever larger segment of the intelligentsia for the ideology of Marxism-Leninism." But he acknowledged "the active spread of Islam" among Senegalese intellectuals and underscored the importance of explaining "to these intellectuals who, consciously or unconsciously, fall victim to the mystico-religious depression," that the introduction of Sharia law has failed to solve the urgent problems either in Iran or the Sudan, and that there is "ultimately no real alternative to the organized struggle" for socialism. (*WMR*, December 1985.)

On the international front, Senegal continued to develop friendly relations with Marxist states, despite its generally Western orientation. In February, Senegal signed a two-year cultural agreement with China for the exchange of students, films, and radio and television programs. At the end of 1985, Senegal had signed similar accords on cultural cooperation with the Soviet Union for 1986 and 1987, which grant Soviet scholarships to Senegalese students and provide for cooperation and exchanges between the two countries in the fields of books, the cinema industry, and sports. In August, a delegation of the National Assembly of Senegal was warmly welcomed in Moscow for an official visit at the invitation of the USSR Supreme Soviet.

Larry Diamond
*Hoover Institution*

# South Africa

**Population.** 33,241,000
**Party.** South African Communist Party (SACP)
**Founded.** 1921
**Membership.** No data
**Chairman.** Joe Slovo
**Leading Organs.** Composition unknown
**Status.** Proscribed
**Last Congress.** Sixth, late 1984 or early 1985
**Last Election.** N/a
**Auxiliary Organizations.** None
**Publications.** *African Communist* (quarterly; published abroad); *Umsebenzi* (published clandestinely in South Africa)

In 1986 the SACP celebrated the 65th anniversary of its founding in Cape Town. In so doing, the clandestine party reconfirmed its commitment to the alliance with the African National Congress (ANC), the country's most prominent African nationalist movement. Both organizations have long histories as legal organizations: the ANC from its founding in 1912 until its proscription in 1960; and the Communist Party of South Africa from its founding in 1921 until the decision of a majority of the party's Central Committee members in 1950 to dissolve it in the face of the impending Supression of Communism Act. Reconstituted underground in 1953 as the SACP, it operated primarily internally until the early 1960s, when heightened government repression forced it and the outlawed ANC increasingly to carry on their activities in exile. Since the 1970s, both the SACP and the ANC have successfully re-established their presence within South Africa; this mobilization was spearheaded by Umkhonto we Sizwe, the military wing of the ANC established in 1961 within South Africa with SACP assistance. Heartened by the rising militancy of opponents of apartheid within South Africa since mid-1984, Joe Slovo, the newly elected chairman of the SACP, stated that "the South African masses are on the move as never before in our history" (*African*

*Communist*, no. 107). As the continent's first Marxist-Leninist party and as South Africa's first nonracial party, the SACP was particularly buoyed by the increasing recognition it has received internally, where "in all parts of the country today the red flag of the Communist Party is being raised by the masses—at funerals and demonstrations in town and country. Epaulettes and flashes bearing the insignia of the Party, the letters SACP, and the hammer and sickle, are proudly displayed by the youth under the very noses of the security police . . . Never has interest in the ideology of Marxism-Leninism been so widespread" (ibid., no. 106).

**Organization and Leadership.** Visible leadership of the SACP remained in the hands of representatives of the older cadre who joined the party during its legal existence in the 1940s and then left the country under party orders in the early 1960s. Working in independent Africa or Europe, they have been actively associated with the exiled leadership of the ANC and its other allied organizations.

Moses Mabhida, the 62-year-old African general secretary, died in Maputo in March. A party member since 1942, Mabhida had been an active trade unionist and prominent in the organization of the South African Congress of Trade Unions (SACTU), which he represented in exile in the early 1960s. In 1963 he turned to full-time work with Umkhonto we Sizwe until his election as general secretary of the SACP in 1978; he continued to hold responsible posts in the ANC and was a member of the National Executive Committee of the ANC until his death. When Mabhida's family refused to accept South African government restrictions limiting any funeral ceremony in South Africa to a family affair, Mabhida was given a state funeral in Maputo by the Mozambican government with President Samora Machel as the leading speaker. By the end of 1986 there had been no party announcement of a successor to Mabhida.

Shortly after Mabhida's death, the SACP announced that Joe Slovo, a 60-year-old Lithuanian-born white barrister, who had also been active in the party since the 1940s, had been elected chairman, a post vacant since the death of Dr. Yusef Dadoo in 1983. Describing the division of labor among top party officials, a writer in the party journal commented: "Traditionally in the Party, the chairman has been the premier diplomatic and public presence, while the general secretary has been the principal political and administrative figure. Despite the public apparent separation of functions, the chairman nevertheless shares the responsibilities of political leadership and the formulation of policy; his functions are far more political than decorative" (ibid.). In the eyes of the same commentator, Slovo "has, in recent years, become acknowledged as the party leader, who makes many of the important keynote speeches of the organization . . . he has certainly become the movement's foremost writer on themes of military-political strategy and the draftsman of many crucial theses which have shaped the present strategy and tactics of the whole South African revolution" (ibid.).

Since 1964, Slovo has been a member of the Revolutionary Council of the ANC in exile, where he combined day-to-day administrative and organizational work with his theoretical writing. "It is for his unique combination of practical tasks with his theoretical leading role that he was chosen chief of staff of Umkhonto we Sizwe and in 1985 was elected to the National Executive Committee of the ANC—the first South African white to be so honored" (ibid.). For the SACP, Slovo's election "symbolizes the new era in which our Party lives and fights: the era of revolutionary struggle for the final liberation of the South African people, the era of deep fraternal unity with the ANC and collabora-

tion in action of communist and nationalist freedom fighters, the era of Umkhonto we Sizwe and of the young men and women—the township revolutionaries—who are at the spearhead of the revolutionary upheaval now poised for victory in South Africa" (ibid.).

Questions concerning the nature of the links between the SACP and the ANC engaged spokesmen of both organizations, particularly in response to commentary in the American and European press alleging SACP domination of the ANC and the publication in June by the South African government of "Talking with the ANC," a brochure quoting liberally from statements of both banned organizations. Designed simultaneously to demonstrate ANC subservience to the SACP and to encourage African nationalist rejection of it, the brochure made the claim that 23 of the 30 members of the National Executive Committee of the ANC were members of the SACP.

Refusing "to join in this game of which the late Senator Joe McCarthy was such a staunch apostle," Slovo asserted that "the alliance between the Communist Party and the ANC has no secret clauses. Only those who have other axes to grind or who are victims of the stereotype image of communists and communist parties see in this relationship [something] sinister . . . It is precisely because it has always been based on a complete respect for the independence and integrity of the internal democratic processes of both organizations, that the alliance has continued to flourish despite unending onslaughts against it from many quarters" (ibid., no. 107). Slovo recognized that the present situation required "the broadest possible front of struggle against the racist autocracy. And a front, by definition, contains disparate forces. The ANC-led liberation alliance, representing the main revolutionary forces is the key sector of this front . . . at the same time there must be no ambiguity about the primary place which the ANC occupies in this line-up and, broadly speaking, the immediate future can only be positively determined under its umbrella" (ibid.). Noting that "both the ANC and the Party emphasize the dominant role of the working people in the coalition of class forces which constitute the liberation front," Slovo delimited a distinctive role for the SACP: "unlike the ANC, which does not and should not commit itself exclusively to the aspirations of a single class, the Party owes allegiance solely to the working people. And it is our prime function both as an independent Party and as part of the alliance to assert and jealously safeguard the dominant role of this class whose aspirations we represent. In our book this does not imply that the Party itself must seek to occupy the dominant position in the liberation alliance. On the contrary, if correct leadership of the democratic revolution requires the strengthening of the national movement as the major and leading mass organizational force, then this is precisely the way in which a party exercises its vanguard role in the real and not the vulgar sense of the term" (ibid.).

For their part, prominent ANC leaders have also defended participation of communists in the ANC. Invoking the longtime overlapping of membership between the two organizations, stretching back to the 1920s, ANC president Oliver Tambo asserted: "ANC members who are also members of the SACP make a very clear distinction between these two independent bodies. We cooperate a lot, but the ANC is accepted by the SACP as leading the struggle. There is absolute loyalty to the position. It is often suggested that the ANC is controlled by the Communist Party . . . by communists. Well, I have been long enough in the ANC to know that that has never been true" (Cape Times, 4 November 1985). In complementary analysis, Tambo's eulogy at Mabhida's funeral praised the late general secretary of the SACP for his determination to maintain the historically open character of the ANC: "none among us was more conscious than he [Mabhida] that the African National Congress could only carry out its historic mission if it maintains the character it has come to assume. That character was that of a parliament of all the people of our country, representative of our future, the negation of the divisions and conflicts that racial arrogance and capitalist greed have imposed on our people. That is why Comrade Mabhida fought hard and long to ensure that nothing should turn the ANC into a rabble of black chauvinists or a clique of leftist demagogues" (Sechaba, May). ANC general secretary Alfred Nzo reiterated that stance: "The African National Congress will continue to defend the right of any South African who chooses to belong to the South African Communist Party. So shall we respect the right of any of our compatriots to belong to any party of their choice as long as that party is not a vehicle for the propagation of racism and fascism. Our democratic perspectives impose these obligations on us" (ibid., September).

Collaboration between SACP members and the ANC has taken place in the widely scattered centers on the African continent and in Europe where members of both organizations are concentrated, as well as more clandestinely in South Africa in the major urban centers where both organizations have had their greatest support. Undoubtedly for the SACP in its vanguard role, the tasks of coordination of a farflung, but probably not large, membership pose daunting organizational problems, particularly within South Africa. In its estimation, "at the center of our efforts lies the task of further strengthening our Party inside the country, extending its links with the workers and the broad masses, and drawing into its ranks the best revolutionary representatives of our people" (African Communist, no. 105).

**Domestic Activities and Attitudes.** Within South Africa, the ever more assertive role of black workers and the locally based activities of civic associations and youthful township militants engage strong support from the SACP. The formation of the multiracial Confederation of South African Trade Unions (COSATU) in November 1985 was hailed as a "decisive advance" that "should enable the workers to act nationally, as a united force, dealing not only with economic questions, but also acting to advance the democratic struggle" (ibid.). With parallel enthusiasm the SACP also pointed to the widespread strikes, boycotts, and stay-at-homes (before the renewed midyear declaration of a state of emergency) as evidence of growing class consciousness among a "black working class, [which] is increasingly assuming its position as the leading social force of the national democratic alliance" (ibid.). The often interconnected moves to discredit and destroy government administration and community councils in the townships and to replace them with locally established autonomous structures is endorsed not only as a success for the strategy of making the townships ungovernable and apartheid unworkable, but also as the emergence of "people's communes" that could provide the genesis of an alternative civil power. Cumulatively, "the masses of the people have engaged in struggles which have resulted in the emergence in some areas of the country of what has been described as an insurrectionary situation. These areas have many features of a mass revolutionary base, with the people highly conscious and active, with well-developed mass legal and semi-legal organizations, and an acceptance by the broad masses of the leading role of the ANC-led liberation front in the democratic revolution" (ibid.).

From this perspective, much of the widespread violence that has occurred is viewed as confirmation that "the idea of a people's war has taken root . . .

Reflecting a popular response to the reactionary violence of the enemy, these armed actions are carried out by combat groups with rudimentary weapons in the majority of cases. Nevertheless, the revolutionaries who have conducted these actions have themselves attained a high level of political awareness and consciously as the combat forces of the revolution, subjecting themselves to the program of the revolutionary movement and its leadership. They represent the further expansion of the people's army, Umkhonto we Sizwe, whose units have also continued to escalate the popular offensive against the apartheid regime" (ibid.).

Faced with the collapse of its authority in many areas, an ever more determined opposition, and a widening economic crisis, the South African government is characterized as being in a state of confusion. "It can no longer claim to have a policy and certainly lacks both the ideas and the means to extricate the apartheid system from its crisis . . . The divisions within the white power bloc have continued to increase. Contradictions between the ruling class, the bourgeoisie and the Botha regime have emerged. Worried by the revolutionary threat to the capitalist system, the bourgeoisie is beginning to indicate a readiness to act on its own and in its interests without waiting for its political representatives to move at a pace which the bourgeoisie considers as unacceptably slow" (ibid.).

In light of these developments, the much-publicized contacts between South African businessmen and ANC leaders, discussion of a national convention (supported by the Progressive Federal Party and Chief Gatsha Buthelezi of Kwazulu), and suggestions by the government of the possibilities of negotiation can be understood but also rejected at present. "While the movement cannot rule out negotiations for all time, we believe that if negotiations have to take place, they will come about only as a result of decisive all-around struggle by the people—when the regime is forced to acknowledge the actual power of the democratic forces. In such a situation Botha will understand why he has to discuss the mechanism of transfer of power, why he has to release all political prisoners and detainees, unban the ANC and its allies, [and] dismantle the repressive apparatus. He will understand why, if a national convention has to be held, it should be elective, sovereign, and truly constituent" (ibid.).

In the assessment of Slovo, "nor should we underestimate the internal and external resources which the regime can still muster in an attempt to keep the majority from opening the gates of political power. But at the same time, the possibility of a people's breakthrough is growing stronger by the day. It follows, therefore, that while continuing to focus our sights on a protracted conflict, we must also prepare and be ready to adjust them to a much swifter transformation involving insurrectionary ingredients" (ibid., no. 107). As other SACP spokesmen have done in the past, Slovo reiterated the SACP's commitment to a program of "democratic transformation along the lines of the Freedom Charter," particularly emphasizing the necessity of "one united South Africa based on the will of the majority . . . Equality must be between individuals (if need be, safeguarded by a constitutional mechanism) and not between race or ethnic groups as such" (ibid.). Slovo stated explicitly that "undoubtedly" there would be a mixed economy after the demise of apartheid, which might, "if political domination of the old ruling class is ended and the new state apparatus is constructed within the framework envisaged by the Freedom Charter, . . . facilitate rather than hinder the continuing drive toward a socialist future; a drive which, within a truly democratic framework, could well be settled in debate rather than on the streets" (ibid.).

**International Views and Activities.** The SACP "has always taken a stand in support of the Soviet Union and the other socialist countries who constitute the sheet anchor of the world revolutionary process," according to the SACP Central Committee (*IB*, July). Its longtime affinity with the Soviet Union and its close allies was manifest in the fraternal appearance of Slovo before the Eleventh Congress of the Socialist Unity Party of the German Democratic Republic (GDR) in April (*Neues Deutschland*, 22 April), followed by his receiving the Order of the Friendship of the Peoples of the USSR on the occasion of his 60th birthday on 22 May. In a sharp contrast, after decades of hostility to the Chinese Communist Party, a SACP delegation headed by Slovo visited China in September for a visit of at least ten days, at the end of which the delegation was received by General Secretary Hu Yaobang (NCNA, 18 September).

On the African continent the SACP continued to identify with Marxist-Leninist parties, both ruling and nonruling. The *African Communist* (no. 106) reported that its representative participated in an international roundtable sponsored by the *World Marxist Review* and the Independence and Labor Party of Senegal; "for the first time in the history of black Africa such a conference was hosted by a

Communist Party." Although representatives from the Soviet Union, the GDR, and Ethiopia were denied entry, delegates from the Communist Party of France, various Nigerian organizations, and Senegalese political parties, including the ruling Socialist Party, participated. The "historic seminar" represented "a sign, however tiny, that many forces in Africa now recognize that they have to work together with communists. That communists in Africa are not 'foreign' but the flesh and blood of the oppressed and exploited masses of our continent" (ibid.).

Special enthusiasm was also evident in reportage of the Second Congress of the Angolan MPLA-PT, at which Slovo in his fraternal address characterized the congress as a "special event . . . because you belong to that small band of African revolutionaries who are working to create conditions for the eventual construction of a socialist way of life . . . There was no simple formula for you to pull out of the archives of Marxist learning. There was no ready-made answer in any communist book for you to apply. The problems of the transition period in conditions such as yours are, as you are aware, filled with enormous complexities. And in your courageous efforts to move toward a socialist path, you are adding to the storehouse of Marxism-Leninism" (ibid., no. 105).

**Publications.** Since its inception in 1959, *African Communist* has been published "in the interests of African solidarity and as a forum for Marxist-Leninist thought throughout our continent." Printed in the GDR and distributed from an office in London, the magazine primarily considers developments in South Africa and the world communist movement from a SACP perspective, but it also devotes attention to statements by African communists and Marxist-Leninists as well as, less frequently, those of communists from other continents. Within South Africa the party publishes more irregularly a clandestine paper, *Umsebenzi*; its title is the Zulu/Xhosa word for worker and invokes the similarly named paper that was the Communist Party of South Africa's legal publication from 1930 to 1936. In addition, the underground SACP has disseminated propaganda flyers and leaflets when possible under the severe constraints of the state of emergency.

SACP publications are complemented by those of the ANC: *Sechaba*, the "official organ," which is also printed in the GDR and distributed from London; and other publications produced in Africa. The ANC also sponsors Radio Freedom, which gives broadcasts of up to several hours that are carried by the government shortwave services of Angola, Ethiopia, Madagascar, Tanzania, and Zambia.

Sheridan Johns
*Duke University*

# Sudan

**Population.** 22,932,000
**Party.** Sudanese Communist Party (al-Hizb al-Shuyu'i al-Sudani; SCP)
**Founded.** 1946
**Membership.** 9,000 (estimated)
**General Secretary.** Muhammad Ibrahim Nugud Mansur

**Secretariat.** 7 members. Muhammad Ibrahim Nugud Mansur, Ali al-Tijani al-Tayyib Babikar, Izz-al Din Ali Amir, Abu al-Quasim (Gassim) Muhammad, Sulayman Hamid, Al Gazuli Said Uthman, Muhammad Ahmad Sulayman (Suleiman)

**Central Committee.** Sudi Darag, Khad(i)r Nasir, Abd-al-Majid Shakak, Hassan Gassim al-Sid, Fatima Ahmad Ibrahim, Ibrahim Zakariya, and the 7 members of the Secretariat

**Status.** Legal

**Last Congress.** Fourth, 31 October 1967, in Khartoum

**Last Election.** 1986; 5 seats in Constituent Assembly (2 in geographical and 3 in "graduates" constituencies) (Khartoum Radio, 14 April; *FBIS*, 15 April; *WMR*, November)

**Auxiliary Organizations.** Democratic Federation of Sudanese Students (DSFS; affiliated with International Union of Students); Sudanese Youth Union; Sudan Workers' Trade Federation (SWTUF; operates with quasi-official standing); Sudanese Defenders of Peace and Democracy (presumably a World Peace Council [WPC] affiliate); Union of Sudanese Women

**Publications.** *Al-Maydan* (newspaper that reappeared in July 1985 after longtime ban); *Al-Shuyuiy (The communist)*

A small group of intellectuals at Khartoum University founded the SCP in 1946. For reasons of security, it adopted the name Sudanese National Liberation Movement. Its familiarity with communist doctrine came largely through Sudanese who had studied in Egypt and had access to Marxist works translated into Arabic. The party became a leading force in the popular struggle for Sudanese independence from Britain, which was achieved in 1956. The SCP was the only political party in Sudan to oppose the military regime under General Ibrahim Abbud that seized power in November 1958 in a coup d'état. Abbud arrested all the Sudanese communist leaders he could locate and forced party members still at large to go underground. The Abbud regime foundered, however, because of its inability to bring the war in southern Sudan under control.

On 25 May 1969, Colonel Jaafar Numeiri seized control of Sudan in a virtually bloodless coup. The SCP gave him its support and became the only legal party in the country. The victory of Numeiri and his SCP allies represented a triumph for the left against powerful economic interests and foreign capital in Sudan. In 1970 the SCP's popularity and prestige reached an all-time high. With a membership totaling 5,000 to 10,000, it was the strongest and best organized communist party in Africa. According to a party official, however, certain "liquidationist tendencies" appeared in the leadership and proposed the dissolution of the SCP into a broad political organization of the petite bourgeoisie. The "liquidationists" reportedly were defeated at an extraordinary party congress. (*WMR*, October.)

The failure of Numeiri's socialist policies and Sudan's continuing reliance on Western financial support prompted the regime to move to the right. A moderate faction within the SCP accepted Numeiri's drift rightward and his plan to dissolve the SCP into his newly created Sudan Socialist Union (SSU), which was to be the country's sole political organization. The SCP's more radical faction (strongly represented by procommunist army officers) opposed Numeiri's shift, however. Leftist officers evidently masterminded an abortive 1971 coup, in the aftermath of which Numeiri outlawed the SCP and liquidated most of its leadership. (For more detail on the origins and background of the SCP, see *YICA*, 1985.)

During its prolonged status as an illegal organization, the SCP retained considerable influence among intellectuals, students (especially at Khartoum University), railway workers, sympathizers in the armed forces, and cotton growers. It also amassed particular strength in the trade unions, and communist inroads became visible among the refugees in and outside of Sudan.

After joining the newly formed National Salvation Front (Jahbat al-Inqaz al-Watani) in 1984 and the overthrow of Numeiri by General Abdel Rahman Siwar el Dahab in April 1985, the SCP was legalized by the transitional military government. SCP general secretary Nugud and other party officials then emerged from clandestinity; still others returned from exile.

On 29 November 1985, the SCP convened an enlarged meeting of its Central Committee to discuss the upcoming national elections. Its outgrowth was a statement, published on 24 December, entitled "Turn the Election Campaign into a Drive to Consolidate Our Party." The statement urged the party to focus on the attainment of two principal goals: to rally all the forces involved in bringing down the former regime and mobilize them in support of the SCP; and to get as many communists as possible into the Constituent Assembly. In pursuit of these objectives, the statement declared that "We should exert utmost efforts in all areas—ideological, political, organizational, and administrative . . . We must urge members of the party and its friends and allies to raise funds for the election campaign, launch new slogans, and use novel strategies . . . (*IB*, April). In addition, party members were exhorted to put forth diligent efforts to register voters and ensure them transportation to the polling stations. "Conducting the election campaign is the top-priority political and party task, requiring supreme efforts of the party organizations and cells, of all party members," the statement concluded (ibid.).

The SCP's election platform, dated 6 March 1986, emphasized the need for adoption of a democratic constitution—that is, a charter that would provide ample scope for the enhancement of communist influence in Sudanese society and politics. The platform attributed the country's difficulties to "a political line . . . which opted for capitalist development and curtailment of democracy." The SCP enjoined the Constituent Assembly, to be chosen in the forthcoming election, to prepare a charter embodying the following criteria: an executive power controlled by and accountable to the parliament; a guarantee of basic human rights and democratic freedoms, including racial and religious equality; "personal immunity, inviolability of the home and correspondence, the right to work, education, housing, health care, and the principle of equal pay for equal work"; an independent judicial system; a military establishment barred from any role in domestic politics; a civil service system aimed at "eroding the positions of capitalist bureaucracy"; a decentralization of administration, with maximum local authority for the masses; a democratization of the educational and cultural establishments and state information outlets; and a mixed economy, featuring centralized economic planning and development along with a private sector, especially in agriculture. Among specific measures to be undertaken by the assembly, the SCP called for nullification of "all laws and degrees by the former regime which served to oppress the people"; passage of statutes rehabilitating and providing compensation to the victims of persecution under the old regime; abolition of laws restricting trade union activity; and transfer of the security police from the jurisdiction of the Ministry of Internal Affairs to that of the parliament. (*IB*, June.)

**Domestic Affairs.** In April, a year after Numeiri's downfall, the elections for a Constituent Assembly were held. The Transitional Military Council, under whose auspices the voting took place, subsequently handed over power to the first democratically elected civilian government in seventeen years. Sadiq al-Mahdi, a descendant of the famed nineteenth-century Islamic spiritual leader and military hero El Mahdi, became prime minister. He was the head of the Umma Party, a moderate Islamic organization, which won 48 percent of the popular vote and 99 seats in the assembly. The Umma Party formed a coalition government with the Democratic Unionist Party—like the Umma, a northern-based, moderate Muslim group—which had won 64 assembly seats. The National Islamic Front, a Muslim fundamentalist party, captured 28 seats, and the SCP took two.

Although there are 301 seats in the assembly, only 264 representatives were elected. John Garang, leader of the Sudanese People's Liberation Army (SPLA), boycotted the elections because his movement had not been consulted about them. At any rate, it proved impossible to conduct voting in 37 constituencies in the rebellion-wracked southern Sudan, which thus was unrepresented in the new assembly. The question immediately arose whether the constitution that the assembly was empowered to write would have any validity for the south. Speaking in the aftermath of the elections, Nugud said that the new government should concentrate, inter alia, on repealing the Sharia code and other repressive laws, seeking a democratic solution to the insurgency in the south, and rectifying the incompetence and corruption in the country's banking system (*Al Ayyam*, 23 April).

The new government in Khartoum sought reconciliation between the northern and southern parts of the nation, but was hobbled both by the SPLA's intransigence and by the National Islamic Front, which opposed a revocation of the Sharia statutes and advocated a *jihad* (holy war) against the infidel insurgents. The government's rapprochement with Libya led Moammar Khadafy to close down the Libyan-based radio station of the SPLA, as promised, and otherwise to cease his support of the Sudanese insurgents. Moreover, Libya supplied Sudan with Soviet-manufactured jet aircraft that have been used to bomb SPLA targets. Ethiopia, however, continues to provide Soviet-made arms and logistical assistance to the SPLA, which maintains its headquarters near Addis Ababa and uses Ethiopian territory as a military training ground and staging area. The insurgent forces now number at least 12,000 and perhaps as many as 20,000. (*NYT*, 18 August; *CSM*, 15 October.)

In March, representatives of the National Alliance for the Salvation of the Country (of which the SCP is a member) met with a delegation of the SPLA at Koka Dam, a site not far from Addis Ababa. According to the Koka Dam declaration issued on 24 March, the two sides agreed on the necessity of convening a national constitutional conference. They also called for the lifting of the state of emergency in Sudan, regional autonomy for the south, repeal of the various laws restricting citizens' freedoms, abrogation of military pacts between Sudan and other countries (an apparent reference to Egypt and Libya), and a continuing endeavor to effect a ceasefire in the southern insurgency. (Clandestine radio of the SPLA, in English, 28 March.) In August, however, the SPLA shot down a Sudanese passenger jet, killing everyone aboard. This incident precipitated the end of the dialogue that the insurgent forces had opened with other Sudanese political forces. Muhammad Mahjub 'Uthman, the SCP's representative in talks between the SPLA and the National Alliance, strongly condemned the attack on the plane (Sudan News Agency [SUNA], 24 August).

The SCP stood to benefit as Khartoum and Moscow moved to improve their bilateral relationship. The Soviet and Sudanese governments exchanged greetings in January on the 30th anniversary of the establishment of diplomatic relations between them. In February, a Soviet economic delegation traveled to Khartoum for talks on cooperation in agriculture, rehabilitation of Soviet-built factories and medical services, and possible Soviet financing of dams and other major projects in Sudan (SUNA, in English, 2 February). In August, Sadiq al-Mahdi paid a five-day visit to the Soviet Union, with the avowed objective "to strike a balance in our relations with the West and East" (*Al Sharq Al-Awsat*, 27 June). Sadiq al-Mahdi, the highest ranking Sudanese statesman to journey to the USSR in fifteen years, met with Nikolay Ryzhkov (his counterpart as chairman of the Council of Ministers) and with Soviet officials from the Ministry of Foreign Affairs, the State Committee for Foreign Economic Relations, and the State Planning Committee. The visitor was also given a tour of Tashkent, the Soviet Union's Central Asian showcase for officials from

Muslim countries. No specific economic or other agreements are known to have been signed during Sadiq al-Mahdi's sojourn—perhaps because the Soviets were wary of jeopardizing their alliance with Ethiopia, a foe of Sudan. However, the Sudanese leader publicly lauded the "peace initiatives" of the Soviet Union (Tashkent Domestic Service, in Uzbek, 15 August), and the joint communiqué issued at the end of the visit expressed agreement on such issues as an end to nuclear testing, reallocation of resources from military programs to economic development, the creation of a nuclear-free zone in Africa and removal of foreign military bases from that continent, support for South African and Namibian insurgent groups, and the right of the Palestinians to self-determination and a state of their own (*Pravda*, 18 August). Neither side mentioned the insurgency in southern Sudan in the statements or documents issued during Sadiq al-Mahdi's visit; thus it is unknown whether he appealed to the USSR to stop funneling Soviet weapons from Ethiopia to the SPLA.

**International Views and Activities.** The SCP closely parrots the radical Arab communist line on Middle Eastern politics. "U.S. imperialism" and the "Zionist aggression" of Israel are the villains. The Sudanese communists also condemn moderate Arab countries, such as Egypt, for siding with the U.S.-Israeli "strategic alliance." The SCP chides the United States for its arms sales to Sudan and for making threats against Libya.

At the April meeting of the WPC, the Sudanese representation on the latter's Presidential Committee was increased from one to two (*New Perspectives*, March, June). One of those representatives, Sudan National Peace Council president Hassan al-Bidani (Bodani), attended the Copenhagen Peace Congress in October, along with three of his countrymen (World Congress Devoted to the International Year of Peace, *Preliminary List of Participants*).

The SCP sent representatives to the Eleventh Congress of the World Federation of Trade Unions (WFTU) in East Berlin in September (*List of Participants*); Sudanese Ibrahim Zakariya was reelected general secretary of the WFTU at this meeting.

In December 1984 the SCP had participated in a gathering of world communist parties in Prague under the auspices of the *World Marxist Review* to assess the international situation and formulate communist strategies and tactics for the coming years (*Rudé právo*, 7 December 1984). Another such gathering occurred in the autumn of 1986. Ali Ahmed el Tayeb, the SCP delegate, stated that the ouster of the Numeiri regime had undermined U.S. imperialism in Africa and alleviated the threat of war in the region. He emphasized the need for less developed countries to accelerate their struggle against hunger, illiteracy, and poverty—a struggle that he deemed beneficial for national liberation, social progress, and peace. (*WMR*, October.)

Marian Leighton
*Defense Intelligence Agency*

# Zimbabwe

**Population.** 8,984,000
**Party.** Zimbabwe African National Union (ZANU)
**Founded.** 1963
**Membership.** No data
**First Secretary and President.** Robert G. Mugabe
**Politburo.** 13 members (15 seats). Robert Mugabe, Simon Muzenda (holds 2 seats), Maurice Nyagumbo, Enos Nkala, Emmerson Munangagwa, Nathan Shamuyarira, Didymus Mutasa, Dzingai Mutumbuka, Teurai Ropa Nhongo, Ernest Kadungura, Sydney Sekeremayi, Rex Nhongo, Josiah Tongamirai
**Central Committee.** 90 members
**Status.** Ruling party
**Last Congress.** Fifth, 8–12 August 1984
**Last Election.** 1985, 76 percent, 64 out of 100 parliamentary seats
**Auxiliary Organizations.** People's Militia, Youth Wing
**Publications.** *Moto* (magazine); ZANU has strong influence in all Zimbabwan media.

Real power in Zimbabwe lies with the ZANU Politburo, although ultimate authority rests with Mugabe, who serves as party head. Mugabe's position in both government and party has been greatly strengthened and more centralized as a result of the new party structure established at the Fifth Congress in 1984. There he was unanimously re-elected to the party leadership, with the new titles of first secretary and president. Subsequently, he has begun to press for the creation of a powerful executive presidency for the government, modeled after that of Mozambique. The party congress also gave him a firm mandate to transform the nation into a one-party, ZANU-controlled regime. Mugabe reaffirmed his commitment to the establishment of a one-party socialist state based on Marxist-Leninist lines, but he has assured the population that socialist goals will be achieved through legal means. If anything, the government gave stronger encouragement to businesses in the private sector that generated jobs and foreign exchange. However, Mugabe threatened to expropriate South African assets if the Botha government continued its raids and clandestine activities in Zimbabwe. (*African Economic Digest*, 16 August.)

At the 1984 congress, Mugabe introduced a

"Leadership Code of Conduct" aimed at curbing corruption and nepotism and at instilling greater ideological discipline. It would also discourage party officials from amassing wealth in the private sector. The Marxist prime minister has been concerned that too many ZANU officials are engaging in capitalist activities inimical to the country's socialist goals. In 1986 the code was honored more in the breach, as officials simply transferred their assets to proxy owners. Others left government service for the more lucrative private sector. Maurice Nyagumbo, a top-ranking member of the Politburo, complained that the code was being flouted by a broad spectrum of the civil service. (*Herald*, 10 October.)

ZANU remained a party dominated by the Shona ethnic group, which comprises approximately 80 percent of the population. Mugabe has had little success in attracting more Ndebele, largely because of the government's brutal tactics in suppressing dissident activity in Matabeleland. The few Ndebele who serve in the government have tended to be vehemently anti-ZAPU and have almost no following among their own ethnic group, since the overwhelming majority of the Ndebele have remained in that major opposition party. ZANU's Central Committee has thus continued to be dominated by Shona speakers. Key positions on the Politburo were held by Mugabe's own Zezuru clan of the Shona. Moreover, in 1985 all Ndebele were purged from the recently merged Central Intelligence Organization (CIO) and the Police Special Branch, and many Ndebele officers were prematurely retired from the national army.

ZANU unity was severely tested in 1986, but the party managed to survive the crises and to come through them stronger than ever. The party was shaken by ethnic rivalries and accusations of malfeasance. However, Mugabe was able to defuse the conflict by expelling Herbert Ushewokunze from the Politburo and from his post as secretary for the Commissariat of Culture and by relieving Byron Hove from his position as ZANU secretary for the Midland province, a party stronghold. (Frost & Sullivan, *Zimbabwe Report*, October.) Nevertheless, ethnic tensions between Zezuru and Karanga party members continued to smolder just beneath the surface and threatened to erupt at any time. Mugabe also dealt firmly with party indiscipline among members of the youth wing. The courts reinforced this by sentencing to death the chairman of the youth wing in North Matabeleland province

for killing five members of a small opposition party. (*African Report*, September.)

ZANU's professed Marxism has been substantially diluted since the end of the liberation struggle and its elevation as the ruling party. Mugabe has become more cautious and pragmatic in his policies. He is committed to a mixed economy, has refrained from expropriating private property, and pays fair market prices for all government acquisitions. ZANU tolerates the white-dominated private sector because it is so vital to the economy. Whites continue to play an important, though steadily diminishing, role in public service. After the election in 1985, Mugabe dismissed the highly influential white minister of agriculture, leaving only one remaining white in the cabinet.

The country has been in desperate need of foreign capital and therefore permitted considerable foreign equity control over locally based enterprises. However, ZANU seeks greater state control and progressive expansion of the state in economic development. Toward that end, the government has purchased the major newspapers, a large bank, and a pharmaceutical company and has created a state-owned minerals marketing board. However, it has refrained from nationalizing or expropriating local businesses or multinational enterprises. Top Politburo leaders, notably Maurice Nyagumbo, have asserted that the private sector should be allowed to compete with the public sector and consequently could challenge the latter to be more efficient. In 1986, Information Minister Nathan Shamuyarira accused some ZANU members of Parliament of "ultra-leftist" tendencies for calling for the total nationalization of the press. (*FBIS*, 21 August.) Yet some observers argued that press freedom was severely compromised in 1986 with the dismissal of the *Sunday Mail*'s outspoken editor, who was also a senior member of the opposition ZAPU party. (Frost & Sullivan, *Zimbabwe Report*, October.)

Mugabe would like to acquire white-owned farmlands that are not being utilized, in order to settle more than a hundred thousand currently homeless families. The Land Acquisition Act became law in 1986 and is expected to accelerate the process of land redistribution. (*CSM*, 24 September.) Since independence, only 30,000 out of 165,000 families have been resettled. It is a sensitive issue that has alienated many citizens from the party.

Modest efforts to form agricultural cooperatives have been blocked by prominent civil servants who have a stake in the private sector. Other government officials have secured a $10 million loan from the World Bank to help small businesses in improving management techniques (*African Recorder*, 2–15 July). In the areas of social services and education, the government has introduced free health care for people with low incomes and free education at the primary school level. Consequently, literacy and life expectancy rates have soared. However, state agricultural, industrial, and trading schemes have been delayed because of high capital costs.

Socialist programs in Zimbabwe have been delayed or scaled back by the escalating costs of national security and defense. According to the 1987 budget projections, defense spending would rise by over 26 percent to 16 percent of total expenditures (Zimbabwe Banking Corporation, *Economic Review*, June). It would be second only to education. In 1986, the government was spending nearly $600,000 a day maintaining approximately 20,000 Zimbabwe troops along the strategic corridor to the Mozambique port of Beira (*African Economic Digest*, 26 April). The corridor has been under increasing attack from Mozambican guerrillas seeking to topple the Marxist government in that country. In late 1986, Zimbabwe and five other frontline states agreed to share their intelligence information with Angola and Mozambique in an effort to contain antigovernment guerrilla movements and South African offensives. (*Africa News*, 27 October.) The Mugabe government has also approached the Eastern bloc nations for defensive weapons against South African incursions into Zimbabwe.

In 1986, Zimbabwe and Mozambique established the Beira Corridor Authority to rehabilitate and operate the rail and road routes and to modernize the antiquated port facilities at Beira (*FBIS*, 8 October). Zimbabwe has been desperately searching for alternative avenues of international trade. Currently, nearly 80 percent of the country's trade must pass through South Africa. In 1986, nearly all donor support for the Corridor Authority came from Western, mainly Scandinavian, sources. However, East Germany became the first Eastern bloc donor by pledging a modest $5 million for technical assistance. (*African Economic Digest*, 1 November.) The Americans and Soviets have refrained from becoming too involved for fear of a Great Power confrontation.

Zimbabwe's economy, which had shown signs of dramatic recovery and robust growth in 1985, began to strain under the pressures of political turmoil and uncertainty in the region. The rate of economic growth slowed from more than 6 percent in 1985 to less than 3 percent in 1986. The volume of agricultural production declined moderately, and manufacturing and mining earnings weakened. Inflation accelerated while export expansion slowed, and the visible trade surplus, so great in 1985, began to diminish. Urban unemployment continued to climb and real wages for industrial workers fell, despite the statutory 10 percent hike. The need to service a burgeoning external debt contributed to a severe shortage of foreign exchange, which limited the country's ability to raise import capacity. (Standard Chartered, *Business Trends*, November.)

Early in the year, the government revealed its new, scaled-down, five-year Transitional National Development Plan. The plan envisions more private investment but also calls for more government spending in the public sector. Nevertheless, considerable emphasis is placed on the importance of a mixed economy and the viability of the private sector as an engine for growth. The plan suggests a contraction in the bloated civil service and greater accountability for the parastatals. Recent structural reforms are designed to increase government participation in industrial development through two parastatals: the Industrial Development Corporation, and the huge Zimbabwe Iron and Steel Company. (*African Business*, May.)

**Domestic Affairs.** Zimbabwe's population remained deeply divided over fundamental questions of power and of national purpose and direction. This was reflected in ambivalence and contradictions in economic theory, in development, and in dealings with foreign diplomats and business people. Ambiguities in policy statements caused considerable uncertainty over the future direction of government. The whites, numbering approximately 115,000, were generally against ZANU's social policies but grudgingly cooperated. They were internally divided and politically apathetic; less than half of those eligible voted. Yet in the 1985 elections they gave Ian Smith—the intransigent former Rhodesian prime minister—and his conservative Alliance Party fifteen of the twenty parliamentary seats reserved for whites. However, the parliament and cabinet have become less relevant as power gradually shifts to Mugabe and the ZANU Politburo.

Toward the end of 1986, progress was made in the on-again, off-again unity talks between ZANU and ZAPU. In July, 51 ZAPU leaders were released from detention. In a dramatic conciliatory gesture a month later, the government dropped treason charges against ten senior ZAPU officials, including the national chairman. As unity/merger talks advanced, political turmoil in Matabeleland diminished. Dissident activity declined and fewer government violations of human rights were reported. But confidence had not yet been completely restored, as evidenced by the renewal of the state of emergency that had been in effect since the days of white rule in 1965. As 1986 came to a close, Mugabe and ZAPU leader Joshua Nkomo reached general agreement over a party merger. ZAPU would be awarded seats in the ZANU Central Committee and Nkomo would be made vice president, but ZAPU would have to renounce its name. Most members of ZAPU and ZANU expressed a willingness to accept the arrangement. However, a minority in both parties were bitterly opposed and vowed to continue the struggle. It remained to be seen if the merger would truly succeed.

**International Views and Positions.** ZANU and the government adhered to a policy of nonalignment. In September 1986, the country was host to the eighth summit of the 102-member Movement of the Nonaligned Nations. Ninety-four delegations and 50 heads of state attended. Mugabe was elected to serve as the movement's chairman until 1989. (*NYT*, 12 September.) At the summit, Mugabe condemned South Africa and criticized the United States for its military assistance to guerrilla movements seeking to topple the Marxist governments in Angola and Mozambique. In a declaration, the movement resolved to increase material support to the African National Congress (ANC) of South Africa in its efforts to overthrow the Botha regime and to assist the frontline states in reducing their economic dependence on South Africa. ZANU and the government pledged to support the ANC but assured the rival Pan Africanist Congress of continued support as well. (*African News*, 15 September.)

Zimbabwe's relations with Great Britain and the United States rapidly deteriorated in 1986. The American ambassador cut short his tenure and went home after the government accused the U.S. Central Intelligence Agency of helping South Africa to destabilize neighboring states, including Zim-babwe. In a 4 July speech at the U.S. Embassy in Harare, a government minister attacked the United States for its refusal to impose harsh sanctions against South Africa while imposing them on Nicaragua and Poland. Mugabe refused to apologize for the remarks and the Americans retaliated by suspending the remaining $13.5 million in aid to Zimbabwe. With $370 million already disbursed since independence, the United States had been Zimbabwe's largest donor. (*LAT*, 11 July.)

Zimbabwe's relations with South Africa also deteriorated. The Botha regime responded to Mugabe's strident support of international sanctions by abruptly, though temporarily, slowing cross-border traffic.

Zimbabwe sought to reduce its trade reliance on the West and to diversify its overseas markets to compensate for losses of exports to South Africa. It stepped up its efforts to develop new export markets in other countries, including those in the Eastern bloc. Zimbabwan president Banana's official visits to Poland, Hungary, and Bulgaria in June led to a strengthening of economic and cultural ties (*FBIS*, 22 June). The annual International Trade Fair in Bulawayo was attended by Cuba for the first time. Hungary returned to the fair after a year's hiatus, and East Germany and Poland joined a host of participants from Western countries. This was followed in late October by trips to Hungary, Yugoslavia, Romania, and the Soviet Union for extensive trade talks. (*FBIS*, 8 October.) Nevertheless, as late as December, trade with the Eastern bloc countries remained small and showed only modest growth. Nor had the Marxist countries significantly increased their levels of military, technical, and economic assistance. Zimbabwe's relations with North Korea cooled in 1986 when the Koreans reneged on a joint venture with a mining parastatal. This was preceded by the departure of the North Korean military advisers who had been in the country for several years. (*African Economic Digest*, 1 March.) Nevertheless, Mugabe has cultivated warm personal relations with Soviet leader Mikhail Gorbachev (*WP*, 25 May), and his relations with China also remain strong. A ten-member trade mission, which included Zimbabwe businessmen, returned from Beijing with a multimillion dollar, interest-free loan to finance projects under the new five-year development plan (Frost & Sullivan, *Zimbabwe Report*, October.)

Zimbabwe has continued to play an increasingly important role in the two major regional trade organizations: the Southern African Coordination Conference (SADCC), and the Preferential Trade Area. In August, Mugabe traveled to Angola to attend the seventh summit meeting of the SADCC (*Africa News*, 1 September). Both organizations were remarkably successful in 1986 in garnering international support. They also achieved greater cooperation among themselves in the face of growing turmoil in South Africa and the anticipated effects of international sanctions against the Botha regime.

Richard W. Hull
*New York University*

# THE AMERICAS

# Introduction

Nineteen eighty-six was an uneven year for Marxist-Leninist governments and organizations in Latin America. The ruling parties in Cuba and Nicaragua maintained firm control in their countries, though both were forced to tighten controls over their people as their economies continued to decline. But domestic problems notwithstanding—or perhaps in part because of domestic difficulties—both Cuba and Nicaragua kept fairly high profiles in international affairs.

In the hemisphere as a whole, however, the trend continued toward democratic institutions within which Marxist-Leninist organizations played less important roles. An increasing number of Marxist-Leninist groups in Central and South America responded to their relative impotence by stepping up their level of violence, often with international support. This violence, in national settings already unstable due to widespread economic and social problems, posed threats to several of the fragile emerging democracies.

The focus of international attention remained Central America, and in particular Nicaragua, where U.S.-backed insurgents got a financial boost in their war to cripple or overthrow the Sandinista government. This was the major conflict underway in 1986 in Latin America, wherein approximately 75,000 Nicaraguan regular troops, with strong Soviet-bloc support ranging from several thousand Cuban advisers to Soviet Mi-24 HIND D attack (flying tank) helicopters, fought between 15,000 to 20,000 *contras*, most of whom were based in neighboring Honduras. By the end of the year, Nicaragua was reportedly receiving an estimated $1 million daily in aid from the Soviet Union.

The anti-Sandinista forces operated abroad under the political umbrella of the United Nicaraguan Opposition (UNO). The UNO's three-man directorship included two former members of the Sandinista junta. The primary military force, however, called the National Democratic Force (FDN), was led by former National Guard members as well as former Sandinistas and others, and this remained a source of friction within the movement and an impediment to greater *contra* popularity within Nicaragua. After much debate during the first half of the year, the U.S. Congress narrowly approved $100 million in military and humanitarian aid to the guerrilla forces. Several months later, the scandal over U.S. arms sales to Iran and reported fund transfers to the *contras* fueled internal dissension within the UNO and clouded prospects for additional aid from the Congress in 1987.

Domestically, the Nicaraguan economy continued to deteriorate, with inflation rising to an estimated 300 percent by the end of December. The government continued to reduce the already limited political freedoms in the country, most notably in two ways: by closing down *La Prensa*, a longtime critic of the Somoza dictatorship and the only surviving opposition paper under the Sandinistas, which the Interior Ministry claimed had been "stepping up its level of provocation and disinformation"; and by escalating its attack on the popular Miguel Cardinal Obando y Bravo and the Roman Catholic Church generally. Though the Nicaraguan government claims to be democratic, and points to 1984 elections to prove it, one opposition leader, quoted in the Paris daily *Le Monde* on 24 June, said the nation's legislative assembly was "designed for export purposes . . . In practice it has no power and is a mere sham."

On the darker side, these limitations on political, religious, and other rights were complemented by the retention and torture of political prisoners. Nicaraguan president Daniel Ortega, in an interview with the West German magazine *Der Spiegel* on 28 April, acknowledged that there were approximately 2,700 prisoners; on 3 October the Sandinista party paper *Barricada* admitted that prisoners had been tortured.

In El Salvador, which only a couple of years earlier had been the center of armed conflict in Central America, the military forces of the government maintained the offensive, despite several serious defeats, in their war against the Farabundo Marti National Liberation Front (FMLN) guerrillas. The army penetrated previously secure guerrilla strongholds and forced the insurgents to resort to smaller-scale actions, including terroristic bombings on roads and in cities. The U.S. embassy in San Salvador estimated that the rebels had caused almost $2 billion in damage since the beginning of the war in 1979. Though the government of Christian Democratic president José Napoleón Duarte found many domestic problems resistant to significant improvement, open splits occurred in the Revolutionary Democratic Front (FDR), the political umbrella organization of the guerrillas, and some of its more moderate members returned to the country from abroad to participate openly in political and labor activities. The guerrillas discussed forming a single vanguard Marxist-Leninist party. Although no such party actually emerged, three of five FMLN member organizations—including the Communist Party of El Salvador—attended the Twenty-seventh Congress of the Communist Party of the Soviet Union together and were evidently treated as equals by their Soviet hosts.

Marxist-Leninist groups were much less important in other countries of Central America. In Guatemala, the elected government of Christian Democratic president Vinicio Cerezo was inaugurated in January. The new president, who tried harder than other Central American leaders not to offend the Sandinistas, offered amnesty to Guatemalan guerrillas. Though as many as 2,000 accepted, others did not and conflict increased somewhat during the last half of the year. In Honduras, the military evidently put down an uprising by the small Cinchoneros group in the northern part of the country. According to a report in the *Los Angeles Times* on 6 November, the guerrillas were apparently trained and armed in and by Nicaragua and Cuba. The communist party in Panama, the People's Party (PDP), held its Eighth Congress in January and committed itself to a broad front strategy, with strong praise for the late military strongman Omar Torrijos and condemnation of the United States, which it charges is planning to renege on its agreement to hand the Canal over to Panama.

The Communist Party of Cuba held its Third Congress in two sessions, the first in February and the second in December. Fidel Castro maintained Cuban support for the Sandinistas and for selected Latin American insurgent movements from Honduras to Chile. About 30,000 Cuban troops remained in Angola to defend the government of José Eduardo dos Santos; Castro announced during the year that he would keep those troops in Angola until apartheid has been eliminated in South Africa. Cuba was believed to have military advisers in thirteen countries and civilian advisers in 27 countries worldwide. Relations with the United States remained combative, as in years past, while evidence of differences with Moscow mounted despite the pledge of "indestructible ties of friendship with the Soviet Union" made at the Third Congress.

Although Castro's strongest interests have always been in foreign policy, periodically he has had to focus more on domestic affairs. Such was the case in much of 1986 because of the crisis in the Cuban economy. Statements at the two sessions of the Third Congress, and policies announced in between them, marked a major shift in the nation's domestic policies designed to reverse the continuing decline of the economy. Cuban leaders have emphasized the failure to meet production goals and pointed out the negative impact on production of work stoppages, absenteeism, discontent, incompetence, and unemployment. The always-critical hard currency crisis got worse and is expected to become catastrophic during 1987; Castro said in December that convertible currency was expected to decline from $1.2 billion in 1985 to $600 million in 1987. He blamed the decline mainly on bad weather, the low international market price for sugar (which for 27 years has remained the basis of the nation's essentially monocultural economy), and a decreasing market value of oil (which Cuba imports from the Soviet Union to resell for hard currency on the world market). On 26 December, Castro announced a wide-ranging austerity program that included large cuts in energy available to private and government consumers and confirmed his earlier warnings that 1987 would be the hardest year on Cubans in the 28-year history of the revolution.

Castro's reaction to his perpetual domestic crisis began in 1984, but the response became firm policy in 1986 when he launched a "strategic revolutionary counteroffensive" intended to centralize decisionmaking by concentrating greater power in his own hands, a line that contrasts with the move toward decentralization and modified market economics in other nonproductive, socialist economies, most importantly in the Soviet Union. Castro's emphasis on moral over material incentives seemed to hark back to his disastrous policies of the mid- and late 1960s, when that line made such shambles of the Cuban economy that the Soviet Union had to step in during the 1970s to try—not very successfully—to set things straight. Since Castro's policies ran contrary to Moscow's, the potential for increasing tensions between Cuba and the Soviet Union grew. The danger was increased because, during 1986, Castro continued to call for a diversification of the economy, as he has done off and on with little result since 1959; in contrast, Moscow pushed for Cuba's further integration into the Soviet-bloc Council for Mutual Economic Assistance as a provider of agricultural products and raw materials for the Soviet and East European economies.

Several countries in the Caribbean experienced political and economic changes in 1986 that seemed to open the door to greater activity by Marxist-Leninist movements. The Dominican Republic faced economic difficulties, though the Dominican Communist Party suffered a humiliating defeat in the late 1986 presidential election. Tensions increased in Jamaica, where the government of Edward Seaga continued to disappoint even its supporters, and the leftist opposition, led by democratic socialist Michael Manley, grew to majority levels in the July municipal elections. During his previous administration, Manley, though not a communist, maintained close ties to Castro's Cuba. In Grenada, one of the big political events of the year came with the court's handing down of death sentences to Bernard Coard, Hudson Austin, and twelve other members of the New Jewel Movement who were convicted of the 1983 murder of former prime minister Maurice Bishop and more than 100 others. Jean-Claude Duvalier, Haiti's self-appointed President for Life, fled abroad during 1986, and the volatile Haitian political system opened up wider than it has been in decades.

Violence continued to escalate in several South American countries, most importantly in Colombia, Ecuador, Peru, and Chile. In Colombia, the pro-Soviet Communist Party (PCC) remained the most important member of a leftist coalition called the Patriotic Union. During the 1986 election, the union increased its representation in both the national Senate and House, though its total support—as measured by the party's presidential vote—still stood at only 4.5 percent. The Colombian government tried to maintain its on-again off-again truce with the country's guerrillas. In 1986 the truce was fairly consistently stable with only one group, the PCC's Revolutionary Armed Forces (FARC). With others—in particular the M-19—conflict escalated, and by the end of the year Colombia's new president, Virgilio Barco, had adopted a harder line toward violence and drug trafficking. Right-wing death squads and paramilitary groups reappeared.

In Peru, the spectrum of leftist parties remained broad. The pro-Soviet Communist Party and most other groups were members of in the United Left (IU) electoral front, the second major political force in the nation and the main parliamentary opposition to the ruling American Popular Revolutionary Alliance (APRA). The front was not very united, however, though its overall thrust could be described as intended to press president Alan García to live up to his promise to make Peru an "anti-imperialist state." The primary armed threat to García and Peruvians generally remained the Maoist Sendero Luminoso guerrillas, who claim credit for tens of thousands of incidents over the past six years; in all, about 10,000 lives have been lost. The primary Sendero Luminoso targets in cities have been state offices, particularly local APRA meeting halls, police and military officers, and national infrastructure. Thirty municipal officials were killed between January and September, and more than 100 have been killed in the past five years. By late February a state of emergency, and military control, had been imposed in 23 provinces. Toward the end of the year, García spoke increasingly often of the need to "combat international terrorism with the power of national security forces." According to Lima's *Resumen Semanal* on 24–30 October, he called upon citizens to become "soldiers of the antiterrorist cause."

In Ecuador, the Marxist-Leninist left also participated in electoral politics and at midyear pulled 18 percent of the vote in a national plebiscite expressing lack of confidence in the government. The national insurgency of the Alfaro Vive! group expanded even though four of its top leaders were killed. There was further evidence of ties between the Alfaro Vive! guerrillas and the Colombian M-19, and perhaps including the Peruvian Sendero Luminoso, in an international guerrilla force called the America Batallion, which operates out of southeast Colombia.

In Chile, most revolutionary violence could be traced directly or indirectly to the Communist Party

(PCC), which fifteen years ago was South America's main practitioner of the nonarmed road to power, and in particular to the PCC's Manuel Rodríguez Patriotic Front (FPMR). In 1986, the PCC maintained that all forms of struggle were needed to eliminate the government of President Augusto Pinochet, though its support for violent tactics alienated it from most other groups that advocated the removal of Pinochet. Late in the year, large amounts of FPMR arms were discovered that intelligence sources traced to Cuba and said were intended to make possible a national uprising or civil war. Some 500 bombings occurred in the first eight months of the year alone; the most important incident was the attempted assassination of Pinochet in September.

Parties in other countries considered and utilized varied tactics in their efforts to develop power in their countries. The Argentine Communist Party (PCA) held its Sixteenth Congress in November, which brought important leadership changes. The congress adopted a "people's front" policy and demonstrated considerable admiration for the Nicaraguan experience, thereby seemingly contemplating a more violence-oriented policy than before. The party was regularly critical of Argentine president Raúl Alfonsín's foreign policies. The PCA may be discouraged from absolute hostility toward the government by the fact that the Soviet Union has become one of Argentina's main trading partners. In December, the Argentine Supreme Court upheld sentences handed down in 1985 against former top government leaders for crimes committed during the "dirty war" against leftist guerrillas more than a decade earlier.

In Uruguay, the left continued to operate through a coalition called the Broad Front, which consisted of three predominant factions, the two smaller ones controlled by Marxist-Leninists. The Tupamaros, the best-known urban guerrilla group of the late 1960s and early 1970s (celebrated in the Costa Gavras film "State of Siege"), participated in electoral politics but threatened to resort to more extreme tactics if the government did not deal with human rights violators of decades past, among other matters. However, in December, the Uruguayan Senate passed an amnesty bill for alleged violators by a margin of almost two to one.

Among the parties stressing the electoral road were those in Brazil, where in November three Marxist-Leninist groups won 22 seats in the 487-member National Congress; they undoubtedly would have won more had it not been for alliance complications in São Paulo. The main winner was the Workers' Party, with strong Trotskyist and radical Christian tendencies. Leftist parties in Venezuela began looking toward a coalition for the 1988 elections, while the Venezuelan Communist Party, which may shun the coalition, was on the verge of its fifth split in two decades. The left in Mexico also began working toward unified participation in that country's 1988 national elections. In Guyana, the pro-Soviet People's Progressive Party of Cheddi Jagan continued to be the main opposition to the ruling People's National Congress, while the second significant leftist opposition group, the Working People's Alliance, maintained the more moderate line adopted in the wake of the U.S. move into Grenada. In the United States, the Communist Party focused its attention on defeating Senate candidates that supported President Reagan, while the Socialist Workers' Party won a long-standing legal case against the U.S. government.

William Ratliff
*Hoover Institution*

# Argentina

**Population.** 31,186,000
**Party.** Communist Party of Argentina (Partido Comunista de la Argentina; PCA)
**Founded.** 1918
**Membership.** 70,000 (estimated); 200,000 (claimed)
**General Secretary.** Athos Fava
**Political Commission.** 12 members: Athos Fava, Jorge Pereyra, Patricio Echegaray, Ernesto Salgado, Luis Heller, Fanny Edelman, Guillermo Varone, Miguel Ballato, Eduardo Sigal, Rodolfo Casals, Enrique Dratman, Francisco Alvarez (¿Qué Pasa? 12 November)
**Central Committee.** 100 members, 15 alternates
**Status.** Legal
**Last Congress.** 4–7 November
**Last Election.** 1985 (parliamentary and provincial midterm elections); PCA joined with Movement Toward Socialism (MAS) in the Front of the People (FREPU) coalition; 2 percent, no representation.
**Auxiliary Organizations.** Communist Youth Federation; local branch of the World Peace Council; Committee in Solidarity with Nicaragua; the party effectively controls the Argentine Permanent Assembly on Human Rights.
**Publications.** ¿Qué Pasa? (weekly); Nueva Era (monthly). The popular political gossip magazine, El Periodista (weekly) as well as Radio Belgrano, are generally regarded as unofficial outlets for the party.

Argentine democracy continued to weather the nation's serious economic problems in 1986, with no serious challenge either to institutions or to the Alfonsín government apparent from either the left or the right. As in 1985, the administration followed an economic policy that could be regarded very broadly as orthodox, complemented (or balanced) by a Third World foreign policy.

Specifically, President Alfonsín's deflationary economic policies—which were far more austere than anything a military government had ever asked Argentines to endure—included drastic budget cuts; wage and price controls; an increase in revenues through a combination of foreign borrowing and heavier taxation; export promotion; and privatization of large state-owned industries, particularly in steel and petrochemicals. It is not surprising that, for the fiscal year ending June 1986, Argentina was scheduled to receive $400 million in new lines of credit from the World Bank and an amount substantially above that figure for 1987.

In 1985 Alfonsín made headlines all over the world by bringing to trial leaders of the deposed military junta for crimes committed during their campaign against urban guerrillas from 1976 to 1983 (see YICA, 1985). On the penultimate day of 1986 the Supreme Court upheld the convictions handed down in December 1985, though it reduced slightly the length of prison sentences in two cases, citing a legal technicality. Meanwhile, serious controversy developed over the degree to which responsibility should be fixed upon the lower ranks; human rights organizations pursued at least 1,700 charges against some 300 officers, whereas the government attempted to demarcate responsibility more narrowly.

In late December, President Alfonsín signed into law a deadline for prosecution of atrocities committed by the former regime, establishing a 60-day deadline for new indictments. Courts would likewise have a similar period to indict any suspects in crimes by leftist guerrilla groups. Human rights groups called the new law "totally unacceptable" (*WP*, 27 December) and promised to challenge its constitutionality.

As noted in the 1985 *YICA*, some elements of the left who had supported Alfonsín in the 1983 presidential elections were notably disaffected two years later, and in the midterm elections abandoned the ruling Radical Civic Union (UCR) for either the Intransigent Party or the joint list of left-wing groups sponsored by the PCA, denominated FREPU. In 1986 Alfonsín took the unusual step of directly attacking the communists in two speeches, one in April, the other in September. He criticized those who were using "the language of those of the far left, the same who have been expelled by the Nicaraguan Sandinistas" and "some groups that originally believed in the need for a democratic system, even if it is, to them, [only] a bourgeois democracy, [but who] have now moved to the far left." In response, Politburo member and long-time militant Fernando Nadra replied, "The President perceives us as being very leftist, because he stands too far to the right. Since every day he moves farther to the right, he sees us as being farther to the left." In addition, Nadra accused Alfonsín of betraying his own campaign promises and of walking away "from the democratic tradition" of his own party "with his McCarthyist language." (*FBIS*, 26 September.)

**Leadership and Party Organization.** At the Sixteenth Congress of the PCA in Buenos Aires in November, there was a massive shakeup of top leadership. Although Athos Fava was re-elected general secretary, 53 members of the standing Central Committee were replaced; ten of these members had submitted resignations, while others—notably Rubens Iscaro and Oscar Arévalo—were replaced through "the process of self-criticism promoted by the party this year." (*Noticias Argentinas*, 8 November; *FBIS*, 13 November.) Nadra, Iscaro, Irene Rodríguez, and Arévalo were dropped from the Politburo; they were replaced by Jorge Pereyra, Patricio Echegaray, and Ernesto Salgado.

**Domestic Party Affairs.** The Sixteenth Party Congress brought to a head problems that had been simmering beneath the surface for some time. The evident failure of the party to make serious electoral inroads—in 1983 as allies of the Peronists, and in 1985 in conjunction with MAS—led to a lengthy process of self-criticism and the resignation of some key figures in the Politburo. According to one report, the internal critique pointed at the party's slavish subordination to the Soviet Union; its apparent indifference to the experience of other (that is, more successful) Latin American communists, as in El Salvador or Nicaragua; and, above all, its tactical error of having lent at least tacit support to the military regime after 1976 and its refusal to join the Peronists in resistance to that regime (see *YICA*, 1983). In particular, the self-criticism of Nadra was "one of the harshest . . . Argentine observers remember hearing from a communist militant." (AFP, 17 May; *FBIS*, 28 May.)

Veteran party leader Iscaro was removed from all leadership positions because, according to reports, he had expressed opposition on several occasions to Fava and particularly to the younger and more radicalized sector of the party headed by Echegaray (*Noticias Argentinas*, 11 December; *FBIS*, 18 December). Among other things, Iscaro had made a speech on 1 May (Labor Day) that was regarded as "anti-Peronist" and for which he was publicly reprimanded by PCA leaders.

The congress thus marked a turn by the party "to the left" (EFE, 9 November; *FBIS*, 13 November), characterized by serious frontal assaults on the Alfonsín administration, particularly its economic policies, but also, for the first time, its *bona fides*. For example, in April, Fava accused the government of "maintaining the repressive labor laws of the dictatorship, the same judges, and the same repressive mechanisms," and in November he characterized the administration as "bourgeois and controlled by monopolies of the great bourgeoisie . . . as a result of this, the government is implementing an increasingly unpopular policy . . . in keeping with the dictates of the IMF" (*Noticias Argentinas*, 8 November; *FBIS*, 13 November). Sharp criticisms were levied at the second round of the so-called Austral Plan (see *YICA*, 1985), immigration policies, and the wage freeze. At the same time, Fava took on the traditionalist leadership of the Peronist unions, who, he alleged, were entering into "sweetheart contracts" with employers to prevent communist groups from establishing a foothold in some industries and shops.

In spite of its differences with the Peronists, the PCA nonetheless endorsed their call for a general strike in June to protest the Austral Plan. The party also joined forces with the Peronist Youth and the militants from the Intransigent Party to protest the visit of banker David Rockefeller to Buenos Aires in January—an event that dissolved into the worst street violence Argentina had witnessed since its return to democracy a little more than two years before.

The party's new long-term strategy was unveiled shortly after the adjournment of the Sixteenth Congress: a "people's front" was to be part of an electoral strategy for the 1987 parliamentary and provincial elections. The front would attract "antiimperialist and antioligarchical sectors" of the Justicialist [Peronist] and Radical parties, especially the Radical youth. Such groups would somehow join the front "but without losing their identity . . . the more advanced leftist sectors [for example, the PCA] will make up the core of the front" (*FBIS*, 21 November). Precisely how the communists could acquire power or even influence electoral politics without subordinating these cadres to a single list on the ballot was unclear. In general, therefore, the new course seemed nothing more than a restatement of the PCA's oldest dream: to recapture those sectors of the working and lower-middle classes lost more than forty years ago to Peronism and, later, to the Radical Party.

**Auxiliary and Front Organizations.** The Committee in Solidarity with Nicaragua had another extremely active year. In July Peronist congressman Eduardo Vaca and his Intransigent colleague Miguel Monserrat proposed the formation of a parliamentary commission to show support for the Sandinista government. The proposal was seconded by Colonel Horacio Ballester of CEMIDA (Military Center for Democracy in Argentina), clergymen, human rights groups, and the Mothers of the Plaza de Mayo.

In September some five thousand people marched through downtown Buenos Aires to express support for the Sandinista government, including leaders of virtually all of the major parties: Peronist, Radical, Intransigent, Socialist, and Christian Democratic, as well as the PCA and its Trotskyist ally MAS. The committee also launched a fund-raising campaign to send a "Ship for Solidarity and Peace" to that republic.

**International Views, Positions, and Activities.** In spite of the evident rapprochement between Argentina, the Soviet Union, and some members of the bloc (see below), PCA leaders were unremitting in their opposition to Alfonsín's foreign policy, particularly his respect for existing international obligations and continued collaboration with the International Monetary Fund. In August, General Secretary Fava repeated his demand that the Argentine government declare a moratorium on the foreign debt; at the same time, he denounced the new accords reached with Brazil intended to advance economic integration between the two subregional powers. These accords, he held, "embrace the interests of the great transnational monopolies, to the detriment of the workers and of the two countries' peoples." (*FBIS*, 4 August.)

There was relatively little interparty activity in 1986. A PCA delegation headed by Iscaro, who was then a Central Committee and Politburo member, visited Hungary in late January and early February; a Communist Party of the Soviet Union delegation headed by K. N. Brutents, deputy chief of the Central Committee International Section, visited Buenos Aires in late September.

**Relations with the Soviet Union and Other Bloc Members.** Argentine-Soviet relations, which have been at least correct and active under all administrations, including ostensibly anticommunist military juntas (see previous editions of *YICA*), were considerably intensified in 1986. The 40th anniversary of diplomatic relations afforded the opportunity for a state visit to the Soviet Union by Alfonsín in October—the first ever by an Argentine chief of state. This event was characterized by effusive expressions of cordiality, intensified cultural exchanges, and the conclusion of new commercial pacts.

One important qualitative change in relations since 1983 has been the gradual shift from hardcurrency transactions to barter for at least a portion of the Argentine harvest. For example, several hydroelectrical complexes have been built with Soviet assistance, and Argentina has begun exchanging foodstuffs for machinery and heavy industrial equipment, particularly fittings for the petroleum and chemical industries. In addition, the Argentine State Railroads have let a contract worth $170 million to Soviet concerns for the upgrading of suburban Buenos Aires commuter lines. In February a group of Soviet naval engineers led by Fleet Admiral Vladmir V. Aristarkhov visited Argentina to submit a proposal for the dredging and remodeling of the port of Bahía Blanca, one of the country's largest fluvial outlets for the grain trade. In July a far-reaching fisheries accord authorized ships flying Soviet and Bulgarian flags access to Argentine territorial waters and granted those countries port facilities, including crew changes, repair, and provisions.

As a result of Alfonsín's visit to the Soviet Union,

Moscow agreed to purchase four million tons of wheat (valued at $400 million) over the next five years. (During the same period, Argentina agreed to purchase Soviet capital goods amounting to $60 million, double the amount purchased in a similar time period prior to Alfonsín's assumption of power.) The new Soviet commitment was an important development, since it preempted the threat represented by a decision of the U.S. Senate in August to subsidize the export of American cereals. This move was the occasion for new Argentine attacks on U.S. Central American policy, support for the Soviet position on nuclear testing, and a reiteration of Alfonsín's policy of providing credits to Cuba. It may also have inspired the Argentine president's decision to visit Cuba itself on his way home, where he carefully avoided criticism of the Castro regime, stressing instead joint economic concerns and the Latin American debt.

Juan Carlos Pugliese, president of the Chamber of Deputies, visited the Soviet capital and Leningrad in May, and in June Vice President Víctor Martínez was an honored guest in Warsaw, the highest Argentine official ever to visit Poland. Radical Party leader Roberto E. Rodríguez visited Hungary in July, and army chief of staff general Héctor Ríos Ereñú and a delegation from the directorate general of military factories journeyed to the People's Republic of China (PRC) the same month. In May the PRC invited Alfonsín to make a future trip to that country.

Cuban vice president Carlos Rafael Rodríguez made a "technical stop" in Buenos Aires in May en route to Uruguay, and the same month a delegation of senior officials from the Soviet Maritime Fleet arrived in the Argentine capital to undertake the fourth round of "consultative negotiations" on maritime transport.

**Other Leftist Groups.** Mario Firmenich, leader of the Montonero guerrilla group, remained in prison awaiting the completion of judicial proceedings (see *YICA*, 1984, 1985). In February, Firmenich, Fernando Vaca Narvaja, and Roberto Per-

dia were elected to the executive board of the "Revolutionary Peronist Faction," the first two in absentia. In September the faction proposed Firmenich as a candidate for national deputy, along with the congressional precandidacy of Pablo Unamuno and two other personalities destined for the Buenos Aires City Council. After much controversy over Firmenich's eligibility, he voluntarily withdrew from the race in October.

Although Firmenich and his supporters were generally regarded as outside the pale of respectable Argentine politics, no one in the mainstream of Peronism thought it worth the effort to read them out of the party; as Unamuno pointed out, Congressman Carlos Grosso, one of the two leaders of "renovated" Peronism, posed no objection to the existence of a "revolutionary caucus" within the party or even to the idea of Firmenich's candidacy (*FBIS*, 9 October).

Argentine authorities continued to contradict one another on the purported resurgence of subversive activity in the country. In August, Facundo Suárez, head of the Secretariat for State Intelligence (SIDE), said in a radio interview that his agency "has not recorded the entrance" of presumed foreign guerrillas in Argentina, contrary to a detailed news report earlier in the month that claimed Suárez had met to discuss the subject with Foreign Minister Dante Caputo and Defense Minister Horacio Jaunarena (*Noticias Argentinas*, 19 August; *FBIS*, 20 August). Likewise, though Prosecutor Juan Romero Vitorica claimed that Firmenich was organizing a subversive comeback from his prison cell in Villa Devoto, Interior Secretary Antonio Tróccoli categorically denied that this was the case. In October, Ríos Ereñú publicly seconded the view that there was no cause for alarm, though in April he himself had charged that subversive groups were infiltrating the Intransigent Party (*Latin American Weekly Report*, 2 May).

Mark Falcoff
*U.S. Senate Foreign Relations Committee*

# Bolivia

**Population.** 6,638,000
**Party.** Communist Party of Bolivia (Partido Comunista de Bolivia; PCB), two factions
**Founded.** 1950 (split, 1985)
**Membership.** 500 (claimed)
**General Secretary.** Simón Reyes Rivera (majority faction); Carlos Soria Galvarro (minority)
**Status.** Legal
**Last Congress.** Fifth, 9–13 February 1985; Extraordinary 26–29 April
**Last Election.** July 1985; the United People's Front (FPU), the electoral coalition supported by the PCB, won 4 of 130 seats in the Chamber of Deputies
**Auxiliary Organizations.** Communist Youth of Bolivia
**Publication.** *Unidad* (majority and minority editions)

The most important events in Bolivia during 1986 were the accomplishment of—and reactions to—the new economic policy of the government of President Victor Paz Estenssoro, and the campaign of the government to curtail the cocaine export problem. The communists participated in leading opposition to all or part of both these programs.

The PCB was founded in 1960 by a group of young people who broke away from the country's first pro-Stalinist party, the Left Revolutionary Party (Partido de Izquierda Revolucionaria; PIR), which had collaborated with conservative governments of the 1946–1952 period. After the Bolivian National Revolution, led by the Nationalist Revolutionary Movement (Movimiento Nacionalista Revolucionario; MNR), the PCB remained a minor force in national politics and the labor movement. However, in the twenty years following the overthrow of the MNR regime in 1964, the communists became the largest single political group in the organized labor movement and particularly among the tinworkers of the Miners' Federation (FSTMB).

During the elections of 1978, 1979, and 1980, the PCB formed part of the Popular Democratic Union (UDP), a coalition that backed the candidacy of ex-president Hernán Siles Suazo of the Left MNR (MNRI). After Siles was finally inaugurated

as president in October 1982, the PCB was represented in his cabinet by two ministers, those of Mines and Labor. However, as a result of a long cabinet crisis, beginning late in 1984, the communists finally left the government in January 1985.

**Split in the PCB.** The Fifth Congress of the PCB met in La Paz on 9–13 February 1985. There were three tendencies in that congress; one was headed by Jorge Kolle Cueto, the long-time general secretary; another by Ramiro Barrenechea, deputy and former minister of labor under President Siles; and the third by Simon Reyes, a leading figure in the FSTMB and the Bolivian Labor Central (Central Obrera Boliviana; COB).

However, the Fifth Congress did not resolve the party's problems. Subsequently, the PCB split into two different organizations, both calling themselves the Communist Party of Bolivia and issuing newspapers called *Unidad*. Apparently the larger and more influential of the factions was that headed by Reyes as first secretary; the other, led by Carlos Soria Galvarro, had its principal following among party units in Cochabamba, Santa Cruz, and Potosi. (*Unidad*-Reyes, 23 December 1985.)

The majority-faction PCB held an extraordinary congress in April 1986. The principal item of discussion was a political report submitted by Reyes. The report called for drastically different economic policies from those being followed by the Paz Estenssoro government, and it "pointed to the need to unite all the country's left-wing forces to oppose the onslaught of reaction and defend political and trade-union freedom." Reyes was re-elected as first secretary of his party. (*FBIS*, 1 May.)

**Programs of the Government.** Paz Estenssoro launched new economic, social, and political policies when he took office in August 1985. These policies were designed to deal with a situation in which inflation had reached the annual rate of almost 12,000 percent during the first half of 1985; a crisis in the country's two major export industries, tin and petroleum, with falling international prices and increasingly unproductive mines; and a more than $5 billion international debt in default.

The government program, backed by the MNR and ex-president Hugo Banzer's National Democratic Action (Acción Democrática Nacionalista; ADN), provided for a "shock program" against inflation, including freezing wage increases for nine months; devaluation of the peso; and moves to bring the national budget more into balance by drastically increasing taxes, particularly by introducing a value-added tax, reducing the number of government employees and trying to rationalize money-losing government firms. The program also involved longer-range goals for the government to "decentralize" the state mining corporation COMIBOL; dispose of unprofitable mines and other enterprises; shift emphasis from mining of tin to lead, silver, and other metals; and establish conditions conducive to renewed private investment, both domestic and foreign.

Within a year, Paz Estenssoro's new economic program had one notable success: restraining inflation. From the high point of an annual rate of 23,447 percent in September 1985, inflation fell so that the annual rate by September 1986 was 94 percent.

However, the restraint of inflation was costly to much of the population. Real incomes of workers with stationary wages fell drastically, and unemployment increased substantially, including the dismissal of 7,000 miners (*NYT*, 24 August). Furthermore, the prospect of longer-run economic changes proposed by the government caused considerable worry among many workers. Understandably, both actual experiences and worries about the future

generated considerable opposition among many groups of Bolivian workers.

When the miners organized a march in late August from Oruro to La Paz of several thousand people to protest government policies, the government declared a three-month state of siege. This was ratified by Congress two weeks later. At the time of the declaration of the state of siege some 161 people were arrested, and the Interior Ministry announced that they "include mostly union leaders and members of the Communist Party and the Democratic Convergence" (EFE, 29 August).

Another part of the government's program was to try to curb the cultivation and export of coca and its derivatives (including cocaine), which were virtually uncontrolled when Paz Estenssoro took office. To this end, in mid-year, he accepted cooperation from a small number of U.S. soldiers, with their equipment. This, too, aroused some vocal opposition.

**Communist Attitudes and Campaigns.** During the year, the communists generally expressed strong opposition to the policies and programs of the regime. This stance helped them to overcome the considerable discredit they had received for their participation in the government of Paz Estenssoro's predecessor, Hernán Siles, when they had sought to restrain labor militancy.

The basic attitude of the PCB to the regime's program was stated in a document of the PCB Central Committee published in January. It claimed that "the whole content of the new economic policy of Paz Estenssoro's government testifies that it is a serious attempt to bolster and restructure the system of dependent capitalism, geared to U.S. imperialism, and to slow down our country's independent development. That being so, the Bolivian people, led by the working class, must join in organized struggle to defend the country's interests and to fight the antinational economic 'model'" (*IB*, January).

The PCB also opposed a new electoral law that the government pushed through Congress in May. In the Chamber of Deputies, Reyes spoke for the party, denouncing the new law as being designed "for the benefit of the ruling Nationalist Revolutionary Movement, ADN, and Jaime Paz Zamora's Movement of the Revolutionary Left, which will control all the electoral organization" (*EFE*, 27 May).

**The PCB and the Labor Movement.** The principal center of trade-union influence of the Reyes

PCB was in the FSTMB. Although the communists had suffered a defeat in the September 1984 congress of the country's central labor organization, the COB, at the hands of a coalition of supporters of long-time FSTMB executive secretary Juan Lechin, various Trotskyist parties, and other groups, the situation moved in the PCB's favor in 1986.

In June, Lechin announced that he would resign as executive secretary of the FSTMB, a post he had held for more than forty years and to which he had recently been re-elected. His resignation was accepted a few days later, and Reyes was chosen to succeed him (AFP, 14 June).

Reyes' tenure as executive secretary, however, was of short duration. Early in September, Reyes and other FSTMB leaders negotiated with the government concerning the future of the state mining corporation, COMIBOL, and reached an agreement on the subject. However, a special congress of the FSTMB on 27 September repudiated the agreement, as a result of which Reyes resigned; Filemón Escobar also resigned as conflicts secretary. Escobar explained that repudiation of the FSTMB agreement with the government "reflects a lack of confidence in the FSTMB executive board" (*Red Panamericana*, 29 September).

Subsequently, Victor López Arias was chosen to succeed Reyes. It was reported that he had been chosen as a result of negotiations between the Reyes PCB and several other left factions in the FSTMB (AFP, 26 October).

**International Relations of the PCB.** It was clear that the Reyes faction of the PCB had the Moscow franchise in Bolivia. A Communist Party of the Soviet Union (CPSU) delegation headed by P. K. Luchinskiy, candidate member of the CPSU Central Committee and second secretary of the Tadzhik Communist Party, brought greetings of the CPSU to the Bolivian party's Extraordinary Congress in April (*Pravda*, 25 April). A delegation from the North Korean Communist Party was also present (AFP, 22 July). Erich Honecker, general secretary of the East German Socialist Unity Party (SED), sent a wire of congratulations to Reyes upon the latter's re-election as first secretary of the PCB (*Neues Deutschland*, 6 May). Humberto Ramirez of the Reyes PCB presented its greetings to the Eleventh Party Congress of the SED in April (*Neues Deutschland*, 23 April). At various times, material of the Reyes PCB appeared in international publications of the pro-Moscow parties (*IB*, January;

*WMR*, May). The PCB also maintained contacts with the pro-Soviet parties in other Latin American countries.

**Other Radical Groups.** Although the Reyes PCB remained the largest single Marxist-Leninist element in Bolivian politics, it competed in the labor movement and elsewhere not only with the Soria PCB faction, but also with several other groups. These included at least two factions of the Movement of the Revolutionary Left (Movimiento de Izquierda Revolucionaria; MIR), a Maoist party, and several Trotskyist groups. There were also reports during the year of the continued existence of guerrilla-oriented factions.

The faction of the MIR headed by Antonio Aranibar Quiroga had allied itself with the PCB in the 1985 elections. It continued to be associated with the Reyes group after the election, and this coalition sought to expand its alliance into a wider grouping of the Bolivian left (*WMR*, May), but apparently without any notable success.

The Marxist-Leninist Communist Party (PCB-ML), headed by Oscar Zamora Medinacelli, which had been formed in 1964 as a Maoist offshoot of the PCB, continued to exist. Although it did not play any major role in national politics during the year, Senator Zamora, one-time president of the Senate, accused the parties associated with the Paz Estenssoro government of treason for allowing U.S. troops to operate in the country against the coca drug operators (AFP, 5 August).

Bolivian Trotskyism, which had once been the largest element in the far left, remained splintered throughout the year. There were at least four different groups proclaiming loyalty to Trotskyism. The most significant faction was the Revolutionary Labor Party (POR), led by Guillermo Lora. It was influential in the student federation of San Andres University in La Paz (AFP, 18 April), and it also still had influence among the miners. It was not affiliated with any faction of International Trotskyism.

Another faction of the POR, the so-called United POR (POR-U), was affiliated with the United Secretariat of the Fourth International. It had been formed by a merger of two other groups in 1983.

The Bolivian affiliate of the "Morenoite" faction of International Trotskyism is the Socialist Workers' Party (PST), originally established as a faction of the Socialist Party of Marcelo Quiroga in the late 1970s. It had some influence in the teachers' unions and the factory workers of La Paz. Finally, the tiny Trotskyist-Posadist POR (POR-TP), headed by

Felix Aranda Vargas, continued to exist as the Bolivian affiliate of the faction of International Trotskyism founded by the late J. Posadas.

Throughout the year, reports of actual or potential far-left guerrilla activity continued to surface. In March, Interior Minister Fernando Barthelemy asserted that "subversive groups are operating in several areas of our country," but he was vague on the details of these groups (*El Diario*, 12 March). In that same month, there was a dynamite attack on the U.S. Embassy in La Paz, for which an unknown group, the "People's Command," claimed responsibility (AFP, 27 March). In September, the Interior Ministry claimed that elements of the Peruvian extremist group Shining Path had been operating within Bolivia and had infiltrated student groups at San Simon University in Cochabamba (*Red Panamericana*, 2 September).

Robert J. Alexander
*Rutgers University*

# Brazil

**Population.** 143,277,000
**Parties.** Brazilian Communist Party (Partido Comunista Brasileiro; PCB), pro-Soviet; Communist Party of Brazil (Partido Comunista do Brasil; PCdoB), pro-Albanian; Workers' Party (Partido dos Trabalhadores; PT), strongly Marxist-Leninist-Trotskyist.
**Founded.** PCB: 1922
**Membership.** PCB: 20,000; roughly 80 percent under the age of 30 (*WMR*, Janaury)
**Top Official.** PCB: General Secretary Giocondo Dias; PCdoB: President João Amazonas; PT: President Luis Inacio "Lula" da Silva
**Executive Committee.** PCB: Giocondo Dias, Hercules Correa, Givaldo Siqueira, Almir Neves, Salomão Malina, Teodoro Melo, Roberto Freire, Ivan Pinheiro, José Paulo Neto, Regis Frati, Paulo Elisario, Sergio Morães, Amaro do Nascimento
**Central Committee.** PCB: reportedly will have 101 members; 66 members elected at January 1984 congress.
**Status.** All legal
**Last Congress.** PCB: Seventh, January 1984
**Last Election.** 15 November, for governors, state legislature, and 487-member National Congress; elected Congress will become Constituent Assembly in 1987. Members of 487-seat Congress: PCB: 2; PCdoB: 3; PT: 16.
**Publications.** PCB: *Voz de Unidade*, João Aveline, director; PCdoB: *Tribuna da Luta Operaria*, Pedro de Oliveira, director

Popular support for the government of President José Sarney grew significantly in 1986 as a result of successful steps taken to reactivate the economy and control inflation. The governing coalition, comprising the Party of the Brazilian Democratic Movement (Partido do Movimento Democratico Brasileiro; PMDB) and the Liberal Front Party (Partido do Frente Liberal; PFL) swept the November elections, with landslides for the PMDB. (The PCB and the formerly pro-Maoist, now pro-Albanian, PCdoB [which split from the PCB in 1961] each elected three federal deputies on various coalition tickets with the PMDB, but both suffered greatly from that party's refusal to cooperate in the key state of São Paulo. The PT, a labor party with heavy Trotskyist, Marxist-Leninist, and radical church influence, elected sixteen deputies, also below expectations.) The progovernment euphoria ended with the introduction of new austerity measures a week after elections. These were greeted with demonstrations, some rioting, and a not altogether successful general strike called by the two major labor confederations on 12 December.

**PCB.** Although membership drives and the installment of party organizations in 20 percent of the districts in each state were immediate objectives, the party continued to promote a broad democratic front to support the process of democratization in Brazil. According to Executive Committee member Freire, the PCB played a significant role in bringing down the military dictatorship through its work in the PMDB and the Democratic Alliance (see *YICA*, 1985): "This has taught us to wage our struggle within a well-organized and strong movement and convinced us that the party's democratic course is correct and realistic" (*WMR*, October). He also stressed the importance of that experience in training a cadre for the newly legal PCB, a cadre comprising not only members from the underground but also parliamentary and labor representatives and medium-level leaders in mass organizations (ibid.).

The PCB attaches great weight to the Constituent Assembly to be seated in 1987 and had hoped to elect ten members. (It elected only two, one from Bahia and one from Pernambuco.) The meager results stemmed directly from the São Paulo fiasco, where the party actually lost three deputies, and indirectly from the general confusion surrounding the complicated and extensive elections. Under the proportional representation system, the substantial numbers of spoiled and blank ballots benefited the large parties. In any case, General Secretary Dias said that a congress would be held, "probably some time next year, to analyze new political facts brought into being by the Constituent Assembly. Everything indicates that a democratic system will be established. To relate ourselves to this new reality, we must reanalyze it and determine what policy we will take toward popular democracy, a democracy that might make it possible to start a socialist movement" (*Trybuna ludu*, 7 May; *JPRS*, 7 July).

In March, the PCB presented an hour-long television program celebrating its 64th anniversary. Disaffected former general secretary Luiz Carlos Prestes was not mentioned, and discussion of the Soviet Union was confined to the 1917 Russian Revolution. Writer Jorge Amado and architect Oscar Niemayer were among those participating.

**Auxiliary and Front Organizations.** The National Coordinator of the Working Classes (Coordenação Nacional das Classes Trabalhadores; CONCLAT) in late March became the General Workers' Central (Central Geral dos Trabalhadores; CGT). Like CONCLAT, the CGT comprises unions dominated by the PMDB, the PCB, and the PCdoB. Joaquim dos Santos Andrade, a "traditional" unionist of the São Paulo metalworkers, remained as president. The PCB's José Francisco da Silva, head of the agricultural confederation CONTAG (Confederação Nacional dos Trabalhadores na Agricultura) became vice president, and Valdir Vicente of the 8 October Revolutionary Movement (Movimento Revolucionario 8 de Outubro; MR-8) and the Rio de Janeiro metalworkers, became general secretary. (The MR-8, a former Guevarista guerrilla movement, has registered as a civic group acting within the PMDB.)

The CGT was less critical of the government than the rival Single Labor Central (Central Unica dos Trabalhadores; CUT) controlled by the PT. When the first Cruzado Plan (so called because the currency name was changed from cruzeiro to cruzado) appeared in February, CONCLAT initially called for a general strike but quickly dropped the position in view of growing popular support for the measures. Adjustments to the plan came almost immediately after the administration's landslide victory in November. The selective lifting of rent and price controls, a new method of calculating inflation, and the liquidation of some state enterprises (and the jobs they provided) were popularly seen as a betrayal and provoked violent demonstrations in several cities. Tanks were used to control rioting in Brasilia.

The CGT called for a 13 December interunion plenary to discuss the possibility of a general strike. The CUT acted more quickly, approving a 12 December strike date and inviting the CGT to participate in the action. Despite the maneuvering and rivalry, it was the first large-scale joint effort of the labor centrals and the first general strike against the Sarney administration. The strike was 80 percent effective in São Paulo but had little impact in the rest of the country, and the feared violence did not materialize.

**International Views, Positions, and Activities.** PCB leaders were active in many parts of the globe in 1986. Deputy Haroldo Pinto traveled in President Sarney's delegation to Argentina in August, using the occasion to call for elimination of the Brazilian government's six military ministries (EFE, 7 August; *FBIS*, 8 August). Executive Committee member Nascimento was received the same month by Dimitur Stanishev, secretary of the Bulgarian Communist Party Central Committee in Sofia (BTA, 1 August; *FBIS*, 8 August). In Bucharest in September, Dias met with Romanian president Nicolae Ceauşescu, who stressed, among other ideas, the need for a new type of unity of communist and worker parties, grounded on full equality and noninterference in domestic affairs (*Agerpres*, 16 September; *FBIS*, 17 September). Executive Committee members Frati and Morães visited China in March as a first step toward restoring relations between the Chinese Communist Party and the PCB, which had broken 24 years earlier. Frati said the rapprochement had been prompted by the renewed understanding between the Soviet Union and China: "a sign of greater unity in the international communist movement" (*O Globo*, 17 March; *FBIS*, 19 March).

The 22-year break in relations between Cuba and Brazil ended on 25 June. Sarney's government carefully kept the leftist parties at a distance during the negotiations and emphasized commercial, rather than political, benefits to be derived from the restoration of relations. According to the newsweekly *Veja*, however, the Cuban government has received "a dozen caravans of communist and PT militants who are to give three-month courses in theory in Havana; Castro thus pursues his old obsession of training a revolutionary elite in Latin America... in the 1960s with the PCs [communist parties] and the guerrillas, in the 1970s with the PCs and terrorism, now with the PCs and the courses..." (*Veja*, 2 July; *JPRS*, 31 July).

**PCdoB.** Like the PBC, the PCdoB was hurt in São Paulo, traditionally the strongest state of both parties, by the PMDB refusal to form coalitions with the communists. In alliances with the PMDB elsewhere, the PCdoB elected two deputies in Bahia—Haroldo Lima and Lidice da Mata—and one in Rio de Janeiro. The PCdoB continued its claims of being the original communist party, and no official settlement has been reached.

The hour-long national television program of the PCdoB in April cautiously praised the economic and agrarian reforms promoted by the current government. Party leader Ronald Freitas called the agrarian reform an "important instrument because it expressly determines priority areas for implementation... but limited in that it does not propose the end of latifundia." According to Lima, the economic reform and monetary correction were necessary to fight inflation, but the reform will have "untoward results in the medium term" because it fails to address the problems of high bank interest and the foreign debt. PCdoB president Amazonas closed the program with a defense of "scientific socialism" and blamed capitalism for "the moral decay of society." (*Folha de São Paulo*, 24 April; *FBIS*, 30 April.)

PCdoB activist Gisela Mendonça was elected president of the National Student Union (União Nacional dos Estudantes; UNE) in 1986 on a coalition ticket including the PMDB and the Socialist Party. The PCdoB has controlled the UNE since 1979 and is frequently blamed for its current irrelevance: only 115,000 students, 10 percent of the total, voted in the June election, and the formerly combative organization now receives government funding (*O Estado de São Paulo*, 29 June).

**PT.** The PT grew out of the São Paulo labor movement of the late 1970s and shelters a number of small ultra-left parties and radical Catholic elements. Performance in the November election was below the party's expectations, and this increasingly radical image may have been responsible. The PT national president, former labor leader Luis Inacio "Lula" da Silva, was elected to the Chamber of Deputies with an impressive individual vote, but only seven others were elected with him in the party's home state of São Paulo, for a total of sixteen deputies nationwide. PT gubernatorial candidates Eduardo Suplicy in São Paulo and former guerrilla Fernando Gabeira in Rio de Janeiro came in a distant fourth and third, respectively. (Suplicy won almost 20 percent of the total vote when he ran for mayor in 1985, opposed to about 10 percent in 1986.)

Even before the general strike and the violent demonstrations that greeted the second Cruzado Plan in November, the government, striving to maintain a delicate wage-price balance, had lost patience with the PT-dominated CUT and its heavy strike activity. In some cases this activity was exacerbated by vandalism in the factory and abuse of nonstriking workers. The PT was absolved of charges that it had started the violence in which two people were killed during a migrant farmworkers' strike, but it continued to promote land invasions by the *sem terra* (landless) groups. The sem terra are likewise supported by the church's Pastoral Land Commission (CPT) and the Basic Christian Communities (Comunidades Eclesiais de Base; CEBs). By mid-year more than one hundred people had died in land clashes, and polarization has grown. In many cases, invaded property has been subsequently expropriated for agrarian reform, and landowners have accused the government of adopting the methods of Salvador Allende in Chile. Two groups—one of delegates from the CPT, CEBs, and PT, and another of Brazilian bishops—had planned trips to observe agrarian, health, and educational sectors in Cuba and Nicaragua.

Six members of the Brazilian Revolutionary Communist Party (Partido Comunista Brasileiro Revolucionario; PCBR) were arrested in connection with two bank robberies in Bahia. The PCBR has been one of the independent extreme left parties harbored by the PT (see descriptions in *YICA*, 1986). Former air force sergeant Antonio Prestes de Paula, leader of the group, said the money was to have been invested in small businesses until the time came to use it for formation of a revolutionary vanguard. De Paula was reportedly arrested on a farm belonging to a regional director of the PT in Goiás (*O Estado de São Paulo*, 25, 28 June). The PT expelled the individuals involved, but, from available reports, the status of the PCBR under the PT umbrella is not clear. According to *O globo* (27 April; see also *JPRS*, 27 May), the seven clandestine parties together have less than 3,000 members but control 35 percent of the PT national directorate and command several regional directorates, including Pernambuco, Pará, and Rio Grande do Sul.

Carole Merten
*San Francisco, California*

# Canada

**Population.** 25,644,000
**Party.** Communist Party of Canada (CPC); Communist Party of Canada (Marxist-Leninist) (CPC-ML); Revolutionary Workers' League (RWL)
**Founded.** CPC: 1921; CPC-ML: 1970; RWL: 1977
**Membership.** CPC: 2,500; CPC-ML: 500; RWL: 200 (all estimated)
**General Secretary.** CPC: William Kashtan; CPC-ML: Hardial Bains; RWL: John Riddell
**Central Committee.** CPC: 77 members
**Status.** All legal
**Last Congress.** CPC: Twenty-sixth, 5–8 April 1985, in Toronto; CPC-ML: Fourth, 3 April 1982, in Montreal; RWL: Sixth, 28 July–3 August, in Montreal
**Last Federal Election.** 4 September 1984; CPC: 52 candidates, average vote 162; RWL: 5 candidates, average vote 127; no representatives

**Auxiliary Organizations.** CPC: Parti communiste du Quebec, Canadian Peace Congress, Conseil québecois de la paix, Association of United Ukrainian Canadians, Congress of Canadian Women, Young Communist League, Workers' Benevolent Association of Canada; CPC-ML: People's Front Against Racist and Fascist Violence, Revolutionary Trade Union Opposition, Democratic Women's Union of Canada, Communist Youth Union of Canada (Marxist-Leninist), Canada-Albania Friendship Association; RWL: Young Socialist Organizing Committee, Comité de la jeunesse révolutionnaire

**Publications.** CPC: *Canadian Tribune* (James Leech, editor), *Pacific Tribune*, *Combat*, *Communist Viewpoint*, *Le Communiste*, *Rebel Youth*, *Jeunesse militante*; CPC-ML: *Marxist-Leninist*, *Le Marxiste-Leniniste*, *Voice of the Youth*, *Voice of the People*, *Democratic Women*, *People's Front Bulletin*, *Canadian Student*, *BC Worker*; RWL: *Socialist Voice* (John Steel, editor), *Lutte ouvrière*

A number of Marxist-Leninist organizations exist legally in Canada. The oldest, largest, and best organized is the CPC. Founded in 1921, it has always adhered faithfully to a pro-Moscow line. The CPC-ML began in 1970 as an ardent follower of the Chinese brand of communism, but since then it has eschewed Beijing for the Albanian model. In addition, there are several Trotskyist groups functioning, the most active of which is the RWL.

Since Brian Mulroney's resounding victory in the 1984 federal election, the political fortunes of the Conservative government have taken a decided turn for the worse. The Conservatives have seen their popular support steadily erode while that of the Liberals and the New Democratic Party (NDP) climbs. This sharp shift indicates the uncertain and unstable Canadian economic recovery and the inability of the prime minister to deliver on his election promises. High unemployment (over 9 percent), a depressed energy sector, and tumbling world wheat prices have been deeply felt, particularly in Western Canada, which witnessed the failure of two regional banks. The government's ongoing efforts to reduce the deficit via cuts in social services, deregulation, and the privatization of certain crown corporations have also created a backlash from organized labor and various interest groups. Meanwhile, Ottawa's highly touted "free trade" talks with Washington have not progressed smoothly. Indeed, they could well be dashed on the hard reality of American protectionism.

Concomitantly, there has been growing controversy in Canadian-American military cooperation. Canada's future involvement in the Strategic Defense Initiative (SDI), continued testing of cruise missiles on Canadian territory, and the proposed overhaul of the Distant Early Warning (DEW) line have mobilized nascent peace groups into forming a loosely knit lobby organization, the Canadian Peace Alliance (CPA). Composed of some 40 affiliates, including Operation Dismantle, Physicians for Social Responsibility, and the Canadian Labour Congress (CLC), the CPA has launched vigorous campaigns for an "independent Canadian foreign policy of peace," which among other items calls for an abrogation of Canada's North American Air Defence Command (NORAD) agreement and the establishment of Canada as a Nuclear Weapons Free Zone (*Peace Courier*, April).

**CPC.** The CPC operates from its national office in Toronto on a meager budget of approximately $300,000 (Canadian) a year. In the 1984 federal election the party fielded 52 candidates, electing none and garnering just over 8,000 votes. During 1986 it ran candidates in four provincial elections. In Manitoba, all five CPC candidates, including the provincial party leader, Paula Fletcher, were defeated, receiving a negligible vote. A similar fate awaited Alberta's party leader, David Willis, and four of his colleagues in the Alberta contest; indeed, they managed an average of only 33 votes. Kimball Cariou was the only candidate representing the party in the Saskatchewan provincial election; he obtained only 71 votes in Regina Centre. In addition, three CPC candidates faced the electorate in the British Columbia provincial election; all were defeated (average vote of 211), including Maurice Rush, the party provincial leader. The only electoral success the CPC obtained during the year was at the municipal level, where the Committee of Progressive Electors (COPE)—an alliance of CPC members, trade unionists, and left-wing NDP members—managed to win a number of seats on the city council and on the board of education in Vancouver (*Canadian Tribune*, 10 February).

There has been no general meeting of the CPC since its Twenty-sixth Congress held in Toronto in April 1985. However, the Central Committee did convene in Toronto on 23–25 May 1986 with more than 70 members present from across Canada (ibid., 2 June). Also, the British Columbia branch of the CPC held a convention 17–20 May with approximately 70 delegates in attendance representing 35 party clubs (ibid., 26 May).

New recruitment continues to be a high priority for the CPC, as does increased circulation of the *Canadian Tribune*. The party has set a goal of 5 percent overall increase in membership and a yearly target of 15 percent growth in the newspaper's subscription (ibid., 1 September). In the latter case, the aim is to eventually produce a daily rather than a weekly. As with the membership drive, this appears to be a difficult task, although as of 4 August the Toronto-based newspaper had moved into larger offices and purchased new equipment designed to modernize the editorial facilities (ibid., 14 July). The *Tribune* also appointed a Berlin correspondent—Gerry Van Houten, a former research director for the CPC's central office in Toronto—and hired Miguel Figeroa to provide "systematic coverage" of the Maritimes and Newfoundland from its Halifax bureau (ibid., 30 June). The *Tribune's* 51st Annual Labour Festival took place on 24 August at Camp Palermo, Ontario, attracting some 3,000 people (ibid., 1 September).

During the year, General Secretary Kashtan attended the Twenty-seventh Congress of the Communist Party of the Soviet Union (CPSU) in Moscow 27 February–6 March (ibid., 31 March). In July he visited Romania and met with President Nicolae Ceauşescu, general secretary of the Romanian Communist Party (ibid., 8 September). More recently, Eduard Shevardnadze, the Soviet foreign minister, met with Kashtan while on an official state visit to Canada. Meanwhile, William Stewart represented the CPC at the Thirteenth Congress of the League of Communists of Yugoslavia in Belgrade 25–28 June, and Edward McDonald and Claude Demers were sent by the party to the Seventeenth Congress of the Communist Party of Bulgaria in Sofia (ibid., 11 August, 12 May).

In March, prominent CPC member Joe Zuken died. He had been an energetic member of the Manitoba Committee of the CPC and a 42-year veteran on the Winnipeg School Board and city council (ibid., 31 March). Another well-known party stalwart, Peter Krawchuk, president of the Association of United Ukrainian Canadians and vice president of the Canadian Society for Ukrainian Labour Research, was awarded the Order of Friendship of Peoples by the Presidium of the Supreme Soviet of the USSR for his "activities in strengthening friendship and cooperation between Canadian and Soviet peoples" (ibid., 25 August).

While the CPC rejoiced in the downward slide of the Conservatives in public opinion polls—which, according to the party, reflect doubts by Canadians about the prime minister's ability to cope with the basic economic and social problems confronting the nation—the CPC decried what it believes has been the unabashed "sell out" of Canada, primarily to U.S. interests (ibid., 13 January, 3 February). Citing the "give away" of the crown-owned de Havilland Aircraft Company to Boeing and of the Montreal Gulf Refinery to Ultramar, as well as the replacement of the Foreign Investment Review Act with Investment Canada, the CPC accuses the government of providing a "welcoming committee for transnationals wanting to extend or recarve their ownership of Canada" (ibid., 27 January).

Of particular concern to the CPC was the prime minister's "free-trade" initiative. Numerous editorials in the *Canadian Tribune* called for a termination of the negotiations, arguing that any agreement would be at the cost of Canadian jobs, especially in the textile, shoe, food, auto, communications, publishing, pharmaceuticals, lumber, and service industries (ibid., 28 April, 8 September). Moreover, the CPC maintained that in the long run the initiative would result in the loss not only of Canada's economic but also its political independence. What Canada needs, instead, the party suggested, is a policy to develop multilateral trade and the nationalization "under democratic control" of U.S. transnationals operating in Canada (ibid., 28 April).

The CPC was also critical of Conservative agricultural policy that "does inestimable harm to a large sector of the Canadian people" (ibid., 14 April). Noting that the wheat prices were the lowest in seven years (due to the U.S. Farm Bill, which boosted subsidies to American farmers while driving down the world price of wheat), the party lambasted Ottawa for doing nothing to protect the farmer. The party's own program included guaranteeing farmers parity prices while providing interest-free loans to low-income family farmers, free crop insurance, a moratorium on farm debts, and an end to foreclosures. To achieve these aims, the party called for "worker-farmer unity" against the government, banks, and other monopolies" (ibid.).

On the domestic scene generally, the CPC was highly critical of the Tories; it accused the Mulroney administration of a "neoconservative drive to dismantle the public sector, ravage social services, and shift an ever larger share of the social wealth into the hands of the transnational corporations" (ibid., 21 July). It labeled Minister of Finance Michael

Wilson's proposed tax reforms—the core of which was a Business Transfer Tax (BTT)—as "totally inappropriate." If implemented, the party averred, the BTT would result in increased prices and additional burdens on the people, particularly those with low incomes (ibid., 15 September). The CPC's tax-reform platform advocated the elimination of income taxes for people earning less than $25,000 a year and an increased corporate tax based on the "recognition that corporations and banks do not carry a fair share of the tax burden (ibid.).

To combat these and other "disasterous" policies of the Mulroney government, the CPC urged the formation of a "people's majority outside of Parliament." In this regard, the party favored a broad coalition of communists with the NDP, left Liberals, and the trade-union movement ("Insight," *Canadian Tribune*, May). While guarding against the Liberal Party becoming the main beneficiary of discontent with Tory policies, the CPC endeavored to press the NDP to advance a "more coherent program against state monopoly capitalism," to oppose deregulation and privatization, and to do battle for Canadian independence (*Canadian Tribune*, 3 March). In the provincial elections this meant that CPC candidates appealed to New Democrats to adopt a "minimum program of unity" while they ignored the top leadership of the NDP (ibid., 26 February, 26 May). A similar strategy was followed with the CPC's approach to trade unions, particularly the CLC. The party recognized that, as the largest organized section of the working class, the CLC "offers the potential to lead the nation into a fundamentally new path for peace, independence, and social progress" ("Insight," *Canadian Tribune*, May). In a show of solidarity with organized labor, the *Canadian Tribune* gave wide coverage to two bitter disputes: the protracted Gainers strike in Edmonton, Alberta, between Peter Pocklington, owner of the meat packing company, and the 1,100 members of the United Food and Commercial Workers Union; and the Newfoundland Association of Public Employees' confrontation with Premier Brian Peckford's government (*Canadian Tribune*, 21 July, 15 September).

The CPC wholeheartedly endorsed the Soviet Union's fifteen-year peace proposals (announced 15 January), which called for a three-stage plan to eliminate nuclear weapons by the year 2000 (ibid., 27 January). The party also applauded Mikhail Gorbachev's announcement that the USSR would extend its test-ban moratorium until 1 January 1987—the fourth such extension since the uni-

lateral test ban was first declared 6 August 1985 (ibid., 25 August). These proposals, the CPC maintained, underline the Soviet Union's genuine commitment to promoting world peace and international security and cooperation. It is in this context that the party has continued to support the activities of the CPA.

The main threat to the achievement of peaceful coexistence and a globe free of nuclear arsenals, according to the CPC, has been American imperialism (ibid., 31 March). The Reagan administration, it argued, has not only scorned the Soviet offers (most recently at the Reykjavik mini-summit) but is also pursuing a confrontationist policy of "trying to provoke new situations and areas of tension" (*IB*, March). The CPC maintained that the U.S. objective is to achieve military superiority in space (via the SDI) while economically wearing down the Soviet Union and the socialist countries in order to exact concessions from them. Indeed, the SDI is seen as an "extremely dangerous drive by U.S. imperialism for obtaining . . . a first-strike capability" (ibid.). Such a course, the party postulated, will "drastically destabilize the globe, bring about an uncontrollable arms race, and ultimately push the world to the brink of catastrophe" (ibid.). "trying to provoke new situations and areas of tension" (*IB*, March). The CPC maintained that the silent, and complicit" (*Canadian Tribune*, 25 August). It was chagrined that the prime minister signed a five-year renewal of NORAD in March, "giving Canada the status of pawn in the hands of Reagan's Star Wars plotters" (ibid., 31 March). The party saw this as "back door" participation in the SDI and Canada's drift into the U.S. "military orbit" (ibid., 17 March). Numerous editorials in the *Canadian Tribune* reiterated CPC demands that Canada halt the testing of cruise missiles on Canadian territory; that the government reject all plans to upgrade NORAD and the DEW system; that it publish all secret U.S.-Canada military agreements (especially those withheld from the recent parliamentary committee reviewing Canada's role in NORAD); and that Canada ultimately pull out of both NORAD and the North Atlantic Treaty Organization (NATO) (ibid., 24 February, 17 March). In the case of NATO, the CPC was particularly opposed to the proposal that NATO establish a "tactical fighter weapons training center" at Goose Bay, Labrador (ibid., 24 February). The above actions are necessary, the party contended, if Canada is to develop an independent foreign policy rather than be reduced "to a U.S. power monkey" (ibid.).

In international affairs generally, the CPC has followed a two-tiered line of stoutly supporting the Soviet position while condemning that of the United States. All facets of U.S. foreign policy were stridently attacked—from President Reagan's refusal to apply "full" sanctions on the "racist" South African government, to Washington's "aggressive machinations" in Central America. Editorials in the *Canadian Tribune* have particularly chastised American support of the *contras* in their war against Daniel Ortega's regime in Nicaragua and the continued U.S. backing of the El Salvadoran government in its struggle to subdue the insurgent guerrilla army (ibid., 28 April). The CPC expressed outrage, as well, at the U.S. miliary operation against Libya, labeling it "dive-bomber diplomacy" and a "most dangerous provocation" (ibid., 31 March).

The CPC also accused the Canadian government of becoming an accomplice to "American adventurism" by surreptitiously condoning U.S. actions around the globe (ibid.). Canada's ambassador to the United Nations, Stephen Lewis, was a focus of ridicule for his "Pavlovian capacity" when he defended the U.S. right to expel one-third of the Soviet U.N. Mission staff and severely criticized the continued Soviet occupation of Afghanistan (ibid., 24 March). In line with the Soviet press, the party also had harsh words for the Western media on their reporting of the Chernobyl accident, stating that they "indulged in a good deal of . . . Soviet-bashing" (ibid., 5 May).

In general, the CPC divides the world into two camps with their respective results: that of the United States, which means confrontation and aggression leading to war and possible nuclear annihilation; or that of the Soviet Union, which strives toward peaceful coexistence, détente, and disarmament. Such a black-and-white scenario has not proved fruitful in soliciting support from Canadians for the party's policies. Indeed, the CPC's traditional link with the USSR remains its greatest problem and ensures the party's relative insignificance on the Canadian political scene.

**CPC-ML.** The CPC-ML operates from its national headquarters in Montreal. Although there has been no party congress since 1982, First Secretary Bains has been active writing a number of polemical pamphlets and giving lectures to a Marxist-Leninist study group at the University of Guelph. The party continued to produce *Marxist-Leninist* both as a daily paper and a weekly magazine that, in fact, appeared irregularly throughout 1986. The CPC-ML also resumed publication in May of *Voice of the Youth*, the organ of the Central Committee of the Communist Youth Union of Canada (Marxist-Leninist), after a hiatus of several months. During the year, the CPC-ML did contest one provincial election; running under the People's Front banner, five Marxist-Leninist candidates received a paltry average of 82 votes in the British Columbia campaign (*Toronto Globe and Mail*, 24 October).

The CPC-ML has remained a doctrinaire organization which believes that the transformation of society from capitalism to socialism can only be ensured through "revolutionary violence" (*Marxist-Leninist*, 17 March). While concluding that the class struggle has deepened in Canada, the party acknowledged that there has been some confusion among the workers, who have been diverted from the true Marxist-Leninist course by "class-collaborationists" and "labour-aristocrats" (ibid., 4 May). For this state of affairs the party blamed the NDP, which "desires that the proletariat should make their peace with the bourgeoisie," and the CLC for its "30 year tradition of collaboration with the bourgeoisie and betrayal of the working class" (ibid.). The CPC-ML particularly chastised the new president of the CLC, Shirley Carr, for "preferring to spend time hobnobbing with the monopolists rather than to be with the workers on the shop floor" (ibid.). Both the NDP and the CLC, the party maintained, have attempted to shackle the workers by making them wage the "class struggle" within the confines of the collective bargaining system and the bounds of bourgeois parliamentary democracy (ibid.). The CPC-ML argued that no such limits or constraints can be imposed on the proletariat if it is to develop its "leading and hegemonic role" (ibid., 17 March).

On domestic issues, the CPC-ML accused the Mulroney government of condoning increased American economic and military domination of Canada. It condemned the free-trade talks as a "national betrayal" and saw closer military cooperation with the United States as a direct threat to Canada's sovereignty. It urged Ottawa to withdraw from NATO and NORAD, to refuse further testing of the cruise missile on Canadian soil, to oppose the overhaul of the DEW system, to prohibit any American military bases in Canada's north, and to reject completely the SDI program (ibid., 17 March, 4, 11 May). To make its views known, the CPC-ML organized a number of "militant pickets" and demonstrations in Toronto, Montreal, Quebec City,

Winnipeg, and Vancouver as part of its "mass actions on May Day" (ibid., 4 May).

On the international level, the CPC-ML saw U.S. imperialism, together with Soviet "social imperialism," as "the greatest enemy of the struggles of the peoples for national and social emancipation" (ibid.). According to the party, the two superpowers have been engaged in ruthless and bloody counterrevolutionary activities around the globe as part of their rivalry for world hegemony. The invasion of Grenada, the bombing of Libya, and Reagan's "counterrevolutionary crusade" against the government of Nicaragua were cited as examples of American "lawlessness" and "terror" designed "to prevent the peoples from casting off the imperialist yoke" (ibid., 4, 11 May). At the same time, the party accused the USSR of cynically trying to capitalize on the worldwide indignation against U.S. aggression by representing itself as the natural ally of the national liberation struggle (ibid., 4 May). It maintained that Moscow collaborated with Washington in the attack on Libya (that is, the United States informed the Soviet Union in advance of its intention to launch the 15 April raid) and points to the "war of occupation against the people of Afghanistan" as further proof of the Kremlin's imperialistic nature. Gorbachev's peace proposals are labeled "deceptive" and "insincere," since "the people must have no illusions that one superpower can provide protection against the other" (ibid.). In general, the CPC-ML believes that the two superpowers have been engaged in war preparations to redivide the globe.

The death of Albania's strongman, Enver Hoxha, "the guardian of Marxist-Leninist purity," has not caused an ideological shift within the CPC-ML. The party has remained committed to Albania as the "touchstone of proletarian internationalism" and fully endorsed Hoxha's successor, Ramiz Alia, first secretary of the Central Committee of the Party of Labor of Albania. Nevertheless, most Canadians have never heard of the CPC-ML. Sixteen years after its founding, the party has remained very much on the political fringe with a tiny (albeit hardcore) following.

**RWL.** The RWL is a member of the Trotskyist Fourth International. In 1986 it underwent considerable reorganization due to a decrease in membership and financial difficulties. Consequently, it closed its Vancouver office and operated solely out of Montreal and Toronto (*YICA*, 1986). The RWL held its sixth convention in Montreal, 28 July–3 August, where it decided to "launch a new pan-Canadian revolutionary youth organization" and to step up the league's participation in selected "solidarity campaigns," particularly in support of the striking meatpackers at the Gainers plant in Edmonton, Alberta. To this end, two RWL leaders, Beverly Bernardo and Joe Young, participated on the Gainers strikers' picket line (*Socialist Voice*, 8 September). The league also announced its intention of building factions in two pan-Canadian industrial unions: the Amalgamated Clothing and Textile Workers Union, and the United Steelworkers of America (ibid.). A spring campaign to sell issues of the *Socialist Voice* and *Lutte ouvrière* resulted in 346 subscriptions, which surpassed the countrywide goal of 310 (ibid., 8 September, 20 October).

On domestic issues, the RWL noted with evident satisfaction that support for the NDP both in English Canada and Quebec has been on the rise. Although quite critical of the New Democrats in the past, the RWL believes that the NDP can be reformed to assume a truly "pan-Canadian character" (ibid., 20 October). The Quebecois, the league maintained, are an oppressed nationality who are kept in second-class status as a result of institutionalized discrimination based on their language. The return of the Liberals to power in Quebec (after nine years of separatist Parti Quebecois rule) was seen as a victory for the pro-federalist forces over the goal of Quebec self-determination. The league proposed the creation of a new, trade-union-based party in the province (ibid., 8 September, 30 November).

In foreign affairs, the RWL was pro-Soviet and anti-American, focusing primarily on U.S. activities in Central America, particularly the Reagan administration's war against Nicaragua. Under the slogan "Boycott South Africa, not Nicaragua," the league denounced apartheid and, while noting Mulroney's antiapartheid rhetoric, pointed out that Canada signed an agreement with South Africa to sell it wheat (ibid., 8 September). In general, the RWL saw U.S. imperialism as the main obstacle to world peace and criticized the Canadian government for kowtowing to American interests. Like the CPC-ML, the RWL has been very much on the political periphery, with no more than about 200 members throughout the country.

**Other Groups.** The Trotskyist League (TL) and the International Socialists (IS) are two other Marxist-Leninist groups that appeared to operate, at least nominally, in Canada. The TL believes in "permanent revolution," has denounced all other Trotskyist organizations, and has advocated a re-forged Fourth International; it was founded in 1975 and publishes *Sparticist Canada*. The IS has been more populist in nature, calling for the building of socialism from below by the establishment of well-organized branches in major cities; the group issues a monthly paper, *Socialist Worker*. Whether through lack of funds or personnel, however, the activities of the TL and IS during the year seem to have been negligible. At any rate, there is insuffi-cient information available to provide a reliable, cogent overview.

Jaroslav Petryshyn
*Grande Prairie Regional College*

The author wishes to express his thanks to the Grande Prairie Regional College Library staff, Professor Scott McAlpine of the Department of Humanities and Social Sciences, and Mr. Mark McAlpine of Kitchener, Ontario, for their aid in locating some of the material for this article.

# Chile

**Population.** 12,261,000
**Party.** Communist Party of Chile (Partido Comunista de Chile; PCC)
**Founded.** 1922
**Membership.** 20,000 (estimated)
**General Secretary.** Luís Corvalán Lepe
**Politburo.** 20 members (clandestine and in exile)
**Secretariat.** 5 members (clandestine and in exile)
**Central Committee.** Over 100 members (clandestine and in exile)
**Status.** Illegal, but functions underground and through front groups.
**Last Congress.** Sixteenth, June 1984, held clandestinely in Chile and simultaneously outside the country; clandestine Central Committee plenum held in Santiago in January 1986.
**Last Election.** March 1973, 16 percent, 23 of 150 seats in lower house
**Auxiliary Organizations.** Communist Youth (illegal); National Trade Union Coordinating Committee (CNS; headed by a Christian Democrat); Popular Democratic Movement (MDP; includes part of the Socialist Party and the Movement of the Revolutionary Left [MIR]); Manuel Rodriguez Patriotic Front (FPMR; terrorist group with independent lines to Havana and Moscow)
**Publications.** *El Siglo* (clandestine newspaper); *Principios* (clandestine theoretical journal)

The PCC has continued to function clandestinely since the 1973 coup in Chile. However, the front group that the party created in 1983, the MDP—which also includes the faction of the Socialist Party headed by Clodomiro Almeyda in East Berlin and the extremist MIR—was active despite having been declared unconstitutional by the Chilean Constitu-tional Tribunal in early 1985. The PCC has influ-ence in the labor movement through the CNS, which in turn participates in the highly visible National Labor Command that leads protests and demonstrations, but the party's principal base is now in the shantytowns (*poblaciones*) in and near the major cities.

Since 1980 the PCC has been committed to the thesis of "popular rebellion" and "all forms of struggle." Through a related group, the FPMR, founded in December 1983, the party has been able to carry out bombings, sabotage, blackouts, and kidnappings. Through the MDP, it has also called for joint action with the centrist parties of the Christian Democratic–dominated Democratic Alliance (AD) and argues that it is not committed to militaristic solutions, but to forcing the removal of President Augusto Pinochet by making the country "ungovernable."

In November 1985, the cooperation between the MDP and the centrist AD in a peaceful protest had seemed to indicate that relations between the two groups were improving. However, two events in 1986—the discovery of large weapons stockpiles clearly intended for use by leftist guerrillas, and an unsuccessful assassination attempt by the FPMR against Pinochet—fundamentally altered the relation of the democratic opposition to the Marxist-Leninist parties.

At the beginning of the year, the PCC Central Committee issued a manifesto in which it called for "social mobilization" of workers, youth, students, and slumdwellers using "all methods of struggle" to overthrow Pinochet. It endorsed "common action by Marxists and Christians" and "agreement to struggle among all the opposition forces, be they from left, center, or right." (Radio Moscow, 28 January; *FBIS*, 21 February.) Informal conversations were later held between MDP leaders and representatives of the Briones faction of the Socialist Party as well as the Radicals, both of which were members of the AD. The Christian Democrats at the University of Chile also formed a common slate with the MDP that was victorious in the student elections. However, these parties were under continual attack for their relations with the left, both by government propagandists and by Andres Allamand, the leader of the National Union Movement (MUN) on the right, which had been a cosigner of the church-sponsored National Accord in August 1985 that called for a return to civilian government. Moreover, there was an upswing in the number of bombings and blackouts attributed to the FPMR, and most observers felt that the FPMR was, if not an arm of the PCC, at least closely related to it.

The problem of formal relations between the centrist and leftist parties was finessed with the creation of the National Civic Assembly (Asamblea Nacional de la Civilidad) in April. The assembly claimed to represent 250 social and professional organizations, and it included groups of many different political orientations, some of them communist. Its manifesto, La Demanda de Chile, called for the termination of the state of emergency and the adoption of a democratically legitimated constitution as well as a series of social welfare measures to help low-income groups. The assembly called a nationwide strike in July that was only partially successful, and when the government reacted by imprisoning its top leadership, the assembly ceased to be a major political force.

The use of violence and terror increased in 1986 with dramatic actions by the FPMR. These included a blackout of 800 square miles of Chile in March, 500 bombings between January and August (including the house of the former head of the intelligence agency), the radio broadcast of a communiqué during a soccer game in May, and the kidnapping and later release of chief of protocol of the Chilean army in August. Chilean analysts argued that the PCC had its own special combat forces trained in the use of violence (Santiago, *La Tercera*, 4 May; *FBIS*, 13 May) and that one should distinguish between the Rodriguista militias, which operated in the shantytowns and gave young unemployed leftists a focus for their opposition to the government, and the much more selective front itself, which carried out the blackouts and bombings. The analysts also argued that the old guard of the PCC was either in exile or had been killed by the regime (especially in 1976–1977, when there had been a systematic attempt by the Pinochet government to eliminate the internal leadership) and that it was now under pressure from a much more violence-prone younger generation. (*La Segunda*, 3 October.) There was also debate as to whether the adoption of "popular rebellion" by the PCC in 1980 had been primarily a response to internal pressures from the younger party members or a Moscow-decreed shift in imitation of the policy that had led to the Sandinista victory in Nicaragua in 1979.

In August the debate on the relation of violence and social mobilization in the strategy of the PCC took a dramatic turn with the discovery of large stockpiles of arms mainly in the north of Chile. The weapons included 3,000 M-16 rifles, later identified by U.S. State Department investigators as having been sent to Vietnam in the late 1960s; 3 million rounds of ammunition; 114 Soviet-made rocket launchers; and 2,000 grenades and other explosives of Bulgarian manufacture that were similar to those used by the M-19 guerrillas in Colombia in the assault on the Palace of Justice in Bogota in 1985.

There was so little confidence in the statements of the Pinochet government that its initial revelations of the arms caches were not widely believed, but when the arms were placed on exhibit and their origins identified, the discovery of *los arsenales* had a profound effect on Chilean politics. It was clear that such massive amounts of arms and ammunition were not designed simply for sporadic guerrilla actions such as had occurred up to that time. They seemed to be aimed at a possible future civil war or national uprising—again on the Nicaraguan model—in which those who had access to military equipment could have a decisive advantage. This cast doubt on the desirability of cooperative action between the democratic center and a Marxist-Leninist left that was following a two-faced policy. The result was the termination of negotiations by the centrist parties and the rejection by the Christian Democrats of a common ticket with the MDP in the university elections. (The Christian Democrats subsequently defeated the MDP by a narrow margin.)

Although the FPMR denied any connection with the arms, it did take responsibility for the attempted assassination of Pinochet as he was returning from a weekend retreat on 7 September. Pinochet escaped, but a number of his drivers and bodyguards were killed and the attack demonstrated an organizational and logistic capacity proving that the FPMR was a well-financed terrorist group with considerable outside support. Investigation of the assassina-

tion attempt and of the arms caches revealed in both cases a Cuban connection: in the first case, the training of several of the assassins in Cuba; and in the other, the presence of Cuban fishing trawlers off the coast between May and July that were believed to have been the sources of the arms.

Further negotiations between the AD and the MDP ceased, but the question of present and future relations with the left remained. When an attempt was made in August to broaden and deepen the National Accord through the establishment of a more specific program, both the right-wing MUN and the Christian Left refused to sign. Luis Maira, the head of the Christian Left, made no secret of his intention to act as a link between the center and the left and, many suspected, to run in any future free election as the candidate of the left. The continued intransigence of Pinochet, and his obvious desire to run as the single candidate of the junta in a 1989 plebiscite, led foreign observers to worry about the "Nicaraguanization" of Chile in the coming years, especially if the arms that had been discovered were only a fraction of what had been brought into the country and concealed. This concern led U.S. policymakers to press harder for a political opening in order to deny the communists the support that Pinochet's policy has provided them.

At the end of the year, the government lifted the state of siege imposed at the time of the assassination attempt, and it promised to allow most exiles to return.

Paul E. Sigmund
*Princeton University*

# Colombia

Population. 29,956,000
Party. Communist Party of Colombia (Partido Comunista de Colombia; PCC)
Founded. 1930
Membership. 16,000 (estimated)
General Secretary. Gilberto Vieira
Secretariat. Gilberto Vieira, Manuel Cepeda, Teofila Forero, Alvaro Vasquez, Jesus Maria Villegas;
    alternate members: Hurtado Alvarez, Roso Osorio (*Voz*, 22 November 1984)
Executive Committee. 14 members
Central Committee. 80 members
Status. Legal
Last Congress. Fourteenth, 7–11 November 1984
Last Elections. 1986: presidential, 4.5 percent; municipal and state assembly, 1.4 percent; congressional, 1.4 percent, 5 of 114 senators, 9 of 199 representatives
Auxiliary Organizations. Trade Union Confederation of Workers of Colombia (CSTC); Federation of Agrarian Syndicates; Communist Youth of Colombia (JUCO), claims 2,000 members
Publications. *Voz* (weekly), 40,000 circulation; *Margen Izquierda*, political journal; Colombian edition of *World Marxist Review*, 2,000 circulation; JUCO publishes a monthly supplement to *Voz*.

The communist movement in Colombia has undergone transformations in both name and organization since the party's initial formation in December 1926. The PCC was publicly proclaimed on 17 July 1930. In July 1965, a schism within the PCC between pro-Soviet and pro-Chinese factions resulted in the latter's becoming the Communist Party of Colombia, Marxist-Leninist (PCC-ML). Only the PCC has legal status. It has been allowed to participate in elections under its own banner since 1972. In 1986, the PCC participated in municipal council, state assembly, congressional, and presidential elections as the leading member of a leftist coalition called the Patriotic Union (Unión Patriótica; UP). The UP was formed in 1985 on the initiative of the Revolutionary Armed Forces of Colombia (FARC) as a broad front to achieve political and social reforms. From the day the movement was founded, the PCC has been active in its leadership and work. The UP won or shared five senate and nine house seats in the March elections (compared to one senate and three house seats for the Democratic Front

coalition in 1982). It also elected a total of nineteen deputies in twelve departmental assemblies (compared to eight in 1982), and 323 councilmembers (compared to 108 in 1982). The UP's presidential candidate, Jaime Pardo Leal, received 4.5 percent of the popular vote in the 25 May presidential election, which represents the highest level of support for the left in Colombian history in terms of number of votes (328,641).

According to U.S. intelligence sources, the PCC has 18,000 members, including communist youth. Although the party contends that its ranks have increased in recent years, the party's growth has been less rapid than its leaders had hoped, especially outside the Federal District of Bogotá. The PCC exercises only marginal influence in national affairs.

The highest party authority is the congress, convened at four-year intervals. Gilberto Vieira, the general secretary of the PCC, is 75. A major source of the party's influence is its control of the CSTC, which is reportedly Colombia's largest trade-union confederation and a member of the Soviet-front World Federation of Trade Unions. The CSTC's president, Gustavo Osorio, and its general secretary, Angelino Garzón, are members of the PCC's Central Committee.

The PCC's youth organization, the JUCO, plays an active role in promoting party policy among university and secondary school students. The JUCO held a plenum in Bogotá on 18–19 January at which it discussed the formation of Patriotic Youth Committees and concerns for its own growth (*Voz*, 23 January). The JUCO organized a National Patriotic Youth Council in February to support the UP and Pardo Leal's candidacy (ibid., 27 February). The JUCO's Central Committee met on 23–24 August to review its role as an auxiliary organization of the PCC and to plan its strategy for dealing with the new government of Virgilio Barco Vargas (ibid., 28 August). The JUCO's general secretary is José Anteguera.

**Guerrilla Warfare.** Although not a serious threat to the government, guerrilla warfare has been a feature of Colombian life since the late 1940s; the current wave began in 1964. The four main guerrilla organizations are the FARC, long controlled by the PCC; the M-19, a guerrilla organization that began as the armed hand of the National Popular Alliance (ANAPO); the pro-Chinese People's Liberation Army (EPL), which is the guerrilla arm of the PCC-ML; and the Castroite National Liberation Army (ELN). Other, smaller guerrilla movements that have emerged in recent years include the Trotskyist-oriented Workers' Self-Defense Movement (ADO); the Revolutionary Workers' Party (PRT); the Free Fatherland (Patria Libre), which some observers believe to be a spin-off of the EPL; and the Quintín Lamé, a pro-Indian group that operates primarily in Cauca department. In late 1985, leaders from the various guerrilla organizations that no longer observe the 1984 cease-fire agreements, or, in the case of the ELN, that did not agree to them in the first place, formed the National Guerrilla Coordinating Board (CNG). The principal leadership within the CNG is provided by the M-19. Among the guerrilla columns functioning under the umbrella of the CNG's coordinated command is the so-called America Battalion, said by its leaders to consist of leftist rebels from Colombia, members of the Alfaro Lives movement of Ecuador, and guerrillas from the Tupac Amaru II movement of Peru. In April, the Quintín Lamé command confirmed that it had broken away from the general leadership of the M-19 and announced its withdrawal from the CNG because of the latter's "unwillingness to engage in any dialogue with the government" (*El Tiempo*, 30 April).

**FARC.** According to the FARC's principal leader, Manuel Marulanda Vélez, the movement has some 6,000 (other estimates range as high as 15,000) operating on 27 fronts. The FARC has expanded its areas of influence in recent years to include portions of the departments of Huila, Caquetá, Tolima, Cauca, Boyacá, Santander, Antioquia, Valle, Veta, Cundinamarca, and the intendance of Arauca. The FARC's general headquarters is located at La Uribe. Jacobo Arenas is Marulanda's second in command; other members of the FARC's central staff are Jaime Guaracas, Alfonso Cano, and Raúl Reyes. Although Marulanda has never confirmed officially that the FARC is the armed wing of the PCC, it is widely believed that the leadership mechanisms and general policy of the FARC are determined by the PCC's bylaws, and political resolutions emitted at party congresses and plenums are presumably transmitted to the fronts through Marulanda's directives.

Discussions between FARC leaders and the government's National Peace Commission culminated on 2 March with a formal agreement to continue the peace process signed at La Uribe on 28 March 1984. The government pledged to provide FARC with the guarantees and liberties necessary for its members to take part in political activity through the UP. For its part, the FARC pledged to integrate itself into civilian life and to uphold its agreements to honor the truce, regardless of the outcome of national elections. The FARC further agreed to condemn kidnapping and extortion, and to declare itself against drug trafficking, personal attacks, torture, and "disappearances," regardless of their origin (*El Espectador*, 2 March). The FARC-UP's coordinator, Braulio Herrera, said the new truce would "consolidate the national reconciliation process and pacify nearly 90 percent of the country." According to the president of the National Peace Commission, John Agudelo Ríos, the FARC had already demobilized more than 2,400 men, and "hundreds" of its members were engaged in political activities through local committees organized by the UP (ibid., 3 March).

The commander of the army reported in April that various FARC fronts were continuing to violate the truce by kidnapping and blackmail (*El Tiempo*, 26 April). FARC leaders, in turn, warned President

Betancur about the "risk of civil war" if the army continued its hostile actions. Arenas called for the creation of special commissions from the attorney general's office "to go to each region and clear up the situation" (*Voz*, 24 April). Colombia's minister of defense subsequently confirmed that the army had clashed with FARC fronts operating in Caquetá, Antioquia, and Santander departments.

Alberto Rojas Puyo, Central Committee member and the PCC's representative to the National Peace Commission, called Virgilio Barco's election "a step forward to consolidate the peace process" and announced that the FARC was prepared to collaborate with the new government (ibid., 5 June). Shortly after his inauguration on 7 August, President Barco stated that his government would continue "an honest and open dialogue with the FARC's top command" (*El Tiempo*, 10 August).

Representatives of the new government and FARC leaders held their first meeting on 18 September. In October the president's adviser for rehabilitation and reconciliation said the government had "reliable information" that the FARC was not abiding by the cease-fire agreement. He added that the government would "adopt whatever measures are necessary to guarantee security" (*El Espectador*, 6 October). The commander of the army's 10th brigade claimed the FARC "continues to recruit students and peasants and is increasing in number, in violation of the peace accords." He reported that two fronts used to operate in Cauca, but "now there are four composed of more than 400 men." He added that "left-wing rebels continue to receive aid from socialist-bloc countries and drug traffickers" (*El Siglo*, 21 October). In November, the FARC asked President Barco to appoint a new peace commission, charging that the presidential adviser for reconciliation "cannot possibly cover all the problems throughout the national territory that deal with the peace process." The FARC also asked that the truce process be supervised by a verification commission because "any momentary lapse could be harmful to the truce" (*El Tiempo*, 3 November).

Iván Márquez, UP congressman from Caquetá, warned in November that "if the government does not control the activity of paramilitary groups, it may lead to a break in the truce." According to Márquez, right-wing death squads and paramilitary groups have killed over 300 UP activists and leaders since April 1985, including three congressmen and twenty municipal council members. He added that the 3,000 local UP committees have been instructed to organize security groups in response to the ad-

vance of "militarism" in Colombia (ACAN, 10 November). On 18 November, government representatives and the FARC's high command issued a joint communique announcing the continuation of the peace process and agreeing to extend direct contacts to all FARC fronts. During the two-day meeting at La Uribe, it was established that the attacks on UP leaders are carried out "by the enemies of change and pluralist democracy." The government agreed to punish the guilty "to the full extent of the law." Arenas reiterated the FARC's commitment to continue the truce and to "take the next steps to definitely restore peace in the country." The FARC accepted in principle the government's position that "the armed forces is the only constitutional army in Colombia," and, as such, it has "all the right to operate in every part of the country" (*El Espectador*, 19 November).

Javier Delgado (alias José Fedor Rey), commander of the Ricardo Franco Front, a FARC splinter group, admitted on 3 January that he had ordered the deaths of 138 "subversives" after it was "proven" that they had infiltrated the group. He claimed that the executions were the result of an "unsuccessful elimination plan" directed by the FARC general staff against its dissidents. Delgado added that he would not be intimidated by death threats "made by traitors at the service of the PCC" (*El Tiempo*, 17 January). The CNG rejected Delgado's explanation for the killings and expelled the Ricardo Franco Front for "atrocities against revolutionaries" (ibid., 23 January). In a pamphlet sent to the press in November, the Ricardo Franco Front disclosed that it had killed several FARC-UP militants for "selling out to the oligarchy" and warned that it would "continue taking actions against the bourgeoisie militants of the UP" (ibid., 11 November). At year's end, the Ricardo Franco Front announced that it was reorganizing its combat units and would continue the armed struggle in 1987 (ibid., 13 December).

**Domestic Attitudes and Activities.** The PCC recognizes the experience of the Communist Party of the Soviet Union (CPSU) as an ideological source, but it also takes "maximum account of the national characteristics and revolutionary and democratic traditions of the Colombian people." This has enabled the party to devise its own tactics, which combine diverse forms of struggle ranging from electoral campaigns to guerrilla warfare. The documents and declarations approved by the PCC's Fourteenth Congress indicate that the strategy and tactics of the PCC will continue to be a combination of all forms of struggle. However, party statements criticize "adventurist and terrorist practices," such as the M-19 seizure of the Palace of Justice in November 1985, that militate against the unity of the masses and "provide the military with the pretext to embark on a reign of terror" (*WMR*, July).

The PCC believes that the political crisis in Colombia is "permanent and general." It argues that the nation's development is being increasingly slowed down by "obsolete institutions, the absolutism of presidential power, and, chiefly, by the predominance of the traditional biparty system" (ibid., May).

The PCC held a plenary session in Bogotá on 10–11 January to consider the political situation in the country, the party's tasks in the March–May election campaigns, and internal party matters. Vieira emphasized that the party must intensify its propaganda effort and expose "reactionary plans" aimed at undermining the democratization process. He exhorted party members to "close their ranks" and to "work to win the confidence of the masses" (*Voz*, 16 January). The Central Committee's report called for the organization of "thousands" of committees in urban and rural areas to broaden the base of popular support for the UP. In offering the PCC's support for Pardo Leal's candidacy, Vieira stated that, "For we communists the UP is not the party of the FARC, but the beginning of a movement that will lead to the Broad Front needed to bring about the democratic changes that the people demand" (ibid., 6 February).

Following the March congressional elections, the PCC claimed electoral "victory" for the UP as the "new democratic option." Support for the UP was especially strong in Arauca, Meta, Antioquia, and Santander. Coalitions between the UP and sectors of the Liberal Party received strong support in Bolívar, Caquetá, Huila, Tolima, and El Valle, where UP candidates won two alternate positions in the Senate and four in the House. In his analysis of the March elections, Vieira stated the UP would continue its policy of alliances with Liberal sectors in developing its parliamentary strategy in the "extraparliamentary mass struggle" (ibid., 20 March). At a meeting with President Betancur, the UP's congressional delegation accused units of the armed forces and paramilitary groups of conducting "criminal actions" against the PCC, the UP, and the FARC. The delegation appealed to the president to lift the state of siege, dissolve paramilitary groups and death squads, and cease repressive actions against regions that gave electoral support to the UP (ibid., 15 May).

At the Central Committee's plenum on 6–8 June, Alvaro Vásquez reported that the UP's electoral results, while not spectacular compared with those of the traditional parties, represented "a significant advance by the left." He added that in the May presidential elections the left succeeded in "consolidating its positions, enhancing its influence among the masses and winning their active support" (*Voz*, 12 June). For the first time, PCC and UP candidates were permitted access to national television and radio networks. In the course of the campaign the party sought to broaden its social base by establishing local committees to serve as focal points for political work. According to Hernando Hurtado, the UP's electoral activity reached approximately 80 percent of Colombia's municipalities (ibid., 29 May). The party maintains that the election results do not reflect accurately the actual alignment of social and political forces in Colombia, arguing that "threats and intimidation" prevented half the electorate from voting. The PCC claims to have made considerable gains in rural areas, especially in the zones of guerrilla activity, and in the large cities, particularly Bogotá.

PCC leaders admit that the electoral campaign also exposed some of the party's weaknesses. A *Voz* editorial criticized the improvisational character of party propaganda and weaknesses in party organization. It cited continued evidence of sectarianism within party circles and a tendency to downplay the role of the PCC within the UP to the point of failing to represent adequately the communists' viewpoints (ibid., 19 June). In August the UP became the third Colombian political party acknowledged by the National Elections Council. Its legal status will allow the UP free access to state media for established political purposes.

Between the March elections and September, twenty UP elected officials were assassinated, including congressman Leonardo Posada, a member of the PCC's Central Committee. Party leaders blame paramilitary groups, while others believe that the crimes were committed by active members of guerrilla groups taking revenge on those who abandoned the guerrilla struggle. In September, UP leaders and the government agreed on the creation of a special panel of civilian judges to investigate the killing of UP and PCC party members. A government communiqué deplored the murders and reiterated the government's determination to "grant all possible guarantees to UP leaders and activists"

(*El Siglo*, 2 September). President Barco himself denounced the wave of political killings on 16 September, saying that they "demand the strictest and most efficient investigation" (ibid., 17 September). Attempts to intimidate UP members have been most frequent in the more remote departments of the country where the UP received its strongest support in the March elections. The PCC helped organize a march in Bogotá on 26 September to protest against the "slow pace of government reforms" and the administration's "failure to denounce killings by right-wing death squads" (*El Espectador*, 27 September). In mid-November, the UP's congressmen announced their withdrawal from Congress until personal guarantees for their safety could be provided.

On 15 December, Octavio Vargas, alternate member of the House and secretary of the PCC in Meta, was killed after attending a political meeting. In a press communiqué, the UP demanded that the government find an "efficient solution" to the killings and called for self-defense "to stop those who want to annihilate us politically and physically" (Reuter, 15 December; *FBIS*, 19 December). A UP delegation comprised mainly of PCC leaders met with President Barco on 19 December to express their concern that the assassination of Guillermo Cano, director of *El Espectador*, might become a pretext for the government "to intensify its repression against the progressive democratic forces of the left." They asked the president to appoint a Permanent Commission on Human Rights and said that "continued promises" of criminal investigations would no longer suffice (ibid., 21 December).

The PCC defines its political line and organizes its activity on the basis of work among the masses. An essential task of the party is to "accelerate the mass struggle, broaden the labor movement, and forge a realignment of all those who seek an effective, democratic solution to the national crisis" (*Voz*, 19 June). With regard to the trade union movement, the PCC's purpose is to ensure unity of action by the working class and "put an end to the fragmentation that is the principal weakness of the revolutionary process." The party admits that past circumstances compelled it to support the formation of an independent trade union association, the CSTC, which has become the principal base of the struggle for working-class unity (*WMR*, May).

According to Vásquez, an essential element in raising the people's consciousness is the struggle against militarism. This means the party's continued opposition to the state of siege, paramilitary actions, disappearance of popular leaders, persecution of the UP, discrimination against the labor movement, and militarization of the universities and popular barrios (*Voz*, 19 June). The PCC has repeatedly denounced the military's Condor Plan and charges that military intelligence carries out some of its actions under cover of the Ricardo Franco group, which it claims is acting in the name of the FARC. In its struggle against militarism, the PCC has also denounced the "criminal policy of repression" directed by the North American Military Mission. According to Vieira, militarism in Colombia is "above all at the service of North American imperialist interests." The only way to defeat it, in the party's view, is through the broadest patriotic coalition possible, and "that is what we [the PCC] are promoting in Colombia through the work of the UP" (ibid., 31 July).

**International Views and Positions.** The PCC faithfully follows the Soviet line in its international positions and insists that it is impossible to remain neutral in the "great international struggle" between socialism and capitalism. The party therefore "enthusiastically" supports the socialist countries and particularly the Soviet Union "because it defends genuine socialism, despite its imperfections" (*YICA*, 1986). At the same time, the party claims that it is not dependent on Moscow, Havana, or "any foreign place," nor does it serve as the agent for the international policy of any foreign country. The PCC wants a Colombian international policy that is "independent and autonomous." The PCC believes that its experience in employing all forms of popular action is proving useful in other Latin American countries.

At the Twenty-seventh Congress of the CPSU in March, Vieira reaffirmed the PCC's unwavering support for "the anti-imperialist struggle of the peoples for peace, democracy, social progress, and national independence, for nuclear disarmament, and for the establishment of normal relations among all countries" (*WMR*, May). He proclaimed Mikhail Gorbachev's political address "the most extraordinary political document of our time" (*Voz*, 6 March).

The PCC is consistently internationalist and invariably displays solidarity with the struggles of fraternal parties and peoples. The party proclaims its unconditional support for the Cuban revolution and solidarity with the Nicaraguan Sandinistas. At the Central Committee plenum on 6–8 June, the party adopted resolutions against "the bloody dictatorships" of El Salvador, Chile, and Paraguay, and against "the impositions" of the International Monetary Fund. It also passed resolutions in support of the World Labor Federation; the "continental struggle" against payment of foreign debt; the New International Economic Order; and Latin American integration (ibid., 12, 19 June). According to Vieira, the U.S. "industrial and military complex" gravely threatens world peace, while the world socialist system, headed by the Soviet Union, works to defend it (ibid., 31 July).

**The Maoists.** The PCC-ML is firmly pro-Chinese, although recently the party has looked more toward Albania for political guidance. Its current leadership hierarchy is not clearly known. The PCC-ML has an estimated membership of one thousand. Unlike the PCC, it has not attempted to obtain legal status, and its impact in terms of national life is insignificant. Its official news organ is *Revolución*. The Marxist-Leninist League of Colombia publishes the monthly *Nueva Democracia*. PCC-ML statements are sometimes found in Chinese publications and those of pro-Chinese parties in Europe and Latin America.

The PCC-ML's guerrilla arm, the EPL, was the first to attempt a "people's war" in Latin America. The EPL has conducted only limited operations since 1975, although according to Colombian intelligence it still has an estimated 350 guerrillas organized in four fronts. The EPL operates mainly in the departments of Antioquia, Córdoba, and Risaralda, with urban support networks in several of the country's larger cities.

The EPL was among the guerrilla movements to conclude a peace agreement with the government in August 1984. However, the murder of several prominent EPL leaders in late 1985 led the movement to disavow the truce. In February 1986, the EPL announced it would boycott the March elections in protest against the absence of guarantees. It also announced plans to create three new combat fronts in honor of its leaders killed in 1985 (*El Siglo*, 20 February). In May, the EPL claimed credit for killing a policeman in Bogotá as part of a campaign to sabotage the presidential elections (AFP, 8 May). At a press conference in Managua, Sonia Martínez, EPL leader, and Luís Gómez, PCC-ML Central Committee member, denounced the FARC for its "revisionist attitude" and "electoral ambitions." They also blamed the FARC for "promoting the demobilization of the Colombian guerrilla movement" (ACAN, 29 July). The EPL has denied any

responsibility for the murders of UP congressional leaders. In September, the army reported that seven EPL members were killed during a skirmish in Cacayunal, Antioquia (*El Siglo*, 6 September). The EPL claimed responsibility for guerrilla actions in Santa Ana, Risaralda, where one solider was killed and several wounded (*El Tiempo*, 22 September).

The Independent Revolutionary Workers' Movement (MOIR) has aspired since 1971 to become the first mass-based Maoist party in Latin America. Its leadership and organization are indpendent of those of the PCC-ML. The MOIR has no military branch and has been unable to strengthen its political position in recent years. The MOIR's general secretary is Francisco Mosquera. The MOIR's Central Executive Committee issued a communiqué in December accusing the FARC of murdering one of its leaders, Raúl Ramírez. It also stated that the MOIR's policy toward the Barco government would depend on whether or not the administration can "protect the country against the onslaught of Soviet-style imperialism, protect national production against abuses by lending agencies and foreign companies, and meet the just demands for a better life by the hard working masses" (ibid., 14 December).

**The M-19.** The M-19, which first appeared in January 1974 as the self-proclaimed armed branch of ANAPO, takes its name from the contested presidential election of 19 April 1970. Since 1976, the M-19 has been actively involved in Colombia's guerrilla movement, pursuing "a popular revolution of national liberation toward socialism." Estimates on the movement's size range from 1,500 to 8,000.

The M-19 held out for what it considered a "broader peace agreement" from that reached by the government with the FARC. For most M-19 leaders, the peace accord signed with the government on 24 August 1984 constituted an agreement to end hostilities in order to open the way to a "national dialogue." Unlike the FARC, the M-19 has lacked a consistent policy regarding the cease-fire, the national dialogue, or its political future. In addition, the movement's loss of leadership in recent years has created internal dissension. Since resuming guerrilla activities in June 1985, the M-19 has been engaged in continuous warfare with the armed forces. The M-19 supplies most of the manpower and leadership for the guerrilla columns operating through the self-styled CNG, including the America Battalion.

The M-19 concentrated most of its activity during the early part of the year in the southeastern departments of Cauca and Valle. Heavy fighting occurred near Popayán in January involving guerrilla columns estimated at more than 500 men (*El Espectador*, 25 January). Six days of fighting between the army and an estimated 300 guerrillas on the outskirts of Cali in mid-March left more than 30 guerrillas and eleven soldiers dead, according to the military (*Latin America Weekly Review*, 28 March). Official sources stated that some 245 people were killed during the first three months of the year, including 96 guerrillas, 79 policemen, and 39 army troops, with the most serious clashes taking place between regular troops and the America Battalion (AFP, 1 April).

Carlos Pizarro assumed command of the M-19 following the killing of its principal leader, Alvaro Fayad, in Bogotá on 13 March. In an official announcement, the M-19 admitted that Fayad's death was a major setback for the movement and that dissension had occurred over the succession of leadership. As head of the CNG and leader of its America Battalion, Pizarro is considered a military strategist, but lacks Fayad's political and ideological depth (*Latin America Weekly Review*, 28 March). In addition to Pizarro, the M-19 announced a new Central Command of Antonio Navarro and Gustavo Arias, and a High Command comprised of Germán Rojas Patiño, Marco Chalita, Vera Grave, Pedro Pacheco, Rosemberg Pabón, Israel Santamaría, and Libardo Parra (*El Siglo*, 19 March). In May, the army confirmed Santamaría's death during a clash in Antioquia.

The military carried out extensive counterinsurgency operations in May as part of a plan to cut off supply channels for M-19 columns fighting in Valle and Cauca. The commander of the army's 3d brigade said that military and police forces in the region were "determined to eliminate once and for all the guerrilla scourge" (*El Espectador*, 19 May). According to the rebel publication *Oiga Hermano*, Pizarro admitted that military forces had inflicted heavy casualties on the movement (*El Tiempo*, 24 May). Miliary officers in charge of the antiguerrilla struggle admit that the problem requires not only a military solution, but also "a political, economic, and social solution."

The M-19 claimed responsibility for the 17 June attack against government minister Jaime Castro, blaming him for the failure of the peace process and calling him one of the "visible heads of the official extermination policy" (*El Tiempo*, 2 July). Military sources reported in July that Arias, the M-19's second in command, was killed during an attack on a police station in Caldas (ibid., 25 July).

In August, President Barco rejected the possibility of holding talks with the M-19, although the new defense minister said that the armed forces would support any new negotiations with the guerrillas that the president might propose (*El Espectador*, 9 August). At a summit meeting in Añorí, leaders of the CNG proclaimed their opposition to the new administration and announced the formation of the Trilateral Guerrillas, an alliance of the ELN, the Free Fatherland, and the PRT (*El Tiempo*, 20 August). Military sources reported on 26 August that during the first three weeks of Barco's government, 49 soldiers and 74 guerrillas died in armed clashes. In response to the escalation of guerrilla activity, the army launched its most impressive military offensive in recent years, deploying a reported 10,000 troops, mainly in Cauca, Valle, and northern Santander (ibid., 27 August). In September, the M-19 announced that a new guerrilla group made up of amnestied people had been created to support the operations carried out by the America Battalion. The so-called Liberty Battalion will operate in the departments of Caquetá, Huila, and Cauca, and in part of the Putamayo region (ibid., 10 September).

An M-19 clandestine communiqué distributed to news media in Bogotá in October asserted that continued dissension among the movement's leaders had led to Pizarro's departure from the country. According to guerrilla member Hernán Jaramillo, Pizarro's arbitrary leadership has taken a heavy toll. Some 111 M-19 rebels have died during clashes with the army in southwestern Valle, where Pizarro has centered his operations with the America Battalion. An additional 148 guerrilla members have been arrested and are now in jail. The situation reportedly has reached the point where some M-19 units have now divided into small groups comprised of six or seven members. The M-19's crisis has caused what appears to be the disintegration of the CNG. In fact, some observers now believe that the ELN has assumed coordination of the CNG's activities, while the M-19 seeks to regroup (AFP, 16 October; *FBIS*, 22 October). Although it would be premature to predict the M-19's demise, by the end of the year the movement had clearly lost most of its political direction and whatever was left of its popular image.

**ELN.** The ELN was formed in Santander in 1964 under the inspiration of the Cuban revolution.

It undertook its first military action in January 1965. Once recognized as the largest and most militant of the guerrilla forces operating in Colombia, the ELN has never recovered from the toll exacted on its leadership and urban network by an army offensive in 1973. According to Colombian intelligence, the ELN has approximately 500 men. It operates in a vast region of northeastern Colombia, in North and South Santander, Bolívar, Cauca, and Antioquia, and in the intendance of Arauca. The ELN was the only major guerrilla movement that did not sign a cease-fire agreement with the government in 1984. The Simón Bolívar and Antonio Nariño fronts accepted a peace agreement with the National Peace Commission in December 1985. Members of the Gerardo Valencia Caño front, which operates in Cauca, Nariño, and a large sector of the Atlantic Coast, signed a similar agreement in April (*El Tiempo*, 23 April).

Most of the ELN's operations throughout the year were directed against foreign oil companies working in the eastern Llanos. ELN units carried out more than twenty attacks against the Caño Limón-Covenas oil pipeline, dynamiting pumping stations, destroying equipment, and kidnapping workers. In a communiqué sent to radio stations in Bucaramanga, the ELN said that attacks on oil installations were intended to "punish the one-sided contract to extract crude oil" between the state-owned Ecopetrol and Occidental Petroleum (EFE, 16 July; *FBIS*, 17 July). Following the destruction of a Chevron pumping station in September, the ELN announced that it would continue dynamiting the pumping stations of foreign companies as a sign of its opposition to oil exports. ELN guerrillas also attacked military and police installations on the border with Venezuela (*El Siglo*, 30 September). In December, Colombian armed forces and police units initiated air and land surveillance over 765 kilometers of the main oil pipeline in an effort to counteract ELN sabotage (ibid., 3 December).

In other actions, ELN columns attacked the towns of Santa Rosa, Bolívar department, and Simití, Antioquia, in May, killing six soldiers and wounding ten. In June, the ELN claimed credit for the attack on a Venezuelan National Guard post in the border state of Apure that left three soldiers dead. According to an ELN communiqué, the attack was to protest the delay in the signing of the Contadora agreement, the impasse in the bilateral discussions between Colombia and Venezuela, and the mistreatment of Colombians who cross the Venezuelan border (*El Espectador*, 8 June). The ELN also took credit for bombings in Pereira and Calarcá that caused property damage to military installations, police substations, and U.S. churches (*El Siglo*, 27 June). Seven soldiers were killed and two wounded by a dynamite explosion set by ELN guerrillas operating in Santander, according to military reports (ibid., 13 August). Army troops patrolling the Valle-Chocó border clashed with ELN guerrillas in September, killing ten (*El Tiempo*, 1 October). In November, army units fought with an ELN column that dynamited three electric pylons and caused a blackout in northern Santander (*FBIS*, 19 November). ELN guerrillas also occupied the town of Zaragoza in northern Antioquia, destroying a bridge linking Medellín with the Atlantic Coast. In pamphlets left at the scene, the ELN stated that it would continue similar attacks in "its name and that of the CNG" (*El Espectador*, 23 November).

**Peace Prospects.** It is clear that Colombia's political leaders are increasingly nervous about the escalation of guerrilla, military, and drug-related violence in 1986. The hope generated by former president Betancur's commitment to peace in 1982 has been replaced by apparent resignation to a period of intense conflict between the armed forces and insurgents. The Barco administration is less tolerant of cease-fire abuses than the previous government and inclined to coordinate its policy more closely with the military.

The threat to peace in Colombia has been exacerbated by the reappearance of right-wing death squads and paramilitary groups. The government vigorously rejected a report issued by Amnesty International in July, which said that members of the Colombian armed forces may be involved in paramilitary groups that are carrying out a "dirty war" of "kidnapping, torture, and political murder." Although military spokesmen have admitted the "possible existence" of such groups, they reject categorically any connection between them and the armed forces (*El Espectador*, 21 November).

While internal dissension and factionalism continue to disrupt the principal guerrilla movements in Colombia, smaller guerrilla groups are proliferating under the umbrella of a loosely coordinated guerrilla command. A major challenge to the government in 1987 will be to preserve its peace agreement with the FARC while conducting a vigorous counterinsurgency campaign against those guerrilla groups still actively seeking to overthrow it. Although President Barco appears committed to supporting the truce with the FARC, that agreement seems increasingly fragile, especially as the FARC-UP, the PCC, and other leftist movements become the targets for assassination, bombings, and harassment. While the FARC-UP still remains committed to the peace process, it will be reluctant to move toward the critical stage of disarmament so long as its partisans are threatened and the armed forces are kept on the offensive by the continued armed resistance of other guerrilla groups.

Daniel L. Premo
*Washington College*

# Costa Rica

**Population.** 2,714,000

**Party.** Popular Vanguard Party (Partido Vanguardia Popular; PVP). A splinter faction is the Costa Rican People's Party (Partido del Pueblo Costarricense; PPC), led by PVP founder and former general secretary Manuel Mora Valverde and his brother Eduardo. Other secondary leftist parties are the Movement of the New Republic (Movimiento de la Nueva República; MNR)—formerly the Revolutionary People's Movement (Movimiento del Pueblo; MRP)—led by Sergio Erick Ardon, and the Costa Rican Socialist Party (Partido Socialista Costarricense; PSC).

**Founded.** PVP: 1931; PPC: 1984; MNR: 1970 (as MRP); PSC, 1972

**Membership.** PVP: estimated at 3,500 to 10,000 prior to 1984 split of PPC. Other left parties have only minuscule memberships.

**General Secretary.** PVP: Humberto Vargas Carbonell; PPC: Manuel Mora Valverde

**General Undersecretary.** PVP: Oscar Madrigal; PPC: Eduardo Mora Valverde

**Central Committee.** PVP and PPC each have 35 members, 15 alternates

**Status.** Legal in all cases

**Last Congress.** PVP: Fifteenth, 15–16 September 1984, in San José; PPC: Fourteenth, 10–11 March 1984, in San José

**Last Election.** 1986: Popular Alliance (Alianza Popular; AP), less than 1 percent of the presidential vote, 1 legislator elected; United People (Pueblo Unido; PU), less than 1 percent of the presidential vote, 1 legislator elected

**Auxiliary Organizations.** Unitary Workers' Central (Central Unitaria de Trabajadores; CUT); General Workers' Confederation (Confederación General de Trabajadores; CGT); National Peasants' Federation (Federación Campesina Nacional; FCN); Costa Rican Peace and Solidarity Council (umbrella group of approximately 50 union and solidarity committees)

**Publications.** PVP: *Libertad Revolucionaria* (weekly), Francisco Gamboa Guzman, director; PPC: *Libertad* (weekly), Eduardo Mora Valverde, director

Political parties on the left in Costa Rica had contradictory experiences during the presidential election year of 1986. On the one hand, the political infighting among the groups that led to the formation of separate political coalitions meant that each presented a presidential candidate. The immediate effect of the split significantly diminished the representation of the left, with the subsequent election of only two deputies in the Legislative Assembly, whereas four deputies had been elected in 1982. On the other hand, the vote of the left was significant in determining which of the mainline party candidates would win. Thus, while the various parties of the left suffered dramatic electoral defeat, the impact of the left's political inclinations were clearly felt in their indirect support of Oscar Arias Sanchez, candidate of the National Liberation Party (Partido Nacional de Liberación; PLN), instead of Rafael Angel Calderón of the Social Christian Unity Party (Partido Unidad Social Cristiana; PUSC). As a result, the potential impact of the left in Costa Rica remains viable for the future.

**Domestic Activities.** A bitter dispute among principals of the PVP led to a division of the party in 1983 that established the basis for the representation of two leftist coalitions in the February 1986 election. The split had evolved when a group of party leaders, headed by Arnoldo Ferreto and Humberto Vargas, challenged the founder of the PVP, Manuel Mora Valverde, at the Third Extraordinary Congress in November 1983 (see *YICA*, 1985). The disagreement focused on whether or not the necessary conditions already existed in Central America and in Costa Rica for a communist takeover. Mora took the position that the struggle had to pass through several stages, while his challengers proposed that conditions already existed to initiate concrete actions to achieve their principal objective: "to take power" (San José, *Rumbo Centroamericano*, 7–13 February). Thus, the left was represented in the 1986 election by the AP, which included the Ferreto-Vargas faction, and the PU, which included the Mora faction.

The AP coalition included the Broad Democratic Front and the PVP (minus the Mora faction). It presented Dr. Rodrigo Alberto Gutiérrez Sáenz as its candidate for president, Luisa Gonzalez Gutiérrez for first vice president, and Rodrigo Urena Quirós for second vice president. Gutiérrez had also been the presidential candidate of the PU in 1982. In its platform the AP proposed drastic economic measures to confront Costa Rica's economic crisis, including: growth and modernization of the agricultural and agroindustrial sectors as a basis of economic development; nationalization of foreign investment; state control of imports, exports, wages, and prices; and no payment of foreign debt in excess of 10 percent of export income. The platform also proposed a wide range of social programs to improve the standard of living of the poor. (*Libertad Revolucionaria*, 10–16 January.)

The PU emerged in 1985 as an alignment of the PSC, the MNR, and the PPC led by Manuel Mora following the split in the PVP. On the 1986 electoral ballot, the PU was identified as a "coalition of Costa Rican socialist and workers' parties." Its slate of candidates included Alvaro Eduardo Montero Mejía for president, José Joaquín Gutiérrez Mangel for first vice president, and Sergio Erick Ardon Ramírez for second vice president. Alvaro Montero had been professor of economics at the University of Costa Rica and was elected to the Legislative Assembly in 1982 as a member of the PSC. Like the PVP, the PU's platform called for drastic economic measures to confront Costa Rica's economic crisis, including a moratorium on payment of the external debt and a minimum salary based on cost of living (*Libertad*, 11–17 December 1985, 10–16 January).

The formalization of two separate coalitions took its toll on the outcome of the vote for the left with the election of only one legislator from each: Humberto Vargas for the AP, and Javier Solís for the PU. Solís declared that his parliamentary tasks would be twofold: "First . . . to be the voice of the poor, the disinherited, the unemployed, and the oppressed—those who do not have a voice in the legislature; and second, to defend the institutional democracy of Costa Rica . . . against whatever foreign power" (*Libertad*, 7–13 February). The election of 29 legislators for the PLN, however, gave it a simple majority (of the 57 seats), which diminished the leverage that the left might have hoped to enjoy.

An analysis of the electoral returns demonstrates that a significant percentage of the left's presidential vote went to Oscar Arias of the PLN, rather than to the candidate of either the AP or PU. For example, in San José, the largest province, the AP received 12,728 votes for legislators and only 3,718 for presidential and vice presidential candidates. Similarly, the PU received 15,428 votes for legislators and 2,624 for president and vice president. Differences were even more exaggerated in the regional provinces. The total difference between the legislative and presidential votes of the two leftist coalitions was 41,639 votes, or 3.7 percent of the total vote. Arias won by 6.7 percent, and while it is impossible to attribute all of the irregular party vote of the leftist coalitions to the PLN, it is clear that a crossover vote from the left would have been more attracted to Arias. During the electoral campaign, Arias was perceived as being closer to the left on both domestic and international issues (*Rumbo Centroamericano*, 7–13 March).

The post-election analysis by the factions of the left in Costa Rica has forced a re-evaluation of the direction and alliances of the various parties (ibid., 7–13 February). Parties from the left must repay their campaign debts and plan for the next election.

Public financing of political campaigns is based on a percentage of performance in the prior campaign. Based on the 1982 campaign, funds were appropriated to all the parties. However, none of the parties of the left reached the required five percent minimum vote in 1986, and they were therefore required to pay back advances that had been given to them. In July, according to Deputy Minister of Finance Edgar Gutiérrez, three parties negotiated a repayment schedule to spread the amount owed over a 20–25 month period. The PVP owed 14 million colones, and the Workers' Party faction of the PU owed 4.7 million colones. The provincial party Alajuelan Democratic Action was also attempting to renegotiate a debt of 1.6 million colones. If the campaign debt is not repaid, these parties may be suspended from participating in the 1990 election by the Supreme Electoral Tribunal (San José, *Tico Times*, 18 July). It is likely that new coalitions will emerge on the left between 1986 and 1990. One party that has already begun a process of renewing its registration with the Supreme Electoral Tribunal is the Radical Democratic Party (PRD), which supported the PU coalition in 1986. A prime mover within that party is Juan José Echevarría Brealey, who was a controversial minister of public security during the Rodrigo Carazo administration at the time of the Sandinista revolution in Nicaragua. While Echevarría sees himself as a social democrat (*Rumbo Centroamericano*, 26 December–2 January 1987), his political and economic connections with Cuba and Nicaragua are extensive.

Following the elections, attention was also focused on the domestic economy. Labor unions pushed President Arias on his campaign promises of new housing, jobs, and redistribution of wealth. On 23 August, Arias and numerous cabinet ministers met with representatives from the confederations of the CUT, Costa Rican Workers, Workers' National, Democratic Costa Rican Workers, Authentic Democratic Workers, Teachers' Union, Federation of Limón Workers, and other independent unions. Together these unions formed the Permanent Workers' Council and have demanded higher wages to meet the cost of living. The government proposed goals of a five percent growth rate, domestic savings of 24 percent of production, and a 12–15 percent growth in exports annually, all of which are consistent with current International Monetary Fund demands. The council, however, categorically rejected the government's proposal. It demanded across-the-board salary increases, price freezes on basic products and a rollback of recent increases, prompt implementation of the housing project, respect for collective bargaining agreements in the public and private sector, and a total moratorium on the foreign debt and support for the New International Economic Order (*Central American Report* [CAR], 12 September).

Labor unrest was evident throughout September and October following the lack of agreement between the government and the unions. Strikes, slowdowns, and public demonstrations occurred across economic sectors and in numerous industries as well as public institutions, including the social security institute, the electric company, the port authority, and educational institutions (*CAR*, 31 October). Protests erupted into violence in mid-September, when nearly a thousand farmers demonstrated in downtown San José and were confronted by Civil Guardsmen with force (*Tico Times*, 19 September). By October, four of the seven principal unions had agreed to modest government increases in salary increases, but widespread labor discontent was still evident (*CAR*, 31 October).

**International Views and Positions.** A sharp distinction may be drawn between the parties of the left and the mainstream political parties of Costa Rica with respect to international views, principally: Costa Rica's relations with Nicaragua and the United States. Whereas Arias was viewed as less anti-Sandinista than his principal opponent, Rafael Calderón, both the AP and the PU were clearly pro-Sandinista and anti–U.S. interventionism in Costa Rica and in all of Central America.

Both coalitions repeatedly charged that the visits of U.S. warships, the presence of U.S. Army engineers involved in construction projects, and the Costa Rican government's tacit acceptance of the presence of Nicaraguan counterrevolutionaries (*contras*) undermined the government's declared neutrality and directly contradicted the tenets of the Costa Rican Constitution. *Libertad Revolucionaria* (21–27 February) included headlines such as "Military Engineers and Warships Threaten Our Peace," with photographs of the U.S. military, and "Normalized Relations with Nicaragua," with photographs of President Ortega. The newly elected Arias commented that, if he were President Reagan, he would sent $100 million in economic aid to Costa Rica, El Salvador, and Honduras instead of to the *contras*; this was met with enthusiastic support from the left (*Tico Times*, 21 February).

Another headline frequently noted in the party newspapers was "*Contras* Prepare Provocation to Disturb Normalization with Nicaragua" (*Libertad*, 28 February–7 March). Throughout 1986, leaders from all the parties on the left were concerned that U.S. involvement in Costa Rica was literally paving the way for an invasion of Nicaragua and was a clear violation of the Costa Rican government's declared neutrality (ibid., 14–20 March). In March, the U.S. Army Corps of Engineers sent 180 troops to build or repair five bridges in the western province of Puntarenas, despite protests from local engineers (*Tico Times*, 1986 Review). The revelation in September of a "secret airstrip" in Guanacaste that was allegedly used by the *contras* (*NYT*, 26, 29 September), the subsequent revelations of the U.S. scandal concerning the sale of arms to Iran, which may have involved a transfer of funds to the *contras*, and the sudden departure of U.S. ambassador Lewis Tambs, who was identified as being intimately involved with the *contra* supply network, all fueled allegations from the left that it was the United States that threatens Costa Rican peace, not the Sandinista government of Nicaragua (ibid., 26 December).

The existence of drug traffic through Costa Rica compounded that government's concern about armed clandestine groups operating in its national territory and expanded U.S. policy concerns in Costa Rica. In addition to armed Nicaraguan counterrevolutionary groups, Costa Ricans from both the right and the left organized private paramilitary forces. In April 1985, for example, a department of the Ministry of Public Security had alleged that the MNR was involved in a bank robbery of 5.5 million colones. Although the case was never proven, former minister of public security Benjamin Piza argued that the evidence to connect the group was clear; MNR leader Ardon, however, categorically denied such charges and alleged that the charges were political machinations of the right (*Rumbo Centroamericano*, 25 April–1 May). The Ministry

of Public Security also investigated the possibility that at least twenty Costa Ricans were training in Libya, a fact that came to light following the investigation of an attack on the U.S. Consulate in April (*FBiS*, 21 April).

The expansion of U.S. concerns about control over the flow of illegal drugs from South America to the United States drew attacks from the left in Costa Rica. Stemming drug traffic through Costa Rica was dramatically shown to be a high priority in 1985 with the arrest in Costa Rica of Mexican kingpin Rafael Caro Quintero, who was allegedly involved in the murder of a U.S. drug enforcement officer in Mexico. U.S. aid to Costa Rica for drug enforcement increased in 1986 with the donation of high-speed patrol boats, the training of eight captains at the U.S. Southern Command in Panama, and technical assistance to the Organization of Investigative Justice (OIJ). Public Security Minister Hernán Garrón confirmed that a small naval port in the west coast area of Puntarenas and another in Puerto Limón would be built to increase antidrug traffic vigilance (*CAR*, 8 August). In December, the PVP charged that the U.S. government had submitted a plan to the Costa Rican government to put the antidrug forces of the OIJ under direct control of the U.S. Drug Enforcement Agency (*Libertad*, 18 December). Although the technical assistance was met with enthusiasm from Costa Rican government officials (*CAR*, 16 January 1987), the extent of the cooperation was seen as a violation of Costa Rica's sovereignty by the PVP.

Overall in 1986, the political parties of the left suffered defeats politically and economically. The split in the PVP proved to be an electoral disaster. Nevertheless, the continuation of Nicaraguan *contra* activities, both military and political, as well as significant U.S. economic and military involvement in and around Costa Rica, will prompt continued opposition to the government by leftist groups. In addition, it is possible that these issues may prompt the various factions to set aside their differences and unite for a greater cause when the 1990 elections loom closer on the horizon.

Jennie K. Lincoln
*Mershon Center,*
*Ohio State University*

# Cuba

**Population.** 10,221,000
**Party.** Communist Party of Cuba (Partido Comunista de Cuba; PCC)
**Founded.** 1965
**Membership.** 450,000 (estimated); 523,639 including candidates (*Granma*, 10 February)
**First Secretary.** Fidel Castro Ruz
**Politburo.** 14 members: Fidel Castro Ruz, Raúl Castro Ruz (second secretary), Juan Almeida Bosque, Julio Camacho Aguilera, Osmany Cienfuegos Gorrián, Abelardo Colomé Ibarra, Vilma Espín Guillois, Armando Hart Dávalos, Esteban Lazo Hernández, José R. Machado Ventura, Pedro Miret Prieto, Jorge Risquet Valdés-Saldaña, Carlos Rafael Rodríguez, Roberto Veiga Menéndez; 10 alternate members.
**Secretariat.** 9 members: Fidel Castro Ruz, Raúl Castro Ruz, José R. Machado Ventura, Jorge Risquet Valdés-Saldaña, Julián Rizo Alvarez, José Ramón Balaguer Cabrera, Sixto Batista Santana, Jaime Crombet Hernández-Baquero, Lionel Soto Prieto
**Central Committee.** 146 members, 77 alternates (*Granma*, 10 February).
**Status.** Ruling party
**Last Congress.** Third, two sessions: 4–7 February, 30 November–2 December
**Last Election.** 1986, all 499 members of the National Assembly of People's Power PCC approved.
**Auxiliary Organizations.** Union of Young Communists (Unión de Jovenes Comunistas; UJC), Union of Cuban Pioneers (Unión de Pioneros de Cuba; UPC), Federation of Cuban Women (Federación de Mujeres Cubanas; FMC), Committees for the Defense of the Revolution (Comités de Defensa de la Revolución; CDR), Confederation of Cuban Workers (Confederación de Trabajadores de Cuba; CTC), National Association of Small Farmers (Asociación Nacional de Agricultores Pequeños; ANAP)
**Publications.** *Granma* (six days a week), official organ of the Central Committee; *Juventud Rebelde* (daily), organ of the UJC.

The Cuban Revolution in 1986 was in the midst of the most serious economic, institutional, and moral crisis of its existence. The Castro regime, which took power on 1 January 1959, was, by its own admission, bankrupt and rotten to the core. It also conceded, more clearly than before, that Marxist Cuba could not function at all, even at its current mediocre economic level, except for a large (albeit somewhat diminishing) Soviet dole. That assistance—estimated at more than $4 billion in 1986—appeared to be an open-ended gift from Moscow, which could never hope to recuperate its Cuban investment; by the end of 1986 that total investment was believed to be over $30 billion. Moreover, the situation will be even worse in 1987 and at least for the rest of this decade, according to President Fidel Castro. But even though Castro repeatedly admitted deep, intractable problems in every sector of the country's society, including the PCC, the government, and the much-touted "socialist youth," he did not fault the Marxist system he had imposed on Cuba.

As a result of mounting internal woes, Cuba's external position deteriorated in 1986. For many in Latin America, even for Castro's ideological followers and friends, the Cuban dictator became a relic and, despite the fact that his regime continued to be strongly entrenched, an irrelevent caudillo. Castro celebrated his 60th birthday in August, and there were no indications that his grip on power was any weaker than before. On the contrary, he continued to set the agenda for his regime and the PCC. His speeches provided guidelines for the country on every conceivable subject: for example, the economy, politics, medicine, agriculture, foreign trade, and journalism. He repeatedly conceded that the very fabric of the country's structure was being corroded by "social vices," including crime, corruption, enrichment of officials, and juvenile delinquency, all of which he had declared eradicated only a few years earlier. Thus, throughout the Western Hemisphere and in Western Europe the Cuban Revolution was becoming stigmatized as an economic and social failure. Proofs of continued violations of human rights by the Castro government added to that negative image.

**Leadership and Party Organization.** Even before the opening of the Third Party Congress—which consisted of two sessions, 4–7 February and 30 November–2 December—changes in the government announced late in 1985 indicated that an unprecedented shake-up of the Cuban leadership was being planned. Replaced in December as minister of interior was Ramiro Valdés Menéndez, one of the closest associates of Castro and member of the Politburo. Two other Politburo members and veteran commanders of the Castro guerrilla force—Sergio del Valle, health minister, and Guillermo García, transportation minister—also lost their jobs. In Castro's closing remarks at the regular session of the National Assembly of People's Power on 28 December 1985, he repeatedly spoke about labor discipline problems in the country. Closing the first part of the Third Congress on 7 February, Castro was blunt: "We know the party has problems," he told 1,790 delegates to the gathering.

The composition of the new Politburo and the Central Committee indicated more than interparty troubles. The reorganization of the party leadership that took place was the most comprehensive since the PCC was founded in 1965. Four senior members of the Politburo—Valdés, García, del Valle, and Blas Roca—were removed. Six of the nine alternate members were also replaced, among them Armando Acosta Cordero, chief of the PCC's mass organizations department, and Jesús Montené Oropesa, head of the PCC's foreign relations department; Montené was also dropped from the party Secretariat. A third of the 146-member Central Committee and of its 79 alternate members were also replaced. Vilma Espín, wife of Fidel Castro's younger brother and officially designated

successor, the 54-year-old Raúl Castro, became a full Politburo member. So did trade-union leader Roberto Veiga and black PCC leader of the Santiago de Cuba province Esteban Lazo. General Abelardo Colomé, who has been Raúl Castro's right-hand man as first deputy defense minister, was also made full Politburo member.

All in all, the changes strengthened the position of Raúl Castro by eliminating a number of veteran Fidelistas from the top party leadership and by situating there, in addition to his wife, several key supporters and subordinates. "The changes in party leadership often used to be merely symbolic, but this time it was necessary to renovate," Fidel Castro told the congress. He explained that "the important concept of broad renovation of party leadership bodies was based on a strong injection of women, blacks and mulattoes, and youth." Recognizing that, in the past, the Cuban party leadership has not been a paragon of equal ethnic opportunity, Castro said that the PCC "must include those compatriots of proven revolutionary merit and talents who in the past had been discriminated against because of their skin color." (*Granma*, 7 February.)

The Cuban leader placed the membership of the PCC at 523,639, including candidate members. There were 38,168 grass-root party organizations. During the last five years, PCC ranks increased by 92,779, he said. Sixty percent of members were engaged in production and services. Defining the present role of the party in Cuba, Castro said: "During this [five-year] period we have tried to relieve the party of everything that implies the duplication or overlapping of functions that correspond to other institutions. The party will thus be better able to play its role in Cuban society as the genuine educator, organizer, and guide of the masses, and to demand that each institution do its job. We have struggled, with encouraging results, against all manner of bureaucracy, superficiality, formalism, routine, and other trends that are incompatible with the life and the work of the party." (ibid.).

Castro stressed the party role in ideological work, which he described as efforts "to instill in our people a political awareness characterized, above all, by unflinching loyalty to the principle of socialism and unwavering moral integrity." Since the educational levels of party members, albeit improved, continued to be relatively low (only 72.4 percent passed the ninth or a higher grade), Castro emphasized the propaganda aspect of the party's ideological work. Newspaper printing was being modernized (with the cooperation of the Soviet Union) and *Granma* was being printed simultaneously in various provinces rather than its copies being transported from Havana. Editora Politica, the PPC's editorial house, had published 746 titles, with over 60 million copies, among them fifteen speeches and interviews by Castro. Cuba, according to Castro, had one of the highest ratios of newspapers per readers among Third World countries: about 400 million copies of national newspapers and 90 million of provincial ones; 62 million copies of magazines; and 13 million copies of foreign publications were distributed in the country annually. At the same time, he said, electronic media coverage was increased. Cuba now had five national, seventeen provincial, and thirty local radio stations. Two television channels were broadcasting, and a third, cultural program was planned for Havana. In the near future, Castro said, Cuba will be broadcasting Cuban television programs via satellite so that they may be picked up, free of charge, in Latin America and in most of the African countries.

Speaking of media coverage, Castro indicated that criticism of some aspects of Cuban life would be allowed, although only up to a point. "In a worker's state like ours, criticism of the deficiencies or mistakes in economic and administrative activities is not made to destroy anybody or damage the people's trust in the revolution, but rather to . . . point the way to corrective action. The party's capacity and authority to wage the struggle against ideological inconsistencies within our society depend on the prevalence of timely and fraternal criticism and self-criticism within the party. We will, of course, continue to wage an unyielding struggle against any enemy attempt to weaken the people's fighting morale and patriotic spirit or diminish their confidence in the revolution" (ibid.).

**Auxiliary Organizations.** At the Third Congress, Castro reviewed the state of auxiliary "mass" organizations existing in Cuba under the control of the PCC. Nearly three million Cubans, representing 99.5 percent of all workers, were members of various unions composing the CTC, he said. The FMC had 3,100,000 members, but the problem of women's equality was far from being solved, Castro reported. Women represented 13.8 percent of PCC membership and the figure was lower at the executive level of the party and the government. The CDR was the largest mass organization in Cuba, according to Castro, with 6,537,000 members. The

Federation of University Students (FEU) and the Federation of Senior High School Students (FEEM) had a combined membership of 459,000. The José Martí Pioneers' Organization had 1,722,306 members, or 99.5 percent of total elementary and secondary school enrollment. The UJC increased its membership in five years by 175,000 for a total of 597,853 members and candidates, Castro told the congress. (Ibid., 10 February.)

**Economic and Social Problems.** The major emphasis of Castro's February address to the Third Congress, as well as his other speeches during the rest of the year, was on the economic and social problems facing Cuba. The litany was seemingly endless: Cuba's growth during 1981–1986 was "sluggish where most needed: exports of goods and services and import substitution." Some delivery commitments to Soviet bloc countries "were not met." Cuban merchant fleet was both "inadequate" and underutilized, and the port, shipyard, and air-terminal operations were "inefficient." The targets of sugar production—the mainstay of the Cuban economy—"were not met because of insufficient planting and unsatisfactory agricultural yields; inadequate soil preparation and short supply of machinery." Cattle raising "has been affected by inadequate land management." During the greater part of the five-year period, the budget "continued to be ineffective." Prices in maintenance, construction, and transportation sectors "are scandalously high, covering up for inefficiency, over-staffing, and over-spending." (Ibid.)

Castro's revelations of these problems at the Third Congress were only the beginning of other similar statements uttered by him during the rest of 1986 that indicated the gravity of the situation. In April, Castro revealed that as a result of the decline in the price of oil, Cuba, which has been re-exporting part of the Soviet annual petroleum allotment, recently lost hundreds of millions of dollars in hard currency. In 1985, re-exports of Soviet oil, averaging some 40,000 barrels per day, earned Cuba about $470 million, or 42 percent of its export revenue. In 1986, the value of re-exports—which were expected to be smaller in volume in view of reduced Soviet supplies—was estimated to be about $200 million. Re-exports of crude oil have been directed to Spain, Belgium, and Italy. Petroleum products refined in Cuba have also been sold to West European countries to cover Cuban purchases there.

The population needs to make "greater sacrifices," Castro continued; "We have people who seek privileges, who seek easy money, not from work but from shady deals, speculation, and illicit trade. I don't want to mention many, but there are those who put us to shame, who have earned 100,000 pesos a year [about $120,000 according to the official rate of exchange] and more through apparently legitimate means—come now, in a socialist society—because I know that there are those who paint and sell paintings or do decorating work, mostly for state agencies, who have even earned over 200,000 pesos a year. I don't think it is a fruit of labor because, let's face it, the paintings are not by Picasso or Michelangelo" (*Granma*, 27 April).

On a larger economic scale, Castro complained that some directors of state enterprises had become "capitalist-like entrepreneurs," who charged exorbitant prices for doing service jobs for other state agencies, and who even for a fee lent much-needed state equipment for repairs or building of private houses. In many factories, he complained, "inefficiency and disorganization" is "concealed" by employing unnecessary persons. (Ibid.)

Also in April, Cuba notified its foreign creditors of the cancellations of payments due in May. Havana explained that the move was due to a "big drop" in its export earnings and the destruction in agriculture caused by the November 1985 Hurricane Kate, which totaled one billion pesos in damages. The announcement said that Cuba wanted a twelve-year payment period, including a six-year grace period. Cuba's overall debt to Western banks was estimated between $2.8 and $3.5 billion. The bulk of the debt was held by French, Canadian, Spanish, and Japanese banks. Cuba was seeking an additional $500 million loan to cover its shortfall in short-term hard currency payments. (*NYT*, 11 July.) At the year's end, negotiations were continuing between Cuba and the so-called Paris Club, an informal group of Western creditor governments.

The Castro government was also confronted with a serious social problem at home. At a 22 May meeting, the Politburo "analyzed the problem of crime and anti-social behavior, in particular in the city of Havana and Havana province," an official announcement said. "Measures were also approved to immediately strengthen and gradually improve the effectiveness of the battle against various types of crime affecting social and personal property, citizens' rights and personal safety, measures to neutralize and strongly punish the aggressive behavior, violence against persons, and gangster-like conduct occurring in the capital" (*Granma*, 1 June).

The measures, which became known as Castro's "program to sanitize the capital," included mobilization of hundreds of police recruits to patrol Havana streets and try to put down a wave of burglaries in private homes, including residences of foreign diplomats. Most of the "delinquents, hoodlums, and bullies," as Havana called them, were young Cubans brought up under the rule of Castro. According to press reports from Havana, there were thousands of youths in the capital who neither worked nor studied, but just hung around on many street corners during the day, planning to steal anything sellable on the black market at night.

Speaking in the capital on 6 June, Castro indicated the problem would not be solved by sweeps of Havana streets. "The struggle against common crime is much more complex, difficult, and protracted" than originally thought, and "it would be illusory to believe that crime would disappear in the course of the transition from capitalism to socialism and from socialism to communism." He also referred to "tough guys" who "have surfaced under socialism although this is a capitalist phenomenon, [and] who gather around outdoor beer stands." (During the summer, sale of beer was banned on the beaches in Cuba.) (Ibid., 15 June.)

In his criticism of various segments of Cuban socialist society, Castro also singled out the working class. Many workers, he said, adopt an "individualist position resorting to various tricks to obtain privileges and get rich" at the cost of others. Signaling a major policy shift, he said that "it would be a mistake to think material incentives are the only way to get people to do things . . . Socialism must be built with awareness and with moral incentives; it must be built with a lot of awareness. And I say this because everything I know about the revolution shows that the best things done by the revolution have been based on moral factors." (Ibid.)

In another speech, Castro said that the Cuban Revolution had "created a class of newly rich who are doing as they please everywhere." Among these he mentioned some physicians who were selling medical certificates enabling people to obtain early medical retirement, giving them "freedom to make a lot of money." And money, he said, was "the center of activity of many people," including those who "have become rich in the free peasant market." (Ibid., 13 July.)

Late in June the Politburo announced a series of measures that in effect ended a two-year-old liberalization trend in the Cuban economy and marked the return to orthodox economic policies, which have been rejected today by most countries in the

Soviet bloc. Free peasant markets were summarily closed, and there was a clampdown on the activities of artists, craftsmen, tradesmen, and street vendors, as well as on owners of trucks who worked independently and on small private restaurants. Private sales of houses became illegal and building of private homes was curtailed. State control over the economy, somewhat relaxed since 1980, was tightened anew. A new policy was initiated to reduce salaries by cutting awards of bonuses for good production results. Explaining the measures at the 25–26 June meeting in Havana of the managers of state enterprises, Castro said that the free peasant markets gave birth to many small private industries in which people using stolen raw materials were manufacturing items that were scarce in official shops; the items were to be sold at the free markets at high prices. A number of state enterprises, he said, became involved in these activities and a "free-trade mentality has sprung up . . . A new sector of industrialists and peasants sprouted all over the place." He added that after closing the free peasant market and eliminating street vendors, it was also decided to revitalize the house construction "mini-brigades" to solve the "serious housing problem." (Ibid., 6 July.)

A plenary meeting of the PCC Central Committee on 17–19 July found that the economic situation had deteriorated during the first six months of 1986. Work productivity had lowered by 1 percent while wages went up by 3 percent. Oil consumption had increased by 4.4 percent, and there was a "considerable shortfall" in the production of export goods. There was "indolence and complacency in the trade union structure," the committee found, saying that the solution to most problems could be summed up with one word: work. Castro, who addressed the meeting, also criticized the country's media. He called on the press to "abandon hackneyed stereotypes and empty boasting." (Ibid., 3 August.) Castro also told the committee that he had compiled a book of "economic irregularities" where "every paragraph is a calamity." He found that at a textile factory in Santiago 1,500 workers out of 6,000 employed there were absent daily. He said that the country invested hundreds of millions of dollars in the Moa nickel plant, which employed 13,000 people and which had yet to produce the first kilo of nickel.

Although Castro extolled the year-long sessions of criticism and self-criticism as a sign of his regime's strength, and although there were some changes in the PCC and government personnel, in reality, by the year's end, nothing really changed. In the 1970s, after the failed effort to produce ten million tons of sugar in 1970, similar chestbeating took place in Cuba. Then, as in 1986, Castro, his brother Raúl, and the communist system introduced by them in Cuba, were untouchable. It was as though limited, public admissions of failings were made by Castro to pay lip service to the reported admonishments by Moscow, which pays most of the bills for the repeated failures of the Cuban leader and his men.

At the concluding session of the Third Congress, delegates approved the so-called party program, which outlined basically political and economic goals for the 1986–1990 period. The party was told to step up monitoring of the country's economic activity. The country was to emphasize the maximum production of goods for export, reduce imports from Western countries, and further integrate its economy with those of the Soviet bloc countries. The 1986 sugar production was estimated at 6.75 million tons, about one million tons less than in 1985. The outlook for 1987 did not appear very promising, according to Castro and other Cuban leaders who refrained from monitoring production goals.

A proof of further belt-tightening in Cuba came at the end of 1986. Addressing the National Assembly in Havana, Castro announced a series of austerity measures to be put into effect in 1987, some on 1 January, others, on 1 March. The prices of city bus rides went up from five to ten cents, and the cost of electric power was increased by 40 percent. The price of rice, meat, black beans, and vegetables—all of which have been rationed for years—was also raised 40 percent. The sick saw their milk and beef rations cut by one-third; snacks were substituted for free meals at schools, and for many government employees free lunches were ended; the gasoline allocated for national consumption was cut by 20 percent; television programming was limited to five hours daily to conserve petroleum; evening sports were rescheduled to daylight hours; office workers saw their on-the-job coffee breaks eliminated. The stated economic reasons for these and other planned measures were to reduce imports from Western countries by 50 percent.

**Foreign Relations.** The Third Congress defined Cuban foreign policy as being guided first by "indestructible ties of friendship with the Soviet Union" and second, in politico-economic terms, by aiming at a "speed-up of the process of Cuba's economic integration with the Council for Mutual Assistance." The PCC platform also expressed "admiration" for Nicaragua, which it said "is fighting an aggression" from the U.S.-backed contras. Cuba offered "resolute backing" to Nicaragua in its fight, "solidarity" to the Salvadoran guerrillas and the "Chilean patriots," "unshakable support" for the Puerto Rican people's struggle for independence, and "solidarity" to Argentina in its demand for sovereignty over the Falkland Islands. The PCC congress expressed its full agreement with "positive policy steps of the People's Republic of China" and noted that "hostility and acts of force by that country against Vietnam are an obstacle to a sincere improvement of relations between Cuba and China." (Ibid., 10 February.)

Cuba-U.S. relations, 25 years after the Bay of Pigs invasion, were as tense as ever. In July the two sides met in Mexico City to try to reactivate the December 1984 bilateral immigration agreement, under which Cuba was to accept 2,700 of the "Mariel criminals," Cubans who are being held in U.S. prisons, and the United States was to admit annually 20,000 Cubans eligible for emigration as close relatives of Cuban-born U.S. citizens or permanent residents. Castro ended the agreement in May 1985 to protest the starting of Radio Martí, a Voice of America program aimed at Cuba. With the exception of a few long-term political prisoners, the Reagan administration has refused to process Cubans in Havana.

The Mexico City talks broke down over the request by Cuba for a clear AM radio frequency to broadcast its programs to the United States and thus compensate for the Radio Martí broadcasts. A month later, on 22 August, President Reagan cut off virtually all Cuban emigration to the United States by prohibiting the processing of visa applications even to those Cubans entitled to visa quotas in third countries, such as Mexico, Panama, and Spain. Later in the year, the order was eased slightly, but at the same time Washington imposed additional controls on U.S. trade with Cuba in an effort to seal tightly the economic blockade established a quarter of a century earlier.

The stringent immigration measures by the administration prevented about 1,000 Cuban political prisoners and their families from coming to the United States despite indications that Havana was willing to let them leave. In August, after strong pressure brought to bear by the American Catholic Conference of Bishops and Cuban exile groups, 69 former prisoners were flown from Havana to Miami. In October, the last imprisoned member of the Bay of Pigs invasion force was released and returned to Miami, and in December, following the November visit to Havana of Felipe González, president of the Council of Ministers of Spain, Castro released Eloy Gutiérrez Menoyo. The Spanish-born Gutiérrez Menoyo, leader of a guerrilla force that overthrew the Batista regime in 1958, was initially an ally of Castro. But he broke with Castro over the growing influence of the PCC—which at the time Castro denied—and left for the United States. In 1965 Gutiérrez Menoyo landed in Cuba as the head a small guerrilla group, wanting to overthrow the Castro regime. He was captured a month later and spent 21 years in jail until his December release.

A proof of Castro's duplicity—his public statement in 1959–1960 professing allegiance to democratic principles and denying communist influence in the government while he was actually conspiring with the communists against democracy—is contained in a book by Tad Szulc, *Fidel: A Critical Portrait*, published in October. Szulc discloses that in 1959 Castro began talking with an emissary of the Soviet government in Havana. At the same time, with seventeen other close associates and a number of Cuban communist leaders, Castro set up a secret "parallel" shadow government to draft Marxist measures and sweeping anti-democratic reform, bypassing the official Cabinet of Ministers made up of center-left politicians. "Publicly, Fidel Castro was rejecting accusations at home and abroad that 'Communism' was creeping into his 'humanist' Revolution," Szluc writes.

In July, Cuba re-established diplomatic relations with Brazil, two months after it was accepted as observer at the Latin American Integration Association, a grouping of South American countries hoping to form a common market. Cuba now has embassies in ten Latin American countries: Argentina, Brazil, Ecuador, Guyana, Mexico, Nicaragua, Panama, Peru, Uruguay, and Venezuela. The country has gone a long way in breaking its diplomatic isolation in Latin America, which began in 1964 when its membership was suspended in the Organization of American States. In October, Cuban and Colombian foreign ministers met at the U.N. headquarters in New York to consider resuming diplomatic relations.

**Foreign Contacts.** Fidel Castro traveled to Moscow late in February to attend the Twenty-seventh Congress of the Communist Party of the

Soviet Union. He met with Mikhail Gorbachev and participated in talks about Soviet-Cuban cooperation through the year 2000. Castro also visited North Korea before returning home by the middle of March. In August, when Castro became 60 years old, he received multiple decorations from socialist countries, including his third Order of Lenin. In September, Castro traveled to Harare, Zimbabwe, to attend the eighth summit of the conference of Non-Aligned Nations. From there, he flew to Angola on a two-day visit, disclosing that Cuba had 30,000 troops there, 10,000 more than recently estimated.

In October, Soviet foreign minister Eduard Shevardnadze visited Cuba, and later that month Argentine president Raúl Alfonsín paid a twenty-hour visit to Havana. President González of Spain was in Havana in November, the month during which Castro made his second trip to Moscow in 1986.

George Volsky
*University of Miami*

# Dominican Republic

**Population.** 6,785,000
**Party.** Dominican Communist Party (Partido Comunista Dominicano; PCD)
**Founded.** 1944
**Membership.** 500–1,000
**General Secretary.** Narciso Isa Conde
**Central Committee.** 27 members
**Status.** Legal
**Last Congress.** Third, 15–17 March 1984
**Last Election.** 1986, 0.23 percent, no representation
**Auxiliary Organizations.** No data
**Publications.** *Hablan los Comunistas* (weekly)

In 1986 the PCD suffered one of the most embarrassing setbacks since it was founded 42 years earlier. In the 16 May presidential election, in which PCD general secretary Narciso Isa Conde was a candidate, the party obtained only 0.23 percent, or about 5,000 votes of over 2 million cast. In 1982, when the PCD with other Marxist parties supported a leftist (though non-Marxist) candidate, they had polled 7.1 percent of the vote.

Isa Conde attributed his electoral fiasco principally to what he called the divisionary tactics of Juan Bosch, who was at one time the left's favored son. Bosch, who is 80 years old, was also the factor in giving the victory—and for the fifth time the presidency—to Joaquín Balaguer, who obtained about 40 percent of the vote. The third major candidate, Jacobo Majluta, obtained 33 percent of the vote. Thus, Majluta's party (the left-of-center Dominican Revolutionary Party [PRD]) and that of Bosch (the Dominican Liberation Party [PLD], also considered of the non-Marxist left) polled almost 52 percent of the presidential vote. Isa Conde accused Bosch of selling out to Balaguer and of dividing the leftist opposition. At the same time, the communist leader was trying to maintain a posture of loyal and legal opposition to the Balaguer government. In a newspaper interview, he praised the "pragmatism" of the president and indicated that he would not be adverse to serving in a national unity government should the deteriorating economic situation force Balaguer to name one. (*Hablan los Comunistas*, 5–12 June.)

The communists were not the only ones who took a beating in the election. Balaguer leads the Social Christian Reformist Party (PRSC), which may disappear when he does from the political scene. At 79, Balaguer is functionally blind. He was elected because many Dominicans remembered the "good old days" of his second presidency twenty years earlier, which were the times of prosperity for the Caribbean republic. But economic problems of the 1980s have been more intractable than those of the 1960s, when Dominican sugar was sold for more than ten cents a pound and a barrel of oil— which the country must import—cost $2.50. In 1986, inflation was more than 35 percent: purchasing power of the Dominicans had declined 5 percent in the previous two years. Unemployment was about 20 percent in the cities, close to 60 percent in the countryside. There was no easy solution to those problems, and Balaguer, having been elected by only 40 percent of the Dominicans, could be the object of their wrath should he not produce one soon.

Fortunately for the president, his opposition was more divided than ever. The PRD was split into two, maybe three factions, and Bosch's PLD may also disintegrate with the demise of its octogenarian leader.

Some observers saw a possibility—given the volatility of Dominican political life—of a leftist coalition in which elements from the PRD, PLD, and Marxist parties would join forces under a new, younger leader. Meanwhile, Balaguer has governed with an energy that surprised even his critics. Two months after his August inauguration, he "retired" 23 generals from active service in what was called the beginning of the farthest-reaching anticorruption drive in the history of the republic.

Although Dominican Marxists have tried to capitalize on the country's perennial socio-economic difficulties, they have not been able to gain strength. This has been principally due to the fact that their rhetoric is by and large negative. They have attacked the government and the nonleftist opposition—and often other extreme left groups—but have not presented a coherent plan for solving the country's ills. In a country where parties proliferate like mushrooms after rain (in the 1986 presidential elections there were sixteen parties on the ballot), the Marxist groups, operating legally, have become part of the chaotic national political scene. In 1986, there were said to be more than 25 extreme-left organizations in the Dominican Republic with a total of over 2,500 members. They were largely quarrelsome minigroups, sometimes with two dozen members each. There have been a few attempts over the last several years to unite all Marxist factions, but nothing tangible has come of them, as the PCD fiasco at the polls in 1986 clearly showed.

George Volsky
*University of Miami*

# Ecuador

**Population.** 9,647,000

**Party.** Communist Party of Ecuador (Partido Comunista Ecuatoriano; PCE), pro-Moscow, participates in elections as part of the Frente Amplio de Izquierda coalition (FADI); Marxist-Leninist Communist Party of Ecuador (PCE-ML), participates in elections as the Movimiento Popular Democrático (MPD); Socialist Party (Partido Socialista Ecuatoriano; PSE)

**Founded.** PCE: 1928; PCE-ML: 1972; PSE: 1926
**Membership.** PCE: 500; PCE-ML: 100 (both estimated)
**General Secretary.** PCE: René Mauge Mosquera; MPD: Jaime Hurtado (National Director)
**Central Committee:** PCE: Milton Jijón Saavedra, José Solís Castro, Efraín Alvarez Fiallo, Bolívar Bolanos Sánchez, Ghandi Burbano Burbano, Xavier Garaycoa Ortíz, Alfredo Castillo, Freddy Almeidau (*YICA*, 1985)
**Status.** Legal
**Last Congress.** PCE: Tenth, 27–29 November 1981, in Guayaquil; FADI: Second, December 1985, in Guayaquil
**Last Election.** 1 June 1986 (for provincial deputies to Congress); FADI: 2 of 59 seats; MPD: 3 of 59 seats; PSE: 6 of 59 seats. Total representation in Congress: FADI: 3 of 71 seats; MPD: 4 of 71 seats; PSE: 6 of 71 seats.
**Auxiliary Organizations.** PCE: Ecuadorean Workers' Confederation (Confederación de Trabajadores del Ecuador; CTE), comprises about 20 percent of organized workers; Ecuadorean University Students' Federation (Federación de Estudiantes Universitarios del Ecuador; FEUE); Ecuadorean Indian Federation (Federación Ecuatoriana de Indios; FEI)
**Publications.** PCE: *El Pueblo*; MPD: *Patria Nueva*

The deepening economic crisis, an aborted military uprising, and the outcome of elections seriously undermined the rightist government of President León Febres-Cordero in 1986 and strengthened the hand of center-left and leftist parties in the opposition. Notwithstanding this change in the balance of political forces, the country wrestled with many of the same problems that have wracked it since the inauguration of Febres-Cordero in 1984. Serious conflicts between executive and legislative branches, chronic tensions over the interpretation of the Constitution, and the continuing presence of a guerrilla movement contributed to the highly charged atmosphere of Ecuadorean politics. The armed forces re-emerged as a central political actor, making public pronouncements during clashes between the Congress and the president and taking center stage with the unsuccessful antigovernment revolt of General Frank Vargas Pazos in March. Adding to the political tumult of 1986 was the economic downturn caused by plummeting prices for oil, Ecuador's primary export, on the international market. In response to the deteriorating economic situation, the government stepped up its liberalization of the economy. The austerity and liberalization measures were vigorously opposed by the center-left majority in Congress and triggered yet another fierce legal battle between the government and the opposition.

**Domestic Affairs.** In the face of widespread opposition to his attempt to postpone the midterm elections for provincial deputies, Febres-Cordero reversed himself and scheduled the congressional elections for 1 June. To divert attention from the elections and to promote his plan of amendments to the constitution, he included a plebiscite issue on the ballot, despite legal challenges from the opposition parties that questioned his authority to do so without prior congressional approval. The question posed in the referendum asked voters to decide whether independent candidates should be allowed to stand for elective office. Under the prevailing law governing political parties, only candidates officially affiliated with a legally recognized party were permitted to participate in elections. A number of factors motivated the administration's decision to pursue the plebiscite; the government saw the referendum as a means to revitalize flagging popular support, capture the loyalties of "independents" in the electorate, and strike a personal blow to ex-president Osvaldo Hurtado, an outspoken leader of the opposition and one of the original authors of the political parties law in 1978.

Public attention was quickly diverted away from the electoral process in March, however, by a series of dramatic events that exposed deep divisions within the armed forces and troubled relations between that institution and the Febres-Cordero administration. After General Vargas's dismissal as head of the armed forces, he took over the coastal air force base at Manta on 7 March. Vargas charged the administration with corruption and named Defense Minister General Luis Piñeiros and Army Chief General Manuel Albuja in the misappropriation of funds involving the purchase of a Fokker airplane from a Dutch firm. About two hundred officers and soldiers joined Vargas inside the air base (*NYT*, 10 March). News of the uprising triggered popular support, and hundreds of pro-Vargas demonstrators began to surround the base during the weekend. On 10 March, Febres-Cordero issued an ultimatum to Vargas in a televised address to the nation. He told Vargas to surrender or face an armed takeover of the base. The first phase of the crisis concluded the next day with the surrender of Vargas, who announced that Piñeiros and Albuja would resign as part of the conditions of the settlement (*El Comercio*, 11, 12, 13 March).

The affair took a strange turn upon Vargas's arrest and transfer to the Quito air base to face charges in a military tribunal. The government announced that no deals had been made with Vargas in exchange for the surrender; Vargas responded by taking over the Mariscal Sucre air base where he was being held captive on the evening of 14 March. Embarrassed and infuriated, Febres-Cordero declared a state of emergency and retook the air base by force a week later. The toll of the 45-minute assault on the base was officially reported as four dead and nine wounded; Vargas survived the attack (*Vistazo*, 21 March).

Opposition parties kept a low profile during the Vargas affair, but were able to capitalize on the deterioration of the government's image. Rather than being seen as traitorous, Vargas had captured the popular imagination and became a political cult hero (*NYT*, 10 June). This worked to the advantage of the opposition in the June congressional elections and plebiscite. During the course of the campaign, Osvaldo Hurtado's Christian Democratic Party (Democracia Popular; DP) became linked in the public mind to the Vargas incident; rightists charged that Hurtado supported the uprising, and René Vargas, brother of Frank Vargas, ran on the DP list (*Expreso*, 18 March). The government responded to the growing opposition by a fierce attack on the DP that included a four-day imprisonment of three leading candidates (including Vargas). Meanwhile, the DP joined with other parties of the opposition to campaign for a rejection of the government referendum (*Hoy*, 19 April).

Disenchanted with the predominant role given to so-called independents in the Febres-Cordero administration and worried about their political future, party leaders within the government's own coalition of parties, the National Reconstruction Front, declined to campaign on behalf of the "No" vote. Only the president's own party, the Social Christians (Partido Social Cristiano) and the Liberal Party (Partido Liberal) officially endorsed a negative vote on the plebiscite (*Expreso*, 18 May).

The elections produced a definitive defeat for the government and demonstrated the increasing electoral appeal of parties of the left. The plebiscite question was defeated in every province; 69 percent of the voters nationwise rejected it. Taken together, the FADI, MPD, and PSE turned in a strong performance. They took 18 percent of the vote, in contrast to the 13 percent they had received in 1984. The PSE and MPD registered the biggest overall percentage gains on the left, with their strength concentrated in sierra provinces (ibid., 4 June).

The elections produced a new opposition majority in the Congress that convened in August. After having been progressively eaten away by individual defections and the breakdown of party alliances, the Frente Progresista (the congressional coalition of center and left-wing parties) became the majority force in Congress once again with 40 of the 71 seats in the unicameral legislature. The coalition elected Andres Vallejo of the Social Democratic Party (Izquierda Democrática) as its chairman and Enrique Ayala of the PSE as vice-chairman (*Weekly Analysis of Ecuadorean Issues* [*WAEI*], 15 August). The left was also assigned important congressional committee assignments: Jorge Moreno of the MPD was chosen to head the Committee on the Economy, and René Mauge of the FADI and PCE was appointed to chair the Labor Committee.

With the opposition in power, serious conflicts between the executive and the legislature erupted immediately across a number of issues. As had been the case throughout the Febres-Cordero administration, these policy conflicts highlighted the still unresolved ambiguities in Ecuador's new constitutional order concerning the proper spheres of authority of each of the branches of the national government. In response to the economic measures taken by the government in August, which included devaluation and currency flotation, the Frente Progresista bloc began impeachment proceedings against Minister of the Economy Alberto Dahik and threatened to include the ministers of foreign affairs, agriculture, interior, and public works. Febres-Cordero disputed the legal right of Congress to engage in such procedures. Aggravating the crisis were other conflicts between the president and Congress, which included a congressional grant of amnesty to Frank Vargas and the fugitive mayor of Guayaquil, Abadallah Bucaram, who was being pursued by authorities for his criticism of the armed forces. This renewed round of constitutional crisis was not so much resolved as it simply fizzled; both sides backed away from a showdown over the issues. When Congress voted for the impeachment of

Dahik, the president refused to recognize the impeachment but did allow Dahik to resign. Congress dropped plans for further impeachments, and the question of the legality of the amnesty was referred to the courts. Looming behind the opposition's decision to back off from continued confrontation was its concern that the constitutional order not be breached and that the presidential elections of 1988 take place as scheduled. The armed forces' pronouncement in favor of the administration's antiamnesty position was a forceful reminder to the opposition that the military was monitoring the behavior of the opposition and would permit these parties to operate only within certain bounds (*WAEI*, 4 November).

**Auxiliary Organizations.** Mobilization against the administration and its economic program was the focal point for popular class organizations in 1986. The Frente Unitario de Trabajadores (FUT), the umbrella organization that unites the three major trade union confederations (CTE, CEDOC, and CEOSL), joined with the Frente Popular in calling for opposition to the administration's wage policy and its commitment to pay the foreign debt (*Hoy*, 4 January). Antigovernment street demonstrations broke out, and a rally sponsored by the FUT and Frente Popular drew between eight to ten thousand protesters to the university stadium in Quito (*Hoy*, 17 January). The first of May was another occasion for protest. The FUT joined again with the Frente Popular to sponsor antigovernment marches in Quito and Guayaquil. At the Quito rally, labor leaders urged workers to vote "No" in the June plebiscite (*El Comercio*, 2 May).

The FUT met in a national convention in Quito to approve a new 22-point platform. In its program, the organization came out in favor of a consumer-protection law and an increase in the monthly minimum wage to 20,000 sucres with automatic cost of living adjustments. The FUT also complained of human rights violations by the government. Opposition to the government's plan to privatize state enterprises, continued payment of the debt, and modifications of the regulations on foreign investment figured prominently in the platform (*Expreso*, 29 July).

The largest popular mobilization of the year came in September following the administration's announcement of its new economic measures. The FUT joined with other labor and student organiza-tions in calling for a nationwide general strike for 17 September. Over one hundred arrests were made during the strike. The minister of labor estimated that only 20 percent of the work force participated in the protest, but news reports claimed that industries, schools, and universities in Quito and Guayaquil were entirely shut down (*WAEI*, 22 September).

**Guerrilla Activity.** Like neighboring Colombia and Peru, Ecuador was faced with growing guerrilla activity. The group known as Alfaro Vive! continued its antigovernment actions in 1986. There were reports linking Alfaro Vive! and Colombia's M-19 to the creation of a cross-national guerrilla group, the America Battalion, located in southeast Colombia (*El Comercio*, 27 January). In January, five men and two women identifying themselves as part of the "Jorge Lima Trujillo" Commando of the battalion took over Radio Atahualpa and broadcast a message calling for unions, student groups, and left-wing parties to form a Front of Opposition to the Oligarchy (Frente de Oposición a la Oligarquía) (*El Universo*, 28 January). In March, police reported that they discovered a safe house of the group, where they found plans for kidnapping Marcel Laniado, the minister of agriculture (*El Comercio*, 28 March). In August, two policemen and an agent of the International Criminal Police Organization (Interpol) were killed when Alfaro Vive! members stormed the Eugenio Espejo hospital in Quito to rescue a fellow member being held there (AFP, 20 August; *FBIS*, 22 August).

Four of Alfaro Vive!'s top leaders—Arturo Jarrín, Fausto Basantes, Hamed Vásconez, and José Flores—were killed in battles with police in 1986. One of the best known remaining leaders, Rosa Cárdenas, was imprisoned along with an estimated 80 other guerrilla members. (*WAEI*, 4 November.) Adding to the organizational problems of Alfaro Vive! was an internal split that produced a new guerrilla organization calling itself the Free Homeland Montoneras (Montoneras Patria Libre; MPL). In its first action outside of Quito, the group disarmed police and raised a red flag over a monument (*Latin American Weekly Report*, 21 January). In May, the MPL group kidnapped Enrique Echeverría, a member of the Tribunal of Constitutional Guarantees, and demanded that the tribunal undertake proceedings against Febres-Cordero for violations of the Constitution. The kidnapping was condemned by political parties, and even Alfaro Vive! joined in the pleas for Echeverría's freedom. He was held for five days and released after negotiations produced an agreement with the MPL in which the tribunal ensured the kidnappers' physical safety and a fair trial. (AFP, 25 May; *FBIS*, 27 May.)

Accompanying this new wave of guerrilla activity were increasing complaints and legal suits filed by local human rights organizations. They accused the government of violations of civil rights, assassinations, and the use of torture in police interrogations of alleged subversives (*El Comercio*, 19 February).

**International Views and Positions.** The Febres-Cordero administration maintained its foreign-policy line of close alliance with the United States, which drew a steady stream of criticism from parties on the left (*El Pueblo*, 24 January).

Catherine M. Conaghan
*Ohio State University*

# El Salvador

**Population.** 5,105,000
**Major Marxist-Leninist Groups**
- Communist Party of El Salvador (Partido Comunista de El Salvador; PCES)
**Founded.** 1930; destroyed two years later; reorganized in late 1940s.
**Membership.** Less than 1,000
**General Secretary.** Jorge Shafik Handal
**Governing Body.** Central Committee
**Last Congress.** Seventh, April 1979
**Status.** Illegal
**Fronts and Auxiliary Organizations.** Political front, Nationalist Democratic Union (UDN); military force, Armed Forces of Liberation (Fuerzas Armadas de Liberación; FAL)
**Publications.** *Voz Popular* (paper), *Fundamentos y Perspectivas* (theoretical journal); both irregular

- Farabundo Martí Popular Liberation Forces (Fuerzas Populares de Liberación Farabundo Martí; FPL)
**Founded.** April 1970, by dissidents from the PCES led by former general secretary Salvador Cayetano Carpio and Central Committee member Melida Anaya Montes ("Ana Maria")
**Membership.** Fewer than 1,000 cadres and fighters; about 20,000 civilian dependents and supporters
**Leadership.** Leonel González, first secretary since August 1983—when Ana Maria was murdered and Cayetano Carpio reportedly committed suicide, both in Nicaragua—and commander of the Popular Liberation Army; Dimas Rodríguez; Ricardo Gutiérrez; Salvador Guerra.
**Governing Body.** Central Committee, membership unknown except for above leaders.
**Status.** Illegal
**Last Congress.** Seventh Revolutionary Council, August 1983

**Front and Auxiliary Organizations.** People's Revolutionary Bloc (BPR), includes unions and professional groups; guerrilla force, Popular Liberation Army (EPL)

**Publications.** *El Rebelde* (irregular), and *Farabundo Martí Weekly Informative* (published abroad). The BPR publishes *Juan Angel Chacón Bulletin* in El Salvador and *Weekly Popular Combat* abroad; the FPL controls the second most active FMLN radio station, Radio Farabundo Martí.

- People's Revolutionary Army (Ejército Revolucionario del Pueblo; ERP)

**Founded.** 1971, as The Group (El Grupo), took present name in 1975.

**Membership.** About 1,500 cadres and fighters; as many as 20,000 civilian supporters and dependents

**Leadership.** Main leader Rene Cruz (alias Joaquín Villalobos)

**Political Commission.** Villalobos, Ana Guadalupe Martínez, Ana Sonia Medina Arriola ("Mariana"), Mercedes del Carmen Letona ("Luisa"), Claudio Rabindranath Armijo ("Francisco"), Juan Ramón Medrano ("Balta"), Jorge Meléndez ("Jonas")

**Status.** Illegal

**Last Congress.** Plenum, July 1981

**Fronts and Auxiliary Organizations.** Party of the Salvadoran Revolution (PRS); Popular Leagues–28 February (LP-28); both largely defunct

**Publications.** Controls FMLN station, Radio Venceremos.

- Armed Forces of National Resistance (Fuerzas Armadas de la Resistencia Nacional; FARN)

**Founded.** May 1975, after ERP purges, by dissidents from PCES, FPL, and Christian Democratic Party

**Membership.** Less than 1,000 cadres and guerrillas; some 10,000 civilian supporters and dependents

**Leadership.** Eduardo Sancho Castañeda (alias Fermán Cienfuegos), and "Luis Cabrál"; main body is the seven-member National Leadership.

**Status.** Illegal

**Fronts and Auxiliary Organizations.** United People's Action Front (FAPU); Party of National Resistance (PRN); both ineffectual

**Publications.** *Pueblo Internacional*, *Parte de Guerra* (war bulletin)

- Revolutionary Party of Central American Workers (Partido Revolucionario de los Trabajadores Centro Americanos; PRTC)

**Founded.** January 1976, in Costa Rica, as regional Trotskyist party with expected branches in Costa Rica and Guatemala, which were never formed, and in El Salvador and Honduras, which were formed but became independent in October 1980

**Membership.** Fewer than 200 members, mostly urban; some 1,000 sympathizers and dependents

**Leadership.** Supreme leader Roberto Roca with Jaime Miranda in Mexico, Central Committee members Mario González ("Mario"), urban terrorist leader Ismael Dimas Aguilar ("Ulysses"), and María Concepción Valladares ("Nidia Díaz")

**Status.** Illegal

**Guerrilla Front**

- Farabundo Martí National Liberation Front (Frente Farabundo Martí de Liberación Nacional; FMLN)

**Founded.** 1979

**Membership.** PCES, FPL, ERP, FARN, PRTC

**Status.** Illegal

**Last Congress.** Fourth, September 1986

**Fronts and Auxiliary Organizations.** The legal National Union of Salvadoran Workers (UNTS), Msgr. Oscar Arnulfo Romero Mothers' Committee for Political Prisoners and the Disappeared (COMRADES)

**Radio Stations.** Radio Farabundo Martí, controlled by FPL; Radio Venceremos, controlled by ERP.

**Political Front**

- Revolutionary Democratic Front (Frente Democrático Revolucionario; FDR), an umbrella alliance including the guerrilla organizations of the FMLN, their parties and fronts, and a few minor civilian parties, including the allegedly social-democratic National Revolutionary Movement (MNR), led by Guillermo Ungo, a vice president of the Socialist International, and a smaller splinter of the Christian Democratic Party, the Social Christian Popular Movement (MPSC), led by Rubén Zamora.
  **Founded.** 1980
  **Membership.** A few hundred intellectuals and internationally connected professionals
  **Leadership.** Guillermo Ungo, Rubén Zamora
  **Politico-Diplomatic Commission.** Members include Ungo (MNR), Zamora (MPSC), and representatives of the front organizations of four guerrilla groups: Mario Aguinada (UDN); José Rodríguez Ruiz (FAPU), Ana Guadalupe Martínez (LP-28), and Salvador Samayoa (BPR).
  **Status.** Illegal

The main developments within the Salvadoran left during 1986 were the first open splits within the FDR-FMLN umbrella, continuous decline in the FMLN's military capabilities, and steady steps by the five FMLN member organizations toward forming a unified, "vanguard" Marxist-Leninist party.

The most active reassessment of its alliance with the guerrillas, or at least of the opportunities available in El Salvador, came from the MPSC. Middle- and lower-level cadres of that party started taking advantage of the promises of tolerance by Napoleón Duarte's government (*NYT*, 22 January). Indications abounded during the year that Ungo's party, the MNR, would follow. Both parties, however, denied the existence of any strategic differences with the FMLN and justified their new approach as "a greater division of labor within the FDR-FMLN coalition" (*Latin American Weekly Report*, 7 February). In fact, it appears that the open return of MPSC cadres to El Salvador was both the expression of differences with the FMLN and a more sophisticated approach to take advantage of the tolerance of the government to infiltrate and manipulate existing legal organizations, particularly the newly radicalized unions.

Within the FMLN, 1986 was dominated by claims of growing unity among the five politico-military organizations. Whereas 1985 had been defined as a year when the insurgents "have taken more serious and solid steps in [the] unification process" (*FBIS*, 3 January), by October Villalobos claimed that they were "at a historic peak in the organization of the moving forces of the revolution" (ibid., 16 October). According to Cabrál of the FARN, the steps toward "ideological and organiza-tional unity" within the FMLN were based on the unified "single political and military line approved by [the] general command at its last meeting in May–June 1985" (ibid., 6 February). The concrete demonstration that greater unity now prevails within the FMLN's traditionally divided ranks, and that it goes beyond joint statements by the supreme commanders of the five groups, was the composition of the FMLN delegation to the Twenty-seventh Congress of the Communist Party of the Soviet Union (CPSU) in Moscow. The three major members were Handal, Cienfuegos, and Nidia Díaz, who were treated as equals by the Soviet media. Both Handal and Cienfuegos addressed the Congress, and their speeches were published in *Pravda* (4, 5 March); an interview with Díaz appeared in *Izvestiia* on 8 March. Moreover, Handal and Cienfuegos together met other delegations at the congress, including that of Czechoslovakia, led by Vasil Bil'ák (*FBIS-Eastern Europe*, 5 March).

In light of the fact that until recently the PCES had practically a monopoly on relations with the USSR and Eastern Europe, the prominent role played by noncommunist leaders indicates that both communists and noncommunists in El Salvador are now increasingly being perceived as part of the same organization, ideologically as well as politically and militarily. Also, the leaders' statements demonstrate that old resistance to Soviet ties is crumbling within some FMLN groups. The most significant fact regarding the Salvadoran delegation to Moscow, however, may well be that neither of the two largest groups within the FMLN—the FPL and ERP—was represented directly, at least at a high level. This, combined with the well-documented influence that the ERP has over the FPL and that the PCES has over the PRTC and FARN, suggest that the unity of the FMLN may well remain bipolar, with Handal and Villalobos each expanding their influence at the expense of the other, smaller partners.

On the political front, the greater success of the FDR and FMLN seems to be their renewed ability to infiltrate and mobilize for their own ends significant sectors of organized labor—an ability they appear to have lost in 1980. The main such instrument is the UNTS, whose opposition to the Duarte government is more political than economic. It is significant in this respect that the UNTS-organized march of 4 October copied exactly the propeace slogans of the FDR and FMLN, opposed the war, (but only as it was waged by the government), and denied the democratic legitimacy of the regime (*FBIS*, 7 October). As a result, the Christian Democratic Party openly accused the UNTS of being a "terrorist front" (San Salvador, *La Prensa Grafica*, 4 October), an accusation that was angrily, but not convincingly, rejected by the union leaders.

While the UNTS has been the most significant recent legal front of the insurgents, some older fronts continued to be active, particularly among the self-proclaimed human rights organizations. The most prominent of these was COMRADES, which was directly accused by guerrilla defector Luz Janet Alfaro of being an FMLN front (*LAT*, 24 September). In addition, President Duarte personally accused the rector of the Central American University, Ignacio Ellacuria, of being a guerrilla spokesman and threatened him with expulsion (San Salvador, *El Mundo*, 6 September).

On the military scene, 1986 continued to demonstrate the growing ability of the army to penetrate areas previously under solid FMLN control. During the first two months of the year, the military succeeded in capturing and, for the first time, in holding Guazapa Hill, one of the oldest guerrilla strongholds in the country. That operation also resulted in a serious blow to the prestige and military strength of the FPL, the main victim of the offensive. Even more damaging, from the guerrillas' point of view, was the military's decision to prevent civilians from returning to areas under FMLN control, thus denying the rebels their recruiting ground and the ability to return.

The FPL, however, was not the only guerrilla group that suffered casualties. In January, a top FARN leader, Pedro Serrano Casco ("Carlos") was captured, and the following month a whole urban cell of the PRTC, including financial and medical experts, was destroyed after the capture of all its members (*FBIS*, 5 February). In October, the military also captured Julio Cesar Ramos ("Alejandro") a member of the PCES Political Commission and a founder of the party. Trained in the USSR, Ramos was one of the organizers of the September FMLN Fourth Congress in Morazan (ibid., 6 October). These spectacular captures indicated significant improvements in the military's intelligence and a weakening of the insurgents' ability to move their cadres outside the areas under their direct control.

Regardless of their accuracy, army-provided casualty figures for the various insurgent groups seem to indicate that the relative size of the five groups has remained unchanged, with the FPL still the largest, followed by the ERP, PCES, FARN, and PRTC. The rebels' ability to inflict casualties on the military continued, but most of those were the result of mines rather than direct contact. While the extensive use of mines had an impact on military morale, it also weakened the civilian support for the insurgents as more and more peasants, including children, were maimed (*NYT*, 10 August). In fact, Handal himself admitted that the FMLN mines were designed to maim rather than kill (ibid., 10 November).

While the war continued, both the guerrillas and the government tried to take political advantage of the general public's desire for peace, and they blamed each other for the failure of the meeting scheduled to take place in Sesori in September. Even after a mediation effort by the Roman Catholic Church and preliminary meetings in Peru, Panama, and Mexico, the FDR-FMLN leaders failed to show up, claiming lack of security.

The massive earthquake that produced great damage and many victims on 10 October in San Salvador was also used by both sides for their political aims. The FMLN and UNTS accused the government of not doing enough to help and of refusing Cuban offers of aid. At the same time, FMLN foreign supporters, including groups in the United States, tried to take advantage of the disaster to resupply the rebel forces under the guise of humanitarian aid, while the government tried to maintain control over the distribution of foreign aid.

Michael Radu
*Foreign Policy Research Institute, Philadelphia*

# Grenada

**Population.** 92,000
**Party.** Maurice Bishop Patriotic Movement (MBPM)
**Founded.** 27 May 1984
**Membership.** No data
**Chairman.** Kenrick Radix
**Status.** Legal
**Last Congress.** October 1985
**Last Election.** 3 December 1984; 5 percent, no seats
**Auxiliary Organizations.** The Maurice Bishop and Martyrs of October 19, 1983, Memorial Foundation; The Grenada Foundation, Inc.; The Maurice Bishop Youth Organization (MBYO)
**Publications.** *The Indies Times* (weekly), *The Democrat* (biweekly)

The most important event of 1986 in Grenada was the sentencing, on 4 December, of the eighteen defendants in the Maurice Bishop murder trial. A high court jury found fourteen former members of the People's Revolutionary Government (PRG) guilty of the murder of former prime minister Bishop, several of his cabinet ministers, and more than a hundred other Grenadians. Three other defendants, former members of the People's Revolutionary Army (PRA), were found guilty of manslaughter, and a fourth former PRA soldier was acquitted.

Among those sentenced to be hung for murder were former PRG deputy prime minister Bernard Coard and his wife Phyllis (a member of the central committee of the New Jewel Movement [NJM]); PRA commander Hudson Austin (chairman of the Revolutionary Military Council that assumed power after Bishop's assassination); PRG mobilization minister Selwyn Strachan; and Leon Cornwall, PRG ambassador to Cuba. Also sentenced to death was Soviet-trained PRA Lieutenant colonel Ewart Layne. Declaring that he had acted alone in ordering the executions, Layne proclaimed that his "entire life has been dedicated to the revolution" (*Washington Times*, 5 December).

Death sentences for the Coards and other members of the Stalinist wing of the PRG effectively put an end to the NJM as a distinct Grenadian communist party. Former PRG police commissioner Ian St. Bernard, who has served as the NJM's de facto party leader since 1984, made little attempt during 1986 to recruit new members for the NJM or reorganize the party. The NJM's demise leaves MBPM as Grenada's sole communist party.

**Domestic Affairs.** In January, MBPM deputy chairman George Louison was detained by Grenadian police for questioning in connection with the arrest of nine former PRA members charged with illegal military training. Louison's detention was alleged to have been due to concern by Grenadian authorities over increased underground activities by the MBPM.

In July and August, 32 Grenadians returned from Cuba after completing various professional educational programs in Cuban universities. Among the ten Cuban-trained doctors returning to Grenada was Bowen Louison, younger brother of both George Louison and former PRA chief of staff Einstein Louison. (Caribbean News Agency, 1 August; *FBIS*, 4 August.)

**International Views, Positions, and Activities.** In apparent recognition that the NJM no longer represented a viable political force in Grenada, the Soviet Union forged closer links with the MBPM. In March, George Louison addressed the Twenty-seventh Congress of the Communist Party of the Soviet Union (CPSU) in Moscow as an official delegate. Referring to the NJM defendants, Louison blamed the death of "staunch revolutionary Maurice Bishop" on "the actions of traitors, leftists, and splittists." Toward the close of his speech, Louison conveyed "most ardent combat greetings from Grenadian revolutionaries" and gratitude for Soviet "support and solidarity both in the past and in the present" (*Izvestiia*, 7 March). Following the CPSU congress, Louison addressed the Eleventh Party Congress of the East German communist party (*Neues Deutschland*, 23 April).

The MBPM finished the year as a recognized, albeit still minimal, force in Grenadian politics. The party's domestic political strategy is based on presenting itself as a moderate socialist alternative to the ruling New National Party coalition (*Financial Times*, 11 December). However, the MBPM leadership remains committed to revolutionary doctrine and has rebuilt the international communist alliances developed by its NJM predecessor.

Timothy Ashby
*The Heritage Foundation*

# Guadeloupe

**Population.** 334,000
**Party.** Communist Party of Guadeloupe (Parti Communiste Guadeloupéen; PCG)
**Founded.** 1944 as section of the French Communist Party (PCF), 1958 as independent
**Membership.** 3,000 (estimated)
**General Secretary.** Guy Daninthe
**Politburo.** 12 members
**Status.** Legal
**Last Congress.** Eighth, 27–29 April 1984
**Last Election.** 16 March, French National Assembly; 28 September, Regional Council, 10 of 41 seats
**Auxiliary Organizations.** Union of Guadeloupan Communist Youth (UJCG); Union of Guadeloupan Women (UFG); General Confederation of Guadeloupan Labor (CGTG)
**Publications.** *L'Etincelle* (PCG weekly); *Madras* (UFG monthly)

The PCG did better in the 1986 elections than its parent party in France, and perhaps because of growing opposition to French party leadership from within the party or because of the popularity of the independence movement in Guadeloupe, the PCG tended to downplay its ties with the PCF. The Guadeloupan party found itself in a defensive posture against the attacks of local nationalists; as a result, party programs focused on economic programs rather than on making political choices.

**Leadership and Party Organization.** On 28 December 1985, General Secretary Guy Daninthe was honored by the party for his 60th birthday. On that day the Soviet Union accorded him its Order of Friendship Among Peoples. At the end of 1986, the party again hailed its longtime leader. Ernest Moutoussamy, PCG member and deputy of the French National Assembly, published a book, *Guadeloupe: The Communist Movement and Its Députés Under the IVth Republic.* Dr. Henri

Bangou—cardiologist, historian, mayor of Pointe-à-Pitre since 1965, and one of the founders of the independent PCG in 1958—was elected to the French senate to replace Marcel Gargar, an ally of the PCG who chose not to run again. The festival of *L'Etincelle* celebrated the 42nd anniversary of the party's newspaper in June, and, as usual, a delegation from Cuba attended.

**Domestic Affairs.** The independence movement, led by the Popular Union for the Liberation of Guadeloupe (UPLG) and the Movement for an Independent Guadeloupe (MGI), constantly attacked the communists. The movement's newspaper unceasingly criticized the communists for being reactionary and traitors. Hardly an issue of the PCG newspaper did not contain a communist response to an attack.

Unlike the nationalists, the PCG proclaimed its faith in local institutions such as the Regional Council, which, in the communist view, could lead the islands toward "democratic and popular autonomy" as a step on the path to independence and socialism. Thus, in cooperation with the socialists, the party presented its list of candidates to the voters on 16 March. Its program emphasized agricultural reform, such as irrigation programs, modernization of sugar mills, guaranteed minimum price for bananas, absorption by the government of small planters' debts, an increase in food crop production, development of the fishing industry, and increased government attention to industrialization as a way to provide jobs. In the Regional Council elections the PCG won 10 out of the 41 seats, a loss of one, but the socialists, who did much better than their fellows in metropolitan France, won 12, a gain of 3 seats. With a total of 22, the communist and socialist alliance chose a socialist as president and a communist, Jérome Cléry, as first vice president. Under the new electoral system, parties won seats in proportion to the percentage of votes.

Moutoussamy led the PCG list for seats in the French National Assembly. In response to a call for a boycott issued by the nationalists, and because of a traditional indifference to elections, the rate of abstention was over 52 percent (*Le Monde*, 19 March). Moutoussamy received 23.9 percent of the votes cast, up from 22.6 percent in the previous elections (*L'Etincelle*, 22 March). He and one socialist took two of the four seats allotted to Guadeloupe. The biggest winner was the candidate of the Rally for the Republic, the party of Jacques Chirac, who subsequently became prime minister.

The PCG announced its firm opposition to Chirac initiatives and criticized Bernard Pons, French minister for overseas departments and territories, during his July visit to Guadeloupe.

As a cap to his long career in politics, Henri Bangou was elected by the 774 town mayors and councillors to the French senate on 28 September. The socialists supported him.

Auxiliary organizations, such as the UJCG, UFG, and CGTG, worked for the election of PCG candidates. The candidates were also allowed to use the party's Radio Gaïac.

**International views.** In addition to the usual visits to the Soviet Union—to the Twenty-seventh Congress of the Communist Party of the Soviet Union (CPSU), for example—the PCG had new contacts with and showed a renewed interest in South Africa and Haiti. A representative of the African National Congress visited Guadeloupe on 20–22 May and was interviewed on Radio Gaïac. More important, as the situation in Haiti began to change at the beginning of 1986, was the expression of PCG solidarity with the Haitian people and the United Party of Haitian Communists.

A meeting was held in Pointe-à-Pitre to discuss Haiti, and on 8 February, a day after the flight of Haitian dictator Jean-Claude Duvalier, the PCG issued a statement of solidarity with that country. René Théodore, general secretary of the Haitian party, the PUCH, stopped in Pointe-à-Pitre on 17 March during his return to Haiti after eighteen years in exile. During his one-hour stopover, he met with PCG representatives. It is likely that the PCG will try to help Théodore organize, although most Haitians tend to disdain Guadeloupans for their continuing ties with France. Haitians are more likely to be sympathetic with nationalist forces in Guadeloupe than with communists there.

Brian Weinstein
*Howard University*

# Guatemala

**Population.** 8,600,000
**Major Marxist-Leninist Organizations**
- Guatemalan Party of Labor (Partido Guatemalteco del Trabajo; PGT), in three factions
**Founded.** 1952
**Membership.** Probably under 500 in all factions
**Leadership.** "Camarilla" faction: Carlos Gonzales; National Leadership Nucleus faction: Daniel Rios; Military Commission faction: unknown
**Status.** Illegal
**Last Congress.** Fourth, December 1969
**Auxiliary Organizations.** Autonomous Federation of Guatemalan Trade Unions (FASGUA), Patriotic Youth of Labor (JPT)
**Publication.** *Verdad* (irregular; published abroad)

- Rebel Armed Forces (Fuerzas Armadas Rebeldes; FAR)
**Founded.** 1962, though largely inactive 1968–1978
**Membership.** 1,000 (estimated)
**Leadership.** Jorge Ismael Soto García (alias Pablo Monsanto)
**Status.** Illegal
**Auxiliary Organization.** National Committee of Trade Union Unity (CNUS), now practically defunct
**Publication.** *Guerrillero* (irregular; published abroad)

- Armed People's Revolutionary Organization (Organización Revolucionaria del Pueblo en Armas; ORPA)
**Founded.** 1971
**Membership.** 1,000 (estimated)
**Leadership.** Rodrigo Asturias Amado (alias Gaspar Ilom), son of Nobel Prize–winning novelist Miguel Angel Asturias
**Status.** Illegal
**Auxiliary Organizations.** Infiltrated the FAR's CNUS and the EGP's CUC
**Publication.** *Erupción* (irregular)

- Guerrilla Army of the Poor (Ejército Guerrillero de los Pobres; EGP)
**Founded.** 1972
**Membership.** 1,000 (estimated)
**Leadership.** Rolando Morán (alias Ricardo Ramírez de León)
**Status.** Illegal
**Auxiliary Organizations.** Peasant Unity Committee (CUC), January 31st Popular Front (FP-31), Revolutionary Christians Vicente Menchu and Robin García Revolutionary Student Front (FERG)
**Publications.** *Compañero* (irregular; published abroad), *Informador Guerrillero* (irregular)

## Umbrella Organization

- National Revolutionary Unity of Guatemala (Unidad Revolucionaria Nacional de Guatemala; URNG)

**Founded.** February 1982, but has never successfully unified its members, all of which continue to act independently

**Membership.** The PGT (National Leadership Nucleus faction), FAR, ORPA, and EGP, their respective fronts, and other sympathetic groups such as the Guatemalan Church in Exile

**Bases.** Operates largely out of Mexico, Nicaragua, and Cuba

**Publication.** *Noticias de Guatemala*; also press agency CESGUA, which serves as a political and diplomatic front for insurgent groups

For Guatemala as a whole, 1986 was a year of uncertain expectations. On 14 January the new civilian president, Christian Democrat Vinicio Cerezo Arévalo, was inaugurated; he is the first freely elected president of Guatemala since 1970 and only the second civilian to occupy the office since 1966. During his first year in office, Cerezo demonstrated considerable political skills in retaining the support of the military, controlling guerrilla activities, attracting significant amounts of foreign aid, and avoiding demagogic but highly damaging economic policies.

Cerezo's charisma and popular following, his foreign and domestic policy successes (including the establishment of normal, if not overly cordial, relations with Nicaragua), and the government's unwillingness to restrain the army's anti-insurgency campaign have combined to force the left to reassess its tactics, if not to change its ultimate goals.

On the insurgency front, the government has continued to press the guerrillas in their traditional areas of operations in the northern departments and to use the services of counterinsurgency experts, despite vocal demands from the legal (and illegal) left for their dismissal and accusations of human rights abuses. The amnesty program of the previous government has also continued, with as many as 2,000 former insurgents taking advantage of it, according to the president.

Another example of continuity, and one that similarly has put the insurgents of the URNG at a disadvantage, was the successful attempt to improve relations with Mexico, thus weakening the guerrillas' rear bases of support and logistical lines. By avoiding a confrontation with Nicaragua, the Guatemalan government has denied that country any additional incentives to increase its support for the URNG. Those two issues—rapprochement with Mexico and quasineutrality with regard to Nicaragua—are closely related, since Mexico is well known to have pressured successive Guatemalan governments into a policy of noninvolvement in Central America's conflicts by combining threats and economic incentives. Cerezo's trip to Mexico in July resulted in reaching an understanding by which Mexico would continue to provide oil at concessionary prices, on easy credit, and to speed up the removal of refugee camps from the border areas to inland locations far from the region. This has been a particularly important issue for Guatemala, since the refugee camps in Chiapas are known to have served as guerrilla rear bases and safe havens. In exchange for such concessions, Guatemala would, at least informally, be expected to stay uninvolved in the Nicaraguan civil war and, by controlling its own guerrilla activities, to insure the peace of Mexico's southern border areas.

Historic Guatemalan claims to leadership in Central America, Cerezo's own ambitions, Mexican incentives, and nationalist feelings that have often turned anti-American all combined to convince the new government that it would have a chance to play an important role in the region. This strengthened the policy of noninvolvement in military terms, and in political terms it took the form of the Central American summit of Esquipulas in May. During the meeting, however, the irreconcilable differences between Nicaragua on the one hand and El Salvador, Costa Rica, and Honduras on the other came to light again, and Cerezo's proposal for a Central American Parliament was received with cool politeness. By the end of the year, moreover, the relative consensus regarding the wisdom of Guatemala's neutrality had broken down, and in December the conservative Guatemalan National Liberation Movement (MLN) claimed that it had trained and prepared 8,000 fighters to join, if asked, the anti-Sandinista forces in Nicaragua (*Washington Times*, 16 December). Among the ruling Christian Democrats there has been no sympathy for the Sandinistas and much sympathy for the struggling Social Christian Party in Nicaragua; in addition, Salvadoran president Napoleón Duarte, a foe of Nicaragua, has influenced his fellow Christian Democrats in Guatemala City.

**Guerrilla Activities.** Throughout 1986 the various guerrilla organizations sent conflicting signals, which were perhaps an indication of their own lack of unity regarding attitudes toward the new government. On the one hand, various personalities within the URNG—including two of the supreme leaders of the insurgents, Rolando Morán and Pablo Monsanto—have given the impression that they are prepared to negotiate (see below); on the other, the fighting continued.

By June the insurgents were active in eight departments: the ORPA in Suchitepequez with the Xavier Tambriz and Luis Ixmata fronts (the latter also in Solola), and in San Marcos with the Manuel Tambriz front; the EGP in Huehuetenango with its Marco Antonio Yon Sosa front and in El Quiche with the Ho Chi Minh front; the FAR in Peten with the Lucio Orantes, Feliciano Argueta, Luis Francisco Toltov, and November 13th fronts (the latter also in Alta Verapaz), and the Mardoqueo Guardado front in Alta Verapaz (*Central America Report*, 20 June). In addition, there were sporadic attacks during the first half of the year in the departments of Baja Verapaz (EGP), Izabal, Quetzaltenango (ORPA), Guatemala, and Santa Rosa (probably PGT). Most of these activities involved attacks against oil installations (for example, in Alta Verapaz and Peten) and brief occupations of farms, followed by gunpoint indoctrination of the population.

By the second half of the year the army's "Consolidation '86" offensive had started producing significant results, and guerrilla activities disappeared in Izabal, Santa Rosa, and Alta Verapaz while declining sharply in Peten (*CAR*, 31 October). The largest offensive attempt by the insurgents took place in the central highlands of Chimaltenango and Quetzaltenango, led by the ORPA, in which a number of commanders were killed in May (*FBIS*, 7 May). The hardest hit, however, was the FAR, particularly in its Peten hideouts, where a protracted anti-insurgency campaign resulted in a drastic decline of guerrilla activities and the highest decoration for the commander in Poptun, Colonel Pablo Nuila Hub (*CAR*, 31 October). Perhaps the best description of the situation is, ironically, that provided by an ORPA document: "...strategy of permanent repression and constant military offensive against the general population and the revolutionary

movement" (ibid.). In fact, with regard to the military's behavior toward the civilian population, and despite continuous claims to the contrary from guerrilla fronts and sympathizers, it appears that there was a significant degree of improvement, which may explain the willingness of the U.S. Congress to renew military aid to Guatemala after many years of interruption.

Most of the army-guerrilla encounters during 1986 were instigated by the former, and all were limited in numbers of both combatants and casualties. Renewed military aid to Guatemala, and particularly the acquisition of spare parts needed to redeploy fifteen helicopters, indicate that increased mobility for the anti-insurgency forces could spell further defeats for the guerrillas in the future.

**Peace Prospects.** The election of Cerezo produced new dissensions within the already disorganized ranks of the URNG, with different organizations taking different approaches to the new government at different times. There is also apparently growing pressure from Cuba and Nicaragua on the insurgents to at least show interest in reaching a negotiated end to the 24-year-old civil strife in Guatemala.

In December or late November 1985, when it became apparent that a new civilian government would be elected, the CUC, presumably speaking for the EGP, issued a strong statement in Mexico dismissing the electoral process as "window dressing" and demanding what amounted to a unilateral disarmament by the Guatemalan army (text in *IP*, 10 February). Less than one month after Cerezo's inauguration, however, FAR supreme leader Pablo Monsanto stated in Havana that the URNG "will not obstruct the new president . . . from carrying out his democratic promises." Yet Monsanto also claimed that "we have the duty of continuing the struggle. To stop or to lay down our weapons would be a crime" (*FBIS*, 13 February). The statement, vague as it was, started a debate in Guatemala; some Christian Democrats and the left-of-center Social Democrats interpreted it as a truce offer, but the army rejected such an interpretation (ibid.). The president stated that he would need one year to consider talking to the insurgents, provided the latter lay down their arms, and that unless they do so, "a democratic government has a right to defend its democracy within the law" (ibid., 18 February).

On 5 March, the URNG offered a two-year "demilitarization" and justified its offer by the "historic moment when there have been important changes that make it possible to overcome existing inequalities" (ibid., 6 March). The offer was promptly denied by Monsanto, who accused the army of continuing its anti-insurgency operations (*Latin American Weekly Report*, 14 March). In Havana, Fidel Castro claimed that he supported a negotiated settlement in Guatemala—an implicit offer immediately rejected by the president of the Guatemalan Congress, Alfonso Cabrera (*JPRS-LAM*, 25 March). Interestingly enough, however, the same Pablo Monsanto who dismissed the previous offer of a truce personally made one of his own at the Havana meeting, but again in conditional terms: "We will continue our armed struggle, but we would like to negotiate a truce" (ibid.). It is unclear if Monsanto had to make the offer because of Cuban pressures, perhaps combined with hopes for a truce that would take some heat off of his forces in Peten. In May the URNG made a more specific offer to the government in a statement in San Jose by two of its civilian leaders, Arturo Jiménez and Ramón Ortiz: if certain conditions were fulfilled by the government, the insurgents were prepared to engage in talks. The conditions were: massive purges of the military; reorganization of the armed forces and police "in keeping with the true national and popular interests"; elimination of the paramilitary forces and "private armies"; punishment for the "death-squad" members; dismantling of the most effective anti-insurgency tool in the countryside, the civil patrols; and freedom of association in the rural areas, tantamount to unlimited right of recruitment by the guerrillas (*FBIS*, 12 May). These points were to become part of the guerrilla propaganda in the countryside, as admitted by a bulletin of the ORPA's Xavier Tambriz front in Suchitepequez (*FBIS*, 11 August).

By the middle of the year, the URNG had renewed offers to open discussions with the government and even suggested various locations for such talks, mostly in guerrilla-controlled areas like Peten, Sierra Madre, and Sierra de Chama, but also in Mexico. However, the president agreed only to talk to exiles in Mexico "as Guatemalans" rather than as partners in negotiations. (*El Grafico*, 1 July.)

Toward the end of the year it became increasingly clear that neither side truly wanted to negotiate. On the URNG's part this was abundantly demonstrated by reiteration of the same unrealistic preconditions, which were always matched by promises to continue fighting. At the same time, President Cerezo flatly rejected negotiations other than on the condition that the insurgents surrender.

The last group to mention the possibility of negotiations was the PGT, which did so in October, on the anniversary of its 37th year of existence. Like other groups of the violent opposition, however, the PGT also accused the president of "drawing a smokescreen over the infamous, genocidal regime that has ruled the country for the past 32 years" (*Latin America Regional Reports: Mexico & Central America*, 30 October). Furthermore, only a few weeks later the PGT claimed that Nicaraguan *contras* were being trained in Izabal, dismissed Guatemala's neutrality on Central American conflicts as a false pretense, and even denied the democratic legitimacy of the government (*El Grafico*, 10 November). Two of the factions of the PGT flatly refused to have anything to do with the negotiations. At the end of October, large arms caches were discovered by the army in San Marcos, apparently an indication of the guerrillas' intention to retake the offensive, and the EGP murdered seven military men in Quiche and mutilated the bodies. The latest episode prompted the president to publicly doubt the ability of the URNG to represent or control the guerrillas in the field, and he formally rejected any peace talks in the near future (*FBIS*, 6 November).

Michael Radu
*Foreign Policy Research Institute, Philadelphia*

# Guyana

**Population.** 771,000
**Party.** People's Progressive Party (PPP); Working People's Alliance (WPA)
**Founded.** PPP: 1950; WPA: organized in 1973, became formal party in 1979.
**Membership.** PPP: 100 leaders and several hundred militants above non-Marxist rank and file (estimated): WPA: 30 leaders (estimated)
**General Secretary.** PPP: Cheddi Jagan
**Politburo.** PPP, 12 members: Cheddi Jagan, Janet Jagan, Ram Karran, Feroze Mohamed, Pariag Sukhai, Clinton Collymore, Narbada Persaud, Isahak Basir, Rohit Persaud, Cyril Belgrave, Reepu Daman Persaud, Harry Persaud Nokta; WPA, 5 members: Eusi Kwayana, Clive Thomas, Walter Omawale, Moses Bhagwan, Rupert Roopnarine
**Status.** Legal but sometimes harassed
**Last Congress.** PPP: Twenty-second, 3–5 August 1985
**Last Election.** 9 December 1985. PPP: 45,926 votes, 16.84 percent, 8 of 53 seats in National Assembly; WPA: 4,176 votes, one seat in National Assembly
**Auxiliary Organizations.** PPP: Progressive Youth Organization (PYO), Women's Progressive Organization (WPO), Guiana Agricultural Workers' Union (GAWU)
**Publications.** PPP: *Mirror* (weekly), *Thunder* (quarterly); WPA: *Dayclean* and *Open Word* (weeklies)

Following the death of Comrade Leader Linden Forbes Sampson Burnham in August 1985, the presidency of Guyana and the leadership of the ruling People's National Congress (PNC) passed to his vice president and close adviser, Hugh Desmond Hoyte. Hoyte won a state-engineered victory in national elections held 9 December 1985, and in 1986 he steered the PNC government through a series of gradual domestic and foreign policy changes aimed at regaining private sector cooperation and Western investment, but without jeopardizing the PNC's 22-year reign. The United States, the English-speaking Caribbean nations, and neighboring Venezuela responded positively, to the detriment of the major opposition, the PPP and WPA. Both parties, which had historically been stationed to the left of Burnham's socialist, authoritarian PNC, found themselves in the ironic position of joining the minuscule right and the churches in demanding democratic guarantees and free elections in order to keep a hand in the game.

Burnham had led the minority-based PNC to power in 1964, two years before independence, and dominated the country from that point on by capitalizing on the unique composition of the Guyanese political landscape in the context of geopolitical reality. By shrewdly projecting the PNC as the sole alternative to the larger, Moscow-oriented PPP and, later, to the radical WPA, he was able to secure control of the government and all repressive sectors of the state, contrive and install a personalized model of Third World socialism, and establish close ties with the Eastern bloc and Third World revolutionary states without incurring a decisive U.S. counteraction. Utilizing the great flexibility inherent in a declared position of nonalignment, he strategically maneuvered the PNC through both right and left orientations and succeeded in maintaining leverage on both sides of the East-West power equation.

In large part, then, the Burnham legacy that confronted the PPP and WPA in late-1985 and 1986 was a state dominated by socialist-oriented PNC elites, some more radical than others but all schooled in adjusting to shifts in the geopolitical balance in order to preserve power at home. It was in this context, and in the context of a destitute economy, that the post-Burnham era began.

Soon after Burnham's death, the United States signaled that it would be open to better relations with Guyana by openly subscribing to the general belief that Hoyte was more pragmatic and less ideological than his predecessor. During the 1970s, Burnham had found in the atmosphere of detente, and in the Carter administration's wider acceptance of ideological pluralism in international affairs, the opportunity to push forward a strongly Marxist agenda and draw closer to the Eastern bloc. After the Reagan administration cut off economic aid in 1982, however, he discovered that the Soviet Union was unwilling to substantially subsidize his self-styled cooperative socialism. In January 1985, with the economy nearly bankrupt, he invited the PPP for dialogue, an initiative designed to impress Moscow, but one that can also be interpreted as a Burnham-style maneuver to scare Washington into once again aiding the lesser of evils in no-win Guyana. The Moscow-line PPP accepted Burnham's offer to talk, but the United States was still calling his bluff when he died.

Hoyte seemed receptive to Washington's gambit; the PNC government quickly softened its foreign policy rhetoric and abstained from supporting Vietnam on the Cambodia (Kampuchea) issue at the United Nations. Then, after announcing elections for December, Hoyte suggested that there was "genuine interest on both sides, certainly on our side" for better U.S.-Guyana relations (*NYT*, 15 December 1985). However, he also publicly invited PPP general secretary Cheddi Jagan to his office to discuss electoral reform and a PPP proposal for a National Patriotic Front government comprising all left and democratic forces. When the elections turned out to be even more blatantly rigged than in the past, that meeting appeared to have been a maneuver to remind Washington of the threatening alternatives to a PNC securely in power.

PNC leaders were pleased, then, when the United States—which had described elections under Burnham as "marred by fraud and intimidation" (*NYT*, 9 December 1985)—issued a statement saying that while there had been irregularities at the December polls, they were not of "a magnitude to have changed the results" (*Latin American Weekly Report* [*LAWR*], 10 January). Soviet approval was enthusiastic: congratulations flowed in from Eastern bloc countries, and the Soviet ambassador in

Guyana went so far as to praise Guyana's "sound economy" (ibid.). *Izvestiia* ran a story that applauded Hoyte for "resolutely rejecting attempts at imperialist dikdat" and promised stronger cooperation and continued training of Guyanese "national cadres" in the Soviet Union (*FBIS*, 17 December 1985).

Superpower approval outweighed the chorus of protest from Guyana's fellow members in the Caribbean Community (CARICOM). Yet Hoyte acted with confidence in coming down on his domestic opponents, busting the PPP's strike attempt, deporting priests, and raiding the offices of the Catholic, Presbyterian, and Moravian churches that had denounced the elections as fraudulent. Meanwhile, other longtime PNC leaders utilized the opportunity to flex some leftist muscle. Prime Minister Hamilton Green stated that he would continue to "work toward the creation of the new socialist society" (Caribbean News Agency [CANA], 14 December 1985), and Foreign Minister Rashleigh Jackson marked the fifteenth anniversary of Soviet-Guyana diplomatic relations by exchanging messages with Soviet foreign minister Eduard Shevardnadze and declaring it "necessary to consolidate and expand our relations" (ibid., 19 December 1985).

By the beginning of 1986, however, Hoyte was steering back toward the center. In public statements and a New Year's address, he stressed strict nonalignment and replaced socialist rhetoric with an emphasis on private sector and foreign involvement in reviving the economy, which was the main item on the national agenda (CANA, 2 January). Under Burnham, state control of the economy had reached 80 percent and per capita income had sunk to the third lowest level in the hemisphere after Haiti and Bolivia.

At the end of January, after a meeting between Hoyte and East Caribbean leaders, there was a stunning turnaround in Guyana's relations with fellow CARICOM countries, and Hoyte said he looked forward to better relations and increased trade with the CARICOM countries. (*Caribbean Insight*, February.)

After returning home, Hoyte remained uncompromising in his attitude to the Guyanese opposition. In response to their continuing outcry and pleas for international support, he said he did not expect them to get "any encouragement at all" and chastised them for "trying to vilify Guyana" (ibid.). The *Catholic Standard* newspaper, traditionally a thorn in the side of the PNC, suggested that Hoyte's new image and the "spectacular somersault" performed by CARICOM leaders were the result of U.S. influence. Hoyte, the United States, and CARICOM leaders denied the suggestion.

During the next few months and into the spring, the Hoyte government established the two-track policy approach in both domestic and foreign affairs that it pursued throughout the year. On one side of the ledger, it introduced reforms to relieve the economic isolation imposed by Burnham's self-sufficiency policy. Offshore banking legislation was passed by the PNC-dominated National Assembly, and Hamilton Green led delegations to the United States to promote American and other foreign investment in agriculture, tourism, mining, and joint oil exploration. Barter agreements were made with Venezuela, one of the first countries to congratulate Hoyte after the election, and congenial talks were held on the longstanding border dispute between the two countries. Trade delegations were cordially received throughout the CARICOM countries, and it was announced that "every effort is being made to return to the eligibility of the [International Monetary] Fund" (*LAWR*, 28 March).

Coinciding with the economic liberalization, the government took measures to appease the opposition. It was announced that the *Catholic Standard* and the PPP newspaper *Mirror* would be allowed for the first time to receive donations or purchase newsprint and printing presses from abroad, and that a private-sector-sponsored newspaper would be permitted. Also, David Hill (aka Rabbi Washington, American fugitive and leader of the House of Israel sect that acted as a paramilitary arm of the PNC under Burnham) was tried and convicted on a 1977 murder charge.

In the area of foreign affairs, Hoyte continued to alter the positions taken by his precedessor on issues of particular interest to the United States. In an interview with a Venezuelan newspaper he dodged questions about Burnham's solidarity with Nicaragua and instead expressed support for the Contadora process; when asked about his policy toward Moscow and Washington, he responded, "Equidistant between each of the two superpowers" (*El Nacional*, 23 June; *FBIS*, 3 July). On the issue of the U.S. bombing in Libya, Guyana stood out in the Third World when it remained silent. Then, in July, speaking at an American Independence Day reception, Hoyte expressed readiness for "positive dialogue, increased cooperation, and good relations" with the United States (*Caribbean Insight*, August).

The United States responded in August with a partial resumption of aid—the donation of 25,000 tons of wheat flour—in recognition of Hoyte's "pragmatic and forward-looking policies" (ibid., September) and "measures which have produced a better balance in foreign policy and an end to anti-American rhetoric" (AFP, 10 August; *FBIS* 13 August). Resumption of the U.S. aid program cut off in 1982 was discounted, since Guyana remained too far in arrears. However, when France and Britain moved to block further aid from the Caribbean Development Bank, CARICOM leaders came to Guyana's defense, stating that if European countries wished to help the Caribbean, "they must help Guyana" (CANA, 24 March; *FBIS*, 25 March).

On the other side of the ledger, however, apart from the policy shifts that many observers were labeling the "de-Burnhamization" of Guyana (*Caribbean Insight*, August), Hoyte was quietly overseeing an internal PNC ideological training program; restructuring the secretariat to consolidate the fusion of the party with the machinery of government; and maintaining good relations with the Eastern bloc and revolutionary states and movements in the Third World. Regarding the government's policy shifts, he emphasized to the PNC party leadership that they "do not represent a change of direction, but rather a different style of leadership" (*LAWR*, 26 June). Foreign Minister Jackson explained the "different style" to mean "new tactics recognizing concrete realities" (ibid.).

A measure of Hoyte's position on internal PNC affairs was the promotion in early February of Ranji Chandisingh to deputy party leader, second only to Hoyte. Chandisingh, a Soviet-trained ideologue and former PPP leader, was made PNC secretary general by Burnham after he switched parties in 1976. At the 21st anniversary of the PNC in government, Hoyte announced that one of the main areas of focus in the party during 1986 would be a comprehensive program of ideological training, particularly within the party secretariat, to be prepared and directed by Chandisingh (*New Nation*, 9 February; *JPRS*, 27 March). Emphasis on the secretariat is significant because by virtue of the most recent PNC constitution, largely authored by Hoyte in 1983 at the request of Burnham, the secretariat is the mechanism through which the PNC ensures that its policies are being implemented by all levels of the government ministries—the concrete manifestation of Burnham's concept of party "paramountcy" in government.

Internationally, the government reinforced the links forged by Burnham with the Eastern bloc and radical states. The Soviet Union, East Germany, and Cuba in particular seemed happy to accommodate Guyana despite Hoyte's courting of the United States. Party-to-party relations remained intact as PNC delegations attended both the Cuban and the Soviet party congresses in February and the German Unity Party (SED) congress in April. New trade and technical cooperation pacts were signed with all three countries during the course of the year, and for the first time Guyana and the Soviet Union established trade representation as an integral part of each other's embassies. Cultural agreements were renewed as well, including training programs for PNC cadres. Approximately 100 Cuban medical and agricultural technicians remained in Guyana (*Foreign Report*, 20 March), and Jackson stated, "Washington must not push us away from our nonaligned position, nor insist upon modifications to our relations with Cuba" (*LAWR*, 26 June). Trade and cooperation talks also took place with Nicaragua and North Korea.

In the domestic arena, although the easing of press restrictions was welcomed, Hoyte ignored the year-long opposition campaign, led by the PPP and the WPA, for electoral reform and local elections to be monitored by international observers. It had been widely reported that Hoyte had given assurances regarding local elections, which had not been held since 1970, to the Caribbean leaders at the January meeting (*Catholic Standard*, 23 November; *Caribbean Insight*, December). When Hoyte suddenly announced in November without any discussion that municipal polling would take place the first week in December, the opposition stated they would boycott in protest. Their appeals for international support were to no avail, however, as Hoyte promptly swore in the PNC slate of 91 candidates a week later.

With the approach of 1987 it was clear that Hoyte's PNC had solidified its hold on the government while successfully parlaying domestic and foreign policy adjustments into better relations with the United States and the West, without disturbing its ties with the Soviet Union and the East. The economy appeared to be showing signs of life, and government hints of a currency devaluation suggested a return to the IMF fold. Venezuela began to extend credits to the private sector in November, and further U.S. aid seemed possible when a State Department official said, "We think Hoyte is moving in the right direction. We are inclined to be helpful" (InterPress Service, *Carib News*, 4 November).

Hoyte's two-track policy reveals, however, that he and the PNC remained positioned for a move back to the left in the event of further geopolitical shifts. On the one hand, it could be argued that cultivating a new image is a tactical device to revive the economy in preparation for completing a socialist agenda. Internal PNC affairs, the promotion of Marxist-Leninist ideologue Chandisingh to deputy leader, and the strengthening of Eastern bloc ties are strong indications of such a strategy. On the other hand, it is possible that Hoyte believes in a more Western orientation in domestic and foreign affairs and that he needs for the time being to placate the radicals in the PNC. Even if that were the case, however, he would still be impeded by the ideological fetters of the 1980 national constitution installed by Burnham to guarantee the building of socialism.

In either case the West would have no alternative but to continue nurturing the identifiable shifts that have taken place under Hoyte's direction. Because of its initial success, the PNC can be expected to maintain its two-track approach in 1987, which is bad news for the PPP and WPA because it leaves them out.

**PPP Domestic Activities.** During the meeting with Hoyte prior to the December 1985 election, Cheddi Jagan submitted the proposal for a national front government that had been incorporated into the PPP platform at the August party congress (*WMR*, December 1985). He explained, "I believe that President Hoyte should summon the three political parties—PPP, PNC, and WPA—which have admitted to the goal of socialism, to work out a detailed socialist-oriented action program and a reasonable power-sharing formula for a national patriotic front government" (CANA, 11 October; *FBIS*, 16 October). The proposal was turned down, as was a subsequent proposal that elections be postponed pending further discussions.

Prior to the balloting, the PPP held meetings with the WPA and issued joint demands for reforming the electoral system, but discussions about a joint slate of candidates came to nothing. On the afternoon of the polling day, the PPP withdrew from the proceedings and Jagan claimed the PNC had "carried out the rawest and most open rigging ever seen in the sad history of recent elections in Guyana." His accusation was later supported by a joint statement from the Anglican and Catholic churches, four trade unions, the Guyana Bar Association, and the Guyana Human Rights Association, which said that the poll had been marked by a "familiar and sordid catalogue of widespread disenfranchisement, multiple voting, ejection of polling agents, threats, intimidation, violence, and collusion by police and army personnel." (*Caribbean Insight*, January.)

Days after the election, Jagan summoned a five-party opposition meeting to call for "strikes and demonstrations to bring down the government" (CANA, 16 December 1985; *FBIS*, 17 December 1985). Only the PPP-controlled GAWU responded, but its actions were limited by police and military intervention.

When the PNC issued the official results, the PPP found itself with eight seats in the National Assembly, down from the previous ten. Jagan threatened not to occupy them but reconsidered "in the interest of unity of action with the WPA," which had decided to take the single seat it received (*Caribbean Insight*, January).

In January the PPP and WPA were joined by three tiny centrist parties—the Democratic Labor Party (DLP), the National Democratic Front (NDF), and the People's Democratic Movement (PDM)—in forming the Patriotic Coalition for Democracy (PCD). Jagan said that the PCD would demand genuine and regular elections supervised at all levels by an independent electoral commission and that it would push for a Caribbean human rights covenant stressing the need to comply with the national constitution to stop the PNC remaining in power indefinitely. (*LAWR*, 31 January.) He said the coalition's goal was "a political environment which will favor a pluralist political system and a strong parliamentary democracy in Guyana" (InterPress Service, *Carib News*, 21 January).

At the end of January, as President Hoyte was returning from the meeting with East Caribbean leaders, a PCD delegation led by Jagan embarked on a tour of the Caribbean region to plead their case. Received by the prime ministers of Barbados, St. Vincent and the Grenadines, and St. Lucia, the PCD asked for a "detailed investigation by a responsible group of Caribbean observers of the conflicting claims relating to the poll of December 9" and recognition of the PCD as a nongovernmental organization with consultative status with the CARICOM secretariat and regional governments (*Caribbean Insight*, February). Although the prime ministers said they were "open to receiving further representation," the PCD expressed profound unease over the change of heart among Caribbean leaders who appeared willing to give Hoyte a chance and over the widespread view in the Carib-

bean that the January meeting had been held at the behest of the United States (*LAWR*, 21 February).

In February, eight PPP representatives—Cheddi Jagan, his wife Janet Jagan, Reepu Persaud, Harry Nokta, Cyril Belgrave, Clinton Collymore, Isahak Basir, and Feroze Mohamed—were sworn in at the National Assembly, but they boycotted Hoyte's speech at the ceremonial opening of parliament. Jagan stated that there was no mood of optimism in the country and criticized Hoyte's address for containing "nothing about socialism" (*Guyana Chronicle*, 7 February; *JPRS*, 27 March). In an apparent move to placate Jagan, the PNC arranged for the election of PPP representative Persaud to the relatively powerless position of deputy assembly speaker.

Throughout the spring the PPP was the major force in attempting to hold PCD rallies keyed to economic issues, particularly the fuel rationing program stemming from the government's inability to pay foreign oil distributors. When the government only provided permits for demonstrations to be held on the outskirts of the capital of Georgetown, the PCD resorted to "Days of Rest" job actions, which were limited by the deployment of riot police. Jagan warned that harsh economic measures "could lead to riots" and that if police used violence to quell unrest, "the people of Guyana could start an armed revolution to overthrow the government" (CANA, 22 February; *JPRS*, 24 March). He tempered these threats, which had been part of his repertoire for years, by saying he preferred peaceful revolution through "mass action" (ibid.).

In March, Jagan rejected an offer from the PNC for continuation of informal talks, saying that the PNC refusal to consider PCD demands for electoral reform meant prospects for a political solution had been dashed and that "influence by outside forces" had negated the possibility of a national unity government (CANA, 19 March; *FBIS*, 20 March). In April, following speculation that the IMF was to declare Guyana eligible for World Bank aid as an impoverished nation, the PPP issued a statement accusing the PNC of "selling out to the IMF," evidence that a "U.S.-Guyana deal had been struck" (CANA, 7 April; *FBIS*, 9 April).

In May, Jagan criticized the PNC for allowing Guyana to be exploited at the expense of "political and economic independence" (*LAWR*, 16 May) and stated that "Guyana should look to the Cuban model of development" (CANA, 1 May; *FBIS*, 2 May). In June, Jagan complained that the PNC was passing laws in the National Assembly without any prior discussion, and he declared prospects for a national unity government "to be virtually nil . . . Not only did the United States make clear its opposition to any PPP participation in government, but [Hamilton] Green has made clear the PNC's determination to institutionalize further its paramountcy" (*LAWR*, 26 June).

On the anniversary of Burnham's death, Jagan declared that there had been no fundamental changes under Hoyte, "a lot of window dressing but nothing new," and that "going back to the IMF in our view without tackling the fundamental problem of democracy, the question of extravagance, corruption, and discrimination—nothing will come out of it" (CANA; *Carib News*, 9 September).

When the government suddenly announced in November that municipal elections would be held in four weeks, the PCD immediately opted to boycott and stated, "By fixing the dates for nominations and elections without meeting [with] the PCD for discussions, the government has shown its contempt for opposition and public opinion and its unwillingness to hold free and fair elections" (*Catholic Standard*, 23 November). The coalition had written letters to Hoyte in May and October asking for a meeting to discuss their electoral demands, but he ignored them. The demands were: an independent electoral commission to conduct the process; counting of ballots at polling places immediately after closing; abolishment of proxy voting; the presence of international observers; exclusion of the military from the process; and guarantees against the molestation or eviction of opposition candidates and polling agents (ibid.).

At the end of the year, the government decided to scrap plans for the permanent display of Burnham's body. The body was due back from Moscow, where it had spent sixteen months being prepared for display in a $3.5 million mausoleum. Citing maintenance costs, the government planned to inter the body in the structure instead. The PCD welcomed the decision but complained that the money already spent was a waste. (InterPress Service, *Carib News*, 5 January 1987.)

**PPP International Activities.** While Cheddi Jagan was still on tour in the Caribbean with the PCD, Janet Jagan led a PPP delegation to the Cuban Communist Party congress in early February. PPP delegations also traveled to the Communist Party of the Soviet Union congress at the end of the month and to the German Unity Party (SED) congress in

April. At all three events, the PPP had to share billing with PNC delegations. In East Germany, PPP delegate Clement Rohee found that the PNC delegation was led by former PPP comrade Chandisingh.

In his presentation, Chandisingh thanked the SED because "your example guides us" (*Neues Deutschland*, 24 April). He stated that the PNC was on "the path of self-determination" and looked forward to the "socialistic strengthening of our friendship" with the SED (ibid.). Rohee countered, stating that "the crisis that has taken over our country has never been worse" and that the only solution was the "formation of a National Patriotic Front to create a revolutionary democracy" (ibid.).

In April the PPP condemned the U.S. raid on Libya as "an act of international terrorism" and picketed in front of the U.S. Embassy in Georgetown (CANA, 16 April; *FBIS*, 18 April). The PNC allowed the demonstration to take place. However, when Jagan sought to have the issue debated in the National Assembly as "a matter of urgent public importance," he was disallowed by assembly speaker Sase Naraine of the PNC (ibid.).

In July, Jagan was received in Sofia by Bulgarian leader Todor Zhivkov. The two condemned U.S. policy in Central America and the Caribbean, especially in Nicaragua, and agreed on the "determination to consolidate further the unity of the international communist and workers' movement on the basis of the principles of Marxism-Leninism and proletarian internationalism" (Sofia, BTA, 25 July; *JPRS*, 29 August).

**WPA Domestic Activities.** While participating with the PPP in the direction of the PCD, the WPA took a less confrontational approach toward the government. In recent years the party had moderated its radical positions and seemed to be hoping that, faced with rising unrest, the PNC would run aground and the West would find the WPA a better alternative to the PPP. However, because of its relatively small following and the continued dominance of the PNC, the WPA could not afford to go it alone in 1986.

In a mid-year interview, WPA leader Eusi Kwayana explained how after the 1980 murder of WPA founder Walter Rodney, who had advocated the removal by any means of the PNC, and with the arrival of the Reagan administration, the WPA had to rethink its strategy: "We began to think in terms of the Reagan doctrine, that any violent revolution would be put down . . . Grenada having been obliterated, we had to rethink our entire perspective . . . We decided that we now had to engage in a full-scale campaign for free and fair elections" (*IP*, 28 July). Kwayana also seemed to endorse, without specific mention, the PPP's national front proposal, stating that prior to the 1985 elections, "We were prepared to enter a government of national unity on the basis of a free and fair election (ibid.).

The WPA joined the PPP in withdrawing from the proceedings on the afternoon of the December 1985 elections, but following the release of official results the party announced that Kwayana would take the seat, stating that to remain outside parliament would be to play into the hands of "the dictatorship" (*Caribbean Insight*, January). Kwayana said that he would "represent the legitimate interests of trade unions and of unorganized toilers" (ibid.).

In 1986, Kwayana utilized his seat to introduce legislation and attempt to modify that of the PNC. While the PPP categorically rejected the PNC's off-shore banking initiative, as well as most other PNC bills, Kwayana sought to guarantee Guyanese shareholding in the new law. He also introduced legislation on lifting press restrictions, electoral reform, the national budget, labor rights, and an investigation into the assets of the late Forbes Burnham. Despite being overridden on every attempt by the PNC majority, he sustained the effort throughout the year.

The WPA actively supported the PCD demonstration attempts during the spring, stating it was "time for civil disobedience in Guyana" (CANA, 18 March), but Kwayana also contributed to establishing the legal basis for the coalitions demands. In January the WPA filed a high court writ seeking a declaration that the election was invalid and an order for a fresh election. Kwayana was also instrumental in preparing the documentation for making the PCD case on the CARICOM tour. (*Caribbean Insight*, February.)

In May the WPA central committee reported steady growth in membership, although no figures were released. It said the drive for party expansion would continue and that members would no longer be required to be activists. Particular attention would be paid to rural areas as well as to the party's urban base. The multiracial aspect upon which the party had been founded was re-emphasized, and the belief that Guyanese were tired of choosing be-

tween the African Creole–based PNC and the East Indian–based PPP was reasserted. (*Dayclean*, 17 May.)

In August, the WPA issued an assessment of President Hoyte's first year in office. The report stated that Hoyte wished to be seen as "an enemy of Burnhamism" by everyone except the military, that the costly mausoleum under construction was a concession to the armed forces to whom Burnham "was a father"; and that Hoyte no longer spoke of "paramountcy" because his strategy was to completely "institutionalize the PNC" without appearing to do so. Regarding Hoyte's foreign policy, it was stated that "Guyana's emerging relationship with the United States must be carefully watched," as Washington was now prepared "to ignore electoral fraud and other human rights abuses . . . This reservation equally applies to the Socialist countries." (CANA; *Carib News*, 9 September.)

At the end of the year, regarding the return of Burnham's body, Kwayana described PNC plans for a second funeral as a "farce" and objected to the government declaration of Burnham as a national hero (InterPress Service, *Carib News*, 5 January 1987).

**WPA International Activities.** In January, while Kwayana formed part of the PCD CARICOM tour, WPA international secretary Andaiye traveled to the United Kingdom and Canada, where she met with human rights groups, Socialist International representatives, and the British Labour Party (*Open Word*, 20 January; *JPRS*, 24 March). The WPA had recently become a "consultative member" of the Socialist International, and so it was represented at that body's world conference in Lima in June by central committee member Roopnarine.

Later in the year, Kwayana issued a proposal for a "Caribbean Development Parliament" to be comprised of trade unions and other nongovernmental organizations, intellectuals, and government representatives. He said that such an organization could lead to a "genuine Caribbean initiative" that would not be dependent on the U.S.-sponsored Caribbean Basin Initiative. (InterPress Service, *Carib News*, 25 February.)

Douglas W. Payne
*Freedom House*

# Haiti

**Population.** 5,870,000
**Party.** United Party of Haitian Communists (Parti Unifié des Communistes Haïtiens; PUCH)
**Founded.** 1934 (PUCH, 1968)
**Membership.** 350 (estimated)
**General Secretary.** René Théodore
**Politburo.** René Théodore, Emmanuel Frédérick, Max Bourjolly
**Status.** Legal since 1985; in the open in Haiti with the return of Théodore in March 1986
**Last Congress.** First, 1979
**Last Election.** 1957
**Auxiliary Organizations.** No data
**Publication.** Publications in Créole forthcoming

The flight into exile of Haiti's so-called president for life in the early hours of 7 February opened the door to radical political change. Leaders of the republic's minuscule communist party, the PUCH, lost no time in returning home even though their status was less secure than that of other groups.

On 17 March, PUCH general secretary Théodore and his close associates Bourjolly and Frédérick returned home after eighteen years in exile in France and elsewhere. French Communist Party notable Charles Ledermann accompanied them to show solidarity and for a measure of personal protection, since membership in the communist party during the rule of Jean-Claude Duvalier had been punishable by death. In an interview with the author in May, Bourjolly said the leadership was still afraid someone might try to kill communists in Haiti. Nonetheless, the PUCH opened an office in downtown Port-au-Prince and raised a huge red banner across the busy main street proclaiming its return in no uncertain terms.

PUCH proposals for a new Haitian political system were not radically different from proposals of some of the other myriad of political parties that suddenly emerged. This fact is probably a sign of the weakness of the communists. For example, they suggested that the Constituent Assembly, which was preparing a new constitution, provide for a national assembly whose powers would include removal of the president and cabinet members. Such a provision would be at odds with a long Haitian tradition of authoritarian heads of state, but others agreed that such a proposal might help the republic to break out of a dismal string of vicious dictators. In many speeches PUCH leaders urged followers to work with neighborhood committees and new labor organizations that have complained that their members have been harassed and dismissed by factory owners. However, the PUCH opposed calls for strikes and other mass action against the transitional government for fear of a reaction against the workers. The party also called for close cooperation with the Roman Catholic Church hierarchy, an important force for change in Haiti since the pope's visit in 1983. The PUCH claimed that the Church had been inspired by liberation theology, which legitimized the party and directed its actions.

The PUCH called for an opening of diplomatic ties with communist countries, particularly neighboring Cuba. In September a dance and music group composed of Cubans of Haitian origin visited the country; Martha Jean-Claude, a famous singer, led the group. Because there are no direct air routes between Havana and Port-au-Prince, the artists had to fly via Panama. Théodore traveled to Havana in November after a trip to East Germany the previous month. In interviews and speeches he called for a popular front; he hailed the Twenty-seventh Congress of the Communist Party of the Soviet Union and thanked that country for what he called its expression of solidarity with the Haitian people.

In an interview with the author, Bourjolly called for land reform, claiming that much of Haiti's best land was owned by the government and private landowners living in the capital. When asked if plans were being made to build an organization of communists outside Port-au-Prince, Bourjolly responded affirmatively but added that the party leadership feared for the safety of members outside the cities. Decades of officially inspired antagonism toward the communists and hostility toward radical change of any kind were a threat to communist recruitment. During a visit to Cap Haitien, Théodore was obliged to cut short his press conference after threats to the hotel where he held it were received. During a visit to neighboring Dominican Republic, PUCH member Professor Gérard Pierre-Charles was arrested and allegedly beaten.

It appeared to this observer that, because of the 40 years of suppression of communists and the old Duvalier claim that his opponents were communist inspired, some Haitians were interested in the PUCH and what it might accomplish as a legal party, while others saw a communist takeover behind any suggestion for meaningful change. The true role of the PUCH will only emerge after the election and installation of a new president in a new political system in February 1988.

Brian Weinstein
*Howard University*

# Honduras

**Population.** 4,648,000
**Major Marxist-Leninist Organizations**
   • Communist Party of Honduras (Partido Comunista de Honduras; PCH)
   **Founded.** 1927, dismantled by 1932, re-established 1954
   **Membership.** Probably less than 200
   **General Secretary.** Rigoberto Padilla Rush
   **Status.** Illegal ,
   **Last Congress.** Fourth, January 1986
   **Publications.** *Vanguardia Revolucionaria*; *Voz Popular* (both irregular, published abroad)

   • Revolutionary Party of the Central American Workers (Partido Revolucionario de los Trabajadores de Centro America; PRTC)
   **Founded.** 1976 in Costa Rica, as Honduran branch of regional party, became independent in 1979
   **Membership.** Probably less than 100
   **Leadership.** Wilfredo Gallardo Museli
   **Status.** Illegal
   **Last Congress.** No data
   **Publications.** No data

   • Morazanist Front for the Liberation of Honduras (Frente Morazanista para la Liberación de Honduras; FMLH)

**Founded.** 1969 claimed, but was inactive until 1980
**Membership.** Claims a few hundred
**Leadership.** Octavio Pérez, Fernando López (both aliases)
**Status.** Illegal
**Last Congress.** No data
**Publications.** No data

- Lorenzo Zelaya Popular Revolutionary Forces (Fuerzas Populares Revolucionarias Lorenzo Zelaya; FPR-LZ)
**Founded.** 1980
**Membership.** 100 (estimated)
**Leadership.** No data
**Status.** Illegal
**Last Congress.** No data
**Publications.** *Lorenzo Zelaya* (irregular, published in Mexico)

- "Cinchoneros" Popular Liberation Movement (Movimiento Popular de Liberación Cinchoneros; MPL-Cinchoneros)
**Founded.** 1981, as successor to the People's Revolutionary Union, established in 1980 as Honduran front for the Salvadoran Popular Liberation Forces
**Membership.** Less than 200
**Leadership.** No data
**Status.** Illegal
**Last Congress.** No data
**Publications.** No data

**Umbrella Organization**
- Unified Directorate of the Honduran Revolutionary Movement (Dirección Nacional Unificada del Movimiento Revolucionario Hondureño; DNU-MRH)
**Founded.** 1982, though largely ineffective
**Membership.** All the above parties, as well as the Socialist Action Party (Partido de Acción Socialista de Honduras; PASOH), led by Virgilio Carias, headquartered in Nicaragua

The most important developments of the year inside the Honduran revolutionary left were the PCH congress in January and the Cinchoneros' attempt to establish a guerrilla base (*foco*) in the northern part of the country. Both events were part of the overall geopolitical and ideological struggle in Central America in which Honduras is an increasingly essential, albeit reluctant, participant.

The PCH Fourth Congress took place in January "in conditions of clandestinity" (San Jose, *Libertad*, 7–13 February); in fact, it is most likely that the meeting took place abroad. Although no details are known, available information indicates that the debates were intense between the followers of General Secretary Padilla Rush, who were mostly exiles, and the largely Honduras-based faction of Mario Sosa Navarro (see *YICA*, 1986). The main debate centered on the strategy to be followed by the party: violence or political activity. As PCH Central Committee member and the party's representative to the

*World Marxist Review* Randolfo Banegas admitted, the number of participants was strictly limited to "an essential minimum of the most tempered and prestigious Communists" (*WMR*, September), implying that heated arguments had been expected. That they did occur despite such a selection of delegates is demonstrated by the admission of "inner party divergences" since 1980 and the description of the debates as "a tense ideological struggle" (ibid.). Such debates and conflicts were the reasons why it took over eight years for the party to organize a new congress after the third one in 1977.

It seems clear that the congress was in fact little more than another attempt by the Padilla Rush faction to impose its views on the party strategy upon the rest of the party—in other words, to formalize the 1980 decision to engage in violence. Padilla's own keynote speech was a long list of accusations against the United States, matched by an equally long litany of praises for the Soviet Union. Not only did Padilla and the delegates "express deep profound gratitude" to the USSR and the communist bloc, but they also gave their support to Fidel Castro's position on international debt, to the Salvadoran insurgents, and to the Nicaraguan regime.

Analyzing the situation in Honduras, the congress concluded that the country was under foreign, that is, U.S. "military occupation" and that the "repression" against the left had become just another instrument for complying with Washington's desires. As for the tactics to be adopted, "The PCH believes that in the prevailing circumstances the liberation process will follow the channel of revolutionary armed violence in a people's revolutionary war. This conclusion, which takes national and international experience into account, is by no means tantamount to a negation of other forms of struggle, including a parliamentary struggle" (ibid.). The newly adopted Platform of Patriotic and Democratic Struggle clarified the main target of the party's activities: the close ties between Honduras and the United States. Thus, the first and foremost point of the document was a call for the withdrawal of all U.S. troops and the "Somoza gangs" from Honduras (ibid.). The platform was described as a minimum program for a united front coalition that would include all "patriots," including members of the business community, the clergy, and even the military; this was a transparent attempt to inflame and take advantage of the Honduran uneasiness with the presence of the Nicaraguan insurgents and U.S. forces in the country. The document also called for reneging on the external debt, cutting the military budget, and declaring Honduras to be neutral (*WMR*, March).

Throughout the congressional documents and related materials published by Padilla, the Central Committee, and Banegas during the year, the major theme was solidarity with Nicaragua. Indeed, as Padilla put it, "By defending our country's sovereignty, the Honduran communists are supporting socialist Cuba and revolutionary Nicaragua as well as the just struggle of the peoples of El Salvador [and] Chile . . ." (ibid.).

Prior to its congress, the PCH had been badly split and highly ineffectual; the internal faction had retained a high degree of autonomy in practice, if not in theory, from the external leadership under Padilla. The importance of the congress—underscored by the attention paid to it by the Soviets, who understood the need for "rallying the ranks" of the party (*Pravda*, 2 February)—lay in the reassertion of Padilla's leadership over the internal wing. The victory of the exiles was not total, however, since they had to accept a combination of political and military tactics; this stressed the role of united front activities, which would strengthen the position of the internal wing. It was even more significant that, although Padilla was re-elected general secretary and there was talk about the inevitability of a revolutionary war, the party itself announced in June that there were "plans for extensive participation in the forthcoming electoral battle." (*Information Bulletin*, June). The overall impression conveyed by the documents of the Fourth Congress was that of a weak party trying to make its impact felt and in desperate search of domestic allies.

**Guerrilla Activities.** At the beginning of the fall, elements of the Cinchoneros infiltrated the northern province of Atlántida and established a guerrilla base in the Nombre de Dios mountain range. It was the group's first known attempt at classic insurgency, a departure from its previous tactics of largely urban terrorism. According to the Honduran military, the group had ties with Colombian guerrillas, who provided the Cinchoneros with cocaine—a large shipment of which was captured in the La Ceiba area (*Central America Report* [CAR], 31 October). The group, estimated at 80 guerrillas (Guatemala City, *La Prensa Libre*, 26 October), was detected on 11 October in the Yaruca area, and during a first clash with anti-insurgency forces two guerrillas and one soldier were killed (*CAR*, 31 October). The departments of Atlántida, Gracia a Dios, Colón, and Cortés were put on alert, and the army continued to pursue the insurgents. By the end of the month, large quantities of weapons had been captured and the incipient network of civilian sympathizers was dismantled (Guatemala City, *El Grafico*, 23 October). By the end of year, however, it appeared that the guerrilla offensive was a failure, as were the 1984 FPR-LZ attempt to establish a base and the 1983 PRTC invasion from Nicaragua. As in the other instances, the insurgents were apparently trained and armed in and by Cuba and Nicaragua, but were almost immediately betrayed by one of their own, who informed the military of the column's whereabouts (*LAT*, 6 November). The insurgents thus failed to establish themselves as a viable force.

Michael Radu
*Foreign Policy Research Institute, Philadelphia*

# Jamaica

**Population.** 2,288,000
**Party.** Workers' Party of Jamaica (WPJ)
**Founded.** 1978
**Membership.** 75 (estimated)
**General Secretary.** Trevor Munroe
**Status.** Legal
**Last Congress.** Third, December 1984
**Last Election.** 1983, Legislative, WPJ boycotted; 1986, Municipal, no representation
**Auxiliary Organizations.** No data
**Publications.** *Struggle*

The economic crisis that began in Jamaica in the early 1970s continued during 1986. In October, it was announced that the country's gross domestic product had fallen 4 percent in the previous year and that "the government is reassessing its policies to reduce dependence on bauxite and to force local industry to become more efficient" (*Latin America Regional Reports–Caribbean*, 2 October).

The economic crisis continued to have political repercussions. In 1972, it had resulted in the victory of the democratic-socialist People's National Party (PNP), headed by Michael Manley, which remained in power until 1980, when the opposition Jamaica Labor Party (JLP) won a landslide victory and its leader, Edward Seaga, became prime minister. The tenure of Seaga and the JLP in power was confirmed in a quick election in 1983—two years early—which the PNP boycotted because of Seaga's refusal to prepare a new electoral roll, which gave the JLP all the members of the Lower House.

However, in July 1986, municipal elections provided the first clear contest between the two major parties. The PNP won a 53 percent majority and control of eleven of the country's thirteen local governments. A disturbing element was the outburst of violence between supporters of the two major parties during and just after the elections. Leaders of both parties stressed their opposition to these violent actions.

**Leadership and Organization.** The WPJ has had the Moscow franchise in Jamaica. The rival Jamaica Communist Party was organized in 1975 by Chris Lawrence, but the only attention it received during the year centered on allegations that during the Manley regime it had sent members to Cuba for guerrilla training (*Daily Gleaner*, 1 June).

The WPJ emerged from study circles established in the early 1970s at the University of the West Indies and a few other places; these groups studied Marxism-Leninism and began to publish a theoretical periodical, *Socialism!*, and a newspaper, *Struggle*. In 1974, the various groups were brought together in the League for the Liberation of the Workers, which was considered "the germ of a proletarian party." The league had strongly supported the PNP in the 1976 election, and its principal leader was Dr. Trevor Munroe, a professor at the University of the West Indies.

The league was converted into the WPJ at a congress in December 1978. That session "put forward as the main tasks the questions of party construction, the expansion of the mass base, the strengthening of positions in social organizations, and the achievement of unity among the leftist and anti-imperialist forces" (Moscow, *Latinskaya Amerika*, February).

The Third Congress of the WPJ was held in

Kingston in December 1984. Some 32.4 percent of the delegates were workers, as compared to 23.1 percent in the Second Congress in 1981. The party was also apparently older: 54.3 percent of the delegates were 30 or older, as compared to only 22.3 percent three years earlier. Munroe claimed that 43 percent of the delegates were leaders in nonparty organizations. (*WMR*, June 1985.)

It was claimed that "the mass social organizations are the main source of support for the WPJ" and that "its representatives participate in the work of youth, student, and women's organizations and movements, trade union associations, and communal councils" (*Latinskaya Amerika*, February). However, the principal organization in which the WPJ continued to have influence was the union of workers of the University of the West Indies, where Munroe was located and which has been his base from the beginning.

**Domestic Attitudes and Activities.** Much of the WPJ's activities in 1986 centered on participation in the municipal elections. These were the first contested elections in the country since the parliamentary poll of 1980, which first brought Prime Minister Seaga to power, and the second in which the WPJ ran its own nominees for municipal office. In the 1976 and 1980 general elections, the WPJ had given critical support to the PNP, and it joined the PNP in boycotting the election of 1983.

In 1986, the WPJ ran fourteen candidates throughout the island, none of whom were elected. This compared with only two nominees the party offered five years earlier, who received 15 and 13 percent of the vote, respectively, in their constituencies. (Bridgetown, Caribbean News Agency [CANA], 2 July.)

During the year, the WPJ became increasingly critical of the PNP and of Manley, with whom they had formerly allied themselves. Although Manley continued to state that, when his party came back to power, it would renew diplomatic relations with Cuba (which had been cut by Seaga [*FBIS*, 26 September]), he also strongly emphasized that a new PNP government would work closely with the private sector (*Daily Gleaner*, 8 August). The WPJ accused the PNP of being too soft on the Seaga government. A typical claim was that PNP policy was "to pressure the Seaga government by rousing the masses to the least extent possible and by doing everything to avoid confrontation" (*IB*, July).

There was no indication during the year that the WPJ had much influence beyond its original trade union base. However, it gave its support to the rest of the labor movement, especially to a teachers' strike early in the year (ibid.).

**International Views, Positions, and Activities.** The WPJ maintained fairly close relations with other pro-Soviet parties in 1986. A representative of the party, Elean Thomas, participated in at least two sessions of the editorial council of the *World Marxist Review* in Prague. She was reported as arguing that "Jamaica's economic and social problems cannot be solved without socializing the basic means of production and deep changes in the relations of production; the road of reform within the framework of neocolonialism is getting narrower" (*WMR*, October). Thomas also delivered a message for the WPJ to the Eleventh Party Congress of the East German Socialist Unity Party in April (*Neues Deutschland*, 23 April).

Only once during the year did the WPJ evidence any criticism of the USSR. This was after the nuclear power plant accident in the Soviet Union in April, when Munroe sent Mikhail Gorbachev a telegram of sympathy, but added, "The Workers' Party and all Jamaicans are disappointed at the apparent slowness of Soviet publicity about the tragedy and look forward to full reports as well as implementation of adequate measures to avoid similar accidents in the future" (*CANA*, 30 April).

Overseas pro-Moscow parties sought during the year to maintain contact with the PNP as well as with the WPJ. For example, a Communist Party of the Soviet Union (CPSU) delegation, led by N. S. Peru of the CPSU Control and Central committees, attended the Forty-eighth Conference of the PNP in September (*Pravda*, 21 September).

**Revolutionary Marxist League.** The third and smallest Marxist-Leninist organization in Jamaica is the Revolutionary Marxist League (RML). It was organized in the late 1970s and identifies itself as Trotskyist. It is, however, aligned with the Revolutionary Socialist League in the United States, which repudiates the traditional Trotskyist position that the Soviet Union and other Soviet-bloc states remain "workers' states." In 1982, the two groups proclaimed their intention of forming an "internationalist tendency" within the Trotskyist movement.

Robert J. Alexander
*Rutgers University*

# Martinique

**Population.** 328,000
**Party.** Martinique Communist Party (Parti Communiste Martiniquais; PCM)
**Founded.** 1921 (PCM, 1957)
**Membership.** Under 1,000
**General Secretary.** Armand Nicolas (61; French citizen)
**Politburo.** 3 members
**Secretariat.** 4 members.
**Central Committee.** 33 members.
**Status.** Legal
**Last Congress.** Eighth, 12–13 November 1983
**Last Election.** 16 March 1986; in Regional Council, 3 of 41 seats
**Auxiliary Organizations.** General Confederation of Martiniquan Labor (CGTM); Martiniquan Union of Education Personnel (SMPE-CGTM); Union of Women of Martinique (Union des Femmes de la Martinique); Martiniquan Committee of Solidarity with the Peoples of the Caribbean and of Central America
**Publications.** *Justice* (weekly newspaper)

The PCM obligingly followed its senior partners in the left coalition, the Progressive Party of Martinique (PPM) and the Socialist Federation of Martinique (FSM). Although the independence movement has been blunted in Martinique by the PPM, which seems to be a nationalist organization, the communists have been attacked for their continuing loyalty to the political status quo.

**Leadership and Organization.** According to *Justice*, the party newspaper, Nicolas traveled to Paris to meet with left-wing elected officials from Guadeloupe, Réunion, and Guyana, France's other overseas departments, but no new initiatives came out of the meeting.

The CGTM held its fifth congress on 26–27 April and re-elected Philibert Duféal as general secretary. During the congress, speakers made ambiguous references to "national liberation." The Union of Women of Martinique celebrated its 43d birthday in 1986, and all party leaders met for the annual festival of *Justice* on 6 and 13 July.

**Domestic Party Affairs.** In the elections to the Regional Council and to the French National Assembly on 16 March, the PCM followed the lead of the PPM's Aimé Césaire and of the socialists. On 4 January, the left parties had met and agreed to present a united list for the elections. The voting system had been changed to proportional representation, which meant that parties would gain seats according to their percentage of the vote. Césaire led the list.

The PCM electoral program made no reference at all to independence; it emphasized instead economic development, such as increasing food production, undertaking land reform, and reducing the 27 percent unemployment rate. The PCM used its radio, Radio Kan Lanbi, for its electoral messages.

In the National Assembly vote, four seats were at stake. The left won two of them: one went to Césaire, and the other to the socialist Maurice Dougué. The left won 21 seats (out of 41) in the Regional Council, but of those only three were allocated to the PCM; one went to Nicolas, who was also named third vice president of the council. The rate of abstention was 41.48 percent of the registered voters (*Le Monde*, 19 March).

**International Views.** Nicolas and other members traveled widely in Eastern Europe in 1986. Representatives also went to Havana in February for the Third Congress of the Communist Party of Cuba. Nicolas went to Moscow for the Twenty-seventh Congress of the Communist Party of the Soviet Union, and other representatives went to congresses in Czechoslovakia, Bulgaria, and East Germany.

The changes in Haiti sparked interest in Martinique. *Justice* reprinted a *L'Humanité* interview of René Théodore, general secretary of the United Party of Haitian Communists.

Brian Weinstein
*Howard University*

# Mexico

**Population.** 81,709,000
**Party.** United Socialist Party of Mexico (Partido Socialista Unificado de México; PSUM)
**Founded.** 1919 (PSUM, 1981)
**Membership.** 40,800 (*IB*, no. 15)
**General Secretary.** Pablo Gómez Alvarez
**Political Commission.** 21 members: Pablo Gómez Alvarez, Sabino Hernández Tellez, Gilberto Rincón Gallardo Meltiz, Manuel Stephens García, Jorge Alocer Villanueva, Rolando Cordera Campos, Ivan García Solís, Arnaldo Martínez Verdugo, Eduardo Montes, Manzano, Pablo Pascual Moncayo, Marcos Leonel Posadas Segura, Gerardo Unzeuta Lorenzana, Miguel Angel Velasco Muñóz, Leopoldo Arturo Whaley Martínez, Valentín Campa Salazar, Eduardo González Ramírez, Adolfo Sánchez Rebolledo, José Woldenberg Karakowsky, Amalia García, Gustavo Adolfo Hirales, Enrique Semo
**Secretariat.** 7 members: Pablo Gómez Alvarez, Sabino Hernández Tellez, Gilberto Rincón Gallardo Meltiz, Manuel Stephens García, Jorge Alocer Villanueva, Jesús Sosa Castro, José Woldenberg Karakowsky
**Central Committee.** 74 members
**Status.** Legal
**Last Congress.** Second, 9–14 August 1983
**Last Elections.** 1985 midterm elections. 3.24 percent of the vote for, and 12 of 400 seats in, the Chamber of Deputies (lower house of the Mexican Congress)
**Auxiliary Organizations.** Youth/Student Section of the PSUM; Independent Center of Agricultural Workers and Peasants (CIOAC); Sole National Union of University Workers (SUNTU); Single Union of Workers of the Nuclear Industry
**Publications.** *Asi Es* (irregular fortnightly, Mexico City)

The PSUM, recognized by the Soviet Union as the official communist party of the country, was formed in 1981 as the product of a fusion between the Mexican Communist Party (Partido Comunista

Mexicano; PCM) with four smaller groups: the Popular Action Movement (Movimiento de Acción Popular; MAP); the Mexican People's Party (Partido Popular Mexicano; PPM); the Revolutionary Socialist Party (Partido Socialista Revolucionario; PSR); and the Socialist Action and Unity Movement (Movimiento de Acción y Unidad Socialista; MAUS). In 1984, however, the PSR had withdrawn from the PSUM in protest against its style of leadership, and in 1985 the PPM had made a de facto break with the party over allegations that the group from the PCM was monopolizing all the leading positions and acting autocratically. General Secretary Gómez has not formally recognized the withdrawal of the PPM, and so the PSUM's composition, along with its membership figures, remain in flux. However, it is the third largest party in Mexico after the ruling Institutional Revolutionary Party (PRI) and the National Action Party (PAN). The PSUM has a base of support among some workers and intellectuals.

The PCM was the most cohesive and well organized among the plethora of leftist parties in Mexico and the only party with a nationwide apparatus and support structure. Ideology has been less important in dividing the various leftist groups than has the emergence of strong personalities, each wanting to dominate his own organization rather than dilute his power in a cooperative venture with like-minded parties.

Beginning in the summer of 1986, gubernatorial and municipal elections took place in several Mexican states; the electoral season will extend until presidential elections are held in July 1988. The ruling PRI has never lost a governorship, but it was charged by the PAN of rigging the vote in the Chihuahua state election when its candidate won a victory over the popular PAN contestant. Aside from capturing the governorship, the PRI claimed victory in the mayoralty races in the state's two largest cities—Chihuahua and Ciudad Juárez. The PAN had elected mayors there in 1983. Although the elections in Chihuahua generated the heaviest publicity (for example, PAN members there staged large street demonstrations that blocked the Rio Grande bridges linking Mexico with the United States), the PRI was accused of widespread electoral fraud in other locales as well. PSUM Political Commission member Martínez remarked, "The economic crisis and the social aggravation of unemployment led people to anticipate riots and strikes . . . But instead, the crisis erupted where least expected—in the fraudulent electoral system that peo-

ple had long accepted but were suddenly no longer willing to tolerate. We're now seeing the beginnings of civic insurgency" (*NYT*, 22 October).

On 20 September, the federal district committees of the PSUM, the Mexican Workers' Party, the Revolutionary Patriotic Party, the People's Revolutionary Movement, and the Communist Left Unity held a meeting aimed at forging a unification of the country's left-wing movement. Representatives of the PSUM and other organizers of the meeting stated that the Mexican working class "should have a more efficient instrument to face the government's anti-popular policy" (Madrid, EFE, 22 September). They expressed hope that the Mexican left wing would participate in the 1988 national elections as a single party (perhaps with the exception of the Revolutionary Workers' Party, a Trotskyist group).

In the meantime, the PSUM leadership reiterated that the party "strives to rely on a policy of alliances and searches for common ground with other forces on a national scale" (*WMR*, June). During an interview in the *World Marxist Review*, PSUM Political Commission and Secretariat member Rincón Gallardo said that "our party cooperates with all trade union currents and is gradually overcoming the previously isolated position of the left in this sector . . . we strive to conduct diverse and flexible work among the masses." However, he stressed that "the struggle against sectarianism" was an indispensable precondition for the PSUM's effective participation in mass organizations; "without it, all our policy goals and objectives will be 'suspended in mid-air'" (ibid.).

Rincón Gallardo emphasized the necessity of seeking organizational forms that would be compatible with situations in various areas of endeavor. "For example, it is clear that we should not work in the same way at industrial enterprises where only small party groups exist so far and in Indian communities where conditions are ripe for the establishment of mass organizations. Medium-size groups have been set up in residential areas and neighborhoods. We have not yet taken up the establishment of PSUM committees in electoral districts, something that is dictated by the specific exigencies of the political struggle" (ibid.).

Rincón Gallardo noted that the PSUM was fashioning an alternative economic program for Mexico, including "a project for Latin American integration that would counter the 'anti-crisis' policy the government conducts in the spirit of the IMF [International Monetary Fund] recommendations." He declared that the initiation of a "moratorium on external debt servicing" was particularly important. In addition, he proposed strict control over currency exchanges in the country's northern states to combat "the rightist offensive . . . connected with big U.S. capital that has gained a firm foothold in the region and is using cheap Mexican labor." He also stated that the PSUM's Central Committee had established a special section to deal with the distinct local conditions in the north. A propaganda bureau within the section directs its efforts at Mexicans in the seven border states as well as at the millions of Mexicans residing in the United States. (ibid.)

The PSUM's international activities have focused heavily on developments in the hemisphere and on issues of peace and disarmament. On 19 April, hundreds of leftist demonstrators held a march in Mexico City to protest alleged U.S. aggression against Nicaragua and Libya. PSUM general secretary Gómez addressed the crowd at the end of the march. He advocated a moratorium on Mexico's foreign debt servicing, movement toward internal democratization of the country, and unity among the left to combat what he regarded as the growing influence of reactionary forces in the Mexican government. (Mexico City, *El Dia*, 19 April.)

In May, the PSUM sponsored a three-day festival that *Pravda* (20 May) called a "traditional [and] significant event in the political life of the country." The festival featured political workshops; slogans calling for the unity of the working class, solidarity in the struggle for peace, and other favorite communist themes; displays of Marxist-Leninist classics, documents from the recently held Twenty-seventh Congress of the Communist Party of the Soviet Union (CPSU), and similar literature; recordings of revolutionary songs; and folk music ensembles and artistic performances representing the culture of people from various parts of Mexico. In addition, the festival provided an occasion for meetings and political discussions between PSUM officials and a variety of foreign delegations. The delegations represented, inter alia, members of friendly governments, "fraternal" parties, editors of Soviet and East European newspapers, and revolutionary organizations from Central and Latin American countries. In a public statement during the festival,

Gómez urged the Mexican people to display solidarity in the struggle to overcome the country's economic crisis, protect its national sovereignty, and resolutely oppose U.S. "imperialism." He also expressed strong support for the embattled people of Nicaragua, who were beset by U.S.-backed insurgents. (*Pravda*, 18, 20 May.)

In July, First Secretary B. K. Pugo of the Latvian Communist Party led a Soviet delegation to Mexico in connection with the expanding ties between the CPSU and the PSUM. The delegation met with Gómez and other PSUM leaders, as well as with leaders of other parties in the coalition of leftist forces that the PSUM helped create. The Soviets and Mexicans exchanged information about the situation in Mexico—particularly the alleged U.S. interference in the country's domestic affairs—and about the struggle for peace and nuclear disarmament. (*Pravda*, 27 July.)

In September, a group of PSUM members from the federal Chamber of Deputies and other elected bodies in Mexico visited the USSR. According to *Pravda* (3 September), the visitors were received at the Supreme Soviet, the CPSU Central Committee organs dealing with party organization work and international relations, and the CPSU committees at the city level in Moscow and Riga. The Soviet Committee for Solidarity with Latin American Peoples and the USSR Writers Union were among the other organizations that held meetings with the Mexican delegation. The visitors voiced special praise for the USSR's moratorium on nuclear weapons testing.

Soviet foreign minister Eduard Shevardnadze paid an official visit to Mexico in October—the first ever by a Soviet official of his rank. Although no specific agreements were announced during Shevardnadze's stay, prospects for increased economic and trade relations appeared bright. Shevardnadze singled out Mexico for praise as a member of the so-called Group of Six (Mexico, Argentina, India, Greece, Sweden, and Tanzania), which was created to press for a ban on nuclear testing and other measures leading toward disarmament.

Marian Leighton
*Defense Intelligence Agency*

# Nicaragua

**Population.** 3,342,000

**Major Marxist-Leninist Organizations.**

- Sandinista Front of National Liberation (Frente Sandinista de Liberación Nacional; FSLN)

**Founded.** 1961

**Membership.** 4,000 (estimated)

*National Directorate.* 9 members: Daniel Ortega Saavedra, Humberto Ortega Saavedra, Víctor Tirado López, Tomás Borge Martínez, Bayardo Arce Castano, Henry Ruiz Hernández, Jaime Wheelock Román, Luís Carrión Cruz, Carlos Núñez Téllez

**Executive Commission.** 5 members: Daniel Ortega Saavedra (coordinator), Bayardo Arce Castano (deputy coordinator), Humberto Ortega Saavedra, Tomás Borge Martínez, Jaime Wheelock Román

**Status.** Ruling party.

**Last Congress.** FSLN Assembly, August 1986

**Last Election.** 4 November 1984; presidential race, 63 percent; Constituent Assembly, 61 out of 96 seats

**Auxiliary Organizations.** Sandinista Defense Committees (Comités de Defense Sandinista; CDS), estimated membership 150,000, led by Leticia Herrera; Sandinista Youth–19 of July (Juventud Sandinista 19 de Julio; JS-19), led by Carlos Carrión; "Luisa Amanda Espinosa" Association of Nicaraguan Women (Asociación de Mujeres Nicaraguenses Luisa Amanda Espinosa; AMNLAE), led by Glenda Monterrey; Sandinista Workers' Central (Central Sandinista de Trabajadores; CST); Farmworkers' Association (Asociación de Trabajadores del Campo; ATC)

**Publications.** *Barricada* (party daily, circulation 110,000); *El Nuevo Diario* (government daily, 60,000); *Nicarahuac* (ideological journal); *Segovia* (army journal); *Bocay* (Interior Ministry monthly); all television stations and the two major radio stations—Radio Sandino and La Voz de Nicaragua—are party-controlled and owned.

- Socialist Party of Nicaragua (Partido Socialista de Nicaragua; PSN), oldest pro-Soviet communist party in the country

**Founded.** 1937 (first official congress, 1944)

**Membership.** Unknown

**General Secretary.** Gustavo Tablada

**Political Commission.** Gustavo Tablada, Domingo Sanchez Salgado, Luis Sanchez Sancho, Adolfo Evertz, José Luis Medina, Juan Gaitán

**Status.** Legal

**Last Congress.** Eighth Plenum, July 1985

**Last Election.** November 1984; less than 2 percent, two seats in Constituent Assembly

**Auxiliary Organizations.** General Confederation of Workers–Independent (CGI)

**Publications.** *El Popular* (weekly)

- Communist Party of Nicaragua (Partido Comunista de Nicaragua; PCN)

**Founded.** 1970, as splinter of PSN

**Membership.** Unknown
**General Secretary.** Eli Altamirano Perez
**Politburo.** 7 members: Eli Altamirano Perez, Ariel Bravo Lorio, Allan Zambrana Zalmeron, Angel Hernández Zerda, Rene Blandón Noguera, Manuel Pérez Estrada, Alejandro Gutiérrez Mayorga
**Status.** Legal
**Last Congress.** Second, June 1986
**Last Election.** November 1984; less than 2 percent, two seats in Constituent Assembly
**Auxiliary Organizations.** Central for Trade Union Action and Unity (CAUS)
**Publications.** *Avance* (weekly, circulation about 20,000)

- Nicaraguan Marxist-Leninist Party (Partido Marxista Leninista de Nicaragua; PMLN), until 1986 called Popular Action Movement–Marxist-Leninist (Movimiento de Acción Popular–Marxista Leninista; MAP-ML)

**Founded.** 1970, as splinter of FSLN
**Membership.** Unknown
**General Secretary.** Isidro Téllez
**Other Party Leaders.** Fernando Malespin, Alejandro Gutiérrez, Carlos Cuadra, Carlos Lucas
**Status.** Legal
**Last Congress.** National Conference, September 1985
**Last Election.** November 1984; less than 2 percent, two seats in Constituent Assembly
**Auxiliary Organizations.** Workers' Front (Frente Obrero; FO)
**Publications.** *Prensa Proletaria* (bi-monthly)

In 1986 the developments in Nicaragua followed patterns already familiar since 1984: continuing civil war against the anti-Marxist insurgents (*contras*); further reduction in the political space available to opposition parties on either the left or right of the ruling FSLN; a more drastic than usual attack against the Catholic Church; and growing association with the Soviet bloc, ideologically as well as militarily and politically. Relations with various Western democracies have deteriorated, and ties to the Nonaligned Movement have failed to provide Nicaragua with its hoped-for prominence, respect, or influence. In particular, relations between the Managua regime and both its neighbors and the United States continued to deteriorate, despite good-will displays by Guatemala and continued reluctance by Costa Rica to engage in an openly anti-Sandinista policy.

**Domestic and Party Affairs.** The FSLN was in a strong position to dominate Nicaraguan politics. This was done in large part through the use of state organs of power, which are controlled by Sandinista leaders. Among the FSLN members who hold top positions in important state institutions are: Daniel Ortega, president of the republic; Humberto Ortega, minister of defense; Borge, minister of the interior; Luís Carrión, deputy minister of the interior; Ruiz, minister of planning and external cooperation; Wheelock, minister of agrarian reform; and Núñez, president of the Constituent Assembly.

Even more than during 1985, domestic politics in 1986 was dominated by the FSLN's successful attempts to cow the existing legal parties into submission. This was done primarily by using the threat of U.S. intervention as an excuse to interpret any dissent as treason, by ruthlessly manipulating the party's majority in the Constituent Assembly, and by intimidating and co-opting members of the non-Sandinista organizations. The main victim of intimidation was the Liberal Independent Party (PLI), the most outspoken opposition party in the assembly. In June, the PLI accused the government of arresting 32 provincial party members (Costa Rica, *Rumbo*, 13–19 June), and in September, one of the vice presidents of the party, Bayardo Guzmán, was arrested and jailed for two weeks without charges (*FBIS*, 18 September). Even more significant were the FSLN attempts to divide the legal opposition, whether by discreetly encouraging parliament members to disobey their groups, as in the case of the Christian Democrat Leoncio Rayo, or by forging temporary alliances with some groups against the others. However, those attempts created near unanimity among the opposition—for example, PCN general secretary Altamirano accused the Sandinistas of a policy of "hostility and division" (ibid., 23 September), and the PLI accused them of manipulation.

The main domestic debate during the year centered on the draft of the new constitution, which was to become law by January 1987, "with or without the participation of other political parties," as Carlos Núñez Téllez has openly stated (ibid., 5 September). Indeed, using its majority in the assembly and tactical alliances with small parties on the far left, the FSLN imposed its will on every issue, prompting the Popular Social-Christian Party leader, Luis Humberto Guzmán, to admit that the oposition had little influence in the parliament. PLI leader Godoy claimed that "the Legislative Assembly was designed for export purposes . . . In practice it has no power and is a mere sham." (*Le Monde*, 24 June.)

Following the FSLN's refusal to open a dialogue with the legal opposition and the September publication of the constitutional draft, most of the opposition parties decided to boycott the constitutional debate. Moreover, a group including the Communist, Socialist, Liberal, Conservative, and Popular Social-Christian parties also demanded that the parties that did not participate in the 1984 elections be part of a new dialogue with the FSLN (*Latin American Weekly Report*, 18 September). By the end of the year, those five parties decided to run as a coalition in the forthcoming 1987 local elections (*NYT*, 8 December).

*Other Marxist-Leninist Parties.* The far-left Workers' Revolutionary Party (Partido Revolucionario de Trabajadores; PRT) and its close ally, the Central American Unification Party (Partido de Unificación Centro Americana; PUCA), are spin-offs of the Revolutionary Party of Central American Workers. Both of the former, minuscule parties operate on the margins of legality; neither was allowed to participate in the 1984 elections, but they are still tolerated. Bonifacio Miranda is the leader of the PRT, and Alejandro Pérez Arevalo heads the PUCA.

*Party Building and Ideology.* The Sandinista Assembly, which is supposed to meet annually, convened in August. Daily FSLN affairs are handled by seven departments: general affairs (led by Rene Núñez), organization (Lea Guido), agitation and propaganda (Carlos Fernando Chamorro), political education (Vanessa Castro Cardenal), international affairs (Julio López), finances (Plutarco Cornejo), and studies of Sandinismo (Flor de María Monterrey).

The slow process of transforming the FSLN into a typical vanguard, Marxist-Leninist party continued during 1986 with a restructuring of the FSLN party leadership committee within the Interior Ministry, which was an important step considering the role and importance of that ministry, the prominence of its leader, Tomás Borge, and the fact that it is the only ministry to include two of the nine National Directorate members (Borge and Luís Carrión). Both Borge and Carrión were dropped from the committee in order to make it more effective, since they have many other functions. The new members are Omar Cabezas (chief of the Political Directorate of the ministry and the committee), Rene Vivas, Doris Tijerino, Lenin Cerna, Manuel Calderón, Walter Ferrety, and Manuel Rivas (*Bocay*, March). It appears that the Interior Ministry's reorganization was seen as a model for the other ministries and FSLN-controlled bodies, such as the JS-19. Yet the Sandinista Assembly's fifth meeting in August concentrated on economic matters rather than on political and party issues.

The public self-description of the FSLN ideology varied, as in previous years, according to the nature of the audience. Speaking at a press conference in the Dominican Republic, Daniel Ortega implicitly denied being a Marxist and described his ideological evolution as follows: "I am a Sandinist. Christian feelings caused me to begin opposing Somoza . . . I believe in a Christ who favors the poor and justice. The first doctrine that I was familiar with was the Christian doctrine. Later I encountered Sandino and, even later, Marx. Marx has also fostered the workers' well-being. So, the two are not incompatible" (*FBIS*, 19 August). In contrast, National Directorate member Víctor Tirado defined the FSLN thinking as "an ideology that sums up the experience and thought of the great ideologists of liberation in Latin America and throughout the world, such as Bolívar, Sandino, Marx, Lenin, Ho Chi Minh, Mao Zedong, Martí, Morazán, and all those who struggled against imperialism and influenced the theory of national liberation and the economic development of the underdeveloped countries" (ibid., 22 October).

Nevertheless, it became even clearer during the year that the FSLN ideology was incompatible with certain existing autonomous institutions and rights in Nicaragua. A spectacular example of this was the 26 June closing of the historically independent and influential newspaper *La Prensa*. The Interior Ministry claimed, among other accusations, that the newspaper "has not at any time met its social, ethical, or professional responsibilities" and that it had been "stepping up its level of provocation and disinformation" (*Barricada*, 27 June). Soon thereafter, Sandinista mobs attacked *La Prensa's* building and workers, and President Ortega called for a 30-year jail sentence for the newspaper's owner, former postrevolutionary junta member Violetta Chamorro.

Another frontal attack on old Nicaraguan institutions came with the sharpening of the FSLN–Catholic Church clash. On 1 January, the Church's Radio Católica was closed down by the Interior Ministry; on 28 June, the spokesman for the archdiocese of Managua, Reverend Bismarck Carballo, was expelled; and on 4 July, the vice president of the Nicaraguan Bishops' Conference, Bishop Pablo Antonio Vega of Juigalpa, was forced to leave for Honduras. The latter action brought a sharp rebuke from Pope John Paul II, who described it as belonging to "the dark ages" (*NYT*, 6 July). The fact that, only a few months before, Borge himself had described Vega as having "a more realistic and open attitude, with great frankness and clarity of positions" (*Barricada Internacional*, 16 January), clearly demonstrates that the action was a warning to the Church as a whole, rather than a specific discontent with the Juigalpa bishop. In any case, these acts against the Church alienated even some hitherto sympathetic groups (such as the U.S. Catholic bishops) from the Managua regime, and they definitively isolated the small number of Marxist priests and former priests in Nicaragua who have enthusiastically supported the anti-Catholic crackdown. Since both Carballo and Vega were Nicaraguan-born, their expulsions represented a step farther than the previous expulsions of foreign-born priests.

The attacks against the media and the Church were part of a general worsening of the human rights situation in Nicaragua, a situation generally blamed by the government on the United States. In April, Daniel Ortega admitted that there may be 2,700 political prisoners in Nicaragua (*Der Spiegel*, 28 April) and that there were no more than 300 persons "murdered or missing." In July, Borge claimed that there were 8,523 prisoners in Nicaragua, of which 4,014 were common criminals and the rest *contras*, Somocistas, or Sandinist soldiers (*FBIS*, 24 July). In July, Ortega claimed that the 3,500 political prisoners were only *contras* and Somoza National Guard members (*Rumbo*, 25–31 July). Finally, in October, the government admitted that Interior Ministry operatives were involved in torturing prisoners (*Barricada*, 3 October). This admission came after the International League for Human Rights described torture and mistreatment of prisoners in Nicaragua (*NYT*, 13 July) and Ortega denied the existence of torture (ibid., 24 August).

**The Economy.** Throughout 1986, the economy continued to deteriorate, which the regime blamed on the United States and internal enemies in the private sector. In fact, one of the reasons for the deterioration was the politicization of the economy; as Agriculture Minister Wheelock put it, the FSLN "cannot look at the problem simply from the production standpoint; we must also consider the unjust distribution" (*Barricada*, 4 March). As a result, the situation in the country reached the point where half of the enterprises were state-owned and the other half did "everything the government tells us to do," according to the head of the Private Sector Council (COSEP) (San José, *La Nacion*, 1 February). Some indications of the stress in the economy were provided by the simple fact that, during 1985 alone, the population of Managua grew by just 6 percent, yet the government admitted being unable to cope with the influx (*JPRS-LAM*, 19 June).

The inflation rate was widely estimated at over 300 percent (*LAT*, 7 July). The average monthly salary was between 12,000 and 27,000 córdobas (Madrid, *Epoca*, 16 May), while the cost of Soviet-bloc products was officially established at such prices as 24,000 córdobas for a pair of sport shoes, 60,000 for a radio, and 9,900 for a blanket (*La Prensa*, 31 March). A head of cabbage cost as much as 500 córdobas, and one pound of fish cost 1,000 (ibid.). In early 1986 the exchange rate of the córdoba to the dollar, officially 70 to 1 or 1,200 to 1 on the parallel market, had reached 2,000 to 1 on the flourishing black market (ibid.). The gross national product per capita had shrunk to less than $500, half the 1979 level (*Forbes*, 25 August).

The government's solution to this situation was to trim public investment to some extent, organize a new census for ration-cards receivers, and, as Ortega claimed, "actually impose heavy taxes" on the private sector (*Barricada*, 25 June). At the same time, and as a result of the general conditions prevailing in the country, police chief Doris Tijerino admitted in July that one crime was committed in Managua every hour, with 50 percent of all crimes being committed in the capital, as a result of "immigration, alcoholism, war-provoked traumas, social inadequacies, and the economic crisis" (*JPRS-Latin America*, 25 July).

*The Army.* According to the new Constitution to be implemented in 1987, the president of the republic is the commander in chief of the armed forces (the Sandinista People's Army [EPS]), against the almost unanimous opposition from all other parties. On 1 July, the last memories of the former guerrilla force that defeated Somoza were erased with the presidential decree establishing formal ranks in the EPS; the first, that of army general, went to the president's brother and defense minister, Humberto Ortega. The next day Humberto Ortega promoted Colonel Joaquin Cuadra, the EPS chief of staff, to major general, and brigade commanders Hugo Torres, Julio Ramos, and Leopoldo Rivas to the rank of colonels. (*Barricada*, 24 August.) The fact that Borge and other Interior Ministry cadres were not promoted was widely seen as a further weakening of Borge's position and strengthening of the Ortega brothers' powers. Nonetheless, despite intensive politicization, the EPS recruits under the national draft still demonstrated high levels of desertion and inability to adapt to civil life once demobilized (*NYT*, 12 September).

The EPS capabilities were enhanced during the year by the delivery of additional SAM-14 (GREMLIN) Soviet-made antiaircraft missiles and as many as fifteen new Soviet-made MI-17 helicopters (ibid., 10 July). Progress was also made toward imitating Cuba's military structure with the formation of Irregular Warfare Battalions (BLI) and Frontier Guard Troops (TGF); the latter were under Interior Ministry control, probably as a concession to Borge, who also controlled the 2,000-strong Pablo Ubeda Battalion, the elite internal security force (*Epoca*, 12 May). While expanding and strengthening its potential, the EPS also remained the most ideologically outspoken organization in Nicaragua. Hugo Torres claimed that "There will not be enough trees or lampposts in Nicaragua from which to hang the [U.S.] Marines if they dare enter our country" (*FBIS*, 4 August).

One little-noticed development regarding the EPS that was important for the conduct of the civil war was the open use of foreign volunteers, who are formally allowed to carry weapons, as were the Swiss Ivan Leyvraz and Frenchman Joel Fieux, both killed by the insurgents (*WP*, 21 August). This was an important factor, considering that there were over two thousand "internationalists" of Western origin in Nicaragua.

The ongoing civil war continued unabated during the year, with both sides making extravagant claims. The new aspect of the war was the EPS shift toward a strategy of denying the insurgents their previous freedom of moving into Nicaragua at any time. This new strategy was manifested in Nicaraguan army attacks against the *contras* rear bases in Honduras, some of which were major incursions, and extensive deployment of mines along the Honduran border. The *contras* used land mines as well, with the intention of denying BLI patrols the ability to engage in long-range reconnaissance. The majority of victims were civilians, and both sides blamed each other for the deaths of noncombatants.

*The contras.* On the insurgents' side, the most important developments in 1986 were the apparent steps toward greater unity, both within the United Nicaraguan Opposition (UNO) and between it and the other armed anti-Sandinista groups. The UNO's three main leaders managed to reach some compromise in dividing their influence and control, but the two who control few or no fighters, Alfonso Robelo and Arturo Cruz, had to accept the formation of a military council led by the main ally of the third director, Adolfo Calero. U.S. insistence on unity among the insurgents was given more weight by the U.S. congressional decision to allocate $100 million in mostly military aid. Significant steps were then taken to coordinate the operations of the Nicaraguan Democratic Force (FDN), the UNO's main military branch, with those of the Indians of the Atlantic Coast—the largest of which is still KISAN—and the southern fighters previously led by Edén Pastora. The main institutional body established in this respect was the Military Commission, which included the leaders of the three main fighting forces: Enrique Bermúdez of the FDN, Adan Artole of KISAN, and Fernando "El Negro" Chamorro of the UNO–Southern Front (*FBIS*, 30 May). Such steps did not, however, prevent fierce struggles for supremacy among all three military organizations. Thus, KISAN strengthened its supremacy over the Indian and Creole fighters by further weakening rival claims from the remnants of Steadman Fagoth's supporters and marginalizing the declining force of Brooklyn Rivera (*WP*, 24 August; *LAT*, 30 August). Despite such internecine fights, the number of Indian fighters joining the armed opposition continued to grow during the year. Differences within UNO reemerged at the end of the year in the wake of the Iran-Contra scandal.

One significant long-term development within

the insurgency was the final departure from the scene of the most consistent and destructive element preventing coordination, if not unity among the insurgent forces: Edén Pastora Gómez. In May, six of Pastora's military commanders—unhappy with his style, incompetence, and inability to obtain military and financial support—decided to join the UNO forces (*NYT*, 11 May). On 16 May, Pastora and some fifty of his followers gave up the struggle and asked for political asylum in Costa Rica; "We withdraw from the armed struggle because we believe that there is no possibility of achieving military victory," said Pastora (*FBIS*, 19 May). Pastora's erstwhile allies in the Southern Opposition Bloc (BOS) clearly did not miss his presence; in June, they signed a pact of cooperation with the UNO providing for the two organizations' members to fight "together but not side-by-side" (*La Nacion*, 28 June; *FBIS*, 20 August). The agreement was signed by Calero, Cruz, and Robelo for the UNO and by Alfredo Cesar, Francisco Fiallo, Alvaro Jerez, Bayardo Lopez, and Adolfo Chamorro for the BOS. With these accords, the tenuous unity of the insurgents was completed and the competition for U.S. funds was on; the BOS, for example, was slated for $5 million. By the end of the year, despite the *contras*' relative inactivity due to retraining in the United States and resupply problems, the war was still continuing on the Honduran and Costa Rican borders and, according to both sides, in the departments of Jinotega, Matagalpa, Zelaya, Nueva Segovia, Madriz, Boaco, Chontales, Chinandega, Esteli, and Rio San Juan. The incoming deliveries of U.S. military aid and the expected arrival of the first U.S.-trained officers at the beginning of 1987, as well as Honduran pressures to move the insurgents into Nicaragua, indicate that a major flare-up in the fighting may occur in the first months of 1987.

**International Views and Contacts.** The general orientation of the Managua regime can be best gauged from its foreign policy, which was characterized during the year by close alignment to the Soviet bloc and radical Third World regimes, declining ties to Western Europe and consistent hostility to the United States, and generally uncooperative attitudes toward other Central American nations.

An attempt was made to maintain normal relations and receive some aid from China; Daniel Ortega visited Beijing in September, at which point the Chinese promised a $20 million aid package,

mostly of food (*NYT*, 15 September; *FBIS-China*, 17 September). The most active and frequent exchanges, however, took place between Managua and the Soviet bloc and radical Third World states. Such ties varied from Henry Ruiz's 29 July–2 August visit to Kampuchea, Laos, and Vietnam, to far more extensive and important trips by other National Directorate members to Soviet bloc states. The most important were visits to the USSR, such as that of Bayardo Arce to the Twenty-seventh Congress of the Communist Party of the Soviet Union (CPSU) in March, where he compared the Bolshevik civil war with the current war in Nicaragua, supported every Soviet foreign policy and arms control initiative, and expressed "gratitude to the Soviet people, the CPSU, and the Soviet government for their effective solidarity and cooperation" with the FSLN (*FBIS-Soviet Union*, 19 March). On 6 November, an FSLN-CPSU cooperation agreement for 1986–1987 was signed in Managua by Arce and CPSU Central Committee member V. M. Kamentsev (*Pravda*, 9 November). Perhaps even more important was Managua's admission that oil by-products imports would increase in 1986 by 13 percent (*El Nuevo Diario*, 23 April), but that supplies "will be met by the Soviet Union" (ibid.).

In March, Luís Carrión visited Czechoslovakia and was received by Gustáv Husák; in August, according to Czechoslovak ambassador Gustáv Stopka, that country had granted $250 million in credits and grants to Nicaragua (*FBIS*, 24 August). However, that figure differed from the one given by Czech chargé d'affaires Vlastimil Kalecki, who had claimed that the grants given by Czechoslovakia in 1980–1986 totaled just $100 million, mostly in shoe factories, trucks and tractors, textiles, and advice (ibid., 28 July). In June, Leticia Herrera visited Hungary for an exchange of experiences, and in November, as part of his worldwide trip, Daniel Ortega also traveled to Prague. During August and September, Ortega visited Zimbabwe (for the Nonaligned Movement summit), Ghana, the Congo, Burkina Fasso, North Korea, and East Germany.

During the Nonaligned Movement summit in Harare, Ortega tried to become the next host, and chairman, of the movement with a speech exclusively directed against the United States. He did not succeed, despite close ties between Nicaragua and the most radical movement members, including Libya, Iran, Cuba, and Vietnam.

Relations with the United States continued to deteriorate, particularly following the U.S. congressional vote for $100 million in military and other aid to the *contras*, the capture of U.S. citizen Eugene Hasenfus as he was delivering arms to the insurgents, and the capture of another American citizen, Daniel Hall, while he was allegedly spying for the insurgents. Hasenfus, after being sentenced to 30 years in jail, was pardoned by Daniel Ortega just before Christmas, and Hall was released in January 1987.

Relations with the rest of Central America were clouded by the debates of the Central American governments at the Esquipulas summit, by incursions into Honduras, by threats against Costa Rica, and by Honduran and Salvadoran claims that Nicaragua was sponsoring guerrillas in their countries.

Michael Radu
*Foreign Policy Research Institute, Philadelphia*

# Panama

**Population.** 2,227,000
**Party.** People's Party (Partido del Pueblo; PDP)
**Founded.** 1930 (PDP, 1943)
**Membership.** 750 (estimated)
**General Secretary.** Rubén Darío Sousa (or Souza)
**Politburo.** Includes César Agusto De Leon Espinosa, Miguel Antonio Porcella Peña, Anastacio E. Rodríguez, Clito Manuel Souza Batista, Luther Thomas (international secretary), Felix Dixon, Darío González Pittí
**Central Committee.** 26 members
**Status.** Legal
**Last Congress.** Eighth, 24–26 January 1986
**Last Election.** 1984, less than 3 percent, no representatives
**Auxiliary Organizations.** Panama Peace Committee, Committee for the Defense of Sovereignty and Peace, People's Party Youth, National Center of Workers of Panama (Central Nacional de Trabajadores de Panamá; CNTP), Union of Journalists of Panama, Federation of Panamanian Students (Federación Estudiantil de Panamá; FEP), National Union of Democratic Women
**Publications.** *Unidad* (weekly), C. Changmarín, director

For the PDP, the major event of 1986 occurred in January with the holding of its Eighth National Congress, the first since February 1980. The congress institutionalized a long-term program for nationwide party expansion and a broad front alliance strategy in the wake of a negligible showing in the 1984 national election. Moreover, careful attention was paid to the traditionally weak PDP and its congress by the Communist Party of the Soviet Union (CPSU); communist party delegations from the Far and Middle East, Latin America, and the Eastern bloc participated; and as an invited observer, the Democratic Revolutionary Party (Partido Revolucionario Democrático; PRD)—the political front and ruling instrument of the Panamanian Defense Forces—attended.

The congress and subsequent party activities during the year took place in a domestic context of further militarization of government institutions and mounting tension between the ruling sector and an angry center-right opposition representing approximately half the country. In an increasingly divisive atmosphere, government demands for national unity against alleged U.S. attempts to abrogate the 1978 Canal treaties clashed with opposition charges of government repression and calls for a complete return to representative democracy. President Eric Arturo Delvalle, who was installed by the Defense Forces in 1985 after the removal of Nicolás Ardito Barletta, managed to last the year but had marginal impact on the country's political developments.

Portions of the reshaped PDP program revealed that efforts would continue to secure the party's place on the evolving political scene by accenting positions shared with the military-dominated government, in particular on the issue of the Canal and the escalating tension in U.S.-Panama relations. Greater emphasis was also clearly placed on forming a united front with non-Marxist groups, nationalist sectors of the military, and other leftist organizations in order to press for a return to the path of the late General Omar Torrijos Herrera from which the PDP claimed Panama had strayed. Through this dual strategy, the party sought in 1986 to begin elevating its status from longtime bit player to a more effective instrument of Soviet influence and possible power broker in the event of escalating national polarization and/or a power shift within the restive Defense Forces. The forces have been controlled since 1983 by the corrupt and opportunistic General Manuel Antonio Noriega.

**The Eighth National Congress.** Following the PDP's failure in the May 1984 elections to garner the 3 percent of the vote required for representation in the National Assembly, which had been a setback for the party following its legalization in 1981, it announced that a National Congress would be held in 1985. After a CPSU delegation led by Karen Brutents, deputy chief of the CPSU Central Committee International Department, met with the PDP leadership in Panama in December 1984, preparations began (TASS, 5 December 1984; *FBIS*, 6 December 1984). Subsequently, the congress was confirmed for 24–26 January 1986.

The PDP affirmed that over 300 representatives from all the country's provinces assembled in Panama City under the motto, "For a party capable of defeating imperialism and the oligarchy." Present "for the first time in the history of the PDP" were delegates from the communist parties of the German Democratic Republic, Costa Rica, Cuba, Guyana, Jamaica, Colombia, the Dominican Republic, Venezuela, Lebanon, the Soviet Union, Palestine, Japan, and the FSLN [Sandinista Front of National Liberation] of Nicaragua. (*FBIS*, 31 January; *WMR*, July.)

The PDP Central Committee report presented to the congress by longtime general secretary Rubén Darío Sousa, and the unanimously adopted resolution of approval, asserted that the 1978 Canal treaties "formally eliminated the U.S. colonial enclave in Panama . . . opening a new phase in the democratic national liberation revolution in this country." However, following the death of Torrijos, there had emerged "a tendency toward conciliation and compromise with imperialism" that would allow "U.S. imperialist policy to make sure that our country does not wrest itself free of imperialist domination once the Panama Canal is decolonized." (*Unidad*, 29 January–4 February.)

In order to ensure the completion of the national liberation phase, the PDP advocated "a new realignment of forces under the Torrijist banner" (*IB*, June). The party declared that it was "going to work for the formation of a Democratic National Liberation Front, which presupposes the achievement of strategic mutual understanding between military men loyal to Torrijism and their political organization, the Democratic Revolutionary Party, on the one hand, and the PDP and the rest of the left parties and working people's organizations on the other" (*WMR*, July).

In another published article, Sousa reiterated that "The idea of broad alliances, advanced by Lenin and tested in the course of socialist construction, is of special significance to us at this stage and serves as a guide in our struggle for advanced democracy" (*WMR*, February). Although no alliance was forged during the course of 1986, the PDP was pleased that the many of the parties targeted for the proposed front, particularly the PRD, accepted invitations to send delegates to the final session of the congress. Joining the PRD, which was also present for the opening session, were the Panameñista Party (PP) and the Popular Broad Front Party (FRAMPO)—both members of the Democratic National Union (UNADE), the five-party government coalition led by the PRD—as well as the leftist Socialist Workers' Party (PST) and the Trotskyist Workers' Revolutionary Party (PRT). (*Critica*, 28 January; *FBIS*, 31 January.)

Many points of the PDP program, especially the raising of the mantle of Torrijos and the call to join in guaranteeing "his nonaligned course" against "U.S. neocolonialism," seemed geared to impressing the PRD and other non-Marxists in attendance. During 1986, the PRD used similar rhetoric as a new member of the Socialist International and at the Nonaligned Movement meeting in Zimbabwe in September, which reflected the more leftist positions of the new PRD leadership that had emerged at the end of 1985 (*Latin American Weekly Report* [*LAWR*], 10 January; *FBIS*, 26 August). Further, the PDP played down Marxist-Leninist rhetoric in favor of avid promotion of "the consistent peace policy of the socialist community led by the Soviet Union." The proposal for complete nuclear disarmament by the year 2000 made on 15 January by Soviet leader Mikhail Gorbachev was hailed and the U.S. Strategic Defense Initiative (SDI) was condemned. Marxism-Leninism was stressed only as the organizational principle upon which the PDP would turn itself into a "mass party" in order to fulfill its "vanguard role" in the completion of national liberation. (*IB*, June.)

Regarding the military, the PDP declared that "Our party has invariably held that in Latin America the army must side with the people." It shrewdly stressed that it would continue to "cooperate with the patriotic officers" and called upon them "to consolidate the popular and liberationist nature" of their organization and form a national army to defend the country's interests and guarantee U.S. withdrawal from the Canal. (*Unidad*, 29 January–4 February; *WMR*, July.) In a similarly careful statement during an interview prior to the congress, Sousa acknowledged that "General Noriega has experienced leadership problems" but suggested that they were related to U.S. efforts "to undermine the leadership of Torrijist officers by applying pressure on them in order to infiltrate the Defense Forces" (*JPRS*, 25 February).

The congress endorsed a novel position on Panama's foreign debt, which in 1986 approached $4 billion. The PDP stated that "Loans are one of the instruments used by imperialism for dominating and exploiting the peoples of developing countries." However, it concluded that "Panama must uphold its international credit but not by submitting to the dictates of the U.S. administration, the IMF [International Monetary Fund], the IDB [Inter-American Development Bank], or other transnational banking agencies." Therefore, "What must be repaid is only that part of the debt which the Torrijos government used for the real development of the country." The PDP denied that its position was at odds with Fidel Castro's call for a complete debt moratorium and said it would support all developing countries against international lending institutions. (*WMR*, July.)

During the congress, it was announced that Sousa had been unanimously re-elected and that there had been changes made in the composition of the Central Committee in accord with the new National Plan of Organization. The Central Committee resolution passed by the congress stated that "We need to turn the PDP into a large party, a Marxist-Leninist vanguard capable of exerting influence on the policymaking process" and that "For the PDP to become a mass party necessitates a systematic retraining of current, and training hundreds of new, party workers, as well as conscious and consistent recruiting of new members in critical strategic areas, primarily among the working class and the peasantry." The addition of banana worker Darío González Pittí to the Politburo seemed to reflect the party's aspiration to expand popular support beyond traditional university strongholds. (*Unidad*, 29 January–4 February.)

Soviet news agency TASS reports on the congress appeared daily in *Pravda* (25, 26, 27, 28 January), beginning with the arrival of the CPSU delegation led by Mikhail A. Ponomarev, member of the CPSU Central Committee and deputy chairman of the Central Committee Party Control Committee. During the proceedings, the CPSU Central Committee in Moscow sent a lengthy message of "fraternal greetings" to the congress, which was published in full in *Pravda*. It is significant that nearly half the message was reserved for promoting "Soviet peace-loving initiatives," in particular the Gorbachev disarmament proposal, and applauding the PDP's support for the measure at the congress. (*Pravda*, 26 January.)

**Domestic Affairs.** In March, President Delvalle succeeded in forcing through the National Assembly three new economic laws—regarding labor, both industrial and agricultural—which were similar to those proposed by his predecessor the year before to comply with IMF and World Bank requirements. General Noriega supplied key support, unlike in 1985, for the measures designed to deal with Panama's $3.8 billion national debt.

While criticizing the new laws generally as "measures imposed on the backs of the people" (*Unidad*, 22–28 January), the PDP focused its efforts on attacking the restrictions of the new labor law. The party called for the unity of all workers against "this scheme of imperialism and the oligarchy," and the PDP-controlled CNTP enthusiastically participated in the mass demonstrations sponsored by the National Council of Workers Organizations (Consejo Nacional de Trabajadores Organizados; CONATO), the largest Panamanian union federation. (*Unidad*, 22–28 January; *LAWR*, 21 March.) The PDP again supported CONATO demonstrations in October to protest the arrival in Panama of representatives of the IMF and World Bank.

It was in the context of escalating tension in U.S. Panamanian relations, however, that the PDP was able to take positions more in line with the government, though support for the Noriega-Delvalle administration was tacit at best. Prior to the summer of 1985, relations between the two countries had been cordial. But with the removal of Barletta in September, the United States had expressed its displeasure by reducing economic aid. Noriega and Delvalle then accused the U.S. Department of State, U.S. Senator Jesse Helms, and the two major Panamanian opposition parties—the Authentic Panameñista Party (PPA) and the Christian Democrats (PDC)—of collusion in a plot to eliminate the Torrijista state apparatus and undermine the Canal treaties.

The White House became increasingly concerned about Panama's ability to maintain and defend the Canal after the year 2000, its strength as a strategic ally against the spread of revolution in Central America, and its role in international drug trafficking. In December 1985, the U.S. government had appealed directly to General Noriega for a reorientation of Panamanian policy, but with little effect (*Miami Herald*, 14 June). In June 1986, when a series of scathing articles on Noriega's activities, written by Seymour Hersh and leaning heavily on official sources, appeared in the *New York Times*, it appeared that the U.S. had opted for a more indirect approach.

The articles cited Noriega's long-term involvement in narcotics trafficking, most recently in the money-laundering side of the business, and evidence of Defense Forces cooperation with Cuba in assisting Latin American guerrilla organizations. They also highlighted Noriega's history of supplying the Cubans with intelligence information and Panama's involvement in Cuba's efforts to circumvent the U.S. trade embargo through Panamanian front companies. Finally, evidence was cited directly linking Noriega to the fixing of the 1984 presidential elections and the 1985 murder of opposition figure Hugo Spadafora. (*NYT*, 12, 13, 22 June.)

The *Times* series served to further delineate the division in Panama's domestic political landscape. While the major opposition parties treated the articles as justification for their position and called on Noriega to resign, the PRD-led government coalition denounced the news stories as a U.S.-sponsored campaign of lies against Panama, rallied around the Defense Forces, and accused the opposition parties of treason. Noriega denied the charges but appeared shaken.

The PDP condemned the United States and the opposition, stating, "This is open Yankee intervention in our internal affairs. The reaction of the oligarchy, the imperialists' docile peons, has been to put two and two together in order to attain power aboard the spacecraft of the *Times*'s accusations and the other strategems planned by Reagan's agents." It is significant that the PDP did not address the veracity of the accusations against Noriega, but instead called on the military "to inform the people of their position: either they take up the patriotic Torrijista flag; defend popular achievements; stop IMF interventions; refuse to accept new antipopular adjustments; revise antiworker, anticonstitutional Law No. 1; [and] defend national sovereignty, true nonalignment, and peace, or they surrender to the treacherous attacks from the darkest forces of imperialism and the internal reaction." (*Matutino*, 14 June; *FBIS*, 16 June.)

Sousa later reiterated the PDP position that the *Times* articles were part of a plan by the United States to maintain domination over Panama beyond the year 2000, and then he asserted that, "Should they fail through political means, the Americans will use terrorism to physically eliminate the Defense Forces' commander in chief" (*Matutino*, 24 June; *FBIS*, 25 June).

The following autumn, possibly in an attempt to appease the United States, Noriega hosted a meeting in Panama of military chiefs from the Central American Defense Council (CONDECA) countries. Established in 1963 with U.S. assistance for the region's collective security, CONDECA included all the Central American countries except

Costa Rica, which had abolished its military in 1948. The organization had been inactive since the overthrow of Somoza in Nicaragua in 1979. At the meeting called by Noriega, El Salvador, Honduras, and Guatemala were represented, but not Nicaragua. Noriega asserted that CONDECA was necessary for guaranteeing the Contadora process for resolving Central American conflict.

Disfavor over the initiative was expressed on both sides of the political fence in Panama, but for an assortment of reasons. PRD leaders warned that reactivating CONDECA "would give the nefarious image that the military prevails over Panamanian society," while the major opposition parties asserted that Noriega's behavior proved exactly that. The PDP, meanwhile, declared that the measure was a U.S. effort "to create mechanisms for intervening in Nicaragua," and it warned that the Panamanian military was in danger of succumbing to "imperialist domination." (*La Prensa*, 25 November; *FBIS*, 26 November.)

During the last two months of 1986, cracks began to appear in the Noriega-Delvalle administration. The PDP kept its distance, seemingly awaiting the outcome of the internal disturbance. In mid-November, Delvalle was forced by the PRD to carry out his first cabinet reshuffle, despite his insistence that it was unnecessary. The changes dictated by the PRD seemed to reflect the consolidation of power of the left wing within the party. That consolidation, and differences over CONDECA and other issues, had apparently caused a rift between the PRD and the military, but it is doubtful the PRD could have bullied Delvalle without at least Noriega's tacit approval. (*Central America Report*, 28 November; *LAWR*, 4 December.)

In December, opposition newspaper *La Prensa* reported that, according to sources within the Defense Forces, mid-level officers had plotted "to overthrow the government of President Delvalle and end the democratic system which is unworkable and very costly," but had been restrained by Noriega (*La Prensa*, 13 December; *FBIS*, 15 December). Although the opposition clearly had an interest in abetting unrest within the ruling sectors, it was nonetheless true that young officers in the Defense Forces had long been unhappy over the general's manipulation of the promotions system and retention of close associates beyond the retirement age.

At the end of 1986, Delvalle nonetheless remained in place, although his administrative authority had been weakened by the PRD and his job

was no less dependent on Noriega. The general, in turn, was working overtime to ensure the continued success of his international and domestic balancing act.

**International Views and Activities.** A PDP delegation attended the Third Congress of the Cuban Communist Party in Havana the first week in February. The delegation then traveled to Managua for the 11–12 February "Continental Meeting in Solidarity with the Sandinista Revolution," which was attended by communist parties, revolutionary political-military organizations, and non-Marxist political parties from 33 Latin American and Caribbean countries. (Havana Radio Reloj, 8 February; *FBIS*, 11 February.)

At the end of February, a PDP delegation attended the Twenty-seventh Congress of the CPSU in Moscow. Afterward, Felix Dixon represented the PDP at a meeting in Prague of approximately 30 communist parties from around the world to consider the program guidelines laid down by the CPSU congress and the "Soviet peace program and the efforts of the communists to avert the nuclear threat and ensure disarmament." The participants stressed the objective "to strengthen the coalition of peace and intelligence uniting all who are opposed to the nuclear threat." Regarding Latin America, it was affirmed that "the Communist Party of Cuba and other fraternal parties in the region are trying to raise the level of interaction and cooperation between various socio-political forces, in the first place with Social Democrats and Christians." (*WMR*, July.) It was further noted that PDP representative Dixon agreed with the delegates from Turkey and Egypt that "The struggle of the peoples in their countries for the removal of the U.S. military bases . . . is a concrete manifestation of the concurring goals of the antiwar and national liberation movements" (*WMR*, October).

Through the FEP, the PDP participated in October in the Second Cuban-Panamanian Youth Meeting held in Panama City. Following a celebration of the 43rd anniversary of the FEP, the participants issued a document condemning U.S. policy in Central America and advocating disarmament and peace. (Havana International Service, 29 October; *FBIS*, 30 October.)

In November, Sousa led a PDP delegation to the celebration in Managua of the 25th anniversary of the FSLN. The FSLN affirmed that non-Marxist leaders joined 45 general secretaries of communist parties from around the world for the gathering. (Miami, *Diario Las Americas*, 6 November.)

*Soviet Contacts*. Despite an absence of formal diplomatic or trade relations, the Soviet Union in 1986 displayed increasing interest in Panama. In February, a Soviet delegation headed by Vladimir Kassimirov, chief of the First Latin American Countries Department of the Soviet Foreign Ministry, arrived in Panama to explain to government officials the recent Gorbachev proposal for nuclear disarmament by the year 2000 and to warn that the U.S. SDI program "entails serious risks for mankind." The delegation also visited officials in Venezuela, Colombia, and Mexico, which are the other three Contadora-group countries, as well as in Costa Rica. (*FBIS*, 12 February.)

In May, Viktor Vol'skii, director of the Soviet Institute of Latin America, paid a visit to Panama University rector Ceferino Sánchez and gave media interviews and lectures on Soviet–Latin American relations and nuclear disarmament (*Matutino*, 24 May; *FBIS*, 5 June). In December, Nikolai Kalmykov, director of the Soviet Institute of Universal History, and Valentin Kuchin, director of the Soviet Committee for the Defense of Peace, visited Panama as guests of the PDP-controlled Panamanian Committee for the Defense of Sovereignty and Peace; they met with union, peasant, and academic groups (*Critica*, 11 December; *FBIS*, 12 December).

In October, Karen Brutents, deputy chief of the Central Committee International Department, headed a CPSU delegation to Panama for the second time in two years for meetings with the PDP leadership and a number of party organizations. *Pravda* reported on 6 October that "The Panama-nian comrades declared complete support for the Soviet peace initiatives based on new political thinking and corresponding with the realities of the nuclear and space age." Significantly, it further reported that the delegation also met with the leadership of the PRD.

In November, opposition newspaper *Extra* reported that, according to foreign ministry sources, the Panamanian government was seeking to have Soviet leader Gorbachev extend a scheduled service stop in Panama to an official state visit during his 1987 Latin American tour (*Extra*, 4 November; *FBIS*, 5 November). Government officials denied the story.

A few weeks later, *Extra* reported that, again according to government sources, Soviet airline Aeroflot had been granted permission to begin operations in Panama in 1987 as a prelude to establishing diplomatic and trade relations between the two countries (*Extra*, 20 November). The Soviet Union had pressed for diplomatic relations and an Aeroflot agreement with Panama during the 1970s, but Torrijos had been reluctant, fearing a negative effect on his position in the Canal negotiations. In December, Civil Aeronautics director Major Pascual González confirmed that a Soviet application had been accepted, although it had not yet been determined when Aeroflot would begin operating (Televisora Nacional, 3 December; *FBIS*, 4 December). Opposition newspaper *El Siglo* subsequently revealed that a PRD delegation had traveled to Moscow a week before the official announcement (*El Siglo*, 10 December; *FBIS*, 12 December). The PRD denied that there was a connection.

Douglas W. Payne
*Freedom House, New York*

# Paraguay

**Population.** 4,119,000
**Party.** Paraguayan Communist Party (Partido Comunista del Paraguay; PCP)
**Founded.** 1928
**Membership.** 4,000 (estimated)
**General Secretary.** Julio Rojas (acting); Antonio Maidana (official) is under arrest.
**Status.** Illegal
**Last Congress.** Third, 10 April 1971
**Last Election.** N/a
**Auxiliary Organizations.** No data
**Publications.** *Adelante* (underground weekly)

"A doddering regime in agony," was how Rogelio González, a Central Committee member of the PCP, described the dictatorship of General Alfredo Stroessner in his August article for the *World Marxist Review*. There was evidence to support his view. Stroessner and General Augusto Pinochet of Chile were the only military rulers left in southern South America. The international environment was no longer friendly; neighboring governments considered Stroessner something of a pariah, and more distant, but equally important, countries such as West Germany and the United States were treating him with increasing coolness. President Reagan promised to use U.S. influence to encourage democratization in Paraguay, and, in furtherance of this policy, U.S. ambassador Clyde Taylor met with various opposition leaders and even took part in a 24 April protest rally by striking doctors and hospital workers. (*Latin American Weekly Report* [*LAWR*], 9 May.)

Taylor was also active in supporting a "national dialogue" being mediated by the Roman Catholic hierarchy, which aimed at bringing together a broad spectrum of groups to search for a peaceful transition to democracy. In each of his meetings with these groups, Taylor expressed his country's commitment to promoting democracy, but pointed out that initiatives for reform had to come from within

Paraguay. However, he promised U.S. aid for groups that worked toward bringing about democracy. The PCP dismissed all such efforts as being concerned only with cosmetic changes, just as in Haiti the fall of Jean-Claude Duvalier had left his generals still holding onto power. (USSR, *International Affairs: Latin America and the Caribbean*, 15 May.)

The Authentic Radical Liberal Party (PLRA) supported the strike by doctors and hospital workers, which was characterized by large public demonstrations and clashes with the police. In June, the PLRA's exiled leader, Domingo Laíno, was badly beaten at the Asunción airport while he was trying to re-enter the country. Besides these incidents, university students added to the regime's problems with strikes and marches in April; peasants in the department of Caaguazú staged several demonstrations for land reform during the year; and the opposition Workers' Inter-Union Movement (Movimiento Intersindical de Trabajadores) staged a May Day protest rally that was broken up by the police.

The regime was plagued by inflation, unemployment, growing foreign indebtedness, and declining exports. There were also scandals, the most serious being the embezzlement of approximately $100 million by top officials at the Central Bank. Nevertheless, the government lashed back at its critics, accusing Taylor of interfering in local politics and dismissing all the agitation as being inspired by the communists.

The PCP remained quite isolated, however. The National Accord parties continued to keep it at arm's length, and González admitted that the PCP was weak and cut off from the masses; the situation was attributed to former leader Oscar Creydt, who was accused of injecting "opportunistic attitudes" and "sectarianism" into the apparatus. According to González, the PCP has been undergoing self-criticism to combat "liberalism, . . . passiveness, spinelessness, and apathy . . . indiscipline, breaches of party secrets, cliqueishness and rumor-mongering," which are "disorders that have plagued a sizeable section of the party organism and have been caused mainly by the long years of struggle in exile, deep underground, ceaseless persecution, and inadequate ideological training" (*WMR*, August).

The remainder of Paraguay's opposition to Stroessner was hardly better off, and for similar reasons. Consequently, no one was predicting the regime's imminent downfall. Stroessner's regime is not a simple military dictatorship, like Pinochet's; a political party is in power. It is perhaps in recognition of this important fact that Taylor told a group of political dissidents that the democratization of their party was the key to a peaceful political transition. (*LAWR*, 9 May.)

Paul H. Lewis
*Tulane University*

# Peru

**Population.** 20,207,000
**Party.** Peruvian Communist Party (Partido Comunista Peruano; PCP)
**Founded.** 1930
**Membership.** 2,000
**General Secretary.** Jorge del Prado Chavez
**Central Committee.** 15 members: Gustavo Espinoza Montesinos, Guillermo Herrera, Asunción Caballero Mendez, Jorge del Prado Chavez, Olivera Vila, Isidoro Gamarra, Roberto Rojas, Valentín Pacho Quispe, Julián Serra, Jaime Figueroa, Víctor Checa, Antonio Torres Andrade, César Alva, Carlos Bonino, Alfonso Barrantes Lingán
**Status.** Legal
**Last Congress.** Eighth Extraord., 24–26 January 1982; Fourteenth Plenary, 8–9 June, 1985
**Last Election.** 1985 presidential and parliamentary. The PCP has six delegates and is part of a coalition of the United Left that has 26 percent of the delegates in the Chamber of Deputies. The PCP has two senators in the coalition that has 25 percent of the representation in the Senate.
**Auxiliary Organizations.** Confederation of Peruvian Workers (CGTP), Peruvian Peasant Confederation (CCP)
**Publications.** *Unidad* (newspaper of the PCP); *El Nuevo Diario* (leftist newspaper).

The PCP has been an important participant in the Peruvian political system since democracy was restored in 1980. As a founding component of the political front, the United Left (Izquierda Unida; IU), the pro-Moscow PCP has gained in influence as the IU has become the second major political force in the nation and the leading parliamentary opposition to the ruling social democratic party, the American Popular Revolutionary Alliance (APRA).

In the 1985 presidential elections, the population overwhelmingly rejected the neoliberal policies of the governing party, Popular Action (Acción Popular), which had presided over the worst economic recession of the century and had failed to deal effectively with either the root causes or the violent manifestations of the major guerrilla movement, Sendero Luminoso. The APRA and IU together captured 80 percent of the vote and a mandate for radical change. President Alan García Pérez's first eighteen months in office were spent initiating some of those changes, which included pursuing a militant anti-imperialist foreign policy, reviving nationalist economic policies with a new emphasis on agricultural development, decentralizing government operations and resources, and combating terrorism through expanded social and economic programs in the Andean highlands.

To attain his goals, García needed the support of his party, the control of the military, and the tacit cooperation of the IU. As 1986 ended, however, those conditions were in question. APRA infighting was rife as the dynamic president's rhetoric and reforms alienated some of his party's old guard. The military was chafing under budget cuts, congressional inquiries, press criticism, criminal charges, and personnel changes. The IU spent the year on the brink of disintegration as it struggled with defining its internal organization, its space within the Peruvian political system, and its ideological position in relation to the progressive García administration.

**Leadership and Party Organization.** The IU is composed of three political parties, three coalitions, various small groups, and individuals. The parties are the PCP, the social democratic Revolutionary Socialist Party (PSR), and the Revolutionary Communist Party (PCR). The major coalitions are the Unified Mariateguista Party (PUM), the Maoist Union of the Revolutionary Left (UNIR), and the Trotskyist Worker, Peasant, Student, and Popular Front (FOCEP). The front is coordinated by a National Directive Committee composed of Jorge del Prado Chavez (PCP), Enrique Bernales (PSR), Manuel Dammert (PCR), Javier Diez Canseco (PUM), Jorge Hurtado (UNIR), and Genaro Ledesma (FOCEP). The leadership of the committee rotates among these individuals, although the

front's president is Alfonso Barrantes Lingán, who was elected mayor of Lima in 1983.

The IU is, above all, an electoral front that fitfully coalesces to compete for office and spends the intervening periods trying to determine the viability of its long-term existence. Each party recognizes that a unified front is the only way to compete with the APRA and rightist political parties. Although none of the groups could realistically go it alone, they remain roughly equivalent to one another, so that in the front's six-year existence no one has been able to dominate. In fact, the consolidation has produced coalitions of the smaller parties that can hold their own against the three main parties of the IU. The equilibrium is so delicate that, despite great discontent and public debate, the IU leadership is still in the hands of Barrantes, an independent who represents no party.

Analysts have consistently proposed converting the IU into a political party built from the base up, with individual members who would identify with the party rather than with any component part. The underlying question is, which group or individuals would define the party? The major division of the IU during 1986 was one of cooperation with, or radical opposition to, the APRA. This could be translated into a pro- or anti-Barrantes position as well.

Barrantes, along with Lima prefect Henry Pease García, the PCP, the PSR, and the PCR, represent the sectors of the front most amenable to cooperating with the APRA, not fearing a loss of identity by doing so. On the one hand, they are more ideologically disposed to cooperation, and on the other, their political successes have reinforced a pragmatic approach. Pease stated, "We support the duty of political forces to find points of coincidence in great national problems. But such concertation does not imply co-government nor does it facilitate cooptation" (*Resumen Semanal*, 12–18 December).

Those with a Barrantista orientation place the IU's unity above the needs of any of its parts. They are concerned that it remain a viable political alternative through which the masses can express their Marxist ideals electorally. They also conceive of the IU as a bulwark in the Peruvian political system, that is, an organization that maintains a civilian, constitutional government, which specifically means not undermining García. This group does not define the APRA, or at least García, as the enemy. The Barrantistas have condemned the path of violence taken by Sendero Luminoso and the Revolutionary Movement of Tupac Amaru

(MRTA). They want to avoid identification with a disloyal, subversive opposition and its attendant repression and loss of political rights. They argue that the best way to do this is to support García on those issues where they have coinciding interests. (Ibid.)

Those who oppose cooperation with the APRA accuse Barrantes of destroying the IU platform, supporting the militarization of Peru, and having reformist tendencies because of his own electoral desires (Lima Panamericana Television, 11 August; *FBIS*, 14 August). When Genaro Ledesma took his turn as leader of the National Directive Committee in November 1985, the FOCEP and PUM pushed for a clear separation from the APRA, which they defined as "reformist" and "militarist." The program adopted by Ledesma and the committee included: 1) the non-payment of foreign debt and the non-remission of foreign exchange abroad; 2) the formation of a temporary civilian government in the emergency zone, amnesty for political prisoners, and the resignation of the minister of defense; 3) the creation of regional governments; and 4) increases in wages and salaries. (*El Diario de Marka*, 14 November 1985; *JPRS*, 14 January.)

The objectives of this program were not a problem for the Barrantes group; rather, it was the rejection of any APRA moves in these directions and the radicalization of some sectors within the IU that caused the tension. Whereas Barrantes saw the APRA initiatives as steps toward socialism, the radical factions of the IU saw such measures as deceptions, rhetoric without action, or only half-hearted efforts that would ultimately be sabotaged by the APRA groups over which the president had no control.

At a meeting in Chiclayo of the National Popular Assembly, which included representatives of the leftist popular organizations, unions, parties, and independents, a series of proposals were made for grass-roots discussions. With regard to the APRA, they proposed defining the party as "pro-imperialist and . . . bourgeois." This was a compromise position, since some had wanted to call it "fascist." In contrast, an attempt to condemn the terrorist activities of Sendero Luminoso as "mistaken" for its "polarization and antidemocratic tendencies" was rejected, and the assembly decided on a statement that "armed struggle in appropriate circumstances" was "a legitimate way to achieve power." (*Latin American Weekly Report* (*LAWR*), 18 September.)

Tension between the radicals and the Barrantistas was particularly evident in the electoral cam-

paign of 1986. For example, there was a notable lack of communication between the National Directive Committee and Barrantes. Initiatives were uncoordinated and confusion existed as to whether individuals spoke for themselves, for their party, or for the IU (Lima, *Quehacer*, 44, p. 18). In June, the National Elections Jury published the IU inscription for the November elections with only the PCP, the PCR, and the PSR listed. A few days later the front made amends and substituted the combined list. (*Resumen Semanal*, 4–10 July.)

Barrantes's penchant for cooperation remained a bone of contention, and subsequently there were moves to find an alternative candidate for the mayor of Lima. PUM leader Diez Canseco felt Barrantes would not be a good leader with what he saw as the increasing militarization of the APRA government. Nevertheless, on 9 August, Barrantes was selected as the candidate with favorable votes from the PCP, PCR, PSR, and FOCEP; the PUM and UNIR abstained. The crisis of leadership and unity was not resolved, however, and the front had parallel lists in Iquitos, Tacna, Pisco, and Piura. (Ibid., 1–14 August.)

In fact, the November municipal elections provided a good illustration of the IU's disarray. It is suspected that the PUM and UNIR abstained in Lima, thus perhaps contributing to Barrantes's defeat. As of the year's end, the official election results had not been published, and the charges of irregularities were such that several races may be nullified, including that in Lima where the APRA candidate, Jorge del Castillo, declared himself the victor over Barrantes by a narrow margin (ibid., 21–27 November).

Unofficially, the APRA won 42 percent of the national vote, the IU 32 percent, and the Popular Christian Party (PPC) 17 percent. For the IU this was an increase from the 1985 presidential elections, when they captured only 25 percent of the vote, but because fewer parties participated in 1986 (for example, Popular Action did not compete), this was tantamount to an electoral reverse. More crucial, the IU lost many district and provincial mayors' seats. In some areas, losses were directly attributed to internal disputes, such as in Tacna, where the UNIR campaigned for the PPC against the IU. In Cuzco, the popular Marxist mayor's defeat was attributed to the direct intervention of President García and his municipal development funding (*LAT*, 28 November). Insiders claimed that other factors were weak organization, unattractive candidates, ignorance about essentially local matters, confusion created by too many lists, and ineffective campaigning on accomplishments (Lima, *Quehacer*, 44, p. 7). Yet the IU did increase its absolute number of voters. It has remained the second largest front in the nation, and more politicians have become accustomed to the participation of IU representatives.

**Domestic Affairs.** There are some important reasons for cooperation between the IU and the APRA. As Barrantes argued, "the grave economic crisis and the phenomena of terrorism...obligate the political parties to look for fundamental coincidences to overcome the economic crisis and defeat terrorism...." (*Resumen Semanal*, 24–30 October). Since both the APRA and the IU have claimed to be the party of the masses, they compete to organize some of the same grass-roots sectors. Their programs are similar in direction, emphasizing nationalism and anti-imperialism, but as the competition has become more intense, the IU's positions grow ever more radical. The PCP and IU role has been to pressure García to live up to promises he made for "an anti-imperialist state" with "socialism in freedom." This effort was particularly evident in agricultural development, economic policies, labor relations, and dealing with terrorism.

Agricultural development was one area that was sorely neglected under Fernando Belaúnde Terry, and both the IU and the APRA see it as key for bringing about a national recovery and stemming rural violence. The PCP believes that agrarian poverty has induced desperate people to support Sendero Luminoso, whose "erroneous orientation and terrorist methods...cause grave damage to genuine revolutionary struggles and a pretext for crackdowns and genocide" (*WMR*, October).

The PCP has stood resolutely on the side of agrarian reform as initiated by Velasco's progressive military government. It has directed and supported a defense of the reform by strengthening the rural labor organizations, the CCP and the National Agrarian Confederation, and by helping create the National Agrarian Unitary Council in 1983 to coordinate rural struggles and urban trade union concerns. With regard to agriculture, the IU, and the PCP especially, called on García to respect and restore the gains of the agrarian reform, to aid peasants, communes, and cooperatives by providing adequate financial and credit facilities, to nationalize agrarian related industry, to alleviate tax burdens, and to provide guaranteed prices. (Ibid.)

García has taken some steps to stimulate agricultural production and has demonstrated his concern through a series of meetings at which local leaders made known their demands. Over 500 representatives from the southern departments attended the meeting in Puno. There the president heeded demands to continue the 1969 reforms, and he personally turned over titles for 500,000 hectares to 300 communities (Paris, AFP, 22 September; *FBIS*, 25 September). Nevertheless, the PCP feels García's efforts have been half-hearted, often blocked by unsympathetic middle-sector APRA members, and not aimed at solving the basic crisis in agriculture (*WMR*,October).

The economic situation in Peru improved in 1986. Slowly but steadily, inflation was cut to 44 percent from 158 percent, the growth rate was increased to 6.5 percent, and salaries rose 150 percent from August 1985 to October 1986, thus outpacing inflation (*Resumen Semanal*, 17–23 October). To some extent this improvement was the short-term result of García's international economic stance. By limiting external debt repayments to 10 percent of export earnings, García was able to increase public sector wages, which in turn stimulated demand for food and simple goods and helped to revive the domestic market. Manufacturing was up 20 percent in García's first six months, output up 8 percent in first-quarter comparisons, and employment up 4.4 percent in the first eight months. Although some critics saw this "supply-side" stimulus diminishing because idle capacity expansion was limited and new foreign investment appeared unlikely under present circumstances, popular enthusiasm for the president's policies remained high (*South*, August).

Labor unrest under García has been less than it was under Belaúnde. The organized sectors have held off national strikes in favor of negotiations on a union-by-union basis. In February and May, there were walkouts by miners, doctors, teachers, and state employees; negotiated settlements were achieved in all cases. The relative labor calm can, in large part, be attributed to García's willingness to become personally involved. His commitment to increasing real wages and his success in stopping rampant inflation have won him worker support. The largest labor organization, the procommunist CGTP, was accused of being passive with regard to the APRA government, but workers did not want to jeopardize their chances for salary increases and their leaders did not want to lose membership to the rival APRA confederation, the Confederation of

Peruvian Workers (CTP). (*El Nacional*, 3 November 1985; *JPRS*, 2 January.) García has actually been relatively nonpartisan in his labor relations. In May, he was the first president to ever meet with the Unitary Peruvian Educators Union (SUTEP) leader, Carlos Salazar Pasache (*LAWR*, 30 May), and in June, he granted political amnesty to the 35 campesino leaders who had participated in the national agrarian strike in November 1982 (*Resumen Semanal*, 13–20 June).

In terms of labor legislation, García's job-stability law has been the most progressive yet in Peru; it changed from three years to three months the length of time an employee needs to work before receiving benefits and job security. Despite a generally positive view, CGTP leader Valentín Pacho complained that the labor-stability law also expanded the reasons to legally dismiss workers. More important, he noted that food prices were outpacing other items in inflation and there were still great shortages of basic items (*LAWR*, 30 May).

García's popularity ran at 70 percent approval most of the year, and he carried his party through the November municipal elections to an overwhelming victory in which APRA candidates won in 18 of 24 departmental capitals. His persona is such that the press agency UPI named him one of the most important figures in Latin America in 1986 (*Resumen Semanal*, 12–18 December). García's charisma has certainly renewed the Peruvian national spirit and fueled optimism in his first eighteen months in office, but the next three years may be much more difficult for him. The major disappointment has been the administration's inability to stem terrorism, which, if anything, had grown worse by the end of 1986.

Barrantes has been consistent in his denunciation of violence and his willingness to work with all groups to alleviate the problem. He stated, "Terrorist violence does not express the popular will. The Peruvian population has a pacific vocation utilizing democratic channels and through them has converted the left into a force with the possibility of governing . . . The peaceful way is possible as we have demonstrated in municipal government; without appealing to violence we have resolved a series of community problems" (ibid., 24–30 October).

A major initiative was undertaken by Barrantes to create the Front for the Defense of Life which would include the Catholic church and the APRA as well as the leftist political parties. Although many professed to be in favor of the idea, it faltered when

most of the opposition came from within the IU. The other IU leaders saw no reason to cooperate with those "responsible for state terrorism" or to recognize the parties of the right (ibid., 24–30 October). The split between the Barrantistas and radicals of the IU became even more acute after the tragedy of 18–19 June.

On 18 June, Sendero Luminoso members in three separate prisons in the Lima area mounted a coordinated uprising and made a series of demands on the government, the most important being to cancel their transfer to a new maximum security prison, Cantogrande. The situation in the jails was lamentable. The government had no real control over what had become "liberated zones," where Senderistas trained and organized inmates, most of whom had not been tried for their offenses. The provocation was timed to embarrass García as the Socialist International congress met in Lima and the world press was focused on Peru. Despite speculation that the Senderistas wanted a military overreaction to demonstrate state repression, it is hard to imagine that they desired the massacre that ensued. The military forces sent to quell the riots did meet some resistance from several guns, homemade bombs, and "fortified" cellblocks; but the death toll of 271 prisoners to 4 members of the armed forces was stark testimony to the excesses committed (ibid., 18–24 July). Moreover, a hostage who survived in Lurigancho prison detailed the murder of inmates who had surrendered (*El Comercio*, 25 June).

Those who had hoped that García's approach to combating terrorism would be markedly different from Belaúnde's were bitterly disappointed by this turn in events. It demonstrated either a reliance on the military solution or a president who did not have firm control over the military. Yet while leftist dissatisfaction was deep, García emerged almost unscathed in popular judgement. Lima polls showed 75 percent of the population approved his decision to use the military against the rioters and supported his subsequent commitment to punish those who committed the excesses. (*Resumen Semanal*, 21–26 June, 27 June–3 July.)

On 21 June, the National Directive Committee of the IU expressed "the most energetic condemnation of the events in the prisons." It demanded a parliamentary investigation, asked why mediation was not tried, and charged that the government had fallen into the "logic of violence" (ibid., 21–26 June). However, the PCP, and other IU reformists were attuned to the public fear of terrorism in Lima and to the possibility that a García abandoned by the moderates would have only the military hardliners to rely upon; thus, they pragmatically advised their colleagues not to push constitutional censure of the cabinet (*LAWR*, 17 July). Instead, they advocated pressing García to do as he promised and go "as high up as necessary" to punish those responsible. Some heads did roll: Republican Guard commander Máximo Martínez Lira resigned, 95 men were placed under arrest, the minister of justice and 22 officials left their posts, and the head of the prisons resigned (Madrid, EFE, 28 June; Paris, AFP, 1 July; *FBIS*, 30 June, 1 July). The IU, along with the other opposition parties, demanded that the cabinet submit to questioning and a special congressional commission be named to investigate the events. Eventually, the government survived an IU motion to censure it and a PPC motion of no confidence, but by the year's end no satisfactory investigation had taken place and the members of the armed forces had not been tried. (*Resumen Semanal*, 12–18 September.)

By the end of 1986 in fact, it had become more difficult for the IU to support García's responses to terrorism as his commentary and actions increasingly resembled those of Belaúnde. García's rhetoric had certainly changed. He spoke more often of the "need to combat international terrorism with the power of national security forces." While criticizing excesses, he emphasized Sendero Luminoso's attacks on innocents and asked citizens to become "soldiers of the antiterrorist cause" (ibid., 24–30 October). In addition, he sanctioned the creation of vigilante groups (*rondas campesinos*) in rural areas. Although this was supported by CCP leader Andres Lunas Vargas, the IU and PCP generally regarded the vigilantes as adding to the spiral of arbitrary violence (ibid.).

The IU—as represented by Diez Canseco, a member of the Senate Human Rights Committee—has consistently demanded that the government observe human rights in its confrontation with the guerrillas. The front has asked for: 1) civilian investigations of genocide; 2) the repeal of the Antiterrorist Law with its vague definition of a terrorist; 3) a ban on the use of military courts for armed forces personnel charged with human rights abuses; and 4) the rejection of all proposals to revive the death penalty. Some gains were made in 1986 in these directions. In December, the IU supported a law that defined genocide, torture, secret arrests, arbitrary executions of prisoners, and sexual violations as crimes to be tried by civilian courts.

Thus, the military and police could no longer claim that such offenses were "crimes of duty" to be tried in military courts. But while human rights offenses were defined as civilian concerns, the Senate also proposed the creation of special tribunals for terrorism, segregating these crimes from the regular judicial system (ibid., 12–18 December). This tactic was borrowed from the Italians, and it was intended to avoid judicial intimidation and speed up trials (Lima Television Peruana, 1 November; *FBIS*, 5 November). The IU, however, worried about the possible abuse of such special tribunals, since they might affect all political opposition.

After the APRA's overwhelming victory in the municipal elections, IU leaders began to worry about it monopolizing power at all levels and abrogating democratic rules. For example, there had been corruption during the municipal election campaign, the executive had made 97 decrees that had not been published in the official record, restrictions were placed on public meetings of political parties under the state of emergency legislation, and there was increased talk of a constitutional convention to alter the limit on presidential succession. (*Resumen Semanal*, 5–11, 12–18 December). Most troublesome, however, was increased partisan violence.

Just as in the Belaúnde era, frustration with lack of success against the terrorists has led to charges that the parliamentary opposition condones violence. By mid-June, fourteen different IU congressmen had been accused of supporting Sendero Luminoso; eight had actually been charged by the national prosecutor with provoking public disorder on Lima's streets during the state of emergency. Four more deputies were suspended as they scuffled with APRA members during a hunger strike at the congress. (Ibid., 16–22 May, 30 May–5 June.)

APRA charges of IU support and cooperation with Sendero Luminoso brought violent confrontations between militants of both parties. The most tragic was in Huancayo, where the son of an APRA deputy killed a young communist student. Thereafter, violence erupted in Lima with two members of the APRA killed. Barrantes and APRA general secretary Armando Villanueva sought a pact to avoid such confrontations with little success. At the same time as Barrantes was trying to create a national accord, IU members Diez Canseco, Rolando Ames, and Guillermo Herrera deplored what they saw as efforts to polarize the nation and to give the military primacy. They challenged García's seriousness about such an accord, saying that he should lift the state of emergency. But García, who had imposed that state of emergency in Lima and Callao in February, bringing to 23 the number of provinces under military control, did not feel confident enough by the end of 1986 to lift the limitations on citizens' political and civil rights. (*Resumen Semanal*, 26 September–2 October, 10–16, 24–30 October.)

**International Views and Positions.** The PCP and IU have found little fault with García's foreign policy initiatives. They have encouraged him to pursue his announced anti-imperialist and non-aligned orientation with concrete actions. In fact, because his rhetoric has earned him descriptions abroad as "socialist" and even "Marxist," the IU has been at pains to differentiate their goals and plans from the president's.

García has focused on unity among the Latin American and Caribbean nations and solidarity with the Third World. He has been consistently outspoken in his defense of national sovereignty and condemnation of great power intervention, especially with regard to Nicaragua. García announced in June that Peru "would break diplomatic relations with any imperialist power which attempts military aggression in Nicaragua" (*IB*, June).

García's policy of strengthening relations within the region was best represented by the restoration of diplomatic relations with Cuba. Despite insulting criticism of García when he was elected president, Fidel Castro's government moved to alleviate signs of competition between the two charismatic leaders and heal what had been a six-year breach in relations. Through 1986, bilateral ties were improved with technical cooperation on 26 projects that included assistance with agriculture, sports, fishing, energy, and transportation (*El Comercio*, 29 March, *JPRS*, 7 July).

Continental unity was an underlying theme regarding the international economic community, intervention in Central America, and confronting drug traffic and terrorism. García urged Latin American cooperation on all fronts, including the creation of a truly Latin American and Caribbean organization, "an OAS without the U.S." that could act jointly (*Insight*, 8 December ). Relations with most of Peru's neighbors improved in 1986. Joint ventures with Colombia and Ecuador against drug trafficking were launched, and Allan Wagner Tizon made the first trip ever of a Peruvian foreign minister to Ecuador (*El Nacional*, 15 June; *JPRS*, 14

August). García himself traveled to Argentina and Uruguay, and in turn he received Tomás Borge of Nicaragua in March and Guillermo Ungo of El Salvador in June at the Socialist International meeting. Relations with Chile were mixed; the military government to the south charged Peru with harboring and assisting revolutionary elements. Yet high-level military talks took place in an effort to limit arms expenditures by both nations (*World Press Review*, August).

Relations with the United States remained strained through 1986 because of García's independent stance on foreign debt and his forthright criticism of the Reagan administration's policy in Central America. Peruvian controls on the remittance of profits by U.S. investors, takeovers of U.S.-owned industries, delayed repayments on assistance loans, and lack of sufficient progress against drug trafficking all complicated and restricted the flow of U.S. aid. Of the $74 million for economic aid and $25.8 million in military aid for counterterrorism requested in the U.S. budget for Peru, analysts felt only a fraction would actually survive approval (*Latin America Update*, November/December).

As a member of the Contadora Support Group, García attacked the U.S. congressional approval of $100 million in aid to the Nicaraguan *contras* as a "clear violation of the principle of nonintervention," and he deplored its consequences as a "disintegrating factor in the negotiation processes" of the Contadora Group (Madrid, EFE, 2 July; *FBIS*, 3 July). IU criticism mounted at the end of 1986 as the front called on García to act on this declaration and break relations with the United States and Honduras as revelations of illegal (even by U.S. standards) involvement in Nicaragua became public (*Resumen Semanal*, 5–11 December).

García's position with regard to external debt has been the most radical position in the world in practice. His commitment to repay only 10 percent of Peru's export earnings toward the debt meant that Peru paid only $35 million of its $180 million obligation to the International Monetary Fund (IMF) on 15 August. This resulted in the nation being declared ineligible for further credit from the international institutions. Thereafter, García called for a "resistance economy to face imperialism" by emphasizing domestic investment. His chances of doing this have been improved by the accumulation of foreign reserves amounting to $2.5 billion, up from $700 million when he took office (*Le Monde*, 7 May; *FBIS*, 13 May).

The PCP supports García's position toward the foreign debt. Del Prado argued that the debt has injured every sector of Peruvian life; therefore, it has given rise to a broad anti-imperialist movement advocating a new economic policy and new international economic relations to which the PCP and IU respond (*WMR*, February). The IU has asked for a moratorium on the external debt and charges García with economic orthodoxy by submitting to repayment plans of the IMF and the World Bank (*Resumen Semanal*, 17–23 October).

However, the president argues that the IMF must be viewed in two parts: one that undermines national sovereignty with its directives, the other a bank to which Peru owes money. García accepts the debt but demands flexibility in its repayment. At the Latin American Economic System (SELA) meeting in October, García's "communiqué de Lima" argued that "external debt is an imminently political problem whose solution implies profound reform of the international financial system, so that each country has the sovereign right to decide the manner of payment without affecting interests of development" (ibid.). One means of flexible payment that has worked well for Peru is to repay in kind. Proposals have been made to fifteen of 280 foreign banks in the United States, Europe, and Japan to make deals similar to those by which Peru paid $343.7 million to the USSR, Romania, Czechoslovakia, Hungary, Yugoslavia, Israel, and Panama during 1984-1985 with minerals, cotton, textiles, and engines (Paris, AFP, 15 August; *FBIS*, 19 August).

Good ties with the communist bloc nations were maintained as IU leaders made several trips in 1986. Del Prado went to Romania in April, and Barrantes, with other IU representatives, went to Cuba for the Third Communist Party Congress there and then to Managua for anniversary celebrations of Sandino's death (*Agerpres*, 24 April; *JPRS*, 13 May; Paris, AFP, 2 April; *FBIS*, 4 February). The García administration also cultivated good trade relations. Agreements with China were signed that provided for the exchange of iron and cotton for rice and a plant to assemble light tractors (*Resumen Semanal*, 21–26 June). Fishing agreements with the Soviet Union were renewed under somewhat better terms for Peru with regard to percentage of the catch to stay in that country (ibid. 5–11 September).

Peru's visibility in global circles was enhanced when García was elected a vice president of the Nonaligned Movement at the Zimbabwe meeting in September and Foreign Minister Wagner was selected chair of the World Conference on South Africa, which was organized by the U.N. Special Committee on Apartheid (*South*, August). The international limelight dimmed, however, when the host to the Socialist International congress in June found himself embroiled in the gravest human rights abuses in Peru since the guerrilla movement began. The congress expressed consternation at the excesses of the military's response to the prison revolts but confidence in García's social democracy to pursue an inquiry. The congress itself was almost canceled and many important figures did not come. (*LAWR*, 3 July.)

A strange international event occurred in June when a Danish boat, the *Pia Vesta*, sailed into Callao harbor. Without docking, it then went to Panama, where officials boarded it to inspect the cargo and found weapons and trucks aboard from East Germany. The Panamanians searched the ship on a request from the Peruvian government, which had been tipped off by the United States. Speculation as to the intended recipients of contraband included Sendero Luminoso, El Salvador, the *contras*, the Chilean rebels, the Peruvian navy, and the APRA. Relations became strained with East Germany, and the Peruvian ambassador was recalled when it was believed that there was a Sendero Luminoso connection. Later investigations, however, suggested that more evidence existed to point to the Peruvian navy or the *contras*. An arms dealer in Miami, Florida, maintained that he sold the cargo to Peruvian navy vice admiral Nicolini. The War Ministry denied this (*Resumen Semanal*, 29 August–4 September; *WP*, 29 August; *LAT*, 31 August). It was also argued that the weapons were purchased to supply the *contras*. An 18 July *Wall Street Journal* article quoted Lieutenant Colonel Oliver North of the U.S. National Security Council as saying that weapons from the Socialist bloc were used to supply the *contras* to give the image that they were captured from the enemy. That the United States had tipped off the Peruvians was seen as an indication of North American infighting over aid to the *contras* (*Resumen Semanal*, 15–21 August). Finally, retired general Jorge Fernandez Maldonado, a cabinet minister under Velasco, charged that the U.S. Central Intelligence Agency had carried out the incident to antagonize negotiations between Peru and East Germany on the construction of a plant to maintain and repair Soviet military equipment (ibid., 5–11 September; Paris, AFP, 11 September; *FBIS*, 11 September).

**Terrorist Activities.** When García took office, there was a great deal of optimism that the spread of terrorism might be halted with policies that placed primary emphasis on social and economic development rather than military elimination of the enemy. Many people felt that this would diminish the appeal of the violent revolution and, at the same time, alleviate the human rights violations that had turned military control of the emergency zones into a counterproductive effort.

García pledged to assist the highlands and made them a top priority for development by earmarking $350 million in assistance for these departments in the central sierra. He emphasized small local projects to raise income and stem emigration. On the political front, he remained committed to a Peace Commission to advise him of ways to address the spiral of violence in the nation, even though the first two commissions had resigned in frustration. He investigated charges of massacres and sought punishment for those responsible.

However, the spread of violence seemed to bear no relationship to these initiatives. By November, 9,690 persons had been killed in the revolutionary struggle launched by Sendero Luminoso in May 1980 (*Resumen Semanal*, January–November). The areas affected by violence extended from La Libertad in the north to the Amazonian basin in the west, to Puno in the south, and in all the coastal metropolitan areas. Strength estimates vary, but Sendero Luminoso itself claims 15,000 members and has taken credit for 300,000 actions in six years (*San Francisco Chronicle*, 13 August).

Analysts seeking to understand this faction, which split from the PCP in 1964, have characterized it as a persistent guerrilla movement, not a fleeting fanatic gang; they no longer emphasize the Incaic aspects of the group, but rather its Maoist stages of development (see *YICA*, 1984, 1985, 1986). In 1986, Sendero Luminoso was said to have entered the fourth stage, the "Great Assault," during which enough liberated zones are supposed to appear to create a provisional revolutionary government that would achieve international recognition (Lima, *Quehacer*, 42, p. 33).

The clandestine group had been notable for its shunning of publicity, disregard for international connections, and resistence to intelligence penetration. In 1986, some observers questioned these assumptions, arguing that as Sendero Luminoso expanded its range of activities, it was cooperating with other revolutionary groups in Peru, making international communications, and providing more information about itself, especially in the wake of the prison massacres. It was suggested that Sendero Luminoso's strength was growing, given successful recruitment of rural and urban poor and the use of legal fronts such as so-called people's schools and various unions (*LAWR*, 7 February).

Using almost the same evidence, the military argued that they were making progress against the terrorists in the first six months of 1986. They saw weakness in Sendero Luminoso's retreat from its original base in Ayacucho to areas in which it had not been previously organized. They saw desperation in the increased failures of urban operations as poorly trained individuals were killed by malfunctioning explosives or were captured. The military also noted the return to combat of intellectual leaders, citing that Julio César Mezzich, reputed to be second in command to founder Dr. Abimael Guzmán, had been seen leading a column of Senderistas (Paris, AFP, 9 June; *FBIS*, 11 June).

The apparent contradiction in interpretations could perhaps be explained by the government's tendency to identify all unattributed activities to Sendero Luminoso, which has created the impression of greater coherence than actually exists. In addition, the group's reputed tight control and coordination of its cells now is questionable. At Sendero Luminoso's fourth central committee meeting held in April and May, analyst Raul González reported on what appeared to be the mysterious Abimail Guzmán's attempt to maintain control of the party and root out "deviations in the urban campaign." Deviations were defined as "cooperation with the MRTA, communication with Cuban and Soviet revisionists," and "confiscations" that had not been authorized by the central committee. The Lima metropolitan committee was reorganized for its failure to follow the prescribed program.

A pamphlet distributed at the meeting, "To Develop the Popular War Serving World Revolution," reiterated the long path to build popular committees, the bases of support, and then the Popular Republic of New Democracy. It also emphasized the primacy of expanding the rural campaign to neighbors north and south (Cajamarca to Puno) over the urban campaign. In the committee meeting, the leaders also clearly underscored their singularity in the world. Calling the Sandinista revolution a "farce," they argued that they were the only movement in the world that did not have foreign or superpower connections. (Lima, *Quehacer*, 44, pp. 49–53.)

If the fourth committee meeting was any guide,

the intensity of the urban campaign in Peru in 1986 may have reflected the spawning of individual terrorist units over which Sendero Luminoso had little or no control, but who considered themselves Senderistas. In any case, during the year there was a quantitative and qualitative change in the urban violence.

Major targets in the cities continued to be state offices, especially local APRA meeting halls. More than 100 municipal officials have been killed in five years, but 30 of those assassinations took place between January and September 1986 (Paris, AFP, 9 September, *FBIS*, 12 September). The result has been mass resignations in some areas, which have created liberated zones by default.

After local authorities, the major targets were police and military officers. By October, nine high-ranking officers had been assassinated, including the retired commander of the navy, Vice Admiral Gerónimo Cafferata Marazzi, who was then the president of the Industrial Bank. (*Resumen Semanal*, 10–16 October.)

The terrorists continued to strike the national infrastructure, but in urban settings the shopping centers, cinemas, hotels, and restaurants also became targets, placing many innocent bystanders in jeopardy and increasing the terror that had previously plagued only the highland areas. For the first time, churches and foreigners were targets. In June, the tourist train to Machu Picchu was bombed; eight persons, including foreigners, were killed, and 35 were injured. In September, an attack on a shop in Callao injured six Soviet fishermen, one critically. Although the left claimed it was right-wing violence, the minister of war blamed Sendero Luminoso, which has never shown any reticence about bombing the Soviet embassy (ibid., 29 August–4 September). The difference, of course, was that the victims were not government representatives of any sort.

The urban violence led to the declaration of a state of emergency on 10 February in Lima and Callao, which for the first time suspended all constitutional guarantees for the metropolitan area and invoked a curfew. Despite the curfew and the state of emergency, terrorist activities mounted in May and June. Within four weeks, 100 persons died, including four persons who were killed in an attack on APRA's third highest party official, the national secretary for organization, Alberto Kitazono. The next day, the longest railroad bridge in Peru was blown up, causing $3.5 million damage and derailing 30 cars. In early June, eight presumed terrorists were arrested inside the congressional building, and at a public ceremony on Plaza Bolognesi on 7 June, one bomb went off before García spoke and two exploded afterward, killing three people in a restaurant. (Ibid., 23–29 May, 6–12 June.)

By mid-year there was heightened pressure from the military and APRA hardliners to restore the death penalty. This, plus García's concern for his image at the convening of the Socialist International in Lima, led to the overreaction in putting down the coordinated prison riots mounted by Sendero Luminoso on 18 June. Although many in the military felt the elimination of the prison training areas and of Senderista headquarters would be a debilitating blow to the organization, that was hardly the case. Those killed were not the backbone of the organization. In fact, the most significant results were diminished Peruvian international prestige; a shift in focus from Sendero's excesses to the military's genocide; new investigations, trials, and imprisonment of military personnel; popular backlash; and finally, Sendero Luminoso's threat to kill ten APRA members for every Senderista who died in the massacre. In fact, assassinations of civilian authorities in the three months after the riots numbered 52, compared to 30 in the three months previous (*WP*, 20 November).

In Puno, Sendero Luminoso tried to exploit the demands of the landless, who did not benefit from Velasco's agrarian reform, by encouraging invasions, stealing animals, and "distributing" them to the peasants. Between 21 and 26 June, Senderistas ransacked sixteen cooperatives and haciendas and forced peasants to accept stolen animals. It was reported the peasants killed the animals immediately to sell the meat and avoid terrorism charges. Military reprisals, however, fell heavily upon the peasants who had followed Sendero Luminoso's orders. (*Latin American Regional Reports*, 31 July.)

In the atmosphere of generalized urban violence, new groups emerged that took credit for their activities—such as the Los Amigos Revolucionarios and the Comando Revolucionarios del Pueblo. The latter is believed to be a split from the MRTA, the second most important party that pursues a violent path to revolution (Paris, AFP, 1 October; *FBIS*, 20 October). The MRTA also altered its previous patterns in 1986.

The MRTA had granted García a two-month truce when he took office, but rescinded it claiming that the APRA had failed to resolve the problems of hunger and poverty and had only "enacted measures which disguised the conditions of the majority"

(Paris, AFP, 24 February; *FBIS*). The MRTA defines the APRA as reformist, and it has few programmatic differences from the IU. It demands that the foreign debt not be paid, that oil and mining be nationalized, that food shortges be resolved, that the state of emergency be lifted, and that political prisoners be freed (ibid.). Although the MRTA advocated the use of violence, until 1986 their activities had been confined to urban areas and had involved only property damage, but in June an officer was killed as the guerrillas seized a police mess hall in Lima (Paris, AFP, 10 June; *FBIS*, 11 June). The following month they made their first attack outside an urban area in Huancayo (Paris, AFP, 30 July; *FBIS*, 31 July).

Although the MRTA had confined itself to metropolitan areas, it did have international contacts. In 1986, the organization announced it had sent three squads to join the American Battalion, which operates in Colombia with members of M-19 and Ecuador's Alfaro Vive! (Madrid, EFE, 28 February; *FBIS*, 4 March).

The large department of Puno poses a crucial challenge for the guerrilla movement's survival and for the IU. They both advocate revolutionary change, but the efficacy of the violent versus the electoral path is being tested in that region. The guerrillas are still a small force facing well-organized popular organizations that have articulated the demands of the peasants and workers since the 1970s. The IU's goals are to keep the military, the APRA, and Sendero Luminoso out of the area. The IU wants to avoid a declaration of emergency that would limit the functioning of the popular organizations it influences. It also wants to maintain civilian autonomy and regional administration of government benefits so that the IU receives the credit, not the APRA. Finally, the IU desires national legislation that addresses the needs of the population so that the electoral route would remain promising. This means that any moves toward militarization, or even the appearance of monopolization of powers at the municipal level by the APRA may lead to such discontent within the IU that the radical faction would split. Although such a split would also not be in García's best interests, his ability to deal with urban terrorism will be one of his party's foremost concerns in 1987, and the hardliners' demand for firm political and military control may be unavoidable.

Sandra Woy-Hazleton
*Miami University*

# Puerto Rico

**Population.** 3,300,520
**Party.** Puerto Rican Socialist Party (Partido Socialista Puertorriqueño; PSP); Puerto Rican Communist Party (Partido Comunista Puertorriqueño; PCP)
**Founded.** PSP: 1971; PCP: 1934
**Membership.** PSP: 150; PCP: 125 (both estimated)
**General Secretary:** PSP: vacant; PCP: Franklin Irrizarry
**Leading Bodies.** No data
**Status.** Legal
**Last Congress.** PSP: Second, 1979; PCP: none known

**Last Elections.** 1984; PSP: 0.3 percent, no representatives
**Auxiliary Organizations.** No data
**Publications.** PSP: *Claridad* (weekly)

Puerto Rico's Marxists continued to be an insignificant force in the island's political life. Their principal slogan, Independence for Puerto Rico, has not gained them followers beyond a small percentage of voters. The majority of Puerto Rican Marxists seek independence by powerful means. However, in the most recent election in November 1984, the *independentista* ticket—for which both Marxists and non-Marxists vote—obtained only 3.5 percent of the total.

The issue before the island's electorate in November 1988 will not be independence, but the degree of autonomy from Washington. Even the ruling Popular Democratic Party (PDP) has been divided on its autonomy platform for the 1988 election. Some PDP leaders have wanted Puerto Rico to demand new powers, ranging from control over immigration and broadcasting to a virtually new status, similar to that of the associated Republic of Micronesia in the Pacific. Governor Rafaél Hernández Colón, the PDP's top leader, has been verbally noncommital, trying to avoid divisive intraparty dispute. By his actions, however, he indicated in 1986 that he would like Puerto Rico to have a larger say in its destiny, especially with regard to foreign relations. Although Washington has not hidden its displeasure, Hernández Colón has established economic and cultural relationships with a number of foreign countries in an apparent effort to establish Puerto Rico in the international arena as a semiautonomous country.

The New Progressive Party (NPP) has based its 1988 campaign on the pledge of converting Puerto Rico into the 51st state of the Union. NPP rejects the associated-republic status, under which all relations with the U.S. would be severed except common currency and defense.

In the political debate, which is expected to become more heated in 1987, Marxists have had limited participation or impact. One reason is that Hernández Colón has adopted populist policies and preempted in part strong anti-U.S. rhetoric of the left with his opposition to some of the Reagan administration actions. The governor indicated his opposition to proposals to train Nicaraguan rebels in the Commonwealth and warned Washington that such a program would create significant political problems on the island.

Nevertheless, militant groups fighting for independence continued to be active in 1986. In October, two bombs exploded outside a U.S. military base in Puerto Rico and eight more were defused in a campaign claimed by three clandestine *independista* groups. One person was slightly wounded and a truck was destroyed in the bombings. A caller to a San Juan radio station said the bombs were placed by the terrorist group Los Macheteros (Machete Wielders) as protest against plans to train the Nicaraguan *contras* in Puerto Rico. A communiqué about the bombings, found later, attacked the U.S. government for actions against the island's independence and for plans to allow commercial harvesting of trees in the tropical rainforests of El Yunque. The communiqué was signed jointly by Los Macheteros, the Organization of Volunteers for Puerto Rican Independence, and the Armed Forces of People's Resistance. (*Miami Herald*, 10 October.)

The principal Marxist group is the PSP, a pro-Cuban organization with some 150 members. Its leader and former general secretary, Juan Mari Bras, is a personal friend of Fidel Castro, whom he frequently visits in Havana. Since 1982, when the 58-year-old Mari Bras resigned the position he had held for many years, the party has been reorganizing its top leadership. The PSP publishes the weekly newspaper *Claridad* in San Juan and advocates the establishment of Puerto Rico as a socialist state.

Equally small, with some 125 members, is the PCP, which is pro-Moscow and closely associated with the Communist Party USA. Even smaller in membership are two Trotskyist parties, the International Workers' League and the Puerto Rican Socialist League.

George Volsky
*University of Miami*

# Suriname

**Population.** 381,000
**Party.** 25 February Unity Movement, or Standvaste (25FM), pro-military; Revolutionary People's Party
(Revolutionaire Volkspartij; RVP), pro-Cuban; Communist Party of Suriname (KPS), pro-Albanian
**Founded.** 25FM: 1983; RVP: 1981; KPS: 1981
**Membership.** 25FM: 25,000 (claimed, but figures inflated); RVP: 100 (estimated); KPS: 25 (estimated)
**Leadership.** 25FM: Desire (Desi) Delano Bouterse (chairman), Harvey Naarendorp (secretary general,
Organizing Committee); RVP: Edward Naarendorp, Glenn Sankatshing, Lothar Boksteen; KPS: Bram
Mehr was executed in 1982, current leadership unknown.
**Status.** Restrictions on political parties were lifted in the fall of 1985.
**Last Congress.** 25FM: First, 12 May 1984; KPS: First, 24 July 1981

Since the military coup that brought Lieutenant Colonel Bouterse to power in February 1980, he has remained adept at maintaining power by alternating alliances with radical Marxist elements in Surinamese society and the more moderate private sector. The 25FM chaired by Bouterse was launched as a mass movement called Steadfast (Standvaste in Dutch) on 12 May 1984, the date of its First Congress. The 25FM was conceived as replacing its predecessor, the Surinamese Revolutionary Front (SRF), which had been founded as a loose coalition of small, left-wing parties, including the RVP, the trade union movement, and the military.

When Bouterse formally announced the 25FM's formation in June 1983, he envisioned a vanguard socialist party similar to the other national liberation movements. At its inaugural congress in 1984, movement leaders were appointed and seven sections were set up: youth, women, production, labor, defense, propaganda, and foreign relations. Bouterse was unanimously entrusted with leadership of the movement and proclaimed the "Defender of the Revolution" with the honorific title of commander.

The pro-Cuban RVP was headed by Edward Naarendorp, the cousin of the once-powerful Bouterse aide and co-founder of the 25FM, Harvey Naarendorp. The party chose to dissolve itself in 1983 and incorporate into the new movement. How-

ever, it has still maintained a quasi-independent existence. Eight of its cadre were involved in the creation of the 25FM's militia, and its leadership controlled the faculty of the National University.

Bouterse was faced in 1986 with an economy badly hit by the falling demand for bauxite and with the cut-off of a $1.5 billion development package from the Netherlands after the execution of prominent democratic leaders in 1982. He had promised to include in his first government representatives from the "old political parties" and to steer the country toward an ambiguously defined democratic future. By the year's end, however, Bouterse faced the most powerful challenge yet to his rule in the form of an escalating guerrilla war in eastern Suriname, a war-damaged bauxite industry, and a severe conflict between moderate cabinet ministers and 25FM militants. While Libya furnished the military advisers for his counterinsurgency campaign against the guerrillas of the Surinamese Liberation Army (SLA), his civilian advisers sought to placate the concerns of neighboring Latin American countries, such as Brazil and Venezuela, by pledging an early return to civilian rule.

Although political parties were authorized to resume activity in 1985 and a return to representative government was promised for April 1987, Bouterse remained the dominant force in Surinamese politics. Civilians from all sectors were appointed to the fourteen-member cabinet and the 31-member national assembly, but Bouterse continued to head the military council and the Topberaad, the supreme decisionmaking council.

**Domestic Affairs.** Bouterse continued in 1986 to implement his plan to create "permanent democratic structures." On 25 February, the government put an end to the state of emergency that had been in force throughout the country since September 1980. Bouterse announced the elimination of all ranks in the army with the exception of commander of the revolution and commander of the army, both of which he possesses. (EFE, 25 February; *FBIS*, 26 February.)

In 1985, representatives of the three principal political parties of the country—the National Party of Suriname (NPS), Progressive Reform Party (VHP), and Kaum Tani Persuatan Indonesia (KTPI)—had reached an agreement with the government by which they would be integrated into the Topberaad. In May 1986, the three parties finally accepted full participation in the council, including former prime minister Henck Arron, who had been deposed by the military in 1980. However, their participation was limited to political and administrative affairs. The parties continued to demand general and secret elections before April 1987, which is the target date for the end of the transitional phase and the start of civilian rule. (Paramaribo International Service 8, 28 May; *FBIS*, 15, 30 May.)

On 16 July, Bouterse named a new government headed by Prime Minister Pretapnaarian Radhakishun, a rice exporter and a member of the VHP. Radhakishun was appointed in part because he was the general secretary of the Union of Surinamese Industry and Trade (VSB) and was known to appeal both to the 25FM militants in the government and to moderates in the private sector. Despite the military's revolutionary rhetoric, Bouterse was aware that Suriname had no alternative to bauxite and alumina as a foreign exchange earner, and support of the VSB was considered critical to bolster confidence of investors in the economy. Shortages of food, medicine, and household items have become commonplace in the once prosperous country. (Caribbean News Agency [CANA], 24 July; *FBIS*, 25 July; *Caribbean Insight*, August.)

The Radhakishun government appointed by Bouterse will remain in office until 31 March 1987. However, the government program presented by the new prime minister on 24 July made no specific mention of elections and gave few details on the planned April 1987 return to civilian rule. Reports throughout the year suggested that progress on the constitution was slow and that it was not known the degree to which the military would play a preponderant role in the executive.

In an interview given to Agence France-Presse on 23 July, Bouterse maintained, "I have always been the promoter of the revolutionary process, and that has special meaning . . . The military must determine how long their commander should serve the country." He promised that "in the next nine months the Constitution will be finished and the Surinamese people will hold a referendum deciding whether they want elections." (AFP, 23 July; *FBIS*, 24 July.)

The Surinamese army, which numbers 2,000–3,000 (only 300 of whom are professionals), experienced significant changes in 1986. Of the original group of sergeants who seized power in February 1980, only Bouterse and Captain Ivan Graanogst, the army chief of staff, remained by year's end. In March, Captain Etienne Boerenveen, the second in command and secretary of the 25FM, was arrested in Miami on drug conspiracy charges. He had demanded $1 million from undercover U.S. Drug Enforcement Administration agents for each air shipment of cocaine from South America to the United States. Suriname agreed to provide facilities for shipment of the ether used to refine cocaine. According to federal agents, Boerenveen and his accomplices offered government protection and logistical assistance to drug smugglers. In September, he was convicted by a Miami Grand Jury and sentenced to twelve years in prison. The Surinamese Foreign Ministry warned that the case would "seriously impair" relations with the United States. (*NYT*, 26 March.)

Two military officers, Major Artie Gorre and Paul Bhagwandas, resigned from the military council headed by Bouterse. Bhagwandas was one of the original group of sergeants who seized power in 1980, and he had reportedly been in charge of the unit that killed a number of democratic opposition leaders in December 1982. The removal of Gorre and Bhagwandas left a vacuum of trained officers and forced Bouterse to appoint Major Riumveldt, a welfare officer, as commander of the military. (*Caribbean Insight*, July.) The breakdown in troop morale and discipline became obvious when guerrilla forces defeated the Cuban-trained Echo Battalion in August and Major Henk van Randwijk, the successor to Gorre, defected to the insurgents (Council for the Liberation of Suriname, *Bulletin*, August).

The Bouterse regime had turned back several coup attempts in the past; in 1986, however, it faced the emergence of a small but tenacious guerrilla group, the SLA, which heightened pressure on the regime and proved successful enough to force the Surinamese leader to make contingency plans for a possible forced flight out of the country. It also forced him to cancel his scheduled trip to Libya and and the Nonaligned Movement summit in September in Zimbabwe.

The SLA is believed to number from 120 to 600 guerrillas and is led by 25-year-old Ronny Brunswijk, a former bodyguard and chauffeur to Bouterse. After being drummed out of the military for his criticism of corruption and a pay dispute, Brunswijk returned to his village, Moengo-Tapoe, in the Patamacca jungle near the border with French Guiana where he worked in the timber business. After a series of 1985 bank robberies were attributed to him, he was arrested and put in Fort Zeelandia, from which he escaped.

During the first week of June, Brunswijk traveled to Holland, where he met with former minister Andre Haakmat and members of the Council for the Liberation of Suriname (CLS) and received financial support from wealthy exiles residing in the Netherlands and the United States. In his many broadcasts smuggled out of Suriname by Dutch journalists, Brunswijk claimed he would transfer power to the CLS if he toppled the regime. In his demands to the government, he repeatedly proposed negotiations on neutral territory and elections within six months of successful talks. In December, it was reported that former Surinamese president Henk Chin A Sen traveled inside the country to hold talks with Brunswijk as the insurgency escalated. (*Caribbean Report*, 2 October; CLS, *Bulletin*, August, September; *Washington Report on the Hemisphere*, 1 October; *Journal of Commerce*, 2 December.)

Brunswijk's guerrilla army began its armed activities on 22 July when it hit the military post of Stolkertsijver, a village along the Commewijne River, and then escalated attacks on other remote military outposts in eastern Suriname. In early September, the SLA managed to take government outposts at the tourist town of Albina and to ground a Brazilian helicopter. Although the government claimed to have destroyed the SLA base and inflicted casualties on the guerrillas, the Surinamese army had to send nearly a quarter of its troops to reinforce the government's shaky position in the northeastern sector of the country. (*Washington Report on the Hemisphere*, 1 October.)

After an initial strategy to demoralize the military, the guerrillas enlarged their activities to disrupt and attack economic targets. By the end of the year, the guerrillas had effectively taken control of Suriname's eastern region, closed down the mines, and threatened to jeopardize the remainder of the crucial bauxite industry, on which the country depends for 78 percent of its foreign earnings.

In November, the SLA warned against attacks on the Zanderij Airport, 50 kilometers south of Paramaribo, and spread its operations closer to the capital, causing serious power outages and blowing up transformer stations about 30 kilometers south of that city. After the government had evacuated the inhabitants of the border town of Albina and the mining town of Moengo, the guerrillas seized those sites. The military regained control, however, and the government began the forced relocation of and indiscriminate attacks against the populations on the French Guiana frontier. By mid-December, 5,000 refugees had poured across the border. (*De Volkskrant*, 16 October; *NRC Handelsblad*, 1 November; CANA, 13 November; *Economist*, 15 November; Bonaire Trans World Radio, 20 November, 15 December; *CSM*, 18 November; AP, 4 December; *Journal of Commerce*, 4 December; *FBIS*, 29 October, 6, 14, 21 November, 16 December.)

The inability of the Surinamese military to cope with the deteriorating security situation provoked sharp splits within the government and among the population. Throughout the autumn, Prime Minister Radhakishun announced his desire to mediate between the government and Brunswijk and expressed his annoyance at the lack of information concerning the military situation. Radhakishun and other cabinet ministers complained about Foreign Minister Henk Herrenberg's preference for an escalated conflict and his antagonism toward the Netherlands, France, and the United States. Herrenberg and the 25FM called for arming the population and eliminating the guerrillas. (Paramaribo International Service, 23 September, 31 October; *De Volkskrant*, 29 October; Bonaire Trans World Radio, 1 November; *FBIS*, 24 September, 3, 4 November.)

In November, Bouterse rejected a request from the Council of Christian Churches in Suriname to negotiate an agreement with the SLA. The following day, Internal Affairs Minister Jules Wijdenbosch summoned the church leaders to his office and accused them of thwarting government policy. A week later, the leader of C-47, the most powerful trade union federation in Suriname, announced that unless the government made good its promises on the restoration of democracy, the union members, including the bauxite workers, would hold demonstrations in the streets. (Reuter, 24 November; *De Volkskrant*, 26 November; *New York City Tribune*, 2 December; *FBIS*, 25 November, 2 December.)

Despite earlier claims that the insurgency would stall the planned transition to civilian rule, Bouterse announced before a 25FM rally on 12 December that general elections would be held pending the approval of a new constitution. The constitution is scheduled to be drafted by the National Assembly by the end of March 1987, after which it would be voted on in a national referendum. The 25FM has proposed general elections to be held on 1 October 1988. Bouterse also announced a "Christmas offensive" to expel the guerrillas from their bases in eastern Suriname, and he claimed that the insurgents had caused $53 million worth of damage. However, that offensive against the guerrillas failed. (*De Volkskrant*, 26 November; *FBIS*, 2 December; *Latinamerica Press*, 1 January 1987.) Also in December, a state of emergency was declared in the districts of Maroni, Commewijne, Brokopondo, Para, and in part of Sipaliwini, an area comprising three-quarters of the national territory (AFP, 4, 5 December).

**Foreign Relations.** Brazil was embarrassed by the possibility of being caught in the escalating guerrilla conflict as a supplier of both commercial credits and military assistance to Bouterse. Since 1983, Brazil has been Suriname's main ally, claiming that its assistance encouraged the Surinamese military to maintain its independence from Havana. Brazil has given Suriname a $70 million credit line, part of which was used to import eleven Brazilian amphibious lorries and armored cars, as well as a large amount of rockets and ammunition to bolster the flagging military. In the autumn, the downing of a private Brazilian helicopter and the SLA's warnings about guerrilla attacks against northern Brazil stimulated more diplomatic efforts by Brasilia to pressure the Bouterse regime to hasten the democratization process. Although Bouterse's personal envoy, Henricus Heidweiller, the former ambassador to the United States, did not receive assurances of Brazilian military assistance, he did meet with Brazilian officials in late December to

solicit political support for the regime. (*YICA*, 1985; CANA, 18 February; *O Estado de Sao Paulo*, 6 September, 24 December; *FBIS*, 25 February, 8 September.)

There were contradictory reports on Brasilia's policy toward Suriname. On the one hand, it was reported that in return for Bouterse's acceptance in principle of a Brazil-style political solution for his country—in which civilian parties would be allowed a heightened role in government while the military withdrew to the background—Brazilians would provide military support in civilian guise to eradicate guerrillas. However, according to Jair Krische, the director of the Justice and Human Rights Movement in Brazil, Brazilian military officers were involved in the shipment of French and Dutch military equipment to the SLA. It was reported that, in early December, Brunswijk had a meeting in Rio de Janeiro with agents of the National Information Service "to discuss details on the transport of arms through Brazilian territory." (*Caribbean Insight*, 6 October; *Latin American Weekly Report* [*LAWR*], 15 January 1987.)

Any prospects for the normalization of relations with Holland evaporated in 1986 as Paramaribo continued to accuse the Hague of destabilizing the country. Bouterse accused Dutch authorities of encouraging the aborted July invasion of the country by American mercenaries and claimed that Dutch embassy officials facilitated Brunswijk's escape to the Netherlands Antilles in June and his secret trip to Holland on a Dutch passport. Foreign Minister Herrenberg attempted to solicit from the Nonaligned Movement leaders, who met in Zimbabwe in September, a statement condemning Dutch interference in Surinamese affairs, but this failed miserably. Prime Minister Radhakishun, who had criticized Herrenberg's behavior toward the Dutch, met with Netherlands foreign minister Hans Van Den Broek at the end of September for talks on the possible resumption of Dutch development aid, which the Hague has linked to a timetable for the restoration of democratic rule. (CANA, 14 July, 3 September; AFP, 31 July; Bonaire Trans World Radio, 1 November; Paramaribo International Service, 10 November; *FBIS*, 15 July, 4 August, 4 September, 3, 12 November.)

In late November, J. B. Hoeman, the Netherlands foreign ministry's director general for international cooperation, made a secret visit to Suriname to investigate ways of channeling humanitarian aid to guerrilla-controlled areas in the eastern part of the country. Van Den Broek rejected Surinamese accusations of Dutch support for the guerrillas, and he expressed concern about reports that government forces had killed civilians during the five-month-old guerrilla war. (*Journal of Commerce*, 26 November; *Caribbean Insight*, January 1987.)

In December, the French government denied the suggestion that it was massing troops in French Guiana with a view to invade Suriname, and it pledged cooperation with Bouterse in his counterinsurgency drive. Yet Herrenberg had told the appointed National Assembly in mid-December that reinforcements had been flown to French Guiana from Guadeloupe and Martinique and that warships carrying helicopters had been seen off the coast. Throughout the year, French government support for the SLA had been rumored; sources claimed that the French resented Bouterse's support for the separatist movements in Martinique and Guadeloupe and feared Libyan surveillance of the European space program, Ariadne, at Kourou in French Guiana. (*LAWR*, 23 October; *CSM*, 18 November; *AP*, 10 December; *Caribbean Insight*, January 1987.)

During his late December visit to refugee camps in French Guiana, French Minister of Overseas Territories Bernard Pons claimed he warned Brunswijk that if he were arrested by the French, he would be returned to Suriname. Following the reports of an impending French invasion of Suriname, the French military attaché in Paramaribo, Pierre Annoi, met Herrenberg and Graanoogst for discussions, during which the French promised to make every effort to prevent Brunswijk from escaping into French Guiana. Annoi told Surinamese officials that French troops had been mobilized along the Marowijne River to receive and assist nearly 5,000 refugees from the conflict areas. (Paramaribo International Service, 29 December; *FBIS*, 30 December; *Caribbean Insight*, January 1987.)

Amid reports of civilian casualties in eastern Suriname and the presence of Libyan military advisers in the conflict zones, U.S. under secretary of state for inter-American affairs Elliott Abrams claimed that Libya was directing subversive operations from Paramaribo throughout South America and the Caribbean. On 16 December, U.S. secretary of state George P. Shultz expressed concern that Surinamese government forces may have violated the human rights of the civilian population in the area of the insurrection. (CANA-Reuter, 16 December; *FBIS*, 18 December; *WP*, 18 December.)

Bouterse sent condolences to Moammar Khadafy after the U.S. bombing raids of Tripoli and Benghazi, and he announced plans to visit Tripoli prior to the Nonaligned Movement summit in Zimbabwe to discuss the $100 million Libyan grant initialed in 1985. Plans to accompany the Libyan leader to the summit were postponed as the guerrilla war worsened. Government officials continued to proclaim that reports of a Libyan presence in the country were part of a disinformation campaign; however, in an interview with a Dutch journalist for *NRC Handelsblad*, Henk van Randwijk, the commander of the elite Echo Battalion who defected to the guerrillas on 22 August, claimed that 50–60 Libyans were in Suriname, the majority of whom came under "cultural exchanges" to act as instructors for the military. Van Randwijk maintained that Russian arms caches supplied by the Libyans were deposited throughout the country and that Libyans were stationed at Albina to monitor international telephone traffic through Kourou and to follow the developments of the European space program. He also maintained that the Libyan military agreements were intended to replace the Cuban pact that ended shortly before the U.S. operation in Grenada in 1983. (*YICA*, 1986; Paramaribo International Service, 18 April; *Journal of Commerce*, 18 August; CANA, 3 September; CLS, *Bulletin*, October; *FBIS*, 22 April, 4 September.)

Reports varied as to the number of Libyan military instructors and their involvement in the counterinsurgency efforts. Reports in the Dutch newspaper *NRC Handelsblad* in October claimed that the number of Libyans assisting the military had dramatically increased after the latter's failed offensive in September. There were said to be 200 instructors in the country, and groups of 45 and 60 Libyans, respectively, arrived in two airplanes in October. Emigrés report that some of these Libyans have been given Surinamese citizenship and travel on Suriname passports. In October, Libyan soldiers were reported to have engaged in attempts to stave off guerrilla attacks against the mining town of Moengo and, later, against attacks on the civilian population near the French Guiana border. (*NRC Handelsblad*, 13 October; *AFP*, 4 December; *FBIS*, 27 October, 5 December.)

Although Bouterse continued his verbal support for the Nicaraguan revolution in press interviews, Suriname maintained low-profile relations with the Sandinista Front of National Liberation. Suriname donated $400,000 worth of lumber to the Managua regime to reinforce the Puerto Cabezas pier on that country's Atlantic Coast. (Managua Domestic Service, 28 February; *FBIS*, 5 March.)

The Soviet Union continued to capitalize on its 1985 efforts to increase influence in the Surinamese trade union movement. In March, Vladimir Nikitin of the foreign relations section of the Soviet labor movement spent a week in Suriname as the guest of the trade union federation De Moederbond. The federation's closer ties with the Soviet Union and its acquiescence to the Bouterse regime provoked an official inquiry by the International Confederation of Free Trade Unions (ICFTU). After an extended investigation, the ICFTU voted in November to suspend De Moederbond from membership for "actions deemed . . . to be in contravention of the [ICFTU] Constitution or against the interests of world labor." While the ICFTU requested its affiliate to act to "effectively isolate the military regime of Suriname," the Soviet Union invited the powerful C-47 trade union federation to the 80th congress of Soviet labor at the end of February 1987 and pledged total cooperation with that union. A relatively subdued Soviet press reported in *Izvestiia* that Suriname's regime had international unity behind its attempt to quell the guerrillas. (Paramaribo International Service, 19 March, 26 December; *Izvestiia*, 28 October; *FBIS*, 31 March, 5 November, 30 December; AFL-CIO, *Bulletin*, January 1987.)

After bilateral talks in Beijing in late April between Herrenberg and Wu Xueqian, China agreed to provide Suriname with a $5 million interest-free loan; they later signed cooperative agreements in agriculture and shrimp farming (Paramaribo International Service, 18 April, 24 November; CANA, 23 May; *FBIS*, 22 April, 30 May, 25 November).

In intergovernmental organizations, Suriname continued to decrease its isolation and rehabilitate its image. In February, after a decision to strengthen ties with Trinidad-Tobago, the government announced plans to seek membership in the Caribbean Community (CARICOM). Suriname also strengthened ties with the Nonaligned Movement by holding a conference in July in Paramaribo that was attended by delegations from Egypt, Indonesia, Guyana, and the Netherlands Antilles. At the meeting, Bouterse stressed that his foreign policy was within the framework of the movement. For the first time, Suriname was chosen to be one of the vice chairmen of the United Nations, where Bouterse addressed the 41st General Assembly. In his speech, he used restrained rhetoric in supporting SWAPO in Namibia, the African National Congress in South Africa, and the Contadora peace process in Central America, and in calling for the demilitarization of the Caribbean. Despite concerns raised by the United States, Suriname won muted support for its pledge before the Organization of American States' sixteenth regular session to move toward a democratic system. (CANA, 5 February, 13 November; Paramaribo International Service, 15 August, 18 September; *FBIS*, 25 February, 18 August, 22 September, 18 November.)

R. Bruce McColm
*Freedom House, New York*

# United States

**Population.**  240,856,000
**Party.**  Communist Party USA (CPUSA)
**Founded.**  1919
**Membership.**  15,000–20,000

**General Secretary.** Gus Hall
**Political Bureau.** Gus Hall, Henry Winston (recently deceased), Arnold Bechetti, James West, George Meyers, Charlene Mitchell, James Steele, Betty Smith, Louis Diskin, Lee Dlugin
**Central Committee.** 83 members
**Status.** Legal
**Last Congress.** Twenty-third, 10–13 November 1983, in Cleveland, Ohio
**Last Election.** 1984 presidential, under 0.1 percent
**Auxiliary Organizations.** U.S. Peace Council, National Alliance Against Racist and Political Repression, Trade Unionists for Action and Democracy, National Congress of Unemployed Organizations, Young Communist League, Women for Racial and Economic Equality
**Publications.** *People's Daily World* (Mike Zagarell, ed.), *Political Affairs* (Barry Cohen, ed.)

The CPUSA is the premier Marxist-Leninist organization in the United States. Founded in 1919, the CPUSA achieved its greatest influence in the years from 1935 to 1950. In this period it had a significant role in the labor movement, particularly in the Congress of Industrial Organizations (CIO), and had a measure of influence within liberal and labor political circles in a number of states. The CPUSA reached its greatest organizational strength in the late 1930s with a membership of nearly 100,000. As the Cold War developed and domestic anticommunism increased following World War II, the CPUSA became politically isolated and was driven from most labor unions. The federal government prosecuted a number of CPUSA leaders in the late 1940s and early 1950s, and the party sent many of its leading cadre underground. The 1956 revelations of Stalin's crimes by Soviet leaders, along with the suppression of the Hungarian revolution, prompted a number of party leaders and the bulk of its members to leave the CPUSA. From a low point of a few thousand members in the late 1950s, the party has regained membership slowly and steadily, showing its greatest growth in the last decade.

**Leadership and Party Organization.** Gus Hall, age 76, has served as general secretary since 1959 and has led the CPUSA longer than any individual in its history; he is one of the longest tenured communist party leaders in the world. Henry Winston, who had been national chairman since 1966, died in Moscow on 12 December at the age of 75. Other prominent leaders are Arnold Bechetti (organizational secretary), James West (Central Review Commission chair), George Meyers (Labor Commission chair), Charlene Mitchell (Commission on Afro-American Equality chair), James Steele (Legislative and Political Action Department chair), James Jackson (Central Committee secre-tary), Si Gerson (Legislative and Political Action Department chair), Scott Marshall (Trade Union Department secretary), Sid Taylor (party treasurer), Jarvis Tyner (New York Communist Party head), Sam Webb (Michigan Communist Party head), and Ted Pearson (Illinois Communist Party head).

The party achieved a long-discussed goal of merging its two daily newspapers into a single national journal with regional and state editions. Mike Zagarell, editor of the East Coast *Daily World*, became editor of the merged *People's Daily World* (*PDW*), and Carl Boice, editor of the West Coast *People's World*, became associate editor. The new journal is slightly longer and uses more color and pictures than its predecessors, but is otherwise little changed. The party's authoritative ideological journal is *Political Affairs* (*PA*). The party's various auxiliary organizations also publish newsletters and journals aimed at specialized audiences.

The CPUSA has emphasized stricter personal standards for members in recent years. James West stated that "the fight for revolutionary moral standards has become both a party question and a question of the class struggle, of the mass fight for peace. It is a party question for the CPUSA because our party . . . does not live in a vacuum. Its members, living in the most aggressive decadent imperialism, surrounded by ubiquitous bourgeois degeneracy day in and day out, are subject to corrupting and opportunist pressures and influences without letup." West announced that in *To Be a Communist*, the party's new book on membership standards, "vigilance against the work of the class enemy, against antiworking class influences on personal behavior and in the party are . . . given attention, including the use of drugs, drunkenness, family and personal life, [and] male supremacy . . . The booklet condemns the use and dissemination of pornography [and] opposes sexual promiscuity, conduct which leads to alienation and hostility between men and women, undermining mutual respect and unity in the struggle for common betterment." (*WMR*, September.)

**Domestic Party Affairs.** The CPUSA ran a few candidates for public office in 1986, but these campaigns were usually for local office and were not of great concern to the party. Instead, the CPUSA placed its major effort on the defeat of congressional candidates who supported President Ronald Reagan. In a single speech, Hall described Reagan as "a hypocritical racist," "stealing food from the mouths of hungry children and destitute, poor people," "evicting the poor from shelter," "ploughing under what is left of family farms," "expelling students and depriving youth of education," "shutting the sick and dying out of hospital emergency rooms," and "picking the pockets of the elderly and infirm" (*WMR*, May).

In a discussion of political strategy, Henry Winston stated that "U.S. Communists are adopting the tactic of building the All People's Front . . . *It is many sided in character.* The Front involves people of different classes and political persuasions opposed to nuclear war and other policies of the Reagan administration. This year's congressional elections are of critical importance. A shift of just four members in the Senate could move it away from Reagan and his policies" (*PA*, July).

James Steele announced that "the struggle to end Republican control of the Senate and shift the political balance in the Congress is the best context for making a breakthrough in electing trade union, working-class, Afro-American and other minority, and women candidates." He described the election as a way "to draw the class and social forces of the All People's Front into a common struggle for common objectives." Steele stated that "in this election it is especially necessary to combine the tactic of working with forces in the two-party system with tactics of developing political independence . . . We must be an important factor for unity in the nitty-gritty organizational work as well as on the policy level. But to play this kind of qualitative role we have to position ourselves among the broad left, progressive, liberal, and center forces involved in the electoral struggles. We have to be active participants in coalitions, in grass-roots mobilizational work." He concluded that "unity, clarity, and joint action of the broad forces of the All People's Front

are the key to shifting the political balance in Congress." (*PA*, March.)

Just before the autumn political campaigns got under way, Steele reminded his comrades that the time was not right for communists to work outside the two-party system. Steele called for "working with the mass forces of political independence still inside the Democratic Party" and picked out the Rainbow Coalition of Jesse Jackson for special praise as well as lauding the New Directions conference of left-wing Democratic Party activists organized by Michael Harrington of the Democratic Socialists of America (*PA*, August). In a speech to the CPUSA 1986 national conference, Hall stated that the party's major emphasis was on operating within the broader political arena and for the near term eschewed independent political action. He told the 700 delegates that progressive forces were growing in America and that communists "must . . . recognize and work with the broader, more spontaneous and less organized sectors" of this progressive movement (*PDW*, 7 August). After the elections, the party expressed great pleasure in the Republican Party's loss of control of the Senate and attributed the victory to the growing power of labor and progressive forces. Hall proclaimed the election to be a vindication of communist views and asserted that "the forces of political independence emerged as the strongest forces in the country" (*PDW*, 26 November).

The party's journals provided extensive coverage of strikes and internal trade union matters, and the CPUSA appeared to place major emphasis on gaining a larger role in union affairs. The *Daily World* reported that the party was distributing ten communist party shop newsletters within different unions at various plants. Hall also called for a re-emphasis on the party's policy of industrial concentration (that is, placing large numbers of party members in a single plant) and greater use of shop papers in those plants picked for the concentration strategy. Without claiming any organizational credit for the CPUSA, Hall spoke with great enthusiasm about the "growth of a Left trend and Left forces, on both rank and file and leadership" in the AFL-CIO, and praised the friendly attitude of William Winpisinger, national head of the Machinists' Union, toward the communist party and the Soviet Union (*PA*, March). The *People's Daily World* also published a lengthy interview with Winpisinger regarding his views on politics, unionism, and communism as part of its May Day edition.

In March, the party sponsored a special trade union conference with attendance reported at "nearly 200" to discuss the party's progress in trade union circles (*DW*, 27 March). George Meyers stated that, in the trade union movement, "class partnership and pro-imperialist policies are still present, but they have been put on the defensive," and he pointed to the growing criticism of defense spending, support for the Sandinistas, antiapartheid actions, and willingness to meet with Soviet trade unionists by leading AFL-CIO figures as signs of the growth of healthy trends in the labor movement (*WMR*, August).

One of the party's clear areas of advance in 1986 was its progress in establishing an accepted role in academia. It had won a limited presence on college faculties in the 1930s and 1940s, but had almost entirely lost that position in the 1950s. Over the last few years, however, there has been a noticeable increase in the number of faculty identified with the CPUSA that write for its journals, teach in its party schools, or associate with its auxiliary organizations. For example, in April, the *Daily World* announced a May Day centennial conference sponsored by the American Institute for Marxist Studies, a body long associated with the CPUSA, and by 28 faculty members from eighteen colleges.

In recent years, the chief organization linking collegiate faculty with the CPUSA has been the Marxist Education Press (MEP). The MEP, which uses the Anthropology Department of the University of Minnesota, Minneapolis, as its mailing address, is led by Irwin Marquit, a physics professor at the university and the party's 1974 candidate for governor of Minnesota. The MEP and scholars associated with it have sponsored academic conferences on Marxism-Leninism for several years; the first was in 1976, the fifth in 1980. In recent years, however, the MEP has spread beyond the Midwest with a national Marxist scholars conference in Cincinnati in 1983, a West Coast conference in 1984, a national conference at the University of Chicago in 1985, a national conference on philosophy and ideology at the University of Minnesota in 1985 (jointly sponsored by the MEP and the Academy of Sciences of Cuba), a Southeast conference at the University of South Florida in 1985, and a Pacific Northwest conference at the University of Washington, Seattle, in April 1986. The Seattle conference reportedly had an attendance of 500 and heard from such communist academic stars as Herbert Aptheker (a historian on the faculty of the University of California, Berkeley,

law school and editor of the party-aligned journal *Jewish Affairs*) and Angela Davis (who teaches ethics at San Francisco State University and was the party's 1984 candidate for U.S. vice president). (*MEP News*, April.)

**Auxiliary Organizations.** The U.S. Peace Council is one of the most active of the CPUSA's associated organizations. Michael Myerson is its executive director and its chairman is Mark Solomon of the History Department of Simmons College. After years of being isolated due to its communist connections and partisanship for the Soviet Union, it is slowly winning acceptance by major American peace organizations. The council has been particularly successful in developing ties with religiously oriented peace organizations; for example, Reverend Tony Watkings, Religious Circles coordinator of the council, served at one time on the executive committee of the National Nuclear Freeze Campaign and as disarmament coordinator of the Clergy and Laity Concerned. Also showing some signs of life after many years of near dormancy is the National Council of American-Soviet Friendship (Rev. Alan Thomson, director).

The Young Communist League (YCL), of which John Bachtell is national chairman, held a convention in July with a reported attendance of nearly 200 delegates from eighteen states and 50 cities. The *People's Daily World* (10 July) stated that 25 percent of the delegates were Afro-Americans, 20 percent were Latino, 63 percent were under the age of 25, 45 percent were working youth, 34 percent were students, 13 percent were unemployed, and 38 percent had been YCL members for less than a year.

The YCL held its first national school for organizers in 1986 and publishes the journal *Dynamic*. The conservative organization Accuracy in Academia reported YCL chapters at the University of Texas, Austin; Wayne State University, Detroit; Brooklyn College; City College of New York; University of Washington, Seattle; University of Arizona; University of Dayton; Youngstown State University; University of Massachusetts, Amherst; and the University of Florida (*Campus Report*, September).

**International Views, Positions, and Activities.** The CPUSA supports the Soviet Union without deviation on all issues and in all arenas. In a report to a party conference, Hall expressed satisfaction with the increasing acceptance of the Soviet view on arms control by American peace groups, pointed with pride to the success of the Goodwill Games in Moscow between Soviet and American athletes, praised the success of the Mississippi Peace Cruise by a joint delegation of Soviet and American peace activists, and expressed his pleasure that U.S. trade union leaders met with a delegation of Soviet trade unionists over the objections of Lane Kirkland, head of the AFL-CIO. Almost every issue of the *People's Daily World* included one or two articles praising some aspect of Soviet culture, technology, agriculture, politics, or government.

CPUSA support for Soviet views included a defense of Soviet actions in the Chernobyl nuclear accident and a persistent and defiant defense of the Soviet destruction of a Korean airliner. Hall simply stated that "who can now believe that the Korean airliner was not a U.S.-CIA directed Spy Plane?" (*PDW*, 23 November). The *People's Daily World* movie reviews were quick to take offense at any films that present the Soviet Union or communism in a hostile light; for example, the journal strongly condemned the highly popular film *Top Gun* for its glorifications of a U.S. Navy fighter pilot who shoots down Soviet Mig aircraft. CPUSA support for the Soviet Union extended even to history; *Political Affairs* published an article justifying without caveat the Hitler-Stalin Pact of 1939.

The CPUSA sent official delegates to a number of communist conferences around the world. Hall attended and spoke to the Twenty-seventh Congress of the Communist Party of the Soviet Union (CPSU) and met briefly with Mikhail Gorbachev. Other foreign communist party meetings attended by CPUSA delegates included the Third Congress of the Cuban Communist Party (Henry Winston), the Thirteenth Congress of the Communist Party of India (Betty Smith), the Seventeenth Congress of the Communist Party of Czechoslovakia (Louis Diskin), the Thirteenth Congress of the Bulgarian Communist Party (James Jackson), the Eleventh Congress of the Socialist Unity Party of East Germany (James West), the Nineteenth Congress of the Mongolian People's Revolutionary Party (Lee Dlugin), the Eighth Congress of the West German Communist Party (Sam Webb), and an informal meeting with the leadership of the Hungarian Socialist Workers' Party (Lee Dlugin). John Pittman also represented the CPUSA at a special meeting of the editorial council of the *World Marxist Review* that met in Prague to consider program guidelines laid down by the CPSU Congress. A CPUSA delegate also attended a June meeting in Ulan Bator, Mongolian People's Republic, where nineteen communist parties met to plan a formal conference of Asian and Pacific communist parties for 1987.

**Other Marxist-Leninist Organizations.** Although it has only about 2,000 members, the Socialist Workers' Party (SWP) is the largest and most active Marxist-Leninist body independent of CPUSA. The SWP, founded in 1937, is associated with the international Trotskyist organization, the United Secretariat of the Fourth International. Jack Barnes is SWP national secretary. The party publishes *The Militant* (Doug Jenness and Margaret Jayko, co-editors), a sister Spanish-language paper, *Perspectiva Mundial*, and a Marxist theoretical journal, *New International. Intercontinental Press*, an SWP journal emphasizing international affairs, was merged with *The Militant* in August. The SWP also sponsors a publishing house, Pathfinder Press, and an associated chain of bookstores. The SWP's youth affiliate, the Young Socialist Alliance (YSA), publishes *Young Socialist*. YSA national secretary is Jackie Floyd, and the national chair is Mark Curtis.

The SWP and YSA were deeply involved in the antiwar movement of the Vietnam War era and absorbed a number of antiwar activists. Jack Barnes and other SWP leaders, for example, had been student radicals at Minnesota's elite Carleton College. In contrast to the CPUSA, the SWP reflects many of the interests and priorities of the New Left of that period and the broad left movement of today, particularly in an emphasis on homosexual rights, abortion rights, and radical feminism. As part of its concern with feminism, the SWP sponsored an educational conference emphasizing a new Pathfinder Press publication, *Cosmetics, Fashions, and the Exploitation of Women*. This book finds that standards of beauty are set in capitalist societies in such a way that the cosmetics industry is able to "rake in profits" (*The Militant*, 9 May, 7 November).

Along with the SWP's abandonment of traditional Trotskyism has come a markedly more pro-Soviet stance. The party now calls for reform of communist regimes and has largely put aside its call for the revolutionary transformation of such states. Although still critical of Soviet and communist actions at times, the SWP takes a generally benign view of the Soviet Union and regards "American imperialism" as the world's chief problem.

In part due to conflict over the SWP's emphasis of matters that were not part of the traditional agenda of Trotskyism, a large number of SWP members and long-time leaders either quit or were expelled in 1984. Some of those who left formed an organization and a journal entitled *Socialist Action*; another group, associated with the veteran SWP leader George Breitman (who died in April 1986), formed the Fourth International Tendency and published the *Bulletin in Defense of Marxism*; and a third group followed Peter Camejo, the SWP presidential candidate in 1976, into a body called the North Star Network.

One element of the broad left movement that the SWP has not adopted is enthusiasm for the religious left. Doug Jenness, editor of *The Militant*, stated that "'liberation theology' simply reflects the attempt by some clergy to accommodate their religious beliefs to the popularity of socialism among the toilers they are trying to influence" and that "working people are driven to strike and organize unions, and some day will wage a revolutionary struggle to overturn capitalist rule, *in spite of, not because of*, their religious views" (*The Militant*, 28 November).

Two issues absorbed most of the SWP's attention in 1986: support for the Sandinista government in Nicaragua, and the strike of United Food and Commercial Workers Local P-9 against the Hormel Corporation. The SWP has supported without significant criticism the policies of the Sandinista regime and has taken a prominent role in American protests against the Reagan administration policy toward Nicaragua. The SWP's concern with feminism and abortion rights, however, has colored even its view of Nicaraguan events. *The Militant*, in a 28 February report on a speech by Jack Barnes to the SWP National Committee, noted that Barnes placed events in Nicaragua at the center of world politics and went on to state that "the discussion and debate that have opened up in Nicaragua over whether to legalize abortion . . . is another front in the war against imperialism."

The SWP's attitude toward the P-9 strike and its differences with the CPUSA illustrate the contrasting strategies of the two parties. Both parties, along with almost all radical organizations, enthusiastically supported the long and bitter strike by packinghouse workers against Hormel's flagship plant in Austin, Minnesota. The strike was lost, however, and the national leadership of the United Food and Commercial Workers eventually took over Local P-9 in an attempt to salvage something from the debacle and to retain union recognition at the plant. The suspended leadership of local P-9

refused to give way, attempted to continue the strike, and created a rival union, the North American Meat Packers Union. The SWP supported the new union's defiance of the parent international union, but the CPUSA denounced the new body as a dual union that threatened labor unity.

Also in contrast to the CPUSA, the SWP followed an independent political course in 1986 rather than working within the Democratic Party. The party ran 62 candidates for public offices in 23 states, mostly for congressional seats. None received a substantial vote. For the longer term, the SWP has stated that "experience will convince workers that, to challenge the employers effectively, a political movement is necessary that can go beyond the important but limited battles in each plant, industry, city, or sector of the working class, a movement that would mobilize millions of working people to fight their exploiters. The most likely initial form for such a movement in the United States will be a labor party based on the trade unions, which would champion the interests of all working people" (*The Militant*, 7 November).

For the SWP, the most heartening event in 1986 was a decision by Federal Judge Thomas Griesa that the Federal Bureau of Investigation's long-standing inquiry into the SWP was illegal; he granted the party $250,000 in damages. The case, *Socialist Workers' Party v. Attorney General*, was originally filed in 1973 and is expected to be appealed by the government.

Besides the SWP, there are a number of other Marxist-Leninist organizations, but none have more than a few hundred members. Other organizations that have their origins in Trotskyism include the Workers' League (a body associated with the Workers' Revolutionary Party of the United Kingdom), the Freedom Socialist Party (a feminist splinter of the SWP in the Pacific Northwest), the Workers' World Party (the product of a 1958 split in the SWP), and the Spartacist League. In March, three small organizations coming out of the Trotskyist tradition—the International Socialists, Workers' Power, and Socialist Unity—merged into a new body entitled Solidarity. The new body does not call itself Trotskyist and prefers the label "revolutionary democratic socialists." The International Socialists grew out of the "third camp" position, which defined the Soviet Union and the United States as equally oppressive. The new organization reflects this view in a statement of support for Polish Solidarity and the Nicaraguan Sandinistas. Solidarity opposed working within the Democratic

Party and is associated with a new journal, *Against the Current*.

The United States has several small organizations with an ultrarevolutionary and vaguely Maoist orientation. The Revolutionary Communist Party, led by former Berkeley student radical Bob Avakian, was formed in 1975 from the Bay Area Revolutionary Union. The Marxist-Leninist Party, USA, publishes *The Workers' Advocate*, and its Detroit branch publishes a literary journal entitled *Struggle*. A third group, the League of Revolutionary Struggle, was once a leading Maoist organization but now disclaims the Maoist label, although it still professes admiration for Mao.

Other Marxist-Leninist groups include the Democratic Workers' Party, which appears to have disintegrated in 1986; the Communist Workers' Party, best known for the fact that five of its members were killed in a gun battle with Nazis and Klansmen in Greensboro, North Carolina, in 1980; the Progressive Labor Party, a body known for its use of physical disruption as a tactic; the Communist Labor Party; and a pro-Soviet group called Line of March, whose journal *Frontline* had the distinction of being twice chastised by the CPUSA for ideological errors.

John E. Haynes
*St. Paul, Minnesota*

# Uruguay

**Population.** 2,947,000
**Party.** Communist Party of Uruguay (PCU)
**Founded.** 1920
**Membership.** 7,500 (estimated)
**General Secretary.** Rodney Arismendi
**Secretariat.** Rodney Arismendi, Jaime Perez, Alberto Altesor, Thelman Borges, Leopoldo Carlos Bruera, Ramon Cabrera, Felix Diaz, Leon Lev, Esteban Valenti (*La Hora*, 23 December 1983)
**Status.** Legal
**Last Congress.** Twentieth, December 1970 (National Conference, December 1985)
**Last Election.** November 1984; PCU ran within Frente Amplio coalition, 6 percent, no seats.
**Auxiliary Organizations.** Union of Communist Youth
**Publications.** *La Hora*; *El Popular* (newspaper)

The year did not start out to be a dramatic one in Uruguay. The newly restored civilian democratic government completed its first year in office on 1 March. President Sanguinetti and his Colorado Party could be justifiably proud of an administration that had completely restored civil liberties. The successful renegotiation of the foreign debt, an economy that grew by almost 4 percent, and a 30 percent increase in exports gave the government reason to feel good about itself. A brilliant foreign policy engineered by Foreign Minister Enrique Iglesias had even won the respect of the left. The year ended, however, with the dramatic and controversial eleventh-hour passage of a law granting amnesty to the armed forces and police for human rights violations committed during the almost twelve years they were in power.

The Frente Amplio, or Broad Front, is a coalition of leftist parties and movements in Uruguay. It continued to be divided into three main tendencies:

first, a social-democratic wing dominated by List 99, which is headed by Hugo Batalla and includes the Socialist Party led by José Pedro Cardoso, and the Christian Democratic Party, which did extremely poorly in the 1984 elections and is led by Héctor Lescano; second, to the left of the first group, the PCU, which is still run by Arismendi and his heir apparent Jaime Pérez; and third, on the far left, a smattering of very small groups, the most well known of which is the Izquierda Democrática Independiente (IDI), headed by Alba Roballo.

The first group wants the Frente Amplio to become a viable alternative to Colorado or Blanco rule. It wishes to see the Frente Amplio replace the Partido Nacional (Blancos) as the second most important party in the country and eventually challenge the Colorados for control of government. The PCU continues to practice an opposition, anti-system politics and would probably like the Frente Amplio to continue in this mold. The far-left continues to be as unrealistic as it is unimportant in the scheme of party politics.

During 1986 the Frente Amplio restructured itself. The front's new by-laws create three governing bodies: a Congress, a National Plenary, and a Political Board. The regular Congress will meet every two and a half years, and a special Congress will meet six months before national elections. The National Plenary is a sort of central committee that must hold at least one session every two months. The Political Board will conduct the day-to-day business of the front. What remains unclear under the new stucture is the freedom of individual factions and parties to adopt an independent position on issues in which there has been a lack of consensus within the Political Board or at the level of the National Plenary. But such ambiguity is a frequent reality for political coalitions, especially on the left. The Frente Amplio consists of such disparate elements that it is difficult to conceive of smooth internal governance.

The Frente Amplio's decision to not allow General Seregni to accept President Sanguinetti's invitation to accompany him on the state visit to Washington, D.C., was criticized harshly by the Socialist and Christian Democratic parties. What is most interesting about the decision is that it was reached by consensus within the political committee of the Frente Amplio despite the objections of Seregni himself, the Social and Christian Democratic parties, and List 99, which by itself had received 40 percent of the front's votes in the 1984 election. Thus, the decision is a good example of how the far-

left inside the Frente Amplio frequently can force the coalition into negative and uncooperative stances. Many moderates within the left publicly argue that the decision had hurt the credibility of a movement that was trying to present itself as a "real alternative" political party for the country. The Socialists especially felt that the Frente Amplio had lost an opportunity to legitimize its role as a leftist opposition coalition capable of interacting with Washington.

In late September, a government-backed proposal of amnesty for human rights violations during the military dictatorship was defeated in the opposition-dominated Parliament. Subsequently, a proposal by the Blancos, the principal opposition party to the Colorado government, also failed when both the Colorados, who thought it went too far, and the Frente Amplio, who thought it did not go far enough, refused to support it. The political stalemate got progressively worse and reached its nadir on 14 November, when, for the first time in Uruguay's history, Parliament could not pass the budget authorization for the following year. The Sanguinetti government threatened to call for early congressional elections (the presidency would not be at stake) unless the budget and human rights stalemate could be overcome. By early December, the budgetary impasse had been resolved amidst rumors that the Colorados and Blancos were close to agreement on an amnesty bill.

Shortly thereafter, the military commanders during the dictatorship issued a declaration in which they admitted that "transgressions" had occurred while they were in power. Vice President Tarigo immediately proclaimed the statement to be a human rights abuses confession by the military. The Sanguinetti government also hinted that Uruguay was still in a less than perfect transition period from dictatorship to full democracy. Such an admission, albeit oblique, was enough to give Wilson Ferreira Aldunate, leader of the Blancos, the excuse to support an amnesty bill, which he had vigorously opposed only months earlier, by claiming that his party was voting for the bill in order to ensure the stability of Uruguay's fragile democracy.

On 22 December, by a vote of 60 to 37, the Uruguayan Senate passed an amnesty bill that was promptly signed by Sanguinetti. The legislation in effect prevents the prosecution of any human rights violations committed by military and police personnel from 1973 to 1985. In addition, the law terminated the 38 cases already pending in the courts.

The legislation was only passed, however, after

bitter debate in both houses of Parliament, fistfights between legislators, and violent street demonstrations. It took effect just one hour before Colonel José Nino Gavazzo was due to appear in court to testify in a case concerning the 1976 abduction of Uruguayan journalist Eduardo Rodriguez Larreta in Argentina and his removal to a detention center in Montevideo. Gavazzo and the entire military institution had made it clear that they would not participate in any trials and would ignore or resist any subpoenas to do so. Such refusal would have created a full-blown constitutional crisis between the executive and the military authority in Uruguay.

Labor relations remained problematic during 1986. The general labor confederation in Uruguay, known as the PIT-CNT, continued vigorously to support strikes and work stoppages. A general strike was held on 17 June, the day that Sanguinetti met with President Reagan at the White House, to protest U.S. policy in Central America. The PIT-CNT, which is controlled by the left and dominated by individuals closely associated with the PCU, was opposed to the amnesty legislation as well as to the government's policy of declaring some areas (such as port facilities) "essential services" in order to prevent strikes or to declare them illegal. It remains to be seen whether the labor movement, the PCU, and the entire Frente Amplio will increase their opposition to government programs and policies or continue their "critical support" in the name of protecting and strengthening the redemocratization process.

In May, Cuban vice president Carlos Rafael Rodríguez visited Montevideo and met with Sanguinetti and Iglesias. These were the first high-level contacts between the two governments in 21 years. Uruguay's democratic government had restored diplomatic relations with Cuba in October of 1985.

The PCU celebrated its 66th anniversary in September. The document released during the celebration contained an extensive analysis of the economic situation and made the following recommendations:

Real increases in salaries, wages, and pensions; elimination of the VAT charges on products in the basic family basket to reduce the cost of living; control of prices of basic commodities; preferential electricity and water rates that will benefit low-income neighborhoods; an appropriate rent law; the renegotiation of the foreign debt to cut the flow of resources being sent out of the country; the reorganization of the private banking system to orient credit toward basic activities; the freezing of nonresident deposits and those of large depositors; the review and correction of the dealings in the selling of portfolios and compulsory deposits in foreign currencies that the private banking system has deposited with the Central Bank; the reorganization of the meatpacking industry and the stimulation of the strategic industrial initiatives that come under the jurisdiction of the state; the implementation of a surcharge system on exports to protect national industries; the selective treatment of the internal debt to avoid the selling of agricultural land and factories to foreign investors; the exploitation of the reduction in international oil prices to reduce production costs; and the modification of the rural tax system and the appropriation of land of large debtors to be given to aspiring colonists. (*La Hora*, 21 September; *FBIS*, 9 October.)

In an interview early in 1986, Eleuterio Huidobro, one of the leaders of the former guerrilla movement, the Movimiento de Liberación Nacional (MLN-Tupamaros), conceded that past failures of the movement indicated that it had failed to establish links with the masses. In addition, he admitted that the organization had adopted a militarism that caused it to forget the essentially political substance of its actions. The MLN-Tupamaro's political platform was described as based on three fundamental pillars: agrarian reform, nationalization of banking, and the nonpayment of the foreign debt.

On 29 July, the executive board of the MLN-Tupamaros issued a warning that, if the government and people were being held hostage by the military over such issues as a full account of human rights violations during the dictatorship, then the Tupamaros might have to reconsider their current political position. This veiled threat of renewed subversive or armed activity was immediately denounced by the rightists and the government. *El Día*, a major progovernment newspaper controlled by Tarigo, criticized the Tupamaros for their contribution to violence and instability that brought on the dictatorship, and it chided them for apparently reviving their old ways of thinking, if not of acting. *El Día* also strenuously denied that the government was under pressure from the military concerning the impending human rights court cases, although those denials seemed less creditable as the year progressed.

Martin Weinstein
*William Paterson College*
*of New Jersey*

# Venezuela

**Population.** 17,791,000
**Parties.** Communist Party of Venezuela (Partido Comunista de Venezuela; PCV); Movement to Socialism (Movimiento al Socialismo; MAS)
**Founded.** PCV: 1931; MAS: 1971 (as splinter from PCV)
**Membership.** PCV: 4,000 (estimated)
**Top Leaders.** PCV: Alonso Ojeda Olaechea (general secretary); MAS: Pompeyo Márquez (president)
**Politburo.** PCV: 7 members: Alonso Ojeda Olaechea, Jesús Faría, Pedro Ortega Díaz, Eduardo Gallegos Mancera, Trino Melean, Silvino Varela, Ali Morales. 3 alternates: including Luis Ciano and José Manuel Carrasquel
**Central Committee.** PCV: 65 members
**Status.** Both legal
**Last Congress.** PCV: Seventh, October 1985; MAS: Sixth National Convention, June–July 1985
**Last Election.** 1983; PCV: 3 of 195 deputies; MAS: 10 of 195 deputies, 2 senators
**Auxiliary Organizations.** PCV: United Central of Venezuelan Workers (Central Unitaria de Trabajadores Venezolanos; CUTV); Communist Youth (Juventud Comunista; JC)
**Publication.** PCV: *Tribuna Popular*, Américo Díaz Nuñez, director

The PCV in 1986 seemed to be on its way to what could become the party's fifth major split. Other leftist parties, however, began to speak of unity for the 1988 national elections. The Revolutionary Left Movement, (Movimiento de Izquierda Revolucionário; MIR), a 1960 splinter of the governing Democratic Action (Acción Democrática; AD), visualized a broad front similar to the January 23 Movement (1958), as well as an outright merger of the three democratic socialist parties. This idea was being studied by the other two parties concerned: the MAS and the People's Electoral Movement (Movimiento Electoral del Pueblo; MEP), a 1967 AD splinter.

**The PCV.** Organizational reforms introduced at the Seventh Congress for the purpose of promoting internal democracy failed to quell dissension. Discontent throughout 1986 from the "renovation" faction culminated in sanctions applied to three PCV leaders in November by the fifth plenum of the Central Committee (CC). Radamés Larrazábal, federal deputy and PCV militant for 42 years, was removed from the Politburo permanently and from the CC for one year. He was replaced on the Politburo by first alternate Ali Morales. Two former general secretaries of the JC and members of the CC were also sanctioned: Noel Sirit was banished from the CC for one year, and Simón Rodríguez received only public censure. All three have left the PCV, and Larrazábal has been attempting to form a new movement. Among others, fifteen regional directors of the PCV in Lara resigned to join him.

A PCV statement explained the sanctions as a response to "a long process of statutory violations and factional activities against party leadership; when this leadership was upheld in the Seventh Congress, the dissidents turned against the PCV itself, publicly slandering the party and inciting the desertion of members" (*El Nacional*, 6 November). A PCV spokesman later said the party had no other choice but to sanction the rebels who were violating the principle of "democratic centralism, without which no communist party can exist" (ibid., 17 November).

According to Rodríguez, however, the "Faría

group" characterized "any discrepancy with orthodox opinion as divisive . . . preventing any understanding of new realities" (ibid., 4 November). For Sirit, the sanctions were "the latest step in the systematic elimination of innovative opinion within the PCV" (ibid.). Larrazábal admitted that in the past he was guilty of the same dogmatism but felt justified in correcting his errors now: "Dogmatism has turned our revolutionary doctrine into cookbooks and prayer books (*recetarios y recitarios*) . . . present leadership is incapable of assimilating new and creative developments of Marxism-Leninism worldwide . . . it has converted the PCV into a sect isolated from the masses, from the left, and from the revolutionary process" (ibid.).

In other areas, the PCV continued to criticize Venezuelan laws that are "dictated abroad," such as government assumption of the exchange risk for payment of private foreign debt, and settlement of claims against expropriated foreign petroleum companies. A statement from the Politburo called the foreign debt agreement "a betrayal of national interests . . . with no contingency clause in the case of natural or financial disaster . . . The waiver of immunity against foreign embargo is unconstitutional" (ibid., 11 April).

At the ninth congress of the CUTV in November, president elect José Manuel Carrasquel (age 40) promised to work for labor unity, greater political consciousness of workers, and a reduction of political party interference in the labor unions. Items approved by the congress included nonpayment of the foreign debt; support for the Contadora peace efforts in Central America; a demand for freedom of political prisoners in Chile; and an annual CUTV conference, with participation at various levels, to promote internal democracy. Later, the CUTV criticized a new government package of economic measures as unrealistic, antipopular, and inspired by the International Monetary Fund (ibid., 25 November, 2, 9 December). In a seminar on draft legislation to amend the labor law, Pedro Ortega Díaz said that proposed restrictions on the right to strike are unacceptable.

Regarding the U.S. congressional approval of aid to the Nicaraguan *contras*, Ortega Díaz said the money itself was not so important, since the *contras* get it anyway, but the congressional support could give President Reagan courage to invade Nicaragua (ibid., 1 July). According to the PCV, the U.S. arms sales to Iran and the channeling of the proceeds to the *contras* were "manifestations of the profound decomposition of Reagan's government, of its ter-

rorist character, and of the adventurism of its foreign policy" (ibid., 15 December).

The car of PCV deputy Raul Esté was destroyed by a bomb in August. Esté has been an active gadfly in ongoing corruption and human rights scandals and has received many threats.

**The MAS.** With two rather turbulent years of self criticism and reorganization behind it, the MAS projected a calmer, less arrogant image in 1986. President Pompeyo Márquez conceded that any leftist alliance in 1988 would have to include the PCV, which had been a distasteful concept to the MAS in 1983 (ibid., 24 March). After the MIR launched its unity proposal, MAS general secretary Freddy Muñoz said that the idea of a merger of the socialist parties was positive, if complex, and deserved study (ibid., 4 December). This sobriety may not survive when the party lifts its ban on discussion of presidential candidates in February 1987. Juvencio Pulgar has not left the party and still favors an independent unity candidate of the center or an alliance with AD or the Social Christian Party (COPEI).

Teodoro Petkoff, the MAS presidential candidate in 1983, insisted that the country needs an entirely new development model, an integrated promotion of small and medium industry and agriculture in order to diversify the petroleum economy. In the short term, he felt the government was far too timid with its foreign creditors, accepting their demand for exchange guarantees on the private foreign debt and getting no concessions in return, neither reduced interest rates nor payments limited to a lower percentage of export earnings (ibid., 12 December).

Two major policy statements were published in 1986: the "orange paper" in January offered solutions to the economic crisis, and the "blue paper" in August addressed the issue of political reform. In line with current liberal opinion, the MAS would decentralize the Venezuelan system by introducing, among other things, direct elections for state governors; nominal, rather than party, ballots for all elected posts; full autonomy of municipal councils; separation of national and regional elections; and norms for the democratization of political parties. Much the same measures were recommended by the official Commission for the Reform of the State, but AD has been slow to approve the changes.

The MAS has one seat on the executive committee of the AD-dominated Venezuelan Labor Confederation (Confederación de Trabajadores Venezolanos; CTV), which represents about 90 percent of organized labor. In a November upset, a MAS slate defeated AD candidates in the election of the important Graphic Arts Union.

At various times during the year, the MAS condemned Reagan's Central American policy as well as the U.S. attack on Libya. In November, Petkoff attended a seminar on U.S.–Latin American relations in Atlanta that was organized by former president Jimmy Carter.

**Other Marxist Parties.** Since its tenth national convention in 1985, the MIR, headed by General Secretary Moisés Moleiro and President Hector Pérez Marcano, has defined itself as socialist, revolutionary, and democratic. The national council of the MIR almost unanimously supported Moleiro's proposal for a merger of the MIR, MAS, and MEP. Above their differences, Moleiro says, the three share the concept of socialism as the foundation of a more profound democracy and none is subordinate to any foreign center; the PCV is a respectable party, but ideological differences are too great. Moleiro thinks the combined strength of the three could represent about 10 percent of the population. (Ibid., 27 November.) AD and COPEI leaders also feel that such a step would be quite useful to Venezuelan democracy (ibid., 10 December).

A parallel proposal called for the formation of a broad electoral alliance that would not exclude even militants of AD and the COPEI. "The contest in 1988" according to Moleiro, "is not between left and right, but between the nation and those who have governed it so badly" (ibid.). The Moral Movement, or Independents' Movement, which was formed a year ago with the aim of joining other groups and parties to defeat the two-party monopoly, welcomed the signs of left unity (ibid., 28 November).

Differing opinions on electoral strategy were voiced by MEP vice president Jesús Angel Paz Galarraga and secretary general Adelso González. (Founder Luis Beltrán Prieto is still president of the party.) González received the proposal for a MIR-MAS-MEP merger with real pleasure, recounting how he had promoted socialist integration for the past eight years (ibid., 28 November). Paz Galarraga considered the idea worthwhile but still a long way down the road; in his opinion, the immediate task is formation of a national alliance as an option to AD and the COPEI (ibid., 9 December).

The MEP had only four federal deputies, but its labor sector was the strongest of the left, with two seats on the CTV executive committee. CTV executive secretary Pablo Castro, an MEP delegate, urged the labor confederation to abandon its dialogue with the government and begin mobilizing: "Workers cannot continue to bear the weight of the crisis while authorities keep on conceding benefits to businessmen, to pay their debts and increase their capital" (ibid., 25 November). CTV secretary general César Olarte, also of the MEP, will head a committee of union delegates to study the new economic package.

**Guerrillas.** Colombian guerrillas, narcotics dealers, smugglers, and common criminals have stepped up activity in the Venezuelan-Colombian border zone. Kidnappings and sabotage have made the region virtually uninhabitable for ranchers and oil contractors. The Venezuelan army is protecting some petroleum installations in the area, but oil companies in Colombia have been asked to organize their own defense as military forces are insufficient to patrol permanently.

Guerrillas of the Colombian National Liberation Army (Ejército de Liberación Nacional; ELN) attacked the Los Bancos army command in the Venezuelan state of Apure, killing three soldiers and wounding eleven. They said the raid was a reprisal for mistreatment of Colombian farmworkers. An earlier attack on a National Guard post in Zulia by the Colombian Popular Liberation Army (Ejército Popular de Liberación; EPL) left one soldier and one guerrilla dead. In the worst of many scandals in 1986, it seems that authorities were secretly selling small arms to the Colombian guerrillas through the state-owned arms and munitions company, Cavim. Whether this was the work of former guerrillas in the country's security forces or a network of corrupt officials is not known. Military courts have been conducting the investigation so far, and some eighteen people have been arrested. (*Latin American Weekly Report*, 27 November; *Veneconomy*, 5 November.)

Carole Merten
*San Francisco, California*

# ASIA AND THE PACIFIC

# Introduction

Much of continental Asia is ruled by the states of North Korea, the People's Republic of China (PRC), Vietnam, Cambodia (formerly Kampuchea), Laos, and Mongolia. Leadership problems have beset, in particular, the first three.

In the Philippines, the communist party and its army, the New People's Army, have become powerful in recent years, and in late 1986 cease-fire negotiations between the government and communist party representatives were held.

Elsewhere in the region, communist activities merely replicated those of recent years, with minor variations that can be highlighted by classifying communist activity as follows: states with ruling communist parties, states with legal communist parties in opposition, and states with banned communist parties.

**States with Ruling Communist Parties.** In Mongolia, the Nineteenth Party Congress met 28–31 May to consolidate changes made after Jambyn Batmonh became general secretary in August 1984. The Laotian People's Revolutionary Party held its Fourth Congress in 1986, and the leadership affirmed its "strategic alliance" with Vietnam. Conditions in Cambodia remained much the same as in the past.

In North Korea, Kim Il-song and his son, Kim Chong-il (45), toured the country while the father sought to guarantee a smooth transfer of power to the son. The defections of film director Shin Sang-ok and his actress wife Choe Eun-hi, who took their annual stipend of some $2.5 million with them to the U.S. embassy in Vienna, most certainly hurt Kim Chong-il's succession prospects by giving credence to the rumors of his privileged lifestyle. Then, in late October, the unannounced visit of Kim Il-song to Moscow to consult with Mikhail Gorbachev also seemed to be linked to his difficulties in ensuring the full transfer of power to his son (*WSJ*, 19 January 1987). These developments, as well as the normal flow of intelligence information, probably account for the announcement by the South Korean government on 16 November that its organs had heard broadcasts along the demilitarized zone stating that Kim Il-song had been assassinated while riding on a train. The next day, the broadcasts were said to have reported that Kim Chong-il had taken power, and the day after, that O Chin-u had "seized power." But on 19 November, Pyongyang was able to film Kim Il-song welcoming Mongolian leader Jambyn Batmonh to the capital.

In China, 1986 began with two of the largest party meetings held in recent years. Vice-Premier Tian Jiyun's key speech at the 6–9 January meeting of 8,000 party and state officials answered the question of whether reform would lead to capitalism: his answer was "an unequivocal no." He pointed out that the new private sector accounted for just 0.6 percent of the total national industrial output. The fourth session of the Sixth National People's Congress met from 25 March to 12 April and endorsed "in principle" the Seventh Five-Year Plan and Premier Zhao's report of that plan.

Although events remained normal the rest of the year, December brought a major challenge to the party leadership. Beginning on 7 December and lasting until the end of the month, student demonstrations for greater democracy and political reform broke out in Hefei (Anhui), Wuhan (Hubei), Shanghai (Jiangsu), Shenzhen (Guangdong), Jinan (Shangdong), Chongqing (Sichuan), Xian (Shaanxi), Peking (Hebei),

Kunming (Yunnan), Tianjin (Hebei), Suzhou (Jiangsu), and Hangzhou (Zhejiang). Wall posters appealing for the same appeared in Changsha (Hunan), Hengyang (Yunan), Chengdu (Guizhou), Taiyuan (Hebei) and Canton (Guangdong). (*FEER*, 7 January 1987.) The regime resorted to threats, appeals, and some selective arrests of student leaders. On 23 December, the *People's Daily* appealed to the students not to endanger the progress of the reforms over the last eight years.

Similarly, in Vietnam the regime continued to be plagued by serious economic troubles and declining social morale. Major leadership change occurred at the top echelon of the party, indicating that a general consensus had approved new blood to direct the party and try to lead the country out of its problems. Of the Politburo's inner circle of five, only one member, Pham Hung, remained on the job by the end of 1986. In mid-December, the Sixth Party Congress took place, and leaders were selected who are more pragmatic in their orientation to solving economic problems. The congress also called for a massive self-criticism (Kiem Thao) emulation movement and urged that younger party members be recruited. The congress' political report frankly admitted the party's inability to achieve the goals set over the past decade and blamed much of the trouble on the economic woes that have long beset the country.

Vietnam's war with Cambodia was conducted at a relatively low level during 1986, compared to previous years, and there was no dry-season military offensive. The resistance forces returned to more traditional guerrilla tactics and moved deeper into the countryside, claiming many successful attacks on Vietnamese installations. Hanoi's pledge to remove all troops from Cambodia by 1990 was repeated on several occasions by officials speaking with foreigners in Hanoi and abroad.

Relations with the United States during the year were largely confined to technical visits by U.S. officials in pursuit of the resolution of casualties information. Some remains of American dead were returned by Vietnamese officials.

**States with Legal Communist Party Opposition.** Bangladesh, India, Nepal, Sri Lanka, Japan, Australia, and New Zealand have allowed communist parties to be active so long as they obey the nation's laws. In Bangladesh, voters elected six Communist Party of Bangladesh members to the newly revived National Assembly. The party had aligned with other, "bourgeois" parties to mobilize votes for its candidates. The Japanese Communist Party activities were unchanged; the party remained dedicated to the path of advocating a peaceful, or parliamentary, road to power. In India, the communists, like other opposition parties, stepped up their criticism of Prime Minister Rajiv Gandhi.

In Nepal, the first half of 1986 was marked by election campaigns. The communists remained divided on whether to participate: all pro-Moscow groups and the Marxist-Leninist faction of the pro-Beijing group decided to participate, while all other pro-Beijing factions and the neutralists decided to boycott the elections. In Australia and New Zealand, the communist parties have small memberships, but some party members hold high positions in several large unions that can play a major role in national politics. In Australia, the communist party was willing to work with the ruling Labour Party, thus hoping to use state resources to influence public opinion.

In Sri Lanka, the violence between the government and the largest ethnic minority group, the Tamils, dominated the year's events. Peace negotiations were conducted between the two sides during the year, and by year's end the government had mapped out a peace plan that had been accepted, in principle, by the nonviolent Tamil United Liberation Front. The pro-Moscow Communist Party of Sri Lanka and the Trotskyist Lanka Sama Samaja Party played a limted role in these peace negotiations.

**States with Banned Communist Parties.** Burma, Thailand, Malaysia, Singapore, Indonesia, the Republic of China on Taiwan, South Korea, and the Philippines have outlawed communist parties and any activity to create groups supportive of those parties. Except for the Philippines and Burma, communist activity has been on the decline or virtually eliminated.

The Burmese Communist Party's clandestine radio broadcasts finally reached the outside world in February to announce that the party's third congress in 47 years had been held between 9 September and 2 October 1985 with 170 delegates attending. They elected a new central committee of 29 members and pledged to rely on Marxism, Leninism, and Mao Zedong's thought to formulate a new party line.

In Indonesia, the communist party's top leaders remained in exile with no signs of organized activity in the country throughout 1986. Little reliable information surfaced about the communist party in Thailand.

In Malaysia, the party's central committee announced that Chin Peng was still alive and mentioned him as the head of the Central Committee. Other than this new information, the outlawed communist parties in both Malaysia and Singapore had little influence in politics or society in 1986.

The Philippines, however, was quite a different case. The New People's Army (NPA) under the leadership of the communist party is a fighting force ranging in size from 16,500 to 32,000. It operated on as many as 60 fronts around the country, sometimes at company size of 200- to 300-man operations. Its shadow government embraced 10–15 percent of the country's villages.

**Soviet Activity in the Region.** Soviet military and economic aid to Vietnam continued as in the past. In spite of the Soviet Union's expression of interest in warmer relations with the PRC, the Beijing leadership has remained skeptically cautious. On 28 July, Gorbachev made an important speech at Vladivostok in which he proposed to withdraw Soviet troops from Mongolia and Afghanistan, undertake negotiations with the PRC for a reduction of troops on the Sino-Soviet border, and accept the Thelwag principle for determining the international boundary along the Amur River. He also expressed willingness to cooperate with the PRC in space, including the provision of training Chinese astronauts. Chinese foreign minister Wu Xueqian met the chargé d'affaires of the Soviet embassy in Beijing to discuss Sino-Soviet relations. Even Deng acknowledged that there were positive elements in Gorbachev's speech and indicated that China would carefully study all its contents. As of the end of 1986, however, the Chinese still insisted on seeing Soviet actions before serious negotiations could begin.

Ramon H. Myers
*Hoover Institution*

# Australia

**Population.** 15,800,000 (*World Factbook*, July 1986)

**Parties.** Communist Party of Australia (CPA); Socialist Party of Australia (SPA); Communist Party of Australia–Marxist-Leninist (CPA-ML); Socialist Workers' Party (SWP); Socialist Labor League (SLL); Spartacist League of Australia and New Zealand (SLANZ)

**Founded.** CPA: 1920; CPA-ML: 1964; SPA: 1971; SWP: 1972; SLL: 1972

**Membership.** CPA: 1,000; SPA: 500; CPA-ML: 300; SWP: 400; SLL: 100; SLANZ: 50

**Leadership.** CPA: Judy Mundey, general secretary; SPA: Peter Dudley Symon, general secretary, Jack McPhillips, president; CPA-ML: Edward Fowler Hill, chairman; SWP: Jim Percy, national secretary

**Status.** Legal

**Last Congress.** CPA: Twenty-eighth, 4 November 1984; SPA: Fifth, September 1984

**Last Election.** 1 December 1984; negligible vote for communist parties; no representatives elected to Parliament

**Publications.** CPA: *Tribune* (weekly), *Australian Left Review* (quarterly); SPA: *Socialist* (fortnightly), *The Guardian* (weekly); CPA-ML: *Vanguard* (weekly), *Australian Communist*; SWP: *Direct Action* (weekly)

Australia's communist parties have small memberships, hold no seats in the federal Parliament, and received few votes in the last election. Nevertheless, they exert a disproportionate influence on Australian politics because communists hold high positions in several large unions. These unions—both white-collar and blue-collar—are generally affiliated with the ruling Australian Labor Party (ALP) and are the primary power base for ALP's well-organized Socialist Left faction, whose members hold over one-fourth of the ALP's seats in Parliament. In addition, although members of communist parties are barred from joining the ALP, communist-designated union delegates form a considerable voting bloc within the Socialist Left faction at the ALP's platform-drafting national conferences. (*Social Action*, February, October.)

Prime Minister Bob Hawke, the charismatic leader of the ALP, has moved his party's economic and foreign policies to the right since his election in 1983. Moreover, to undercut the power of the Socialist Left, Hawke brought four moderate trade unions back into the Victorian (State) Labor Party, challenging the Socialist Left in its stronghold. In 1986, the Socialist Left countered by forming an alliance—called the Broad Left—with the more moderate communist parties and political action groups, and by pressuring Hawke to reincorporate traditional socialist policies into the ALP platform before the next election, which must be held by April 1988.

In March 1986, a Broad Left conference drew 1,600 participants to Sydney—quite a feat by Australian standards—but polarized Australian communists into two camps. On the one hand, the CPA has decided to work with the ruling ALP and hopes to use the government's resources to change public attitudes (ibid., March). In this effort, the CPA has been joined by several political action groups of former communists, such as the Association for Communist Unity (ACU), a Sydney-based group of pro-Soviet union officials who were expelled from the SPA in the early 1980s for resisting the authority of the party's Central Committee, and the Socialist Forum, a Melbourne group with over 200 members, whose founders left the CPA in 1984 and which has reportedly become the "ideological pacemaker" of the ALP Socialist Left (ibid., October).

On the other hand, the SPA, the SWP, and the CPA-ML reject cooperation, maintaining that the ALP is a "liberal capitalist party" that has abandoned its socialist roots and is as oppressive of the working class as its rival, the Liberal-National coalition (see the *Tribune*, 19 February). According to a moderate trade union publication, Soviet interests are supporting both the SPA-SWP axis, which proposes a unified Marxist party distinct from the ALP, and the CPA-ACU–Broad Left group, which intends to work within the mainstream party to gain "control over political and industrial labor" (*Social Action*, March, October).

**The CPA.** Although the CPA has remained the largest communist party in Australia, its membership declined from a peak of 23,000 in 1945 to approximately 1,000 in 1986. Moreover, the originally pro-Soviet party has gradually backed away from the USSR, partly because the Soviet invasions of Hungary in 1956 and Czechoslovakia in 1968 cost it so many members. As a result, the now "Eurocommunist" CPA suffers many of the same problems as its counterparts in Western Europe (*YICA*, 1986, pp. 458–59). Many of its most talented ideologues have defected to hard-line parties, such as the SPA, the SWP, or the CPA-ML (*Social Action*, March). As moderates have gained control of the party and committed it to achieving socialism through the country's existing democratic processes, the CPA has lost its distinctively communist character and has had to compete for members with the stronger ALP. Moreover, in the 1980s the CPA has become the home of a disparate group of leftists whose primary commitments are to feminism, homosexual rights, environmental protection, antinuclearism, and abolishing racism. The party therefore lacks a clear sense of direction.

Nevertheless, the CPA influences Australian politics by maintaining its ties with several unions, including Australia's largest, the Amalgamated Metal Workers and Shipwrights Union (AMWU). The CPA counts as one of its recent trade union successes persuading leaders of the Australian Council of Trade Unions (ACTU; the equivalent of the AFL-CIO in the United States) to derail the Hawke government's 1985 plan to impose a nationwide sales tax (*Tribune*, 26 March). The CPA has also joined forces with the ALP Socialist Left on issues of mutual interest, such as protesting the

government's August 1986 decision to resume sales of uranium to France—reversing a ban enacted in 1984 to protest French nuclear testing in the South Pacific—and staging demonstrations against joint U.S.-Australian defense facilities (see *Tribune* advertisement and coverage of rallies).

The CPA's decision to work with the ALP Socialist Left in organizing the Broad Left conference incurred the wrath of the more dogmatic communist parties because the conference ignored three major issues: Hawke's expulsion of maverick union leader Bill Hartley from the Victorian Labor Party, Hawke's deregistration of the rebellious, strike-prone Builders Laborers Federation (BLF) from the ACTU, and his use of the 1983 Price and Wage Accord between the ACTU and the government to restrain wage growth. The SPA, SWP, and CPA-ML have formed a Left Consultation, or Left Alternative, organization to formulate a strategy for reversing these trade union losses.

**The SPA.** The pro-Soviet SPA splintered from the CPA in 1971 because the latter party had condemned the Soviet invasion of Czechoslovakia. In 1975, Moscow publicly recognized the SPA as the only Marxist-Leninist party in Australia and has been rewarded with SPA support for Moscow's foreign policy initiatives, including the imposition of martial law in Poland. The SPA's weekly newspaper, *The Guardian*, features reports from Central Committee members on communist party congresses they attend in such countries as the Soviet Union, Czechoslovakia, Bulgaria, and India. In addition, the SPA has apparently taken under its wing Bill Hartley and his support for the radical Muslim nations in the Middle East (*Social Action*, May; *The Guardian*, 12 February, 12 March, 9, 16 April, 7 May).

The SPA is tightly organized and its Central Committee does not hesitate to oust members who defy its authority. In 1983, for example, the SPA expelled the popular Pat Clancy, a former party secretary, even though the move cost the party its largest union connection, the Building Workers' Industrial Union. The SPA has retained ties with several smaller unions, including the Australian Federation of Locomotive Enginemen and the Transport Workers' Union.

Targeting youth, the SPA organizes numerous conferences, meetings, and rallies, such as the 1985 regional conference of Asian/Pacific Students in Sydney, a 1986 conference for university newspapers on their role in the peace and disarmament campaign, and—together with the World Federation of Democratic Youth (WFDY)—a 1986 conference on unemployment and youth wages (*The Guardian*, 29 January).

The SPA also assists the Soviet-front World Federation of Trade Unions in its activities in the South Pacific (*Quadrant*, August 1985), facilitates Soviet-bloc friendship societies in Australia, and runs left-wing bookshops (see *The Guardian* advertisements).

The SPA condemns the CPA's decision to work with the ALP and calls on Australian socialists to form a single Marxist party and win seats in their own name, saying the ALP will never implement socialism (*The Guardian*, 9 July). The SPA boycotted the Broad Left conference in March, and in April the party took the lead in creating the Left Consultation. In July, this coalition of parties sponsored the National Fightback Conference in Canberra and in September and October held Fightback public meetings in at least four Australian cities.

**The SWP and Other Trotskyist Parties.** In 1985, the SWP broke with the Trotskyist Fourth International because the latter has insisted that the working class does not hold power in the Soviet Union, China, Eastern Europe, Cuba, or other existing communist countries, but instead is oppressed by the bureaucracy in each. The SWP, in contrast, supports what it terms the "anti-imperialist axis" and believes pragmatism is needed to foster revolution (*Intercontinental Press*, 24 February, 23 September 1985). Together with the SPA, the SWP supports revolutionary movements in Central America by organizing Southern Cross Brigades of leftist students, academics, unionists, and public servants who donate their summer holidays doing manual labor in Cuba and Nicaragua. The SWP's youth wing, Resistance, has been active on at least five Australian university campuses (Michael Danby, journalist, Working Paper).

On domestic issues, the SWP has been active but not effective. In 1985, for instance, the SWP badly bungled an attempt to take over the single-issue Nuclear Disarmament Party—which won over 6 percent of the popular vote in December 1984—and in the process split that party into at least four factions.

Like the SPA, the SWP believes that Australia needs "a real communist party," not a Broad Left movement "that no one will join" (*Social Action*, February). The SWP allowed its members to attend the Broad Left conference but afterward joined the

SPA and CPA-ML in forming the Left Consultation. The smaller Trotskyist groups—the SLL and SLANZ—also participated in that coalition. (*Social Action*, August.)

**The CPA-ML.** With only 300 members, the pro-Beijing CPA-ML has had negligible influence on Australian politics. The party, which broke away from the CPA in 1964 because of the rift between the Soviet Union and China over Marxist ideology and practice, appeals primarily to university teachers and students. Its highly theoretical newspaper, *Vanguard*, offers weekly lessons in Marxist-Leninist-Maoist thought but carries almost no advertisements of rallies, meetings, films, or the like.

In 1986, the *Vanguard*—like the CPA *Tribune*—found itself twisted into intellectual knots to approve Beijing's opening of its economy to competition and simultaneously to disapprove Canberra's moves to the right on economic issues (*Vanguard*, 29 January, 4 June; *Tribune*, 6 August). More significantly, the CPA-ML suffered a body blow when its one sizable union connection, the BLF, was deregistered from the ACTU and prohibited from organizing workers. Although the CPA-ML initially encouraged its members to attend the Broad Left conference (*Vanguard*, 19 February), the party afterward quickly threw its support to the more strident Left Consultation, warning that the successful "smashing of the BLF would set a dangerous precedent that would expose the union movement to further attacks" (*Vanguard*, 28 May).

**Outlook.** Despite the dedication of the Left Consultation, the coalition will almost certainly have no success in reversing the Hartley expulsion, the BLF deregistration, or wage restraint under the 1983 accord. All three issues have widespread support in the general electorate and majority support in the ALP.

If the CPA dissolves into the Broad Left, the voting strength of Australia's communist-designated parties would wane from negligible to nil. As for industrial support, the ultraleft parties could then count on only the Food Preservers' Union, elements of the Plumbers' Union and the Victoria Electrical Trades' Union, a few public sector unions, the remnants of the outlawed BLF, and a dwindling number of university student associations (see *Social Action*, October).

The communist-inspired Broad Left, however, will probably remain powerful. It currently has the support of the AMWU as well as three other communist-controlled unions—the Building Workers' Industrial Union, Federated Engine Drivers' and Firemen's Association, and Miners' Federation—that are negotiating a merger that would cover over 100,000 workers and become the largest single union in Australia's history (ibid., May). In addition, the unions of meatworkers, liquor trades, municipal employees, miscellaneous workers, railways, teachers, and clerical officers support the Broad Left (ibid., February, October).

The Broad Left coalition would probably disintegrate if the Hawke government lost the next election, but an independent CPA would also probably find it difficult to regain support. Traditional communist goals have not been popular with today's Australians, most of whom consider themselves middle class. Moreover, frequent or violent strike activity—a traditional tactic of Australian communist parties—is becoming intolerable to many Australians. World prices for Australia's primary exports (agricultural and mineral commodities) are declining, bringing economic hardship to the country. Australia therefore finds itself needing to become more competitive, which would involve reforms of the labor market opposed by all of Australia's communist parties.

Joanne P. Cloud
*Herndon, Virginia*

# Bangladesh

**Population.** 104,205,000
**Party.** Communist Party of Bangladesh (CPB)
**Founded.** 1948 (as East Pakistan Communist Party; banned in 1954; re-emerged in 1971 following the establishment of Bangladesh)
**Membership.** 3,000 (estimated)
**General Secretary.** Muhammed Farhad
**Secretariat.** 10 members
**Central Committee.** 26 members
**Status.** Legal
**Last Congress.** Third, 1980
**Last Election.** 7 May 1986; CPS won 5 of the 300 contested seats in the parliament (Tatiya Sangsad)
**Auxiliary Organizations.** Trade Union Centre, Cultural Front, Chatra Union, Khetmozdur Samiti, Mahila Parishad, Jubo Union
**Publication.** *Ekota* (in Bengali)

In May, the CPB scored a major political breakthrough when Bangladeshi voters elected six CPB candidates to seats in the newly revived Parliament. Ever since martial law was declared in March 1982, the CPB had been in the forefront of a broad-based opposition campaign to topple the army regime of Lieutenant General Hussain Muhammed Ershad. The CPB strategy called for an escalating series of strikes and protests designed to force Ershad's resignation. To achieve this goal, the CPB aligned itself with so-called bourgeois parties and a handful of pro-Moscow splinter parties. On three occasions, Ershad bowed to opposition pressure and canceled scheduled elections after reasoning that an opposition boycott would render the polls meaningless.

In March 1986, the CPB abandoned its strategy of confronting the government in the streets after Ershad vowed to carry out elections with or without opposition participation. CPB strategists feared that the party would be relegated to the political wilderness if Ershad succeeded in making the transition from martial law to elected civilian government. Accordingly, the CPB agreed to contest the election as part of an eight-party, center-left alliance headed by the powerful Awami League (AL).

Although the alliance could not prevent Ershad's supporters from gaining a parliamentary majority, the CPB viewed the May election as a watershed in the party's history. This was the first time CPB candidates won national office. Now that it has gained a parliamentary foothold, the CPB is in a position to exert political influence within the AL-led parliamentary opposition. Simultaneously, the party plans to step up antiregime activities outside of parliament and build up the party's organizational base.

**Organization and Leadership.** The CPB is the successor party of the East Pakistan Communist Party, which separated from its Indian parent organization after the subcontinent was partitioned in 1947. Because of its weak organizational base, the CPB traditionally operated within the ranks of the AL, the pre-eminent vehicle of Bengali nationalism. In 1957, the CPB broke with the AL over the issue of Pakistan's entry into U.S.-sponsored military pacts and aligned itself with all-Pakistan opposition alliances. In 1967, the CPB split into pro-Moscow and pro-Beijing wings. The CPB was legalized after independence in 1971. As with most leftist parties in Bangladesh, the CPB has suffered factional disputes based on ideology, tactics, and personalities.

With an estimated membership of 3,000 activists, the CPB exercises political influence out of proportion to its popular following by coordinating its activities with a variety of front organizations and pro-Soviet factions. Muhammed Farhad, the CPB general secretary, is a longtime Moscow loyalist who works closely with the Kremlin in mapping the party's strategy. In March, Farhad attended the Soviet party congress in Moscow. Observers speculated that the Soviets were instrumental in altering the CPB's political strategy. Within a month after Farhad's return to Dhaka, the CPB agreed to participate in parliamentary elections (*FEER*, 3 April). Farhad again met with Soviet party officials in December to lay the groundwork for the CPB's Fourth Party Congress scheduled for February 1987.

Moni Singh is the octogenarian CPB president and theoretician. Singh is in poor health. Now that the party has entered Parliament, young CPB members are lobbying to replace Singh with a more vigorous leader. Other party stalwarts include Saifuddin Ahmed Malik (secretary of labor and industry), Abdur Salam (secretary of agricultural affairs), and central committee activists Ajoy Roy, Matiur Rehman, and Manzuru Hasan Khan.

The CPB supports a variety of front organizations that carry the party's message to targeted constituencies. The CPB student front, the Chatra Union, commands a strong following at Dhaka University. On several occasions during the year, armed CPB cadres clashed on campus with proregime student associations and Islamic militants. Communist student groups have provided the CPB with a ready reserve of supporters for use in strikes and demonstrations. The peasant front, the Khetmozdur Samiti, has a shallow base of support—a decided liability in a country where 75 percent of the population resides in the countryside. Other fronts include the Trade Union Centre (workers), the Cultural Front (intellectuals), the Mahila Parishad (women), and the Jubo Union (youth). *Ekota*, the party organ, was shut down by the government after the paper called for another election boycott. When the CPB reversed its strategy, the paper resumed publication. *Sangbad*, an English-language daily, is not under exclusive CPB control, though it consistently promotes CPB and Soviet policy lines.

On the international front, the CPB participates in Soviet-sponsored organizations such as the World Peace Council and the World Federation of Trade Unions. The CPB adheres to Soviet policy pronouncements and criticizes the Ershad government's pro-Western orientation (see, for instance, *Pravda*, 6 January). The CPB also maintains fraternal ties with pro-Soviet parties abroad, particularly in India. The CPB regards the Chinese party as heretical.

**Electoral Maneuvers.** At the outset of 1986, the political situation in Bangladesh was deadlocked. Ershad reaffirmed his determination to stage national elections over the objections of the deeply divided opposition. On 1 January, Ershad formed the Jatiya Party, a personal political vehicle composed of proregime elements and a smattering of opposition defectors. Ershad then called parliamentary elections for 26 April. The opposition refused to participate in a poll held under the shadow of martial law and lined up behind the five-point demand put forward in September 1983. The opposition called for: (1) the lifting of martial law; (2) the restoration of political rights and basic freedoms; (3) the holding of free and fair elections; (4) the release of political prisoners; and (5) the installation of a neutral caretaker government to oversee the return to democracy. To back up its demands, the opposition staged a massive rally on 24 February. The rally was billed as an opening round of protests leading up to a nationwide strike to coincide with the fourth anniversary of the Ershad coup on 24 March.

Behind the scenes, however, Ershad initiated a political dialogue with opposition leaders. The mainstream opposition parties are grouped into two alliances. The first is a fifteen-party combine (soon reduced to eight parties) that includes the CPB and ten pro-Moscow fringe parties. The driving force behind the alliance is Sheikh Hasina Wazed, the AL head and daughter of Bangladeshi founding father Sheikh Mujibur Rahman. The second alliance is an eight-party grouping (later reduced to five parties) dominated by the Bangladesh National Party (BNP). Begum Khaleda Zia is the BNP head. The two alliances differ sharply over tactics and strategy. Ershad reasoned that sections of the alliances could be induced to participate in the elections in the hope of winning a share of power.

Ershad's strategy of exploiting opposition disunity paid off as the 21 March deadline for filing candidate nominations approached. After Ershad pleaded on national television for opposition participation, Hasina announced that the AL alliance would contest the election. In return for AL participation, Ershad agreed to reschedule the poll for 7 May to allow for opposition campaigning. In addition, Ershad pledged not to use his powers as president and chief martial law administrator to influence the outcome of the balloting.

Hasina's dramatic decision to contest the election created a storm of controversy within the opposition ranks. The BNP refused to participate in any election held under martial law. Fearing that a major split in the opposition would guarantee a Jatiya Party landslide, the CPB attempted to forge a semblance of opposition unity. The CPB proposed that Hasina and Begum Zia personally contest all 300 parliamentary seats, thereby transforming the election into a head-on contest between the combined opposition and the regime. Both opposition leaders scoffed at the proposal. Ershad, leaving nothing to

chance, then promulgated a martial law ordinance that prohibited candidates from standing for election in more than five constituencies (*FEER*, 3 April).

Five pro-Moscow parties within the AL alliance refused to comply with Hasina's decision and quit the alliance. These parties included the Bangladesh Sramik-Krishak Samajbadi Dal, the Workers' Party, a faction of the Jatiya Samajtantrik Dal, and two factions of the Bangladesh Samajbadi Dal. None of these parties commands much popular support. Their decision to break with the AL put the CPB in a ticklish position. Under Moscow's urging, the CPB leadership enthusiastically endorsed Hasina's decision. Although the CPB came under fire from pro-Moscow parties and militant cadres within the party itself, the CPB hoped to enter Parliament on AL coattails. General Secretary Farhad justified the party's tactical reverse by arguing that Ershad "should not be allowed to score in a one-sided game" (*FEER*, 3 April).

The eight parties that remained in the AL alliance agreed to coordinate their campaign activities. The CPB fielded nine candidates. In all, 28 parties fielded over 1,000 candidates for the 300 seats. As is often the case in Bangladesh, the elections were marred by violence. The press reported eleven persons killed and 800 injured during the three-week campaign (*CSM*, 7 May). After banning antielection activities, Ershad ordered the arrest of Begum Zia and 800 opposition leaders. Estimates of voter turnout varied considerably. Most independent observers agreed, however, that Ershad and his supporters blatantly rigged the balloting. According to the *Times* of London, Ershad's handling of the election amounted to a "massive nationwide effort to destroy any pretence of a return to democracy" (9 May). The CPB joined the entire spectrum of opposition parties in crying foul. In the end, however, the CPB resigned itself to entering Parliament.

Ershad's Jatiya Party secured 153 seats in the 7 May election. Although the victory allowed Ershad to form a government without coalition partners, the government fell short of the two-thirds majority needed to amend the constitution. The AL won 76 seats. In addition to the five CPB candidates who won office, seven pro-Moscow splinter parties won 19 seats. Since the AL and its partners controlled fewer than one-third of the seats, the parliamentary balance was held by a handful of independents and Islamic fundamentalists.

Ershad convened Parliament on 10 July. The

AL-CPB members decided to boycott the session, however, since martial law was still in force. On 26 August, Ershad improved his position in Parliament when his candidates won all eight seats in a by-election. Once again, Ershad's supporters rigged the election by capturing voting booths and intimidating opposition candidates. Hasina accused Ershad of unleashing a "reign of terror" (Hong Kong, *AFP*, 25 August; *FBIS*, 27 August).

After securing his position in Parliament, Ershad then pressed ahead with his plan to engineer his own election as a civilian president. On 31 August, Ershad resigned his commission as chief of army staff, though he retained effective control over the political process in his dual role as president and commander in chief of the armed forces. On the same day, the *London Observer* ran a lengthy article alleging that Ershad had amassed a personal fortune in Swiss bank accounts. Although Ershad denied the charges, the revelations further damaged his public image. Ershad called a presidential election on 15 October.

The opposition reasoned that Ershad would win the presidency in a walkover. Consequently, the CPB and its partners refused to participate in the poll. Undeterred, Ershad banned antielection activities, arrested 1,000 opposition party activists, and dispatched security personnel to maintain order. As expected, Ershad won the contest handily. In a lackluster field of twelve candidates, Ershad garnered 83 percent of the vote. The government claimed a voter turnout of 55 percent; the opposition cited a turnout of 15 percent or less (*NYT*, 16 October).

The year's final test of strength occurred on 10 November when Parliament reconvened. Prior to fulfilling his pledge to remove martial law, Ershad demanded that Parliament pass an indemnification act validating all actions taken by the military during the martial-law era. The parliamentary opposition refused to legitimize Ershad's seizure of power and boycotted the session. Press reports maintain that the CPB was prepared to take its place in Parliament but joined the AL-led walkout in deference to Hasina's wishes (*FEER*, 27 November). Ershad narrowly secured a two-thirds majority for the bill.

**Foreign Policy.** Relations with the Soviet Union remained cool but correct. The two sides negotiated a barter trade protocol in March. Two-way trade has declined in recent years, however (Dhaka, *BSS*, 17 March; *FBIS*, 21 March). The Ershad government remains suspicious of the Kremlin's close ties with the CPB and India.

Relations with China remained extremely close. In March, Chinese president Li Xiannian conducted a four-day state visit to Bangladesh. Both sides expressed a close identity of views on international issues and pledged to strengthen bilateral ties. Ershad termed China a "time-tested friend" and a "major partner in progress" (Dhaka Domestic Service, 8 March; *FBIS*, 10 March). Maoist revolutionaries, once a potent force in Bangladesh, have receded into obscurity in recent years. Primarily for geopolitical reasons, China lends full support to the Ershad regime.

Douglas C. Makeig
*Rockville, Maryland*

# Burma

**Population.** 37,651,000
**Party.** Burmese Communist Party (BCP)
**Founded.** 1939
**Membership.** 3,000 (1979); estimated armed strength 8,000–15,000
**Chairman.** Thakin Ba Thein Tin
**Politburo.** Believed to include: Thakin Ba Thein Tin, Pe Tint, Khin Maung Gyi, Myo Myint, Tin Yee, Kyaw Mya, Kyin Maung
**Central Committee.** 29 members: Aye Hla, Aye Ngwe, Thakin Ba Thein Tin, Bran Ba Di, Khin Maung Gyi, Kyauk Mi Lai, Kyaw Mya, Kyaw Myint, Kyaw Zaw, Kyin Maung, Mya Thaung, Myint Min, Myo Myint, Ni Tu Wu, Pe Thaung, Pe Tint, Po Ngwe Sai, Po Tint, Sai Aung Win, San Tu, Saw Ba Moe, Saw Han, Soe Hein, Soe Lwin, Tin Yee, Tint Hlaing, Tun Lwin, Ye Tun, Zaw Mai (VOPB, 7 February; *FBIS*, 12 February)
**Status.** Illegal
**Last Congress.** Third, 9 September–2 October 1985
**Last Election.** N/a
**Auxiliary Organizations.** None identified
**Publications.** None identified; broadcasts over the Voice of the People of Burma (VOPB), apparently located along the Sino-Burmese border inside Burma

The BCP's third congress of its 47-year existence was held 9 September–2 October 1985 and attended by over 170 delegates "in a liberated area in Burma," according to the BCP clandestine radio, the VOPB. Due to a long break in VOPB transmissions, first word of the congress reached the outside world only in February 1986 (VOPB, 7 February; *FBIS*, 12 February). The congress elected a new Central Committee of 29 members, named in the press release. No election of a new chairman was noted in congress material available in 1986, although other VOPB broadcasts have indicated the BCP is still led by 77-year-old Thakin Ba Thein Tin. Although Thakin Ba Thein Tin has been described as in poor health (*YICA*, 1985; *FEER*, 22 May), the VOPB reported he attended the Third Congress and submitted the Political Report (VOPB, 7 February; *FBIS*, 12 February); other sources claimed he met a delegation of the National Democratic Front (NDF) at BCP headquarters at Pang Hsang in early 1986 (Bangkok, *The Nation*,

14 July; *FBIS*, 17 July). There has been no mention of the Politburo in available congress material, although seven names previously identified as members appeared on the new Central Committee list. One previously identified member of the Politburo, Yeba Taik Aung (*YICA*, 1985), was not included in the new list of Central Committee members. Previous indications of a devolution of BCP leadership authority appear to be supported by the congress press release statement that a "panel of chairmen . . . which included the original Central Committee led by Chairman Thakin Ba Thein Tin" presided over deliberations (ibid.).

**Party Internal Affairs.** The Third Congress was held "in accordance with Marxism, Leninism, and Mao Zedong thought" adapted for "concrete conditions" in Burma. The congress laid down the "tactical line" for the party—"armed struggle as the main form of struggle"—and approved the "continued firm flying of the combat banners of internal peace, democracy, and national solidarity while waging the armed struggle." There was a need "to build up and strengthen an extensive revolutionary united front, including people from various classes and all strata of life opposed to the military government in nonliberated areas." The congress also approved the (still undefined) "nine future programs of the party." (VOPB, 7 February; *FBIS*, 12 February.)

According to the VOPB, the congress approved Central Committee political and financial reports. Broadcast of the Political Report by the VOPB commenced on 16 March (*FBIS*, 18 March) and was not complete as of the end of the year. At least three chapters and some additional material were broadcast that analyzed imperialism, society, and revolution in Burma as well as BCP tactics (VOPB, 1, 15, 22 June, 12 July; *FBIS*, 4, 24 June, 2, 16 July).

The BCP acknowledged that the party's past in general has seen reverses. In commemorating the party's founding, it was noted that the party "has experienced numerous twists and turns and ups and downs along its tortuous revolutionary path" (VOPB, 17 August; *FBIS*, 8 September). In commemorating the start of the BCP's insurrection, the party asserted "although there have been errors and deviations by the party during these 38 years of armed revolution, it has never betrayed or turned its back on the people of Burma" (VOPB, 29 March; *FBIS*, 3 April).

The BCP analysis of Burma itself, however, was far more critical. According to that analysis, "Burma is a semicolonial and semifeudal society" dominated by the "three evil systems: imperialism, feudal landlordism, and bureaucratic capitalism." Commentary on the Burmese economy, which followed a pattern of fairly elaborate attacks on government policy based on government economic statistics, claimed that the Rangoon government "mercilessly oppresses and exploits the working people at home, becomes more dependent with time on imperialists and reactionaries abroad, maintains and safeguards imperialism and feudal-landlordism locally, and promotes in relation to Burma's standards, the growth of monopolistic bureaucratic capitalism." (VOPB, 23 March; *FBIS*, 31 March.)

Attacks on government policy continued. The BCP singled out the government's 3 November demonetization of 100, 50, and 20 kyat notes, which was aimed by the government at the flourishing black market; the action was "an unjustifiable act of banditry" that should show the people "they must direct their opposition to their common enemy— the military government—and their struggle for immediate and full refund for their . . . demonetized currency notes must be integrated with other forms of struggle. For the people, unity is strength; unity is victory" (VOPB, 15 February; *FBIS*, 20 February).

Not directly reflected in this commentary was the probable effect of the demonetization on the BCP, which has been forced increasingly to support itself from black-market trading in recent years (see *YICA*, 1986). Another government action, which elicited no BCP commentary but probably affected the party, was the destruction of more than 30,000 acres of opium during the first half of 1986, as reported by Prime Minister U Maung Maung Kha (Hong Kong, AFP, 13 October; *FBIS*, 16 October). A visit by the Thai prime minister to Burma in February also reportedly resulted in agreement to step up cooperation in suppression of drug trafficking along the Thai-Burma border (*The Nation*, 28 February; *FBIS*, 3 March). The BCP has reportedly derived funds from the opium trade since the late 1970s (*YICA*, 1981).

**The Insurgency.** The BCP statement on the anniversary of the insurrection maintained that "the armed struggle must be the main form of struggle and it must be integrated with other forms of struggle" (VOPB, 29 March; *FBIS*, 3 April). Commemorating the party's founding, the VOPB said the BCP must "keep military tasks as the central pillar; strengthen and build the party, the army, the cadre force, and the base area; expand while strengthening our own forces; carry out extensive guerrilla warfare behind enemy lines and build up guerrilla bases; and unanimously unite with all the armed revolutionary forces as well as the patriotic forces throughout the country" (VOPB, 17 August; *FBIS*, 8 September). This appears to leave little prospect for the "three banners" first proclaimed in 1981 (see *YICA*, 1982), and currently elaborated as the BCP's three-point plan, on the basis of which the party asserts its willingness "to discuss and exchange views with any patriotic persons and political organizations." The three points are: cessation of civil war and establishment of internal peace; dismantling of the single-party dictatorship and giving democratic rights to the people; and immediate end to national discord and re-establishment of national unity." (VOPB, 23 February; *FBIS*, 25 February.)

The major development in the insurgency in 1986 appeared to be the on-again off-again alliance with the NDF. The NDF is an alliance of nine ethnic insurgent groups, of which the most important are the Kachin Independence Organization (KIO) and the Karen National Union (KNU). The NDF, and in particular the KNU, have been under pressure from a three-year Burmese government push into Karen base areas that has cut off much of the Thai-Burma border smuggling traffic upon which Karen finances have long depended. The consequent search for allies reportedly led an NDF delegation to the Sino-Burmese border early in 1986 to seek "moral support" from China, but it was refused entry by the Chinese. It then proceeded to BCP headquarters at Pang Hsang for talks with the BCP Central Committee. (*The Nation*, 14 July; *FBIS*, 17 July.) These talks lasted from 17 to 24 March and resulted in an agreement to coordinate military operations against the Rangoon government (*FEER*, 22 May). The agreement was marked by a joint-statement broadcast by VOPB on 17 April (*FBIS*, 21 April). However, at an August NDF meeting held at KNU headquarters to ratify the agreement, the KNU balked, arguing that the delegation had exceeded its mandate. Further, the KNU reportedly cited the BCP objective of taking over the country under a one-party system, and communist involvement in the narcotics trade, as reasons against the pact (*FEER*, 11 December). Representatives of the KIO, which has been allied with the BCP since 1976, indicated that their own military cooperation with BCP would proceed and denied that the agreement would support a one-party system or drug trafficking. "It is strictly a military pact to fight against the common enemy—Rangoon" (ibid.).

The military conflict continued in 1986, although the BCP still avoids the large-unit action that it tried unsuccessfully in the mid-1970s and that was renounced as "the military line of leftist adventurism" in 1979 (*YICA*, 1981). While the government offensive against the KNU appeared to be Rangoon's major anti-insurgency effort, government operations against the BCP and its putative NDF allies have also been reported (*FEER*, 22 May). Combat reports are sparse. The few exceptions include a mine attack on a Burmese Army unit on 17 March (VOPB, 20 April; *FBIS*, 23 April); the communist attack on an Arakan state police station on 8 May (reported by Rangoon); and the surrender to the government between May and August of a total of 200 insurgents, including 59 BCP members (*FEER*, 25 September).

Reports continued of a BCP presence near the Thai border, although those reports were fewer than in recent years. Possibly in consequence, no expressions of Thai leadership concern were noted in 1986. Reports on a September campaign by Wa insurgents against Shan United Army positions and heroin refineries in the Doi Lang area, which is on the Thai-Burma border opposite Thailand's Chiang Mai province, asserted that BCP troops had joined the Wa effort (*Bangkok Post*, 17 September; *The Nation*, 19 September; *FBIS*, 17, 19 September). Thai border police reported a 9 October clash along the Burmese border with a small group of Burmese insurgents, who, according to captured documents, were BCP members (Bangkok, *Siam Rat*, 10 November; *JPRS–Southeast Asia*, 25 November).

Arms smuggling continued along the Thai border, evinced by the 5 June seizure by Thai police of a large amount of ammunition and rockets in Chiang Mai province. The weapons were reportedly in the hands of a gun-running organization that served minority groups. One report connected the shipment to Kuomintang remnants along the border. (Bangkok, *Matichon*, 6 June; Hong Kong, AFP, 6 June; *FBIS*, 9 June.)

**International Positions and Activities.** The available documentation from the Third Congress has shown no sign of the long-rumored BCP estrangement from China. Rather, the Political Report declares, "It is obvious that in the 36 years since liberation, China—a socialist country—has experienced successes in all spheres, including agriculture, industry, science, and national defense." In contrast to the previous Political Report in 1978, the 1985 document sharply reduced its political denunciation of the superpowers and concentrated on criticism of economic problems in the West, the Soviet Union, and Eastern Europe. (VOPB, 16 March; *FBIS*, 18 March.)

Although the BCP's China orientation apparently remained intact, Chinese relations with Rangoon also appeared to have prospered. A protocol on the first joint inspection of the China-Burma border was signed in Beijing on 7 November (Rangoon Domestic Service, 7 November; *FBIS*, 14 November). Several official visits took place during 1986. Prime Minister U Maung Maung Kha visited China in April. (*FBIS-China*, 14, 16, 17 April; *FBIS-Asia and the Pacific*, 21 April.) A delegation led by Minister of Industry U Tint Swe visited Beijing in July (*FBIS*, 15 July). The governor of Yunnan province visited Rangoon in March and met with the Burmese prime minister (Rangoon Domestic Service, 12–13 March; *FBIS*, 14 March).

Soviet purchases of 180,000 tons of Burmese

rice in 1985 and early 1986 reportedly made the Soviet Union Burma's largest customer during this period (*FEER*, 10 April), and TASS reported a further purchase of 60,000 tons (16 October; *FBIS*, 17 October). A flurry of Soviet cultural visits was also noted, although the Burmese have yet to reciprocate or indicate that they intend to change their cool relations with Moscow (*FEER*, 10 April).

On 18 December, the VOPB commented on cease-fire negotiations in the Philippines between the Aquino government and the New People's Army, which is headed by the Communist Party of the Philippines. The truce was called "a victory for the people." (*FBIS*, 19 December.)

**The VOPB.** The VOPB went off the air on 16 April 1985 but resumed broadcasting in late January 1986. A 31 January broadcast was the first

picked up by *FBIS*, which noted that the VOPB gave no explanation for its break in transmission (*FBIS*, 7 February). Broadcasts in 1986 were said to be coming from a mobile station on the Burmese side of the Sino-Burmese border (*FEER*, 27 March). The new transmissions appeared to be less powerful than previous ones. Consequently, *FBIS* was unable to transcribe at least one complete VOPB broadcast, and the incidence of unintelligible sections of other broadcasts was also noticeably greater than before the transmission break.

Charles B. Smith, Jr.
*U.S. Department of State*

Note: The views expressed here are the author's own and do not necessarily represent those of the Department of State or the U.S. government.

# Cambodia
# (Formerly Kampuchea)

**Population.** 6,388,000 (July 1986). Average annual growth rate is 2.2 percent.
**Major Parties**
- Kampuchean (or Khmer) People's Revolutionary Party (KPRP)
**Founded.** Traces its origins to the (Khmer) Kanapak Pracheachon (Khmer People's Party) founded in June 1951.
**Membership.** 7,500 (*FBIS-Asia and the Pacific*, 21 October 1985; *WMR*, February)
**General Secretary.** Heng Samrin (b. 1934, former Khmer Rouge official and military commander; fled Cambodia 1977–1978 after an abortive revolt against the Pol Pot leadership; returned December 1978 with the invading Vietnamese army).
**Politburo.** 9 full and 2 candidate members: Heng Samrin (b. 1934, chairman, Council of State); Chea Sim (b. 1932, chairman, National Assembly; chairman, National Council of the Kampuchean United Front for National Construction and Defense); Hun Sen (b. 1951, chairman, Council of Ministers; prime minister; chairman, KPRP Foreign Relations Commission); Say Phuthong (b. 1925, secretary, KPRP Central Committee; vice-chairman, Council of State; chairman, KPRP Central Control Commission); Bou Thong (b. 1938, vice-premier; vice-chairman, Council of Ministers); Chea Soth (b. 1928, minister of planning; vice-chairman, Council of Ministers); Men Sam-An* (b. 1953, chairman, KPRP Central Organization Commission; member, Control Commission); Mat Ly* (b. 1925, vice-chairman, National Assembly; chairman, Cambodian Federation of Trade Unions); Ney

Pena* (first deputy minister of the interior); Chan Seng* (b. 1935, candidate member; member, Control Commission); Nguon Nhel* (candidate member; secretary, Phnom Penh municipal KPRP committee). *Indicates new members selected at the Fifth Party Congress.

**Secretariat.** Heng Samrin, chief; Hun Sen; Bou Thong; Men Sam-An; Ney Pena

**Control Commission of the Central Committee.** Say Phouthong, president; Chan Seng; Sim Ka; Men Sam-An; Say Chhum; Mean Sam-An; El Vansarat

**Central Committee.** 31 full and 14 candidate members: Bou Thong (b. 1938, vice-premier; vice-chairman, Council of Ministers); Chan Phin (minister of finance; minister for local and foreign trade); Chan Seng (b. 1935, member, Control Commission of the Central Committee); Chay Sangyum (commander, Third Military Region of the Khmer People's Revolutionary Armed Forces [KPRAF]); Chea Chantho (b. 1941?, candidate member; minister of planning); Chea Sim (b. 1932, chairman, National Assembly; chairman, National Council of the Kampuchean United Front for National Construction and Defense); Chea Soth (b. 1928, vice-chairman, Council of Ministers; chairman, Central Inspection Commission); Chhay Than (candidate member; minister of finance); Chheng Phon (b. 1934, candidate member; minister of information and culture); El Vansarat (deputy minister of defense; chief, general political department of the KPRAF); Heng Samkai (brother of Heng Samrin; secretary, Svay Rieng provincial KPRP committee); Heng Samrin (b. 1934, chairman, Council of State); Ho Nan (female; deputy minister, cabinet of the Council of Ministers); Hul Savoan (commander of the KPRAF fourth military region); Hun Neng (candidate member; secretary, Kompong Cham provincial KPRP committee); Hun Sen (b. 1951, chairman, Council of Ministers; prime minister); Ke Kimyan (deputy minister of defense; chief of the general staff, KPRAF); Kham Len (candidate member; member, Council of State); Khoy Khunhuor (secretary, Preah Vihear provincial KPRP committee; chairman, Central Propaganda and Education Commission); Kim Ying (director general, Voice of the Cambodian People Radio); Kong Korm (b. 1942, foreign minister); Koy Buntha (b. 1952, minister of defense); Lak On (female; secretary, Ratanakiri provincial KPRP committee); Lim Thi (candidate member; secretary, Kandal provincial KPRP committee); Mat Ly (b. 1925, vice-chairman, National Assembly; chairman, Cambodian Federation of Trade Unions); Mean Sam-An (female; b. 1956, chairwoman, Association of Revolutionary Women of Kampuchea); Men Sam-An (female; b. 1953, chairwoman, KPRP Central Organization Commission; member, Control Commission); Neou Sam-On (candidate member; vice-chairman, KPRP Central Organization Commission; chairman, Cambodian-Laotian Friendship Association); Ney Pena (minister of the interior); Nguon Nhel (secretary, Phnom Penh municipal KPRP committee); Pen Navut (candidate member; minister of education; chairman, Kampuchean Committee for Scientific Research); Runphlam Kesan (secretary, Koh Kong provincial KPRP committee); Ros Chhum (candidate member, general secretary National Council of the Kampuchean United Front for National Construction and Defense; deputy minister of planning); Sam Sarit (candidate member; director, General Department of Rubber Plantations); Sam Sundoeun (b. 1951, secretary, provisional committee of the People's Revolutionary Youth Union of Kampuchea; president, Association of Revolutionary Youth of Kampuchea; member, commission for cultural and social affairs of the National Assembly); Sar Kheng (chief of cabinet, KPRP Central Committee); Say Chhum (secretary, Kompong Speu provincial KPRP committee; member, Control Commission; minister of agriculture); Say Phuthong (b. 1925, vice-chairman, Council of State; chairman, KPRP Central Control Commission; secretary, KPRP Central Committee); Say Siphon (candidate member; vice-chairman, Cambodian Federation of Trade Unions); Sim Ka (minister for control of state affairs; member, Control Commission); Som Kim Suor (female; b. 1949, editor in chief, *Pracheachon*); Som Sopha (candidate member; deputy secretary, Stoeng Treng provincial KPRP committee); Tie Banh (b. 1945, candidate member; minister of communications, transportation, and posts); Thong Khon (b. 1941?, candidate member; mayor of Phnom Penh; president, Phnom Penh municipal KPRP committee); Yos Son (chairman, foreign relations commission of the KPRP Central Committee).

**Status.** Sole authorized political party in all areas of Cambodia controlled by the regime in Phnom Penh. As in other Marxist states, party and government are synonymous, and KPRP leaders serve concurrently as key officials in the governing apparatus of the People's Republic of Kampuchea. The

KPRP has been heavily influenced by the Vietnamese Communist Party, and its present dynamics and key decisions remain under the close tutelage of Vietnamese advisers.

**Last Congress.** Fifth, 13–16 October 1985, in Phnom Penh. Attended by 250 delegates from 22 subordinate party committees representing the provinces, municipalities, and armed forces in the People's Republic of Kampuchea.

**Last Election.** May 1981, National Assembly. The KPRP was unchallenged by any political opposition. Out of 148 candidates running for office, 117 were elected.

**Auxiliary Organizations.** Cambodian Federation of Trade Unions (80,000 members); Association of Revolutionary Women of Kampuchea (1.3 million members); People's Revolutionary Youth Union of Kampuchea (37,000 members); Association of Revolutionary Youth of Kampuchea (80,000 members; vice-president, Im Suosdei); Kampuchean United Front for National Construction and Defense (KUFNCD), formerly called the Kampuchean National United Front for National Salvation (KNUFNS), KUFNCD National Council deputy general secretary Min Khin, vice-chairman Tep Vong.

**Publications.** *Pracheachon* (People), semiweekly of the KPRP Central Committee, founded October 1985, circulation 37,000, editor in chief Som Kim Suor, deputy editor Pen Panhnha; *Kongtap Padevoat* (Revolutionary army), weekly of the KPRAF, editor in chief Ros Savanna; *Phnom Penh*, weekly of the Phnom Penh municipal KPRP committee; *Kampuchea*, weekly of the KUFNCD, editor in chief Khieu Kanharith; *Neak Khousna*, monthly magazine. The official news agency is SPK (Sar-Pordamean Kampuchea), general director Em Sam An, deputy director Sum Mean. SPK publishes *Daily Bulletin* in Khmer and French, and *Angkor*, a monthly magazine, in Khmer.

- **Party of Democratic Kampuchea (PDK).** Formerly the Kampuchean (or Khmer) Communist Party (KCP), which was the political instrument of the Khmer Rouge, who governed Cambodia harshly from April 1975 to December 1978, when they were driven from power by the Vietnamese invasion.

**Founded.** Traces its origins to the (Khmer) Kanapak Pracheachon (Khmer People's Party) founded in June 1951. The KCP was replaced by the PDK in December 1981.

**Membership.** No data. The only large PDK mass organization known to be extant is the National Army of Democratic Kampuchea (NADK), a guerrilla force numbering 30,000–35,000 armed personnel. Most combatants, however, are probably not formal party members.

**General Secretary.** Pol Pot possibly still the dominant figure, in spite of his official retirement in August 1985. In late 1986, he was allegedly terminally ill and undergoing treatment in Beijing (*NYT*, 7 December).

**Secretariat.** Possibly no longer functioning.

**Control Commission.** Possibly no longer functioning.

**Politburo.** Party organizations, except for the NADK, lapsed into inactivity when the KCP converted to the PDK (Floyd Abrams, *Kampuchea After the Worst: A Report on Current Human Rights* [New York: Lawyers' Committee on Human Rights, 1985], p. 182). A Supreme Military Commission of the NADK was reportedly disbanded with Pol Pot's retirement and may have held its final meeting at that time.

**Central Committee.** Possibly no longer functioning.

**Status.** The PDK represents the Khmer Rouge, which is the dominant partner in a tripartite anti-Vietnamese front with the Khmer People's National Liberation Front (KPNLF) of Son Sann, and the National United Front for an Independent, Neutral, Peaceful, and Cooperative Cambodia (Front uni national pour un Cambodge indépendant, neutre, pacifique et coopératif; FUNCINPEC) of Prince Sihanouk. The front took the name Coalition Government of Democratic Kampuchea (CGDK) in mid-1982. PDK authority extends to its refugee and insurgent camps along the border with Thailand and Laos and probably to a zone of control in the Cardamon Mountains of Koh Kong province in southwestern Cambodia.

**Last Congress.** Third (and last), 14 December 1975, in Phnom Penh

**Last Election.** 20 March 1976, for the People's Representational Assembly of Democratic Kampuchea. Elected were 150 peasants, 50 workers, and 50 soldiers.

**Auxiliary Organizations.** No information available. An Association of Democratic Kampuchean Youth may be in existence.

**Publications.** Voice of Democratic Kampuchea (VODK), clandestine radio broadcasting station.

**Leadership and Party Organization.** *KPRP.* Party leadership and organization remained unchanged in 1986. In March, however, changes were announced in a number of senior government positions. Interior Minister Khang Sarin became president of the People's Supreme Court. Chan Min was appointed chief judge of the court. KPRP Politburo member Ney Pena went from deputy to minister of interior. Central Committee members Say Chhum and Chhay Than were promoted to minister of agriculture and minister of finance, respectively (Berkeley, California, *Indochina Chronology* [*IC*], January–March).

In December, three other influential KPRP figures lost some of their government functions. Caught in the shakeup were Hun Sen, who relinquished the portfolio of foreign minister; Bou Thong, who was relieved as defense minister; and party veteran Chea Soth, who gave up the position of planning minister. Their places were taken by Kong Korm as foreign minister, Koy Buntha as defense minister, and Chea Chantho as planning minister (*FBIS-AP*, 10 December). All three of the new appointees had previously been deputy ministers in their respective ministries. Although analysts speculated that the relief of Bou Thong could have been related to the uninspired performance of the KPRAF in the field, reasons for the overall shuffle remained unclear. The changes could have been intended to divest the former incumbents of the heavy workload caused by their concurrent service in several top-echelon positions. However, the shakeup also showed the growing confidence of the KPRP and People's Republic of Kampuchea (PRK) in the training and appointment of second-echelon officials to top leadership positions, and their willingness to assign substantial responsibilities to the new appointees. In a less obvious manner, these latest promotions could also strengthen the ranks of a new, rising generation of party leaders with neither Khmer Rouge nor Vietnamese antecedents (*JPRS–Southeast Asia Report* [*SEA*]-86-142, 15 August).

*PDK.* Party dynamics remained concealed from outsiders. However, the apparent waning presence of Pol Pot may have given rise to a measure of disunity among top-echelon PDK leaders. The maverick of this leadership group remained Ta Mok, the most radical KR commander, who may

not have accepted the authority of Son Sen, Pol Pot's designated successor, as supreme military commander of the NADK. In 1986, Ta Mok commanded a guerrilla force of about 10,000 men and was in charge of a Khmer Rouge military zone extending from the Thai border to the northern shores of the Tonle Sap and northern suburbs of Phnom Penh. He has reportedly set himself farther apart from other PDK leaders/Khmer Rouge military commanders by refusing to cooperate with the noncommunist factions of the CGDK (*FEER*, 6 March).

**Domestic Party Affairs.** *KPRP.* In 1986, the party set about implementing the measures prescribed by the Fifth Congress in October 1985. Among these reforms was promulgation of the nation's First Five-Year Plan, which would run from 1986 to 1990. The plan emphasized development in four key sectors: the cultivation of rice and rubber, and the exploitation of forest and aquatic resources. Development of these four "economic spearheads" was given renewed impetus at the seventh national agricultural conference, which was held in Phnom Penh in April (*IC*, April–June).

Regarding political matters, General Secretary Heng Samrin in a keynote article stressed two important personnel tasks confronting the party: the need for continued recruitment of high-caliber members to serve as a vanguard of the working class in Cambodia, and the necessity of dispatching cadres to build up the KPRP's grass-roots organization in the countryside (*WMR*, February). Both are essential tasks if the party is to extend the writ of the PRK to all corners of Cambodia and lessen dependence on its present mentor, the Vietnamese Communist Party.

The KPRP held two plenums of its Fifth Congress during the year. The Second Plenum, held in mid-January, called for increased struggle against the resistance factions of the CGDK, solidarity among the Indochinese countries, and continued efforts to meet the goals of the 1986–1990 five-year plan for socio-economic development (*IC*, January–March). The Third Plenum, which met in a lengthier session in mid-July, passed a resolution on "building the Cambodian working class into a genuine vanguard class in the cause of the Cambodian revolution." This was a turgid concept earlier defined by Heng Samrin as a party task that would make the KPRP "an organization dedicated to the interests of our working people and the ideas of proletarian internationalism." (*WMR*, February; *IC*, July–September.) The Third Plenum also set forth KPRP policy toward intellectuals. It discussed the political and economic training tasks of Central Committee members, listened to reports on developments implemented during the first half of the year, and set targets to be met during the second half of 1986.

The KPRP also held a meeting in late December. Details of the session are lacking. However, items on the agenda included a report by Heng Samrin on the Sixth Congress of the Vietnamese Communist Party in Hanoi, an assessment of Soviet-Cambodian relations, and a report by Chea Sim on his brief sojourn in Albania. The Politburo also expressed its support for an Indochinese summit conference to be held in 1987 (*FBIS-AP*, 29 December).

Some activity was also noted in the KPRP-dominated government organs of the PRK. The First National Assembly held its tenth session in February and ratified the Cambodia-Vietnam border treaty signed in December 1985. It also approved the state plan for 1986 and extended current assembly tenure until 1991, in view of the postponed elections (*IC*, January–March). At its eleventh session in July, the assembly heard a number of presentations on various domestic developments. Among the reports submitted to the delegates were those on the implementation of tasks for 1986, the state of the national budget, the Supreme Court and General Procurator's office, foreign affairs, the defense works on the Thai border, party-building efforts, and reaffirmation of party policy toward intellectuals (*FBIS-AP*, 22 July). The assembly also took note of the four revolutionary tasks facing the PRK: fighting the nation's enemies, winning over protestors to the government side, expanding production, and building the KPRAF (ibid.). The assembly took time to reject the eight-point proposal submitted by the CGDK to end the insurgent war in Cambodia, denouncing the effort as "concocted by Beijing in an attempt to return the genocidal Pol Pot clique to power to massacre the Cambodian people again (ibid., 30 July).

A number of ceremonial events also marked the KPRP calendar in 1986. In February, party functions attended by top-echelon KPRP officials and foreign dignitaries from the Socialist bloc were held to celebrate the 56th anniversary of the Indochinese Communist Party and the seventh anniversary of the Treaty of Peace, Friendship, and Cooperation with Vietnam. In June, similar celebrations were held in honor of the KPRAF Armed Forces Day and to mark the 35th anniversary of the KPRP.

*PDK.* Party activities are unknown. Fragmentary reports continued to hint at a draconian regime imposed by the PDK on villages and insurgent/refugee camps under its control.

**Military Issues.** *KPRP.* The KPRAF is the military instrument of the nation and party, and it numbers 30,000–35,000 personnel. It consists of the regular army, regional forces, and village militia. The regular army comprises six understrength divisions (including the 4th, 6th, 196th, and 286th) and a number of independent regiments. Three of the divisions are headquartered in Battambang city, Sisophon and Treng in Battambang Province, and western Cambodia, with subordinate units reportedly deployed in stationary blocking positions near the Thai border (Singapore, *Indochina Report* [*IR*], October 1984; *Asian Defense Journal*, August 1985).

Military analysts have rated the KPRAF poorly as a fighting force. Morale was low and desertions were rampant; some of the rank and file subsequently joined or collaborated actively with the resistance. PRK authorities were compelled to disband the 2d division because of a wave of mutinies in its ranks. Because of their unreliability and inexperience, KPRAF units have usually been relegated to rear-echelon security duties, and most combat operations against the insurgents have been mounted by the ten to twelve Vietnamese divisions in Cambodia. Overall, the KPRAF was also lacking in high-caliber party cadres and poorly trained in military skills. Vietnamese and Soviet advisers, however, have been attempting to correct this latter deficiency with a network of newly established military schools around Phnom Penh. Some Cambodian officers have also been sent to Vietnam and the Soviet Union for training. Domestically, KPRP directives have stressed the correct ideological training of armed forces members and have spurred provincial military command committees to strengthen regional and militia units and to assign military tasks to all subordinate echelons. In spite of all recruitment efforts, though, the KPRAF has been chronically undermanned since its inception. With a shallow manpower base to draw from and the need to keep KPRAF personnel strength at a credible level, the PRK has extended the period of conscription from two to five years for able-bodied males 18–30 years of age (*Le Monde*, 4–5 May).

In an effort to prevent infiltration of refugees and insurgents from Thailand, the PRK has forged ahead on the construction of a cleared zone of military obstacles, ditches, minefields, and fortifications along its western border. Each district (*srok*) in Cambodia has been assigned responsibility for clearing a segment of the border and must itself draft the personnel to dispatch this task. In mid-1986, 60,000–120,000 men from 18 to 45 years of age were thus engaged for three-to-six-month tours of duty, frequently under conditions of great hardship, and watched by KPRAF units (ibid.).

This forced labor project, which has touched all corners of Cambodia under control of the PRK, has reportedly engendered considerable disaffection among the rural population toward the government in Phnom Penh. In the absence of dry-season offensives for the past two years, the construction of the defense works along the Thai border was the most sustained military-related activity pursued by the Hanoi and Phnom Penh regimes in 1986.

*PDK.* The NADK remained the most formidable fighting force confronting the KPRAF and the Vietnamese military forces in Cambodia. It was amply supplied with Chinese small arms and conducted small-scale operations from the Tonle Sap area to the suburbs of Phnom Penh. In 1986, the noncommunist members of the resistance coalition reported increasing cooperation from NADK units belonging to Khieu Samphan and Ieng Sary; in March, a joint operation involving the armed forces of all three factions was mounted against Battambang. Maverick NADK hardliner Ta Mok has reportedly held aloof from such cooperation and on several occasions deliberately attacked military units of the noncommunist coalition partners.

**Auxiliary and Front Organizations.** *KPRP.* Information concerning auxiliary organizations of the KPRP was confined to a few official announcements of meetings and ceremonial events in 1986. In July, the People's Revolutionary Youth Union of Kampuchea celebrated its 31st anniversary with a mass meeting of 2,000 attendees in the national stadium of Phnom Penh (*JPRS-SEA*-86-121, 22 July). The organization was later authorized by the National Assembly to hold a congress at all governmental levels (province, district, and municipality) in Cambodia to expand membership and set targets and goals for implementation (*FBIS-AP*, 18 August). For its part, a committee of the Cambodian Federation of Trade Unions met to discuss the strengths and weaknesses displayed by the organization in the first half of 1986. The committee resolved to stimulate workers and other personnel to greater efforts and to emphasize the building of a "family-run economy," which it considered a "significant economic grouping for improved livelihood." Politburo member Chea Sim addressed the committee and exhorted the participants to share their experiences in meeting goals set by the organization (ibid., 14 August). A delegation of the Cambodian Federation of Trade Unions also traveled to Laos in March to attend a conference of trade unions of all three countries in Indochina (ibid., 18 March).

*PDK.* There was no information concerning auxiliary or front organizations maintained by the PDK in 1986.

**International and Regional Issues.** *KPRP.* In the search for a negotiated settlement to the insurgent war in Cambodia, KPRP and PRK officials in 1986 forfeited the initiative to their opponents in the CGDK. Speaking from Beijing, President Norodom Sihanouk, in a bold gambit in March, announced an eight-point plan to bring about a resolution of the turmoil in the war-ravaged country. The plan encompassed eight steps that would be implemented sequentially to break the present deadlock in Cambodia. The steps included the negotiated withdrawal of Vietnamese troops in stages, to be followed by a cease-fire and the establishment of a transitional government composed of the four Cambodian parties to the dispute (the KPRP/PRK, KPNLF, FUNCINPEC, and PDK). The transitional government would then hold free, United Nations–supervised elections to restore Cambodia to the family of nations as an independent, nonaligned state. The last two steps were an appeal to all nations to help rebuild Cambodia and the negotiation of a treaty of nonaggression and peaceful coexistence with Vietnam (*FBIS-AP*, 18 March).

Predictably, officials in Phnom Penh lost no time in denouncing the CGDK plan as "a new farce staged in Beijing," and they labeled it an effort "to keep alive the genocidal Pol Pot clique" and permit its return to power in Cambodia (ibid., 25 March). In contrast to the plan set forth by Prince Sihanouk, the PRK submitted its own proposal to solve the

Cambodian problem. As articulated by Politburo member and prime minister Hun Sen, the gambit reaffirmed by Cambodia, Vietnam, and Laos consisted of a multilateral conference between the states of Indochina and the Association of Southeast Asian Nations (ASEAN) at which "problems of peace and stability in Southeast Asia" could be discussed (Moscow, *New Times*, 42, 1986). In a bid to drive a wedge between the two noncommunist partners of the Khmer resistance and the Khmer Rouge of the PDK, newly appointed PRK foreign minister Kong Korm reaffirmed his government's willingness to talk with resistance leaders so long as they were willing to discuss "how to dismantle the Pol Pot group" (Hong Kong, *Asiaweek*, 14 December). This exclusion of the Pol Pot faction from any resistance dialogue with Vietnam and the PRK has remained the negotiating stance of both Hanoi and Phnom Penh over the years.

On a global scale, the regime in Phnom Penh in 1986 was recognized by about 40 states and revolutionary movements, including the Soviet Union and India (*WMR*, February). The trend in the relationship with Moscow has been the establishment of direct bilateral ties, bypassing (at least overtly) Vietnam as an intermediary. In 1986, the PRK negotiated a five-year trade and aid agreement with the Soviet Union. Under the terms of the pact, Moscow will provide Phnom Penh with petroleum products, chemical fertilizer, and motor vehicles such as tractors, in exchange for Cambodian rubber, timber, and various agricultural and industrial products such as lacquer (*IC*, January–March). Several high-level visits also reinforced the friendly relationship between the two countries. KPRP general secretary Heng Samrin attended the Twenty-seventh Congress of the Communist Party of the Soviet Union, and Politburo member Chea Sim led a delegation on a friendship visit to the USSR in August. In turn, Soviet officials of the Soviet-Kampuchean Friendship Society visited Phnom Penh in April, and a Soviet Foreign Ministry delegation traveled to Cambodia in August.

The United States does not recognize the PRK on the grounds that it was put in place by the Vietnamese invasion of 1979. Washington, in the recent past, has provided limited, nonlethal aid to the two noncommunist partners of the CGDK.

Cambodian party and state relations with Vietnam remained tilted asymmetrically in favor of Hanoi. There is an increasing body of evidence that Vietnamese officials exercise oversight authority over all PRK decisionmaking, a state of affairs that has become increasingly chafing to their Cambodian counterparts. Vietnamese advisers are stationed at all levels of the PRK and KPRP, even down to district levels. Vietnamese settlers have reportedly been returning to Cambodia after their expulsion dating back to the early 1970s. Areas of Vietnamese colonization have reportedly included the eastern provinces of Svay Rieng and Prey Veng and around the Tonle Sap lake of western Cambodia. (*Etudes*, February; *IR*, July–September.)

*PDK.* The party's main international backer has been China, which has maintained long-standing and friendly ties with Pol Pot. In 1986, observers looked for signs that Beijing might be stepping back from supporting the primacy of the Khmer Rouge in any negotiated settlement to the conflict in Cambodia. There was a flurry of speculation to this effect late in the year. As one example, Indonesian foreign minister Mochtar Kusumaatmadja reported that, in a dialogue with Chinese officials, he had been assured that Beijing "would accept anything the Khmers would agree to, among themselves" and that the Chinese now seem to be fully backing Sihanouk (*Asiaweek*, 14 December). Chinese premier Zhao Ziyang himself had declared earlier that Beijing supported "the establishment of a quadripartite coalition government headed by Samdech Sihanouk following the total withdrawal of the Vietnamese troops" (Islamabad, *Muslim*, 16 September).

The PDK made an effort to strike a higher international profile on behalf of the coalition government. The party threw its support behind Prince Sihanouk's eight-point proposal, and leading PDK figures such as Khieu Samphan and Ieng Thirith journeyed abroad to gain international backing for the plan. CGDK delegations led by Khieu Samphan visited the Philippines and Japan in April and seven nonaligned countries in Africa later in the year for that purpose.

Russell R. Ross
*Library of Congress*

# China

**Population.** 1,045,537,000 (July 1986)
**Party.** Chinese Communist Party (Zhongguo gongchan dang; CCP)
**Founded.** 1921
**Membership.** 44 million (Xinhua, 25 September; *FBIS*, 26 September)
**General Secretary.** Hu Yaobang
**Standing Committee of the Politburo.** 5 members: Hu Yaobang, Chen Yun, Deng Xiaoping, Li Xiannian (president, People's Republic of China [PRC]; chairman, National People's Congress [NPC]), Zhao Ziyang
**Politburo.** 20 full members: Hu Yaobang, Chen Yun, Deng Xiaoping, Fang Yi, Hu Qiaomu, Hu Qili, Li Peng, Li Xiannian, Ni Zhifu, Peng Zhen, Qiao Shi, Tian Jiyun, Wan Li, Wu Xueqian, Xi Zhongxun, Yang Dezhi, Yang Shangkun, Yao Yilin, Yu Qiuli, Zhao Ziyang. 2 alternate members: Chen Muhua, Qin Jiwei
**Secretariat.** 11 members: Hu Yaobang, Chen Pixian, Deng Liqun, Hao Jianxiu, Hu Qili, Li Peng, Qiao Shi, Tian Jiyun, Wan Li, Wang Zhaoguo, Yu Qiuli
**Central Military Commission.** Chairman: Deng Xiaoping; permanent vice-chairman and secretary-general: Yang Shangkun; deputy secretary-general: Hong Xuezhi; other members: Yang Dezhi, Yu Qiuli, Zhang Aiping
**Central Advisory Commission.** 162 members. Chairman: Deng Xiaoping; permanent vice-chairman: Bo Yibo; vice-chairmen: Song Renqiong, Wang Zhen
**Central Commission for Discipline Inspection.** First secretary: Chen Yun; second secretary: Wang Heshou; permanent secretary: Han Guang; secretaries: Chen Zuolin, Han Tianshi, Qiang Xiaochu
**Central Committee.** 210 full members and 133 alternate members (since September)
**Status.** Ruling party
**Last Congress.** Twelfth, 1–11 September 1982, in Beijing (but a rare National Conference of Party Delegates was held 18–23 September 1985 in Beijing)
**Last Election.** 1981, all 3,202 candidates were CCP approved
**Auxiliary Organizations.** The All-China Women's Federation, led by Kang Keqing; the Communist Youth League of China (50 million members), led by Hu Jintao; the All-China Federation of Trade Unions, led by Ni Zhifu; the People's Political Consultative Conference (CPPCC), led by Deng Yingchao.
**Publications.** The official and most authoritative publication of the CCP is the newspaper *Renmin ribao* (People's daily; *RMRB*), published in Beijing. The theoretical journal of the Central Committee, *Hongqi* (Red flag), is published approximately once a month. More influential in recent years, however, is *Liaowang* (Outlook), the weekly publication of Xinhua (the New China News Agency; NCNA), the official news agency of the party and government. The daily paper of the People's Liberation Army (PLA) is *Jiefangjunbao* (Liberation Army daily). The weekly *Beijing Review* (*BR*), published in English and in several other languages, carries translations of important articles, editorials, and documents from these publications and from other sources. *China Daily* (*CD*), the first English-language national newspaper in the PRC, began official publication in Beijing and Hong Kong on 1 June 1981. It began a New York edition in June 1983.

**Domestic Affairs.** The year 1986 was one of international consolidation, following the dramatic changes across the spectrum in recent years, particularly in the immediately preceding year. This restraint with regard to further changes for the time being was underscored in October at the Sixth Plenum of the Twelfth Central Committee at which only a single promotion (from alternate membership to full) was registered. This does not mean that further reforms were not undertaken; as the year wore on, a number of important changes were recorded, particularly in response to the criticisms of foreign businessmen who earlier in the year had begun to voice their frustrations more openly. There was considerable talk about the need for further political reforms during the year, but such reform was deferred to the following year, at least. This hesitancy over political reform apparently helped fuel massive university student demonstrations in December. In addition to demands for the correction of lesser grievances, students called for more political democracy, often going beyond the political reforms which party leaders have in mind.

The year began with two of the largest party meetings to be held in recent years. These meetings of 6 and 9 January were attended by 8,000 senior party, army, and government officials in the Great Hall of the People without prior public announcement. General Secretary Hu Yaobang gave the keynote speech, but the young reformists led by Hu Qili dominated the conference. Announced at the meeting was a new campaign against corruption at senior levels. The leadership of this new campaign was given to a new group, rather than to the Central Commission for Discipline Inspection (CCDI). The new anti-corruption team was headed by Qiao Shi, who had become secretary of the important Commission of Political Science and Law in August 1985 and was promoted to the Politburo in September 1985. Chen Yun, first secretary of the CCDI, did not attend the meeting. However, neither did Deng Xiaoping and Li Xiannian. (*FEER*, 23, 30 January.)

Vice-Premier Tian Jiyun's speech to the participants on 6 January was subsequently given widespread publicity abroad, carried first in two installments in the *Beijing Review* on 27 January and 3 February, and then again as a slightly abridged entire document in the 10 February issue, entitled "On the Present Economic Situation and Restructuring the Economy." Tian emphasized that on the question as to whether the reform will lead to capitalism the answer is "an unequivocal no." He said

that public ownership will continue to be regarded as the foundation of the national economy, pointing out that the entire new private sector as a whole only accounts for 0.6 percent of the total national industrial output.

On 28 January, Peng Zhen, in a speech at Zhejiang University, discussed the relationship between the ongoing reforms and Marxist-Leninist tenets. He objected to the suggestion that a person is considered conservative and an opponent of reform if he stresses Marxism-Leninism. He argued that "It is the theories of the capitalist class and its apologists that are conservative and ossified. Bourgeois thoughts may look very fresh and jaunty today, but they serve only to defend capitalism's status quo" (*BR*, 19 May).

The Fourth Session of the Sixth NPC was held from 25 March to 12 April. The session endorsed "in principle" the Seventh Five-Year Plan and Premier Zhao's report on the plan. This was the first time since 1949 that such a plan had been discussed and adopted by the NPC before it was promulgated and implemented. Of the previous five-year plans, the first (1953–1958) and the sixth (1981–1986) had been the most successful and were made known to the public. But the first plan was not approved until 1955, and the sixth was not approved until December 1982. The intervening five-year plans had each been formulated late and were never promulgated.

The Seventh Five-Year Plan gives priority to reform, meaning specifically reforms in three areas. First, enterprises, especially state-owned, large and medium-sized ones, are to be made more independent and solely responsible for their losses and profits. Second, the socialist commodity market is to be further developed and the market system gradually perfected. Third, the state management of enterprises is to change gradually from direct to indirect control and a new "socialist macro-economic management system" is to be established.

The plan also sets an average annual economic growth rate (total industrial and agricultural output value) of 6.7 percent, and the GNP at an average annual rate of 7.5 percent. Social investment in fixed assets will be 70 percent more than during the previous five-year plan. The average accumulation rate stands at 30 percent, which is on a par with that of the Sixth Five-Year Plan, but lower than the 1985 level. The actual rural and urban consumption level will increase 5 percent each year, corresponding to the expected rate of increase of the national income. The plan also attaches importance to the development of science, technology, and education, and it holds that equal attention is to be paid to the promotion of cultural and ideological advance as well as material progress. (Excerpts from the Seventh Five-Year Plan are in *BR*, 28 April.)

The Fourth Session of the Sixth NPC also endorsed the General Principles of the Civil Code to come into force in 1987, the Law Governing Compulsory Education, which became effective 1 July, and the Law Governing Enterprises with Foreign Capital, which became effective upon publication. The NPC also adopted a State Council plan for economic and social development in 1986 and a state budget for the coming year. The NPC Standing Committee was empowered to examine and endorse the final 1985 accounts. Qiao Shi was appointed the fifth vice-premier of the State Council. Song Jian, minister in charge of the State Scientific and Technological Commission, was appointed state councillor. Five additional members were elected to the NPC Standing Committee. (*BR*, 21 April.)

On 9 April, Hu Yaobang spoke at a forum on rectifying the party's style of work. He categorized the many contradictions that exist in the party into those between different views on work and understanding on the one hand, and those between personal interests and the interests of the party and the people on the other. The main deviation in the party at present, he said, is the second type of contradiction. This, and the inability to handle it, has resulted in a "flabbiness" in the party's work style. (*BR*, 14 July.)

Prominent conservative leader Hu Qiaomu was acutely embarrassed and placed on the defensive during the year, following the arrest and imprisonment of his son, Hu Shiying, for "embezzling education funds" on 7 March (Hong Kong, *Pai hsing*, 1 May; *FBIS* 12 May). But there were other cases of sons and daughters of leading cadres who were brought to justice, along with many others during the year. In February, three children of senior Shanghai party officials were executed for rape and hooliganism. In June, 31 criminals were shot to death in Beijing for crimes ranging from rape and armed robbery to theft, constituting the largest single mass execution since the current anticrime campaign was launched in 1983. (Beijing, AFP, 25 June; *FBIS*, 26 June; see also Beijing, *Zhongguo xinwen she*, 19 February; *FBIS*, 21 February.)

On 31 July, Vice-Premier Wan Li spoke before a national research symposium in Beijing on "soft science" or policy research. He acknowledged that

in order to develop a scientific approach "it is necessary first to create a political environment in which democracy, equality and the free exchange of views and information are the norms of life." He said that "Leaders must respect other people's democratic right to air their opinions without fear, including, of course, those that contradict their own." This was all the more important, he went on, for soft science research "because it comprises mental work involving political as well as academic questions." (*BR*, 29 September.)

More than 130 researchers and responsible persons from the Central Committee and the State Council participated in a symposium to discuss the theory of political structural reform from 10 to 12 July in Beijing. The discussions focused on the basic aim of decentralizing power in China. This included discussion of the functions of the CCP itself. It was reported that most of the participants held that the "overconcentration of power finds expression mainly in party organizations so that generally speaking, the party functions in place of the state." (Hong Kong, *Liaowang Overseas Edition*, 21 July; *FBIS*, 23 July; Chi Fulin, "Symposium on Theory of Political Structural Reform," *BR*, 17 November.)

On 5 July the exchange rate of the renminbi was suddenly devalued by 15.8 percent. Prior to the devaluation the exchange rate of renminbi to the U.S. dollar was 3.21; afterwards it became 3.71. This was the biggest devaluation in the PRC since 1949. (Stephen Morgan, Annie Lam, Yan Meining, and Ivan Lo, "Special Report," *Hong Kong Standard*, 13 July; *FBIS*, 16 July.)

In August an explosion-prevention equipment factory in Shenyang became the first enterprise to be declared bankrupt. Its license was revoked and its assets scheduled for auction (see *BR*, 8 September). The event was unprecedented and sent a shock wave throughout China's economy.

On 2 September, Deng Xiaoping was interviewed by Mike Wallace on CBS's "60 Minutes" program, during which he made a number of his usual candid comments. Deng said he hoped that the Soviet Union would urge Vietnam to end its aggression in Cambodia. He advised the United States "to take a wiser approach to the Taiwan question." (See text in *BR*, 22 September.)

On 9 September the State Council promulgated four sets of regulations on reforming China's labor system. According to He Guang, minister of labor and personnel, the aim of the reform was to eliminate the defects of the "iron rice bowl" practice and to establish the relationship between workers and enterprises on a rational basis in order to meet the needs of a planned commodity economy. (Interview in *BR*, 15 September.)

Following a five-day preparatory meeting, the Sixth Plenary Session of the Twelfth Central Committee was held on 28 September, attended by 199 of its members and 126 alternate members. Also present were members of the Central Advisory Commission and of the CCDI. At the lengthier preparatory meeting, participants had been briefed by Yao Yilin on the current economic situation and economic work. The Sixth Plenum made only one minor personnel change: Yin Changmin, a former alternate member, was promoted to full membership on the Central Committee.

The principal task of the Sixth Plenum was the adoption of a resolution (of about ten thousand characters) on the "guiding principles for building a socialist society with an advanced culture and ideology." The basic guiding principle of the resolution is that such an effort must be capable of pushing forward China's modernization, promoting the all-around reform and the opening to the outside world, as well as embodying the four cardinal principles. The resolution declares: "As a basic, unalterable state policy, opening to the outside world applies to our efforts to achieve cultural and ideological progress as well as to our work for material progress." "Taking economic development as the key link," the resolution says that "China is to continue to reform its economic and political structure and at the same time speed up the country's cultural and ideological progress, making sure that these aspects of work are coordinated and promote each other. The cultural and ideological progress provides a powerful guarantee for the correct orientation of the material progress." (*BR*, 6 October.) The resolution, even though it highlights economic development as the key link, was seen as something of a victory for ideological conservatives. This was especially the case inasmuch as the plenum did not address the urgent question of political reform. A subsequent *People's Daily* commentary reported that the government will be putting forward a practical plan for reform in one year's time, ostensibly in time for the Thirteenth Party Congress in October 1987. (*BR*, 22 December.)

Beijing and Taipei held their first face-to-face negotiations in 37 years following the hijacking of a Taiwan Boeing 747 cargo plane to Guangzhou on 3 May. The talks were held in Hong Kong and resulted in the reclaiming of the aircraft by the government of Taiwan. (Hong Kong, AP, 19 May; *NYT*, 20 May.)

Hu Ping, the governor of Fujian province, said in May that his province has made preparations for expanding trade with Taiwan. "The key," he said, "lies on the Taiwan side." (Hong Kong, *Kuang Chiao Ching*, 16 June; *FBIS*, 30 June.)

Deng Xiaoping expressed disappointment to a visiting Philippine delegation in June that Taiwan's leaders had not responded to his offer of a "Hong Kong formula" to reunify China. Deng said, reportedly, that "Problems can be postponed but they cannot be ignored forever . . . When patience runs out and peaceful compromise is refused, there is no other way but force." (Hong Kong, *South China Morning Post*, 22 June; *FBIS*, 23 June.)

On 12 November some ten thousand persons attended a rally in Beijing honoring the 120th birthday of Sun Yat-sen. They heard NPC chairman Peng Zhen stress that China wanted to negotiate with the Nationalist Party and was willing to negotiate with others in Taiwan as well. Peng noted that some people "with ulterior motives" were supporting a Taiwan independence movement and the concepts of two Chinas or one China and one Taiwan, thus pointing to the need for the Nationalists to discontinue their procrastination. Peng's speech was seen as an apparent response to recent moves in Taiwan to end martial law in 1987 and allow the formation of opposition parties.

The Democratic Progressive Party in Taipei, which jumped the gun in forming its organization before it could legally do so, reportedly had ratified a platform supporting more independence for native Taiwanese (Beijing, AP; Hong Kong, *South China Morning Post*, 13 November). Subsequently, on 2 December, opposition leader Hsu Hsin-liang landed at Chiang Kai-shek International Airport, but was not allowed to disembark (even though there was a 1980 warrant for his arrest on sedition charges) and had to return to Manila on the same plane. An earlier attempt similarly failed when Cathay Pacific Airways refused to allow Hsu to board their flight in Tokyo on 30 November because of the Taiwan government's warning that he would not be allowed to disembark. More than 3,000 troops surrounded the Taipei airport to prevent Hsu's supporters from entering the airport to welcome him (*FEER*, 11 December). The opposition Democratic Progressive Party went on to win several legislative

Yuan seats in the 6 December elections (Tokyo, *The Japan Times*, 8 December).

After being delayed for nearly two years, the book *Apology of Humanism*, a collection of philosophical essays by Wang Ruoshui, formerly a deputy editor in chief of the *People's Daily*, was made available to the public (Beijing, *CD*, 12 August; *FBIS*, 14 August).

*Amnesty International Report 1986* expressed concern about prisoners of conscience in China, including Catholic priests. It reported that Father Shen Baishun, 82, died in detention this June while serving a ten-year sentence. Father Shen, a Jesuit, had been released in the late 1970s after about twenty years in detention, but was rearrested in 1981 and sent to a labor camp in Anhui province. The Amnesty report also said several groups of Protestants were arrested and tried for propagating religion or conducting "house churches," a practice that has been spreading widely in China in recent years (Hong Kong, *South China Morning Post*, 13 November).

The Central Committee and the State Council from 8 to 12 November sponsored a national conference in Beijing on rural work. Vice-Premier Tian Jiyun warned that enterprises and government departments should not capitalize on the increased incomes of peasants by charging more for their services, nor should unwarranted charges be levied on farm products. He promised that the cost of raising crops would not increase in the coming year. He said that, if conditions permitted, other reform measures would be undertaken to increase economic benefits in the countryside. He noted that the development of a commodity-producing economy was the best way to increase peasant income. In 1987 the three goals for agriculture will be to increase grain production, to continue to readjust the economic structure, and to open more channels to accelerate the circulation of rural commodities. Despite natural disasters, a bumper grain harvest was reported for 1986. Remaining problems included the difficulties in implementing readjustment of agricultural production under the responsibility system based on the household, and the improving of links between production and sales (Beijing, *CD*, 26 November.) Vice-Premier Wan Li later called on peasants to update their old beliefs and to clear away the last remnants of feudalism. He noted that many of the new economic activities directly contradict traditional moral concepts. For example, looking down upon merchants has hindered the development of a commodity economy. He also said that feudal superstitions, mercenary marriages, expensive and wasteful marriage and funeral ceremonies, and gambling and other economic crimes remain among the problems in rural China. (Beijing, Xinhua; Beijing, *CD*, 27 November.)

A proposed bankruptcy law was reconsidered at the eighteenth session of the NPC Standing Committee in November, after having been rejected at its previous session two months earlier.

Also presented at the session was a motion calling for the formation of a state commission for the machine-building industry that would replace the existing ministries of machine-building and ordnance industries. The purpose of the move, according to Premier Zhao, was "to strengthen the unified management of national machine-building and military enterprises and the implementation of a policy to integrate the armed forces with civilian management (Beijing, *CD*, 28 November).

After a sharp drop in the number of private businesses in the first half of the year (from 11.71 to 11.35 million by June 1986), private enterprises recovered in the second half. The downturn in the first half of the year was a nationwide phenomenon, and was the first such decline in private commerce since it was permitted in 1979. However, beginning in July, the State Administration of Industry and Commerce, which oversees private enterprises, ordered its provincial agencies to make conditions more favorable for private businesses. As a result, the total number of employees in the private sector is said to have reached 17.66 million, an increase of 470,000 between June and November. According to the overseas edition of the *People's Daily*, this was on a par with the record figure at the end of 1985. (Beijing, *CD*, 26 November.)

In his speech to the NPC Standing Committee on 25 November, Peng Zhen criticized those who denigrated the communist ideal. He defended the superiority of socialist democracy and urged that the socialist legal and democratic systems be strengthened so that they "are not subject to change with the change of leadership, or changes in the views and attention of the leaders." Some suspected that such warnings of the danger of personal rule are directed against Deng Xiaoping and Zhao Ziyang. Peng Zhen is seen by some, most notably veteran China-watcher Father Louis LaDany in Hong Kong, as building an institutional base in the NPC from which to challenge the Deng leadership, which now controls key party organs. Peng's speech, along with the NPC's extensive debate on the bankruptcy law and other reformist measures in sessions of the

NPC Standing Committee this year, is seen as evidence of the LaDany thesis (*FEER*, 11 December). (Full text of Peng Zhen's speech in *BR*, 17 November.)

It was reported in December that a recent circular of the Central Committee's Department of Organization urged that all regions and departments mobilize their rank and file to make public assessments of the abilities, moral character, conscientiousness, and achievements of leading officials at the county level and above during the winter and coming spring. This followed initiatives by the Guangdong Provincial and the Beijing Municipal party committees which suggested the use of public opinion polls to determine the performance of officials. (*BR*, 22 December.)

The first Chinese edition of the *Complete Works of Karl Marx and Frederick Engels* was published by the People's Publishing House. The 50-volume collection was translated from the Russian edition, reportedly with only slight differences (*BR*, 1 December). Earlier in the year, the third volume of the *Selected Works of Chen Yun (1956–1985)* was published (Beijing, Xinhua; *FBIS*, 27 June). A new edition of 68 articles by Mao Zedong, written between 1921 and 1965, was scheduled for publication in September, the tenth anniversary of the late chairman's death (*BR*, 25 August).

In December students who had become increasingly restive in the recent weeks began demonstrating openly in several cities, a phenomenon which persisted through the end of the year. Beginning in provincial cities, the movement reached Shanghai on 20 December when as many as 30,000 students marched "for democracy" through the city. The march was considered the largest student demonstration in China since the Cultural Revolution. The official media finally broke weeks of silence regarding other recent prodemocracy demonstrations on Chinese campuses, indicating that it was "understandable that college students should be concerned about the restructuring of the political system and hope to express their views on these issues" (Beijing, AP; *Honolulu Star Bulletin*, 20 December). However, on 21 December, authorities banned further demonstrations unless they had police permission. But students in Shanghai continued to demonstrate. On 23 December some two thousand students again marched on city hall and, while they were turned away by police, the event was peaceful. Some banners in Shanghai asked, "Xiaoping, where are you?" The movement then began to spread to Nanjing and to Beijing. Some four thousand students demonstrated at Qinghua University, after which about one thousand marched to Peking University. (Shanghai, AP; *Honolulu Star Bulletin*, 23 December.)

By 26 December, Beijing officials had banned unauthorized demonstrations, even as the official media backed the calls for greater democracy. It was stressed, however, that desired changes are to be made through existing channels. The *Workers' Daily* in Beijing warned against the idealization of Western institutions, holding that the Western election system "is in reality manipulated by a few financial groups" (Beijing, AP; *Honolulu Star Bulletin*, 26 December). He Dongchang, the senior vice-chairman of the Ministry of Education, said on 30 December that as many as 40,000 students had participated in the demonstrations in ten cities, but not one student had been arrested (Beijing, AP; *Honolulu Star Bulletin*, 30 December).

**Auxiliary and Front Organizations.** The fourth session of the sixth national committee of the People's Political Consultative Conference (CPPCC) was held almost simultaneously with the Fourth Session of the Sixth NPC in March and April. Cheng Zihua, CPPCC vice-chairman, reported to the session on 24 March on the organization's extensive work in people's diplomacy. Since 1983, eleven delegations had visited foreign countries, while the National Committee had in return received nine visiting foreign delegations and 1,100 people from 50 countries and organizations. Vice-Chairman Yang Chenwu on the same day reported on the CPPCC's work in collecting historical data. He said that CPPCC organizations have collected 500 million characters of information since 1959. More than 200 types of selected historical data and 100 "special data" have been published. A new series of books based on the personal experiences of former Kuomintang generals is now in preparation, according to Yang. He said that former industrialists and business people will be organized by the CPPCC to collect similar data relating to foreign trade, finance, banking, and Sino-foreign joint ventures. Such data will also be collected among compatriots in Hong Kong, Macao, and Taiwan, and among Chinese nationals residing abroad, he added. (*BR*, 31 March.)

A resolution passed by the session pointed out that "as an organization of the patriotic united front of the Chinese people, the CPPCC represents a major venue for developing socialist democracy in the country's political life, and that with its vast body of experts in various fields and its links among the people the CPPCC will continue to play an important role in economic development and the promotion of socialist culture and ethics." Among its other missions, CPPCC members are called upon to "expand their ties with compatriots in Taiwan, Hong Kong and Macao and overseas Chinese, [and] promote the peaceful reunification of the motherland." (*BR*, 21 April.)

**International Affairs.** The year saw continued vigorous implementation of the open-door policy. Prominent leaders made well-publicized visits abroad, and Beijing hosted many important leaders from around the globe. In March, President Li Xiannian visited Bangladesh, Sri Lanka, Egypt, Somalia, and Madagascar. In June, General Secretary Hu Yaobang visited the United Kingdom, the Federal Republic of Germany, France, and Italy. In July, Premier Zhao visited Romania, Yugoslavia, Greece, Spain, Turkey, and Tunisia.

It was reported that more than 20,000 students from 114 countries around the world have studied in China since 1973. China reportedly was planning to enroll 2,400 foreign students this year, 400 more than in 1985. (*BR*, 6 October.)

Beginning 1 February the Chinese government increased the number of areas open to foreigners from 107 to 244 (Beijing, Xinhua, 30 January; *FBIS*, 31 January).

Principal features of China's foreign policy were articulated in State Councillor and Minister of Foreign Affairs Wu Xueqian's address to the 41st session of the United Nations General Assembly in New York on 24 September. He proclaimed China's opposition to the arms race and its extension to outer space. He referred to China's reduction of its armed forces by one-fourth, the annual reduction of its military expenditures, and the shifting of much of its military industry to civilian production. With regard to Asia, he first discussed Vietnam's occupation of Cambodia, expressing support for the eight-point proposal for a political settlement put forward by the coalition government of democratic Kampuchea in March. He said that the occupation of Afghanistan by foreign troops poses a grave threat to the security of adjacent countries and peace in Asia. China supports North Korea's "positive efforts" for the independent and peaceful reunification of Korea and its "reasonable proposals and

demands for dialogue between the North and the South, tripartite talks and the withdrawal of U.S. troops from South Korea."

In the Middle East, China "consistently supported the just struggle of the Arab countries and Palestinian people . . . Israel must abandon territories occupied since 1967, while the right to existence of all countries in the Middle East should be recognized." With regard to the Iran-Iraq war, Wu said that both countries were China's friends.

In Central America, Wu affirmed China's support for the principles put forward by the Contadora group for solving the region's problems and his hope that the group will succeed. Wu inveighed against the South African regime. He referred to the "increasingly imbalanced and irrational" state of international economic relations. He said that a boost given to the economic growth of developing countries "will contribute both to the common prosperity of the world economy and to world peace and stability." (Full text in *BR*, 6 October.)

The 29 June issue of the *People's Daily* (in English in the 7 July issue of *Beijing Review*) carried an article by Lian Yan on the CCP's relations with other parties. The author affirmed that the experience of the postwar world communist movement has demonstrated that a leading center and a leading party are not necessary. "No party is entitled to place itself above the others," he said. He said that the four principles of independence, equality, mutual respect, and noninterference in each other's internal affairs applied to the CCP's relations with other communist and progressive parties. He acknowledged that the CCP has made mistakes in handling its relations with other parties, and that these mistakes have "negatively affected certain parties." But he claimed that the party has learned from such mistakes and has been open about acknowledging and correcting them. He said that the CCP is "a party of patriotism and internationalism, and it advocates the integration of the two." Looking ahead, he held that "no matter how many difficulties and hardships may appear, with the concerted efforts of all communist parties, the international communist movement will have a bright future." (*FBIS*, 10 July; *BR*, 7 July.)

Despite considerable public criticism in Hong Kong, seven contracts were signed on 23 September for China's largest joint venture to date, the Daya Bay nuclear power plant project (*FEER*, 2 October).

Queen Elizabeth II and Prince Philip visited

China from 12 to 18 October and, except for some tactless remarks by Prince Philip, it was reported a successful historic event, symbolizing the Sino-British agreement on the transfer of Hong Kong to Chinese sovereignty in 1997.

The fifth meeting of the Sino-British Joint Liaison Group was held in Beijing 25–28 November. Agreement was reached on means to ensure that Hong Kong will remain in the International Maritime Organization and the International Telecommunications Union when it becomes a special administrative region of China. Also the two governments exchanged a memorandum on the continued use of the certificates of identity now used by Hong Kong residents. (*BR*, 8 December.)

China was formally admitted to the Asian Development Bank (ADB) on 10 March. The president of the Bank of China, Chen Muhua, subsequently attended the nineteenth annual meeting of the ADB board of governors in Manila on 2 May, and expressed regret that representatives from Taiwan had not attended the meeting (*BR*, 12 May). Later, on 13 May, Premier Zhao told a visiting ADB delegation led by ADB president Masao Fujioka that, because of China's size and role in the Asia-Pacific region, the issue of China's seat on the board of the ADB should be resolved soon (*BR*, 26 May).

Chinese were accused of racism by African students in China following a confrontation between 40 Africans and their guests at a campus party in Tianjin and a crowd of 400 irate Chinese. The incident was the most prominent among many less dramatic slights that Africans say they have endured while studying or residing in China. On the other side, some of the resentment of the Chinese stems from the privileges which Africans, along with other foreigners, enjoy in China. (*NYT*, 10 June.)

China and Portugal held two rounds of talks on Macao in September and October leading to an agreement on the return of Macao to China, although no firm deadline was established. China undertook to guarantee that Macao can retain its capitalist system for another 50 years. (*CSM*, 23 October.)

China officially applied on 11 July for resumption of full membership in the General Agreement on Tariffs and Trade (GATT) as an original signatory, and indicated its readiness to enter into substantive negotiations on tariff concessions (*BR*, 21 July). Approval of the application is likely to take at least one year. (Separately, Hong Kong became the nineteenth contracting party to the GATT on 23 April, having theretofore been represented in the GATT by Great Britain.) (*BR*, 5 May.)

China joined in the 10th Asian Games held in Seoul from 20 September to 5 October and won the most gold medals of any of the participating nations (*BR*, 13 October).

China was actively engaged in providing labor services abroad. China has secured $5.1 billion worth of contracts in the past seven years. More than 59,000 Chinese engineers, technicians, and workers are currently active in overseas projects (out of 170,000 people sent abroad in economic and technical work in the past few years). More than 60 Chinese companies have been involved in over 2,600 projects in 85 countries and regions (*BR*, 10 February; Wulan Mulun, "Economic Co-operation Expanded Abroad," *BR*, 3 March). This year a Hungarian automobile company undertook to hire 350 Chinese workers to help in the production of 12,000 trucks for China in the next five years. This represents the first instance of Chinese workers being hired in Europe (Beijing, *Jingji cankao*, 5 September; *FBIS*, 19 September).

On 11 October the State Council published a 22-article document entitled "Provisions for the Encouragement of Foreign Investment" designed "to improve the investment climate, facilitate the absorption of foreign investment, introduce advanced technology, improve product quality and expand exports in order to earn more foreign exchange and develop the national economy." This was in response to increasingly vocal complaints by foreign businessmen and investors in China. (*BR*, 20 October; full text in *BR*, 27 October.)

Gu Ming, general director of the Economic Legislation Research Center under the State Council, said in Hong Kong on 26 November that China was to enact a fairly complete set of economic laws during the 1986–1990 period to protect the legal interests of foreign investors. Gu noted that China had formulated more than 300 economic laws since 1978, many aimed at promoting joint ventures and other businesses involving overseas investment. In 1986 two regulations were published on balances of foreign exchange for joint ventures and further preferential treatment to encourage overseas investment. Gu said that the training of legal personnel was being accelerated. At present China has only 20,000 lawyers (compared to 700,000 in the United States), he said. Furthermore, in 1986 the State Council established an advisory group to cut red tape in making economic decisions, and several major cities have set up joint offices to make such decisions regarding foreign economic relations. This has purportedly reduced delays from a year or two to less than three months. Similarly, foreign-funded businesses can now import materials or components for production without repeated approval from authorities. China also published four documents this year enabling all business managers and factory directors to have the final say in personnel matters. Furthermore, joint ventures now have the right to dispute charges or refuse to pay additional or unreasonable charges imposed by local departments, a matter which has long incensed overseas investors. Finally, Gu noted that the 10–15 percent income tax imposed on joint ventures in the special economic zones is among the lowest in the world. (Hong Kong, Xinhua; Beijing, *CD*, 27 November.)

China is considering joining the United Nations' Convention on the Recognition and Enforcement of Foreign Arbitral Awards (known as the 1958 New York Convention), and is also considering revision of the country's arbitration procedures. The joining of the convention is seen, as Premier Zhao told the NPC Standing Committee in November, as a necessary part of China's policy of opening to the outside world. He said it will be beneficial to the development of the country's economic and trade relations with foreign countries. Vice–Foreign Minister Zhu Qizhen said that by having China join the convention foreign investors and businessmen would be assured of fairness. And, conversely, Chinese themselves would be similarly assured of the enforcement of an arbitration in their favor. (Beijing, *CD*, 28 November.)

*Relations with the USSR.* Despite the general improvement of Sino-Soviet relations in 1985, the new year began with China digging in its heels on the political issues that divide the two parties and nations. This reaction followed a meeting between Soviet leader Gorbachev and Chinese vice-premier Li Peng on 23 December 1985 in Moscow, at which Gorbachev offered to restore party-to-party relations and the exchange of top-level leaders. As Deputy Foreign Minister Qian Qichen put it in a review of Chinese foreign relations in late December 1985, the Soviet Union had been "unwise and unrealistic" in seeking to avoid discussion of the three obstacles that China holds stand in the way of such improved political relations. (*CSM*, 10 January.)

On 15 January, China publicly rejected a Soviet proposal for a mutual nonaggression treaty, indicating that the Soviet Union had more concrete ways of improving relations if it chose to do so (*NYT*, 16 January).

However, further progress in the relationship could be discerned in the agreement reached during a visit to China by Soviet first deputy premier Ivan V. Arkhipov in March, whereby the Soviet Union undertook to open special new offices in Beijing to help China on economic matters and on science and technology (*LAT*, 20 March).

That the Soviet Union was taking China more seriously was suggested in the appointment of Oleg Troyanovskiy as ambassador to Beijing in April. Troyanovskiy had been ambassador to Japan and to the United Nations, and is an alternate member of the CPSU Central Committee. (*Issues & Studies*, September.)

Then, on 28 July, Soviet leader Mikhail Gorbachev undertook a new initiative toward China in an important speech at Vladivostok. This initiative included proposals to withdraw Soviet troops from Mongolia and Afghanistan, to undertake negotiations with China for a reduction of troops on the Sino-Soviet border, and to accept the Thelwag principle for determining the international boundary along the Amur River, and an expression of willingness to cooperate with China in space, including the provision of training for Chinese astronauts.

The Chinese response was skeptically cautious although, on 13 August, Foreign Minister Wu Xueqian met with Fedotov, the acting charge d'affaires of the Soviet Embassy in Beijing, to discuss Sino-Soviet relations. Wu said that China "attaches importance to" Gorbachev's statement at Vladivostok and "expresses welcome to it" (*BR*, 18 August). Deng Xiaoping also acknowledged "there were positive elements in Gorbachev's speech and indicated that China will carefully study all its contents." On 2 September, during his interview with Mike Wallace, Deng went further, saying that he would meet with Gorbachev in Moscow if the "main obstacle" to normalization, i.e., the Cambodian issue, were removed. Deng explained that China and the Soviet Union were "actually in a state of confrontation . . . which takes the form of pitting Vietnamese armed forces against China." On the following day Deng told a Komeito delegation that the proposed withdrawal of Soviet troops from Afghanistan was unsatisfactory because those withdrawn represented only 5.7 percent of Soviet forces there. However, Deng acknowledged some new points in the proposal and approvingly noted that for his part Gorbachev had acknowledged a territorial dispute which might lead to negotiations. Subsequently, at the UN General Assembly session in New York, Foreign Ministers Wu Xueqian and Eduard Shevardnadze agreed to resume in early 1987 border talks which originally had begun in 1969 (but were suspended in June 1978) at the vice-ministerial level. (*FEER*, 13 November.)

For the first time in about 25 years the Soviet Union began transporting goods to China by means of the Amur River. A trade agreement reportedly provides for Soviet ships to bring goods from China and for Chinese rivermen to call at Soviet ports (Moscow, "Vremya" newscast, Moscow Television Service, 6 August; *FBIS*, 8 August).

However, in July a Chinese soldier was killed and another wounded in a border firefight with Soviet soldiers. The Soviets claimed that the Chinese had invaded Soviet territory. Protest notes were exchanged, but the affair was kept quiet by both sides because of the mutual interest in reconciliation. (London, *Daily Telegraph*, 23 August; *FBIS*, 26 August.)

In September, Soviet deputy prime minister (and Politburo candidate) Nikolai Talyzin visited China, the highest-level Soviet official to do so for two decades. The visit was especially relevant to the growing mutual economic interests of the two countries. In this regard, Soviet deputy foreign minister Igor Rogachev separately spoke of a de facto coordination of the Soviet and Chinese five-year plans (*FEER*, 13 November). Incidentally, the appointment of Rogachov as vice–foreign minister in August may be seen as another indication of the greater attention the Soviet Union is now paying to the China relationship, inasmuch as Rogachov is a China specialist.

During the ninth round of Sino-Soviet talks held in Beijing from 6 to 14 October between Vice–Foreign Minister Qian Qichen and Rogachov, the Soviets discussed the Cambodia issue for the first time. However, little progress was made. The Soviets apparently sought to persuade the Chinese to negotiate with Vietnam on the issue. Following the talks, the Chinese reportedly said that the Soviets had implicitly rejected the offer by Deng Xiaoping to visit the Soviet Union if the latter pressured Hanoi to withdraw from Cambodia. (*The Indonesia Times*, 3 November.)

On 2 November the *People's Daily* went further than Deng's earlier expressed skepticism, charging that Moscow had sought to deceive world opinion with its heralded troop withdrawal from Afghanistan in October. In fact, the paper said, Moscow had reinforced its military presence. While the Soviet Union had, with much publicity, withdrawn 8,000 troops, it had earlier moved in 15,000 troops equipped with modern weapons. (*The Indonesia Times*, 3 November.)

Nevertheless, the Soviet Union won two major contracts to supply ten 210-megawatt generating units for four Chinese power stations, and equipment and material for two long-distance power transmission lines. The deal is to be conducted on a barter basis, so that the Soviets will not be taking hard currency from the Chinese. The contracts will involve the sending of Soviet technicians to China once again. (Beijing, *The Straits Times*, 29 October.)

The USSR trade and industry exhibition was scheduled to be held in Beijing 12–28 December. The exhibition delegation consisted of about 130 members. All kinds of products and equipment were to be exhibited. The only previous exhibition of this kind was held in 1954. (Beijing, *CD*, 27 November.) The Chinese had held an economic and trade exhibition in Moscow in late July and August, the first since 1953 (*BR*, 11 August).

*Relations with the United States.* The U.S.-China relationship remained on an even keel throughout the year. American businessmen in China began to complain loudly about their frustrations early in the year, but were greatly mollified by further concessions made by the Chinese government as the year wore on. There were indications that the military relationship between the two countries was becoming yet closer.

After being detained for nearly a week on suspicion of espionage, *New York Times* correspondent John F. Burns was expelled from China for disregarding the laws of China and deliberately violating the law governing aliens in China. Burns and Edward McNally, a lawyer on leave from the U.S. Department of Justice who was teaching constitutional law at Peking University, were accused of breaking into a military restricted zone and taking "innumerable" photographs. (Hong Kong, AP, 23 July; *NYT*, 24 July.)

A letter of intent was signed in April by US TERESAT Inc. and China's Ministry of Aeronautics Industry to have the China Great Wall Industry Corporation launch two communication satellites for the United States (*BR*, 19 May).

In August the Chinese government denounced U.S. plans to sell to Taiwan $260 million worth of equipment to modernize S2 sub hunters (Beijing, AFP, 12 August; *FBIS*, 12 August). A Foreign Ministry spokesman also denounced a resolution adopted by the U.S. House of Representatives that criticized China's population policies and human rights violations and that also called for the peaceful resolution of the Taiwan issue. (Beijing, AFP, 5 August; *FBIS*, 6 August.)

U.S. defense secretary Caspar Weinberger met Deng Xiaoping on 9 October in Beijing during a four-day visit to China. Both expressed pleasure over the prospects for further development of U.S.-China relations (*BR*, 20 October).

Three American naval vessels, a guided-missile cruiser, a guided-missile frigate, and a destroyer, visited Qingdao on 5 November, the first such visit to China since 1949. The vessels arrived in full dress regalia with a brass band playing "Happy Days Are Here Again." (Qingdao, AP; *Honolulu Star Bulletin*, 5 November.)

On 8 November, Defense Minister Zhang Aiping called for stronger military cooperation with the United States, Britain, and other "friendly nations." This remark, made to British field marshal Sir Edwin Bramall, coincided with the visit of the American naval ships, and followed an announcement that China had signed an agreement to purchase about $500 million in advanced American avionics equipment for 50 F8 jet interceptors. This sale was only the third, but by far the largest, U.S.-China arms deal. (Beijing, UPI; *Bangkok Post*, 10 November.)

U.S. Army chief of staff general John Wickham visited China for one week in mid-November. He was the first American army head to make such a visit. (Beijing, AP; Hong Kong, *South China Morning Post*, 17 November.)

Deng Xiaoping met John Phelan, chairman of the New York Stock Exchange, on 14 November, following a week of top-level talks between Wall Street and Chinese financial leaders during a symposium on financial markets held in Beijing. Deng jokingly told Phelan that the main purpose of the symposium "was to exploit you," to which Phelan rejoined: "Then it's a great honor to be exploited." China had opened small capital markets in three cities during 1986. (Beijing, Reuter; *South China Morning Post*, 15 November.)

China expressed indignation at the listing of Tibet as a separate country in a recent amendment to the U.S. Export-Import Bank Act of 1945. The U.S. Congress was accused of "wanton interference in the internal affairs of China." The Chinese government, however, took note of a statement by President Reagan in signing the amendment that the United States recognized Tibet as part of the People's Republic of China. (*BR*, 3 November.)

*Relations elsewhere.* At the end of September, the CCP and the Japan Communist Party (JCP) ended secret negotiations on the normalization of relations after failing to reach an agreement, according to Tetsuzo Fuwa, chairman of the JCP (Tokyo, *Kyodo*, 14 November; *FBIS*, 17 November). The two parties broke off formal relations in 1967.

Interestingly, Zhou Erfu, the vice-president of the Chinese People's Association for Friendship with Foreign Countries and a prominent author, was expelled from the party "for transgressing disciplinary codes for conduct in foreign affairs." Zhou's transgressions had occurred during a visit to Japan in October and November 1985, during which time, among other instances of improper behavior, he visited the Yasukuni Jinja Shrine. "In so doing . . . Zhou tarnished the national integrity and dignity of a socialist country," according to the announcement of the party's Central Commission for Discipline Inspection. (*BR*, 10 March.)

Prime Minister Yasuhiro Nakasone's hurried visit to China on 8–9 November appeared to be a successful one. The textbook revision issue had abated, particularly following the sacking of Japanese minister of education Masayuki Fujio. But there were economic problems. These had been discussed with the 163-member Japanese delegation to China in late May, but were not resolved. (Beijing, *CD*, 28 May; *FBIS*, 29 May.) The Chinese continued to be displeased with the 1986 estimated trade imbalance of $4 billion. Nakasone explained that a chief reason for the imbalance is that China did not export suitable products. However, the Chinese complained about the inadequate level of Japanese investment. Nakasone is said to have ordered his Ministry of International Trade and Industry to look into this matter upon his return to Japan. (*FEER*, 20 November.)

Subsequently, the deputy foreign ministers of both China and Japan agreed to hold a working-level mixed-trade committee meeting to discuss ways of boosting Japan's imports from China. The mixed-trade committee was set up under the 1974

Japan-China trade agreement but has not been convened since November 1978. The meeting was to be held as soon as possible and prior to a bilateral meeting of government ministers set for 1987. (Tokyo, Xinhua; Beijing, *CD*, 29 November.)

The third session of the 21st Century Committee for China-Japan Friendship was held at Oiso in Kanagawa Prefecture from 22 to 24 September. Wang Zhaoguo led the Chinese delegation. The first session had been held in Japan in 1984, the second in China in 1985. (Beijing, *RMRB*, 23 September; *FBIS*, 25 September.)

China's warming ties with Eastern Europe were much in evidence in 1986. Foreign Minister Wu Xueqian visited East Germany and Hungary in May and June (the first such visit by a Chinese foreign minister in over 30 years), and Premier Zhao visited Romania and Yugoslavia in July. General Wojciech Jaruzelski, first secretary of the Central Committee of the Polish United Workers' Party and chairman of the Council of State of the Polish Republic, made a working visit to China in late September. He met with Deng Xiaoping and Hu Yaobang. The meeting with Hu constituted the first meeting between Chinese and Polish party leaders for more than twenty years. (*BR*, 6 October.)

Similarly, the goodwill visit to China by Erich Honecker, the leader of the German Democratic Republic, in late October was the first visit to China by the head of the East German government in the 37 years since the two countries first established diplomatic relations (*BR*, 27 October).

It was also expected that high-level talks would soon ensue between the leaderships of China and Czechoslovakia. In the meanwhile, a trade agreement was signed by the two countries that provided for 2.9 times more than the mutual trade of 1981, and 12.7 times more than in 1950. The provisions include, for the first time, export to Czechoslovakia by China of four ocean-going vessels. (*BR*, 8 December.)

Vice-Premier Tian Jiyun made a two-week tour of Singapore, Malaysia, the Philippines, and Thailand in October (*BR*, 10 November).

During the New Year's holiday, Hu Yaobang made an inspection visit to Chinese troops stationed on the Paracel Islands (claimed by both China and Vietnam) in the South China Sea (*CSM*, 10 January). The Vietnamese border remained tense, with intermittent clashes throughout the year. On 28 January, China claimed to have "wiped out" intruding Vietnamese forces that had killed or wounded 65 Chinese soldiers and civilians during that month

(Beijing, UPI; *San Francisco Sunday Examiner & Chronicle*, 2 February). In August, China harshly rejected Hanoi's offer "to enter negotiations anywhere with China at any level," phraseology that echoed Soviet leader Gorbachev's expression of willingness to talk with China (28 July) (*CSM*, 22 August). Another sharp increase in fighting immediately followed the conclusion of the Sino-Soviet talks in Beijing in October. Hanoi reported that it had "wiped out" more than 100 Chinese troops in company-sized attacks (*Hong Kong Standard*, 17 October). On 22 November, Zhao Ziyang in Nanning said: "As long as Vietnam continues its anti-China activities and aggression against Kampuchea... China will not change its policy of exerting pressure on Vietnam along the border. And our troops must be ready to take necessary actions at any time." He referred to recent "high-sounding words for peace" from Vietnamese authorities, but said that, in fact, they do not intend to abandon their basic policy of aggression against Kampuchea and opposition to China. The only way for Vietnam to extricate itself from its predicament, he said, "was to pull its troops out of Kampuchea and stop opposition to China." (Nanning, Xinhua; Beijing, *CD*, 24 November.)

The seventh round of Sino-Indian border talks ended in Beijing on 23 July without any real success, although both sides planned to continue the discussions in New Delhi in the near future (*BR*, 4 August). However, since the July talks, Indian sources have repeatedly accused China of intruding into Indian territory in the Sumdorong Chu Valley area along the eastern sector of the international boundary. In fact, New Delhi has claimed that this is the most serious intrusion since the 1962 border war. The Chinese have denied any such intrusions, holding that the particular district in dispute has always been Chinese territory. (*BR*, 1 September.) Indians, incidentally, were upset at the time that the Soviet Union was not giving media attention to this issue. Nor, according to Indian sources, were the Soviets taking note of Indian press reports that China was intensifying its support for insurgents in the Indian state of Nagaland (*FEER*, 16 October). On 8 and 9 December, the Indian Parliament passed a bill upgrading the union territory Arunachal to the level of a state, even though the area is in dispute between China and India. On 11 December, the Chinese government strongly protested this action, declaring it illegal and a serious violation of China's territorial integrity and sovereignty. (*BR*, 22 December.)

Nicaraguan president Daniel Ortega Saavedra visited Beijing in September and received from the Chinese an interest-free loan of $18.9 million, which was added to a loan of about $10 million the previous December, as well as some assurance of political support. However, the relationship was reportedly kept on a state-to-state basis. (*FEER*, 2 October.)

Stephen Uhalley, Jr.
*University of Hawaii*

# India

**Population.** 783,940,000
**Parties.** Communist Party of India (CPI); Communist Party of India-Marxist (CPM)
**Founded.** 1928
**Membership.** CPI: 479,000 (*IB*, June); CPM: 361,000 (*India Today*, 31 January)
**General Secretary.** CPI: C. Rajeswara Rao; CPM: E. M. S. Namboodiripad
**Politburo.** CPI: Central Executive Committee, 9 members: C. Rajeswara Rao, Indrajit Gupta, Indradeep Sinha, Jagannath Sarkar, N. Rajasekhara Reddi, N. E . Balaram, M. Farooqi, A. B. Bardhan, Homi Daji; CPM: 10 members: E. M. S. Namboodiripad, B. T. Ranadive, M. Basavapunnaiah, Harkishan Singh Surjeet, Jyoti Basu, Samar Mukherjee, E. Balanandan, Nripen Chakravarty, Saroj Mukherjee, V. S. Achuthanandan
**Central Committee.** CPI: National Council, 125 members; CPM: 70 members
**Status.** Legal
**Last Congress.** CPI: Thirteenth, 12–17 March in Patna; CPM: Twelfth, 25–30 December 1985, in Calcutta
**Last Election.** 1984. CPI: 2.71 percent, 6 seats; CPM: 5.96 percent, 22 seats (out of 509 contested in 544-seat Parliament)
**Auxiliary Organizations.** CPI: All-India Trade Union Congress, All-India Kisan Sabha, All-India Student Federation; CPM: Centre for Indian Trade Unions, All-India Kisan Sabha, Students' Federation of India
**Publications.** CPI: *New Age* (Indradeep Sinha, editor), Indian-language dailies in Kerala Andhra Pradesh, West Bengal, Punjab, and Manipur; CPM: *People's Democracy* (M. Basavapunnaiah, editor), Indian-language dailies in Andhra Pradesh, Kerala, and West Bengal

Indian communism, which has been confined to a few regional areas, continued its national decline in 1986. This situation was discussed at the party congresses held by the two major communist parties: the pro-Moscow CPI at its Thirteenth Congress in March, and the more independent and larger CPM at its Twelfth Congress at the end of 1985. The leadership of both parties seemed unsure about how to restore national momentum to Indian communism.

During 1986, Indian communists, like other opposition parties, stepped up their criticism of Prime Minister Rajiv Gandhi following a year-long political honeymoon that had characterized the Indian political scene in the wake of his assumption of power in late 1984. The communists generally gave him high marks for defusing ethnic crises and for his "progressive" foreign policy, but they attacked his domestic economic policies. Gandhi has not subscribed to the socialist nostrums advanced by the political elites that assumed control of the country at the time of independence in 1947. More than any previous Indian prime minister, he had in his first two years in office sought to enhance the role of private industry and to reduce the power of the "license raj" system that has come to stifle Indian productivity. (*FEER*, 31 June.) In addition to their apprehensions regarding the government's commitment to socialism, the communists were concerned that Gandhi's economic policies might veer India toward the West.

Perhaps most disturbing to the communists was the Seventh Five-Year Plan (1985–1989) drawn up under Gandhi's guidance. Such plans set in motion trends that have a long-lasting effect. In seeking significantly higher growth rates, this plan has assigned to the private sector the major role in future development for the first time. Private sector investment levels are to be raised substantially to 52 percent of plan outlays. In contrast, the public sector is to concentrate on consolidation, with emphasis on improving the management and efficiency of existing units and on selective development of power and transportation. The communists also criticized Gandhi's efforts to lure foreign investment for joint ventures. His government put together a panoply of investment incentives, such as tax breaks, subsidies, cheap credit, import and foreign exchange allocation concessions, and infrastructural support. Such efforts, the communists fear, will strengthen India's ties with the West, since it is the West more than the Soviet Union that possesses both the technology and the capital India wants. Only 30 of the 770 collaboration agreements involving technology and design during the 1985–1986 fiscal year were with Eastern bloc countries. (Ibid.)

The communists were not the only group alarmed by Gandhi's shifts in economic policy. Organized labor feared losing its protected status. Political parties on the right agreed with the communists that liberalization might give foreign powers an undue influence in Indian affairs. Many intellectuals claimed that Gandhi's economic policies would primarily benefit the top 15 percent of the population that constitutes India's consumer society. Indeed, many members of his own party echoed some of these charges, and Gandhi in his second year slowed the pace of reform.

However, the communists have not been able to capitalize on the opposition to Gandhi's economic policies. In part, this may be due to his caution in implementing the policies. He has refined the "license raj" system, not abandoned it. More important, the communists have not been able to appeal to the growing regionalism, which incorporates economic issues with regional demands for greater local power. Some regional parties have done relatively well in mobilizing support for greater state's rights, while the communists, except in their own regional base of West Bengal, have not.

Also harming the communist effort to mobilize support have been the continued divisions in Indian communism. Although the two major parties did selectively cooperate, they were still kept apart by personal differences among their leaders and by policy differences. They were generally agreed on the "correctness" of the Soviet Union's foreign policy but were less united on the role of China in world affairs. The CPI has traditionally taken a more critical stance regarding China than has the CPM. However, with the warming of Sino-Soviet relations, the CPI has begun to take a more conciliatory attitude toward China. Both communist parties supported Sino-Soviet rapprochement as underlined in a speech by Gorbachev on 28 July, but so far they have been silent about the possible difficulties this might create for Indian foreign policy. The visit of Chairman Mikhail Gorbachev to India on 25–29 November, his first to a Third World country, provided an opportunity for both communist parties to praise Soviet foreign policy. By the end of the year, however, neither party had spoken out about the cooling relations between India and China. Not only did the seventh round of border talks at Beijing in July not go well, but the Indians charged that the Chinese had established forward positions in territory that New Delhi claims are south of the McMahon Line at the Bhutan/Indian/China trijunction. Should Sino-Indian relations continue to deteriorate, both parties would be forced to take difficult foreign-policy stands.

Regarding Gandhi's foreign policy, both the CPI and the CPM described it as "progressive," in marked contrast to their criticism of his domestic policies. In part, this may be influenced by the obvious Soviet effort to woo Gandhi. For the first time, Moscow dispatched a delegation, led by Viktor Afanasyev, editor of *Pravda*, to attend centenary celebrations of the ruling Congress Party in late 1985. While there, Afanasyev stated that the Communist Party of the Soviet Union (CPSU) wanted to establish a relationship with the party. (Ibid., 30

January.) To further this objective, the CPSU invited a Congress Party delegation to its Twenty-seventh Congress. Arjun Singh, the Congress Party vice president who represented his party, even addressed the CPSU conclave. (*FBIS*, 20 March.) Moreover, Gorbachev heaped praise on Gandhi during his November visit to India. For its part, New Delhi has been careful to maintain cordial relations with Moscow.

**The CPM.** *Organization and Leadership.* At its Twelfth Congress, the CPM decided to provide the two strongest state units—West Bengal and Kerala—increased representation on the highest party organs. It also took steps to reduce the chances of these two units dominating party decisions. The Politburo was enlarged from eight to ten; the two new members were Saroj Mukherjee and V. S. Achuthanandan, general secretaries of West Bengal and Kerala, respectively. The Central Committee was doubled in size, though four of the 70 seats were left vacant to be filled later. Only four of the sitting members were dropped and that because of "leftist adventurism." The 66 members of the new Central Committee included the previous eight Politburo members, 27 of the 31 previous Central Committee members, and all permanent invitees to the previous Central Committee. E. M. S. Namboodiripad was re-elected general secretary for a third term. The Politburo continued to be represented by men who had been prominent since the communist split in 1964. Most of its members are over 70. Achuthanandan, at 60, is its youngest. Thus, the party did not fulfill its pledge at the prior congress to induct "new blood" into the highest ranks, though some effort was made on this score at the state level.

Party statistics underscore the increasingly regional nature of the CPM. Over 80 percent of the party membership growth of 89,581 between 1981 and 1985 was from West Bengal and Kerala; West Bengal accounted for well over half the total increase (*India Today*, 31 January). Less than 3 percent of the new members were from the Hindi-speaking states, where the party has failed to develop roots, and where it must do much better if it is ever to have aspirations for national power. Few of the 361,000 members come from the Hindi-speaking heartland of the country, where over half the Indian population lives.

The party's mass organizations reveal a similar pattern of regional concentration. Over the past several years, well over half the new members—a four million increase to a new total of fourteen million—came from West Bengal. (Ibid.) Of the 1.8 million members in the CPM's Centre for Indian Trade Unions, 1.2 million are in West Bengal. Almost 80 percent of the 2.5 million members of the party's Democratic Youth Federation are West Bengali. The well-oiled West Bengal unit employs almost 6,000 paid workers, far more than anywhere else.

To prevent West Bengal from dictating national policy, the central committee changed party rules so that no state unit could summon an extraordinary party congress even if it were backed by one-third the membership, the current requirement. To call such a congress, a state needs the backing of at least one other state, in addition to one-third the membership. Some party leaders talk of growing "federalism" in the CPM, a thinly veiled reference both to the potential danger of regional dictation of national policy and to regional freedom of action. This rule may have also reflected fears regarding the commitment to the party's ideology on the part of the many new members added by the party since 1977, when it set about to expand membership rapidly.

The CPM congress signaled a major shift of tactics by revising the former political line of "left and democratic" unity to unity of "left and secular" forces. This new tactic was adopted to exclude parties allegedly responsible for the increasing interethnic strife in the country. Party leaders pointed to developments in Punjab, Assam, and Gujarat to stress the need for secular credentials for a political partner. All three states had witnessed major intercommunal conflicts. This policy would rule out working with the large Hindu-oriented Bharatiya Janata Party because of its alleged role in heightening Hindu-Muslim tensions. It would also block participation with various Muslim political parties and with specifically ethnic parties like the Akali Dal, which represents Sikh political interests in Punjab. The CPM congress even noted that the ruling Congress Party was not a "totally secular party" because of its presumed "conciliatory attitude" toward communalism. This stance was to create problems in some state units, where segments of the local CPM wanted electoral alliances with the proscribed parties to enhance the party's electoral success.

The new approach toward parties defined as communal produced a split in the party's powerful Kerala unit. A faction led by one of its most popular political figures, E. M. Raghavan, set up a separate party—the Communist Marxist Party—when the state Politburo ruled against an alliance with the Muslim League in the forthcoming 1987 state elections, a decision backed by the national leadership. In defense of his view, Raghavan pointed out that the CPM had earlier identified the Congress Party as communism's main enemy and asked that tactics be shaped to ensure its defeat at the polls. (*FEER*, 7 August.) Namboodiripad did not disagree that this had been earlier policy, but he pointed out that past party tactics were not "sacrosanct" (*Times of India*, 30 June). The national situation now demanded a tough anticommunal line because of changed circumstances. The party could point to its defeat at the hands of communal parties in Assam and Punjab. In addition, the CPM-led government in West Bengal was challenged by a surge of Nepali identity in the northern districts of the state. Communism, the CPM chiefs decided, did not flourish in a setting of interethnic strife, and it stood to lose support if it tried to cooperate with communal parties because such parties gained more than the communists. Politburo member M. Basavapunnaiah argued in a speech at the Twelfth Congress that the CPM was prepared to cooperate with the Congress Party to defeat communalists. He even suggested that Congress Party control of the federal government might be necessary until a viable democratic and secular alternative was available. (*Statesman*, 28 December 1985.)

Namboodiripad went out of his way to isolate Raghavan, apparently recognizing that Raghavan's stand has been appealing in the pre-election period leading up to the state polls in Kerala for 1987. The general secretary's vehemence also suggested that the leadership fears that Raghavan's views have a resonance in other states. The general secretary vowed to block any of Raghavan's supporters from entering the CPM-led left front coalition (*Times of India*, 18 August). This stand, however, could make it difficult for the left front to win a majority, since the popular Raghavan has threatened to contest all 140 seats if denied admission (ibid.). The revolt in Kerala may damage the CPM in a state where the margin of victory is often thin.

The CPM has rejected the weaker CPI's call for unity. On the eve of the party congress, Namboodiripad stated that a "gulf of difference" separated the two parties (*Times of India*, 26 December 1985). This stand may have irritated the CPSU, which appears to want a unification of the two major communist parties. The CPSU did not send a message of greeting to the Twelfth Congress, even though some other parties affiliated with the CPSU did so. Another indication of Soviet displeasure was the decision to seat the CPM delegation attending the CPSU's Twenty-seventh Congress in the audience, while the general secretary of the CPI was placed with other representatives of fraternal parties. No one from the CPM addressed that congress, even though representatives from the CPI and even the Congress Party did so. The Soviets may also have calculated that they could score points with Gandhi by demonstrating a cool attitude toward the CPM, which had stepped up its criticism of him.

*Issues: Domestic and Foreign.* As Gandhi's market-oriented policies became clear, the CPM became increasingly hostile toward him. The party congress enacted an Economic Resolution that claimed Gandhi was "taking India toward greater privatization, opening doors to multinational corporations, and downgrading the role of the public sector" (*FEER*, 24 April). The CPM opposed his relaxation of the licensing system, his lowering of individual and corporate taxation, and his liberalization of import policies. In addition to criticizing these policies, the party called for the nationalization of the jute industry, which is concentrated in West Begal and has been in recession for several years.

However, the party had to reconcile its opposition to Gandhi's liberalized economic policies with the espousal of similar programs by the CPM-led government of West Bengal. West Bengal's high unemployment rates and declining industrial base have harmed the party in urban areas, where the Congress Party has a growing appeal. For several years, the West Bengal government of Chief Minister Jyoti Basu has appealed to private capital, both domestic and foreign, to invest in his state. Basu has traveled overseas selling his state to multilateral corporations as a safe place in which to invest, and he has had some notable successes. He has also had some success in luring Indian private capital by encouraging the establishment of joint companies with mixed private and public investment. Under this arrangement, the state holds 29 percent of the equity, the private sector 25 pecent, and the remainder is sold as shares to the public. The state has not hesitated to keep labor in line, and it has used the communist unions in West Bengal, the state's largest, to further this objective. It has even sold some unproductive units to the private sector.

Some of the delegates at the party congress grumbled about West Bengal's economic policies.

Party leaders felt compelled to respond that, because the state government "operates within the framework of the capitalist economy, it is not a government free to attack property relations" (*FEER*, 24 April). On the eve of the congress, CPM leaders rebuked the CPI, whose central executive committee had criticized West Bengal for its joint venture policy (*Statesman*, 11 December 1985). The CPM leaders reminded their CPI counterparts that the latter was a partner in the West Bengal government, and that such criticism might damage the public image of the left front there. Some CPM leaders stated that the CPI criticism might be a tactic designed to show the Congress Party that it was not necessarily tied to the CPM-led government in West Bengal. (Ibid.) In a statement bound to infuriate the CPI, West Bengal commerce minister Nirmal Bose told a foreign journalist that "We are ready to work with private entrepreneurs, ready to work with multinationals" (*WSJ*, 28 February).

The party congress generally backed Gandhi's foreign policy, though some delegates warned that his market orientation might erode ties with the socialist world. Some even offered amendments questioning India's nonaligned policy, but they were all rejected. (*Statesman*, 28 December 1985.) Rather, the party ruled that Gandhi has not deviated in any significant way from the foreign policy of the USSR, that he supported the goals of the nonaligned movement, and that he was opposed to "imperialism" (*Telegraph*, 23 December 1985).

Some delegates, probably from the party's potent pro-China wing, expressed apprehension that the CPM was tilting too much toward the USSR. Perhaps to give greater balance, the International Resolution noted that the PRC was "truly communist" and moving in the correct international direction. (*Times of India*, 27 December 1985.) The party congress also applauded closer Sino-Soviet relations. Some delegates even questioned whether Vietnam was correct to occupy Cambodia and whether the government installed there could be called socialist (ibid.).

The CPM congress put its stamp of approval on the proposal that communal forces endanger national unity and are therefore to be avoided. The party had learned from hard experience that escalating ethnic tension worked to undermine support for the communists, a development that had occurred in Punjab and Assam. The party itself has been faced with rising ethnic discord in the two states it rules: West Bengal and Tripura. The Nepali population, concentrated in the northern districts of West Bengal, have been increasingly backing the call of the Gurkha National Liberation Front (GNLF) for a separate Nepali-speaking state. Tensions mounted in September as the GNLF battled communist cadres opposed to the call for a separate state. Gandhi and other central government spokesmen criticized the CPM government for neglecting the Nepali-speaking areas. (*FBIS*, 29 September.) The prime minister also argued that the Nepali movement was not antinational, a stand rejected by the CPM. This verbal jousting may have been a tactical effort of each to embarrass the other in a state that goes to the polls in 1987.

Against a backdrop of rising Indian concern about Pakistan's nuclear program, party leaders have supported India retaining the option of assembling nuclear weapons (*Patriot*, 26 December 1985). The CPM also blamed Pakistan for supporting Sikh militants in Punjab, where several party workers have been killed by the extremists.

**The CPI.** *Organization and Leadership.* Representatives from 36 fraternal parties, including the CPSU, attended the CPI Thirteenth Congress in March. The CPSU delegation was led by P. N. Demichev, minister of culture and candidate member of the Politburo, a lower-level representation than at previous conclaves. The new CPI National Council comprises 125 members, of whom about one-fifth are new members. Some of General Secretary Rajeswara Rao's rightist critics who advocated closer ties with the Congress Party, such as Mohit Sen, H. K. Vyas, and K. S. Shukla, were dropped from the council, underscoring Rao's continuing hold on the party machinery. Rao was re-elected general secretary for his sixth consecutive term, and his nine-member Central Executive Committee remained much as it was before.

At the party congress, the leadership was particularly harsh in its criticism of the continuing decline of party activism and strength. One senior party figure claimed that members were now "more oriented to bourgeois parliamentary institutions of all types" (*India Today*, 15 April). The leadership advised the CPI membership to revive a "militant fighting party of the toiling masses" to enable the party to survive as a viable political force (ibid.). Among the signs of decay was the declining number of party local committees and branches. The former had diminished from 1,926 in 1983 to 1,805 in 1985, and the latter slid from 25,125 to 23,607 over the same time period. (Ibid.)

The party's right wing advocated closer ties with the Congress Party, but it made no headway at the Thirteenth Congress and even suffered reverses, as reflected in the dropping of its most prominent national spokesmen from the National Council. The CPI was still living down its support of Indira Gandhi's 1975–1977 state of emergency, a stand that has harmed the party at the polls. Rao, who has been identified with the turn away from the united-front line, has opposed a policy that would probably quicken the pace of decay, even though the Soviets, seeking improved state-to-state ties, would clearly like it to move closer to the Congress Party. Rao's deliberate policy of ignoring Soviet advice on this score could also help the party reject charges that it is guided by Moscow. For their part, the Soviets did put pressure on Rao to alter party policy. At the CPI's 60th anniversary celebrations in December 1985, the CPSU representative urged the CPI to unite all "left, democratic, and national patriotic forces" to strengthen India's independence, unity, and territorial integrity (*FEER*, 31 January). The "national patriotic forces" part of that formulation was a code phrase for the Congress Party. That same month, the CPSU sent a prestigious delegation to the Congress Party's centenary celebrations, and it heaped praise on Gandhi and his party.

Instead of toning down criticism of the Congress Party, Rao was harsher than in the past, perhaps even harsher than the CPM. The anti–Congress Party line was retained with 590 to 93 votes and 10 abstentions (*Economic and Political Weekly*, 19 April). Later in the year, Rao called for a massive agitation to protest Gandhi's policies and did not rule out cooperating with other parties to oust him from power (*FBIS*, 2 October). The CPI leadership repeatedly called for closer ties with the CPM and among the various front organizations of the two parties. Central Committee member N. K. Krishnan wrote that such unity was retarded by the "narrow partisan attitudes of the CPI (M) leadership" (*WMR*, July).

*Issues: Domestic and Foreign.* Like the CPM, the CPI opposed Gandhi's domestic policies, especially his economic program, while generally characterizing India's foreign policy as "progressive." The Economic Resolution at the Thirteenth Congress pointed out that the previous party congress had predicted that Indira Gandhi's economic policies would lead India away from self-reliance and social justice. Her son's policies were identified as even worse. On other domestic matters, the party

congress urged lowering the voting age to 18, radical land reform, protecting rights of Muslims, nationalization of monopoly businesses, state control of wholesale trade in foodgrains and essential goods, and a moratorium on foreign debts to "U.S.-dominated agencies." In contrast to the CPM, the CPI conclave advocated abandoning the nuclear option.

The CPI, again like the CPM, generally backed Gandhi's foreign policy. However, the party congress did criticize the government for occasionally equating the two superpowers and for seeking closer economic ties with the West. As expected, the CPI was almost totally supportive of the USSR's foreign policies; however, for the first time in almost two decades, the party took a rather benign view of China. The Political Resolution of the congress welcomed "some of the changes in the attitude of the People's Republic of China." Also for the first time in many years, the congress did not formally mention Chinese assistance to Pakistan.

In contrast, the United States was blamed for a wide variety of problems, including the militarization of the Indian Ocean, the regional arms race, and help to various extremist forces in India such as the Sikh militants. Like the CPM, the CPI has been adamantly opposed to the goals and tactics of the militants. The National Council on 1 October resolved to "fight to the finish" with the Sikh extremists and even requested that the government issue to its workers licenses for semiautomatic guns, the weapon favored by the militants. (*FBIS*, 2 October.)

**Other Communist Parties.** Small communist parties and groups exist on both the left and right of the two major communist parties. On the right is the All-India Communist Party (AICP), established by S. A. Dange, a Lenin Peace Prize recipient who left the CPI in a disagreement over its decision to abandon the united front policy with the Congress Party. The AICP has been virtually ignored by the CPSU, perhaps because of its anemic electoral performance. Moreover, its separate existence is apparently in opposition to the CPSU's desire for a united Indian communist party. In 1986, the moderate Communist Marxist Party emerged in Kerala because of the parent CPM's policy of avoiding any relationship with communal parties.

To the left of the CPI and CPM are a number of small Maoist parties, often collectively called Naxalites—a reference to a district in West Bengal where radical communists tried to establish a rural base of operations in the late 1960s. Some of these parties have retained their revolutionary orientation and others have begun to operate by the rules of India's parliamentary system. The efforts begun in 1985 by several of the seventeen factions of the late Charu Mazumdar's Communist Party of India (Marxist-Leninist) are still blocked by ideological squabbles regarding the international role of China and the USSR as well as by differing views regarding revolutionary tactics. At least six of these Naxalite groups, brought together in 1985 by Kanyu Sanyal, have continued to function under the name Communist Organization of India (Marxist-Leninist). It is opposed to the "terrorist and anarchist" line of other Naxalite groups.

The press in 1986 reported an increasing number of incidents between police and radical Naxalites in Andhra Pradesh, West Bengal, and Bihar. One report noted that almost half of the state police in Andhra Pradesh, where the Naxalites appeared to be most active, were engaged in anti-Naxalite activities (*The Week*, 20–26 July). However, that report also noted the highly fragmented nature of the Naxalite movement there. The most militant of these groups has called itself the Marxist-Leninist War Group and was active in the relatively backward Telegana area of Andhra Pradesh (*Statesman*, 16 January).

Walter Andersen
*Arlington, Virginia*

# Indonesia

**Population.** 176,764,000 (*World Factbook*, 1986)
**Party.** Indonesian Communist Party (Partai Komunis Indonesia; PKI)
**Founded.** 1920
**Membership.** 1,000–3,000 (estimated) in country (*World Factbook*, 1986); 100–300 in exile
**General Secretary.** Pro-Moscow: Satiadjaya Sudiman; pro-Beijing: Jusuf Adjitorop
**Leading Bodies.** No data
**Status.** Illegal
**Last Congress.** Seventh Extraordinary, April 1962
**Last Election.** N/a
**Front Organizations.** None identifiable in Indonesia
**Publications.** None known in Indonesia

The aging leaders of the PKI living in exile remained on the fringes of international communist activity. In Indonesia, the outlawed party had no role in domestic affairs, but the party's remnants remained a source of concern to the country's leaders.

**Leadership and Party Organization.** Little is known about the Moscow or the Beijing branch of the exiled party. While Indonesian delegations were listed as participants in several international communist meetings, in almost all instances no individual names were given. Two exceptions were meetings in Prague attended by Satiadjaya Sudiman, who is believed to be general secretary of the party's Moscow wing, and the contribution of an article to *World Marxist Review* by Tomas Sinuraya, who was listed as a leadership member of the PKI (for details on Sinuraya, see *YICA*, 1985, pp. 189–90).

**Domestic Party Affairs.** There were no signs of organized PKI activity in Indonesia during 1986. Nevertheless, leading government officials remained on the alert for a possible resurgence of the once-powerful party, and their concerns were nourished by several events.

In April, during a visit to the West Kalimantan border area, armed forces chief General Benny Murdani said that there were still communist remnants in remote jungle areas along the Sabah border and that Indonesia would continue its military operations to crush them. Several communist terrorists were reported arrested during army operations in the area, and the military also seized hundreds of guns and other arms (Indonesian News Agency, 28 April; BBC, 30 April).

Later in the year, a parliamentary commission called on the government to keep an eye on some 10,000 ethnic Chinese in West Kalimantan believed to be communist sympathizers. The report to the Indonesian House of Representatives said that the supervision of former detainees in the region belonging to the 30 September Movement of the PKI was generally going smoothly and that some of them would be allowed to vote in the 1987 general elections. However, the report also called for an upgrading of the regulation governing the supervision of former detainees and recommended adequate funds be made available for the program. (Jakarta, *Berita Buana*, 6 November; *FBIS*, 13 November.)

The military commander of Central Java disclosed the arrest there of four Indonesian communists trained abroad. Three of the group had received military training before infiltrating the country and the fourth even succeeded in getting enrolled in the police academy in the provincial capital. One suspect, Hans Dimyati, reportedly went to school in Moscow and underwent military training in Nanking before coming to Indonesia. Another, Sambungan Simanjuntak, allegedly entered through Hong Kong after receiving military training in Albania, Burma, and China. The third, Tangis Darmono, came to Indonesia from Cambodia after receiving military training in Vietnam. There were no details on the fourth detainee, Tohari. (Hong Kong, AFP, 15 July; *FBIS*, 17 July.)

The Indonesian veterans' administration stripped 144 veterans of their status as "honored veterans of the war for independence" because of alleged links with the banned PKI more than twenty years earlier. Another 104 veterans of the 1945–1949 independence war against the Dutch faced similar action, depending on proof of their alleged PKI links (*FEER*, 6 February).

In a seminar marking the twentieth anniversary of the Suharto government, General Murdani spelled out the parameters of the debate in preparation for the May 1987 general elections. He ruled out Western-style liberal democracy on the grounds that it could open the way for a revival of communist activity. "Unlimited freedom," he said, "will only give birth to various types of anarchy and . . . the revival of communist forces" (Reuters, 9 March). On another occasion, Murdani said the main constant threat to Indonesia was communism through the remnants of the 30 September Movement of the PKI and "its latent force." At the same time, he noted that another major threat to the country was religious extremism (Jakarta Domestic Service, 15 November; *FBIS*, 21 November). Probably most troubling of all to the government were rumors that leftist students appeared to be seeking links with Muslim opposition groups (Hong Kong, AFP, 11 October; *FBIS*, 15 October).

Nine former communist leaders who had been sentenced to death more than fifteen years earlier were executed in late September. The most prominent of the executed prisoners was Kamaruzaman, who, as head of the PKI's Special Bureau, had joined dissident military officers in organizing the 1965 coup attempt. The others executed were Abdullah Alihamy, Bono, Amar Hanafiah, Kamil, Sudiono, Supono, Tamuri Hidayat, and Wirostomodjo. Among the fifteen or twenty communists under sentence of death remaining in prison were Ruslam Wijayasastra, formerly number six in the party hierarchy, and Sukatno, who had been a communist youth leader. (AFP, 8, 11 October; BBC, 10 October; *FBIS*, 15 October; *FEER*, 20 November.)

The executions took place despite protests and appeals from the Dutch government and the European Community, among others (Reuters, 9 October; Xinhau, 14 October). In addition to the predictable reactions from the world communist press, there were vigorous protests against the executions by free world groups (Vilna, *Volkskrame*, 10 October; *Neues Deutschland*, 10 October; Reuters, 10 October; AFP, 11 October).

**International Activities.** There were no surprises in Indonesian communist activities abroad; the customary participants—now scarcely a handful—appeared at the usual international meetings. Meanwhile, in Indonesia the staunchly anti-communist government sought to strengthen its economic ties with communist countries.

The PKI was represented at several international communist meetings; the names of the Indonesian delegates were not given. Delegations from the PKI attended the Seventeenth Congress of the Czechoslovakian Communist Party in April; the Eleventh Congress of the Socialist Unity Party (SED) of the German Democratic Republic, also in April; the Mongolian party congress in June; and the Ninth Congress of the Albanian Workers' Party in December. At this last, the listing of the Indonesian delegations was conspicuous for omitting the delegates' names.

Satiadjaya Sudiman attended the special meeting in Prague of the editorial council of the *World Marxist Review*, which was convened to consider the program guidelines of the Twenty-seventh Congress of the Communist Party of the Soviet Union and the strategy of other fraternal parties to build up world security. There was no indication of his having taken any role in the discussions (*WMR*, July). Sudiman was also listed as a participant in the international symposium in Prague marking the 70th anniversary of Lenin's "Imperialism, the Highest Stage of Capitalism" (ibid., September).

Tomas Sinuraya, a major figure in the Moscow wing of the party, contributed an article to *WMR*, "Disperse the Clouds of Tension in Southeast Asia." In it, he attacked U.S. attempts to "turn the peoples of the Asian and Pacific region into vassals of U.S. imperialism and involve them in the U.S. strategy of aggression directed against the Soviet Union and other socialist countries . . . Our people are also concerned about growing U.S.-Chinese military cooperation."

A speech by the Indonesian delegate to the SED congress appeared in *Neues Deutschland*; it followed traditional lines and contained the standard expressions of optimism. The speaker thanked the SED for the invitation to participate in the congress, seeing it as a sign of SED's solidarity with the PKI, which was toiling under the difficult conditions of illegality. Speaking in the name of the leaders of the PKI, the delegate said that for the past two decades, the PKI had fought in a responsible fashion for fundamental democratic rights that "in our nation are trampled underfoot." But better times were coming, because "all patriotic democratic forces from all elements of society and various political groups have taken such a position . . . Our party, which is using all means available, is directing its efforts for uniting the progressive forces on the basis of common challenges." The speaker also stated that Indonesia's debt had been growing, and social differentiation had increased while economic development, based on dependence on multinational monopolies, had fluctuated dramatically. Hence, the achievement of a democratic way of life as an alternative to the present situation was seen as an unconditional necessity. Indonesia had traditionally belonged to the progressive nations that support the fight for independence and world peace. Through the so-called imperialist policy of the current regime, it had been isolated for twenty years from the progressive force of the world. "Our nation in its inclination as a developing country is closely tied objectively with the countries of the Third World and the socialist countries" (*Neues Deutschland*, 21 April).

In Indonesia, the economy reflected the impact of the sharp decline in its oil revenues, with the price for Indonesian oil dropping from $28.53 a barrel early in 1986 to $12.31 in the closing months of the year (*Jakarta Post*, 10 December; *FBIS*, 18 December).

Indonesian trade and industry representatives exchanged visits with several East European delegations during the year, and a succession of high-ranking Soviet visitors sought means of improving trade relations between the two countries. The Soviets also announced their desire to buy more Indonesian non-oil commodity goods (Jakarta Domestic Service, 12 August; *FBIS*, 18 August). In addition to visits by representatives of the Soviet Chamber of Commerce and Industry, Jakarta was host to a team of high-ranking Soviet officials on a foreign-relations tour of the Association of Southeast Asian Nations (ASEAN). Akil Salimov, deputy chairman of the Supreme Soviet Presidium, told reporters that there were "many similarities of views" between Indonesia and the USSR. "There is no dispute between the Soviet Union and Indonesia; on the contrary, relations between the two countries have been going well" (*Antara*, 30 May; Hong Kong, AFP, 1 June; *FBIS*, 3 June).

Despite Indonesia's commercial overtures to communist countries, suspicions of Soviet intentions remain. Most Indonesian ports are closed to Eastern bloc naval vessels. In September, the military commander for Central Java, General Hartas, said that Soviet submarines had recently been detected in Indonesian territorial waters and that Soviet aircraft often violate Indonesian airspace. The Indonesians claimed that the submarines had come from the Indian naval base in the Nicobar Islands, which Soviet experts have been helping to build. Hartas's statement, coming just before visits to Indonesia by India's prime minister and the Soviet foreign minister, was thought in some quarters to be meant as a first warning to Delhi and Moscow (Hong Kong, AFP, 15 September; *FBIS*, 16 September).

Indonesian trade with China had resumed in June 1985 with the signing of a memorandum of understanding between the chambers of commerce of the two countries. The trade balance in the first year of direct trade with China was heavily in Indonesia's favor. Indonesian exports to China were $200 million while imports from China were $50 million, according to an executive of the Indonesian Chamber of Commerce. Normal diplomatic ties between the two countries have yet to be resumed, but Indonesia's foreign minister expressed his willingness to hold direct talks with the Chinese on the latest developments in Cambodia. He would do so, he explained, in his capacity as interlocutor for the ASEAN countries (Hong Kong, AFP, 7 August; *FBIS*, 18 August).

Jeanne S. Mintz
*Washington, D.C.*

# Japan

**Population.** 121,048,923 (*Japan Times,* 11 November)
**Party.** Japan Communist Party (Nihon Kyosanto; JCP)
**Founded.** 1922
**Membership.** 470,000 (*World Fact Book,* 1986)
**Central Committee Chairman.** Kenji Miyamoto
**Presidium Chairman.** Tetsuzo Fuwa
**Central Committee.** 206 members
**Status.** Legal
**Last Congress.** Seventeenth, 19–25 November 1985
**Last Election.** July 1986 (9 percent of popular vote in House of Representatives) 12 seats of 250 in House of Councillors; 27 seats of 512 in House of Representatives.
**Auxiliary Organizations.** All-Japan Student Federation, New Japan Women's Association, All-Japan Merchants' Federation, Democratic Foundation of Doctors, Japan Council of Students, Japan Peace Committee, Japan Council Against Hydrogen and Atomic Bombs
**Publications.** *Akahata* (Red banner), daily circulation 550,000, Sunday circulation 2,450,000, total readership, 3,000,000; *Zen'ei* (Vanguard), monthly theoretical journal; *Gekkan gakushu* (Education monthly), education and propaganda magazine; *Gikai to jichitai* (Parliament and self-government), monthly; *Bunka hyoron* (Culture review); *Sekai seiji shiryo* (International politics); *Gakusei shimbun* (Students' gazette), weekly

The role of the Japan Communist Party (JCP) remained generally unchanged in 1986. The party's position was consistent or predictable on virtually all major political issues. The JCP's relationship with the other opposition parties worsened somewhat during the year. Because of this, plus the fact that the JCP made gains in the election in July while the other opposition parties lost ground, JCP leaders could argue that the other parties' "turn to the right" and their "anti-JCP actions" hurt them at the polls. JCP leaders were less convincing, however, when they argued that the big victory for the conservative Liberal Democratic Party (LDP) did not represent a shift to the right in Japanese politics.

The JCP did not veer from its path as a "Eurocommunist" party—one that advocates the peaceful or parliamentary road to power. However, the party's image was to some extent hurt by the activities of other Marxist and communist parties and terrorist and other radical groups on the left. Although these groups generally have no ties with the JCP, the JCP is often implicated by association in the mind of the public. The number of cases of highly publicized violence committed by these groups increased in 1986.

The JCP's relations with the Communist Party of the Soviet Union showed signs of improving, especially after a JCP delegation visited Moscow and held talks with General Secretary Gorbachev. Negotiations were held with the Chinese Communist Party, but nothing was accomplished, and events toward the end of the year suggested that relations were not going to improve and, in fact, had gotten worse.

**Party Leadership and Meetings.** Kenji Miyamoto, who has been top leader of the JCP since the mid-1950s, retained the position of chairman of the Central Committee and was throughout 1986 the party's ranking member and its spokesman on major issues. Tetsuzo Fuwa remained chairman of the party's Presidium and did much of the day-to-day work, with Miyamoto concentrating more on theoretical and broad policy issues. Mitsuhiro Kaneko, head of the Secretariat, is considered the number three ranking party member and by some its rising star.

The JCP held a national conference of prefectural committee chairpersons and secretaries on 25 and 26 January in Tokyo. At that meeting party leaders discussed the JCP's successes during 1985 in blocking the proposed state secrets protection bill and opposing a bill on reapportionment in the Diet. On the latter issue Miyamoto criticized the other opposition parties' position on a disparity of three to one in vote value between rural and urban areas, stating this was "unacceptable" to the JCP, and he reiterated the JCP's position that it should be two to one or less.

Miyamoto also discussed the "five nuclear goals" (presented at the Seventeenth Party Congress in November 1985) and a "nonnuclear government." He hit the ruling LDP for omitting any reference to "prohibition of A and H bombs" from its program and called the Nakasone cabinet a "pronuclear government"—having voted against six UN nuclear disarmament–related issues and abstained on nine (of a total of 27). He also assailed port calls in Japan by U.S. nuclear submarines. In connection with the nuclear issue, Miyamoto claimed that 913 units of local government had declared themselves "nuclear-free peace cities" and that the nuclear-disarmament movement was growing rapidly. (*Akahata*, 27 January.)

The party convened its second plenum Central Committee meeting at its headquarters in Tokyo on 15 March for four days. Party leaders discussed a number of issues, including relations with the Philippines and China, Diet debates, the July election, the Zushi and Miyakejima struggles (against U.S. bases in Japan), the celebration of the 60-year reign of the emperor (which the JCP protests), opposition to privatization of the Japanese National Railways (JNR), the spring labor struggle, problems of small companies resulting from revaluing the yen upward, and bullying in schools. (*Akahata*, 15 March.)

A proposal for implementing decisions made at the Seventeenth Party Congress of November 1985 was passed. A goal of 10 to 20 percent of the vote in all districts (ibid.) was set for the House of Councillors election in the summer.

The JCP held its fourth plenum meeting of the Central Committee on July 19 for three days. This was the first important party meeting since the second plenum (the third plenum being limited to election campaign planning). The agenda of the fourth plenum included assessing the results of the July Diet election, strengthening the party's mass movements, getting ready for the spring 1987 simultaneous local elections, and increasing readership of the party newspaper *Akahata* by 30 percent above mid-1983 (a goal stated a number of times in the last three years). (*Akahata*, 1 August.)

A party resolution passed at this meeting noted that the LDP had gained 54 seats in the Diet in the July election because of other opposition parties "giving help to the politics of the LDP." The resolution also attributed the LDP victory to Prime Minister Nakasone's "false propaganda and grandstand play as Reagan's adjutant" and to his "concealing arms expansion and cooperation in U.S. preparations for nuclear war." The resolution went on to note it would be a "fundamental mistake" to conclude that an era of conservativism had begun. (Ibid.)

The resolution also expressed regret that only 61 percent of party members had read the resolution of the third plenum and that in eleven constituencies JCP incumbent Diet members lost in the election. An "over-optimistic approach" was blamed for the defeats. (Ibid.)

Regarding future concerns and policies, the JCP leadership cited opposition to or concerns about the following: privatization of the JNR, revision of the education and taxation systems, reorganization of the industrial structure in response to the Reagan administration's demands, a new state secrets protection bill, defense cooperation with the United States, and cuts in welfare and education budgets. Concern was also expressed over the Japan Socialist Party's split with the JCP-supported World Conference against Atomic and Hydrogen Bombs. (Ibid.)

**Domestic Affairs and Issues.** The special issues of concern to the JCP during 1986 were: the nuclear issues (both weapons and nuclear power, as well as compensation for victims of World War II), the Strategic Defense Initiative, Japan's military spending, the defense pact with the United States, taxes, and welfare. The JCP also expressed concern about the future of the nation's railroads and unemployment in the context of the falling yen.

In his January New Year's address, Central Committee Chairman Miyamoto declared that the privatization of the JNR would be "counter to the development of [Japanese] history." He went on to declare that it would be "outrageous" to sell the JNR, "the property of the people," to major enterprises just to please them, while shifting the burden of JNR debt, caused by bad government planning, onto the shoulders of the people. (*Akahata*, 1 January.) Throughout the year the JCP continued to oppose LDP efforts to sell part of the national railroads in order to lower government subsidies to the railroads and make them more efficiently run.

JCP leaders also railed for lower taxes throughout the year, including income and resident taxes, as well as sales taxes. Party leaders reasoned that by lowering income taxes (which the ruling conservative LDP sought to do also) the government would be forced to cut defense spending (assuming other government programs were maintained). The party took a position similar to that of the other opposition parties in attacking the ruling party's plan to raise sales taxes (which the JCP labeled a regressive tax), though there was little in the way of coordinated efforts of policies. (Tokyo, *Japan Times*, 6 December.)

The JCP took a strong stand throughout the year consistent with its past policies of opposition to nuclear weapons. In May, Chairman Miyamoto stated that the idea that the elimination of nuclear weapons is harmful to Japan is "brazen and outrageous." He made similar statements about the LDP's contention that war will break out if nuclear weapons are eliminated. Miyamoto underscored the JCP's role in the antinuclear movement, which he noted had more than nineteen million signatures in Japan, while half of the population is living in municipalities that have declared themselves nuclear free. (*Akahata*, 5 May.) While this issue proved to be a good one for the party, there were difficulties in that the other opposition parties did not cooperate with the JCP, most importantly the Japan Socialist Party (JSP). The latter carried on a number of protest demonstrations without JCP participation. (See, for example, *FBIS*, 22 July, 25 August.)

The JCP also took an adamant position against nuclear power in Japan, which it viewed as being related to the nuclear-weapons issue. Party leaders made a special issue of nuclear power plants in Japan in the wake of the Chernobyl accident in April. JCP leaders cited their 1975 "Proposal for Atomic Power Development in the Interest of the People, with Priority Given to Safety" and chided the government for building nuclear power plants with "many fatal defects" while not ensuring the safety of the people. (*Akahata*, 27 May.) JCP leaders also noted that the other parties did not cooperate in this effort and, in fact, supported the ruling LDP on the issue of nuclear power (*Akahata*, 17 June).

The JCP opposed Japan's participation in the U.S. Strategic Defense Initiative (SDI), which the government decided upon in the late summer. The JCP's position was that SDI would endanger Japan and constituted militarizing outer space and an escalation of the arms race (*FBIS*, 10 September). Unlike the majority of the population of Japan (according to opinion polls), the JCP linked SDI to the issue of nuclear weapons.

Meanwhile, JCP Diet members initiated an amendment to a relief law enacted to aid victims of the 1945 atomic bombs dropped on Hiroshima and Nagasaki that would expand social and medical benefits to these people. The measure, however, did not win sufficient support to pass. (*Japan Press Weekly*, 26 April.)

In June the JCP put forth a proposal for a "Non-nuclear Government to Save Japan from the Threat of Nuclear War." This embodied the positions of the party mentioned above, plus called for nuclear-free zones in Asia and international efforts to deal with the "nuclear threat to mankind." The proposal strongly condemned the ruling LDP's policies and called on the other opposition parties to do something about the issue. (*Akahata*, 17 June.)

The JCP maintained its stand on a number of other issues, including: criticizing "money politics" and the corruption of the ruling LDP, pushing environmental protection, opposing legislation that would favor big business over small companies and small businesses, and advocating increased spending for social welfare, unemployment, and education. Party leaders specifically opposed policies that reduced the work force in the name of increasing productivity and allowing the yen to be revalued upward (under pressure from the United States). (See *Akahata*, 5, 7 May.) The party also continued its opposition to the U.S.-Japan security treaty (alone among the political parties in Japan), visits by U.S. naval vessels, and security ties with South Korea. The JCP opposed defense spending generally, but oddly not as strongly as a large segment of the JSP.

**Auxiliary Organizations and Splinter Groups.** The JCP maintains close ties with or controls a number of affiliate organizations. (See previous issues of *YICA* for details on these groups.) There are also a number of splinter groups that were once part of the JCP and broke from the JCP, and there are some groups that have never had any tie with the JCP that are sometimes identified with the JCP. Events during 1986 mostly involved the splinter or unaffiliated groups.

The Japanese Communist Party (Left), headed by Masayoshi Fukuda and called the Fukuda clique by the JCP, celebrated its twentieth anniversary in 1986. It began as a pro-China breakaway party, but switched to become pro-Albania in the 1970s. Three other small parties are outgrowths of the Japanese Communist Party (Left): the Japan Labor Party (referred to as the Okuma clique by the JCP); the Japan Workers' Party, led by Shosaku Itai; and the Japanese Communist Party (Marxist-Leninist), headed by Kuraji Anzai. The Japan Workers' Party

publishes the newspaper *Jinmin shinpo* and the Japanese Communist Party (Marxist-Leninist) publishes *Proletariat*. Neither paper has a large circulation. The JCP attacks these groups in its publications (for example, see *Akahata*, 11 May).

Another party, which the JCP refers to as the Shiga clique, broke from the JCP 22 years ago when differences escalated between the JCP and the Communist Party of the Soviet Union, possibly at the instigation of Khrushchev. In the spring of 1986 the Shiga clique joined with several other small parties or political organizations, including the Socialist Unity Party, the Liberation Research Institute, and a group called Knowledge and Labor. They announced jointly forming a "vanguard party," later saying it was the "reconstruction of the Japanese Communist Party as a vanguard party." The JCP also made a special effort to criticize these efforts. (*Akahata*, 26 May.)

The reason the JCP gave not inconsiderable attention to these splinter groups during 1986 was the fact it was the twentieth anniversary of the formation of the Fukuda clique and that it, as well as the other splinter parties, was a topic of discussion during talks with the Communist Party of the Soviet Union and the Chinese Communist Party. In addition, the splinter parties took a strong anti-JCP position during the July elections and in so doing caused some embarrassment and difficulty for the JCP.

In addition to publicity generated by these groups during the year, a number of radical and terrorist groups (most never having any real connection to the JCP) were in the news. In March the Japanese Red Army threatened to "act against" the 60th anniversary celebrations of Emperor Hirohito's ascendance to the throne. Since the early 1970s the Japanese Red Army has acted as an auxiliary to George Habash's Popular Front for the Liberation of Palestine. However, the release of Kozo Okamoto, the lone survivor of the terrorist squad that carried out the Lod Airport massacre in 1972, may have given the group new life. In any event, Japanese security officials took the threat seriously. (*Insight*, 31 March.)

In April the Revolutionary Workers' Council claimed responsibilty for two rockets fired at a state guesthouse that was to be the venue of the May summit talks among the leaders of the major industrial countries (*FBIS*, 2 April). This followed similar firings on the Imperial Palace, the U.S. Embassy, the Osaka prefectural police headquarters, and Akasaka Palace. According to the Public Security Investigation Agency, these attacks were carried out by Chukakuha (Middle Core Faction), which has a membership of 3,200; Kakumaru (Revolutionary Marxist Faction) with 2,000 members; Kyuosando (Communist League) having 1,500; a following of the Fourth International with 1,200 supporters; and Kakurokyo (Revolutionary Workers' Council) with 1,200. Fewer than 20 percent of the member of these groups are students according to authorities. (*KDK Information*, April 1985.)

In April signal and communications lines of the Japanese National Railways were bombed in western and central Japan. The Middle Core Faction claimed responsibility. (*FBIS*, 20 April.) In May rockets were fired at the building where the seven-nation summit meeting was being held, though they missed the building. The heads of state of seven nations, including President Reagan, were there at the time. The firings occurred in spite of 30,000 Japanese police on duty and on guard against such an incident. (*FBIS*, 5 May.)

In November a member of the Japanese Red Army, released from jail in 1977 after members of the organization hijacked an airplane and held 151 hostages, was suspected of firing projectiles at the U.S. and Japanese embassies in Djakarta, Indonesia. In neither case was the embassy damaged or its personnel hurt. The evidence was based on fingerprints found at the scene. (*FBIS*, 23 June.)

**Elections.** Dual elections (of both houses of the Diet) were held on 6 July. The JCP received 9.5 percent of the popular vote in the House of Councillors proportional representation constituency (in which the voters cast votes for parties) and 11.4 percent in the local constituencies. Both were higher than in the previous national election: up from 8.9 and 10.5 percent, respectively. The JCP won a total of nine seats (five in the national constituency and four in local constituencies) for a gain of two seats. This made the JCP the fourth-ranking party in the House of Councillors in terms of seats. (*FBIS*, 8 June.)

In the more important House of Representatives election, the JCP won 27 seats from 9 percent of the popular vote. In number of seats in the lower house, the JCP finished with the same amount as at the time of dissolution. Its popular vote declined slightly from the 1983 election, when it won 9.6 percent of the total votes cast. However, the JCP passed the Democratic Socialist Party to become the number

four ranking party in number of seats because of losses by the latter. (Ibid.)

JCP leaders claimed an election victory for a number of reasons. Secretariat Chief Mitsuhiro Kaneko won in a Tokyo constituency after losing to an anti-JCP coalition of opposition parties in the 1983 election. Presidium Vice-Chairman Hiromu Murakami also won in his Osaka district. More important, however, the party won the largest number of votes ever in the House of Councillors national constituency, an increase of 1.27 million over the 1983 election. (*Akahata*, 17 July.)

The JCP also performed well, considering poor relations and lack of cooperation with the other opposition parties prior to and during the campaign. In fact, JCP leaders claimed with some credibility that the JCP had become the only true opposition party. Poor showings by the other major opposition parties, which JCP leaders claimed was a result of their anticommunist, pro-LDP line, also increased the importance of the JCP's performance. JCP leaders also contended that the ruling LDP had launched an anti-JCP campaign (*Akahata*, 8 July). The dual election and the high voter turnout (71.4 percent compared to 68 percent in the 1983 election) likewise did not favor the JCP, which depends more upon good organization and party loyalty than do the other political parties in Japan.

JCP leaders could also boast of electing seven women to the Diet (of a total of sixteen elected). (Ibid.) However, the voter preference in the election for the ruling LDP and a strong showing for Prime Minister Nakasone seem to reflect a conservative shift by the electorate and weigh against the JCP expecting more influence in Japanese politics as a result of the election.

The JCP's platform centered on workers' rights and the nuclear issue, both of which according to party leaders helped the party at the polls (*WMR*, September). JCP candidates also campaigned on all of the domestic and international positions taken by the party. It was a hotly contested election with quite a lot of name-calling. Presidium Chairman Fuwa called Prime Minister Nakasone a "fascist politician" and an *Akahata* editorial referred to him as "Japan's Hitler" (*Akahata*, 22 July 1985).

Late in the year JCP leaders began planning for the April 1987 election of the Tokyo governor, an election which a joint JCP-JSP candidate has frequently won in the past. However, the JSP declared that it would not sponsor a candidate jointly with the JCP, and it appeared the JCP was having difficulty finding a candidate it could sponsor alone. (Tokyo, *Japan Times*, 6 November.)

**International Views and Activities.** The major international issue of importance to the JCP in 1986 was a better relationship with the Soviet Union. Better relations, however, seemed in large measure an outgrowth of Soviet efforts to improve relations with the Japanese government and to exploit the nuclear issue in Japan.

In January the JCP commented favorably on a joint communique issued at the end of talks between Japanese foreign minister Abe and Soviet foreign minister Shevardnadze. Party spokesmen also hailed a proposed visit between Prime Minister Nakasone and General Secretary Gorbachev. Party leaders, causing some uneasiness, however, suggested that sensitive territorial issues be put on the agenda of future talks, particularly talks that might lead to a peace treaty between the two countries. (*FBIS*, 21 January.)

In February a three-member JCP delegation headed by Presidium Chairman Fuwa traveled to the Soviet Union. Fuwa met with General Secretary Gorbachev and discussed arms talks between the United States and the Soviet Union, a nuclear arms ban, and the international antinuclear movement, among other issues. (*FBIS*, 11, 13 August.) Fuwa later stated that his accomplishments in the meeting with Gorbachev included getting the Soviet Union's commitment to join the Hiroshima-Nagasaki appeal adopted in February at a Hiroshima peace meeting in which twelve countries participated and which eighteen international organizations and 133 groups from various countries supported. (*FBIS*, 27 August.) Fuwa also said that Gorbachev had agreed that a joint statement between the two parties made in 1984 on the subject of nuclear weapons was still applicable, that the two had agreed on ways to strengthen peace and security in Asia, and that the dissolution of existing military blocs should not lead to their replacement. (Ibid.)

The JCP engaged in talks with the Chinese Communist Party throughout most of the year. According to Japanese newspapers, the JCP set two conditions for the restoring of relations: a Chinese admission that it interfered in the internal affairs of the JCP during the Cultural Revolution in the late

1960s, and a promise that it would break its ties with the Japan Labor Party (a party of about 5,000 members formed by JCP members who broke with the party in 1966 when the JCP opposed China's united front against the United States and the Soviet Union). (*FBIS*, 14, 15 January.) However, in March Miyamoto reported that no progress had been made in the talks (*FBIS*, 13 March).

In October the JCP attacked China for suggesting that it would be all right for Prime Minister Nakasone to visit Yasukuni Shrine in Tokyo if Class-A war criminals' names were removed (General Hideki Tojo and twelve others). Party spokesmen said this attitude is "tantamount to approving of Japan's militarism [during World War II] and violates the constitutional principle of freedom of religion and the separation of politics and religion." (Tokyo, *Japan Times*, 15 October.) This seems to have been the prelude to a break in talks the next month, though the JCP said it was because the Chinese Communist Party would only admit to a "few mistakes" and would not comply with the JCP's request to break relations with the Japan Labor Party (Tokyo, *Japan Times*, 15 November).

In October it was reported that the JCP was helping finance the purchase of weapons from Vietnam by the New People's Army in the Philippines. The founder of the Philippine Communist Party, José Maria Sison, had, according to the reports, traveled to Japan and met with JCP leaders who offered financial help. The JCP subsequently sent a protest note to the Philippine embassy and denied the allegations. (*FBIS*, 28 October; *Washington Times*, 12 November.)

The JCP received delegations from Czechoslovakia and Romania during the year, as well as from a number of other communist parties (*FBIS*, 15 August, 29 September). The JCP sent delegations to the Middle East and to Eastern Europe (*JPRS*, 1 October). JCP leaders protested the visit of Japan's crown prince to South Korea in the fall, stating that the visit gave the impression of recognizing the South Korean government as legal (*KDK Information*, June).

John F. Copper
*Rhodes College*

# Korea: Democratic People's Republic of Korea

**Population.** 20,543,000
**Party.** Korean Workers' Party (Choson Nodong-dang; KWP)
**Founded.** 1946 (a united party since 1949)
**Membership.** 2.5 million
**General Secretary.** Kim Il-song
**Presidium of the Politburo.** 3 members: Kim Il-song (DPRK president), Kim Chong-il (Kim Il-song's son), O Chin-u (minister of People's Armed Forces)
**Politburo.** Kim Il-song, Kim Chong-il, O Chin-u, Kang Song-san (DPRK premier), Pak Song-chol, Yim Chun-chu, Yi Chong-ok, So Chol, Yon Hyong-muk, Kim Yong-nam (foreign minister), Ho Tam, Kim Hwan, O Kuk-yol, So Yun-sok, Yi Kun-mo (new premier), Hong Song-nam, and others; alternate members Kye Ung-tae, Chon Pyong-ho, Hong Si-hak, Kim Pok-sin, Choe Kwang, Chong Chun-ki, Hyun Mu-kwang, Kang Hui-won, Cho Se-ung, Yi Sun-sil, and others
**Secretariat.** 15 members: Kim Il-Song, Kim Chong-il, Kang Song-san, Ho Tam, Yon Hyong-muk, Hyun Mu-kwang, An Sung-hak, Hwang Chang-yop, Ho Chong-suk, Chae Hui-chong, So Kwang-hui, Kim Yong-sun, Pak Nam-ki, Chon Pyong-ho, Choe Tae-bok
**Central Committee.** 145 full and 103 alternate members
**Status.** Ruling party
**Last Congress.** Sixth, 10–15 October 1980, in Pyongyang
**Last Election.** 2 November 1986. 100 percent participation reported for Eighth Supreme People's Assembly, all 706 candidates on the slate elected
**Subordinate and Auxiliary Organizations.** General Federation of Trade Unions of Korea, Union of Agricultural Working People of Korea, Korean Democratic Women's Union, Socialist Working Youth of Korea, Friends' (Chondogyo religion) Party, Korean Democratic Party, Committee for the Peaceful Reunification of the Fatherland, many others
**Publications.** *Nodong sinmun* (Worker's daily, *NDSM*), KWP organ; *Minju Choson* (Democratic Korea); *Kulloja* (The worker), party theoretical organ; *Choson inminkun sinmun* (Korean people's army news); many others. English-language publications include the *Pyongyang Times* and *Korea Today*; in Japan *The People's Korea* generally follows the North Korean line. The official news agency is the Korean Central News Agency (KCNA).

Politics in the DPRK in 1986 continued to move within the general confines of the Kim Il-song ruling system, established in 1946 and now entering its fifth decade, and the specific decisions of the Sixth Party Congress in 1980, which designated Kim's son, Kim Chong-il (45), as his successor. This continuity nonetheless could not mask serious strains in the leadership over the succession, punctuated by a flurry of rumors in November that Kim Il-song had been assassinated. Continuity also marked the economic program, which remained committed, as it has been since the 1940s, to a heavy-industry-first strategy; the diminishing returns of this approach were marked by a year-long lag between the old and new seven-year plans. In foreign relations, the DPRK greatly deepened the tilt toward Moscow that has governed its strategy since 1983.

**Leadership and Organization.** In 1986 Kim Il-song and Kim Chong-il as usual toured the country, individually and together, visiting workers and peasants. In February, Kim Chong-il gave instructions on improving combat capabilities to air force, naval, and artillery units; he stopped in at a dairy plant as well, urging a big boost in egg production. In March he toured several plants, including the Yongsong Bearing Factory, which has recently gotten advanced technology from the USSR, and where many Soviet engineers and advisers are posted.

Kim Chong-il came under public scrutiny when on 13 March his filmmaking friends, director Shin Sang-ok and Shin's actress wife, Choe Eun-hi, formerly of the South, defected to the American Embassy in Vienna. They took their annual stipend of some $2.5 million, reportedly provided by Kim Chong-il himself, with them. After appropriate preparations in Washington, the couple held a press conference in Baltimore in mid-May, during which they revealed that Chong-il was rather a movie buff, possessing a personal collection of some 20,000 films (*NYT*, 15 May).

Unquestionably this episode was the worst blow to Kim Chong-il since the succession had been arranged; it reinforced rumors about his high-living ways, garnered much bad publicity, and cost the cash-short regime a large amount of foreign exchange. Chong-il had long been referred to as "the dear guide" (*chinaehanun chidoja*), but that sobriquet increasingly gave way to "the dear comrade" (*chinaehanun tongmu*). Observers differed over whether this was a demotion.

Over the years many reports have surfaced about opposition to the succession: that somebody tried to run over Kim Chong-il with a truck, injuring his head and requiring brain surgeons from Japan; that some generals opposed to the succession sought to bring off a coup but failed and fled to China; and so on. No such report has ever been verified. In 1984 Amnesty International reported that 1,096 people had been purged for opposing the hereditary succession, but the organization admitted that its information was sketchy. Foreign visitors routinely find sentiments of all-out support for Chong-il.

Two important documents in May and June suggested that the succession might be in trouble. Kim Il-song on 31 May came forth with a classic speech on party building that he might have given at any point in the past 40 years in terms of its major themes of the mass line, the *chuche* (self-reliance) idea, a monolithic party, and the importance of the top leadership. But, in a somewhat unusual reference, he said that "loyalty to the party is life itself to the revolutionary armed forces," perhaps an indication that elements in the military were restive about the succession. He concluded this long speech with unusual bluntness, saying that "the leader's position and role should be inherited by the successor without change," that "our party has satisfactorily solved the problem of inheriting the revolutionary cause," and that the party had rallied "against all phenomena gnawing at the party's unity and cohesion" (*FBIS*, 9 June). That the regime felt it necessary for Kim to say all this himself was particularly noteworthy.

When the succession was first broached publicly in 1980, the North Korean press was full of an odd political language redolent of outdated, corporatist, organic politics: the body politic, the party as the "heart" of the body politic, and the leader as the "great heart" of the party. These emphases returned in a special article in the party newspaper in June (*NDSM*, 21 June), where it was argued that "society is like an organ," the party was "the heart of society," a "central organ" making society move "with one breath and one pulse." The article gave Kim Chong-il especial credit for such ideas; the association with the succession could not have been clearer. Both documents taken together suggested, at minimum, the need to reinforce the succession policy.

Since 1980 the North Koreans in one picture after another have depicted a traveling threesome: Kim Chong-il gesticulating to some worker, and behind him his father accompanied by the defense minister, O Chin-u, an ally of Kim Il-song going back to the guerrilla struggle in the 1930s. This was obviously meant to demonstrate the military's support for the succession. From mid-July onward O Chin-u rarely appeared in public, and rumors floated about that he had been injured in an automobile accident in late August. (Seoul, *Korea Herald*, 29 October.) General O is two years senior to Kim Il-Song and, after the death in 1984 of Kim Il, is thought to be the one remaining old guard member who can speak bluntly to Kim. Observers also detected a decline in public appearances by Chong-il in this period.

During the fall of 1986 O Chin-u was not reported to have appeared in public, except at the elections for the Supreme People's Assembly (SPA) on 2 November, when he was said to have voted in his local district (KCNA, 3 November). He did not appear at any of the party, military, or diplomatic functions that would usually require his presence, including the state visit of East German leader Erich Honecker in October.

The SPA elections followed the usual DPRK practice, with 100 percent of the registered voters turning out and electing the candidates slated by the regime. Although the regime did not give the total number elected, there were at least 706 district elections, suggesting that the SPA had grown a bit from its previous total of 615 members.

The leadership lineup in party and government, as reported at election time, showed few if any changes (KCNA, 3 November). O Chin-u was still ranked third; after him came the premier, Kang Song-san, and Pak Song-chol and Yim Chun-chu.

On 16 November, South Korean sources claimed to have heard broadcasts along the DMZ stating that Kim Il-song had been assassinated while riding on a train: "Our leader Kim Il-song flows in the river as a leaf." The next day the broadcasts were said to have reported that Kim Chong-il had taken power. The following day the South Korean Defense Ministry announced that O Chin-u had seized power, again citing DMZ broadcasts. (*NYT*, 20 November; Seoul, *Korea Herald*, 17–20 November.)

On 19 November, however, the KCNA reported that Kim Il-song had welcomed the Mongolian leader, Jambyn Batmonh, to Pyongyang; KCNA supplied video clips of the airport ceremony, and foreign diplomats who turned out said that Kim looked healthy and fit. The North Koreans later denounced Seoul's reports as a "malicious big lie."

The South Korean Defense Ministry suffered a high degree of embarrassment in the aftermath. American units stationed along the DMZ had not heard the broadcasts, and the U.S. government did not back up South Korea's information. Seoul could not produce tapes of the broadcasts, only edited transcripts. Foreign observers generally thought that the broadcasts had in fact been made by the North. Then the question became, why? Why would a regime that treats Kim as a virtual deity concoct false reports of his demise?

One answer is that the broadcasts were the work of disgruntled military units who sought and failed to pull off a coup. It seems unlikely, however, that such people, after killing his father, would then turn around and support Kim Chong-il. Perhaps they might support O Chin-u, but there has never been any evidence that O was opposed to the succession; instead, for years he has lent his prestige to it.

Another answer is that the broadcasts were part of a disinformation scheme with two goals: first, to make fools of the South Koreans and call the world's attention to Kim Il-song; and, second, to prepare resurrection myths for domestic consumption. A third possibility is that no such broadcasts were made, the South inventing them to distract attention from Seoul's domestic political crisis.

If there was indeed a power struggle in the North, it may well have been between a younger generation backing the son and wishing the succession to take place sooner and an old guard faction with doubts about the son's capabilities and maturity, wishing it to take place later or not at all. It is not impossible to imagine that Kim Il-song might be part of the second group. Korean history has several examples of kings who originally sought to promote their sons to power, only to grow disillusioned—even to the point of starving the son to death, in one memorable case. The defection of the film stars would have been just the sort of episode to draw the opprobrium of a stern father.

As for O Chin-u, he still has not been seen in public. On 24 November, in an unusual statement to foreign reporters, a North Korean official said he had "heard" that General O was "the victim of a road accident" and was then recuperating (according to Pyongyang), or in a coma (according to the Western reporters) (*FBIS*, 24 November, citing Hong Kong, AFP, 24 November).

In late December the twelfth plenary session of the sixth KWP Central Committee convened. Yi Kun-mo replaced Kang Song-san as premier, and Yi and Hong Song-nam were promoted to the Politburo (KCNA, 27 December). Kang Song-san did not seem to be in any disgrace, however, since he was posted to the Secretariat of the Central Committee. Yi Kun-mo generally has been associated with economic affairs. During the year there were other personnel shifts, all of them minor.

As the year ended, a mass rally in Pyongyang hailed the re-election of Kim Il-song as president of the DPRK; regime pundits said everyone was "holding in high esteem dear comrade Kim Chong-il as the great successor to the revolutionary cause of *chuche* and as the sagacious leader of our party and revolution." Pyongyang reported on some new silicate factories which were the "fruits of the wise leadership and solicitude" of Kim Chong-il (KCNA, 31 December). It seemed that business was back to usual in the DPRK as Kim Il-song began his 41st year in power.

**Domestic Activities.** Kim Il-song's 1986 New Year's address continued the pattern of recent years in being brief, schematic, and generally uninteresting. If any theme could be cited, it would be the perennial one of more energy recovery for more heavy industry, with special attention to coal. As ever, the emphasis was on investment rather than consumption, despite the lip service to improving the people's livelihood.

In April the finance minister, Yun Ki-jong, came forth with the annual budget report, and as usual it was full of ersatz percentage figures and aggregates that were of little utility. Revenues and expenditures were expected to climb 4 percent in 1986; defense was to drop from 14.4 percent of total expenditures in 1985 to 14.1 percent in 1986 (American and South Korean sources put the real total closer to 30 percent). Untangling transport bottlenecks continues to be a regime priority in that the heavily used railway system was to get a 10 percent increase in funds to reinforce existing railways and to build a new rail line in the north. The biggest increase went to "scientific work," a 30 percent jump in funds for mechanization, automation, and even robotization. Coal, metals, and chemicals also got big increases (12 to 20 percent); all three are lumped together in North Korea as the real or synthetic fuels and materials of industrialization under the policy of self-reliance.

In recent years North Korea has shown interest in the economic reforms going on in China and passed a rudimentary joint venture law in 1984. But one sensed that even this tepid interest cooled during 1986 as relations with the Chinese generally soured. The DPRK does appear to have two joint ventures underway with French concerns for a new international hotel and a satellite facility.

Kim Chong-il has usually been associated with high technology, such as it is in the North, so it was no surprise to see him turn up early in March at the satellite facility, termed the Earth Station for International Satellite Communications, newly installed in Pyongyang with the help of the French. But much of this seems to be for show. North Korea has not begun to make the basic reforms of enterprises, taxes, foreign exchange regulations, and the like done by China in the past decade.

The DPRK did begin a limited program of foreign tourism in 1986. It is now possible to book a two-week tour and several groups did so—a West German group at the start of the year and a British group in March. But the low priority given to foreign travel (there are only six flights per week from the USSR and China combined) suggests that this, too, is hardly a regime priority and nothing compared to the massive tourism in China now. Perhaps more noteworthy is the fact that Pyongyang established direct train service with Moscow for the first time in many years.

A more likely model for North Korea is East Germany. Kim Il-song toured some of the new *Kombinates* during his visit to East Germany in 1984, and Kim Chong-il is said to have gotten part of his education there. Some observers now say that limited experimentation with East German reforms began in the DPRK in 1986, mainly to loosen some central controls on enterprises and give plant managers some autonomy, while formally encouraging complementary industries to coordinate their operations.

The regime continued to worry about transportation and supply bottlenecks, which reportedly have caused frequent delays in meeting production schedules. The party newspaper came out strongly in late May for efficient organization of "supply work" so as not to hinder "the enhanced zeal of the masses" (*NDSM*, 27 May).

1986 also saw the completion of one water project and the beginning of another. It is such grand water projects to remake nature and irrigate rice fields that do much to associate Kim's rule with the classic model of the Asiatic mode of production or "oriental despotism." For five years the North Koreans have been talking about the Nampo Lockgate, a large dam with three locks on the Taedong River, which winds up from the coast into Pyongyang; they completed it in June 1986 to much fanfare. Basically it creates lakes and reservoirs from river water to irrigate paddies and reclaim tidal coastlands for agriculture. Toward the end of the year the South Koreans made much of the North's new water project in the Diamond Mountains near the DMZ, which South Korea believes would threaten its defenses, were the North to break the dam in time of war and flood the South (see below).

In November the regime announced the Third Seven-Year Plan (1987–1993) after an unexplained eighteen-month lag since the stated completion of the previous plan. Most likely, the targets of the old plan had not in fact been met until recently. The new plan was designed, the regime said, to achieve the "ten long-term objectives" set out by Kim Il-song at the Sixth Party Congress in 1980. These include plans to produce annually 15 million tons of steel, 120 million tons of coal, 15 million tons of grain, and 7 million tons of chemical fertilizers. But elsewhere this was labeled a "strategic target," that is, a guide to developmental efforts but not necessarily one that will be achieved at the end of the third plan (KCNA, 29 December).

Kim Il-song heralded the new plan with a speech claiming that it would bring the DPRK economically into the ranks of the advanced countries in the world and make "decisive progress" toward "the complete victory of socialism." Priority was given, as ever, to "a rapid development of mining, power, metal, and machine-building industries and transport"; the plan promised "the complete irrigation, chemicalization, and comprehensive mechanization of agriculture." Then came light industry and the task of "completely solving the problems of food, clothing, and housing of the people." Nonetheless, as the year ended Pyongyang made an unusual reference to the economy's advance in spite of "the complicated situation" in 1986—which "situation," of course, was given no elaboration. (KCNA, 27 December, 1 January 1987.)

The DPRK was estimated to have a gross national product of $23 billion in 1984, yielding a per capita figure of about $1,200. (CIA, *World Fact Book*, 1986.) Even if we halve the DPRK's claimed growth rates in the past two years, we would get a per capita figure of about $1,400. That is well below the South's, which stands at more than $2,000, but it is not a figure suggesting that North Korea is an economic disaster. Its per capita output of cement, coal, electric power, and minerals is on a par with several East European economies. It is clear that the DPRK for a number of years has faced problems of diminishing returns from a heavy-industry-first program that worked well for the first two decades, weakly for the last two. But the new seven-year plan gives little indication of any change in economic priorities.

On other fronts, some important developments occurred domestically in 1986. In late March the DPRK held the sixth congress of the General Federation of Literature and Arts Unions, an organization that had not held a congress for a quarter century. This organization looks after all the writers, artists, musicians, composers, and other cultural workers. But the timing of the congress is probably explained by one other group it includes—filmmakers. The DPRK has a large and high-quality film industry, and the sixth congress came right on the heels of the defection of Shin and his wife, Choe, and was no doubt intended to ensure that no such thing happens again.

Throughout the year Pyongyang continued to cite the addition of new sports facilities as part of its attempt to co-host the 1988 Olympics. Yanggak Island, just southeast of the capital, is the site of the new hotel being built with French help; under construction also are a 30,000-seat sports stadium, indoor swimming pools, and other facilities. Kim Chong-il was said personally to have designed some of them, such as the downtown Pyongyang skating rink, shaped to look like a ski cap (according to regime scribes).

**Relations with South Korea.** North-South interaction during the year began on a hopeful note, continued apace into the summer with indications that tensions might relax, only to dissolve as the year ended in acrimonious fighting over Kim's alleged demise and the Diamond Mountain water project.

Persistent rumors in late 1985 and through the early months of 1986 had it that Ho Tam, former DPRK foreign minister, was meeting secretly with high South Korean leaders, in Seoul and elsewhere, seeking to arrange a summit between Kim Il-song and South Korean president Chun Doo-hwan. One report said that Ho had met eight times with Chang Se-dong, the leader of South Korea's National Security Planning Agency (*FPI International Report*, January). These reports were given credence early in the year when Kim Il-song called for high-level North-South talks.

When the United States and South Korea began extensive military maneuvers in February, the North Koreans, as they have in recent years, suspended any discussions about North-South talks. In late May the rumors began again, this time citing alleged meetings between the two premiers, Kang Song-san and Lho Shin-yong. One report said that Kim Il-song had sent an emissary to Chun to apologize for the 1983 terrorist bombing of Rangoon, which nearly killed Chun and blasted his cabinet, saying that it had been done without Kim's approval by hotheaded young officers, who had since been executed.

In early June, North and South Korean negotiators met with Olympics officials in Lausanne, Switzerland, seeking to break a deadlock on hosting the 1988 Olympics. The DPRK wants joint equal co-hosting; South Korea wants no DPRK involvement unless it is necessary to get China or the USSR to participate, in which case it wants to limit co-hosting to the bare minimum. The meetings in Lausanne seemed to have achieved an agreement whereby the North would hold a couple of minor events in return for not blocking Soviet or Chinese participation. Later it appeared that there was no such agreement.

While attempting to arrange some measure of co-hosting, Pyongyang also issued all manner of invective about the very idea of holding the games in Seoul. At the end of July, for example, the North said Seoul was always "threatened with death and disaster," claiming among other things that the "satanic disease" of AIDS had infected 600,000 people in South Korea; thus Olympics sportsmen "can hardly escape death from AIDS" (KCNA, 31 July). Pyongyang has been harping on AIDS and grossly inflating the number of sufferers in the South for some time although independent sources cite little incidence of the disease in South Korea.

On June 18 South Korean defense minister Yi Ki-paek said he had received an "unprecedented" letter from DPRK Defense Minister O Chin-u, offering to hold high-level military talks aimed at reducing tension on the peninsula (Seoul, *Korea Times*, 18 June). Certainly the letter contained something new: the first DPRK use of the American commander's formal title as the head of United Nations forces. Neither South Korea nor the U.S. had much use for the proposal, however, and it went nowhere. Meanwhile, Kim Il-song claimed to have withdrawn 150,000 soldiers from units stationed near the DMZ as an earnest of his peaceful intent. Foreign observers hastened to point out that this was routine practice for the North, which frequently employs large numbers of soldiers in economic construction. (For example, Kim lauded the army for its aid in building the Nampo Lockgate.)

The North alternated these hopeful overtures with a steady drumbeat about the developing political crisis in the South and claims of the imminent demise of the Chun regime. It is unquestionable that the North sees in the growing strength of the opposition, the radicalization of students, and the continued problems of legitimacy of the Chun government a major opportunity to exert influence on the South. At the same time, however, as opposition leaders in the South are wont to note, the North seems to come forth in moments of crisis with proposals for summits and high-level talks, thus bolstering the man in power in Seoul. It did this in 1972 with Park Chung Hee, and then did it again in 1986 with Chun. There was no move, however, to resume either the Red Cross talks, held sporadically in past years, but with several important exchanges in 1985, or the unprecedented economic talks that began in 1984.

North-South relations plunged to their nadir of the year over South Korea's too-hasty reports of Kim's assassination, and soon after that the South began harping on the North's Diamond Mountain hydroelectric project. The South alleged that once the dam was completed it would reverse the southward flow of the critical Han River, running through Seoul; it would also hold "no less than twenty billion metric tons of water" and, if unleashed suddenly, "the consequent floods would not only imperil the survival of the fifteen million inhabitants in the Han River Valley in the south but also virtually isolate our armed forces units deployed north of the river." The North was warned to stop work on the project. Foreign diplomats wondered what all the flurry was about, since the dam project had been known in the South for some time, was five years from completion, and would take another ten years to fill up. The North Koreans predictably denounced the South for creating more obstacles to North-South talks; it termed the South's worries "a queer anticommunist commotion . . . by those who have lost reason." (Seoul, *Korea Herald*, 7 November; *NYT*, 30 November; KCNA, 4 November.)

In December the DPRK continued to call for a reconvening of talks in Lausanne on co-hosting the Olympics (KCNA, 26 December). As the year ended, Kim Il-song at the first session of the Eighth Supreme People's Assembly called for the convening of "North-South high-level political and military talks" (KCNA, 1 January 1987), thus ending the year on the same note on which it had begun.

**International Views, Positions, and Activities.** From beginning to end, 1986 witnessed a deepening of Korean-Soviet relations, a trend begun in 1983 that has carried with it a drawing down of the previously close relationship with China. It is important not to overestimate this tilt, however. Relations with the Soviets are still not particularly warm, and China remains a close ally of North Korea. Furthermore, the warming of relations between China and the USSR has provided space within which Pyongyang can mend its relations with Moscow without offending Beijing.

Former premier Kang Song-san visited Moscow as 1985 ended and secured a pledge from his counterpart, Nikolai Ryzhkov, to visit North Korea at an unspecified later date. At this time the Soviets released a report detailing their recent aid to the Korean economy, citing loans of unspecified amounts, technical aid, and engineering advisers posted at several factories. Among the plants mentioned were the Pukchang Thermal Plant, the Chongjin Thermal Plant, the Yongsong Bearing Plant, and an unnamed new aluminum factory. The Soviets said trade with North Korea was growing, mentioning Korean exports of rolled steel, cement, small motors, batteries, and other items (*FBIS*, 27 December 1985). Such Soviet help has generally gone unmentioned in the North Korean press.

Various exchanges with the Soviets proceeded throughout the year. Foreign Minister Eduard Shevardnadze visited Pyongyang in January, and the important Soviet Far Eastern expert, Mikhail Kapitsa, arrived in May. From 6 to 9 July a Korean air force squadron flew a goodwill mission to the USSR, no doubt in thanks for the MIG23s that the Soviets finally consented to provide to Pyongyang in 1985. A week later the 25th anniversary of the DPRK-USSR Treaty of Friendship, Cooperation and Mutual Assistance was greeted with a high degree of fanfare.

The Soviets sent a delegation to Pyongyang headed by Yuriy Solovyev, an alternate member of the Politburo. They toured various sites in Pyongyang and participated in a mass rally to commemorate the treaty. Meanwhile, a Soviet Pacific fleet squadron visited the port of Wonsan, one of an increasing number of Soviet port calls in North Korea. Kim Il-song hailed the treaty as "a new high stage" in "the relations of class alliance" between the two parties (*FBIS*, 15 July).

A few days later Pyongyang commemorated the 25th anniversary of a similar treaty with China, but with much less fanfare and with very tepid verbiage, especially when compared to the warmth of the Sino-Korean relationship in the late 1970s and early 1980s. Still, the Koreans referred many times to ties with China as "sealed in blood," "a friendship in blood," etc. (*NDSM*, 11 July), which are references to the Chinese sacrifices during the Korean War and, by implication, to the absence of similar sacrifice by the Soviets. Pyongyang also sent a reasonably high-powered delegation to Beijing for commemoration ceremonies there, led by sixth-ranking Politburo member Yi Chong-ok. Chinese party leader Hu Yaobang received the delegation on 11 July and continued the Chinese practice of recent years in wishing long life to both Kim Il-song and Kim Chong-il, which the Soviets generally refuse to do (KCNA, 13 July).

The celebrations of the 41st anniversary of the liberation from Japan in mid-August underlined the warming trend with Moscow. For years Pyongyang refused to acknowledge any Soviet participation in the liberation of Korea, but now the Koreans keep the graves of fallen Soviet soldiers clean and tidy, and this time Kim Il-song referred to "defeating Japanese imperialism jointly with the Soviet Army" (*FBIS*, 15 August)—still a historical revision of some note, but from the Soviet standpoint much better than the old formula.

In late October Kim Il-song abruptly made a five-day visit to Moscow, despite his advanced age (74) and his reputed fear of flying. There was no advance notice and little of substance was reported in the aftermath. No joint communiqué emerged, and Secretary Gorbachev pointedly remarked that although relations with Korea had "accumulated a good momentum over recent years," there was "still ample room for growth in our cooperation." Some sources had it that Gorbachev expressed displeasure with misuse of Soviet aid by the North (*NYT*, 18 November; Hong Kong, *South China Morning Post*, 1 November). Still, Soviet-Korean trade is booming. The 1986 figure probably totaled about $1.1 billion, a 50 percent increase over 1985. This is roughly one-quarter of the DPRK's total trade— about half of which is with noncommunist countries. (CIA, *World Fact Book*, 1986.)

Pyongyang also courted close allies of Moscow, mainly Fidel Castro of Cuba and Erich Honecker of East Germany, although Olympics politics were also at stake (East Germany and Cuba field unusually strong athletic teams). Some press reports treated Castro's state visit to Pyongyang in March as if it were a meeting of old friends and comrades at arms, but in fact it was Castro's first visit and signaled a thaw in DPRK relations with Cuba after many years. North Korea has been at particular odds with Cuba in Africa, in its close relations with Mugabe in Zimbabwe, for example, where the USSR and Cuba supported the Nkomo forces; and especially in Angola, where Pyongyang backed the Roberto Holden faction against the Cuban-backed eventual victor in the Angolan civil war, Neto.

A decade later relations are much better. Castro explicitly thanked Kim for supplying Cuba with "100,000 automatic rifles and tens of millions of rounds of ammunition on very favourable terms of loan and price." He also signed a twenty-year treaty of friendship and cooperation while in Pyongyang, a routine event in Korean diplomatic relations (there are many such treaties with Third World countries). The more important part of the visit was securing Castro's pledge not to send a team to the Seoul Olympics if co-hosting arrangements agreeable to Pyongyang cannot be reached. Since Castro also has influence in the Nonaligned Movement, Pyongyang no doubt hoped to signal its noncommunist Third World friends to do likewise (*FEER*, 17 April).

Honecker visited Korea from 17 to 22 October and Kim Il-song undoubtedly sought more German economic aid and support for Pyongyang's position on the Olympics. Honecker was described as "our intimate friend" at the conclusion of his visit. The German-Korean friendship was said to have "entered a new high stage," but there was little indication that the Germans were willing to step out in front of their Soviet allies in their relations with Korea (*NDSM*, 23 October). This may be why Kim abruptly flew to Moscow just as Honecker left North Korea.

It will be clear that Pyongyang's relations with Moscow and East Germany will have reached what Gorbachev would term effective cooperation, should the North make overtures to Vietnam. Ties with this former close friend have varied from hostile to cool since the Vietnamese invasion of Cambodia (which Pyongyang publicly denounced). Kim Il-song still provides spending money and a lavish villa to Prince Sihanouk, leader of the Cambodian resistance. In June the prince attended a big dinner in Pyongyang with his wife, Monique, and Kim's wife, Kim Song-ae, reciprocated with a rare public appearance (KCNA, 18 June). Kim has for many years let Sihanouk and his entourage wander the world and come home to the comfort of his Korean villa; he even funded several films directed by Sihanouk.

North Korea continued its active courting of its reasonably extensive group of friends and allies in the Third World. In March the last group of Korean military advisers departed from Zimbabwe, after reportedly training a 25,000-strong paramilitary militia, as well as the so-called Fifth Brigade, which earned a reputation for brutality against civilians during counterinsurgency campaigns. A stream of African leaders visited Pyongyang: the leaders of Mali and Senegal visited in June, the leaders of the Ivory Coast and Benin later in the year. North Korea supplies advisors and/or weaponry to a number of African countries: Algeria, Libya, Tanzania, Mo-zambique, Somalia, the Seychelles. (North Korean guards headed off a coup in the latter country in 1981.)

North Korea developed a Middle Eastern policy and presence after the Iran-Iraq war began in 1981. It found much profit in recycling weapons for oil and other Iranian exports. Pyongyang became Iran's main arms supplier, loading up Iran's Boeing 747 transports with both domestically produced and Chinese weapons. In 1986 it remained first among those selling arms to Teheran. There were reportedly about 300 North Korean advisors in Iran in 1986.

Pyongyang has long been active in the Nonaligned Movement, often presenting Kim Il-song as a founder and natural leader of the group. But the North Koreans could not have been pleased with the results of the Harare Summit, which included a stunning denunciation of the ineffectiveness of the group by Libya's Khadafy. A twenty-page joint communiqué from Pyongyang virtually pleaded with the members to unite and work together against imperialism and the countries of "the North" (KCNA, 21 June).

Relations with Japan remain informal, but they improved in 1986. There were rumors that Prime Minister Nakasone was playing a go-between role in trying to arrange talks between North and South Korea and between North Korea and the United States, and he has lifted tight visa restrictions, enabling more North Koreans to visit Japan. After the United States issued visas to three North Korean visitors in 1985, observers thought that a mild thaw might be occurring. But there was no progress on this front in 1986. North Korea seemed particularly incensed by the appointment of a new American ambassador to Seoul with a long CIA background, Robert Lilley. The North Koreans again complained loudly about the large military exercises mounted in February. There has been a distinct diminution of anti-American rhetoric, however, at least by Pyongyang standards, and at the end of the year Kim Il-song reiterated his call for three-way talks between the United States and the two Koreas. (KCNA, 27 December.) This proposal has been on the table since January 1983; the Chinese have supported it but the Soviets have not, since it would tend to leave Moscow out of the negotiations.

Bruce Cumings
*University of Washington*

# Laos

**Population.** 3,679,000
**Party.** Lao People's Revolutionary Party (Phak Pasason Pativat Lao; LPRP)
**Founded.** 22 March 1955
**Membership.** 44,000 (Radio Vientiane, 13 November; *FBIS*, 13 November)
**General Secretary.** Kaysone Phomvihane (66, Lao-Vietnamese, premier)
**Politburo.** 13 members: Kaysone Phomvihane, Nouhak Phoumsavan, Souphanouvong (president), Phoumi Vongvichit (acting president), Khamtai Siphandon, Phoun Sipaseut, Sisomphon Lovansai, Sisavat Keobounphan, Sali Vongkhamsao, Maichantan Sengmani, Saman Vi-gnaket, Oudom Khatti-gna (alternate), Chounmali Sai-gnakon (alternate) (Radio Vientiane, 15 November; *FBIS*, 17 November)
**Secretariat.** 9 members: Kaysone Phomvihane, Khamtai Siphandon, Sisavat Keobounphan, Sali Vongkhamsao, Maichantan Sengmani, Saman Vi-gnaket, Oudom Khatti-gna, Chounmali Sai-gnakon, Somlak Chanthamat (ibid.)
**Central Committee.** 51 full members, 9 alternate members (for names, see *FBIS*, 17 November)
**Status.** Ruling and sole legal party
**Last Congress.** Fourth, 13–15 November, in Vientiane
**Last Election.** 1975; all 46 candidates were LPRP approved
**Auxiliary Organizations.** Lao Front for National Construction (LFNC)
**Publications.** *Pasason* (The people), LPRP central organ, published in Vientiane (daily); *Alun Mai* (New dawn), LPRP theoretical journal, published in Vientiane (quarterly); the official news agency is Khaosan Pathet Lao (Pathet Lao News Agency; KPL).

At the LPRP's Fourth Congress in 1986, the leadership affirmed its adherence to the "strategic alliance" with Vietnam and consolidated the gains of a mixed economy of state and private enterprises. The year also saw the Laotian leaders making rapid strides toward normalizing relations with both China and Thailand. At the same time, serious constitutional issues have remained unresolved since President Souphanouvong was forced by ill health to give up his positions, at least temporarily.

**Leadership and Party Organization.** As a result of elections at the Fourth Congress, the LPRP Politburo was enlarged by the addition of four full and two alternate members. Sisavat Keobounphan, secretary of the Vientiane municipality party committee; Sali Vongkhamsao, chairman of the State Planning Commission; Maichantan Sengmani, head of the party-government central control commission; and Saman Vi-gnaket, head of the party central organization committee, were elevated to the Politburo. All were party Central Committee secretaries. Oudom Khatti-gna, secretary of the Xieng Khouang provincial party committee, and Chounmali Sai-gnakon, a vice-minister of national defense, also joined the Politburo as alternates.

The party Secretariat remained at nine members, but three senior members—Nouhak Phoumsavan, Phoun Sipaseut, and Sisomphon Lovansai—gave up their membership in favor of younger party leaders. Somlak Chanthamat, the party's central propaganda and training chief, was added for the first time.

The party Central Committee (CC) was raised

from 47 full and 6 alternate members to 51 full and 9 alternate members. The new CC comprises 55 men and 5 women. Their average age is 52, with a range of from 33 to 77. Nine CC members were also members of the former Indochinese Communist Party (ICP), the LPRP's parent party. Over the past ten years, according to the announcement of the election results, the members of the new CC have gone through short- and long-term training on Marxism-Leninism at the intermediate and higher levels, and 15 percent of them hold university- or preuniversity-level technical knowledge. Listed in 35th position in the new CC was Thongvin Phomvihane, Kaysone's wife. One of Souphanouvong's sons, Khamsai, was listed as an alternate CC member. (Radio Vientiane, 15 November; *FBIS*, 17 November.)

Overall, the new party leadership exhibited the same stability as in the past. This was especially true of the pre-eminence of its general secretary, who was reported to be extremely active; he attended provincial party congresses, oversaw the work of the Lao People's Democratic Republic (LPDR) government and its various commissions, and traveled extensively abroad to attend important party meetings and consult with the leaders of Vietnam, the Soviet Union, and bloc countries.

Deaths of political leaders in 1986 included those of Faidang Lobaliayao, on 12 July in a Vientiane hospital at the age of 76, and Khamsouk Saignaseng, on 29 July in a Moscow hospital at the age of 71. Faidang, a member of the Hmong tribe, was the most famous of the tribal leaders whose allegiance was crucial to the party-directed resistance first against French forces in Laos and later against those of the royal government, and he had held positions as vice-chairman of the Supreme People's Assembly and of the LFNC Central Committee (Radio Vientiane, 13 July; *FBIS*, 16 July). Khamsouk had been a member of the LPRP CC and chairman of the Laos-USSR Friendship Association (Radio Vientiane, 8 August; *FBIS*, 14 August).

**Domestic Party Affairs.** After extensive preparations throughout much of the year, the Fourth Congress of the LPRP opened with hardly any advance public notice on 13 November and was attended by 303 delegates. A bust of Ho Chi Minh, founder of the ICP, as well as portraits of Karl Marx and Lenin and a photograph of Kaysone, adorned the congress hall. (Radio Vientiane, 13 November; *FBIS*, 13 November.)

Some historical details filling in gaps in knowledge of the party were provided at the congress. The First Congress was officially said to have convened in Houa Phan (Sam Neua) province between 21 March and 6 May 1955, with the participation of 22 delegates representing 400 party members. The Second Congress convened in Viang Sai district of Houa Phan province on 3–6 February 1972, with the participation of 125 delegates representing 21,000 members. At that congress, the name of the party was changed from Lao People's Party to Lao People's Revolutionary Party. The Third Congress convened in Vientiane (which remained the capital of Laos following the LPRP seizure of power and proclamation of the LPDR on 2 December 1975) on 27–30 April 1982, with the participation of 225 delegates representing 35,000 party members. (Ibid.)

At the opening session of the Fourth Congress, acting president Phoumi Vongvichit, Kaysone, Nouhak Phoumsavan, and Sisomphon Lovansai all spoke. Among the accomplishments claimed after eleven years of party rule in Laos were the following: rice production in 1985 exceeded 1.39 million tons, making Laos basically self-sufficient (although considerable imbalances between surplus and deficit areas exist and there is much local trade in rice); irrigated farmland in 1985 reached 130,000 hectares; there were 3,400 agricultural cooperatives encompassing 53 percent of peasant families and 52.3 percent of total farmland; roads extended for 12,980 kilometers, including 2,460 of national highways and 6,200 kilometers of provincial roads; and 99 out of 122 districts are linked to provincial capitals by these highways and roads. (Ibid.)

The major crisis that threatened the stability of the LPDR in 1986 was the sudden, and medically unexplained, illness of its first and only president, Souphanouvong. This required that Phoumi Vongvichit be named acting president, according to a four-paragraph decree issued on 29 October (Radio Vientiane, 30 October; *FBIS*, 30 October).

Souphanouvong had followed what appeared to be a normal schedule of activities and speech-making until August. On 27 August, he was reportedly seen off at Vientiane's Wattay airport at the head of the LPDR's delegation to the Nonaligned Movement summit meeting in Harare, Zimbabwe (Radio Vientiane, 28 August; *FBIS*, 29 August). Foreign Minister Phoun Sipaseut, second-ranking member of the delegation, was reported to have stopped over in Moscow on 28–29 August, but Souphanouvong was not mentioned (*Izvestiia*, 30 August; *FBIS*,

4 September). According to press reports, Souphanouvong never showed up in Harare (*FEER*, 13 November). On 11 September, Phoun returned to Vientiane in the capacity of leader of the LPDR delegation (Radio Vientiane, 12 September; *FBIS*, 12 September).

Souphanouvong was reportedly not seen in public in the capital thereafter. Although his name appeared as a signatory of congratulatory messages to foreign heads of state, such as on that to Chinese leaders on 1 October (Radio Vientiane, 1 October; *FBIS*, 2 October), this would have been in accordance with customary practice in communist countries. (Souphanouvong's signature was on the message sent by the Vientiane leaders on Vietnam's national holiday, 2 September, although ostensibly he was in Harare on that day.)

It was not until the end of October that Souphanouvong's undisclosed illness became a serious enough matter for the LPDR to make a public announcement, which came in the form of a decree issued by the LPDR president, the Supreme People's Assembly (SPA), and the LPDR Council of Ministers (Radio Vientiane, 30 October; *FBIS*, 30 October).

The mystery surrounding the circumstances of the brief announcement was heightened by the fact that the official news agency, KPL, in the original English version of its 70-word report on the decree, used the words "a new president" and "in place of President Souphanouvong" in describing Phoumi Vongvichit (KPL, 31 October; *FBIS*, 31 October). However, the following day the same report was published with the words changed to read "the acting president" and "at the proposal of President Souphanouvong" (KPL, 1 November; *FBIS*, 3 November).

Souphanouvong retained his other state position, that of chairman of the SPA, until 25 November, when a communiqué announced the appointment of Sisomphon Lovansai to the position of acting chairman (Radio Hanoi, 30 November; *FBIS*, 1 December). Laotian spokesmen emphasized to Western reporters the "temporary" nature of these changes (Bangkok, AFP, 31 October; *FBIS*, 31 October).

The potential gravity of the constitutional situation arises from the fact that the LPDR has as yet not adopted a constitution. A commission of the SPA has been working at the task of drafting a constitution for some years, but progress has apparently been slow. Souphanouvong announced at the opening session of the annual SPA meeting in January that a report on "the execution of the central task of writing the draft constitution and the draft election law, the former of which has already been compiled," was under examination (Radio Vientiane, 30 January; *FBIS*, 4 February). But in his speech closing the meeting, he was able only to promise that "we will further discuss the contents of the draft constitution and the draft election law" (Radio Vientiane, 1 February; *FBIS*, 6 February). A resolution adopted at the meeting said the party would "continue intensifying efforts to fulfill the historic tasks entrusted by the national congress of people's representatives to the end—that is, to complete the drafting of the first constitution of the LPDR, to promulgate the election law" (Radio Vientiane, 2 February; *FBIS*, 7 February).

It would seem from the evidence at hand that drafting a constitution in Laos, as was the case in the People's Republic of Kampuchea (PRK), is a task fraught with difficulty. In the PRK, the process dragged from the end of 1978, when a constitution was first promised by the leaders of the new government installed by the Vietnamese, until 1981. In the process, several drafts were announced, produced by different commissions, and contained at times sharply divergent wordings. This was not too surprising, in view of the intricate relationship between the present leaders of both the PRK and the LPDR and the Vietnamese Communist Party (VCP). This relationship raises a whole host of issues involving nationalism and dependency, sovereignty, and proletarian internationalism. Since a constitution establishes the official version of the history of the emergence of party and state to their present status of powerful arbiter of the people's livelihood and thinking, it is possible that the drafting process may lead to divergent interpretations within the top leadership itself. In any event, by the end of 1986 there was no indication of when the LPDR would have a constitution, or of whether the recent shifts of persons responsible would further delay, or possibly speed up, the process of drafting one.

**Auxiliary Organizations.** The LFNC, the party's principal mass-mobilization organization, was seldom in the news beyond the holding of routine meetings.

**International Views, Positions, and Activities.** As they have done in the past, LPRP leaders gave pre-eminence to Vietnam in the litany of their relations with foreign friends. They stressed at every occasion the common front of the two parties in the successive struggles against the French and the Americans, claimed to perceive in the future a continued strengthening of these bonds, and hinted at new forms of integration yet to be disclosed.

The most significant indicator of the state of relations between the LPRP and VCP were the speeches by party leaders at their respective congresses, which took place about one month apart. Even before this, however, there were unmistakable signs that the "special relationship" between Laos and Vietnam, consecrated in dogma as the heritage of Ho Chi Minh, had been publicly elevated by the two parties to the level of "strategic alliance." Chu Huy Man, a senior old-line VCP Politburo figure, had given an authoritative reading of the situation in an article near the end of 1985. He saw the ICP's attempt to duplicate the party's seizure of power in Vietnam across the mountains in Laos as "the first great achievement of the alliance." The formation of an independent government in Laos in 1945 was largely the work of noncommunist nationalists and, in any case, was of short duration. Subsequently, although the "objective requirements of the revolution" led to the founding of separate Marxist-Leninist parties in each country in place of the ICP, Chu Huy Man wrote, the alliance was once again an important factor in the defeat of the French. Finally, the alliance became "a historical reality" in the fierce, prolonged war against the United States.

Tracing the evolution of the alliance in the post-1975 period, Chu Huy Man wrote that "this alliance has developed into a state-alliance." He described the summit conference of Vietnam, Laos, and Kampuchea held in Vientiane in February 1983 as having given "a full legal basis" to the "militant strategic alliance of the three Indochinese states." From the military point of view, the strategic alliance implies that in the event of war all Indochina "is to be a single battlefield." Any attempt to divide the countries from one another, he concluded, goes against pure proletarian internationalism and is a manifestation of "narrow-minded nationalism." (Hanoi, *Vietnam Courier*, no. 11, 1985.) Kaysone reiterated this theme in his speech to the VCP congress (Radio Vientiane, 17 December; *FBIS*, 18 December).

In his political report to the LPRP congress in November, Kaysone declared: "Our alliance with Vietnam in defending the country is growing with every passing day."

The Vietnamese delegation to the LPRP congress was led by Pham Van Dong, Nguyen Van Linh, and Dang Thi. In his speech, Pham Van Dong said that "the militant solidarity, fraternal friendship, and all-around cooperation between Vietnam and Laos, painstakingly fostered by President Ho Chi Minh," had become "a priceless asset of our two peoples and the law governing the survival and development of each country's revolution."

While he was in Vientiane, Pham Van Dong also paid a visit to Souphanouvong and wished him restoration to good health (Radio Hanoi, 12 November; *FBIS*, 14 November).

Among the practical matters in relations between the LPDR and Vietnam, one of the most significant has been the delineation of their common border as called for in the 1977 treaty of friendship and cooperation (see *YICA*, 1978). Steps were reportedly taken in this regard during 1986, following years of negotiations that have been described as "hard-fought and at times heated" (Martin Stuart-Fox, *Laos* [Boulder, Colo.: Lynne Rienner, 1986], p. 177). On 24 January, LPDR foreign minister Phoun Sipaseut and Vietnamese foreign minister Nguyen Co Thach signed a protocol on the planting of border markers (Radio Vientiane, 27, 30 January; *FBIS*, 29 January, 3 February). On 19 September in Hanoi, the LPDR and Vietnam exchanged ratification documents legalizing the border treaty and its protocol (Radio Vientiane, 20 September; FBIS, 22 September). None of these documents had been published as of the end of the year.

A conference on the border situation was reportedly held in Hue City in 1986. Attending were representatives of the central border committees of each country and of the border provinces on each side: Bolikhamsai, Xieng Khouang, Savannakhet, Khammouane, Sedone, and Attopeu for the LPDR, and Nghe Tinh, Binh Tri Thien, Quang Nam-Danang, and Gia Lai-Cong Tum for Vietnam. The conference "unanimously endorsed a plan for the inspection of the situation along the entire border and repair or replacement of a number of damaged border posts." (Radio Hanoi, 25 November; *FBIS*.)

The LPDR's alliance with Vietnam rather tightly circumscribed the former's relations with other countries. This fact made the major initiatives taken by the LPDR during 1986 to improve relations with China and Thailand all the more significant.

The turning point came with Mikhail Gorbachev's 28 July speech in Vladivostok, the importance of which was being emphasized by LPDR spokesmen within a matter of days. Deliberations were also going on internally within the LPDR government and between the LPDR and Vietnam.

The communiqué of the twelfth regular conference of foreign ministers of Vietnam, Laos, and Cambodia, held in Vientiane on 23–24 January, said with respect to China that "only through negotiations can differences among the parties be solved"; the communiqué of the thirteenth such conference, held in Hanoi on 17–18 August, added to this statement of principle a specific endorsement of an LPDR initiative: "The conference welcomes the reasonable position of the government of the LPDR advocating the normalization of its relations with the People's Republic of China (PRC) on the basis of mutual respect for each other's national independence, sovereignty, and territorial integrity, of mutual nonaggression, of noninterference in each other's internal affairs, and of peaceful coexistence" (Embassy of the LPDR, Washington, D.C., *News Bulletins*).

The communiqué of the eleventh plenary session of the third LPRP CC, held 30 September to 7 October, declared that the session "maintained that there is a new development in the relations between the Soviet Union and China and considered it an important contribution to the defense of peace and international security" (Radio Vientiane, 9 October; *FBIS*, 9 October). The message from Kaysone and Souphanouvong to the PRC leaders on 1 October was a warm one, extending "sincere congratulations and best wishes to the National People's Congress, the PRC government, and the entire Chinese people" (Radio Vientiane, 1 October; *FBIS*, 2 October).

China, which was reported to be receptive to the LPDR initiative (see, for example, Tokyo, *Kyodo*, 25 November; *FBIS*, 25 November; *FEER*, 4 December), responded by sending equally warm congratulations to the LPDR on its national day (KPL, 6 December; *FBIS*, 9 December). Although the Chinese Communist Party was not listed among the nineteen delegations from fraternal parties attending the LPRP congress in November, Kaysone's remarks on China in his political report were markedly subdued.

However unsettling the prospect of a Soviet-Chinese rapprochement may have been to the VCP leaders with respect to carrying out Ho Chi Minh's final instructions concerning the satellization of Laos and Cambodia, the Laotians lost no time in seizing the grand opportunity offered them by Gorbachev's speech. Barely a month after their congress, the LPDR leaders announced that Chinese deputy foreign minister Liu Shuqing would visit the LPDR soon (Radio Vientiane, 18 December; *FBIS*,

18 December). A simultaneous announcement in Beijing set the dates of the visit as 20–25 December (*NYT*, 18 December).

According to a Laotian report on the talks, both sides "reaffirmed their aspirations to restore and normalize the relations between the two countries for the benefits of both Lao and Chinese peoples as well as for the interest of peace and security in Indochina and Southeast Asia," indicating that the talks had touched on the Sino-Vietnamese conflict. The LPDR delegation was led by First Deputy Foreign Minister Khamphai Boupha. Liu Shuqing paid a courtesy call on Foreign Minister Phoun Sipaseut in the course of his visit, and visited unspecified economic and cultural sites. Liu also invited Khamphai to visit China to hold further talks, and Khamphai "gladly" accepted the invitation. (KPL, 25 December; *FBIS*, 29 December.)

In an interview in Bangkok before returning home, Liu confirmed that his talks with the LPDR had briefly touched on the Sino-Vietnamese conflict. "I said that times have changed. In past years Vietnam was a victim of aggression and we supported Vietnam's fight against the aggressors. Now Vietnam is committing aggression against Cambodia. We can only stand with the victim of aggression." (Bangkok, *Xin zhong yuan ribao*, 26 December; *FBIS*, 29 December.)

Liu also said he had assured the Laotians that "there is no question of China supporting the Lao resistance groups" (ibid.). In the past, China has given unofficial support to anti-LPDR resistance groups, particularly of the Hmong tribe.

For his part, Khamphai said in an interview after conclusion of the talks that both sides found them "beneficial and concretely appropriate." He added: "The Lao side affirmed the LPDR's principled policy and plan to do its best to restore and develop fine, neighborly relations of friendship and cooperation with the PRC on the basis of the five principles of peaceful coexistence, thus contributing to peace and stability in Indochina and Southeast Asia. The Lao side finds it necessary to stress that the absence of a peaceful situation caused by China's policy toward Vietnam as well as China's assistance to the forces of Pol Pot and other Cambodian reactionaries opposing the PRK affects the LPDR's security and the speedy normalization of Laos-China relations." (Radio Vientiane, 2 January 1987; FBIS, 2 January 1987.)

The LPDR's normalization of relations with Thailand in 1986 was a development of almost equal importance. The border situation with Thailand is more difficult than with China, since there have been repeated armed clashes over the years, culminating in a serious incident on the Sayaboury-Nan border in 1984 involving rival claims to three villages. An exacerbating element has been the presence of antigovernment rebels in border sanctuaries on both sides. Nevertheless, a dialogue between the two countries had never been broken off, even at the height of tensions, and in 1986 apparently both countries felt the time had come to seek a modus vivendi.

The first sign of a better atmosphere, perhaps, came in September, when the traditional boat races between the two countries resumed at Chiang Khan on the Mekong River after a suspension of two years; a team from Sayaboury took part. The following week, the LPDR Foreign Ministry formally proposed a new round of talks with Thailand and requested the opening of more border checkpoints to facilitate trade (Radio Vientiane, 25 September; *FBIS*, 25 September). On 18 October, boat races were resumed downriver at Nong Khai, near Vientiane, "in a carnival atmosphere" (*Bangkok Post*, 19 October; *FBIS*, 20 October).

Previous negotiations on improving relations had been held alternately in Vientiane and Bangkok. The dates for the visit of a Thai delegation were reported in the Thai press as being 27–29 November (*Bangkok Post*, 4 November; *FBIS*, 4 November), and an official announcement in Vientiane specified that the talks would be at the level of "high-level technical delegations" (Radio Vientiane, 22 November; *FBIS*, 24 November).

Deputy Foreign Minister Souban Salitthilat expressed his satisfaction with the outcome of the talks, saying "each side has demonstrated the good intentions of its government of establishing good relations with each other." The two sides also reaffirmed their adherence to the joint statements by their prime ministers of 6 January and 4 April 1979 "as a good basis for the relations between the two countries," Souban said. (Radio Vientiane, 28 November; *FBIS*, 1 December.) These two statements are notable in that they pledge the two sides to prevent anyone from using their territory "as a base for interference, threats, or aggression against the other, or to carry out subversive activities against each other in whatever form." The relatively large (23-member) Thai delegation departed from Vientiane on 29 November with an acceptance by the Laotian side to continue the talks in Bangkok.

Hopes for further improvement of relations with the United States, whose embassy in Vientiane was still maintained at the chargé d'affaires level, was also expressed by Kaysone in his political report. He noted the "actual deeds" to the LPDR's credit in this respect, especially in the form of cooperation in searching for remains of missing U.S. servicemen. The latest such excavation of an aircraft crash site was completed by a joint team on 24 February in Savannakhet province.

Kaysone made a number of visits to the Soviet Union during 1986. On 27 February, he made the LPRP speech to the Twenty-seventh Congress of the Communist Party of the Soviet Union (CPSU) in Moscow (*Pravda*, 2 March) and met Gorbachev (KPL, 3 March; *FBIS*, 7 March). On 8 September, Kaysone reportedly returned to Vientiane from the Soviet Union following a one-month vacation at the invitation of the CPSU CC (TASS, 8 August; *FBIS*, 11 August; Radio Moscow, 8 September). On 15 October, Kaysone was again in Moscow for another meeting with Gorbachev (Radio Vientiane, 17 October; *FBIS*, 21 October). An editorial in the party daily *Pasason* extolled the close relations between the LPRP and the CPSU, and said they would continue "to bear more fruit and grow incessantly" (Radio Vientiane, 22 October; *FBIS*, 24 October).

The CPSU delegation to the LPRP congress was headed by Geydar A. Aliyev and included the newly arrived Soviet ambassador to the LPDR, Yuriy Mikheyev, who is the author of a book on Laos (*Les Débuts du Socialisme au Laos* [Moscow: Novosti Press Agency, 1985]).

Kaysone attended Le Duan's funeral in Hanoi at the head of a party-state delegation, and the LPDR observed a five-day mourning period (Radio Vientiane, 11, 13, 15 July; *FBIS*, 11, 14, 15, 17 July). Kaysone and Sisomphon Lovansai led the LPRP delegation to the VCP congress (Radio Vientiane, 14 December; *FBIS*, 15 December).

**Biography.** *Souphanouvong.* Prince Souphanouvong was born in Luang Prabang on 13 July 1909, the son of the viceroy of the Kingdom of Luang Prabang, Boun Khong (died 1914) and of his eleventh wife, Mom Khamouane. As such, he was a half-brother of Prince Phetsarath, who held the title of viceroy until his death in 1959, and of Prince Souvanna Phouma, several times prime minister of the independent Kingdom of Laos between 1953 and 1975, who died in 1984. Souphanouvong studied in Hanoi and in Paris, returning to Indochina in 1936 with the degree of Ingénieur des Ponts et Chaussées. Assigned to a Public Works job in Vietnam, he married Le Thi Ky Nam, a Vietnamese, in Nha Trang.

Although details about his early communist associations are sparse, he is reported to have met Ho Chi Minh in Hanoi at the time of the August Revolution of 1945. He was sent by the Viet Minh leaders to Savannakhet and Thakhek and founded a Liberation Committee for South Laos. At the end of October, he arrived in Vientiane and merged his committee with the newly formed Lao Issara independent government headed by Phetsarath, of which he was named foreign minister and commander in chief of the liberation army.

He was severely wounded in fighting against the French at Thakhek in March 1946 and escaped across the Mekong to Thailand, where he remained for the next few years with the Lao Issara government in exile. In November 1949, after splitting with the Lao Issara over the issue of dependence on the Viet Minh, he left Bangkok for Vietnam, traveling overland through Burma and China. In March 1951, he participated in the formation of an alliance among the Viet Minh, the Pathet Lao, and the Khmer resistance. After the granting of independence to Laos by the French and the 1954 Geneva Conference, Souphanouvong remained in the Pathet Lao base area of Sam Neua.

Between 1955 and 1962 he took part in numerous negotiations with the royal government, and as titular head of the Pathet Lao faction he assumed ministerial posts in coalition governments among rightists, neutralists, and the Pathet Lao. At one point in this period (May 1958), he was elected to the National Assembly with an overwhelming majority in Vientiane. Following the outbreak of renewed hostilities between the Pathet Lao, backed by North Vietnam, and the royal forces, in 1959 he was imprisoned along with other Pathet Lao deputies. He escaped from prison in 1960 and made his way on foot back to Sam Neua.

When a third coalition government was negotiated in 1974, Souphanouvong returned to Vientiane for the first time in more than ten years. The public demonstrations that accompanied his arrival attested to the fact that he was virtually the only Pathet Lao leader who possessed popular appeal among the lowland Lao. His popularity was mistrusted by the party leadership to the point where they made sure he was absent from the capital when the mass demonstrations demanding the dissolution of the coalition in May 1975 marked a decisive turning point in the LPRP seizure of power. In December 1975, with the proclamation of the LPDR, Souphanouvong was unanimously elected president, after having joined with his half-brother, Prince Souvanna Phouma, in a successful personal appeal to King Savang Vatthana to abdicate the throne.

Arthur J. Dommen
*Bethesda, Maryland*

# Malaysia and Singapore

**Population.** Malaysia: 15,820,000; Singapore: 2,584,000 (*World Factbook*, 1986)
**Party.** Communist Party of Malaya (CPM); Communist Party of Malaysia (MCP); North Kalimantan Communist Party (NKCP)
**Founded.** CPM: 1930; MCP: 1983
**Membership.** CPM: estimated 2,000 armed insurgents on Thai side of border; estimated 200 full-time inside peninsular Malaysia. NKCP: estimated fewer than 100 in Sarawak; estimated 200-500 in Singapore (*World Factbook*, 1986)

**General Secretary.** CPM: Chin Peng; MCP: Ah Leng; NKCP: Wen Ming-chuan
**Politburo.** no data
**Central Committee.** CPM: no data; MCP: Chang Chun (chairman), San Cheng Ming, San Sen, rest unknown
**Status:** Illegal
**Last Congress.** CPM: 1965 (last known)
**Last Election.** N/a
**Auxiliary Organizations.** CPM: Malayan People's Army (MPA), Malay Nationalist Revolutionary Party of Malaya (MNRPM), Islamic Brotherhood Party (Paperi), Malayan People's Liberation Front (MPLF), Barisan Sosialis, People's Liberation Organization (the last two based in Singapore); MCP: Malaysian People's Liberation League (MPLL)
**Publications.** No regular periodicals known; CPM: Voice of Malayan Democracy (VOMD), clandestine radio station broadcasting from southern China; MCP: Voice of the People of Malaysia (VOPM), clandestine radio station, location unknown.

**Leadership and Party Organization.** All indications are that Chin Peng remains the leader of the CPM. The party's Central Committee issued its customary New Year's greeting in his name and, in the party's broadcast celebrating the 56th anniversary of its founding, he was referred to as head of the Central Committee. (VOMD, 31 December 1985, 28 April; FBIS, 7 January, 13 May.)

In April, Malaysia's inspector general of police confirmed his understanding that Chin Peng was probably still alive and remained the CPM's general secretary, although his whereabouts were unknown. The inspector general did not elaborate on his reasons for this assumption but cited evidence from the 1960s and 1970s. The same official said the authorities had also identified three other guerrilla leaders operating in peninsular Malaysia. They were Toe Kah Lim, leader of a faction operating mainly from southern Thailand; Chong Chor, head of the 6th Assault Unit based in West Pahang; and Ah Soo Chye, leader of the 5th Assault Unit in Perak (Kuala Lumpur, *New Sunday Times*, 27 April; FBIS, 1 May).

A Thai military report on the seizure of a key guerrilla camp near Betong on the Malaysian-Thai border said that one of the inhabitants who fled along with the rest of the camp at the approach of the government troops was the party's general secretary, Chang Chung-Ming. Although the newspaper account referred to the camp as a CPM base, it may have belonged to the MCP, since Chang Chun is chairman of its central committee. The same dispatch identified the camp leader as Lee Yuan, whose party position was not identified. (*Bangkok Post*, 20 June; FBIS, 1 July.)

Little is known of the organization of the North Kalimantan People's Forces (Paraku), but the leader of a group who surrendered to government forces late in 1985 was identified as 60-year-old Ubang Anak Huing. Others who surrendered included several high-ranking Paraku commanders, six regional committee members, and three party branch chiefs (Kuala Lumpur Domestic Service, 27 January; FBIS, 30 January). The overall commander of an NKCP unit captured in May was identified as Chong Ah Wah, age 46 (Kuala Lumpur, *Bernama*, 1 June; FBIS, 4 June).

**Domestic Party Activities.** The outlawed communist parties appeared to remain essentially irrelevant to the mainstream of Malaysian politics in a year marked by national elections and some restructuring of the United Malays National Organization (UMNO), the major partner in the ruling coalition.

The CPM continued to address its appeals to all ethnic groups in an effort to play down its traditional identification as a Chinese party. The party's 1986 New Year's greeting was addressed to people of all nationalities and called on them to unite more closely. The statement referred to the Malay people's mass movement establishing "close solidarity with the Chinese, Indians, and others." Although the statement acknowledged that 1985 had been marked by misery and problems of revolutionary struggle, it also spoke of valuable successes, such as the revolutionary armed struggle having "continuously quelled all the enemy army's eradication campaigns," and it noted unity and cooperation between party members and the people's army as well as revolutionary members throughout the country (VOMD, 31 December 1985; FBIS, 7 January).

The New Year's statement decried the economic deterioration in Malaysia and Singapore and the economic crisis haunting the capitalist world, and it cited the progress of "development in the socialist countries, such as the PRC [People's Republic of

China]," which "has achieved tremendous success." The statement ended with an exhortation to "all members of the party and army as well as the people of all nationalities in the country" to "unite more closely" and to work toward creating "a democratic coalition government."

An editorial celebrating the 56th anniversary of the establishment of the CPM continued to stress the role of the "revolutionary people of all nationalities" and spoke of the party's "great influence because it is deeply rooted in the masses of all nationalities in the country." Similarly, the CPM-led MPA was described as "a strong pillar for the people of all nationalities whose rights and interests it is defending." (VOMD, 28 April; *FBIS*, 13 May.)

The anniversary statement reaffirmed the party's commitment to the special program it had outlined in 1985. It pointed to the "deteriorating" domestic economic situation, various financial scandals plaguing the country, the in-fighting among UMNO factions, and the "sharpening conflict of interests between the Kuala Lumpur and Singapore ruling cliques," while "opposition parties and people's organizations are stepping up the struggle against corruption, poverty, and the violation of human rights." It noted that "various patriotic and democratic forces" have been showing a greater tendency to unite, which led to the conclusion that the 56th anniversary of the founding of the CPM was being celebrated in a favorable situation.

Following the August general elections, which even TASS reported as a "convincing victory" for the ruling coalition since it won 148 of the 177 parliamentary seats (*Pravda*, 5 August), the CPM and its auxiliary, the MNRPM, extended warm congratulations to the opposition parties and in particular the Pan-Malayan Islamic Party. The CPM encouraged the struggle of the opposition parties in Parliament, whereas the MNRPM called for the immediate establishment of "a broadly based united front to systematically counter the Barisan National government" (VOMD, 11, 15 September; *FBIS*, 15, 17 September).

The rival MCP had issued a call for a broad united front in a major statement in April in which it attacked the government's buildup of "the new Malay compradors and bureaucratic capitalist class." The national culture policy was described as a policy of assimilation. Steps the regime has taken "under the pretext of applying Islamic values" were all said to be aimed at attaining the political and economic targets of the Malay comprador and bureaucratic capitalist class. At the same time, the

Chinese and Indian nationalities were described as stepping up their struggle against racial discrimination and oppression. An increasing number of Malay figures in the religious, political, labor, and intellectual domains were said to be freeing themselves from narrow traditional thinking to sympathize with and support the struggle of the non-Malays.

The statement cited conflicts between the comprador and bureaucratic capitalists class and the working class, between the national bourgeois class and the feudal class, and among compradors and bureaucratic capitalists from different nationalities. The most serious conflict, however, was between the comprador and bureaucratic capitalists class and the working class. It is these growing conflicts that may inevitably give rise to the growth of the revolution.

Noting that the country cannot "depend on one single community in our efforts to overthrow the UMNO-led Barisan national government," the statement concluded by calling on the oppressed people of all nationalities to "establish a broad united front of patriotic and democratic forces" and draw up a plan of action encompassing "the interests of various nationalities" to be agreed upon by all sides on "the basis of racial equality" (VOPM, 23, 25 April; *FBIS*, 1 May).

MCP attempts to identify itself with Islamic groups included a broadcast by its clandestine radio station of a manifesto of the Malaysian United Islamic Front. The manifesto contained a broad attack on the UMNO and sought to "establish priorities for protecting the interests of Muslims." It argued that, of the commandment to all Muslims to "obey God, obey the Apostle, and those charged with authority among you, . . . only the commandment to obey God and the prophet is absolute . . . it is not essential to obey the government; absolute obedience and support should be pledged only to a fair, just government." The manifesto called for upholding Islamic values, spreading "the nucleus of Islamic philosophy," preserving Islamic morality while fighting against oppression and exploitation . . . and opposing all evil deeds of the ruling group which outrage Islamic values" (VOPM, 28 July; *FBIS*, 1 August).

The other manifestation of communist activity, the guerrilla forces, were the object of a series of Malaysian-Thai military operations conducted throughout the year (Bangkok, *The Nation*, 12 February; Bangkok Domestic Service, 12 March; *Bangkok Post*, 20 June; *FBIS*, 12 February, 13

March, 1 July). The operations were not in response to increased communist activity, but were initiated in an attempt to reduce the number of guerrillas (Bangkok, *Naeo Na*, 20 February; *FBIS*, 21 February). Thai military spokesmen said that, despite a reportedly higher rate of defection, there were still 1,500 CPM guerrillas operating in Thailand after 40 years and they remained an irritant to the authorities (Bangkok, *Siam Rath*, 22 May). In the familiar lament of those seeking guerrilla units, the Thai military noted that the guerrillas have generally fled the area before their camps are penetrated.

Although the capture of a communist communications platoon's stronghold netted the unit's mobile radio station—a transmitter for the VOPM—another transmitter was back on the air a few months later (*The Nation*, 19 February; *FBIS*, 19 February).

Malaysian communist guerrillas on the Thai border were said to be extorting protection money from local individuals and companies and mounting small sniper attacks on government supporters' outposts. Some of the units were reportedly trying to combine forces and reorganize under a new name. (Bangkok, *Matichon*, 21 March; *FBIS*, 24 March.)

Although the number of communist guerrillas on the Thai-Malaysia border remained fairly static, Malaysian authorities said there were fewer than 200 left in peninsular Malaysia (*Bernama*, 22 September; *FBIS*, 23 September). In June, Sarawak's First Division was declared free of any communist threat following the capture of sixteen communists by Indonesian authorities the previous month and the surrender of three others shortly thereafter. There were then only 46 known communist terrorists operating in the Sibu area, compared with the 500 operating in Sarawak at the height of their struggle. Officials expressed the hope that the just treatment accorded former communists who returned to society would induce the remaining terrorists to give up their struggle. (*Bernama*, 1 June; *FBIS*, 4 June.)

Despite the dwindling number of communists within Malaysian borders, the authorities continued to warn of the danger they could still pose to national security. The deputy home affairs minister warned of a new breed of "modern communists" who had infiltrated the community in villages and towns. He said the government was checking to see whether these new communists had infiltrated societies and other organizations, especially those with foreign links. The communists, he said, might also have links with Zionists (Kuala Lumpur, *New Straits Times*, 20 October; *FBIS*, 23 October). The reference to Zionist influence came at a time when the Malaysian government was protesting against the visit of the president of Israel to Singapore. The deputy home minister also charged that Indonesia's communist party was assisting the CPM. He spoke of the pro-Russian communist movement operating within the country that was assisted by seventeen former leaders of the Indonesian communist party who had fled to Beijing after their abortive coup in 1965 and had since settled down in Europe (*Bernama*, 2 November; *FBIS*, 4 November.)

**International Activities and Views.** In 1986, as in previous years, the CPM did not figure in international communist gatherings. The MPC in its brief existence does not appear to have developed links with either Moscow or Beijing. Neither party in its major statements for domestic consumption made reference to the USSR, and China was only cited in passing by the CPM as an example of socialist economic success.

During the year, both the Malaysian and Singaporean governments increased their largely economic ties with Warsaw Pact countries and China. A high-level Soviet delegation visiting Southeast Asia cautioned the region's noncommunist countries against keeping Moscow at arm's length. "The Soviet Union is not only a European country but also an Asian country," the team's leader said. He accused the United States and Japan of trying to form a military bloc in Southeast Asia, but said that China was not considered a threat in this regard. "As far as we are concerned, China is not interested in closed groups." (Hong Kong, AFP, 2 June; *FBIS*, 6 June.)

A senior Singapore diplomat visited the Soviet Union in October, the first high-ranking Singapore official to do so since Premier Lee Kuan Yew's planned visit in 1980 was canceled. The purpose of the talks was apparently to improve economic relations with Moscow, which had taken a downturn in the past year with Singapore losing place to Malaysia and Indonesia in trade with bloc countries (Hong Kong, AFP, 8 October; *FBIS*, 10 October).

Relations with China appeared to ease somewhat in response to China's assurance to leaders of the Association of Southeast Asian Nations (ASEAN) that it would support a neutral government in Kampuchea. Malaysian officials spoke hopefully of China's identity of interests with the Third World during the Chinese vice-premier's visit to Kuala

Lumpur. (*Bernama*, 15 October; International Service, 15 October; *FBIS*, 16 October.)

In November, the Malaysian government further relaxed its restrictions on Malaysian businessmen wishing to visit China for trade and economic purposes. The move was one of several taken to step up bilateral trade with China following Prime Minister Mahathir's visit there in 1985. (*Bernama*, 20 November; *FBIS*, 21 November.)

Jeanne S. Mintz
*Washington, D.C.*

# Mongolia

**Population.** 1,942,000
**Party.** Mongolian People's Revolutionary Party (MPRP)
**Founded.** 1921
**Membership.** 88,150 (*Novosti Mongolii*, 29 May; *FBIS Supplement*, 11 July); 30.3 percent women, 69.7 percent men; 33.2 percent workers, 16.8 percent Agricultural Association members, 50 percent intellectuals
**General Secretary.** Jambyn Batmonh (60)
**Politburo.** 7 members: Jambyn Batmonh (chairman, Presidium of People's Great Hural), Dumaagiyn Sodnom (premier), Bat-Ochirym Altangerel, Bujyn Dejid, Demchigiyn Molomjamts, Tserendashiyn Namsray, Tumenbararyn Ragchaa; 3 candidate members: Nayamin Jagbaral, Sonomyn Lubsangombo, Bandzaragchiyn Lhamjab
**Secretariat.** 6 members: Jambyn Batmonh, Tserenpilyn Balhaajab, Paavangiyn Damdin, Bujyn Dejid, Demchigiyn Molomjamts, Tserendashiyn Namsray
**Central Committee.** 85 full members; 65 candidate members
**Status.** Ruling party
**Last Congress.** Nineteenth, 28–31 May, in Ulaanbaatar
**Last Election.** 22 June; of 370 seats in People's Great Hural, 346 went to members or candidate members of the MPRP
**Auxiliary Organizations.** Mongolian Revolutionary Youth League (over 200,000 members), Ts. Narangerel, first secretary; Central Council of Mongolian Trade Unions, B. Lubsantseren, chairman; Committee of Mongolian Women, L. Pagmadulam, chairman
**Publications.** *Unen* (Truth), MPRP daily organ, published Tuesday–Sunday; MONTSAME is the official news agency.

**Leadership and Party Organization.** The Nineteenth MPRP Congress, held in May, consolidated the changes made since Jambyn Batmonh replaced Tsedenbal in August 1984. Just before the congress, on 21 May, the Central Committee replaced party secretary M. Dash with Bujyn Dejid, former head of the party's Control Commission, and made Bandzaragchiyn Lhamjab a candidate member of the Politburo and new head of the Control Commission. Politburo member and party secretary D. Gombojob, who retired in December, was not replaced on the Politburo. D. Yondonsuren was elected chairman of the MPRP Central Committee Auditing Commission. (MONTSAME, 31 May; *FBIS Supplement*, 18 July.)

There were also few changes in the state organs.

In October, the People's Great Hural abolished the Ministry of Irrigation and released its head, D. Janjaadorj, and replaced the minister of agriculture, S. Sodnomdorj, with S. Gungaadorj (MONTSAME, 22 October; *FBIS*, 27 October). The new Hural was elected in June, and nearly 70 percent of its members were elected deputies for the first time. The leadership of the Hural and the Council of Ministers remained essentially as before, although Politburo member Tumenbararyn Ragchaa was appointed first deputy chairman of the council (MONTSAME, 26 June, 2 July; *FBIS*, 27 June, 3 July).

**Domestic Affairs.** Besides holding the party congress, Mongolia also began its Eighth Five-Year Plan in 1986. Mongolia's leaders generally claimed success for past performance, but there was considerable criticism of agricultural performance. A review of the economic goals set forth in the most recent plan indicates that those goals have been substantially reduced when compared with the past (*FEER*, 29 May). Mongolia remains heavily dependent on agriculture, which accounts for about one-fourth of national income but over 60 percent of the value of exports. Mongolia imports twice as much as it exports, and the country has just concluded a new trade agreement with the USSR that will increase trade by 25 percent over the next few years; consequently, it is important that agriculture perform well. (MONTSAME, 27 August; *FBIS*, 3 September.)

Concerns about improvements in economic performance and the influence of Mikhail Gorbachev's reform agenda at the Twenty-seventh Congress of the Communist Party of the Soviet Union (CPSU) were noticeable in statements made by Batmonh and other leaders. At the MPRP congress, Batmonh strongly attacked bureaucratism and sloth, and he demanded that party members begin to think and work in new ways (MONTSAME, 31 May; *FBIS Supplement*, 18 July).

At year's end, a session of the People's Great Hural issued documents claiming that the "material and spiritual" needs of the people were being met. Personal cash income in 1986 was said to have risen by 5 percent over 1985 and would grow another 5 percent during 1987. The per capita consumption of food was also said to be increasing, with improved supplies of meat, eggs, and dairy products. Health, housing, and education were also improving. (MONTSAME, 9 December; *FBIS*, 11 December.)

**Auxiliary Organizations.** In March, the Committee of Mongolian Women sponsored a ceremony honoring the 75th anniversary of International Women's Day. Chairman Pagmadulam hailed Gorbachev's voluntary ban on nuclear testing and praised the contribution of Mongolian women to building socialism. According to Pagmadulam, 40 percent of the "shock workers" in the current five-year plan are women. (MONTSAME, 7 March; *FBIS*, 12 March.)

Also in March, Ulaanbaatar hosted the first meeting of Asian Socialist Parliamentarians, which included representatives from North Korea, Laos, Cambodia, Vietnam, and the USSR. As could be predicted, the representatives praised Soviet initiatives and condemned the United States for stirring up tension and trouble in the region. The Soviet delegate, for example, called for putting an end to "imperialist intrigues aimed at alienating Asian states and peoples" (MONTSAME, 27 March; *FBIS*, 28 March).

In spite of its strong denunciations of U.S. policies, Mongolia indicated that it wished to normalize relations with the United States, and talks between U.S. and Mongolian officials were held at the United Nations. Some observers believe that this is the best prospect for normalizing ties between those two countries since the establishment of the Mongolian People's Republic in 1924 (*CSM*, 21 October).

At Soviet behest, Mongolia took steps to improve relations with China. Soviet foreign minister Eduard Shevardnadze visited Ulaanbaatar in January and clearly indicated that moves would be taken to improve relations with China (MONTSAME, 24 January; *FBIS*, 30 January). In April, Mongolia concluded a new long-term trade agreement with China. Just two weeks after Gorbachev's Vladivostok speech heralding a new Soviet approach to Asia, Chinese deputy foreign affairs minister Liu Shuqing traveled to Ulaanbaatar to conclude a consular convention (AFP, 8 August; *FBIS*, 8 August). Liu was the highest ranking Chinese visitor to Mongolia since 1960. A Chinese friendship delegation visited Mongolia in September; new agreements were reached over border trade, rail service, and a resumption of air service; and, for the first time in 28 years, Mongolian acrobats performed in China.

**International Views and Affairs.** Mongolia continued to adhere closely to Soviet policy and centered its own policies around Soviet client states. Polish leader Jaruzelski visited Ulaanbaatar in September, and East German leader Honecker visited a month later. In addition to visiting the USSR on several occasions, Batmonh made official visits to Czechoslovakia and North Korea. Mongolia further cemented its ties with communist regimes in Asia and Eastern Europe with several new agreements in trade and cultural affairs. The first official visit made by an Italian government representative to Mongolia occurred in May, when Foreign Ministry undersecretary Bruno Corti met with Mongolian officials to improve economic and cultural ties (ANSA, 20 May; *FBIS*, 21 May). Mongolia also normalized relations with the Ivory Coast.

Close adherence to Soviet positions was indicated by Mongolia's harsh propaganda line towards the United States. Mongolia denounced the Strate-

gic Defense Initiative and accused the United States of trying to make propaganda out of the Chernobyl nuclear accident. The government officially denounced the U.S. bombing of Libya and even went so far as to claim that the space shuttle Challenger disaster resulted from U.S. efforts to achieve space and military supremacy over socialist countries (MONTSAME, 3 February; *FBIS*, 5 February). Mongolia strongly supported various Soviet initiatives, such as the nuclear-test moratorium, and consistently voted with the USSR in the United Nations.

William R. Heaton
*Dumfries, Virginia*

# Nepal

**Population.** 17,422,000

**Parties.** Nepal Communist Party (NCP), with two neutralist factions; Nepal Communist Party (Marxist-Leninist) (NCP-ML), with four pro-Beijing factions; Nepal Communist Party/pro-Moscow (NCP/M), with four pro-Moscow factions; Janabadi Morcha (Democratic Front)

**Founded.** NCP: 1949; NCP-ML: 1978; Janabadi Morcha: founded in 1980 as radical democratic organization but turned Che Guevarist in 1985

**Membership.** 5,000 (estimated), with pro-Chinese and neutralist factions accounting for almost 75 percent of members.

**Leadership.** NCP/neutralist factions—Man Mohan Adhikary, Mrs. Sahana Pradhan (Pushpa Lal's widow); NCP-ML/pro-Beijing factions—Radha Krishna Mainali and Mohan Chandra Adhikary, Fourth Congress: Mohan Bikram Gharti, Mashal: Nirmal Lama, Nepal Workers' and Peasants' Organization: Narayan Man Bijukchhe 'Rohit'; NCP/M (pro-Moscow factions)—Rayamajhi faction: Dr. Keshar Jung Rayamajhi, Manandhar faction: Bishnu Bahadur Manandhar, Varma faction: Krishna Raj Varma, Tulsi Lal faction: Tulsi Lal Amatya, Janabadi Morcha/Che Guevarist: Ram Raja Prasad Singh

**Politburo.** No data

**Secretariat.** No data

**Central Committee.** 35 members in NCP/M (Rayamajhi faction); no data on other factions

**Status.** Proscribed

**Last Congress.** 1961 (last pre-split congress)

**Last Election.** 1959, 7.5 percent, 4 of 109 seats

**Auxiliary Organizations.** Neutralist: Nepal Progressive Student Union; pro-Beijing: All-Nepal National Free Student Union, All-Nepal National Teachers' Organization; Anti-imperialist Front; pro-Moscow: Nepal National Student Federation, Nepal National Youth Federation. In addition to these organizations, pro-Beijing and neutralist communists have shadow organizations within the government-sponsored labor and peasant organizations.

**Publications.** Neutralist: *Naya Janabad* (New democracy) and *Nepal Patra*; NCP-ML: *Barga Sangharsha* (Class struggle) and *Mukti-Morcha* (Liberation front); pro-Beijing: *Mashal* (Torch); NCP/M: *Samikshya Weekly* (reflects views of all pro-Soviet factions)

The political situation in Nepal in the first half of 1986 was marked by election campaigns for the Rastriya Panchayat (National Assembly). In late January, the election commission announced that national elections would be held in May to choose 112 members for that assembly (*FBIS*, 30 January). The outlawed democratic socialist party, Nepali Congress, decided to boycott the elections (*FEER*, 20 February); the communists, however, were divided on the issue. All pro-Moscow groups and a Marxist-Leninist faction of the pro-Beijing group decided to participate, whereas all other pro-Beijing factions and neutralists chose to boycott (*FBIS*, 11 March). Meanwhile, the government headed by Prime Minister Lokendra Bahadur Chand resigned to facilitate "fair and impartial" elections, and King Birendra formed a ten-member interim government, led by former prime minister Nagendra Prasad Rizal (ibid., 21 March).

Despite the announced boycott, several communist cadres of junior ranks contested the election, defying party directives and warnings (*FEER*, 8 May). All opposition candidates openly charged the government candidates with corruption and inefficiency and described the Panchayat system as an undemocratic system that has not served the people. The Panchayat candidates, however, asked the people to vote for them to protect national integrity and serve the country and the king (ibid.). Participating communist candidates vigorously attacked the Panchayat system as "fascist" and called for change through "people's power." Some opposition candidates were arrested by the government for their public criticism of the system (*FBIS*, 6 May).

By October, all groups had started to focus their attention on the upcoming April 1987 Panchayat elections for local and district bodies. Nepali Congress leadership continued to be divided over the question of participation; party secretary Girija P. Koirala desired participation, senior leader Ganesh Man Singh advocated a boycott, and Krishna Prasad Bhatterai was neutral on the issue. Singh said that Nepali Congress would start a mass movement against the Panchayat system rather than participate in its elections (ibid., 3 November). The Marxist-Leninist and pro-Moscow factions of the NCP, however, began active preparations to contest elections for local bodies (*FEER*, 2 October). Faced with Marxist pressure, the Panchayat government permitted Nepali Congress to hold its regional meetings and rallies while cracking down on the leftist activities.

**Leadership and Organization.** The history of the NCP is one of factionalism. Despite the organizational weakness of the NCP, factional groups remain capable of attracting increasing numbers of Nepalese to their ranks, thus making it possible to portray themselves as a powerful alternative to the present order if they could form a single unified party. In 1986, however, party unification remained unimpressive.

In 1985, there had been a split in the pro-Moscow group led by Bishnu Bahadur Manandhar and Krishna Raj Varma; Varma left the group holding Manandhar responsible for the split in the anti-imperialist movement in Nepal. In April 1984, Keshar Jung Rayamajhi's group had convened its sixth conference in Patan, which was attended by 167 delegates from 57 districts of Nepal. The conference re-elected Rayamajhi as president of the NCP/M for the fifth term and also formed a 75-member national assembly and a 35-member central committee. Another pro-Soviet group was led by Tulsi Lal Amatya, a former communist member of the 1959–1960 parliament; that group occasionally rears its head by issuing statements against the government.

Since 1984, the pro-Beijing Man Mohan Adhikary faction has changed its political and ideological line; it decided to remain neutral in the ideological conflict between the Chinese and the Soviet communist parties. The Adhikary group's party platform also dropped the term "Mao Zedong thought." Similarly, a former Maoist group led by the late Pushpa Lal (now led by his widow, Sahana Pradhan), has avoided embracing either Beijing or Moscow. That faction has continued to capitalize on its close relations with the Communist Party of India-Marxist (CPM) in order to extend its contact with both the Chinese and the Soviet parties, but the result has been negligible.

The Fourth Congress group, formerly led by Mohan Bikram Gharti, was divided into the Nirmal Lama and Gharti factions in 1984. The split was apparently caused by Gharti's conclusion that China had abandoned fundamental principles of communism in the post-Mao era and that true communism did not exist anywhere in the world. Gharti and his group have reportedly put their faith in the thought and activities of China's disgraced "Gang of Four." Lama's group, known as the Mashal faction, decided to continue the struggle against the anti-China line. Thus, the Fourth Congress, which was formerly recognized as a pro-Chinese extremist group, is divided into Maoists (led by Gharti) and Dengists (led by Lama).

Another pro-Beijing group, led by Narayan Man Bijukchhe 'Rohit,' has functioned under the name Nepal Workers' and Peasants' Organization, and it has been influential in the Bhaktapur district and surrounding areas. The Rohit faction differs with other Maoists in that it believes in both covert and overt strategy to achieve its objectives, and it has participated in the Panchayat elections. One of the Rastriya Panchayat members representing the Bhaktapur district, eight miles east of Kathmandu, is alleged to be sponsored by Rohit.

The NCP-ML, an offspring of the Indian Naxalite movement, has been particularly active in eastern Nepal since the early 1970s, when it launched a "class annihilation" movement against the so-called exploiting class. The ideological line of this group is unclear; it hovers between Maoism, Lin Biaoism, and the ideas of the Gang of Four. The leadership is considered to be immature by other communist factions. Nevertheless, the group enjoys a significant amount of influence among the radical university students.

The Janabadi Morcha, which made headlines in the summer of 1985 by exploding bombs in different parts of the country, is led by a lawyer and former national legislator, Ram Raja Prasad Singh. The group is violence prone, extremely anti-monarchist, and puts its faith in Che Guevarist-type revolution. The rank and file in the Janabadi Morcha come from Nepal's lowlands, and its headquarters are in an undisclosed location in India.

**Domestic Party Affairs.** The main issue of division in the communist parties since the mid-1950s has been the problem of identifying the main enemy and creating a united front against that enemy. Sino-Soviet disputes appeared to be an issue only in the mid-1960s, especially after the beginning of the Cultural Revolution in China. The Maoists belonging to the Fourth Congress and the Mashal group regard the king and Nepali Congress as enemies of equal proportions, and hence they reject the idea of any form of united front with Nepali Congress. The NCP-ML had regarded the monarchy as enemy number one but also ruled out the possibility of a united front with Nepali Congress; that group, according to the NCP-ML, was a puppet of both the international comprador capitalism and the reactionary Indian government. By 1986, however, the NCP-ML had changed its line and participated in the political process it had previously condemned. Among the neutralist factions, Adhikary's activities seem to be guided more by the ideology of radical socialism than by Marxism-Leninism. His program envisages the replacement of the Panchayat system by a democratic system rather than the overthrow of the monarchy. Another neutralist faction, the Pradhan group, advocates the overthrow of the monarchy by a broad-based, united front of all progressive and democratic elements, including Nepali Congress. The pro-Soviets, in contrast, see different roads to democracy and hence advocate both covert and overt strategies.

The unity talks between these factions continued throughout 1986. The Adhikary and Pradhan groups reportedly decided to unite, although they could not reach a decision on future programs or on the composition of the united central committee (*Nepal Press Digest* [*NPD*], 6 October). The pro-Moscow Tulsi Lal and Varma factions were also reported to have decided to merge. In a joint statement, they announced the formation of a fourteen-member coordination committee to implement the decision, and they called for unity of all leftist groups (ibid., 10 November).

The leaders of the four factions of the NCP/M decided to contest national elections for the Rastriya Panchayat and fielded 36 candidates. Varma described the general election as a historic event that he believed "would provide an opportunity for all people to exercise their democratic right to elect representatives to the national legislature through universal franchise (*FBIS*, 11 March). The pro-Beijing, Rohit and Mashal factions also decided to participate in the elections, while the two neutralist factions and the Fourth Congress decided to boycott them (ibid.).

In the general elections, communist candidates, mostly belonging to the NCP-ML factions, won approximately sixteen out of 112 seats. Prominent among them were Padma Ratna Tuladhar, Bhim Prasad Shreshta, Jagrit Prasad Bhetuwal, Dron Prasad Acharya, and Som Nath Pyasi. These members have openly and repeatedly demanded the re-introduction of the multiparty political system. Emboldened by their electoral success in May, the NCP-ML has been actively preparing to contest elections for local bodies in April 1987 (*FEER*, 2 October). The group has come to believe in utilizing Panchayat elections to help the cause of people's politics and promote public consciousness. The NCP/M groups have also decided to participate in the upcoming elections.

The merged neutralist faction, however, did not participate in the May elections and has declared a boycott of those in 1987. The group reportedly expelled some of its workers who had participated in the national elections either directly or indirectly (*NPD*, 29 September). In late August, the group held a Zonal Conference, somewhere in the Kathmandu valley, which was attended by about 150 peasant representatives from the Kathmandu, Lalitpur, Bhaktapur, Kabhre, Sindhupalchok, and Dhading districts. At the conference, Adhikary called for unity between Nepali Congress and leftists to attain a multiparty system in the country; he described the multiparty system as a "stepping stone for communism" (ibid., 8 September).

**Auxiliary and Front Organizations.** The central committee of the All-Nepal National Free Student Union demanded an immediate end to the nationwide wave of arrests and repression and the release of all arrested students and political workers (ibid.). The committee also delivered a protest note to the British embassy against the dismissal of 111 Gurkhas who had served in the British army. The note declared that such an action had hurt the dignity of Nepal and the Nepali people and that it justified the demand for the abrogation of the Nepal-British agreement on Gurkha recruitment (ibid., 15 September).

The seventh national preparatory conference of the Nepal National Student Federation issued a statement appealing to the student community to struggle for cheaper education and for democracy

(ibid., 3 November). The statement charged that, at the suggestion of American imperialists, the Nepali government had turned education into an instrument of private profit. The statement, finally, expressed solidarity with all peace-loving and anti-imperialist countries, including the Soviet Union, and with all liberation movements (ibid.).

**International Views, Positions, and Activities.** No change was recorded in international views and positions of the divided factions of the NCP. Differences of opinion, however, surfaced over the issue of supporting or opposing the Gurkhaland agitation in northern West Bengal of India for a separate homeland for the people of Nepali origin. The Gharti group and the Democratic National Unity Forum (an auxiliary of Mashal) issued statements supporting the Gurkhaland movement (ibid., 8 September). Some groups, however, did not support the agitation. Nilamber Acharya, a member of the Manandhar faction's politburo, stated that his group could not support the Gurkhaland movement because of its separatist character.

Indian president Giani Zail Singh made a five-day state visit to Nepal (*NPD*, 28 July). Although the visit was described as successful and fruitful by official media, Nepali officials were disappointed that they could not secure India's support for King Birendra's proposal to declare Nepal a "zone of peace." Nepal's relations with China remained cordial, with several exchanges of high-level official visits. Newly elected Nepali prime minister Marich Man Singh Shrestha, while opening a Chinese artistic handicraft exhibition in Kathmandu, said "Nepal should strive hard to strengthen the Nepal-China relations in various aspects and make them more meaningful and productive" (*FBIS*, 23 September).

**Notable Figures and Newsmakers.** M. M. Adhikary, who is in his late-60s, continued to be a prime newsmaker because of his charismatic personality. It should be noted, however, that Adhikary is more popular among noncommunists, since his speeches are balanced and lack orthodox Marxist-Leninist jargon.

Chitra K. Tiwari
*Arlington, Virginia*

# New Zealand

**Population.** 3,266,200 (New Zealand Department of Statistics, *Information Release*, 30 September)
**Parties.** Communist Party of New Zealand (CPNZ); Socialist Unity Party (SUP); Socialist Action League (SAL); Workers' Communist League (WCL)
**Founded.** CPNZ: 1921; SUP: 1966; SAL: 1969; WCL: 1980
**Membership.** CPNZ: 50; SUP: 300; SAL: 100; WCL: 50 (all estimated)
**Leadership.** CPNZ: Richard C. Wolfe; SUP: George Jackson (national president since 1 May, previously national secretary); SAL: Russell Johnson (national secretary); WCL: Graeme Clark
**Status.** All legal
**Last Congress.** CPNZ: Twenty-third, 1984; SUP: Seventh, 26–27 October 1985; SAL: Eleventh, 26–31 December 1986; WCL: Third, June 1986
**Last Election.** 14 July 1984 (parliamentary), no representatives elected; 11 October 1986 (local government), no representatives elected
**Auxiliary Organizations.** SUP: Youth in Unity (inaugural meeting 23 August 1986), Peace Council New Zealand, New Zealand–USSR Society; SAL: Young Socialists, Socialist Forum, Latin America Committee, Cuba Friendship Society, Committee for a Workers' Front, Nicaragua Must Survive Committee
**Publications.** CPNZ: *People's Voice* (weekly); SUP: *NZ Tribune* (bimonthly), *Socialist Politics* (every two months); SAL: *Socialist Action* (bimonthly), *Socialist Action Review* (periodically); WCL: *Unity* (monthly)

New Zealand's four main communist parties have only some 500 members and exert little direct political or economic influence. However, the SUP has influenced the trade union movement, and communist influence in that area may currently be greater than at any previous time in New Zealand's industrial history. The SUP, SAL, and WCL also have influence disproportionate to their small memberships in the much broader-based radical movements opposed to nuclear testing, ANZUS, U.S. involvement in Nicaragua's civil war, sexism, and racism. All have welcomed and supported the New Zealand Labour government's ban on U.S. nuclear ship visits and its boycott of South Africa.

**The CPNZ.** After 40 years of faithfully following the lead of the Communist Party of the Soviet Union (CPSU), the CPNZ broke with Moscow in the early 1960s and supported the Chinese in the Sino-Soviet dispute. Following China's détente with the West, the CPNZ aligned itself with the Albanian Party of Labor, which the CPNZ regards as "leading the only socialist country in the world" (*People's Voice*, 21 July). The factional infighting and splits that accompanied each realignment reduced the CPNZ to an aging handful of members who exert no discernible influence even on the extreme left of New Zealand politics. The party still admires Stalin. It raises, by donations, about $6,000 annually and publishes from its Auckland headquarters a small weekly newspaper, *People's Voice*. The introduction to the CPNZ's constitution, adopted by the Twenty-third National Conference in 1984, claims that "the CPNZ has maintained a clear and unequivocal stand in opposition to the . . . Khrushchevite revisionists . . . [and] Chinese revisionism." The party sees itself as a revolutionary vanguard that rejects as impossible the peaceful transition from capitalism to socialism by gradual parliamentary means. (Ibid.)

**The SUP.** The SUP was formed at a conference in Auckland on 1–2 October 1966 by a number of former CPNZ members who opposed that group's pro-Chinese direction. Since then, the SUP has identified totally with the Soviet Union and in return has been supported by the CPSU. The SUP's version of its history is found in *Communism in New Zealand, an Illustrated History*, a 40-page booklet published in 1986 to mark the 65th anniversary of the founding of the CPNZ and the 20th anniversary of the SUP's establishment. Celebrations to mark the latter anniversary were held in Auckland, Wellington, Christchurch, and Dunedin and were addressed by SUP president George Jackson and two visitors from the Soviet Union, the historians Eugene Dobrotin and Valeri Kudinov. Another visitor was Victor Perlo, a member of the Central Committee of the Communist Party of the United States (CPUSA).

In 1986, a number of prominent SUP members visited the Soviet Union. In March, for example, G. H. "Bill" Andersen, at that time party president, and Jackson attended the Twenty-seventh Congress of the CPSU in Moscow. In September, an SUP delegation led by Bruce Skilton, a Central Executive member, and John Mitchell, one-time chairman of the Auckland region of the SUP and former editor of the *NZ Tribune*, returned from the USSR.

The party's national officers changed as of 1 May. Jackson replaced Andersen as SUP president. Andersen, who is president of the Auckland Trades' Council and secretary of the Northern Drivers' Union, resigned from the executive of New Zealand's Federation of Labour (FOL) to make time to become the SUP national secretary. However, the Central Committee announced in July that it had reversed the decision to appoint Andersen secretary because of the necessity of retaining him as a full-time trade union leader. No alternative appointment was made, and throughout the latter part of 1986, the party's assistant general secretary, Marilyn Tucker, was acting secretary.

Ken Douglas, secretary-treasurer of the FOL and arguably the most capable and influential trade union leader in New Zealand, represented the SUP at an international working-class conference in Moscow during the year. He was elected national chairman of the SUP, and Ella Ayo is vice-chair. The other Central Committee members in 1986 were Richie Gillespie (Wellington regional secre-

tary), Doug McCallum (chairman and organizer of the Auckland region), Bernie O'Brien, Jack Marston, Frank McNulty, Jackson Smith, and Skilton. There are four candidate members: Dave Arthur, Joe Tonner, Simon Wallace, and Alan Ware. On 23 August, a new SUP youth group, Youth in Unity, was formed, with an executive of three: Wayne Ruscoe, Sandy Rickard, and Conal Tuohy.

Several SUP candidates stood for election in the New Zealand local government elections in October. The inability of the SUP to attract electoral support was indicated by the votes received for its most successful candidate, Steve Bradley, who stood in the central city ward of Auckland. Bradley, who has a master's degree in politics and is education officer for the Auckland Trades' Council, polled a mere 281 votes of the 6,483 total votes cast for the three candidates.

The SUP's Fighting Fund Appeal for 1985 exceeded its target of NZ$45,000 by NZ$106. The same target in 1986 appeared to be more difficult to achieve and by early November stood at only NZ$35,041.

In the propaganda areas of activity, the SUP publishes fortnightly a twelve-page newspaper, the *NZ Tribune*, and every two months a theoretical journal, *Socialist Politics*. The party held a summer school over four days in January and was active in organizing a symposium in October on the theme "Co-Existence or Non-Existence," which was officially sponsored by the New Zealand–USSR Society. The symposium was addressed by Victor Linnyk (*Pravda*), Dmitri Urnov (USSR Academy of Sciences), Albert Tunis (Soviet Trade Mission), Sonya Davies (prominent trade unionist and chair of the Aotearoa Committee for the U.N. International Year of Peace), Fran Wilde (Labour member of Parliament), Dr. Ian Prior (national secretary of the International Physicians for the Prevention of Nuclear War), and Alistair Macfarlane (New Zealand Dairy Board). It is intended that the symposium will become an annual fixture and that Moscow might host a future event.

The SUP's unpublished 113-page draft resolution, which was presented to its seventh triennial national conference held in Auckland on 26–27 October 1985, and the subsequently published party program detailed the party's activities over the previous three years. The documents analyzed the political, economic, and strategic situation and suggested a future plan of action in what the party sees as an increasingly destabilized New Zealand economy and society and an equally destabilized Southwest Pacific. Party leaders discussed such matters as SUP activities among trade unionists, the unemployed, women, youth, Maoris, and Pacific Islanders—especially the Kanaks—whose countries must be freed from "colonial bondage"; they also examined ways by which the "class collaborationists" in the Labour government might be prevented from harming the living standards of wage-earners. The SUP documents devoted a great deal of attention to ways in which the New Zealand peace movement could be used to enhance the image of the USSR, to stop the United States from creating a "second front" against the Soviet Union in the Pacific, and to shift New Zealand into the Non-aligned Movement. Considerable success was claimed already in working toward these objectives, since the party had conducted its so-called cadre schools in 1984 and 1985 on the theme of "Building the United Front in Today's Conditions."

The major united front that had been identified and discussed in some detail was the peace movement, which the SUP claimed to have influenced in such a way as to have effected "significant change in the country's foreign policy" over recent years. The peace movement was used especially to facilitate "extensive education on the Soviet Union's position, on its tremendous consistency in fighting for peace since it was a fledgling state in 1917." In 1986, which was proclaimed the International Year of Peace, there would be ample opportunity for "a massive worldwide campaign" in support of Soviet proposals at the Geneva arms control negotiations, and "all branches [of the SUP] should be active in the local Peace groups or helping to establish them where they don't exist." Hiroshima Day (6 August) and World Peace Day (1 September) would require special efforts.

Indeed, throughout 1986 the SUP did concentrate on consolidating its influence in the trade union movement and on encouraging broad-based support for the New Zealand Labour government's antinuclear foreign policy and the Soviet Union's disarmament proposals.

**The SAL.** The SAL grew out of the student protests against the Vietnam War, is influenced by the theories of Leon Trotsky, and belongs to the Fourth International. Although the party has a policy of infiltrating and influencing the union movement—particularly the engineers, food and chemical workers, and meatworkers—its major efforts go into radicalizing young students and workers around such issues as Nicaragua, South Africa,

Maori grievances, women's liberation, nuclear disarmament, and support for the Palestine Liberation Organization. The SAL has links with Cuba and thinks highly of Fidel Castro. It operates through a number of popular front organizations and was successful, during 1986, in persuading several Labour Party members of Parliament to participate in public forums. A major aim, according to its most influential leader, Russell Johnson, is for the SAL as "the Marxist revolutionary vanguard" to wage a "massive class fight to transform the Labour Party" into "part of the broader working-class movement" through the antiapartheid, antiwar, and union movements (*Socialist Action*, 9 May).

The SAL has a twelve-person National Committee elected each December at its national conference. Among the most prominent of the leaders, other than Johnson, are Neil Jarden (probably second to Johnson in influence), Eileen Morgan (director of SAL trade union work), Mike Tucker (editor of *Socialist Action*), and Etuale Sua-Filo (national coordinator of the Young Socialists). In mid-1986, the National Committee admitted that recruitment had been small over the previous four years and that total membership had declined slightly (*Socialist Action*, 11 July). As a result, the Hastings branch was closed and the membership consolidated into three branches: Auckland, Wellington, and Christchurch. *Socialist Action*, which has been published for the past eighteen years, continued as a fortnightly paper, but was reduced from twelve pages to eight. It remains the most attractively presented and best written of the various communist newspapers published in New Zealand and reflects the great importance placed by the SAL on education and propaganda. The paper relies on sales and a NZ$40,000 fund collected annually (by 14 August only $24,907 had been received).

The Young Socialists held their tenth national conference in Christchurch on 31 May–2 June. It was attended by representatives of the Japanese Communist Youth (Miyasita Tomoyuki), the U.S. Young Socialist Alliance (Lisa Ahlberg), and the Australian Socialist League (Megan Martin).

**The WCL.** Formed in 1980 by a merger of two pro-Chinese communist groups that had split from the CPNZ, the WCL is located primarily in Wellington. It is the most secretive of New Zealand's Marxist-Leninist parties and does not reveal its leaders' names, although it is known that the leadership consists of an equal number of men and women. The WCL's most influential member,

Graeme Clark, visited China and the Philippines in April and May. The party has some influence in the Wellington Trades' Council, in the Wellington Unemployed Workers' Union, and among some young university graduates; its objective is "the building of a strategic alliance between the working class, the struggle for women's liberation, and the struggle for Maori self-determination" (*Unity*, 5 December 1985). It sees racism and sexism as distinct from the class structure and asserts that "the overthrow of capitalism . . . will not in itself bring about the liberation of women and Maori people" (ibid.). The WCL national conference in June agreed that "the central strategy of the WCL over the next two years [will] be to promote the conditions for, and the development of, political unity amongst communist and other revolutionary groups and individuals"

(ibid., 14 November). To that end, the party was involved in a number of forums throughout 1986 attended not only by WCL members but also by members of the SUP, SAL, and a recently formed Revolutionary Communist League located at Canterbury University in Christchurch. Formal talks of an exploratory nature were held, particularly between the WCL and the SAL. The objective was to create a socialist alliance or "ecumenical left" to reach into the Labour Party and thus, it was hoped, to influence government policy. In addition to its emphasis on class, racism, and sexism, the WCL is pro-Palestinian, pro-Sinn Fein, and pro-Nicaragua.

Barry Gustafson
*University of Auckland*

# Pakistan

**Population.** 101,855,000
**Party.** Communist Party of Pakistan
**Founded.** 1948
**Membership.** Under 200 (estimated)
**General Secretary.** Ali Nazish
**Status.** Illegal
**Last Congress.** First, 1976 (clandestine)
**Leading Bodies.** No information available
**Publications.** None

On 30 December 1985, President Zia-ul Haq told a joint sitting of the National Assembly and the Senate that martial law was being lifted on that day. Thus, emergency power was removed from the executive for the first time since 1965.

The opposition parties were therefore confronted with a new and unexpected political situation. The multiparty Movement for the Restoration of Democracy (MRD) maintained throughout 1986 that neither the president nor the members of the

legislatures elected in 1985 under martial law regulations had a right to exercise power, since they were not selected in accordance with the provisions of the 1973 constitution. However, there were minorities within the MRD and the Pakistan People's Party (PPP) that disagreed with this stand. Two groups broke away from the MRD and PPP, respectively, and registered as new political parties.

The MRD's call for new elections took shape with the 10 April return to Pakistan of Benazir

Bhutto, head of the PPP, from exile in Europe. She was greeted in Lahore by crowds estimated by the press as between five hundred thousand and one million people (*FEER*, 24 April). In her travel around the country in the following month, an estimated ten million people turned out for her rallies (ibid., 5 May). Bhutto's central themes were the demand for new elections and the resignation of President Zia. As early as 31 December 1985, one day after martial law was lifted, she had called the decision an "act of camouflage" to dupe the West (*NYT*, 1 January). However, her campaign assumed a moderate tone toward the United States and she successfully kept the crowds peaceful in most places.

Indeed, to the surprise of many of her followers, Bhutto adopted a relatively moderate approach toward the new political order put together in 1985. Although she suggested that Zia follow the examples of Jean-Claude Duvalier and Ferdinand Marcos and flee, she also offered to cooperate with Prime Minister Mohammed Khan Junejo to hold new elections (*LAT*, 12 April). Her initial conciliatory attitude toward Junejo was perhaps a tactic to drive a wedge between him and Zia. Her moderate approach was questioned by many within the PPP as well as other constituents of the MRD. In addition, some MRD elements grumbled that her rallies were used by the PPP to advance its interests alone. Her attitude toward Junejo hardened, however, after he traveled to the United States in June.

**Party Affairs.** The tiny CPP generally supported the domestic activities of the MRD and adhered faithfully to the foreign policy stands of the USSR. At the Twenty-seventh Congress of the Communist Party of the Soviet Union (CPSU), a CPP delegate blasted Zia's close ties with the United States and adhered to the Soviet position on Afghanistan (*Pravda*, 5 March). On the eve of the lifting of martial law, the CPP's Central Committee had called for the "broadest possible single front," comprising the MRD and other parties, to work for the "restoration of democracy." It also called for the "intensification of the struggle" of the working class and the continued independence of the CPP. (*WMR*, December 1985.) The CPP, which is not a constituent of the MRD, exercises negligible influence on its own, but Marxists outside the CPP played some role among the PPP's militant left (not its dominant element) and among three leftist constituents of the MRD: the Qaumi Mahaz Azadi, the Pakistan Socialist Party, and the Pakistan Progressive Party.

Perhaps the most important initiative taken by the Pakistan left during 1986 was the amalgamation in July of four parties—the Mazdoor Kisan Party (MKP), the National Democratic Party (NDP), the faction of the Pakistan National Party (PNP) led by Latif Afridi, and the Sindhi Awami Tehrik (SAT)—to form the Awami National Party (ANP). The constituent parties all had their bases outside Punjab. Indeed, their leadership tended to emphasize minority rights more than class struggle. (*FEER*, 7 August.) The largely rural SAT, led by Rasool Bux Palejo, combines Sindhi nationalism with Marxism. The MKP and the NDP draw their support from the North-West Frontier Province, and the PNP from Baluchistan. Lacking strength in Punjab, the ANP cannot aspire to be a national party.

The ANP is led by Abdul Wali Khan from the former NDP and General Secretary Shaukat Ali from the MKP, which is the staunchly pro-Soviet party that pushed the notion of uniting. Both men participated in highly publicized visits to Eastern bloc countries during the year. Ali went to East Berlin in September to participate in the eleventh congress of the World Federation of Trade Unions as representative of the All-Pakistan Federation of Trade Unions. While there, Ali reportedly attacked those calling Abdul Wali Khan a "communist agent" simply because he wants a peaceful resolution of the Afghan situation (*Muslim*, 16 September).

On his part, Khan visited Moscow in late August as the guest of the Soviet Committee for Afro-Asian Solidarity, and he received high-level attention (*FBIS–South Asia*, 2 September). Moscow may have deliberately intended to give such attention to these two ANP leaders to bestow legitimacy on the new party. Earlier in the year, the Soviet leadership had met with Benazir Bhutto and PNP leader Ghaus Bux Bizenjo. This trail of visitors suggests that the USSR is not reluctant to have direct access to opposition politicians now that Pakistan has a more open political system. The ANP thus far has taken a pro-Soviet line on foreign policy issues; it criticizes the United States and Pakistan's cooperation with the United States, and it opposes the government's refusal to talk directly with Afghanistan in the Geneva proximity talks. Domestically, it supports greater autonomy for Pakistan's provinces and backs the MRD.

Nevertheless, the formation of the ANP aroused the ire of other leftist politicians. For example, Bizenjo argued that he would not participate in the new ANP because of ideological differences (*Muslim*, 2 August). He maintained that the ANP is an "opportunistic alliance" of self-serving politicians. He even accused its leaders of being involved in a conspiracy of "imperialism" because of the party's alleged promotion of a "Paktoon buffer" between Pakistan and Afghanistan. He argued that the United States wanted such a buffer because of problems in a democratic Pakistan. This outburst probably reflected Bizenjo's efforts to tar a competitive leftist party with the brush of "imperialism." He himself had been invited to attend the Soviet Union's Twelfth World Youth and Students' Festival in August as its guest of honor. This squabble among leftist politicians underscores the difficulty in getting the ANP and Pakistan's highly personalized leftist parties to establish a broad alliance, which has been the tactical goal of the CPP.

**Foreign Affairs.** Relations between Pakistan and the USSR remained cordial. Moscow funds several showcase industrial projects, such as the Karachi steel complex and the Multar thermal project. Relations were strained somewhat by the 16 September assassination of Fedor Gorenkov, the Soviet assistant defense attaché, but after a few formal broadsides from Moscow, the incident seems to have receded from memory. The USSR also publicly criticized Pakistan's nuclear program, the treatment of the non-Punjabi language groups, and the country's approach toward the Afghan civil war. An article in the 27 July issue of *Pravda* even implied that no settlement in Afghanistan would be likely so long as Zia remained in power. Gorbachev's 28 July Vladivostok speech did not include Pakistan as an Asian state to be included in his Asian security scheme.

The major divisive issue between the USSR and Pakistan remained the Afghan question. Pakistan insisted that Soviet troops pull out and thus permit the Afghans to form their own government. The USSR claimed that the civil war continues because of interference from Pakistan. Pakistan refused to negotiate directly with the Kabul regime at the periodic U.N.-sponsored proximity talks in Geneva. At those talks, the major unresolved issue was a timetable for Soviet troop withdrawal; Pakistan wanted a timetable of a few months, whereas the USSR proposed several years. During the year, Pakistan complained about increased incidents of air incursion and cross-border firing from Afghanistan. It was not impressed by Gorbachev's 28 July announcement that the USSR intended to withdraw six regiments from Afghanistan. Prime Minister Junejo, in a 22 July speech in New York before the Foreign Policy Association, argued that the Soviet presence in Afghanistan is a violation of international law. (*FBIS–South Asia*, 30 July.) At the United Nations, Pakistan again submitted the annual resolution calling for the withdrawal of foreign troops from Afghanistan.

In contrast to the frequent suspicions and mutual recriminations that have characterized Soviet-Pakistani relations, Islamabad's tie with Beijing remained a cornerstone of Pakistan's foreign policy. China is viewed as a valuable ally that has stood by Pakistan since the 1960s. It remains a major source of military equipment. The importance of the bilateral relationship was underscored by the attendance of Premier Zhao Ziyang at the 15 September signing of the peaceful nuclear accord between the two countries (Beijing, Xinhua, 19 September). Other signs of the cordial relationship were the visit of president Li Xiannian to Karachi in March and the visit of Chinese warships to Karachi (and other Indian Ocean ports) at the end of 1985, the first such naval deployment to the Indian Ocean since the communists came to power.

Walter K. Andersen
*Arlington, Virginia*

# Philippines

**Population.** 58,091,000
**Parties.** Communist Party of the Philippines (Marxist-Leninist) (CPP); Communist Party of the Philippines (Partido Komunista ng Pilipinas; PKP)
**Founded.** CPP: 1968; PKP: 1930
**Membership.** CPP: 15,000 (estimates range from 10,000 to over 30,000); PKP: 200
**Leadership.** CPP: Rodolfo Salas (chairman), Rafael Baylosis (general secretary), Antonio Zumel (Politburo member and head of the National Democratic Front), Juanito Rivera (commander of the New People's Army), Benito Tiamzon, Benjamin De Vera, Ignacio Capegsan (Central Committee members); PKP: Felicismo C. Macapagal (general secretary); Alejandro Briones, Jesus Lava, José Lava, Merlin Magallona (Central Committee members)
**Status.** CPP: Illegal, but negotiations to legalize the party were started in December; PKP: legal
**Last Congress.** CPP: unknown; PKP: Eighth, 1980
**Last Election.** Not applicable
**Auxiliary Organizations.** CPP: New People's Army (NPA); National Democratic Front (NDF); May First Movement; Nationalist Youth (KM); League of Filipino Students (LFS); Youth for Nationalism and Democracy (YND); Christians for National Liberation (CNL); Nationalist Health Association (MASAPA); Nationalist Teachers' Association (KAGUMA); Union of Democratic Filipinos (KDP); Justice for Aquino–Justice for All; August 21 Movement; Association of Concerned Teachers; Ecumenical Movement for Justice and Peace; Movement of Attorneys for Brotherhood, Integrity, and Nationalism. PKP: National Association of Workers (Katipunan); Democratic Youth Council of the Philippines; Philippine Committee for Development, Peace, and Solidarity (PCDPS); Association of Philippine Women Workers; Philippine Printers' Union; Agricultural Workers' Union
**Publications.** CPP: *Ang Bayan* (The nation), monthly; NPA: *Pulang Bandila* (Red flag), bimonthly (started in 1985); NDF: *Liberation*, monthly; *Taliba ng Bayan*, biweekly; *NDF-Update*, bimonthly, published in the Netherlands; *Ang Katipunan*, irregular, published in Oakland, California; PKP: *Ang Komunista*, irregular

After a decade of rapid expansion, the Philippine communist insurgency was slowed in 1986 by a broad-based, reformist movement that forced Ferdinand Marcos into exile and propelled Corazon Aquino and her "People Power" coalition into a new government after the fraudulent elections and civil disobedience campaign in February. Aquino has pursued a policy of reconciliation with the rebels, despite some contrary views in her cabinet and the military. On 10 December, a 60-day ceasefire began, ending over seventeen years of hostilities between government forces and communist guerrillas. Government and rebel representatives began negotiations over highly contentious issues, including the legalization and demilitarization of the CPP and NPA, amnesty for the rebels, power-sharing by the CPP in the new Aquino government, redistribution of wealth and power concentrated during the Marcos years, and the status of U.S. bases in the Philippines. By the start of 1987, it remained uncertain whether agreement on basic differences would be reached before the resumption of hostilities.

As in the case of the Huk Rebellion of the 1940s and 1950s, the current radical insurgency is rooted in poverty and injustice. It increased substantially after Marcos declared martial law in September 1972, and accelerated rapidly during the early 1980s when the country experienced a prolonged economic decline and increased corruption, political repression, and military abuses. The insurgency reached crisis proportions after the assassination of opposition leader Benigno S. Aquino, Jr., at Manila International Airport on 21 August, 1983.

The success of the CPP was also due to a new generation of radical nationalist leaders who developed a new political strategy for achieving power. They have developed a distinctly Philippine version of Maoist revolutionary theory. In brief, it calls for a nationalist, rural-based, protracted people's war carried out through highly self-sufficient and decentralized guerrilla fronts combined with widespread political mobilization.

However, in the aftermath of the dramatic rise of the Aquino government, the CPP has been undergoing an overhaul of leadership and strategy. (For major new studies of the history and development of the CPP, see Richard J. Kessler, "The Politics of Rebellion in the Philippines" [Manuscript, Carnegie Endowment for International Peace, 1986], and Gareth Porter, "Insurgency and Counter-Insurgency in the Philippines" [Manuscript, American University, 1986]. For recent articles on current developments, see Larry A. Niksch, "The Communist Party of the Philippines and the Aquino Government: Responding to the 'New Situation,'" in Carl H. Lande, ed., *The Philippines and U.S. Policy* [Washington, D.C.: Washington Institute, 1987], and William M. Wise, "The Communist Insurgency in the Philippines Since the February Revolution" [Paper presented at the Conference on a New Road for the Philippines, Medford, Mass.: Tufts University, Fletcher School, 5–7 October, 1986].)

**The New People's Army.** The NPA is a political and propaganda force as well as a fighting force. Its first objective, according to its basic document, is to help recruit and train communist party members; second, to carry out agrarian reforms; third, to build rural bases or guerrilla fronts and to engage in armed struggle; and fourth, to help mobilize support for the NDF.

Most NPA members are not soldiers; they are political workers, social workers, agricultural advisers, paramedics, and teachers. They work in rural barrios and poor urban centers, in factories and on plantations, in churches, and even in government offices. Accordingly, a guerrilla front is not just a military unit. It is a provisional local government. It provides a regular exchange of material benefits for political support.

The strategy is summarized in the party slogan, "centralized leadership and decentralized operations." The Central Party Committee formulates general policies and guidelines. The local committee, or guerrilla front, has the flexibility to experiment with different tactics for implementing general policy. As a result, guerrilla fronts have been created in almost every ethnolinguistic and geographic region of the country, from Mountain Province in the North to Mindanao in the South.

From a total force of a few thousand armed guerrillas in 1980 , the NPA has grown to probably over 23,000 regulars and a larger number of part-time irregulars. NPA force estimates range from 16,500 (according to the Pentagon) to 32,000 (according to the NPA). These forces were operating on as many as 60 fronts around the country, including occasional company-level (200–300 men) operations. The NPA reportedly has shadow governments in 10–15 percent of the country's villages. Some level of NPA activity exists in almost all of the country's 73 provinces. (*CSM*, 6 January 1987.)

The NPA and CPP have expanded into the sugar-producing regions of Negros and Panay islands and into northern Mindanao, where firefights and general strikes occurred with regularity and where shadow governments were formed in the hinterland villages (*Asia 1986 Yearbook*, pp. 221–22). The NPA also began expanding outside the mountainous province regions in northern Luzon to provinces such as Ilocos Sur on the western side and Nueva Viscaya and Nueva Ecija to the east. It also now has some units in the Zambales mountains close to the U.S. Subic Bay Naval Base. Cebu, the bastion of traditional moderate political opposition factions, also became a target for expansion. (Ibid.) Before the February "snap revolution," CPP spokesmen predicted a strategic stalemate on Negros Island by 1987. CPP and NPA members can enter and leave the seaport capital of Bacolod under cover and freely roam sugarcane fields just outside city limits. Masses of unemployed peasants and workers are still ripe for the rebels. (For a recent account of the persistent causes of insurgency, see James Clad, "An Island Without Joy," *FEER*, 25 December.)

During the Marcos years, the military initiative clearly rested with the NPA. Its guerrillas were supplied almost entirely with weapons captured, and occasionally purchased, from the Philippine armed forces. The United States estimated that, from 1983 to 1986, the NPA was growing at a rate of 20 percent a year, constrained only by the shortage of arms and money, not recruits. (Senate Select Committee on Intelligence, "The Situation in the Philippines," 1 November, 1985.) Before the Aquino government, the NPA had planned to step up operations. Guerrilla units in the most advanced NPA areas, such as Mindanao, had already been told to launch operations at least four times a week. By 1987, the NPA aimed to have 60,000 fighters in all and daily operations in its more advanced zones. It planned to attack and briefly hold major provincial towns. (Paul Quinn-Judge, "Insurgency in the Philippines Could Provoke Full-scale War Unless Growth Is Checked," *CSM*, 15 October, 1985.)

Although infiltration and operations did increase in the metropolitan Manila area, rebel activities there were few compared to some rural areas, such as Davao City, where the NPA clashed daily with government forces until the December 1986 cease-fire.

Corazon Aquino's People Power revolution of February 1986, however, caught the CPP unprepared and has forced an intensive "rectification campaign" among leaders and rank and file of the CPP and NPA.

**The National Democratic Front.** The NDF, the political front created and led by the communist party, has developed significant support among some radical Christian groups, labor organizations, student groups, and others. NDF influence is evident in Bayan (Nation), a legal opposition coalition founded in April 1985 that grew out of the Coalition for the Restoration of Democracy, which emerged after Benigno Aquino was killed. Bayan encompasses elements of the Marxist left in addition to cause-oriented groups and traditional nationalist politicians, academics, and businessmen. A conflict over leadership structure and the role of CPP supporters led to the departure of important supporters, including Agapito "Butz" Aquino, the brother of Benigno Aquino, and José Diokno, an elder statesman of Filipino nationalism.

In areas where guerrilla fronts have been established, the NDF functions as the government authority. It collects taxes, implements land reforms, organizes public works and schools, and administers "revolutionary justice." The NDP has been able to spread its anti-Marcos and anti-American views among both radical and moderate opposition groups and in both rural and urban areas. In 1986,

the NDF represented the armed insurgents in negotiations with the Aquino government.

**Government Response.** The communists made a grave mistake in underestimating popular support for Aquino's bid for power. She formed a new coalition for political change with strong support from the Catholic Church, the business community, and almost every socioeconomic group in the country. Her campaign rekindled the democratic spirit of the country and gave her a manifest electoral victory that could not be denied by widespread electoral graft, violence, and corruption by the Marcos forces. The Marcos government was immobilized by defections from within and noncooperation from without. Aquino also won over important allies in the military, including Secretary of National Defense Juan Ponce Enrile and Deputy Chief of the Armed Forces Fidel Ramos. On 26 February, abandoned by all but his most faithful supporters, Marcos gave up power and left the country with a minimum of violence. He left with two of the most prominent targets of opposition criticism, Fabian Ver, chief of the armed forces, and Eduardo Cojuangco, the richest of the crony capitalists.

Despite Aquino's enormously popular campaign for nonviolent civil disobedience, the left was unable or unwilling to support her effort to oust Marcos. Hence, the election not only forced Marcos out of power, but it also split the anti-Marcos opposition into two separate political forces, one in power and the other in disarray.

In order to defuse the persistent insurgency, Aquino began her government by fulfilling her campaign pledges of political reconciliation. Her first proclamation was to abolish the government's power to detain people without charge, a practice that Marcos had used widely in purported cases of subversion, sedition, and conspiracy.

Over 500 political prisoners were ordered released by the Aquino government, despite some objections from top military officials. Those released included José Maria Sison, founder of the CPP and a former English professor at the University of the Philippines, and Bernabe Buscayno, also known as Commander Dante, son of a poor farm family and reportedly the former head of the NPA. Both had been imprisoned for nearly ten years. Also released were Alexander Birondo, alleged chief of the Armed City Partisans in Manila, and Ruben Alegre, who had been captured in a shoot-out with police in Manila in June 1985.

Although the official CPP remained illegal, in

1986, Sison, Buscayno, and other Filipinos organized a new legal leftist party, the People's Party (Partido ng Bayan). It has the support of the May First Movement, a leftist labor federation that claims to have about half a million members, the largest in the country. (*NYT*, 22 December.)

Aquino dismissed many generals eligible for retirement, including nearly all senior commanders. She said she would cut the military intelligence budget and demobilize the Civilian Home Defense Forces. But those early moves made some military officers apprehensive, including Enrile, who publicly criticized Aquino's military reform proposals and her policy of reconciliation with the rebels. After numerous rumors of a military coup, a farcical attempt to grab power by Marcos' former vice president, Arturo Tolentino, which involved several Marcos loyalists in the military, and some mysterious bombings around Manila, Aquino finally replaced Enrile with Rafael Ileto, a loyal and competent military leader with extensive counterinsurgency experience from the Huk Rebellion of the 1950s. Ileto appears well suited to bridge the gap between Aquino's cabinet and the military. Not only is he a former officer highly respected within the military, but he also believes in the primacy of civilian government, unlike his politically ambitious predecessor, Enrile. He is expected to place far greater stress on discipline throughout the armed forces.

Aquino's economic goals aim to reduce the country's poverty—including unemployment and underemployment—which is an essential task to defuse the communist insurgency. Finance Minister Jaime Ongpin calls the economic program "private enterprise with a social conscience." It gives top priority to increasing domestic food production and only secondary support to export promotion. Land reform, however, was not addressed in the first few months of the new Aquino government.

Negotiations between the new government and the communists began fitfully, with numerous conflicts within and between both camps. On 5 August, Aquino opened cease-fire talks with a proposal for a 30-day truce. The NDF broke off negotiations, however, after government forces arrested CPP leader Rodolfo Salas. Cease-fire talks were resumed on 10 November, when Aquino instructed her negotiators to reach an agreement by the end of the month. Two days later, Rolando Olalia, a prominent left-wing labor leader, was assassinated. Again, NDF negotiators broke off talks and said they would not resume negotiations until his killer

was found. On 23 November, after two weeks of open conflict within the government and growing restlessness within the military, Aquino announced a major shake-up in her cabinet, including the resignation of Defense Minister Enrile. In the same speech, Aquino set a deadline of 30 November for the communists to agree to a cease-fire and resume the talks. If they did not, she warned, she would step up military operations. On 25 November, the NDF came back to the negotiating table.

Chief negotiators for the NDF included Antonio Zumel, chairman of the front and former news editor of the defunct *Manila Chronicle*. He had gone underground when martial law was declared in September 1972 (*FEER*, 23 May 1985). Another negotiator and journalist-turned-revolutionary was Saturnino Ocampo, former assistant business editor of the *Manila Times*, whose 5 May escape from custody ended nine years of military detention. His ordeal of torture and solitary confinement had become the rallying cry for numerous human rights groups, both locally and abroad (ibid.).

Ocampo commented on how the country's austerity affected CPP finances. "The leadership of the movement is devising ways and means by which to raise funds and among these are what we call revolutionary taxation. The basic idea is to impose some taxes on the big corporations, whether foreign or local, that are exploiting the natural resources and human resources of the country, like the mining areas, logging areas that are denuding the forest, or the huge plantations in Mindanao" (*FEER*, 2 January).

But revolutionary taxation has been an unpopular CPP policy and may have been a factor in leading the party into negotiations. "The more the communists squeeze the incomes of wealthier peasants, the more they risk losing their support in the revolution" (*CSM*, 29 December). The CPP believes in the basic idea of class struggle, but it also realizes that it needs to form class alliances. This is a widespread dilemma among party leaders. How much should they compromise their ideals with the so-called middle forces in order to win power? How much should they compromise on land reform goals? As of 1986, their land reform demands have been modest, usually limited to raising the share of the crop for tenant farmers or raising worker wages. Rarely is land confiscated outright. The party has dealt with large and small landlords rather gently; confiscation has been used only where persuasion, protest, and boycott fail. "We are not going to establish a communist society quite yet. That is still several generations away," said Jaime Lanoy, party secretary for southeast Mindanao. "In the meantime, we will allow even anticommunists to coexist with us." (Ibid.)

Half of the cease-fire period had been taken in reaching agreement on a still ambiguous agenda for negotiations. It was uncertain whether substantial progress would be made in the talks to lead either side to propose an extension of the cease-fire beyond its scheduled expiration date of 8 February 1987. The talks at least gave the Aquino government a chance to win popular support away from the guerrillas and to organize a comprehensive counterinsurgency program. Her cabinet approved a $50 million rebel rehabilitation program, but it appeared unlikely that it would be implemented during the 60-day cease-fire.

Some observers see the cease-fire as a strategic advantage for the communists. "They will use the new 'democratic space' to expand their political contacts among centrist elements, recruiting new members, and trying to further infiltrate the government, and developing foreign connections both for future material and ideological support"; hence, "both the communists and the military see the cease-fire as an opportunity for war, not peace" (Kessler, "Politics of Rebellion").

If political reconciliation and economic recovery are inadequate to stop the communist insurgency, then Aquino has vowed to use military force where necessary to put down armed rebellion. Unfortunately, the Philippine armed forces are ill prepared for this, according to many reports. The defense budget equals only 1 percent of the gross national product, the lowest in Southeast Asia. Shortages of supplies and equipment—such as trucks, aircraft, uniforms, food, and fuel—are endemic. Pay is poor and medical care is often nonexistent. A disproportionate number of units are concentrated in Manila rather than sent into the field against the NPA. Equipment maintenance is inadequate, and there is no logistical system worthy of the name. Morale and mobility are both low. Perhaps most important, leadership is often poor and there are no central training facilities, with the result that troops are frequently sent into the field with inadequate training. Many of the best officers and technically skilled personnel have left the armed forces to take higher-paying jobs as mercenaries with armies in the Middle East. It will take many years to solve all the military's organizational, training, and materiel problems. Despite its many current weaknesses, however, the military is likely to remain a powerful national institution in the post-Marcos period, given the persistent threats to internal security.

If Aquino's popularity continues, if the new constitution is approved in February 1987 as expected, and if the military curbs its abuses and becomes a more effective fighting force, then the insurgency is unlikely to increase. It is unlikely to decrease or dissipate until major economic and social reforms are implemented, including comprehensive agrarian reform.

In the meantime, Aquino's policy of reconciliation may have some limited appeal, especially among Catholic clergy, nuns, and religious workers who supported or joined the rebels during the Marcos years (Vermont, *Burlington Free Press*, 11 October). A notable example is Conrado Balweg, a former rebel priest, NPA commander, and popular Filipino folk hero to some. Balweg was perhaps the most widely known rebel in the Philippines. During the Marcos years, military authorities said he was one of their most wanted fugitives; they offered an $11,000 reward for his capture, dead or alive. A member of the Society of the Divine Word until he joined the rebels in January 1980, Balweg is from the minority Tinggian tribe, which has been fighting government reclamation projects and a big logging company to retain its ancestral lands. When Balweg joined the Cordillera guerrillas, they had 32 fighters. By 1984, their Luzon mountain area forces were believed to have grown to 700. He said that their forces tripled in 1984 despite a 1,000-man government military operation against them, and that 99 percent of the recruits were from mountain villages. (*San Diego Union*, 28 April 1985.) After the February revolution, Balweg remained as an NPA commander until he broke away to form the Cordillera People's Liberation Army in northern Luzon.

On 13 September, Aquino made a dramatic surprise visit to the Cordillera Mountains north of Manila, where she met with Balweg in an animist ritual truce ceremony. Balweg gave Aquino a tribal spear; Aquino gave Balweg a Bible, a rosary, and an M-16 rifle tied with a yellow ribbon. The government agreed to halt work on a dam construction project and a paper mill that had been the major causes of the insurgency. The proposed new constitution also allows greater autonomy for the Cordillera region. (*NYT*, 14 September; *FEER*, 2 October.)

The proposed constitution also allows greater autonomy for another area of past and potential rebellion, the southern Muslim region of the country. Philippine government representatives have been meeting in Jidda, Saudi Arabia, with Nur Misuari, head of the Moro National Liberation Front (MNLF), one of the main Muslim insurgent groups. Misuari has dropped his demand for a separate state, but it was uncertain whether the MNLF would support the form of autonomy proposed in the constitutional referendum scheduled for 1987. (*NYT*, 7 January; *FEER*, 11 September; for an analysis of the Muslim insurgency since the February revolution, see Lele Garner Noble, "Muslim Grievances and the Muslim Rebellion," in Carl H. Lande, ed., *The Philippines and U.S. Policy* [Washington, D.C.: Washington Institute, 1987].)

**U.S. Interests.** Clark Air Force Base and Subic Bay Naval Base are the most visible manifestations of the U.S. presence in the Philippines. The NPA has viewed the bases as symbols of the "Marcos-U.S. dictatorship" and an affront to Philippine sovereignty. In the December cease-fire negotiations, removal of the bases was a major rebel demand. The bases are located in an area of intense NPA activity, and perimeter security is poor at both. NPA leaders boast that they can walk on and off Clark and Subic at will. As of the end of 1986, however, there had been no effort by the NPA to target either the bases or U.S. personnel.

The bases agreement comes up for review in 1988 and for possible renegotiation in 1991. In anticipation of the continued polarization of Philippine politics and the renegotiation of the agreement, U.S. officials have begun to make detailed contingency plans in order to relocate navy and air force units from the Philippines to Guam, Okinawa, and other Pacific locations (*NYT*, 25 January). The United States also leased 18,000 acres on the Marianas Islands of Tinian and Saipan for possible replacement of Philippine facilities, and the Pentagon began considering hiring shipyards in Singapore and South Korea (*Burlington Free Press*, 10 December 1985, 19 January).

During her September state visit to the United States, Aquino said she would keep all her options open for the U.S. bases until the renegotiations. However, one major change may occur if the new constitution is approved in 1987, because it would allow for legislative and popular referenda on the continued presence of the bases in the Philippines, in addition to the previous method of renegotiating through executive agreement. In the meantime, Philippine and American government officials emphasized that the issue of the future of bases in the Philippines should be postponed until the Aquino government can first respond to the pressing crisis of reinvigorating the economy and defusing the radical insurgency (Michael Armacost, "The Philippines and the United States," *Current Policy No. 876* [U.S. Department of State, Bureau of Public Affairs, October 1986]).

According to Admiral James Lyons, commander of the U.S. Pacific fleet, there is no concrete evidence of any ties between the NPA and the Soviet Union or any other foreign communist country (*CSM*, 11 December).

David A. Rosenberg
*Middlebury College*

# Sri Lanka

**Population.** 16,638,000
**Parties.** Communist Party of Sri Lanka (CPSL, pro-Moscow); Lanka Sama Samaja Party (LSSP, Trotskyist); Janatha Vimukthi Peramuna (JVP, Maoist)
**Founded.** CPSL: 1943; LSSP: 1935; JVP: 1968

**Membership.** CPSL: 5,000 (estimated); LSSP: 2,500 (estimated); JVP: unknown
**General Secretary.** CPSL: Kattorge P. Silva; LSSP: Bernard Soysa; JVP: Lional Bopage
**Politburo.** CPSL: 11 members, including Kattorge P. Silva, Pieter Keuneman (chair)
**Status.** CPSL, LSSP: legal; JVP: illegal
**Last Congress.** CPSL: Twelfth, 27–29 January 1984
**Last Election.** 1977, parliamentary: CPSL, 2.0 percent, no seats (1 member elected in by-election); LSSP, 3.6 percent, no seats; JVP, did not contest. 1982, presidential: CPSL, did not contest; LSSP, 0.9 percent; JVP, 4.2 percent.
**Auxiliary Organizations.** CPSL: Federation of Trade Unions (24 affiliated unions), Public Service Worker's Trade Union Federation (100 affiliated unions), Communist Youth Federation, Kantha (women's) Peramuna; LSSP: Ceylon Federation of Labour (16 affiliated unions), Samasamaja Kantha Peramuna, Youth League
**Publications.** CPSL: *Aththa* (newspaper; B. A. Siriwardene, editor; circulation 17,500)

The violence between the government of Sri Lanka and the largest ethnic minority group, the Tamils, dominated Sri Lankan society in 1986. The United National Party (UNP) government of President Junius Richard Jayawardene continued to focus its energy on a resolution of the conflict and to reject opposition party demands for general elections before their scheduled 1989 date. For the first time since the violence escalated in 1983, the negotiations between the government and the Tamil representatives narrowed the differences between the two sides. By the end of the year, the government had mapped out a peace plan that had been accepted, in principle, by the nonviolent Tamil United Liberation Front (TULF). The major obstacle to the plan was the opposition of the largest of the numerous violent Tamil youth groups commonly called "tigers." The proposed agreement called for a devolution of power to provincial councils. These councils would have revenue-generating power and the ability to control police and government activities in their provinces. Local autonomy has been a major demand of the Tamil leadership.

**Party Leadership and Affairs.** As members of the opposition, the pro-Moscow CPSL and the Trotskyist LSSP played a limited role in the peace negotiations. On several occasions, including a political parties' conference on the ethnic issue held on 25 June and attended by eight opposition parties, they were consulted by the government for their opinions on the conflict. The CPSL and LSSP took strong stands in support of a negotiated settlement of the conflict and in making concessions to the Tamils. They differentiated themselves from the other Sinhalese-dominated leftist parties by supporting the general direction of the government's peace initiatives. These government initiatives involved negotiations with not only the TULF but also

several of the violent tiger organizations. The Sri Lanka Freedom Party and the Sri Lanka Mahajana Party opposed the concessions made by the government in these negotiations. However, the CPSL and LSSP have criticized the government for not recognizing the Tamils' right to regional autonomy within the framework of a united Sri Lanka. In September, the CPSL made a number of policy proposals, including an end to discrimination and firings of Tamils in government institutions, a halt to sweep arrests and detention of Tamil youths, and a recognition of the right of the Tamils to preserve and develop their own culture and language.

The only significant change in either party in 1986 was the serious blow to the CPSL caused by the death of Sarath Muttetuwegama in a car accident on 18 May. Muttetuwegama was a CPSL Politburo member and the party's only member of Parliament. He represented a new generation of communist party leadership and was one of only a few of his generation to reach the higher levels of party leadership. He was an articulate spokesman in Parliament not only for his own party but for the other opposition parties as well. His eloquence, integrity, and intellect had won him the respect of even the most anticommunist members of the governing UNP.

The parliamentary vacancy caused by Muttetuwegama's death created a brief struggle within the party for the right to represent the party in Parliament. Under the constitution of 1978, parliamentary seats belong to the party, not to the member of Parliament holding the seat. As a result, vacancies are filled by a nomination by the party unless that party decides to not fill the seat, in which case the vacancy is filled in a by-election. A number of party members supported Muttetuwegama's wife, Manouri, for the vacancy. She is the general secretary of the Women's Front of Sri Lanka and has been active in CPSL activities; under the old constitution's system of by-elections, she would have probably been selected to represent her party in the by-election. However, the CPSL Central Committee selected D. E. W. Gunasekera, a younger member of the Politburo, to take the seat. Gunasekera is from Matara district in the south, a CPSL stronghold that has produced a disproportionate number of CPSL leaders. Muttetuwegama was from the Kandyan hill country in Ratnapura district, an area that, although supportive of the CPSL, has not been well represented in the party's leadership.

**Trade Union Activity.** Since 1977, when the UNP came to power, the trade union movement in Sri Lanka has been dominated by progovernment unions. Other unions have been unable to strike successfully against the government or private companies. Attempted strikes have generally resulted in the proscription of the union and the loss of the union members' jobs. Since many of the major unions and trade movement associations are controlled by or sympathetic to the parties of the left, the weakening of the unions has also weakened the CPSL and LSSP. Union activity in 1986 was marked by a partially successful strike by the Public Service United Nurses' Union in March and April. The government initially banned the union and threatened to fire all striking nurses, but finally backed away from its threat and negotiated a partial settlement with the union. This action—as well as labor unrest among estate workers, the Government Medical Officers' Association, and university faculty— marked a major increase in labor activity and the possibility of the return of influence and power among the CPSL and LSSP unions.

**The JVP and the Tigers.** The Marxist JVP continued to be proscribed and its leadership remained in hiding in 1986. There were a number of reports, however, indicating that the JVP was gaining strength and was involved in violent attacks against government targets in the southern regions of the country. The accuracy of those reports and the strength of the JVP cannot be verified. A splinter group of the JVP did break away from the main organization and is known to have made contact with one of the largest tiger organizations, the People's Liberation Organization of Tamil Eelam (PLOTE). Several JVP members were arrested during the year while fighting for the PLOTE. In addition, there were unconfirmed reports that they were involved, on their own, in attacks against government targets in the predominantly Sinhalese area of North Central province.

The numerous tiger organizations continued to carry out armed attacks against the government during the year. Several of the most prominent of the groups—the Eelam Revolutionary Organization of Students, the Eelam People's Revolutionary Liberation Front (EPRLF), and the PLOTE—espouse Marxist ideologies. These Marxist groups and the Tamil Eelam Liberation Organization (TELO) suffered a serious setback in intergroup fighting that began in April. The Liberation Tigers of Tamil Eelam (LTTE) was involved in a number of clashes—with the PLOTE in April and May, with the TELO in May, and with the EPRLF in December—in which the LTTE inflicted a large number of casualties on each group. The rise to dominance of the LTTE, a non-Marxist group, propelled the most militant of the tiger organizations to the forefront of the battle for an independent Tamil state in Sri Lanka.

**International Relations.** Sri Lanka's pro-Western foreign policy did not change during the year. However, the government continued to establish friendly relations with communist nations. In March, a state visit by Chinese president Li Xiannian to Sri Lanka resulted in verbal Chinese support for the government in the ethnic conflict with the Tamils. Relations with the Soviet Union warmed up considerably with a visit of several Soviet technicians and a pledge of support from the Soviet Union for the Mahaweli irrigation and dam project. A July visit to Moscow by President Jayawardene was canceled in June and, as of the year's end, had not been rescheduled.

Robert C. Oberst
*Nebraska Wesleyan University*

# Thailand

**Population.** 52,438,000
**Party.** Communist Party of Thailand (CPT)
**Founded.** 1942
**Membership.** 500–700 (estimated)
**General Secretary.** Pracha Tanyapaiboon (pseudonym), not confirmed
**Leading Bodies.** No data
**Status.** Illegal
**Last Congress.** Fourth, March and April 1984, clandestine
**Last Election.** N/a
**Auxiliary Organizations.** No data; all organizations reportedly dissolved
**Publications.** None

Among the most significant events in Thailand in 1986 were the government's loss on a parliamentary bill and the consequent parliamentary election on 27 July, the fashioning of a new administration under the continued leadership of Prime Minister Prem Tinsulanond, the ouster of General Arthit Kamlang-ek (the nation's most powerful military leader), economic difficulties related to the price of rice, the threat of foreign trade protectionism, and a tenuous relationship with communist neighbors. Because these events were managed adroitly, by the end of the year the stability and continuity of the government remained intact.

Reliable information on the CPT was scarce in 1986 largely because 1) the CPT is illegal; 2) no party congress has taken place since the abortive Fourth Congress in 1984; 3) the number of CPT members has decreased from an estimated 12,000 ten years ago to only 500–700; and 4) there are no longer any party publications or radio broadcasts from which to analyze current leadership, tactics, or ideology.

Since 1979, the CPT has declined in numbers and activities. The demise of the party stems from the ending of support from neighboring communist governments in China, Laos, and Vietnam; the internal factions that emerged following the Chinese invasion of Vietnam and Laos and the consequent split between pro-Chinese and pro-Soviet forces; the government's 1980 amnesty program, which resulted in the return of thousands of CPT members; the disillusionment of former student leaders, who had joined the party following the 1976 military coup d'état, with the rigid CPT leadership; and the government's "politics over military" counterinsurgency strategy and emphasis on economic development in sensitive areas of the kingdom. By 1982, the Thai government had proclaimed victory over the insurgency.

Given this optimistic assessment, there was no surprise at army commander in chief General Chaovalit Yongchaiyut's announcement that the communists were once again on the offensive and constituted a direct threat to the security of the nation. In a report to Prime Minister Prem, he stated that the CPT and its fronts had developed and grown stronger. He noted that their objective is to resort to an armed struggle, to prepare to launch a new war, and to spread a war atmosphere. He implied that former CPT members who had defected and become elected members of the Parliament were infiltrating the political process. Chaovalit's assessment was especially noteworthy since he had been the architect of the successful "politics over military" policy, is considered a moderate on the issue of insurgency, and is currently director general of the drive to suppress communist insurgency.

Chaovalit claimed that the army and government had failed to press on with their political offensive to uproot the CPT and had allowed the banned party to take the offensive. He cited the success of the CPT in enlarging its "front activity" at an "alarmingly rapid rate" (*Nation*, 2 November; *FBIS*, 5 November). He suggested that, although the CPT's strongholds and the Thai People's Liberation Army's regular and guerrilla forces had been liquidated, their armed units in other forms remained intact and in hiding.

National unity must be effectively created, according to Chaovalit. He added that it is necessary to move the government's emphasis from the development of democracy to the fight to defeat the communists (ibid.). Politicians elected in the 27 July parliamentary elections were quick to denounce the speech as a threat to the kingdom's democratic institutions. They accused Chaovalit of reviving the "armed struggle" as an excuse to expand the army's budget and as a threat to former CPT members who had been elected to the Parliament. The threat was of particular significance because of the infighting and consequent instability among the coalition partners in Prem's new administration. Moreover, the political leaders condemned Chaovalit's speech for its lack of specific evidence.

In a 31 October speech over national radio, Chaovalit mentioned five conditions favorable to the CPT: 1) the guerrilla fighters wear different disguises and have been more difficult to destroy; 2) the liberation army is fully equipped with hidden weapons that can be used at any moment; 3) the idea of the armed struggle still exists; 4) conflicts among factions in the CPT have been settled; and 5) the current political and economic situation has fostered excellent conditions for the CPT to increase its united fronts and prepare its liberation army (Bangkok, First Army Division Radio, 31 October; *FBIS*, 3 November).

**Leadership and Party Organization.** There was no definitive information in 1986 on the leadership and organizational structure of the CPT. Most analysts believe the party structure has collapsed, with regional pockets of scattered armed insurgents. The military arm of the party, the Peo-

ple's Liberation Army of Thailand, comprises just 500–700 men; only occasional armed clashes with government troops are reported. Army chief of staff General Wanchai Ruangtrakun said the CPT now has about 570 armed men: 50 in the central plains, 100 in the northeast, 120 in the north, and 300 in the south.

**Domestic Party Affairs.** The most significant concentration of armed insurgents is in the southern provinces, although the arrest of party leaders has undermined insurgent activity there. Chamnan Banjongkliang is reputed to be the regional secretary. Five or six operational areas have been set up, each with a leader in charge of 40 to 100 persons. Relations with Muslim separatist movements and the Communist Party of Malaysia in the four southern provinces complicate the insurgency situation. In the northeast, the regional secretary is Prachuab Ruangrat. Like the south, the northeast is divided into operational areas covering various provinces.

The north, with three operational areas, is led by Waitoon Sinthuwanich. Insurgency problems there are related to hill tribesmen and linkages to the Burmese Communist Party on the border. For the central plains region, which has two operational areas, no information is available about the party secretary.

For about seven years, there have been reports of a faction of the CPT, the Thai People's Revolutionary Movement, popularly known as the Pak Mai (New party), with headquarters in Laos. It is not clear who leads the group and what its precise relationship is to the CPT. The Pak Mai was reportedly supported by Vietnam, Laos, and the Soviet Union and had about five hundred armed members (*YICA*, 1986). The Pak Mai group has apparently not yet reached the armed phase of its struggle. Instead, it has limited its activities to armed propaganda in the northeast provinces (*FEER*, 9 January).

The CPT has traditionally been pro-Chinese, because of support from China and the Sino-Thai leadership that has dominated the party since its inception. In the past two years, there was speculation that much of the Sino-Thai leadership had died or resigned and Chinese support had evaporated. Hence, the hard-line Maoist leadership and tactics have seemingly evolved to a more "authentic Thai party," with emphasis on urban infiltration rather than on armed struggle in the rural areas. Thai counterinsurgency experts suggest that the CPT is now more pro-Soviet, which reflects the Soviet Union's dominance in neighboring Laos, Cambodia, and Vietnam, as well as the bankruptcy of the Maoist doctrine adhered to by the CPT for over 40 years.

Chaovalit views the CPT as having moved from armed struggle to infiltration of political parties and front groups; that is a new policy he sees as even more insidious and dangerous than before. Although the CPT has yet to form a national united front, according to Chaovalit, it has laid stress on expanding mass activities among workers, the poor, students, and intellectuals. Also targeted are political parties, patriotic organizations, and religious and charitable foundations (*FEER*, 9 January).

The *Bangkok Post* reported on 13 July that the CPT set up its headquarters in Bangkok to operate an urban insurgency, infiltrate domestic and international organizations, and set up a front called the Thai Democratic Solidarity Group (TDSG). Allegedly, five prominent but unidentified communists who came out of the jungle were identified as leaders of the underground activities. The TDSG has reportedly infiltrated organizations set up by public-spirited people to combat official corruption, fight for human rights, and strive for a more just society. Among the groups the TDSG reportedly contacted is Amnesty International. No evidence was provided, however, to support the allegations.

**The Counterinsurgency.** Until 1980, when Prime Minister Prem promulgated the "politics over military" policy, Thai counterinsurgency tactics were primarily military. It was not until the Fifth Five-Year Plan (1982–1986) that Thailand's defense requirements were built into development planning (*FEER*, 17 April). Chaovalit himself stressed the importance of guaranteeing economic justice for all, "for eliminating those who create injustice in society, and those who are corrupt and misbehave in the bureaucracy" (*Bangkok Post*, 13 November; *FBIS*, 17 November). To achieve that goal, the Sixth Five-Year Plan (1987–1991) emphasizes "volunteer self-defense and development villages, particularly near the border areas." Between 1982 and 1986, 970 million baht were provided to 4,000 such villages. Under the program, the army organizes armed village units and teaches development techniques (*FEER*, 17 April). Development villages were planned along the Thai-Malaysian border to help fight the banned Communist Party of Malaya (CPM).

**International Positions.** After two years of acrimonious relations between Laos and Thailand stemming from a conflict over three remote border villages, steps were taken in 1986 to improve ties. At a meeting of representatives from both nations, agreement was reached to stop verbal attacks on each other, urge their governments to refrain from using force to settle disputes and to keep in contact when conflicts arise, further discuss future plans to improve relations, and lift the Thai embargo on strategic products destined for Laos.

Relations with Vietnam, however, continued to be tense because of the occupation of Laos and Cambodia by Vietnamese troops. Throughout the year, Vietnamese troops intermittently struck at various points on the border between Cambodia and Thailand. China and Thailand negotiated several agreements, including the trade of agricultural products, increased commercial flights between Bangkok and Beijing, and continued support by China for the Thai position on the withdrawal of Vietnamese troops from Cambodia.

In December, Thailand announced that it was closing Khao I Dang, the refugee camp on the Cambodian border that housed some 26,000 Cambodians. The closing will result in those persons losing their legal status as refugees; instead, they will become "displaced persons" who can be returned to Cambodia. Prasong Soonsiri, general secretary to the prime minister, announced that all refugee camps would be closed in the near future, and that Thai authorities would move the camp's population to settlements closer to the border.

Clark D. Neher
*Northern Illinois University*

# Vietnam

**Population.** 61,944,000 (*World Factbook*, 1986)
**Party.** Vietnam Communist Party (Dang Cong San Vietnam; VCP)
**Founded.** 1930 (as Indochinese Communist Party)
**Membership.** 1.7 million (Indochina Archive estimate, December 1986); 20 percent women; ethnically, almost entirely Vietnamese; average age in mid-40s; 40 percent *ban co* (poor peasant); 25 percent peasant/farm laborer; 15 percent proletariat; 20 percent other
**General Secretary.** Nguyen Van Linh (b. 1915)
**Politburo.** Nguyen Van Linh (b. 1915), Pham Hung (b. 1912), Vo Chi Cong (b. 1912), Do Muoi (b. 1917), Vo Van Kiet (b. 1922), Le Duc Anh (b. 1910?), Nguyen Duc Tam (b. 1920), Nguyen Co Thach (b. 1920), Dong Sy Nguyen (b. 1920?), Tran Xuan Bach, Nguyen Thanh Binh, Doan Khue, Mai Chi Tho (b. 1922), Dao Duy Tung (alternate)
**Secretariat.** Nguyen Van Linh, Nguyen Duc Tam, Tran Xuan Bach, Dao Duy Tung, Tran Kien, Le Phuoc Tho, Nguyen Quyet, Dam Quang Trung, Vu Oanh, Nguyen Khanh, Tran Quyet, Tran Quoc Hoang, Pham The Duyet
**Central Committee.** 124 full and 49 alternate members
**Status.** Ruling party
**Last Congress.** Sixth, 15–18 December 1986
**Last Election.** 1981, the Seventh National Assembly, 97.96 percent, 496 of 614 seats, with all candidates VCP endorsed (Indochina Archive)
**Auxiliary Organizations.** Fatherland Front (Huynh Tan Phat, chairman); Ho Chi Minh Communist Youth Union (Vu Mao, secretary general)
**Publications.** *Nhan Dan* (The people), VCP daily, Hong Ha, editor; *Tap Chi Cong San* (Communist review), VCP theoretical monthly; *Quan Doi Nhan Dan* (People's army), army newspaper.

The year 1986 for Vietnam was largely devoted to anticipatory waiting by party members, government leaders, and the general public. It was as if the society had been suspended in time pending the outcome of the important Sixth Party Congress, which, after several postponements, was convened in mid-December. Throughout the year, important matters of state in which policy choices existed, such as the war in Cambodia or relations with China, were held in abeyance. Hence, the year witnessed few leadership initiatives and no bold foreign policy overtures by the ruling Politburo. Even the economic sector, badly in need of firm and decisive policymaking, appeared to be on hold.

Adding importance and a sense of urgency to the upcoming congress was the death of party secretary Le Duan, 79, on 10 July. Although known to be in failing health—he was rumored to have died in Moscow in February—Le Duan had appeared to be active during the year. His death was a signal that the old original leadership, dating from the earliest days of the Communist Party of Vietnam/Indochina, was nearing its end. Le Duan was buried with customary pomp, but only the Soviet Union and neighboring Cambodia and Laos were invited to send official party delegations.

An emergency plenum on 14 July named Truong Chinh acting general secretary with the central task of supervising preparations for the Sixth Congress.

As with earlier party congresses, the meaning of the Sixth Congress will unfold slowly; its full import will not be known for perhaps a year, and complete assessment will not be possible for several years. Both cadres and the general population were prepared for change, if only for reasons of age and physical vulnerability; the aging leadership, always few in number, had been at the helm for three generations. Of the Politburo's inner circle that began the year (Le Duan, Pham Van Dong, Truong Chinh, Le Duc Tho, and Pham Hung), only Pham Hung remained by the year's end. The sense of the congress was clearly that renewed determination was essential to address the nation's central problem: its many economic difficulties. To that end, the congress approved significant changes in the membership of the Politburo and Central Committee. The operative principles at work in the selection process appeared to be twofold: to choose individuals with somewhat more pragmatic and less ideological orientations toward economic problem-solving; and to draw from the corps of party figures with long experience in the South, so as to better tap the human resources and potential contributions represented by that region.

The unspoken theme that appeared to dominate the congress was rejection of the economic methods of the past decade, which had not worked. But, while few at the congress seemed willing to defend the status quo, there was not a clear shared vision of what economic measures and approaches should be substituted. Determining these will be the primary task of the new leadership.

**Leadership and Party Organization.** The Sixth Congress resulted in significant change in the top level of party leadership. Judged by standards of change in communist parties elsewhere, these might not seem extensive, but they are in terms of VCP history. Changes in the VCP during the past several decades have been confined largely to the few caused by death. Those effected by the Sixth Congress were more far-reaching and significant than anything witnessed in the past.

Added to the Politburo were Tran Xuan Bach, Nguyen Thanh Binh, Doan Khue, Mai Chi Tho, and Dao Duy Tung. Tran Xuan Bach is an obscure figure whose career has been associated with the newly elevated party Central Committee Secretariat. Since 1971 he has been known to be the chief administrative figure within the highest level of party leadership. Press reports have described him as involved in overseeing civil administration in Cambodia. Nguyen Thanh Binh is a People's Army of Vietnam (PAVN) major general who has held no military assignments since 1962. He appears to be

an important figure in the science-technology area, working out of the Central Committee Secretariat. He has been minister of water conservancy and has had economic assignments on various state inspection/financial commissions. He appears to be knowledgeable about economic administration, trade, and agricultural development. Doan Khue is a lieutenant general whose military commands have been chiefly in the South (Da Nang region) as political commissar. Mai Chi Tho, brother of Le Duc Tho, served for years as a major party figure in Ho Chi Minh City, much of it as chairman of the People's Committee, or "mayor," as he was informally called. Much of his work involved supervising internal security in that city, and much of his career has been associated with party activities in the South. Dao Duy Tung, the alternate member, is a long-time figure in the Central Committee's Department of Propaganda and Training and, since 1982, its director. He is the former editor of the party theoretical journal, *Tap Chi Cong San*, and is considered an intellectual party theoretician.

Dropped from the Politburo were Truong Chinh, Pham Van Dong, Le Duc Tho, To Huu, Van Tien Dung, and Chu Huy Man. Truong Chinh, 79, was the party ideologue and chairman of the Council of State who took over the party secretaryship at Le Duan's death (see biographical sketch in *YICA*, 1984). Pham Van Dong, 80, was prime minister (chairman of the Council of Ministers), whose age and poor health were apparently responsible for his departure from the leadership. Le Duc Tho, 76, had been the long-time leader of a powerful Politburo faction due to his political skill and the support of his constituency, the party organization cadres. To Huu, 66, was removed from his government position earlier in the year, apparently as a result of his role in the currency change that resulted in uncontrolled inflation. Senior General Van Tien Dung, 69, Vietnam's principal military figure, had been minister of defense and the commander of the armed forces since the retirement of General Vo Nguyen Giap. Van Tien Dung remains on the Central Committee. Senior General Chu Huy Man, 66, was chief of the PAVN Political Directorate, associated with Le Duc Tho, and also supported by Le Duan. His deputy, Lieutenant General Dang Vu Hiep, was also removed from the Central Committee.

It was announced a few days after the congress that the retiring Politburo members would assume the newly created roles of "consultants to the Politburo," apparently so they could retain party seniority. Although it had been anticipated that Truong Chinh and Pham Van Dong would relinquish their state posts, this did not happen. Rather, National Assembly elections were scheduled for the spring of 1987, after which the new assembly will meet to name a new chief of state and prime minister.

Although personalities changed at the highest level of VCP leadership, institutionalism continued. Still in place, it appeared, was the principle of collective leadership, which holds that decisions at the Politburo level must be acceptable to all and that, in terms of actual political power, all are more or less equal. When Nguyen Van Linh began his tenure, he was not even "first among equals," as Le Duan had been.

The process of convening a party congress in Vietnam has always been considered by the leadership to be even more important than the congress itself. It is regarded as a means by which new spirit can be injected into the rank and file. Political strength is mobilized and harnessed, basic-level personnel changes are effected, and provincial/district-level leadership is rejuvenated.

Preparatory work began on 11 March with a VCP Secretariat directive ordering the start of the party election process. This began in June at the grass-roots level and involved some 8,000 basic-level party units. Representatives were chosen for some 400 district-level congresses, urban wards, and regimental levels in the PAVN, at which representatives were named to the provincial-level (or equivalent) congresses. There the 1,129 individuals were chosen to go to Hanoi to attend the national congress. Most district-level congresses were completed by the end of September, the provincial congresses by early November.

There was some delay in convening the Sixth Congress, apparently because the leadership in Hanoi had difficulty in agreeing on the makeup of the new Politburo and Central Committee membership and in determining the exact language of the policy guidance to be given the congress.

In mobilizing the party faithful during the preparatory period, great use was made of the general secretary's draft Political Report, a basic statement of the new party line. Initially, the draft of the report was presented to the party's Tenth Plenum (Fifth Congress) in May, then sent to lower congresses for discussion. After being amended by this process, the report was read to the party congress itself.

The Political Report contained generalized policy enunciation and specific recommendations for internal change within the party system. It stressed the need for economic improvements in Vietnam and solicited ideas on how this could be accomplished. Among the recommendations were a larger allocation of resources to agriculture; increased consumer goods manufacturing; more energy production; improved and enlarged public transportation; and "price stability" (that is, control of inflation, at the time running about 700 percent per year). The report detailed the rise of "negative phenomena" in the society, meaning corruption and antiregime activity, and called for greater indoctrination efforts and more agitprop and emulation movement work within the party as well as with the general public. The report stressed the need to take more seriously the criticisms and suggestions of party members and to act on them accordingly. To this end it endorsed a massive *kiem thao* (self-criticism) emulation movement.

With respect to internal party needs, the report called for the lowering of the average party age through recruitment of young members and through retirements. Singled out for extended treatment was the party's younger "right arm and reserve force," the Ho Chi Minh Communist Youth Union. The report said that the organization had declined in both membership and prestige in recent years, which was one of the reasons for the increased juvenile crime in Vietnam. The youth union, it said, needed to be both augmented and "raised from moral decline."

The Political Report, as well as speeches by high officials during the year, frankly acknowledged the party's inability during the past decade to achieve the goals set for itself, taking onto the party much of the blame for the economic troubles that had descended on Vietnam. The report itself was subsequently criticized as being "still too far from reality" and for its vagueness and lack of precision as to exactly what kinds of new policies were required.

Party leaders met in three plenums during the year. The Tenth Plenum convened in Hanoi on 19 May for an unusually long (nineteen-day) session. Its agenda included the upcoming congress, economic problems, and what was termed "the cadre issue," meaning poor performance or misbehavior by party cadres. There was an unnumbered emergency plenum in July to name Truong Chinh interim general secretary (following the death of Le Duan), and the Eleventh Plenum (Fifth Congress) met in Hanoi on 20 November, as the "unity plenum." Most of its work was devoted to the final preparations for the Sixth Congress.

Deaths during the year of high-level VCP officials, in addition to Le Duan, included Senior General Hoang Van Thai, 79, one of the original PAVN old guard, 2 July in Hanoi; Senior General Le Trong Tan, 72, PAVN chief of staff, 7 December of a heart attack; Tran Quoc Hoan, 79, former security chief in the earlier Hanoi years and Politburo member until 1982, who died in December; and Trinh Dinh Thao, 85, a major figure in the Fatherland Front, who died in Ho Chi Minh City on 31 March. The Socialist Republic of Vietnam (SRV) minister of engineering and metals, Nguyen Van Kha, and eight other officials were indicted in early September on charges of graft involving an automobile assembly plant in Ho Chi Minh City, according to the Hanoi trade union newspaper, *Lao Dong*. This was the first time a criminal charge had been made against a standing cabinet official. The trial had not been held as of the end of the year.

**Domestic Party Affairs.** Throughout the year, the VCP carried on an unremitting campaign against "negative tendencies" that have "lowered the quality of socialist life" in Vietnam. Much of the blame was assigned to "bureaucratic authoritarianism" in the basic-level party organizational structure. Throughout the grass-roots level of the party, it was charged, discipline was poor and corruption high. As in the past, there was a tendency to single out the party cadre as whipping boy and subject him to steady editorial attack by the party press. *Nhan Dan* (19 March) declared that all party members who violate party regulations and state laws "must be expelled so as to keep the party pure and clean." On 25 April, the paper carried an extraordinarily harsh article on party and state cadres in the legal sector who it said were guilty of "theft, corruption, complicity, and degeneracy." *Nhan Dan* also declared that party cadres and state officials manipulated justice so as "to hand down right-tilting but unjust verdicts," handled some legal cases through "internal settlement" (that is, transferring individuals charged with white-collar crime acts rather than pressing charges), and generally provided an umbrella of legal protection for one another. A terse *Nhan Dan* report on 21 June said that two provincial-level party officials were to go on trial for "corruption and incompetence." Only one of the two provinces involved, Thanh Hoa, was named. There was no subsequent report on the trial.

On 21 June, Radio Hanoi broadcast details on the SRV Council of State communiqué announcing the appointment and dismissal of officials from nine ministerial level positions. They were Vo Chi Cong, replacing To Huu as vice-chairman of the Council of Ministers; Bui Danh Luu, replacing Dong Sy Nguyen as minister of communications/transport; Doan Duy Thanh, replacing Le Khac as minister of foreign trade; Hoang Minh Thang, replacing Le Duc Thinh as minister of home trade; Vu Tuan, replacing Chu Tam Thuc as minister of finance; Vu Tuan, relieved as minister of food; Nguyen Chan, relieved as minister of mines and coal; Nguyen Van Hieu, relieved as minister of culture; and Lu Minh Chau, replacing Nguyen Duy Gia as governor general of the State Bank.

Rank and file party members were also subjected to a good deal of attention by the hierarchy during 1986, in the form of special campaigns designed to improve their performance, commitment, and morals. A massive emulation movement in the name of criticism/self-criticism was launched early in the year and pressed steadily throughout. This venerable institution for self-examination was managed by a permanent cadre corps numbering some 35,000 *kiem thao* cadres who work chiefly at the grass-roots level through village and ward chapter meetings. Their duties were a cross between hearing religious confession and staging protests. Individual members were encouraged, even required, to criticize themselves, their peers, and their superiors in the party. Written reports on the substance of these sessions were then sent to higher headquarters for such action as deemed necessary.

In 1986, the *kiem thao* principle was extended to the general population, which was encouraged to criticize whatever it wished through the mechanism of letters to Vietnamese newspapers, chiefly in Hanoi and Ho Chi Minh City, and with the promise there would be no recriminations against the critic. The response was enthusiastic. Some 1,300 letters in one weekend arrived at a Ho Chi Minh City newspaper. The overwhelming number of complaints had to do with the economy. The second greatest number of complaints dealt with officious or corrupt party cadres and state bureaucrats accused of high living, nepotism, and using public office for personal gain. Typical of these letters was one signed by two young engineers who listed these charges: "State organs are cumbersome in operation, inefficient, and impractical; party cadres are incompetent; deviationists and opportunists have wrecked the economy; party cadres are often mean, wicked people who form their own cliques with secret connections to protect their own behinds and who with subtlety and cunning restrict or eliminate those cadres who are upright persons working effectively with good technical skills, because they are afraid of the competition of younger cadres with technical skills" (*Saigon Moi*, 12 June). Many of the letters adversely contrasted party cadre behavior during the Vietnam War and the postwar period. The great outpouring of criticism conjured up the picture of a failed sociopolitical system largely run by incompetents and thieves, as well as a general lack of understanding by the public as to basic causes of its social malaise.

Throughout the year, a systematic and concerted effort was made to improve the quality of the party membership and its lower-level leadership by altering its demographic structure. Party Directive 80 (May) enlarged the size of district/precinct party committees by about one-third. The directive also ordered the lowering of the average age of committee members at this level, and it ordered more women admitted to leadership positions as well as an increase in the number of women party members in general. A year-end report said that the average age in 60 percent of the district/precinct committees had been reduced to below 40 years, and the number of women in these committees increased by 2 percent. Overall, female membership in the party, said the report, had been increased from 15 percent to 20 percent in two years and the number of members with some post-high school education raised to 32 percent.

The country's economic problems during the year continued to be addressed by the leadership with essentially the same policies as had been set down by the Eighth Party Plenum (Fifth Congress) in June 1985. This program was restated and redefined in January 1986 with Politburo Resolution No. 28/NQ-TW dealing with "price policies." The program essentially had three major purposes: to abolish "bureaucratic centralism," meaning to transfer some of the decisionmaking and economic planning from Hanoi to the provincial level; to abolish "the mechanism of subsidy-based management," meaning to end the cumbersome wartime system of subsidizing wages and salaries with payment in kind; and to "shift to socialist economic accounting and business transactions," meaning to adopt more efficient cost accounting methods and inventory record keeping. Politburo Resolution 28 (28 April) on production and trade set forth what was termed the "basic economic unit's right to autonomy in production and business," which meant the extension of authority in certain economic planning and management activities to the provincial-level party and state apparatus.

Other important party/state directives during the year included Politburo Resolution 26 (4 July) to improve the party's youth activities; Secretariat Directive 79 (11 March) ordering a nationwide *kiem thao* emulation campaign; and Secretariat Directive 80 (circa April), which amended Directive 79 by specifying that the self-criticism campaign was to include "direct criticism of upper echelons of authority."

**Front Organizations.** The Fatherland Front, under the leadership of Presidium chairman Huynh Tan Phat and General Secretary Nguyen Van Tien, as with other institutions in Vietnam during the year, came in for a good deal of official criticism. VCP Secretariat Directive No. 17 (4 August) said Fatherland Front work of the past several years had been less than adequate. It set forth a five-point program to improve the front as the party's chief instrument for mobilizing the Vietnamese general population.

A new united-front anniversary was proclaimed during the year and is to be observed annually. The date 18 November 1930 was fixed as the day when the anti-imperialist association was created by the Indochinese Communist Party and is to be called Vietnam United Front Day. The proclamation in effect asserts that the Indochinese Communist Party organized and controlled the united-front movement in Indochina throughout the 1930s, thus claiming for the party greater centrality and influence than outside historians are willing to ascribe to it.

**International Positions.** Party and state foreign relations did not change appreciably during the year. The association with the USSR remained close and, at year's end, Moscow announced that its economic assistance for the SRV's 1986–1990 five-year plan would be double that of the previous plan (which would mean about $750 million a year, or $3.75 billion for the entire period).

Le Duan was in Moscow in February for the Twenty-seventh Congress of the Communist Party of the Soviet Union (CPSU) and for medical treatment, his last trip abroad before his death in July. His interim successor, Truong Chinh, flew to Moscow in late July, a few weeks after his appointment, where he was quoted by TASS (26 July) as saying that Vietnam had wasted and mismanaged Soviet aid and that rectification measures were underway. In late December, the new party secretary, Nguyen Van Linh, accepted an invitation to visit Moscow in early 1987.

In February, Vietnam and the USSR signed a five-year educational development agreement under which the USSR will begin training large numbers of Vietnamese economic cadres. Hanoi officially gave enthusiastic endorsement to the USSR's 23 April policy statement on Asia and the Pacific. It was less enthusiastic in its response to CPSU general secretary Mikhail Gorbachev's 28 July speech at Vladivostok. Prime Minister Pham Van Dong told TASS that the speech "contained initiatives that have a realistic significance" and added that he interpreted the speech to mean that Vietnam could continue to count on the support of the USSR (*FBIS*, 4 August). This cool treatment apparently resulted from the fact that the speech largely ignored the Cambodia problem.

Vietnam continued its integration into the socialist world's economic system by hosting in January the thirty-seventh session of the Council for Mutual Economic Assistance (CMEA) Committee on Cooperation in Planning. Delegates from nine countries attended, including the USSR's state planning commission chairman, who used the occasion to continue work with Vietnam's planning chairman, Vo Van Kiet, on coordinating the 1986–1990 five-year plans of the two countries. There were indications of dissatisfaction on the part of the USSR and demands for better economic performance in the use of aid and greater increase of exports to the Soviet Union to redress the lopsided trade balance.

Relations with China remained in the gray area somewhere between cold war and small-scale limited war. Border clashes and other military activity in what the Vietnamese called the "multifaceted war of sabotage" continued unabated during the year, culminating in a serious border battle in late December that left 1,500 Chinese dead, according to Hanoi.

Vietnam's war in Cambodia was conducted at a relatively low level during 1986, compared to previous years. There was no PAVN dry-season offensive. The resistance forces returned to more traditional guerrilla tactics and moved deeper into the countryside, claiming many successful attacks on Vietnamese installations. Hanoi's pledge to remove all troops from Cambodia by 1990 was repeated on several occasions by officials speaking with foreigners in Hanoi and abroad.

Relations with the United States during the year were largely confined to technical U.S. visits in pursuit of the resolution-of-casualties issue. Some remains of American dead were returned by Vietnamese officials.

**Biography.** *Nguyen Van Linh.* Nguyen Van Linh is one of the most secretive figures in the entire hierarchy of the Vietnamese communist movement. Hence, his sudden elevation to the post of party secretary by the Sixth Party Congress understandably came as a surprise and triggered great speculation about his personality, his earlier political activities, and his abilities as a leader.

Linh is not simply a revolutionary who has lived and operated in the shadows. Rather, he is one who has moved in a deeply clandestine manner throughout most of his career, obscure even to most party members.

Linh either supplanted or succeeded Le Duc Tho as the party leader responsible for party organization and for the important task of supervising cadre assignments and promotions in what is collectively termed the "central agencies apparat," meaning cadre and rank and file party members at the party center, in Hanoi. This element was Le Duc Tho's chief constituency and power base within the party/ state political structure, and apparently it was inherited by Linh.

Linh was born in 1915 in Hanoi into a petty bourgeois family from Hung Yen province (now Ha Bac) just south of Hanoi. His official biography says he took part in revolutionary activities while a student and was arrested by the French; he joined the Indochinese Communist Party in 1936, after release from prison under an amnesty. He did party organizational work in Saigon and central Vietnam until his second arrest in 1941. Released in 1945, he resumed party work in the Saigon-Cholon area and was reportedly the agent in charge of party political struggle operations in the South throughout the Viet Minh War. He headed the Central Office in South Vietnam (COSVN), although the area he supervised was at the time something of a military backwater, since the Viet Minh War was largely fought in the North.

With the party's 1959 decision to resume armed struggle in the South, Linh was named to head the reconstituted COSVN. However, the South Vietnamese government's strategic-hamlet program in 1961–1964 cut into the party's southern apparat, and Linh, who was considered responsible for the failure to meet this challenge, was replaced in 1964 as chief of COSVN by General Nguyen Chi Thanh; Linh became Thanh's deputy. After Thanh was killed, his place was taken by Pham Hung, and Linh stayed on as his deputy. Throughout the Vietnam War, Linh operated under various aliases in the South, including Nguyen Van Cuc, Nguyen Van Muoi, Muoi Cuc, and other variations of these names. It was not clear until after the war that all of these names represented one individual.

After victory, Linh was assigned various high-level duties in Ho Chi Minh City, and he became secretary of the city's party committee in 1976. Much of his work had to do with security. He was also generally responsible for reconstituting the city's social structure, which was considered part of "breaking the machine" in the South. He also supervised the economic coup d'état of 1978 that destroyed the existing southern trade and distribution system, for which many southerners have never forgiven him.

Linh was admitted to the Politburo by the Fourth Party Congress in December 1976. For reasons that are still not clear, he was dropped without announcement from the Politburo at the Fifth Congress in March 1982. There were virtually no press references to him between that time and 1985; he had apparently become something of a nonperson within the party. Then, also without announcement, he was returned to the Politburo sometime between April and July 1985.

Much of Linh's day-to-day work over the years has been associated with the mass organizations that act as the chief instruments for mobilization and motivation of the general Vietnamese population. These include the Fatherland Front, the Confederation of Vietnam Trade Unions, and friendship organizations with ties to the USSR, Eastern Europe, and Japan. He appears to be regarded as an individual with well-developed mobilizational skills. He seldom goes abroad and what trips he has taken apparently have been only to socialist countries.

Little is known by outsiders about Linh's personality, and virtually nothing is known about his private life.

Douglas Pike
*Berkeley, California*

# EASTERN EUROPE AND THE SOVIET UNION

# Introduction

The most important event in Moscow, with repercussions not only for the USSR and Eastern Europe but also for the world communist movement, was the CPSU congress held during the early part of 1986. Six of the eight East European ruling parties also held congresses in 1986, all after the Soviet one. Despite the call by M. S. Gorbachev for intensification of economic growth, the neighboring client states found it impossible to adopt the kind of radical reform measures that would accelerate developments in the right direction.

**The Soviet Union.** Overshadowing all other news during the year was the Twenty-seventh CPSU Congress, held from 25 February through 6 March. It did not prove to be as exciting as the Twentieth Congress in 1956, at which N. S. Khrushchev made a secret speech denigrating his predecessor and the Stalinist repression of loyal communist party members during the Great Purge and later.

As a matter of fact, although the five thousand party delegates approved Gorbachev's suggestions for economic reform, the general inertia and bureaucratic opposition may represent obstacles to implementation. Open disagreements over special privileges for CPSU members suggest that even the elite has not been captured by Gorbachev's vision.

CPSU organizations in Central Asia (Kirghizia and Uzbekistan) as well as Moscow itself were accused of mismanagement and corruption. However, despite replacement of every third regional party secretary, only two candidates for Politburo membership, aged 85 and 80, were retired. Fewer than half of the Central Committee members could be ousted.

Regarding the domestic economy, Gorbachev suggested specific improvements for agriculture, which he had supervised (1978–1985) as one of the CPSU national secretaries. The Central Committee adopted a resolution on 29 March that provided both collective and state farms with incentives and more autonomy. Effective in 1987, these measures should allow the sale of produce at higher prices through cooperatives and private markets.

More precise guidelines for other parts of the economy were spelled out by N. I. Ryzhkov, the chairman of the Council of Ministers. Draft targets, published in October 1985, remain unchanged. They cover the 1986–1990 period as well as the longer-term plan through the year 2000. It is probable that the drop in world prices for crude oil and the consequences from the accident at Chernobyl will affect Soviet hard currency income as well as the output of electricity from nuclear power stations.

The new CPSU leader had not been exposed to external affairs prior to 1985, and only about one-sixth of his speech at the Twenty-seventh Congress dealt with foreign policy. Peace and security could be guaranteed, he said, only if the Soviet plan to eliminate all nuclear weapons by the year 2000 was accepted.

This proposal, first enunciated by Gorbachev on 15 January, is claimed to be the cornerstone of USSR foreign policy.

Apart from repeating standard communist propaganda charges against the United States and the West in general, the CPSU general secretary expressed the idea that global interdependence is a growing trend. Nevertheless, he accused the "right-wing" group in Washington, D.C., and "fellow travelers" in NATO of supporting a policy of force. Gorbachev described Western Europe as the fundamental sector in Soviet policy.

Asia and the Pacific are of increasing importance, with the Middle East and Central America, as well as southern Africa, described as "hotbeds." Only the war in Afghanistan received more detailed treatment by Gorbachev. He suggested that the Soviet military presence would be withdrawn once "foreign" interference had ceased. Removal of USSR troops is one of three obstacles to basic improvement of Moscow's relations with Beijing. The others are the military buildup along their common borders and the Vietnamese occupation of Cambodia. The rest of the Third World received mention by Gorbachev in terms of countries with a "socialist" orientation, revolutionary democratic parties, and the nonaligned movement.

The CPSU general secretary was able to "retire" just one of his opponents on the Politburo, D. A. Kunaev, who was dropped from his position as CPSU leader in Kazakhstan in mid-December. Replacing Kunaev with an ethnic Russian precipitated demonstrations by "hooligans," mostly university students in Alma Ata. (This did not prevent Kunaev's dismissal from the Politburo on 29 January 1987.) The second CPSU secretary for the republic is a native Kazakh.

Otherwise, the campaign against corruption continued. In addition to Central Asia and the Caucasus, "violations of socialist legality" were uncovered at Voronezh as well as Novosibirsk. The city of Moscow did not remain immune, as local officials were purged for covering up poor administration. The "second economy" flourished, nevertheless. A decree issued in November allows taxi drivers and repairmen to moonlight.

*Glasnost'*, or openness, included news about the existence in the USSR of drug abuse, prostitution, racial antagonism, and even AIDS. The publicized release of Anatolii Shcharansky and Yuri Orlov in February brought firsthand estimates to the West that 15,000 to 20,000 prisoners of conscience are being held in the USSR. Gorbachev also telephoned Nobel laureate Andrei Sakharov in mid-December to reveal that he would be allowed to live in Moscow after seven years of exile in Gorky. Only a week earlier, this distinguished academician had been referred to as a "criminal" by the deputy chairman of the USSR Supreme Court.

Much of the foregoing was done to impress the West favorably with the new Soviet leadership. Gorbachev's invitation to President Reagan for a mini-summit at Reykjavik broke the impasse over the set-up arrest of *U.S. News and World Report* journalist Nicholas Daniloff, who was exchanged for a KGB intelligence officer. It is not improbable that the Politburo had decided that its leader should not go to Washington, D.C., in 1986. That may explain Gorbachev's behavior in Iceland. A massive expulsion of USSR diplomats from the United States resulted in an official ban against Soviet citizens working at the U.S. embassy and consulates in the Soviet Union.

**Eastern Europe.**   Despite the Chernobyl nuclear power plant explosion, which contaminated several of the countries bordering the Ukraine, no official protests or claims for damages were made by any of the East European client regimes. Moscow television broadcast a speech by Gorbachev in mid-May that expressed gratitude to those governments for acceptance of the Soviet misfortune as their own.

The Council for Mutual Economic Assistance (CMEA) summit, held during November in Moscow, agreed to direct links between producers throughout the bloc. Trade has increased sixfold within the East European and Soviet area since 1971, and the USSR and other CMEA governments have signed about 100 bilateral agreements for machine building alone. Economic growth, however, has been disappointing. In addition, the total foreign debt in hard currency stood at almost $114 billion in 1986.

The military alliance, the Warsaw Treaty Organization (WTO), continued modernization of its equipment, with the USSR delivering advanced weapons systems. The WTO Political Consultative Committee met at Budapest in June and issued an appeal to "all other European countries, the United States and Canada" for substantial reductions of manpower as well as armaments between the Atlantic and the Urals.

By the early 1990s, it proposed, each side should have 500,000 fewer troops. Not mentioned was the fact that the Mutual and Balanced Force Reduction talks, now in their fourteenth year and covering only Central Europe, have not reached any agreement to date.

Albania, in neither the WTO nor CMEA, has been outside the bloc since 1961. It held a party congress that confirmed Ramiz Alia as successor to the late Enver Hoxha, who had ruled the country over a 40-year period. Continuity was emphasized in the leadership composition. Whether the atmosphere will improve, after providing material incentives, remains to be seen. Tirana refuses to have any contacts with Moscow—party or government.

Todor Zhivkov, the communist leader in Bulgaria, has been in office for 32 years. At age 75, he was re-elected to all posts and received the Order of the October Revolution from the Soviet Union. Almost every sector of the Bulgarian economy is now closely linked with the USSR. The party congress in April at Sofia seemed to emulate the one in Moscow, with campaigns against alcoholism and corruption pursued vigorously. Only the *glasnost'* did not appear to be genuine.

By contrast, the Czechoslovak leadership paid only lip service to reforms at its party congress in March. Criticism could be heard from the podium, although change probably will come slowly. The fact that about 80 percent of all foreign trade is with other communist-ruled states (more than half of that with the USSR) indicates that the Prague regime is in a straitjacket. Gustáv Husák obviously will do Moscow's bidding, as he has done ever since he replaced the reformist Alexander Dubček.

The best economic performance throughout the bloc is being registered by the German Democratic Republic, which does not plan any reforms to speak of. More than half of its electronic component production is sent to the USSR. Here, too, party leader Erich Honecker, even at age 73, is in firm control— as shown by his performance at the communist party congress in April that Gorbachev attended. As long as expansion continues, it is doubtful that the East Germans will emulate the changes introduced by the Soviet Union.

Once the showplace of the bloc, Hungary's standard of living has declined. It showed no growth in either 1985 or 1986. This last year marked the 30th anniversary of the revolution that gave the people a modicum of freedom—until crushed by the Soviet tanks that brought with them János Kádár. Some of the Hungarian economic reforms have been adopted by the USSR. However, the European Economic Community's ban on agricultural products from Budapest after the Chernobyl accident negatively affected hard currency income.

The same situation occurred in connection with Polish food exports to Western Europe. A congress of the ruling communist party in Warsaw, attended by Gorbachev, proclaimed "normalization" after the 1980–1981 Solidarity interlude. The last 225 political prisoners were not released until September. However, some are known to remain in prisons. Serious economic problems exist, compounded by the tighter integration with CMEA. Regime exhortations that people should work harder seem to fall on deaf ears; hearts remain with the underground Solidarity movement.

Only in Romania does the regime continue to raise economic targets that will never be met. The policy of forced industrial growth is accompanied by a linking of wages with plan fulfillment, resulting in lower pay. Food is rationed and frequently unavailable. An austerity program has reduced imports from abroad. Party leader Nicolae Ceaușescu's "cult of personality" now includes his wife, Elena, who is in charge of key personnel assignments. The radioactive fallout from Chernobyl affected relations with the Soviet Union, which continues to offer crude oil to Romania in exchange for low-priced food.

The only CMEA "associate" member, the one that never joined the Warsaw Pact, is Yugoslavia. Its party congress in June heard speeches deploring disunity among communist leaders and complaints about the situation in Kosovo, where some 80 percent of the population is Albanian. The latter have been accused of terrorist tactics against other ethnic groups. The new party leader, Milanko Renovica, visited Moscow in December. Trade between the two countries has been growing, although the USSR has never provided Yugoslavia with any hard currency credits.

In conclusion, one could say that it will be difficult for the Soviet Union and its East European client-states to apply economic "intensification" effectively and successfully. The bloc appears to be stable enough, with no leadership changes occurring in 1986. As mentioned, the military and economic summits during the year apparently were well orchestrated in advance. Only in the case of Romania could any deviation be detected, namely the refusal to accept any "joint enterprises" with the Soviet Union. That may come later, if the USSR is willing to pay the price, perhaps in larger crude oil and natural gas deliveries.

In general, the year 1987 may be much the same as its predecessor, both for the Soviet Union and its "allies" in Eastern Europe.

Richard F. Staar
*Hoover Institution*

# Albania

**Population.** 3,020,000 (World Factbook, 1986)
**Party.** Albanian Party of Labor (Partia ë Punës ë Shqipërisë; APL)
**Founded.** 8 November 1941
**Membership.** 147,000 regular party members; 39.8 percent workers; 29.5 percent cooperativists (peasants); 31.3 percent civil servants. Women constitute 32.2 percent of the membership. (*Zeri i Popullit*, 4 November.)
**First Secretary.** Ramiz Alia
**Politburo.** Thirteen full members: Ramiz Alia (first secretary, president of the republic, and supreme commander of the armed forces), Adil Çarçani (prime minister), Besnik Bekteshi (deputy prime minister), Foto Çami, Lenka Çuko, Hekuran Isai (minister of the interior), Hajredin Çeliku (minister of industry and mines), Rita Marko (deputy chairman of the Presidium of the People's Assembly), Simon Stefani, Pali Mishka (chairman of the People's Assembly), Manush Myftiu (deputy premier), Prokop Mura (minister of defense), Muho Asllani (party chief of Shkodër); five alternate members: General Kiço Mustaqi (deputy defense minister, chief of the General Staff), Llambi Gjegprifti (chairman of the executive council, Tirana district), Pirro Kondi (party chief, Tirana district), Qirjako Mihali (party chief, Durress district), Vangjel Çerava (ATA, 8 November; *FBIS*, 10 November)
**Secretariat.** Five members: Ramiz Alia, Foto Çami, Lenka Çuko, Simon Stefani, Vangjel Çerava.
**Central Committee.** 85 members, 46 alternate members
**Status.** Ruling party
**Last Congress.** Ninth, 3–8 November 1986, in Tirana
**Last Parliamentary Elections.** 1982, all 250 candidates of the Democratic Front. Only one ballot was cast against the front candidates.
**Auxiliary Organizations.** Albanian Democratic Front, Nexhmije Hoxha, chairwoman; Central Council of Trade Unions (UTUA), approximately 610,000 members as of 1984, Sotir Kocallari, chairman; Union of Labor Youth of Albania (ULYA), approximate membership 500,000, Mehmet Elezi, first secretary; Women's Union of Albania (WUA), Lumturi Rexha, chairwoman; Albanian War Veterans, Shefqet Peçi, chairman; Albanian Defense of Peace Committee, Musaraj Shefqet, chairman
**Main State Organs.** Council of Ministers (20 members). The People's Assembly (250 members) is constitutionally the leading body of the state, but in reality it rubberstamps decisons reached by the party's Politburo or Central Committee.
**Publications.** *Zeri i Popullit*, daily organ of the Central Committee of the APL; *Rruga ë Partisë*, monthly theoretical journal, organ of the Central Committee of the APL; *Bashkimi*, daily organ of the Democratic Front; *Puna*, weekly organ of the UTUA; *10 Korik* and *Lluftetari*, biweekly organs of the Ministry of Defense; *Nendori*, literary monthly, organ of the Albanian Writers' and Artists' League; *Laiko Vema*, daily organ of the Greek minority. The Albanian Telegraphic Agency (ATA) is the official state news agency.

The Albanian communist party was founded on 8 November 1941 on the initiative of Marshal Tito of Yugoslavia, who was acting on Comintern instructions. In early October of the same year, two Montenegrin communists, Miladin Popović and Dušan Mungoša, ventured to Tirana with explicit instruc-

tions to forge several regional groupings of communist agitators into a "national" communist party. As
far as Tito and the Comintern were concerned, the
formation of an Albanian communist party was a
prerequisite to the commencement of any meaningful resistance against the German-Italian
occupation.

A total of fifteen individuals, claiming to represent existing communist organizations in the cities
of Korçë, Shkodër, and Tirana, assembled in a
private house in the old part of the city, under the
tutelage of Mungoša and Popović. Although accounts of what transpired in the "founding congress"
differ widely, enough has been written from all sides
to reconstruct events rather accurately.

The two Yugoslavs impressed upon those present the need to start early the anti-Nazi resistance—otherwise it could be preempted by Albanian nationalists who were, as in neighboring
countries, actively resisting the enemy or preparing
to do so. Invoking proletarian internationalism and
the duty to defend the motherland of socialism, the
two Yugoslavs managed to unite the factions into a
single organization. Compromises were made by
all present. The first compromise was made by the
leaders of the three regional communist groups. It
was agreed that none of them should be named
provisional secretary. The second was the selection
of Enver Hoxha, a teacher of French from
Gjoricastër. Hoxha had spent time in Korçë, but in
1936 had moved to Tirana, where he opened a
tobacco shop. A seven-member Central Committee
was created, consisting of Enver Hoxha, Qemal
Stafa, Koçi Xoxe, Tuk Jakova, Kristo Themelko,
Ramadan Çitaku, and Gjin Marku. (Hoxha, *Kur
lindi Parti* [When the Party Was Born], p. 220.)

Enver Hoxha, the son of a mullah, was elected
provisional secretary, since he was acceptable to
all factions. The Yugoslavs made sure that Koçi
Xoxe was keeping a watchful eye over him.
(*Hellenic Review of International Affairs*, vols. 3
and 4, p. 94.)

The dominant element of the Albanian communist party was the Korçë group, whose origins are
traceable to the work of two Comintern operatives,
Lazar Fundo and Ali Kelmendi. Two tinsmiths from
the same city, Koçi Xoxe and Pilo Peristeri, had
founded the communist cell "Puna" (Work) in 1931
in collaboration with fellow travelers from the
Greek communist party. Peristeri, currently the
chairman of the Central Committee's Control Commission, sponsored the admission of Hoxha to the
Puna cell.

A second significant group of Albanian communists had been in existence in the city of Shkodër
and active (though in a disorganized manner) since
the mid-1920s. Due to its proximity, it had maintained close relations with Yugoslav and Austrian
communists. The Shkodër group was led by the
prominent Albanian intellectual Zejfula Mal-
eshova, one of the first victims of Enver Hoxha's
permanent purge.

The third component of the Albanian communist
party came from the youth organization, Zjari
(Fire), originally formed in Athens by an obscure
Albanian personality, Andrea Zisi. Once established in Tirana, Zjari was taken over by Anastas
Lulo and Sadik Prempte. From the outset, Zjari was
suspected of reflecting the views of the Greek communist party—an organization notorious for its
docility to Moscow and internationalist militancy.
(*Hellenic Review of International Affairs*, vols. 3
and 4, p. 89). The Zjari group had come under
Hoxha's influence as of 1936, but Prempte and Lulo
maintained some control until the founding congress. Once brought under the umbrella of the nationwide party organization, the leaders of Zjari
were targeted for elimination. Their alleged crimes
were "opportunism" and "divisiveness." After a
vain attempt by Prempte to etablish a rival party
organization in the port city of Vlorë, he fled the
country. Lulo was captured and executed.

Upon the creation of the communist party, the
Yugoslav emissaries instructed their Albanian
counterparts to form armed units and commence
resistance against the foreign enemy. For the duration of the war and until the Tito-Stalin break the
Albanian communist party was under de facto
Yugoslav control, with Svetozar Vukmanovic-
Tempo as overall supervisor of its military and
political activities. At its first regular congress (1
November 1948) the name of the party was changed
to the Albanian Party of Labor, and Enver Hoxha
was elected as its first secretary, a post he held until
his death on 11 April 1985. It is worth noting that by
1948, all seven members of the party's first Central
Committee had been purged or executed. Only one,
Qemal Stafa, was killed in action.

The First APL Congress legitimized the break
with Yugoslavia, "exposed the plots of Xoxe and
other Titoites," and unleashed the harshest form of
class struggle known in communist annals. Xoxe
and hundreds of his followers were executed, while
others were given harsh and lengthy prison terms.

Instability at the highest ranks and inability to
find permanent friends among ruling communist

parties have been the two dominant characteristics of the Albanian Party of Labor. Five major and numerous smaller purges were orchestrated by Enver Hoxha after 1941. A total of 47 party leaders who had reached the rank of Central Committee member (two-thirds of whom were also full or alternate Politburo members) have been physically eliminated since 1941.

The latest housecleaning involved Mehmet Shehu (prime minister for 28 years), sixteen members of his cabinet, hundreds of his followers and family members, and several hundred high-ranking officers of the armed forces and security service. Shehu was formally accused of being a "triple agent," working simultaneously for the CIA, KGB, and the Yugoslav intelligence service, the UDBA.

Historically, the Albanian purges followed the classic Stalinist model: first purge the enemies or suspected enemies, then purge the purgers of enemies for "excessive zeal," but never admit error or rehabilitate any of the victims. Political patterns suggest that Hoxha had a well-founded fear of his own instruments of oppression, the secret police and the military, if we are to judge from the fate that has befallen their leaders. With the exception of himself, all defense and interior ministers since 1948 have been politically banished or physically eliminated. The current minister of the interior, Hekuran Isai, who was placed in charge of security after the removal of the "Shehu protégé," Kadri Hazbiu, seems to have held his own in the post-Hoxha leadership. But there are signs that, like his predecessors, his power is diminished.

The post-Hoxha leadership of the APL has made the transition to power with minor, but potentially significant, changes in style, ideological orientation, and the composition of top party organs. Although Alia's consolidation of his position was facilitated by the massive purges orchestrated by Hoxha against the so-called Shehu gang, he nevertheless was quite busy throughout 1986 to establish his own leadership pattern and to fend off potential challenges to his authority. A distinct Alia style of leadership emerged from his numerous appearances before mass organizations and festivities, characterized by an unusual degree of pragmatism and (by Albanian standards) openness (*Zeri i Popullit*, 9 January). His New Year's address to the nation, replete with blunt criticism of poor economic performance, is a case in point (ibid.).

As a first, and perhaps prerequisite, step toward power consolidation Alia assumed his position as commander in chief of the armed forces and kept a

close watch on the activities of the organs of internal security. Although his military experience is limited (his wartime activities consisted exclusively of ideological work, see *YICA*, 1983), he nevertheless observed firsthand several military exercises involving military-civilian coordination of coastal defenses. He reviewed a massive summer exercise involving the Durrës garrison that was intended to test the application of the doctrine of "total people's defense." Alia used the opportunity to denounce the Shehu-Hazbiu-Baluku strategy of "retreat to the hinterland" in case of an invasion. (Tirana radio, 10 July; *FBIS*, 11 July). In a similar appearance in the region of Permët (close to the Greek border), he reaffirmed the Hoxha doctrine of mass involvement in the defense of the country and "transformation of the plains into highlands" through the construction of fortifications (*Zeri i Popullit*, 21 October). Attention to military and security affairs is not unusual in a country so thoroughly militarized and internally controlled. Alia's attention to these matters, however, is coupled with an emphasis on "legality" and a warning to the security apparatus to be both *vigilant* and *fair*.

In his report to the Ninth Party Congress, the first secretary advised the state organs to act within the framework of the constitution and the laws and warned that the party will see to it "that the state organs at all levels carry out their activities on the basis of the constitution and the laws derived from it" (*Zeri i Popullit*, 4 November). In a pointed reference to the role of the organs of the Ministry of the Interior, Alia admonished them to bear in mind that "they must act justly and strictly, defending the interests of the state and society, but also the *rights*, *lives*, and *property* of citizens" (ibid.). Absent from his speech were past ritualistic references to "state organs" as the instrument of the dictatorship of the proletariat and the class struggle.

Perpetuation of the Hoxha legacy has been a constant theme in party life throughout the year. Furthermore, the personality cult of the late dictator is carefully cultivated. Several of his books were published posthumously by the Institute of Marxism-Leninism, which is directed by his widow (ATA, 16 October; *FBIS*, 16 October). Despite the persistence of the Hoxha cult, divergences with past approaches appeared in two critical areas: the economy and the treatment of young people.

Several editorials and "scientific" studies criticized the past policies of restricting the role of the private plot in a socialist economy. Elimination of private plots and privately owned livestock was a central theme of the Eighth APL Congress, the last one under Hoxha. In his report to the Eighth Congress, Hoxha had demanded that the party and state "further restrict private plots in order to strengthen the organization and management of production" (*YICA*, 1982). In a noticeable reversal, perhaps dictated by economic realities, Alia and several other party members criticized the "failure to understand fully party directives concerning the formation of small flocks and herds of sheep held on the cooperative workers' private plots . . . which led to considerable damage and slaughter of much livestock" (*Zeri i Popullit*, 4 November). Alia's criticism was reiterated by Foto Çami, a rising personality in Albanian politics, who deplored the "misunderstanding and misapplication of policies concerning private plots, causing bad consequences on production levels and farm output in several districts" (ibid., 6 November). Çami went a step further and admonished the participants in the Ninth Congress to take under serious consideration "the fact that general principles and fundamental laws of socialism cannot be carried out in a mechanical manner, at all times, under all circumstances and in the same way under all conditions" (ibid.). If we take under consideration that "total socialism" and "scientific" orthodoxy were the central theme of the Eighth Party Congress, the nuances that pervaded Alia's and Çami's reports to the Ninth Congress may be indicative of new trends in party politics and the economic affairs of Albania.

As in previous years, problems with the attitudes of the young emerged and perhaps intensified during 1986. To judge from the content of Alia's comments on the subject, the distinct impression emerges that he intends to channel youth energies in a way that could neutralize pressures from the older generation of leaders, who feel more comfortable in their paternalistic approach toward demands of the younger generation. In a major editorial, reflective of the Central Committee's views, the APL daily criticized the outmoded mentality of party and state authorities toward Albanian youth. "Young people do not need everything to be dictated to them and do not need to be watched by a teacher on duty at every evening dance on the supposed ground that they will make mistakes" (*Zeri i Popullit*, 19 February). Speaking to the students and faculty of the Alexander Xhuvani Institute of Elbasan (named after Alia's father-in-law), the first secretary recommended to "once and for all get rid of the tutelage and all other methods allegedly used to *discipline* the cultural, artistic, and sporting activities of young people—even their entertainment—because they artificially hinder the drive, skills, and initiative of the young" (ibid., 7 May). Further, Alia advised the youth to "ignore the inhibiting opinions of lazy people [and] of those who have limited horizons" (RFE, RL *Background Report* 79, 5 June).

**Internal Party Affairs.** Preparations for the Ninth Party Congress, held in Tirana (3–8 November), dominated the agenda of party and state organizations during the entire year. This was the first congress since Hoxha's death. As usual in conjunction with an anticipated party congress, a massive drive for "frontal attack on economic problems" was spearheaded by the regional and local party organizations, who aimed at fulfilling the goals of the Seventh Five-Year Plan. But despite intense ideological effort, economic problems persisted throughout the year, and new approaches to their solution crept into Albanian Marxist orthodoxy. Another look at the value of the private plot and the introduction of incentives emerged as distinct options for the post-Hoxha era.

Veiled criticism of a policy initiated by Hoxha and the former chairman of the State Planning Commission, Petro Dode (*YICA*, 1982; *Zeri i Popullit*, 27 March 1981) constituted a significant aspect of reports by Alia, Çami, and Prime Minister Çarçani. Conveniently, 1981 policies regarding private plots were blamed on the "Shehu gang" and on the "failure of lower party organs" to properly interpret the party's intent on this matter. The issue of incentives, a prominent feature in Eastern European economic models, has acquired a new significance in the Albanian context; they are looked upon as a better method to increase productivity and to assure the fulfillment of the Eighth Five-Year Plan, whose draft directives were approved by the Ninth APL Congress.

In a lengthy article, the APL theoretical journal proposed an "innovative" approach to productivity based on fine-tuning three interrelated elements of economic policy: a new wage policy, refinement of pricing mechanisms, and appropriate manipulation of financing and investment policies (*Rruga ë Partisë*, July). Departing from past emphasis on an egalitarian approach to compensation, the theoretical journal recommended that wages be determined by the "importance and difficulty of work, required level of skills, results attained in production, and savings achieved in resources" (ibid.). Further, the author of the article recommended the use of pricing as a tool to influence "supply and demand." The policy of incentives was affirmed by the Ninth Congress and constituted an important part of Alia's report on the state of the economy (*Zeri i Popullit*, 11 November).

Economic problems had dominated the concerns of local party organizations in previous years as well. What is different in this post-Hoxha era, however, is the frankness of criticism and the sharpness of Alia's attack on "bureaucratism," "technocratism" and "formalism." *Zeri i Popullit* on numerous occasions singled out several districts for gross failure to fulfill their plans and for permitting waste of resources by careless managers and cadres. Kruje, Durrës, and Librazh were made examples for their failure to fulfill production quotas of tobacco, a key export (ibid., 11 September). Similarly, Qirjako Mihali, alternate member of the Politburo and party chief of the second largest district, Durrës, chided those who ignore the value of "mass action" to increase productivity, and referred to studies that have "reached the conclusion that within particular enterprises and sectors there are still failures to fulfill the plan and major unused reserves and opportunities that must be exploited" (ibid., 2 June).

In a 1985 speech before a congress of innovators held in his hometown of Shkodër, Alia had expressed his impatience with the pervasiveness of bureaucratism and technocratism and had denounced those who hamper innovation. This theme was repeated on several occasions during 1986. In early January, *Zeri i Popullit* denounced the bureaucrats for viewing the "innovators as maniacs who cause work and worry and disturb the peace and quiet and routine of ordinary desultory labor" (ibid., 9 January). "Bureaucrats have created an intellectual elite with 'rare abilities,'" according to the party organ, "and have even transplanted technical language into party and mass organizations, which is barely understood by members" (ibid.). Alia used similar verbiage in his report to the Ninth Congress, and he identified the main threats to socialist production as liberalism, sectarianism, bureaucratism, and technocratism (ibid., 4 November), all of which have persisted in Albanian life. Support for the still fragile tendency toward openness came from several major party figures during the congress, including Foto Çami and Besnik Bekteshi, a young deputy premier and new member of the Politburo.

Çami alluded to a lack of frankness on the part of cadres, who ignore a "tradition of the party to speak frankly with the people everywhere . . . as it has done in the past when it discussed the problems of our land openly." Up to that point his remarks could be viewed as a euphemism, but Çami broke new ground when he argued for a more meaningful approach to communications and the use of propaganda, with "more information, more ideas and knowledge, more facts and arguments" (ibid., 6 November). Bekteshi, emerging as a new economic tsar at age 47, took to task those who pursue "centralization for centralization's sake." In his view, "centralization does not presuppose that all powers be concentrated and controlled by higher bodies" (ibid., 7 November).

Besides an obvious change in the atmosphere of party life during the past year, there have also been changes and additions to the higher party organs that underscore the consolidation of gains by the postrevolutionary generation of leaders.

For the first time since 1981, the Politburo has its full complement of thirteen members. Geographically this body is still dominated by southerners; only four members can be considered to belong to the revolutionary generation (Alia, Çami, Mura, and Myftiu). The three new members of the highest party body were elevated to that position from the list of alternates. They are Besnik Bekteshi, Foto Çami, and the defense minister, Prokop Mura (ibid., 9 November; *FBIS*, 10 November). By themselves, the changes in the composition of the Politburo suggest continuity and renovation. It is noteworthy that two prominent party personalities, Nexhmije Hoxha and Qirjako Mihali, failed to advance in the new party hierarchy. Mihali continues to be an alternate member of the Politburo; Madame Hoxha was relegated to the position of chairwoman of the Democratic Front. Analyses published in the West presented her new position as a "promotion." The Democratic Front, however, is only a "transmission belt," and its chairmanship traditionally has been an honorary position (RFE, *Background Report* 43, 23 March; *NYT*, 12 October).

Among the alternate members of the Politburo are at least three who have obviously benefited from the downfall of Shehu and to some extent played a role in it. One is General Kiço Mustaqi (chief of the General Staff), who replaced Prokop Mura (elevated to full membership) in that position. The other two are Pirro Kondi, party chief of Tirana, and Vangjel Çerava (from the district of Korçë), who was elevated to the party secretariat in 1982.

Hekuran Isai, minister of the interior, was the only member who was not re-elected to the Secretariat.

The Central Committee of the party offers a new portrait as well. The size of this body increased from 81 to 85 full members, while the alternate membership increased from 40 to 46. A total of 22 new members were elevated to full membership; 12 were drawn from the list of alternates, and 10 are new faces (*Zeri i Popullit*, 17 November). Fourteen members of the old committee failed to be re-elected. The alternate list has 33 newcomers among its ranks. The new party bodies, according to Alia, reflect the growth in membership and social composition of the party and a desire to rejuvenate the ranks (ibid., 4 November).

Membership in the party has grown at an annual rate of 6 percent since the last party congress. As indicated in the first secretary's report, the party consists of 147,000 full members (ibid.; *Pravda*, 6 November). There are no figures given about the number of candidate members. According to Alia, the membership will continue to grow at the rate of 6,000 new members annually. Sociologically, 80 percent of the membership of the APL comes from the "production sector." Women constitute 40 percent of the members (an increase of 2.5 percent as compared to 1981); 29.5 percent of the members are classified as "cooperativists"; 39.2 percent are of working class origin; and 31.4 percent are white-collar workers. The latter category shows a decline of 1.4 percent as compared to 1981 (*Zeri i Popullit*, 4 November). Over 80 percent of the party membership is under 40, and those over 51 years of age constitute only 8 percent of the total.

There are no fundamental changes in the criteria used to select and admit party members. "The political past and present perspective of the candidate's family, his social origin, his professional abilities, and his productivity are taken into account, along with his personal traits and social responsibility and his behavior as a citizen" (ibid., 4 November).

Reflective of Alia's pragmatism and emphasis on youth (he started off his political career as first secretary of the party's youth organization) were the remarks on "vigilance," and "patriotism," and willingness to innovate that he incorporated in his report to the Ninth Congress.

"Vigilance" was the central theme of the brief report given by the minister of the interior, Hekuran Isai, who told the participants of lurking dangers and a need to continue the class struggle. In a speech reminiscent of the harshest days of the Hoxha era, Isai warned of threats to socialist Al-bania from "new enemies and people who degenerate in our ranks owing to the vestiges of the past and the outside bourgeois-revisionist pressure" (Tirana Radio Domestic Service; *FBIS*; 7 November). Although Alia assured the congress that the damages caused by the "Shehu gang" had been repaired, Isai warned of "external and internal enemies striving to introduce new influences, ideas, and concepts that could lead to the degeneration of the people, particularly of the young people" (ibid.). In what appears to be a contradiction in tone and content to Isai's report, Alia and Çami advised party members to avoid "mechanical application of Marxist-Leninist principles" and asked the cadres to "strive for things that are new and progressive and never become slaves of formulas, habits, styles, and methods that have become outmoded" (*Zeri i Popullit*, 4 November). In this context, Alia invoked "patriotism" as a concept "that never ages or rusts"—while Isai invoked class struggle.

**Party-Military Relations.** The year under review was characterized by symbolic militarization of the top party leaders. Ramiz Alia, a theorist and ideologue, made several appearances in his capacity as commander in chief of the armed forces (ibid. 10 July). The defense minister, Prokop Mura, who had been handpicked by Hoxha to deal with the "Shehu gang," was promoted to full membership in the Politburo. Although a civilian and economist by profession, he donned a general's uniform and assumed tighter control of the military, perhaps on Alia's behalf (RFE, RL *Background Report* 163, 13 November). Mura's position in the alternate list of Politburo members was taken by General Kiço Mustaqi. Two deputy defense ministers, Simon Balabani and Ali Vukatana (often referred to as the general secretary of the Ministry of Defense), retained their positions as members of the Central Committee (*Zeri i Popullit*; 11 November).

Alia's report to the APL congress was rather thin in its treatment of the military. He simply repeated clichés regarding the need to maintain a military "with an all-round political, military, psychological, technical, and physical training, consistent with the requirements of our military art of people's warfare" (ibid., 4 November). Although he was quite harsh in denouncing the damage done to the security forces by the "Shehu gang," Alia omitted such references in the two paragraphs he devoted to the military, suggesting that purges of senior officers accused of "praetorianism" and "Shehuism" have gone far enough. However, other senior defense officials with high standing in the party have kept the anti-Shehu rhetoric alive and intense.

Ali Vukatana warned against praetorianism and antiparty mentality in the military on several occasions. In a major article, he derided past attitudes among staff officers, who prompted the slogan "the army can survive without the party, but not without the staff" (*Rruga ë Partisë*, July). Similarly, a major editorial prior to the Ninth Congress complimented Alia for maintaining party supremacy over the military and for supporting "free military schools" where young schoolchildren from the age of fourteen are trained in military arts (*Zeri i Popullit*, 21 October).

In one area, allocation of resources, the military has been affected negatively during the past year. The defense budget for 1986 was reduced by 43 percent as compared to the previous year. The proposed budget stands at 978 million leks (1.7 billion for 1985). The cost cuts could well have been dictated by economic necessities. In an appearance before senior officers, Alia demanded greater contribution "by the military to the economic life of the country without compromising defense" (RFE, RL *Background Report* 106, 26 July). Defense Minister Prokop Mura reiterated support of the party line in his brief report to the APL congress and parroted Alia's slogan, "without strong economy there can be no strong defense" (*Zeri i Popullit*, 6 November).

**Auxiliary and Mass Organization.** In a ritualistic and redundant manner, all mass and auxiliary organizations were mobilized to "fulfill economic tasks" in preparation for the APL congress. Espousing the slogan "turning grief for the loss of Enver into strength," party and mass organizations sought to invigorate an apathetic public and turn it into a force for the improvement of the social and economic conditions of the country.

The Democratic Front, the largest mass organization, fields candidates for public office under the direction and control of the party. During 1986 the front was preoccupied with the preparation for and conduct of the 27 April elections for people's district, city, and village councils and for people's judges (ATA, 28 April; *FBIS*, 29 April).

At a March meeting of the General Council of the Democratic Front, First Secretary Ramiz Alia nominated Madame Nexhmije Hoxha for the position of chairman of the mass organization (*Zeri i Popullit*, 2 March). This post had been held by her late husband but traditionally has been an "honorary" position with little real power. Contrary to some Western analyses that the assumption of the post by Madame Hoxha was a "promotion," it seems that her election to the chairmanship of the Democratic Front effectively removes her from direct access to the inner circles of political power (*RFE, RL Background Report* 43, 20 March). Supporting evidence of this was her failure to be elected to the Politburo, as predicted by certain Western and Yugoslav analysts. Her role is now limited to "furthering links between the party and people" rather than acting as power broker, as suggested in Yugoslav and Western news stories (*NYT*, 12 October). In pursuance of its role as a "bridge between party and masses," the central committee of the Democratic Front was called into session by its chairman to analyze the results of the regional and local elections (ATA, 4 June; *FBIS*, 6 June). In early October, Madame Hoxha called a meeting of the front's presidium to discuss the work and policies of *Bashkimi*, the second most important newspaper in Albania (*Bashkimi*, 5 October; *FBIS*, 16 October).

Throughout 1986 youth organizations and the school-age generation were subjected to contradictory messages from party officials and leaders of ULYA. An editorial addressed to Albanian youth advised greater control of their cultural tastes and vigilance against any compromise "with foreign tastes and manifestations" (*Zeri i Popullit*, 9 August). However, the first secretary of ULYA, Mehmet Elezi, proposed diverse "angles" to reach the youth, which has been increasingly subject to alien influences. In Elezi's view, "monotony and one-sidedness in the internal life of youth organizations are created not only by repetition and formalism, but also by failure to find a specific angle of tackling the problems [of the young] (*Zeri i Rinisë*, 25 December 1985; *JPRS Eastern Europe* 86-022, 15 February).

Ramiz Alia devoted a significant part of his report to the Ninth Congress to issues of the post war generation. Although he proposed closer ties between ULYA and the party, some of his remarks seemed intended to harness the energies of the young to fend off potential opponents of his leadership and policies. In his address to the faculty and student body of the Institute of Higher Learning in Elbasan, Alia criticized unnamed party officials for their paternalistic attitudes and for a tendency "to exert unnecessary control over the work and, in particular, the activities of the youth" (*Zeri i Popullit*, 7 May). His report to the APL congress continued the same theme and invited the young "to remain constantly in the frontline of the struggle against the vestiges of outdated and backward customs and against the dissipative and degenerative influence of the capitalist and revisionist world" (ibid., 4 November).

ULYA, like other mass organizations, was mobilized in 1986 to contribute to fulfillment of economic goals in preparation for the congress. In an effort to revive the old militant spirit, Alia presided over a "passing of the baton ceremony" in commemoration of the 40th anniversary of the construction by voluntary youth labor of the first railroad line (Kukës-Peshkopi) (ATA, 6 June; FBIS, 11 June).

The Seventeenth Plenum of ULYA's central committee occupied itself with an analysis of economic matters and youth's contribution to achieving assigned tasks and preparations for the Ninth APL Congress (ATA, 18 June; FBIS, 19 June). After the congress, youth representatives from throughout the country ventured to Tirana to celebrate the 45th anniversary of the founding of their organization. Elezi gave the main address to the gathering; Alia and other senior Politburo members were in attendance and advised the ULYA representatives to fend off "alien manifestations" but at the same time to pursue innovation and skill acquisition (ATA, 24 November; FBIS, 25 November). A recurring theme concerning youth has been the pervasive reluctance on their part to pursue training in hard sciences and their propensity to drift towards social sciences and humanities (Zeri i Rinisë, 9 August; RFE, RL Background Report 118, 29 August). Furthermore, nepotism and "backscratching" continue to frustrate party officials in their efforts to channel youth energies in a pre-determined direction. These problems were also singled out by Alia in his report to the Ninth APL Congress where he advised party members not to remain indifferent "when faced with lack of order and discipline, favoritism and back-scratching, with demands for privileges, and unfair claims" (Zeri i Popullit, 4 November).

The Central Council of Trade Unions of Albania (UTUA) came under criticism, unusually open and direct, for its failure to maintain discipline in the workplace. The need for discipline was underlined in a major editorial in the UTUA organ, Puna, which pointed to serious shortcomings affecting labor organizations during the past several years. Among the problems that required correction by "persuasion and administrative measures" were "failure to keep work schedules, unapproved departures [from work], failure to utilize work schedules, poor quality production, production below stipu-

lated quantities, alien manifestations among some of the younger and immature workers," and so on (Puna, 6 December 1985; FBIS, 27 December 1985).

As in previous years, the UTUA continued its international contacts. A visit to Vietnam at the invitation of its union counterpart was undertaken in midsummer, and several African delegations visited Tirana at the invitation of the UTUA (ATA, 22 June; FBIS, 24 June).

Upon conclusion of the work of the Ninth Congress, a plenum of the central committee of the labor organization was called into session in Tirana to examine "the tasks set forth for the Trade Union Council" by the APL congress and the directives of the Eighth Five-Year Plan. Central among the "tasks" was better control of the working class, higher levels of discipline, and increased productivity (ATA, 24 November; FBIS, 25 November).

**Domestic Politics.** There were no surprises during the first post-Hoxha year in domestic Albanian political developments. The Hoxha personality cult continued unabated, with Madame Hoxha the main proponent of her husband's national "sanctification." At least five books by Enver Hoxha were published posthumously by the Institute of Marxism-Leninism (directed by Nexhmije Hoxha) with such diverse titles as The Superpowers, On Woman, and Always Vigilant (ATA, 7 March, 30 October; FBIS, 7 March, 4 November). It is worth noting that the highly polemical Always Vigilant was published on the eve of the Ninth APL Congress—an apparent warning to those who had hidden thoughts about changing the Hoxha line. Madame Hoxha's vested interest in perpetuating the cult of her late husband is apparently shared by other high-ranking members of the party hierarchy. Foto Çami, a clear beneficiary of the demise of both Hoxha and Shehu, in a major article declared Enver Hoxha to be "synonymous with Albania" (Zeri i Popullit, 11 April). In light of Çami's call for more frankness in his address to the APL congress (ibid., 6 November), his unusual eulogy of Hoxha on the first anniversary of his death is at best puzzling.

Elections for district, city, and village people's councils and for people's judges at all levels were held on 27 April under the auspices of the Democratic Front (ATA, 27 April; FBIS, 29 April). A total of 1,796,948 registered voters (voting is mandatory) participated, with the predictable result: 99.99 percent voted for the front's candidates. As compared to the 1982 parliamentary elections, when only one vote was cast against front candidates, this time more opponents surfaced. Ten opposed the candidates for district people's councils, but only one opposed the candidates for city councils. However, for the village councils, a total of 123 voted against the front candidates, 41 against the list of people's judges, and 14 opposed the slate of assistant judges. (Ibid.)

Problems of "socialist legality" and the pervasiveness of foreign influences among the youth occupied the attention of party, state, and mass organizations during the entire year. Certain ministries (among them the Ministry of Industry and Mines) were criticized for failure to enforce laws and, as a consequence, violation of production directives (Zeri i Popullit, 3 January). More alarmingly, the paper noted a casual attitude toward the meaning of laws and directives, as reflected in the fact that in some ministries the "work of a jurist is performed by the engineer or economist, while the jurist in some other enterprises performs the work of the one who establishes quotas and of the economist" (ibid.).

In an effort to mobilize economic forces, or perhaps to make better utilization of high party organs, several top-ranking officials were assigned to key regional positions. Qirjako Mihali, an alternate member of the Politburo, was assigned as party chief of the Durrës district. Lambi Gjegprifti was demoted from deputy premier to chief executive (mayor) of the people's council executive committee of Tirana. Muho Asllani, a Politburo member, was sent to Shkodër as district party chief. On the other hand, Pirro Kondi, a vociferous Stalinist, received the critical post of party chief for Tirana (replacing Foto Çami), where he leads a party force of 24,000 members (ibid., 7 November). The reassignment of Mihali, Gjegprifti, and Asllani may indicate more than just an attempt by Alia to better manage the three largest districts.

**Social and Economic Issues.** It is obvious from Albanian literature and official statements that the leadership has had serious problems in containing liberalization trends manifested in an increasingly rebellious youth. This concern has dominated the agenda of mass organizations, labor groups, party officials, and society in general. As usual, blame is placed on foreign influences that have penetrated Albanian society and are no longer possible to contain. Reception of foreign television and radio broadcasts is possible and young people have been "absorbing decadent capitalist culture reflected in screaming jazz and vulgar television shows" (ibid., 9 August; Zeri i Rinisë, 5 February). Zeri i Popullit lamented the lack of "healthy public opinion to control the penetration of foreign influences and the viewing of "foreign, tasteless, distorted, and totally worthless programs" on portable televisions (Zeri i Popullit, 9 August). In a polite way, the Central Committee organ lamented the reluctance of "healthy-minded" citizens to be informants on the listening habits of their neighbors. Zeri i Rinisë attacked those who consider Albanian music and art inferior to the "screaming jazz" of decadent capitalism (Zeri i Rinisë, 5 February).

Generational issues apparently are inevitable in a country whose population grows at an average rate of 2.3 percent annually and has a median age of 25. The demographic trends have created serious difficulties in the absorption of entry-level laborers into the economic mainstream (Adil Çarçani's "Report of the Eighth Five-Year Plan," Zeri i Popullit, 5 November). The Albanian population surpassed the 3 million mark in 1986 and party and state organs project a population of 4 million by the year 2000 (ATA, 3 March; JRPS-Eastern Europe 86-065, 25 April). Over one-third of the population is under the age of 15, making it imperative for the Albanian economy to grow at a pace capable of absorbing 200,000 new entrants to the labor force during the next five years (Rruga ë Partisë, August). Although it is anticipated that approximately 87,000 workers will be pensioned between 1986 and 1990, the economy will still face serious stresses in accommodating the new labor force. The results of the Seventh Five-Year Plan (the first plan to be based on domestic forces only) are not encouraging in that respect.

Prime Minister Çarçani and Alia were both frank in admitting failure of the plan in several key sectors. Although they both tried to put the best face forward and blamed the failures on adverse weather conditions and the "treachery of the Shehu gang," the seriousness of shortfalls could not be hidden. Thus, growth in social product for the five-year period (1980–1985) stood at 18 percent instead of the planned 34-36 percent (for "Directives of the Eighth APL Congress on the Seventh Five-Year Plan," see Zeri i Popullit, 6 November 1981). Industrial production increased by 26 percent during the same period, instead of the projected 36–38 percent; similarly, capital investment grew by 14 percent instead of 24 percent; and the national income grew 16 percent instead of the projected 35–37 percent (Bashkimi, 4 July). Despite the failures of the previous five years, the Eighth Five-Year Plan and the respective directives seem to be characterized by the same ambitions as the Seventh Five-Year Plan. Emphasis is placed on increased exports, while per capita income is expected to grow by only 7–9 percent (*Zeri i Popullit*, 4 July, 5 November). Growth in the social product is set at 31–33 percent, exports at 44–46 percent and growth in national income at 35–37 percent (ibid., 6 November).

Three new elements have characterized Albanian party and state policies vis-à-vis economic matters during the past year: first, the recognition of the value of incentives to spark higher productivity; second, the open, often specific, criticism of mismanagement, "elitism," and bureaucratism that have plagued the social, political, and economic life of the country; and, third, an acknowledgment of problems with the younger generations, who persist in adopting "alien" styles and thumb their noses at state and party tutelage.

Highly placed state and party organs firmly supported the notions of "incentives" to the "qualitative and quantitative level of productivity by individual workers." *Rruga ë Partisë* and *Zeri i Popullit* kept up a campaign for broadening the party policy of "linking remuneration of labor with plan indicators [for the purpose of] increasing efficiency in production" (*Rruga ë Partisë*, November). The policy of incentives, taken in context with the re-examination of the role of privately owned plots and livestock by cooperativists, suggests a retreat from Hoxha's Stalinist orthodoxy. *Zeri i Popullit* was often critical of managers and directors of enterprises for their failure to "properly utilize model workers" and for not recognizing the importance of "granting them appropriate rewards and recognition" (*Zeri i Popullit*, 11 July). The Ninth APL Congress affirmed the desirability of "remuneration according to labor" and, at least for the time being, one should expect the expansion of this policy (*Rruga ë Partisë*, November).

Mismanagement, corruption, nepotism, and bureaucratic elitism were issues identified as major causes of the poor performance by the economy. Specific examples of losses due to inefficiency were cited, and calls for public pressures to keep the bureaucrats in check were issued by high-level party and state officials (*Bashkimi*, 22 January). Examples were cited: restaurant managers who locked customers out to be served in peace by their own staff (*Zeri i Popullit*, 11 June), distributors who took the first crack at quality products (ibid.), workers who caused losses of 279,000 leks in the district

of Kruje by failing to load cement. Party organizations were not spared criticism along the same lines.

The Thirteenth Plenum of the Central Committee of the party was devoted, to a large extent, to the problem of "cadre discipline" and abuses of power. A major editorial reminded base organizations that "authority does not mean unlimited rights" (ibid., 7 February). As the party organ sarcastically stated, "there is no lack of cases of cadres who consider their jobs and the authority that goes with them to be the prize for their 'rare' qualities" (ibid.).

Youthful rebelliousness, conveniently attributed to alien manifestations, was also viewed as a factor in economic failures and the emergence of "unhealthy public attitudes" in general. Party officials and news media sought to spark a "social movement" in opposition to "wrongdoers, usurpers of common socialist and individual property, rumormongers, people who behave badly toward their families, society, and work" (*Zeri i Popullit*, 23 February). A major party and state concern was the refusal of the youth to pursue educational goals directly linked to production and industry. *Zeri i Rinisë* admonished the youth to follow the "party directives" in choosing careers, since society needs "engineers, as well as philosophers and lawyers" (*Zeri i Rinisë*, 9 August; RFE, RL *Background Report* 118, 29 August).

There were no significant departures in the allocation of resources and budgetary policies in 1986 (except for defense) as compared to previous years. The 1986 state budget (excluding district expenditures) projected an income of 9.3 billion leks, expenditures of 9.25 billion leks, and a surplus of 50 million leks (*Zeri i Popullit*, 15 January). Expenditures for social and cultural programs are set almost at 2.7 billion leks and, for maintenance of the administrative apparatus, at 141 million leks (ibid.). As indicated above, the defense budget was reduced to approximately the 1984 levels from the high of 1.7 billion leks allocated in 1985. The 1986 defense appropriations (which do not include the security forces) were set at 978 million leks.

*Human Rights.* During the past year, the Albanian government was again singled out for human rights violations and the maintenance of a system of internal exile, labor camps, and imprisonment for reasons of conscience.

The United Nations Commission on Human Rights has refused to exempt Albania from its list of "gross violators" of the rights of individuals (*Jour-*

*nal de Geneve*, 28 August). Escapees from Albania describe persistent political oppression and state-initiated antireligious activities (*NYT*, 2 September). The Italian missionary agency, AIMIS, has traced a pattern of officially sanctioned antireligious persecution going back to the end of World War II. This repression persists today, as evidenced by the imprisonment of twenty monks and Roman Catholic priests (there are no known Greek-speaking priests alive; most died in prison or were executed), including the 69-year-old apostolic bishop of Durrëss, Monsignor Nikoll Troshani (AFP in English; *FBIS*, 21 December). Ramiz Alia rejected all criticism that minorities are oppressed in Albania (*Zeri i Popullit*, 4 November). In a speech to the inhabitants of Dropuli, Foto Çami praised the contributions of the Greek minority to Albanian society and promised broadening of its contacts with Greece, "including human contacts" (*Zeri i Popullit*, 2 June).

Although the Albanian authorities did not acknowledge the existence of political prisoners, they declared a broad amnesty, which de facto confirmed their presence. The amnesty, issued in commemoration of the 40th anniversary of the founding of the People's Republic and the adoption of its Stalinist constitution, included individuals who had been "imprisoned for up to six years" for such political acts as "agitation and propaganda against the state," and "treason against the fatherland, in the form of attempts to escape outside the state," and so forth. Excluded from the amnesty were "repeat offenders" (ATA, 10 January; *FBIS*, 13 January). The types of crimes "pardoned" show that the Albanian authorities, like leaders of other East European regimes, have adopted an interpretation of the term "political"—and human rights—which is contrary to the Universal Declaration of Human Rights.

A persistent criticism of the Tirana government has been related to its policies aimed at the assimilation of non–Albanian-speaking minorities. Two laws enacted in 1975, Legislative Decree No. 5354/11 (November 1975), "Concerning the Mandatory Changes of Certain Names," and Legislative Decree No. 225/9 (September 1975), "Concerning the Changes of Names of Certain Villages in Sarandes and Korçe" (Greek Orthodox–inhabited areas), are apparently being enforced, according to the Albanian daily *Rilindjia* of Prishtina, Kosovo. (For a Western source for these decrees, see *NYT*, 27 February 1976.) Recently, the Tirana authorities have reissued a *Dictionary of Personal Names*, first published in 1982, to "assist" parents in choosing "culturally acceptable names" for their offspring (*Rilindjia*, 18 October; *FBIS*, 24 October).

**Foreign Policy.** The post-Hoxha foreign policy of the Albanian government has been characterized by a careful, judicious, and selective expansion of relations with West European and Third World countries and a similar approach in its state-to-state relations with members of the Warsaw Pact.

In pursuing a policy line of broadening contacts with the West, Tirana spokesmen reiterated the known, and politically safe, clichés of Enver Hoxha, which were intended to counter the image of Albanian "isolationism" often repeated in Western news media.

The first secretary of the APL, Ramiz Alia, in his New Year's address reaffirmed the Hoxha line in economic and foreign policy matters and expressed his satisfaction with the improvement in Albania's standing in the world arena (ATA, 1 January; *FBIS*, 2 January). In a subsequent commentary, *Zeri i Popullit* reaffirmed the policy line set forth in Alia's Korçe speech of 27 August 1985, and denounced those who interpret normal diplomatic acts of the independent and sovereign state as "opening up of Albania," or as a tendency to get close to this or that side (*Zeri i Popullit*, 4 January). Yet, despite verbal adherence to the Hoxha line, the Alia regime showed a high degree of self-assurance in its ventures to broaden relations with the West, without any significant evidence of softening its stand vis-à-vis the two superpowers.

*Western Contacts.* During the past year, full diplomatic relations were established with Spain (ATA, 12 September; *FBIS*, 12 September) and negotiations were conducted with Britain toward the same objective. Two issues that have prevented the establishment of relations with London have not been resolved, but there are indications of a willingness to compromise by both sides. First is the matter of the return of approximately two tons of Albanian gold held by Britain; second is London's demand for Albanian reparations for the sinking of a destroyer in the Corfu channel with loss of life and the damaging of a second ship in 1946 (RFE, RL *Background Report* 21, 7 February).

In the London-Tirana negotiations the United States is an indirect partner, since technically the Albanian gold is under the control of the U.S.-French-British Tripartite Commission. On the matter of reparations for the sinking of the British destroyer, Tirana has consistently denied responsibility and has rejected the International Court of Justice decision favoring the British.

Negotiations with West Germany to establish diplomatic relations (extensive economic ties were established several years ago; see *YICA*, 1983) were held in Vienna and it appears that during 1986 the two countries inched closer to an agreement on the critical issue of war reparations demanded by the Albanian government (RFE, RL *Background Report* 42, 20 March). Apparently, Albania has dropped its demand for reparations, while West Germany expressed a willingness to finance industrial projects and to offer other types of technical assistance to the Tirana regime (UPI, 10 March; Hamburg, DPA in German, 13 March; *FBIS*, 13 March).

In February 1986, a Norwegian delegation headed by a deputy foreign minister visited Tirana to conclude an agreement for the purchase of Albanian chrome (approximately 100,000–150,000 tons annually) worth 10 million dollars and the training of Albanian specialists by Norwegian universities (*Aftenposten*, 13, 14 February; *FBIS*, 19, 20 February). Finland and Albania continued their close state-to-state relations. A large Finnish parliamentary delegation visited Albania and was received by high-level state and party officials (ATA, 17 January; *FBIS*, 20 January). To facilitate West European contacts, Albania and Switzerland established air links (ATA, 16 March; *FBIS*, 17 March), and Austria continued to be one of Albania's favorite trade partners. In March, an Austrian delegation signed a six-year trade pact providing for the export from Albania of chrome, iron, nickel, electric power, and agricultural products, in return for chemical products, spare parts, and machinery (ATA, 7 March; *FBIS*, 11 March).

During 1986 Albania was active in international organizations, suggesting a feeling of security and maturity in its approach to world affairs. Foreign Minister Reiz Malile attended the opening of the U.N. General Assembly and put forth the basic principles of Albanian foreign policy. While in New York, Malile met with a dozen of his counterparts (mostly from Third World countries) and used the opportunity to woo the U.S.-Albanian community (ATA, 1 October; *FBIS*, 3 October).

The Albanian Minister of Health, Ajli Alushani, attended the 39th meeting of the World Health Organization in Geneva (ATA, 18 May; *FBIS*, 19 May), and the director general of FAO visited Tirana and several agricultural areas of the country to assess the status of agricultural production (ibid.).

Despite the growth and deepening of relations with the rest of the world, and particularly with the West, Ramiz Alia and other leaders continued to criticize the major powers and ritualistically referred to the "difficulties created for Albania" by an imaginary imperialist blockade (*Zeri i Popullit*, 9 November).

*Italy.* Relations between Tirana and Rome failed to develop further during 1986, despite the promise of earlier years. In March Albania cancelled tourist visas for a group of Italians as a retaliation for the refusal of the Italian government to turn over to Albanian authorities a six-member family which had sought refuge in the Italian embassy in Tirana (Prishtina radio, 10 March; *FBIS*, 12 March; see also *YICA*, 1986). Alia's speech to the Ninth APL Congress contained a perfunctory reference to Albanian-Italian cooperation in trade and cultural matters. He did not refer to the specific issues that had caused a cooling of the ties, thus leaving the door open for a face-saving resolution of the problems caused by the Albanian family that had sought asylum on 12 December 1984.

*Greece.* Greek-Albanian relations continued to improve during 1986, despite the inability of the two governments to resolve several technicalities related to the termination of the state of war that had existed since 1940. Alia praised the Greek leadership for the improvement of relations and expressed the hope that remaining differences would be resolved through mutual efforts (*Zeri i Popullit*, 4 November). In the same speech, he referred to the close relations between the "Greek and Albanian people, the two autochthonous and most ancient inhabitants of the Balkans" and to the need for minorities to maintain their spiritual links with their nations of origin" (ibid.). Increased contacts between the Greek minority in Albania and Greece have been pursued by the Greek government with mixed results. During 1986 approximately one thousand ethnic Greeks, mostly handpicked communists, were allowed to cross the borders (statistics provided by the Greek Immigration Service). The two countries pursued the implementation of agreements reached in Tirana during the visit there by Karolos Papoulias, the Greek foreign minister, in December 1984 (*Athena*, January).

In January, Ioannis Papandoniou, Greek deputy minister of national economy, visited Tirana and signed a trade protocol of one year's duration (ATA, 9 January; *FBIS*, 10 January), and a tourist agreement was put into effect in February (ATA, 13 February; *FBIS*, 13 February). In addition, a postal service agreement was signed that made Ioannina the transit point for Albanian mail to West European capitals (ATA, 7 January; *FBIS*, 8 January). During the summer, the secretary general of the Greek Foreign Ministry traveled to Tirana, reportedly for the purpose of resolving "technical difficulties" related to formal lifting of the state of war (*Kathimerini*, 28 July). In the fall the Greek communist composer, Mikis Theodorakis, visited Albania and was received by several high-level officials, including Alia (*Zeri i Popullit*, 6 September). Finally, in late November, the Albanian Telegraphic Agency (ATA) and its Greek counterpart, the Athens News Agency (ANA), signed an agreement for the exchange of news and information (ATA, 24 November; *FBIS*, 25 November).

Fundamental disagreements on the status of Albania's Greek minority between the ruling socialist party of Greece and the main opposition party, New Democracy, have impeded further development of Greek-Albanian relations. Prime Minister Papandreou assured the Greek parliament that his policy "gives us now the opportunity to defend the human rights of the Greek minority there more effectively than before" (*Parliamentary Minutes*, 23 April, p. 6370; *NYT*, 11 May). However, New Democracy leader Constantine Mitsotakis accused the government of seeking to improve relations by "trading away internationally recognized Greek interests and obligations vis-à-vis the minority in return for Albanian goodwill" (ibid.). On 21 December, the New Democracy Party issued a formal declaration opposing the lifting of the state of war until the status of prewar treaties and obligations by both sides is defined (*Kathimerini*, 23 December). For its part, the Albanian government considered the issue of minority rights "resolved by the Albanian constitution" (*Zeri i Popullit*, 4 November), and thus far, has avoided specifying the existing "difficulties" alluded to by Alia and Çami. The Greek press on several occasions has raised the issue of unacceptable activities by the Albanian secret police and the expansion of its espionage network in Greece (*Vradini Kyriakis*, 16 March).

*Yugoslavia.* During 1986 Yugoslav-Albanian relations failed to show any significant improvement at the ideological level. Despite the fact that Yugoslavia remains Albania's largest trading partner, Tirana has continued to attack "Titoist revisionism" and the "oppressive policies" of Belgrade toward Albanian ethnics in Kosovo (BBC, *Current Affairs Research Report*, no. 3). Alia's speech at the Ninth APL Congress repeated the known Albanian positions of a desire to improve relations with Belgrade coupled with a demand for better treatment of the Albanian minority in that country (*Zeri i Popullit*, 4 November). Alia, however, saw no prospect for improvement in relations because, in his view, Yugoslav policy has "been guided by a sort of feudal mentality that they ought to impose their dictates and tutelage over Albania" (ibid.).

The Albanian press ran several critical articles on the Thirteenth Congress of the Yugoslav party and accused the "revisionists" of Belgrade of seeking to detract attention from serious domestic problems by conducting a "savage anti-Albanian campaign" (ibid., 14 May). As in previous years, the Albanian press criticized the Yugoslav intellectual establishment for allegedly seeking to "falsify history" concerning the role of the Albanian nation and the origin of the Albanian minority in Yugoslavia (ibid., 4 July). Similarly, the Albanian press attacked the social policies of Belgrade "which have caused approximately 125,000 unemployed Albanians" in Kosovo and have undermined the prospect for a new cultural agreement between the two countries. The Tirana government objected to Yugoslav demands to add a supplement to a draft agreement "seeking to defend the cultural rights of the Slav minority in Albania" (ATA, 19 July; *FBIS*, 20 July). The Yugoslav press, too, maintained a polemical tone throughout the year and criticized the Albanian government for teaching "anti-Yugoslav policy" in its schools (Tanjug in English, 11 April; *FBIS*, 15 April). Despite the intense nationalistic warfare, the two countries took some steps to smooth trade relations. The long-delayed Shkodër-Titograd rail line was finally inaugurated, linking Albania with the rest of Europe. A trade protocol was also signed between the two countries (*WP*, 7 August). On 1 September, transportation of goods commenced, and in October a new Yugoslav ambassador was appointed to Tirana (ATA, 2 September, 19 October; *FBIS*, 3 September, 20 October). The new rail line will permit Albania to transport approximately 600,000–700,000 tons of goods to various European points. A new long-term trade agreement (1986–1990) envisages an increase in trade between the two countries of 25 percent over the next five years (RFE, RL *Background Report* 197, 8 August).

*Eastern Europe.* Albanian relations with East European states, have, generally speaking, continued to be proper and correct at the state-to-state level, without any indication that party-to-party relations are about to improve. The APL theoretical journal as well as members of the academic and political elites persisted in their criticism of the "neocolonial relations" that the East European leaderships maintain with the Soviet Union (*Rruga ë Partisë*, November). Such unequal relations, the journal argued, "would have not been achieved without their [Eastern Europe's] superstructure degeneration, without the creation of a fifth column in these countries" (ibid.).

Despite the general criticism of East European communist parties, the Tirana regime continued a trade policy that is overwhelmingly oriented toward communist-ruled states. Thus the 1986 trade figures, which show a decline in exports of approximately 10 percent over the previous year, demonstrate that East European and socialist states are the primary trading partners of Albania. From a total trade of $678.5 million, $346.5 million was with CMEA countries, $80 million with Yugoslavia (a decline of almost 40 percent since the troubles in Kosovo started), and $252 million with Western countries (Belgrade, *NIN*, 21 December). Multiyear trade protocols were signed with all East European states, but it appears that a "gradation" of Tirana's political preferences is emerging. Romania and Bulgaria have in the past year inched closer to the new Tirana regime. Their press coverage of Albanian affairs referred positively to the leadership of Ramiz Alia and the "achievements under socialism"; they "regretted" the disruption of relations in the 1960s and completely ignored Enver Hoxha (Bucharest, *Lumea*, August; *FBIS*, 7 August; Sofia *Otechestven front*, 7 August). In the case of Romania, relations have been conducted at higher levels than those with other East European states. Several visits by Albanian officials were reciprocated by their Romanian counterparts, including a visit by the Albanian minister of foreign trade, Shane Korbeçi (ATA, 20 October; *FBIS*, 26 October). Indicating an approval of Romania's independent foreign policy vis-à-vis Moscow, a major editorial appeared on the anniversary of Romania's national day (*Zeri i Popullit*, 23 August).

There were no substantive changes in the type of trade conducted between Albania and the East European states during 1986. The usual Albanian exports (chrome, agricultural products, nickel, knitwear) were exchanged for machinery, chemical products, synthetic rubber, and consumer goods. Commercial agreements with Poland (ATA, 19 October; *FBIS*, 20 October), Czechoslovakia (ATA, 31 January; *FBIS*, 5 February), and Vietnam (ATA, 26 February; *FBIS*, 27 February) were signed by second-echelon functionaries. However, a GDR delegation that visited Tirana to sign a trade protocol was received by Prime Minister Çarçani in addition to several ministers dealing with economic matters (ATA, 23 June; *FBIS*, 24 June). Similarly, a Hungarian health delegation was received by several high-level officials and an agreement was concluded on the "medical and curative climatic treatment of sick people in the two countries" (ATA, 21 October; *FBIS*, 24 October).

*Third World and Muslim Countries.* Albania, officially an atheist state but predominantly a Muslim country, maintained cordial relations with Third World, Arab, and Muslim countries. Relations with Turkey continued their upward trend in 1986, with several high-level visits in each direction. The Albanian minister of energy, Lavdosh Memetaj, visited Smyrna (and Ankara) to participate in the opening of the 55th annual trade fair, in which Albanians participated ( ATA, 28 August; *FBIS*, 12 February). The Turkish deputy minister for foreign affairs, Necet Telez, visited Tirana and was received by high-level state officials, including Reiz Malile (ATA, 10 June; *FBIS*, 12 June). Ramiz Alia's greetings on the Turkish national day were indeed warm and emphasized the "cultural traditions that the two peoples share" (ATA, 29 October; *FBIS*, 29 October), and *Zeri i Popullit* praised the "support that Ataturk had given to the new Albanian state" (*Zeri i Popullit*, 29 October). Relations with Algeria intensified during the past year, and Albanian support for Libya's Khadafy continued to be strong (ATA, 16 April; *FBIS*, 16 April).

Early in the year, an Algerian petrochemical group visited Tirana to "exchange opinions about the strengthening of trade relations between the two countries" (ATA, 13 February; *FBIS*, 13 February). During the same month Reiz Malile, Albania's foreign minister, visited Algeria, where he was received warmly by the country's leaders (ATA, 11 February; *FBIS*, 12 February). Subsequently, a large parliamentary delegation headed by Pali

Mishka, chairman of the People's Assembly, visited Algiers in return for a similar visit by Algerian parliamentarians in the previous year (ATA, 27 March; *FBIS*, 2 April). In July a five-year trade protocol was signed in Tirana by the Algerian minister of trade, Mostefa Benamar (ATA, 21 July; *FBIS*, 1 August).

Albanian spokesmen and mass media were outspokenly critical of U.S. actions and policies against Libya and denounced the U.S. air raid against that country (ATA, 16 April; *FBIS*, 16 April). However, Alia's message on the occasion of Libya's national day was formalistic and lacked the warmth that characterized similar messages to Turkey, Egypt, and Iran (ATA, 31 August; *FBIS*, 2 September).

Relations with Egypt remained pragmatic, with some emphasis on broadening the "traditional" ties between the two countries (ATA, 12 July; *FBIS*, 15 July).

In an ironic twist, the Albanian-language daily of Kosovo, Yugoslavia, accused Iranian "support" of Albanian nationalism and Albanian policies of being a "cover" for exporting Islamic fundamentalism to the Albanians of Kosovo (*Rilindjia*, 18 April).

*USSR.* The year was characterized by renewed efforts on the part of Moscow to bring Albania back into the bloc. For several years after the Hoxha-instigated break with Moscow, the Soviet press characterized the Albanian leadership as adventurous and anti-Soviet. During the Brezhnev era the USSR chose to ignore the Albanians altogether. In 1986, however, the Soviet press and officials adopted a new, more refined approach toward Tirana. They increased positive coverage of the "achievements of Albanians under socialism," with an emphasis on the early years; the Soviets emphasized the benefits Albania had received from its past association with Moscow and the CMEA countries; they reminded Tirana of Soviet support for Albania during critical times; they avoided any reference to the role of Enver Hoxha; and they factually covered the activities of First Secretary Ramiz Alia. Finally, the Soviet press repeated the theme that "relations have been abnormal since 1961," but that the Soviet Union desires normalization for the "benefit of socialism, peace, and mutual advantages" (Moscow radio, 20 November; *FBIS*, 21 November). *Pravda*, *Izvestiia*, *Novyi mir*, Moscow radio and television, and other organs covered factually and with a positive slant the proceedings of the Ninth APL Congress (*Pravda*, 6, 7, 9 November). The Soviet press was equally generous with praise of Albania's antifascist resistance on the occasion of the Albanian national day (*Pravda*, 28, 29 November). Significantly, the new Soviet press coverage included even routine activities of the APL, such as Central Committee plenary sessions, and the Soviet media quoted directly from speeches of Albanian leaders (*Pravda*, 1 July, 4 October; RFE, RL *Background Report*, 11, 21 January). To all appearances the Soviet press treated Albania as another socialist state with which relations were only temporarily abnormal. It must be noted that the positive coverage of Albanian affairs by the Soviet press is initiated by East European news media, particularly the Bulgarian press.

All Soviet overtures, however, were rejected by the post-Hoxha leadership. Alia's speech to the Ninth Congress, intense criticism of the Soviet and East European parties, and formal celebration of the anniversary of the 1961 Albanian-Soviet rift, suggest that Moscow initiatives had no visible impact on Tirana.

In contrast to the Soviet coverage of the APL congress, the Albanian Telegraphic Agency announced the commencement of the Twenty-seventh CPSU Congress as a "revisionist congress" opening under Gorbachev (ATA, 26 February; *FBIS*, 27 February). A lead article condemned the Gorbachev leadership for the "continuation and advancement of the revisionist and social imperialist course" (*Zeri i Popullit*, 9 March). *Rruga ë Partisë*, in a pointed rejection of Soviet overtures on the occasion of the APL congress, dismissed the Gorbachev leadership as a "Khrushchevian clique" pursuing neocolonial policies toward Eastern Europe (*Rruga ë Partisë*, November). A persistent point of criticism in the Albanian press was related to U.S.-USSR relations. All U.S.-Soviet contacts were depicted in Tirana as a superpower conspiracy "to carve the world into spheres of influence at the expense of smaller states" (*Zeri i Popullit*, 4 January). Albania's intention to continue the "Hoxha path" (no relations with either superpower) was reflected in all major speeches to the Ninth APL Congress and the posthumous publication of two characteristically anti-Soviet books by Hoxha, *On Superpowers* and *Always Vigilant*. The policy was further affirmed by Foreign Minister Malile's U.N. speech, in which he denounced the Soviet occupation of Afghanistan and Moscow's colonial behavior toward the socialist states (ATA, 1 October; *FBIS, 3 October)*.

*United States.* Relations between Albania and the United States remained unchanged during 1986. Foreign Minister Reiz Malile and the Albanian press reiterated adherence to Hoxha's "principled foreign policy of no relations with either of the two superpowers," and Ramiz Alia made this position part of his official report to the Ninth Congress (*Zeri i Popullit*, 4 November, 26 January). A target of Albanian criticism has been President Reagan's Strategic Defense Initiative and Washington's attempt to involve the Europeans in its development (ibid., 26 January). With intense anti-American rhetoric the Albanian mass media and officials denounced American action against Libya and demanded the removal of U.S. and Soviet forces from the Mediterranean (ibid., 18 September). Along with denunciations of U.S. policies, the Albanian government rejected the notion of collective security and repeated its intention to ignore such gatherings as the Stockholm Security Conference, because they are seen as "means by which the two superpowers seek to divide the world into spheres of influence" (*Bashkimi*, 29 September; *Zeri i Popullit*, 14 October).

In October a "scientific conference" titled "On the Hegemonic Policy of Superpowers and the Stand of APL" was held in Tirana at the Institute of Marxism-Leninism and was presided over by Madame Hoxha (ATA, 14 October; *FBIS*, 15 October). In this gathering, intended to set the form for the Ninth APL Congress, the United States came under severe criticism. In a paper titled "The Mediterranean and the Balkans in the Plans of the Superpowers" an unidentified author demanded removal of U.S. presence from the area.

Although Tirana emphasized its intention not to establish relations with either Washington or Moscow, it nevertheless engaged in indirect trade with both during 1986. According to the Yugoslav weekly *NIN* and London's *Economist*, during 1986 Albania exported goods worth $12 million to the United States and received U.S. imports worth $4 million (Belgrade, *NIN*, 21 December). Furthermore, there was an increase of visits by U.S. citizens of Albanian ancestry to their country of origin during 1986. An Albanian-American journalist was given a guided and guarded tour of the country (*Boston Herald*, 19–24 August). It must also be noted that the United States is an indirect participant in the British-Albanian negotiations concerning the return of the Albanian gold held by the Allied Tripartite Commission.

*Vietnam and China.* Albanian relations with the Asian ruling communist parties have been far better than relations with European parties. The Vietnamese were the only delegation from a ruling party to be invited to the Ninth APL Congress (*Zeri i Popullit*, 10 November). State-to-state relations between Hanoi and Tirana continued to be cordial. A five-year commercial agreement was signed in February and several Albanian delegations (including a UTUA group) visited Hanoi (ATA, 26 February; *FBIS*, 27 February). The Vietnamese minister of health, Dang Hoi Xuan, paid an official visit to Tirana (ATA, 15 March; *FBIS*, 17 March). Upon the death of Le Duan, Vietnam's party chief, the entire Politburo of the APL visited the Vietnamese embassy to register its condolences (ATA, 15 July; *FBIS*, 15 July).

Relations with China continued to be pragmatic and businesslike, without any indication of significant change. Messages between the two countries were formal and correct, and a five-year commercial agreement was put into effect (ATA, 1 October; *FBIS*, 2 October). But the reception for the occasion of the Chinese national day was attended only by second-level officials, led by Sokrat Pliaka (deputy foreign minister). Pointedly, Ramiz Alia received the new Chinese ambassador to Tirana in his capacity as chief of state; no mention of party-to-party relations was made on this occasion.

**International Party Contacts.** The Albanian Party of Labor continued to assert its claim that it is the true defender of Marxist-Leninist doctrine, and it avoided any formal contacts with most ruling communist parties, with the exception of Vietnam. A total of fourteen splinter Marxist-Leninist groups from Third World and West European countries followed the proceedings of the APL congress. Their representatives included several individuals from France, the United States, Canada, Tanzania, and the Pan-African Congress. The Albanian press, radio, and television ignored all East European commentary and coverage of the congress, but gave prominence to Albanian speakers who attacked the "Khrushchevites and social-imperialists."

Nikolaos A. Stavrou
*Howard University*

# Bulgaria

**Population.** 8,990,000 (July 1986) (The World Factbook, 1986)

**Party.** Bulgarian Communist Party (Bŭlgarska komunisticheska partiya; BCP)

**Founded.** Bulgarian Social Democratic Party founded in 1891; split into Broad and Narrow factions in 1903; the Narrow Socialists became the BCP and joined the Comintern in 1919.

**Membership.** 932,055. According to information presented at the Thirteenth Party Congress in April, 44.36 percent of members are classified as industrial workers, and 16.31 percent are classified as agricultural workers (*Bŭlgarska telegrafna agentsiya*, 5 April; *FBIS*, 8 April). Bulgaria no longer publishes data on ethnic minorities; ethnic Turks and Gypsies, the two largest minority groups, are believed to be underrepresented in the party in proportion to their numbers in the general population.

**General Secretary.** Todor Khristov Zhivkov (b. 1911)

**Politburo.** 11 full members: Todor Zhivkov (chairman, State Council), Chudomir Alexandrov (b. 1936), Georgi Atanasov (b. 1933, prime minister), Milko Balev (b. 1920, member, State Council), Ognyan Doynov (b. 1935, chairman, Economic Council), Dobri Dzhurov (b. 1916, minister of national defense), Grisha Filipov (b. 1919), Pencho Kubadinski (b. 1918, member, State Council; chairman, Fatherland Front), Petŭr Mladenov (b. 1936, minister of foreign affairs), Stanko Todorov (b. 1920, chairman, National Assembly), Yordan Yotov (b. 1920, editor in chief, *Rabotnichesko delo*); 6 candidate members: Petŭr Dyulgerov (b. 1929, chairman, Central Council of Trade Unions), Andrey Lukanov (b. 1938, first deputy prime minister), Stoian Markov (b. 1942, first deputy prime minister; chairman, State Committee on Research and Technology), Grigor Stoichkov (b. 1926, deputy prime minister), Dimitŭr Stoyanov (b. 1928, minister of internal affairs), Georgi Yordanov (b. 1931, chairman, Council on Intellectual Development)

**Secretariat.** 9 members: Chudomir Alexandrov, Milko Balev, Grisha Filipov, Emil Khristov (b. 1924, member, State Council), Stoyan Mikhailov (b. 1930), Dimitŭr Stanishev (b. 1924), Vasil Tsanov (b. 1922), Yordan Yotov, Kiril Zarev (b. 1926)

**Central Committee.** 195 full and 145 candidate members

**Status.** Ruling party

**Last Congress.** Thirteenth, 2–5 April 1986, in Sofia; next congress scheduled for 1991

**Last Election.** 8 June 1986. All candidates run on the ticket of the Fatherland Front, an umbrella organization (4.4 million members) comprising most mass organizations. Fatherland Front candidates received 99.9 percent of votes cast. Of the National Assembly's 400 members, 276 belong to the BCP and 99 to the Agrarian Union; 25 are unaffiliated (most of these are Komsomol members). The Bulgarian Agrarian National Union (BANU; 120,000 members) formally shares power with the BCP. It holds 3 of the 27 places on the State Council; the ministries of justice, public health, agriculture and forests; and fills about one-sixth of the people's council seats. BANU leader Petŭr Tanchev's post as first deputy chairman of the State Council makes him Todor Zhivkov's nominal successor as head of state.

**Auxiliary Organizations.** Central Council of Trade Unions (CCTU; about 4 million members), led by Petŭr Dyulgerov; Dimitrov Communist Youth League (Komsomol; 1.5 million members), led by Andrey Bundzhulov; Civil Defense Organization (750,000 members), led by Colonel General Tencho Papazov, provides training in paramilitary tactics and disaster relief; Committee on Bulgarian Women (30,000 members), led by Elena Lagadinova

**Publications.** *Rabotnichesko delo* (*RD*; Workers' cause), BCP daily, edited by Yordan Yotov; *Partien zhivot* (Party life), BCP monthly; *Novo vreme* (New time), BCP theoretical journal; *Otechestven front* (Fatherland front), front daily; *Dŭrzhaven vestnik* (State newspaper), contains texts of laws and decrees. Bŭlgarska telegrafna agentsiya (BTA) is the official news agency.

Todor Zhivkov demonstrated that his power in Bulgaria has not been diminished by changes in the Soviet leadership. He dominated the party's Thirteenth Congress, and, as he has in the past, avoided designating a successor. The accusation that Bulgarian agents had been involved in the attempted assassination of Pope John Paul II was finally laid to rest by an Italian court. But, on the negative side, Bulgaria's party and state leaders continued to grapple with major economic problems without apparent success.

**Leadership and Party Organization.** The report of the BCP's Central Committee to the Thirteenth Congress stated that since the previous congress in 1981 party membership had grown by 12.8 percent, from 825,876 to 932,055. Between the congresses 157,837 new members were added to the BCP, of whom it was reported that "more than 90 percent" held at least high school diplomas, 70 percent were under 30, and 44 percent were women. Information presented about the total party membership indicated that 44.36 percent of members were classified as industrial workers and 16.31 percent as agricultural workers. The remaining 39.33 percent were not identified, but presumably fell into the white-collar category. In age distribution, 11.9 percent of members were under 30, 26.7 percent between 30 and 40, 22.0 percent between 40 and 50, and the remaining 39.4 percent were over 50. About a third (32.7 percent) of party members were women, and about two-thirds (64.6 percent) had completed at least secondary education. Between the congresses only 8,545 members were expelled; 38,452 had been expelled during the preceding five-year period. The low number of expulsions and the substantial influx of new members indicate that some relaxation of standards had occurred, and during the year the party press did indeed urge local party committees to exercise increased vigilance regarding the political and moral character of their members (BTA, 4 April; *FBIS*, 8 April; *RFE, Situation Report*, 22 April).

*The Zhivkov Succession.* Todor Zhivkov has been in power longer than any other leader in the Soviet bloc. His age, combined with reports of friction with CPSU leader Mikhail S. Gorbachev, provoked speculation in the foreign and émigré Bulgarian press about Zhivkov's future. Reports appeared that Zhivkov would retire or be forced from office at the party congress, or that he would be elected to an honorific position and would surrender power to Grisha Filipov or Chudomir Alexandrov, thought to be his most likely successors. (See *YICA*, 1986; *CSM*, 11 March; RFE, *Situation Report*, 17 February, 12 March.) In any event, the reports of Zhivkov's political demise proved premature. In the months before the BCP congress, Zhivkov supervised several shake-ups among the leadership, made a vigorous and prominent appearance at the congress of the CPSU in Moscow, and displayed a firm command of the Bulgarian political landscape. He was re-elected general secretary at the Thirteenth BCP Congress, and in September he celebrated his 75th birthday—apparently fully in control, without even a clear heir apparent.

At a plenum of the BCP Central Committee held on 24–25 January, Todor Bozhinov was dismissed as a full member of the Politburo and Stanish Bonev was dropped from candidate membership. Neither move was surprising, since both men had previously been demoted in the government hierarchy and had been publicly held responsible for shortcomings in the country's economic performance (see *YICA*, 1986). Bozhinov had headed a "superministry" in charge of energy and raw-material resources, and Bonev had been chairman of the State Planning Commission. Bozhinov was later appointed chairman of the Committee on Protection of the Environment, a position not totally without influence, but he was not given the ministerial rank that had been held by his predecessor. Bonev's fate was not made public, although both he and Bozhinov retained their membership in the BCP Central Committee after the Thirteenth Congress.

The Central Committee plenum raised Stoyan Markov to the rank of candidate member of the Politburo. A 43-year-old electronics specialist, Markov had also been the chairman of the State Committee on Scientific and Technological Progress, which was reorganized and renamed the State Committee on Research and Technology. Politburo member Chudomir Alexandrov was also made a party secretary and was relieved of his position as first deputy prime minister (BTA, 25 January; FBIS, 27 January; Sofia Domestic Service, 27 January; RFE, *Situation Reports*, 17 February, 12 March).

Shortly before the opening of the party congress, a second Central Committee plenum and the National Assembly made several changes in the party and state hierarchy. Grisha Filipov was dismissed as prime minister and made a member of the party Secretariat, to which Politburo member Yordan Yotov was also added. Georgi Atanasov and Ognyan Doynov left the Secretariat, but in neither case did this represent a loss of influence. Atanasov was named the new prime minister and was raised from candidate to full membership in the Politburo. Doynov was appointed to head the new Economic Council, making him the dominant official in this field (BTA, 20 March; FBIS, 21 March).

No further changes in either the Politburo or Secretariat were made at the Thirteenth Congress. As a result, the question of Zhivkov's successor remained as cloudy as ever. One candidate, Grisha Filipov, was eclipsed, and the remaining front-runner, Chudomir Alexandrov, was given one new rival in Georgi Atanasov and possibly another in Ognyan Doynov. Zhivkov's formal successor as head of state is an Agrarian, Petŭr Tanchev, who is not in line for the key position of BCP general secretary.

*The Central Committee.* Of the 197 full members of the Central Committee elected at the Twelfth Congress in 1981, one, Mircho Spasov, was purged for corruption (see *YICA*, 1983), and eleven others died. Of the 185 surviving members, the Thirteenth Congress re-elected all but 24. Those dropped included Alexander Lilov, who was excluded from the Politburo in 1983, and several former district party secretaries who were purged shortly before the congress opened (see below). The congress promoted 25 candidate members to full membership and elected 8 entirely new full members, to bring their total number to 195. Among the new full members were Zhivkov's son, Vladimir, and his cousin, Khristo Maleev. The relatively minor changes in personnel at this level meant that the average age of full members was about 60, whereas in 1981 it was 57.5. Only 12 of the full members of the Central Committee were women, and only 2 could be identified as ethnic Turks. The number of candidate members grew from 139 to 145, including 18

women and 5 ethnic Turks (*RD*, 6 April; *FBIS*, 9 April; RFE, *Situation Report*, 22 April).

*District Party Committees.* In the months before the party congress, an unusually large number of shake-ups occurred at the district level. Nine first secretaries and 38 secretaries were replaced in the country's 28 district party organizations. In three cases the changes at the level of first secretary involved promotions to higher posts, but in the remaining six the previous leaders were subjected to harsh criticism. The leadership in Vidin was called to account for lagging in the effort to introduce new technology and for permitting a low level of labor discipline. In Kyustendil the party leadership was charged with "overwhelming inertia" and held responsible for severe setbacks in agriculture. In Pazardzhik and Sliven, district party leaders were accused of allowing a sharp decline in the profitability of industry and a diminution in the area of land under cultivation (*RD*, 28 February, 1, 7, 8 March; *FBIS*, 15, 25 March; RFE, *Situation Report*, 27 March).

The most unusual development on the district level involved the leadership of the Sofia City Committee. At the report-and-election conference held on 12 March, Georgi Atanasov, about to be raised from candidate to full membership in the Politburo at the Thirteenth Congress, delivered a long indictment of the failures of the Sofia leadership in several areas, including economic planning and investment, transportation, housing construction, and the functioning of public utilities. Atanasov also referred to the emergence of "enchanted circles" among the city's party elite, who were unconcerned with the welfare of the inhabitants of the capital; he called these circles "the work of Satan." This criticism was puzzling, however, because Georgi Georgiev, ousted as first secretary of the Sofia City Committee, was made chairman of the Committee of State and People's Control and was elected a full member of the BCP Central Committee at the Thirteenth Congress. Petŭr Mezhdurechki, removed as mayor of Sofia, was named Georgiev's first deputy and was re-elected to the Central Committee. Consequently, it appeared that the real target of Atanasov's criticism must have been Chudomir Alexandrov, who had held the post of Sofia first secretary until his elevation to the Politburo two years previously. Since Alexandrov appeared the most likely of Zhivkov's successors, the events of the Sofia conference may have been engineered to diminish some of his political luster. Anastasi Donchev was named the new district first secretary. He had previously led the Razgrad district committee (*RD*, 13 March; BTA, 10 March; *FBIS*, 11 March; RFE, *Situation Report*, 27 March).

**Internal Affairs.** Bulgaria usually takes its cue from the Soviet Union, and during the year a number of initiatives were put forward reflecting some of the new themes of Gorbachev's Russia. One was an intensified campaign against alcohol and tobacco addiction. The party press announced in January that it would encourage in the factories the creation of brigades composed of workers who had sworn off alcohol and tobacco. The press preached the virtues of abstinence, and Zhivkov linked this to Bulgaria's goal of carrying through the scientific-technological revolution, but there were no reports that the government had moved to reduce the supply or availability of either alcoholic beverages or tobacco (RFE, *Situation Report*, 12 March).

Bulgarian authorities also grappled with the theme of *glasnost'*, or openness, but were clearly not at home with it. *Glasnost'*, which is a Bulgarian as well as Russian word, was discussed in the Central Committee's report to the Thirteenth Congress in connection with the desirability of giving greater publicity to cases of corruption. Radoslav Radev, the first deputy editor of *Rabotnichesko delo*, engaged in self-criticism, stating, "We do not throw enough light on phenomena that are even as serious as robbing from the state. We did not report the stealing by some of the leading officials in Sofia and its districts, and it was not until long after the most incredible rumors had begun to circulate, that we reported about the fraud which the former chairman of the Soccer Federation had been engaged in." Later in the year, popular writer Georgi Mishev published a strongly-worded article in the cultural gazette *Narodna kultura*, stating that until recently there had been a tacit prohibition against printing details about official corruption. He added that now that this prohibition had been lifted the press was still too timid, and he gave as an example the unreported case of a high-ranking official who was caught stealing hundreds of thousands of leva, but who was tried in secret and received only a mild sentence. In this call for greater openness, Mishev himself did not print the name of the official or the details of his crime (*Narodna kultura*, 5 September; RFE, *Situation Report*, 25 September; 20 November). Nor did there appear to be significant improvement in the reporting of crime, accidents, or other disasters. In November a major fire and explosion took place at a chemical combine near Varna, but the published reports gave only sketchy details (Sofia Domestic Sevice, 12 November; *FBIS*, 12 November; *WP*, 2 November). For the time being, it appeared that calls for *glasnost'* were being merged into the traditional campaigns urging Bulgarians to work harder and be more honest.

*The Economy.* Coping with serious economic setbacks provided the principal challenge to party and state leaders. The severe drought that afflicted Bulgaria last year created enormous problems in agriculture and some sectors of manufacturing. The decreased volume of water flowing in Bulgaria's rivers reduced the production of hydroelectric power and aggravated an energy shortage to which a decline in Soviet oil exports to Bulgaria also contributed. According to the annual report on plan fulfillment, the 1985 increase in domestic net material product was only 1.8 percent, the lowest increase ever recorded and far short of the plan target of 4.1 percent. Total industrial production rose 4.0 percent against a target of 5.2 percent, but within this category there were several major setbacks. The generation of electrical power, scheduled for a 3.5 percent increase, actually fell by 6.8 percent. And coal production, targeted for a 14.2 percent increase to make up for shortfalls in other energy sources, fell by 4.3 percent. No data were published on total agricultural production, but some reports indicated an approximate 9 percent decline. The annual report stated that it had become necessary to import agricultural goods to meet the needs of the population and the need of fodder for livestock.

Capital investment, usually the state's highest priority, also failed to achieve plan targets. Real per capita income was reported to have risen 2.7 percent, close to the target of 3.0 percent, but housing construction, as usual, lagged well behind plan goals. The 1986 plan called for growth by 4.0 percent in domestic net material product, 4.5 percent in industrial production, and 2.7 percent in real per capita income. Growth in agriculture was targeted at 7.4 percent, an increase that would still leave it below the 1984 level (*RD*, 1 February; RFE, *Situation Report*, 17 February). Although optimistic in tone, the report on plan fulfillment at the three-quarter mark indicated that recovery was far from complete. Significant increases were claimed in most categories of production, but only in comparison with the first three quarters of 1985. Moreover, the generation of electricity failed to reach even last year's level (*RD*, 30 October; *FBIS*, 12 November). The press reported an unusually large number of shortages in a wide range of consumer articles, ranging from foodstuffs to pencils, but placed the blame on local authorities and managers rather than the national leadership (RFE, *Situation Report*, 25 September).

In the largest sense, Todor Zhivkov's response to Bulgaria's economic problems has been to urge that the country carry through a "scientific-technological revolution." In a speech delivered to the Politburo on 7 January, Zhivkov described this revolution as requiring the restructuring of the planning process in the interest of greater innovation and efficiency, mastering advanced computer technology and biotechnology, educating and training citizens for work in new industries, and improving ideological work to inculcate the virtues of dedication, diligence, and patriotism in the population (*RD*, 18 March; *FBIS*, 20 March). Zhivkov's formulations provided the central themes for an expanded plenum of the Central Committee at the end of January and for the BCP's Thirteenth Congress (*RD*, 6, 7 April; *FBIS*, 30 April).

However appealing Zhivkov's goals may be in the abstract, their translation into practice has not been easy and has been marked by several changes of course. At the end of January, the National Assembly approved a number of measures aimed at streamlining economic planning and administration. Several ministries were closed down or subsumed into three new councils: an Economic Council, a Social Council, and a Council for Science, Culture, and Education. The third was soon renamed the Council for Intellectual Development (RFE, *Situation Report*, 17 February). In March, almost all of the economic ministries were abolished, to be replaced with trusts or combines described as "self-managing organizations" that would coordinate enterprises in the various industrial sectors. The model for this apparently was the Agro-Industrial Union that had replaced the Ministry of Agriculture and Food Industries in 1979. However, the Agro-Industrial Union was itself abolished and replaced by a Ministry of Agriculture and Forests (*RD*, 18 March; *Dŭrzhaven vestnik*, 9 May; *JPRS-Eastern Europe*, 7 October). In July the BCP Secretariat and the Council of Ministers held a conference to discuss the production of consumer goods. Although Zhivkov's speech to this conference was not published, *Rabotnichesko delo* reported that it had criticized a number of practices frequently engaged in by Bulgarian enterprises.

These included reclassifying products from "ordinary" to "deluxe" in order to disguise price increases, producing for the plan rather than for the real needs of the population, and indifference to the consumer. *Rabotnichesko delo* called upon managers to take action without waiting for specific instructions from above, but offered no clear guidelines (*RD*, 7 July; RFE, *Situation Report*, 6 August). The leadership of the chemical trust, established in the March restructuring, was purged in October, accused of being unable to adapt to new ways of operating. It was taken over by a team from the Economic Council, the State Planning Commission, and the Committee for Research and Technology. At the same time, articles in the economic press complained that the government had not defined with sufficient clarity the status and functions of the trusts and combines it had created (RFE, *Situation Report*, 20 November).

*Elections.* Elections were held on 8 June to select the members of the National Assembly and people's councils. At the same time, mayors and jurors for district and regional courts were also elected. As usual, the election campaign was organized by the Fatherland Front, whose committees selected the lists of candidates. It was reported that at pre-election meetings, 331 of the 75,636 candidates were rejected and replaced by others. These were all candidates for the lower offices, and no candidates for the National Assembly were involved. The official election report stated that 99.9 percent of eligible voters had cast ballots and that "practically all" had voted for the front list. Zhivkov was unanimously elected to the National Assembly by his home district in Sofia. Of the 400 delegates elected to the National Assembly, 276 were BCP members (an increase of 5 compared with the last election in 1981), 99 belonged to the BANU (unchanged), and 25 were unaffiliated. Most of the "unaffiliated" were in fact Komsomol members. In the 1981 elections, 14 of the deputies could be identified as ethnic Turks. Owing to the Bulgarianization of Turkish names, the number of "former" Turks in the new assembly could not be determined. Of the 54,496 people's councilors elected, approximately 56 percent were BCP members, about the same as in 1981 (*RD*, 22 April, 14 May; *FBIS*, 9, 11 June; *JPRS-Eastern Europe*, 19 June).

When the new assembly convened on 17 June it dropped Alexander Lilov and Peko Takev from membership in the State Council. Both men earlier had been purged from the Politburo and other high-ranking positions (See *YICA*, 1984 and 1983). Tsola Dragoicheva, who retired from the Politburo in 1984, was also dropped (RFE, *Situation Report*, 7 July).

*The Turkish Minority.* In April, Amnesty International published a report on the forcible assimilation of ethnic Turks in Bulgaria. It estimated that between December 1984, when the assimilation campaign apparently began, and March 1985, approximately 900,000 Bulgarian citizens of Turkish origin were forced to adopt Bulgarian names. The report also stated that at least 100 people had been killed by Bulgarian security forces in outbreaks of violence that accompanied the name-changing campaign, and that it possessed the names of more than 250 individuals who had been imprisoned for opposing it (Amnesty International, *Bulgaria: Imprisonment of Ethnic Turks*). Bulgarian spokesmen branded the report as "completely false," but the general outline of Amnesty International's description was confirmed in a second report by the Helsinki Watch Committee (*Destroying Ethnic Identity: The Turks of Bulgaria*). The reports were verified throughout the year by ethnic Turks who had found the means to leave Bulgaria and by the impressions of some observers who made contact with ethnic Turks inside the country. During the summer, Halil Ahmedov Ibishev, a former member of the National Assembly, defected to Turkey and gave an extensive description of the campaign. He added that he had attempted to protest to Prime Minister Grisha Filipov, but was told that the decision had been made by Zhivkov himself and that it was final (*WP*, 8 April; RFE, *Situation Report*, 9 September).

The drive to assimilate the ethnic Turks has also included ending the publication of Turkish-language periodicals, proscribing the use of Turkish in schools or other official places, and the prohibition of traditional customs such as circumcision and the washing of the dead before burial. (The prohibition of circumcision was apparently not extended to the country's small Jewish population.) The government also mounted a "patriotic" campaign in areas of heavy Turkish settlement, calling upon its agitators to win the confidence of the people and to introduce among them Bulgarian customs, dances, celebrations, and so on to make them more aware of their Bulgarian identity (RFE, *Situation Report*, 9 September).

The position adopted by the government was that the Turks in Bulgaria were not truly Turks at all, but the descendants of Bulgarians who had been forcibly converted to Islam and "Turkicized" during the centuries of Ottoman domination. Consequently, what is taking place is the "reclaiming" of a genuine Bulgarian heritage. In defense of this position, the government produced historical and anthropological studies aimed at proving that the ethnic Turks were Bulgarians all along. In addition, a number of prominent ethnic Turks, with new Bulgarian names, were rallied to express their gratitude to the government for helping them to find their real identities. At the BCP's Thirteenth Congress Yasen Ustrenski (formerly Fahri Ilyazov), who during the year became one of the most vociferous spokesmen for Bulgarianization, stressed ancestral ties to Bulgaria and called the campaign a "great historic act" that would free the minorities from fanaticism and conservatism. The government also took pains to declare that the campaign of Bulgarianization was not directed against the practice of Islam, and it produced a number of Muslim religious leaders to state that complete freedom of religion prevails in the country (*NYT*, 20 April; RFE, *Situation Report*, 27 May).

The primary cause of the Bulgarianization campaign appeared to be the government's fear that demographic trends were working strongly against the ethnic Bulgarian population. In recent years the regime has attempted to raise incentives for Bulgarian couples to have more children, but apparently without result. The population in areas known to be heavily Turkish continued to grow rapidly.

**Auxiliary Organizations.** On 24 March a plenum of the Komsomol's central committee elected Andrei Bundzhulov, described as a 30-year-old sociologist, to the post of first secretary. His predecessor, Stanka Shopova, had held this position since 1981, and was rewarded for her work by promotion to the secretariat of the Sofia City Committee of the BCP. In his speech to the BCP congress, Bundzhulov stressed the need for improving ideological work among youth, calling present methods "outdated." He emphasized the importance of struggling against two trends that have made strong inroads among Bulgarian youth: "a consumer mentality," and "the uncritical imitation of all things foreign" (RFE, *Situation Report*, 27 May).

The Bulgarian Agrarian National Union held its Thirty-fifth Congress on 19–21 May. As usual, it followed close upon the BCP congress and was

largely devoted to confirming the BANU's allegiance to the policies announced there. Petŭr Tanchev, age 66, was re-elected to the leading post of
secretary. His speech stressed the need for intensified political/ideological work in the agricultural
sector to further technological modernization, and
he called for the preservation, and even the expansion, of private plots as a means of raising the
standard of living. As has become traditional, following the congress the BANU hosted an international conference of noncommunist, left-wing parties. Delegates from parties and organizations from
84 countries heard an address from Zhivkov supporting a restructuring of the world information
media to overcome the "information terrorism"
practiced by Western imperialism (BTA, 22 May;
*FBIS*, 23 May; *RD*, 20 May; RFE, *Situation Report*, 7 July).

**International Affairs.** On 29 March an Italian
court acquitted three Bulgarians of charges that they
had been involved in a conspiracy to assassinate the
pope. Two of the defendants—Todor Aivazov, who
had been cashier at the Bulgarian embassy in Rome,
and Lieutenant Colonel Zhelio Vasilev, who had
been the embassy's assistant military attaché—had
returned to Bulgaria before charges were lodged,
and they were tried in absentia. The third, Sergei
Antonov, the Rome representative of the Bulgarian
airline (Balkanair), had been held since his arrest in
November 1982.

Originally described as "the trial of the century,"
the proceedings were expected to produce evidence
of Bulgarian, and by implication Soviet, participation in Mehmet Ali Agca's attempt on the life of
Pope John Paul II in May 1981. The ten-month
trial, however, failed to produce any evidence to
corroborate the testimony of Agca, upon which the
case almost entirely rested. Since Agca changed his
testimony many times, both before and during the
trial, adding assertions that he was the reincarnated
Christ and an "angel in human form," the absence
of corroboration was decisive. Even the prosecution
in its summing up of the case admitted that the
charges remained unproven and called for an
acquittal as the appropriate verdict. Three Turkish
defendants were also acquitted. In a 1,200-page
explanation of their verdict, the judges stated that
no evidence was produced that linked the "Bulgarian matrix" to the "Turkish matrix" (*Washington
Times*, 22 November).

During the trial Bulgarian spokesmen accused
Western intelligence agencies of fabricating the

case against Antonov and the others to discredit the
socialist camp. Later in the year Vitaly Yurchenko,
a high-ranking KGB official who defected to the
United States and then redefected to the USSR,
stated that while he was in the hands of the Americans the CIA sought to prepare him to give testimony at the Rome trial, playing the role of "Mal-
enkov," the Soviet agent said by Agca to have been
the paymaster in the conspiracy against the pope
(*WP*, 9 August). There was no evidence to substan-
tiate this charge, and it appeared that the principal
factor that led to the trial was the pressure from
right-wing journalists and Italian politicians for
whom the existence of a "Bulgarian connection"
was a matter of faith. American journalist Claire
Sterling and former National Security Council staff
member Paul Henze conducted an extensive campaign in the media that not only asserted a Soviet-
bloc origin for the attempt on the pope's life, but
also accused Western leaders who had illusions of
coexisting with communism of seeking to suppress
the case. Another factor seems to have been the
sloppy investigative procedures employed by the
prosecutor, Illario Martella, who allowed Agca access to materials containing information that the
Turk later incorporated into his testimony. Following the trial, Antonov returned home to his family
and to a hero's welcome at the Thirteenth Party
Congress (*WP*, 30 March; BTA, 29 March; *FBIS*,
31 March).

On the negative side, Bulgaria's two-and-one-
half year campaign to have Sofia selected to host the
1992 Winter Olympics ended in failure when the
International Olympic Committee voted to assign
these games to Albertville in France (RFE, *Situation Report*, 6 November).

*The Soviet Union.* In 1985, reports of difficulties in Bulgaria's relationship with the USSR and in
Zhivkov's personal relationship with Soviet leader
Gorbachev were widespread (see *YICA*, 1986). This
year, however, Bulgarian-Soviet relations resumed
their traditionally harmonious appearance and, if
real difficulties existed, they were successfully concealed from public view. Zhivkov led the Bulgarian
delegation to the Twenty-seventh Congress of the
CPSU, where he was chosen to address the congress on behalf of the other Warsaw Pact leaders. It
was also reported that he had a long meeting with
Gorbachev devoted to the theme of economic and
scientific cooperation (Sofia Domestic Service, 6
March; *JPRS-Eastern Europe*, 31 March). The Soviet government presented Zhivkov with the Order

of the October Revolution on the occasion of his 75th birthday and stated that he deserved "the profound admiration of all communists" for his work toward the modernization of Bulgaria and the development of Soviet-Bulgarian friendship (*Pravda*, 7 September). Gorbachev personally presented this award to Zhivkov at a ceremony in the Kremlin in November (*Pravda*, 11 November). The USSR also honored Bulgarian Politburo member and minister of defense Dobri Dzhurov with an Order of Lenin on the occasion of his 70th birthday (Sofia Domestic Service, 10 March; *FBIS*, 11 March).

The Bulgarian press took pains to minimize the significance of the nuclear disaster at Chernobyl, probably owing to the fact that the country possesses two major Soviet-built atomic power complexes along the Danube. Although stating that increased radiation levels in the country were not dangerous, the government halted the sale of sheep's milk and recommended that leafy vegetables grown in the open not be eaten for the time being. Bulgaria also protested the ban imposed by the Common Market on the importing of Bulgarian agricultural products (RFE, *Background Report*, 23 May).

*Other East European and Balkan Countries.* During the year Turkey continued to apply diplomatic and economic pressures in defense of Bulgaria's ethnic Turks, with the result that relations between the two countries steadily deteriorated. Turkey raised the issue of Bulgaria's persecution of its Turkish minority at several international forums and bilateral diplomatic meetings, doing significant damage to Bulgaria's reputation in the Islamic world. In January a meeting of the Islamic Conference Organization in Fez adopted a resolution calling attention to the plight of the Bulgarian Turks that was subsequently published by the United Nations. The Turks also boycotted some Bulgarian goods and sought to develop direct ferry links with Romania and Italy that would allow them to avoid the land route across Bulgaria. For its part, Bulgaria characterized the Turkish efforts as unjustified interference in the affairs of a neighbor and mounted a campaign criticizing abuses of human rights in Turkey. The Bulgarian press focused on historic issues, such as the massacre of the Armenians, and current ones, such as Turkey's persecution of its Kurdish minority. In May Bulgaria accused Turkish authorities of torturing to death a Bulgarian citizen who had been accused of espionage. Later in the year, Bulgaria released the

film *Midnight Express*, calling on all citizens to see "the endless labyrinths of violence and cruelty that are modern-day Turkish prisons." (RFE, *Situation Reports*, 27 March; 6 August; 9 September.)

Perhaps because of the mounting hostility with Turkey, relations with Yugoslavia quietly improved, and polemics over the Macedonian question were minimal. Stanislav Stojanovic, executive secretary of the Yugoslav League of Communists Central Committee Presidium, spent four days in Sofia in January, meeting with members of the Politburo and government officials. At the conclusion of his visit, a two-year program of cooperation between the Yugoslav League of Communists and the BCP was agreed upon. Stojanovic stated that the two countries had made significant strides in developing "a spirit of good-neighborliness and mutual respect" (BTA, 24 January; *FBIS*, 27 January; Tanjug, 25 January). In March the governing bodies of radio and television in the two countries signed an agreement to expand cooperation and to exchange news and other programs (Tanjug, 18 March; *FBIS*, 19 March).

Prime Minister Andreas Papandreou of Greece paid a state visit to Bulgaria in September, during which he characterized Greek-Bulgarian relations as "surpassing the conventional borders of good-neighborliness." At the conclusion of his visit, he and Zhivkov signed a "Declaration on Friendship, Good Neighborliness, and Cooperation," which was seen in some quarters as a near alliance directed against Turkey or Yugoslavia. In fact, the declaration contained little that was new and explicitly stated that it was not aimed at any third party and did not affect the membership of Bulgaria in the Warsaw Pact or of Greece in NATO. For Papandreou, the main purpose in signing the declaration seems to have been to mollify his left-wing supporters at home. The benefit for Zhivkov is that he appears to be engaged in an active Balkan policy. Trade between the two countries has actually declined nearly 50 percent since Greece entered the Common Market in 1981 and, although Papandreou and Zhivkov pledged to increase it, the opportunities for doing so appeared quite limited (*RD*, 13 September; *FBIS*, 21 September; RFE, *Situation Report*, 6 November).

Bulgaria always has stressed its loyal and active participation in the Warsaw Pact and the CMEA. Zhivkov led the Bulgarian delegation to the Warsaw Pact meeting in Budapest in June where he expressed full support for Soviet disarmament proposals (BTA, 17 June; *FBIS*, 19 June). Foreign

Minister Bohuslav Chnoupek of Czechoslovakia spent three days in Sofia in June. Following his visit and meeting with Zhivkov, he announced that the volume of trade between Czechoslovakia and Bulgaria has more than doubled during the last five years (Prague Domestic Service, 7 June; *FBIS*, 9, 16 June; *RD*, 8 June).

*The Third World.* While attending the CPSU Congress in Moscow, Zhivkov met with Cuba's Fidel Castro to sign an accord covering economic and scientific-technical cooperation until the year 2000. A protocol implementing this agreement for the period 1986 to 1990 was signed at Sofia in May. It called for a 22 percent increase in trade in comparison with the previous five-year period (*RD*, 16 May; *FBIS*, 5 June).

Bulgaria continued to pursue an active policy toward Africa. Canaan Banana, president of Zimbabwe, visited Sofia in June. He and Zhivkov condemned South Africa, and President Banana invited Zhivkov to pay a future visit to Zimbabwe (*RD*, 22 June; *FBIS*, 26 June). A two-year agreement was signed with Tanzania providing for an expansion of cooperation in science, education, culture, and sports (*RD*, 6 June; *FBIS*, 17 June). A protocol calling for the acceleration of projects already agreed upon was signed with Ethiopia in August (BTA, 24 August; *FBIS*, 25 August).

During a visit to Sofia in June, Foreign Minister Shankar of India described his country's relations with Bulgaria as "excellent." After meeting with Zhivkov, he stated that he expected economic and cultural relations with Bulgaria to continue to expand rapidly (BTA, 12 June; *FBIS*, 16 June).

*Western Europe and the United States.* West Germany is Bulgaria's largest trading partner among the Western nations. In May Foreign Minister Petŭr Mladenov spent three days in Bonn, where he met with his counterpart, Hans-Dietrich Genscher, and with Chancellor Helmut Kohl. The two sides found little agreement on general political issues, and Mladenov protested the restrictions that the Common Market had placed on the import of Bulgarian agricultural products in the wake of the Chernobyl disaster. They did agree, however, that bilateral German-Bulgarian relations were developing satisfactorily (BTA, 20 May; *FBIS*, 21 May). In August a West German parliamentary delegation met with Zhivkov and other officials at Sofia to discuss measures to increase trade. It was reported that in the first six months of 1986 West Germany increased its trade with Bulgaria by 7.2 percent, while its trade with Eastern Europe as a whole declined by 6.3 percent (RFE, *Situation Report*, 9 September).

Bulgaria traditionally has had good relations with Austria. In 1986 the two countries signed an agreement to cooperate on the upgrading of their communications links with a view toward establishing a major electronic communications route between Western Europe and the Middle East (BTA, 7 March; *FBIS*, 10 March).

Bulgaria protested American naval maneuvers in the Black Sea, accusing the United States of violating Soviet and Bulgarian territorial waters to gather military intelligence and "test the diplomatic nerves" of the two countries. According to the military newspaper *Narodna armiya*, this was the fourth American violation of Bulgaria's territorial waters in the past four years (BTA, 20 March; *FBIS*, 21 March; *Narodna armiya*, 22 March; *FBIS*, 28 March).

John D. Bell
*University of Maryland Baltimore County*

# Czechoslovakia

**Population.** 15,542,000
**Party.** Communist Party of Czechoslovakia (Kommunistická strana Československa; KSČ)
**Founded.** 1921
**Membership.** 1,675,000 (*Rudé právo*, 25 March)
**General Secretary.** Gustáv Husák
**Presidium.** 11 full members: Vasil Bil'ák, Petr Colotka (deputy prime minister), Karel Hoffman (chairman, Revolutionary Trade Union Movement), Gustáv Husák (president of the republic), Alois Indra (chairman, Federal Assembly), Miloš Jakeš, Antonín Kapek, Josef Kempný, Josef Korčák (deputy prime minister), Jozef Lenárt, Lubomír Štrougal (federal prime minister); 6 candidate members: Jan Fojtík, Josef Haman, Vladimír Herman, Miloslav Hruškovič, Ignác Janák, František Pitra
**Secretariat.** 9 secretaries: Gustáv Husák, Mikulás Beno, Vasil Bil'ák, Jan Fojtík, Josef Haman, Josef Havlín, Miloš Jakeš, František Pitra, Jindřich Poledník; 2 members-at-large: Zdeněk Hořeni, Marie Kabrhelová
**Control and Auditing Commission.** Jaroslav Hajn, chairman
**Central Committee.** 135 full and 62 candidate members
**Status.** Ruling party
**Last Congress.** Seventeenth, 24–28 March 1986, in Prague; next congress scheduled for 1991
**Slovak Party.** Communist Party of Slovakia (Komunistická strana Slovenska; KSS); membership: 436,000 full and candidate members; Jozef Lenárt, first secretary; Presidium: 11 members; Central Committee: 91 full and 31 candidate members
**Last Election.** 1986, 99.94 percent, all 350 National Front candidates; 66 percent of seats reserved for KSČ candidates
**Auxiliary Organizations.** Revolutionary Trade Union Movement (Tenth Congress, April 1982), Cooperative Farmers' Union, Socialist Youth Union (Third Congress, October 1982), Union for Collaboration with the Army, Czechoslovak Union of Women, Union of Fighters for Peace
**Main State Organs.** The executive body is the federal government, which is subordinate to the 350-member Federal Assembly, composed of the Chamber of the People (200 members) and the Chamber of the Nations (150 members). The assembly, however, merely rubber-stamps all decisions made by the KSČ Presidium and Central Committee.
**Publications.** *Rudé právo*, KSČ daily; *Pravda* (Bratislava), KSS daily; *Tribuna*, Czech-language ideological weekly; *Predvoj*, Slovak-language ideological weekly; *Život strany*, fortnightly journal devoted to administrative and organizational questions; *Práce* (Czech) and *Práca* (Slovak), Revolutionary Trade Union Movement dailies; *Mladá fronta* (Czech) and Smena (Slovak) Socialist Youth Union dailies; *Tvorba*, weekly devoted to domestic and international politics; *Nová mysl*, theoretical monthly. Československá tisková kancelář (ČETEKA) is the official news agency.

The KSČ developed from the left wing of the Czechoslovak Social Democratic Party, having co-opted several radical socialist and leftist groups. It was constituted in Prague and admitted to the Communist International the same year. Its membership in the Comintern, however, was an uneasy one until in 1929 the so-called bolshevization process was completed and a leadership of unqualified obedience to the Soviet Union assumed control. During the First Czechoslovak Republic (1918–1939), the KSČ enjoyed legal status, but it was banned after the Munich Agreement. After the war, it emerged as the strongest party in the postwar elections of 1946, although it did not poll a majority of votes. In February 1948, the KSČ seized all power in a coup d'état and transformed Czechoslovakia into a communist party-state of the Soviet type. The departure from Stalinist practices started later in Czechoslovakia than in other countries of Central and Eastern Europe, but it led to a daring liberalization experience known as the Prague Spring of 1968. A Soviet-led military intervention by five Warsaw Pact countries in August of the same year ended the democratization course and imposed on Czechoslovakia the policies of so-called normalization—a return to unreserved subordination to the will of the Soviet Union and the emulation of the Soviet example in all areas of social life.

**Party Internal Affairs.** The most important event in the life of the KSČ during 1986 was the Seventeenth Party Congress, held in Prague during 24–28 March. It was preceded, as usual, by plenary meetings of regional and municipal party organizations in all ten regions of the country and in the capital cities of the two republics, Prague and Bratislava (Radio Prague, 13 February), as well as by the congress of the Communist Party of Slovakia (Bratislava, *Pravda*, 17 March). This latter congress confirmed Jozef Lenárt as KSS first secretary and re-elected most other functionaries of the party's governing bodies.

Observers expected more important personnel changes to happen at the national congress of the KSČ. They also wondered to what extent the congress would respond to the new course gradually taking shape in the Soviet Union under Mikhail S. Gorbachev. Steps toward a penetrating reform of the economic system were often cited among the decisions that the congress might take (Belgrade, *Borba*, 23/24 November 1985). This appeared to be all the more likely, as the KSČ congress was to follow shortly after the Twenty-seventh Congress of the CPSU in Moscow. The Soviet party was represented in Prague by a Politburo member and chairman of the CPSU Control Committee, Mikhail Solomentsev, who in his speech stressed the unanimous view of the Soviet leadership that "the entire system

of Soviet planning of the economy must be improved in a radical way" (*Rudé právo*, 26 March).

On the subject of possible innovations in the sphere of economic management and planning, General Secretary Gustáv Husák declared in his talk at the regional party conference in Hradec Králové that Czechoslovak communists "were not afraid of any reforms." They followed closely what their comrades in the Soviet Union were doing, said Husák, but "looked for their own solutions" (Radio Prague, 15 February). When the congress convened on 24 March, it became clear that many of the expectations would remain unconfirmed and many of the urgent questions facing the party would stay open. Husák's inauguration speech, three hours long, indicated that present party leaders continued to reject all ideas of reform that might depart from ideological orthodoxy. It also suggested that personnel changes would be limited to lower party echelons. (*Rudé právo*, 25 March.) Lubomír Štrougal, a KSČ Presidium member and the federal prime minister, specifically addressed the issue of economic reform. Although he admitted that efforts made to improve the performance of the Czechoslovak economy in the previous five years had "foundered on compromises and a half-hearted approach to the tasks at hand," and that "the government in its entirety, its individual members as well as leading officials in other agencies, simply have failed to adjust the style and the methods of their work to the new economic conditions," the organizational innovations and changes in economic management that Štrougal announced did not seem in tune with the radical nature of his criticism (*Rudé právo*, 26 March). They were ambiguous, to say the least; it remains to be seen whether they were mere window dressing or whether they represented the first step toward a genuine reform, as some Western analysts inferred (*WP*, 29 March).

Official media coverage of the congress reserved an important place for a new version of the party statutes adopted at the congress. Their full text, published in *Rudé právo* on 3 April, indicated, however, that little will change in the way the party is ruled. Since the rejection of the statutory revision proposed by the Dubček leadership in 1968, which would have had party officials regularly elected by a majority vote from grass-roots organizations, the leading cadres have been renewed by simple co-optation. Comments on the new statutes emphasized that the revised version would "facilitate the expansion of party activities and help enforce its leading role in all parts of the country's life"(*Rudé právo*, 14 January). The congress also approved two documents, "The Main Direction of Economic and Social Development in the ČSSR for 1986–1990" and "The Outlook for the Period up to the Year 2000," both of which had been widely distributed and discussed in the precongress party gatherings. A substantial part of these publications was devoted to economic problems and reflected the same measure of inconsistency as the reports submitted by Husák and Štrougal. In its social and cultural section, the first document summed up the development of the country during the previous fifteen years (since the Fourteenth Party Congress in 1971, the first after the Soviet-led military intervention of 1968) and claimed that the party had succeeded in "bringing true socialist democracy to the toiling masses" (*Rudé právo*, 3 April).

The congress did not carry out any significant changes in the composition of top party organs. The number of Presidium candidates was enlarged by three, and the Central Committee was increased by twelve full members and seven candidates (Radio Prague, 28 March). Party membership had grown notably since the Sixteenth congress in 1981. The total of 1,675,000 includes, as General Secretary Husák pointed out, every seventh Czechoslovak citizen aged 18 and over (*Rudé právo*, 25 March). The mass character of the Czechoslovak communist party has long been an established fact. Although previously large membership rolls seemed on occasion to embarrass the leaders and to draw criticism from the Soviets (for being incompatible with the Leninist notion of the party as an elite avant-garde of the working class), this growth in 1986 appeared to be a source of pride. Yet it may not always be an unmixed blessing. As the first secretary of the KSS, Jozef Lenárt, revealed later in the year, some 1,486 members had to be expelled from the party because they "misused their positions" and in some instances even "violated the laws and engaged in criminal activities" (Bratislava, *Pravda*, 4 July). On the other hand, including so many elements from all walks of life in the membership seems unintentionally to provide a platform for voicing unorthodox opinions that are widely shared by the population at large. This came to the fore especially in the precongress debate (*Rudé právo*, 1 February; Radio Prague, 15 February).

The year 1986 marked the 65th anniversary of the founding of the KSČ (the preparatory congress was held in May 1921; the merger congress in October–November 1921). The anniversary was also commemorated in the Soviet party press; however, any elaboration on what kind of party the original KSČ had been, before it was successfully "bolshevized" in 1929, was carefully avoided (Moscow, *Pravda*, 28 March).

**Domestic Affairs.** The population of Czechoslovakia increased by 39,000 (0.25 percent) between July 1985 and July 1986 (*World Factbook*, 1986). This year's growth was below the average of 0.3 percent. As in previous years, this birthrate, only slightly above the reproduction minimum, was even lower in the Czech lands than in Slovakia. The fact that the Gypsies increased their numbers far faster than other ethnic groups seemed to be a source of particular concern to the authorities (*Smena*, 6 August). An interesting demographic study undertaken by independent scholars in Czechoslovakia and published in the exile publication *Listy* at Rome (no. 5, December 1985) shed some light on the possible factors contributing to the low population growth. According to the findings of this study, Czechoslovakia during the last twenty years lost 234,638 people (more than 1.5 percent of the total) through emigration, both legal and illegal.

During 23 and 24 May 1986, elections to federal, state, and municipal legislative and executive bodies were held. As could be expected, the single ballot ot the National Front with 66 percent of its candidates representing the KSČ was elected unopposed; only the majority it mustered was incredible, even by the usual communist standards. According to the official count, no less than 99.94 percent voted for the National Front (Radio Hvezda, 24 May). The National Assembly and two National Councils (the parliaments of the Czech and of the Slovak republics respectively) that issued from the elections endorsed the new federal government, as well as the governments of the two republics. Only minor changes were effected in their composition, compared with the previous executive organs. The appointment of Czechoslovakia's permanent representative to the CMEA, Rudolf Rohlíček, to the post of first deputy prime minister of the federal government seemed to indicate an emphasis on economic issues and perhaps an intention to seriously tackle the problem of economic reform during the new legislative period. At the inauguration ceremony of the new government, President Husák made some remarks that appeared to confirm this impression (ČETEKA, 16 June).

The economic difficulties that Czechoslovakia has been experiencing since the 1960s were not, to be sure, the only problems with which the party and the government had to deal in 1986. Among the most serious was the pollution threat to which all industrial nations of the world have been exposed, but which in the countries of the Soviet bloc—and particularly in Czechoslovakia—has been exacerbated by decades of neglect. Only recently has the topic of protection of the environment become admissible in official utterances and the media. The problem has been most acute in the Czech provinces, especially in Bohemia, where soft coal has been the principal source of heat and industrial energy, but the situation in Slovakia, too, has been rapidly deteriorating. It is expected that by 1990 the forest area destroyed or threatened by sulphuric oxide emission will double (*Práce*, 17 August). Some Czechoslovak experts claimed that the country was approaching the so-called ecological barrier, beyond which any further economic development can be bought only at the price of irreparable damage to the natural environment (*Podniková organisace*, no. 8). Having gradually become aware of these risks, the government approved (in November 1985) a special comprehensive document on environmental protection. The final version of this document was incorporated into the two already mentioned economic publications of the Seventeenth Party Congress. It was made public two months later (*Hospodářské noviny*, 16 May). The success of the planned measures, however, will depend on the ability of the system to adapt to new ways of government and management. Some Western commentators noted that in Czechoslovakia statistics on the environment continue to be treated as state secrets (*Die Welt*, 7 February).

Heavy dependence on soft coal and sulphur-rich Soviet oil could be reduced by further development of nuclear capacities. Czechoslovakia has made considerable progress in this direction, but has inevitably had to face the problem of the safety of nuclear energy, as well as its rising costs (*Finance a úvěr*, no. 9). The seriousness of the problem was dramatically illustrated by the fallout—real as well as political—of the nuclear accident at Chernobyl in the Ukraine. As a model satellite, Czechoslovakia under Husák's leadership faithfully endorsed the Soviet line on this tragic event. Party spokesmen, especially during the parliamentary election campaign, echoed the Soviet charges and condemned "the cynicism with which political officials and propaganda in some NATO countries misused the tragic event at Chernobyl for political ends" (Radio Prague, 19 May). They admitted, however, that as a consequence of the Chernobyl accident "a number of people were unnecessarily alarmed, and this still continues in some places" (ibid., 21 May).

Less spectacular, but nevertheless significant, was the admission by official sources that the problem of drug abuse does exist in Czechoslovakia. Implicitly, this fact was conceded by Czechoslovak signature of the 82-nation plan for an antidrug campaign, worked out at a U.N.-sponsored conference in Vienna (Reuters, 1 August). Yet the media continued to claim that drug addiction in Czechoslovakia, although spreading, has not become a mass phenomenon (*Průboj*, 11 April; *Učitelské noviny*, 15 May). According to Western analysts, however, in 1984 there were no fewer than 500,000 drug addicts in the country, that is, more than 3 percent of the entire population (RFE/RL Research, *Situation Report*, no. 2, 6 February 1984).

On the other hand, the problem of illegal abortions appeared to ease, so that political decision makers submitted new, more relaxed legislation in 1986. These new regulations no longer require permission from two physicians and a social counselor; the decision is left entirely to the pregnant woman, who must have the abortion performed within the first twelve weeks of pregnancy (Czechoslovak Television, 20, 22 October). This legislative change met with strong opposition from Christian believers, especially Catholics, who organized a petition campaign while the bill was under discussion in the Czech and the Slovak National Councils. Although the police detained and questioned some of the petitioners, 14,598 signatures were collected (Prague, AFP, 25 September, 20 October).

As for more directly political problems, regime representatives admitted on several occasions that the system had to deal with continuing tensions among ethnic groups, especially with the delicate relations between the Slovak majority and the Hungarian-speaking minority in Slovakia. Often they attributed these tensions to the actions of "foreign anticommunist forces," who allegedly tried "to resuscitate nationalism and to exploit it as an instrument for the destabilization of political conditions" (*Nová mysl*, no. 9). Ethnic Hungarians nevertheless continued to perceive their situation in Czechoslovakia as somewhat disadvantageous; the argument that the Slovak-speaking citizens of neighboring Hungary were not faring much better as far as their ethnic aspirations were concerned seemed to be of little comfort. The Hungarian minority interpreted the restrictions imposed on travel from Czechoslovakia to Hungary—motivated mainly by economic considerations—as another form of discrimination, an attempt to impede contacts with their families and relatives south of the border (Radio Prague, 8 February). The recent experience of the Hungarian ethnic group's leader, Miklós Duray, who was imprisoned and released in 1985, may have reinforced the mistrust of the ethnic Hungarians in Czechoslovakia (see *YICA*, 1986).

*Economy.* Data published in early 1986 regarding the 1985 performance of the Czechoslovak economy indicated that plan targets had on the whole been met or exceeded, with the exception of a few important sectors, such as housing and agriculture. Fulfillment of the production plan in the course of the year had been irregular, and the number of enterprises that failed to meet the planned gross production increase of 15.4 percent was higher than it had been in 1984 (*Rudé právo*, 25 January). The Eighth Five-Year Plan (1986-1990), unlike previous plans, was based on a long-term perspective of fifteen years and took into consideration the anticipated capacities and needs of the year 2000. Furthermore, some of its aspects had to be adjusted to the targets of the economic plans of other CMEA countries, so that its final version was delayed and made public much later than on previous occasions (*Rudé právo*, 28 February). However, introducing a wider time span into the planning process was not an isolated innovation. There had been a consensus for some time about the necessity to reform the operation of the Czechoslovak economy. Some two years earlier, a program of what was called "intensification" (sometimes "acceleration") of production had been adopted. Officials were rather disappointed about the results of this experiment (*Práce*, 30 December 1985). The intensification campaign was formalized in the "Main Direction of Economic and Social Development," which was hailed as "the charter of intensification" (*Rudé právo*, 11 January).

Whether this blueprint for the improvement of economic performance will be more successful after its incorporation into the resolutions of the last party congress remains to be seen. Both Czechoslovak and foreign observers familiar with the problems of the economy recognize that much will depend on the willingness of the party to depart from established dogmatic principles, especially from its aversion to stimulating private initiative and responsibility by creating opportunities for profit.

These dogmatic views are very deeply rooted in the leadership that came to power in the wake of the Soviet-sponsored "normalization" after the military intervention of August 1968, which negated all innovative ideas, including that of a "socialist market economy" (*Selected Papers Submitted to the Joint Economic Committee of Congress*, vol. 3, 28 March, pp. 95–97; *NYT*, 20 June).

The weak areas of the economy were found especially in housing (Moscow, *Statistical Yearbook of the Member Countries of the CMEA*, 1985; *Soviet Studies*, no. 3, July) and in the service sector (Bratislava, *Pravda*, 7 January; *Rudé právo*, 30 January; Radio Hvězda, 11 August; *Rudé právo*, 29 August, 2 September). The system of wages prevailing in Czechoslovakia, too, has often been blamed for insufficient economic performance. Therefore a new system of remuneration was initiated, the Czech acronym for which is ZEUMS (for "Perfecting the Economic Effectiveness of the Wage System"). Its application, however, met with resistance on the part of the workers. In one officially reported case a strike occurred in the tractor factory "Agrozet" at Uherský Brod in Moravia (*Rudé právo*, 10 March). Although the party daily blamed the work stoppage on the plant managers who allegedly "implemented the new system in an improper and insensitive way," and called the strike "essentially understandable," the truth is that the striking workers were actually protesting the principle of remuneration according to individual performance. Thus, they challenged the very objective of the wage system reform.

The unrest in Uherský Brod was symptomatic of the predilection for wage egalitarianism among the Czechoslovak labor force—which had been instilled by long decades of centralist industrial management and planning of the most dogmatic Stalinist type. It also suggested how difficult it may be to bring the Czechoslovak economy to a higher level of efficiency, even if party leaders seriously set their minds to this goal. The egalitarian mentality has reduced labor mobility so that, for example, there were no fewer than 750,000 job vacancies, almost 10 percent of the entire work force. In many instances, enterprises competed with one another for available and willing workers, whom they sought to win over with better facilities or fringe benefits—a wholly unsocialist approach (*Rudé právo*, 2 September). The obverse side of the egalitarian wage principle had been the virtually guaranteed security of employment. Most enterprises keep everyone on their payroll, regardless of the actual need for manpower. This certainty of keeping one's job under any circumstances, combined with the knowledge that pay will remain the same regardless of the quality of work performed, has bred widespread indifference and low labor productivity.

Economic decision makers have for some time contemplated the possibility of efficiency-justified mass layoffs in the nationalized industry. The short-term unemployment that inevitably would result from such measures is obviously still a taboo subject and, therefore, is not called by its true name; instead, Czechoslovak economists have been talking of "introducing the criterion of rationality into employment policies." This rational employment should have precedence over "employment as such." It has even been argued that, while socialism and full employment are indivisible, "rational employment" is more congenial with socialism than "employment for employment's sake" (Bratislava, *Pravda*, 24 February).

The egalitarian wage system practiced in the past went hand in hand with strict price controls, each facilitating the other. Nevertheless, an inflation of 17.7 percent occurred during the years of the Seventh Five-Year-Plan. It was the lowest inflation rate in Eastern Europe and allowed for a steady, although modest, growth of real wages (ČETEKA, 9 July). Economic statistics for the first half of 1986 indicated that performance during the first six months had been mixed. According to this report, "the state plan's intentions in most quality indices have not been fulfilled in the first half of the year, although they improved in comparison with 1985" (ČETEKA, 25 July). The 1986 harvest statistics were not good. While the previous year's crops had been almost a record—second-best in the last twenty years—the 1986 yields were unsatisfactory, in some places even 30 percent below average and the "smallest in ten years" (*Rudé právo*, 26 August). The failure was blamed chiefly on bad weather. However, various comments in the press on this subject admitted that other factors may have been responsible: excessive use of chemicals, neglect of organic fertilizers, soil erosion caused by heavy agricultural machinery, and so on (*Rudé právo*, 9 September).

*Culture, Youth, and Religion.* Czech literature in 1986 suffered a great loss when poet Jaroslav Seifert, Czechoslovakia's first Nobel Prize laureate, died on 10 January at the age of 84. His death, not unlike his receipt of the prestigious prize in 1984, created a somewhat uneasy situation for the communist regime. Seifert, although a convinced socialist of working-class origin, had always been critical of the Czechoslovak communist party, before as well as after its coming to power. He made a courageous address denouncing the crimes of Stalinism at the Second Congress of Czechoslovak Writers in April 1956, and offered a bold answer to an invitation from the chief "normalizer," Gustáv Husák, after the Soviet invasion: "If we writers accept, we will forfeit our moral legitimization, and thus will be of no use to you!" Seifert was among the first known personalities to put his signature to the Charter '77 proclamation. The party retaliated by ignoring him and preventing publication of his works. He was given a state funeral; however, friends and readers who shared his views were prevented from attending the ceremony (Prague, Reuters, 21 January; *NYT*, 22 January).

Seifert's appeal to the Czech public, especially to the young was one of many unmistakable signs of the failure of the communist establishment to win genuine public trust and allegiance. This failure was implicitly admitted by several party spokesmen in their public statements during the year. Speaking to a delegation of the Socialist Youth Federation at the Prague Castle, General Secretary Gustáv Husák pointed out that "socialist awareness does not crop up automatically, but it requires a purposeful influence by word and deed." He complained that "a certain part of youth is also manifesting certain unfavorable traits." The party must, Husák continued, "effectively ward off the attempts to introduce in our country various harmful, so-called fashionable, trends from the West" (*Rudé právo*, 25 June).

By these "harmful trends," the general secretary obviously meant also the enthusiasm of young Czechs and Slovaks for modern Western music, especially rock. The regime has been waging a losing battle with rock music for many years. Recent police and court measures against various rock musicians and groups have only underscored the inability of the communists to counteract their popularity. At the end of 1985, seven young people, all blue-collar workers, received prison sentences because they had held a rock concert without written official authorization (*Informace o Chartě*, no. 7, April). At the same time it seemed as if the regime were willing to accept rock if it did not threaten the communist cultural monopoly. Josef Trnka, director of the Institute for Cultural and Educational Activities, wrote that a green light would be given only to rock music that met the ideological and aesthetic criteria of socialist society. An ideal solution, according to him, would be to let the clubs for youth music operate within the framework of the SFY (*Mladá fronta*, 22 July). In fact, the regime allowed a rock festival to be held in Prague under official sponsorship, but with the participation of many underground rock groups, on 29 and 30 June (*Večerní Praha*, 28 April).

Yet there was no real consistency in the approach to the problem of Western music. Communist authorities continued to persecute the lovers of jazz, especially the members of the former jazz section of the Czech Union of Musicians. This section had been disbanded in 1983, although it had several thousand members and its periodicals had reached a readership of no fewer than 100,000 persons. The section had also been registered with UNESCO, which insured it international recognition. Spokesmen protested aginst the dissolution at the European Cultural Forum at Budapest in 1985. They had planned another protest action for the CSCE follow-up conference in Vienna during November 1986, but were prevented by the police (Prague, AFP, 1 September). The chairman and six other members of the section were arrested. It was assumed that they would be put on trial early in 1987 (*NYT*, 12 December).

Music was not the only area in which regime propaganda had to admit defeat and lack of influence. Several official commentators concluded that almost forty years of concentrated effort were not enough to re-educate young people in the spirit of communism or gain their acceptance of the Marxist view of history. Writing in the party ideological review, Slovak historians Samuel Cambel and Marian Škaldány stated that "despite the purposeful efforts of Marxist historiography to crush legends, such as the ones of [T. G.] Masaryk and Štefánik, all of them, and even the most reactionary ones, suddenly emerged in full nakedness in the late 1960s, and were partly greeted with applause." Significantly for the current situation in Czechoslovakia, they added: "It is surprising how deeply these legends are engraved on the collective mind of society. They have a tough life. Despite almost forty years of work on our socialist education, they succeed in infecting some young people." (*Nová mysl*, no. 9.) Not even on this issue—the "Masarykian legend" that allegedly infects Czech and Slovak youth—did offical policy seem consistent. The 100th anniversary of the birth of T. G. Masaryk's son, Jan Masaryk (minister of foreign affairs in the last Czechoslovak government before the communist takeover, who died under mysterious circum-

stances in March 1948) was, surprisingly enough, remembered in all main organs of the party press (*Rudé právo*, 13 September; Bratislava, *Pravda*, 13 September; *Tribuna*, no. 36, 10 September; *Tvorba*, no. 36, 10 September). Even more surprising was a statement in one of the articles that Jan Masaryk was to be commended for having tried "to preserve the genuine legacy of T. G. Masaryk," in contrast to the politicians of the noncommunist parties who allegedly betrayed this legacy (*Rudé právo*, 13 September).

In 1986, the ideological supervisors worried also about other possible deviations to which the youth might succumb. One of them was pacifism. This, too, seemed curious: peace and peace slogans have since the start been the stock-in-trade of communist propaganda. Yet the party ideological weekly argued that pacifism "could erode socialism from within" (*Tribuna*, no. 38, 24 September). This danger, said the writer, stemmed from so-called independent peace movements in socialist countries with whom "selected pacifist organizations in the West seek to intensify contacts." He seemed to refer to one concrete incident that happened in the spring of 1986, when five Austrian students joined Czechoslovak students in their protest against the risks of insufficiently secured nuclear reactors. The Austrians were arrested and later expelled from the country (ČETEKA, 30 May).

Another phenomenon observed among youth—and among adult generations—preoccupied party leaders. Not unlike the persisting "historical legends," forty years of systematic atheistic propaganda have not ended the practice of religion. There has been a net decline in the total number of people going to church or associated with various denominations and congregations, but this trend could be attributed with considerable plausibility to the advancing secularization characteristic of all industrial societies. It could even be argued that the crude methods applied by the system against what is called "religiosity" have, instead of eradicating religious faith, solidified the remaining core of believers. In a certain sense, religion appeared to assert itself more powerfully than ever, especially in Slovakia. The regime seemed alarmed by the existence and proliferation of various informal groups meeting and worshiping outside the framework set by the state, calling them "illegal, secret church bodies" (*Nová mysl*, no. 9). Equally frightening to the authorities was the unusually large attendance at religious pilgrimages that has been observed for several years. In 1986 some 100,000 Catholics gathered in July at the shrine of Our Lady in Levoča, in northeastern Slovakia (BBC, *Current Affairs Research*, 7 July), while 40,000 members of the Greek Church participated in the pilgrimage to Lutina, near Prešov, in the same region, on the feast of the Assumption (*Informace o církvi*, no. 10). Authorities had tried to prevent or to impede the gatherings by various means, including police harassment (Vienna, *Neue Kronen Zeitung*, 14 August).

Regime pressure against the churches continued through the year. The Catholic primate of Czechoslovakia, František Cardinal Tomášek, appealed to the Western public for moral support "in this struggle for the survival of the Church" (ibid., 9 February; *Kurier*, 30 July). Persecution of the clergy took various forms, but most often the authorities withdrew vocational licenses from individual priests, making more acute the already critical shortage of ecclesiastical personnel (Radio Prague, 28 March; Prague, AFP, 26 November; *Deutsche Tagespost*, 15 May). Some religious activists were arrested (*Le Monde*, 21 January) or committed to psychiatric institutions (Prague, UPI, 13 January). At the same time, more refined means were applied in the effort to neutralize the impact of religion. Government spokesmen cited statistics about churches, parishes, and graduates of theological seminaries as proof of "unrestricted freedom of religious exercise" (*Rudé právo*, 18 April), and occasionally brought up the subject of a possible "Marxist dialogue with Christians" that had been discussed—in a radically different political climate, to be sure—before and during the Prague Spring. They pointed out, however, that such a dialogue could take place, on the communist side, only with "well-trained and firm Marxists." The topics of the dialogue should be "specific and positive"; they should not concern so much matters of theory or ideology as concrete joint action, such as the "fight against imperialism" (*Nová mysl*, no. 7/8).

*Dissidence.* Open dissent in Czechoslovakia continued to center chiefly on two groups: the civil rights defense body called Charter '77 (to remind the regime of the obligations it had assumed by having signed the Final Act at the Helsinki Conference), and the VONS (the Czech acronym for the "Committee for Defense of Unjustly Persecuted Persons"). Other groups were active in this field in 1986; their objectives usually were more specific: to monitor the situation of the churches, to speak for the freedom of scientists and writers, and so on. All

continued to be exposed to relentless pressure and persecution on the part of the regime. Party spokesmen on several occasions declared that independent opinions on political or social issues or criticism of the system in any form would not be tolerated, "not even under the guise of the defense of civil and human rights" (*Rudé právo*, 25 March). The Czechoslovak government prepared, for the July session of the United Nations Committee on Human Rights at Geneva, a report on compliance with the requirements of the International Covenant on Civil and Political Rights. According to this report, "no discrimination exists in Czechoslovakia against any citizen for reason of political or other opinion. Suppression of any of these rights or freedoms would constitute a violation of legal standards instituted by Czechoslovak law." It was further argued in the report that "Czechoslovakia's laws and regulations actually provide civil and political rights in excess of what is required by international law" (New York, RFE *Correspondent's Report*, 4 July).

The dissidents in the country, however, seemed to know better. They persevered in their uneven struggle despite persecution. At the start of the year, three new spokesmen for Charter '77 were appointed: Martin Palouš, Anna Šabotová, and Jan Štern—replacing Jiří Dienstbier, Eva Kantůrková, and Petruška Šustrová (*Informace o Chartě*, no. 1). In the course of the year, the group published several documents on important issues and problems of the time, such as the social and moral situation of Czechoslovak youth (Vienna, *Kurier*, 24 March); the purpose and mission of Charter '77 (*Informace o Chartě*, no. 4); parliamentary elections (ibid., 13 May); the nineteenth anniversary of the Soviet-led military intervention against the Dubček leadership (ibid., 20 August); and the misuse of work relationships for the purpose of political control of society (in the form of an open letter to the government and the Federal Assembly, 15 August). Some initiatives of the charter group drew the particular attention of Western observers. In March, an open letter signed by ten chartists, dated December 1985 and addressed to the president of Nicaragua, Daniel Ortega, circulated in Prague and was published in the West. The letter protested the curtailment of human and civil rights by the Sandinista regime, and invoked the previous record of Charter '77 as a constant supporter of the struggle of small nations for independence, including the Sandinista revolution (*Intercontinental Press*, 24 March).

Western media also registered with appreciation

the dignified and well-balanced reply of the charter group to the invitation from the World Peace Council to participate in the peace conference at Copenhagen scheduled for mid-October. Charter '77 declined the invitation, partly for practical considerations (fear that the regime might prevent the delegates from returning to Czechoslovakia after the conference) and partly for reasons of principle (disagreement with the World Peace Council about what constitutes the real threat to peace—not only the existence of nuclear weapons but also the unwillingness of political regimes to live with a plurality of views and opposition) (*Informace o Chartě*, no. 5).

The world press paid considerable attention to a joint appeal made by dissidents from four Central and East European countries—Czechoslovakia, East Germany, Hungary, and Poland—on the 30th anniversary of the Hungarian uprising. The appeal cosigned by 24 Czechoslovaks, emphasized that the 1956 events in Hungary were a model of the struggle for independence, democracy, and neutrality. The signatories pledged to continue the struggle until these goals were achieved (Reuters, 23 October). Charter spokesmen also assessed the follow-up conference on CSCE in Vienna. In an open letter, they stressed the need to pursue the efforts begun at Helsinki ten years earlier (Vienna, *Die Presse*, 17 November). The charter group also maintained contacts with the Polish Solidarity movement. In April, *Informace o Chartě* carried an interview with a former Solidarity official, Janusz Onyszkiewicz. In May, four Polish interest groups associated with Solidarity offered to cooperate with Charter '77 in specific unofficial actions and the exchange of information. They pointed out that overcoming the isolation among oppositional activists in countries under Soviet domination was the most important task of the day (*Informace o Chartě*, no. 9).

Less conspicuous but equally important were the activities of other independent groups, especially those engaging in scientific and artistic work not subject to government supervision and control. Their efforts are best known from the unofficial publications that for many years have appeared in Czechoslovakia as periodicals and monographs. This literature is usually labeled samizdat, a Russian term that, on the whole, corresponds to its special character. It covers practically the entire field of cultural activity: prose, poetry, the creative arts, scholarly studies, philosophy, and religion. One unofficial or "independent" publication that created great interest not only in Czechoslovakia but also in the West included an opinion survey based on 300 respondents. The questionnaire covered topical and controversial subjects, such as dissidence, economic reform, relations between Czechoslovakia and the USSR, and political pluralism. The survey indicated, among other things, that the present support for the KSČ among the population is relatively limited and that in truly free elections the party would probably not poll more than 10 percent of the vote (a report on this survey was published by an exile in Paris; see *Svědectví*, no. 78).

All these independent publications continued to lead an uneasy existence in the "gray zone" between what the regime may be willing to tolerate or to ignore and what it is determined to suppress. Much depends, of course, on the nature of the subjects these publications treat; yet none can consider itself safe. The ambivalent relationship between the system and those who dare to say they do not share its views were reflected in the manner in which the establishment dealt with nonconformists and dissidents during 1986. As in previous years, leading personalities of the rights groups were subject to questioning and harassment (Prague, AFP, 22 September). Some were arrested and imprisoned (VONS, *End-of-the-Year Report*, 3 January; *NYT*, 6 July) or confined to insane asylums (Radio Vatican in Czech, 18 January). On the other hand, the regime's approach was not quite consistent. A representative of the West German federal parliament for the Greens' Party, Milan Horáček (himself an erstwhile Czechoslovak dissident and exile), noted during a visit to Czechoslovakia that opponents of the regime were treated with a certain discrimination. Unauthorized religious activities, for instance, were repressed more harshly than activities in defense of human rights (*Frankfurter Rundschau*, 11 January). Although there may have been an element of subjectivity in this observer's judgment, it would seem that the regime did make distinctions among the dissidents. Similarly, it appeared to distinguish among the various individuals and groups of political exiles living in the West. This was evident from the way various party press organs occasionally reported about them (*Jihočeská pravda*, 21 February; *Zemědělské noviny*, 26 May; *Rudé právo*, 21 July).

**Foreign Affairs.** As from the very beginning, communist Czechoslovakia faithfully followed the Soviet line in foreign policy. This was especially evident in relations with the West, particularly the United States. Czechoslovak diplomatic representatives and delegates to international organizations all backed the positions taken by their Soviet colleagues. Party spokesmen and media commentators did the same. They blamed the American government for not having accepted the offer of General Secretary Gorbachev, made early in the year, to eliminate all nuclear weapons by the year 2000 (Radio Prague, 30 March). After the U.S. raid on Libya, regime-controlled mass organizations staged a demonstration in front of the U.S. embassy in Prague protesting "the murder of innocent women and children." The raid was condemned as a "criminal and aggressive action, ordered by the White House" (*Rudé právo*, 16 April). Interestingly enough, on the same day, Czechoslovakia and the United States signed a cultural and scientific exchange agreement for 1986 and 1987. This could be viewed as an improvement of the climate, which otherwise was characterized as being "only slightly above the freezing point" (*NYT*, 3 April). Official comments nevertheless continued to criticize President Reagan's Strategic Defense Initiative as an attempt to "ensure U.S. supremacy in the world," which could only be in the interest of "the industrial military complex and the richest people" (ČETEKA, 14 October; Czechoslovak Television, 18 October). Czechoslovakia also hosted a meeting of the editorial council of the *World Marxist Review* that was devoted exclusively to the "Soviet Peace Program and the Efforts of Communists to Avert the Nuclear Threat and Ensure Disarmament" (*WMR*, July).

Relations with other Western powers were not without problems. Rapport with two noncommunist neighbors, the German Federal Republic and Austria, was strained by several incidents in which Czechoslovak border guards shot not only individuals trying to escape but also people in German and Austrian territory who came too close to the Iron Curtain (AP, 20 September; *Die Welt*, 2 October). The memories of these incidents overshadowed gestures of political goodwill, such as the visit of President Rudolf Kirschschläger of Austria to Bratislava (*Rudé právo*, 1 February) or the meeting of the Czechoslovak minister of foreign affairs, Bohuslav Chňoupek, with his Austrian counterpart in Vienna, after the follow-up conference of CSCE (Radio Prague, 7 November). Foreign Minister Hans-Dietrich Genscher of West Germany went to Karlovy Vary to meet with Chňoupek. Their talks, as the party central organ pointed out, were supposed to provide evidence that "the East-West dialogue is not only the affair of the superpowers" (*Rudé právo*, 6 February).

In the fall, Presidium member and secretary of the KSČ Central Committee Miloš Jakeš traveled to Bonn, where he "conducted negotiations with political and economic figures of the German Federal Republic" (ibid., 9 October). This visit signaled the recent interest in communist quarters for contacts with the social democrats in Bonn and indicated that Jakeš's political star may be rising. Many observers have identified Jakeš as the most likely successor to Gustáv Husák as general secretary.

Federal Prime Minister Lubomír Štrougal visited Greece in October. He was received by his Greek counterpart (Bratislava, *Pravda*, 23 October). This state visit followed the trip to Prague of the Greek interior minister, who was Štrougal's guest in the Hrzán Palace (Radio Prague, 24 June). The Czechoslovak premier also sent a message expressing his government's solidarity with the delegates at the Conference for the Immediate Independence of Namibia, held at Vienna (Radio Prague, 8 July). On the occasion of the meeting of the nonaligned nations in Zimbabwe, President Husák sent greetings to the host and chairman of the conference, Prime Minister Robert Mugabe (ČETEKA, 31 August).

The Venezuelan foreign minister visited Prague to discuss matters of common interest with various members of the Czechoslovak government (Prague Television, 8 July). The foreign ministers of Egypt and Iran came to Prague in close succession. "Traditional relations of long standing" and "mutual understanding" were stressed on these occasions (ČETEKA, 13 June; Radio Prague, 25 June). The Syrian prime minister arrived in Prague and was received by President Husák and Prime Minister Štrougal (ČETEKA, 22 August).

Among government-level contacts with countries of the Soviet bloc, the most important was the visit to Prague of the Hungarian prime minister, who was received by the entire presidium of the federal government and the president of the republic. One of the main points on the agenda was the coordination of the five-year economic development plans of the two countries (Budapest, MTI, 19 May). Foreign Minister Chňoupek traveled for "an official friendly visit" to Moscow and met with his Soviet colleague, Eduard Shevardnadze (Radio Moscow Domestic Service, 26 April). The Polish minister of foreign affairs, Marian Orzechowski, went to Prague on Chňoupek's invitation. The joint communiqué issued on this occasion stressed the importance for the whole socialist community of friendship and cooperation between Czechoslovakia and Poland (Radio Prague, 7 September). President Husák sent a message of greeting to President Ortega of Nicaragua on the 25th anniversary of the foundation of the National Liberation Front (ČETEKA, 7 November).

*Foreign Trade and Foreign Debt.* The problems with which Czechoslovakia has had to deal in the area of foreign trade have persisted since the oil crisis of the 1970s. The country has shared these problems with all members of the Soviet bloc. They are not merely problems of payment balance; on this point Czechoslovakia has fared better than the remaining members of the CMEA. Its foreign debt, especially in hard currencies, has been moderate: at the start of 1986, it amounted to $2.3 billion. Some $1.4 billion, or more than a third of the debt owed in 1980, has been paid (*Financial Times*, 19 February). It is expected that Czechoslovakia will shortly change its status of hard currency debtor to that of a creditor (*Journal of Commerce*, 8 April). Although less than a fourth of Czechoslovakian imports and exports are oriented toward the West and the Third World, a solid reserve of convertible currencies is vital to the economy. Czechoslovakia's relatively advanced and diversified industries need raw materials that can be purchased only outside the Soviet orbit. Further increase in the supply of hard currencies will depend, above all, on the ability of Czechoslovak enterprises to successfully compete in Western markets. Here, however, the record has been rather unsatisfactory. The quality of products often does not meet international standards; the reputation for servicing the durables, such as cars or capital goods, is bad.

These are serious obstacles to any significant expansion of trade with the West, even if the heavy dependence on the Soviet Union did not intervene. In 1986, nevertheless, managers of Czechoslovak industry tried to bring some improvement in this area. Recently they seem more disposed to seek credits in the West. Also, first steps were taken in 1986 toward the realization of joint economic ventures with Western entrepreneurs. The federal minister of foreign trade, Bohumil Urban, disclosed in London that negotiations were being conducted with prospective Western partners about eight joint enterprises. In these ventures, foreign investors will be allowed to own up to 49 percent of the capital and to repatriate their share of the profits (*Financial*

*Times*, 12 June). Previously, Czechoslovakia had experimented only with formulas less objectionable from the ideological point of view, such as coproduction or joint research (*Svĕt hospodářství*, 6 May). Over a hundred such contracts had been implemented by the end of 1985.

Close cooperation with members of the Soviet bloc and the USSR, of course, has not been neglected because of overtures to the West. The most important agreement in this respect concerned Czechoslovak participation in the construction of an iron-ore treatment plant at Krivoi Rog in the Ukraine. The Czechoslovak share in the project will represent the value of 408 million convertible rubles (the unit of currency used in transactions within the CMEA), for which Czechoslovakia will be compensated by free delivery of 1.3 million tons of iron pellets annually over a period of ten years (*Večerní Praha*, 24 June). Attention was also paid in 1986 to cooperation with CMEA partners in agriculture. For some agricultural products, such as barley, Czechoslovakia assumes the role of an exporting country (East Berlin, *Internationale Zeitschrift der Landwirtschaft*, no. 1). The Czechoslovak government manifested its solidarity with the predominantly agricultural economies of other CMEA countries by condemning the ban imposed after the Chernobyl nuclear accident by the European Economic Community. The media asserted that the decision not to import produce from the fallout area was "linked with a campaign of lies against the socialist countries" (ČETEKA, 13 May; *Rudé právo*, 17 May).

Individual trade agreements and treaties of economic and technological cooperation were concluded in 1986 with China (Radio Prague, 2 June); Cyprus (ČETEKA, 25 August); Ethiopia (Radio Prague, 20 August); and Syria (Radio Prague, 22 August).

**International Party Contacts.** As for relations among the communist parties within the Soviet bloc, the attention of the Czechoslovak public and of Western observers focused on the possible impact of changes in policies introduced or contemplated in the USSR by the Gorbachev leadership. It was expected that some indications of this impact would be found at the meeting of secretaries from central committees of ruling communist parties who had gathered at Bucharest in December 1985. However, the final resolution of the meeting contained little more than reiteration of the desiderata spelled out in the communiqué of the Warsaw Pact summit meeting at Sofia (*Intercontinental Press*, 1 February). The critical statements made at the Twenty-seventh Congress of the CPSU about the state of the USSR economy and society seemed to shock some Czechoslovak communists, who even protested against "exaggerating Soviet problems and difficulties... in front of the whole world" (*Rudé právo*, 3 June). However, the attitude of the KSČ leadership has on the whole been a "wait-and-see" one, especially since no spectacular changes of any kind seemed to follow the harsh criticism at the CPSU congress. This impression was confirmed by later developments during 1986. In October, talks between a Czechoslovak delegation composed of KSČ ideological secretaries and editors in chief of the party dailies and their Soviet counterparts took place in Moscow. On this occasion, Presidium candidate and party secretary Jan Fojtík wrote an article in which he endorsed Gorbachev's call for "openness" (*glasnost'*) in the media (Moscow, *Pravda*, 20 October). However, except for the reprint of his article by the Czechoslovak party press, not much openness could be noticed in the daily media.

Foreign observers attributed some significance to the October meeting of KSČ Presidium member Miloš Jakeš and Mikhail Gorbachev, if for no other reason than Jakeš's image as the most probable candidate for the post of KSČ general secretary. Although officially this trip was for the purpose of discussing the agenda of the forthcoming CMEA council meeting in Bucharest (TASS in English, 21 October), some analysts speculated that Gorbachev might have wanted to find out the chances of his idea for "reconstruction" being adopted also in Czechoslovakia. These speculations could not be substantiated or refuted in the remaining weeks of the year. No radical changes in the political line of the KSČ followed the meeting in Moscow of General Secretary Husák with Gorbachev and the heads of the communist parties of Hungary and Vietnam, János Kádár and Truong Chinh (*Neues Deutschland*, 13 November).

Another blocwide meeting held in 1986 was the conference of the presidents of academies of sciences in socialist countries, held at East Berlin in July. Czechoslovakia was represented at this conference by Professor Josef Říman. The delegates issued a proclamation "To All Scientists of the World" calling for peace and cooperation, and especially for disarmament and joint efforts in protecting the environment and fighting poverty (*Neues Deutschland*, 3 July).

As for bilateral party contacts, the Czechoslovak presence at the Twenty-seventh Congress of the CPSU received the largest coverage in official media (Moscow, *Pravda*, 28 February; *Rudé právo*, 28 February). The KSČ sent a high-ranking delegation, headed by Presidium candidate and secretary František Pitra, to the rally of the communist party of Portugal at Cacem in June (Lisbon, *Avante*, 3 July). Later in the year, a delegation from the communist party of Spain came to Prague. Thus relations between the two parties, broken in 1969 after Soviet imposition of the "normalization" course upon the KSČ, were renewed. Disagreements over the interpretation of the Prague Spring, the USSR military intervention of August 1968, and the notion of "Eurocommunism," however, continued despite this gesture (Radio Prague, 24 October). In the same month, a delegation from the communist party of France visited Czechoslovakia. This party had shared, though in a more moderate form, the reservations of the Spanish communists about the Soviet military action against the reformist leadership of the KSČ, but the French communists have gradually moved closer to the official USSR position (Radio Prague, 3 October).

Georgi Razumovsky, secretary of the Central Committee of the CPSU, traveled to Prague to inform KSČ secretary Vasil Bilák about implementation of the decisions of the Twenty-seventh Congress and to be informed about the realization of political tasks set by the Seventeenth KSČ Congress (Radio Prague, 29 July). The KSČ was represented at the Nineteenth Congress of the Mongolian communist party in Ulan Bator by a delegation led by Presidium member Antonín Kapek (Radio Prague, 2 June). General Secretary Jambyn Batmonh thereafter visited Prague and was received by the KSČ general secretary, Gustáv Husák (Radio Prague, 20 August). The Cuban communist party sent a delegation, headed by party secretary Jaime Crombet, to Prague. The delegation toured the country and visited some of the model socialist enterprises in the Gottwaldov region (Radio Prague, 12 July). Representatives from Israel's communist party also visited Czechoslovakia (Radio Prague, 18 June). General secretary of the Moroccan Progress and Socialism Party, Ali Yata, and Michal Štefanák, member of the Central Committee of the KSČ, signed a joined declaration during Yata's trip to Prague. The statement condemned the efforts of the U.S. government to revive the Camp David accords, which were, according to this declaration, "part of the strategic aims for international imperialism, Zionism, and racism" (ČETEKA, 19 September). The KSČ also dispatched a delegation to meet with the communist party of Japan (Radio Prague, 25 September). In October, a two-year agreement on cooperation was signed in New Delhi between the KSČ and the Communist Party of India—Marxist. This party represents the smaller, pro-Soviet splinter from the once unified Indian communist party (ČETEKA, 2 October).

One party paper remembered two important, albeit somewhat delicate, anniversaries in the history of the world communist movement: the Hungarian uprising of 1956 and the erection of the Berlin Wall in 1961. Writing about the earlier event,

*Rudé právo* (23 October) said that "the plot against the Hungarian people, and against socialism, just as in the case of Czechoslovakia in 1968 and Poland at the beginning of the 1980s, could not achieve the objectives set by the international reaction." The Slovak paper *Smena* praised the Berlin Wall, which "with a decisive action, in the course of one single day, determined the normal status of border relations between the western and the eastern parts of Berlin" (13 August).

Zdeněk Suda
*University of Pittsburgh*

# Germany:
# German Democratic Republic

**Population.** 16,692,000
**Party.** Socialist Unity Party of Germany (Sozialistische Einheitspartei Deutschlands; SED)
**Founded.** 1918 (SED, 1946)
**Membership.** 2,304,121 members and candidates; 58.1 percent workers, 4.8 percent peasants and farmers on cooperatives, 22.4 percent intelligentsia, 14.7 percent other (*Neues Deutschland* [*ND*], 18 April)
**General Secretary.** Erich Honecker (74)
**Politburo.** 22 full members: Erich Honecker (chairman, State Council), Hermann Axen (70), Hans-Joachim Böhme (55; first secretary, Halle regional SED executive), Horst Dohlus (61), Werner Eberlein (66; first secretary, Magdeburg regional SED executive), Werner Felfe (58; member, State Council), Kurt Hager (74; member, State Council), Joachim Herrmann (58), Werner Jarowinsky (59), Heinz Kessler (66; defense minister), Günther Kleiber (55; deputy chairman, Council of Ministers, and permanent representative to CMEA), Egon Krenz (49; deputy chairman, State Council), Werner Krolikowski (58; first deputy chairman, Council of Ministers), Siegfried Lorenz (55; first secretary, Karl Marx Stadt regional SED executive), Erich Mielke (79; minister of state security), Günter Mittag (60; deputy chairman, State Council), Erich Mückenberger (76; chairman, Central Party Control Commission), Alfred Neumann (77; first deputy chairman, Council of Ministers), Günter Schabowski (57; first secretary, East Berlin regional SED executive), Horst Sindermann (71; deputy chairman, State Council, and president, People's Chamber), Willi Stoph (72; chairman, Council of Ministers, and deputy chairman, State Council), Harry Tisch (59; member, State Council, and chairman, Free German Trade Union Federation); 5 candidate members: Ingeborg Lange (59), Gerhard Müller (55; first secretary, Erfurt regional SED executive), Margarete Müller (55; member, State Council), Gerhard

Schürer (65; deputy chairman, Council of Ministers, and chairman, State Planning Commission), Werner Walde (60; first secretary, Cottbus regional SED executive)

**Central Audit Commission.** Kurt Seibt, chairman (78; president, GDR Solidarity Committee)

**Secretariat.** 11 members: Erich Honecker, Hermann Axen (international relations), Horst Dohlus (party organs), Werner Felfe (agriculture), Kurt Hager (culture and science), Joachim Herrmann (agitation and propaganda), Werner Jarowinsky (church affairs, trade, and supply), Egon Krenz (security affairs, youth, and sports), Ingeborg Lange (women's affairs), Günter Mittag (economics), Günter Schabowski (East Berlin)

**Central Committee.** 165 full and 57 candidate members (1986)

**Status.** Ruling party

**Last Congress.** Eleventh, 17–21 April 1986

**Last Election.** 8 June 1986, 99.94 percent, all 500 seats won by National Front

**Auxiliary Organizations.** Free German Trade Union Confederation (FDGB), 9.1 million members, Chairman Harry Tisch; Free German Youth (FDJ), 2.3 million members, First Secretary Eberhard Aurich; Democratic Women's League of Germany (DFB), 1.4 million members, Chairwoman Ilse Thiele; Society for German-Soviet Friendship (DSF), 6.0 million members, President Erich Mückenberger

**Publications.** *Neues Deutschland*, official SED daily; *Einheit*, SED theoretical monthly; *Neuer Weg*, SED organizational monthly; *Junge Welt*, FDJ daily; *Tribüne*, FDGB daily; *Horizont*, foreign policy monthly. The official news agency is Allgemeiner Deutscher Nachrichtendienst (ADN).

In contrast with other East European countries, where party members frequently voice self-criticism at official meetings, delegates to the Eleventh SED Congress heard nothing but praise for their ruling party's achievements. M. S. Gorbachev added his personal imprimatur in a speech heard also by representatives from 144 "fraternal parties and other revolutionary parties and progressive organizations and movements from 106 countries." (*Pravda*, 18 April.)

**Leadership and Party Organization.** The new SED Politburo has four additional members. Two were promoted from candidate status: Werner Eberlein and Siegfried Lorenz, both regional SED first secretaries. Hans-Joachim Böhme took over the equivalent position for Halle, and Heinz Kessler has been defense minister since December 1985. The number of candidate members dropped by two because of Eberlein's and Lorenz's promotions. One person, Günter Schabowski, was added to the Secretariat. The average age in the Politburo is 64, although eight members are more than 70 years old.

These developments indicate a consolidation of power for Erich Honecker, who reportedly had been the target of an attempted coup the previous year (Hamburg, *Bild*, 24 July). Konrad Naumann and Herbert Häber, the alleged organizers of the coup, were dropped from the Politburo on 23 November 1985. Soviet endorsement of the SED leadership at the Eleventh Party Congress certainly strengthens Honecker's position.

The Central Committee increased by nine full members; 14 were dropped and 27 new ones were appointed (13 had passed through the probationary stage of candidate membership). Some of these changes may have been related to the Naumann/Häber plot, if indeed there had been one. From all outward appearances, it would seem that Egon Krenz remains the heir apparent. Whether he will be patient enough to wait until 1991 and the next SED congress before attempting to succeed Honecker is another matter.

The rank-and-file party membership seems stable, with only 63,000 having been expelled and 25,000 resigning compared with an increase of 12,000 over the most recent five-year period (*ND*, 9 January).

Among the 2.3 million members, more than half (58.1 percent) are workers, almost one-fourth (22.4 percent) represent the intelligentsia, and fewer than one-twentieth (4.8 percent) farm the land (ibid., 18 April).

**Domestic Affairs.** Elections for the 500 seats in the parliament were held on 8 June, and only 7,512 (0.06 percent) votes were cast against the National Front ticket (East Berlin radio, 9 June; *FBIS*, 9 June). Four subordinate political groupings, the Democratic Farmers' Party (DBD), Christian Democratic Union (CDU), Liberal Democratic Party (LDPD), and National Democratic Party (NDPD), are represented in the People's Chamber, with a total of 52 seats allocated among them. (See the table in

*Staat und Recht* 35, no. 4, April.) Others with representation include the trade unions, the Women's League, the ruling SED's youth movement, a Cultural League, and a Farmers' Mutual Aid association.

This legislature rubber-stamped the five-year economic plan (FYP), first approved at the party's Eleventh Congress. Submitted by Prime Minister Willi Stoph, the plan assumes that current growth rates will continue through 1990 and that "comprehensive intensification" remains the key to success (see *ND*, 23 April, for the full directive).

Central planning will concentrate on the new technologies, with a target of some 90,000 computer systems to be installed for industry by the end of the current FYP. Automation may displace up to 1.3 million industrial workers and would involve restructuring of the labor force. Almost 3.5 billion East German marks will be allocated for investments, compared with 2.6 billion spent during 1980–1985 (*RL Background Report* 63, 30 April).

Despite an excessively labor-intensive system, low capital productivity, inadequate scientific and technological progress, spiraling costs of material inputs, and wasteful use of resources, the East German economy has performed better than that of any other bloc member. It is held up as a model. Hence, the choice is continuity rather than reform (U.S. Joint Economic Committee of Congress, *East European Economies*, 28 March, p. 113).

The East German regime attempts to manipulate the Evangelical Church as it does the subordinate political groupings. A retired bishop, Dr. Albrecht Schönherr, described the "unequal partnership" between church and state in a speech (East Berlin, *Die Zeit*, 12 February). Not mentioned, or perhaps censored out, was discussion of atheistic indoctrination and a resigned mood among the faithful. Although the church once claimed half the population as members, the number has dropped to an estimated 1.5 million, of whom almost half are past retirement age. (*RL Background Report.*)

The Roman Catholic Church, with a membership of about 1.2 million, maintains its allegiance to Rome. Joachim Cardinal Meissner has warned that Christians should become witnesses and not fellow travelers. The first Catholic convention ever permitted will be held in July 1987 at Dresden. It is hoped that Pope John Paul II may visit East Germany at that time. The vacuum created by Marxism-Leninism may be contributing to a revival of religion (ibid.).

Despite protests from religious organizations, paramilitary sports contests for youth continue to be held every summer. They include exercises with rifles, hand grenades, machine guns, and radio communications that serve as preparation for universal military service. The Free German Youth (FDJ), patterned after the Soviet *Komsomol*, now includes 2.3 million boys and girls (107,000 are candidates for SED members; *ND*, 27 March). The FDJ coordinates militarization of the school curriculum.

The East German defense minister, General Heinz Kessler, was appointed toward the end of 1985. He had been the army's chief commissar during the preceding seven years as head of the Main Political Administration. In his current position, he also supervises the paramilitary program in the schools. (See his article in *Einheit* 16, no. 3, March; and his biography in Moscow's *Krasnaia zvezda*, 4 May.)

**Foreign Policy.** *Intra-German Relations.* Instead of the party/state chief, Erich Honecker, the East Germans sent Horst Sindermann, third-ranking Politburo member and president of the People's Chamber on an official visit to the Federal Republic of Germany (FRG). Sindermann's visit included talks with his hosts, West German Social Democrats Willy Brandt and Hans-Jochen Vogel, as well as discussions with leaders of the Greens in the West German parliament (East Berlin radio, 20 February; *FBIS*, 21 February). Perhaps more importance should be attached to the meeting at Stockholm on 15 March between Chancellor Helmut Kohl and Honecker. The latter had planned to visit West Germany in September 1984, but the plans reportedly were blocked by Moscow.

A second SED Politburo member, Günter Mittag, went to Bonn in the spring. He held political talks with Chancellor Kohl, Social Democratic opposition leader Johannes Rau, and CSU chairman Franz-Josef Strauss (East Berlin radio, 10 April; *FBIS*, 11 April). Deputy foreign ministers from the two German governments met at Vienna in midsummer, during preparations for the Helsinki review conference.

These contacts have not resulted in a relaxation of the controls that prevent an estimated half-million East Germans from emigrating to the West. The Berlin Wall, symbol of this repression, marked its 25th anniversary on 13 August. Since mid-1962 the FRG has purchased the freedom of about

40,000 political prisoners from the East at $20,000 to $60,000 in goods and services per head (*NYT Magazine*, 16 February). This practice continues, although it is not publicized.

Perhaps to distract Western public opinion from this traffic in human beings, the East German regime began dumping Third World refugees into West German transit camps at the rate of 100,000 per year. Interflug flights from countries like Sri Lanka and Ghana brought asylum seekers by the planeload to the East Berlin airport at Schönefeld. From there they were guided into the divided city's western sectors. During the fall of 1986, after FRG protests, the dumping stopped (*CSM*, 22 September).

Official contacts between the two Germanys are supplemented by a continuing "dialogue" among SED and Social Democratic Party (SPD) functionaries. These take place on both sides of the border. Disinformation and propaganda were also disseminated by East German "professors," eight of whom met their SPD counterparts at a resort in the Black Forest (Hamburg, *Der Spiegel* 40, no. 11, 10 March).

Johannes Rau, the man favored by the East for FRG chancellorship after the January 1987 elections, was received by Honecker and other politburocrats in East Berlin (*ND*, 8 May). The SED chief also met with H. J. Vogel, chairman of the SPD parliamentary group in the West German parliament (*Pravda*, 31 May). An exchange of opinions also took place in West Berlin between SPD politicians and SED central apparatus officials from the other side of the wall (*ND*, 13–14 September).

The culmination of this campaign occurred the following month in Bonn, where Politburo member Hermann Axen and SPD ideological adviser Egon Bahr issued a joint communiqué. Based on an agreement between Honecker and Willy Brandt signed in East Berlin on 19 September 1985, two working groups had developed a set of "Principles for a Nuclear-Weapons-Free Zone in Central Europe." The zone extends 150 kilometers on each side of the border. (For text, see ibid., 22 October.)

*Westpolitik.* In addition to the Federal Republic, East Germany maintained active contacts with other West European governments and their communist parties. A delegation from the French Communist Party met with Politburo member Kurt Häger in East Berlin, and communist youth members from France held a rally at Eberswalde (ibid., 3 July, 21 August).

Horst Sindermann traveled to Italy, where he was received by that country's president (ibid., 26 June). Politburo member Horst Dohlus informed an Italian Communist Party delegation about decisions made at the Eleventh SED Congress (ibid., 5–6 July). Another politburocrat, Günter Mittag, met in East Berlin with the chairman of the Italian private industry association (ibid., 16, 17 September).

Hermann Axen led an SED delegation to visit the prime minister of Greece, at the invitation of the ruling PASOK socialist party (ibid., 26–31 August). The respective foreign ministers exchanged views, and simultaneously Honecker received the president of Greece in East Berlin (ibid., 16 September).

Erich Honecker himself visited Sweden, where he met with the prime minister, King Carl Gustaf XVI, and the heads of both communist organizations recognized by Moscow: the Left Party Communists as well as the Communist Workers' Party (ibid., 26–29 June).

*Third World.* East Germans have frequently acted as surrogates for the USSR, and this continued during 1986. Hermann Axen paid a lengthy visit to Latin America. He called on the president of Uruguay, the general secretary of that country's communist party, and the head of the left-wing Broad Front, a political umbrella organization. Axen then stopped off to call on the president of Argentina, everywhere delivering messages from Honecker (ibid., 31 October–3 November). The leader of the Nicaraguan junta, Daniel Ortega, received a pledge of 30,000 tons of grain and the equivalent of $20 million in aid after he met at East Berlin with Honecker—to whom Ortega awarded the Order of Sandino (*ND*, 18 September; *CSM*, 18 September).

East Germany had more contacts with the Middle East, beginning with visits by Algerian and Egyptian foreign ministers (East Berlin radio, 6 May, 15 June; *FBIS*, 7 May, 16 June). They were followed by their counterparts from Kuwait (*ND*, 10 September). Iran's prime minister held talks with Willi Stoph on bilateral relations (ibid., 13 October). Axen received the leader of the Socialist Progressive Party from Lebanon earlier that same month (ibid., 3 October).

Activities in Africa south of the Sahara included

a shipment of medical supplies to Luanda (East Berlin, *Horizont* 19, no. 2, February), a rally of Angolan and East German students at Halle (*ND*, 26 September), and SED-MPLA consultations in East Berlin (ibid., 27–28 September). Politburo member Egon Krenz received the Angolan interior minister (ibid., 30 September); their discussions may have dealt with East German training of the Angolan secret police.

Ethiopia's party/state leader attended the SED congress, where he vowed that East German assistance would never be forgotten (ibid., 19 April). Agreements on expansion of economic cooperation were also signed (East Berlin radio, 28 August; *FBIS*, 29 August). The following month, the same type of agreement was made with Mozambique at Maputo (*ND*, 10 September).

Oliver Tambo, leader of the African National Congress (ANC), was received by Honecker, who called for the release of Nelson Mandela (ibid., 11–12 October). A "solidarity" shipment of bicycles and textiles was sent to the ANC through the East German ambassador in Dar es Salaam, Tanzania (ibid., 25–26 October).

Honecker's visits to North Korea, mainland China, and Mongolia were the first by any top East European leader to those countries. His stop at Pyongyang resulted in a trade agreement, discussion of party-to-party relations, and a statement in support of Soviet foreign policy (ibid., 21 October). Honecker's visit to Ulan Bator, en route home from Beijing, was publicized only by an exchange of toasts between the two party/state bosses (ibid., 27 October).

From 21 to 26 October Honecker received an inordinate amount of space in *Neues Deutschland*, which carried many photographs. On the last day of his visit to the People's Republic of China, Honecker signed a fifteen-year agreement for economic cooperation. The emphasis throughout the stay in Beijing was on harmony, although it is known that differences exist. The Soviets may not have been altogether satisfied with the visit (*RL Background Report* 155, 31 October).

**International Party Relations.** The SED commemorated the tenth anniversary of the "Conference of Communist and Workers' Parties of Europe," held during 29–30 June 1976 in East Berlin (*ND*, editorial, 5–6 July), as if conditions a decade ago had been less difficult for the world communist movement. The East Germans sent delegations to the Soviet, Polish, and Yugoslav ruling party congresses. They were not invited to the one in Albania, although trade relations exist between the two countries.

Many of the "fraternal" movements dispatched representatives to the Eleventh SED Congress. One of these, Fidel Castro, appeared in a page-one photograph in *Neues Deutschland* (4 March) that depicted Castro and Honecker smiling at each other. The East Germans, of course, are heavily committed to the bloc's aid program for Cuba.

Special ties exist with the CPSU, whose general secretary paid tribute at the SED congress to the East German model of economic achievement. In actuality, this success has been possible because of favorable economic relations with West Germany. Despite that, both Honecker and Gorbachev attacked the Federal Republic in a special statement after the congress. The situation in Europe could only improve, they said, if "the FRG were really to embark on the path to détente." Bonn, unfortunately, is moving "in the opposite direction" (TASS, 22 April; *RL Background* Report 63, 30 April; see also *ND*, 19 April, for Gorbachev's speech to the SED congress).

Jadwiga M. Staar
*Stanford, California*

# Hungary

**Population.** 10,624,000
**Party.** Hungarian Socialist Workers' Party (Magyar Szocialista Munkáspárt; HSWP)
**Founded.** 1918 (HSWP: 1956)
**Membership.** 870,992 (Thirteenth Congress Report, 1985). Women make up 30.5 percent of the membership. The average age is 46.9 years. Active and retired industrial workers (including foremen) make up 42.6 percent of the membership; active and retired collective farm workers and supervisors represent 7.8 percent; active and retired intellectuals and white-collar workers, 42.4 percent; other occupations, 7.2 percent; 80.3 percent of members have joined the party since the 1956 revolution.
**General Secretary.** János Kádár (74, worker)
**Politburo.** 13 members: György Aczél (69, intellectual), Sándor Gáspár (69, worker), Károly Grósz (56, worker), Ferenc Havasi (57, worker), Csaba Hámori (38, technical intelligentsia), János Kádár, György Lázár (62, technical intelligentsia), Pál Losonczi (67, farmer), László Maróthy (44, technical intelligentsia), Károly Németh (64, worker), Miklós Óvári (61, educator), István Sarlós (65, educator), István Szabó (62, farmer)
**Secretariat.** János Kádár (general secretary), Károly Németh (deputy general secretary), János Berecz (55), Ferenc Havasi, István Horváth (51, jurist), Miklós Óvári, Lénárd Pál (60, scientist), Mátyás Szűrös (53)
**Central Committee.** 105 full members (listed in *JPRS*, 17 May 1985)
**Status.** Ruling party
**Last Congress.** Thirteenth, 25–28 March 1985
**Auxiliary Organizations.** Patriotic People's Front (PPF), general secretary, Imre Pozsgay; Communist Youth League (CYL), 926,000 members, first secretary, Csaba Hámori; National Council of Trade Unions (NCTU), 4,399,000 members, chairman, Sándor Gáspár; National Council of Hungarian Women, chairwoman, Mrs. Lajos Duschek; National Peace Council
**Last Election.** June 1985; 387 seats (35 national list, 352 multicandidate constituencies. Approximately 70 percent of deputies are party members.
**Main State Organs.** Presidential Council, chairman, Pál Losonczi; Council of Ministers, chairman, György Lázár
**Publications.** *Népszabadság* (People's freedom), HSWP daily, deputy editor, Péter Rényi; *Társadalmi Szemle* (Social review), HSWP theoretical monthly, editor, Valéria Benke; *Pártélet* (Party life), HSWP organizational monthly; *Magyar Hirlap*, government daily; *Magyar Nemzet*, Patriotic People's Front daily; *Népszava*, National Council of Trade Unions daily. The official news agency is Magyar Távirati Iroda (MTI).

The Hungarian Section of the Russian Communist Party (Bolshevik) was founded in Moscow in March 1918 by Béla Kun (1886–1939) and a few other Hungarian prisoners of war. The Communist Party of Hungary came into being in Budapest in November 1918. Kun was the dominant figure in the communist–left socialist coalition that proclaimed the Hungarian Soviet Republic on the collapse of Mihály Károlyi's liberal-democratic regime. The red dictatorship lasted from March to August 1919.

During the interwar period, the party functioned

as a faction-ridden movement in domestic illegality and in exile. The underground membership numbered in the hundreds. With the Soviet occupation at the end of World War II, the Hungarian Communist Party (HCP) re-emerged as a member of the provisional government. Kun had lost his life in Stalin's purges, and the party was led by Mátyás Rákosi (1892–1971). Although the HCP won no more than 17 percent of the vote in the relatively free 1945 elections, it continued to exercise a disproportionate influence in the coalition government. Thanks largely to Soviet-backed coercive tactics, the HCP gained effective control of the country in 1947. In 1948, it absorbed left-wing social democrats into the newly named Hungarian Workers' Party.

Rákosi's Stalinist zeal was exemplified by the show trial of József Cardinal Mindszenty and the liquidation of alleged Titoist László Rajk. The New Course of 1954–1955 offered some relief from economic mismanagement and totalitarian terror; inspired by some of Stalin's successors, it was led in Hungary by the moderate communist Imre Nagy (1896–1958). De-Stalinization undermined the party's authority and unity, and the replacement of Rákosi by the equally doctrinaire Ernö Gerö (1898–1980) did not halt the rising tide of popular opposition. Following the outbreak of revolution on 23 October 1956, Imre Nagy became prime minister for the second time and eventually headed a multiparty government that withdrew Hungary from the Warsaw Pact. On 25 October, János Kádár (1912– ) became leader of the renamed party, the HSWP. The Nagy government was overthrown by the armed intervention of the Soviet Union on 4 November.

Since the end of the 1956 revolution, the HSWP has ruled unchallenged as the sole political party, firmly aligned with the Soviet Union. After an initial phase of repression that culminated in the final collectivization of agriculture (1959–1960), Kádár's rule came to be marked by his conciliatory "alliance policy" and by pragmatic reforms, most notably the New Economic Mechanism launched in 1968.

**Party Affairs.** In 1986 expressions of confidence in the stability and permanence of communist rule and of the reformed economic mechanism were mixed with concern about the party's weaknesses and growing evidence of economic and social stress. In an interview in *Time* (11 August), party leader János Kádár asserted that the political and economic foundations of Hungarian society were firm and that the Soviets "understand and appreciate that we search for new solutions to present problems." The reforms, indicated Kádár, would be preserved by his successors. Speculation is rife regarding the aging Kádár's potential successor. While the party issues no official comment on the question, Károly Grósz and János Berecz are considered to be leading contenders, along with Károly Németh and László Maróthy.

Weaknesses in the party's grass-roots support and debates about its leading role have been acknowledged by leading figures. Berecz identified three contradictory strains of criticism: from liberals, who argue that the party still interferes too much; from conservatives, who deplore its relative withdrawal from public administration; and from those who claim that there is no national consensus and that the party does not enjoy the trust of the people. Berecz conceded that economic and social problems had strained the earlier consensus and that patient, tolerant party work was needed to regain popular support. The leading role of the party was beyond question, and the economic reforms were fundamentally sound, but more attention had to be directed to the plight of the underprivileged. (*Társadalmi Szemle*, no. 2; RFE *Research*, 25 March.) A deep ideological malaise was diagnosed in a debate by party experts, who observed that the "propaganda idealizing bourgeois freedom, the principle of the private individual, and the romanticism of retreating into the personal sphere have found reception in certain layers of our public opinion." Emphasis was placed on the need to integrate the creative intelligentsia into the party by improving its capacity for open debate and ideological innovation. The experts noted the positive stimulation offered by Soviet reformist tendencies and by developments in China. (*Pártélet*, no. 5.)

The economic reforms are radical in regional perspective, and are suffering from a decline in domestic popularity as the economy stagnates. Party spokesmen therefore tirelessly reassert the validity of reforms. István Huszár, the director of the Party History Institute, insisted that "our greatest leap forward was the decision taken in 1968 to abolish a planned economy" and to make central planning rely on market laws. Notwithstanding Stalinist theory, he said, state and collective ownership were equivalent. The reforms also affected the political system, notably in the demands they made on workers. The single-party system would not be changed, said Huszár, but the "trade unions must be given a new role, while autonomous groups must be given more liberty and expression of various social interests [must be] allowed." Economic growth is a precondition for social progress, and countries possessed of different interests need not imitate the solutions of others. Huszár observed it was "difficult to imagine that the private sector of the [Hungarian] economy could endanger socialism." (*Danas*, 3 December 1985; RFE *Research*, 3 January.) Károly Grósz, who is often portrayed as tough-minded, also delivered a spirited defense of private initiative and of income differentials that reflect differences in energy, talent, and productivity (*Siker*, September; RFE *Research*, 31 October).

The governing elite's internal problems were aired at the first national conference on "party democracy," held 21–22 November 1985 in Budapest with some 300 senior party functionaries in attendance. In his keynote address, Deputy General Secretary Károly Németh reiterated the requirements of the Leninist principle of democratic centralism: active involvement by the rank and file in policy development, the obligation of the minority to accept majority decisions, and party unity. He insisted that the distortions of the Stalinist past had been superseded but admitted that the equality of all party members was not always respected, since there was a tendency to restrict policy discussions to leading bodies and experts. There was a need for broader involvement of members and patience in answering their questions. Debate in party forums should be encouraged and attendance at party meetings not regarded as a burdensome obligation. Németh also called for "growth in the independence and responsibility of every political institution and state, economic, and social body" to express a variety of interests. (*Népszabadság*, 22 November 1985.)

Mikhail Gorbachev's stress on rejuvenation of the nomenklatura probably reinforced the Hungarian party's review of cadre policy. The Central Committee at its 18 March session heard a report on the matter from Németh. The selection of cadres had become more systematic and democratic, but "subjectivism" and "personal connections" still created problems, and more rapid promotion and turnover were needed to bring younger people, particularly women, into leading positions. The old criteria of political and moral orthodoxy, professional distinction, and leadership qualities remained in force. Although commitment to support the party's policies was essential, nonparty members were welcome to most positions of responsibility. A Committee for Cadre Policy was established

by the HSWP Central Committee to oversee implementation of these guidelines. (*Népszabadság*, 20 March.)

Complaints that the progressive scale of membership dues was too burdensome in the context of declining real wages impelled the leadership to reduce the scale across the board and set the upper limit at 4 percent of income, effective 1 January 1986. The upper limit previously was 5 percent, higher than that prevailing in other East European parties. Before the change, the party derived 69.5 percent of its income from dues, 17.3 percent from "other sources," and 13.2 percent from the state. The shortfall anticipated as a result of the scale reduction will be met from state funds. (*Pártélet*, no. 12, 1985.)

The thirtieth anniversary of the Hungarian revolution of 1956 compelled the regime to address questions that normally it takes pains to avoid. The media published articles presenting the official version of events, noting the abuses of the Rákosi era, the justified grievances of the workers, the exploitation of all this by radical counterrevolutionary elements and Western propaganda agencies, and the return to rule of a reformed party under Kádár with the fraternal assistance of the Soviet Union. Low-key commemorative ceremonies were held in Budapest and, on 4 November, in Szolnok. According to the official history it was in the latter city that the Kádár regime was born. In fact, it came into being under Soviet auspices in Uzhgorod in the Soviet Ukraine. The main speaker at Szolnok was János Berecz, who has acted as the official historian of the revolution. He told Western journalists that "because the Hungarian experience of 30 years ago includes bitter memories, we lower our flags modestly when we mark the day, and we do not make it a holiday" (*NYT*, 5 November). Security was tightened in Budapest on the anniversary, and there were no disturbances. A new regulation was enacted prohibiting visits to the unmarked graves of freedom-fighters on the anniversary and on All Saints' Day.

**Mass Organizations and Government.** The Patriotic People's Front, which is the party's main agent for organizing elections and for mobilizing nonparty interest groups (such as the churches) and the population at large, held its Eighth Congress on 13–15 December 1985. General Secretary Imre Pozsgay conceded that corruption and abuses had multiplied but insisted that the social tensions and inequalities and the decline in the standard of living were temporarily unavoidable. Shortages and unfulfilled plans were responsible for "spoiling the good political mood," said Pozsgay, who called for a more independent and active role for the PPF in socioeconomic policy development. He warned that the support of the intelligentsia had to be actively courted and recommended state aid for the temporarily unemployed. Pozsgay also raised the minority issue, indicating that Hungary's national minorities enjoy exemplary rights, and Hungary expected ethnic Magyars in the neighboring countries to enjoy language and cultural rights and to strengthen their ties with Hungary. The congress stressed the need to preserve and expand the economic reforms and called for faster social integration of Gypsies as well as for measures to halt the decline in Hungary's population. Pozsgay was reelected general secretary, and Gyula Kállai was reelected chairman of the Patriotic People's Front. (*Magyar Nemzet*, 16 December 1985.)

Mobilization of the 4.4 million members preceded the Twenty-fifth Congress of Hungarian trade unions, held 14–16 February. At the lower-level elections, the local membership could opt for a secret ballot, and over half of the shop stewards and higher union officials were elected by this method. One-third of the successful candidates were chosen for the first time. Attending the congress were 803 delegates and numerous foreign observers, including, after a long absence, a trade union delegation from the People's Republic of China. The chairman of the National Council of Trade Unions, Sándor Gáspár, is a powerful and conservative member of the party leadership, and in his speech he alluded to economic weaknesses and the inadequate integration of the second economy. In the preparatory meetings and at the congress, numerous grievances were aired concerning wages, full employment, excessive overtime, and the new enterprise work collectives. Despite the views expressed by some that socialism was getting weaker and that the unions should be more forceful in advancing demands, Gáspár said, the NCTU's "action program" was the official five-year plan. Lajos Faluvégi, a deputy premier and chairman of the National Planning Office, assured the congress that the government wanted to cooperate more closely with the unions in policymaking. The final resolution was an anodyne appeal for the assertion of union rights and for improvement in the standard of living. There were 21 negative votes and 21 abstentions on the initial version of the resolution. Gáspár was reelected chairman, and Tibor Baranyai was reelected general secretary of the NCTU.

The failure of mass organizations in socialist systems to satisfy the needs of their members is a chronic problem, and young people are even more alienated than union members. The young join the Communist Youth League (CYL) mainly to improve access to higher education, and local units occasionally offer material incentives such as housing. However, as was admitted at the CYL central committee meeting on 15 November 1985, many of the members are indifferent and inactive (*Népszabadság*, 16 November 1985). At the Eleventh CYL Congress, held 23–25 May, First Secretary Csaba Hámori reported that the influence of the organization was declining, partly because of the general economic and social malaise. Nominally, membership had risen to 926,000 (from 874,000 at the last congress), with relative increases among working youth and secondary school students and a decrease among postsecondary students. The university and college section of the congress noted the alienation of students from the CYL and their concern with issues of ecology, poverty, and Hungarian minorities abroad. The leadership's frustration was reflected in Hámori's call for more stringent membership criteria and his invitation to other bodies to set up their own youth organizations. (*Magyar Nemzet*, 26 May.)

Indeed, the party leadership is acutely aware of political alienation, dissatisfaction with wages and housing, and delinquency among young people. The shortcomings of the CYL had already impelled the National Council of Trade Unions to announce the creation of a new organization for young workers on 25 October 1985. The organization aims to represent the special interests of some 1.5 million young workers, one-third of the total membership. All union members under 30 will belong to "youth sections" of the basic trade union groups, and the work of these sections will be coordinated by youth councils under the aegis of trade union councils. The NCTU and the CYL blame each other for the problems of dealing with dissatisfied youth, but neither can offer concrete remedies. The new organization's purpose is political mobilization and publicity and not the provision of financial aid.

Marginal democratization of the political system remains on the regime's agenda, and the media publish guarded discussions of the meaning of pluralism in a socialist system, of the need for more autonomy and organized expressions of interests, and, more concretely, of the possibility of holding local plebiscites to determine investment priorities (*Mozgó Világ*, no. 1985; *Élet és Irodalom*, 13 December 1985). The National Assembly chairman, István Sarlós, reports that in consequence of the new electoral system the deputies were more active in parliamentary sessions and standing committees, and were more critical and demanding of government officials and agencies (*Izvestiia*, 24 June; *JPRS*, 7 August). On 20 March, the National Assembly overrode the finance minister's objections and amended a bill in order to reduce the property transfer tax. The attempts to enhance the parliament's image include the creation of a National Assembly press office and a new rule allowing deputies to speak during session without previous written request. In August, the Council of Ministers issued a decree requiring all state organs (except the defense and interior ministries) to respond to deputies' requests for information.

**Economic Affairs.** Despite the favorable image it enjoys abroad, Hungary's economic system suffers from severe stresses induced by domestic circumstances as well as external factors. A measure of the crisis was given by the report on the sixth five-year plan (1981–1985) (*Népszabadság*, 1 February). National income had increased by 7 percent instead of the planned 14–17 percent (and had in fact fallen by 1 percent in 1985). Real wages declined by 5 percent, although per capita real incomes rose 7–8 percent, thanks to second jobs, private enterprise, and additional social benefits. Industrial production rose by 12 percent over the five years, whereas the plan called for an increase of 19–22 percent. In hard currency trade exports were up 22 percent (mostly agricultural products) and imports 11 percent, but the terms of trade deteriorated by 8.2 percent. The pace of privatization accelerated, with 12 percent of shops and 40 percent of catering establishments transferred to contractual operation.

The plan for 1986 anticipated a 2.3–2.7 percent rise in national income, a 1–1.5 percent increase in per capita real income, a 0.5 percent rise in real wages, and a $350–400 million surplus in hard currency trade (MTI, 29 December 1985; *FBIS*, 7 January). Within a few months it became apparent that these targets, which are part of the seventh five-year plan, were in trouble. Faluvégi voiced dissatisfaction with industrial productivity and the restructuring of the weaker branches, and there appeared to be no consensus within the leadership over the respective merits of incentives and decentralization, and of more forceful central intervention (*Magyar Nemzet*, 4 April). The hard currency trade balance had slid from a $400 million surplus in 1984 to an over $400 million deficit in 1985, and an even greater deficit was forecast for 1986. The officially reported net hard currency debt had meanwhile risen by $2.4 billion, to $7.4 billion. The results for the first half of 1986 reinforced the gloomy predictions. (*Népszabadság*, 8 October.)

Consumer prices rose by nearly 40 percent between 1980 and 1985, and since real wages (not to speak of pensions) did not keep pace, the government has been trying to follow an anti-inflationary policy in order to induce better management and, in the words of Ferenc Havasi, to "strengthen political stability" (ibid., 18 January). However, the state directly sets prices for only 43 percent of consumer goods and services, and by August the consumer price index had overshot the annual target.

The meeting of the Central Committee on 19–20 November produced no new answers to these problems. The economy's inadequate performance was attributed to unfavorable world market prices, bad weather, and labor and management problems. Government and party oversight of the economy also received its share of criticism. The recommended remedies were technological modernization, greater labor discipline and productivity, cost-cutting, and the phasing out of inefficient production units. Among the modest prescriptions for the 1987 plan were a 2 percent rise in national income, a 2.5–3 percent growth in industrial production and a 4.5–5.5 percent in agricultural production, the stabilization of the 1985–86 living standard, and a major improvement in the hard currency trade balance. The Central Committee resolution anticipated a new personal and enterprise income tax system and a greater role for credit and financial tools in economic management. (MTI, 21 November; *FBIS*, 24 November.)

Various new measures are designed to induce the streamlining and modernization of an economic system that is still characterized by inefficiency, technological obsolescence, an unmotivated labor force, and a conservative managerial class. A presidential decree on 1 September gave Hungary the first genuine bankruptcy law in Eastern Europe, designed to provide for the liquidation or reorganization of insolvent enterprises. The drive to eliminate inefficient operations has led to the liquidation of a few small agricultural cooperatives and, not without labor controversy, to the shutting down of the big Rába enterprise's Red Star foundry. The government is providing unemployment benefits for redundant workers awaiting relocation. Officially, Hungary suffers from a shortage of manpower, but low labor mobility, housing problems, and the distribution of skills makes economic reorganization politically problematical.

Reform of the financial sector has already brought about a bond market, and a two-tier banking system will come into being on 1 January 1987. The National Bank will remain the central reserve bank, responsible for foreign exchange and the money supply, and the central clearing bank. In the second tier will be five commercial banks and ten specialized development banks, linked by stock ownership to the central bank. After six months, enterprises will be free to choose their bank, and the latter will have to compete for customers. Profitability will determine the banks' credit policies, and they will be allowed to set differentiated interest rates. It is expected that by the multiplier effect this diversification of the banking system will generate more capital for investment. The electronic equipment of the reorganized system was funded in part by a World Bank loan. Also from 1 January 1987, a new State Development Bank will issue government bonds to finance the budget deficit.

Hungary's energy supply is also bedeviled by internal and external problems. The country produces 23 percent of the oil and 64 percent of the natural gas currently consumed. Only the coal reserves are substantial, for domestic sources of oil and natural gas will be depleted by the beginning of the next century. The government is promoting conservation, substitution, and exploration programs but lacks adequate funds to modernize and expand production. As a consequence, the country's dependence on foreign, mainly Soviet, energy supplies is growing. In December 1985 Hungary joined other CMEA members in a project to build the new "Progress" natural gas pipeline from Siberia. By 1990 the Soviet Union is expected to supply 50 percent more natural gas to Hungary. The Soviet pricing mechanism for oil, a five-year moving average, is gradually reflecting the collapse of world market prices, and in August the Hungarian prices of oil products were lowered by 11–16 percent. There were simultaneous increases in the producer prices of coal and electricity; the effect on consumers was reduced by subsidies.

The coal industry, meanwhile, is in a state of crisis, suffering from antiquated equipment, an overworked labor force, and chronic shortfalls in production. The congress of the mine workers union in November–December 1985 submitted a "package plan" of grievances over wages, housing,

and overtime to the party and government. Havasi acknowledged the shortcomings and promised new investments. Coal (and uranium) miners were given a 10 percent wage raise for 1986, double the planned average increase. A plan to restructure the industry, close down unprofitable pits, and lengthen working hours was announced by the government on 17 July, prompting 600 miners in the Miskolc area to resign in protest.

In September the third reactor came on line at the Paks nuclear power plant, which supplies 15 percent of the country's electricity. A fourth reactor will become operational in 1987, and a Hungarian-Soviet agreement signed in February provides for the construction of two more, larger reactors. When these are completed in the 1990s, Paks will satisfy 40 percent of the projected electrical power needs. There are doubts, however, whether domestic uranium supplies will last beyond the turn of the century. The accident at the Chernobyl nuclear power plant in April prompted official assurances that Paks was of a different and safer Soviet design, but no comment was made on the accident itself. The ensuing temporary ban by Austria and the European Community on the importation of Hungarian foodstuffs caused severe loss of trade and bitter official complaints. Farmers were given compensation.

At the Forty-second Session of the CMEA Council in Bucharest on 3–5 November, Prime Minister György Lázár complained about problems with the CMEA's "Mir" electrical power pool, referring to shortages that had caused "extremely serious harm to the Hungarian economy." (Hungary imports 30 percent of its electricity.) Lázár also urged reform of the CMEA's system of bilateral clearance by product group, claiming that it adversely affects Hungary's trade. (RFE *Research*, 21 November.) In May, Austria and Hungary signed an agreement for Austrian financing (approximately $400 million) and participation in construction of the Gabcikovo-Nagymaros hydroelectric dam on the Danube. The dam is to be completed by 1993, and repayment will take the form of two-thirds of the electricity generated for twenty years. Final decision on the dam, a joint Austrian-Czechoslovak-Hungarian project, had been long delayed by environmental concerns on the part of many Hungarians, including a powerful ecological lobby. This "Danube Circle" group had addressed a petition against the project to the Austrian parliament in June.

A major investment in public relations and tourism was the organization of the first Formula One

Grand Prix car race in Eastern Europe, near Budapest in August.

**Social and Cultural Affairs.** The malaise pervading Hungarian society is drawing growing attention from not only political dissenters but also established authorities. Prominent sociologist Elemér Hankiss diagnosed the problem, observing that chaotic circumstances undermined the individual's self-respect and sense of identity. He identified a chronic uncertainty induced by arbitrary reinterpretations of history and national identity and by the double standards prevailing in Kádár's "market socialism," as in the case of the worker whose main job is in the centrally planned economy and whose second job is in the market economy. (*Valóság*, February.) Other observers claim that severe stress is caused by self-exploitation through overwork and that half of the population suffers from some form of neurosis (*Ötlet*, 24 April). The decline in the standard of living was the subject of a confidential study, which found that 7.3 percent of Hungarians live below the minimum subsistence level and 19 percent below a "modest but socially still acceptable" level (*Beszélö*, no. 15, 1985). Nearly half of the country's 2,260,000 pensioners live at or below the subsistence level; the lowest pensions were raised 5 percent on 1 January.

Taking stock of the dismal record of ideological indoctrination, the Central Committee's Agitprop Committee called in 1982 for the modernization of the teaching of Marxism in universities and colleges. One result is the introduction in 1986 of a course on Hungarian history (1918–1975) to replace one on the history of the "workers' movement" (*Ifjúkommunista*, 4). A new history textbook for university students has been published presenting a more objective picture of the precommunist era. The stress on the "revolutionary workers' movement" is attenuated, and the pre-1944 Horthy regime is no longer branded as fascist, in recognition of the limited pluralism and trade union rights that prevailed at the time. There are limits to this marginally more tolerant treatment of the past. When a publishing house decided to reprint the major prewar Hungarian encyclopedia, it received over 70,000 subscriptions, but the authorities belatedly banned publication on the grounds that it contained objectionable historical and ideological views.

A new press law, claimed to be more democratic, was passed by the National Assembly on 20 March. It prescribes the responsibility of the press to provide timely and accurate information, and the responsibility of all state bodies to respond promptly to journalists' inquiries. However, all publishing activity still must have official permission, and national security and enterprise secrecy can serve to prevent the publication of information. The party's cadre authority, official guidelines on information, and the self-censorship imposed on all who write for publication ensure that freedom of the press will not extend to the questioning of "real existing socialism." Although officials deny that censorship exists, the authorities intervene regularly when the unspoken guidelines are transgressed. A new magazine, *Liget* (Parkland), was withdrawn from circulation, probably because of critical articles concerning the 1956 revolution and its aftermath. A poem alluding to the revolution was the likely reason for withdrawing the July issue of the provincial cultural review, *Tiszatáj*.

The *Tiszatáj* affair was aired at the seventh general assembly of the Hungarian Writers' Union, convened 29–30 November. The congress was marked by heated debate, including a harsh speech by Berecz, who warned the writers that their union would be dissolved if they did not toe the party line, and critical rejoinders by writers complaining of censorship and constraints on freedom of thought. A 71-member executive board was elected by secret ballot, and the party's preferred candidates were all defeated. The leading officers chosen were not party men, and the congress only aggravated the tense relations between the HSWP and the writers. (RFE *Research*, 23 December.)

Although the Kádár regime is eager to be regarded in the West as a model of tolerance, the scope for dissent is strictly limited. The cultural director in the village of Lakitelek, Sándor Lezsák, organized one in a series of literary meetings in October 1985 on the anniversary of the revolution. At the meeting he criticized the repression of freedom of speech in Hungary and Romania. The trade union paper, *Népszava* (30 October 1985), carried an article praising Lezsák, but the party daily, *Népszabadság* (1 November 1985), denounced this praise, and Lezsák was dismissed from his job. The police broke up a small and peaceful demonstration of Austrian and Hungarian environmentalists in Budapest on 7 February, and on the national holiday, 15 March, they intervened with force to disperse an unofficial march by hundreds of young people.

The police have multiplied their raids on samizdat publishers, and it has been reported that in June the Politburo ordered a weekly blacklist of dissidents who published abroad or in samizdat

(UPI, 26 July; RFE *Research*, 29 August). István Csurka, a leading writer who had visited the West, published essays in the United States, and allowed Radio Free Europe to broadcast one of his lectures, was accused of disloyalty, and his works were banned from publication (*Magyar Nemzet*, 9 August). There were 52 Hungarians among the 122 East European dissidents who on 19 October issued a joint declaration commemorating the 1956 revolution. The signatories asserted that the basic demands of the Hungarian and other East European revolutions have not been satisfied and proclaimed their determination to struggle for democracy, national independence, and minority rights. Some of the Hungarian signatories were subsequently subjected to punitive measures.

László Cardinal Lékai died on 30 June. Over ten years he had forged a modus vivendi with the state, though not without incurring some criticism for being too ready to compromise. Thirty Catholic and Marxist intellectuals from East and West met in Budapest on 8–10 October for a dialogue on "Society and Ethical Values." The meeting, in the course of which Kádár met Austria's Franz Cardinal Koenig, was organized by the Institute of Philosophy of the Hungarian Academy of Sciences and the Papal Gregorian University of Rome.

**Foreign Affairs.** Hungary's official perspective on international issues was summed up by State Secretary Gyula Horn's comment on the Geneva summit of December 1985: improvement in Soviet-American relations creates "more favorable conditions" for Hungary and other small countries (RFE *Research*, 6 December 1985). Secretary of State George Shultz visited Budapest on 16 December 1985 in the course of a ten-day European tour. The visit testified to the relatively favorable view taken by Washington of Hungary's human rights record and economic reforms. Shultz avoided suggesting any American interest in dividing the Soviet bloc and praised Kádár as a wise man. The meeting produced agreement on the positive development of bilateral relations and on the need to continue that dialogue (*LAT*, 17 December 1985). Hungary is actively seeking more trade and joint ventures with the United States, whose share of Hungary's exports to the West has risen from 3 percent in 1977 to 8 percent in 1984. It also wants a longer-term guarantee of most-favored-nation tariff status but is not likely to get it. An instance of the Hungarian disposition to display openness in dialogue was the inclusion of Mark Palmer, assistant secretary of

state for European and Canadian affairs at the State Department (subsequently named U.S. ambassador to Hungary), in a roundtable discussion with Soviet, West German, and Hungarian officials on disarmament and other international issues, broadcast on Hungarian television on 8 May.

At the Conference on Security and Cooperation in Europe (CSCE) review conference that opened in Vienna in November, Hungary apparently intended to follow up on issues raised at the earlier Budapest Cultural Forum, including freer exchange of newspapers and translated books from smaller nations and the establishment in Budapest of a European Folklore Center named after composer Béla Bartók (Radio Budapest, 14 November; RFE *Research*, 21 November). These initiatives are inspired in part by concern for the Hungarian minority in Romania (see below). Ten Hungarian dissidents signed a memorandum to the Vienna conference by the "European Network for East-West Dialogue." The memoranadum addressed peace and security, democracy, the environment, and cultural cooperation.

Among the more notable state visits in 1986 were those of President Kenan Evren of Turkey in June and of President Richard von Weizšacker of West Germany in October.

*Communist Relations.* The party's foreign affairs spokesman, Mátyás Szürös, continued to profess a loose interpretation of socialist internationalism. Communist unity and its ideological base are not a steady state but a process marked by varying approaches, and "only time and practice will tell who is right and who is wrong." There is, insisted Szürös, "no universally applicable or binding model of socialism or way to socialism." (*WMR*, 4.) In another lecture, delivered in Finland, Szürös reiterated the Hungarian view that small nations have a special role to play in European détente. He also observed that, in the spirit of Helsinki, the Hungarian minorities in Eastern Europe can serve better understanding between neighboring countries through their dual bond to their states and their ethnic group. Said Szürös, "Caring for them is a special task of Hungarian foreign policy." (*Valóság*, July.)

Cordial relations with the Soviet Union remain the cornerstone of Hungarian foreign policy, and great weight is placed upon Moscow's continuing endorsement of Kádárism. An article in *Pravda* (22 January) reflected positively on Hungary's achievements and on the closer economic and commercial relations with the Soviet Union and the CMEA. It warned against Western trade and tourism serving as a channel for "antisocialist propaganda" and noted that the quality of Hungarian exports to the Soviet Union was not always satisfactory. In an interview, Mátyás Szürös construed the article not as criticism but as an accurate and friendly appraisal of achievements and problems. He praised Gorbachev's "efforts for renewal and dynamic change," notably with respect to the democratization of party life, as realistic, and observed that any progress in the Soviet Union would also benefit Hungary. (Radio Budapest, 27 January; RFE *Research*, 3 February.)

In early January the Soviet-Hungarian Committee on Economic, Technical, and Scientific Cooperation met in Budapest, and 28 agreements were signed on economic specialization and cooperation. At the Twenty-seventh Congress of the CPSU in February, Kádár praised the "realistic and open" policies adopted by Gorbachev. He observed later that there was a similarity between the two parties' approaches and that more dynamic development in the Soviet Union meant that "we, too, can breathe more easily." Szürös, who was a member of the HSWP delegation, found encouragement in the CPSU's Leninist nationality policy of harmonious coexistence. (*Népszabadság*, 27 February, 6, 8 March.) Gorbachev paid a "friendly working visit" to Budapest on 8 June, on the eve of the meeting of the Warsaw Pact's Political Consultative Committee. The communiqué claimed full identity of views on economic cooperation and foreign policy. Speaking to workers at a Csepel factory, Gorbachev said that he followed with "attention and respect" the Hungarian economic reforms and emphasized the need for reversing the decline in the rate of economic growth in the Soviet Union. (ibid., 10 June.)

KGB chairman Viktor Chebrikov visited Budapest on 23–24 April and met with Kádár, Central Committee Secretary István Horváth, and Interior Minister János Kamara for talks about "important questions" of cooperation. Among prominent Hungarian visitors to the USSR were János Berecz (23 April) and Mátyás Szürös (12 May). Kádár attended the meeting of CMEA party leaders in Moscow on 10–11 November and held further talks with Gorbachev.

The Hungarian-Romanian dispute over the circumstances of the 2 million Magyars in Transylvania continued to intensify. The controversy had resurfaced at the Budapest Cultural Forum in October–November 1985, and critical articles appeared in Romania (notably in *Contemporanul*, 6 December 1985) charging that Hungarian commentaries on the history of Transylvania were marked by deviationism, chauvinism, and revisionism. The Budapest press noted the closing down of a long-established Hungarian magazine in Romania, *Müvelödés* (Culture), and its replacement by a Romanian magazine with a Hungarian section. The apparent suicide of Transylvanian Hungarian actor and dissident Árpád Visky was also reported. Despite official Romanian protests, a play by the distinguished Transylvanian author András Sütö, which had been banned in Romania, was staged in Budapest. In January, the International PEN Club congress in New York criticized Romania's repression of minorities; the meeting was attended by two Hungarian dissident writers, Sándor Csoóri and György Konrád.

At the CSCE follow-up conference on human contacts, held in Bern from 15 April to 27 May, the Hungarian delegation defended the right of ethnic minorities, notably the Hungarians in neighboring countries, to develop links with their main national group. A Yugoslav proposal to the same effect was vetoed by Romania, which was the principal Warsaw Pact spokesman (along with the Soviet Union) and generally took a hard line. High-level visits between Bucharest and Budapest are infrequent. Deputy Premier Gheorghe Oprea held talks in Budapest with László Maróthy, also a deputy premier, on 26–28 May, and reference was made to the need for closer relations and the scope for more economic exchange.

Confronted in an interview with the claim that Hungarians were dissatisfied with their government's inability to induce improvement in the lot of the minority in Romania, Culture and Education Minister Béla Köpeczi admitted that the possibilities for cooperation with Romania on cultural relations were receding (*Mozgó Világ*, June). There has been official criticism of the very limited availability of Hungarian newspapers in Romania (which purchases some 12,000 copies of Hungarian press material annually, compared with over 100,000 for Czechoslovakia, which has a much smaller Hungarian minority). *Népszabadság* (29 October) deplored the complaints of the "domestic nationalist opposition" about the regime's inaction but acknowledged that there were "differences of views" between the two governments.

Indicative of a progressive normalization of relations was the visit of China's foreign minister, Wu Xueqian, who is also a member of his party's Politburo, on 2–4 June. He met Kádár and brought both government and party greetings, but there are still no official interparty relations. Wu said in an interview that Hungary's experience with economic reform was "very useful to China" (*Magyar Hirlap*, 6 June). A technical and scientific cooperation agreement was signed on the same occasion. Trade has been expanding, Hungarian exports to China having grown by 75 percent from 1984 to 1985. Deputy premier Lajos Faluvégi visited China in August. It was reported that the Rába engineering works will be employing 350 Chinese guest workers in 1987. (There are already some 8,000 Polish guest workers in Hungary.)

Prime Minister György Lázár paid an official visit to Yugoslavia on 10–11 December 1985. The resulting communiqué expressed satisfaction with relations, trade and economic cooperation, and the status of the two countries' respective ethnic minorities. Trade is projected to rise 50 percent by 1990, and there are plans for cooperation in the supply and storage of energy. (*Népszabadság*, 12 December 1985.) Other socialist meetings in 1986 included the visit of Lázár to Czechoslovakia in May, of Gustáv Husák to Budapest in November, of Foreign Minister Péter Várkonyi to East Berlin and of Szürös to North Korea in May; and of head of state Pál Losonczi to Syria in September. Alessandro Natta, the general secretary of the Italian Communist Party, visited Budapest from 29 September to 1 October and held "cordial comradely talks" with Kádár, reviewing their "traditionally good interparty relations" (MTI, 1 October; *FBIS*, 2 October).

Bennett Kovrig
*University of Toronto*

# Poland

Population. 37,546,000 (December 1985)
Party. Polish United Workers' Party (Polska Zjednoczona Partia Robotnicza; PZPR)
Founded. 1948
Membership. 2,125,762; workers, 38 percent; farmers, 9 percent; intellectuals, 53 percent (*Polityka*, 5 July 1986)
First Secretary. General of the Army Wojciech Jaruzelski
Politburo. 14 full members: Kazimierz Barcikowski, Józef Baryła, Józef Czyrek, Jan Głowczyk, Czesław Kiszczak, Zbigniew Messner, Alfred Miodowicz, Włodzimierz Mokrzyszczak, Zygmunt Murański, Marian Orzechowski, Tadeusz Porębski, Florian Siwicki, Zofia Stępień, and Marian Woźniak; 5 alternate members: Stanisław Bejger, Bogumił Ferensztajn, Janusz Kubasiewicz, Zbigniew Michałek, Gabriela Rembisz
Central Committee. Approximately 200 members and 70 alternate members. Secretaries of the Central Committee include Józef Baryła, Henryk Bednarski, Stanisław Ciosek, Kazimierz Cypryniak, Józef Czyrek, Jan Głowczyk, Zbigniew Michałek, Tadeusz Porębski, Andrzej Wasilewski, and Marian Woźniak.
Status. Ruling party
Last Congress. Tenth, 29 June–3 July 1986

**Last Election.** 1985. The regime claimed that 78.81 percent of Poles had voted; an independent estimate indicates that not more than 60 percent voted.

**Publications.** *Trybuna ludu* (*TL*), party daily; *Nowe drogi* and *Ideologia i polityka*, party monthlies; *Zycie partii*, fortnightly party organ; *Zołnierz wolności*, army daily. Polska Agencja Prasowa (PAP) is the official news agency.

Although it has consolidated its political power with the help of oppressive measures, the ruling communist party in Poland has been unable to arrest the decline of the Soviet-like state. The key difference between the Soviet model of the state and any other is that the communist state bears the entire responsibility not only for the political apparatus but also for the economy, social affairs, and education. The issue of Poland's decline is complicated by the fact that, according to Lenin, Soviet-type states should now be in the last stages of transition from socialism to communism rather than in a retreat from socialism.

Evidence of that retreat is the general attempt by the communist states to free themselves from total economic control, specifically by fostering private enterprise, introducing the so-called market mechanism within the socialist sector of the economy, and continuing to stress the political pluralism highly visible in Poland's party-church relationship.

The essence of the problem is not limited to the methods recently employed by the communist regimes. It also includes the meaning and relevance of such concepts as "class struggle," "rule of the working class," the "dictatorship of proletariat," and the "leading role of the party." In short, the question of political legitimacy is at stake. This basic question was discussed by the Polish communist party—the Polish United Workers' Party—during its Tenth Congress held in June and July.

**The Party.** The debates of the Tenth Party Congress focused on three issues: first, the results of "normalization"—the stick-and-carrot policy adopted by General Jaruzelski after martial law was introduced in December 1981; second, the long-range development program, including the sensitive issue of social acceptance; and, third, the need for a new framework to steer the economy during substantial private sector growth and declining political control over publicly owned enterprises.

It was obvious during the congress that the party needed to project optimism and to demonstrate with renewed force its vitality, creative strength, potential, and ability to attain a new level of so-

cioeconomic development. The popular image of the party is that its skills are limited to conspiring with Moscow against the Polish nation—and that the current stage of socialism is a form of stagnation without precedent in the nation's history.

Preparations for the congress began on 20 December 1985 when the Central Committee met for its Twenty-third Plenum. Apparently, the purpose of this plenum was to give the current leadership full credit for the allegedly healthy state of the national economy. The three-year national socioeconomic plan that began in January 1983 was nearly completed, and the party decided to praise itself for the benefits of economic reform. It was a tactic designed to flush out possible opposition within the party before the congress, during which criticism would be more difficult to control.

The party credited itself with increases of 10 to 12 percent in national income, 16 percent in industrial production, and 17 percent in housing construction. It was stressed that the increase in individual income had been achieved exclusively by increasing productivity. The material intensiveness of production was, according to the official view, reduced in the three-year period by about 6.3 percent, and the energy intensiveness of this production was reduced by about 5.5 percent. The only unfavorable development mentioned was the increase in the population's cash income, which was estimated to have risen 57 percent in the three-year period. (*TL*, 21–22 December 1985.) The authorities admitted the existence of inflationary tendencies (officially referred to as a "price movement in excess of the plan") in the Polish economy, but failed to admit to at least a doubling of prices since 1982.

Also avoided by the official statement on the national economy was any reference to the huge deficit Poland has accumulated since 1980. The shortage for fiscal year 1985 was estimated to be $150 billion złoty ($.75 billion according to the official rate of exchange), and a slightly higher deficit was anticipated in fiscal year 1986. This amounts to 8,000–9,000 złoty ($615–690) of deficit per employed citizen annually. This relatively large deficit is a direct result of continuing heavy subsidies for socialized enterprises, and for 1986 it forced the authorities to increase the income tax by 19 percent despite estimates that national income would grow no higher than 3.4 percent (Warsaw Domestic Service, 29 December 1985.)

Nevertheless, the Central Committee evaluated the results of the three-year plan positively, giving General Jaruzelski and his leadership high marks for management of the nation's economy during the post-1980 crisis period. With this conclusion, the plenum officially opened a campaign to prepare for the Tenth Congress.

The Twenty-fourth Central Committee Plenum, held in Warsaw on 1–2 February, marked the first official step in the precongress campaign. Again, the party decided to evaluate the state of Poland's educational system in the most orthodox ideological manner. The authorities had shown no concern for the quality of eduation, which had been in decline for at least a decade. Rather, their undivided attention was focused on "preparing the young generation for active participation in constructing a socialist society." (TL, 7 February.)

The Central Committee often has discussed the education of young people in Poland, stressing an unfavorable level of ideological consciousness among the Polish youth, especially in acceptance of communist ideas. Effectiveness of ideological indoctrination was analyzed by five plenums in the last five years. This time, however, the party felt strong enough to define a program of action that includes the following "working guidelines": more dynamic party leadership in education; elaboration of educational goals in the context of the party's ideological resolutions; teaching Marxism-Leninism at all levels of the educational system by Polish and, if necessary, guest instructors— particularly from the Soviet Union; strengthening the socialist and lay nature of schools and universities; strengthening all party organizations at educational institutions; and supporting educational institutions through communist youth organizations, the Society of Polish-Soviet Friendship, the National Defense League, and other communist-run organizations. Needless to say, the party is fostering procommunist and "internationalist" attitudes in order to streamline its administrative control over the academic curriculum and instructors.

This ideological prelude to the Tenth Congress followed the bloc-wide tendency toward ideological orthodoxy and concern about Western influence on young people. It is doubtful, however, that the Polish government has sufficient resources to implement this expensive scheme (RFE, Polish SR/3, 19 February). The current program is not just a Soviet echo, but a repetition of similar attempts over the past few decades to strengthen the "socialist" content of education.

This is just one example of the recently adopted Soviet convergence policy, which indicates that the "national road to socialism" approach, accepted in October 1956, has been modified. The trend is, then, toward a greater degree of uniformity in order to "reach the next stage of socialist development." The experience of the USSR, the "most advanced socialist state," will apparently be followed closely. (Zycie partii, 26 February.)

The plenum removed the more independent-minded members of the so-called Central Committee problem commissions and replaced them with less capable, but unquestionably loyal, party hacks, thus establishing a pattern to be followed by the congress. For example, the Economic Reform and Policy Commission removed well-known economists Kazimierz Barcikowski, Stanisław Kukuryka, and Janusz Obodowski, substituting them with regional party secretaries. Also, Jerzy Wiatr, a well-known sociologist, was dropped from the Science and Education Commission, a step fully consistent with General Jaruzelski's "better red than expert" cadre policy. (TL, 3 February.)

The Twenty-fifth plenum (13–14 March), the last before the Tenth Congress, was scheduled right after the Twenty-seventh Congress of the Soviet communist party—to pay tribute to Moscow and set guidelines for strengthening the "socialist foundations of a secure, economically efficient, modern and law-abiding Poland" (Radio Warsaw, PAP, 14 March; FBIS-Eastern Europe, 14 March). It was an important gathering, because it was the first after General Jaruzelski's meeting with Mikhail Gorbachev in Moscow, a meeting that was officially characterized by "mutual understanding." In communist jargon, that implies mutual unwillingness to understand each other despite certain disagreements. (Le Figaro, 14 March.)

General Jaruzelski's statement at the plenum was a restrained adulation of the Soviet Union, Poland's "first ally and partner," with which Polish communists are "in the same Leninist concert," but which should recognize that Poland is at a "different stage of development and in different realities." The entire international communist movement, General Jaruzelski stated, should be guided by "unity in versatility" and realizations of the universal principles in the historically shaped, national conditions."

In conclusion, speaking on behalf of the Polish communist party, General Jaruzelski pledged Poland's faithfulness to Marxism-Leninism (as just defined by Moscow), the Soviet Union, the Warsaw Pact, and the CMEA and defined Poland as a partner contributing to "the common treasury of socialism." (Radio Warsaw, PAP, 15 March; *FBIS-Eastern Europe*, 18 March.) Then, having stressed both loyalty and self-identity, the PZPR was ready for its own show.

The Tenth Congress had been prepared carefully to project an image of a thoughtful and harmonious organization unequivocally committed to ideology and common sense. It was the first party congress since the 1980–1981 crisis. It focused on the prospects of "socialist renewal"—the strategy for the socioeconomic "path into the 21st century." (*TL*, 5 July.) Also very different from the extraordinary Ninth Congress in 1981 was the party itself. At the beginning of 1980 there were over 3 million members and candidates; by 1986 more than 1 million had been expelled or had resigned. Between the congresses, the party admitted 160,000 candidates: 1,200 in the second half of 1981; 7,500 in 1982; 17,000 in 1983; 35,000 in 1984; 63,000 in 1985; and more than 30,000 in the first half of 1986. Consequently, party membership at the time of the Tenth Congress totaled 2,125,762. Since 1980, the proportion of workers has decreased from 44.8 to 38.2 percent; peasants decreased from 9.5 to 9 percent; intellectuals increased from 44 to 51.5 percent; and young party members (up to the age of 29) decreased from 15.6 to 7.5 percent. (*Polityka*, 5 July.) More than ever the party has become an organization of professional careerists or apparatchiks, that is, employees of the defense and interior ministries. More than 68 percent of Ministry of Internal Affairs functionaries are either members or candidate members of the PZPR, and in the security services the figure exceeds 90 percent (*TL*, 4 June).

Some 1,776 delegates attended the congress, of whom 51.5 percent were workers and peasants; 85 percent of the delegates came from families of workers and farmers. There were 356 women (20 percent), 781 delegates with higher education (44 percent), and 324 delegates (18 percent) were members of the youth organizations. (Radio Warsaw, PAP, 25 June.) As these figures indicate, the congress had been carefully prepared to confirm the "class essence" of Jaruzelski's party.

Political programs adopted by the congress for 1986–1990 demonstrated that nothing new could be invented from the old discredited organization and its ideology. The five-year plan assumes that the Polish economy can achieve a major rise in labor productivity and, by 1990, attain living standards comparable to those of 1979. Social goals formulated by the party for the next five-year period include hopes to increase food consumption by about 12 percent; achieve self-sufficiency in food production; increase the supply of industrial goods by 17 percent; increase national income; reduce inflation to less than 10 percent by 1990; solve the housing problem by increasing the number of new apartments by 10 to 12 percent; and halt the process of the destruction of the natural environment. (*TL*, 14 July.)

A resolution adopted by the Tenth Congress, entitled "On Increasing Management Efficiency and Improving the Standard of Living, on Enhancing Socialist Democracy, on Consolidating Poland's International Position," created the impression that the party was particularly concerned with improving the nation's standard of living, especially the desperate housing shortage. By 1990 more than a million apartments should be built and another million modernized to satisfy the most urgent needs. But, according to more independent sources, the country's housing situation is not likely to improve for at least 65 years! (RFE, Polish SR/11, 22 July.)

Founded on two mutually exclusive premises, the entire new program is dominated by a lack of realism. On the one hand, the party celebrated its victory over the Polish nation by congratulating "all functionaries of the Citizens Militia and Security Service for their effective action to defend and safeguard the state's internal security" (*TL*, 14 July) and by promising toughness in dealing with every form of social disorder or "counterrevolutionary" activity. Yet at the same time it expressed hope for an improved economic situation and increased productivity. There is nothing in the resolution to indicate an inclination to address the effects of Poland's political, social, and economic crises. As so many times before, the party has established high social and economic goals in a vacuum; that is, without a realistic assessment of social reality and economic resources, and with the expectation that discipline and ideological militancy will provide an adequate substitute for a dialogue with the nation. For example, the 1986–1990 plan assumes that a 16 to 19 percent increase in national income is possible and that such an increase would raise per capita consumption 9 to 11 percent. The increases are contingent, however, on a 7.5 to 9.5 percent decrease in consumption of production materials, a

9 to 11 percent decrease in energy consumption, and, simultaneously, a 16 percent increase in productivity.

It is also evident that the five-year economic program will perpetuate the lopsided nature of Poland's economy. An accelerated rate of investment outlays in some branches of heavy industry and electronics is to be achieved at the expense of agricultural modernization; microelectronics, computer science, automation, biotechnology, and so forth are top-priority investments. "Scientific-technological progress" is to be the driving force of economic development into the next century.

Agricultural development has one of the lowest priorities: investments may not increase beyond that recommended for the entire economy and, as always, such investments would subsidize the least-productive, collective sector of agriculture. Moreover, the party will continue to advocate unpopular policies "encouraging socialist changes in farming," specifically, promoting collectivization through various forms of cooperative production and concentration of farmlands. (*TL*, 14 July.) As one delegate pointed out, such policies make the "peasant unsure of the permanence of the [private] form of land ownership" and has a detrimental effect on productivity. (RFE, Polish SR/11, 22 July.)

The party's entire energy has been focused on perfecting the state apparatus and centralizing party decisionmaking. The Tenth Congress affirmed as "inviolable" the discredited principles of democratic centralism and officially reversed all democratic procedures followed five years ago by the Ninth Congress—such as voting by secret ballot, nominating more than one candidate for a position, rotating the leadership cadre, and free discussions. The party again has acquired an anti-intellectual, socially narrow, and dogmatic character and is guided by selfish parochial interests. An excessive dependence on Moscow is the only option for the unpopular regime. In his address, Gorbachev—the only Soviet-bloc leader to attend the gathering—reiterated the USSR's commitment to the notorious Brezhnev Doctrine of limited sovereignty, that is, the Soviet right to invade other communist-ruled states. The "socialist gains are irreversible," stated Gorbachev, and "to threaten the socialist order, try to undermine it from the outside, and tear one country or another from the socialist community means encroachment not only on the will of the people but also on the entire postwar order and, in the final analysis, on peace." (*FBIS-Eastern Europe*, 1 July.)

USSR influence is particularly evident in Poland's foreign policy goals, which stress "concerted actions" with Moscow rather than independent actions within the broad framework of Soviet foreign policy. Attacks on the United States and West Germany were frequent. At one point General Jaruzelski attacked the "militarist and imperialist" West for plundering other nations, including Poland. At the same time, Jaruzelski gave his unconditional support to the "Soviet peace initiatives and to Comrade Mikhail Gorbachev's personal involvement, to his far-seeing, brave, wise, and honest policy aimed at removing the threat of nuclear annihilation." (RFE, Polish SR/11, 22 July.) *Trybuna ludu* (1 July), the Central Committee's daily, pointed out in its commentary that "we cannot fail to notice how many assessments and conclusions from [Gorbachev's] speech . . . are in common" with those of the Central Committee report on the Tenth Congress. In particular, the newspaper quoted two conclusions made by the Soviet leaders:

> Close cooperation and alliance between Poland and the USSR, two of the largest European socialist states, is an essential condition for favorable development of our countries and for stability and peace in Europe.
>
> We will provide the firmest resistance to the adventurist and destructive activity of the United States. One cannot let U.S. imperialism decide the fate of the world according to its own whims.

Unrestrained anti-U.S. propaganda dominated Polish and Soviet statements at the congress. Not for the first time, General Jaruzelski depicted the United States as an "unscrupulous, evil-minded power threatening Poland and all of humanity," forgetting that his ambition to lead the country into the twenty-first century would be nothing more than a pipe dream without U.S. economic aid.

This party convention showed how willing the regime is to sidestep the main issues facing Poland today. General Jaruzelski devoted five years of his leadership to rebuild and centralize the party, but failed to reach agreement with the Polish people. In international affairs he reduced Poland to a Soviet puppet eager to serve Moscow at the expense of its own national interest. Consequently, the congress will have no effect on Polish society. Its purpose was to strengthen Jaruzelski's leadership to make it easier for him to apply pressure against both the party masses and society as a whole. As a Solidarity spokesman, Janusz Onyszkiewicz, pointed out, the Tenth Congress indicated the organic weakness of the party as the "tool which controlled all areas of social life. This tool is now unusable and the control must be exercised through other means, chiefly through the police." (*Svenska Dagbladet*, 30 June; *FBIS-Eastern Europe*, 9 July.) At the end of the five-day party congress a new fifteen-member Politburo was selected by the Central Committee. Seven members of the old Politburo were removed, primarily individuals who might be characterized as liberals. The new Politburo includes four generals: Jaruzelski, the first secretary; Florian Siwicki, the defense minister; Czesław Kiszczak, the minister of interior; and Józef Baryła, the party secretary responsible for security affairs. The current Politburo also includes Alfred Miodowicz, chairman of the trade union that replaced Solidarity. These promotions to membership in the ruling Politburo give little substance to the claim that the new union is independent from the state.

Like his victory over Solidarity, the Tenth Congress was another short-range success for General Jaruzelski. Temporarily, it will bring about ideological consolidation and concentrate power in General Jaruzelski's hands, but it is most unlikely to accelerate the country's economic development. The congress had no psychological impact on the public, contributing nothing to the solution of such pressing issues as the nation's lack of confidence and passivity—to say nothing of waste and bureaucratic red tape.

For the time being, General Jaruzelski and his ambiguous program of socialist renewal—a line of accord, reforms, and struggle—are triumphant. With Soviet blessings and a victory over the party hard-liners he is likely to gain more room for maneuvering within the party organization and the government, gaining new momentum in building "garrison socialism" in Poland.

**The Church.** Relations between church and state in Poland continue to deteriorate as the party recovers from the 1980–1981 disaster. Inflammatory, doctrinal attacks on the church increased in 1986, indicating an increasing polarization of these two key institutions. A recently adopted party strategy calls for discrediting the church.

The regime claims that the church does not respect the principle of ideological tolerance and demands instead that only the church's outlook has a right to exist. This alleged Catholic totalitarianism strives to replace civil authorities in Poland with "medieval ecclesiastical authority," which would rule over the ignorant masses that are "swayed only by primitive emotion." According to the officially encouraged view, the church is determined to convert Poland into a "colony of the Vatican." (*Argumenty*, 8 June.)

The second principle supposedly violated by the church is that of the separation of church and state. The church is accused of conducting political activities and engaging in moral edification and political crusades against Leninism. Any attempt to criticize the authorities is immediately interpreted as unwarranted interference in political affairs and a violation of the constitutional right to be an atheist. In this manner the regime seeks to undermine the church's credibility and shift responsibility for the lack of state-church cooperation onto the church.

Church authorities meet this challenge with various levels of sophistication. The typical parish priest calls communism the "red dragon" and condemns "three systems in the world which threaten human life: Communism, Hitlerism, and the killing of unborn children." The communist system, according to some militant priests, is "based on the principles of plundering, organized robbery, and thievery." (*Żołnierz wolności*, 5–6 April.)

More prudent clergymen argue that the communist authorities are alien, serving Soviet rather than Polish interests, and determined to perpetuate their ideology without regard to the consequences for the Polish nation. During the so-called Mass for the fatherland, a monthly service initiated by Father Jerzy Popieluszko (the dissident priest murdered in 1985 by Polish secret service police), the regime was criticized for its unwillingness to establish a dialogue with Polish society and for "manipulating" official propaganda to "discredit those who think differently by branding them as national enemies." The great majority of priests (especially younger ones) have no hope for a meaningful and durable reconciliation between the communist state and the church because "what peace or freedom can there be for a people that has no guaranteed role in public life, that is governed by a single party which sees its interests as those of the state?" (Radio Paris, AFP, 27 January.)

Despite its difficulties, the church carries on with its historical mission of protecting the Polish nation from the effects of Sovietization and sustaining Poland's European heritage. While the regime emphasizes that Poland is part of the socialist commonwealth of nations headed by Soviet Russia, the church is defending Poland against "Asiatization"—the acceptance of totalitarian and imperial order founded and enforced by coercion rather than the consent of the governed. With equal anxiety, the church struggles against the "socialist laicization" promoted by the authorities, which stresses technological progress over moral progress and the dignity of man. In the opinion of the church this reduces the individual to the role of a machine.

According to the church, the right to express Christian values is a testimony to Poland's national sovereignty, because the Marxist-Leninist view of materialism runs counter to millenniums-old Polish cultural values; "values on which our nation relies and which give it the strength to live must not be violated" (the late Stefan Cardinal Wyszyński, quoted in *Przeglad katolicki*, 21 September). The church is struggling to preserve Polish individuality and personality and demanding respect for the freedom to choose political and moral values over administratively enforced atheism.

The right to be a Catholic is a fundamental right of every Polish citizen, the church argues, and, under the current geostrategic situation, the only safeguard for the independence and cultural self-identity of Polish society. The promotion of Soviet ideology, an accelerated pace of discrimination against the Catholic press, and highly restricted access to radio and television networks is impoverishing national culture and subjugating Poland to foreign ideology, according to the church. Stressing the economic implications of the civil rights issue, the church warns that the problems facing the country will not be solved without full respect for human rights. Until Poles are free to live according to their own values the church will continue to carry on its "liberating mission." (*Tygodnik powszechny*, 11 May.)

The right and duty of believers to foster Catholic ideas was expressed by the pope in a sermon to Polish pilgrims:

Catholic laymen have the right and duty to shape the order on this earth in the spirit of the Holy Gospel and, regardless of external difficulties, to bear witness to their faith in public life, in jobs, and in professions. It is their duty to be bold in reacting to features of moral wrongdoing. Guided by Christian conscience in their activities, they should have a sense of dignity regarding the rights of the political community and show the necessary solicitude for the correct development of the organization of social life. (*Tygodnik powszechny*, 7 September.)

On the 30th anniversary of the 1956 Poznań incidents that initiated the process of demoraliza-

tion in Poland and testified to the political and moral awareness of the working class, the leading Catholic weekly discussed the symbiotic unity of Poland and Christianity:

In Poland Christianity has become the content of the nation's self-knowledge and the determinant of its ethical awareness. It endows our culture with a certain specific tone peculiar to Poland. The church has turned out to be the heir and trustee of the 1,000 years of national tradition. In dividing up the goods, Christianity has become the spokesman for the working man on both the personal plane and on the social plane. Defending human rights it gives human work the highest value, not only economic and social value but also ethical and superinstrumental value. (*Tygodnik powszechny*, June.)

In its official pronouncements, the regime admits that the majority (up to 90 percent) of the Polish citizens are believers, but rather than give political rights to the Catholic majority in Poland, the party is guided by the principle that the interests of the "*socialist* [emphasis added] Fatherland . . . are supreme to ideological cleavages" (*TL*, 31 June).

In practice, this demands that the church accept the leading role of the communist party and laicization as historical necessities. Officially, atheism is gaining popularity in Poland and the church hierarchy is overreacting to its declining popularity (*Sztandar młodych*, 26–28 September).

In effect, both the church and the party claim an ideological monopoly in Poland, and continue to dispute which is the better patriot. Both sides' inflammatory and aggressive rhetoric indicates a deepening polarization that usually is symptomatic of approaching crisis. The church today is stronger than ever before; it claims almost the entire population, regardless of religious convictions, and acts as guardian of a nation deprived of true representation.

The outcome of Poland's historic church-state rivalry will determine the future of the nation. If the party ever prevails over Catholicism in Poland, sovietization will no longer be opposed within and eventually the country could face incorporation into the Soviet state. As long as the communist-Catholic dualism continues, neither institution will have exclusive control over Polish society nor the exclusive right to speak for the nation. At this moment, however, the church is stronger, not only because of its enormous popularity, which includes active support from many nonbelievers, but also because of its ideological flexibility—a luxury that is unavailable to the conservative, dogmatic party. The church-state confrontation includes every aspect of Polish existence; it is a total war between incompatible systems.

The new ideological campaign authorized by the Twenty-fourth Plenum of the PZPR Central Committee was specifically aimed at rolling back the church's influence. First, the regime ordered a nationwide "verification" or "sociopolitical review" of teachers' political qualifications, involving a "self-evaluation questionnaire" that included the following questions: "How do I promote lay customs in my school's daily life?"; "How do I promote lay customs in the life of my own family?"; "Why do I not belong to the party?"; and "What action would I take if students put up crosses in my school?" (*Znaki czasu*, no. 2.) At the second stage of verification, each teacher is interrogated by the Verification Commission, which includes at least one member of the local party apparatus (ibid., no. 7).

General Jaruzelski justified this policy by referring to an "axiom" that the next generations will live in "socialist" Poland. However, according to an independent poll, only 3.6 percent of Polish young people favor socialism (RFE, Polish SR/9, 5 June).

The second part of the current effort to check the church's influence on the younger generation requires all academic institutions to introduce a mandatory course entitled "religious science." The course's entire program was published in *Wychowanie obywatelskie*, and includes lessons on the "class origin" of religion, the study of Christianity and Catholicism in the context of their "attempted adjustment to the capitalist social order," analysis of Zionism as a political phenomenon, and so forth. Recommended reading for the course includes works by Marx, Engels, and Lenin, but not a single religious book—the Bible, for example—is suggested. Finally, the course was elaborated not by Polish academic institutions, but by a Soviet-educated member of the Central Committee's Social Science Academy (RFE, Polish SR/10, 27 June).

This new form of ideological indoctrination met with strong criticism from the Catholic hierarchy as well as from civilian academic institutions. The church questioned the desirability of adding another course to the already overburdened curricula, and pointed out that scientific knowledge of religious phenomena and Marxist knowledge are two different things. In the Marxist view religion is moribund, and the educational system should accelerate the process of decay by imparting the "socialist and scientific (atheistic)" world outlook (*Przeglad katolicki*, 31 August).

More independent criticism of the proposed religious education program calls attention to its political rather than academic character and its lack of consideration for the great majority of students who are practicing Catholics. The course has no educational merits, such as the development of a comprehensive vision of the world (including a religious vision), nor does it stimulate intellectual inquiry into the social sciences and humanities. Its purpose is to channel communist propaganda, which is equally offensive to believers and nonbelievers, because it is "degrading the atheistic convictions of the students who are indifferent to religion." A Warsaw University professor, Edward Ciupak, expressed deep concern over plans to introduce the course with the help of "enthusiastic" teachers trained in "emergency" sessions. (*Polityka*, 2 August.) The "religious science" course is therefore another case of General Jaruzelski's "storming" approach to social and economic problems. He continues to apply administrative and police methods to social and economic problems.

In the long term the church's political program aims to institutionalize pluralism in Poland, including official sanction for youth organizations, clubs, and even the Christian Workers' Federation—an independent quasi–trade union association. Tadeusz Mazowiecki, a prominent member of Solidarity, summarized these pluralist aims: "The church has become the representative of the workers generally in this country, though that doesn't mean it can fix things for them . . . And the freedom of the individual in Poland has become irrevocably linked to the freedom of the church." (*WP*, 14 December.)

Cardinal Glemp and General Jaruzelski's first "summit" meeting produced mixed results. The church agreed to cooperate with the regime on "combating social pathology . . . [and] concern for the natural environment." The church would also play the leading role in maintaining the "patriotic ties joining Poles abroad to their country." Both sides agreed that "restrictive measures against Poland [Western economic sanctions], which harm the nation, should be completely abandoned." (*TL*, 25 April.) A second "summit" in December focused on preparations for a third visit by Pope John Paul II to Poland in June 1987 (Radio Warsaw Domestic Service, 27 December; *FBIS-Eastern Europe*, 23 December.)

Both meetings failed, however, to make any

progress on two essential issues: establishing diplomatic relations with the Vatican and the church's legal right to pastoral activities (*Le Figaro*, 25 April). The church also has abandoned its four-year effort to break from the regime's agricultural foundation because the authorities were unwilling to modify their demand for an "organic" relationship between the foundation and the government. Such an arrangement "would mean *diktat* by the state administration, which would run counter to the assumptions of the foundation, particularly its autonomy" (Radio Vatican City, International Service in Polish, 3 September; *FBIS-Eastern Europe*, 4 September).

**Society.** In the five years since General Jaruzelski deployed military power to crush Solidarity, he has been unable to overcome the deadlock between the regime and Polish society. The Hungarian and Czechoslovak uprisings against communist rule were followed by much more brutal repressions than Poland's martial law, but, unlike those two previous "normalizations," the Warsaw regime has been unable to bribe society by offering a higher standard of living. Unlike Kádár in Hungary or Husák in Czechoslovakia, General Jaruzelski has compromised with his subjects by making political rather than economic concessions. It is quite clear that the regime cannot eliminate political opposition or curb the church. Instead, Warsaw's method of dealing with an unruly society involves tough measures directed against some prominent individuals, followed by equally sudden retreats and calls for reconciliation. This peculiar hit-and-run strategy has produced neither reconciliation nor dispersion of the opposition. Solidarity has been broken, but the line between the union and society has ceased to exist. Opposition is no longer organized on a national level; it is fragmented and preoccupied with micro-social problems, but it includes almost the entire Polish nation. The communist regime in Poland is no longer facing an organized but unarmed foe vulnerable to police methods; it is now confronted by a reluctant nation that by and large ignores its leadership.

The political stalemate in Poland offers hope that one day the regime will again step down from its ivory tower and negotiate with the opposition. Jacek Kuroń, a leading member of Solidarity, explained that, first, the Soviet Union may find the situation in Poland too unstable and accept the idea of limited political pluralism; second, factional struggles within the Polish communist party may open new opportunities for opposition; and, third, Poland may become one of the major East-West issues, and new international compromises may alter the domestic situation (*Dagens Nyheter*, 17 June).

The Polish issue, according to Solidarity, is no longer an internal problem. Not only is Poland an "Afghanistan of Europe," but accelerating political instability and economic collapse is exacerbating international tensions that threaten peace in Europe. This internationalization of the Polish crisis should eventually result in a new status for Poland in European politics, an arrangement that would take into account the political aspirations of the Polish nation. That is, there will be a permanent détente in Europe until the Polish problem is solved. (*Perspektywy*, 11 April.) Sovietization of Poland has failed and is unlikely to succeed in the future; the party has power but is unable to govern. The need to prevent total disintegration of the social order may eventually convince leaders in Warsaw and Moscow that pluralism in Poland would be a "lesser evil" than a violent national revolt.

There are indications that General Jaruzelski's regime is now aware of the gravity of the political situation in Poland and, above all, of the limits of his power. In December, the regime agreed to create a consultative council to advise the Council of State, Poland's collective presidency. The new council, whose membership includes ten individuals nominated by the church, ten individuals nominated by the communist party, and ten nonpolitical independent members, is a "new, experimental form, broadening the platform of search for dialogue, civil initiatives and co-responsibility," according to General Jaruzelski (*NYT*, 7 December).

The regime also has made some concessions to the idea of pluralism in general. Rejecting the concept of pluralism as advocated by Solidarity because it was "borrowed from a different sociopolitical formation," *Trybuna ludu* admitted that the "Polish community is pluralistic" (10 October), and that the socioeconomic situation will continue to deteriorate without political changes. A noted Catholic writer addressed this issue in *Tygodnik powszechny*:

There is no doubt that Poland is crumbling, and he who refuses to believe with his own eyes that this is true should read the dailies. However, what is interesting in this connection is that the Polish press in question describes only effects and avoids like a plague the need to present causes and proto-causes of these effects. Is curing the results of diseases instead of the sources of diseases a right and effective therapy? (5 October.)

Six years after the August 1980 agreement between the communist authorities and Solidarity, none of the major national problems have been solved, and this inability to govern has created a political vacuum and a social demand for opposition. As an organization, Solidarity is destroyed; however, it is alive as an inspiration for reform—as "the search for effective paths to reform, for the best reform" (Lech Wałesa in *Der Spiegel*, 5 November). Ludwik Dorn, another member of Solidarity, perceives the union not so much as an organization but as a movement that is constantly "in the stage of exploration and self-creation," and whose purpose is to organize society "into self-government" bodies of various kinds. Thus, martial law has only a limited and temporary adverse effect on the union. (*Znaki czasu*, no. 1.) The brief legal existence of Solidarity, followed by five years of underground and semilegal activities, have not reduced the popularity and social support of this authentically Polish attempt to change the artificial reality constructed on orders from Moscow. Solidarity today is a Polish version of the "wars of national liberation." Wide social acceptance of the need to find new and effective forms of government has enabled Solidarity to survive.

Solidarity "exists as an ideal deeply rooted in the population," observed Cardinal Glemp. (*Le Monde*, 13–14 April.)

In the first half of 1986, the underground suffered several setbacks. Parallel to the show of strength at the party congress, the regime put five members of the Confederation of Independent Poland (known by its Polish acronym, KPN) on trial. Unlike Solidarity, which claims to be a trade union, the KPN aspires to be a political party openly demanding the "free elections Poland was promised at Yalta." Its leader, Leszek Moczulski, who in the 1970s had a successful career as a historian, advocated overthrowing the communist system in Poland by such nonviolent means as elections. In 1979 he published an article entitled "Revolution Without Revolution," in which he proposed the establishment of a "parallel state" by means of a "creeping revolution" that would slowly erode the communist monopoly of power and eventually lead to total independence—and even a return to the Polish com-

monwealth of nations that included Lithuania, Belorussia, and the Ukraine. The KPN claimed 60,000 members in 1981. (RFE, Polish SR/6, 4 April.)

The leaders of this group were first sentenced by military tribunals in October 1982, but they were released from prison under the July 1984 amnesty. They immediately returned to political activities and were jailed again and sentenced to as many as four years for "membership and leadership of a banned organization" and "incitement to public disorder." (Radio Paris, AFP, 27 April.)

The authorities' biggest success was the 31 May arrest of Zbigniew Bujak, who for four-and-a-half years headed the underground Provisional Coordinating Commission (TKK) of the outlawed Solidarity. He was immediately portrayed as a man "controlled and inspired by Western special services and centers of ideological subversion," and responsible for "actions [that] had led to many tragic events in our state." (Radio Warsaw, PAP, 2 June; *FBIS-Eastern Europe*, 3 June.)

The TKK became famous in Poland for organizing strikes, demonstrations, and boycotts of official elections, as well as for private broadcasts and interviews in underground and foreign newspapers. Bujak's capture by the secret police was described by Lech Wałesa as "one success in a record of failure" by the regime to destroy the underground. (*NYT*, 1 June.) Bujak's ability to avoid police became legendary, and for many he is a national hero, the "most outstanding and courageous fighter for human rights and Solidarity in Poland." Accused of preparing a coup against the communist state, Bujak faced a possible ten-year prison term. At one time, government spokesman Jerzy Urban even alleged that the TKK, in addition to activities aimed at overthrowing the constitutional order, had an "intelligence character," implying that the sentence could be longer. (Radio Warsaw, PAP, 3 June.)

Most embarrassing for the authorities was the TKK's ability to conduct coordinated activities on a national scale. In 1986, several public demonstrations took place in Poland, most notable of which was the so-called counterdemonstration on 1 May, and the celebration of the 30th anniversary of the October 1956 events in Poland. Bujak's arrest, as well as arrests of numerous other leaders, had not affected the TKK's ability to stage demonstrations.

Once political activists began to fill up Polish prisons, Jaruzelski's normalization again acquired the characteristics of martial law. With more than 350 opposition leaders behind bars and facing show trials, Poland could hardly qualify for Western economic help. A successful crackdown on the opposition presented General Jaruzelski with new choices: full-fledged trials that would be highly provocative to Polish and world opinion; negotiations with the opposition that could expose the regime to the public scrutiny it received in August 1980; or retreat and ignore the opposition. Knowing that most of the public is apathetic, the regime chose the third alternative. On 11 September the Polish government announced that it would free all prisoners, including Zbigniew Bujak and Leszek Moczulski. The amnesty embraced everyone accused of political offenses except those charged with espionage, terrorism, sabotage, or treason, and nineteen individuals accused of serious and capital acts (*NYT*, 12 September). Members of the independent pacifist movement, Freedom and Peace (WIP), which challenges the military draft and ties to the Soviet Union (particularly subordination of the Polish armed forces to the Soviet commanders) were not initially released, because they were considered to be common criminals.

Referring to the amnesty, General Jaruzelski stated that it was time to stop playing "hide and seek" (*NYT*, 28 September), while Lech Wałesa reminded the authorities that "only the road of social pluralism can lead to a situation in which prisons will not be refilled very soon again with political prisoners" (*NYT*, 12 September). The amnesty resulted in the release of about 20,000 common criminals out of a total prison population estimated to exceed 100,000 (*San Francisco Examiner*, 14 September).

The amnesty, portrayed as a purely humanitarian gesture, was intended to have internal and external effects. General Jaruzelski decided to assume a conciliatory line and to persuade Poles to take the initiative, especially in economic affairs. No doubt he also hoped to create the conditions necessary to lift Western economic sanctions against Poland. As Michael Kaufman observed in the *New York Times*, the Polish government decided "to show that Western nations no longer have human rights issues as a reason to continue their economic and political isolation of General Jaruzelski's government. This has been appended to the older government's argument that stability in Poland is essential to the peace of Europe and that such stability required the new investment credits that had been blocked since martial law was declared" (15 September).

Solidarity's reaction was a mixture of caution and hope. As with all three previous amnesties, the accused political activists had no right to reject the clemency and demand a trial to prove their innocence. Also, Solidarity believed that the political purpose of the amnesty was to demonstrate that the opposition is ineffective and no longer dangerous to the system. However, the TKK and its clandestine leadership emerged from hiding and established the union's Temporary Council, which includes seven members of the TKK and four other members of Solidarity—with Lech Wałesa acting as chairman. The Provisional Council petitioned the court for a legal restoration of the union, but the authorities concluded that the council was not covered by Polish legislation, and, since its activities could "constitute a danger to public order," its existence would not be legalized. Wałesa chose to ignore the court order, stating that "the decision does not concern us as the council is not a new organization, for we never recognized the government's dissolution of our union." The right of the council to exist is "guaranteed by the Polish Constitution as well as by international conventions signed by Poland," according to Wałesa.

Without legal recognition, the council proceeded to resume political activities, including the establishment of a panel of economic experts. The regime condemned the council as illegal, but has refrained from any harsh measures, especially since Wałesa again asked the United States to lift economic sanctions. Only *Trybuna ludu* published a lengthy attack on Solidarity, calling it "incapable of working out a real program of action," and consequently limiting "themselves to negative destruction, and making their presence known by trying to prevent normal life in the country" (15 October).

As in the past, the regime's attempt to isolate the opposition includes support for the new union that replaced Solidarity. In five years, the membership of this government-sponsored organization has grown to 6.5 million, or 60 percent of the membership Solidarity claimed at the peak of its popularity in 1981. In 1986, the new union was finally permitted to organize on a national level—into the National Alliance of Trade Unions (OPZZ), which is supposedly independent and self-governing. (Radio Warsaw, PAP, 12 August). In 1987 this organization is expected to elaborate a sample collective labor agreement that each factory branch will adapt to its local conditions. This collective labor agreement will regulate the relationship between employee and employer—including pay, health care, social assistance, vocational qualifications, and work standards. Alfred Miodowicz, a member of the Politburo and OPZZ chairman, expects that this new practice will strengthen the new union, although the "administration will not find this a very comfortable state of affairs." He continued, "We must abandon this practice of allowing an official in a ministry to decide about the vital interests of a work force. Today, to live in accordance with the reform, decisions cannot be made at the top for work force and independent enterprises" (*TL*, 13 August).

Despite gains in union membership, the psychological barrier between workers and the authorities persists. The majority of the people are aware that the party "has brought our country to poverty." (Premier Zbigniew Messner over Radio Warsaw Domestic Service, 3 October; *FBIS-Eastern Europe*, 8 October.)

One of Poland's most painful social problems is the housing shortage. It is the principal element of the so-called progressive pauperization, which includes a waiting period of more than twenty years for a new apartment, and collective occupancy of the same flat by several families. The household-to-housing unit ratio in Poland is approximately 120 to 100—worse than in some underdeveloped states. (RFE, Polish SR/6, 6 April.) There are also unofficial reports that Poland has more than 500,000 homeless, 50,000 of them in Warsaw (RFE, Polish SR/2, 2 February). Yet housing construction continues to decline by approximately 12 percent annually (*TL*, 16 April).

Housing construction has become the new union's rallying cry. Under the new collective bargaining agreements, economic enterprises would be required to construct apartments for employees (Radio Warsaw Domestic Service, 6 August; *FBIS-Eastern Europe*, 7 August). Control over housing would provide the union with a powerful blandishment for attracting new membership. Monopolistic control over employment, pay, vacation, and housing will make membership mandatory for everyone employed by the government, while the unions' political role would not deviate from Lenin's recommendation that trade unions should be a "transition belt" between the party and the working class.

Progressive subordination of all social and political institutions to the party has been evident in the agenda of the Sejm (Polish parliament), which in 1986 very closely followed the political program prepared by the party. Numerous legislative acts adopted in 1986 aimed at consolidating and centralizing decisionmaking in the hands of communist authorities, simplifying court proceedings to expedite and facilitate convictions, and implementing the party's economic program without modification. Despite Jaruzelski's assurances, expressed a few years ago, that the party intended to distance itself from daily politics and to give governmental bodies more autonomy, real democratization of political processes never took place. The only significant development is a greater openness of political life, owing to the breakup of the state's information monopoly.

The Polish press is relatively frank about social and economic matters except when they involve criticism of the party apparatus or political and economic relations with the USSR and other Soviet-bloc states. It also makes rather frequent attacks on the West—especially the United States—and Solidarity. As a commentary by Warsaw's *Polityka* stated, the diversity of views is fully legitimate in every pluralistic society, but there are areas in which encroachment is harmful to Poland's international position and East-West relations. Poland's political system should encourage "rival ideas and questioning of the system within the limits of national interest" and, one may add, within the rather narrowly defined "loyal opposition" (5 October).

This unusual freedom of information for a communist-ruled state is necessitated by several factors, including: the enormous popularity of Radio Free Europe and the Voice of America; the social role of the church, including several outstanding Catholic publications; a very active underground press; and opportunities to publish abroad. Because it is almost impossible to conceal facts from the public, the regime is compelled to come up with its own interpretations. The regime continues to discriminate against the church by limiting Catholic publications to less than 2 percent of all material published and denying the church access to radio and television. Occasionally the censor will pass publications that are highly critical of the regime, which is a major embarrassment for the system.

The best-known such incident in 1986 was an article written by Bohdan Urbankowski, deputy chief editor of *Poezja*, in which he summarized postwar Polish literature. Urbankowski called the introduction of communism "crimes committed against the entire nation and its present and future life," because the "Soviet model" of socialism was forcefully imposed on Poland. Urbankowski wrote that genuine Polish culture had been destroyed by the "red encyclopedists and inferior" survivors of World War II who agreed to collaborate with the "new class" that took political power in Poland (*Poezja*, no. 3.)

After three months of procrastination, *Trybuna ludu* (26 June) issued a strong attack on Urbankowski. He was accused of promoting "reactionary and chauvinistic values" and publication of "worthless thoughts," and promptly was dismissed as deputy editor upon the request of the Warsaw branch of the Union of Polish Writers and the regional party organization. Unable to control all Polish publications, the regime expects self-censorship and strikes those who exceed the limits of tolerance.

The quality of the Polish underground press has improved its focus by shifting from criticism of the regime to examination of social ills. Hopelessness and impoverishment are credited with responsibility for spreading alcoholism, prostitution, drug abuse, profiteering, bribes, and illegal trade. It finds most alarming the rapid sovietization of the Polish youth, which is characterized as a "general lowering both of national culture, and resistance to totalitarianism," and a "care-less" attitude. Poland is not in danger of russification, these writers state, because the Russians are despised—but this may not prevent the younger generation from acquiring characteristics of Homo sovieticus, an individual whose life has no meaning and purpose. (*Vacat*, no. 27, April 1985; in RFE, RL *Polish Underground Extracts*, 17 January.)

Poland's catastrophic social degeneration has been well documented by governmental and private sources. Alcoholism should be regarded as the foremost peril. In 1985 per capita alcohol consumption was 8.5 liters per annum; including illicit consumption, the rate would total 11 to 12 liters. And consumption continues to increase. The number of crimes has increased 100 percent since 1982. There are more than 150,000 drug addicts according to the artificially low figures, and some 900,000 young people (5 percent of the population under 30 years of age) are considered to be maladjusted children. The so-called "moral health" of the nation is tragically low as a result of "the negligible extent to which social consensus has been achieved." Many sources suggest that the current situation threatens the physical existence of the Polish nation. (*Znaki czasu*, no. 2; *Rzeczpospolita*, 18 June; RFE, Polish SR/7, 25 April.)

Preoccupied with power, the communist regime is fully responsible for Poland's social decay. There is no realistic plan to arrest social plagues: ideological campaigns are least likely to curb drinking and other social problems. Communism's degradation of the individual is the primary reason for the proliferation of alcoholism, drug abuse, and criminal behavior. Meanwhile, the regime invests in alcohol production to reap huge profits. Polmos, the state-owned producer of vodka and other hard spirits, tops the list of 500 Polish enterprises. Every złoty invested in Polmos yields 2,400 percent profit! (*Zycie Warszawy*, 8 July.)

**Economy.** The economy continues to be the major weakness of Jaruzelski's Poland. It is widely known that the Polish economy is in a very serious decline despite claims of 3 percent real growth in 1986. The regime is condemning inefficiency, low productivity, and outdated industrial practices.

Rising apathy, and the prevailing feeling that the economic situation will continue to deteriorate, inhibits productivity: it is impossible to convince skeptical people to work harder without the prospect of higher real wages. The idea that people should work for future generations is no longer popular as a result of the Polish experience over the past 40 years. To redress the apathy problem, the government continues to increase national income over output, supply of goods to the marketplace, and labor productivity—fueling an unfavorable imbalance of supply and demand. Average earnings in 1986 were 22.7 percent higher than in 1985, causing at least a 19 percent inflation (*TL*, 15 December). Stagnation is perpetuated by strong political pressure to raise wages, the policy of assigning large funds to projects, and structural changes that will produce increased consumption in two or three decades. Poland's economic outlook for the year 2000 is pessimistic. As one commentator noted, the country is likely to find itself "outside the European economy" (*Polityka*, 26 July, 1986).

The inflationary tendencies of the Polish economy are exacerbated by public disengagement from public affairs. This "escape to privacy" fosters economically harmful attitudes, such as "grabbing" goods above the actual need to beat inflation. In addition, the general political inertia of the population manifests itself in an abdication of the responsibility for public property and in poor performance at work. Consequently, public apathy in Poland breeds inflation and low productivity. (*Tydzień pol-*

*ski*, April.) A Polish worker's productivity is one-sixth that of a Swedish worker and half that of a Spanish worker (*CSM*, 14 July).

With the exception of discontinuing the "equal wages" policy (in response to public outcry), the Polish government has not developed effective anti-inflation measures. Ironically, egalitarianism was officially found to be in conflict with the socialist principles of "to each according to his work" and "true justice." Socialism, according to the new perspective, postulates rivalry, competition, and risks, that is, it should provide equal opportunities and rights to everyone, but not an equal share regardless of contribution. Warsaw's *Rzeczywistość* called equal wages "sham equality" and an "unjust exploitation of individuals and teams whose performance is above-average" (20 July; *Polityka*, 12 July). It would be difficult to deny that this form of "socialism" closely resembles the philosophy of free enterprise.

Another reason for Poland's economic failure is the primacy of politics over the economy. The economic reform initiated in 1981 guaranteed autonomy, self-government, and self-financing for state enterprises, and made the managers responsible to the workers' council. Management and the workers were to think and act independently, take initiative, and assume responsibility. Continuing inflationary pressure compelled the authorities to recentralize control over key heavy industries and to deprive workers' self-management bodies of their right to influence decisions on wages and investments. (*WP*, 1 December). These new restrictions indicate that the enterprises' initiative and independence cannot be reconciled with centralized planning and that the economic system has returned to the traditional Stalinist model. This mechanical repetition of old practices is also evident in the expansion of subsidies for enterprises that are supposed to be self-sufficient. The total amount of subsidies for enterprises and consumer goods is estimated to be $8 billion annually. (*WP*, 20 December.)

This return to Stalinist centralized management does not mean that Poland could repeat the Stalinist pattern of extensive economic growth. In 1986–1990, the country will experience the lowest increase in manpower since World War II: about 340,000 individuals. By comparison, Poland's labor force increased 1.6 million from 1971 to 1975 and 1.2 million from 1976 to 1980. The next four years will be complicated further by a large increase in the number of pensioners and young people of school age, while the supply of fuels and basic raw materials will be only two percent higher (*Nowe drogi*, April).

In contrast, Poland's private economic sector has performed well. Deficiencies in services and supplies of numerous goods create spectacular opportunities for private initiative. According to official statistics, the nonagricultural private sector is contributing 5 percent to national income, 4.7 percent to employment, and 2.3 percent of goods for retail sale. However, it is producing 35 percent of the goods for the market. The private sector's biggest role has been in providing 55 percent of Poland's basic services; in some areas, such as passenger taxis, the private sector provides nearly 100 percent of services. (*Zycie Warszawy*, 28 August.)

A special place in Poland's economy is occupied by the 683 Polonia firms. These foreign-financed, private companies operate throughout the country and employ 46,900 people. When Poland opened its doors ten years ago to foreign capital, profitability of investment was very high. Also, the government promised to eliminate bureaucratic difficulties and to exempt these firms from taxes for at least two years. Numerous restrictions, taxes, and other legal obstacles introduced since 1982 have adversely affected the popularity of the Polonia firms. For example, 142 such firms were established in 1984, but only 50 in 1985. Also, it was originally expected that 50 percent of Polonia production would be exported, earning hard currency for the country. However, once these firms were forced to sell 50 percent of their foreign exchange profits to the state—without deducting the costs for imported materials—export became unprofitable, and now exports account for merely 5 percent of overall production. (*Słowo powszechne*, 11 August.)

Equally detrimental was the 1985 directive issued by the Council of Ministers obligating Polonia firms to employ Polish citizens only, hired through governmentally operated employment agencies. Because the rank-and-file workers of Polonia firms earn up to five times more than employees of the government-owned enterprises, a mass exodus of highly qualified specialists had to be stopped by administrative measures.

Facing a decline in both the popularity and export potential of these firms, the Warsaw government reversed some of the most oppressive regulations in a new law enacted on 1 July. Now between 15 and 25 percent of the foreign exchange profits must be sold to the state. Employees with foreign citizenship are entitled to have half their salaries paid in hard currency that can be taken abroad without taxation. (*Rzeczpospolita*, 13 July.)

It is yet to be seen whether the new law will increase foreign investments in Poland. The prevailing attitude of Poland's communist establishment is that this "capitalist" sector is a permanent element of the socialist economy yet a bad example for the working class. Many local officials have instigated "witch-hunts," inspecting private enterprises and exposing their allegedly "criminal" activities. (BBC, 14 June.) In any case, official policy is capricious and arbitrary. And, despite the officially stated commitment to make the private sector a permanent element of Poland's economy, the Polonia firms have a very limited degree of approval. For this reason, Poland is likely to continue to show the lowest rate of investment in the world.

By some estimates, 1986 was a relatively good year for agricultural production. The total sales of all foodstuffs increased by about 6 percent—the result of propitious weather, not structural improvements in the agricultural sector of the economy.

Despite the increase in production for 1986, agriculture's economic situation has deteriorated. Poland has one of the most primitive and inefficient agricultural programs in Europe, for three basic reasons. First, agriculture continues to be one of the lowest state priorities. Only 22.1 percent of investments are destined for agriculture and the food economy, rather than the 30 percent envisioned by the national plan, and investment increases run 50 percent lower in agriculture than in the economy as a whole. Second, technological development is very low; only 6 percent of overall industrial production is designated for agriculture. Consequently, supplies of machines, spare parts, fuels, fertilizers, and other chemicals are inadequate. Third, 75 percent of Poland's farmland is cultivated by private farmers who produce more than 80 percent of all foodstuffs. Private farms are approximately 13 percent more productive than the state farms, yet the latter continue to receive preferential treatment from the government. (*Zycie gospodarcze*, 22 June; *Słowo powszechne*, 10 June.)

Officially, difficulties experienced by Polish agriculture and food processing industries are blamed on economic sanctions imposed by the United States following the Polish government's imposition of martial law in December 1981. The government claims that the agriculture sector alone lost more than $7 billion as a result of restrictions on imports of grain, fodder, and fertilizers. In effect, per capita consumption of meat decreased by 35 pounds in the last five years. (PAP, 30 September; *FBIS-Eastern Europe*, vol. 2, no. 19.)

Recently published statistical data indicate the weaknesses in Poland's rural infrastructure. For example, only 17 of every 1,000 farmers have a telephone; water mains are available in only 20 percent of Poland's villages; only 44 percent of rural roads are hard surfaced; and only 27 percent of rural communities are accessible by paved roads. (*Le Figaro*, 29 January.)

To address some of these problems, in 1982 the church offered to organize and administer an independent agricultural foundation designed to help private farmers. With money provided by Western churches and private organizations and deposited in Western banks, the foundation was to help Polish farmers purchase farm machinery, fertilizers, spare parts, and other badly needed items unavailable in Poland. The church promised to channel more than $2 billion in the course of five years, providing that the assistance would be given only to private farmers, and that the foundation would be autonomous from the state.

After four years of negotiations between the church and the state, talks collapsed in September 1986, and the church officially abandoned its effort to raise hard currency and set up the foundation. While the church considered the foundation a social and economic project, for the regime it became a major political concern. The government welcomed the opportunity to have $2 billion invested in the national economy, but would not accept the idea of an independent foundation. Compromise became impossible when the regime made establishment of the foundation conditional on an investment procedure that required foreign capital collected by the church to be channeled through the state apparatus to both collective and private farms. As in the case of Solidarity, the communist state found it unacceptable to allow an independent organization to function within its framework. (*Przeglad katolicki*, 5 October.)

Officially, the regime expressed regrets about the church's decision and promptly alleged that the real reason for the demise of the foundation was a lack of funds. According to official sources, the church had collected no more than $28 million, that is, slightly more than 1 percent of the original estimate. (*Zycie Warszawy*, 9 September.) The church, on the other hand, never revealed how much money it had at its disposal, but indicated that it would be willing to discuss the idea in the future if the government agreed to drop political conditions.

After four years of intensive negotiations, Poland was readmitted to the International Monetary Fund (IMF) in 1986. Although the country was among the 45 original members of the IMF, Moscow forced Poland to withdraw its membership in 1950. Consequently, the decision to return to the IMF was a political one, because it implied that Poland would not be able to progress without Western assistance. To become eligible for new loans, Poland would be required to open its books to Western creditors. Of the communist-ruled states, only Hungary, Romania, and China are members of the IMF, all of which have the status of developing countries. The official rate of exchange in September 1986 was set at 200 złoty per dollar; thus, per capita income in Poland is about $900. This would place Poland among the poorest states in the world. However, according to the IMF, Poland's per capita income was $3,730 in 1980 and currently is about $3,400.

On the other hand, membership in the IMF is proof of Poland's economic creditworthiness and permits access to large, medium-term (3–5 years) credits. Poland's contribution was set as the equivalent of 680 million Special Drawing Rights (SDR), which could entitle the country to borrow as much as $800 million ($1.17 per SDR). In some cases, Poland could borrow as much as 450 percent of its SDR share, that is, almost $4 billion.

The original share assigned to Poland in 1950 was $125 million. By now it would have increased ten times, enabling the country to borrow as much as $8 billion. Also, had Poland been a member of the IMF in the 1970s, when it borrowed more than $20 billion from Western creditors, the irrational use of these funds most likely would have been prevented. (*Tygodnik powszechny*, no. 22; RFE, Polish SR/10, 27 June.)

In 1987 Poland could be eligible to borrow several billion dollars through the IMF program, but this is conditional on the implementation of four drastic steps intended to stabilize the nation's economy. First, the government must cut subsidies for industry and consumer goods to $5 billion from the current $8 billion. Second, heavily subsidized prices for utilities and raw materials such as coal must be increased by 26 percent, to bring prices closer to the cost of extraction. Third, more realistic exchange rates between the Polish złoty and hard currencies must be introduced. Finally, the government would have to stop runaway inflation by placing a ceiling on wage increases. From 1982 to 1985, wages increased by almost 80 percent rather than the anticipated 50 percent. (UPI, 20 December; *TL*, 21–22 December.)

Poland's membership in the IMF and its relatively good crop in 1986 is not reason enough to be optimistic about the performance of the Polish economy. The foreign debt continues to increase, reaching $31.2 billion plus $5.3 billion in transferable rubles as of March 1986. Polish exports to the West fell 5.3 percent from a year earlier, while imports increased by 1.2 percent. Warsaw continues to devalue its currency to promote exports. In 1986 alone, the Polish złoty was devalued twice: in early February from 147 to 170 to the dollar, and in September to 200 to the dollar. The dollar's black market value in 1986 was up to 850 złotys—100 złotys higher than the previous year. The ruble is worth 91 złotys. (*WSJ*, 2 September.)

While the Polish government is short on hard currency, it is estimated that up to $3 billion is privately held. Over $800 million is deposited in about three million hard currency accounts used to purchase goods provided by 634 hard currency shops (PEWEX). In 1985 a $300 million turnover was recorded; as much as half of that was accounted for by the sale of alcohol. This "internal export" system, which makes all kinds of goods available to customers who receive hard currency from abroad, is frequently criticized as incompatible with the socialist system, but the popularity of these stores and their high profit margin provide a convenient instrument for channeling privately owned hard currency into the state treasury. (RFE, Polish SR/7, 25 April.)

Warsaw registered substantial hard currency losses as a result of the accident at the USSR's Chernobyl nuclear plant and Poland's consequent radiation risk. The radiological situation in Poland is still unclear. Government sources claim that up to 500 times normal radiation levels were recorded and that the iodine content of milk samples exceeded by as much as 72 percent the recommended "emergency level" for children. Yet data provided by Solidarity and by Polish officials to the International Atomic Energy Agency in Vienna reported radiation levels 6,000 times higher than normal. (RFE, Polish SR/10, 27 June.)

Sixteen West European countries, plus the United States, Canada, and Japan, imposed restrictions on food imported from countries within 600 miles of Chernobyl. Polish officials estimate that the country lost $35–56 million in foreign sales and tourism. A fraction of these losses was recovered when Moscow bought 12,000 tons of Polish beef with hard currency. (*WP*, 25 July.) The export of Polish food to the West was one of the few positive developments in Poland's foreign trade. Poland earned $642 million from food exports in 1981, $711 million in 1983, $829 million in 1984, and $938 million in 1985. In 1986 Poland expected to earn $1 billion rather than the planned $1.5 billion. (*TL*, 13 May.)

In conclusion, the Polish economy continues to decline on all fronts. The government simulates economic reforms and the people simulate work. There have been no changes in the five-year political-economic impasse: the regime is unwilling or unable to compromise with the people, and the opposition has been too weak to obtain meaningful changes. This is an old story in Poland's 40 years of communist rule, and it has always produced the same result—violent confrontation. Many believe another explosion is imminent, and for this reason General Jaruzelski and his supporters have recently been nicknamed the "scapegoat team."

**Foreign Affairs.** The past five years were very difficult for Poland's foreign policy. The imposition of martial law to break Solidarity left the regime isolated in the international arena without any means to balance Soviet pressure. The West's political and economic boycott of the Jaruzelski regime intensified socioeconomic difficulties and complicated "normalization." The regime has been unable to regain its proper place internationally, especially the considerable prestige it had enjoyed in the 1970s when Warsaw was a very important link in East-West détente. Edward Gierek, first secretary of the ruling communist party, was a frequent visitor in West European capitals and in Washington, and Warsaw hosted numerous international meetings. Solidarity's sixteen months of international attention focused world opinion on Polish affairs, but Poland's international relevance declined almost simultaneously with the termination of both détente and the nation's experiment with democracy.

Solidarity destroyed Poland's prestige in Moscow and other Soviet-bloc states sensitive to any spontaneous social movement, and the restoration of the Soviet-type system with the help of terroristic measures discredited the regime's prestige in the West. Poland suddenly became identified with the USSR and, like Soviet republics, became totally irrelevant in international affairs.

The process of rebuilding Poland's international position has been slow and is far from completed. It appears that Jaruzelski's domestic policies gained cautious acceptance in Moscow, but relations with the West are yet to be mended. Warsaw has managed to reactivate links only with such neutral European states as Finland, Austria, and Greece. Considering Poland's economic situation it was much easier for the regime to broaden contacts with such Third World countries as India, Libya, Algeria, and Tunisia, which are interested in low-quality and low-priced industrial goods manufactured in Poland.

The dubious internal legitimacy of Poland's communist regime pressures Polish authorities to show that their regime has full and unconditional recognition from leading Western states—above all the United States. In addition, contacts with the United States are the major source of the technological knowledge and hard currency that determine the pace of Poland's economic development and the internal acceptance of the regime. Western economic sanctions resulted in the worst economic regression and political instability since World War II. As long as U.S. sanctions are in force—especially the moratorium on new loans and the suspension of the most-favored-nation clause—and until the heads of major Western states visit Warsaw or Polish leaders visit Western capitals, Poland will not regain respect, nor will the regime command respect at home. The international position of Poland improved in 1986, but Poland's isolation is still intact.

Officially, Poland's foreign policy has three priorities. First, the prime focus of Poland's foreign policy is the tie with Moscow and other Soviet-bloc states. "In the divided world," explained Poland's foreign minister, Marian Orzechowski, "ties with the socialist community provide the opportunity to live in peace, and are a foundation of our national security" (Radio Warsaw, PAP, 13 June; *FBIS-Eastern Europe*, 17 June). He failed to admit that Soviet ties are the only guarantee that Poland's communist elite can rely on to stay in power. Second, Poland's relatively successful Third World policies forced the regime to identify itself with developing states and to place relations with countries in Asia, Latin America, and Africa above contacts with the West. This reorientation is artificial and somewhat demeaning to the Polish national pride, because the country cannot ignore its advanced neighbors in Western Europe and North America. It is merely an exotic way of pretending that Polish diplomacy is as busy as ever. Third, there is the policy of "peaceful coexistence" with the Western states. This policy is dependent on mutually beneficial relations and is "based on respect for the principles of international law"—a phrase used by the Soviet-bloc states to characterize Western criticism of their politics as unlawful interference in domestic affairs.

Poland appears to be the most faithful Soviet servant in international affairs. Official statements in the press are saturated with the glorification of the USSR, the Warsaw Pact, and the Soviet-controlled CMEA. In January, Jaruzelski recalled Poland's ambassador to the Soviet Union, Stanisław Kocio-łek, a hard-line opponent of Jaruzelski's domestic policies, and replaced him with career diplomat Włodzimierz Natorf. Kociołek is a notorious Stalinist who was responsible for the bloody suppression of strikes in 1970. He is highly antagonistic to Solidarity and the church. Preoccupied with personal conflicts and opposition to Jaruzelski, Kocio-łek was ineffective in shoring up USSR economic support for Poland (*LAT*, 4 January). Like Foreign Minister Orzechowski, the new Polish envoy to Moscow is a graduate of a Soviet university; both enjoy Moscow's confidence and support. The Soviet agreement to replace Kociołek "signaled a measure of support for the Polish policies of the party and economic change" (*NYT*, 4 January).

Soviet-Polish economic and scientific exchange intensified in 1986 as a direct result of improved relations and implementation of the 1984 "Long-Term Program for Development of Economic and Scientific-Technological Cooperation Between the PPR and USSR Until the Year 2000." That agreement placed Poland's economy into Soviet hands, and it is expected that Soviet-Polish trade will increase by 35 percent in the next five years (*TL*, 9 January). The agreement specified 219 areas of cooperation, of which 160 have been formalized. The scientific and technological research program covers 85 research problems and involves the cooperation of 93 Polish and 180 Soviet institutes. Of the 44 agreements envisaged, 33 have been signed. (Radio Warsaw, PAP, 20 October; *FBIS-Eastern Europe*, 21 October.)

USSR assistance became crucial for the functioning of the Polish economy and significantly tightened Moscow's control over Poland. The Soviet economic invasion of Poland over the past five years has great political and economic significance, because Moscow can manipulate Warsaw by economic means. A large part of Polish industry is directly linked to Soviet enterprises and appears to be independent of its own government.

This submission to Moscow, especally in foreign policy and economic areas, was rewarded by a restoration of Poland's status as the first major ally of the Soviet Union. During the Twenty-seventh Party Congress of the CPSU, General Jaruzelski was treated with special respect and personal attention by Mikhail Gorbachev, who was the only head of a ruling communist party to visit Warsaw for the PZPR's Tenth Congress. The Soviet foreign minister, Eduard Shevardnadze, arrived in Warsaw before the Polish congress to express Soviet approval of Jaruzelski's policy. Moscow received new assurances and the means to influence Warsaw, but also "came to accept Polish nationalism as a fact of nature and of honor." (*NYT*, 9 March.)

For the sake of Polish public opinion, the alliance with the USSR is presented as an expression of the most vital national interest. The authorities imply that everything Polish, including Poland's liberation from the Nazi occupation, its current borders, international status, and development, is made possible by the "friendship and alliance" with the Soviet Union (Foreign Minister Orzechowski, in *Gazeta lubelska*, 19–20 April). This official assessment of mutual relations failed to recognize that Poland's sovereignty is severely limited by the Soviet Union and that the country depends excessively on a military giant that is economically backward and weakened internally by ideological and social crises.

As expected, Poland followed USSR foreign policy in global and regional matters without any attempt to show independent initiative. Foreign policy statements delivered by Polish officials, for example, Orzechowski's 25 September speech at the U.N. General Assembly session in New York, were no more than an echo of the Soviet line.

Poland's relations with the Soviet-dominated states of Eastern Europe have followed closely the general trend toward military-economic integration set by Moscow. Intrabloc diplomatic activities have concentrated on methods of implementing the comprehensive programs planned for bilateral cooperation up to the year 2000. Poland signed long-term economic agreements with East Germany and Hungary for joint industrial production, research, and specialization concerning mutual enterprises. The general framework of cooperation was elaborated during General Jaruzelski's December 1985 visit to East Berlin, followed by Premier Zbigniew Messner's talks with East Germany officials in October 1986. (Radio Warsaw, PAP, 8 October; *FBIS-Eastern Europe*, 9 October.) Political terms of the Polish-Hungarian economic exchange were worked out during the March "working visit of friendship to Poland" by János Kádár, general secretary of the Hungarian communist party (*TL*, 29–31 March). Specific conditions for implementing the "comprehensive program" of developing relations between Poland and Hungary were formulated during Messner's visit to Budapest in September. (Radio Warsaw, PAP, 5 September; *FBIS-Eastern Europe*, 9 September.)

Polish trade with East Germany and Hungary is expected to increase by 30 percent during the next five years, largely stimulated by Soviet credits made available to Poland. The total amount of these credits has not been published. However, it is known that during the next two years the country will receive Soviet credits amounting to about 1.7 billion rubles (Radio Warsaw Domestic Service, 3 March; *FBIS-Eastern Europe*, 4 March), and it is very likely that Poland's intrabloc debt of 6 billion rubles will double by the end of this decade.

By comparison, Polish-Czech relations are developing slowly, owing to Prague's lack of confidence in Jaruzelski's liberal approach to the opposition. Foreign Minister Orzechowski's visit to Czechoslovakia in September resulted in nothing more than a statement of support for Soviet foreign policy. (Radio Warsaw, PAP, 7 September; *FBIS-Eastern Europe*, 9 September.)

The ultraconservative Czech regime is highly apprehensive about the state of political affairs in Poland. On 16 August *Rudé právo*, Czechoslovakia's Central Committee daily, published a lengthy article entitled "Postcards from Kraków," which attacked the political climate at Jagiellonian University. The article claimed that current party membership among students is now minimal after a two-thirds drop in membership during 1980–1986. The article also claims that "thus far, neither Marxism-Leninism, nor scientific communism, nor other disciplines they were teaching prior to the crisis have been reinstated." Moreover, while activities of the officially recognized student organizations are rare, the "church is setting up clubs at local churches, in which young people can comprehensively develop their personalities [and] it arranges summer camps for parents and children almost gratis." It is evident that the Czech leaders, who are currently the most orthodox in the Soviet bloc, are uneasy with General Jaruzelski's "normalization," which permits tampering with pluralism. A more repressive regime in Poland would add legitimacy to the harsh political reality in Czechoslovakia.

The Polish press and radio in 1986 was, by and large, paying little attention to Czechoslovakia, and from time to time one could find criticism of Prague's discrimination against Polish tourists, who were charged high fees for repair work and currency exchange, and were sometimes even refused assistance. (Radio Warsaw Domestic Service, 5 August; *FBIS-Eastern Europe*, 6 August.)

Returning from the CPSU party congress, General Jaruzelski met with Lithuanian communist party officials on 28 February and 1 March in Vilnius (*TL*, 1–2 March). This highly controversial and emotional foreign policy initiative required personal approval by the Soviet leader, since it evoked memories of the Polish-Lithuanian commonwealth that for four centuries had contained Russian expansion to the West. Just two years ago Poland celebrated the 200th anniversary of its union with Lithuania. Vilnius was a Polish city until 1939 and was the birthplace of many patriots who distinguished themselves in the struggle against Russian domination. Jaruzelski's trip to Lithuania had strong nationalistic overtones and demonstrated that the Soviets had a high degree of confidence that he would not exceed the limits of the USSR's tolerance for nationalistic expression.

The Polish leader's "working" visit to China at the end of September was an even more significant political event. Originally, General Jaruzelski was scheduled for talks in Mongolia and North Korea; only three weeks before his departure, China was added to his itinerary. Most likely, Warsaw did not want to be left behind in the Chinese effort to improve relations with Eastern Europe, so General Jaruzelski promptly arranged a visit to Beijing before East German leader Erich Honecker's announced "official goodwill visit" in October and Hungarian leader János Kádár's visit planned for early 1987. (BBC, *Caris Talks*, no. 105/86, 26 September.)

The significance of General Jaruzelski's visit to Beijing was strongly emphasized by the Polish press, which continually stressed bilateral "summit" dialogue between the two countries and unconditional support for methods of internal modernization in both China and Poland. Polish-Chinese economic cooperation had been developing rapidly, and in 1986 Poland became China's second-largest trading partner among the Soviet-bloc states, after the Soviet Union. (*TL*, 1 October.)

Another purpose of Jaruzelski's visit was to act as a Soviet proxy. General Jaruzelski was the first East

European leader other than Nicolae Ceauşescu to visit China in the past 30 years, and his visit should be "regarded by the Chinese as conciliatory gestures by Moscow itself and as indirect Soviet diplomatic signals of a readiness to improve interparty political and ideological relations" (RFE, RL *Background Report* 144, 3 October).

In addition to China, Polish officials traveled to Australia, the Philippines, and Egypt; representatives of several less-developed countries, including the Yemen Arab Republic, Iraq, and Zimbabwe, visited Warsaw to conclude economic agreements. Every such foreign exchange is described by Polish officials as an important step in breaking through the isolation imposed by the West after Poland's imposition of martial law.

Relations between Poland and major West European states were confined to a number of low-level contacts and visits to Warsaw by former heads of state. The most embarrassing, perhaps, was the "postponement" of an official trip to Britain by Foreign Minister Marian Orzechowski owing to Britain's attempt to "downgrade the visit" by refusing to set up appointments for Orzechowski with leading British officials (*NYT*, 10 April). Orzechowski's visit to the Federal Republic of Germany proceeded as planned and resulted in follow-up visits by West German businessmen and other officials. The expansion of economic relations had little positive effect on political ties. Polish–West German relations are complicated by such controversial issues as the interpretation of history in schoolbooks, the finality of the Oder-Neisse border, the question of "revanchist" West German territorial claims against Poland, and the size of the German minority in Poland. No progress has been achieved in any of these areas. In fact, Orzechowski described his visit to Bonn as limited in purpose. "We tried," he stated, "to work out a balance sheet of sorts of all these matters to 'clear the foreground' to define and name all that is harmful to our relations, all that hinders them or is necessary to give them new impulses" (*TL*, 8 April).

Although the Polish government has not overcome its isolation, the primate of Poland, Józef Cardinal Glemp, has been received very much like a head of state in Paris and Rome. The church—for the time being at least—has assumed a quiet but effective role representing the Polish nation abroad. It may even appear for a time that a *sui generis* division of labor has been established between the party and the church in Poland, with the party

assuming primary responsibility for relations with the Soviet Bloc and the Third World, and the church particularly active in the West. Representatives of the Polish Catholic hierarchy are frequent visitors in Western capitals, and without exception they are received by state authorities and frequently by heads of state—while those from the Warsaw government are not welcomed at all.

Polish-U.S. relations in 1986 can be divided into two periods: before and after the amnesty law came into force in Poland. At the beginning of the year, Poland's attitude toward the United States had been unusually hostile. For example, the Polish authorities exploited the *Challenger* tragedy by linking the U.S. space program with arms in space. Following the U.S. air strike against Libya, the Polish press accused Washington of piracy and state terrorism. Government press spokesman Jerzy Urban concluded that "U.S. aggression against Libya constitutes a challenge to the entire international community. It is a glaring example of arrogance and contempt for world opinion" (Radio Warsaw Domestic Service, 15 April; *FBIS-Eastern Europe*, 16 April). *Żołnierz wolności*, the official newspaper of the Polish Armed forces, assailed President Reagan for escalating "neoglobalism," "feverish adventurism," and a "gunboat party" (January 16). These crude statements were aimed at characterizing U.S. actions as a campaign for military superiority in order to coerce smaller nations such as Poland into obedience.

These and many other unceremonial attacks on the United States precluded the improvement in relations expected after the March visit to Warsaw of Walter J. Stoessel, Jr., a former ambassador to Poland, the Soviet Union, and West Germany (*LAT*, 27 March). His unofficial negotiations with Polish officials, including a meeting with General Jaruzelski and Cardinal Glemp, were expected to produce a turnaround in relations. Yet, except for the United States' tacit agreement to accept Poland's application to the International Monetary Fund, the Stoessel mission failed to reduce tensions. Instead, relations deteriorated in the spring and summer because of two unexpected incidents.

The first incident was a somewhat comical development that involved the U.S. Senate's resolution to send 50,000 tons of dry milk to Poland when the Chernobyl accident caused Polish milk to become radioactive. Before the milk was shipped, however, Senator Jesse Helms introduced an amendment restricting American milk deliveries to *private* Polish organizations—primarily the church—for distribution among the people. Warsaw was offended, but not enough to decline the milk, and reciprocated with the "humanitarian" gift of some 6,000 blankets and sleeping bags for the American homeless. The sleeping bags were never delivered, because the U.S. Customs Service imposed a tariff of up to $100,000 for the Polish gift. (*WSJ*, 7 July.) Needless to say, the sleeping bag affair did not improve Polish-American relations.

More serious and embarrassing for the U.S. authorities was the publication in the Polish press of the so-called Kukliński affair. Colonel Kukliński, member of the Polish general staff until he left Poland in November 1981, informed the United States in detail about plans concerning the introduction of martial law. However, U.S. authorities failed to warn Solidarity. While Washington decided to ignore this controversy, implying that by withholding the information it had prevented civil war in Poland, Warsaw used the Kukliński affair as an example of American duplicity and lack of scruples. (*Polityka*, 25 July.)

In June the second volume of *A Policy of the United States of America Towards Poland in the Light of Facts and Documents (1984–1985)* was published in Poland. Like the first volume, the political work accused the United States of blackmailing Poland by means of economic sanctions, interfering in internal affairs, supporting organizations struggling to overthrow Poland's constitutional system, propaganda aggression, and attempting to isolate Warsaw in the international arena. The book reiterated the Polish claim that American economic sanctions resulted in $15 billion in losses from 1981 to 1985. The U.S. sanctions have become a convenient scapegoat for economic problems caused by gross mismanagement. By enumerating alleged American sins against Poland, Warsaw appeared to be advancing preconditions for normalization. Polish authorities repeatedly have insisted publicly that the United States should reverse its policy toward Poland, and have privately wondered why Poland, still the most liberal state in Eastern Europe, continues to be on top of the blacklist while more oppressive regimes such as Romania enjoy U.S. trade

and credits. It should be noted, however, that while trade with the United States is certainly important for the Polish economy in terms of access to high technology and hard currency, such trade has never exceeded 3.3 percent of Poland's total foreign trade (RFE, Polish SR/12, 13 August). For the most part, good relations with the United States are a source of political prestige for the Warsaw regime: using the "American card" augments Poland's internal legitimacy and earns Soviet respect. Poland's unconditional amnesty, which freed virtually all political prisoners, also opened new opportunities in Polish-American relations.

The United States did not respond immediately, apparently in order to ensure that Warsaw would not rearrest the freed political prisoners and proceed with the show trials. After Washington was convinced that the amnesty was permanent, and as the result of appeals by nine Polish intellectuals (RFE, Polish SR/17, 18 November) the U.S. Department of State announced that Deputy Secretary of State John C. Whitehead would visit Warsaw in late January or early February 1987 to "continue our dialogue with the government of Poland, which we are in the process of reinvigorating" (*WP*, 31 December). If this visit is successful, Polish-American negotiations may slowly improve and may lead to the exchange of ambassadors, a withdrawal of the remaining economic sanctions (especially the ban on new government-guaranteed credits), and the reinstatement of Poland's most-favored-nation status.

In conclusion, during 1986 Warsaw acquired some room for maneuvering in international affairs by gaining credibility in Moscow, expanding the scope of its economic and political relations with the Third World and Western Europe, and creating conditons for, eventually, a full normalization with the United States. One may wonder, however, whether the Polish authorities are not doing too little too slowly to surmount the economic and social crises that threaten Polish national identity.

Arthur R. Rachwald
*U.S. Naval Academy*

# Romania

**Population.** 22,830,000
**Party.** Romanian Communist Party (Partidul Comunist Român; PCR)
**Founded.** 1921
**Membership.** 3,557,205 (31 December 1985)
**General Secretary.** Nicolae Ceauşescu
**Political Executive Committee (PEC).** 21 full members, 7 of whom belong to the Permanent Bureau: Nicolae Ceauşescu (president of the republic), Emil Bobu (chairman, Council on Problems of Economic and Social Organization), Elena Ceauşescu (first deputy prime minister, chairwoman, National Council of Science and Instruction), Constantin Dăscălescu (prime minister), Manea Mănescu (vice president of the State Council), Gheorghe Oprea (first deputy prime minister), Gheorghe Rădulescu (vice president of the State Council); other full members: Iosif Banc, Virgil Cazacu, Lina Ciobanu (chairwoman, Central Council of the General Union of Romanian Trade Unions), Ion Coman, Nicolae Constantin (deputy prime minister), Ion Dincă (first deputy prime minister), Miu Dobrescu (chairman, PCR Central Collegium), Ludovic Fazekas (deputy prime minister), Alexandrina Găinuşe (deputy prime minister), Paul Niculescu, Constantin Olteanu (first secretary of the Bucharest PCR Municipality Committee), Gheorghe Pană (chairman of the Committee for People's Councils' Affairs), Ion Pățan (chairman, State Committee for Prices), Dumitru Popescu (rector of the "Ştefan Gheorghiu" PCR Academy); 26 alternate members: Ştefan Andrei (chairman, Council of Workers' Control and Economic and Social Activities), Ştefan Bîrlea (chairman, State Planning Committee), Nicu Ceauşescu (first secretary of the Central Committee of the Communist Youth Union, minister of youth), Leonard Constantin, Gheorghe David (minister of agriculture), Petru Enache (vice president of the State Council), Mihai Gere, Maria Ghiţulică, Nicolae Giosan (chairman, Grand National Assembly), Suzana Gâdea (chairwoman, Council of Socialist Culture and Education), Mihai Marina, Ilie Matei, Vasile Milea (minister of national defense), Ioachim Moga, Ana Mureşan (minister of domestic trade), Elena Nae, Marin Nedelcu (minister of machine-building industry), Cornel Pacoste (deputy prime minister), Tudor Postelnicu (head of the State Security Department), Ion Radu, Ion Stoian, Gheorghe Stoica, Iosif Szasz (vice-chairman, Grand National Assembly), Ioan Totu (minister of foreign affairs), Ion Ursu (first vice-chairman, National Council of Science and Technology), Richard Winter (minister of wood industry and building materials)
**Secretariat.** 11 members: Nicolae Ceauşescu, Ştefan Andrei, Iosif Banc, Vasile Bărbulescu, Emil Bobu, Ion Coman, Silviu Curticeanu, Petru Enache, Maria Ghiţulică, Constantin Radu, Ion Stoian
**Central Committee.** 265 full and 181 alternate members
**Last Congress.** Thirteenth, 19–22 November 1984, in Bucharest; next congress scheduled for 1989
**Last Election.** 17 March 1985; of the record number of 15,733,060 registered voters, 15,732,095 (97.8 percent) cast their votes for the candidates of the Socialist Democracy and Unity Front (SDUF), while 356,573 (2.3 percent) voted against them (which is 125,962 more than in 1980). Next elections are scheduled for 1990.
**Auxiliary Organizations.** Union of Communist Youth (UTC, 4 million members), Nicu Ceauşescu, first secretary; General Union of Romanian Trade Unions (7 million members), Lina Ciobanu, chairwoman of the Central Council; National Council of Women, Ana Mureşan, chairwoman; Councils of Working

People of Hungarian and German Nationalities, Mihai Gere and Eduard Eisenburger, respective presidents; Socialist Democracy and Unity Front (SDUF), Nicolae Ceauşescu, chairman, Manea Mănescu, first vice-chairman, Tamara Maria Dobrin, chairwoman of the Executive Bureau

**Publications.** *Scînteia*, Ion Mitran, editor in chief, PCR daily (except Monday); *Era Socialistă*, PCR theoretical and political biweekly; *România Liberă*, SDUF daily (except Monday); *Lumea*, foreign affairs weekly; *Revista Economică*, economic weekly. Agerpres is the official news agency.

The Romanian Communist Party (PCR) was founded on 8 May 1921, in Bucharest, as a section of the Communist International. It operated legally until April 1924, when it was outlawed by the Liberal government then in power. After its delegalization, a party center continued to operate underground in Romania, while a parallel leading center was established in Moscow. Throughout all its clandestine years, the PCR evinced a total and unconditional support for the Stalinist international strategy. Primarily composed of militants belonging to ethnic minorities, the PCR failed to espouse and endorse Romanian national aspirations. It was therefore widely perceived as an alien political body, profoundly and consistently committed to promoting the expansionist designs of the Soviet Union. The party lacked an organic basis within the Romanian working class and was adamant in its anti-intellectual stances. Compared to other East European communist parties, the PCR was strikingly powerless and sectarian, a radical minority with no genuine national roots.

Following the occupation of the country by the Soviet Army, the PCR played an increasingly influential role. Benefiting from external support and the general post-Yalta conditions, it managed to gain national stature. The PCR was instrumental in the neutralization and then suppression of traditional political parties. It engineered the destruction of the Romanian parliamentary system. The establishment, under Soviet pressure, of a left-wing government led by fellow traveler Petru Groza on 6 March 1945, as well as the rigged elections of November 1946, facilitated the task of Romanian communists. The PCR was committed to implementation of a so-called people's democracy, which was only another name for totalitarian dictatorship. Internecine struggles within the party leadership resulted in the elimination of the Muscovite faction headed by Ana Pauker and Vasile Luca (May–June 1952) and the triumph of "national" communists grouped around Gheorghe Gheorghiu-Dej.

The PCR was extremely active in the anti-Yugoslav campaign that followed the Cominform resolution in June 1948. It can be surmised that Gheorghiu-Dej succeeded in ingratiating himself with Stalin personally and thus received the Soviet dictator's blessing for his masterful coup against the Muscovite faction. This denouement of the struggle for power within the Romanian communist elite should be interpreted in the light of the anti-"cosmopolitan" witch-hunt waged by Stalin in his later years. The headquarters of the Cominform was moved from Belgrade to Bucharest, and Romanian leaders were adamant in their support for Soviet politics.

Nicolae Ceauşescu's political career was marked by his decades-long association with Gheorghiu-Dej. He had been directly involved with various purges, including the rabid anti-intellectual campaigns of 1957–1958. He also benefited by elimination from the Politburo in June 1957 of a powerful rival and one of the very few intellectuals in the PCR leadership, Miron Constantinescu. At the First Congress of the Romanian Workers' Party (Partidul Muncitoresc Român; PMR), Ceauşescu was elected a member of the Central Committee. At the Second Congress in 1955, he was promoted to the Politburo and became a national secretary.

Under Gheorghiu-Dej, the PCR opposed any attempt at liberalization and implemented a harsh Stalinist program of industrialization. Forced collectivization of agriculture took a heavy toll on the Romanian peasantry and further alienated the regime from the population. Incessant persecution aimed at intellectuals and party dictatorship over literature and the arts enabled the ruling elite of the PCR to gain undisputed control over the country. Gheorghiu-Dej and his partisans were suspicious of Khrushchev's calls for de-Stalinization and resented Soviet plans to establish a supranational, "integrated socialist economic system." It was under Gheorghiu-Dej that a statement of the PCR's position on relations between communist-ruled countries was published in April 1964, at a moment when the Sino-Soviet polemic had become open. This declaration emphasized national values and condemned attempts to violate the principles of equality, sovereignty, and independence. Romanian communists under Gheorghiu-Dej first normalized and then intensified relations with Tito's Yugoslavia. Prime Minister Ion Gheorghe Maurer's visit to Paris in 1964 encouraged many observers to think that Romania was headed toward a self-styled East European "Gaullism." The autonomist temptation was conspicuous in the Romanian reluctance to support Soviet anti-Maoist stances. There were even signs of moderate relaxation in domestic policy: Western art exhibitions opened in Bucharest, the dogma of socialist realism was gradually abandoned, and a certain cultural diversity was tolerated by the party.

Nicolae Ceauşescu succeeded to the PCR leadership in March 1965 and enhanced Gheorghiu-Dej's politics of economic autonomy vis-à-vis the Soviet Union. After a short-lived liberalization between 1965 and 1971, the regime reasserted its Stalinist legacy both in socioeconomic and cultural policy. No genuine reform developed in Romania, and ideological orthodoxy maintained its tight grip over all intellectual life. Certain spectacular foreign policy initiatives were presented as proof of the country's much trumpeted independence: diplomatic relations with Israel after 1967, diplomatic relations with West Germany established before Ostpolitik, condemnation of the Warsaw Pact invasion of Czechoslovakia in August 1968, an overture toward the nonaligned movement, and so forth. In 1971, following Ceauşescu's visits to China and North Korea, a new wave of Stalinism struck Romania: it seems that the general secretary was particularly impressed with the political advantages resulting from an all-pervasive cult of personality. This artificially inspired phenomenon has become the main source of authority and legitimacy for the Romanian leader.

A dogmatic approach to economic issues and a systematic refusal to acquiesce in any form of market-oriented experiments generated serious difficulties during the late 1970s and early 1980s. The working class was increasingly dissatisfied with low salaries and permanent food shortages, while the "new agricultural revolution," proclaimed by Ceauşescu as a panacea for the country's agricultural crisis, failed to improve living standards in the rural areas. Unfavorable economic conditions and an unswerving commitment to bureaucratic centralism dramatically worsened socioeconomic conditions in Romania. Ceauşescu's ambitious decision to pay off all foreign debts by 1990 resulted in a draconian program of austerity that severely affected the life of the whole population.

An increasing estrangement between the general secretary and the party's rank and file has been accompanied by an unprecedented concentration of power in the hands of the Ceauşescu clan. The exacerbated cult of Ceauşescu's personality has transformed political life in contemporary Romania into a mockery. Persistent rumors circulated in 1985 and 1986 concerning a deterioration in the health of the general secretary, and there were speculations regarding preparations for a dynastic succession. National apathy and universal distress are phenomena noticed by foreign observers (*NYT*, 30 November). The general impression offered by Romania at the end of 1986 is that "of a nation perennially standing in line with empty shopping bags and returning home with bags scarcely fuller" (ibid., 4 January 1987). The dominant opinion in Romania is that the country is experiencing the worst economic and political crisis in its history. Consequently, the prevailing mood is one of bitter skepticism and unconcealed anguish.

**Leadership and Organization.** In the documents of the Central Committee plenum, held during 1–2 April, there are detailed statistics on the numerical strength and social composition of the party. According to these data, on 31 December 1985, the PCR consisted of 3,557,205 members, almost 15 percent of the country's population. Of the total, some 61 percent came from the ranks of the workers and more than 15 percent from those of the peasants. The number of women in the PCR reached 1,185,351 (33 percent) at the end of 1985 (*Scînteia*, 8 April). Speaking at the Bucharest meeting on the 65th PCR anniversary, Nicolae Ceauşescu referred to the role of the party in contemporary Romania: "Drawing the necessary conclusions from its long-standing activity, we must act with great determination to constantly strengthen its unity and organizational and ideological strength in order to continuously increase, in keeping with the new conditions, its political role in all fields of activity." (*FBIS*, 21 May.)

Ceauşescu's cult of personality intensified, particularly on such occasions as his birthday (26 January) and his carefully staged visits to local economic units. In a letter addressed to Ceauşescu by the Political Executive Committee (PEC) on 26 January, the sycophantic language reached Byzantine servility: "The deep gratitude for the everlasting merits you have in creating such a party have been and are strongly expressed in the ardent and resolute will of all the communists and the entire nation which, by electing you at the 9th PCR Congress to the supreme leading position in the PCR, have brilliantly and unanimously reasserted this historical option at all the following congresses, strongly demonstrating the will of all the sons of the homeland to have you always at the head of the party and country and of the struggle waged to build Romania's new socialist and communist destiny. During this period of heroic struggle and great achievements which is recorded in history with golden letters, for centuries on end, bearing the name of its great founder—"Nicolae Ceauşescu Era"—with legitimate pride, all our nation views you, much esteemed and beloved Comrade Nicolae Ceauşescu, as the wise and clearsighted leader who unites and guides all the nation's creative power toward fulfilling a great target and toward attaining unprecedented achievements in its millenia-old existence." (*Scînteia*, 27 January.) According to these paeans, the general secretary would be the greatest personality in all Romanian history, the guarantor of the country's progress and independence, the visionary architect of its future.

This avalanche of worshipful rituals compels the members of the party elite to reaffirm their association with Ceauşescu, preventing them from any attempt to keep a low profile and thus to shun further compromising their careers (RFE, *Situation Report*, 24 February). No one feels secure in contemporary Romania, and there are reasons to believe that high-ranking party officials may resent the most outrageous features of the Ceauşescu cult. It seems quite obvious that members of the upper stratum of the Romanian nomenklatura are upset by their growing job insecurity (ibid., 11 September). The perpetual game of musical chairs practiced by Ceauşescu continued in 1986. On 18 January, Ion Cioara was replaced by Eugen Tarhon as the minister of forestry. On 6 May, Ion Păţan, the minister of light industry and a member of the PEC, was replaced for "health reasons" by a former deputy prime minister, Alexandrina Găinuşe. Five weeks later, Păţan was appointed chairman of the State Price Committee, replacing Aneta Spornic, who was promoted to the position of deputy prime minister. The most puzzling and significant demotion concerned former prime minister Ilie Verdeţ, who was eliminated from the PEC and the Central Committee in connection to his "election" to the honorary position of chairman of the Central Auditing Commission. There were rumors in Bucharest that Verdeţ had managed to antagonize Elena Ceauşescu, primarily because of his less rigid approach to economic matters. Reliable sources in Bucharest described Verdet as embarrassed by Mrs. Ceauşescu's attainment of control over the party

bureaucracy. A witness of Nicolae Ceauşescu's early career under Gheorghiu-Dej and his close associate before Elena's irresistible ascent, Ilie Verdeţ shares responsibility with the general secretary for the main political decisions made after the Ninth Congress in 1965. His ouster is indicative of Nicolae Ceauşescu's growing distrust of people once supposed to represent the mainstay of his power. Another meaningful personnel change was the appointment of Ceauşescu's brother-in-law, Vasile Bărbulescu, as a Central Committee secretary. (*FBIS*, 23 October.)

The other beneficiary of the personality cult is the general secretary's wife. Elena Ceauşescu is not only a first deputy prime minister and chairwoman of the National Council on Science and Instruction, but also head of the party's Commission for Cadres. This last position enables her to exert direct control over all organizational activities and to facilitate the careers of people closely associated with the presidential clan. Furthermore, it should be kept in mind that Elena Ceauşescu is mainly responsible for the promotion of certain women to top party and government functions, including the national party Secretariat. Alexandrina Găinuşe, Lina Ciobanu, Maria Ghiţulică, Tamara Dobrin, Elena Nae, Aneta Spornic, and other prominent women in the PCR hierarchy owe their current positions directly to Mrs. Ceauşescu and represent a potential power base for her. Emil Bobu, the national secretary in charge of security police affairs, is also one of Mrs. Ceauşescu's protégés. The same appears to be true of Tudor Postelnicu, chief of the security police (Securitate). On the occasion of her birthday, Mrs. Ceauşescu was portrayed as a personality as prominent as her husband. She was praised as a providential leader of the nation, "the party's torch," "the woman-hero," "the hero of the fatherland," and "our tricolor." The message sent by the PEC to Mrs. Ceauşescu took care to emphasize her merits in international politics as well: "Serving with self-denial the interests of the country, of the Romanian people, and the cause of socialism on the Romanian soil, you, much esteemed Comrade Elena Ceauşescu, have also asserted yourself as a tireless promoter of the most thrifty ideals of understanding, cooperation, and peace among nations and as a brilliant militant for defending the fundamental rights of the nations and of the peoples to life, to a free and dignified existence, to independence, sovereignty, and peace." (RFE, *Situation Report*, 10 January.)

Another peculiar Romanian development consists of the spectacular rise to political prominence of Nicu Ceauşescu, the couple's youngest son. At the Thirteenth RCP Congress in November 1984, Nicu was elected an alternate member of the PEC. His wife, Poliana Cristescu, was promoted to full membership on the Central Committee. Confronted with the growing apathy and dissatisfaction of Romanian youth, Nicu obediently follows the directives of his father. As one Western journalist noted, Ceauşescu blames "outside influences" for the disaffection of young people with his regime, and he has cracked down on "unsuitable" Western movies or music groups outside the officially approved performances attuned to the authorities' political needs and tastes (*CSM*, 4 April). Trying to foster an international image for himself, Nicu indulged in restless external contacts. In April he led a delegation of the Union of Communist Youth (UTC) to a consultative meeting in Moscow with leaders of youth organizations in socialist countries. In June he visited Poland and had talks with Polish party and government officials. In September Nicu Ceauşescu attended an international "Youth and Peace" seminar at the Black Sea resort of Costineşti. In November he made a trip to the Middle East and developed contacts with officials in Iraq and Jordan (*FBIS*, 10 November). That same month, he headed the UTC delegation to a meeting of the World Federation of Democratic Youth in Budapest (*Scînteia*, 30 November). Nicu Ceauşescu was assigned the task of mobilizing Romanian youth for the fulfillment of huge economic projects. In September he took the floor during a festivity marking the conclusion of activities on the national youth building site of the Poarta Alba-Midia-Năvodari canal.

Other members of the family have been placed in key party and government positions: Lieutenant General Ilie Ceauşescu, one of the president's brothers, remains deputy minister of defense and head of the Higher Political Council of the Armed Forces. Another brother, Nicolae A. Ceauşescu, performs an influential function as chief of the cadres department of the Internal Affairs Ministry. A third brother, Ion Ceauşescu, is first vice-chairman of the State Planning Committee and a de facto member of the government.

There is no doubt that all these measures are bound to enhance the power of the hegemonic group and to strengthen Ceauşescu's domination over the party apparatus. Members of the nomenklatura are disgruntled with the preeminent role granted to Mrs. Ceauşescu and tend to question both her revo-

lutionary credentials and the legitimacy of her power. There is no coherent and consistent party line in contemporary Romania, except the often contradictory and confusing "indications" of the general secretary. Western correspondents describe the current Romanian course as characterized by "erratic financial tactics and extreme domestic policies" (*WP*, 28 October). The possibility of an imminent succession seems to have preoccupied foreign embassies in Bucharest, and particularly the Soviet ambassador, Yevgeny Tyazhelnikov. The USSR reportedly has intensified its watch over Romania, developing contacts with party officials and dispatching more advisers to supervise the ailing Romanian economy (*Insight*, 21 July).

**Domestic Affairs.** The structure of party and government institutions in Ceauşescu's Romania is often disconcerting. The general secretary has favored a policy of formal economic reorganization instead of pursuing genuine reforms. As a result, mixed party-government bodies have emerged that are supposed to coordinate PCR decisions with government legislation.

The main aim of Romania's economic plan for 1986 was to boost industrialization. At the April Central Committee plenum, Nicolae Ceauşescu expressed sharp criticism of Romania's economic performance. This criticism was not accompanied by a daring strategy of economic liberalization, but by routine political urges for yet tighter control and more centralization. Ceauşescu's plans to reduce manpower by up to 40 percent in certain industrial units and on state farms met with criticism, on the grounds that it might bring about unemployment (RFE, *Situation Report*, 2 July). The dire economic situation in Romania was noted by foreign journalists, including observers from neighboring Yugoslavia. A commentary about the situation in Romania and Bulgaria began by asking "whether Ceauşescu has anything new to say in international relations or might he be drawing closer to Moscow in order to get some major help because of Romania's even worse internal situation." (Ibid., 19 August.) Romanian opposition to any reformist attempts was voiced by party ideologues who echoed Ceauşescu's conservative approach to the issue of economic decentralization. The regime clings to obsolete Stalinist economic dogmas and unflinchingly defends its theoretical orthodoxy. (Ibid., 11 August.)

Since all events in Romania are usually attributed to Ceauşescu's personal initiatives, it is surprising that he was proclaimed a "Hero of the New Agricultural Revolution." In a speech delivered on Harvest Day (19 October), Nicolae Ceaușescu announced that Romania had harvested 28,000,000 tons of grain in 1986. Some remarks by Ceaușescu to party activists in the agricultural field suggest that the figures for cereal output may have been manipulated. According to the general secretary, the harvest "victory" was the result of efforts to modernize agriculture through mechanization, the use of chemical fertilizers, irrigation, land reclamation, and a generally better use of land. Romanians tend to be skeptical about the party's claim of great achievements in agriculture, since it seems unlikely that they would necessarily translate into improved food supplies for the population. (Ibid., 6 November.)

Unlike other communist leaders, Nicolae Ceaușescu has made repayment of the foreign debt, a result of irrational economic investments in his early years in power, a first priority. The whole economy works now to reduce Romania's debt, and harsh measures of austerity have been imposed on the population. Since 1982, Romania has approximately halved a foreign debt estimated at its peak to have reached $14 billion (*NYT*, 4 January 1987).

*Increasing Repression.* Ceaușescu continued his ambitious project to restructure the center of Bucharest and thereby destroy valuable historical monuments. In October he announced his intention to turn Tirgoviste into the second capital city of Romania. His vainglorious approach to historical matters and the egregious nationalism displayed by party propaganda further aggravated relations between the leadership and various social and ethnic sectors. The plight of the Hungarian minority in Romania is already well documented and has provoked an intensification of the now open polemic between Bucharest and Budapest (*Contemporanul*, 6 December 1985). Speaking on Budapest television on 3 September, several prominent Hungarian journalists strongly criticized Romanian authorities for their failure to eliminate severe disruptions in tourist traffic between the two countries. Unveiled criticism of Romania was allowed to appear in official Hungarian publications and Romanian media did not hesitate to reply (BBC, *CARIS report*, 5 September). Increasing discontent was also expressed by representatives of the German minority in Romania.

Human rights groups in the West decry religious persecution in Romania and have urged the U.S.

Congress to revoke or suspend the most-favored-nation trading status that Romania has enjoyed for the past ten years. According to various human rights groups in the United States, the Romanian regime has consistently restricted the religious freedom of evangelical Christians through arrests, fines, and restrictions on freedom of assembly. Clandestine efforts to import the Bibles needed to service the expanding number of Protestant converts in Romania have been met with beatings and imprisonments (*CSM*, 18 August). A semiannual report on human rights in Eastern Europe, issued by the U.S. State Department in June, said that "Romania's observance of basic human rights continues to be poor" (*NYT*, June 4). A new trend toward activism in defending church rights seems to have developed among lower-level Orthodox clergy in Romania. Most of these active priests are followers of Father Gheorghe Calciu, who emigrated to the United States in 1985 after many years of imprisonment and persecution. Contacts with foreigners were reduced to a minimum as a result of a new decree on preservation of state secrets. To quote the title of an essay by Dorin Tudoran, an exiled Romanian intellectual, "frost and fear" are the lot of the Romanians forced to struggle for survival under the Ceaușescu dictatorship. The title of a *Scînteia* editorial sums up the atmosphere of stifling suspicion so characteristic of the regime in recent years: "Strengthening Vigilance and Militancy in Protecting State Secrets and the People's Revolutionary Achievements—a Priority Patriotic Duty of Each Citizen" (*Scînteia*, 6 August).

**Foreign Affairs.** The major initiative adopted by Ceaușescu in 1986 was his organization of a national referendum on a 5 percent reduction in military spending (for manpower and arms). At a mass meeting in November, the general secretary announced that immediately after the referendum Romania would reduce its armed forces by 10,000 men, 250 tanks and armored vehicles, 130 artillery and grenade launchers, and 26 combat planes and helicopters. Military spending for 1987 would be curtailed by $130 million, according to Ceaușescu. The Romanian leader made this proposal to various Warsaw Pact organs, but his ideas were not applauded by other communist leaders. The Romanian voter turnout was reported nearly perfect; only 228 eligible citizens did not take part in the plebiscite. All Romanians at least fourteen years old were required to vote and sign their ballots (*NYT*, 23, 25 November). The referendum was staged as a major propaganda show aimed at revamping Ceauşescu's image as an adamant champion of peace and an opponent of superpower diplomacy.

*Communist Regimes.* Relations with the USSR seemed to improve, primarily because of Romania's dramatic need for energy supplies and raw materials. Nicolae Ceauşescu attended the Twenty-seventh CPSU Congress in February and subsequently visited Moscow again in May. A long-term program for the development of economic, scientific, and technical cooperation between the USSR and Romania through the year 2000 was signed by Ceauşescu and Gorbachev on that occasion (*FBIS*, 6 June). The latest Soviet foreign trade statistics indicate a massive expansion of Romanian food exports to the USSR. At the same time, Romanian agricultural exports to the West have been significantly declining. Meat constitutes almost half of food exports to the Soviet Union, and Romania ranks third as the USSR's supplier of vegetables and fruit. This trend is apparently the result of Soviet insistence that increased deliveries of energy and raw material be compensated partly by deliveries of foodstuffs (RFE, *Situation Report*, 19 August). In the same direction, Romania appears to have made more extensive commitments than any other CMEA country to the development of energy and raw materials resources in the Soviet Union for the 1986–1990 period.

Contacts with other communist regime leaders included a June visit to Romania by Premier Zhao Ziyang of China. The communiqué issued at the end of his visit emphasized the willingness of both countries to develop and intensify their party and state relations. The following month Romania received the visit of the Yugoslav foreign secretary, Raif Dizdarević (*FBIS*, 9 July). Also in July, Ceauşescu received East German Politburo member and Central Committee secretary Egon Krenz. In October a meeting of foreign affairs ministers of the Warsaw Pact states took place in Bucharest. Taking the floor during a reception for the delegations, Nicolae Ceauşescu voiced strong Romanian support for the USSR position taken during the summit in Iceland. His perspective, however, was a bit different from the Soviet one with respect to the continuation of negotiations between the superpowers: "We believe that the issue of nuclear weapons in Europe can be solved without linking them to the whole package of problems, and they are in no way connected to the question of the

1972 treaty and virtually can be approached and solved independently" (*FBIS*, 21 October).

During his official visit to Romania in October, the Soviet minister of foreign affairs, Eduard Shevardnadze, informed Nicolae Ceauşescu about the content of the Reykjavik summit between Mikhail Gorbachev and Ronald Reagan. Following Shevardnadze's visit, the Romanian leader avoided reiterating his controversial views on the "linkage" issue. In November Ceauşescu received Nikolai Ryzhkov, chairman of the Council of Ministers of the USSR, who headed the Soviet delegation to the forty-second CMEA meeting in Bucharest (*FBIS*, 4 November). In November Romania received the official visit of President Sinan Hasani of Yugoslavia. In December Nicolae and Elena Ceauşescu met with Bulgarian party and state leader Todor Zhivkov (*Scînteia*, 19 December). On that occasion Zhivkov was awarded one of the highest Romanian state decorations.

*Western Contacts.* In April Ilie Văduva, then Romania's foreign minister, visited West Germany. The two main issues on the agenda were economic relations and Romania's German minority. It seems Bonn made it clear to Romanian officials that human rights and minority problems are closely linked to increased economic cooperation (RFE, *Situation Report*, 26 May). Prime Minister Turgut Ozal of Turkey visited Bucharest in June and was received by Nicolae Ceauşescu. In September Didier Bariani, secretary of state at the Ministry of External Relations of France, visited Bucharest. Also in September, Prime Minister Andreas Papandreou of Greece visited Bucharest. In his toast during the official reception, the Greek statesman expressed admiration for Ceauşescu's policy and described the Romanian leader as "a personality who influenced the world's outlook on independence, peace, and progress" (*FBIS*, 12 September). Romania and Greece tend to share a common view of the role of the Third World in international politics and have similar anti-Western resentments.

*Middle East.* The increasing orientation of Romanian foreign policy toward the Third World was illustrated by extensive contacts with political personalities from the Middle East. The president of Lebanon visited Romania in June. In September Ion Stoian, Romanian Central Committee secretary in charge of international affairs, visited Damascus and was received by President Hafez al-Asad. Yasir Arafat, the chairman of the PLO, is one of Ceauşescu's favorite partners in political talks. Romanian media describe the PLO leader as a personal friend and comrade of the PCR general secretary. In both February and August Arafat was an official guest in Bucharest, and in September Ceauşescu received the deputy supreme commander of the "Palestinian Revolution Forces" (*FBIS*, 22 September). Attempting to play a more significant role in Middle East politics, Ceauşescu invited representatives of the PLO and of the Israeli-Palestinian Dialogue Committee to a meeting in Romania in November, but no impressive results came from that gathering (*FBIS*, 7 November). In December President Hosni Mubarak of Egypt visited Bucharest and conferred with Ceauşescu.

*Third World Relations.* Romania's relations with the nonaligned movement constitute a pillar of Ceauşescu's foreign policy. Ceauşescu often tends to perform as a Third World rather than a communist leader. He seems to be fascinated by the prominent position Tito held as a promoter of nonalignment and would like to inherit the late Yugoslav leader's authority in the Third World. Foreign Minister Ion Totu attended (as an observer) the summit meeting of nonaligned countries in Harare, Zimbabwe, in September. Since 1976 Romania has been a member of the Group of 77 and has acquired the status of a permanent guest of the nonaligned movement. There are indications that this Third World trend in Romanian diplomacy expresses the ideological preference of Elena Ceauşescu, "whose political proclivities are for the sort of radical, left-wing, and independent-minded states that can be found in the Third World." (RFE, *Situation Report*, 11 September.) In October, Nicolae Ceauşescu reiterated his disapproval of the Vietnamese occupation of Cambodia and called for making that country "an independent nonaligned state" (ibid., 6 November).

**International Party Contacts.** A Romanian delegation participated in the Seventeenth Congress of the Italian Communist Party in April. In May Ion Stoian, the Romanian party official in charge of international relations, was received by Meir Vilner, general secretary of the Communist Party of Israel, and held conversations with leaders of the Labour Party in that country (*JPRS-Eastern Europe*, 5 May). In May Nicolae Ceauşescu received Jorge del Prado, general secretary of the Peruvian Communist Party. Also in May, Ceauşescu had a friendly meeting with Santiago Carrillo, head of one of the competing Spanish communist factions and former general secretary of the Communist Party of Spain. In July, an PCR delegation led by Ion Coman visited Portugal and met with Alvaro Cunhal, general secretary of the Portuguese Communist Party. A Romanian delegation attended the festivities organized in Spain in October to mark the 50th anniversary of the International Brigades. The delegation was received by the general secretary of the Communist Party of Spain, Gerardo Iglesias. In October, Nicolae Ceauşescu met Alvaro Cunhal on the occasion of the latter's visit to Romania.

A willful style of political leadership, compounded with a hoarding power in the hands of a tiny group of people surrounding the party's general secretary, has brought Romania to the brink of social and economic disaster. Economic and political mismanagement are obvious to any independent observer of the situation in the country. For the time being, however, there are no suggestions that cogent alternatives to the country's domination by the Ceauşescu clan have been formulated or envisioned within the party apparatus. That political group seems no less confused and powerless than other social sectors in a climate of false enthusiasm and profound despair over the future.

Vladimir Tismaneanu
*Foreign Policy Research Institute, Philadelphia*

# Union of Soviet Socialist Republics

**Population.** 278.7 million (TASS, 1 January); 279,904,000 (CIA, July); 281 million (AP, 19 December).
**Party.** Communist Party of the Soviet Union (Kommunisticheskaia Partiia Sovetskogo Soiuza; CPSU)
**Founded.** 1898 (CPSU, 1952)
**Membership.** 18.5 million (*Pravda*, 4 June 1984); 44.1 percent workers; 12.4 percent peasants; 43.5 technical intelligentsia, professionals, administrators, and servicemen; women, 27.6 percent of all party members, 33 percent of candidates; estimated total membership as of 1 January 1987, 19.1 million
**General Secretary.** Mikhail S. Gorbachev
**Politburo.** (Unless otherwise indicated, nationality is Russian; first date given is year of birth, second date is year of election to present Politburo rank.) 11 full members: Mikhail S. Gorbachev (b. 1931, e. 1980), Geidar A. Aliev, Azerbaijani (b. 1923, e. 1982, first deputy chairman [first deputy prime minister], Council of Ministers), Viktor M. Chebrikov, Ukrainian (b. 1923, e. 1985, chairman, Committee for State Security [KGB]), Andrei A. Gromyko (b. 1909, e. 1973, chairman of the Presidium [president], Supreme Soviet), Egor K. Ligachev (b. 1920, e. 1985), Nikolai I. Ryzhkov (b. 1929, e. 1985, chairman [prime minister], Council of Ministers), Vladimir V. Shcherbitsky, Ukrainian (b. 1918, e. 1971, first secretary, Ukrainian Central Committee), Eduard A. Shevardnadze, Georgian (b. 1928, e. 1985, foreign minister), Mikhail S. Solomentsev (b. 1913, e. 1983, chairman, Party Control Committee), Vitali I. Vorotnikov (b. 1926, e. 1983, chairman, Russian Soviet Federated Socialist Republic [RSFSR] Council of Ministers), Lev N. Zaikov (b. 1923, e. 1986); 7 candidate members: Piotr N. Demichev (b. 1918, e. 1964, first deputy chairman of the Presidium [vice-president], USSR Supreme Soviet), Vladimir I. Dolgikh (b. 1924, e. 1982), Nikolai N. Slyunkov (b. 1929, e. 1986, first secretary, Belorussian Central Committee), Sergei L. Sokolov (b. 1911, e. 1985, minister of defense), Yuri F. Solovyev (b. 1925, e. 1986, first secretary, Leningrad oblast party committee), Nikolai V. Talyzin (b. 1929, e. 1985, first deputy chairman [first deputy prime minister], Council of Ministers), Boris N. Eltsin (b. 1931, e. 1986, first secretary, Moscow city party committee)
**Secretariat.** 11 members: (* indicates members of Politburo): *Mikhail S. Gorbachev (general secretary), *Egor K. Ligachev (ideology and personnel), *Lev N. Zaikov (economy), *Vladimir I. Dolgikh (heavy industry), Aleksandra P. Biryukova (b. 1929, light industry), Anatolii F. Dobrynin (b. 1919, international affairs), Aleksandr N. Iakovlev (b. 1923, propaganda), Vadim A. Medvedev (b. 1930, ruling communist parties), Viktor P. Nikonov (b. 1929, agriculture), Georgi P. Razumovsky (b. 1936, cadres), Mikhail V. Zimianin, Belorussian (b. 1914, culture)
**Central Committee.** 307 full and 170 candidate members were elected at the Twenty-seventh CPSU Congress. The Central Committee apparatus is organized under 21 departments; key department heads include Anatolii F. Dobrynin (international), Nikolai I. Savinkin (b. 1913, administrative organs), Vladimir A. Karlov (b. 1914, agriculture), Nikolai E. Kruchina (b. 1928, administration of affairs), Anatolii I. Lukyanov (b. 1930, general), Georgi P. Razumovsky (party organizational work [cadres]).
**Status.** Ruling and only legal party
**Last Congress.** Twenty-seventh, 25 February–6 March 1986, in Moscow
**Last Election.** Supreme Soviet, 4 March 1984; more than 99.9 percent of vote for CPSU-backed candidates, all 1,500 of whom were elected; 71.4 percent of elected candidates were CPSU members.

**Defense Council.** The inner circle of the leadership concerned with national security affairs; only the chairman is publicly identified. Chairman: Mikhail S. Gorbachev; probable members, as of 1 January 1987: Andrei A. Gromyko, Lev N. Zaikov, Marshal Sergei L. Sokolov. Possible members or associates: Nikolai I. Ryzhkov, Egor K. Ligachev, Viktor M. Chebrikov, Anatolii F. Dobrynin, and Marshal Sergei F. Akhromeyev (b. 1923), the chief of staff and first deputy minister of defense.

**Government.** 98 members of Council of Ministers, including three first deputy chairmen (first deputy prime ministers), ten deputy chairmen (deputy prime ministers), 59 ministers, and 24 chairmen of state committees. Key members of the government not identified above include Vsevolod S. Murakhovsky, Ukrainian (b. 1926, first deputy chairman, Council of Ministers, and chairman, State Committee for the Agroindustrial Complex), Guri I. Marchuk, Ukrainian (b. 1925, deputy chairman for science and technology, Council of Ministers), Aleksandr V. Vlasov (b. 1932, minister of internal affairs), Lev A. Voronin (b. 1928, deputy chairman, Council of Ministers and chairman, State Committee for Material and Technical Supply).

**Auxiliary Organizations.** Communist Youth League (Kommunisticheskii Soiuz Molodezhi; Komsomol), 42 million members, led by Vladimir Mironenko, Ukrainian (b. 1953); All-Union Central Council of Trade Unions (AUCCTU), 132 million members, led by Stepan A. Shalayev (b. 1929); Voluntary Society for the Promotion of the Army, Air Force, and Navy (DOSAAF), led by Admiral Georgi M. Egorov (b. 1918), more than 65 million members; Union of Soviet Societies for Friendship and Cultural Relations with Foreign Countries

**Publications.** Main CPSU organs are the daily newspaper *Pravda* (circulation more than 11 million), the theoretical and ideological journal *Kommunist* (appearing 18 times a year, with a circulation over 1 million), and the semimonthly *Partinaia zhizn'*, a journal of internal party affairs and organizational matters (circulation more than 1.16 million). *Kommunist vooruzhennykh sil* is the party theoretical journal for the armed forces, and *Agitator* is the same for party propagandists; both appear twice a month. The Komsomol has a newspaper, *Komsomolskaia pravda* (6 days a week), and a monthly theoretical journal, *Molodaia gvardiia*. Each USSR republic prints similar party newspapers in local languages and usually also in Russian. Specialized publications issued under supervision of the CPSU Central Committee include the newspapers *Sovetskaia Rossiia*, *Selskaia zhizn'*, *Sotsialisticheskaia industriia*, *Sovetskaia kultura*, and *Ekonomicheskaia gazeta* and the journal *Politicheskoe samoobrazovanie*. TASS is the official news agency.

The Soviet Union experienced several years of leadership disarray in the late 1970s and early 1980s. As the Brezhnev era neared its close, an aging, feeble leadership clung vainly to power. Then came unprecedented instability at the top, with four men successively occupying the post of General Secretary in a period of 28 months. Moreover, under Brezhnev's "business as usual" approach, problems had been allowed to fester. The souring economy, featuring slow growth rates, technological backwardness, and an intractable crisis in agriculture, contributed to a general social malaise, evidenced by rampant alcoholism and corruption, low birthrates, and a noticeable decline in popular morale. Finally, the apparent foreign policy successes of the 1970s were followed by a series of setbacks in the 1980s, and the world "correlation of forces" seemed to be turning against the USSR.

Against this background, the Soviets had opted for a new course with the March 1985 election of Mikhail S. Gorbachev as General Secretary of the CPSU. For the remainder of that year, Gorbachev set a blistering pace, cajoling the citizenry to greater efforts, cracking down on corruption and alcoholism, and grasping the reins of power more quickly than had any previous Soviet leader. An impressive performance at the November Geneva summit conference stamped Gorbachev as a highly competent and articulate new leader on the world stage.

The year 1986 was not as kind to the new leader as 1985 had been. The Twenty-seventh CPSU Congress further consolidated Gorbachev's authority, but perhaps not to the extent anticipated. Conservative opposition to some aspects of Gorbachev's reform program apparently increased during the year. Moreover, it was still not clear how far Gorbachev wished to go in reforming the system. His tentative answer for the economy—"intensification"—was considered by most foreign economists to be inadequate to achieve the desired results. And a flood of criticisms and exhortations in the official press indicated that progress was not really satisfactory on any front. The Chernobyl disaster in April provoked a maelstrom of complications at home and abroad and provided the first real test of the policy of *glasnost'* (openness), a test that the leadership initially failed. The blow-up of the Reykjavik summit in October was not necessarily a failure from the Soviet viewpoint, but Gorbachev seemed thus far unable to derive tangible benefits from his fresh approach to superpower diplomacy, since negotiations yielded no arms control agreement that might relieve political and economic pressures at home.

**Party Congress.** The Twenty-seventh CPSU Congress met in Moscow from 25 February to 6 March. The congress was attended by 4,993 registered delegates and by 152 delegations from 113 foreign countries (*Pravda*, 26 February).

As the first congress under Gorbachev's leadership, the conclave marked a milestone in the transfer of power from the "old guard" to a somewhat younger, and certainly more vigorous, cadre corps. Its principal business was the endorsement of the new course plotted by Gorbachev, rallying of support for the five-year and fifteen-year economic plans, and formal ratification of the new CPSU program, which replaced the discredited document adopted at the Twenty-second CPSU Congress in 1961.

The tone and major theme of the congress were indicated at a press conference on the eve of the convocation conducted by Leonid Zamyatin, who enjoyed a "last hurrah" as head of the International Information Department of the CPSU Central Committee. "The CPSU holds," Zamyatin said, "that, in present-day domestic and international conditions, all-around progress of Soviet society can be insured along the lines of accelerating socio-economic development. This is the party's strategic course which is directed toward a qualitative remaking of society." Major contributing factors in the achievement of this broad aim would be "the renovation of the material-technical base on the basis of the achievements of the scientific and technological revolution" and "the refining of social relations, first and foremost, in the economy" (TASS, 24 February).

Major speakers at the congress emphasized "intensification" of the economy, technological development, and the restoration of discipline and accountability in party, state, and society. In all this there was general agreement—not surprising in view of the carefully planned and controlled agenda and the need to present an image of a monolithic

party to the general public. However, there were important differences in emphasis and some overt disagreement, evoking doubts about the degree of consensus among the hierarchs on major aspects of the renovation drive. As usual, the congress was highlighted by two key speeches, the political report delivered by the general secretary and the report on the economy presented by the prime minister.

In his marathon opening address, Gorbachev frankly acknowledged economic shortcomings of recent years and called for "intensification" and restructuring of economic activity. He admitted that "production of most types of industrial and agricultural output in the Eleventh Five-Year Plan did not reach the levels which were outlined by the Twenty-sixth Congress" (*Pravda*, 26 February). The long-range problems of the economy Gorbachev largely attributed to concentration upon "extensive" development long after such an approach had become outmoded:

> The forms of production relations, the system of running and managing the economy currently in force gradually took shape in the conditions of an extensive development of the economy. Gradually they became obsolete; they began to lose their role as incentives, and here and there they turned into impediments. Currently, we are striving to change the thrust of the economic mechanism, to overcome its cost-intensive nature, to target it toward enhancing quality and efficiency, accelerating the progress of science and technology and strengthening the role played by the human factor. (Ibid.)

As he had done in previous speeches, Gorbachev spoke of "restructuring," "acceleration," and "intensification." Although the general secretary, in the course of his five and one-half hour address, provided many details on the economy, he failed to offer anything resembling a complete blueprint. The sum total of his proposals and projections certainly did not amount to "radical reform," a phrase used by Gorbachev in his speech and which represented an escalation of his rhetoric on economic recovery. Attitudes of officials, managers, and workers again drew major attention; foot-draggers on restructuring were likened to a Gogol character who conceived "all sorts of wild schemes" but in practice "did nothing and changed nothing." Laggards and opponents of his program were sternly warned: "Personnel who adopt such a position can expect no peace. We are simply not going the same way. Our path has even less in common with those who hope that things will settle down and go back into the old rut. There will be none of that, comrades." (Ibid.)

Gorbachev did adumbrate two important economic departures. While stressing the importance of increased autonomy for individual enterprises under the general direction of Gosplan, an oft-repeated Gorbachev position, the general secretary added a special twist for agriculture. Farmers would be assigned fixed five-year production targets; any surplus could be disposed of "according to the farmer's own judgment." Gorbachev also acknowledged that there should be more emphasis upon commodity-money exchange as opposed to administrative fiat: "It is time to overcome the bias against commodity-money relations and their underuse in planning practice." (Ibid.)

The speech also contained extensive remarks on retooling of the economy and the upgrading of consumer goods and services. But, on the whole, the keynote address maintained Gorbachev's cautious approach to actual changes in the economy. There was certainly no hint of movement toward a "market economy" or the Chinese and Hungarian "mixed" models of socialism. Most observers concluded that Gorbachev was either reserving more radical remedies for later, in case "intensification" did not work, or had been forced to mollify elements in the leadership (probably including Ligachev, Gromyko, and Ryzhkov) who were suspicious of widespread experimentation. Some Western sovietologists, however, noted that Gorbachev appeared to display greater confidence than previously in his insistence upon the need for change and his adamant position that nothing would be allowed to slow the momentum of "restructuring."

The international section of the report was fairly predictable. The United States was blamed for most international tensions and for the lack of progress on arms control; the Strategic Defense Initiative (SDI) continued to be the centerpiece of criticism of the Reagan administration. Two potential areas of agreement were suggested: accords on the halting of nuclear tests and the "elimination of U.S. and Soviet missiles in the European zone." Moscow's goal of detaching Western Europe from the United States, to whatever extent possible, was lightly touched upon: "The CPSU considers one of the basic sectors of its foreign policy to be the European one. Europe's historic chance, and its future, lies in

peaceful cooperation between the states of that continent." (Ibid.)

Gorbachev emphasized that "the Asian and Pacific sector is of growing importance." In that sector, he said, there are many "tangled knots and contradictions." Beginnings of efforts should be made, Gorbachev continued, to "remove the acuteness of military confrontation in different areas of Asia" and then to stabilize those situations.

There was no real clue in the speech indicating that Gorbachev had opted for either side in the debate reportedly going on behind the scenes in Moscow between officials who stressed the priority of superpower relations and those who wanted relations with the United States downplayed, with more emphasis upon Western Europe and medium-range powers elsewhere. Gorbachev did, however, firmly endorse continued tactical flexibility and expressed a willingness to accept the support of left-leaning elements in both the developed countries and in the Third World that might support Soviet foreign policy goals: "The Soviet public is prepared to continue developing links with noncommunist movements and organizations, including religious ones, which come out against war." (Ibid.)

Ryzhkov's economic report was necessarily more detailed than the political roundup; it was also a more conservative speech. Notably, in two areas where Gorbachev had hinted at innovations—more flexible prices and the extension of wholesale trade in consumer goods—Ryzhkov was reticent or unenthusiastic (*RL Research*, 3 March). Details of the "restructuring" set out by Gorbachev in broad terms might have been expected in the economic report but were strikingly missing. The prime minister strongly defended "centralized planned leadership" and scoffed at "the hopes of bourgeois ideologists that we will retreat from this fundamental principle" (*Izvestiia*, 3 March).

Most of Ryzhkov's speech consisted of repetition of figures and goals set out in economic documents adopted in 1985. There were, however, three major points of interest. First, he claimed that the slowdown in economic growth had been halted by the "acceleration" set in motion by the April 1985 plenum of the Central Committee. Second, he gave some new estimates on investment: in the Twelfth Five-Year Plan, total "productive" investment is to grow by 25 percent. The plan set a figure of 18 to 21 percent for total investment. Thus, "nonproductive investment" (hospitals, schools, housing) will have, at best, small increments. Finally, both fixed productive capital and growth of the labor force will decline during the period of the Twelfth Five-Year Plan, while virtually all of the projected increase in production during the years 1985–1990 must come through increased factor productivity.

Perhaps the most interesting moments of the congress came in the speeches, on successive days, by the new Moscow party chief, Boris N. Eltsin, and by a party secretary and Politburo member, Egor K. Ligachev. The two men offered remarkably different views on the contemporary domestic political situation. Eltsin was quite outspoken about popular complaints, especially those relating to special privileges for the elite, and he was sharply critical of past abuses. In a matter seemingly far removed from his own responsibilities, Eltsin rebuked the Party Organizational Work Department of the Central Committee for alleged longstanding shortcomings. The department had not functioned properly, according to Eltsin, because it had taken on a multitude of functions outside its assigned sphere. Since Ligachev headed this department for nearly two years and has had general oversight over it since April 1985, this unexpected sally into Central Committee matters could be interpreted as a slap at the party's so-called second secretary. Even more startling, however, was Eltsin's ringing summation of his call for reform and reinvigoration of the system, one of the frankest public expressions from a leading Soviet politician in decades: "We must not be mesmerized by the steady political stability of the country. How many times can one allow the same mistakes and not take into account the lessons of history?" (*Pravda*, 27 February.)

The speech by party organizational overseer Ligachev was mainly concerned with personnel matters. He explained that the widespread practice under Gorbachev of transferring officials from the center and moving cadres between regions was desirable for the faster transmission of "experience." The practice, of course, also serves to break up, or prevent the formation of, local patronage networks, an aim clearly pursued by Gorbachev and Ligachev. Adding to earlier Gorbachev assurances against a general purge, the "second secretary" went to some lengths to deflect any fears that the extensive personnel turnover of 1985–1986 would lead to a Khrushchev-style "instability of cadres": "In the past, as you know, comrades, in these matters we had both hard frosts and thaws, but what we need is stable good weather." (Ibid., 28 February.)

The expression "stable good weather" apparently meant that regional officials would be reasonably secure in their *nomenklatura* tenure provided they stamped out corruption in their bailiwicks, were reasonably successful in meeting regime goals, and did not form local patronage networks with low accountability to the center.

On the issue of elite privileges, Ligachev countered Eltsin's thrust of the previous day. *Pravda*, shortly before the congress, had published a letter critical of the special stores and other privileges enjoyed by officials (ibid., 13 February). As so often in the past, Viktor Afanasyev, editor in chief of *Pravda*, was serving as a lightning rod, attracting controversy and serving as the point man for "reform" elements in the party. Ligachev did stress the accountability of party organizations, even listing his home base, Tomsk obkom, among key organizations not immune to criticism, but he drew the line at threats to the party's elite status. *Pravda* was strongly reprimanded for going too far (ibid., 28 February).

It had been widely expected that Kazakhstan party leader Dinmukhamed Kunaev would be dropped from the leadership after a scathing attack by *Pravda* (9 February) on that republic's party organization two weeks before the opening of the congress. Somehow, Kunaev temporarily held on to his party posts; part of the price was apparently an act of contrite self-criticism before the assembled delegates and vigorous support for Gorbachev's program. "We accept in a party-like manner," he said, "the criticism leveled against us." Further, Kunaev told the congress that the targets set by the party can be reached "only on the basis of intensification." (Ibid., 27 February.)

The congress adopted, with minor textual changes, the draft program approved by the Central Committee in the fall of 1985 (ibid., 7 March). Carefully avoided were the utopian projections of the previous program, which had been a source of embarrassment ever since economic decline set in during the midpoint of Brezhnev's tenure. The new program does emphasize the economic goals set for the year 2000, the realism of which is open to question, but it sets no timetable for the achievement of communism or the definitive surpassing of the advanced capitalist countries.

Ideologically, the program is a rather strange blueprint for the communist movement and offers little in the way of energizing goals. Replete with standard formulas and stock slogans, it avoids the more controversial aspects of contemporary socialist ideology (for example, there is no hint in the document of the remarkable 1983–1984 debate on the "contradictions of socialism").

The most notable feature of the new program is its overwhelming pragmatism and emphasis upon the specific problems and prospects of economic development in the Soviet Union. Chiding the Brezhnev leadership for the recent loss of momentum, the program concentrates upon the "restructuring" and "intensification" of the Soviet economy. It makes clear that Soviet society is at an earlier phase of development than previously indicated; the country is merely at the outset of the stage of "developed socialism." On international affairs, the standard line on "peaceful coexistence" and arms control is restated; international tensions are attributed to "imperialism," and the United States is depicted as the nefarious leader of imperialism. The program stresses the accountability of cadres and offers some hope for intraparty democracy. But there is no indication of any general liberalization in Soviet society: among other things, "socialist realism" in the arts is strongly reaffirmed.

The congress also adopted a new version of the party rules, notable mainly for the absence of radical changes that had been forecast in some quarters (ibid.). There had been some speculation that an age limit would be set for party office holding, but no such rule was adopted, perhaps due to the opposition of Ligachev, who later in the year expressed relief that the party had not acted to impose an age limitation.

The final major action of the congress was the election of the Central Committee (ibid., 5 March). The new Central Committee has 307 full members and 170 candidates. As expected, turnover was greater than under Brezhnev: 60 percent of full members elected in 1981 were re-elected, against an 80 percent holdover rate at the Twenty-sixth Congress. However, among candidate members, the retention rate dropped only from 34 to 30 percent. Additionally, 23 candidate members elected in 1981 were promoted to full membership.

Since membership in the Central Committee is largely determined by positions held elsewhere, changes in its composition reflect the extent of personnel turnover carried out since the last congress, mostly by Andropov and Gorbachev. Regional secretaries remain the largest single bloc in the committee, accounting for 110 members, or more than one-fifth of the total. Notably, representation for the military declined from 41 to 30 members. Average age of full members of the new Central Committee is about 60. (*RL Research*, 10 March.)

A strange footnote to the new composition of the Central Committee was provided by the re-election of several figures prominent in the Brezhnev era who had since lost their principal positions. Nikolai A. Tikhonov, 81, former prime minister, and Nikolai K. Baibakov, 75, former head of Gosplan, both lost their posts in the fall of 1985, but they remained full members of the Central Committee. So did Boris N. Ponomarev, 81, whom the new Central Committee dropped from his post as party secretary and his rank as candidate Politburo member. Also retained was Vasili V. Kuznetsov, 85, first deputy chairman of the Supreme Soviet, who lost his candidate membership on the Politburo. However, the recently deposed Moscow party chief, Viktor V. Grishin, and Konstantin V. Rusakov, who "resigned" as party secretary for ruling communist parties a week before the congress, were not re-elected. Some observers attributed the re-elections of Tikhonov, Baibakov, and Ponomarev to a desire on the part of Gorbachev and associates to avoid the appearance of a "purge." It was perhaps more likely that the re-elections of Tikhonov and Baibakov were tied to a deal whereby the former's "honorable" retirement was assured in 1985. Ponomarev's continuing elite status may have been due to the still strong, if declining, influence of his longtime companion-in-arms, Andrei Gromyko, the Soviet president.

**Party Leadership and Organization.** A major change occurred in the top leadership on 25 December 1985 when Viktor V. Grishin, who had held the post since 1967, was fired as first secretary of the Moscow city party committee (*Pravda*, 26 December 1985). Grishin had reportedly been a major figure in a last-minute drive to deprive Gorbachev of the leadership, and he had been identified by the Western press as the "Old Guard" opposition's alternative candidate for general secretary. After the summary dismissal of his political ally, Grigori Romanov, in July 1985, it was evidently only a matter of time before Grishin felt the full weight of the Gorbachev steamroller. Following his dismissal as Moscow party chief, Grishin was forced to endure the humiliation of widespread publicity in the press and at party meetings concerning corruption in and inadequacy of public services in Moscow during his tenure. His successor as Moscow first secretary, Boris N. Eltsin, 54, came to the post from a Central Committee secretaryship and had earlier served nine years as first secretary of Sverdlovsk obkom.

An unusual plenum of the Central Committee, ostensibly called to complete preparations for the party congress, formally dismissed Grishin from the Politburo a week before the congress began (BBC Caris, 18 February). The plenum also elected Eltsin a candidate member of the Politburo. At the same time was announced the retirement of Konstantin V. Rusakov, 76, the secretary for liaison with ruling communist parties (*Pravda*, 19 February).

Several changes were announced in the composition of the upper party elite (Politburo and Secretariat) following the first meeting of the new Central Committee (ibid., 7 March). The changes appeared likely to strengthen the general secretary's authority over the central party apparatus; most, if not all, of the new appointees bore a distinct Gorbachevian stamp.

Party Secretary Lev N. Zaikov, 62, was the only new full member of the Politburo; like his colleagues Ligachev and Ryzhkov in the previous year, he was elevated directly to full membership without going through candidate status. Zaikov had served as "mayor" of Leningrad for nine years before succeeding Grigori Romanov as Leningrad first secretary in 1983, when the latter was named a secretary of the Central Committee. At the time, Moscow rumor insisted that Zaikov was chosen because he was "the only honest man in the Leningrad leadership"; notably, Zaikov was personally installed by Gorbachev as the Leningrad leader, without the attendance of Romanov. Called to Moscow in July 1985 to be a secretary of the Central Committee, Zaikov had assumed responsibility for the defense industry and military affairs. His election as a full Politburo member raised him immediately to the number three position in the party hierarchy, and it appeared likely that he would take on general responsibility for the economy.

Two candidate members were added to the Politburo: Yuri F. Solovyev, 61, first secretary of the Leningrad party organization since July 1985, and Nikolai N. Slyunkov, 56, first secretary of the Belorussian party organization since January 1983. Vasili V. Kuznetsov, first deputy chairman of the Supreme Soviet Presidium, and Boris N. Ponomarev, party secretary and head of the Central Committee's International Department, were dropped from candidate membership.

Noteworthy was the continued absence of military representation among the full Politburo members; the defense minister, Marshal Sergei L. Sokolov, remained a candidate member. There are now three full members of the Politburo with high military rank—General Chebrikov, General Aliev, and General Shevardnadze (in all three cases, the ranks were awarded for service in the police and security forces)—and no representative of the military leadership. This is ironic but not surprising in view of Gorbachev's strong reliance upon the police and security forces and the apparent downgrading of the political influence of the military since the summer of 1984.

Boris Ponomarev was retired from both his party secretaryship and the position of head of the International Department. Ivan V. Kapitonov, 72, party secretary for consumer affairs and a longtime associate of Grishin, was kicked downstairs to the largely honorific post of chairman of the Central Auditing Commission.

New appointments to the Secretariat drew more attention than did the additions to the Politburo. Most important of these was the naming of Anatolii F. Dobrynin, 66, to be a party secretary and head of the International Department after 24 years as Soviet ambassador to the United States. Dobrynin subsequently emerged as the chief architect of Soviet foreign policy and apparently played a key role in the massive shakeup of Foreign Ministry personnel during the year (see below).

Aleksandra P. Biryukova, 56, became the first woman to be included in the party's top leadership ranks in a quarter-century; she succeeded Kapitonov as secretary for consumer affairs. A trained engineer, Ms. Biryukova had served as a secretary of the USSR Central Council of Trade Unions since 1968 and had been a full member of the Central Committee since 1976.

Vadim A. Medvedev, 55, is the new party secretary for relations with ruling communist parties. Medvedev's career had been spent in ideological, cultural, and educational work; at the time of his election to the Secretariat, he was serving as head of the Science and Educational Institutions Department of the Central Committee. Given Medvedev's total lack of diplomatic experience, his selection as Rusakov's successor at first appeared strange to some observers. The promotion of Medvedev, however, fully accords with Gorbachev's strategy of bringing in "outsiders" to break up entrenched cliques in the foreign policy establishment both in the Foreign Ministry and in Central Committee headquarters on Staraya Ploshad.

Aleksandr N. Iakovlev, 62, head of the Central Committee's Propaganda Department, was also added to the Secretariat. A close associate of Gorbachev since the latter's 1983 visit to Canada, where Iakovlev served ten years as ambassador, the fast-rising former diplomat had been expected to obtain a leadership position. His exact role in the Secretariat was not immediately clear; since he retained his old post, his elevation appeared to render Mikhail Zimianin, 71, party secretary for culture, something of a "superfluous man" in the key party organ. Later in the year, however, it became clear that Iakovlev was playing a major but still unspecified role in foreign policy; he was highly visible at the Reykjavik summit. During the summer, Iakovlev was relieved of his administrative burden as head of the Propaganda Department and was replaced by Yuri A. Sklyarov (Reuters, 5 August).

Other changes in the central party apparatus were effected during the year. The International Information Department was abolished and its head, Leonid Zamyatin, was dispatched as ambassador to Great Britain (see below). Aleksandr G. Melnikov, 55, first secretary of Tomsk obkom, was named head of the Central Committee's Construction Department. He was succeeded in the Tomsk party post by Viktor I. Zorkaltsev, the second secretary, a former inspector of the CPSU Central Committee (*Pravda*, 1 February).

There were unconfirmed reports that Oleg Rakhmanin, notorious for his extreme hard-line views on relations with Eastern Europe and China, had been replaced as first deputy head of the Central Committee department for liaison with ruling communist parties. On two occasions, Georgi Shakhnazarov, 62, a deputy head of that department since 1972, was identified in the press as first deputy head (ibid, 3, 4 October; *RL Research*, 10 October).

There was one early change in an important regional secretaryship. Aleksandr V. Vlasov, named head of the Ministry of Internal Affairs, was succeeded in Rostov by Boris M. Volodin (*Pravda*, 26 January).

A clear-cut victory for opponents of ideological hard-line tendencies came with the ouster of Richard I. Kosolopov, 55, from his position as editor in chief of the party's theoretical journal, *Kommunist* (Belgrade Tanjug, 29 March; BBC Caris, 8 April). Kosolopov had long been identified as an ultraconservative on ideological matters and had been a principal spokesman against "reformers" in the 1983–1984 debate on the "contradictions of socialism." His successor, Ivan T. Frolov, 56, made a striking comeback from the obscurity to which he had been relegated in the 1970s after losing his job as editor of the periodical *Voprosy filosofii* when its expression of anti-Stalinist and other unorthodox views ran afoul of Brezhnev's ideological hatchet man, Sergei Trapeznikov.

Republic party congresses and regional conferences on the eve of the party congress provided forums for the airing of grievances against the former leadership and for some shakeups of personnel. Attracting most attention was the Moscow city party conference in January, attended by members of the Politburo, including Grishin. The city's new first secretary, Boris Eltsin, recounted in detail the shortcomings of the previous leadership and said that it had "lost touch with the masses" and had set itself "above criticism" (*Moskovskaia pravda*, 25, 26 January). A few days later, the Politburo announced that it would be keeping the work of the Moscow party organization under "constant supervision" (Radio Moscow, 30 January; *RL Research*, 31 January).

Eltsin seemed to be the ideal of the new type of party official envisioned by Gorbachev, one characterized by vigor, openness, and close ties with the masses. Reportedly, Eltsin stood in lines at food stores to observe the service at first hand and rode a city bus to check on the much-maligned transportation system (*WP*, 10 February).

The Sixteenth Congress of the Kazakh communist party featured criticisms of economic performance, particularly in agriculture, with a special censure for the Kazakhstan Academy of Sciences (*Pravda*, 9 February). Prior to the congress, more than 500 officials in the republic had been relieved of their duties for reasons that "reflect negatively on them." Dismissals included Asanbai A. Askarov, 63, first secretary of Chimkent province, and Kenes M. Aukhadiev, 47, first secretary of Alma-Ata province, both full members of the CPSU Central Committee. The departure of Aukhadiev was particularly noteworthy; he had been regarded as a possible successor to party leader Dinmukhamed Kunaev and had served since 1984 as chairman of the youth commission of the USSR Council of Nationalities. Delegates were also told that Akan D. Koichumanov, first secretary of Alma-Ata's city committee, had been expelled from the CPSU "for unworthy conduct and abuse of office" (ibid.).

Party leader Inamzon Usmankhodzhaev, at the Twenty-first Congress of the Uzbek communist party, sharply criticized his predecessor, Sharaf

Rashidov, for maintaining a "cult of office," concealing an economic slowdown, fostering corruption, and other abuses (*Pravda vostoka*, 31 January). Later in the year, the premier under Rashidov, Narmakhonmadi Khudaiberdyev, was expelled from the CPSU for "falsification" of economic reports (ibid., 27 July). The former first secretary of the Shakhrisabz raion party committee, Khalil Khalikoy, was sentenced to execution for "embezzlement on a particularly large scale" (*RL Research*, 6 August).

Major changes were carried out in the leadership of the Beloɪ ussian communist party. Those displaced included Vladimir I. Brovikov, premier and member of the party's buro, who was subsequently named ambassador to Poland; I. F. Yakushev, head of the Party Organizational Work Department, and V. I. Liventsev, chief of the Administrative Office of the Central Committee, who both retired; and Yu. P. Smirnov, head of the Department of Research and Educational Institutions, who was "transferred to other work" (*Sovetskaia Belorussia*, 22 January).

The Twenty-seventh Congress of the Ukrainian communist party was highlighted by criticisms: of the republic Council of Ministers, of several republican and regional secretaries and department heads, of Gosplan, and of all agencies, party and state, involved in agriculture. It was announced at the congress that I. Yarkovoi had been relieved as first secretary of Ternopol province "for serious deficiencies in his work" (*Pravda*, 9 February).

The Twenty-seventh Congress of the Georgian communist party heard a lengthy report on corruption in the republic (*Zaria vostoka*, 25 January). A rather bleak picture was painted for delegates to the Twenty-first Congress of the Azerbaijan communist party. Among other things, it was reported that the oil industry was not performing well and that corruption had been found in law enforcement agencies (*Pravda*, 3 February).

Foreign Minister Eduard Shevardnadze was the speaker at the traditional Lenin anniversary celebration in the Kremlin. He hailed improvement in the morale of the Soviet people over the previous year and maintained that the new strategy of development adopted by the Twenty-seventh CPSU Congress would have been impossible without the decisions of the March 1985 plenum of the Central Committee (which brought Gorbachev to power) and the movement of new personnel into key positions in the state and party hierarchies. On foreign affairs, Shevardnadze denounced the United States for the raid on Libya, said that the United States was following a course of militarism and expansionism, and called upon Washington to reconsider its policy of conducting nuclear tests and to provide other tangible evidence of its desire to reduce international tensions (ibid., 23 April).

The June meeting of the Central Committee was mainly concerned with the economy and was a rather dull affair, with no changes in leadership personnel and no policy departures. General Secretary Gorbachev delivered a speech mainly devoted to restatement of his goals on "restructuring" and "intensification." Particular stress was given to the responsibility of ministries and the consequences of past planning failures. "We cannot allow," Gorbachev said, "billions to be invested in obsolete projects that are based on technically unfit solutions." The party leader touched briefly and gingerly upon the Chernobyl nuclear disaster and said that "we will be able to overcome it." Turning to foreign affairs, Gorbachev defended recent Soviet arms control proposals and charged that the "forces of militarism and aggression headed by U.S. reactionary circles" are "waging with increased hostility a struggle against the Soviet initiatives to improve the international situation." (Ibid., 17 June.)

An October meeting of republican and regional party secretaries in Moscow was devoted to problems in the acceleration of socioeconomic development and the "restructuring" of economy, society, and party. Addressing the secretaries, Gorbachev warned that "not all levels of the planning and economic bodies are yet aware of the importance of rapid improvement in the social sphere and of making use for this purpose of existing means and opportunities." Party and soviet organs have the task, he said "to overcome sluggishness and bring about a decisive turning point in the attention paid by ministries and departments to improving the living conditions of the working people." (*Krasnaia zvezda*; *FBIS*, 24 October.)

Much attention was devoted in the press during the year to the "restructuring" of the party, with particular emphasis upon "style of work" and responsiveness of cadres. A front-page *Pravda* editorial on the eve of the Lenin anniversary celebration, entitled "On the Paths of Restructuring," pointed to the new attitudes demanded of cadres:

Ensuring the fundamental restructuring of party work is a matter of paramount importance. That means that an atmosphere of efficiency and initiative, creation, principled exchanges, and self-criticism must be asserted everywhere. That means that a resolute struggle must be waged against departmentalism and localistic tendencies, paper-shuffling, and other bureaucratic obstacles. (*Pravda*, 21 April.)

Earlier (4 February), *Sovetskaia Rossiia*, a standard-bearer of "reform," had published an article by Professor G. Popov of Moscow State University, which charged that voting procedures sometimes permitted the election of candidates without a true majority and implied that existing electoral processes were partly responsible for stagnation of the party. Popov pointed out the consequences of a perfunctory approach to party elections: "A whole generation of leaders has grown up feeling virtually immune to the danger of being voted out. Under those conditions there is an inevitable sense of being free from censure and monitoring from below becomes lax."

Several front-page *Pravda* editorials following the June plenum of the Central Committee heavily accented the new approach to party activity. On 25 June, in an editorial entitled "Restructuring Party Work," *Pravda* noted that, in general, "restructuring" was going well and that a majority of party cadres "have accepted these ideas with understanding and are beginning to incorporate them into practice." However, it was pointed out that the Kursk and Cherkassy party organizations had been chastised at the Central Committee plenum for their "unfit and unacceptable methods of work with the cadres" and stressed the continuing problem of "excess paperwork." The editorial summed up:

In all organizations it is necessary to stress the atmosphere of intolerance for shortcomings. Stagnation of affairs, sham, idle talk, complacency, and parasitism are inadmissible. To combat these and other negative phenomena demands that the mood of criticism be strengthened in the spirit of the Twenty-seventh Congress . . . The criticism must maintain a spirit of unrest and healthy dissatisfaction with what has been achieved.

A 30 June editorial entitled "Against Bureaucracy" praised party committees in Belorussia, Sverdlovsk, Sumy, Donetsk, Lipetsk, Volgograd, and Leningrad for their promotion of "acceleration" in the economy and reform of management methods and party leadership. However, the proliferation of unnecessary paperwork was said to be a continuing general problem: "There has been no reduction in the flow of various directives and other papers sent by party committees, ministries, and departments."

A 5 July editorial, "Closer to People," maintained that "the more profound are the transformations that we seek, the more essential it is to raise interest in them and convince millions of people of their necessity." Effective party ideological work, especially lectures, offered great potential for mobilizing people for tasks "associated with accelerating the development of the nation." Clearly, the existing situation was, in general, unsatisfactory; the editorial repeated a favorite complaint of Brezhnev concerning "ineffective and vague presentations" and drove home the major point: "One must do everything possible to assure that impressive 'results' of propaganda actually reflect a real impact on real people, and that their thoughts and concerns are not lost behind impressive statistics of numbers of people reached by propaganda work." (*Pravda*, 5 July.)

Given the big stick of personnel control wielded at the center by Gorbachev, Ligachev, and Razumovsky, and the continuing tough policing of internal party activities by a revived Party Control Committee, there could hardly fail to be some alteration in the work habits of party cadres. Within the party, however, perhaps even more than in other spheres, the leadership seemed to be relying upon a change in attitude rather than any fundamental structural reform. It remained to be seen whether party cadre ranks, enervated by years of bureaucratic stagnation and ideological erosion, could become a major rejuvenative force in Gorbachev's grand, if somewhat hazy, design for the "restructuring" of Soviet society.

Spectacular events in December showed that the effects of party "restructuring" reached beyond the party's own ranks. The long-expected dismissal of Dinmukhamed Kunaev as party leader in Kazakhstan came on 16 December. The earlier turnover of personnel in the Kazakh party and continuing criticism in the press had marked Alma-Ata as a primary target in the drive for party rejuvenation. But the real surprise came with the announcement of Kunaev's successor: Gennadi V. Kolbin, 59, an ethnic Russian (ibid., 17 December). Kolbin, as second secretary of the Georgian party from 1975 to 1983 and as first secretary in Ulyanovsk province since 1983, had gained a reputation as a dedicated foe of corruption. But his selection came as a shock in Alma-Ata; Kazahk students rioted following the announcement.

In a startling display of *glasnost'* (openness), the

Soviet media reported rather candidly on the events in Kazakhstan. TASS said that a group of students "incited by nationalistic elements" took to the streets to protest the decisions of the Kazakh party's central committee. Deputy Foreign Minister Vladimir Petrovsky said that "hooligan elements" were responsible for the violence that followed a demonstration by the students. The chairman of the Party Control Committee, Mikhail Solomentsev, an old foe of Kunaev, was sent to Alma-Ata, evidently to take charge and to assure that order was restored (TASS, 18, 19 December; AP, *NYT*, 19 December).

Vyacheslav M. Molotov, former premier, Politburo member, and right-hand man of dictator Josef Stalin, died on 8 November at the age of 96 "after a prolonged and serious illness" (*Izvestiia*, 11 November).

**Government.** Turnover in the Soviet government continued apace, as more Brezhnev-era holdovers were replaced by somewhat younger officials. One early major change, however, involved the ouster of an Andropov appointee.

Aleksandr V. Vlasov, 53, succeeded Vitali V. Fedorchuk, 67, as minister of internal affairs (*Izvestiia*, 26 January). Fedorchuk had served in the post since December 1982 and had been interim head of the KGB following Yuri Andropov's transfer to the Central Committee Secretariat in May 1982. Earlier, he had headed the KGB in the Ukraine for twelve years and had earned a reputation as a fierce opponent of dissent. The official announcement said that Fedorchuk had been "transferred to other work"; subsequently, it was reported that he had been assigned as an army inspector (Paris, AFP, 9 March). A highly public figure in the anticorruption drive under Andropov, he had been less visible in recent months, but there had been no hint of his impending downfall.

Vlasov is known to have had close connections with the defense industry. He made his career in the northern Caucasus regions recently dominated by Gorbachev. He served for nine years as party first secretary of the Chechen-Ingush Autonomous Republic before his promotion in July 1984 to the party leadership in Rostov province (*NYT*, 26 January), where he was charged with restoring "discipline" following a major scandal. His vigorous prosecution of corruption in Rostov apparently accounted for his promotion to the top police post. At the time of Vlasov's appointment about one-third of governmental ministers had been replaced since Gorbachev's accession, approximately matching

the turnover rate for middle-level party officials (*FPI International Report*, 29 January).

Viktor V. Dementsev was appointed chairman of the USSR State Bank, replacing Vladimir S. Alkhimov, who retired on pension (Moscow Domestic Services, 10 January). Konstantin I. Brekhov, 78, was replaced as minister of chemical and petroleum machine building by Vladimir M. Lukyanenko, 48, a Ukrainian who had been serving as general director of the Frunze Mechanical Engineering Scientific Production Association (ibid., 11 January).

Two changes were made in key governmental posts in the propaganda field. Valentin M. Falin, 50, replaced the retiring Pavel Naumov as head of the Novosti Press Agency (TASS, 10 March). Mikhail F. Nenashev, 57, was named head of the USSR State Committee for Publishing Houses, Printing Plants, and the Book Trade, succeeding Boris N. Pastukhov, 53, former head of the Komsomol (*Izvestiia*, 25 February). Pastukhov was transferred to the post of ambassador to Denmark (*RL Research*, 16 July).

Two major changes in union-republic governments were made in the weeks immediately preceding the Twenty-seventh CPSU Congress. In Moldavia, which had been the principal geographical base for Konstantin Chernenko, Premier Ivan G. Ustiyan retired "for reasons of health" at the age of 46, and four Central Committee department heads were sacked. Ustiyan was replaced by the chairman of the Moldavian Supreme Soviet Presidium, Ivan P. Kalin, 50 (*Sovetskaia Moldavia*, 25, 29 December 1985). Mikhail V. Kovalev, 60 was promoted from first vice-chairman to chairman of the Belorussian Council of Ministers, replacing Vladimir I. Brovikov, 54 (*Izvestiia*, 12 January), who was subsequently named ambassador to Poland.

Vladimir I. Reshetilov, 48, a Ukrainian, was named USSR minister of construction, replacing Georgi A. Karavayev, who retired. Reshetilov had served since 1985 as USSR deputy minister for construction of heavy industrial enterprises (ibid., 26 January). Seven months later, Reshetilov's assigned domain was carved up into three parts. Reshetilov was appointed USSR minister of construction in the northern and western regions, Arkady N. Shchepetilnikov became USSR minister of construction in the southern regions, and Sergei V. Bashilov became USSR minister of construction in the Ural and West Siberian regions (*Pravda*, 3 September).

V. G. Lomonosov was named deputy chairman of the All-Union Central Council of Trade Unions.

Elected to the AUCCTU Council were Karatai Turysov and M. B. Ryzhukov (ibid., 5 April).

The governmental organization hardest hit by the winds of change was the Foreign Ministry. In late May, a meeting of heads of Soviet missions abroad was held in the Foreign Ministry and heard addresses by Gorbachev and Shevardnadze. They were accompanied by Central Committee secretaries Dobrynin and Iakovlev as well as other officials (ibid., 24 May). The meeting reportedly dealt with a re-evaluation of Soviet foreign policy goals, implementation of new negotiating tatics, and corruption in the Foreign Ministry (*RL Research*, 16 July). Meanwhile, a major shakeup of personnel was in progress. Thirty new ambassadors had been named since Gorbachev's accession (*NYT*, 24 May), and prominent victims of the reshuffle included Vladimir Lomeiko, the son-in-law of USSR president Gromyko (Lomeiko was succeeded as chief spokesman for the Foreign Ministry by Gennadi Gerasimov, editor of *Moscow News*), and a first deputy foreign minister, Viktor Maltsev, who was demoted to the position of ambassador to Yugoslavia. Georgi M. Kornienko, the other first deputy foreign minister, was shifted to the party apparatus, as a first deputy head of the International Department. The only notable party apparatchik other than Shevardnadze named to the top ranks of the ministry was Valentin Nikiforov, deputy foreign minister for personnel, who had been serving as deputy head of the Organizational Party Work Department of the CPSU Central Committee (*RL Research*, 16 July).

The new first deputy ministers are Yuli M. Vorontsov, 56, former ambassador to France and reportedly Dobrynin's closest associate, and Anatolii G. Kovalev, 63, formerly head of the First European Department and, more recently, ambassador to West Germany (*Pravda*, 22 May). New deputy foreign ministers include Boris N. Chaplin, 55, former ambassador to Vietnam (ibid., 27 May); Anatolii L. Adamishin, 51, former head of the First European Department; Vladimir F. Petrovsky, 53, former chief of the International Organizations Department (ibid.; *NYT*, 30 May); and Igor Rogachev (TASS, 13 August; *FBIS*, 13 August).

Prominent ambassadorial appointees included Yuri V. Dubinin (United States), Yuli A. Kvitsinsky (Federal Republic of Germany), Oleg A. Troyanovsky (People's Republic of China), Leonid M. Zamyatin (Great Britain), Nikolai N. Solovyev (Japan), and Yakov P. Ryabov (France). The transfer of Zamyatin from the post of head of the Central

Committee's International Information Department was certainly a demotion and, given the veteran apparatchik's abysmally low standing with Western diplomats and journalists, hardly indicative of a high Soviet priority for improved relations with London. The postings of experienced diplomats Kvitsinsky and Troyanovsky to Bonn and Peking probably reflected the importance attached to relations with those capitals.

Designation of Solovyev, fluent in Japanese and former head of the Second Far East Department, signaled an upgrading of the importance of relations with Tokyo. The appointment of the 56-year-old Ryabov as ambassador to France appeared superficially to be a demotion since he moved from a deputy premiership, but may have instead presaged a wider future role for him in foreign affairs. The most widely experienced Soviet politician of his generation, Ryabov is the young "elder statesman" of the Kirilenko wing of the party and has been closely associated with two other prominent political figures from Sverdlovsk, Premier Ryzhkov and the Moscow party chief, Eltsin.

The summer session of the Supreme Soviet relieved Piotr N. Demichev as minister of culture and elected him first deputy chairman (vice president) of the Supreme Soviet Presidium, succeeding the retired Vasili V. Kuznetsov (*Pravda*, 19 June). Two new deputy premiers were appointed—Gennadi G. Vedernikov, 48, and Vladimir K. Gusev, 54 (*Izvestiia*, 20 July). Vedernikov had been first secretary of Chelyabinsk obkom since 1984, drawing high praise from Moscow for his leadership of the economy in that key region. Gusev served as first secretary of Saratov obkom from 1976 to 1985, surviving sharp criticism from the central authorities during Andropov's tenure to move up to a deputy premiership of the RSFSR in 1985.

In September, another deputy premier was added. Vladimir M. Kamentsev, 58, moved up from the post he had held since 1979 as minister of the fish industry (*Izvestiia*, 3 September).

The long-expected retirement of First Deputy Premier Ivan V. Arkhipov, 79, was announced in October (TASS, 5 October; *FBIS*, 6 October). A hometown crony of the late leader Brezhnev, Arkhipov had survived much longer than expected in his post (to which he was appointed in 1980), perhaps because of the key role he has played in recent years in trade negotiations with China.

Timofei Guzhenko, 68, retired on 28 September as USSR merchant marine minister, apparently because of a Black Sea collision in August that killed

398 people. He was replaced by Yuri Volmer (TASS, 26 October).

Filipp T. Ermash, 63, was replaced in December as head of the state film industry by Aleksandr I. Kamshalov, 54, a former teacher and official of the Komsomol (TASS, 28 December; *NYT*, 29 December). The change was a key personnel move in the *glasnost'* campaign; Ermash's retirement followed the release of a number of films that had been censored during Ermash's fourteen years as head of the cinematography committee.

In view of the apparent symbolic downgrading of the military "brass" since Gorbachev's coming to power, the annual Revolution Day parade attracted particular attention. For only the second time in Soviet history, the defense minister missed the ceremony. Marshal Sergei L. Sokolov, reportedly ill, did not attend the parade, usually considered the military's most importance annual public observance. The real surprise on this occasion was that the military was represented by General Piotr G. Lushev, 63, a deputy defense minister who ranks no higher than fifth, perhaps lower, in the defense ministry hierarchy (AP, 7 November).

The fall session of the Supreme Soviet, 17–19 November, dealt mainly with economic matters, including a new law permitting a measure of private enterprise in certain businesses (*Izvestiia*, 18–20 November).

**Domestic Affairs.** The Gorbachev leadership maintained its drive to get the USSR "moving again," carrying out its offensive on many fronts: "intensification" of the economy, continuing campaigns against alcoholism and corruption, and asserted policies of more openness in public communication and broader public participation in decisionmaking. Gorbachev made symbolic gestures to demonstrate that he was opposed to a new "cult of personality"; however, he appeared to receive more media attention than had Khrushchev and Brezhnev at comparable stages in their tenures.

Meanwhile, the new leader seemed to be following Khrushchev's political strategy of appealing directly to the masses over the heads of hostile bureaucrats. Superficially, the strategy seemed to be paying off, as Gorbachev met evidently friendly, even enthusiastic, crowds in his travels around the country. However, there were reports throughout the year of grumbling among the masses about "more work for less vodka" (News America Syndicate, 1 December) and of some private carping about the Western stylishness and alleged expensive tastes of Raisa Gorbacheva. Ordinary Russians are used to virtual invisibility in their leaders' wives. Moreover, questions posed to Gorbachev by the populace became sharper as the year wore on.

A cardinal feature of Gorbachev's program was the policy of *glasnost'*, or greater frankness in information delivered to the Soviet public; execution of this policy was reportedly entrusted to a party secretary and Gorbachev confidant, Aleksandr Iakovlev. The April disaster at the Chernobyl nuclear power plant brought the first major test of *glasnost'* and the first real political crisis for the new leadership. Initially, there was a paucity of information both at home and abroad, and reportedly there was strong opposition within the top leadership to full disclosure. Ultimately, the full story was apparently mostly revealed, but international agencies were probably given more details than the Soviet public. The policy of *glasnost'* survived, however, as indicated by *Pravda*'s attack on the television program "Vremiia" for its sterile presentation of the news, implying that TV newsmen were culpable for the lack of aggressive, forthright reporting on Chernobyl (*NYT*, 27 July) and by later prompt reporting of events such as the August collision and sinking of a cruise ship in the Black Sea.

Politically, the Chernobyl disaster was a setback for the leadership at home and abroad. The early "circling the wagons" posture of elite spokesmen, including Gorbachev himself, was said to have strengthened domestic critics of the reform program and, indeed, the drive for renewal seemed to lose some of its zip for several months. Economically, it was difficult to assess the long-range adverse effects on agriculture and the environment but it certainly produced short-run pressures in the matter of energy, a growing Soviet concern in recent years. With alternatives in short supply, the leadership subsequently reaffirmed its commitment to the development of nuclear power.

The economy showed some gains during the year and the harvest was reportedly the best in eight years. Party and government spokesmen continuously asserted that "intensification" and "restructuring" would not involve any fundamental departure from the command economy. But in November the Supreme Soviet passed a law, much publicized on Gorbachev's India trip, allowing wider parameters for cooperatives to permit private citizens to join together in setting up small factories (*WP*, 28 November).

On the cultural front, there was some relaxation in the arts and literature. The regime also demonstrated greater flexibility on certain matters of emigration, particularly the reuniting of couples of mixed nationality. The release of Andrei Sakharov and his wife, Elena Bonner, from internal exile in December seemed to open up startling possibilities for the future evolution of the Soviet system, although some Western observers saw the move as a cosmetic public relations gesture. It was unclear how this and other developments related to *glasnost'* would affect the configuration of power among major political structures. But, for much of the year, virtually all foreign observers identified the KGB as one of the principal bulwarks of the Gorbachev leadership; the secret police forces were apparently aligned in a loose supporting coalition with upwardly mobile, young and middle-aged party apparatchiks and with technocrats in the economic institutes, industry, and agriculture.

*Chernobyl.* An explosion at the Chernobyl atomic power station in the Ukraine on 26 April caused major environmental damage both within the Soviet Union and beyond its borders; brought to light the sloppy safety standards and practices of a Soviet nuclear industry whose overriding goal was the rapid "on-line" deployment of plants, usually near large cities; and created a critical situation for the Soviet leadership.

The disaster was revealed on 28 April, after Swedish scientists detected unusually high levels of radiation (AP, 28 April) and officials at Sweden's embassy in Moscow made inquiries of the authorities in Moscow. Soviet spokesmen denied that there had been a nuclear accident in the USSR (Reuters, 28 April; *RL Research*, 2 May) but later in the day Moscow issued its first terse statement about the incident, almost three days after the explosion (Radio Moscow, 28 April). The Soviet public received no details for a week, and Soviet spokesmen put a noncritical gloss on the news that dribbled out. Meanwhile, the fire at Chernobyl raged out of control, a mass evacuation was carried out over a wide area, and radioactivity spread over Scandinavia to Western Europe, finally reaching the western coast of North America. Two commissions were set up, one under Premier Ryzhkov to coordinate handling of the crisis, another under Deputy Premier Boris Shcherbina to investigate (*Pravda*, 30 April).

Ryzhkov and Egor Ligachev were dispatched to the affected area for an on-site inspection, accompanied by the Ukrainian party leader, Vladimir Shcherbitsky (*Izvestiia*, 1 May). Behind the scenes,

Soviet officials were asking Western experts for advice on how to stop the fire. After inspections by representatives of the International Atomic Energy Agency (Moscow Radio, 8 May; TASS, *FBIS*, 9 May) and the arrival of Western medical specialists to help with the victims, "stonewalling" became impossible.

The first detailed statement for the outside world came from Politburo candidate member Boris Eltsin, in West Germany for the congress of the German Communist Party, who revealed that almost 50,000 Soviet citizens had been evacuated from the Chernobyl area, that there was a 30-kilometer exclusion zone around the power station, and that perhaps 40 people had received serious doses of radiation (BBC Caris, 6 May). Meanwhile, Soviet officials and media made a concerted effort to depict Western reports as exaggerated and assailed U.S. "hypocrisy" over the accident (*Sovetskaia Rossiia*, 8 May). And less than two weeks after the explosion, a Soviet spokesman indicated the continuing commitment to nuclear power, a position subsequently reaffirmed by ranking officials, who said that "mankind cannot renounce the peaceful use of atomic energy" (TASS, 8 May; *FBIS*, 9 May).

On 14 May, Gorbachev finally broke his eighteen-day silence with a nationwide televised address about the nuclear disaster. He disclosed that 9 people had died as a result of the accident and 299 victims had been hospitalized. He reassured viewers that the worst danger was over and maintained that the government was fully in control of the situation and had provided timely information on the incident. Striking a belligerent pose, he accused Western governments and media of carrying out "an unrestrained anti-Soviet campaign" about Chernobyl, made up of a "mountain of lies"; its purpose, said Gorbachev, was the undermining of Soviet arms proposals. Notably absent was any expression of regret for the consequences suffered by other countries in Eastern and Western Europe (Moscow Television; *FBIS*, 14 May).

It was clear throughout the crisis that local officials had been slow to react, that evacuations had not been sufficiently expedited, and that serious problems existed in the construction and operation of Soviet atomic plants. The fire at Chernobyl was extinguished after several weeks of herculean efforts by Soviet military and civilian personnel. Then came the postmortem and the political fallout. In July, Evgenii V. Kulov, 57, since 1983 the chairman of the State Committee for Safety in the Atomic Power Industry, was fired (TASS, 18 July). Kulov was succeeded by Vadim M. Malyshev, 54, since 1973 the director of the I. V. Kurchatov Beloyarsk Atomic Power Station (*Izvestiia*, 3 September). Valery Legasov, deputy director of the state's atomic energy institute, was quoted as saying that Chernobyl "forced us to revise once again the concept of the development of nuclear power engineering in the country, the location of nuclear power plants, the level of technical preparedness, and the skill of personnel" (*New Times*, 18 July).

One day after the sacking of Kulov, four other major officials in the nuclear industry were dismissed, and the Politburo issued its report on the investigation of the disaster (*Pravda*, 19 July). Nikolai F. Lukonin, director of the Lenin Atomic Electrical Station in Leningrad, was named to head a new Ministry for Atomic Energy created to monitor safety and to prevent a repeat of the Chernobyl disaster (TASS; UPI, 21 July). Disciplinary action against eight other nuclear industry officials was announced in the following month (*Pravda*, 14 August).

In its 18 July report, the Politburo estimated direct financial losses at $2.8 billion and said that 28 people had died due to the accident, 30 were still hospitalized, and 173 others had been affected by radiation sickness. According to the official report, the accident had disrupted the nation's power supply, forced closing of local factories, and contaminated 400 square miles of land in the northern Ukraine and southern Belorussia. The explosion and fire were attributed to improperly supervised and badly conducted experiments on a turbine generator without proper safety precautions. A sweeping condemnation was issued concerning local, Ukrainian, and national officials responsible for operating the Chernobyl reactor (*San Franciso Chronicle*, 20 July). Meanwhile, the RSFSR government newspaper reported that crops in an eighteen-mile zone around Chernobyl became radioactive during the accident and were unfit for consumption (*Sovetskaia Rossiia*, 18 July).

Ukrainian authorities reported in July that the energy loss from the Chernobyl disaster was mostly being covered by increased use of thermal power and thrifty consumption of energy. It was announced that two nuclear power stations, at Rovno and Zaporozhe, would come into service by the end of the year (TASS; *FBIS*, 26 June). Meanwhile, a crash building program was underway to house Chernobyl residents at a safe distance from the damaged reactor (*Pravda*, 23 July).

In a report prepared by the Soviets for the International Atomic Energy Agency, the nuclear disaster was attributed to workers turning off key emergency equipment while running a test, then ignoring warnings (*NYT*, 16 August). Commenting on the report, U.S. scientists were highly critical of the risk-taking detailed in the document (ibid., 18 August). A second major fire at the Chernobyl plant, nearly a month after the disaster, was reported by a Soviet newspaper in August (*Leninskoe znamia*, 20 August; *NYT*, 21 August). Efforts to seal the damaged number four reactor were reportedly slowed by technical problems, poor design, and a concrete shortage. (*NYT*, 17 August; *CSM*, 22 August), but in September Boris Shcherbina reported that burial of the damaged reactor was nearing completion (*Izvestiia*, 23 September). Reactors one and two, both shut down after the 26 April explosion, were restarted for tests in October and November, respectively (AP, 9 November).

*Economy.* At the outset of the year, the economy was just beginning to function under a newly streamlined governmental management. Several ministries had been eliminated, others consolidated (six in agriculture). The unconsolidated ministries were expected to encounter a higher degree of subordination to Gosplan (whose new chairman, Nikolai Talyzin, had been vaulted to candidate status in the Politburo in the previous October). More autonomy was anticipated for the individual enterprises within their jurisdictions.

This "restructuring" at the top was counted upon to promote the goal of squeezing greater productivity out of the economy, the central thrust of the new five-year plan. Indeed, without a more radical "restructuring" of the economy than the leadership was willing to consider, enhanced efficiency was the only general option available, in view of declining labor inputs, rising costs of resource extraction, increasingly unfavorable terms of world trade, and other negative phenomena. But Western experts concluded that the projected annual growth rate of more than 4 percent in national income would require an unrealizable rise in total factor productivity from −0.5 percent a year in 1981–1985 to +1.5 percent in 1986–1990, thus rendering Gorbachev's "acceleration" program impossible of achievement (*RL Research*, 2 July). Economic growth during the year was surprisingly strong, especially in view of the Chernobyl disaster, but these short-run gains did not improve the rather bleak long-range picture. A persistent major theme of official pronouncements was dissatisfaction with the rate of progress (*NYT*, 3 August).

Figures released in January showed a 3.1 percent increase in national income and a 6 percent rise in consumer goods production in 1985, but oil production dropped 2.9 percent, to 11.9 million barrels a day from 12.3 million barrels a day the year before (*San Francisco Examiner and Chronicle*, 26 January; *WSJ*, 27 January). Severe criticism was leveled at the oil ministry and related departments for the shortfall (*Pravda*, 10 January; *Sovetskaia Rossiia*, 10 January). The precipitous decline in world oil prices (nearly 50 percent in some markets over a two-month period) added energy-related pressures to the Soviet economy, since petroleum was the most important source of hard-currency earnings (*CSM*, 5 February).

Gorbachev announced in a speech at Toliattigrad in April that Soviet industrial output for the first quarter was 6.7 percent higher than in the first quarter of 1985 (Radio Moscow, 9 April; *RL Research*, 15 April). The first quarter of 1985, however, had been one of exceptionally poor performance. Moreover, official Soviet statistics indicated a substantial drop from that high during the second quarter. The Central Statistical Administration report for the first half of the year showed some rises: 3.7 percent in national income and 5.6 percent in industrial output. Labor productivity rose 5.2 percent in industry, 4.9 percent in construction, and 8.9 percent in railroad transportation. Foreign trade turnover reportedly declined 4 percent (*Pravda*, 20 July; *FBIS*, 23 July).

The CPSU Central Committee and the Council of Ministers issued two major resolutions on the upgrading of consumer goods. A May resolution announced a restructuring of planning in light industry (*Pravda*, 6 May); the July resolution on output quality emphasized the testing of products and stated that officials would be held liable for "misrepresenting information on the existing world standard when assessing output quality" (ibid., 2 July).

Managerial bureaucrats received much criticism throughout the year for foot-dragging on the acceleration program. In his major speech to the Central Committee in June, Gorbachev said that the first five months of 1986 had seen some improvement in economic performance, but not nearly enough. "The post-Congress period has shown," he asserted, "that the complicated structure and inefficient performance of our managerial bodies are significantly hindering our progress and the intro-duction of new methods" (*Pravda*, 17 June; *RL Research*, 18 June).

In early August an editorial in the main newspaper of the RSFSR government sharply criticized several ministries at both all-union and republic levels for resisting new methods and impeding reorganization (*Sovetskaia Rossiia*, 5 August; *FBIS*, 11 August). The USSR State Committee on Science and Technology, headed by Deputy Premier Guri Marchuk, was added to the list of censured organizations in September. In his Krasnodar speech, Gorbachev criticized the committee for its role "in the very slow pace of restructuring" (*Pravda*, 20 September).

Following seven years of poor harvests, some of them disastrous, the authorities were understandably nervous over the 1986 crops. In June, the CPSU Central Committee delivered a stinging public rebuke to the first secretaries of the Bryansk and Nikolaev obkoms, Anatolii Voistrochenko and Leonid Sharaev. They were chastised for failure to provide livestock farms with adequate supplies of high-quality fodder and for failure to reorganize the agroindustrial bodies in their oblasts in line with the resolutions of the Twenty-seventh CPSU Congress. The two regional secretaries were held "personally responsible" for fulfillment of the production plan for feed grain and for exansion of output of meat and dairy products (Radio Moscow, 12 June; *RL Research*, 24 June). Two months later, a pessimistic *Pravda* editorial (18 August) on agriculture spotlighted transportation problems adversely affecting crop collection in various parts of the country. Nevertheless, the harvest appeared to be the best in years. In November, the U.S. Department of Agriculture forecast that Soviet grain imports might be the lowest in eight years; analysts boosted their projections on Soviet grain production by 15 million tons to 195 million, still well below the latest Soviet estimates (UPI, 10 November). In December, USDA spokesmen confirmed a Soviet grain harvest of 210 million tons (ibid., 10 December).

Despite emphatic strictures against "unearned income," there was some allowance for an increase in essential private services in the economy (*Pravda*, 28 May; *Izvestiia*, 20 November). Nevertheless, the leadership rather consistently emphasized that there would be no retreat toward a market economy; this had been particularly made clear in Premier Ryzhkov's major speech at the Twenty-seventh CPSU Congress. Therefore, an announced modest reversion to private enterprise came as something of a shock. Most surprising was the highly publicized and detailed exposition of the reform presented by Leonid Abalkin, director of a top economic institute in Moscow, in New Delhi during Gorbachev's November visit to India. Although Abalkin is a leading theorist of Gorbachev's "acceleration" program and the reform had been voted by the Supreme Soviet, issuance of such an important statement by a relatively low-ranking official in a foreign capital indicated a high probability of continuing intense infighting in Moscow over issues of the "marketization" of the economy.

Abalkin said that expansion of existing laws on cooperatives will permit private citizens to join together in setting up small cooperatives. He further elaborated on changes that will allow ministries and enterprises to buy and sell directly overseas. Abalkin estimated that the revised and expanded cooperatives would constitute 10 to 12 percent of the national income within the next decade (*WP*, 28 November).

The lot of Soviet consumers did not improve during the year, and in at least one respect deteriorated. Coffee virtually disappeared from stores and restaurants; a Soviet weekly said that consumers were overreacting to the shortage, which had resulted from droughts in Brazil, frosts in Africa, and panic buying due to a rumored price increase. The hard currency needed to buy coffee at the much higher world market prices was spent for "other serious and socially important reasons," according to the journal *Ogonek* (7 December).

*Social Problems and Policies.* Soviet spokesmen following the Gorbachev line presented a general picture of moral rot, describing a society that, after 69 years of communist rule, had retrogressed in regard to production of the "new Soviet man." The campaign against corruption continued unabated. Regional and union-republic party conclaves preceding the Twenty-seventh CPSU Congress devoted much attention to the toleration of violations of law and social norms in the past and the undiminished necessity for vigilance. The militia continued to be a special target in the clean-up campaign. Further publicity of police abuses followed immediately after the firing of Vitali Fedorchuk as interior minister. Spotlighted were local party and law enforcement officials in Voronezh and Novosibirsk, who were warned by the chief USSR prosecutor, Aleksandr Rekunkov, for violating "socialist legality" in their efforts to combat crime (*Izvestiia*, 22 January). There was no concealment of the fact that the police themselves had been heavily involved in crime, particularly in Novosibirsk, where several police officials were disciplined or fired, and a member of the militia was sentenced to death for the 1984 murder of a public prosecutor (*Pravda*, 22 January; *RL Research*, 23 January). The predominantly non-Russian republics in the Caucasus and Central Asia continued to make news on the anticorruption front, particularly Uzbekistan, where the former leadership of Sharaf Rashidov was castigated again and again, and the former minister of the ginning industry, V. Usmanov, was sentenced to death for embezzlement and bribe-taking (*Pravda*; *FBIS*, 29 August).

The most publicized center was the city of Moscow, where the new party chief, Boris Eltsin, repeatedly denounced the previous Grishin leadership for violations of law, poor administration, and a cover-up of deplorable conditions; a host of local officials fell victim to a vigorous purge. Eltsin depicted a wretched situation in the capital in regard to housing, transportation, medical services, and even food supplies (*RL Research*, 31 January). If conditions were so intolerable in Moscow, traditionally the city with highest priority in matters of consumption, it could be assumed that provincial urban areas were, in most respects, in even worse shape. Eltsin devoted special attention to lax labor discipline and the presence in the capital of persons with no obvious legal source of income. In June, a regulation was announced requiring all Muscovites between 16 and 60 (55, for women) to present the housing department with a certificate from his or her place of work or educational institution. This survey was to be conducted between July and November; those refusing "socially useful work" were to be prosecuted for "parasitism" (*Vechernaia Moskva*, 12 June; *RL Research*, 18 July). In September, a major bribery prosecution was begun against former leaders of the Moscow Gorispolkom Main Administration for Trade (Glavmostorg) (*Sovetskaia Rossiia*, 13 September; *FBIS*, 24 September).

Since no responsible figure in party or state envisioned abolition in the foreseeable future of the "second economy," deemed essential for operation of the civilian sector, it was not always clear where corruption began and acceptable business ended. In a much publicized campaign against "unearned income," authorities attempted to define clearly what was unacceptable—embezzlement, bribery, theft and misuse of "socialist property," and private work on state-paid time (Moscow Domestic Service, 6 June; *FBIS*, 17 June; *Pravda*, 28 June; Moscow

Domestic Service, 6 July; *FBIS*, 10 July). In November a Supreme Soviet decree legalized moonlighting by private citizens as self-employed taxi drivers, restaurateurs, and repairmen (*Izvestiia*, 20 November).

One effect of the "law and order" (*poriadok*) drive, begun under Andropov and reinvigorated under Gorbachev, has been a vast increase in the number of persons imprisoned for crime. The overburdening of existing prison facilities has forced the authorities to change the structure of places of confinement and has led to the creation of a new kind of colony-settlement—a less expensive option than the building of additional modern closed camps. (*RL Research*, 1 September).

The campaign against alcoholism retained its high priority during the year, but there were some sour notes. In January, both party and government spokesmen expressed fears that the drive was running out of steam and noted that enforcement of the campaign had been relaxed in some parts of the country (BBC Caris, 24 January). A June conference at the CPSU Central Committee headquarters brought party, government, Komsomol, and trade union officials together for a conference on alcoholism, featuring a report by Interior Minister Vlasov. It was noted that the sale of alcoholic drinks had fallen by one-third, but that work by many party and state agencies in the antialcohol drive had recently slackened and "an atmosphere of intolerance toward violators has not been created anywhere" (*Pravda*, 11 June).

The price of liquor rose 20 to 25 percent at the end of July to put additional bite into the sobriety campaign. To compensate for the sudden increase, the price of children's clothes, furs, footwear, clocks, motorcycles, and various household goods dropped 20 to 30 percent (Reuters, 31 July). Foreign media reported continued grumbling among consumers about the long queues at liquor outlets; one minor concession by the regime was extension of open hours for wine stores.

*Glasnost'* was remarkably evident in the coverage of drug abuse, formerly a virtually taboo subject, except in regard to Central Asia. Some discussions of drug addiction were quite frank, and it was acknowledged that the problem was growing; some doctors attributed the recent increase to the antialcohol drive. The party committee of the city of Moscow announced a "struggle against narcotics" on 10 April (*WP*, 23 April) and Procurator General Aleksandr Rekunkov, in a May article, pointed to the growing seriousness of the problem. Rekunkov

noted that the problem was much less acute than in the United States, but that cases of drug addiction "are not all that rare" in the USSR and the danger had previously been underestimated. He asserted that investigators had found that many burglaries in Rostov province were committed by drug-takers (*Zhurnalist*, May).

Georgi Morozov, director of the Serbsky Institute and notorious for his association with the forcible administration of drugs to dissidents, called for increased public awareness of the drug problem and advocated a campaign similar to the one being conducted against alcohol abuse (*Sovetskaia kultura*, 20 May; BBC Caris, 4 June; *RL Research*, 14 July). Subsequent articles in the press reflected continuing concern with the problem (*Izvestiia*, 12 August; *Literaturnaia gazeta*, 20 August).

An even more surprising manifestation of *glasnost'*, in view of the traditional puritanical facade of Soviet life, was revelation of the existence of prostitution in major Soviet cities. Some commentaries reflected the old official prudishness, using euphemisms to identify the problem. Prostitutes were said to be operating openly outside leading hotels in the center of Moscow and in the World Trade Center, favored by foreign businessmen. The Komsomol was assigned a major role in combating this no longer secret social evil; police officials complained that they were powerless to arrest anyone for soliciting or engaging in prostitution because there are no laws against it (*LAT*, 10 December). The absence of such laws is presumably due to the formerly asserted ideological position that such practices are a product of bourgeois society and should not be found under socialism, where everyone is guaranteed socially useful work.

Another previously taboo subject (at least at the all-union level), racial tension, was aired when recent instances of "collective hooliganism" involving young Russians and Yakuts in the city of Yakutsk were revealed (Moscow Television First Channel, 25 June). Apparently, racial antagonism has been a by-product of the enormous influx of Russians into the Yakut ASSR in connection with the exploitation of its valuable mineral resources (*RL Research*, 1 July).

A draft decree of the CPSU Central Committee extended the educational reform program (initiated in 1983) to the country's universities (*Izvestiia*, 1 June). The proposed higher education program aims to end the concentration upon narrow vocational and professional specialization and to promote a broader-based education enabling graduates to adapt more readily to new technology. The Ministry of Education is to be granted authority to supervise all college-level institutions, higher education is to be integrated more closely with the economy, and links between universities and research institutes are to be strengthened (*NYT*, 6 July).

*Dissent and Emigration.* Major stories on the dissent front concerned the releases of Anatolii Shcharansky (ibid., 12 February) and Yuri Orlov. Shcharansky, a founder of the Moscow Helsinki group, was convicted in 1978 on a charge of spying for American intelligence. He was permitted to emigrate as part of a deal involving the return of several East European intelligence agents held in the West (ibid., 3 February). Orlov, one of the leaders of the Democratic Movement in the early 1970s, was freed and allowed to leave the Soviet Union in early October as part of the swap that concluded the Daniloff-Zakharov affair (see below).

Shcharansky received tumultuous receptions in both Israel and the United States. In an interview with an American news magazine after he had settled in Israel, Shcharansky estimated that there are 15,000 to 20,000 prisoners of conscience in the USSR (*U.S. News and World Report*, 11 May), well above the estimate of 10,000 usually accepted in the West.

With the pending release of Shcharansky, Gorbachev reaffirmed that the most prominent of the dissidents, Andrei Sakharov, would not be freed. In an interview with the French communist newspaper *L'Humanité*, Gorbachev said that Sakharov "still has knowledge of secrets of special importance to the state, and for this reason cannot go abroad." Responding to Gorbachev's claim that the scientist had committed "illegal acts," Sakharov's family challenged the Soviet leader to put Sakharov on trial (AP, 8 February). Elena Bonner, Sakharov's wife, left the United States in May after a six-month stay for medical treatment and returned to the USSR after several stops in Europe. Prior to her departure, she told U.S. congressmen that she was "desperately afraid of returning to Gorky" (BBC Caris, 23 May). Although she had clearly violated the terms of her agreement with Soviet authorities by granting emotionally charged interviews to Western newsmen, the public response from Moscow was quite restrained, perhaps out of fear that she would not return.

Although Soviet spokesmen hinted at greater flexibility on human rights, early returns indicated that the parameters of *glasnost'* were not wide enough to accommodate critics of regime policies. The general treatment of dissidents apparently was unchanged. In January and February, two seventeen-year-old girls, Irina Pankratova and Anetta Fadeyeva, both members of the unofficial peace organization, the Group to Establish Trust Between the USA and the USSR, were arrested and reportedly confined in psychiatric hospitals (ibid., 3 February). Sixteen members of the group were arrested in Moscow in early February after they tried to hold a meeting, and one woman was reportedly badly beaten by police (*CSM*, 6 February).

The regime's hostility toward religion had become more apparent since the 1985 appointment of Konstantin Kharchev, a 50-year-old engineer and former diplomat, as chairman of the Council of Religious Affairs (BBC Caris, 3 January). A favorite ploy of the authorities has been that of arranging public "recantations" by prominent persecuted believers. In the first quarter of the year, TASS publicized two such "recantations" by Orthodox activists Sergei Markus and Boris Razveyev, and authorities in Estonia announced an official pardon for Lutheran pastor Harri Moetsnik on grounds that he had "confessed his guilt" and "repented" (ibid., 7 January; 9, 16 April).

An underground document made available to two Western reporters by unidentified "officials" created something of a sensation during the summer. The document, an "appeal to the citizens of the Soviet Union," was issued by the "Movement for Socialist Renewal." There was immediate speculation that the *samizdat* "appeal" was inspired by reform elements in the party, perhaps including some members of the leadership (London, *The Guardian*, 22 July). The appeal called for abandoning central controls, turning to a market economy, and introducing Western-style democratic freedoms; the authors maintained that these are the only solutions for the general crisis of the Soviet system. The authors contended that the Soviet standard of living is one of the lowest among industrial countries, that the USSR ranks behind only Mexico and Brazil in foreign indebtedness, that the family as an institution is in decline, and that the Soviet-led community of nations is falling apart (*NYT*, 23 July). After a detailed examination of the seventeen-page document, Radio Liberty analyst Allan Kroncher concluded that the "freedom manifesto" was written by well-informed persons in the Soviet middle-level intelligentsia, not by specialists or members of the scientific or party elites (*RL Research*, 29 July).

There were some indications of a cultural thaw (albeit restricted by prohibitions against certain forms of political criticism) after a quarter-century of enforced, stultifying conformism. There was also contradictory evidence unfavorable to such a trend. Poet Evgenii Evtushenko stated in Helsinki that the Soviet Union is undergoing a literary revival, but he denied that it was a result of Kremlin orders. Evtushenko remarked, "We have the chance to write frankly and clearly, and there is a difference between this thaw and earlier ones. I think this one is here to stay." (UPI, 26 November.)

It was now possible for works that would formerly have been prohibited to be published or displayed, but this was no guarantee against official wrath. Articles in party and government newspapers severely criticized the work of avant-garde artists, whose creations run counter to the style of "socialist realism" reaffirmed in the new CPSU Program (*Moskovskaia pravda*, 20 April; *Sovetskaia kultura*, 5 July; *RL Research*, 22 July).

When the Twenty-seventh CPSU Congress convened in February, emigration from the USSR had actually declined since Gorbachev's accession to power. Yet the regime was able to score public relations points by indications of greater flexibility, by effective publicity on returnees to the USSR, and by promulgation of new regulations governing emigration—which dissidents doubted would have much practical effect.

High-publicity cases drew special official attention. Inessa Fleurov and her family were granted visas so that she could donate bone marrow to her leukemia-stricken brother in Israel (AP, 3 November), and permission was granted for a three-year-old girl, "the world's youngest political prisoner," to rejoin her parents in Sweden, where they had fled in 1984 (UPI, 19 November). The Soviet media also played up "happy" returnees, notably Izrael Glikman and Aleksandr Belikin, who recounted their sad experiences in the United States, which they described as an arena of crime, discrimination, and unemployment lacking the closeness and warmth of Soviet society (*Izvestiia*, 28 October).

Soviet officials said that new visa regulations would ease the process of leaving the country. The new rules, which go into effect 1 January 1987, mostly codify existing practices but do require decisions on visa applications within a month, unless further consideration is necessary. The reunification of families and other hardship reasons are grounds for special consideration, and nine reasons are specified for rejections (*NYT*, 8 November; UPI, 7 December).

The apparent increase in flexibility even extended to some prominent dissidents, although this was mostly a matter of their use as pawns in diplomatic exchanges (see above and below). Tragically, permission to emigrate came too late for one dissident. In November, Soviet authorities offered to release from prison 48-year-old Ukrainian human rights activist Anatolii Marchenko, who had spent almost his entire adult life in confinement (*LAT*, 26 November). Two weeks later, his family was notified that Marchenko had died in the Chistopol prison hospital 600 miles east of Moscow (UPI, 9 December).

Whatever the minor propaganda points scored earlier by the Soviets, any such gains may have been wiped out following the disclosure of Marchenko's death. The dissident had not been allowed to see his wife for two and one-half years prior to his death, and she said that she believed he had been subjected to forced feedings during a hunger strike. Western human rights activists reported that Marchenko had written of beatings and repeated confinements in a cold isolation cell (AP, 10 December).

The ugly face of the Soviet regime was publicly displayed in its celebration of International Human Rights Day. A government-organized rally crowded out a protest of Soviet human rights abuses in Pushkin Square. Plainclothes police arrested members of a divided-families group who had planned to stage a protest elsewhere in Moscow. At a news conference, Deputy Foreign Minister Mikhail Kapitsa attacked alleged human rights abuses in other countries, especially the United States, and Sergei Gusev, deputy chairman of the USSR Supreme Court, dismissed Andrei Sakharov as a "criminal" (*NYT*, 11 December; AP, 10, 11, December).

Suddenly reversing its policy on Sakharov, the Soviet regime on 19 December freed the dissident from internal exile in Gorky and pardoned Elena Bonner, allowing the couple to return to Moscow (AP, 19 December). Gorbachev personally telephoned the Sakharovs in Gorky to announce the decision. Upon his return to Moscow, Sakharov was welcomed by the Academy of Sciences and resumed giving interviews to the Western media.

*Ideology.* The theoretical underpinnings of the new CPSU program, supposedly the ideological guide for Soviet communists, were rather thin, and the cliché-ridden document artfully skirted virtually all recent controversies related to Marxism-Leninism (see above). Moreover, the activist, technocratic mentality of the new leadership was not compatible with the traditional heavy-handed Soviet emphasis on dogma. Nevertheless, there were some interesting turns on the ideological front during the year.

Economist Tatiana Zaslavskaia, author of the celebrated 1983 Novosibirsk Report, published an article in January that struck fiercely at the ideological smugness underlying the concept of "developed socialism," a major contribution of the Brezhnev leadership to Marxism-Leninism. Zaslavskaia was critical of progress toward achievement of the classless society and said that economic opportunity in the Soviet Union is still largely determined by social status, connections, and geographic location (*Sovetskaia kultura*, 23 January). A September article by Professor Vsevolod Davidovich of Rostov University, entitled "Soviet Society: Unity in Diversity," dealt with the persistence of separate group and individual interests under socialism and the possibility that greater clashes of interest may occur in the future. Davidovich's solution was not more pluralism but stronger centralization under the political leadership (*Pravda*, 12 September; *RL Research*, 26 September).

Both articles contained echoes of the remarkable 1983–1984 debate on the "contradictions of socialism." The idea that a diversity of interests may exist under socialism, that these interests may become "antagonistic," and that the conflict of interests may increase in the course of socialist development touches on the basic incompatibility between forced Soviet-style modernization and the original tenets of Marxism. Accordingly, public discussions of recent years have revealed more clearly the ideological vulnerability of the Soviet regime, so often noted by foreign Marxists over the past two decades. Gorbachev has noted the diversity of interests and has said that it must be taken into account, but he seems concerned with a much bigger problem, namely the general retrogression of the Soviet system in terms of social and economic development.

Although the new CPSU program declared that the Soviet Union had "entered" the stage of "developed socialism," Gorbachev in effect discarded the concept and replaced it with a new one, that of "acceleration" (*RL Research*, 19 August). At the Twenty-seventh CPSU Congress, Gorbachev attributed the slowdown in development in the 1970s and early 1980s partially to the "psychology" of resistance to change that prevailed under the Brezhnev leadership (*Pravda*, 26 February). In a July speech, Gorbachev said that "we have weakened somewhat over the past fifteen and a half years" (Radio Moscow, 26 July; *RL Research*, 19 August). The concept of "acceleration" acknowledges the growing gap between the USSR and developed capitalist economies. It calls for a reversal of existing trends by "restructuring" of the economy, intensive (as opposed to extensive) development, technological retooling, and massive change in popular attitudes. "Restructuring equals revolution," Gorbachev said in a 31 July speech at Khabarovsk (*Pravda*, 2 August). Viewed from the perspective of traditional Marxism-Leninism, "acceleration" clearly marks a giant step in increased emphasis on the so-called subjective factor.

That "acceleration" faced strong domestic opposition was candidly admitted by Gorbachev at a conference of social scientists in early October. He said that "an acute, uncompromising struggle of ideas" is going on in the Soviet Union. According to Gorbachev, this struggle pits old ways of thinking against the need for profound, revolutionary change in Soviet society (*Pravda*, 2 October). At the same conference, the party's "second secretary," Egor Ligachev, complained about neglect of "the link between ideology and life and the unity of words and action," and charged that Soviet philosophy has "perhaps departed even further from the real world" than have the social sciences (TASS, 1 October; *RL Research*, 2 October).

The concepts of *sblizhenie* (drawing together) and *sliianie* (merger or fusion), which describe the final phases of national integration in the USSR, were downplayed during the year. A major article in *Pravda* (14 March) by "V. Sergeyev" dealt in very pragmatic fashion with nationalities questions and avoided all references to *sblizhenie* and *sliianie*. A February article by Yuri Katcharava in *Kommunisti*, the Georgian daily, directly attacked the concept of the "merging of nations" and accused certain 1960s scholars of attempting to outrun natural historical processes by claiming that the "complete merging of nations" was a contemporary task. Katcharava stressed that the new party program envisioned the "complete unity of nations" as something for the remote future. He added that this "hypothetical complete unity" does not mean the disappearance of the nationalities' separate identities but rather the eradication of antagonisms between them so that they can coexist within a single state (BBC Caris, 21 March).

**Auxiliary and Front Organizations.** One positive indicator of a less rigid domestic climate under Gorbachev was the Eighth Congress of the Soviet Writers' Union, held in June. The congress voted to turn the former dacha of Boris Pasternak at Peredelkino into a museum honoring the controversial poet and novelist. The congress replaced its longtime first secretary, Georgi Markov, who had led attacks on Aleksandr Solzhenitsyn and other dissidents, with the more moderate Vladimir Karpov.

One-third of the union's 63-member secretariat were new appointees, including Evgenii Evtushenko, who presented the museum proposal; poet Andrei Voznesensky, who has pushed for Pasternak's full rehabilitation; Evtushenko's wife, poetess Bella Akhmadulina; and anti-Stalinist songwriter and singer Bulat Okudjava. Some delegates spoke publicly in favor of the publication in the USSR of the banned novel, *Dr. Zhivago* (BBC Caris, 1 July).

The Komsomol and the All-Union Central Council of Trade Unions (AUCCTU) have traditionally been whipping boys for the leadership, even during the relatively tranquil Brezhnev era. In 1986 the two "transmission belts" received less abuse than did the ministers and managers who were cool or hostile to Gorbachev's "acceleration" program. Both organizations were still identified as problem areas in the party leader's September speech in Krasnodar. "We can raise the issue," Gorbachev said, "of making the Komsomol more independent, more responsible, and more self-sufficient right now." As for the trade unions, he accused some officials of "waltzing and hobnobbing with the managers, instead of being firm with them in the interests of the collective" (*Pravda*, 20 September).

The first half of the year featured striking self-criticism by Komsomol leader Viktor M. Mishin at the Twenty-seventh CPSU Congress (ibid., 1 March) and a later frank admission by him that the Komsomol's campaign against drunkenness among young people had as yet achieved "no appreciable results" (*Komsomolskaia pravda*, 15 April). The Komsomol's central committee on 19 July replaced Mishin, 43, by Vladimir Mironenko, a 33-year-old Ukrainian (ibid., 20 July). Mironenko had headed the Komsomol in the Ukraine since 1983. At the same time, the committee scheduled the Twentieth Congress of the All-Union Komsomol for April 1987. Mishin was transferred to the post of secretary of the AUCCTU.

It was widely believed that Mironenko, an "outsider," had been brought in to supervise a house-cleaning of the youth organization's top ranks. But criticism did not stop with Mironenko's appointment. A month after his election, a *Pravda* editorial (16 August) complained that "many Komsomol workers are still in the grip of bureaucracy and confine themselves to the narrow range of official problems" and that "many party committees lack an efficient system in their work with young people and are dominated by hurried campaigns."

The CPSU Central Committee in February took charge of two AUCCTU branch newspapers, in the civil aviation and merchant shipping industries, because the departmental ministries and the professional trade unions wanted to suppress the criticisms that had appeared in the newspapers (Budapest Domestic Service, 11 February; *FBIS*, 12 February). In addition to this flagrant violation of *glasnost'*, the trade unions were criticized for lagging in their role in the "acceleration" campaign. AUCCTU head Stepan A. Shalayev engaged in self-criticism along these lines at the eleventh AUCCTU plenum in July, saying that "we are advancing too slowly." He cited particularly the trade unions' tasks in socialist competition, the solution of social problems, and the elimination of "obsolete stereotypes" (*Trud*, 5 July; *FBIS*, 17 July).

The Fourteenth General Assembly of the World Federation of Scientific Workers was held in Moscow in July; as expected, Soviet "peace" initiatives were played up, particularly Gorbachev's recent arms proposals. The conference was attended by physicists, chemists, biologists, oceanologists, geographers, historians, and sociologists from Europe, Asia, Africa, and America (*Krasnaia zvezda*, 23 July; *FBIS*, 28 July).

The Fifth All-Union Report and Election Conference of the USSR-USA Society, held in Moscow on 29 May, was also dominated by propaganda for Soviet arms control policies; an appeal was addressed to the U.S. public to help "liberate mankind from the pernicious arms race and establish lasting peace on the planet." Academician N. N. Blokhin was elected as chairman of the organization (*Pravda*, 31 May; *FBIS*, 3 June).

**International Views, Positions, and Activities.** Gorbachev's impressive performance at the November 1985 Geneva summit had demonstrated in a striking manner the altered image of the USSR in world affairs traceable to the new leader's activist approach. Upon coming to office, Gorbachev had initiated a whirlwind of activity on various fronts in an attempt to overcome the relative isolation of the USSR and to carry out his apparent mandate to effect a reversal of unfavorable trends in the world "correlation of forces." This involved changes in both strategy and tactics.

Tactically, the new leadership sought to convey the impression of a more conciliatory and open diplomacy, corresponding to the approach of *glasnost'* and greater flexibility on the home front. This had already been evident during 1985 as the new foreign minister, Eduard Shevardnadze, brought a fresh approach to international negotiations that contrasted starkly with the stubborn, stodgy posture of Soviet diplomacy for nearly three decades under the tenure of Andrei Gromyko. In terms of policymaking, however, Shevardnadze was kept on a short leash; Gorbachev made clear that policy would be formulated by the party leadership and that the independence the Smolensk Square establishment had attained under Gromyko would not be tolerated.

The new year brought further proof of the leadership's commitment to an overhaul of style and organization in the foreign policy realm. Brezhnev holdover Konstantin Rusakov, the Central Committee secretary for relations with ruling communist parties, "retired" on the eve of the Twenty-seventh CPSU Congress. At the conclusion of the congress, octogenarian Boris Ponomarev was replaced as party secretary and head of the International Department by Anatolii Dobrynin, longtime ambassador to the United States. Subsequently, a thorough housecleaning of personnel was carried out in both the Foreign Ministry and the departments of the Central Committee concerned with foreign policy (see above). Reportedly, the purse was supervised by Dobrynin, who was quickly recognized as Gorbachev's principal adviser on foreign affairs. According to some sources, he was given an office near Gorbachev's inside the Kremlin.

Overall Soviet strategy appeared to encompass these major goals: (1) achieve an arms control agreement with the United States that would obviate future overwhelming strains on Soviet resources; (2) pursue, to whatever extent possible, the "uncoupling," politically and militarily, of Western Europe and the United States and defuse wherever possible hostile relations with other powers and even minor states on the Soviet empire's periphery; (3) restore the stability of the East European bloc under the undisputed leadership of Moscow; (4) maintain the USSR's status as a superpower and reject emphatically denials of the USSR's claims and capacity to sustain interests in all parts of the world; and (5) reduce the costs, both political and economic, of Soviet commitments in the Third World, while concentrating on the preservation of existing footholds in key areas. The inner consistency of this apparent strategic framework was open to some question; particularly obvious was a certain degree of tension between goals (1) and (2).

Persistent rumors circulating in Moscow indicated a split among Gorbachev's advisers on foreign policy strategy. Dobrynin was reported to place highest priority on a stable relationship with the United States and conclusion of a satisfactory arms control pact. Another influential Central Committee secretary, Aleksandr Iakovlev, was said to advocate downgrading of the relationship with the United States and enhanced emphasis on Western Europe and the "borderlands." During 1985, Gorbachev had appeared to favor the Iakovlev strategy until the Geneva summit; after the summit, he made a dramatic attempt to influence West European opinion.

For most of 1986, relations with Washington assumed central status, but it was not clear how much Dobrynin's influence affected this. The pressure of events obviously exerted an unavoidable impact. For much of the year, the Soviets sought to obtain maximum propaganda leverage on arms control issues and coyly played the summit card, displaying recalcitrance on the timing and even evoking doubts about the holding of the promised superpower meeting. In a dramatic turnabout, the superpowers agreed to a "preparatory" summit in Iceland in October, moving with almost unseemly haste to organize a major conference in a few days time. The Americans' rush to confer may have been partially explained by domestic political considerations, with the midterm congressional elections less than a month away.

On the Soviet side, the seemingly high price paid for resolution of the Daniloff-Zakharov affair (see below), a prerequisite for holding of the conference, suggested a sense of urgency and strong Kremlin pressures on Gorbachev to show some results from his new-style foreign policy. Further, Gorbachev's uncharacteristic reliance on position papers aroused speculation that he was acting on strict Politburo instructions and that his independent authority in foreign affairs, flaunted at the Geneva summit, had undergone considerable erosion.

Before the Reykjavik summit broke up over the American refusal to forego testing of SDI weapons, both sides had made startling and unprecedented concessions on arms control matters that reverberated around the world, bringing into question existing security policies of all major powers. Gorbachev carefully left the door open for future agreements with the United States but the possibilities for major arms control pacts with a lame-duck American president adamant on SDI (and soon to be severely wounded politically by revelations of the Iran arms fiasco) were highly problematical. Moreover, it was by no means certain that Gorbachev could hold his own troops in line for an arms agreement that Washington would accept.

Hopes for cultivation of a "European" attitude that would make Moscow a more acceptable partner for West European governments—and Washington a less welcome one—were dealt a severe setback by Chernobyl, described by most Western observers as the worst public relations disaster for the Kremlin since the Korean airliner incident of 1983. The effects of radioactive fallout in Western Europe and the Soviets' handling of information on the catastrophe evoked a firestorm of censure from Western governments and even harsh criticism from some communists, especially in Italy. Moreover, the prospect of substituting neutralist and antinuclear policies of leftist political parties for the fizzling "peace" movement appeared rather bleak at year's end, particularly in Britain, where, after an earlier surge in the polls, the Labourites fell behind Margaret Thatcher's Conservatives, primarily because of the former's radical stance on nuclear matters.

The East European bloc remained relatively quiet during the year but there was little, if any, evidence that the Kremlin had made progress in resolving the contradictions underlying recent instability in the region.

In the Near East, the Soviets could count little, if any, gain in influence. Loud Soviet protests followed the U.S. bombing of Libya, but Moscow made rather plain its unwillingness to take any real military risks for Moammar Khadafy, the erratic Libyan leader. Lebanon's chaotic politics continued to frustrate Moscow, as Syria pursued its own independent line. However, there was some prospect at year's end that the return of the PLO to Lebanon, and Western diplomatic shunning of Damascus over the issue of terrorism, would enhance Soviet leverage over Syria's Assad. Further east, overtures to Iran seemed to offer some hope for at least minimal normalization of relations, and Moscow showed signs of giving higher priority to these efforts after America's second Iranian debacle within a decade.

The diplomatic offensives for reduction of ten-sions with two major border states, China and Japan, were still at best in the early stages, with no real movement on substantive issues. India was a different story. Gorbachev's November visit to New Delhi appeared to be mainly successful; Soviet openhandedness apparently deflected Rajiv Gandhi from his earlier pronounced tilt toward the United States.

The war in Afghanistan entered its eighth year and continued to go badly. According to one report, Gorbachev had concluded that the war was not winnable; Afghanistan, it seemed, had indeed turned out to be Moscow's Vietnam.

All in all, the year provided a crash course for neophyte diplomat Gorbachev in the difficulties of operating the multidimensional foreign policy of a superpower, especially one plagued by domestic vulnerabilities and a tarnished image abroad. Nevertheless, there was the undeniable impression of a new élan and heightened competence in the Soviet diplomatic establishment, permitting Moscow to confront the West with fresh challenges on a variety of fronts.

*U.S.-Soviet Relations.* The overwhelming issue in U.S.-Soviet relations was arms control, with Moscow continuing to insist that SDI was the principal obstacle to a general agreement. In January, Gorbachev offered new proposals, including a phased elimination of all nuclear weapons by the end of the century, and starting with withdrawal by both sides of medium-range missiles in Europe. Britain and France could maintain their current levels of nuclear armament during the first phase, but Soviet SS-20 missiles would remain in Asia until the final stage of disarmament. The United States must abandon its SDI program (*Pravda*, 16 January). At the same time, Gorbachev announced a three-month extension of the Soviet moratorium on nuclear tests. President Reagan and other U.S. officials welcomed the apparently more flexible posture on the Soviet side, but the proposed ban on SDI was, of course, unacceptable. Many U.S. experts were highly skeptical about the Soviet proposals (*NYT*, 17 January).

The Soviet press reported favorable world reaction to the latest Gorbachev proposals (*Pravda*, 17, 18, 19 January). Meanwhile, an expressed Soviet willingness to accept on-site inspections attracted special attention (ibid., 22 January; *NYT*, 24 February). In February, Gorbachev sent a message to the regular meeting of the Geneva disarmament conference, calling attention to the Soviet moratorium and insisting that the United States was obliged to respond. In Geneva, a first deputy foreign minister, Georgi M. Kornienko, asserted that SDI was a violation of the 1972 ABM treaty (*Pravda*, 21 February). In his speech to the Twenty-seventh CPSU Congress, Gorbachev gave highest priority to his arms control proposals (ibid., 27 February).

While Americans and Soviets sparred over arms control in Geneva and elsewhere, a major media event occurred in Moscow. Senator Edward Kennedy appeared in a taped statement and interview on Soviet television. Kennedy noted that the United States and USSR were at odds on Afghanistan, human rights, and other issues but called the Kremlin's recent arms control proposals "constructive." He voiced reservations about SDI but said he was certain that President Reagan was willing to negotiate "a real reduction in nuclear weapons." Upon his return to Washington, Kennedy said that he had spoken forcefully to Soviet officials about the treatment of two prominent dissidents, Anatolii Shcharansky and Andrei Sakharov (*WP*, 10 February). Two days after the Kennedy telecast in Moscow, Shcharansky crossed over to the West in Berlin, the outcome of a deal reported prior to Kennedy's arrival in Moscow (*NYT*, 12 February). The freeing of Shcharansky aroused qualified optimism in some quarters of the West about the possibilities for greater Soviet reasonableness at home and abroad.

But the "Spirit of Geneva," always nebulous, was soon largely forgotten as the wide divergence on policy between Moscow and Washington became more and more apparent. For several months, alternating verbal attacks on Washington and conciliatory gestures, the Soviets made substantial progress in their "peace offensive," enjoying some success in the depiction of the Reagan administration as an obdurate force resisting efforts to reduce world tensions.

In February, the United States rejected Soviet proposals (made at the 40-nation conference on disarmament in Geneva) for an interim agreement barring the spread of chemical weapons (*NYT*, 12 February). In March, the United States ordered the Soviets to reduce their United Nations mission in New York—for many years regarded by American intelligence officials as a major center of espionage—from 275 to 170 Soviet nationals by April 1988 (*WP*, 8 March). The Soviet Foreign Ministry lodged a formal protest in Washington, claiming that the United States had no legal right to limit the USSR's U.N. personnel (*Pravda*, 12 March).

The Soviets issued another protest, for alleged violation of Soviet territorial waters, when the American guided-missile carrier *Yorktown* and the destroyer *Caron* conducted exercises in the Black Sea from 10 to 17 March, apparently for intelligence-gathering purposes (ibid., 19 March). The punitive raid by the United States against Libya that followed a terrorist bombing in West Berlin was denounced by the Soviets in the strongest terms (ibid., 27, 28 March) but, aside from some movements of Soviet intelligence-gathering ships in the Mediterranean, there was no military response from the USSR. With a barrage of words and no action, Moscow made it quite clear that it was unwilling to take even marginal risks for its uncontrollable and sometimes embarrassing ally, Khadafy.

The Soviet delegation at the Geneva arms talks proposed in May that United States and Soviet intermediate-range missiles in Europe be reduced to zero. U.S. officials, however, said that the offer only put into formal language an earlier Soviet proposal and contained the same flaws as Gorbachev's arms control plan outlined in January, namely, failure to deal with Soviet missiles in Asia and insistence on a freeze at current levels of British and French missiles (*LAT*, 16 May). American spokesmen speculated that the Soviet move in Geneva was designed to distract attention from adverse publicity on the Chernobyl incident. Meanwhile, Moscow extracted maximum propaganda advantage from the American resumption of nuclear tests by extending its unilateral moratorium on tests to 6 August, anniversary of the bombing of Hiroshima. When the United States announced its fourth nuclear test of the year in Nevada, the Soviets denounced the test as demonstrating the Reagan administration's unwillingness to listen to "the voice of reason" (TASS, 21 May; *FBIS*, 22 May).

The United States, hoping for a wider agreement, rejected Soviet proposals for limited East-West contacts at the international conference in Bern dealing with these matters. However, the United States welcomed Soviet agreement on the emigration of members of divided families; 36 families and over 100 persons were involved, the largest single reunification of divided families since the United States started pressing such cases in the late 1950s (BBC Caris, 28 May).

As the arms deadlock continued, the United States and the USSR headed for a major confrontation. Following the FBI's 23 August arrest on espionage charges of Gennadi Zakharov, a Soviet physicist assigned to the United Nations (*WP*, 24 August), the Soviets retaliated by arresting Nicholas Daniloff, Moscow correspondent of *U.S. News and World Report* (and a descendant of one of the Decembrists), on the same charge (*NYT*, 31 August). Daniloff, who was scheduled for an early reassignment and departure from the Soviet Union, had reportedly long been a target of the KGB. Western observers almost unanimously concluded that the arrest of Daniloff "in the act of receiving classified documents" was a classic KGB set-up. Some Westerners thought Daniloff's arrest might be an independent KGB action, ignoring the fact that the USSR has usually made "hardball" responses to similar incidents in the past.

Secretary of State George Shultz ruled out a Zakharov-Daniloff swap (ibid., 6 September). Daniloff was formally charged with espionage on 7 September, and the Soviets claimed that he had been engaged in various acts of espionage, including the gathering of intelligence on Soviet military operations in Afghanistan (*Izvestiia*, 8 September). On 12 September, the two accused men were released to the custody of their respective ambassadors, with charges still pending (*NYT*, 13 September). Five days later, the United States ordered the expulsion of 25 U.N.-based Soviet diplomats, claiming that it was a follow-up to the March order and had no connection with the Daniloff case (*WP*, 18 September). Gorbachev, on a visit to Krasnodar, added fuel to the flames by asserting that Daniloff was a "spy caught red-handed" (TASS, 18 September).

President Reagan summoned Shevardnadze, in the United States for the annual fall meeting of the U.N. General Assembly, to the White House on 19 September to "convey the strength of his feelings" about the Daniloff case (*NYT*, 20 September). Several meetings followed between Shevardnadze and Secretary of State Shultz, and on 29 September Daniloff was released. The deal cut by the two sides included a no contest plea by Zakharov and his departure from the United States without a formal expulsion order, the scrapping of the U.S. expulsion order regarding Soviet diplomats (although the United States did subsequently continue the reduction of Soviet diplomatic personnel), and the release of prominent Soviet dissident Yuri Orlov (AP, 29 September).

The most stunning part of the deal was announced the day after Daniloff's departure from the Soviet Union: Reagan and Gorbachev would meet in Reykjavik, Iceland, on 11 October to resume the search for an arms control accord (ibid., 30 September). Both sides characterized the conference as a "preliminary" meeting rather than a formal summit, but the distinction eluded most Western observers. Clearly, both sides were willing to pay a price for resumption of negotiations at the highest level, but the initiative for the "non-summit" came from the Soviets.

That the Reykjavik meeting caught Washington by surprise, but not Moscow, was reflected in the performance of the two delegations. Ten days had obviously not been sufficient for the U.S. delegation to prepare. They arrived in Iceland sans agenda or clearly outlined positions; during the conference there were reports of squabbling among Reagan's advisers and inept staff work. Gorbachev and his new foreign policy team, on the other hand, came armed with carefully prepared positions and position papers, upon which the Soviet leader relied heavily in his talks with Reagan.

In two days of meetings, according to Secretary Shultz, the negotiators had verbally agreed to slash long-range missile and bomber arsenals in half in five years and completely by 1996. In addition, they were prepared to eliminate all but 100 medium-range missiles on each side—including all those deployed in Europe—during the first five-year phase, and the balance of those in 1996 (ibid., 12 October). The potential deal fell apart when the Soviets made it conditional on the limitation of SDI to laboratory research during the ten-year period, with no testing of SDI weaponry (*NYT*, 13 October). With the collapse of the summit, each side initially blamed the other in rather bitter terms (ABC News, 12 October). Both Reagan and Gorbachev, however, subsequently maintained that substantial progress had been made at Reykjavik and said that the arms control process would continue.

The Reykjavik summit had aroused high hopes, partially due to the apparent Soviet violation of a news blackout agreement. The first general reaction to the lack of agreement was one of disappointment and shock around the world. Sober second thoughts soon had their day. In the United States, critics of the negotiations ranged from conservative columnist George Will to Senator Sam Nunn, the principal Democratic spokesman on military matters in the Senate. They pointed out that the United States had nearly agreed to the "uncoupling" of American and West European defenses, a goal long sought by the Soviets (*WP*, 14–17 October). West European leaders publicly supported the United States and shared the optimistic assessment of progress made. Privately, they expressed great uneasiniess at the apparent U.S. willingness to "uncouple" defenses at a meeting from which they were excluded (*NYT*, 19 October).

Faced with mounting criticism (and some uncertainty about what the United States had actually offered), the Reagan administration did some backtracking. Negotiations resumed in Vienna, between the foreign ministers, in the following week. Secretary of State Shultz said that Reagan had offered to eliminate all offensive ballistic missiles during the next ten years and had tried to persuade the Soviets to start negotiating an agreement on medium-range missiles without making all issues contingent on SDI. Shevardnadze said that the president had agreed to eliminate "all nuclear weapons" and that the proposals presented by Gorbachev at Reykjavik had to be considered as a package (*Newsweek*, 17 November). After a five-hour negotiating session, the meeting broke up, and Shevardnadze displayed a bitter reaction to the press. In Moscow, Gorbachev said there could be "no road back" from the positions taken in Reykjavik (TASS, 7 November) and, in Geneva, Soviet negotiators at the soon-to-be-recessed arms control talks closely followed the proposals set out at the summit.

Following the Reykjavik meeting, the United States enforced its March order on reduction of Soviet diplomatic personnel. In response, the USSR ruled that no Soviet citizens would be allowed to work at the U.S. embassy in Moscow. The exodus of housekeeping personnel made it difficult for the embassy to function (*NYT*, 30 November), but Soviet capacity for diplomatic espionage had apparently been greatly reduced, in both Moscow and the United States.

One positive aspect of the Reykjavik meeting that was evidently not affected by the summit breakup concerned the exchange of information. Charles Wick, head of the U.S. Information Agency, disclosed in late October that he had met with a secretary of the CPSU Central Committee, Aleksandr Iakovlev, in Reykjavik and that they had worked out the general outlines of an agreement. Wick said that Iakovlev had offered to stop jamming Voice of America shortwave broadcasts if the Soviets could gain access to the AM radio audience in the United States (UPI, 29 October).

Iakovlev has the reputation among Kremlin-watchers of having a European, rather than a super-power, orientation in his foreign policy views, as opposed to the approach of Anatolii Dobrynin, who is said to give first priority to relations with the United States (see above). It was noted at Reykjavik that, at the outset of the conference, Dobrynin was highly visible but, when Gorbachev met the press following the summit collapse, Iakovlev was seated on his left, Shevardnadze on his right, and Dobrynin was completely out of the television picture. Dobrynin, however, was particularly prominent during Gorbachev's late November visit to India. Whether there was a tug-of-war between Gorbachev's advisers was, of course, impossible to determine. But in the weeks following Reykjavik, the Soviets did play openly for a European audience.

After the United States exceeded the limits set by the SALT II treaty by deploying a B-52 bomber capable of carrying cruise missiles (*NYT*, 29 November), the Soviets refrained from following suit. A Kremlin announcement said that "Washington is making a big mistake" and that, although the USSR had grounds to consider itself free of the treaty, it was not ready to scrap it—"taking into account the immense universal importance of the issue and the need to preserve the key restraint on the strategic arms race" (TASS, 5 December; *Pravda*, 6 December).

Moscow also maintained its unilateral moratorium on underground nuclear testing for two months after the Iceland summit. However, after the United States had carried out 42 tests at its Nevada testing site during the seventeen months the Soviet moratorium had been in effect, Moscow announced in December that the USSR would resume nuclear testing after the beginning of the new year (TASS, 18 December; *Pravda*, 19 December). The Soviet ambassador to the United States, Yuri Dubinin, said on the day following the Moscow announcement that the USSR was prepared to delay resumption of nuclear tests if the Reagan administration would start negotiations on a test ban by 1 January (AP, 19 December). Meanwhile, it was revealed that the Soviet Union was developing plans to defeat an American-based defense system. It would use dummy missiles, countermeasures against lasers, and other steps to improve the survivability of Soviet missiles (*NYT*, 18 December).

Spectacular revelations in November and December concerning the role of the U.S. National Security Council in arms dealings with Iran and diversion of funds to support the *contras* in Nicaragua did not augur well for the arms control process. Gorbachev had invested a great deal of political capital in the push for arms limitations, and a politically weakened U.S. president was unlikely to secure approval at home for an arms control package—witness the fate of SALT II in 1979. On the other hand, Reykjavik made it seem increasingly unlikely that Reagan would ever agree to an arms control agreement that Gorbachev could sell in Moscow, and the president's domestic political woes made more difficult the funding of his pet SDI project.

*Western Europe.* A new "European" orientation of Soviet policy was very much in evidence during the early months of the year. Principally, this involved drumming up support for Soviet arms control proposals and the attempt to use West European antinuclear and "neutralist" sentiment as a lever to pressure the United States in negotiations. The long-range objective appeared to be the "uncoupling" of West European and American defenses and the establishment of closer relations between Moscow and West European states under the rubric of "Europeanism," rationalized in terms of claimed continental interests. The latter goal was especially reflected in the new "open," more flexible approach of Soviet diplomacy and a shakeup of major European ambassadorships.

The Soviet media spotlighted West European support for and "interest" in Gorbachev's January nuclear arms proposals. On the day following Gorbachev's issuance of his arms control plan, the West German foreign minister, Hans-Dietrich Genscher, was reportedly "welcoming" the new Soviet peace initiatives and promising that the FRG and its partners in NATO would "carefully study these proposals." At the same time, Moscow heralded the support of the British "Campaign for Nuclear Disarmament" (TASS, 16 January; *FBIS*, 17 January). By the beginning of February, the Soviet press could report positive responses by governments or "public organizations" in all West European countries. A *Pravda* editorial (4 February) called the Soviet response a "barometer reflecting the general weather of sentiments in the world" and emphasized the "specific continental features" of the Gorbachev plan and the "European aspect of the nuclear problem." *Pravda* remarked, "It is time to cut the Gordian knot and find a way out of the impasse. The European aspect of the Soviet nuclear disarmament plan proposes just such a bold, radical solution."

In early March, Foreign Minister Shevardnadze met with Spain's ambassador to Moscow, Jose Luis Xifra de Ocerin, who said that the Soviet proposals were viewed in Spain as "reasonable and bold" and that Spain "welcomes the complete elimination of nuclear arms as the ultimate objective" (TASS, 7 March; *FBIS*, 10 March). Moscow had high hopes for the Spanish referendum on NATO (*Pravda*, 25 February), which were dashed when Spain's voters, by a narrow margin, opted for continued participation in the Western alliance (ibid., 14 March). Nevertheless, this setback did not slow the Soviets' drive to promote "neutralism."

Prime Minister Ryzhkov represented the USSR at the funeral of Sweden's Premier Olof Palme in Stockholm and conferred with Swedish political leaders and with world figures who attended the rites (ibid., 15 March). Palme had been regarded as Moscow's best friend in ruling government circles in Western Europe, and his loss was keenly felt. But the Soviet press stressed that the new premier, Ingvar Carlsson, was an advocate of a nuclear-free zone in northern Europe and had pledged to continue Sweden's policy of neutrality (ibid., 14 March; TASS, 20 March).

The shakeup in diplomatic personnel was apparently mainly designed to assure implementation of the fresh Gorbachev approach to foreign policy at the ambassadorial level. But the appointment of a new ambassador to the FRG may have had other aims as well. Yuli A. Kvitsinsky had been one of the principal Soviet arms negotiators in Geneva and his assignment to Bonn neatly complemented the Soviet propaganda pitch on nuclear arms to the West German public (Paris, AFP, 8 March; *FBIS*, 10 March). Kvitsinsky replaced Vladimir Semenov, 75, reputed author of the Brezhnev Doctrine.

Subsequently, Yakov P. Ryabov, a deputy premier close to the new leadership in Moscow, was dispatched as ambassador to Paris, and Leonid Zamyatin, head of the soon-to-be-defunct International Information Department of the Central Committee, was appointed ambassador to Great Britain. It was not immediately clear what Zamyatin's qualifications were for his new post except his command of the English language. His appointment was one that did not seem compatible with the new style of Soviet diplomacy; perhaps it was calculated that he could do less harm to East-West relations in London than in Moscow.

Other new ambassadors to West European countries included V. F. Stukalin (Greece), Anatolii I. Blatov (Netherlands), S. K. Romanovsky (Spain), and Boris N. Pastukhov (Denmark) (*RL Research*, 16 July).

The Chernobyl accident and its aftermath were highly embarrassing to Moscow, occurring at the peak of Moscow's antinuclear campaign; the incident strained relations with most West European governments. Moscow was besieged with official and unofficial protests, even coming from the Italian and Belgian communist parties (see below). The major complaint of official West European states' communications to Moscow was the lack of information from the USSR both before and after the spread of radioactivity beyond Soviet borders. Typical was the complaint of Norway, over whose territory the radioactive cloud had passed. The Norwegian ambassador to the USSR, Olav Bucher-Johanessen, told the Soviets "unambiguously" that there should have been a warning about the nuclear accident at Chernobyl (Oslo, *Aftenposten*, 30 April; *FBIS*, 5 May).

Even before the Soviets disclosed details to the home audience, the public relations campaign to repair the damage was underway in the West. Boris Eltsin, new party boss of Moscow, in West Germany for the congress of the German Communist Party, was the point man in this campaign. In interviews with Western newsmen, Eltsin gave the frankest report of the disaster then available and lashed out at Western media coverage of the accident, calling it "slanderous," with "clear and precise aims" (Hamburg, ARD television, 2 May; Paris, AFP, 5 May; *FBIS*, 5 May). A Soviet delegation headed by Ivan Frolov, new editor of *Kommunist*, shortly thereafter visited West Germany at the behest of West German Social Democrats and met with officials of SPD and CDU/CSU fractions of the Bundestag. According to Soviet reports, the delegation emphasized Soviet disarmament propopsals and rebuffed the "anti-Soviet conjectures and insinuations circulated in the West" about Chernobyl (TASS, 13 May; *FBIS*, 15 May).

Meanwhile, a new Social Democratic government came to power in Norway. It was welcomed by Moscow for its avowed intention to "devote much attention to maintaining good relations with the Soviet Union"; however, it was noted in Moscow that Premier Gro Harlem Brundtland had also pledged continuing "cooperation and solidarity" with NATO (*Izvestiia*, 11 May; TASS, 13 May; *FBIS*, 15 May).

In July, Gorbachev welcomed to Moscow President François Mitterrand of France and pushed the pan-European theme. The Soviet leader called on Europe "to speak more definitely and confidently on its own behalf" and "to press for progress on all the ongoing talks" on arms control. In response, Mitterand said that "it is time for Europeans to become masters of their own destiny" (*LAT*, 8 July). Gorbachev pledged that the Soviet Union would abide by the human rights agreement negotiated at Bern but not signed because of U.S. objections to a watered-down document (BBC Caris, 8 July).

Meanwhile, in its approach to West Germany, Moscow played both sides of the street. The conservative government's foreign minister, Hans-Dietrich Genscher, was in Moscow in July for talks with Gorbachev, Shevardnadze, and other Soviet officials. Gorbachev reportedly told Genscher that the interests of the FRG required it to play an active role on disarmament matters that should include, among other things, opposition to SDI. When the FRG followed such a policy, Gorbachev intimated, Bonn would find the USSR a reliable diplomatic partner (*Neues Deutschland*, 22 July). The West German left, Moscow's long-run hope for neutralization of the FRG, was not neglected. The chairman of the SPD, Willy Brandt, long a Moscow favorite, was spotlighted in the Soviet press for his criticism of Western governments' slowness in responding to the USSR's arms control proposals. Brandt was quoted as saying: "The West is wasting time. And this does not only concern nuclear missiles but chemical missiles as well" (*Pravda*, 19 June). Johannes Rau, minister-president of North Rhine–Westphalia and the SPD's designated candidate for chancellor in 1987, was guest of the RSFSR Council of Ministers at the West German industrial trade show in Moscow (ibid., 25 June). But the relatively low-key concentration on West Germany, which contrasted starkly with the heavy-handed Soviet attempts to influence the 1983 FRG elections, was evidently not making the desired headway with the West German public. Despite the frequent political fumbles of the Kohl government, the SPD continued to fare poorly in the public opinion polls.

A major move in the Soviet "peace offensive" in northern Europe was reported by Egor Ligachev in November. Ligachev said that the USSR "over the past months" had removed all intermediate-range nuclear missiles from its major western Arctic base near Murmansk and had reduced the number of intermediate-range missiles in the Leningrad area. The "second secretary" indicated that the action was part of an initiative aimed toward making northern Europe nuclear-free (AP, 13 November).

The velvet glove was most apparent within the framework of the new-style Soviet diplomacy, but Moscow still brandished the stick at times. The Soviet press denounced the signing by Italy of the "Memorandum of Mutual Understanding" concerning participation of Italian firms in the U.S. Star Wars program. "By this act," said *Pravda* (20 September), "Italy officially subscribes to the practical implementation of dangerous plans for creating space-strike weapons." The proposed deployment of 30 Stealth reconnaissance aircraft at the U.S. Air Force base at Lakenheath, Suffolk, brought Soviet threats of retaliation against Britain in the event of their use against the USSR—on the grounds that they could not be distinguished from nuclear-capable Stealths. "Those who hand over their territory for U.S. military ventures," said Moscow, "are taking yet another step toward U.S. nuclear enslavement" and "an extremely dangerous step into 'invisibility'" (*Krasnaia zvezda*, 12 September; *FBIS*, 16 September).

Moscow has lately placed its highest hopes for European detachment from Washington on Britain. The Labour Party, under Neil Kinnock, made a spectacular recovery and adopted far-ranging proposals for a nuclear-free Britain. By December, however, the Labour Party had again fallen behind Margaret Thatcher's Conservatives in the polls.

*Eastern Europe.* The East European bloc was relatively quiet during the year, with the Chernobyl disaster producing only mild ripples on the political surface. Gorbachev appeared to enjoy success in regard to his aims of promoting greater bloc cohesion and of lining up the East European allies behind his world policy. Nevertheless, the underlying problems of the bloc remained, particularly tensions over East European hopes for greater technological and other links with the West, nationalist resistance to Soviet domination, and the "contradiction" inherent in differing levels of domestic conformity to Soviet policies.

As in the West, the Chernobyl disaster caused a stir, particularly in Poland and Hungary. But the Soviets largely ignored the consequences for the USSR's allied neighbors, and Eastern Europe was treated briefly and casually in Gorbachev's 14 May speech on the accident. Gorbachev did not mention fallout beyond the Soviet borders or long-range health threats; he said nothing about delay in reporting the incident; and there were no apologies for the damage resulting from Soviet negligence. The Soviet leader said that the East European states had accepted the Soviet misfortune as their own and that the USSR was grateful for their expressions of sympathy (Moscow Television, 14 May; *RFE Research*, 20 May).

Moscow was more successful in securing formal support for its world and bloc policies than in getting the allies to follow its lead in confronting do-

mestic problems. But it was not immediately clear to the East European leaders how the Soviets' domestic program of renewal would be expected to affect their own policies. From Berlin to Sofia, bloc politicians moved cautiously, keeping a wary eye on Moscow. At the Twenty-seventh CPSU Congress, there were some indications that the new leadership in Moscow looked most favorably on the domestic policies pursued by the Jaruzelski leadership in Poland. General Jaruzelski was accorded more attention than any other East European leader, and Polish officials interpreted Gorbachev's major speech to the congress as meaning that Poland's regime had a "free hand" to implement decentralizing policies and to "try to rid the economy of unproductive failures." The impression of Moscow's strong support for Jaruzelski seemed confirmed by the general's visit to Vilnius, capital of Soviet Lithuania and former Polish territory (*NYT*, 10 March).

East Germany, however, has generally been the East European country held up as an example during Gorbachev's tenure as Soviet leader. (BBC Caris, 9 June). But Soviet satisfaction with East German economic performance was not the only factor in the GDR-USSR relationship. Moscow displayed great uneasiness over the East Germans' drive for stronger links with West Germany. The Soviet drive for tighter integration of the socialist economies, frequently expressed during the year, directly contradicted the pan-European appeal aimed at Western audiences. The resulting tension was obvious throughout the year but was muted at the various gatherings of the bloc leaders, where the appearance of monolithism was maintained.

The country watched most closely by Western observers was Hungary, whose economic reform served as a stimulus in the debates going on in Moscow about organization of the Soviet economy. There were indications that the new Soviet leaders not only rejected the Hungarian reform as a model for the USSR but also were concerned about the potential political effects of this experimentation within Hungary and throughout the bloc. A *Pravda* article (22 January) entitled "The Limits of Mutual Cooperation" (by correspondents I. Vorozheikin and V. Gerasimov) stated that experience with the capitalist countries had convinced our "Hungarian friends" that economic cooperation with the West is profitable "only if accompanied by . . . the all-round development of integration with the CMEA countries." The article also warned that Hungary's booming tourist industry held ideological dangers, saying that many Western tourists "try to use commercial contacts and scientific or cultural exchanges as a channel for introducing bourgeois ideology, antisocialist propaganda."

The January *Pravda* article followed by seven months the much-publicized and hard-hitting June 1985 "D. Vladimirov" article in *Pravda*, which appeared to call for greater subordination of the bloc countries to Moscow. Notably, the January article went further by extending the discussion from commercial exchanges into the field of tourism and personal contacts (BBC Caris, 29 January). The visit to Budapest by KGB chief Viktor Chebrikov in April coincided with a fresh wave of harassment against Hungarian dissidents, many of whom were subsequently fined (ibid., 9 June). And when Gorbachev visited Budapest in June, the official communiqué emphasized the need for further development of cooperation between the two countries and among the "countries of the socialist commonwealth" (*Pravda*, 10 June).

Talks with Hungarian leader Kádár were followed by the regular meeting of the Warsaw Pact countries in Budapest. Most attention was devoted to Soviet "peace" initiatives and, predictably, the organization solidly endorsed Gorbachev's arms control proposals (*Pravda*, 11 June; *NYT*, 12 June). As at the East German and Polish party congresses, when the allies turned to economic matters, the emphasis was on enhanced integration of the bloc.

The stress on Soviet foreign policy goals was also evident at the April congress of the Socialist Unity Party in East Germany, which endorsed the USSR's recent initiatives on arms control. Despite Gorbachev's attendance as chief Soviet representative, the East Germans ignored the drive for domestic renewal in the USSR. Gorbachev called for "bold experiments" in economic relations by the socialist countries and the elimination of excessive bureaucracy, complacency, and "antiquated, stereotyped ways of thinking." SED leader Erich Honecker, on the other hand, in his major speech to the congress promised strict continuity of the conservative internal policies pursued by the East German regime for the past fifteen years (*NYT*, 23 April).

Perhaps the most ominous development for the East Europeans was Gorbachev's speech to the Polish party congress in June. While praising the present Polish leadership, Gorbachev reaffirmed the Brezhnev Doctrine and linked it to the Helsinki Pact. A major lesson of the recent events in Poland, he said, was that "socialist gains are irreversible" and that any attempt "to wrench a country away

from the socialist community" represents a threat to the "entire postwar settlement and, in the final analysis, to peace" (*RL Research*, 30 June; *Pravda*, 1 July). However, for the foreseeable future, East European leaders could expect to confront not massive armed interventions but rather more subtle Soviet political and economic pressure to induce conformity and subordination to Moscow.

*Afghanistan.* The conflict in Afghanistan entered its eighth year in December amid signs that Moscow was more interested than before in a way out of the imbroglio. Pakistan's leader, Zia-ul Haq, said in March that the Soviet Union appeared to be seriously interested in exploring a political settlement of the war (*LAT*, 3 March). Such talk had been heard before, but this time the Soviets began a new round of U.N.-sponsored indirect talks on Afghanistan in May and announced the withdrawal of 6,000 troops from the country. There was considerable doubt as to whether this was a real reduction or merely the regular replacement of troops; Chinese and Japanese officials, particularly, were skeptical (AP, 8 November).

While these moves were making news, the Soviets applied *glasnost'* to the war, with franker discussions of the conflict itself and press reports of the alienation of returning veterans (*CSM*, 13 January; *Sovetskaia Rossiia*, 4 May). The low morale of the Soviet troops was presumably one of the reasons Gorbachev referred to Afghanistan as a "bleeding wound" (*LAT*, 23 January).

Meanwhile, a leadership change took place in Afghanistan. Babrak Karmal had spent the month of April in Moscow; upon his return to Kabul, he was replaced by the 39-year-old former secret police chief, General Najibullah. That the change was inspired by Moscow was indicated by the sudden deployment of Soviet troops at key points in Kabul after Najibullah's election. Official reports stressed the new leader's allegiance to Moscow. "He is known as an internationalist," said TASS, "a great friend of the Soviet Union" (TASS, 6 May; *WP*, 7 May; Reuters, 6 May; *Pravda*, 8 May).

In November, a Soviet offensive resulted in the loss of numerous guerrilla positions in the Kama-Dhaha area of Ningrahar, close to the Pakistan border. U.N. envoy Diego Cordovez arrived in Kabul to try to arrange resumption of the peace talks, once again recessed (AP, 22 November). In December, reports from Moscow reflected gloom about the situation in Afghanistan. Sources in the Soviet capital reported that Gorbachev had decided the war was "not winnable" and was more seriously than ever looking for a way out (ABC News, 11, 12 December). Not only was there no prospect of early victory; the tide of the battle seemed to have turned against the Soviets. One factor was the increasing use of U.S. arms by the rebels. The U.S. State Department reported that Soviet forces had been losing an average of one plane or helicopter a day for the past three months to Afghan resistance forces armed with sophisticated U.S. weapons (AP, 16 December). Lieutenant General Mikhail Sotskov confirmed the use of U.S. Stinger missiles by the resistance fighters and Soviet losses of aircraft since November (UPI, 19 December).

*Japan.* The apparent mild thaw in Soviet-Japanese relations during 1985 was followed by the visit of Foreign Minister Shevardnadze to Tokyo from 15 to 20 January (*Pravda*, 21 January). Willingness of the Soviets to discuss the Northern Territories issue had been a Japanese condition for the issuance of a joint communiqué (*RL Research*, 15 January); the former Soviet foreign minister, Gromyko, had not only refused to talk about the issue, he had also declined all invitations to visit Japan over a ten-year period (*CSM*, 13 January). A week before the Shevardnadze visit, the Soviet deputy foreign minister, Mikhail Kapitsa, had repeated in an article the Soviet view that Japan's claims on the islands were "unsubstantiated and unlawful" (*Pravda*, 8 January). Shevardnadze gave no ground on the territorial issue but, unlike Gromyko, did discuss it, allowing Japan's foreign minister, Shintaro Abe, to agree to a joint communiqué (*FEER*, 30 January).

The two sides agreed to regularize foreign ministerial meetings on an annual basis. Japan ended the sanctions imposed on the USSR following the invasion of Afghanistan, and it was agreed to continue the dialogue with an exchange of invitations between Gorbachev and Premier Yasuhiro Nakasone for each to visit the other's country. The conferees also agreed to return to negotiations over a peace treaty (ibid.).

The Soviet strategy had been to concentrate on economic cooperation and to downgrade the territorial issue. Trade between the two countries had increased by 10 percent in 1985 after a sharp three-year decline. Continuing the economic gambit, the Soviets welcomed the Japanese deputy foreign minister, Reishi Teshima, to Moscow in March for talks with a USSR deputy foreign minister, Aleksei Manzhulo, and the USSR minister of foreign trade,

Boris Aristov (TASS, 11, 12 March; *FBIS*, 13 March). Although Moscow was pleased with evidence of Japanese willingness to resume "normal" trade relations, one major problem remained: the difficulty for the USSR of providing sufficient desirable exports to balance trade with Japan.

Both sides continued to express hopes for a summit meeting between the two nations' leaders, but they moved warily. Gorbachev's July speech in Vladivostok, in which he suggested that "closer cooperation should be promoted in a quiet atmosphere free from the problems of the past," quickened the diplomatic tempo in Tokyo. But the USSR ambassador to Japan, Nikolai N. Solovyev, said that a foremost condition for a summit meeting would be the guarantee of "tangible results" (*FEER*, 14 August). In August, Deputy Foreign Minister Kapitsa traveled to Tokyo for talks with Japanese officials; Kapitsa played up the initiatives regarding Asia set out in Gorbachev's Vladivostok speech (TASS, 28 August; *FBIS*, 29 August).

The appointment of Solovyev, fluent in Japanese, was a clear indication of Moscow's desire to thaw relations with Japan. But there was more change in atmosphere than in substance, with underlying problems largely untouched. A sour note for Moscow was sounded in November when Premier Nakasone met the leader of the Chinese Communist Party, Hu Yaobang, in Beijing. Nakasone and Hu agreed that the USSR was not acting sincerely to resolve the crises in Afghanistan and Cambodia (AP, 8 November).

*China.* China was the centerpiece of Gorbachev's design to promote a new Soviet stance in Asia. As in the case of Japan, Moscow sought a "normalization" of relations with an emphasis on economic ties. But on the three crucial issues for Peking—the concentration of Soviet troops along China's northern frontier, the Soviet occupation of Afghanistan, and Moscow's support for Vietnam's occupation of Cambodia—there was real movement only on the first.

Gorbachev had reportedly offered to restore relations between the Soviet and Chinese parties in a meeting with Vice-premier Li Peng on 23 December 1985, but the Chinese deputy foreign minister, Qian Qichen, dashed hopes for an early thaw two weeks later, when he said that Moscow had been "unwise and unrealistic" in trying to avoid discussion of the three obstacles to normal relations (*CSM*, 10 January). As usual, the Chinese stayed away from the CPSU congress, and Beijing paid it little attention. Nevertheless, Kremlin spokesman Vadim Zagladin said that state-to-state ties had "improved" in recent months and that party-to-party relations would be "restored sooner or later" (Paris, AFP, 8 March; *FBIS*, 10 March).

Moscow soon had its turn in downgrading Sino-Soviet relations. First Deputy Premier Ivan V. Arkhipov traveled again to Beijing in March to inaugurate the Sino-Soviet Commission on Trade and Technological Cooperation, but the visit was overshadowed by the last-minute decision to send Arkhipov instead of First Deputy Premier Nikolai V. Talyzin, who, as a candidate member of the Politburo, held higher rank in the Kremlin hierarchy. Western diplomats saw the substitution as a sign that a more realistic mood was settling in over Sino-Soviet relations (Hong Kong, AFP; *FBIS*, 13 March). For their part, the Chinese publicly endorsed a peace proposal on Cambodia that Prince Norodom Sihanouk announced on the fourth day of Arkhipov's visit (*FEER*; 27 March).

*Pravda* sounded a hopeful note (12 May) when it said that "we can speak with satisfaction of a certain improvement in Sino-Soviet relations," even if "differences remain, notably in the approach to a series of international problems." In July, Deputy Foreign Minister Qian said that although economic relations between the two countries were progressing well, political relations were not, and he ruled out any meeting of foreign ministers during the year. Meanwhile, *Pravda* continued to sound a hopeful note. "Every condition exists," the paper said, "for surmounting the existing difficulties in Sino-Soviet relations" (BBC Caris, 3 July).

Gorbachev's 28 July speech in Vladivostok produced some reaction in Beijing, but evidently not as much as expected. Two weeks after the speech, the Soviets had still not received a formal response from China to the speech, although the Soviet Foreign Ministry's China specialist, Igor Rogachev, said that "the Chinese representatives we deal with stress that the speech is very interesting and important." Rogachev announced that one of the initiatives contained in the speech was being implemented and that discussions would soon be completed with Mongolia on the partial withdrawal of Soviet forces stationed there. Evidently reacting to the Soviet initiative on Mongolia, China signed a consular treaty with Mongolia on 9 August (*CSM*, 11 August).

The remainder of the year saw the exchange of various delegations but glacial movement on major issues. Indicative of the mutual desire for concilia-tion was the treatment of a border incident in which a Chinese soldier was killed. The affair was hushed up by both sides, although its occurrence was finally obliquely admitted by the spokesman for the USSR Foreign Ministry, Gennadi Gerasimov (London, *Daily Telegraph*, 23 August).

The Chinese economic reform continued to be a topic of some controversy in Moscow, but the Soviets apparently did not consider this an obstacle to improved relations. A new round of Sino-Soviet talks began in Beijing in October. Rogachev, appointed a deputy foreign minister on 13 August, was designated the chief Soviet negotiator (Tokyo, *Kyodo*, 24 August; *FBIS*, 25 August). In the fall, East Germany's Honecker and Poland's Jaruzelski visited Beijing, apparently as surrogates for Moscow (*RL Research*, 4 November). No immediate change was noted in Sino-Soviet relations, but the visits indicated that the Soviet leadership was learning that a bit of subtlety is needed in playing the "China card."

*India*. With a lavish outlay of attention and funds, Moscow tilted India back toward a pro-Soviet orientation during Gorbachev's four-day visit (25–28 November), his first trip to a Third World nation since taking office as general secretary in March 1985. During the visit, the USSR announced its largest credit package to India, pledging $1.2 billion to finance four giant hydroelectric, coal, steel, and oil exploration projects. The money is repayable over seventeen years at 2.5 percent interest (AP, 28 November).

Upon Gorbachev's arrival in New Delhi, Prime Minister Rajiv Gandhi praised him as a "crusader for peace." Both Gorbachev and Gandhi blamed Reagan's Star Wars program for the failure of the Iceland summit (UPI, 25 November).

Two days later, in a 30-minute address to the Indian parliament, which repeatedly cheered him, Gorbachev said that the world may be destroyed if the United States pursues its space-based defense program. The Soviet leader urged Washington to negotiate on demilitarization of the Indian Ocean and called for a "star peace" program for the exploration of outer space by the developing nations, with India to play a major role. Gorbachev and Gandhi signed a joint declaration endorsing the principle of complete nuclear disarmament by the end of the century, and the Indian premier described the Soviet leader's disarmament proposals as "remarkable for their sweep and boldness" (AP, *NYT*, 28 November). The visit was marred by demonstrations over

Afghanistan, but Gorbachev spoke of the withdrawal of Soviet troops from that country and any discussions of the issue by the two leaders were apparently low-key (ABC News, 27, 28 November).

*Southeast Asia and the Pacific.* Moscow's commitment to Vietnam was strongly emphasized by the presence of a high-level Soviet delegation, including Premier Ryzhkov and Secretary Dobrynin, at the funeral of Vietnamese leader Le Duan in July (see below). Deputy Foreign Minister Igor A. Rogachev visited Vietnam in August and reportedly sought support for Gorbachev's disarmament and other international initiatives (*Izvestiia*, 29 August). Also in August, Deputy Foreign Minister Mikhail Kapitsa declared that "a people's democratic system is consolidating in Kampuchea" and that "developments there are irreversible" (*RL Research*, 12 August).

Soviet support for Vietnam's occupation of Kampuchea (Cambodia), which had a dampening effect on Sino-Soviet rapprochement, also inhibited Soviet efforts to normalize relations with ASEAN states, especially Thailand. Nevertheless, the Soviets made a major push in the region, emphasizing economic matters. A Soviet trade mission visited Jakarta in early May, taking preliminary steps to promote increased technological and trade exchanges between the USSR and Indonesia (*CSM*, 17 June). In addition to trade negotiations, a Supreme Soviet delegation headed by Deputy Chairman Akil Salimov, an Uzbek, sought to publicize recent USSR foreign policy initiatives during a tour of Indonesia, Singapore, Malaysia, and Thailand in early June (*Vedomosti verkhovnogo soveta SSSR*, no. 27, 2 July). Reflecting the USSR's tactic of presenting itself as a European country to promote neutralism in the West and as an Asian country to thaw relations with border states to the East (a tactic evident in Gorbachev's 28 July Vladivostok speech), Salimov, at a press conference in Singapore, referred to "a common Asiatic heritage" between the USSR and Southeast Asia and emphasized that the Soviet Union is an Asian country. He called upon the states of the region to draw on the Soviet Union's help to resist attempts by Japan and the United States to use their economic dominance to build a "military axis" in the area (*Neue Zürcher Zeitung*, 6/7 July; *RL Research*, 12 August).

The Soviets made a potentially costly bobble by supporting Ferdinand Marcos in the Philippine elections. When Corazon Aquino came to power,

Moscow moved quickly to recognize the new government. First Deputy Foreign Minister Georgi M. Kornienko said that such recognition was automatic and that the USSR maintained relations with the Philippines regardless of who was in power. Central Committee spokesman Leonid M. Zamyatin said that the fate of Marcos showed that it was "dangerous to be a friend of the United States" (Reuters, 28 February).

Recognizing the strategic importance of the South Pacific, the Soviets created a new Pacific Ocean Department in the Foreign Ministry (*Izvestiia*, 29 June) and established diplomatic relations with the island republic of Vanuatu (*CSM*, 4 June). Offering to pay 20 percent over the going rate for fishing rights, Moscow was reportedly negotiating a fishing agreement with Vanuatu, and Fiji was said to be considering such a pact. Kiribati had signed a fishing agreement with the USSR in August 1985, but the Solomon Islands, Tuvalu, and Western Samoa had turned down Soviet economic offers (*RL Research*, 21 July).

*Near and Middle East.* Moscow's relations with erratic ally Moammar Khadafy were even bumpier than usual. The U.S. air raid on Libya in April set off recriminations in Tripoli against the USSR. Libyan officials complained about Soviet nonsupport, citing Moscow's refusal to supply sophisticated radar equipment, and Colonel Khadafy chided Soviet reporters over the USSR's reaction to the raid. The USSR reportedly pulled out several hundred military advisers from Libyan missile bases two days before the U.S. jets struck; a week after the raid, a Soviet warship made an appearance off the Libyan coastline as a "show of solidarity" (*NYT*, 6 May).

Speaking at the SED congress in East Germany, Gorbachev gave the impression that the USSR's response to the United States would be largely rhetorical. Gorbachev called the raid a resort to the "law of the jungle" and warned that U.S.-Soviet relations "cannot develop independently of how the United States behaves on the international scene" (TASS, 19, 20 April), but he did not threaten to call off the projected summit meeting. The rhetorical, no-risk approach remained in evidence when Libya's second in command, Abdel Salam Jalloud, was received in Moscow for talks with Gorbachev and Premier Ryzhkov. Gorbachev said that the raid on Libya "again showed to the whole world what imperialism is" (AP, 27 May), but there was no indication of change in Moscow's policy vis-à-vis Khadafy.

Meanwhile, Moscow was making an effort to mend fences with Libya's hostile neighbor, Egypt. A Soviet parliamentary delegation was received by Egyptian leader Hosni Mubarak, who reaffirmed his "keenness on maintaining friendship and bolstering relations" with the Soviet Union (ibid., 24 March; *RL Research*, 26 March). Mubarak's aim for a more balanced position between East and West was welcomed in Moscow. More tangible proof of improved relations was the visit of Egypt's minister of the economy, Sultan Abu Ali, to Moscow for talks on trade (BBC Caris, 25 March).

Syria evidently remained the principal source of Moscow's concern in the region. Unwilling to give guarantees to Khadafy, the Soviets indicated that a U.S. attack on Syria would be a much more serious matter. Vice president Abd al-Halim Khaddam of Syria arrived in Moscow as Libya's Jalloud met with Soviet leaders, and Khaddam was greeted with a statement from Gorbachev that any attack by Israel or the United States on Syria or the Palestine Liberation Organization would have "incalculable consequences" (AP, 27 May).

But it was not a U.S. threat to Syria that most concerned Moscow; rather, it was the continuing hostility between the Syrian leadership and the Soviets' allies in the PLO. Shortly before his visit to Moscow, Khaddam had described Soviet-Syrian relations as "superb" (Moscow Television, 17 May; *FBIS*, 19 May) but the Soviets experienced continuing frustration in attempts to influence Syria's policies. During the summer, Moscow made efforts to effect some sort of unity among the PLO factions, and in August a first deputy minister of foreign affairs, Yuli Vorontsov, traveled to the troubled region for separate talks with President Hafiz al-Assad of Syria and the PLO's Yasir Arafat (Abu Dhabi, *Al-Ittihad*, 26 August; *FBIS*, 28 August). Vorontsov reportedly put pressure on Assad to normalize relations with Arafat's PLO faction, but apparently the Soviet diplomatic drive to help Arafat had little effect in Damascus. Later in the year, the return of the PLO to Lebanon and Syria's growing diplomatic isolation by Western countries due to its links with terrorism may have increased Moscow's leverage over Assad. However, prospects for major changes in the Moscow-Damascus relationship remained dim.

The January factional fighting in strategically important South Yemen, which ultimately led to the ouster of head of state Ali Nasir Muhammad, apparently caught Moscow off guard. The Soviets quickly recovered, however, and emerged with perhaps greater influence in the country. Prime Minister Hayder Abu Bakr al-Attas, who took over as South Yemen's leader in a successful coup, was reported to have changed sides and abandoned Mohammed while in Moscow for talks with top Soviet officials (*FPI International Report*, 29 January). Subsequently, newspaper accounts indicated that Soviet pilots may have bombed the Aden airport and "turned the scales" in favor of the rebels. Reports from the area noted that as many as a hundred Soviet advisers may have been casualties in the two weeks of fighting between the Marxist factions (*LAT*, 6 February).

Moscow continued its efforts to effect some sort of rapprochement with Turkey. In September, the Soviet chief of staff, Marshal Sergei Akhromeev, returned the 1985 visit by the Turkish chief of staff. Reportedly, Akhromeev was sent to Ankara mainly to try to influence Turkish attitudes toward SDI. There were signs, however, that rapprochement with Turkey was relatively low on the Soviet list of priorities. When Turkey's premier, Turgut Ozal, visited Moscow in August, he was unable to see Gorbachev. (*RL Research*, 18 September).

First Deputy Foreign Minister Georgi M. Kornienko visited Iran from 2 to 4 February (BBC Caris, 5 February). The visit by Kornienko, the highest-ranking Soviet official in Teheran since the establishment of the Khomeini regime, reflected a continuing modest improvement in Soviet-Iranian relations. In late summer, it was reported that deliveries of Iranian natural gas to the Soviet Union, suspended since April 1980, would be resumed in December (*WP*, 26 August; *RL Research*, 2 September).

Following the Reagan administration's embarrassment over disclosures concerning its Iranian arms deal, Moscow seemed to give higher priority to links with Teheran. In December, the USSR and Iran conducted their first high-level economic talks since the 1979 revolution. Iran's mines and metals minister, Mohammad-Reza Ayatollahi, was quoted as saying that his country wanted to expand ties with its neighbors, including the Soviet Union. However, Iran's powerful parliamentary speaker, Hashemi Rafsanjani, again criticized the USSR for supplying weapons to Iraq and for occupying Afghanistan (AP, 9 December). Moreover, strong ideological hostility continued to cloud relations between the two countries, and the December nationalist riots in Kazakhstan may have added an indirect complication for Soviet relations with all neighboring Muslim countries.

*Africa South of the Sahara.* The Soviets in Africa avoided new commitments while seeking to make firmer their existing footholds, which had been subject to increased threats over the previous two years. Ethiopia, strategically important for Soviet access to the port of Assab on the Red Sea, continued to receive Moscow's support. Economic and military backing of the Marxist regime in Addis Ababa reportedly was costing Moscow $3 million a day (*CSM*, 18 February), and Soviet military advisers assisted the Ethiopian ally in a major offensive against rebel forces (ibid., 8 April). A close Soviet link with Addis Ababa was signaled by the presence of Ethiopian leader Mengistu Haile Mariam at the CPSU congress (*Pravda*, 27 February).

In southern Africa, the regional "correlation of forces" had apparently turned against the Soviets in 1984–1985 as revolutionary regimes moved toward accommodation with South Africa. In 1986, renewed opportunities were provided to Moscow by the turmoil in South Africa, U.S. support for Jonas Savimbi's UNITA forces in Angola, and May raids by South Africa against African National Congress bases in Zimbabwe, Zambia, and Botswana (UPI, 19 May). Moscow had already moved to thaw relations with Zimbabwe when Premier Robert Mugabe was welcomed to Moscow in December 1985 (*Izvestiia*, 4 December 1985). Bilateral accords were signed on economic and technical cooperation, and Mugabe hinted that he had discussed the question of military cooperation with his Soviet hosts (*RL Research*, 20 May).

The president of Mozambique, Samora Machel, visited Moscow in March (TASS, 31 March; *Izvestiia*, 3, 4 April). Angola's president, José Eduardo dos Santos, represented the Popular Movement for the Liberation of Angola (MPLA) at the Twenty-seventh CPSU Congress (*Pravda*, 27 February) and then returned for a state visit in May (ibid., 8 May). During the visits, the USSR and its African allies affirmed their unity on the issues confronting southern Africa. The official communiqué on dos Santos's May visit asserted that the Soviet Union and Cuba are ready "to undertake concerted action" with Angola in defense of its "independence, sovereignty, and territorial integrity" (TASS, 10 May; *RL Research*, 20 May).

Soviet military assistance to the MPLA government was reportedly costing around $1 billion per year (*NYT*, 6 March), in addition to annual economic aid of at least $200 million. The military aid has recently included a sophisticated radar network, including advanced surface-to-air missiles (*CSM*, 8 April).

During Machel's visit, Gorbachev reaffirmed Soviet commitments to Mozambique. "The Soviet Union," he said, "has been doing and will continue to do what it can to render Mozambique assistance in economic and cultural development, in training national personnel, and in strengthening its defenses" (TASS, 31 March; *RL Research*, 20 May). Underlining the Soviet stake in Mozambique, Moscow dispatched a high-level delegation led by First Deputy Premier Geidar Aliev to Machel's funeral in October (TASS, 28 October; *FBIS*, 29 October).

*The Americas.* Following his attendance at the fall meeting of the U.N. General Assembly and his wrestling with the Daniloff-Zakharov affair, Foreign Minister Shevardnadze visited Canada (*Pravda*, 4 October) and Mexico (ibid., 5, 6 October). The trip to Ottawa seemed aimed toward influencing Canadian opinion on Soviet "peace" proposals, while the visit to Mexico was clearly related to Mexican participation in the Contadora peace initiatives on Nicaragua.

Moscow gave clear signals that its costly support of the Marxist regime in Cuba would continue. Cuba's leader Fidel Castro led the Cuban delegation to the CPSU congress (ibid., 27 February), where he was the Third World figure attracting most attention. Earlier, Moscow had sent a high-level delegation to the Third Congress of the Cuban Communist Party. The delegation was headed by the Kremlin's second in command, Egor Ligachev, who praised Cuba for its "realistic" economic planning (TASS, 5 February; *FBIS*, 6 February). *Pravda* (8 February) lauded the Cuban communists for their "internationalism and proletarian cohesion," that is, their allegiance to Moscow.

Nicaragua was apparently the Third World country with the most pronounced upgrading of Soviet commitments during the year. Soviet military shipments had been down in 1985 but, at mid-year 1986, the Pentagon estimated that the USSR had already supplied $650 million in military aid to the Sandinistas since 1 January, against a record annual total of $250 million for the year 1984 (*WP*, 27 June). President Ronald Reagan charged that the Sandinistas were taking steps toward becoming a client state of the USSR and said that Russians, Cubans, Bulgarians, East Germans, and even North

Koreans were deeply involved in running all manner of official Nicaraguan institutions (*CSM*, 26 June).

In October, the Pentagon estimated that Soviet arms deliveries during the year had totaled 18,800 metric tons; recent deliveries had included six Mi-24 helicopter gunships, bringing to twelve the number of such "armored flying tanks" in the Nicaraguan arsenal. Moreover, the Soviets reportedly had shifted many of their arms shipments to their own vessels, rather than relying on eastern bloc ships, displaying a more overt Soviet program of support than in the past (AP, 28 October). While evidence mounted of massive increments in Soviet arms shipments to the Sandinistas, future U.S. aid to the *contras* was jeopardized by congressional reaction to the Iran-*contra* arms connection.

**International Party Contacts.** For more than a quarter-century, it has been impossible to maintain even the fiction of the unity of the world communist movement. But it was still important for Moscow to claim that it was the real center of the world movement—without demanding a dominant role, which was impossible of realization. The Soviet desire for a symbolic leadership role required continuing contact with Marxist-Leninist movements of various stripes and consideration of the divergent exigencies confronting the "comradely" parties: the need for parties in the Western industrialized countries to demonstrate at least a formal commitment to democratic politics; domestic pressures on many ruling communist parties to demonstrate a degree of formal independence from Moscow, combined with the need for continued Soviet underpinning to maintain their authority; the requirement among Third World movements for practical, as well as theoretical, support for violent revolution.

The delicate balancing act required for maintenance of an international movement amid these frequently contradictory pressures had been largely entrusted for many years to Secretary Boris Ponomarev. His retirement, announced at the Twenty-seventh CPSU Congress, signaled the end of an era, certainly in terms of style, and probably of substance as well. As always, relations with the world parties were determined ultimately by the national interest of the USSR, but the new leadership in Moscow seemed committed to a new policy agenda and to "restructuring" of the foreign policy mechanisms, with a different "style of work." The priorities of the new leadership included revitalization of the domestic Soviet system; heading

off a runaway arms race with the United States, a race the USSR could conceivably lose; restoration of tight cohesion in the fundamental East European bloc; and "normalization" of relations with several more or less hostile countries bordering the Soviet empire.

Increasingly costly ventures in the Third World appeared to be downgraded, at least in regard to new commitments, although the USSR could not forswear support for "national liberation" movements without some loss of "revolutionary" legitimacy. The apparent policy turn made likely increased tensions with Third World movements and, in some cases, conflicts among such forces made formulation of a coherent approach to "national liberation" increasingly complex. The relatively tough policy toward the East European bloc raised the possibility of additional behind-the-scenes discord with ruling parties in that area; at the same time, bloc party leaders worried that the Soviet renovation campaign and *glasnost'* would set off a "revolution of rising expectations" in the East European countries. Meanwhile, the radical Chinese economic reform added a potential complicating factor to the perennially prickly relations with China's ruling communist party.

Amid this welter of pressures and counterpressures, there was a further important consideration that had to be given considerable weight by decisionmakers in Moscow. Given the admissions of domestic retrogression and implied acknowledgment of unfavorable trends in the world "correlation of forces," it was probably more necessary than ever before for Moscow to establish at least minimal cohesion in the world movement. As usual, the party congress provided a potentially useful forum for demonstrating worldwide revolutionary support for Soviet objectives, and the Moscow propaganda machine played this card skillfully, giving wide publicity to the presence of leading Marxist-Leninists from abroad. According to General Secretary Gorbachev, 152 delegations from 113 countries attended the party congress (*Pravda*, 26 February).

Party leaders of all the East European bloc countries headed their delegations, as did Fidel Castro of Cuba, Babrak Karmal of Afghanistan, Mengistu Haile Mariam of Ethiopia, and Le Duan of Vietnam. Kim Il-song of Korea was represented by a deputy, as were the leaders of nonruling parties in France, Italy, and Japan (ibid., 24, 25, 27 February, 7 March).

Relations with the ruling bloc parties of Eastern

Europe remained of cardinal importance. Czechoslovakia had displayed uneasiness, both official and unofficial, over Soviet plans to counter the NATO missile buildup with deployments in Central Europe. Nevertheless, Czechoslovakia was a much less troublesome ally than others in Eastern Europe and the Kremlin seemed satisfied with the overall record of stability attained by the Czech communist party. The generally satisfactory level of relations seemed evident in the reception accorded the CPSU delegation to the Seventeenth KSČ Congress in March. The delegation was headed by the chairman of the Party Control Committee, Mikhail S. Solomentsev, and also included the CPSU Central Committee secretary for agriculture, Viktor P. Nikonov, and Latvian party leader Boris K. Pugo (Moscow Domestic Service, TASS, 23 March; *FBIS*, 24 March).

The Kremlin has apparently attached greater importance to its Hungarian connections since the election of Yuri Andropov as CPSU general secretary in 1982. Hungary's excellent economic performance, the high level of economic stability, and János Kádár's support for Moscow's bloc and world policies have all been welcomed by the Moscow leadership. At the same time, Hungary's economic experiments have added fuel to Soviet domestic debates over reform and created some uneasiness in the bloc. These considerations were evident in party relations between Moscow and Budapest during the year. In April, János Berecz, Central Committee secretary of the Hungarian Socialist Workers' Party, was in Moscow for talks with CPSU officials (Budapest, MTI, 23 April; *FBIS*, 25 April) at the same time that KGB head and CPSU Politburo member Viktor M. Chebrikov was in Budapest for a visit (Budapest Domestic Service, 24 April; *FBIS*, 25 April). In June, Soviet party leader Gorbachev visited Budapest (*Pravda*, 9 June). His talks with Kádár apparently dealt mainly with economic matters; the official communiqué emphasized cooperation on the basis of "existing resources and requirements" and the acceleration of specialization and coordination of production (Moscow Domestic Service, 8 June; *FBIS*, 9 June; *Pravda*, 10 June).

Poland remained the top trouble spot in the bloc, signaled by Gorbachev's personal appearance at the Tenth Congress of the Polish United Workers' Party in June. In his speech to the congress, Gorbachev praised Polish party leaders for their victory in "the struggle for the very existence of socialism in Poland." In his analysis of the Polish crisis, Gorbachev appeared to reaffirm the Brezhnev Doctrine and link it to the Soviet view of the Helsinki Pact's confirmation of the results of World War II and definitive settlement of boundaries in Europe. A major lesson of recent events in Poland, according to Gorbachev, was that "socialist gains are irreversible" and any attempt "to wrench a country away from the socialist community" represents a threat to the "entire postwar settlement and, in the final analysis, to peace" (TASS, *RL Research*, 30 June; *Pravda*, 1 July).

Bulgaria has traditionally held the position of Moscow's most loyal ally in Eastern Europe, but Sofia's recent feelers to Bonn regarding technological and other sorts of cooperation produced a stir in Moscow. The Kremlin's newly awakened concern for its Bulgarian ties was obvious in the sending of a high-level delegation, headed by Premier Nikolai Ryzhkov and including Secretary Georgi Razumovsky, to Sofia for the Thirteenth BCP Congress in April. Notably, the congress speeches and official communiqués emphasized the results of the Twenty-seventh CPSU Congress, Soviet arms control policies, bilateral economic relations between the USSR and Bulgaria, and bloc integration—but were silent on the subject of Bulgarian economic relations with the West (*Pravda*, 5, 7 April).

Geidar A. Aliev, first deputy premier and Politburo member, led the CPSU delegation attending the Thirteenth Congress of the League of Communists of Yugoslavia (LCY). Other members of the delegation were Anatolii I. Lukyanov, head of the CPSU Central Committee's General Department, and Viktor F. Maltsev, USSR ambassador to Yugoslavia (ibid., 30 June).

The theme of the Eighth Congress of the German Communist Party, held in Hamburg in May, was "For a new world policy: a world without nuclear weapons and with work for all." The congress devoted much attention to SDI and the Soviet moratorium on nuclear testing. In view of the heavy concentration on nuclear matters, it was rather ironic that the congress opened six days after the explosion at Chernobyl. Not surprisingly, the congress was overshadowed by press reports of remarks by CPSU delegation head Boris N. Eltsin (ibid., 3 May) concerning the nuclear disaster in the USSR. Eltsin's revelations constituted the frankest early Soviet admissions concerning Chernobyl, but he soon moved to an aggressive stance, denouncing the "slanderous insinuations and anti-Soviet concoctions" allegedly being circulated in the West about the matter (TASS, 7 May; *FBIS*, 8 May).

A delegation led by Nikolai S. Ermakov, first

secretary of Kemerevo obkom, visited West Berlin in May at the invitation of the Board of the West Berlin Socialist Unity Party (*Pravda*, 8 May; *FBIS*, 9 May).

CPSU relations with the Italian Communist Party (PCI) have been strained for many years over issues such as Eurocommunism, Poland, Afghanistan, and human rights. A visit to Moscow by PCI General Secretary Alessandro Natta and Secretary Giancarlo Pajetta in January (ibid., 28, 29 January) raised the prospect of some sort of rapprochement between the parties. although the Italian party leaders subsequently insisted that wide disagreements remained on substantive issues and that there could be no compromise on the autonomy of the PCI. Hopes for a closer relationship between the parties were jolted by Chernobyl; the PCI newspaper described the Soviet regime's failure to publish prompt and full details of the nuclear disaster as "anachronistic and absurd" (*L'Unità*, 1 May; *RFE Research*, 7 May). Nevertheless, a low-level CPSU delegation from Leningrad province, led by the Leningrad obkom secretary, A. M. Fateev, visited Italy in June at the invitation of the PCI of Lombardy province (*Pravda*, 30 June).

The Belgian Communist Party's newspaper was also highly critical of Soviet reportage about Chernobyl, while French and British communist papers either ignored or belittled the threat posed to Western Europe (*RFE Research*, 7 May). The French Communist Party's newspaper also published in February a lengthy and highly favorable interview with Gorbachev by its editor in chief (*L'Humanité*, 8 February).

While Moscow apparently placed lower priority on Third World commitments in general, partially reflected in the lower incidence of meetings with officials of Third World movements than had been the case during Boris Ponomarev's hyperactive tenure at the International Department, there were notable instances of strong Soviet symbolic and rhetorical public reassurances for key leaders.

At the end of 1985, a plan for interparty ties between the CPSU and Zambia's United National Independence Party (UNIP) was signed in Lusaka (*Pravda*, 24 December 1985; *FBIS*, 26 December 1985). Two other African leaders whose movements in recent years have not been entirely tractable from the Kremlin's standpoint were given demonstrative welcomes to Moscow in the spring: Mozambique's president and head of the FRELIMO party, Samora Machel, in March (TASS, 31 March; *FBIS*, 1 April; *Izvestiia*, 3, 4 April) and Angola's

president and chairman of the Popular Movement for the Liberation of Angola (MPLA), José Eduardo dos Santos, in May (*Pravda*, 8, 11 May). Geider A. Aliev led the Soviet delegation attending the funeral of Machel in October (TASS, 28 October; *FBIS*, 29 October).

Six months after the overthrow of Ali Nasir Muhammad in South Yemen, Yasin Said Numan, PDRY premier and member of the Yemen Socialist Party's politburo, was welcomed to Moscow and given assurances of Soviet support in talks with Nikolai Ryzhkov (*Pravda*, 6 June). With Soviet-Syrian relations remaining complex and frustrating for Moscow, General Secretary Khalid Bakhdash of Syria and several other top officials of the party were invited to Moscow for talks with CPSU Central Committee secretaries Egor Ligachev and Aleksandr Iakovlev and with the International Department's deputy chief, Karen Brutents (TASS, 7 April; *FBIS*, 8 April).

The CPSU dispatched Ligachev to Havana as its representative at the Third Congress of the Communist Party of Cuba in February. In his speech to the congress, Ligachev spoke mainly of the renewal program in the USSR but praised the Cuban communists for a "realistic economic strategy" (TASS, 5 February; *FBIS*, 6 February).

A top-level delegation, led by Premier Ryzhkov and including Secretary Anatolii Dobrynin, represented Soviet party and government at funeral services for Vietnamese General Secretary Le Duan in July (Moscow Television, 12 July; TASS, 13 July; *FBIS*, 14 July).

Vitali I. Vorotnikov, chairman of the Council of Ministers of the RSFSR and member of the Politburo, led the CPSU delegation at the Nineteenth Congress of the Mongolian communist party in May (*Pravda*, 28 May). The busy Geidar Aliev led the CPSU delegation attending the Fourth Congress of the Lao People's Revolutionary Party in November (ibid., 16 November).

Korean communist leader Kim Il-song, who had missed the Twenty-seventh CPSU Congress, visited Moscow from 22 to 27 October for talks with Gorbachev and other officials (ibid., 23, 25, 28 November). Perhaps due to the attempts being made to "normalize" relations with China and Japan, little publicity was given to Kim's visit.

A curious episode marked the August visit of a Japanese communist delegation led by the chairman of the JCP, Tetsuzo Fuwa. The protocol-conscious Japanese were kept waiting for a week to see Gorbachev, apparently to their embarrassment, amid reports that the visitors would return to Tokyo without meeting CPSU officials. Finally, a meeting was set with Secretary Ligachev, and Gorbachev unexpectedly showed up; it was reported that he had been suffering from a cold. Main topics of the meeting were Gorbachev's proposed visit to Japan and the contemporary international situation; the official communiqué stated the full agreement of the parties on arms control issues. (Tokyo, *Kyodo*, 9, 11 August; Moscow Television Service, 11 August; *FBIS*, 11, 12 August).

Y. A. Krasin, prorector of the CPSU Social Science Academy, and D. A. Lisovolik, a sector chief of the International Department, attended a theoretical conference in New York sponsored by the journal *Political Affairs*, organ of the Communist Party USA (*Pravda*, 14 March).

CPSU leader Gorbachev met in Moscow in November with Hungarian leader János Kádár, Czechoslovak leader Gustáv Husák, and Vietnamese General Secretary Truong Chinh (*Neues Deutschland*, 13 November).

**Biographies.** *Lev Nikolaevich Zaikov.* Lev Zaikov, a Russian, was born in 1923. He became a member of the CPSU in 1957 and graduated from the Leningrad Economic Engineering Institute in 1963. Between 1941 and 1961, Zaikov rose through the factory ranks to hold successively the positions of metalworker, group chief, foreman, deputy shop superintendent, shop superintendent, and production chief. From 1961 to 1971, he was director of a plant in Leningrad.

In January 1976, Zaikov was named chairman of the executive committee of the Leningrad City Soviet of People's Deputies (mayor). In 1983, he was the surprise choice to succeed Grigori Romanov as first secretary of the Leningrad province party committee when Romanov was transferred to Moscow as a secretary of the CPSU Central Committee. Gaining a reputation as an honest, efficient administrator, Zaikov again succeeded Romanov in July 1985, when the former Leningrad chief retired from his party posts "for reasons of health." As a secretary of the CPSU Central Committee, Zaikov assumed responsibility for the defense industry and for military affairs.

Following the Twenty-seventh Congress of the CPSU in March 1986, Zaikov was elected a full member of the Politburo. With his new status, he became the number three official in the party hierarchy, with the task of general supervision of the economy.

Zaikov has been a deputy to the USSR Supreme Soviet since 1979 and a member of the CPSU Central Committee since 1981. He holds the decoration of Hero of Socialist Labor.

(Sources: *Pravda*, 2 July 1985, 7 March 1986; *NYT*, 7 March; Boris Lewytzkyj, *Who's Who in the Soviet Union*, Munich, 1984, p. 361.)

*Anatolii Fedorovich Dobrynin.* Anatolii Dobrynin, a Russian, was born in 1919. He graduated from the Moscow Aviation Institute in 1942 and became a member of the CPSU in 1945. He entered the diplomatic service in 1946 and quickly rose to the top ranks of the foreign ministry.

Dobrynin served as USSR assistant deputy minister of foreign affairs, 1949–1952; embassy counselor, then minister, in the Soviet embassy in Washington, 1952–1955; again assistant deputy minister, 1955–1957; deputy secretary general of the United Nations, 1957–1960; board member and then head of the American Department in the ministry, 1960–1962.

In January 1962, Dobrynin was posted to Washington as ambassador, a post that he held for more than 24 years. In March 1986, he was recalled to Moscow when he was elected a secretary of the CPSU Central Committee and named head of the International Department. After his return to Moscow, he became the chief foreign policy adviser to Mikhail Gorbachev and accompanied the general secretary on his trips to Iceland (for the Reykjavik summit) and to India.

Dobrynin was elected a candidate member of the CPSU Central Committee in 1966 and has been a full member since 1971. He has been decorated with the Order of the Red Banner of Labor.

(Sources: *RL Research*, 30 May 1982; Boris Lewytzkyj, *Who's Who in the Soviet Union*, Munich, 1984, p. 78; *Pravda*, 7 March, 28 November; *NYT*, 11 October.)

R. Judson Mitchell
*University of New Orleans*

# Yugoslavia

**Population.** 23,284,000

**Party.** League of Communists of Yugoslavia (Savez Komunista Jugoslavije; LCY). The LCY is the only political party in the Socialist Federal Republic of Yugoslavia (SFRY). However, there are party organizations in each of the six republics—Slovenia, Croatia, Bosnia-Hercegovina, Montenegro, Macedonia, and Serbia—and the two autonomous provinces—Kosovo and Vojvodina—as well as within the Yugoslav armed forces (JNA).

**Founded.** April 1919, as the Socialist Workers' Party of Yugoslavia; disbanded and replaced by the Communist Party of Yugoslavia (CPY) in June 1920. The CPY took the name League of Communists of Yugoslavia at the Sixth Party Congress in November 1952.

**Membership.** 2.1 million (Tanjug, 14 May); roughly 70,000 primary party organizations

**President of the Presidium.** Milanko Renovica, 58, a Serb from Bosnia-Hercegovina, was elected for a one-year term in June 1986.

**Secretary of the Presidium.** Radiša Gačić, 48, a Serb from Serbia (first half of a two-year term). At this time there are seven appointed executive secretaries: Slobodan Filipović, Marko Lolić, Vukasin Lončar, Boris Muževič, Stanislav Stojanović, Uglješa Uzelac, and Ljubomir Varošlija. The number of executive secretaries varies as needed.

**Presidium.** 23 members representing the republics, autonomous provinces, and the LCY organization in the Yugoslav armed forces. Fourteen members of the Presidium hold that job between party congresses. However, there are 9 ex officio members who take part in Presidium meetings by virtue of their positions as presidents of their own territorial League of Communists (LC) or as head of the JNA party organization. Since these presidencies rotate on different schedules—sometimes on a one-, sometimes on a two-year basis—the makeup of the ex officio members can change within any given year. Members: Slovenia, Stefan Korošeč (48) and Franc Šetinc (57); Croatia, Ivica Račan (43) and Stipe Šuvar (50); Bosnia-Hercegovina, Ivan Brigić (50) and Milanko Renovica (58); Montenegro, Marko Orlandić (56) and Vidoje Žarković (59); Macedonia, Milan Pančevski (51) and Vasil Turpurkoviski (35); Serbia, Dušan Čkrebić (59) and Radiša Gačić (48); Kosovo, Kolj Shiroka (64); Vojvodina, Boško Kunić (57). Ex officio members: Slovenia, Milan Kučan (45); Croatia, Stanko Stojčević (57); Bosnia-Hercegovina, Milan Uzelac (54); Montenegro, Miljan Radović (53); Macedonia, Jakov Lazaroski (50); Serbia, Slobodan Milošević (45); Vojvodina, Djordje Stojšić (58); Kosovo, Azem Vlasi (38); party organization in the army, General Georgije Jovičić (59).

**Central Committee.** 165 members: 20 from each republic, 15 for each of the two autonomous provinces, and 15 for the army's party organization.

**Status.** Ruling Party

**Last Congress.** Thirteenth Congress, June 1986

**Last Elections.** 1986. The Yugoslav parliament, the Federal Assembly, has two chambers: a 220-member Federal Chamber and an 88-member Chamber of Republics and Provinces. Elections are conducted by the Socialist Alliance of the Working People of Yugoslavia (SAWPY) via a complex delegate system. In May, Ivo Vrandečić (Croatia) became president of the assembly; Nedjo Borković (a Serb from Kosovo) became vice president. The term of office is one year.

**Auxiliary Organizations.** The Socialist Alliance of the Working People of Yugoslavia (Socijalistički savez radnog naroda Jugoslavije; SAWPY) is an umbrella mass organization that includes all major political/social organizations as well as individuals. SAWPY provides the political machinery for conducting elections and mirrors the tensions reflected in the LCY itself. There is also the Confederation of Trade Unions of Yugoslavia (Savez sindikata Jugoslavije; CTUY), and the League of Socialist Youth of Yugoslavia (Savez socijalističke omladine Jugoslavije; LSYY).

**Governmental Bodies.** An 8-member collective state presidency was elected in May 1984 for five-year terms. The president and vice president serve for one year, and these positions rotate among the membership. In May 1986 Sinan Hasani, 64 (ethnic Albanian, Kosovo) became president of the SFRY; Lazar Mojsov (Macedonia) became vice president. Other members of the presidency are: Slovenia, Stane Dolanc; Croatia, Josip Vrhovec; Bosnia-Hercegovina, Hamdija Pozderac; Montenegro, Veselin Djuranović; Vojvodina, Radovan Vlajković; and Serbia, Nikola Ljubičić. Milanko Renovica meets with the presidency as an ex officio member in his capacity as head of the LCY Presidium. There is also an administrative general secretary of the presidency, Ljubiša Korać. Day-to-day government is in the hands of a 29-member Federal Executive Council (FEC) elected for four years and headed by Prime Minister Branko Mikulić, 58. There are two vice-premiers, Miloš Milosavljević and Janez Zemljarič. Among the most important federal secretaries are Raif Dizdarevic, foreign affairs; Admiral Branko Mamula, defense; Dobroslav Ćulafić, internal affairs; and Svetozar Rikanović, finance.

**Publications.** Main publications of the LCY are *Komunist* (weekly) and *Socijalizam* (monthly); SAWPY's main publication is *Borba*, a daily newspaper with Belgrade and Zagreb editions. Other major dailies include *Politika*, *Večernje novosti*, *Politika ekspres* (Belgrade), *Večernji list*, *Vjesnik* (Zagreb), *Delo* (Ljubljana), *Oslobodjenje* (Sarajevo), and *Rilindja* (Priština). Prominent weeklies are *NIN* (*Nedeljne informativne novine*; Belgrade) and *Dana* (Zagreb). Among the boldest of the youth newspapers is the occasionally banned Belgrade weekly, *Student*; much controversial religious material appears in the biweekly Catholic journal, *Glas koncila* (Zagreb). Tanjug is the official news agency.

## Leadership and Party Organization.

In 1986 the merry-go-round of Yugoslav collective leadership stopped long enough to allow a new crew to climb on board. Of the 165 members of the LCY Central Committee elected at the Thirteenth Party Congress in June, 127 were new to the job. These were regional politicians, selected by party congresses and conferences in Yugoslavia's six republics and two autonomous provinces prior to the federal party congress. Each republic sent forward twenty Central Committee members. The autonomous provinces have fifteen slots, while fifteen members represent the party organization of the Yugoslav armed forces (JNA). Although technically elected by the congress delegates, this election was essentially a ratification of the choices of the military and regional party organizations.

The new Central Committee, in turn, elected 14 members of the LCY Presidium by secret ballot. Votes for individual candidates reportedly ranged from 135 to 161. (Tanjug, 28 June; *FBIS*, 30 June.) The 9 ex officio members were the elected presidents of the republican, provincial, and JNA party organizations. Of the 23 Presidium members, only 4 were holdovers from the former Presidium, and 2 of those 4 were ex officio members (Kučan and Jovičić) who will rotate out of the top party body

when their terms end (as head of the Slovene League of Communists (LC) and the JNA party organization, respectively).

Notwithstanding the warnings of outgoing party president Vidoje Žarković about the weakening of party unity in the face of bureaucratism and nationalistic tendencies (Tanjug, 25 June; RFE *Research*, 17 July), the post-Tito political machinery has worked in organizational terms. It has solved a serious problem of age homogeneity within the party and has largely contained factional struggle during a major generational transition. Although there is disagreement on some individuals, the average age of the Presidium appears to be roughly 50; the average age of the new Central Committee is in the mid-40s. With respect to composition, there were 86 managers and executives in the 1986 Central Committee, 27 workers, 19 women, and 3 farmers. (Tanjug, 18 June; *FBIS*, 18 June.) Despite the ideological awkwardness of a workers' party with that ratio of managers to workers, these figures imply a high level of education and practical economic experience. At the Presidium level, by far the majority of members have university-level professional training.

This educational trend was also reflected in the party rank and file, where by 1986 half the LCY's

2.1 million members had either a university education or a degree from some other institution of higher education. On the eve of the Thirteenth Congress, however, Yugoslav media focused attention on the failure of attempts to strengthen the working-class basis of the party. Reportedly workers made up 34.6 percent of the party: 1.2 percent less than before the 1982 party congress. Equally worrisome, workers had one of the highest dropout rates, accounting for some 43 percent of those who left the LCY for various reasons. (Tanjug, 14 May; *FBIS*, 15 May.) The party was also older. With an average age of 37, young people (those under 21) made up only 34.4 percent of membership—a figure that varied from 16.6 percent in Slovenia to 37.8 percent in Kosovo.

The demographics of party membership have been investigated by researchers at the Center for Marxism in Split, under the auspices of the Social Research Center in Belgrade. That study, "Class-Social Composition of the Membership of the League of Communists, 1981–1985," updated the Belgrade center's earlier work on the LCY's class-social structure from 1968 to 1980. The more recent findings were reported just before the Thirteenth Party Congress in an article entitled "The Party in Social Crisis" (*Komunist*, 6 June; *JPRS*, 30 July). Not surprisingly, discussion of the need to attract more workers and young people re-emerged on the congress agenda.

The new political generation at the top of the Yugoslav party is both the product of and restrained by the "Titoist solution" set in motion when the godfather of Yugoslav communism essentially stage-managed his own succession during the period between the Tenth LCY Congress in 1974 and his death in May 1980. This leadership reflects the federalization of the League of Communists into eight regional party leagues plus the party organization of the armed forces. It is one part of what may be the most elaborate quota system in the world. In fielding political leaders Yugoslavia applies republic/provincial and ethnic keys to most political jobs at all levels and operates within established rotation schedules for many top positions.

This balancing act is based on a 1982 social compact that in 1986 resulted in a party president from Bosnia-Hercegovina, a secretary of the LCY Presidium from Serbia, a president of the state presidency from Kosovo, a president of the Federal Assembly (parliament) from Croatia, a president of SAWPY from Montenegro, and a secretary of SAWPY from Macedonia (Tanjug, 9 April; *FBIS*,

10 April). Reportedly a working group within SAWPY has been charged with producing an amended sequence for the next eight years to prevent a clustering of representatives from Bosnia-Hercegovina and to assure that the job of preparing for party congresses does not fall exclusively to Montenegro and Croatia.

In the policy making arena, LCY leaders in 1986 continued to operate according to the principle of interrepublican consensus, despite vocal dissatisfaction with the results. Increasingly, the question of "what is to be done" focused on proposed constitutional amendments that implied a new approach to relations between the republics, provinces, and the central government. The history of problem-solving by constitutional amendment in Yugoslavia is anything but encouraging. Even leaving aside the political resistance of regional politicians defending their own turf, constitutional change is at best a slow process. Even if the Constitutional Commission gets its recommendations to the SFRY presidency in time for that body to propose the amendments to the national assembly by the end of 1986, passage is projected to take "at least two years" (*Borba*, 18–19 October; RFE *Research*, 20 November).

In short, pinning hopes on an improved constitution is passing the buck. That is perhaps inevitable. Under the existing rules of the Yugoslav political game, the LCY has been reduced to an arena for achieving agreement among powerful republic/provincial political actors. The importance of its contribution to regional compromise should not be underestimated, nor should the central party be blamed for its inability to "harmonize" conflicting interests when the best that could be expected is to contain conflict. The newness of the party leadership has not been an asset in this regard. Consequently, throughout 1986 the leading role of the party was largely symbolic; democratic centralism was more an idealized myth than an organizational principle.

**Domestic Affairs.** The second post-Tito elections took place in May. This complicated representative process began in December 1985 and required Yugoslavs to participate in three electoral roles: as producers, consumers, and citizens. In all three capacities, members of the Yugoslav electorate took part in nominating meetings to select delegates to send to communal assemblies that sent delegates to republic/provincial assemblies charged to send delegates to the Federal Assembly. Inspired by a desire to deprofessionalize the political process and mobilize more grass-roots participation, this complex election machinery remained hopelessly confusing for many ordinary voters. In the 1982 election some 70 percent of the nomination meetings accepted lists of candidates prepared in advance by authorities (*Danas*, 11 February; RFE *Research*, 7 March). If that was an indicator, the new system provides little incentive for individual initiative. Nonetheless, amid considerable complaint, the electoral system in 1986 put in place a new national assembly.

Equally—perhaps more—important, the state presidency sent forward the name of one of its own members, Branko Mikulić, to replace Milka Planinc as prime minister. Notwithstanding reports of his "enthusiastic" endorsement by SAWPY organizations in the republics and autonomous provinces, this breach in rotation etiquette (in which a Croat from Bosnia-Hercegovina replaced a Croat from Croatia) was openly criticized in the Yugoslav press (*NIN*, 12 January; *Vjesnik*, 11 February).

Despite unhappiness about the Mikulić's fait accompli and controversial allegations about his role in repressing Bosnian intellectuals (*Danas*, 22 July; RFE *Research*, 19 August), Mikulić may be a major force in Yugoslav policymaking during his four-year term as prime minister. He is a senior Yugoslav politician who has served on both the party Presidium and state presidency and has held top party and government posts in his home republic of Bosnia-Hercegovina. Another member of the Bosnia-Hercegovina presidency, Milanko Renovica, has the job of president of the LCY Presidium; he is a former colleague with substantially less impressive political credentials. The secretary of the central party is a relatively unknown representative of Serbia, Radiša Gačić, who is ten years younger than the prime minister. Presumably Mikulić works well with those members of the state presidency who nominated him, and he is clearly a more powerful figure than the current president of that body, the Albanian Sinan Hasani. In any case Hasani has only a one-year mandate.

In the new federal government Mikulić retained several key figures, including Admiral Branko Mamula, federal secretary of national defense; Raif Dizdarević, foreign minister; and Dobroslav Culafić, secretary of internal affairs. This continuity, combined with Mikulić's personal authority, make likely an enhanced political role for the Federal Executive Council (FEC). If so, given the newness of the party leadership, the apparent shift in power from party to government bodies may accelerate.

This is not to imply that the Federal Executive Council had a free hand in 1986. Indeed, there were signs of legislative assertiveness. Harsh criticism in committee of the council's request to amend the Law on State Administration (so as to postpone retirement of roughly 60 workers, primarily in the secretariats for foreign affairs and internal affairs, from the June deadline until the end of 1988) led the government to withdraw that proposal (Belgrade Domestic Service, 18 June; *FBIS*, 19 June). The criticism highlighted the self-perceived watchdog function of the assembly, particularly with regard to cadre renewal and apparent abuses of privileges by party/government officials.

Throughout the spring republic party congresses, provincial conferences, and the JNA party conference concentrated on replacing their own leaders, putting together the lists of *their* representatives for federal party posts, and electing delegates to attend the Thirteenth LCY Congress. This process was controversial in its own right. Former prime minister Milka Planinc was abandoned by her Croatian constituents. Charges that fighters against nationalism in 1971 were punished at the republic level for their pains were refuted by the president of the Croatian party, Mika Spiljak (*Borba*, 28 April; *FBIS*, 5 May). There was visible mudslinging involved in selecting the Croatian central committee (*Danas*, 27 May; *JPRS*, 23 July). In Serbia, Miloš Minić, a long-standing voice for cooperation and compromise, was not returned to represent the Serbia LC at the federal level.

The elections, regional party congresses, and preparations for the LCY congress in June provided a political three-ring circus that came with its own sideshow in the form of heated debate on the substance of political reform. These polemics focused on the "Critical Analysis of the Functioning of the Political System of Socialist Self-Management," a document drafted by the Federal Social Council for Affairs of the Social System and circulated by *Delegatski vjesnik* in January (*JPRS*, 5 March). This was the official response to Professor Najdan Pašić's 1982 letter to the LCY Presidium appealing for reform of the political system to prevent "parcelization of power" and paralysis of policymaking (*Politika*, 29 September 1982).

Pašić personally participated in the original fourteen-member working group, which soon expanded into five subgroups. Like Topsy, the project grew: some 217 policymakers, experts, and academics took part. Pašić himself led the Subgroup for Achievement of the Delegate System of Decisionmaking in Assemblies of Sociopolitical Communities. Considering the number of leading cadre who contributed to the "Critical Analysis," its cautious endorsement of the LCY Central Committee (*Borba*, 17 January; *FBIS*, 7 February) was to be expected.

Pašić described the document as "too extensive, too descriptive." He expressed dissatisfaction with the slow progress of the project, attributing it to the attitude that results should not be presented to the public or even to the LCY Central Committee before full agreement had been reached on controversial wording.

Milan Kučan, a high-ranking Slovene representative on the commission who later became a member of the 1986 LCY Presidium, admitted "we failed to overcome the division into the so-called progressive and conservative forces" (*Borba*, 15 January; *FBIS*, 28 January). He questioned the tendency to declare someone "progressive, merely because he advocated change . . . [whether or not such changes] really constitute an advance."

Rather clearly, the "Critical Analysis" had become the victim of the same endemic tensions and procedural problems that the working group had been set up to investigate. The rights of nations and republics/provinces were essentially reaffirmed as basic values to be worked with rather than abandoned. From the perspective of those who were dissatisfied with the highly decentralized political arrangements, the document identified problems but stopped short of solutions. In Serbia it was condemned for "fetishization" of constitutional arrangements. According to the Serbian veterans' organization, the proposed measures were "pale and incomplete" (*NIN*, 4 May; *JPRS*, 17 July).

Conversely, the Slovene LC supported the "Critical Analysis," especially with regard to maintaining the existing constitutional conception of the federation while increasing its effectiveness (*Borba*, 2 April; *JPRS*, 30 April). Boško Krunić of Vojvodina called the document "open and inspiring" and waxed eloquent as to how knowledge "that full national equality of peoples and nationalities . . . in Yugoslavia also appears as the class interest of the entire working class . . . [and] strengthens the awareness of the need for consensus" (*Borba*, 15 January).

Criticism came from scholars, politicians, and veterans, one of whom objected that the language of the document was "abstruse and incomprehensible to an ordinary person" (Belgrade Domestic Service, 27 February; *FBIS*, 28 February). The president of the Veterans' Federation presidium followed up with what might be considered the bottom line: "I do not think this is a scientific document based on Marxism . . . [it] is a political document based on consensus." Perhaps not surprisingly, the concrete proposal to establish a new Chamber of Associated Labor in the SFRY assembly was not in the draft put forward for public discussion.

This debate was yet another round in the tug-of-war between those committed to Yugoslav federalization, who view political reform as getting the kinks out of the "Titoist solution," and Serbian reformers, who increasingly believe that the constitution of 1974 was not the answer but the problem. In general, Serbs favored a Chamber of Associated Labor; those who feared its domination by Serbia opposed the idea.

The stage was set for the Thirteenth LCY Congress at the end of June. This second post-Tito congress mobilized a cast of thousands. Of the 1,553 delegates, 1,083 were elected by local party meetings charged to send forward one delegate for every 2,000 party members. Another 470 members were elected to achieve the agreed political balance: 60 delegates for each republic party organization, 40 for each autonomous province, and 30 soldiers from the army (*Borba*, 25 March; RFE *Research*, 30 June). Some 200 nonvoting delegates from various federal agencies also attended. With guests and the delegations of 120 parties and liberation movements, according to Dimče Belovski, the secretary of the LCY Presidium (Tanjug, 23 June; *FBIS*, 24 June), the total jumped to 2,257. Belovski informed journalists attending his precongress press conference that 1,450 representatives of the Yugoslav news media would be joined by roughly 200 foreign reporters covering the congress. He estimated the cost of this political and media extravaganza at 500 million dinars. As the dinar had just edged over the 400-to-the-dollar mark, the secretary was talking about $1.2 million.

The congress responded to the polemical atmosphere generated by the debate over the "Critical Analysis" with self-criticism and considerable breast-beating. The outgoing president of the Presidium, Vidoje Žarković, took the party to task for lack of unity and ideological direction. He flatly accused "many" organizations of the League of Communists of identifying with "special interests" and sliding into "statist-technocratic tendencies. . . . Bureaucratic, egoistic, and nationalistic inclinations gnawed at the LCY," he warned, "weakening its ideological unity and unity of action" (*Borba*, 25 June; *FBIS*, 30 June). Žarković evenhandedly condemned "bourgeois-liberalist" ideology and "étatist" ideology. He insisted that the legacy of the Yugoslav revolution could only be achieved by strengthening "national equality and working-class power." We can assume that the linking of nation and class reflected the official LCY position in support of the existing constitutional arrangements. That impression is reinforced by Žarković's flat statement that the solution for overcoming "polycentric étatisms" (read misuse of republic/provincial power) should not be sought in "federal étatist centralism" (restoring the central authority that has devolved to the regional level).

In an important aside, Žarković used the congress platform to dissociate the leadership from responsibility for the ongoing economic chaos that harassed Yugoslav housewives and policymakers alike. The party president dated the causes of the current economic crisis to well before the Twelfth LCY Congress in 1982; he attributed problems to the fact that investment expansion in 1976–1980 was accompanied by "carefree and disorganized borrowing and failure to use the loans in an efficient and rational manner." This understandable attempt to shift blame for the sorry state of the Yugoslav economy was hardly complimentary to Tito. Although ritualistic references were made to Tito as an inspiration for party unity and revolutionary action, the Thirteenth Congress added its voice to the de facto de-Titoization underway in 1985.

Like many earlier Yugoslav political assessments, the Thirteenth Congress had an Alice-in-Wonderland quality. Somehow overwhelming problems became less problematical by virtue of being identified, dissected, and discussed. The incoming president of the LCY Presidium, Milanko Renovica, ended the congress on an optimistic note: self-management was not in crisis, rather the mechanisms and methods of implementing the system were inadequate. He described the congress as a "congress of unity and action." (Belgrade Domestic Service, 28 June: *FBIS*, 1 July.) Renovica's remark did not reflect some of the more controversial sessions of the six working commissions, which struggled with the nitty-gritty questions of future policy.

Even a cursory reading of the commission debates revealed deep disagreement and pervasive frustration. The most dramatic exchange took place in the Defense Commission. Defense Minister Branko Mamula attacked "so-called peace movements" for their demands that "we stop arming ourselves" and views "designed to wreck the unity of our armed forces." He was followed by a Slovene delegate, who openly defended the Slovene Youth Movement's attraction to "alternative groups" devoted to pacifist, feminist, and ecological causes, saying they were consistent with the pluralism of self-managing interests. (*NYT*, 30 June.)

At the congress, the LCY admonished its members to offer genuine programs instead of "papers and empty appeals." Yet the mountain of resolutions and papers (produced during months of discussion involving hundreds of expert consultants as well as members of the Central Committee, then intensively debated in the working commissions) contained no clear program of political reform.

Bystanders in downtown Belgrade applauded the elderly man who climbed a tall tree on the opening day of the congress and shouted his opinion—that the political system had brought the country to the brink of ruin. Members of the crowd might not have gone so far, but they may have agreed with Milovan Djilas that the meeting was a "meaningless repetition of similar past events" (*Daily Telegraph*, 27 June). For the more politically concerned there was some disappointment that proposals to elect the LCY Central Committee from a list of multiple candidates had been sidetracked. As for the new party statutes, it remained to be seen if statutory strengthening of democratic centralism would clarify the relationship of the LCY Central Committee to its own Presidium, never mind the tangled web of republic/provincial responsibilities vis-à-vis the federal party.

It is not an exaggeration to say that the Thirteenth LCY Congress demonstrated the ability of such gatherings to serve as political steam valves, which provide increasingly threadbare illusion of unity and little sense of direction. For many ordinary Yugoslavs it was a congress that fulfilled low expectations. As one observer commented, "we are taking a tram into the twenty-first century" (personal communication, Belgrade, 27 June).

*The Economy.* Despite the albatross-like foreign debt of $19.78 billion, the year began on a cautiously optimistic note. There was a positive balance of trade, with 1985 exports up by 7 percent as compared to a 5 percent increase in imports. Industrial production had increased slightly (2.7 percent); tourists spent 12 percent more of the hard currency so essential to meet Yugoslavia's debt-servicing obligations.

Dropping oil prices could be expected to further reduce the outflow of hard currency. Perhaps most important, the decline in the standard of living had been halted in 1985. Reportedly it even grew a fraction, 0.9 percent, over 1984. (Tanjug, 31 January; RFE *Research*, 27 March). In his April report to the Federal Assembly, the FEC secretary for market and economic affairs, Sinisa Korica, revised that figure upward to 2.8 percent (Tanjug Domestic Services, 9 April; *FBIS*, 10 April).

From the point of view of Prime Minister Branko Mikulić, that was the good news. The bad news was that debt servicing still absorbed about 44 percent of total foreign currency. Inflation was an admitted 80 percent, and unofficially thought higher still. Some 1.2 million Yugoslavs were unemployed, an estimated 6.7 percent more than the year before, and bad weather had crippled agricultural production, which was down 8 percent. The uneven distribution of personal incomes between republics and provinces continued to create ambivalence about prescriptions for economic recovery, with some economists arguing that reform unfairly favored the more developed regions. (*Danas*, 11 March.) This may have signaled resentment that Slovene personal incomes had increased well above the Yugoslav average in 1985.

The sense of a lack of equity on the road to economic stabilization reinforced the federal government's drive to gain control over the economy. Undoubtedly foreign currency came high on the list of "economic levers" that Milka Planinc wanted to consolidate in the hands of the federation (interviews with *Borba*, 31 December 1985, 2 January; RFE *Research*, 27 March). The resulting foreign currency law (*Sluzbeni list SFRJ*, 11 December 1985) centralized foreign currency earnings, moving them out of the hands of exporting enterprises into approved banks. Thereby it eliminated what reportedly had been a freewheeling capital market, within which enterprises that had foreign exchange sold it to those who needed it for what the market would bear. Others argue that even here the exchange rate unrealistically favored the dinar.

Somewhat ironically, the foreign currency laws appealed in principle both to the IMF advisors, who wanted a Yugoslav government with enough economic power to influence the economy, and to those Yugoslavs committed to a more egalitarian distribution of resources. It was a high-minded, ideologically appropriate thing to do. The arguments of Slovenia and Croatia that this would have a disastrous impact on the incentive to export were pushed

aside. Mikulić adopted a wait-and-see attitude (speech to the presidium of the Yugoslav Youth Federation Conference, *Oslobodjenje*, 22 January; *FBIS*, 27 January). Indeed, when he became prime minister in May the issue appeared to slide to a back burner.

Taking over as head of government just as the six-year IMF "supervision" of the Yugoslav economy came to an end, Mikulić had somewhat more scope for structuring Yugoslav economic policy than his predecessor. IMF austerity measures had stabilized the country's foreign debts. kept Western credits flowing while debts were rescheduled, introduced a realistic rate of exchange, and brought interest rates on domestic credit somewhat in line with inflation. The cost of these measures had been declining investment, galloping inflation, and high unemployment.

Undoubtedly, the new prime minister's first priorities were to tackle inflation and improve the competitiveness of Yugoslav products on the international market. A new economic package went to the Federal Assembly in June. The dinar was devalued again, making Yugoslav goods abroad more attractive. Interest rates were cut to help staggering enterprises. Conversely, enterprises that wanted to raise prices were told that the government needed four months to consider the matter instead of the previous thirty-day notice. Although these policies did little to control erratic price swings, such as the 60 percent increase in the price of bread in early July that the government temporarily rescinded (Tanjug, 10 July; *FBIS*, 11 July), they signaled Mikulić's willingness to use administrative measures to counter inflation rather than rely on market socialism to do the job.

At first glance, the FEC economic package had something for everyone. But as the implications of its underlying economic philosophy—that inflation is rooted in wage increases that do not reflect rises in productivity—became clear, the program ran into opposition. In midsummer, the prime minister complained that it seemed as if "every measure aimed at transferring obligations from the economy in general to the population is resisted" (speech in Niš, *Večernji list*, 22 July). A wave of strikes largely related to decreasing salaries showed what workers thought of the idea (*Borba*, 6–8 August; *FBIS*, 14 August). Trade unions, which had originally unenthusiastically supported the government, took another look at the consequences of the new intervention law for personal income and decided that it violated the self-managing rights of associated labor organizations that had already signed social agreements on incomes (Belgrade Domestic Service, 18 November; *FBIS*, 20 November).

Yugoslav patience, described by sociologist Josip Županov as a "miracle" in light of buying power that had declined to the 1967 level (*Ilustrovana politika*, 4 March; *JPRS*, 14 July), was wearing thin. It was not helped by a 38 percent increase in the cost of electricity in July and the news that another increase could be expected in October (Tanjug Domestic Service, 10 July; *FBIS*, 11 July). When October arrived, Yugoslav media admitted that, rather than dropping, inflation had reached 100 percent (*Vjesnik*, 21 October; RFE *Research*, 20 November).

The hard fact was that the government's economic package had failed on both counts. Inflation had risen and exports had declined 3.6 percent by the beginning of November (Tanjug, 21 November; *FBIS*, 24 November). There was discussion of increasing imports to bring domestic prices down by competition. That solution would have been counterproductive, however, by destabilizing Yugoslavia's foreign debt and requiring still more hard currency to pay for imports. Slovene pressure for a change in the foreign currency laws continued, but the issue had not re-emerged in the Federal Assembly by the end of the year.

Rather than remove the disincentives to export, a new tack was taken. Changes were proposed in the accounting system and in methods of rescuing and liquidating unprofitable enterprises. A proposed tax reform appeared designed to serve both as an "economic lever" and a revenue producer. The FEC's "Third Basket" to the Federal Assembly included the suggestion that the federation be financed by proceeds from a turnover tax that would go entirely into the federal budget rather than being halved with the republics and provinces as before. The proposed 1987 budget of 1.9 billion dinars amounted to a 37 percent increase over 1986 spending. (*Borba*, 11 November; *FBIS*, 20 November.)

Although the government still resisted a price freeze, Mikulić acknowledged that disturbances in the price sector might warrant such a move. He warned that some 2,000 requests to raise prices 100 to 800 percent were waiting in the wings (speech to the Economic Chamber of the Federal Assembly, *Borba*, 30 September; *FBIS*, 6 October). Under these conditions, one might be excused for wondering if "market socialism" had not somehow withered away. Indeed, frustrated voices inside and outside the government speculated on private enter-

prise as an answer, particularly in the agricultural sector. It was a theme that Mikulić himself had sounded from the beginning (*Borba*, 17–18 May; RFE *Research*, 17 July). The message was dramatized by one of Yugoslavia's "national heroes," Čedo Grbić, when he bluntly declared to the Thirteenth Congress that "Communism can be achieved only by means of the highest labor productivity and a rich working class . . . I did not fight for a socialism of the poor!" (*Duga*, 27 June; RFE *Research*, 27 June).

It sounded fine. But ideological preferences in the West aside, private enterprise is not a panacea for Yugoslavia any more than market socialism or socialist self-management. The problems of the country's domestic economy and Yugoslavia's place in the international political economy are hopelessly intertwined. Policymakers are caught in an unhappy dilemma—measures needed to stimulate exports also jack up the already virtually unbearable inflation. There are no panaceas—only another round of experimental remedies. Mikulić faced that reality when he reluctantly allowed interest rates to rise with inflation. Unfortunately, the prime minister had even less control over ethnic frustrations, which also rose in tandem with rising prices and declining wages.

*The National Question.* Inevitably, the economic crisis worsened national tensions. In the fall of 1985 manifestations of Serbian nationalism escalated. Demands that federal policymakers protect the security of Serbs and Montenegrins in Kosovo so as to prevent their mass migration from the Albanian-dominated province became charges of genocide (*Književne novine*, 15 December 1985; RFE *Research*, 7 March). The original demand had originated as a petition in Kosovo, signed by several thousand Serbs and other nationalities. In January, 212 Serbian intellectuals again petitioned the Federal Assembly and Serbian Assembly: they accused the government of waffling and elaborated on the charge of genocide, linking the present "protectors of Albanian tyrants" to three centuries of Serbian oppression by Turks, Habsburgs, Italian Fascists and German Nazis. The tone and intensity of these petitions reflected anger, alienation, and a dangerous degree of Serbian separatism.

The issue had expanded from one of personal security and harassment to the much murkier problem of communal rights versus individual property rights. In February, a delegation of Serbs from Kosovo complained to the Federal Assembly that

Albanians were buying property in Serbian villages and Serbian communities were being "encircled." There were threats that if the Albanian families were not moved out by the authorities, the entire village would make a mass migration. Indeed, just before the June party congress, Serbian families from the village of Batusi (outside Kosovo's capital of Priština) began the long march to Belgrade, reportedly to pitch their tents on the banks of the Sava River until the government acted.

The estimated number of the migrants varied widely, from 500 into the thousands. But there is no doubt that a Serbian diaspora was threatened and it was taken seriously in Belgrade. Riot police and army vehicles blocked the road. According to the official version, top provincial officials—including the president of the Kosovo Presidium, Azem Vlasi, and members of the Serbian LC leadership— persuaded the marchers to return home. (*Borba*, 23 June; *FBIS*, 1 July.) Journalists and dissident sources in Belgrade said that they had been told by witnesses that the police used clubs and barricades to reinforce persuasion (*WP*, 28 June).

A three-day debate in Kosovo with more than 1,000 speakers defused the incident without producing any answers to the basic questions. How can the government keep Serbs and Montenegrins in Kosovo when they feel they are in physical danger from Albanian nationalists, if not their Albanian neighbors? How can it convince them to come back when the unemployment rate in the province is more than 30 percent, and among young people perhaps as much as 50 percent? Some 20,000 of the 220,000 Serbs and Montenegrins living in Kosovo (according to the 1981 census) reportedly have emigrated. Of the roughly 2,000 who did return between 1982 and 1985, only an estimated 630 found jobs. (RFE *Research*, 27 March.) If the authorities take the current route of promising jobs ("without competition and other formalities"), favorable credits, and land (Tanjug Domestic Service, 10 November; *FBIS*, 12 November), how can they prevent ethnic Albanians from feeling even more like second-class citizens in the province where they form 77 percent of the population? Groups of federal and Serbian officials investigating charges and overseeing decisions regarding Albanians and Serbs hardly demonstrate national equality and can easily be viewed as interfering in provincial affairs (Priština, *Jedinstvo*, 21 June; RFE *Research*, 17 July).

Day by day Kosovo became more polarized. Stung by the steady attacks on Albanian na-

tionalism, Ismail Bajra, a member of the presidency of the Kosovo League of Communists, retorted that Serbian and Montenegrin nationalism itself was "counterrevolutionary" (*Rilindja*, 24 February; RFE *Research*, 17 March). Although Bajra was not renominated to the top provincial, Serbian, or LCY leadership in April, his views were restated in somewhat more moderate terms by the Kosovo presidency, which warned that Serbian and Montenegrin nationalisms had become more organized and were openly attacking national equality and politicizing everyday problems so as to encourage Serbs and Montenegrins to emigrate (Tanjug Domestic Service, 29 September; *FBIS*, 3 October). The perception of the problem varies widely, depending on the set of policymakers involved, never mind unofficial opinions.

By September, the Serbian Academy of Arts and Sciences had joined the debate with a 74-page draft memorandum on "The Crisis of Yugoslav Economy and Society," which was "illegally" distributed by the Belgrade daily *Borba* and finally banned (RFE *Research*, 20 November). The memorandum was a scathing criticism that tied Yugoslavia's political and economic system to the deteriorating position of Serbian people within the country. It derided the slogan "we must separate in order to unite!" and dismissed concerns about Serbian dominance as exaggerations. The constitution of 1974 was blamed for reducing the country to such a state that laws could not be implemented. Croatia and Slovenia were accused of obstructing Yugoslav unity— "thanks to the political position of their leaders," a phrase that slapped directly at both Tito and Kardelj. The problems of Kosovo were seen as a legacy of Stalinism. The charge of Albanian-spawned genocide against Kosovar Serbs was repeated, along with a warning that the "anti-Serb coalition" in Yugoslavia regarded Serbs as "hegemonists, centralizers, and policemen." (Excerpts in *Večernje novosti*, 24 September; RFE *Research*, 16 October.)

This reference to an "anti-Serb" coalition referred to the growing feeling among Serbs that due to Tito (whose father was a Croat, and mother a Slovene) and Kardelj (the Slovene schoolteacher most frequently associated with the theoretical underpinnings of socialist self-management), Croatia and Slovenia had been able to gang up against Serbs and Serbian interests. It was as if the breaking of the Croatian "mass movement" and the purging of the Croatian party leadership in 1971 had never happened.

Whatever one thinks of the factual basis of the memorandum, its tone accurately reflected the increasingly sectarian nature of Yugoslav politics. From the Serbian perspective, the Slovenes had been unsupportive on the painful issue of Kosovo and had even asserted that Albanian irredentism was rooted in the Serbian-Montenegrin nationalism that had ruled in Kosovo for many years. (*Dnevnik*, 9 April; *FBIS*, 15 April.) A Slovene journalist underscored the legitimacy accorded Serbian nationalist demonstrators in Kosovo and Belgrade as compared to the arrests and condemnation of Albanian nationalists, who were dismissed as irredentists and given long jail terms. In Belgrade, public reference to the appearance of a double standard in dealing with conflicting Kosovar nationalisms was *not* appreciated. It sparked a sense of outrage much like the defensive reaction to the "White Book" reportedly distributed by Croatian communists who accused the Serbs of "anarcholiberalism"—an attack on Serbian insistence that anti-Titoism and more democratization is the only way out of Yugoslavia's crisis (RFE *Research*, 20 November).

Yugoslavs worried that Vladimir Bakarić, godfather of Croatian communism, was all too prophetic when he said in 1971 that "Yugoslavia can exist with a Croatian problem, but it cannot exist with a Serbian problem" (*NYT*, 24 October). Time will tell. Throughout 1986 the cauldron of Yugoslav nationalism boiled; it stopped short of boiling over.

*Dissent.* Yugoslav dissent remained inseparable from nationalism. Trials of Albanians continued; district courts handed down sentences from three months to thirteen years to 46 Albanians charged with trying to create an Albanian republic in Yugoslavia. Another 27 members of a dissident Marxist-Leninist group were sentenced in a Priština court (*NYT*, 23 May). From the Serbian view, these calls for an Albanian republic would cut the heart out of historic Serbia. The demand for republic status was condemned as a first step on the road to secession from Yugoslavia and unification with Albania. It was unclear if any connection existed between those being tried and the unofficial accounts in 1985 of a Movement for Liberation financed by Albanian émigrés in the West and rumored to have sympathizers among ethnic Albanian officers in the Yugoslav armed forces (*CSM*, 9 January).

Intellectual protest paralleled national dissent. The case of Dr. Dragoljub Petrović of Novi Sad, who was sent to jail for 60 days for his uncompli-

mentary account of the behavior of Yugoslav communists during and after World War II, became a cause célèbre in which Yugoslav intellectuals put aside their national/ethnic differences. Serbian, Slovene, Muslim, and Croatian writers rallied in Petrović's defense. Comments about "atavistic repression" were at least as unflattering to the current leadership as Petrović's revisionist history was to their wartime predecessors (*Intervju*, 17 January; RFE *Research*, 11 February).

A groundswell of support emerged for Tomăs Mastnak, a young Slovene sociologist charged with "offending another constituent republic"—a crime carrying a possible three-year sentence—for his public suggestion that Branko Mikulić's strong-arm tactics against freedom of academic and religious expression in Bosnia-Hercegovina made him a poor choice for prime minister. Still insisting that he had grounds for prosecution, the prosecutor unhappily dropped the charges as "socially insignificant." (*NIN*, 20 July; RFE *Research*, 19 August.) With respect to this dimension of dissent, party policy had the worst of all possible worlds. It did not silence the criticism, while the very nature of official response increased the number of critics like fleas.

By midsummer some 200 Yugoslav authors, professors, and journalists had started a fund to assist colleagues who had lost jobs due to their political opinions. This financial blow for freedom of expression was announced in an open letter to newspapers and radio and television offices. It was followed in October by a letter to the Federal Assembly from the Committee for the Defense of Freedom of Thought and Expression, a group of nineteen intellectuals led by the most famous living Serbian writer, Dobrica Ćosić. The letter stressed the need for direct elections as a step toward doing away with the one-party state. It suggested that "no one should hold power forever." (AP, 6 October; RFE *Research*, 16 October.)

There was a particularly spontaneous character to both nationalist and intellectual dissent in Yugoslavia. What one could get away with depended very much on which republic and which national/ethnic group was involved. Typically, laws were much more strictly enforced in Bosnia-Hercegovina, where a retired schoolteacher was sentenced to five-and-a-half years in prison for insulting Tito, and defendants were jailed on nationalist offenses for religious activities (*Pravoslavje*, 1 April; *JPRS*, 22 July). Conversely, statements against Tito and the state were viewed much less seriously in Serbia. These differences may have reflected the silent support of the republic party leadership in Serbia for criticisms of the political system that came from Serbian intellectuals, especially those remarks directed against the treatment of Serbs and Montenegrins in Kosovo.

No figures were available for 1986, but according to the federal public prosecutor's department, of the 415 persons charged with political crimes in 1985 only 62 were accused of being a counterrevolutionary threat to society or conspiring to commit acts of enemy activity. The majority, 288, were tried for enemy propaganda or promoting national, racial, and religious hatred; 101 were charged with violating the reputation of the Yugoslav state or disseminating untrue reports. Some 335 were sentenced. (Tanjug, Domestic Service, 16 June; *FBIS*, 17 June.)

**Auxiliary Organizations.** Generally speaking, auxiliary organizations took part in the agonizing reappraisal that racked the party itself. To an extent this was a function of pressure to respond to the "Critical Analysis" coming from policymakers increasingly committed to popular debate. Some considered this democratization, or at least feedback. Others, less flatteringly, implied that it was a form of avoidance behavior by politicians unwilling to make the hard choices. Whatever the intent, there was a pervasive institutional identity crisis and a search for new, sometimes expanded, roles within a fluid political environment.

Inevitably SAWPY was whipsawed by the party's ambivalence about its own self-image. On the one hand, there were those who felt that the Socialist Alliance erred on the side of its transmission role vis-à-vis the LCY (interview with Alexandar Grličkov, president of the Federal Conference of SAWPY, *Borba*, 1–2 February). Franc Šetinc pointed to the danger of SAWPY becoming "more like the party than the party itself . . . a caricature" (Tanjug Domestic Service, 10 October; *FBIS*, 20 October). On the other hand, there were those who thought that communists kept too much to themselves and did not work actively enough within the alliance (Tanjug Domestic Service, 10, 11 September).

Suggestions ranged from the idea that the LCY should wither away within SAWPY (leaving the Socialist Alliance as the core infrastructure of self-managing socialism) to the notion that SAWPY itself should wither away and a new party by implication would eliminate the need for SAWPY as a front

organization (Tanjug Domestic Service, 10 October; *FBIS*, 17 October). As might be expected, the party had little enthusiasm for either scenario. Indeed, concern about the activity of communists within the Socialist Alliance preoccupied an LCY Central Committee session in October. The committee struggled with the problem of how SAWPY could simultaneously advance democratic pluralism and ensure implementation of party policy. There was no answer, only a decision to approve some draft stances to be debated within the party until 15 December. At that time the topic would presumably be thrown open for public debate within SAWPY.

For SAWPY, however, the dilemma was not only how to relate to its communist members, but also how to deal with proliferating "alternative movements." Should peace and environmental movements be co-opted or excluded? From the perspective of political mobilization, there was every reason to welcome young people who took the initiative on issues of peace and international cooperation. Yet peace movements have a way of becoming pacifist, of making demands that are dangerously unacceptable in the opinion of SAWPY members sensitive to the army's need for resources and modernization. (*Borba*, 12 September; *FBIS*, 18 September.)

The Socialist Alliance was a key arena within which spokesmen for the JNA expressed their concern about the impact of economic crisis on the capability of the Yugoslav armed forces to defend the country. It was not only that "some people" went so far as to question the need for social investment in military modernization, or that inflation was eating up the army's budget. Lack of unity in railroads and telephone systems also hindered the country's defense. (*Narodna armija*, 29 May; *FBIS*, 4 June.)

At the Tenth Congress of the veterans' organization, similar worries were voiced about the dangers of "eight isolated economies" and the lack of unity in the LCY. The veterans had both corporate issues, rooted in their unequal treatment in republics and provinces, and societal concerns, such as opposition to more nuclear power plants. (Tanjug Domestic Service, 10 June; *FBIS*, 11 June.) It was not that they intrinsically objected to nuclear energy. Rather, the objection was to increasing Yugoslavia's debt burden to pay the bill. In the speeches of veterans both at the congress and at other meetings during the year, there was a tone of alienation and anger; a sense that their justified criticism was ignored by younger party members who were willing to see the Yugoslavia the partisans had fought for disintegrate into squabbling nationalisms.

A similar alienation and agitation flowed from the Twelfth Congress of the League of Socialist Youth. As one Zagreb commentator put it, this was a congress of contradictions. The delegates floundered between name-calling and high-minded appeals by the Slovene youth organization to march for the unemployed and invest in small production plants rather than spending money on ritualistic Youth Day celebrations. Ultimately, the Slovene petition was transformed into a bland resolution that Youth Day should be "enriched" with new meaning. The more controversial subject of a civilian substitute for military service was sidetracked; the buck was passed to other organs. Demands for democratization at all levels of organization and decisionmaking were met only by an imposed slate of officers put in place by an electoral conference after the congress ended; the process reportedly included numerous irregularities, creating a "delicate situation" (*Danas*, 17 June; *JPRS*, 31 July.)

Nor were workers immune from the frustration that young Yugoslavs and veterans felt with their daily political and economic struggle. According to the Commission of Petitions and Complaints at the Tenth CTUY Congress, "injustice and the feeling of helplessness" were harder to cope with than "financial perils" (Tanjug Domestic Service, 31 May; *FBIS*, 2 June). Workers urged the trade unions to do more to protect their self-managing rights and social property. The congress resolutions reflected this sense of urgency and focused on issues of unemployment, improvement in workers' personal incomes, and the need to eliminate unjustified social differences. A demand to examine the tax policy was put forward.

The report of the Self-management Commission to the trade union congress expressed considerable dissatisfaction with the functioning of the delegate system in recent elections. There was a presentation by a delegate of the Kosovo trade union federation that attacked the negative effects of both Albanian and Serbian/Montenegrin nationalism as "springboards" against socialist self-management. His remarks were followed by a somewhat ambiguous speech referring to contradictions in society that had spilled over into the Yugoslav army. The speaker appeared to reject charges that the army was centralist, with no sensitivity for national considerations. He even more firmly opposed "what we have been offered as an alternative": dissolving the professional military into territorial defense forces

or a national police. (Tanjug Domestic Service, 30 May; *FBIS*, 2 June.) For the CTUY congress, this was an aside. For students of Yugoslav politics, it was an important indicator of an increasingly widespread debate over the political role and military mission of the Yugoslav army.

In terms of the future, the most concrete accomplishment of the congress came in the form of revised CTUY statutes that attempted to be more precise about the status of republic and provincial trade union organizations. It was an effort to find the line between republic/provincial autonomy and the need to implement agreed policy. In that process consensus was abolished at conferences of basic organizations. Although the term of office of the president of the CTUY council remained one year with no re-election, the term of the council secretary was extended to two years with a possible re-election to another two—thereby providing organizational continuity and a clear focus for institutional power.

Other proposed changes were treated much more gingerly by the trade unions. In September, the trade union presidium postponed discussion of introducing a Chamber of Associated Labor into the Federal Assembly. That possibility had been raised at the CTUY congress as well as in many party forums throughout the year. (*Politika*, 26 September; *FBIS*, 9 October.) Notwithstanding the congress pledge to more actively protect worker rights, trade union leaders were openly negative to politicizing the problem of work stoppages by legalizing strikes (*Borba*, 15 October; *FBIS*, 7 November).

Other auxiliary organizations surfaced in public confrontation with the party on both substantive and organizational issues. To some extent, this was a spinoff of differences regarding the boundaries of freedom of expression (see *Dissent*). The Serbian Writers' Association held weekly protest meetings in support of Dragoljub Petrović, who had been expelled from the party and sentenced to 60 days in prison for his revisionist history of LCY wartime and postwar activity. The association also accused Albanian writers in Kosovo of keeping silent on persecution of Kosovar Serbs and Montenegrins. That position brought a rebuke from the LCY leadership, which charged that the Serbian association itself was becoming corrupted with Serbian nationalism and was opposing the policy of national equality. (Tanjug, 14 March; RFE *Research*, 27 March.)

Throughout the year there was continual sniping

between the party and the Slovene Journalists' Association. Slovene journalists campaigned to drop from the charter of the Yugoslav Journalists' Association the requirement of a loyalty oath to the ideas of Marxism-Leninism (*Dnevnik*, 9 October; *FBIS*, 22 October). The suggestion generated polemical discussion, but was considerably further than their colleagues in other areas were willing to go.

**International Views and Positions.** Yugoslav foreign policy reflected the country's economic woes and internal tensions. The post-Tito collective leadership virtually had been forced to rewrite the script and recast the play for domestic politics; in foreign policy Tito's successors had an established part. This was particularly true with respect to Yugoslav nonalignment, where preparations for the Eighth Nonaligned Summit in Harare, Zimbabwe, reinforced federal visibility and importance. The Thirteenth LCY Congress set the stage with extensive bilateral discussions and speeches reiterating the "authentic, original principles" of nonalignment to the Commission on Questions of LCY Cooperation and SFRY Foreign Policy. (*Borba*, 26 June; *FBIS*, 8 July.)

It was the standard package: reaffirmation of nonaligned principles of independence, sovereignty, respect for territorial integrity, and mutual advantage and noninterference in internal affairs as procedural guidelines for international relations; renewed commitment to peaceful resolution of violent conflicts dividing nonaligned nations; repeated warnings to the superpowers not to make the world such a dangerous place for their small and medium-sized neighbors; and pleas for reopening the north-south dialogue in the search for a new international economic order.

There was a shift in emphasis, however. Both the congress resolutions and Hasani's speech to the Harare summit put the nonaligned struggle to build "new international relations free from all domination and hegemony" firmly in its economic context. The Yugoslav president pointedly focused on the burden of debts as a joint problem for creditors and debtors; he called for an expanded three-way discussion that included debtor countries, creditor governments, and international financial and banking institutions. (Tanjug Domestic Service, 3 September; *FBIS*, 5 September.) He was not so blunt as earlier media accounts that accused creditor countries of using their economic power for "exploitation and domination" of developing countries (*Borba*, 11 April). But Hasani's remarks did reinforce sug-

gestions that ways should be found to deal with the ever-growing debt burden of the Third World beyond IMF austerity requirements and rescheduling.

Ironically, this put the Yugoslav delegation on the same side as the Cubans. Ever since Fidel Castro insisted that the socialist countries are the "natural allies" of the nonaligned (a view vigorously refuted by Tito at the Havana summit in 1979), Cuba has been considered the archopponent of the Yugoslav desire for an "authentic, nonbloc" nonalignment. This area of mutual interest may well have contributed to Castro's friendly three-day visit to Yugoslavia on his way home from Harare. The Cuban leader spoke glowingly of his meetings with the "unforgettable comrade Josip Broz Tito" (Havana Television Service, 13 September; *FBIS*, 15 September). Possibly he was trying to make amends for a doctored photograph that had accompanied an article on the 25th anniversary of the first nonaligned summit in Belgrade. Much to Yugoslav annoyance, the photo either inadvertently or intentionally eliminated President Tito, along with several other dignitaries. (Belgrade Domestic Service, 21 August; BBC, 26 August.) Be that as it may, Castro was on his best behavior. There were no references to areas of ideological disagreement, and the tone of Cuban coverage was even more cordial than that of the Yugoslav media.

Although creditor governments and international financial circles had little interest in the proposed dialogue, debtor countries began talking more seriously among themselves. Following the Harare summit, the Tenth Ministerial Meeting of the Group of 77 took up the issue. In November Yugoslavia joined some 36 other debtor countries—members of the nonaligned movement and the Group of 77—in a consultative meeting in Lima, Peru, to debate the debt problem. Experts on finance, economy, and budgetary questions as well as foreign ministry officials and representatives of central banks exchanged their country's specific experiences. (*Review of International Affairs*, 5 December.) This was the first meeting of its kind. Given the global nature of the debt problem, it is a form of south-south cooperation that can be expected to recur.

Although there was general agreement on the broad principles of Yugoslavia's nonaligned foreign policy, internal divisions existed on nonaligned strategy. Slovenes tended to stress the value of neutral and nonaligned activity in Europe. Calls for intensification of the north-south dialogues were criticized by those who felt that the movement would do better to give up dialogue with the deaf and to concentrate on south-south initiatives. Still others rejected the idea of nonaligned self-reliance as hopelessly naive.

Moreover, the actual economics of nonalignment were disappointing. Claims that a two-year slide in Yugoslav's trade turnover with its nonaligned allies had been halted (Tanjug, 17 May; *FBIS*, 19 May) proved premature. By midsummer a foreign ministry spokesman admitted that rather than moving toward the 24 percent target, such trade had slipped to roughly 14 percent (personal communication, 2 July). Efforts to turn the situation around focused on tripartite Yugoslav-India-Egypt economic cooperation, supplemented by attempts to expand what appeared to be a flourishing Yugoslav construction industry in order to compensate for the country's unfavorable balance of trade with developing countries. For example, in 1985 Yugoslav contractors built projects worth an estimated $800 million in Iraq (Tanjug, 6 May; *FBIS*, 7 May). Economic dealing continued with Iran as well, despite signs of strain stemming from Iranian charges of persecution of Yugoslav Muslims and Yugoslav countercharges of "Ayatollah Stalinism" (*Vjesnik*, 14 August; RFE *Research*, 19 August). Indeed, according to some reports, the Yugoslavs were considerably more pragmatic than principled when it came to arms sales to other nonaligned countries, including Iran and Iraq (BBC, 26 August).

Notwithstanding the underlying consensus in support of Yugoslav nonalignment, differences of opinion undoubtedly also existed on cost-benefit calculations concerning the amount of nonaligned activity. This mirrored popular resentment at resources devoted to nonaligned obligations during the troubles that plague Yugoslavia's domestic economy. Meanwhile, demands for cutbacks on official travel did not visibly diminish bilateral nonaligned diplomacy. A steady stream of nonaligned delegations (from Ghana, Egypt, Algeria, India, and Burma, among others) appeared in Yugoslavia. Prime Minister Mikulić visited India in July, and in November, a Yugoslav assembly delegation began a tour of Latin America to discuss the international economic and political situation in Venezuela, Colombia, and Peru.

The effort to maintain Yugoslavia's prestige within the nonaligned world was one foreign policy goal. The drive for hard currency, generated by debt-servicing obligations, was undeniably another. In this regard, Yugoslav relations with the West showed mixed returns.

The decision of the European Community to establish a one-thousand-kilometer "danger zone" around Chernobyl after the Soviet nuclear disaster and to ban food imports from six East European countries, including Yugoslavia, damaged the country's agricultural markets. According to Yugoslav estimates, exporters suffered some $25 million in immediate losses (Tanjug, 31 May; *FBIS*, 3 June). Another blow came when the 30 June meeting of the European Research Agency (EUREKA)—a cooperative program to promote European high-technology industries—rejected Yugoslav membership on the grounds that Yugoslavia did not have a market economy.

Given these setbacks, the Yugoslavs embarked on a campaign of bilateral meetings with West European governments in search of credits, markets, and ways to reduce trade deficits. These efforts were particularly intense with the West Germans, since the trade deficit with Yugoslavia's "second largest economic partner" had grown 12 percent, to reach $716 million (Hamburg, *Cap*, 6 August). Sessions with the FRG's minister of economics, Martin Bangemann, and foreign minister, Hans-Dietrich Genscher, were followed by talks with West German parliamentarians, in an attempt to enlist FRG support against protectionist measures restricting Yugoslav exports to the Common Market (Tanjug, 17 September; *FBIS*, 19 September).

Trade with France increased and showed a decreasing deficit (*Politika*, 2 June; *FBIS*, 6 June). British banks refinanced credits of $92.6 million and 10.4 million pounds sterling on terms "more favorable than last year" (Tanjug Domestic Service, 27 September; *FBIS*, 29 September), and in October the British foreign trade minister, Alan Clark, was in Belgrade for negotiations. Talks were also held with Sweden and Holland in hopes of expanding economic cooperation. With respect to Greece, appeals for neighborly relations alternated with polemics over official Greek policy toward the Macedonian question (*Politika*, 19 June; *FBIS*, 19 June).

Yugoslav-U.S. relations were also tangled in a somewhat different national/ethnic issue. During the year, three Yugoslav-Americans who had maintained dual citizenship were arrested in Yugoslavia for antistate activities. The case of Peter Ivezaj included charges that he had demonstrated in Chicago and Washington, D.C., against Yugoslav treatment of ethnic Albanians. Those charges were dropped when a Michigan representative, William S. Bloomfield, introduced legislation in Congress to revoke Yugoslavia's most-favored-nation trading status, a proposed bill with 150 cosponsors. Ivezaj and the two others were released. (*NYT*, 11 October.)

Although this crisis was averted, the case of Milan M. Nikolić, a Yugoslav sociologist sentenced to five months in prison for a thesis he wrote at Brandeis University, may have set off another round of tensions (*NYT*, 8 December). In the meantime the Yugoslav finance secretary, Svetozar Rikanović, held talks in Washington on Yugoslav-U.S. relations. Emphasis was on joint investment rather than credits, with considerable praise for the modern marketing of the compact car Yugo, whose sales were expected to reach 60,000 by the end of the year. (Tanjug, 25 November; *FBIS*, 26 November.)

Relations with the Soviet Union were cordial and correct, although with the negotiated reduction of Soviet oil prices from $27 per barrel to something closer to world market prices, economic exchanges leveled off—at a projected $36 billion worth of merchandise and services for the next five-year period (Tanjug, 15 May; *FBIS*, 16 May). This was some $4 billion below earlier estimates of a $40 billion trade turnover (Tanjug, 19 June). It was, however, in the context of expanding overall contacts.

In September, a CPSU cultural delegation arrived in Belgrade, followed in October by a delegation of the USSR Supreme Soviet led by First Deputy Chairman Petr Demichev. Demichev tactfully referred to the contribution of Yugoslavia to the victory over fascism at the end of World War II, and even went so far as to assess the decisions by the nonaligned summit in Harare as "positive." (Tanjug, 20 October; *FBIS*, 21 October.) Then, in December, CPSU Politburo member Viktor M. Chebrikov led a delegation of Soviet security officials that arrived almost back-to-back with President Renovica's visit to the USSR (*Izvestiia*, 11 December; *FBIS*, 12 December). In Moscow both sides praised their "all around" cooperation, a prelude perhaps to General Secretary Mikhail Gorbachev's scheduled 1987 visit to Yugoslavia.

Although there was not a great deal of detailed news on Yugoslavia's relations with other East European countries, an agreement to increase trade with Czechoslovakia to $7.6 billion by 1990 was signed in Prague (Tanjug, 14 March; *FBIS*, 17 March). Notwithstanding reports that Yugoslav-Albanian trade had been declining since 1983 (*Borba*, 11 April; *JPRS*, 12 June), a railway cooperative agreement was signed that allows Albania to maintain freight traffic with Western Europe. Otherwise, as might have been expected, Yugoslav-Albanian relations were largely limited to polemical exchanges concerning the ethnic Albanian majority in Kosovo.

Defense Secretary Mamula visited Romania in June. Foreign Minister Dizadarević talked with his Hungarian counterpart in December; the exchange of views included issues raised by the Eighth Nonaligned Summit as well as matters of European security (Tanjug, 5 December; *FBIS*, 8 December). Also in the fall, Prime Minister Mikulić received the Bulgarian minister of finance. Attention was devoted to improving Bulgarian-Yugoslav economic relations, a problem that continued to be exacerbated by the long-standing dispute over what Yugoslavs believe is Sofia's cultural genocide of Macedonians living in Bulgaria.

The Yugoslav-Chinese connection flourished, with several high-level delegations exchanging pleasantries. Radovan Vlajkovic, president of the SFRY presidency until mid-May, visited Beijing the month before he left office. The Chinese prime minister, Zhao Ziyang, made a return visit to Yugoslavia in July at Mikulić's invitation. Although no financial details were released, this appeared to be part of a general expansion of Yugoslav economic relations with China. In 1985 Yugoslav exports to China reportedly rose by 40 percent, totaling $133 million and, equally important, showing a strongly favorable balance of trade (Tanjug, 28 February; *FBIS*, 3 March).

In general, activity related to the international communist movement appeared to be a low priority, with the exception of LCY relations with the Italian Communist Party (PCI). PCI general secretary Alessandro Natta visited Yugoslavia in February, and the two parties confirmed their "broad convergence" of views (*L'Unità*, 19 February; *FBIS*, 24 February).

Thus there were no radical departures in Yugoslav foreign policy. There was what might be considered a proliferation of republic-level foreign policy activity, including a trip to Moscow by the president of the Croatian Chamber of Commerce, the establishment of a Serbian department for economic cooperation with China, and the visit of a Slovene LC delegation to Katowice, Poland, to further cooperation between the two regions. Visiting delegations from abroad more frequently fanned out to visit republic and provincial capitals.

With respect to foreign trade, the result was that Yugoslav enterprises seeking markets were uncoordinated and appeared to sabotage one another. Not surprisingly, the government attempted to restrain this process with registration of enterprises allowed to engage in foreign trade that was to be completed by the end of the year (Tanjug, 14 August; *FBIS*, 15 August). This problem highlighted a somewhat less recognized dimension of the foreign policy dilemmas facing Yugoslav policymakers. Post-Tito federalization created more foreign policy actors in terms of territorial/bureaucratic units. The pressure to export, the obsession with hard currency, has interacted with the legal rights of self-managing enterprises to create literally 1,000 more in the form of enterprises with licenses for foreign trade.

**Biographies.** *Milanko Renovica.* Renovica, 58, is president of the LCY Central Committee Presidium (June 1986 to June 1987). A Serbian, Renovica has a law degree and has been a member of the LCY since 1947. He has held a number of party posts in Bosnia-Hercegovina, including member of the republic LC presidency. He served as premier of the Bosnia-Hercegovina government from 1974 to 1982, when he was elected to the republic presidency. Reportedly many of his positions at the republic level have been in the economic field. (Sources: Tanjug, 28 June; *FBIS*, 30 June.)

*Radisa Gačić.* Gačić, 48, is secretary of the LCY Central Committee Presidium, elected for a two-year term in June 1986. A Serbian, he has been a member of the LCY since 1957. Gačić has a law degree. He worked as a secondary-school teacher until 1970, when he began a political career; he has held various posts in the Serbian League of Communists. Until May 1986 he was secretary of the presidency of the LC of Serbia. (Sources: Tanjug, 28 June; *FBIS*, 30 June.)

*Sinan Hasani.* Hasani serves as president of the SFRY (state) presidency (May 1986 to May 1987). An Albanian, born in 1922 in Kosovo, Hasani belongs to the "club of 1941," having joined the national liberation struggle in that year. He became a member of the LCY in 1942. His political career

has been in the autonomous province of Kosovo, in the republic of Serbia, and at the federal level. At the provincial level he has been president of SAWPY, a member of the provincial LC executive committee, and *Rilindja* director. He has also served on the legislative side as a member of the Kosovo Assembly, the Federal Assembly, and as vice president of the Serbian Assembly. Hasani has diplomatic experience as the former Yugoslav ambassador to Denmark. He is widely published and a member of the Kosovo Academy of Arts and Sciences.

In 1978, at the Eleventh LCY Party Congress, Hasani was elected a member of the LCY Central Committee. In 1981 he became a member of the Presidium of the provincial committee of Kosovo and was elected president of the provincial committee in 1982; he thereby became an ex officio member of the LCY Central Committee Presidium. He was elected to the SFRY presidency in 1984. (Sources: Tanjug, 15 May 1985; *FBIS*, 16 May 1985; *International Who's Who*, 1986–87.)

*Branko Mikulić.* A Croatian, born in 1928 in Bosnia-Hercegovina, Mikulić was educated at a school of business in economic studies. He took part in the national liberation war from 1943 and has been a member of the LCY since 1945. Mikulić has had a number of important party and state posts both at the republic and federal level of the LCY. He has served as secretary of the central committee of the Bosnia-Hercegovina LCY, president of the executive council of the republic assembly, and president of Bosnia-Hercegovina's LC central committee. He has also been president of the Bosnia-Hercegovina republic presidency. At the federal level, Mikulić has been a member of the LCY Central Committee Presidium and a member of the state presidency. (Sources: Tanjug, 6 January; *FBIS*, 7 January; *International Who's Who*, 1986–87.)

Robin Alison Remington
*University of Missouri-Columbia*

# Council for
# Mutual Economic Assistance

A summit of communist party leaders from all ten CMEA member states took place in Moscow toward the end of November, the first such meeting in two and one-half years. The forty-second session of the organization had been convened earlier that same month at Bucharest. In addition, the CMEA executive committee met four times in 1986.

After a six-year hiatus, talks resumed with the European Economic Community to normalize trade. The CMEA suggested bilateral relations between itself and each of the twelve EEC members. A meeting at Geneva of experts from both sides ended in late September without any agreement other than to meet again. The EEC exports goods each year worth about $11 billion more than its imports from the East. (*NYT*, 22 September.)

The economic summit, held at Moscow during 10–11 November, included all ten bloc leaders, whose pictures appeared in *Pravda* on two consecutive days. All participants reportedly agreed that economic development and cooperation must become more dynamic. Direct links between producers will be accompanied by "joint associations, enterprises, design offices, and other international collectives" throughout the CMEA area. (Moscow radio, 15 November; *FBIS*, 17 November.) All of the foregoing presupposes implementation of reforms that will improve price setting, currency/financial relations, and legal aspects.

The groundwork for the summit had been prepared a week earlier in Bucharest. CMEA prime ministers approved a program to build nuclear, electric, and thermal power stations through the year 2000. Bilateral agreements were signed between national economic organizations in the USSR, Bulgaria, Czechoslovakia, East Germany, and Hungary. No mention was made of either Poland or Romania in this connection. (*Pravda*, 16 November.)

Trade within CMEA last year accounted for 54.8 percent of the Soviet total. It has increased sixfold since 1971. For calendar year 1985 the figures, in billions of rubles, were as follows (projected figures for the 1986–1990 five-year plan are given in parentheses): East Germany, 15.2 (66–82); Czechoslovakia, 13.4 (56–73); Bulgaria, 12.5 (52–70); Poland, 12.0 (50–74); Hungary, 9.4 (40–51); Cuba, 7.9 (32–45); Romania, 4.2 (18–30); Mongolia, 1.5 (not available); Vietnam, 1.4 (not available). (Moscow, *Ekonomicheskaia gazeta* 45, November.) The same source indicates that the USSR has signed about eighty multilateral and one hundred bilateral agreements with other CMEA governments on specialization and production-sharing for machine building alone. Yuri Shiriaiev, head of the Research Institute on International Economic Issues in Moscow, gave an interview at Budapest in which he suggested examining "the possibility of partial convertibility of the ruble." (*Magyar Hirlap*, 4 November; *FBIS*, 13 November.) He admitted that this problem had not been solved over the preceding fifteen years.

The East European client regimes are dependent to a large extent upon the Soviet Union for oil and electricity as well as certain raw materials. Prices for a barrel of Siberian petroleum vary: nonmember Finland paid $20, associate member Yugoslavia $27, and full CMEA member Romania $32 in the spring of the year (Vienna, *Die Presse*, 18 March). More than 80 million tons of oil and oil products are sent each year by the USSR to Eastern Europe.

The accident during April at Chernobyl in the Ukraine, leading to the temporary shutdown of all four nuclear reactors, resulted in a temporary loss of 24 billion kilowatt-hours of annual generating capacity and affected Soviet deliveries of electricity to CMEA member states, which had received 20 billion kilowatt-hours the previous year. (*NYT*,

1 May.) This probably led to some anxiety, especially among policymakers in countries that are adjacent to the USSR and those that rely increasingly on nuclear plants for domestic production of electric power: Bulgaria (31.6 percent), Czechoslovakia (14.6 percent), and East Germany (12 percent). (Table in ibid., 31 August.) However, about one-fourth of Eastern Europe's primary energy consumption is based on oil and gas imports, mostly from the Soviet Union.

Economic growth throughout the area has been disappointing, as indicated by results from the 1981–1985 five-year plan (FYP). Over the preceding decade, a massive infusion of hard currency sustained an artificially high level of national income. Area-wide, growth of the average national income had declined to 3.2 percent for 1985, with a target of 4.1 percent over the next FYP (table in *Europäische Rundschau* 14, no. 2).

Although much has been written about reform, especially in the direction of a free-market economy, this hardly seems likely because of ideological constraints. At the same time, about 2 percent of the population occupies the top managerial and bureaucratic posts. This so-called nomenklatura is opposed to any liberalization that might affect the kickbacks derived from "private rationing schemes." According to a Polish newspaper, the latter take away almost half of the consumer durables in the city of Krakow (London, *Economist*, 6 July). A new car brings two and one-half times its original price when sold secondhand.

CMEA hopes to alleviate some of its problems by producing raw materials—through joint construction of an iron-ore processing complex at Krivoi Rog in the Ukraine, another natural-gas pipeline from Western Siberia, as well as petroleum and gas plants in the Caspian basin. The "Progress" natural-gas pipeline will involve building forty compressor stations (Moscow, *Sotsialisticheskaia industriia*, 5 January).

Another approach has been launched by means of a program for scientific and technical cooperation through the end of the century, adopted by CMEA in December 1985. Each of the 93 projects has been allocated to one of the eleven intersectoral organizations that will control research and development, production, marketing, and servicing (Moscow radio, 1 April; *FBIS*, 2 April). The idea apparently is to make the research institutes and production enterprises supranational rather than placing them under the control of each country's bureaucracy.

Whether this will work remains uncertain. Already there have been complaints registered about the lack of cooperation in the electronics industries. The production of microchips in Hungary reportedly stopped completely after an explosion there. East Germany criticizes other CMEA members for delaying software deliveries. (London, *Foreign Report*, 20 November.)

Relations with the West, especially in trade, have been curtailed because of the hard currency debts that were incurred over the years. These now total more than $113 billion, as follows: Poland (29.3 billion), USSR (26.4 billion), Yugoslavia (18.8 billion), East Germany (13.9 billion), Hungary (11.8 billion), Romania (6.5 billion), Czechoslovakia (3.9 billion), and Bulgaria (3.2 billion). (Washington, D.C., *Handbook of Economic Statistics, 1986*, tables 20 and 49.)

Meeting even the interest on these debts has affected East-West trade adversely. Several of the CMEA member states requested a moratorium on or extension of the original repayment schedules. Poland has done the latter several years in a row. One of the consequences of the debt problem is a noticeable shift away from commercial exchange with the EEC and the United States and toward other members of CMEA.

Bulgaria, although its hard currency indebtedness declined between 1979 and 1985, remains dependent upon Moscow for raw materials and fuels. It is caught between the USSR's demand for higher quality goods and its own inability to purchase petroleum from any other country. (*NATO Review* 34, no. 3, June.)

Czechoslovakia, with a low debt and near self-sufficiency in food production, is being driven toward closer economic integration by the Soviet Union due to a worsening trade deficit. This prevents reform and diminishes production capacity as well as the quality of products, making them less than competitive in the West (ibid., p. 19).

East Germany also has redirected its imports from West to East. However, expanded deliveries to the USSR necessitate greater reliance on trade with the Federal Republic of Germany. The manufacture of oil products, on which the East Germans have relied to obtain hard currency, has been affected by the drop in the price of crude petroleum. The Kremlin's respect for East Berlin's economic prowess could be seen when a statue of German communist part founder Ernest Thälmann, the only East European so honored, was unveiled in Moscow (*Pravda*, 4 October). That same newspaper printed three different photographs of Erich Honecker with Mikhail Gorbachev, usually smiling.

Hungary has pursued a policy of restricting demand in order to increase exports and improve the balance of payments. This has led to relative stagnation and, perhaps, to more realism. Here too the trend is against more trade with the West and greater integration with the East. More than three hundred agreements on specialization and production sharing have been signed with the USSR (ibid., 3 June).

Poland's economic crisis has become exacerbated by a shortage of raw materials and manpower as well as low investment and high inflation levels. The West does not appear willing to offer more financial assistance, especially in view of the huge Polish debt. The regime in Warsaw has almost no popular support, and that probably is why it may be impossible to implement the kind of austere policies required. (*NATO Review* 34, no. 3, June.)

Romanian decisionmakers have imposed a form of militarization over their economy. Planning has been too ambitious, and the wrong investments were made. In addition, Romania has committed itself to CMEA joint projects more than any other member state: iron ore from Krivoi Rog, two other

metal mines, the "Progress" gas pipeline, natural-gas fields in Turkmenia and Kazakhstan, plus bilateral agreements in oil field development with the USSR (RL *Background Report* 100, 15 July).

Yugoslavia, only a CMEA associate, nevertheless takes part in the work of almost all specialized commissions. For all practical purposes, it is a full member of the organization. With an inflation rate of 96 percent, unemployment at 15 percent, and a hard currency debt of almost $20 billion, the economy is faced with serious problems. Supposedly a nonaligned country, Yugoslavia has been able to surmount its difficulties with constant new loans from Western banks and international monetary organizations.

In conclusion, there seems to be little real integration within the East European CMEA area and even less with members like Cuba, Mongolia, and Vietnam, all of which survive because of Soviet aid. It is true that some specialization exists. Economic reform has faced obstacles, even in Hungary. The future still depends upon the Kremlin.

Jadwiga M. Staar
*Stanford, California*

# Warsaw Treaty Organization

The Warsaw Treaty Organization (WTO), established in 1955, was renewed in 1985 for 20 years (see *YICA*, 1986). Soviet control of this important instrument of coercion was firmly established under General Secretary Mikhail S. Gorbachev, and its military presence was an effective reminder. The Soviet foreign policy priority was to "strengthen cooperation" and achieve "unity of view" with East European countries in all sectors. Political, military, and economic integration continued. Members experienced economic difficulties due partly to their high military expenditures; Romania announced a 5 percent cut. Moscow's allies endorsed

Gorbachev's arm control proposals and appeals to European states. The Reagan-Gorbachev meeting at Reykjavik was followed by Foreign Minister Eduard Shevardnadze's briefing of the pact's foreign ministers. WTO efforts for an "all-European process" were an obvious attempt to drive a wedge between the United States and its NATO allies.

**Military Developments.** Unlike the previous year, Soviet strategic forces in 1986 experienced "major developments in all major weapon categories." Of the 1,398 ICBM launchers, 72 SS-11s were replaced by the deployment of road-mobile and more accurate SS-25s. Due to its solid fuel, the SS-25 has a shorter launch time. In addition, the SS-X-24, a new ICBM, was tested and was expected to be deployed shortly. The number of highly mobile SS-20 intermediate-range missiles, with three warheads each, stood at 441; after a redeployment of about 36 missiles from Central Asia, 270 SS-20s were capable of striking targets in Europe.

Overall the number of ballistic-missile submarines remained about the same. A new submarine-launched ballistic missile, the liquid-fueled, 10-warhead SS-N-23 had made its appearance in 1985; its range of 8,300 kilometers is similar to that of the older SS-N-20. Combat helicopters, in support of the ground forces, were put under army, rather than air force, command. The ground forces reportedly increased by one motor rifle division and two air assault brigades (International Institute for Strategic Studies, *The Military Balance, 1986–1987*, p. 31). The MiG-29, the most modern and sophisticated all-weather jet fighter, made its first appearance before Western observers in Finland on 2 July (*NYT*, 12 September).

Non-Soviet WTO armies continued modernization, whereas navies and air forces showed minor changes. Czechoslovakia and the German Democratic Republic (GDR) were obtaining SS-21s to replace FROG-7; Bulgaria and the GDR received more Scud SSMs (surface-to-surface missiles); and Bulgaria and Hungary received T-72 MBTs (main battle tanks). The Romanian M-77, modeled on the medium T-55 tank, was believed to be deployed in significant numbers, and Bulgaria reportedly had the SA-13 SAM (surface-to-air missiles).

Naval changes consisted largely of retiring older ships and partially replacing them. Changes in the air forces included completion of one Mi-14 ASW (anti-submarine warfare) helicopter squadron each in Bulgaria and the GDR. "This modernization, though modest, does represent an enhancement of the overall capabilities of the forces concerned. They still, however, remain significantly less well equipped than the Soviet Union's forces in Eastern Europe" (*The Military Balance, 1986–1987*, p. 47).

Czechoslovakia reportedly is planning to construct a "gigantic" new military airport near Brno, the capital of Moravia, for use by WTO air forces. Five villages are to be displaced and their inhabitants resettled over the next five years. (Linz, Austria, *Sudetenpost*; Vienna, *Wiener Zeitung*, 14 November; *FBIS*, 14 November.)

**The Twenty-seventh CPSU Congress.** At the CPSU congress Gorbachev emphasized that the pact's extension was of "great importance," adding that "This treaty has received a second birth, as it were; today, there would be difficulty to imagine world politics without it" (*Pravda*, 26 February).

The first high-level meeting of WTO after the congress took place on 19–20 March in Warsaw. The foreign ministers predictably endorsed Soviet arms control policies, including Gorbachev's 15 January proposals: their communiqué provided no indication of concrete future proposals. Their criticism of Western policies was along familiar lines, but the tone was less aggressive than the one adopted at the CPSU congress (*Pravda*, 21 March).

**Political Consultative Committee.** Gorbachev's 15 January initiative and 18 April arms control proposal at the Eleventh Congress of the SED (the East German communist party) were elaborated on and given endorsement by the WTO's highest governing body, the Political Consultative Committee (PCC). The PCC meeting in Budapest on 10–11 June produced comprehensive and complicated proposals on reduction of military forces in Europe. The communiqué called for the cessation of nuclear testing, liquidation of Soviet and U.S. medium-range missiles in Europe, concrete accords at the Soviet-U.S. talks on nuclear and space arms, elimination during this century of weapons of mass annihilation such as chemical weapons, substantial reduction of armed forces and conventional armaments on global and regional levels, and effective verification in all fields and at all stages of arms reduction and disarmament (*Pravda*, 12 June).

In a major appeal "to all other European countries, the United States, and Canada," the WTO proposed substantial reduction of land forces and tactical aviation, as well as conventional armaments and tactical nuclear arms. The area of the proposed reductions extended from the Atlantic to the Urals. Initially, NATO and the WTO would undertake a one-time mutual reduction of 100,000–150,000 troops plus reductions of tactical aviation within one or two years. Subsequently, each side would continue to decrease ground forces and tactical aviation, so that by the early 1990s the reductions would amount to more than half a million troops on each side, or 25 percent of the present level. The suggested cuts would be by units together with their armaments and military equipment. Simultaneously, tactical nuclear weapons would be destroyed.

Decreases would subsequently continue but involve other European states as well. The PCC proposal provided for "reliable and effective verification" by national technical means and "international procedures," including on-site inspections. In addition, observation of military activity of the remaining forces was proposed, as well as exchanges of data on land forces and tactical aviation in the reductions area. An international consultative commission would include nonalliance countries, whose responsibilities would entail manning of checkpoints at rail junctions, airfields, and ports. The PCC submitted three alternative forums for its proposals: the second stage of CDE; a special forum; or an expansion of MBFR negotiations to include other European states and a change of mandate (ibid.).

The PCC appeal, although providing for on-site inspection, was along the line of traditional Soviet proposals—incorporating vague and sweeping declarations intended for world public opinion, especially West European opinion, rather than initiating serious negotiations on concrete issues. It contained obvious shortcomings. In addition to the disparity in force levels, for example, the proposed verification, while broader than previous measures, was neither sufficiently specific nor extensive. On-site inspection was restricted to "when needed," rather than on demand, as favored by the West. Other elements—tactical aviation, nuclear forces, and armaments—would give the USSR a unilateral advantage due to geographic asymmetry.

The Western allies did not reject the proposal but pointed to these weaknesses and to the ongoing negotiations at Stockholm, Geneva, and Vienna that were already considering these questions. Earlier, on 30 May, the NATO Council, deciding that "bold new steps are required," set up a high-level task force on conventional arms control to pursue the objective of "strengthening stability and security in the whole of Europe" and to take into account Gorbachev's 18 April statement on pursuing conventional force reductions from the Atlantic to the Urals (Department of State, *Bulletin*, August).

Having received the task force's report, the NATO Council on 11 December decided in its Declaration on Conventional Arms Control that "We are ready to open East/West discussions with a view to the establishment of a new mandate for negotiating on conventional arms control covering the whole of Europe from the Atlantic to the Urals" (Brussels, NATO Information Service, 11 December). The declaration was immediately criticized by Moscow for not proposing solutions or even mentioning the Budapest appeal (*Pravda*, 17 December).

Among the plethora of WTO arms control proposals during the year was one for direct contact between NATO's supreme Allied commander in Europe, General Bernard W. Rogers, and the commander in chief of WTO Joint Armed Forces, Marshal Viktor G. Kulikov, and for discussions between NATO secretary general Lord Carrington and WTO plenipotentiary representative G. Królikowski. Both suggestions were declined by NATO. To Moscow this too indicated NATO's "reluctance to begin concrete talks" on reductions of armed forces and armaments in Europe (ibid.).

**The Stockholm Conference.** The WTO, as well as NATO, compromised to reach an accord by the 19 September deadline at the Conference on Confidence and Security-Building Measures and Disarmament in Europe (CDE), which began on 17 January 1984. The purpose of CDE was to reduce the risk of war starting through misinterpretation and miscalculation. The area of application stretches from the Atlantic to the Urals. U.S. territory was not affected. The measures, effective 1 January 1987, include prior notification of military activities, observation of military activities, annual calendars, and verification. The result was important because it was a precedent-setting East-West accord on conventional military forces in Europe and because of the effect it may have on other negotiations as well as on East-West relations (see the document in Department of State, *Bulletin*, November).

Following the Budapest appeal the WTO accepted on-site inspection (*Izvestiia*, 21 August)—the first such provision in East-West security agreements—after having opposed NATO's request for inspections on demand. The final document provides for a "right to conduct inspections," but states must "address a request for inspection," and no participant is obliged to accept more than three "challenges" annually.

Signatories are obliged to issue notification of military exercises at least 42 days in advance if they involve 13,000 or more troops or at least 300 battle tanks. The threshold had been the subject of contention, with the West proposing lower and the WTO higher levels. When maneuvers involve 17,000 or more troops the states should extend invitations to all signatory governments to send observers. Annual calendars of above threshold military activities are to be exchanged with all signatories by 15 November of the previous year—or one year in advance for exercises involving more than 40,000 troops and two years for those involving more than 75,000.

Another disputed provision was NATO's proposal that planes and pilots of neutrals be utilized to transport inspectors. This was successfully countered by Moscow, which insisted that planes and pilots be from the country inspected. The WTO also prevailed on the principle of non-use of force, which was already established in the U.N. Charter and the Helsinki Final Act. The accord was not universally acclaimed. Some critics (for example, *WSJ*, 24 September) were concerned about its "illusions."

**The MBFR Negotiations.** On 5 December 1985 the 37th Round of the NATO-WTO negotiations on Mutual and Balanced Force Reductions (MBFR), which began in 1973 in Vienna, came to an end. At that time the West made an unprecedented move to break the deadlock by abandoning its demand for prior agreement on force levels before initial reductions, despite a discrepancy of some 230,000 WTO forces. Accepting the framework of the East's "Basic Provisions" of the previous February, the West required strengthened verification measures (see *YICA*, 1986).

Prospects for a breakthrough appeared promising when, in his 15 January proposals on arms control, Gorbachev recognized the need for "reasonable verification provisions," including "permanent monitoring points." However, at the 30 January session that began Round 38, the WTO characterized the NATO compromise offer as "one-sided and unrealistic," and attacked especially the West's verification provisions (*MBFR Press Transcript*, 30 January). The West, at this session, distributed to the East a "Table of Associated Measures" as an annex to its 5 December proposal.

On 20 February the East proposed a draft agreement that revised its "Basic Provisions" and provided for lower U.S.-Soviet reductions: within one year, the Soviet Union would withdraw 11,500 and the United States 6,500 ground troops. This would be followed by a three-year no-increase commitment for all military forces and armaments in the reductions area. Verification measures consisted of

noninterference with national technical means (satellites), exchange of information, three to four observation points, requests for on-site inspection, and a consultative commission (ibid., 20 February).

The West was "deeply disappointed" with the Eastern response, especially on verification. For example, on-site inspection would not be a "right" as demanded by the West, but a "request" that could be effectively refused (ibid.). Excluding semiannual rotation of Soviet troops—numbering perhaps 500,000—from exit/entry points, contrary to its own 1983 draft agreement, was counted a "major step backward" (ibid., 27 February). Moreover, proposing an increase of U.S. withdrawals by 30 percent was said to be "without justification" (ibid., 20 March). In effect, WTO had "rejected" the Western proposal and its position had retrogressed in some areas (ibid., 25 September).

From the beginning of the MBFR negotiations the Soviet Union was a reluctant participant, preferring instead a wider forum. As noted above, the PCC in June suggested three possibilities. At the conclusion of the 40th Round on 4 December, the Soviet negotiator, Valerian Mikhailov, called for a "very simple accord" to break the deadlock, then more of a reduction in conventional armed forces and armaments throughout Europe. If this proved impossible, he continued, another way should be found—that is, "all-European" negotiations. The West was opposed to a "symbolic agreement," preferring a "significant agreement" instead (ibid., 4 December). The WTO position was reaffirmed by Mikhailov at a Moscow news conference on 12 December, at which he said "a more favorable atmosphere" would exist in "all-European talks" (TASS, 12 December; *FBIS*, 12 December). On 15 January Gorbachev had expressed hope that "1986 would be a milestone for the Vienna talks." All would agree that it was not.

**Post-Reykjavik Developments.** The WTO foreign ministers met in Bucharest during 14–15 October for a briefing by Foreign Minister Eduard A. Shevardnadze on the Reagan-Gorbachev meeting in Reykjavik, Iceland. In view of the bloc's earlier accusatory language, the ministers' communiqué was more reserved (*Pravda*, 16 October). They urged the United States and NATO to consider the Soviet proposals and "to continue the dialogue." They were "highly appreciative" of Stockholm, citing "the spirit of collaboration, realism, and understanding," and calling the accord "a good start for negotiations on conventional arms and troop reductions in Europe and, equally, for confidence-building measures, inclusive of limitation of military activities."

As expected, the foreign ministers gave full support to Soviet arms control policies (including nuclear disarmament, nuclear testing, chemical weapons, intermediate-range missiles in Europe, and nuclear-free zones in Europe) and underscored the importance of the PCC's Budapest appeal. In underlining the need for specific understandings at the Soviet-American Geneva talks, they demurred from a one-sided attack against the U.S. Star Wars program and stated that the talks "should take into account the interests of both sides." The ministers emphasized the development of an "all-European process" (ibid.).

**Military Council and Defense Ministers.** At its 12–14 November meeting in Bucharest, the WTO Joint Armed Forces Military Council, chaired by Marshal Kulikov, reviewed the results of the Reagan-Gorbachev Reykjavik meeting and discussed military questions. The council specified measures for maintaining army and naval personnel on detachment from the national armies to the Joint Armed Forces "at a level ensuring military parity" between the WTO and NATO. In addition, the conferees heard results of the pact's operational and combat training during the year and established training requirements for next year. Reportedly the council members reaffirmed the need "to expand and deepen further combat cooperation among the national armies" (*Izvestiia*, 15 November).

In an address to the meeting, President Ceauşescu of Romania complimented the members for focusing their debate on the decisions of pact leaders regarding military equipment and measures necessary to improve combat and political training of the armies. He recalled the party leaders who earlier had met in Moscow to assess "the huge military spending that influenced and continues to influence negatively economic and social development." Ceauşescu declared that reductions are necessary, citing the Budapest proposal for 25 percent reduction and pointing to Romania's 5 percent cut in military expenditures. He said that nearly 50 percent of Romanian troops work in economic units, but he assured the council that Romania would continue to maintain its combat capability and to fulfill its pact obligations (Agerpress, 14 November; *FBIS*, 17 November).

The Committee of Defense Ministers held a session, chaired by Defense Minister Florian Siwicki

of Poland, during 1–3 December in Warsaw. Also attending were representatives from the Joint Armed Forces, headed by Marshal Kulikov. The ministers briefed First Secretary Wojciech Jaruzelski on the recommendations "for further deepening and expansion of socialist cooperation," and the "need for strengthening the defensive capabilities of the Joint Armed Forces" (Radio Warsaw, 3 December; *FBIS*, 4 December). In their communiqué the defense ministers emphasized PCC's Budapest conference decision to "reduce substantially the armed forces and conventional weapons in Europe with the corresponding reduction in military spending." Also, the ministers cited the need to further increase military cooperation and strengthen unity. And they agreed on measures to maintain military parity with NATO and increase the combat readiness of the Joint Armed Forces (*Pravda*, 4 December).

**Military Exercises.** Training, especially joint military exercises, continued to play an important role in WTO preparedness. According to the Helsinki Final Act, prior notification of maneuvers exceeding 25,000 troops is required. WTO's implementation was poor with regard to prior notification, the amount of information provided, and the invitation of observers. It was even less efficient on "discretionary" notification of smaller exercises— for example, "Duna 86" in Hungary and an unnamed field exercise in the GDR (*Twentieth Semiannual Report* by the President to the Commission on Security and Cooperation in Europe on the Implementation of the Helsinki Final Act, 1 October 1985–1 April 1986).

Early in the year tactical maneuvers with reservists were held in Hungary, involving the Hungarian, Czechoslovak, and Soviet armies (Radio Budapest, 27 January; *FBIS*, 28 January). Moscow did issue notification of "Zapad 86" [West 86], which was held in the Baltic Military District from 10 to 17 February and involved some 50,000 Soviet troops. Notification also was given of "Kavkaz 86" [Caucasus 86], which was conducted by approximately 25,000 Soviet troops in the southern USSR from 17 to 21 February. Observers were not invited to either of the exercises (ibid.).

Prague gave notification of "Druzhba 86" [Friendship 86], which involved 25,000 troops from Czechoslovakia, the USSR, and Hungary from 8 to 12 September. In the "spirit of Helsinki" observers were invited to the exercises in Czechoslovakia, and 19 countries—NATO, WTO, and neutral—were represented, including the Federal Republic of Germany and the United States. This was the first invitation since 1979 that permitted Western military personnel to observe maneuvers in a WTO country. Western observers had never been allowed on Czechoslovak or GDR territory (DPA, 5 September; *FBIS*, 8 September). Regrettably, observers were severely restricted (*Twenty-first Semiannual Report*). The announced purpose of the exercise was to improve coordination between commanders and units in defense operations (ČETEKA, 14 August; *FBIS*, 19 August). Minister of Defense Colonel General Milan Vaclavik of Czechoslovakia stressed that this training for soldiers was "the fulfillment of their international duty in defense of socialism in union with the armies of the Warsaw Pact" (Bratislava, *Pravda*, 4 September).

Commanders developed cooperation with the air force, artillery, and tank units. Deployment of tank units was featured, as was the Czechoslovak army's maneuvers in a mountainous environment, supported by fighters and helicopters (ČETEKA, 11 September; *FBIS*, 19 September). A water crossing involved Soviet helicopters and Czechoslovak and Soviet rifle units on armored carriers, supported by antiaircraft defense, artillery, and air force, followed by tanks (ČETEKA, 12 September; *FBIS*, 19 September).

On 18 August Moscow and the GDR issued notification, without designation, of a major exercise involving 25,000 Soviet and GDR forces, to be held on GDR territory from 8 to 13 September. Observers were not invited. (*Twenty-first Semiannual Report*, 1 April–1 October.) The announced aim was to perfect the training of staffs and level of combat (ADN, 18 August; *FBIS*, 19 August).

**Differences Within the WTO.** The year began with reports of perceptible strains within the pact, despite a pretense of unity. Soviet control over Eastern Europe was unchallenged, but there were continual references to "the strengthening of unity and cooperation," "consolidation of unity and cohesion," and the need "to strictly observe the national independence and sovereignty, and noninterference in domestic affairs." The style of Soviet control under Gorbachev became more skillful, but dissatisfaction with Moscow's domination and the desire for greater freedom domestically and in foreign policies, especially toward the West, continued. Soviet nuclear missiles in Czechoslovakia and the GDR remained an irritant, and the Chernobyl disaster affected exports from the bloc. The diverse tendencies were likely perceived by Moscow as a challenge to its control. The Twenty-seventh CPSU Congress reflected both concern with diversity and pledges to strive for unity. According to an editorial in *Krasnaia zvezda* (22 March), the "improvement of ties" between the Soviet Union and its allies was of "particular concern" to the CPSU. Of concern also was strengthening the unity of their armies and joint training.

With its massive Soviet military presence, the GDR occupies a special place in Soviet policies and military strategy. Thus, the GDR's behavior is of particular importance to Moscow. General Secretary Erich Honecker's visit to the Federal Republic of Germany was cancelled in 1984, "postponed" in 1985, and did not materialize in 1986—possibly a consequence of the FRG's decision to participate in SDI research.

Depressed economies afflict WTO countries. Romania, probably in the worst crisis, increasingly had been assigning military personnel into the economic sector. As noted above, the PCC suggested reductions in armed forces and armaments, but Bucharest took a unilateral step with its 5 percent reduction in arms, troops, and military spending. In an unprecedented national referendum held on 23 November, the Romanian public officially confirmed Ceaușescu's program. According to the president, the cuts would amount to $130 million, with demobilization of about 10,000 personnel, artillery, planes, helicopters, and 250 tanks and armored vehicles (Agerpress, 24 November; *FBIS*, 25 November).

John J. Karch
*Falls Church, Virginia*

# International Communist Organizations

## WORLD MARXIST REVIEW

This Soviet-controlled international communist theoretical monthly is the only permanent institutional symbol of unity for the world's pro-Soviet and independent communist parties (see *YICA*, 1984, for a full treatment of this subject). In August 1986, its chief editor, Yuri Shklyarov, became head of the CPSU Propaganda Department and Pavel Auersperg, one of its two "executive secretaries" (deputy editors), became the Czechoslovak ambassador to the Netherlands. (In contrast to Shklyarov, Auersperg appears to be on his way down, not having been re-elected to his party's Central Committee at its March Congress.) Aleksandr Subbotin, former international secretary of the All-Union Central Council of Trade Unions, was announced as the new chief editor of the *Review* in late December; Auersperg's replacement is not yet known.

The year also saw the addition of representatives from the Communist Party of Saudi Arabia and Morocco's Party of Progress and Socialism to the *Review*'s editorial council, bringing the number of its members to 69. This means all the Arab communist groups that meet together periodically, except the Tunisian Communist Party and the Bahrain National Liberation Front, are now represented on the magazine and it may thus serve as an Arab communist coordinating mechanism. The magazine's Prague headquarters might be used as a meeting site for these groups (which might explain why the venues of Arab communist meetings are hardly ever mentioned publicly).

## FRONT ORGANIZATIONS

**Control and Coordination.** The international Soviet-line communist front organizations operat-

ing since World War II are counterparts of organizations established by the Comintern after World War I. Their function today is the same as that of the interwar organizations: to unite communists with persons of other political persuasions to support and thereby lend strength and respectability to Soviet foreign policy objectives. Moscow's control over the fronts is evidenced by their faithful adherence to the Soviet policy line as well as by the withdrawal patterns of member organizations (certain pro-Western groups withdrew after the Cold War began, Yugoslav affiliates left following the Stalin-Tito break, and Chinese and Albanian representatives departed as the Sino-Soviet split developed).

The Communist Party of the Soviet Union is said to control the fronts through its International Department (ID) (U.S. Congress, *The CIA and the Media*, 1978, p. 574), and ID sector chiefs have been publicly identified as being involved in front affairs, Yuliy F. Kharlamov for the World Peace Council (WPC) and Grigory V. Shumeyko for the World Federation of Trade Unions and the Afro-Asian People's Solidarity Organization (Washington, D.C., *Problems of Communism*, September–October 1984, p. 73). Such officials appear to operate, however, through the Soviet national affiliate, which usually has a representative at the front's headquarters who gives on-the-spot direction. This person is usually a member of the front's Secretariat, but in some situations it may be a Soviet vice president (*YICA*, 1981, p. 455).

Aside from the CPSU's indirect coordination of the various fronts through its ID, more direct coordination takes place. First, since at least 1981, these fronts, defining themselves as "closely coordinating" international nongovernmental organizations, have met together with the apparent intention of formulating a joint policy.

Second, the WPC, the largest and most important of the international fronts, provides slots in its main bodies for the leaders of most of the fronts so that they are connected with one another. For example, eleven are represented on the current WPC Presidential Committee (Helsinki, *New Perspectives*, no. 5, p. 2), and two others had such representation in the recent past (ibid., no. 5/79, p. 2, and no. 3/86, p. 2). During the 1983–1986 period, the IADL had an organizational slot on the WPC proper while the FISE president was a member of its Sri Lankan delegation (WPC, *List of Members, 1983–1986*, pp. 162, 129).

Finally, there appears to be some sort of coordination performed by the *World Marxist Review*, since it is a Soviet-dominated policy guidance organ of nearly 70 communist parties with a specific Problems of Peace and Democratic Movements Commission that is oriented toward the international fronts (Washington, D.C., *Problems of Communism*, November–December 1982, p. 60).

The report of the 1979 meeting of "closely coordinating" nongovernmental organizations and one of the two reports of 1983 meeting indicated, moreover, that representatives of the *WMR* were participants therein (see chart below). The inconsistency in the 1983 reports may be indicative that such representatives did not have full, official status at the meeting and/or that their presence was not meant to be advertised. This leads one to the conclusion that *WMR* representatives may have attended some or all of the other meetings as well. The *WMR* is not considered with the fronts because, unlike the latter, it is (with one recent exception) fully communist in composition.

It must be pointed out, however, that the fronts themselves occupy a spectrum in this respect, going from such organizations as the WFTU (the vast majority of whose members are affiliated with officially communist trade unions), to the WPC (whose leadership organs have a fairly good balance among communists, socialists, "revolutionary democrats," and independents), to the basically noncommunist CPC.

**Emphases.** Nuclear disarmament remained the main theme of front propaganda during the year, while the opposition to Star Wars (the American Strategic Defense Initiative, or SDI), the main concern of 1985, was relatively de-emphasized (see *YICA*, 1986, p. 398). Cessation of all nuclear testing was urged. The WPC, in the *Peace Courier* in May and in the November–December issue of *New Perspectives*, presented the test ban as an effective

means for halting SDI research. The declaration coming out of the April WPC meeting put forth the test ban as a first step toward the elimination of all nuclear weapons ("Together for a World Without Nuclear Weapons," Helsinki, *Peace Courier*, May supplement).

The October World Congress Devoted to the International Year of Peace, the most important front gathering of 1986, seemed to give SDI and the test ban equal emphasis: "To halt the nuclear arms race on earth and to prevent it in outer space, to eliminate all nuclear weapons, we demand as urgent practical steps: Stop all nuclear-weapons tests immediately! No to star wars!" (*Copenhagen Appeal* brochure). The document coming out of the July General Assembly of the WFSW was basically identical (Moscow, *Trud*, 26 July). The aforenoted April WPC declaration had buried these points in a long statement calling for the gradual elimination of nuclear and chemical conventional weapons, establishment of nuclear-free and chemical weapons–free zones, and the ultimate disbandment of military alliances (together with the foreign basing arrangement they sometimes entail) (Helsinki, *Peace Courier*, May supplement).

The appeal of the WFDY Assembly in November similarly added a call for nuclear-free zones to the anti-SDI and test ban lines and also added an antiproliferation statement (Twelfth Assembly of the WFDY, *Appeal* brochure). By contrast, the report of the Eleventh World Trade Union Congress in October, in a short paragraph on the prevention of nuclear war and elimination of all mass-destruction weapons, only had the anti-SDI clause (Prague, *World Trade Union Movement*, November, p. 24). The report by that congress' Peace and Disarmament Commission, however, called for the test ban and most of the other items noted in the comprehensive April WPC declaration discussed above (ibid., pp. 14–16).

As for secondary themes, front propaganda continued to link Western armament expenditures with reduced funding for economic development and to decry the alleged depredations of Western creditors and other "transnational corporations," all in the context of calling for a "New International Economic Order" (NIEO) to redress the imbalance between the West and the Third World. Western intellectual "exploitation" was decried in the call for a "New International Information Organization" (NIIO). Third World control of its own news sources was the subject of two thematic conferences during the year (AAPSO, April, and IOJ, July) and was, of course, a major focus of the 10th IOJ Congress in October. Finally, there were the inevitable solidarity campaigns for Afghanistan, Cyprus, Libya, and Nicaragua, and for the "peoples" of Chile, El Salvador, Namibia, Palestine, and South Africa. Such solidarity, as well as the NIEO, was stressed at the World Trade Union Congress. (*World Trade Union Movement*, op. cit., pp. 17–20, 25–31.) In the context of these solidarity campaigns, "neo-globalism" and "state terrorism" were terms used to describe certain aspects of U.S. foreign policy.

**Techniques.** The tendency noted in 1985 for conventional fronts and their top leaders to remain in the background while conducting much of their activity continued into 1986 (*YICA*, 1986, p. 398). Nowhere was this better seen than in the World Congress Devoted to the International Year of Peace held in Copenhagen in October. This largest front meeting of the year played down its connection with the WPC even though a WPC spokesman in July 1984 had made what was apparently the first public mention of the congress and even though it was in the triennial cycle of such congresses that the WPC had clearly been sponsoring since 1950 (Copenhagen, *Berlingske Tidende*, 12 October; England, *Soviet Analyst*, 19 November). For the first time, such a congress was separated in time and space from the line-giving and housekeeping sessions of the WPC (held this year at Sofia in April); it was chaired by an individual with no direct connection with the WPC, World Federalist President Hermod Lannung; and only some 200 of the 1,457 listed members of the 1983 WPC could be found among the congress' 2,468 delegates (*List of Members, 1983–1986*; World Congress Devoted to the International Year of Peace, *Preliminary List of Participants*).

The congress attempted to identify itself with the UN and the latter's International Year of Peace (IYP), hence the choice of its title and the solicited support from that world body. This resulted in a warm message of greetings by UN Secretary General Javier Perez de Cuellar and attendance by one of the UN's undersecretaries general and by the head of its IYP Secretariat (*Peace Courier*, November–December; World Congress Devoted to the International Year of Peace, op cit., p. 23). The aforenoted appeal, the main operational document coming out of the congress, attempted to identify the congress with the peace efforts of the "Delhi Six," the nonaligned leaders of Argentina, Greece,

India, Mexico, Sweden, and Tanzania, for it was sponsored by "representatives of public opinion" from these very six countries (*Copenhangen Appeal* brochure). An earlier attempt to identify with the "Delhi Six" had resulted in messages of greetings sent to the congress by Prime Ministers Gandhi of India and Papandreou of Greece, as well as by President Alfonsin of Argentina (Helsinki, *Peace Courier*, November–December).

These efforts were only partially successful at best. The apparent attempt to involve the other strands of the peace movement, most notably those connected with the nonaligned European Nuclear Disarmament (END), failed. Only a sprinkling of such persons attended the congress, and they did so as individuals rather than as a group. (World Congress Devoted to the International Year of Peace, op. cit.) Soviet Peace Committee Chairman Yuri Zhukov had called for cooperation with such groups as a top priority at the April meeting of the WPC and laid principal blame on the WPC Secretariat for not having brought this about (Copenhagen, *Land og Folk*, 3–4 May). Ironically, Zhukov had been the chief culprit in antagonizing the END in early 1983. (See *YICA*, 1984, p. 434). The Copenhagen press went to great lengths to point out the WPC and ultimate Soviet inspiration and control of the congress (see especially *Morgenavisen Jyllands Posten*, 29 June; *Berlingske Tidende*, 12, 16 October). Their efforts were aided by the reports of the failure of Afghan rebels and East European civil rights spokesmen to get a fair hearing at the congress (or even admission to it, in most cases). More circumstantial evidence of Soviet–WPC control was furnished when virtually the whole Soviet mechanism for running the WPC turned up at the meeting (Zhukov, CPSU International Department operatives Vitaliy Shaposhnikov and Yuliy Kharlamov, WPC Secretaries Oleg Kharkhardin and Djanghir Atamali, and WPC Information Center Chief Aleksey Treskin) (*YICA*, 1986, p. 397; World Congress Devoted to the International Year of Peace, op. cit., pp. 18–19, 25). Also present were 19 of the 25 full-time WPC headquarters officers, all but 8 of whom were, significantly, buried in their respective country delegations rather than being included in that of the WPC (ibid., pp. 4–25; Helsinki, *New Perspectives*, November–December, p. 1). Finally, eight of the thirteen "representatives of public opinion" sponsoring the *Copenhagen Appeal* brochure are or were members of the WPC (ibid., p. 2; WPC *List of Members*, pp. 95, 118, 145).

The second major front meeting of the year, the Eleventh World Trade Union Congress held in East Berlin in September, also played down its ultimate front sponsor, in this case the WFTU. In a Moscow television broadcast of 22 July, it was announced that this meeting was to be open to all trade unionists and was not to be the exclusive province of the WFTU (*FBIS*, 24 July). As a result, the 1,014 delegates claimed to represent "almost 300 million" trade unionists (rather than the slightly over 200 million claimed by the WFTU) and the congress could be addressed by ostensibly individual trade unionists, as well as "the WFTU, the ICFTU, the WCL and other international and regional trade union organizations" (Prague, *World Trade Union Movement*, pp. 1, 24). Internal WFTU matters were taken care of exclusively by the congress' fourteenth session, limited to representatives of WFTU affiliates (ibid., p. 3).

Other attempts by the fronts to widen their constituency by concealing their hand could be seen in the First International Conference of the Teachers for Peace Movement (Copenhagen, August) in which the FISE apparently played an important role; the formation of the International Movement of Jurists for the Protection of Peace and Prevention of Nuclear War (Moscow, November), in which the IADL apparently figured; and the World Meeting of Veterans for Peace (Vienna, December), in which the FIR was one of four ex-servicemen's organizations involved. Whether these meetings will result in groups clearly identified with traditional fronts, like the Generals for Peace and the International Trade Union Committee for Peace and Disarmament with their overlapping memberships in the WPC and WFTU, respectively, or whether they will be less easy to categorize, like the International Physicians for the Prevention of Nuclear War, remains to be seen (*YICA*, 1982, p. 532; 1986, p. 399).

## Major International Front Organizations

### Afro-Asian Peoples' Solidarity Organizations (AAPSO)
**President.** Abd-al-Rahman al Sharqawi (Egypt)
**Secretary General.** Nuri Abd-al Razzaq Husayn (Iraq)
**Last Top Meeting.** Sixth Congress (Algiers, May 1984)
**Major 1986 Conferences.** Second Conference on the New International Information Order (Kabul, April); Fourteenth Council Meeting (Moscow, May); Presidium Meeting (Ulan Baator, October)
**Related Organizations.** World Peace Council (interlocking leadership); Organization of Solidarity of the Peoples of Africa, Asia, and Latin America (presumed Latin American extension)
**Publications.** *Solidarity* (monthly), *Development and Socio-Economic Progress* (quarterly), *Afro-Asian Affairs* (quarterly)

### Christian Peace Conference (CPC)
**President.** Bishop Dr. Károly Tóth (Hungary)
**Secretary General.** The Reverend Dr. Lubomir Mirejovsky (Czechoslovakia)
**Last Top Meeting.** Sixth All-Christian Peace Assembly (Prague, July 1985)
**Major 1986 Conferences.** Working Committee meeting (Sofia, March); African CPC meeting (Dar-es Salaam, June); Fourth Latin American CPC Continuation meeting (Quito, August); International Conference on the International Year of Peace (Hannover, October)
**Related Organizations.** Official regional subsidiaries: African CPC, Asian CPC, CPC in Latin America and the Caribbean; complementary organizations (with different religious constituencies but cooperate with the CPC): Berlin Conference of European Catholics, Asian Buddhist Conference for Peace
**Publications.** *CPC* (quarterly), *CPC Information* (semimonthly)

### International Association of Democratic Lawyers (IADL)
**President.** Joe Nordmann (France)
**Secretary General.** Amar Bentoumi (Algeria)
**Last Top Meeting.** Twelfth Congress (Athens, October 1984)
**Major 1986 Conferences.** Meeting of "Socialist Countries" Lawyers' Associations (Moscow, March)

**Related Organizations.** De facto regional affiliates: Arab Lawyers Union (joint affiliation), Anti-Imperialist Tribunal of Our America (TANA)

## International Federation of Resistance Movements (FIR)
**President.** Arialdo Banfi (Italy)
**Secretary General.** Symun T. Viscanesa
**Last Top Meeting.** Ninth Congress (East Berlin, September 1982)
**Major 1986 Conferences.** Consultative Meeting of Member Organizations (Prague, November); World Meeting of Veterans for Peace (Vienna, December), co-sponsored by FIR and noncommunist veterans' organizations
**Publications.** *Résistance unie—Service d'informacion* (monthly), *Cahiers d'informacions medicales, sociales et juridiques* (quarterly)

## International Organization of Journalists (IOJ)
**President.** Kaarle Nordenstrent (Finland)
**Secretary General.** Jiri Kubka (Czechoslovakia)
**Last Top Meeting.** Tenth Congress (Sofia, October)
**Major 1986 Conferences.** Latin American and Caribbean Journalists Seminar (Havana, July); International Seminar on Central America, with WIDF (Managua, November)
**Related Organizations.** De facto regional affiliates: Federation of Arab Journalists (joint affiliations); Federation of Latin American Journalists (joint affiliations); Union of African Journalists (joint affiliations)
**Publications.** *Democratic Journalist* (monthly); *IOJ Newsletter* (semimonthly)

## International Union of Students (IUS)
**President.** Joseph Scala (Czechoslovakia)
**Secretary General.** Georgios Machaelides (Cyprus)
**Last Top Meeting.** Fourteenth Congress (Sofia, April 1984)
**Major 1986 Conferences.** Executive Committee Meeting (Pyongyang, January); Science and Education for Peace Seminar, with IIP (Vienna, April); International Conference of Support for Chilean People (Florence, June); All-European Forum on Education (Helsinki, October); Education and Society, World Student Forum (Prague, November)
**Related Organizations.** De facto regional affiliates (presumed joint organizations): All-Africa Students Union, Latin American Continental Student Organization (OCLAE); World Federation of Democratic Youth (co-sponsor of World Youth Festivals)
**Publications.** *World Student News* (monthly); *IUS Secretariat Reports* (irregular)

## Women's International Democratic Federation (WIDF)
**President.** Freda Brown (Australia)
**Secretary General.** Mirjam Vire-Tuominen (Finland)
**Last Top Meeting.** Eighth Congress (Prague, October 1981) (Ninth Congress to be in Moscow, June 1987)
**Major 1986 Conferences.** Bureau Meeting (East Berlin, March); International Conference on Libya (Athens, June); Seminar for Asian Women (Tashkent, October)
**Related Organizations.** De facto regional affiliates (presumed joint affiliation, all participate with WIDF in WPC activities): Africa Women's Organization; Arab Women's Federation; Continental Front of Women (Against Intervention in Central America)
**Publications.** *Women of the Whole World* (quarterly), *Documents and Information* (frequency unknown)

## World Federation of Democratic Youth (WFDY)
**President.** Walid Masri (Lebanon)
**Secretary General.** Vilmos Cserveny (Hungary)

**Last Top Meeting.** Twelfth General Assembly (Budapest, November)

**Major 1986 Conferences.** International Conference on Arab Peoples (Athens, March); International Youth Meeting on Peace in Asia (Hanoi, May); Latin American Youth Congress for Peace (Managua, July)

**Related Organizations.** Official subsidiaries: International Bureau of Tourism and Youth Exchange (BITEJ), International Commission of Children's and Adolescents' Movements (CIMEA), International Voluntary Service for Friendship and Solidarity of Youth (SIVSAJ); de facto regional affiliates: Arab Youth Union (presumed joint affiliations), Pan-African Youth Movement (joint affiliations)

**Publications.** *World Youth* (monthly), *WFDY News* (semimonthly)

## World Federation of Scientific Workers (WFSW)

**President.** Jean-Marie Legay (France)

**Secretary General.** Stan Davison (U.K.)

**Last Top Meeting.** Fourteenth General Assembly (Moscow, July)

**Major 1986 Conferences.** International Scientists' Forum (Moscow, July)

**Related Organizations.** World Federation of Trade Unions (stated relationship)

**Publications.** *Scientific World* (quarterly), *Bulletin* (about six times a year)

## World Federation of Teachers Unions (FISE)

**President.** Lesturuge Ariyawansa (Sri Lanka)

**Secretary General.** Daniel Retureau (France)

**Last Top Meeting.** Thirteenth Conference (Sofia, May 1985)

**Major 1986 Conferences.** Teachers for Peace Conference (Copenhagen, August; not officially a FISE meeting)

**Related Organizations.** Trade Union International of the World Federation of Trade Unions; de facto regional affiliates: All-Africa Teachers Organization, Federal Arab Teachers, Confederation of American Educators

**Publications.** *International Teachers News* (eight times a year), *Teachers of the World* (quarterly)

## World Federation of Trade Unions (WFTU)

**President.** Sándor Gáspár (Hungary)

**Secretary General.** Ibrahim Zakariya (Sudan)

**Last Top Meeting.** Eleventh Congress (East Berlin, September)

**Major 1986 Conferences.** Annual Consultative Conference of Trade Unions International (Prague, January); World Trade Union Conference on Disarmament (actually sponsored by the "Dublin Committee," Dublin, May); International Trade Union Meeting on Peace, Development and the Social Aspects of Disarmament (actually sponsored by the "Dublin Committee," Geneva, July); Energy Workers Trade Union International Extraordinary Conference (Podbanske, Czechoslovakia, June); Trade Union Conference on Economic and Social Development (Brazzaville, July)

**Related Organizations.** Trade Unions International (TUIs) coordinated by a WFTU department and represented on the WFTU Council: Agriculture, Building Industry, Chemical Industry, Commerce, Energy, Food Industry, Metalworkers, Public Service, Teachers (World Federation of Teachers Unions, treated separately here); Textile, Transport; de facto regional affiliates (high percentage of joint affiliates with WFTU): Permanent Congress of Trade Union Unity of Latin American Workers (CPUSTAL); International Confederation of Arab Trade Unions (ICATU); Organization of African Trade Union Unity (OATUU); Asian and Oceanic Trade Union Coordinating Committee (AOTUCC); International Mineworkers Organization (evolved out of a former TUI of Miners and Energy Workers); International Trade Union Committee for Peace and Disarmament (many WFTU-affiliated personnel)

**Publications.** *World Trade Union Movement* (monthly), *Flashes from the Trade Unions* (weekly)

## World Peace Council (WPC)

**President.** Romesh Chandra (India)

**Secretary General.** Johannes Pakaslahti

**Last Top Meeting.** World Peace Council meeting (Sofia, April)

**Major 1986 Conferences.** International Conference on the Mediterranean (Athens, January-February); Socialist Countries' Peace Committee Meetings (Uzhgorod, USSR, May); World Congress Devoted to International Year of Peace (not officially WPC; Copenhagen, October)

**Related Organizations.** International Liaison Forum of Peace Forces (although Chandra is its head, it involves additional and more innocuous organizations pursuing WPC aims); International Institute for Peace (research body left behind when the WPC moved to Helsinki); International Committee for European Security and Cooperation (pursues WPC aims regionally); Women's International League for Peace and Freedom

**Publications.** *New Perspectives* (bimonthly), *Peace Courier* (monthly), *Disarmament Forum* (monthly)

## Attendance of Meetings and Conferences

| | HOST AND DATE | | | | | | |
| --- | --- | --- | --- | --- | --- | --- | --- |
| | WFDY<br>Mar<br>'79 | IUS<br>Sep<br>'81 | WFTU<br>Mar<br>'82 | CPC<br>Sep<br>'83 | IOJ<br>Feb<br>'84 | WPC<br>Apr<br>'85 | WIDF<br>Sep<br>'86 |
| World Peace Council (WPC) | X | X | X | X | X | X | NA |
| World Federation of Trade Unions (WFTU) | X | X | X | X | X | X | NA |
| Women's International Democratic Federation (WIDF) | X | X | X | X | X | X | X |
| World Federation of Democratic Youth (WFDY) | X | X | X | X | O | X | NA |
| International Union of Students (IUS) | X | X | X | X | X | X | NA |
| International Organization of Journalists (IOJ) | X | X | X | X | X | X | NA |
| Christian Peace Conference (CPC) | X | X | X | X | X | X | NA |
| World Federation of Teachers Unions (FISE) | O | X | X | X | X | X | NA |
| Afro-Asian People's Solidarity Organization (AAPSO) | X | O | X | X | X | X | NA |
| World Federation of Scientific Workers (WFSW) | X | O | O | NA | X | O | NA |
| International Federation of Resistance Movements (FIR) | X | O | O | O | O | X | NA |
| International Association of Democratic Lawyers (IADL) | X | O | O | O | O | O | NA |
| *World Marxist Review (WMR)* | X | O | O | NA | O | O | NA |

X = present    O = absent    NA = not available

SOURCES: East Berlin, *Neues Deutschland*, 21 March 1979; Budapest, MTI, 22 March 1979; Prague, ČETEKA, and Radio Prague, 13 September 1981; *Neues Deutschland*, 16 September 1981; Prague, *Flashes from the Trade Unions*, 23 March 1982, 21 October 1983, 9 March 1984; U.S. Congress, *Religious Persecution Behind the Iron Curtain*, 1985, p. 182; Prague, *IOJ Newsletter*, no. 8, April 1985, no. 21, November 1985; Prague, *CPC Information*, 1 November 1985, 26 November 1986.

Wallace H. Spaulding
*McLean, Virginia*

# THE MIDDLE EAST

# Introduction

Adding still another open conflict to the war-weary Middle East region, the People's Democratic Republic of South Yemen (PDRY) erupted to bloody civil war early in the year. The consequences have been devastating for the ruling Yemeni Socialist Party (YSP) and for the already impoverished PDRY—the Arab world's only Marxist controlled state. Dissension within the YSP Politburo precipitated President 'Ali Nasir Muhammad's preemptive attack that sparked the conflict. His eventual exile along with thousands of his followers, coupled with numerous deaths of party leaders of both factions and the imprisonment of scores of others, has decimated the YSP of much of its core leadership. As a result, control of the country has passed largely from the seasoned old guard of the party to minor figures lacking the charisma and tribal credentials needed to reconstitute vigorous YSP strength. Deep tribal and ideological divisions appear merely to have been papered over, with final scores remaining unsettled. In October, elections to the Supreme People's Council were held for pro forma confirmation of senior government officers, but the far touchier and substantively important convening of the Fourth Congress of the YSP was postponed at least until mid-1987.

Because the former president and leader of the hard-line and most pro-Soviet faction of the YSP, 'Abd al-Fattah Isma'il, and his associates eventually triumphed in the civil war, early assessments tended to view the conflict as Soviet inspired. In fact, initial Soviet support went to the less ideological Muhammad, whose broadening relationships with the moderate states of the Arabian peninsula meant financial help for the PDRY and harmony with Soviet attempts to achieve diplomatic respectability in the region. Because Soviet support shifted to Isma'il during early stages of the fighting and because he had been long regarded as Moscow's man, there was deep concern in Oman, the states of the gulf, and in the Yemen Arab Republic (YAR) that with Soviet support the PDRY would return to its former policies of hostility and subversion. As the full extent of the physical and political devastation unfolded, however, most observers came to see the conflict as a severe setback for Soviet aims in the region. Long-standing Soviet efforts to foster unity between the YAR and the PDRY collapsed as the YAR hosted many of the exiled opposition including Muhammad himself. An estimated 10,000 to 15,000 followers fled to the YAR, and up to 10,000 went to Ethiopia—including the bulk of the PDRY navy, along with its gunboats.

The Ethiopian leadership's continuity of ties with Muhammad and his followers has obviously strained the formerly close relationship between the two Marxist regimes. Moreover, the validity of the PDRY as a model of Marxist stability and triumph over the tribal and other divisions in the Arab world so derided by Moscow has collapsed. The eruption of bloody tribal conflict and the uneasiness of the ensuing truce offer poor testimony to the twenty-plus years of Marxist party control and Soviet presence.

In Soviet-occupied Afghanistan, the People's Democratic Party of Afghanistan (PDPA), also Marxist, continues to be plagued with internal rivalry between its two main wings (Parcham and Khalq) and by its inability to achieve the support of the Afghan masses. Virtually universal assessment by outside observers remains that (1) the PDPA would collapse without direct Soviet military support and (2) the PDPA's national military and Soviet forces control only some of the country's major cities, and even this control is constantly subject to major guerrilla attacks. A case in point was guerrilla destruction of a major ammunition dump near Kabul in late August.

Soviet dissatisfaction with PDPA general secretary Babrak Karmal became increasingly obvious during 1986 when Mikhail Gorbachev failed to receive him during two separate Moscow visits, and by May 4, at the Eighteenth PDPA Central Committee Plenum in Kabul, Karmal resigned for health reasons. Dr. Najib (also called Najibullah) was immediately elected to replace him. Najib had worked particularly closely with the Soviets as head of KHAD, the State Information Service (secret police), and proved to be an efficient administrator. This efficiency was equally apparent following his late 1985 promotion to secretary of the Central Committee with complete responsibility for all security forces. Although a heavy Soviet hand presided over the transfer from Karmal to Najib, with Soviet forces in control of Kabul's streets and Afghan military barracks, there were student riots in Kabul and Jalalabad.

Dr. Najib immediately began a vigorous effort to revitalize and unify the PDPA by recruiting new members and eliminating corruption. For example, he denounced party members for escaping military service through the intervention of influential relatives (U.S. Department of State, *Afghanistan: Seven Years of Soviet Occupation*, Special Report no. 155, December). Characteristically, the PDPA claimed substantial increases in party membership. Najib, for instance, claimed that 9,000 new members were added between May and November. (*FBIS*; Kabul Radio, 24 October). Although no indications of any change in the PDPA's level of popularity supported this claim, Najib expanded the 66-man (with 16 alternates) Central Committee by 31 members and 39 alternates. By December, 11 more members and 14 alternates had been added.

The practice of bringing nonparty members into government continued, but the substantive test—recruiting members of the guerrilla opposition groups—failed. Efforts that were largely show, with the traditional tribal jirgas called to support the regime and to form a National Fatherland Front (NFF), were all boosted by Najib to at least symbolically strengthen the PDPA's support base. There was, apparently, no solid progress.

Although Soviet military effectiveness improved during the year according to some observers, guerrilla forces benefited from the receipt of more sophisticated British and U.S. air defense weapons. Public acknowledgement by the United States that it supported the opposition groups reportedly helped guerrilla morale. By the end of July, the Soviets announced a troop-withdrawal plan as part of a major peace offensive designed to shut off supplies to the guerrillas from Pakistan and strengthen the credibility of the PDPA regime. The sincerity of Soviet intentions was not enhanced when it became evident that, soon after Gorbachev's July announcement of the withdrawal plan, two new Soviet units, obviously not equipped to fight guerrilla warfare, were sent to Afghanistan and then ceremoniously withdrawn in front of Western reporters in October (DoS, *Seven Years*). The Soviets and the PDPA regime clearly see the Geneva proximity talks between the Afghan and Pakistan governments as an avenue to reduce the pressures of international condemnation and gradually undercut the lines of supply to resistance groups.

The Iran-Iraq war and the ideological shock waves of the Iranian revolution continued through 1986 to far overshadow any influence from far-left groups in the gulf region. The Iraqi Communist Party (ICP) became, if anything, even more wholly identified as a Kurdish movement without national appeal. The ICP, isolated with Kurdish resistance groups in northern Iraq, exists in the precarious environment of a Kurdish national movement allied with the communist parties of Iran and Turkey. Thereby, the ICP and its allies court the enmity of the Turkish, Iranian, and Iraqi governments on the dual grounds of communist affiliation and Kurdish separatism. Although the Communist Party of Iran, or Tudeh Party, is exiled and still decimated from Khomeini's total assault in 1983, it has at least the remnants of a far broader national base than the ICP. Efforts by some party members to increase the Tudeh's popular appeal by making the party more independent from the Soviets caused their expulsion from the Central Committee. Despite this dissension the Tudeh managed to hold a national conference during the year (location unknown); it was attended by 100 members, including members of the party's clandestine organization in Iran (*Morning Star*, 23 July 1986). Tudeh propaganda reveled in the news of the U.S. and Israeli arms sales to the Khomeini regime and particularly fastened on reports of the Central Intelligence Agency's role in helping Khomeini in 1983, omitting, of course, the key role of the Soviet KGB defector to the British who identified Tudeh agents. In 1986 there were major exchanges of delegations between Moscow and Teheran accompanied by announced plans for renewed commercial and economic relations. In December the Permanent

Commission for Joint Economic Cooperation resumed activity after a suspension of six years; a protocol was signed covering the resumption of Soviet activities in Iran in a wide range of fields and reportedly including the return to Iran of Soviet experts and technicians. Actual implementation remains to be seen, particularly in the question of resumed sales of natural gas to the USSR. Posed against Iran's urgent, if not desperate, economic needs are Teheran's continuing rage over Soviet support for Iraq's war efforts, Soviet occupation of Afghanistan (which apart from strategic and ideological considerations, burdens Iran with an estimated two million refugees), and the Soviet-Tudeh linkage.

Elsewhere in the gulf, little opportunity opened for an increased role by the tiny and essentially absentee Saudi Arabian and Bahrain communist parties. The Communist Party of Saudi Arabia whose imprint only occasionally surfaces, achieved representation on the Editorial Council of the *World Marxist Review* and sent unnamed delegates to communist party congresses in East Germany and India. The Bahrain National Liberation Front (NLF/B), called "pro-Soviet and revolutionary democratic," conducted more international activity by sending delegates to communist party congresses in Cuba, the USSR, Bulgaria, and East Germany. The NLF/B also signed, as one of eight communist and workers' parties of Arab east countries, a document protesting the arrest of most of the Jordanian Communist Party's leadership in May. The largely foreign focus of the NLF/B was evidenced when the arrest of apparently low-level leaders in Bahrain in July and August caused little activity by members of the Governing Committee, who reside in Damascus or elsewhere outside the gulf.

The Communist Party of Jordan (CPJ) saw its entire leadership arrested in May following student demonstrations at al-Yarmouk University that were in response to the split between King Hussein and PLO Chairman Yasir Arafat and the U.S. bombing of Libya. The demonstrations caused deaths and injuries, and with blame attached to the CPJ, its leadership of seventeen members was not released until September 4. The party remains officially banned, as it was before the arrests, allowing the government to keep tight control of its activities. Jordan's relationship with the USSR remains equally cautious and is largely focused on ceremonial visits like the August visit of the Soviet first deputy foreign minister that resulted in statements supporting international settlement of the Palestinian question.

In keeping with the trend of many Middle East governments to be somewhat on the defensive against worsened economic conditions resulting from oil price declines, against religious fundamentalism, and against extremism unleashed by the gulf and Lebanon wars, Egypt late in the year cracked down on a communist organization calling itself "Revolutionary Current." Its aim, according to the Ministry of Interior, was to use Maoist techniques to impose communism on the country by force. In September, 278 members of leftist parties in nine governates were charged with organizing to overthrow the government. These and other crackdowns evidenced an active but highly splintered Egyptian left and shed little light on the actual involvement of the Egyptian Communist Party per se.

In Lebanon the Lebanese Communist Party (LCP) and the Organization of Communist Action in Lebanon (OCAL) continue to be active in the civil war, particularly in the context of political disintegration where loyalties between factions and militias shift quickly. Overall, the influence of these parties has declined in relation to the growing importance of Shi'ite movements like Amal and Hizb Allah (Party of God). The LCP follows Syria's line for the most part, but given its traditional closeness to Palestinian groups, it finds itself at cross purposes with Amal's efforts to prevent a Palestinian comeback in Lebanon. The OCAL has been similarly hurt by close PLO ties and in the past three years has suffered heavily in battles with both Amal and the Hizb Allah.

James H. Noyes
*Hoover Institution*

# Afghanistan

**Population.** 11 million (estimated) (U.S. State Department, Background Notes, *Afghanistan*, July); refugee flow plus wartime casualties have reduced significantly a population that in 1978 was thought to number 15–17 million.

**Party.** People's Democratic Party of Afghanistan (Jamiyat-e-Demokrati Khalq-e-Afghanistan, literally Democratic Party of the Afghanistan Masses; PDPA). The party has two mutually antagonistic wings: Parcham (Banner) and Khalq (Masses).

**Founded.** 1965

**Membership.** Officially 170,000 (*Pravda*, 5 January 1987; *FBIS*, 5 January 1987). This figure includes candidate members (about half) and is greatly inflated. A maximum probable figure for full members is 40,000, of which only a fraction can be considered reliable.

**General Secretary.** Dr. Najib (Radio Kabul 5 May; *FBIS*, 6 May)

**Politburo.** 11 members: Dr. Najib, Sultan Ali Keshtmand (prime minister of the Democratic Republic of Afghanistan [DRA]). Suleiman Laeq (minister of tribes and nationalities), Nur Ahmad Nur (revolutionary council [RC] Presidium member), General Mohammed Rafi (minister of defense), Anahita Ratebzad (head of the Peace, Solidarity, and Friendship Society and RC Presidium member), Abdul Zaher Razmjo (secretary, Kabul city party committee), Abdul Wakil (foreign minister), General Mohammed Aslam Watanjar (minister of communications), Lieutenant General Ghulam Farouq Yaqubi (minister of state security), Dr. Saleh Mohammed Zeary (RC Presidium member); 5 alternate members: Mahmoud Baryalai (leading party theoretician), Sayed Mohammed Gulabzoy (minister of interior), Mir Saheb Karwal, Farid Ahmad Mazdak (first secretary of the Democratic Youth Organization of Afghanistan [DYOA]), General Nazar Mohammed (first deputy prime minister)

**Secretariat.** 8 members: Dr. Najib, Mahmoud Baryalai, Mir Saheb Karwal, Najmuddin Kawiani (in charge of Central Committee organizational department, RC Presidium member), Dr. Haider Masoud (chairman, State Committee for Radio, Television, and Cinematography), Niaz Mohammed Mohmand (economics expert), Nur Ahmad Nur, Dr. Saleh Mohammed Zeary

**Central Committee.** 103 full and 69 candidate members. This represents more than a twofold increase during 1986.

**Status.** Ruling Party.

**Last Congress.** First, 1 January 1965, in Kabul; National Conference 14–15 March 1982.

**Last Election.** Local council elections, the first of any kind under the PDPA, were held in 1985 and 1986. The regime claimed that 14,190 deputies were elected, of whom 64.7 percent were supposed to be nonparty (*Kabul New Times [KNT]*, 5 October; Bakhtar, 30 October; *Afghanistan Forum*, January 1987).

**Auxiliary Organizations.** National Fatherland Front (NFF) (claims 800,000 members) (Radio Kabul, 14 October; *FBIS*, 20 October). Abdul Rahim Hatef, chairman; Central Council of Trade Unions (claims 285,000 members) (*KNT*, 27 September), Abdus Sattar Purdeli, president; Democratic Youth Organization of Afghanistan (DYOA) (claims 200,000 members), Farid Ahmad Mazdak, first secretary (Radio Kabul, 14 October; *FBIS*, 20 October); Central Council of High Tribal Jirga (154 members), Haji Mohammed Chamkani, chairman (*KNT*, 4 April); All Afghanistan Women's Council (AAWC, formerly Democratic Women's Organization of Afghanistan [DWOA]; claims "over 55,000 members") (ibid.,17

June), Feroza Fedaie, president (ibid., 17 August); agricultural, consumer, and handicraft cooperatives (674 groups, comprising 150,000 members) (ibid., 7 August); Council of Religious Scholars and Clergy; Economic Advisory Council; various militias ("groups for the defense of the revolution"). For the larger groups, the above statistics, like those for PDPA membership, are unquestionably inflated and involve a good deal of double counting.

**Publications.** *Haqiqat-e Enqelabe Saur* (The Saur revolution truth), Central Committee daily organ, claimed circulation 80,000 (Bakhtar, 2 April; *FBIS*, 4 April); *Haqiqat-e-Sarbaz* (The soldier's truth); *Darafsh-e-Jawanan* (The banner of youth), Pushtu and Dari daily, circulation 70,000 per week (*KNT*, 26 May); *Dehqan*(Peasant); *Kabul New Times* (*KNT*), English-language daily; *Storai* (Story), DYOA monthly; *Peshahang* (Pioneer), Pioneer monthly. Total claimed newpaper circulation exceeded 500,000 (Bakhtar, 2 April, *FBIS*, 4 April); combined circulation of weeklies and dailies was allegedly about 12.5 times the pre-1978 circulation (*KNT*, 10 December). In 1984 the DRA claimed to have eleven national newspapers and periodicals, eighteen provincial newpapers of the party, and 42 periodicals "which cater to a diversity of audiences." The regime has a limited television network. The official news agency is Bakhtar.

In 1967, two years after its founding, the PDPA split into opposing Parcham and Khalq wings. Both kept the PDPA name and both were loyal to Moscow, but each maintained a separate organization and recruitment program. Khalq, led by Nur Mohammed Taraki, the PDPA's founder, depended for support on the relatively poor rural intelligentsia and recruited almost solely among the Pushtuns, the dominant (40 percent) Afghan ethnic group. Parcham, more broadly representative ethnically, was urban-oriented and appealed to a wealthier group of educated Afghans. It was led by Babrak Karmal, son of an Afghan general. Both groups focused their initial recruitment efforts on intellectuals, media employees, and especially teachers. When Mohammed Daoud overthrew the Afghan monarchy in 1973, the Parchamis at first collaborated with him and were obliged to refrain from aggressive recruiting. The Khalqis, who remained in opposition, began an intensive recruitment campaign among the military in preparation for the PDPA coup that was to follow five years later. During this period, the Khalqis moved from numerical parity with the Parchamis to significant quantitative superiority.

Under Soviet pressure, Parcham and Khalq formally reunited in mid-1977, and their combined strength was enough to overthrow Daoud and inaugurate the DRA in April 1978. They almost immediately fissioned again, however, with Taraki sending the most prominent Parchamis into diplomatic exile as ambassadors and jailing or demoting most of those who remained in Afghanistan. When a Parchami plot to unseat Taraki was discovered in the summer of 1978, the ambassadors were recalled but disobeyed the order and fled into exile in Eastern Europe.

Meanwhile, popular resistance to Khalq's rigorous Marxist-Leninist rule grew rapidly and soon threatened to topple the new regime in spite of massive Soviet military aid. In September 1979, the Soviets attempted to force another artificial reconciliation between Parcham and Khalq, but their plan to place all the blame for the schism on Taraki's deputy, Hafizullah Amin, backfired when Amin himself seized power and murdered Taraki. Amin, however, could not pacify his rebellious people, and on 27 December 1979, Soviet troops invaded Afghanistan, shot Amin, and restored the Parchamis to power. Babrak (he affects the surname Karmal, "friend of labor" or "Kremlin" for political purposes) became the new leader and tried to heal the breach with the Khalqis on the one side and the Afghan population on the other. In neither effort was he successful, and thanks to a Soviet presence that slowly swelled from 85,000 combat troops in 1980 to about 120,000 by the end of 1984, the regime maintained a tenuous hold on power in a few main Afghan towns (but it was only in those towns and only during daylight hours). Since that time, the Soviet-force strength has remained fairly constant, although there was a marginal decrease in 1986 (U.S. Department of State, *Afghanistan: Seven Years Of Soviet Occupation*, Special Report no. 155, December).

Since the Soviet invasion, the PDPA technically has not been a communist or even a "socialist" (in the Soviet lexicon) party, but the ruling—and so far only permissible—party in a country undergoing the "national democratic stage of revolution." Unlike the avowedly socialist PDPA ideologues of 1978–1979, party spokesmen since the invasion have done their utmost to avoid using the terms *socialist* and *socialism* when referring to

Afghanistan. Nevertheless, the total dedication and subservience of the party to Moscow's interpretation of Marxism-Leninism is unmistakable, as is shown by its devotion to such principles as "internationalism" and "democratic centralism." Article 1 of the party's 1965 constitution declares that the PDPA's "ideology is the practical experience of Marxism-Leninism," and a 1976 history of the party sent to fraternal parties abroad is entitled "Establishment of the Marxist-Leninist Party in Afghanistan" (Arnold, *Afghanistan's Two-Party Communism: Parcham and Khalq*, 1983). Both documents pay homage specifically to Moscow and ignore or criticize the Chinese version of socialism.

**Leadership and Party Organization.** The most important PDPA development during 1986 was the long-awaited political eclipse of Babrak Karmal and his replacement as general secretary by Dr. Najib. In late 1985, Babrak himself hinted that he had been given deadlines for better performance when he warned a police (Sarandoy) audience that they should fulfill their "most urgent, major, and vital revolutionary tasks in two stages, in the course of two and four months... [to establish DRA power] in most of the villages and all of the districts" (*KNT*, 22 December 1985). The timing of this statement implied that one deadline was the Communist Party of the Soviet Union's (CPSU's) Twenty-seventh Party Congress and the other the anniversary of the 1978 PDPA coup. Babrak's failure to produce on schedule was signaled by Soviet general secretary Mikhail Gorbachev's pointed snubbing of him at the former event and confirmed immediately after the latter event, when Najib replaced him as general secretary.

The transition was not expected to be smooth; Babrak supporters, including women probably mobilized by Ratebzad, demonstrated in his support as rumors of his replacement spread (DoS, *Seven Years*). Accordingly, Soviet armor was drawn up around Afghan military barracks and the ministry of interior, Soviet troops patrolled the streets, Afghan soldiers went about without weapons, and newspapers suspended publication for a day (BBC World Service, 6 May; *FBIS*, 7 May). These measures were not adequate, however, to prevent a week-long outbreak of student riots in Kabul and Jalalabad in the wake of the change (Hong Kong *AFP*, 11 May; *FBIS*, 12 May). Other disturbances followed, including an outbreak of violence among pro- and anti-Babrak soldiers in Kandahar (*LAT*, 19 May). The unrest continued into June, as Najib

himself was to confirm when he railed against "provocative slogans... in some of the girls' schools last month," a phenomenon he ascribed to "narrow-mindedness of our intellectual females, the improper stand of parents, the black strivings of factionalists, or the conspiracies of our enemies" (Radio Kabul, 10 July; *FBIS*, 15 July).

Perhaps because of anticipated problems, Babrak at first was allowed to keep his honorary title of president of the RC, his seat on the Politburo, and his chairmanship of the Constitutional Drafting Commission. In November, however, he was retired from all his state and party positions except simple membership in the RC. Official announcements gave bad health as the reason for each dismissal, and the retirement ceremonies included a medal (Order of the April Revolution) and votes of thanks from leading party and state organs (*NYT*, 5 May; *Pravda*, 22 November; *FBIS*, 1 December). Although it is not impossible that Babrak in fact was in poor health, his relative popularity compared with that of Najib—manifested by demonstrations of popular support when he partook in departure ceremonies for Soviet troops in October (*NYT*, 26 January 1987)—was probably a more trenchant reason for his retirement.

Under Babrak, the leadership rarely showed its face outside of Kabul. Najib signaled his departure from his predecessor's customs by making a series of speeches in provincial capitals and inducing other Politburo members to do the same. His basic pitch was for even stronger ties with the USSR and involvement of the provinces and tribes in running the country (Radio Kabul 7 May; *FBIS*, 8 May).

By July, Najib was ready to establish his own team. The Central Committee, which had had only about 66 full and 16 alternate members, was suddenly expanded by 31 full and 39 alternate members (*KNT*, 12 July). In line with Najib's own background and interests, Yaqubi, who had replaced Najib as security chief, was raised to alternate Politburo membership and Laeq, responsible for tribal affairs, was promoted to full Politburo status. In November, as Babrak was losing his last functions, 9 more full and 10 alternate Central Committee members were named (Radio Kabul, 20 November; *FBIS*, 21 November); and in December, another 2 full and 4 alternate members took their seats (Bakhtar, 31 December; *FBIS*, 31 December). Of the 56 new full members, only 16 had been alternates before 1986. Although little is known about most of them, it is safe to assume that most are persons known to and trusted by Najib and that they include a significant number of secret police colleagues. Among those on whom there is a known record, there are several secretaries of provincial party committees (12 added in July) and Central Committee staff employees (5 added in November).

So far, dismissals from the Central Committee have been minimal. Aside from Babrak, four provincial secretaries—two of them Central Committee members—were fired for malfeasance, and the former Khalqi secret police chief, Assadullah Sarwari, long since exiled to Mongolia as ambassador, was dropped with minimal comment (*KNT*, 12 July; Radio Kabul, 7 October; *FBIS*, 19 October). It would not be surprising, however, to see an eventual purge of pro-Babrak elements from that body.

According to official statistics, the rank and file membership of the PDPA continued to climb impressively, from 155,000 full and candidate members in May (*KNT*, 14 May) to 160,000 in October (TASS, 25 October; *FBIS*, 27 October) to 165,000 in mid-December (*Pravda*, 14 December; *FBIS*, 15 December) and finally to 170,000 at the end of the year (*Pravda*, 5 January 1987; *FBIS*, 5 January 1987).

Even so, the reported jump in membership is open to some question. In the past, about 65 percent of the party has been on active duty with one of the security services—the military, police, secret police, or one of the numerous volunteer militias. This figure remained the same in 1986 (*KNT*, 14 May). Also in past years, it has been stated that 65 percent of the security forces are PDPA members, implying that the total enrollment in those services equals total PDPA membership. It is estimated that there are only about 80,000 men under arms for the DRA (DoS, *Seven Years*), which thus becomes the total party figure (including candidate members) as well. If candidates compose half the party, this reduces the full members to 40,000, but even that figure is suspect if the DRA's statistics on regional party membership are correct.

For example, only 570 of Balkh province's 450,000 peasants are enrolled in party organizations, and only 52 of its 6,000 tradesmen and craftsmen have become PDPA members (*KNT*, 2 June). In 1978, then party chief Taraki boasted that most of the PDPA were teachers, but in 1986, Najib was to complain that only 6,691 out of 22,000 DRA teachers—less than a third—were party members (Radio Kabul, 7 October; *FBIS*, 10 October). In a speech in Tashkent, Najib stated that there were 1,300 Afghan Uzbek members of the PDPA (*KNT*, 15 December). In the past, Uzbeks had comprised about one-sixteenth of the Afghan population (Harvey H. Smith, ed., *Area Handbook for Afghanistan*, 1973), and if their party membership is proportional to the total population, this would indicate fewer than 20,000 party members.

Other miscellaneous statistics indicate that 30 percent of the party are peasants, 60 percent are under 30 years of age, and 54 percent of the newly admitted come from the ranks of the DYOA (Bakhtar, 23, 27 May; *FBIS*, 29 May; *KNT*, 26 May). Clearly, the drive to increase party ranks is continuing as it has for the past several years, but with less than total success. On several occasions, Najib complained strongly about failure to enlist DYOA veterans in the PDPA (Radio Kabul, 10 July; *FBIS*, 15 July), and in November, he noted that "the stratum of PDPA and DYOA members among teachers and youth is very tiny" (*KNT*, 23 November). In July, the Politburo instructed the party to "improve the social composition of PDPA candidates," with emphasis on recruiting workers, peasants, tradesmen, soldiers, noncommissioned officers, and members of the DYOA and the DWOA (now the AAWC) (Radio Kabul, 3 July; *FBIS*, 8 July). This comprises most of the Afghan population; about the only significant groups omitted are military/security officers and bureaucrats, most of whom, presumably, are already signed up.

The same instruction enjoined the Ministry of Interior to intensify its education of cadres in a "spirit of patriotism, internationalism, faithfulness to party and people." The implication is that the Ministry of Interior, a stronghold of Khalqi sentiment, had been lacking in these virtues, yet another indication that the feud between Parcham and Khalq continued unabated. There were other such signals as well, most notably the recurrent demand for party unity. In Najib's words, "the main [PDPA] task is to strenghten unity in the leadership and among the party masses" (*Pravda*, 12 July; *FBIS*, 17 July). Almost in the same breath with assurances that the Parcham-Khalq rivalry "belongs to the past" (Radio Kabul, 12 July; *FBIS*, 14 July), Najib complained that "some PDPA members sow discord," and "defiance of unity is treachery" (Radio Kabul, 10 July; *FBIS*, 15 July).

Khalq's position in the party and state apparats remained subordinate to Parcham's, despite the Khalqi majority (about 60 percent) in the party (DoS, *Seven Years*). Personnel shifts in late 1985 and early 1986 seemed to indicate a slight degrading of the Khalqi position: party stalwart Ismail

Danesh, for example, was dropped from the Polit-buro in connection with his posting abroad as an ambassador (*YICA*), Ghulam Dastigev Panjsheri re-tired for reasons of health, and Sarwari, Arian, and Zeary lost their RC Presidium seats (Radio Kabul, 17 January; *FBIS*, 21 January). As soon as Najib took over, however, the Khalqis more than compen-sated for their earlier setbacks: Arian took over the Party Control Commission in May, Panjsheri took his place as head of a renamed Central Inspection Commission in July, and the tacitly recognized head of Khalq, Minister of Interior Gulabzoy, was given an alternate Politburo membership (Radio Kabul, 10 July; *FBIS*, 11 July). Taken in sum, these latter moves seemed to reflect a cautious effort by Najib to mend some fences with Khalq without, however, giving up significant power to the rival faction.

Whatever progress Najib may have made in heal-ing the split with Khalq—and it is not likely to have been great—may have been offset by cleavages within Parcham. Najib has lent an unmistakable Pushtun flavor to the new government, referring to the Pushtuns as "elder brothers" to the other na-tionalities (Radio Kabul, 7 May; *FBIS*, 8 May), a condescension the latter are unlikely to have appre-ciated. At least three factions within Parcham are said to have developed around Babrak, Keshtmand, and Najib (*Afghan Realities*, 16 July). A possible reflection of this division can be found in the fact that management of the PDPA/DRA was ostensibly divided among the three leaders from May to No-vember, with Babrak as chairman of the RC, Kesht-mand president of the Council of Ministers, and Najib as general secretary of the party (DoS, *Seven Years*).

One of the more interesting developments of 1986 was the incorporation into the PDPA of vari-ous small splinter groups, most of them previously unknown. In July, Najib claimed that two of these "leftist and democratic" organizations had already merged with the PDPA, another three were about to do so, and a sixth was thinking about it (Radio Kabul, 21 July; *FBIS*, 23 July).

After an initial period of utter confusion when the various groups seemed to be just one that had donned slightly different names on different occa-sions, five distinct names have emerged: the Revo-lutionary Association of the Working People of Afghanistan (RAWPA), the Vanguard Organization of Working People of Afghanistan (VOWPA), the Vanguard Workers' Organization of Afghanistan (VWOA), the Revolutionary Organization of the Working People of Afghanistan (ROWPA) (*KNT*,

23 November), and the Vanguard Organization of Young Afghan Workers (VOYAW) (Bakhtar, 17 Sep-tember; *FBIS*, 17 September). There is still some question whether these were actually five separate groups or whether some group, or groups, were referred to by more than one name.

The chief of RAWPA, Zaher Ofuq (Ofaq, Ufoq), is known only for his participation as a Khalqi in the factional struggles with Parcham in the late 1960s. He appears to have left the PDPA shortly thereafter. His group has not previously been reported. Spokesmen for VOYAW were Taza Khan Deyal and Abdul Shokur Khushachin, neither of whom is known to have featured in Afghan politics before. (Deyal appears to be identical with Taza Ihan, Taza Wayand, and Taza Khan Wial, a person who was elected to the Central Committee in November while pursuing graduate studies in the USSR [*KNT*, 22 November]). They assert that VOYAW has been in existence since 1970 (*KNT*, 1 November), a claim difficult to verify, especially because even the Afghan English-language outlets cannot agree on the precise title and acronym for the group. (Bakhtar calls it the Vanguard Organization of Young Workers of Afghanistan—VOYWA.)

**Domestic Affairs.** The switchover from Babrak to Najib saw no essential changes in the party line, which continued to push and expand on programs inaugurated by Babrak in late 1985. Babrak's inno-vations at that time did, however, signal a significant departure from policies that had prevailed from 1981 through most of 1985. He put forth ten "the-ses" that consisted of three important points of polit-ical philosophy and appeals for support to seven segments of the Afghan population. The first thesis emphasized that the present stage of Afghan devel-opment would be "long and difficult," with even the temporary goals of freedom and democracy unat-tainable for some time to come. The second was a demand that the PDPA accept the concept of sharing power with nonparty "patriots" in the DRA. There followed the appeals (in order) to workers and peas-ants, capitalists and traders, the intelligentsia, the various nationalities, members of the NFF, religious leaders, and military servicemen. Finally, Babrak's last point was an earnest plea for peace and "all around international cooperation" (Radio Kabul 9 November; *FBIS*, 12 November 1985). It was a classic "united front" approach, one that was in keeping with traditional Parchami philosophy but anathema to Khalqis. Babrak's somewhat apprehensive phraseology implied that he recognized this danger.

The reason for this appeal to persons normally considered class enemies was the inability of the DRA to establish its power in the villages and tribal areas. The resolutely religious and conservative Afghan villager would not heed appeals by the communists but might be persuaded if enough noncommunist collaborators could be found. Thus, the new direction involved a return to the policy of "broadening the base" or "widening the social pillars" of the DRA by introducing nonparty people into the RC and other state organs, a platform that was proclaimed immediately after the Soviet invasion. As in 1980 and 1981, the purpose of the move was to increase the legitimacy of the DRA in the eyes of its citizens without at the same time relinquishing the PDPA's grip on the principal levers of power. The policy failed in the earlier period because the party (and the Soviet occupiers) would not deliver on promises regarding exercise of real power by the state organs and cessation of Soviet interference in running the country.

In practical terms, the RC was suddenly and sharply increased from 69 to 148 members, and its nonparty contingent was jumped from 2 to 58. In the RC Presidium, 6 of 18 members were nonparty, as were nine of thirteen supergrade appointments in the bureaucracy. Fifteen of 21 newly appointed ministers and deputy ministers, 10 of 37 members of an Elections Commission, and 27 of 74 members of the Constitutional Drafting Commission were also nonparty (Radio Kabul, 26 December 1985, 17 January; *FBIS*, 27 December 1985, 21, 22 January; *KNT*, 29 December 1985, 23 January, 11, 22 February).

In parallel with this policy, the PDPA (like its mentor, the CPSU) seemed bent on exposing at least some of its shortcomings via a program of *glasnost'* (candor), on undertaking a "restructuring" (*perestroyka*) of society, and on introducing surface measures of democratization.

Regarding revelations of PDPA/DRA shortcomings, Babrak's unprecedented admissions of party and state failures in March (Radio Kabul, 30 March; *FBIS*, 3 April) were only exceeded by Najib's even more biting criticisms in July and August (Radio Kabul, 11 July; *FBIS*, 14 July). The litany of PDPA/DRA sins included failure of the security forces to cope with the outnumbered guerrillas, shortcomings in work with the border tribes, inability to establish "people's sovereignty" (read DRA power) in the countryside, failure to attract peasants, rejection by some party members (presumably Khalqis) of the policy of sharing power with nonparty figures, official bureaucratism and bombast, corruption and embezzlement in high quarters, ostentatious display of privilege by party higher-ups, ideological shortcomings in the media, front group failures, insufficient "openness," party workers' laziness or proneness to "leaping ahead of phases" (Khalqis again), a foundering economy, and a disunited party.

When repeating these, Najib added heretofore unmentionable topics, such as desertion from the armed forces and the failure of party and state organs to implement military draft orders, charges that were not only announced in the Kabul press but featured in Soviet outlets as well (*Pravda*, 12 July; *FBIS*, 17 July). Leading state and party cadres stood accused of shielding their sons and brothers from conscription, and a new decree on military service made fulfillment of that obligation a prerequisite for study abroad; those already abroad would have to serve their military time immediately on return (*KNT*, 12 November).

From Najib's high orations about these shortcomings, one might have anticipated that a sweeping, ruthless purge of party and state organs was imminent. Such is not the case so far. During 1986, only four individuals lost their seats on the Central Committee, and two of these (Babrak and Sarwari) were merely political scapegoats. A larger housecleaning may impend, but it seems likely that the PDPA is already so short of qualified manpower that it simply cannot afford to fire any but the worst malefactors.

Dismissals are easier in Kabul (where—due to better security—PDPA membership is most dense) than in the outlying regions. A purge of the Kabul city party committee in November apparently in connection with "weak points and shortcomings" (*KNT*, 30 November), resulted in the transfer of 12 former full and alternate members of that body and the appointment of 11 replacements, but no similar actions are known to have occurred elsewhere. It is characteristic of PDPA huddling in Kabul that of 147 claimed full and candidate Central Committee members in July, only 46 were supposed to be working in the provinces (Radio Kabul, 21 July; *FBIS*, 23 July).

In the course of 1986, the PDPA held five plenums. The seventeenth, on 27 March, was devoted to Babrak's report on the CPSU's Twenty-seventh Party Congress, which had taken place a few weeks before, and to a comprehensive critique of PDPA/

DRA performance since the Sixteenth (November 1985) Plenum (Radio Kabul, 30 March; *FBIS*, April). The Eighteenth Plenum, on 4 May, was devoted entirely to Najib's replacement of Babrak as general secretary (Radio Kabul, 4 May; *FBIS*, 5 May); no other business appears to have been transacted during this nervous period. At the nineteenth, on 12 July, Najib expanded the Central Committee, repeated Babrak's critiques of what was wrong with the country, and vowed to move ahead on solving its problems (Radio Kabul, 11 July; *FBIS*, 14 July). At the twentieth (20 November, when Babrak lost his remaining party and state responsibilities), the main thrust of the meeting was to reiterate dedication to fulfilling the resolutions of the Sixteenth Plenum, specifically Babrak's "ten theses" (Radio Kabul, 22 November; *FBIS*, 25 November). Finally, on 31 December, the Twenty-first "extraordinary" Plenum had Najib reporting on Moscow's marching orders and the next steps to be taken, including an attempt to arrange a six-month cease-fire with the resistance (TASS, 1 January; *FBIS*, 2 January 1987).

Thus, the year from November 1985 to November 1986 saw considerable personnel shuffling but no essential changes in policy. For Najib, as for Babrak, the basic political dilemma was how to improve the legitimacy of his discredited government without giving up power. Babrak, in listing his "ten theses," had said that "authority will not be monopolized by the PDPA" (*YICA*, 1986) but he then had been obliged to add that the party "has and will have in the future the mission of leading society and revolution" (*KNT*, 29 January). Najib walked the same tightrope. He maintained that "national compromise" was his goal and that "we agree to officially recognize every kind of organization and group, though they do not join the PDPA, but act according to the laws of the DRA" (*KNT*, 22 July)— yet in laying out the ground rules for compromise, he stated that "we will not retreat one inch from the results of the 1 April [*sic*] Revolution . . . [and] those who come to us should officially recognize the leading role of the PDPA" (Radio Kabul, 22 November; *FBIS*, 25 November).

Nevertheless, some cosmetic efforts were made during the year. The regime continued to declare that Islam was its state religion, and it made much of its contributions to mosque repair and its success in attracting the support of mullahs, some 10,000 of whom it claimed were on the state payroll (DoS, *Seven Years*). Statistics on contruction of new mosques and renovation of old ones were contra-

dictory however. The DRA's efforts to brand the resistance as sacrilegious continued unabated throughout the year but with no appreciable success.

An amnesty for draft dodgers and deserters (Radio Kabul, 29 May; *FBIS*, 30 May) was probably intended both to demonstrate the regime's humane posture and to fill the conscription quotas. Later, Najib was to claim the desertion rate fell "for the first time" in 1986, but his continued exhortations to various party and front groups showed that the problem remained a serious one (Radio Kabul, 7 October; *FBIS*, 10 October).

The private sector of the economy received official encouragment with the establishment of an Economic Consultative Council under Sayed Amanuddin Amin, a nonparty deputy prime minister (DoS, *Seven Years*). Businessmen must have been startled, however, when they heard Babrak declare that "those party and state authorities who create obstacles [to block the] growth and protection of the private sector will be seriously investigated and tried" (*KNT*, 6 January). After Najib came to power, low-interest loans were made available to investors (DoS, *Seven Years*). Statistics released in November showed that the private sector stood at 123.4 percent of the plan, which was 12.8 percent more than the previous year. (This would indicate that the plan originally had called for a decrease in the private sector.) In all, 82.7 percent of all domestic output—including 99 percent of agriculture—was allegedly in private hands (*KNT*, 13 November). The Five-Year Plan envisaged continued growth of private enterprise, at least through 1991 (ibid.), and Najib lent his personal endorsement to its support, noting that there were 70 applications for investments by investors offering more than one billion afghanis (Radio Kabul, 22 November; *FBIS*, 26 November).

In its drive to establish agricultural collectives (always termed "cooperatives" to avoid use of the more inflammatory "collectives") the regime made a point of emphasizing that joining was to be voluntary, even as it called for faster action (*KNT*, 3 April). Land and water reform remained a high-priority propaganda item but apparently had some problems on the ground; late in the year Najib established a joint commission of PDPA Central Committee and DRA RC members under Zeary to examine "a different approach toward distributing land among the peasants" (Radio Kabul, 22 November; *FBIS*, 26 November).

Among the less effective messages the PDPA

and DRA consistently tried to put across during the year was the sanctity of Afghan-Soviet friendship. Even as Babrak and Najib were trying to woo traditional "class enemies," such as mullahs, businessmen, landowners, traders, and tribal leaders, and even as Najib hinted at a coalition government that included opposition figures, he constantly played on the Soviet friendship theme (*KNT*, 9 October).

To lend more weight to the nonparty element in the government, Babrak's state function as RC chairman was taken over on an acting basis by a nonparty figure, Chamkani. The regime seemed somewhat nervous about publicizing this appointment, which surfaced first in the Czechoslovak press service (ČETEKA, 20 November; *FBIS*, 22 November) and only three days later on Radio Kabul (*FBIS*, 25 November). Nevertheless, Najib had no qualms in stating that 38 percent of the 133 new members in the RC, Council of Ministers, and NFF were nonparty (Radio Kabul, 22 November; *FBIS*, 25 November). In any case, neither these lesser lights nor Chamkani ever expressed anything but the party line, including attacks on "American imperialism," acknowledgement of the PDPA's "leading role," and the need for "closing the borders to enemies" (Radio Kabul, 8 December; *FBIS*, 8 December).

As another element of reform, a 74-person Constitutional Drafting Commission under Babrak's chairmanship was established early in the year (*KNT*, 22 February). A draft of the document was supposed to be ready for consideration by the RC in October, but its text remained out of the public domain for the balance of the year. Statements by various leaders indicated that it would provide for the replacement of the RC by either another unicameral People's National Assembly (Hong Kong, AFP, 14 October; *FBIS*, 15 October), or a bicameral group of elected representatives and Council of Nationalities (Radio Kabul, 2 June; *FBIS*, 4 June). Replacement of the RC by a "National Council" was supposed to take place in 1984 (Milan, *L'Unità*, 6 January 1984; *FBIS*, 10 January 1984), but at that time—as is the case today—seemed to be thwarted by the regime's inability to establish believable control in the countryside.

Perhaps the most unusual effort, however, was the establishment of Extraordinary Commissions for National Reconciliation. Ostensibly formed under the aegis of the NFF, such commissions were approved by the Politburo and Presidium in Sep-

tember (*KNT*, 27 September), and allegedly began work on the local level immediately. They were supposed to work with "political groups of a centrist and monarchic persuasion" and even with "the leaders of armed antigovernment groups operating abroad" (TASS, 1 January 1987; *FBIS*, 2 January 1987). By the end of the year, Najib and Chamkani were boasting that the commissions were conducting talks with "417 groups numbering 37,000 people," and that 8,000 persons had "come over to the side of the DRA." Najib hinted at the formation of a coalition government with these various elements. (TASS, 1 January 1987; *FBIS*, 2 January 1987.)

This move had already been telegraphed to refugee circles in Pakistan, who anticipated that the regime might have a limited measure of success among the following small constituencies: secret police penetrations of the resistance, resistance leaders who had indulged in factional brawls, persons who can be deceived by sufficient bribes, some factions of the socialist party, Afghan Mellat, Settam-e-Melli (an anti-Pushtun Marxist splinter group), and Sholay-e-Jaweid (a Maoist group) (*Afghan Realities*, 18 December). The effectiveness of the commissions will not be enhanced by their name, the acronym for which in Russian is CHEKA, the acronym for the first Soviet secret police.

As an offshoot of the reconciliation effort, Najib announced his intention of instituting a unilateral cease-fire, to be in force from 15 January to 15 July 1987 (ibid.). Resistance commanders, however, unanimously rejected his idea.

At year's end, it remained unclear whether the reconciliation campaign was any more serious than patently unacceptable earlier efforts at a "political solution" to the war. Regardless of Najib's intentions, however, the resistance did not intend to quit fighting until the last Soviet soldier had left Afghanistan.

**Election and Front Activities.** Babrak's task of establishing DRA power "in all of the districts and most of the villages" had been under way since August 1985 by means of elections of local deputies. They were supposed to be the prelude to national elections that would follow in September or October. The elections were declared completed as of 17 September 1986 (*KNT*, 15 November), yet new results continued to be published through the rest of the year, and no national elections were scheduled. The regime's intention seems to have been mainly to demonstrate its ability to hold elections throughout the country and thereby to demonstrate some measure of authority, even though in most places it could not muster a majority of votes for the PDPA. As of January, nonparty candidates made up "about 60 percent" of the new deputies (*KNT*, 14 January), a figure that later rose to 65 percent (Radio Kabul, 13 November; *FBIS*, 19 November).

Despite the regime's boast that 14,190 deputies had been voted in by "85 percent of the eligible voters" (*KNT*, 5 October), the elections could scarcely be termed a success. Even in Kabul Province, which was supposedly under regime control by virtue of the Soviet and DRA troops concentrated there, elections had been held in only 180 out of 628 villages by late in the year (*KNT*, 5 November). According to Najib, they had occurred in only one out of three villages "said to be free." The social makeup of the deputies was also unsatisfactory, with too many members of the intelligentsia (4,338, the second largest group after "workers and peasants" [7,424]) and too few representatives of minority nationalities, peasants, artisans, entrepreneurs, nomads, and other groups. As in previous speeches, Najib complained that the elections had not resulted in any practical work on behalf of the DRA by those fortunate enough to have been voted in. (*KNT*, 23 November.)

Front activities during the year reflected the party's policies. In March, the NFF added 33 new members, "representing all ethnic groups," to its Central Committee (*KNT*, 31 March). In line with the ostensible decentralization of authority, the NFF took responsibility for nominating "either directly or through its organizations" all 79 of the new RC members. To no one's astonishment, all were accepted (*KNT*, 15 June). Like the party, the NFF remained concentrated in Kabul, with a claimed 330,000 of its alleged 800,000 members resident in the capital. The tough new PDPA line on rounding up military recruits resulted in an allegedly sharp increase in NFF effectiveness in this field: from 85 "volunteers" it found in all of 1984–1985, the front pushed 1,397 into the regular armed forces and 2,118 into revolutionary defense groups in just six months in 1986 (*KNT*, 30 December). The Second Congress of the NFF, originally scheduled for September or October, has been rescheduled for January 1987.

The importance that the authorities ascribed to work with the tribes was underscored by the formation of the Central Council of the High Tribal Jirga (also called High Jirga of Frontier Tribes), and the appointment of Chamkani as its chief. (Chamkani was later to be named acting chief of the RC when Babrak was dismissed.) The council's basic mission is to secure tribal cooperation with the army and thus to "safeguard the border" (that is, deny passage to the resistance). It is divided into four commissions, headed by vice-chairmen Daud Shah (military), Mohammed Ebrahim Atai (cultural affairs), Wakil Mohammed Hashim Mushwany (liaison), and Safer Mohammed (economic affairs). The executive secretary is Bismullah Akbari. (Radio Kabul, 3 April; *FBIS*, 4 April.) Except for Shah, who is chief of the political department of frontier troops, none of these men is known to be a formal PDPA member, though their allegiances can scarcely be in doubt.

Two other front groups—the DYOA and the DWOA—were also in the news when Najib gave speeches to their respective managements. Under Ratebzad, the DWOA had increased membership from 39,623 in September 1985 to 54,100 in March 1986 (*KNT*, 5 June), but Najib complained that the group's management had made it as hard to join as the party itself. In connection with its August plenum, the name was changed to AAWC and a new management under Feroza Fedaie was installed (*KNT*, 6 August). The real purpose of the change, however, was probably to remove Ratebzad, an intimate of Babrak for many years, from her political power base. She was doubtless held at least partially responsible for the pro-Babrak disturbances that erupted among school girls when Najib replaced him as general secretary.

The DYOA also came in for some criticism and a personnel shakeup. In August, nine full members of its Central Council and four alternates were dismissed. Thirty-four others (eleven of them former alternates) were promoted to full membership and 25 newcomers became alternates (*KNT*, 5 August). Mazdak, however, is an old associate of Najib and retained his position as chief of the organization. Perhaps for that reason, criticism of the front for not adequately supporting border forces was relatively mild (ibid.). Later, however, Mazdak was one of four persons whom Najib criticized by name for failure to recruit more youngsters into the DYOA and for letting youth get away with draft dodging (Radio Kabul, 22 November; *FBIS*, 25 November).

Najib did not address the activities of other fronts

specifically, but indicated that they would be the topic of some scrutiny at a later date (Radio Kabul, 22 November; *FBIS*, 25 November).

**International Views and Connections.** As in the past, the policies of the PDPA and DRA were carefully copied from those of the CPSU and USSR. Gorbachev's campaigns of "glasnost'," his criticisms of the middle levels of Soviet bureaucracy, and his ostensible dedication to democratization of Soviet society were all reflected precisely in Najib's speeches, which, ironically, illustrated exactly the sort of obedience against which the Soviet leader was railing in his campaign to "restructure" Soviet society.

Certainly Najib's explicit policy from the time he took over from Babrak has been the strengthening of Soviet-Afghan ties (Radio Kabul, 7 May; *FBIS*, 8 May). As a leader whose survival depends on the Soviet occupation army, Najib's endorsement of his protectors could scarcely be anything but enthusiastic, and he has been even more solicitous of consolidating Soviet ties than was Babrak. From the Soviet side, their continued hosting of some 10,000 Afghan students in the USSR (*KNT*, 2 November) is clearly intended to guarantee a body of support for the USSR in the future.

On the formal level, CPSU relations with the PDPA were distant and cool until December. Gorbachev snubbed Babrak at the CPSU Twenty-seventh Congress in February/March. The Soviet representative at Saur Revolution Day (27 April) in Kabul was described by only his state—not party—rank, and in September, Vsevolod S. Murakhovsky, a lifelong confidant of Gorbachev and an influential member of the CPSU Central Committee, was described only by his state rank of first deputy chairman and head of the State Agroindustrial Committee of the USSR Council of Ministers during his visit to discuss Soviet-Afghan trade (Radio Kabul, 25 September; *FBIS*, 29 September).

The departure in July of Soviet ambassador Fikrat A. Tabeyev, who had served in Kabul since before the invasion, and his eventual replacement in August by Pavel Petrovich Mozhayev (*KNT*, 10 August) provided the first hint of a possible change, although neither the Soviet nor Afghan press put undue emphasis on the party side of his career. Mozhayev had had a successful career in the Leningrad party apparat, but—in view of Gorbachev's defeat of Leningrad party chief Grigory V. Romanov during the 1985 Kremlin succession struggle—his appointment might have been interpreted as a form of polite exile, Afghan style, rather than a CPSU commitment to the PDPA.

In mid-December, however, seven of the eleven PDPA Politburo members traveled to Moscow, where they were received by most of the CPSU's leading lights: eight of twelve full Politburo members, five of seven alternates, and four of seven Central-Committee secretaries (*Pravda*, 14 December; *FBIS* 15 December). The Afghan delegation included two Khalqis, Zeary and Gulabzoy, but Ratebzad—apparently in political eclipse—and three other Politburo members (Laeq, Razmjo, and Watanjar) were left behind. The concentration of rank on both sides was unprecedented in CPSU/PDPA relations. The party-relations nature of the visit was emphasized by the absence of the DRA's leading nonparty figure, acting RC chairman Chamkani, and by the emphasis given to each Soviet host's party rank.

The reason for this demonstration of Soviet support may have been the effect on the Afghan public of Moscow's withdrawal of occupation forces in October. For the entire week bracketing the main withdrawal, the *KNT* devoted at least one prominent article a day to Soviet-Afghan friendship (*KNT*, 14–21 October), a theme that continued to receive heavy emphasis in Afghan media through the rest of 1986. Although the withdrawal was largely illusory (DoS, *Seven Years*), it probably shook the confidence of DRA supporters and cheered its opponents, and an exhibition of Soviet support was required to offset this trend.

Relations with other countries in the socialist world seemed to be carried on at somewhat lower tempo than in earlier years, with relatively few references to exchange visits in the *KNT*. Party schools in Bulgaria, the USSR, Mongolia, East Germany, and Czechoslovakia received thanks for their contributions to the PDPA Institute of Social Studies (*KNT*, 25 June). Various delegations from Warsaw Pact countries orbited through Kabul on an infrequent basis during the year, appearing to stay only long enough to pay their respects. The higher level of resistance activity may explain Kabul's low attraction for socialist visitors.

The PDPA as a party had few contacts outside the socialist bloc, and DRA relations with the noncommunist world ranged from good (India) to strained (Pakistan). The United States was held responsible for the ongoing war against the resistance.

**Conclusions.** The switch from Babrak to Najib resulted in a good deal of personnel shuffling, some harsh criticisms of party and state performances, and some innovative measures, such as the amnesty for deserters. To date, however, none of Najib's innovations appears to have strengthened the regime's control over its citizens. The war—not covered in the preceding assessment—has, if anything, intensified during 1986, with heavier casualities suffered on both sides and the resistance showing no signs of giving up. Najib's surface democratization—"broadening the base," bows to religion, promotion of private enterprise, and references to a "coalition government"—involve no abrogation of the PDPA's repeated claim to monopolize the leading role in this and any future Afghan government. Until that monopoly is specifically renounced, there is no likelihood of an effective DRA government. Moreover, the life expectancy of Najib, the PDPA, or any other leader or party installed by the Soviets is, and will remain, very low if Moscow decides to remove its troops.

**Biographical Note.** Najib (also known as Najibullah and Mohammed Najibullah) was born on 6 August 1947 (possible 1946) in Malan (Milan), near Gardez in Paktia Province, one of six children. His father, an Ahmadzai Pashtun of the Ghilzai tribe, was a state employee of "average wealth," who subsequently became a trade representative for the Afghan government in Peshawar, Pakistan, in the 1960s. Najib attended Habibia High School in Kabul and joined the fledgling PDPA (founded 1 January 1965) after his graduation from Habibia some time later the same year. He attended Kabul University's medical faculty but his political activities clearly took precedence over his studies. When the party fissioned into two wings in 1967, Najib—nicknamed "the ox" for his large size, booming voice, and enthusiastic participation in student brawls with the rival Khalqi faction—joined the Parchamis. He wrote a number of articles for the faction's newspaper *Parcham* in the late 1960s and was twice jailed (1969, 1970) for his activism. In 1972–1973, he was the spokesman and leader of Parchamis among Kabul University students. In fact, his eventual graduation in 1975 was said to

have been more or less involuntary, a political move by the university administration to remove a troublesome influence. In any case, he is never known to have practiced medicine. At one point, however, he is said to have sat on the same student union council with one of his chief adversaries today, resistance leader Gulbuddin Hekmatyar.

After graduation, Najib served one year in the army but thereafter devoted himself to party affairs. In 1977, when the two wings of the party temporarily papered over their differences in preparation for the coup that was to follow in 1978, Najib became a member of the joint Central Committee and is supposed to have been given responsibility for liaison between the PDPA and CPSU. Following the coup, he was one of the few prominent PDPA members not to receive a ministerial appointment, but he was sent into diplomatic exile along with all other top-ranking Parchamis when Khalq emerged the victor in their internecine struggle. As ambassador to Tehran, he was implicated in a coup attempt against the Khalqis in 1978 and, ignoring an order to return to Kabul, disappeared into Eastern Europe.

Najib returned to Kabul five days after the Soviet invasion and immediately became chief of the secret police, KHAD. He also was chairman of the Central Committee's Tribal Affairs Commission and built a reputation as a clever manipulator of tribal rivalries. He remained chief of KHAD until November 1985 when, in a move reminiscent of Yury Andropov, he quit his state duties to undertake full-time party work as both a Politburo member and general secretary. Under Najib (who was aided by KGB and East German advisers), KHAD acquired a reputation for ferocity and efficiency unmatched elsewhere in the DRA bureaucracy.

His notoriety as chief of KHAD and his unswerving support of the Soviets probably outweigh any political advantage accruing from his family connections with one of the more prominent Afghan tribes. He is married and has three daughters. His languages include English, Urdu, and probably Russian.

Ruth and Anthony Arnold
*Novato, California*

# Algeria

**Population.** 22,817,000
**Party.** Socialist Vanguard Party (Parti de l'avant-guarde socialiste; PAGS)
**Founded.** 1920
**Membership.** 450 (estimated)
**First Secretary.** Sadiq Hadjeres
**Leading Bodies.** No data
**Status.** Proscribed
**Last Congress.** Sixth, February 1952
**Last Election.** N/a
**Auxiliary Organizations.** No data
**Publications.** *Sat al-Sha'b* (Voice of the people) issued clandestinely at infrequent intervals; editor unknown

The Algerian Communist Party (Parti communiste algérien; PCA) was founded in 1920 as an extension of the French Communist Party. It has existed independently since October 1936. Although the PCA participated in the nationalist struggle against France, it was proscribed in November 1962, only four months after Algerian independence. In 1964, dissident left-wing elements of the legal National Liberation Front (FLN) joined with communists from the outlawed PCA to form the Popular Resistance Organization. In January 1966, this group was renamed the Socialist Vanguard Party. No regular party congress has been held since 1952, although the PAGS has held at least one national conference (in 1969) and in July 1981 held a meeting at which a ten-point general platform was adopted. Barely tolerated by the Algerian government, the PAGS is recognized in the communist world as the official Algerian communist party.

**Leadership and Party Organization.** Sadiq Hadjeres is first secretary of the party. Although the precise membership of the PAGS Politburo and Secretariat is not known publicly, prominent members of the party in recent years are believed to include Larbi Bukhali, a former party secretary general; Bashir Hadj 'Ali; Ahman Karim; and 'Ali Malki.

Both Hadjeres and Malki have contributed to the *World Marxist Review* and the *Information Bulletin* on behalf of the PAGS. Malki is on the Editorial Council of the *World Marxist Review* and contributed to its November issue; Hadjeres contributed an article to its September issue.

**Party Views, Positions, and Activities.** The year 1986 marked the fiftieth anniversary of an independent Algerian communist party and the twentieth year since the emergence of the PAGS. The year thus saw a certain amount of retrospective stock-taking, and some statements of current positions and policies, by the PAGS. The party's basic principles were expressed in a resolution adopted by the PAGS Central Committee in December 1985. This resolution supported the emancipation of women, their equality with men, and the right of women to work and to obtain education. At the same time, the party reiterated its commitment to furthering the material, moral, and political interests of the working class and peasants. This included support for the purchasing power of workers, the fair distribution of national income, representative democratic trade unions, and genuine and democratic participation by workers in running and supervising the country. Finally, the

Central Committee resolution defined the crucial problems in Algeria as the consolidation of ties between the PAGS and the working class, the broadening of "unity of action of all patriotic forces," and the buildup of "the anti-imperialist front thoughout the Maghreb, the Arab World, Africa and the world." (*Sawt al-Sha'b*, 26 January; *IB*, June.) On the policy level, the party considered it imperative to defend Algeria's economic independence, reinforce the public sector, raise its efficiency, respect and extend the democratic and social rights of the working class, and safeguard peace and security against "imperialist provocations" (*WMR*, November).

The PAGS generally has viewed the regime of President Chadli Benjedid, which has ruled Algeria since early 1979, as opportunist and reformist compared with the more militant regime of Houari Boumediene (1965–1978) (see *YICA*, 1983). During 1986, several party pronouncements warned of the danger of "the slide to the right" that has occurred in Algeria under the Benjedid regime. Hadjeres argued on this point that "the difficulties spring mainly from the growing economic and political influence of various strata of the bourgeoisie (bureaucratic, parasitic, liberal), which has grown stronger in the presence of the state sector" (*WMR*, September). He argued further that the slide to the right in Algeria has involved, inter alia, liberalization of the economy, weakening of the strong state sector established under the Boumediene regime, worsening of the living conditions of the working class, growing joblessness, a housing shortage, and a growing gap between official institutions and the masses (*IB*, March).

Since the early 1980s, in an effort to defend the achievements of the Boumediene regime and counter the swing to the right, the PAGS has pursued a policy of alliances aimed at bringing about a broad patriotic front. Malki recognized that "this front may also attract certain liberal-minded sections of the bourgeoisie whose positions are endangered by increasing penetration on the part of the transnationals" (*WMR*, November). Support for a broad patriotic front led the PAGS to call for a yes vote in the 16 January referendum on the new edition of Algeria's National Charter, first adopted in 1976. Hadjeres explained that this "was much more a vote in favor of unity of action by the patriotic and progressive circles than a vote for the new ideological content of the Charter" (*WMR*, September).

In terms of foreign policy, Hadjeres called for a "more consistent anti-imperialist thrust." Such a policy requires a confirmation of positions championed by the Boumediene regime, positions that brought Algeria to the forefront of the Nonaligned Movement. As part of this foreign policy, Hadjeres called for effective support for national liberation struggles in Palestine, South Africa and Namibia, the Western Sahara, and elsewhere; promotion of a new world economic order; elimination of the indebtedness of exploited Third World nations; and increased cooperation and solidarity with the world socialist system in "the struggle for peaceful coexistence, against the arms race and for universal peace." (*IB*, March.)

**State Relations with the Soviet Union.** In 1986, Algeria continued its pattern of exchanging high-level visits with the Soviet Union. Of particular importance was the official 25–28 March visit to Moscow of a top-level Algerian delegation led by President Chadli Benjedid (who is also general secretary of the FLN) accompanied by the leading members of his government. During this visit, Benjedid met on March 26 and 27 with CPSU general secretary Mikhail Gorbachev. The meetings allowed a full exchange of views between the two leaders on both bilateral relations and a broad range of international problems of mutual interest. A detailed joint communiqué was issued on March 28, at the conclusion of the visit (Moscow, TASS, in English, 28 March; *FBIS*, 1 April). Gorbachev accepted an invitation to make an "official friendly visit" to Algeria at an unspecified future date. During the discussion of the Arab-Israeli conflict, both sides reaffirmed that a just settlement required Israeli withdrawal from all occupied territories, the inalienable national rights of the Palestinians, and greater efforts by the Soviet Union and Arab countries toward the convocation of an international conference with the equal participation of all sides, including the Palestine Liberation Organization. A series of ministerial meetings produced three signed bilateral documents: a long-term program of economic, trade, scientific and technical cooperation; a protocol on consultations; and an agreement on economic and technical cooperation. (Moscow, TASS, in English, 28 March; *FBIS*, 1 April.) The Benjedid visit, which produced "positive results" according to the Soviet press, strengthened Soviet-Algerian relations, which had declined for a variety of reasons since Boumediene's death in 1978.

In late August, Cherif Massaadia, an important member of the FLN Politburo, followed up the Benjedid visit with a brief visit to Moscow, where he had an exchange of views with CPSU Central Committee Secretary Yegor Ligachev (Moscow, TASS International Service, in Russian, 27 August; *FBIS*, 28 August). In June, a Soviet economic delegation visited Algiers; during this visit, a Soviet-Algerian protocol was signed calling for the expansion of bilateral cooperation in ferrous metallurgy and metalworking, geology, the mining, oil and gas industry, electricity, water resources, forestry, the training of national cadres, and trade (*Pravda*, 26 June; *FBIS*, 1 July). And in late July, a Soviet-Algerian contract worth "tens of millions of rubles" was signed; under the contract Soviet organizations will provide some of the construction of the large Al-Hajjar metallurgical complex, one of the biggest projects of Soviet-Algerian economic cooperation (Moscow, TASS, in English, 29 July; *FBIS*, 5 August).

John Damis
*Portland State University*

# Bahrain

**Population.** 422,000
**Party.** Bahrain National Liberation Front (NLF/B)
**Founded.** 1955
**Membership.** Unknown but believed negligible
**Chairman.** Yusuf al-Hassan al-Ajajai
**Governing Committee.** (incomplete) Members: Ali Naji Abdallah, Yusuf al-Hassan al-Ajajai, Aziz Mahmud, Badir Malik, Aziz Ahmad al-Mudhawi, Jasim Muhammad, Abdallah 'Ali al-Rashid, Ahmad Ibrahim Muhammad al-Thawadi. Alternate: Yusuf al-Hassan
**Status.** Illegal
**Last Congress.** Unknown
**Last Election.** N/a
**Auxiliary Organizations.** Bahrain Peace and Solidarity Committee (affiliated with the World Peace Council), Democratic Youth League of Bahrain (affiliated with the World Federation of Democratic Youth), National Union of Bahraini Students (affiliated with the International Union of Students), Women's Organization of the NLF/B (affiliated with the Women's International Democratic Federation), Federation of Bahraini Workers (affiliated with the World Federation of Trade Unions)
**Publications.** No data

The pro-Soviet and "revolutionary democratic" NLF/B continued a moderately high level of activity internationally during 1986. Delegates were sent to the congresses of the communist parties of Cuba (February), the Soviet Union (February–March), Bulgaria (March), and East Germany (April). Additionally, the NLF/B was one of the eight communist and workers' parties of Arab East countries to sign the May document "End Repression and Terror in Jordan" protesting the arrest of practically the entire leadership of the Jordanian Communist Party (*IB*, July). Relatively little fuss was raised when the NLF/B's own leaders in Bahrain were apparently arrested in July and August; it seems this was because, unlike the arrested Jordanians, these were low-level leaders. None of them appear to have been among the Governing Committee members noted earlier; the latter were apparently either at the organization's presumed Damascus headquarters or elsewhere abroad (see *YICA*, 1986). A protest against these arrests by one Committee for the Defense of Human Rights in Bahrain was carried in the World Federation of Trade Unions' *Flashes from the Trade Unions* (12 September).

Relative to previous years, 1986 was a good year for information on the NLF/B's front activities. In April, the *World Marxist Review* carried an article on the Democratic Youth League of Bahrain, stressing the allegedly effective job it was doing under conditions of repression. Also in April, Abdallah 'Ali al-Rashid, who had just represented the NLF/B at the Twenty-seventh CPSU Congress, was appointed to fill the newly created Bahraini slot on the World Peace Council Presidential Committee (Helsinki, *New Perspectives*, no. 4). Chairman of the Federation of Bahraini Workers, Abdallah Hus-

ayn, together with international secretary, Muhammad Abd-al-Jalil Bawazir, attended the September 11 World Trade Union Congress in East Berlin (Eleventh World Trade Union Congress, *List of Participants*, p. 4), and the Bahraini union was admitted to World Federation of Trade Unions (WFTU) membership at this time (Prague, *World Trade Union Movement* no. 11). Finally, in October, the Bahrain Peace and Solidarity Committee sent three delegates to the Copenhagen World Congress Devoted to the International Year of Peace (The World Congress of the International Year of Peace, *Preliminary List of Participants*, pp. 1–2). Since one other delegate represented the NLF/B per se at this meeting (ibid.), this underlies the fact that once again the NLF/B has been able to organize a separate group to serve as the country's WPC affiliate (see *YICA*, 1986).

Wallace H. Spaulding
*McLean, Virginia*

# Egypt

**Population.** 50,525,000
**Party.** Egyptian Communist Party (al-Hizb al-Shuyu'i al-Misri; ECP)
**Founded.** 1921; revived in 1975
**Membership.** 500 (estimated)
**General Secretary.** (Apparently) Farid Mujahid
**Politburo.** Michel Kamil (chief of foreign relations), Najib Kamil (representative to the *WMR*); other names unknown
**Secretariat.** No data
**Central Committee.** Farid Mujahid, Yusuf Darwish; other names unknown
**Status.** Proscribed
**Last Congress.** Second, early 1985 (possibly 1984)
**Last Election.** N/a
**Auxiliary Organizations.** No data
**Publications.** Circulars under the heading *al-Wa'i* (Consciousness) and leaflets; *al-Yasar al-Arabi* (Arab left; published by Egyptian communists in Paris); information on publications not current.

The communist movement in Egypt dates back to 1921 and the formation in Alexandria of the Egyptian Socialist Party (al-Hizb al-Ishtiraki al-Misri) by Joseph Rosenthal and some former members of a more diverse group founded in Cairo the year before. With its name soon changed to the Egyptian Communist Party, the ECP was admitted to the Comintern in 1923. Suppression by the authorities started almost immediately and has continued sporadically ever since.

The movement, which has also been beset by factionalism, virtually disappeared during the 1920s and 1930s. Numerous communist factions emerged during the early 1940s, and the two largest groups combined to form the Mouvement démocratique de libération nationale (MDLN) in 1947. The MDLN also splintered, with the formation of a Unified Egyptian Communist Party in 1958. Soon, additional splintering meant that no one faction was important enough to be singled out for international recognition. At least two groups heeded Soviet instructions to cooperate with "progressive" single-party regimes by dissolving themselves in return for a commitment by the Egyptian government to tolerate individual communists. Many of the latter occupied important positions in the Arab Socialist Union (ASU) and mass media. But with President Anwar al-Sadat's shift to the right during the 1970s, a new ECP emerged in 1975.

The Egyptian communist movement remains as splintered as ever. Besides the ECP, several groups have surfaced during recent years. These include the Revolutionary Current, the Egyptian Communist Party—8 January, the Egyptian Communist Workers' Party, the Popular Movement, the Armed Communist Organization, the Egyptian Communist Party—Congress Faction, a Trotskyist communist organization called the Revolutionary Communist League, and the Revolutionary Progressive Party. It is possible that some of these are merely descriptive labels rather than formal names of organizations, and it is not known whether there is any relationship between these groups and the ECP. All indications point to the relative insignificance of communist groups in comparison with the threat to the regime posed by militant religious movements.

There were several developments during 1986 relating to communist organizations although in most cases, the organizations were not identified. In June, the Egyptian Supreme Court of State Security concluded the trials begun in 1979 of 34 individuals charged with "creating communist organizations and disseminating ideas of Marxism-Leninism"; all of the accused were sentenced to terms of one to three years forced labor in prison as well as fines (*Pravda*, 5 June; *FBIS*, 11 June).

In September, security forces arrested 278 members of leftist parties in nine of the country's governates. Those arrested were charged with stirring up the masses against the government, calling for general disobedience and strikes in the public services, and forming extreme organizations and cells to overthrow the government (Kuwait, *al-Ra'y al-'Amm*, 22 September; *FBIS*, 24 September). The security forces also seized a large number of pamphlets that were ready for distribution (Cairo, *al-Ahram*, 21 September; *FBIS*, 24 September). some reports referred to the arrested individuals as members of an organization, perhaps meaning that this was a coalition of various groups. But there was no indication of the names of the component groups or of the overall organization.

On 16 December, the Interior Ministry announced that 44 members of the Revolutionary Current (described as a Maoist organization in *YICA*, 1978) had been arrested and that the police were looking for 3 others. The arrests began 12 December with apprehension of 23 members of the group's congress (made up of the Central Committee and seven heads of governate committees—and including its leader, Professor Abd al-Mun'im Talimah of Cairo University) as it met in Giza to plan an effort to seek support within the masses for overthrowing the regime and establishing a communist system. The organization, said to consist of individuals who had been involved in the food riots of 1977 and later released, had planned to penetrate student, worker, and youth groups to incite them to revolutionary activities. With the permission of the Supreme State Security Court prosecutor, security authorities had been monitoring the group and had recorded its proceedings. With the arrests, the Revolutionary Current's archives were seized; among their contents were various secret publications, video and audio recordings, and documents that revealed the names of its members and its organizational structure. (Cairo, MENA, 16 December; *FBIS*, 17 December; *NYT*, 17 December; AP.)

**Leadership and Party Organization.** Little is known about the ECP's leadership and organization. Few party officials have been mentioned in available publications. Official statements by ECP leaders published abroad are mostly anonymous. The name most often mentioned is Politburo member Michel Kamil, obviously because of his position as the party's chief of foreign relations. All indications point to the typical pattern of "democratic centralism," albeit in a rudimentary form resulting from the group's small membership and clandestine character.

**Domestic Party Affairs.** No information is available on meetings of party organs during the year or on statements by party leaders on domestic matters. Statements in previous years typically condemned the increasing gap between the masses and the "big bourgeoisie" and the antidemocratic nature of the regime.

Many members of the ECP are in prison or are repeatedly arrested and retried. According to one source, 12 members of the ECP were included among the leftists arrested in September (Beirut, Voice of Lebanon, 20 September; *FBIS*, 22 September).

Egypt experienced numerous examples of sabotage during the year, but the most violent outburst was the large-scale rioting of conscripts in the State Security Forces in February. These riots were apparently largely or entirely spontaneous, but there were allegations of communist involvement. As a result, Mustafa Kamil Murad, leader of the rightist Liberal Party, pictured most communists as "still operating underground through the secret cell system to which they are accustomed and which they have perfected" and as having infiltrated "the ranks of students, workers, and other groups." He maintained that the riots were the beginning of a series of communist "sabotage plans . . . so as to ride the crest of the wave of unrest in order to return the country to a one-party system." (Cairo, *Al-Ahrar*, 3 March; *FBIS*, 7 March.)

**Auxiliary and Front Organizations.** Little information has come to light about any auxiliary organizations of the ECP. Under present conditions, it seems safe to assume that children's and youth organizations do not exist. In the past, the party was actively concerned with organizing primarily students and workers.

Pointing to the regime's increased dependence on the United States, an ECP statement of 14 October 1985 called for the establishment of "a national democratic front with truly deep popular roots" to struggle for "national and social objectives." It specified the need for forming "the front's committees" in which "the broadest sections of the people and the national political forces" throughout the

country—with emphasis on "students, teachers, and . . . industrial workers"—could exert "massive pressure on the ruling regime" to sever relations with Israel and overcome dependency on the United States. (*IB*, February).

Much more important than the ECP or any other communist organization is the broad, legal leftist opposition front, the National Progressive Unionist Party (NPUP), whose general secretary is longtime Marxist Khalid Muhyi al-Din. (For a biography of Muhyi al-Din, see *YICA*, 1984.) Its deputy general secretary is Rif'at al-Sa'id. Some of the members of the NPUP (organized in 1976 when President Sadat first permitted the formation of leftist and rightist opposition groups) are Marxists; others are Nasserites or other opponents of the nonsocialist pro-Western direction of the regime. The NPUP publishes the weekly newspaper, *al-Ahali* (edited by Muhyi al-Din), which has a large circulation. Before 1980, the party had three seats in the People's Assembly. In the 1984 elections, it got 3.8 percent of the total vote, but application of an 8 percent rule prevented it from getting seats in the newly adopted proportional representation system.

A plenary meeting of NPUP Central Committee was reported in January. It criticized the deterioration of the Egyptian economy and "called for an intensification of the struggle for the interests of the working class." (*Pravda*, 27 January; Jerusalem, *The Soviet Union and the Middle East* 11, no. 1, 1986.)

Along with all the other opposition parties, the NPUP boycotted the 1 October election to fill 70 seats of the advisory Shura (consultative) Council. These parties objected to a new election law that seemed designed to favor the ruling National Democratic Party by providing that no party receiving less than 20 percent of the vote would be eligible for a seat and that a party with an absolute majority in a particular province would get all of that province's seats. (*NYT*, 2 October.)

In April Muhyi al-Din delivered a speech at the Eleventh Congress of the German Socialist Unity Party (SED) of the German Democratic Republic (*East Berlin, Neues Deutschland*, 24 April). When an Egyptian airplane was hijacked to Malta in December 1985, Muhyi al-Din speculated that there was Israeli involvement designed to bring about a confrontation between Egypt and Libya (ibid., no. 1). In January, the NPUP newspaper, *al-Ahali*, published a long interview with Afghani leader Babrak Karmal in which one of the interviewers described Afghanistan as "the target of an 'undeclared' actual war by many foreign forces" (*FBIS*, 23 January).

**International Views, Positions, and Activities.** Representatives of the ECP attended the Twenty-seventh Congress of the CPSU, where they criticized Egypt's ties with the United States (*The Soviet Union and the Middle East* 11, nos. 3–4). In November 1985, communist and workers' parties of the Arab East issued a joint statement emphasizing "profound anxiety" over "the fascist terroristic acts committed by the Israeli occupation authorities." There was no indication of what parties were involved, but the ECP has previously been one of the participants in this grouping. (*IB*, January.) The ECP was listed among the eight communist and workers' parties of Arab East countries that issued a statement calling for an end to repression in Jordan on May 17 (ibid., July). It was also represented by Kamel Magdi at the *World Marxist Review* Commission on the Exchange of Party Experience held in Prague, apparently soon after the Twenty-seventh CPSU Congress, for the purpose of exchanging views on the communist movement in a changing world (*WMR*, October). Farid Mujahid (Mougahed), identified only as a member of the ECP Central Committee, joined Zinen Zorzolilis, a member of the Central Committee of the Communist Party of Greece in a statement attacking the U.S. raid on Libya (*WMR*, June).

Magdi warned that "preparations for [nuclear] war are essentially under way, especially in the Middle East, where Israel has joined the 'star wars' programme, and where US nuclear armed warships are allowed to use the Suez Canal" (*WMR*, October). The United States' "gangster raid" on Libya was described as exemplifying "rabid chauvinism, violence and state terrorism" (ibid., June). It was also said to be "one in a series of US provocations mounted in response to Soviet dynamic peace initiatives" and an attempt "to worsen Soviet-American relations" (ibid.). The May statement of eight Arab communist parties, including the ECP, warned of United States and Israeli "threats of aggression against Syria," continuing intimidation of Libya, and conspiracies against the people of Palestine; the "terror, arrests and repression" of the Jordanian regime against its people were explained as "a glaring indication of the close links between the country's rulers and imperialist quarters" (*IB*, July).

Glenn E. Perry
*Indiana State University*

# Iran

**Population.** 46,604,000
**Party.** Communist Party of Iran (Tudeh Party)
**Founded.** 1941 (dissolved May 1983)
**Membership.** 1,000 –2,000 hardcore members; 15,000–20,000 sympathizers
**First Secretary.** Ali Khavari
**Leading Bodies.** No data
**Status.** Illegal
**Last Congress.** 1986, National Conference
**Last Election.** N/a

**Auxiliary Organizations.** No data
**Publications.** *Rahe Tudeh* (Tudeh path), *Mardom* (People) and *Tudeh News* (in English).

**Domestic Affairs.** In 1986 while still striving to recover from the 1983 onslaught of the Khomeini regime, it appeared that the Tudeh Party also had to cope with the deeper problem of fragmentation. The Nineteenth Plenum decided to expel six members and alternate members of the Central Committee "who attacked the party treacherously" (*Tudeh News*, 1 October). Although it was charged that the purged group had tried to smear the name of the party and compel it to deviate from its principles, it was clear that the real reason for the purge was the group's drive to make the party more independent from the Soviet Union. By expelling these members (Babak Amirkhosravi, Farhad Farjad, Fereydoun Azarnour, Mohammad Azadgar, Saeed Mehr-Eghdam, and Hossein Anvar-Haghighi), the party presumably tried to ensure the purity of its "proletarian internationalism" but in effect only created an appearance of subservience to Moscow, a major reason for the party's persistent lack of popular appeal in Iran.

In 1986, the Tudeh Party suffered still another setback: the death of Gholam Yahya Danesheyan, who had joined the newly formed Tudeh Party in 1941 and was an active member of the party leadership and of the Democratic Party of Azarbaijan and a member of the Tudeh Party's Central Committee. Although Danesheyan had been ill for some time, his death was a blow to the party.

The party, however, was not entirely debilitated, managing to elect Ali Khavari as first secretary of its Central Committee, and succeeding in holding a national conference attended by more than one hundred cadres of the party who came from "all over the world," including the party's clandestine organization in Iran. According to Ali Khavari, the national conference critically analyzed the party's policy before and after the "savage attack" on the party by the Khomeini regime in 1983. In an exercise of self-criticism, it declared that the party should have moved step by step to end the policy of supporting the Khomeini regime once that regime had gained "absolute political power" (*Morning Star*, 23 July). In adopting a "new party programme," the national conference endorsed the idea that, in the struggle against the Khomeini regime, "one must use all forms of struggle from demonstrations to general strikes and also popular armed struggle."

The external activities of the party in 1986 included its participation in the Twenty-seventh CPSU Congress. Addressing this congress, Ali Khavari complained bitterly about the "cruel offensive" of the Khomeini regime against the rank-and-file party members, some of whom had been sentenced to between 10 and 30 years imprisonment. This and other acts of repression, he said, had "brought down" not only the Tudeh Party but also the Fedayeen-e Khalq (majority) and other "progressive" Iranian organizations (*Pravda*, 4 March; *FBIS*, 19 March). Fedayeen-e Khalq First Secretary Farrokh Nekyakhdar joined his Tudeh comrades-in-arms in congratulating "the great party of Lenin" on the occasion of the Twenty-seventh Congress and, as Ali Khavari had done, applauded the Soviet support for his party.

At the regional level, in 1986, the Tudeh Party interacted with the Turkish communists on the one hand and with the Afghan Marxist regime on the other. At the end of a major meeting between the delegations from the Tudeh Party and the Turkish Communist Party, a joint statement was issued. The statement condemned the Khomeini regime, agreed that Turkey's present regime was fascist, and endorsed the efforts of the Tudeh Party to overthrow the Khomeini regime (National Voice of Iran, 22 February; *FBIS*, 25 February and National Voice of Iran, 25 March; *FBIS*, 27 March). Ali Khavari sent a congratulatory message to the new Afghan leader, Mohammed Najibullah, on the occasion of his election as general secretary of the Central Committee of the People's Democratic Party of Afghanistan (PDPA), expressing the hope that the traditional friendship between the Tudeh Party and the PDPA would "become more fruitful and blossoming" under his leadership (Kabul in English to South Asia, 14 May; *FBIS*, 15 May).

No development in 1986 caught the Tudeh Party more by surprise than the news of the covert U.S.-Iran dealings. The Tudeh Party announced the news by broadcasting the text of a statement issued by the Central Committee of Fedayeen-e Khalq. During their visit to Tehran in May 1986, the U.S. delegation, led by former security adviser Robert McFarlane, allegedly discussed with "the officials" of the Iranian government U.S. arms exports to Iran for use in prosecution of the war against Iraq. It also discussed implementation of the "$20-billion arms agreements" that had been made between the shah's regime and the U.S. government, presumably in return for Iran's collaboration in obtaining the release of American hostages in Lebanon and the expansion of economic and political relations between the two countries (Radio of the Iran Toilers, 25 November; *FBIS*, 26 November).

The Tudeh Party viewed the clandestine U.S.-Iran dealings as a reflection of treasonous changes in the domestic and foreign policies of the Khomeini regime. Domestically, the party alleged, the regime betrayed the anti-imperialist goals of the February revolution by serving the interests of "big capitalists and feudal landlords" through suppression of "revolutionary and democratic forces, and an unbridled policy of hostility toward the communists and the Soviet Union." Externally, the Khomeini regime allegedly betrayed the goals of the revolution by conspiring with "Japanese, British, West German, French and Canadian imperialists, and through (its) ideological and political unity with America's lackeys in regions [*sic*] such as Turkey and Pakistan" (Radio of the Iran Toilers, 26 November; *FBIS*, 28 November).

The revelation that truly infuriated the Tudeh Party about the covert U.S.-Iran dealings was that in 1983, the CIA had provided the Khomeini regime with a list of Soviet KGB agents and Tudeh collaborators operating in Iran. As a result, the Khomeini regime executed as many as 200 suspects, closed down the Tudeh Party in Iran, and expelled 18 Soviet diplomats. Although Ayatollah Khomeini had at the time thanked God for the "miracle" leading to the arrest of the "treasonous" leaders of the Tudeh Party, the truth was revealed in November 1986: Vladimir Kuzinchkin, a senior KGB officer in Tehran whose job it had been to maintain contacts with the Tudeh Party, had defected to the British in late 1982 and had been debriefed later by the CIA, giving the United States details of Soviet and Tudeh operations in Iran (*WP*, 19 November). The Tudeh Party attributed this "disgraceful revelation" to a long-standing collaboration between the CIA and the Iranian intelligence organizations. In fact, it was an unexpected intelligence windfall resulting from Kuzinchkin's defection (Radio of the Iran Toilers, 26 November; *FBIS*, 28 November).

This revelation, in my opinion, calls for a reconsideration of the stock interpretation of the crackdown of the Khomeini regime on the Tudeh Party. Until now, the attack on the Tudeh Party had generally been attributed to the resumption of large-scale Soviet arms supplies to Iraq that began in the spring of 1982 after Iran's successful offensive in

March. This new revelation, however, suggests that the attack on the Tudeh Party was a direct result of the CIA providing the Khomeini regime with vital intelligence information, presumably regarding the Soviet-backed infiltration of the Khomeini regime by Tudeh members and KGB agents.

**Foreign Relations.** Unlike any other year since the Iranian revolution, 1986 was marked by an unprecedented improvement in Soviet-Iranian economic and commercial relations. Although some signs of a thaw in the chilly relations between Moscow and Tehran had surfaced in July 1985, there had been no real relaxation of tensions. In 1986, however, there were four major exchanges of visits that eventually culminated in the revival of the Soviet-Iranian Permanent Commission for Joint Economic Cooperation. At the invitation of an Iranian foreign ministry official, Ali Mohammad Besharati, the Soviet first deputy foreign minister, Georgiy Korniyenko, arrived in Tehran on 2 February at the head of a Soviet delegation. He met with President Ali Khamene'i, Prime Minister Mir-Hussein Musavi, Parliamentary Speaker Hashemi-Rafsanjani, Foreign Minister Ali Akbar Velayati, and Oil Minister Gholamreza Aqazadeh. The two sides agreed to reactivate their joint commission, continue talks on improving economic relations, and resume flights from Moscow to Tehran by the Soviet airline Aeroflot (Radio Free Europe, 4 February).

On 11 June a second Soviet delegation, led by Director-General of the Soviet Economic Cooperation Committee Yakubov, arrived in Tehran for a one-week visit at the invitation of Iran's Ministry of Economic and Financial Affairs. The talks were aimed at preparing a draft protocol on economic cooperation, but concrete agreement was reached only on extending the long-term trade agreement for another year (Tehran Domestic Service, 18 June; *FBIS*, 19 June). The third exchange of visits had an upbeat note to it. Deputy Foreign Minister for Economic and International Affairs Mohammad Javad Larijani, who led an Iranian delegation to Moscow, characterized his visit on 10 August as "positive and constructive," adding that "fortunately, there are no major impediments in Irano-Soviet relations" (Tehran, Iran News Agency [IRNA], in English, 10 August; *FBIS*, 11 August).

The fourth and final meeting, which took place in Tehran in December, led to the first breakthrough in the strained relations beween Tehran and Moscow since the Iranian revolution and ended the six-year suspension of activities of the tenth session of the Soviet-Iranian Permanent Commission for Joint Economic Cooperation. According to Chairman of the USSR State Committee for Foreign Economic Relations Konstantin Fedorovich Katushev, who led the Soviet delegation, the two countries considered the fact that the commission sessions had not been held during the previous six years to be "abnormal and contrary to the interests of the two sides." Iranian Finance and Economic Affairs Minister Mohammad-Javad Iravani considered the visit of the Soviet delegation as "a positive step" in the relations of the two countries, one based on "good-neighborly relations, equality, and mutual respect" (Tehran Domestic Service, in Persian, 9 December; *FBIS*, 10 December). The upshot of the session was the signing on 11 December of an economic cooperation protocol that covered commerce, banking, transportation, fisheries, manufacturing industries, housing construction, and technology and construction of steel plants and power stations in Iran and provided for high-level meetings between the two countries every six months to review economic affairs and ways of implementing agreements (*WP*, 13 December; Tehran Domestic Service, in Persian, 11 December; *FBIS*, 12 December). The two sides also agreed that the eleventh session of the commission would meet in Moscow in 1987.

At this meeting, the Soviet Union reportedly agreed to send back to Iran Soviet experts and technicians who had left in May 1985 because of the threat of bombing raids by Iraq (an explanation Iran considered a mere excuse for their departure). More important, even before the tenth session of the commission was held in December, agreements on hydrocarbon issues were reached between Tehran and Moscow. Iran agreed to export 3 million cubic meters of natural gas per day to the Soviet Union beginning in 1986; this amount was to be increased to 80 to 90 million cubic meters per day by March 1990 (Tehran, IRNA, 25 August; *FBIS*, 25 August). The two countries also agreed that the Soviet Union would cooperate with Iran in drilling operations to explore the oil reserves in the southern sector of the Caspian Sea (Tehran, IRNA, in English, 26 August; *FBIS*, 26 August), a joint project that had been conceived more than twenty years earlier and one on which most of the planning and survey work has been completed (*WP*, 26 August). Interestingly, these agreements were being announced around the time that Iranian Oil Minister Aqazadeh was triumphantly disclosing that the Soviet Union had complied with his request in Moscow to cut its oil

exports to Western Europe by 100,000 barrels during the months of September and October, whereas Britain and Norway had refused to cooperate with OPEC in cutting back their oil production in face of the worldwide oil glut and dwindling prices (Tehran, IRNA, in English, 23 August; *FBIS*, 25 August).

The unprecedented improvement in economic relations between Moscow and Tehran in 1986 was paralleled by continued strained relations over the old issues, and the strain was even heightened by tensions over new issues. The Khomeini regime missed no opportunity to register its continuing dissatisfaction with the Soviet military occupation of Afghanistan and Soviet arms supplies to Iraq. At the end of a three-day meeting of the fourth international conference on Islamic thought held in Tehran in January 1986, the lay scholars and religious leaders who were present condemned "the aggression of the USSR forces against Afghanistan and stressed the need for their withdrawal and unconditional departure," preparing the ground for "the establishment of an Islamic government" there. The conference also condemned the war imposed by Iraq on Iran, recognizing "the Ba'thist regime of Iraq as the aggressor" (Tehran Domestic Service, in Persian, 31 January; *FBIS*, 3 February). Not unexpectedly, the Khomeini regime condemned Najibullah's new government in Afghanistan as vigorously as it had that of Babrak Karmal because it viewed "the reshuffle of pawns in Kabul [as] a sign of the Soviet defeat in Afghanistan" (Tehran Domestic Service, in Persian, 5 May; *FBIS*, 6 May). What must have surprised the Russians, however, was the fact that the improvement in their economic relations with Tehran seemed to make no real difference in the hostile attitude of the Khomeini regime toward the Soviet occupation of Afghanistan or the Soviet arms supplies to Iraq.

The new issue that caused the Soviet ideological and political hostility toward the Khomeini regime to surface was the disclosure of the covert U.S.-Iran arms deals. On 1 December, the Soviet government newspaper *Izvestiia* accused Iran of aiding the United States in an undeclared war against Afghanistan, saying that Iran had undertaken "an unbridled hostile campaign" against the Soviet Union over its support of the Afghan government and charging that Iran was participating in "blatant interference" in the internal affairs of Afghanistan. Latching onto a statement by Rear Admiral John M. Poindexter, former national security adviser to President Reagan, *Izvestiia* attacked the Khomeini regime in the toughest terms it had used in over a year. Quoting Poindexter as having said that some of the weapons supplied to Iran by the United States and Israel were intended for the Afghan guerrillas, *Izvestiia* asked, "To whose advantage but that of the United States, the Israeli Zionists and other reactionary forces is the course of the present leadership of Iran?" It went on to say, "In words, it proclaims that it follows anti-imperialist ends, but in fact it cooperates with the forces of imperialism in carrying out an undeclared war against the Democratic Republic of Afghanistan" (*NYT*, 2 December). Most observers believed that the Soviet Union was using the U.S.-Iran arms deal as a warning to Tehran that closer economic ties with the Kremlin come at a certain price. In my opinion, however, the shocked Soviet reaction reflected Moscow's deepfelt concern that its dogged postrevolutionary policy of barring any American re-entry into Iran might have been defeated. When on December 8 Deputy Foreign Minister Alexander Bessmertnykh accused the Reagan administration of having "lied" to the Soviets about its arms supply to Iran, he was attempting to kill two birds with one stone. He was trying to use the arms deal as a means of depicting the U.S. as an unreliable negotiator in U.S.-Soviet strategic talks. He was also trying to secure the Soviet position in the Middle East by exploiting some of the lost credibility suffered by Washington in the Persian Gulf region as the Iran affair unfolded (*WP*, 9 December).

Neither Moscow nor Washington in 1986 seemed to adequately understand the true nature of Iranian overtures to the superpowers. The Soviets believed that Iran's determination to expand economic relations with Moscow simply reflected its desperate economic needs, and the Americans believed that Iran's dealings with Washington simply resulted from its need for American arms and spare parts. Both superpowers failed to note the more important change in the Iranian revolution. Like all historical revolutions, the Iranian one had just begun to undergo an overall mellowing process, resulting partly in a more pragmatic stance in international politics (R.K. Ramazani, *Revolutionary Iran: Challenge and Response in the Middle East*).

R.K. Ramazani
*University of Virginia*

# Iraq

**Population.** 16,019,000
**Party.** Iraqi Communist Party (ICP)
**Date Founded.** 1934
**Membership.** No data
**First Secretary.** Aziz Muhammad (62, Kurdish, worker)
**Politburo.** Zaki Khayri (Arab/Kurdish, journalist), Fakhri Karim; incomplete
**Secretariat.** No data
**Central Committee.** No data
**Status.** Illegal
**Last Congress.** Fourth, 10–15 November 1985
**Last Election.** N/a
**Auxiliary Organizations.** No data
**Publications.** *Tariq al-Sha'b* (People's road), clandestine

Early in 1986, information about the fourth congress in the 52-year history of the ICP began to appear. Held 10–15 November 1985 in a part of Iraqi Kurdistan controlled by the ICP and/or its Kurdish allies, the congress was attended by party leaders from outside Iraq. All delegates successfully avoided capture by Iraqi security forces on their way to and from the congress (*Morning Star*, 30 January). This congress, the first since 1976, has been the most successful activity of the ICP in the past year or two. Even though holding the congress brought to the fore a serious split in party leadership and the editor of *Tariq al-Sha'b* was expelled, the fact that the ICP could hold a congress on Iraqi soil was a pointed reminder to Saddam Husayn's regime of the limits to its domestic control.

**Leadership and Organization.** In the summer of 1984, a plenary meeting of the ICP Central Committee decided to hold the Fourth Congress (*IB*, April). Dissension at this meeting resulted in the dropping of three Central Committee members and one member of the Politburo in 1984 (*YICA*, 1985). Differences within the top echelon of the party continued to such an extent that a Central Committee meeting held in the spring of 1985 failed to find a formula for healing the split, which centered on ICP policy and program concerning the Iraq-Iran War (Kuwait, *Arab Times*, 5 April; *FBIS*, 7 April). During the summer of 1985, the Central Committee met again, this time in an effort to resolve a division in the party signaled by former first secretary Baha al-Din Nuri's decision to leave the ICP (*YICA*, 1985). Finally, First Secretary Muhammad convened an enlarged plenary meeting of the CC during the end of October and early November 1985. This meeting was "attended by a number of leading party workers" who, after analyzing party activity since July 1984, decided "to continue preparation for holding this most important function . . . at the due date" (*IB*, January). In plainer language, Muhammad had assembled the delegate strength he needed to purge the Central Committee, so the Fourth Congress could and did open shortly thereafter, on 10 November 1985.

The tenacity of Muhammad (a Kurd) in holding to a policy of armed struggle in the Kurdish areas of Iraq and of totally opposing the war was a major cause of the split in the ICP leadership. His keynote address to the Fourth Congress "analyzed in detail the course of the Iraq-Iran war." He affirmed the unwavering party position urging an immediate end to the war, a task that "does not contradict contin-uing efforts to mobilize the masses to topple the [Iraqi] dictatorship." (*IB*, April.) His control of the congress is evident in the communiqué's words that "many delegates paid special attention to the Iraq-Iran war, stressing that its immediate end and a deposition of the fascist dictatorship were the primary goals in the struggle of our people and the party" (ibid.).

The Fourth Congress elected "by secret ballot" a new Central Committee, which in turn chose a new Politburo and re-elected Muhammad to the post of first secretary. The only other person named in the communiqué was Politburo member Khayri, who at 75 was the oldest delegate attending. In consequence, the present composition of the leading party bodies is unclear, and due to the ICP's clandestine existence, it may be some time before even a partial roster can be compiled. Certainly there were major changes. As mentioned, four leaders were dropped in 1984. Four others—Amir Abdallah, Majid Abd-al Rida, Abd al-Razzaq Safi, and Nazihah al-Dulaymi—are reported to have been expelled from the party (Kuwait *Arab Times*, 5 April; *FBIS*, 7 April). All of the latter had been on the Central Committee for many years and are Arab (two Shi'a, two Sunni), and at least two of the four who left in 1984 are also Arab. The inference to be drawn from these changes is that Kurds now predominate in the ICP and Kurdish interests now outweigh national interests. In fact, the ICP joined the Turkish Communist Party, the Iranian Tudeh, and the Iranian Fedayeen-e Khalq in the following statement: "Our parties believe that the Kurdish national movement, which is struggling in all three countries to regain its rights, is an important basic force in our countries' communist and worker movement . . . The view is spreading through the Kurdish masses that regaining their rights is tied to the common aims of the national democratic and progressive movements in their countries" (Voice of the Turkish Communist Party, 19 March; *FBIS*, 27 March).

Domestic slogans from the congress point up continuation of Muhammad's party policy of recent years. In addition to calling for an immediate end to the war, three slogans of note were: "The alliance of the workers and peasants led by the working class and its Communist Party is an instrument for carrying out the party program"; "Step up the fight by our people to topple the dictatorship and form a national democratic coalition"; "For democracy in Iraq and real autonomy for Kurdistan." The years of cooperation with the Ba'thist regime (1968–1979) were examined in some detail and an apparently critical report received the delegates' assent (*IB*, April).

From the reaction of an ICP spokesperson, it appears that those dropped from the ICP are working to set up a separate organization. The ICP representative to the *World Marxist Review*, speaking at a meeting on problems in communist movements, pointedly declared that "the Iraqi Communists reject any arguments that could appear to justify the existence or emergence of two parties in one country . . . [because] one of them is moving along the wrong road" (*WMR*, October).

**Domestic Affairs.** Since the outbreak of fighting, the ICP has opposed the war between Iraq and Iran, consistently called for its end, and blamed the government in Baghdad for carrying it on, although it has also assigned responsibility for the war to Iran. The ICP has joined the Iranian Tudeh Party in calling for an end to the war "with no annexations" by either party and no interference in each other's affairs (*YICA*, 1986).

This opposition to the war has had serious domestic consequences for the ICP. Despite such setbacks as the Iranian seizure of Fao in February, the Ba'thist regime has for the most part successfully defended its territory and has mobilized huge military forces. It has demanded and generally received support from the 80 percent of the Iraqis who are Arab. Kurdish allegiance is divided; active rebellion has been in progress in Kurdish regions for years, and the ICP guerrillas are linked with the Kurdish Democratic Party of Iraq (KDP/I) and other Kurds in a Democratic National Front.

In the news coming out of Kurdish Iraq, the major organizations, KDP/I and the Patriotic Union of Kurdistan (PUK), receive the most notice. The former had some successes in 1986; its guerrillas took and held for several days a subdistrict center north of Mosul and have raided other large towns. It and the PUK each control stretches of territory. The two groups agreed, under the aegis of the Iranian-based, Iranian-supported Supreme Assembly for the Islamic Republic of Iraq (SAIRI), to collaborate in action against the Ba'thist regime (Radio Teheran, 12 November; *FBIS*, 13 November). Although the ICP claims its guerrillas participated in some of the larger attacks made by the KDP/I early in 1986, collaboration between the KDP/I and the PUK will put the communists in an inferior posi-tion. They will not be able to expect aid from SAIRI, which continuously emphasizes the Islamic nature of Kurdish guerrilla forces operating in Iraq—a formula that excludes the ICP. The ICP joined the Iranian regime's enemies when it, the Tudeh, the anti-Khomeini Fedayeen-e Khalq, and the Turkish Communist Party criticized Iran and Iraq for continuing the war, Turkey for helping both combatants, and all three states for oppressing the Kurds (Voice of the Turkish Communist Party, 19 March; *FBIS*, 27 March).

**International Relations.** Internal problems have not prevented the ICP from carrying on activity outside Iraq. It joined seven other Arab communist and workers' parties in a statement condemning Jordan's repressive actions against students at Yarmuk University and arrests of Jordanian Communist Party leaders (*IB*, July). In Damascus, the same parties distributed a statement criticizing the U.S. air attack on Libya (Damascus, Syrian Arab News Agency, 15 April; *FBIS*, 16 April). Muhammad visited Aden as head of a delegation of Arab communist and workers' parties (Aden Radio, 15 June; *FBIS*, 16 June), and earlier in the year, at the Twenty-seventh Congress of the CPSU, he delivered on behalf of the ICP an address in which he endorsed the "peace-loving Soviet policy [that] fully corresponds with the interests of the Arab peoples" and called, as did the Fourth Congress of the ICP, for "a democratization of Iraq and real self-government for Kurdistan" (*Pravda*, 2 March; *FBIS*, 20 March). Muhammad also spoke at the Eleventh Congress of the GDR's German Socialist Unity Party, as did Samir Abd-al Wahhab, a member of the ruling Ba'th Party in Iraq (*Neues Deutschland*, 24 April). Muhammad also conferred with General Secretary Zhivkov in Bulgaria (Sofia, BTA, 12 August; *FBIS*, 13 August).

Good state-to-state relations continue between Iraq and the USSR. The latter is a major arms supplier to the Baghdad regime. The USSR and its allies are actively involved in Iraqi economic development projects, and there are frequent visits by East European government delegations to Iraq, visits that are returned by Iraqis.

John F. Devlin
*Swarthmore, Pennsylvania*

# Israel

**Population.** 4,208,000 (not including territories occupied in 1967)
**Party.** Communist Party of Israel (CPI); also called New Communist List (Rashima Kommunistit Hadasha; RAKAH)
**Founded.** 1922
**Membership.** 2,000 (estimated)
**General Secretary.** Meir Vilner (member of the Knesset [parliament]; age: 68)
**Politburo.** 9 members, including David (Uzi) Burnstein, Benjamin Gonen, Wolf Erlich, Emile Habibi, David Khenin, Tawfiq Tubi (deputy secretary general and member of the Knesset), Meir Vilner. 4 alternates (the inclusion of some names on the Politburo and Secretariat lists is based on the assumption that they were re-elected at the last congress).
**Secretariat.** 7 members, including Salibi Khamis, David Khenin, Jamal Musa, Tawfiq Tubi, Meir Vilner, George Tubi
**Central Committee.** 31 members, 5 candidates
**Status.** Legal
**Last Congress.** Twentieth, 4–7 December 1985
**Last Election.** 23 July 1984. 3.4 percent of the vote (with the Democratic Front for Peace and Equality [DFPE]), 4 seats (for DFPE), total number of seats in the legislature: 120
**Auxiliary Organizations.** Young Communist League, Young Pioneers
**Publications.** *Al-Ittihad* (editor: Emile Habibi); *Zo Ha-Derekh* (editor: Meir Vilner); *al-Jadid* (editor: Samih al-Qasim); *Information Bulletin, Communist Party of Israel*

The communist movement in Palestine began in 1920. Two years later, a Palestine Communist Party (Palestinische kommunistische Partei; PKP) was established. It joined the Comintern in 1924. Following the periodic appearance of factional divisions, the PKP split along ethnic lines in 1943, with the Arab breakaway faction called the League for National Liberation. In October 1948, with the new state of Israel gaining control of most of Palestine, the two groups reunited to form the Israeli Communist Party (Miflaga Kommunistit Isra'elit; MAKI).

The movement split again in 1965, partly along ethnic lines. The RAKAH—pro-Moscow, strongly anti-Zionist, and primarily Arab in membership, although with many Jewish leaders—soon eclipsed the almost completely Jewish and increasingly moderate MAKI. The latter's disappearance by the late 1970s left RAKAH as the undisputed communist party of Israel and the internationally recognized successor to the pre-1965 communist organizations. Although the name RAKAH is still used for electoral purposes, there is an increasing tendency to reclaim the designation of MAKI (Mark Segal, "'Palestinization' Alarm Bells," *Jerusalem Post*, international edition). With Arab nationalist parties not permitted (although the joint Arab-Jewish Progressive List for Peace [PLP] emerged in 1984 to espouse the cause of Palestinian self-determination and thus to compete for the Arab vote), RAKAH has served mainly as an outlet for the grievance of the Arab (Palestinian) minority. Almost all of the party's vote—at least 85 percent—comes from the Arab population (the CPI-dominated DFPE got about 50 percent of the Arab vote in 1977, 38 percent in 1981, and 34 percent in 1984). The DFPE has dominated most Arab town councils since the 1970s.

**Leadership and Party Organization.** The organization of the CPI is typical of communist parties in general. According to Central Committee Secretary George Tubi, "All party organisations are to ensure strict observance of the principles of democratic centralism and party rules and to apply unhesitatingly the tested weapon of criticism and self-criticism" (*WMR*, June). The congress normally meets at four-year intervals and chooses members of the Central Committee, the Central Control Commission, the Presidium, and the Secretariat. There are also regional committees, local branches, and cells (the latter based on both residence and place of work). The CPI is said to be the best organized political party in Israel, which gives it an important advantage in its rivalry with the PLP for Arab votes.

George Tubi reported that membership in the CPI increased by 30.2 percent between the nineteenth and twentieth congresses. But he stressed the need to continue gaining members—"especially from among the working class, women and the younger generation." (Ibid.) General Secretary Meir Vilner also called on members to encourage women to join the party and asked "veterans who had built up the party" and "the young" to show mutual respect (*IB*, March). The 600 delegates at the Twentieth Congress represented 90 local party organizations, but the total number of such organizations had reached 95 (up from 86 four years earlier) (ibid.).

Although perhaps 80 percent of the members of the CPI are Arabs, Jews predominate in the top party organs. In recent years, the Jewish general secretary has been balanced by an Arab deputy general secretary. Although the party has been noted as a nearly unique arena of Arab-Jewish amity, there are reports of dissatisfaction on the part of Arabs because of their inadequate representation at the top.

**Domestic Party Affairs.** No information is available on meetings of party organs during the year.

Party leaders stressed economic problems resulting from military expenditures. Ali Ashour, the CPI representative on the *World Marxist Review* (and member of the Central Committee) wrote of "the calamitous economic situation," pointing to the unprecedented unemployment rate approaching 10 percent and a "catastrophically" high inflation rate (without mentioning recent improvements in the latter) and demanded that money be used for food and jobs rather than for armaments and settling occupied territories (*WMR*, January). Vilner spoke of "social programs being decimated and real wages pushed down" (*IB*, July).

Vilner also pointed to "racist campaigns" calling for expulsion of Arabs and to the growth of "the dangerous idea that the country needs a strong man" (ibid.). George Tubi warned of the dangers coming from "Jewish fascist terrorist groups" like Rabbi Meir Kahane's "racist gangs" who "receive covert and overt support from influential circles in the ruling Zionist establishment" (*WMR*, June).

The condition of the Arab minority continued to be a major concern. Emphasis was put on the inadequacy of funding for Arab communities and the neglect of Arab education more than on the expropriation of land (*CSM*, 4 April). Tawfiq Zayyad, Knesset member and the communist mayor of Nazareth, told a Knesset committee that unemployment in Nazareth is "a pressure cooker with the lid coming off" and pointed to a "nearly 30 percent" unemployment rate in the Arab town (*Jerusalem Post*, international edition, 8–14 June).

As usual, the CPI played an important role in organizing the annual Day of the Land (31 March) among the Arabs of Israel and the occupied territories. There were protest demonstrations in various Arab communities, but all were peaceful. Most Arabs did not respond to the PLP's call for a strike but chose to participate in CPI demonstrations demanding "equal rights" (*CSM*, 4 April).

In June, the DFPE was one of five groups in the Knesset that introduced unsuccessful no-confidence motions relating to the issue of two teenage hijackers whose death at the hands of security forces following their arrest in 1984 had been unsuccessfully covered up (*Jerusalem Post*, 29 June–5 July).

Mordechai Vanunu, the Israeli nuclear technician who revealed alleged secrets about his state's nuclear weapons stockpile, was said to have been a member of the CPI (*NYT*, 10 November) but elsewhere as having only "applied for membership" (*Jerusalem Post*, international edition, 16–22 November). In any case, no one has suggested that the party was involved.

President Chaim Herzog met with Vilner in March (*Pravda*, 1 April). As was the case with the president's message of greeting to the Twentieth CPI

Congress, this unprecedented courtesy extended to the party was widely understood to be fitting in the context of ongoing tentative efforts to improve Israeli-Soviet relations.

**Auxiliary and Front Organizations.** The CPI dominates the DFPE, which includes two noncommunist partners: the Black Panthers (an Afro-Asian or Oriental Jewish group protesting discrimination by Jews of European origin) and the Arab Local Council Heads. Aside from the one member of the Black Panthers included in the DFPE delegation in the Knesset, there was formerly (1977–1981) a representative of the Arab Local Council Heads. The fifth member of the list in the 1984 election represented the same group. The DFPE is also organized on the local level, particularly in Arab towns and villages.

According to George Tubi, the twentieth congress "rejected the false assumption. . . about 'progressive Zionism,'" but the party is nevertheless open to "cooperation with Zionist elements on some practical common issues as was the case in the antiwar movement during the Lebanese war" and in fact "calls for the establishment of the widest possible Jewish-Arab front so as to rebuff the racist onslaught and the fascist threat" (*WMR*, June).

The CPI sponsors the active Young Pioneers and the Young Communist League (which, according to Vilner, is growing in membership [*IB*, July]). According to Ashour, communists were active in the formation in 1982 of the Committee Against the War in Lebanon and "formed a note-worthy role in inaugurating the There Is a Limit organisation, which calls upon Israeli servicemen. . . to refuse to serve in the occupation forces in Lebanon." He listed Mothers Against the War, Soldiers Against Silence, and Women for Peace as recently formed organizations with which the CPI cooperates, in addition to "various committees for solidarity with the Palestinian population in areas seized by Israel." (Ibid., January.) At least in the past, the CPI sponsored or actively participated in the Committee for the Defense of Arab Land. Ashour reported that to assure the "growth and unity" of the antiwar movement, the CPI considers support for Peace Now to be "expedient. . . despite the vagueness of its demands and the anti-communism of some of its members" (ibid.). The CPI also participates in the Democratic Women's Movement, the Israel-USSR Friendship Movement, the Israeli Association of Anti-Fascist Fighters and Victims of Nazism, and Arab student committees (which its members have long dominated at some universities). A student organization called "Campus" at Ben-Gurion University in Beersheba (and formerly headed by Vanunu) is said to be (or to have been) affiliated with the CPI and the PLP (*Jerusalem Post*, international edition, 9–15 November).

**International Views, Positions, and Activities.** Eighteen foreign delegations participated in the Twentieth CPI Congress in December 1985, which was opened with greetings to the Palestinian Communist Party and to Palestine Liberation Organization (PLO) chairman Yasir Arafat (Jerusalem, *The Soviet Union and the Middle East* 11, no. 1). There was also a message from Arafat and "from the population of the Golan Heights" (*IB*, March). Zayyad "spoke on behalf of the Palestinian Communist Party" (ibid., July).

The CPI Central Committee designated Vilner and al-Qasim (editor of the magazine *al-Jadid*) to participate in the Twenty-seventh Congress of the CPSU (Tel Aviv, *Ma'ariv*, 25 February; *FBIS*, 26 February).

Vilner also participated in the Eleventh Congress of the Socialist Unity Party of the German Democratic Republic in April. While in Berlin, he met with CPSU general secretary Mikhail Gorbachev for 45 minutes (Tel Aviv, IDF Radio, 23 April; *FBIS*, 24 April). During the same month, Zahi Karkabi, alternate member of the CPI Central Committee, headed a delegation to the Thirteenth Congress of the Bulgarian Communist Party (BCP) and concluded a protocol for cooperation between the two parties during 1986–1987 (Sofia, BTA, 10 April; *FBIS*, 13 May). Also, a three-man delegation of DFPE members of the Histadrut (General federation of labor) visited Prague for talks with the World Federation of Trade Unions (Prague, ČETEKA, 19 April; *FBIS*, 8 May). Vilner received a delegation of the Romanian Communist Party (RCP) that was in Israel to participate in the Labor Party Congress in April (Bucharest, Agerpress, 11 April; *FBIS*, 5 May).

Interviews with David Khenin and Emile Habibi (members of the CPI Politburo) were published in the Prague newspaper *Rudé právo* on 22 May and 6 June respectively (*The Soviet Union and the Middle East* 11, no. 8). Habibi was leading a CPI delegation to Prague at the time and meeting with Czech party leaders (Prague Domestic Service, 17 June; *FBIS*, 19 June).

In June, a CPI delegation consisting of Vilner, Khenin, and George Tubi visited Hungary and met with top party and state officials, including János Kádár. An interview with Vilner was published in *Népszabadság*, with his picture on the front page— indicating that the visit was considered quite important (*The Soviet Union and the Middle East* 11, no. 8).

Ruth Lublitz, a member of the CPI Central Committee, participated in the Tenth Congress of the Polish United Workers' Party (PUWP) and discussed problems related to future CPI-PUWP cooperation (Warsaw, PAP, 9 July; *FBIS*, 5 August). Vilner and Ashour were guests of the RCP (Bucharest, Agerpress, 16 September; *FBIS*, 17 September).

Eliezer Filler, a member of the CPI, along with four non-communist Israelis visited Romania in November for talks with representatives of the PLO. They claimed not to represent any political parties as such. Prime Minister Yitzhak Shamir called them traitors, and Israeli police interrogated them upon their return. (*Jerusalem Post*, international edition, 16–22 November.)

Statements by CPI leaders deplored all aspects of Israeli foreign policy. Vilner desribed the Israeli government as "now fully dependent on the United States" and on military production, exportation of weapons to dictatorships, and "training fascist armies" to the extent that peace would create an economic crisis for the country; the growth of Latin American democracy was described as already producing a "disaster" for Israel. Israel's cooperation with South Africa in economic matters and atomic research was singled out for condemnation, as was its "anti-Soviet position" (*IB*, July).

George Tubi wrote of "the consistent policy of the Soviet Union aimed at preventing nuclear war, curbing the arms race, and strengthening peaceful coexistence" (*WMR*, June). CPI statements generally paralleled Soviet positions, while joint statements with Bulgarian and Czech communist leaders stressed agreement on all issues. In response to an interviewer's question, Politburo member David Burnstein said that his party had "shown interest" in what the interviewer called "prisoners of Zion" in the USSR and had "been asking and trying to find out why these still are being held" but refused to "come out publicly for" their cause (Tel Aviv, *Ma'ariv*, 22 February; *FBIS*, 26 February). George Tubi described the "growing threat of nuclear confrontation and of an intensified arms race brought about by the aggressive global policy of U.S. imperialism and the monstrous plan of the Reagan administration to militarise outer space" (*WMR*, June). The United States attack on Libya was "strongly condemned" by the DFPE delegation to Czechoslovakia (Prague, ČETEKA, 19 April; *FBIS*, 8 May).

On the Arab-Israeli conflict, George Tubi condemned his government's "aggressive policy" and its occupation of Arab territories. He reiterated his party's call for withdrawal from all occupied territories, acceptance of Palestinian self-determination (and in particular of an independent Palestinian state), the right of Palestinian refugees to choose between return and compensation, and the right of both Israel and the Arab states to "sovereign existence and development"; he insisted on the necessity of an international conference, with Israel, PLO, U.S., and Soviet participation, to implement these principles. (*WMR*, June.)

Several statements by CPI leaders strongly denounced Zionism. As a case in point, Vilner described it as "a reactionary movement which cannot be progressive" (*IB*, March).

**Other Marxist Groups.** For information on the Israeli Socialist Organization (Matzpen) and groups that have broken away from it, including the Revolutionary Communist League, see *YICA*, 1982 and 1984.

# PALESTINE COMMUNIST PARTY

**Population.** Over 4,500,000 (estimated) Palestinians, including 930,000 in the West Bank (including East Jerusalem), 560,000 in the Gaza Strip, more than 600,000 in Israel (*Jerusalem Post*, international edition, 27 April–3 May, 2–8 November), and more than 1.4 million in Jordan (East Bank) (estimated)
**Party.** Palestine Communist Party (al-Hizb al Shuyu'i al-Filastini; PCP)
**Founded.** 1982
**Membership.** 200 (estimated)
**General Secretary.** (Presumably) Bashir al-Barghuti (journalist)

**Politburo.** Sulayman al-Najjab, Na'im Abbas al-Ashhab; others not known
**Secretariat.** No data
**Central Committee.** Dhamin Awdah, Mahir al-Sharif, Sulayman al-Nashshab, Ali Ahmad, Mahmud al-Rawwaq, Na'im Abbas al-Ashhab, Mahmud Abu-Shamas; others not known
**Status.** Illegal, but tolerated to a large extent in Israeli-occupied areas
**Last Congress.** First, 1984
**Last Election.** N/a
**Auxiliary Organizations.** Progressive Workers' Bloc (PWB)
**Publications.** *Al-Tali'ah* (The vanguard; weekly newspaper edited by Bashir al-Barghuti)

The roots of the communist movement among Palestinians in the Israeli-occupied West Bank and Gaza Strip and among those in diaspora can be traced to the pre-1948 Palestine Communist Party and particularly to the post-1943 breakaway faction, the League for National Liberation, as well as to the Communist Party of Jordan (CPJ). According to PCP Politburo member Ashhab, one remnant of the League for National Liberation evolved into the Gaza Strip Palestine Communist Party in 1953. Other Palestinians joined communist parties (particularly the CPJ) in the various Arab countries in which they resided. In 1974, the section of the CPJ in the West Bank became the West Bank Communist Organization, and with the addition of members from the Gaza Strip, the group became the West Bank and Gaza Strip Palestinian Communist Organization (PCO). Members of the CPJ in Lebanon became the Palestinian Communist Organization (PCO) in Lebanon (*WMR*, February 1983).

With the approval of the CPJ, the PCP was organized in February 1982. The party was to include communists in the Gaza Strip and the West Bank, members of the PCO in Lebanon, and all Palestinian members of the CPJ except for those living in Jordan, that is, the East Bank.

**Leadership and Party Organization.** Relatively little is known about the organization of the PCP. The First (constituent) Congress met in 1984 and adopted a program and rules for the party, as well as selecting the members of the Politburo, Secretariat, and Central Committee. Several non-PCP sources refer to Barghuti as the party's leader, but there is no evidence that he is necessarily the general secretary.

According to Ashhab, the members of the PCP and of its First Congress tended to be young. Also, about half the members are workers, and this was reflected in the composition of the congress as well, since party rules require that there be one delegate representing each 30 workers while other delegates

each represent 50 nonworker members. (See *YICA*, 1986.)

**Palestinian Affairs.** According to Politburo member Najjab, the PCP "works within and outside the occupied areas" (East Berlin, *Neues Deutschland*, 24 April). As has been emphasized by its leaders, the party has been particularly active within the occupied territories.

The PCP is illegal in the occupied territories, but although concern for security sometimes leads to crackdowns (and there have been reports of individuals arrested at times for possessing communist literature), it is in fact generally tolerated. Barghuti, who was once imprisoned by the Jordanians, now edits the weekly party newspaper, *al-Tali'ah*, in East Jerusalem. There were reports in the past of another PCP newspaper, *al-Watan* (Homeland), presumably published outside the occupied territories. Statements of the PCP are also disseminated by the CPI press, particularly by *al-Ittihad*.

The PCP is not represented in the Palestine National Council (PNC), the Executive Committee, or other organs of PLO, which is an umbrella group for the main organizations in the Palestine national movement. However, the PCP has been actively involved with other Palestinian organizations. In 1984, it joined with the Popular Front for the Liberation of Palestine (PFLP), the Democratic Front for the Liberation of Palestine (DFLP), and the smaller Palestine Liberation Front to form the Democratic Alliance, which undertook an intermediate position in the conflict between PLO chairman Yasir Arafat and the Syrian-backed National Alliance. According to the Aden agreement worked out by the Democratic Alliance and Arafat's supporters in June 1984, the PCP was to be represented in the PNC, thus giving it full recognition within the Palestine national movement. However, the National Alliance rejected the Aden agreement, and when the Seventeenth Palestine National Council finally met in Amman in November 1984, the PCP and its allies in the Democratic Alliance did not participate. Yet three seats on the fourteen-member Executive Committee were left open, possibly to be filled later by groups that boycotted the session, presumably including the PCP.

The PCP condemned the agreement between King Hussein of Jordan and Chairman Arafat in 1985. However, although the PFLP joined pro-Syrian factions to form the National Palestine Salvation Front to oppose the agreement, neither the DFLP nor the PCP did so.

With King Hussein's February announcement that he was ending his effort to work with Arafat on a peace initiative, the PCP was involved in renewed efforts to settle intra-Palestinian differences. Najjab described the 1985 agreement between the PLO's "official leadership" and Jordan as a "deal directed against the national program and aims of the Palestinian people" (*Pravda*, 4 March; *FBIS*, 19 March). But there now seemed to be a possibility that Arafat would renounce the agreement and that this would allow the intra-Palestinian rift to be bridged (*NYT*, 2 March). On 22 February, leaders of the PCP and the DFLP called for rapprochement with Arafat's faction if Arafat would cancel the agreement, convene the PNC, and permit creation of a collective leadership for the PLO (Washington, *Journal of Palestine Studies*, Summer). Fatah, the largest component of the Palestine national movement (and headed by Arafat) was said to be in contact with other Palestinian organizations, including the members of the Palestine Salvation Front (and presumably the PCP), with the goal of convening an emergency PNC to restore Palestinian unity, and some Arab governments and the USSR were being asked to provide their good offices (Kuwait News Agency, 22 February; *FBIS*, 24 February).

Representatives of the PCP and four other groups (Fatah, the Arab Liberation Front, the DFLP, and the Palestine Liberation Front, but not including any components of the Palestine National Salvation Council) reached agreement, apparently at the beginning of August, to convene the PNC within 45 days (*Journal of Palestine Studies*, Autumn). This was apparently related to talks held in Moscow at about the same time and sponsored by the Soviet government. At these talks in which the PCP, Fatah, and the DFLP participated, Ashhab represented the PCP. Progress was reported, with Fatah agreeing to abrogate the agreement with Jordan once the proposed PNC session began in Algiers. But the Palestine National Salvation Front subsequently announced that it rejected any such

PNC meeting unless Arafat renounced the agreement in advance. (Ridgewood, N.J., *Middle East Monitor*, 1 September; *NYT*, 15 August.) And so the reconciliation was aborted.

In line with the PCP's consistent support for the concept of a "two-state" solution to the Palestine conflict, Najjab reiterated its support for "our people's right to a homeland and to the formation of an independent state on the West Bank . . . including the Arab sector of Jerusalem and the Gaza Strip." He invoked the programs adopted by the Fez Arab summit conference of 1982 and Soviet proposals for a settlement. He noted the Israelis' "brutal oppression of our people," the seizure of Arab land, and "fascist activity by bands of Zionist extremists" and warned of "a serious danger of new mass atrocities and the banishment of hundreds of thousands of Palestinians from their homeland." (*Pravda*, 4 March; *FBIS*, 19 March.)

Najjab also reiterated the PCP's acceptance of the PLO "as the sole legitimate representative of the Palestinian people" and called for its participation "on an independent and equal basis" in an international peace conference (*Pravda*, 4 March; *FBIS*, 19 March).

**Auxiliary and Front Organizations.** The PWB, which is closely tied to the PCP, has long dominated the General Federation of Trade Unions (GFTU) in the West Bank. The PWB's hegemony was threatened during the late 1970s and early 1980s by the emergence of increasingly important groups associated with various guerrilla organizations. This led (in 1981) to the formation of a rival GFTU by a Fatah-backed group, and the PWB was also faced with serious rivalry in the original GFTU. Yet as the Israelis detained, imprisoned, and deported leading members of the rival Workers' Unity Bloc during 1985, the PWB was again able to reassert its primacy in elections for the (original) GFTU executive committee in September of that year. (Joost R. Hiltermann, "The Emerging Trade Union Movement in the West Bank," *Merip Reports*, October–December.) The release of PWB leader George Hazboun from town arrest that same September was apparently another tactic used by the Israeli occupation authorities to manipulate rivalry between his group and the non-PCP-related factions.

There is little information on other auxiliary organizations. But PCO or PCP involvement with student and professional groups has been reported in the past.

In effect, the PLO is a government-in-exile. Its supporters and its leadership span the political spectrum. Its dominant component, Fatah, might in a sense be called a united front, since it avoids ideolgy in favor of pursuing a national cause. It contains some Marxists but is dominated by centrists like Arafat and has a history of rivalry with the PCP, which sometimes accuses it of being rooted in the Palestinian bourgeoisie and criticizes its ties with conservative Arab regimes. Small groups like the PFLP and the DFLP are Marxist but are not considered to be communist.

The Palestine National Front was organized in 1973 as an alliance of communists and others in the occupied territories. It gained some importance for a while but withered before the end of the decade (see *YICA*, 1985).

**International Views, Positions, and Activities.** Najjab participated in the Twenty-seventh Congress of the CPSU in February and March (*Pravda*, 4 March; *FBIS*, 19 March) and in the Eleventh Congress of the Socialist Unity Party (SED) of the German Democratic Republic (GDR) in April (*Neues Deutschland*, 24 April). The PLO was also represented at each of these congresses— by Faruq Qaddumi, head of the Political Department, at the CPSU congress (Baghdad, Voice of the PLO, 28 February; *FBIS*, 21 April). Another PCP delegation, headed by Ashhab, visited Bulgaria from 29 September to 4 October as guests of the Central Committee of the Bulgarian Communist Party (Sofia, BTA, 4 October; *FBIS*, 8 October). Ashhab also was the PCP representative at the meeting of the *World Marxist Review* Editorial Council in Prague (*WMR*, July). On 17 May, along with seven other communist and workers' parties of the Arab East countries, the PCP joined in a call for an "End [to] Repression and Terror in Jordan" (*IB*, July). Barghuti was scheduled to participate in an Amnesty International conference in the United States in June, but the Israeli occupation authorities refused to allow him to go (London, *Index on Censorship*, August).

Leaders of the PCP consistently praised the USSR. Najjab told the Twenty-seventh CPSU Congress that the USSR's loyalty to Marxism-Leninism had earned it "the trust of all Soviet people" and proclaimed support for Soviet "initiatives and proposals," particularly those that "envisage the total elimination of nuclear and chemical weapons." Washington was described as "mainly rely[ing] on the aggressive 'strategic alliance' . . . with Israel's rulers" aimed at "patriotic regimes in the region" and as "subordinating the entire region to its military and political domination and turning it into a bridgehead for nuclear missiles aimed at the Soviet Union" (*Pravda*, 4 March; *FBIS*, 19 March). At the SED congress, he praised the German Democratic Republic's "peace policy," described the United States attack on Libya as "the expression of its aggressive policy," called the United States' "strategic alliance with the ruling circles in Israel" a design to prevent "a just solution to the Palestine question," and "welcome[d] the friendly position of the Israeli Communist Party in supporting the just struggle of our people" (*Neues Deutschland*, 24 April).

Glenn E. Perry
*Indiana State University*

# Jordan

**Population.** 2,794,000 (excluding the West Bank and East Jerusalem)
**Party.** Communist Party of Jordan (al-Hizb al-Shuyu'i al Urduni; CPJ)
**Founded.** 1951
**Membership.** Accurate estimate not available
**General Secretary.** Fa'ik (Fa'iq) Warrad
**Leading Bodies.** No data
**Status.** Proscribed
**Last Congress.** Second, December 1983
**Last Election.** N/a
**Auxiliary Organizations.** None
**Publications.** *al-Jamahir, al-Haqiqa*

After the partition of Palestine, the League for National Liberation (the communist party of undivided Palestine since 1943) changed the party's name in June 1951 to the Communist Party of Jordan. The Central Committee headed by Fu'ad Nassar opposed the annexation of eastern Palestine (renamed the West Bank) by King Abdullah and called for establishment of an independent Palestinian state in accordance with the United Nations General Assembly resolution 181 (II) of 29 November 1947.

The CPJ entered the Jordanian parliamentary election campaign of 1951 under the name Popular Front, and three of its candidates were elected. It campaigned on a practical platform that called for legalizing political parties and trade unions, land reform, and industrialization to provide employment.

The Partisans for Peace also provided an outlet for the CPJ, which attracted establishment figures and nationalists. In addition to its official organ, *al-Muqawamah al-Sha'biyah* (Popular resistance), the CPJ issued two others in 1952: *al-Jabha* (The front) and *al-Raye* (Opinion).

The government clamped down by sentencing the CPJ's general secretary, Fu'ad Nasser, to ten years of rigorous imprisonment in December 1951. Two years later, it amended the Law to Combat Communism, making any association with party activities illegal and punishable by a jail sentence ranging from three to fifteen years. Despite these restrictions, the CPJ entered the 1954 parliamentary campaign under the name National Front, organized mass demonstrations against the Baghdad Pact, and together with nationalist parties, helped create the atmosphere in which Jordan terminated the 1948 Anglo-Jordanian Treaty in 1956. The CPJ polled 13 percent of the vote in the 1956 elections and was the first communist party in the Arab East to be represented in the cabinet. A subsequent all-out offensive by King Hussein's army, backed by the Eisenhower administration, led to the ouster of the cabinet, imposition of martial law, dissolution of the parliament, and imprisonment of communist deputies and hundreds of communists, most of whom remained in prison until the general amnesty of April 1965.

During the 1960s, the CPJ aligned itself with Egypt and Syria in accordance with the prevailing Soviet policy of cooperation with the national bourgeois regimes in the Third World. The party benefited from the decision of the Jordanian government to exchange full diplomatic relations with the Soviet Union in August 1963, but it continued to function clandestinely.

The party's 1964 program called for rapid industrialization, social welfare legislation, and a non-aligned foreign policy for Jordan. It endorsed the first Arab summit meeting of January 1964 and the creation of the Palestine Liberation Organization (PLO). But when its new official organ, *al-Taqadum* (Progress), published a front-page article that considered Arab solidarity a positive trend and regarded Jordan as progressive, an internal party rift ensued. Elements responsible for the article were purged as right-wing deviationists.

The 1967 Israeli occupation of the remainder of Palestine and the consequent rise of an independent Palestinian resistance based largely in Jordan provided impetus for the re-emergence of oppositional political forces in the country. The CPJ enjoyed a period of relative toleration by the regime, interrupted by occasional repression. Following the rift between King Hussein and Yasir Arafat in February 1986 and the U.S. aerial raid on Libya that April, student demonstrations at one of Jordan's universities (al-Yarmouk) in which many people were killed or injured provided an opportunity for the government to crack down on the party. In May the government arrested all seventeen CPJ leaders, blaming the CPJ for the student protests. They were released on 4 September, but the party remained officially banned. In July, on the occasion of his sixtieth birthday, the party's general secretary, Warrad, received several congratulatory messages from East European communist parties and was awarded the Order of International Friendship by the USSR Supreme Soviet Presidium (*FBIS*, July 16).

**Party Internal Affairs.** Following a congress of the CPJ in 1970 in Amman, an internal rift in the party produced a faction led by Fahmi Salfiti and Rushdi Shain. This left-wing faction operated under the name of the Communist Party of Jordan–Leninist Cadre and began to publish the newspaper *al-Haqiqa* (Truth—not to be confused with the journal of the same name published by the CPJ).

The CPJ became involved in PLO politics after the 1967 Israeli occupation, and until the formation of the Palestine Communist Party (PCP) in 1982, its work centered on the West Bank.

The 1970 CPJ congress established the Ansar militia to contribute to armed Palestinian resistance against Israeli occupation. Two years later, Nassar was elected to the Palestine National Council (PNC). In 1974, the CPJ published a transitional plan that influenced the posture of the Democratic Front for the Liberation of Palestine (DFLP) and,

ultimately, the PNC decision to struggle for establishment of an independent Palestinian state.

In late December 1981, the CPJ's Central Committee decided to authorize the Palestinian Communist Organization (PCO)—the leading component of the Palestine National Front (PNF) in the occupied West Bank and Gaza—to prepare for establishment of an independent Palestinian communist party (*IB*, March 1982). The PCP, which continued the work of the PNF underground, was established on 10 February 1982 (*WMR*, February). In November 1985, the CPJ's Central Committee issued a major statement declaring that "the unity of the communists of Jordan...has been attained" in accordance with Warrad's May 14, 1985, initiative. The party defined itself as "one of the contingents of the internationalist communist movement" and, simultaneously, of "the Arab national liberation movement" struggling against "any revisionist encroachments on Marxism-Leninism...whether from the right or from the 'left'...against the threat of nuclear war" and working for consolidation of the policy of peaceful coexistence, international détente, and disarmament. (*IB*, February.)

**Domestic Attitudes and Activities.** The CPJ leaders have consistently denounced the Jordanian regime for following a "course aimed at suppressing democracy and civil rights and liberties" (ibid., April). In the first half of October 1984, the Central Committee of the CPJ held an enlarged plenary meeting and adopted resolutions against what it described as a reign of terror in Jordan. It called on "the popular masses and on all national patriotic forces to close their ranks and continue the struggle to end the policy of terror and persecution and ensure healthy and democratic operation of the parliament which will enable the people to exercise their basic rights and freedoms" (ibid.). The resolutions also decried the economic crises manifested in "a drop in production, a decrease of national income...an increase in the deficit of the trade balance and the balance of payments." Jordan is described as a consumerist society dominated by a parasitical bourgeoisie that relies on remittances from the Persian Gulf and by a bureaucratic bourgeoisie that creates state enterprises. The tensions between these two, as well as the growing number of indigenous and foreign laborers deprived of the benefits of social legislation and trade unionism, provide the CPJ with the opportunity to mobilize support among workers, students, women, and the youth. Jordanian communists are represented in the General Secretariat of the Alignment of Popular and Trade Union Forces as well as on the newly established Committee of Political Parties and Organizations. The program of the CPJ congress of December 1983 called on the party membership to work for formation of a "broad national democratic front of workers, peasants, members of the petty and national bourgeoisie and revolutionary intellectuals in order to bring about national democratic rule." (See Fa'iq Warrad's article in *WMR*, July 1984.) The November 1985 statement of the CPJ's Central Committee reaffirmed the call for such a front identifying the national bourgeoisie as that "connected with industrial and agricultural production" (*IB*, February). The statement described the party's strategy as seeking establishment of a "national democratic power" on the basis of economic planning, breaking away from the world capitalist market and from the "Camp David bloc." More specifically, the party's strategy in the internal arena called for termination of the 11 February 1985 Amman Agreement between Hussein and Arafat; ensuring the freedom of assembly and association, including the right to organize trade unions and political parties and to strike; utilization of national resources for industrialization in cooperation with "progressive" Arab countries; pursuit of a radical agrarian reform providing for the confiscation of large landed estates and their distribution among the poor peasantry; and the establishment of equality between the sexes, together with the development of public programs to satisfy educational, health, and social security needs. (Ibid.)

Together with seven communist and workers' parties of the Arab East, the CPJ issued a statement deploring the Framework of Common Action signed by King Hussein and Yasir Arafat on 11 February 1985 (ibid., May 1985). The signatories of the statement called for "a fight to foil it [and] expressed spiritual solidarity with the opposition to it displayed by the patriotic Palestinian masses, organizations and leaders in and outside the occupied territories." Another statement by the CPJ's Central Committee (November 1985) considered the Framework and its antecedent—the October 1984 Amman session of the Palestine National Council—as having had "grave negative results in the political and organizational spheres." It "infringed on the Palestinian people's inalienable national rights, above all its right to the creation of its own independent national state," and it "denied the PLO the right to represent independently the Palestinian people." (Ibid., February.)

**Auxiliary and Mass Organizations.** Jordan's all-out offensive against the PLO in September 1970 and Israel's de facto annexation of the West Bank and Gaza Strip spawned the indigenous nonviolent resistance, under the banner of the PNF, inside the West Bank. Organized in August 1973, the PNF attracted a broad nationalist coalition reminicent of the 1950s. The PNF organized against land expropriation and publicized various grievances under the 1949 Geneva Conventions in the Israeli Parliament through the Israeli communist party. It urged Arab businessmen not to pay taxes to the occupation authorities and organized mass demonstrations against Israeli expulsion of Palestine leaders from the occupied territories. Israel clamped down on the PNF in April 1974 and placed many of its leaders under administrative detention. The Soviet newpaper *Pravda* (18 June), reporting on the arrests in Jordan in connection with the Yarmouk University demonstrations, identified the arrested as activists of the JCP, the Jordanian-Soviet Friendship Society, the Jordanian Committee for Peace and Solidarity and trade unions (*FBIS*, 19 June).

**International Activities and Attitudes.** An October 1983 article by Izhaq al-Khatib, member of the CPJ Politburo, advocated a policy of close relations with the Arab national liberation movement (*WMR*, October 1983). The program of the congress of December 1983 recognized serious difficulties facing the Arab national liberation movement, which it attributed to the "abandonment of radical positions by the majority of patriotic Arab regimes" and the inability of the petty-bourgeois regimes to preserve gains made in the 1960s.

During 1984, however, the CPJ began to distinguish beween various Arab and Third World countries on the basis of the "degree of social development" attained by each country. In countries such as the People's Democratic Republic of Yemen and Ethiopia, the "national democratic revolution has achieved a reasonably high level of development." These countries thus formed "vanguard parties guided by the theory of Scientific Socialism, Marxism-Leninism." In countries such as Jordan and Saudi Arabia, however, where the "national and revolutionary forces are crushed and persecuted," it has been necessary to form a broad coalition of nationalist and leftist parties. "The parties of the working class must therefore assume the chief role at precisely this stage" in order to build socialism (*IB*, March 1984). The 1985 literature of the CPJ, however, recognizes the difficulties facing that prospect: "The 'oil era,' the flood of 'petrodollars,' the growing influence of the oil-producing countries of the Persian Gulf Cooperative Council [have] . . . led to an increase in pressure for capitulationist settlement options, and the growing threat of the United States establishing its control over the regime within the framework of the strategic alliance [with Israel]" (ibid., Feburary).

The CPJ joined a number of communist parties from eastern Europe, the Soviet Union, Latin America, North America, and the Third World at a conference held in Prague to consider the program of the Twenty-seventh Congress of the CPSU (*WMR*, July). Many speakers emphasized the importance of the CPSU's conclusion that it is crucial to "put an end to outdated political thinking and to develop and introduce into international practice a new type of conciousness consistent with the realities of the nuclear age." That conciousness was said to require an entrenchment of the Leninist concept of peaceful coexistence into international relations. "To think of categories of military strength in our day is to accept the possibility of humanity commit-

ting suicide." (Ibid.) The conference condemned the use of military power to attain political objectives: "The arms race unleashed by the USA, its neoglobalist claims and . . . its disguised piracy" are new factors that contribute to the "escalation of international terrorism in the region." The attacks against Lebanon, Tunisia, Grenada, and Libya are milestones of that escalation—"one of the steps towards the assertion in Washington of the dangerous imperial philosophy that it can do anything it likes." (Ibid.)

Relations beween the Soviet Union and Jordan continue to be limited to ceremonial visits often concluded with joint statements endorsing the need for an international settlement of the Palestine question. The Soviet first deputy foreign minister visited Jordan and met with King Hussein and his prime minister on 29 August. Amman's daily *al-Dustour* editorialized thus: "The agreement between Amman and Moscow that achieving peace in the Middle East and solving its problems is possible only through an international conference . . . is one of the major points on which the two countries' viewpoints are identical" (*FBIS*, 2 September).

Naseer H. Aruri
*Southern Massachusetts University*

# Lebanon

**Population.** 2,675,000
**Party.** Lebanese Communist Party (al-Hizb al-Shuyu'i al-Lubnani; LCP). Organization of Communist Action in Lebanon (Munazzamat al-'Amal al-Shuyu'i; OCAL)
**Founded.** LCP: 1924. OCAL: 1970
**Membership.** LCP: 14,000–16,000 (claimed); 2,000–3,000 (CIA, *World Factbook*). OCAL: 1,500 (author's estimate)
**General Secretary.** LCP: George Hawi. OCAL: Muhsin Ibrahim
**Politburo.** LCP: 11 members

**Central Committee.** LCP: 24 members
**Status.** Both legal
**Last Congress.** LCP: Fourth, 1979; OCAL: First, 1971
**Last Elections.** 1972, no representation
**Auxiliary Organizations.** LCP: Communist Labor Organization, World Peace Council in Lebanon, and
a number of labor and student unions and movements
**Publications.** LCP: *al-Nida'* (The call) daily; *al-Akhbar* (The news) and *Kanch* (The call; in Armenian)
weeklies; *al-Tariq* (The road) quarterly. OCAL: *al-Hurriyya* (Freedom) weekly

The LCP was established in October 1924 as the
Lebanese People's Party. During the French mandate over Syria and Lebanon (1920–1946), the LCP
recruited members in both countries, but the Syrian
element dominated the party despite its name.

Initially, the communist appeal in Lebanon was
largely confined to the Orthodox Christians, particularly to the Greek Orthodox community, which
provided the bulk of the LCP's membership, both
leaders and followers. The historic ties between
Russia and the Orthodox communities of the Levant
no doubt explain this fact. In the early 1930s, Armenians also played a role in the LCP, but their
participation declined after 1932 and they were
supplanted by Arab members. For many years, the
factional character of the LCP hindered communist
efforts to attract a following among Lebanese Muslims; however, by the late 1960s, Shi'ite Muslims
had become attracted to the LCP in significant numbers, largely because the socioeconomically disadvantaged Shi'ites found the LCP's antiestablishment
slogans appealing.

The LCP was banned from 1939 until 1970, at
which time it, along with several other leftist organizations, was granted legal status by the Lebanese
government. Despite the LCP's lack of legal recognition prior to 1970, it was tolerated and often
participated (without success) in Lebanese parliamentary elections. On the eve of Lebanon's civil war
of 1975–1976, the LCP entered the leftist, Muslim-
dominated Front for Progressive Parties and National Forces, later known as the Lebanese National
Movement (LNM). The LNM was aligned with,
and often subordinate to, the Palestine Liberation
Organization (PLO).

Both the LCP and the OCAL participated in
Lebanon's civil war and continue to play active roles
in the country's political affairs. Nonetheless, since
the Israeli invasion of 1982 and the resultant decline
in the influence of the PLO in Lebanon, both organizations have found themselves increasingly on the
political and military defensive. In particular, the
ascendancy of Shi'ite movements, such as the Amal
and the Hizb Allah (Party of God), has led to a

palpable deterioration in the influence of the LCP
and the OCAL.

**Leadership and Organization.** Hawi has
served as the LCP's general secretary since 1979,
and Ibrahim has led the OCAL since its foundation
in 1970.

Although the congress, theoretically the highest
organ of the LCP, is supposed to convene every four
years, only four congresses have been held since
1924. The Fifth Congress is scheduled for February 1987 (for the draft Central Committee report
see *al-Nida'*, 6 July). The Fifth Congress may be the
scene for a serious challenge to Hawi's leadership.
His prime challenger is 'Abd al-Karim Muruwwa, a
Shi'ite Muslim, who might, in the current climate of
rampant religious factionalism, depose the Christian Hawi.

Authority is vested in the 24-member Central
Committee, which in turn elects the 11-member
Politburo (for a listing of Central Committee mem-
bers, see *YICA*, 1981).

Lebanese sources indicated that the LCP had
established a radio station in the vicinity of Sidon at
a cost of 18 million Lebanese pounds, about U.S.
$500,000. The station was to begin broadcasting in
September (Middle East News Agency, 7 August;
*FBIS*, 8 August).

The LCP maintains a well-organized and centrally controlled network of clandestine local cells,
which are in turn organized into districts and
regions. Hawi indicates that the LCP resisted
intraparty pressures to abolish the "underground
structure" and channel the party into "legal mass
work." He asserts that by maintaining secrecy the
LCP has managed to frustrate American, Israeli,
and Arab reactionary designs to eliminate the communists (*WMR*, November 1985). Both the LCP
and the OCAL maintain well-armed "self-defense"
paramilitary units that participate actively in street
battles and other "military operations."

**Domestic Views and Activities.** Throughout
the year, the LCP struggled to maintain its steadily

more tenuous position on the violent Lebanese political stage. The party clung to its alliance with the Druze Progressive Socialist Party (PSP) in the face of punishing attacks from the Shi'ite Amal movement. The LCP stressed its support for "fraternal" Syria and hewed closely to the Syrian line (*WMR*, February). On paper, the LCP is aligned with the Amal movement (and the PSP) in the National Union Front (NUF) that was created in 1985, but the alliance seemed devoid of much content during 1986, when the LCP found itself being pummelled by Amal.

The LCP consistently called for continuation of the struggle to liberate south Lebanon from Israeli control (ibid., November 1985). In 1982, the LCP, in cooperation with the OCAL and the Arab Socialist Action Party, created the Lebanese National Resistance Front (NRF). The NRF had achieved notable military successes against the Israeli army and its Lebanese proxy forces in south Lebanon (ibid., February; *al-Nida'*, 6 July); however, many attempts to carry out attacks in south Lebanon were thwarted in 1986 by Amal forces. Although Amal has vehemently denounced the Israeli-maintained security zone in the south, it is anxious to prevent attacks that may prompt retaliation by Israel (see Norton, *Amal and the Shi'a*, 1987). Moreover, the LCP's long-standing support for the Palestinian cause, and its many ties with Palestinian organizations, make it keenly suspect to Amal, which is clearly committed to preventing the re-establishment of an armed Palestinian presence in Lebanon. Despite the fact that the LCP took pains to castigate the "Palestinian right wing," thereby aligning itself with Syria and against Yasir Arafat, it still found itself at odds with Amal, which simply rejects the LCP's assertion that the Palestinians have a political role to play in Lebanon's "national democratic revolution" (*al-Nida'*, 6 July). Throughout the year, the LCP sought to distance itself from Arafat's attempt to re-establish his PLO power base in Lebanon, and when possible, it blamed Palestinian "rightists" for creating problems, as in November when the Central Committee blamed Arafat for clashes in Sidon (Beirut Domestic Service, 8 November; *FBIS*, 10 November).

The LCP continued to call for the enactment of "broad democratic reform" and a "radical sociopolitical restructuring" of Lebanon (*WMR*, November 1985). The principles for this reform, enunciated by Hawi, were as follows: complete eradication of confessionalism in Lebanese politics; electoral reforms, including a system of proportionate balloting; redistribution of powers between the executive and the legislature, with increasing power to the legislature; modernization of the bureaucracy; and a reorganization of the army (ibid.). The LCP demands are consistent with those unsuccessfully promoted by Syria in the Tripartite Agreement of December 1985, which had been signed by Nabih Berri of Amal, Walid Jumblatt of the PSP, and Elie Hobeika of the Lebanese Forces and which were rejected almost immediately thereafter by representatives of the Maronite community. Responsibility for failure of the December agreement was ascribed by Hawi to a group of pro-Israeli and pro-U.S. Maronite politicians who have a stake in a system that "conceals class monopoly" (*IB*, June).

Although LCP officials were critical of the Phalangist's "doctrinal-factional program," (*al-Nida'*, 6 July), they were clearly worried about a trend that they viewed as parallel, namely the Iranian-backed Hizb Allah's campaign to install Islamic rule in Lebanon. Just as Phalangist domination denies many Lebanese their rights, "Islamic hegemony... would be a new form of exploitation and domination making the Islamic bourgeoisie the strongest partner, even though it would certainly cede part of power to the Christian bourgeoisie" (*IB*, June). The LCP Central Committee draft report to the Fifth Congress reveals a clear apprehension that the "doctrinal ideology" of Islamic hegemonists will submerge the "national" ideology of Amal (*al-Nida'*, 6 July).

But if the LCP is concerned lest Berri's Amal lose its power struggle with Hizb Allah, many of the most serious problems faced by the LCP stemmed from Amal. On 7 January, Michel Wahid, an LCP official, was killed after being held—reputedly by Amal—for more than two months. The LCP Politburo declared a general mobilization in January (Voice of Lebanon, 25 January; *FBIS*, 29 January) after the rejection of the Tripartite Agreement. In early February, about a hundred LCP members were arrested by Amal in south Lebanon (Jerusalem Domestic Service, 10 February; *FBIS*, 11 February), apparently to prevent unauthorized military activities and to preclude LCP support for Palestinian fighters in the refugee camps of the south. In apparent reaction to the Amal arrests, clashes broke out throughout West Beirut (Voice of Lebanon, 9 February; *FBIS*, 10 February). Subsequently, 86 of those arrested were released (Beijing, Xinhua, citing Phalangist radio; *FBIS*, 13 February), but LCP sources said 30 leading members were still being held by Amal. Amal later seized fifteen more

LCP members in south Lebanon (Voice of Lebanon, 23 February; *FBIS*, 24 February).

Two prominent LCP officials, Khalil Nawsah and Suhayl Tawilah, were killed in early 1986 (*Pravda*, 3 March; *FBIS*, 20 March). Tawilah, editor in chief of *al-Tariq* and a member of the Central Committee, was found dead in Beirut (Beirut Domestic Service, 24 February; *FBIS*, 24 February). Kidnapped on 23 February by gunmen from Hizb Allah (Voice of Lebanon, 24 February; *FBIS*, 24 February), Tawilah was reputedly executed by Hizb Allah for his failure to hand over the assassins of a Hizb Allah official (Voice of Lebanon, 24 February; *FBIS*, 25 February).

Khalil Na'us, the LCP official responsible for West Beirut, and member of the Central Committee and the Politburo, was killed in West Beirut (Beirut Domestic Service, 20 February; FBIS, 21 February). A report that Amal was involved was denied by LCP sources (Voice of the Mountain, 22 February; *FBIS*, 24 February), but Amal was nonetheless thought to be responsible for the death, in response to which the LCP called a general strike for 21 February. The LCP asserted that isolationist forces were acting in line with the plan of Israel and the United States to distract attention from the main enemy in the south and to divert the campaign to end sectarianism in Lebanon (Voice of the Mountain, 20 February; *FBIS*, 21 February). One report, on the major Maronite radio station, indicated that a new organization, the Communist Revolutionaries Organization (Munazzamat al-Thawriyin al-Shuyu'iyin), had denounced the assassination of Na'us and threatened to punish those responsible in Amal's West Beirut security service (Voice of Lebanon, 21 February; *FBIS*, 21 February).

Hizb Allah and Amal were alleged to have joined forces in West Beirut against the LCP and the OCAL (Voice of Lebanon, 23 February; *FBIS*, 24 February). On 24 February Hizb Allah forces struck at LCP offices and at homes of LCP members. The Progressive Socialist Party ordered its members to protect LCP centers in West Beirut (Radio Free Lebanon, 24 February; *FBIS*, 24 February). Approximately 40 LCP members were arrested in West Beirut by Hizb Allah (Voice of Lebanon, 24 February; *FBIS*, 25 February).

Kamil al-Sabbah, an LCP official, was found murdered in al-Nabatiyah in south Lebanon (Radio Free Lebanon, 7 April; *FBIS*, 8 April), and LCP remained under pressure in the south and in Beirut through the remainder of the year.

**International Views and Contacts.** The LCP remains a strong and consistent supporter of the Soviet Union. The party "emphasizes the great role the Soviet Communist Party is playing in the area of consolidating the unity, power and status of the system of socialist countries" (*al-Nida'*, 6 July). Yet the USSR seems to have attempted to establish a relationship with Amal. In January, for instance, 25 wounded Amal fighters were sent to the Soviet Union for medical treatment (Beirut Domestic Service, 11 January; *FBIS*, 13 January).

The LCP speech at the Twenty-seventh CPSU Congress was delivered by Nadim 'Abd al-Samad, deputy general secretary of the LCP, who pointedly noted the murder of three LCP officials in Lebanon and stressed the importance of the LCP alliance with the PSP (which has enjoyed cordial relations with Moscow) (*Pravda*, 3 March; *FBIS*, 20 March). (Jumblatt represented the PSP at the congress, where he praised the USSR, condemned terrorism of all kinds, and called for the withdrawal of Israel from Lebanon and the maintenance of a truce between Israel and Lebanon following the withdrawal [*Pravda*, 2 March; *FBIS*, 19 March].) The month prior, it had been reported that the Soviets had intervened with Damascus in the question of the assassination of LCP officials in West Beirut (Voice of Lebanon, 26 February; *FBIS*, 27 February).

The LCP condemned the "Camp David deal" and subsequent U.S. proposals to settle the Arab-Israeli conflict. It maintains that the achievement of a lasting and just settlement of the conflict requires the withdrawal of Israel from all Arab territories occupied in 1967. The LCP also calls for an international peace conference, including representatives from the USSR, to settle the Middle East crisis. It rejects the 11 February 1985 agreement between Arafat and King Hussein to pursue a formula for PLO participation on a Jordanian delegation as "ignoring the rights of Palestinians, above all their right to national statehood, and [denying] the PLO its role as the sole legitimate representative of the Palestinians" (*WMR*, November 1985).

In May the LCP joined six other Arab communist parties and the Bahrain National Liberation Front in condemning Jordanian authorities for attacks on student demonstrators at the Yarmouk University (*IB*, July).

In September, Samad met in Warsaw with Polish United Workers Party Central Committee secretary Jozef Czyrek to discuss current developments (Warsaw, PAP, 16 September; *FBIS*, 17 September), and in Sofia with Bulgarian Communist Party Central Committee member Dimitur Stanishev (Sofia, BTA, 21 September; *FBIS*, 22 September).

**Publications.** The principal LCP publications are the Arabic-language daily newspaper *al-Nida'*, whose publisher is 'Abd al-Karim Muruwwa; the weekly *al-Akhbar*, and the quarterly *al-Tariq*. The party also publishes the weekly *Kanch* in the Armenian language. They contain articles on Lebanese political and socioeconomic issues, international and Arab politics, and Marxist-Leninist ideology. These organs often disseminate the news of illegal communist parties in the Middle East, although in recent years their publication or distribution has been disrupted because of the prevailing insecurity in Beirut. The OCAL publishes the weekly *al-Hurriyya* jointly with the Democratic Front for the Liberation of Palestine, a component organization of the PLO. Ibrahim is its publisher. Both the LCP and the OCAL also publish booklets and pamphlets.

**OCAL.** The precursor of the OCAL was the now defunct Arab Nationalist Movement (ANM) founded by Dr. George Habash in 1954. In 1969, as the ANM began to split into various groups after the 1967 Arab-Israeli war, Ibrahim and his colleagues established the Organization of Lebanese Socialists (OLS). In May 1970, the OLS merged with the smaller Socialist Lebanon Organization, led by Fawwaz Tarabulsi and a few dissident communists, to form the OCAL. This newly extablished "revolutionary" organization held its first congress in 1971, elected a Politburo, and designated Ibrahim its general secretary. Tarabulsi acts as the assistant secretary general.

The OCAL was part of the LNM (declared defunct in 1982 by Jumblatt) and, like the LCP, has many ties to the PLO. Although the OCAL was particularly successful in attracting young, politicized Shi'ite Muslims, who have always made up the majority of its rank and file, since the late 1970s it has lost many members and potential members to Amal.

The OCAL has lost a considerable amount of the power it enjoyed prior to the 1982 Israeli invasion, when it benefited from its close ties to the PLO and enjoyed more influence than its numbers necessarily justified. It did, however, play an important role in the anti-Israeli resistance, especially during 1983 and 1984. Since 1984 it has been badly hurt in clashes with Amal and Hizb Allah. After a period of inactivity, prompted by a series of clashes in Beirut and Tripoli, the OCAL re-emerged in early 1986. Despite the efforts of Amal to dominate West Beirut, the OCAL has reportedly organized more than fifteen cells in West Beirut, although it seems destined to play a minor and fading role in Lebanon (Radio Free Lebanon, 20 February; *FBIS*, 21 February).

The OCAL maintains close ties with the Democratic Front for the Liberation of Palestine and other leftist Palestinian groups. Outside of West Beirut, the organization maintains a presence in the northern city of Tripoli and in south Lebanon.

Initially, the OCAL was critical of the LCP, charging that it had become rigid and was not genuinely Marxist (*Arab World Weekly*, 15 May 1971). The OCAL also sided with China in the Sino-Soviet conflict. Since the mid-1970s, however, it has moderated its views and moved closer to the LCP. In May 1984 an agreement was reached between the LCP and the OCAL "to intensify the communist military presence through the two organizations and to set up additional positions along the contact lines" (Radio Free Lebanon, 28 May 1984; *FBIS*, 1 June 1984), but this seems an alliance based on weakness. The OCAL also maintains close contacts with party and state officials in the People's Democratic Republic of Yemen.

**Auxiliary Organizations.** A number of other Lebanese communist and communist-dominated organizations have been mentioned in the news media from time to time; among these, the more significant seem to be the Communist Labor Organization, the Organization of Arab Communists, the Revolutionary Communist Party (Trotskyist), the Lebanese Communist Union, the World Peace Council in Lebanon, and various "Friendship Committees" with East European countries.

Augustus Richard Norton
*United States Military Academy*

Note: Views expressed in this article are those of the author and do not necessarily represent the position of the U.S. government or any of its components.

# Morocco

**Population.** 23,667,000
**Party.** Party of Progress and Socialism (Parti du progrès et du socialisme; PPS)
**Founded.** 1943 (PPS, 1974)
**Membership.** 2,000 (estimated)
**Composition.** Unknown
**General Secretary.** 'Ali Yata
**Politburo.** 12 members: 'Ali Yata, Ismail Alaoui, Mohamed Ben Bella, Abdeslem Bourquia, Mohamed Rifi Chouaib, Abdelmajed Bouieb, Omar El Fassi, Thami Khyari, Abdallah Layachi, Simon Lévy, Mohamed Moucharik, Abdelwahed Souhail
**Secretariat.** 4 members: 'Ali Yata, Mohamed Rifi Chouaib, Omar El Fassi, Mohamed Moucharik
**Central Committee.** 65 members
**Status.** Legal
**Last Congress.** Third, 25–27 March 1983, in Casablanca
**Last Election.** 14 September 1984; 2.3 percent: 2 out of 306 seats
**Auxiliary Organizations.** No data
**Publication.** *Al Bayane* (daily), French and Arabic editions

The Moroccan Communist Party (Parti communiste marocain), founded in 1943 as a branch of the French Communist Party, was banned by the French protectorate in 1952. After three years of open operations in independent Morocco, it was again banned in 1959. Renamed the Party of Progress and Socialism, the PPS was granted legal status in 1974. In the 1976 municipal elections, the party won thirteen seats on the city council of Casablanca. The PPS participated in the Moroccan national elections in the spring of 1977 and won one seat in Parliament. In the last municipal elections, held in June 1983, the PPS won only two seats on the Casablanca city council. In Morocco's last parliamentary elections, held in September 1984, the PPS won two seats in Parliament, where the party is presently represented by Yata and Alaoui.

**Leadership and Party Organization.** The PPS's Third National Congress, held in March 1983, re-elected Yata as general secretary of the party. The congress re-elected 50 of the 57 members elected to the Central Committee by the party's Second National Congress in 1979 and elected fifteen new members. The 1983 congress elected a twelve-man Politburo, all of whose members had been on the thirteen-man Politburo elected in 1979. At the conclusion of the Third National Congress, the Central Committee reduced the party Secretariat from seven to four members. (For details on the Third Congress, see *YICA*, 1984).

**Domestic Party Affairs.** The party's domestic views were articulated by Secretary General Yata at the PPS Central Committee's regular plenum in February 1985 (see *YICA*, 1986). The PPS argues that Morocco has suffered for many years from a deep and continuing social and economic crisis. The party is seriously concerned about the government's moves to weaken the state sector of the

Moroccan economy by denationalization and the transfer of productive enterprises to private ownership. The PPS is determined to continue safeguarding the vital interests of the Moroccan working class. The party supports the democratization of the country's political situation and recognizes the need to strengthen its ties with the masses and to enhance its impact on the social, economic, and political life of Morocco.

The PPS daily newspaper, *al Bayane*, was suspended "indefinitely" on 31 October. The issue that led to the suspension was its support of the position adopted by Morocco's leading opposition party, the Socialist Union of Popular Forces (UNFP), that a Moroccan Jew should not be allowed to sit in the national Parliament. Leading government spokesmen argued strongly in the progovernment press that the right of any Moroccan to be a member of Parliament was at the very heart of Morocco's political system. The position of the opposition had emerged in part as a reaction to the destruction of a monument to Mohammed V, the first king of independent Morocco (1956–1961), in Ashkelon, Israel. (*Jeune Afrique*, 12 November.) At the end of the year, the Moroccan government announced that *al Bayane* would be allowed to resume publication on January 10, 1987, ending an unusually long suspension of more than two months.

**International Views, Positions, and Activities.** In an *al Bayane* editorial at the end of 1985, the PPS voiced its strong support for Morocco's August 1984 Treaty of Union with Libya. The party pointed to a variety of concrete measures—joint ventures for fertilizer processing and fisheries, increased air transport, and the promotion of cooperation in the vocational training, social security, and public health sectors—as evidence of the consolidation of cooperation between the two countries. The party argued that, although the union faced continuing problems stemming from different positions adopted by the two countries, the best way to reinforce the union's structure was through concrete achievements. (Rabat, Maghreb Arabe Presse, in English, 28 December 1985; *FBIS*, 3 January.) On 29 August, King Hassan II canceled the Moroccan-Libyan Treaty of Union in response to a Libyan-Syrian joint communiqué that denounced the visit of Israeli prime minister Shimon Peres to Morocco in July (*NYT*, 30 August).

Along with other opposition papers, *al Bayane*

sharply criticized the American bombing raids of 15 April against Libya, although it stopped short of calling on the Moroccan government to break relations with the United States. In an interview given to the *World Marxist Review*, PPS Politburo member Abdallah Layachi said that the prime motivation of the raids was to teach Libya a "lesson" because of its anti-imperialist policy and strong support for the Palestinians. He argued that Washington's intent was to increase tension throughout the Mediterranean area in order to intimidate the Arabs and force them to accept "imperialist blackmail and dictation." Layachi interpreted the American raids as a counteroffensive to setbacks suffered by U.S. policy in the Arab world since the 1982 Israeli invasion of Lebanon. The PPS views American military acts in the Mediterranean as an integral part of the active U.S. opposition to Third World national liberation movements. (*WMR*, October.)

Layachi went on to argue that the escalation of military activity and the arms race in the Mediterranean is closely linked to U.S. plans for breaking the present military-strategic parity and gaining superiority over the Soviet Union. In his view the United States assumed that an attack on Libya would divert world opinion from Soviet peace initiatives and from the Reagan administration's reactions to those initiatives and would divert attention from American underground nuclear explosions and acceleration of work on militarizing outer space with a Strategic Defense Initiative. Layachi stressed that only through unity could the Arabs defend themselves against the relentless attacks by the United States, Israel, and "local reaction." (Ibid.)

PPS general secretary Yata voiced the party's "total and unconditional support" for the Soviet Union's initiatives in the field of arms control. In an article in the *World Marxist Review*, the PPS leader praised the Soviet pledge against the first use of nuclear weapons, the 1985 decision on a six-month freeze on the deployment of intermediate-range missiles in Europe, and a moratorium on all nuclear explosions. He argued that the Soviet initiatives contribute to "a dynamic development of the prerequisites of peace and to a renewal of the process of strengthening détente." (*WMR*, December 1985.)

In late September, Yata visited Bucharest as a guest of the Romanian Communist Party (RCP) Central Committee. During this visit, he met with President and RCP General Secretary Nicolae Ceauşescu. Both men stressed the need, in the current grave international situation, to accelerate efforts to halt the arms race and move on to disarmament. Ceauşescu reiterated Romania's position on the Arab-Israeli conflict, which calls for a global negotiated settlement and the need to call an international conference, under United Nations supervision, with the participation of all concerned states, including the Palestine Liberation Organization and Israel. (Agerpress, in English, Bucharest, 23 September; *FBIS*, 24 September.)

John Damis
*Portland State University*

# Saudi Arabia

**Population.** 11,519,000
**Party.** Communist Party of Saudi Arabia (CPSA)
**Founded.** 1975
**Membership.** Number unknown but believed negligible
**General Secretary.** Mahdi Habib
**Other Spokesmen Noted Since 1979.** Abd-al-Rahman Salih, Salim Hamid, Hamad al-Mubarak, Abu Abdallah
**Status.** Illegal
**Last Congress.** Second, August 1984
**Last Election.** N/a
**Auxiliary Organizations.** Saudi Peace and Solidarity Committee (affiliate of the World Peace Council and, apparently, the Afro-Asian Peoples' Solidarity Organization), Saudi Democratic Youth (affiliate of the World Federation of Democratic Youth), Workers' Federation of Saudi Arabia (WFSA; associate member of the World Federation of Trade Unions [WFTU])
**Publications.** Apparently exist; titles unknown (see *YICA*, 1984)

The most significant event for the CPSA during 1986 appears to have been its June Central Committee plenum. The account carried in Peace and Socialism International Publishers' *Information Bulletin* (19) indicates that the meeting concentrated on the domestic issues of economic adversity and allegedly related political repression. The economic crisis is blamed not only on the drop in world oil prices (implied to be at least partially the result of Saudi pricing and production policies) but also on "excessive" expenditures for armaments and the security services. The latter are said to engage in repression on behalf of the ruling feudal–"parasitic bourgeois" alliance and against the "workers" and "national bourgeoisie," the elements most hurt by the country's current economic situation. The ultimate problem here is considered to be Saudi Arabia's dependence on the "world capitalist system," especially in its "American imperialist" manifestation. A solution offered was for the country to develop closer relations with the "socialist" nations, which would presumably result from the same sort of coordinated action by "national patriotic and progressive forces" both "at home and abroad" as that advocated by that same meeting for forcing the government to release political prisoners and end other forms of repression. (This is a considerably less ambitious program than the one advocated during the first half of 1985; see *YICA*, 1986.)

Internationally, the most noteworthy event for the CPSA during 1986 seems to have been its admission to the Editorial Council of the *World Marxist Review*, first noted in the July issue of that magazine. The party was a signatory, along with seven other communist and workers' parties of Arab East countries, of a May petition to "End Repression and Terror in Jordan" protesting the arrest of practically the entire leadership of the Communist Party of Jordan (*IB*, 14). Earlier, it had sent "fraternal delegates" to communist party congresses in India (in March) and East Germany (in April), but the persons involved were not publicly identified.

Much of the front activity publicized during the year was connected with the labor movement. Articles on the Saudi labor movement and the WFSA appeared in the two publications of the WFTU, *Flashes from the Trade Unions* (23 March) and *World Trade Union Movement* (April). Alongside these articles there appeared protests at the arrests of leftists in Saudi Arabia (which had actually culminated in October 1985) allegedly made by a group of apparently ad hoc bodies: "Committee for the Defense of Political Prisoners in Saudi Arabia, Committee for the Defense of Freedom in Saudi Arabia, and Committee for the Defense of Human Rights in Saudi Arabia.

Some new identifications were made of Saudi front personalities. Sabri Shaqir al-Khatani, WFSA chairman, was publicized as having attended the WFTU's 11 September Congress in East Berlin along with Majid Ali Zahrani, the source of the aforementioned article in *Flashes from the Trade Unions* (Eleventh World Trade Union Congress, *List of Participants*, p. 32), and Amadri Mahmud was listed as representing the Saudi Peace and Solidarity Committee at the October Copenhagen World Congress Devoted to the International Year of Peace (World Congress Devoted to the International Year of Peace, *Preliminary List of Participants*, p. 17).

Wallace H. Spaulding
*McLean, Virginia*

# Syria

**Population.** 10,931,000
**Party.** Syrian Communist Party (al-Hizb al-Shuyu'i al-Suri; SCP)
**Founded** 1924 (as a separate party in 1944)
**Membership.** 5,000 (estimated)
**General Secretary.** Khalid Bakhdash (74); deputy secretary general: Yusuf Faysal (61)
**Politburo.** Khalid Bakhdash, Yusuf Faysal, Ibrahim Bahri, Khalid Hammami, Maurice Salibi, Umar Siba'i, Daniel Ni'mah, Zuhayr Abd al-Sammad, Ramu Farkha, Ramu Shaykhu (not necessarily complete or up-to-date)
**Secretariat.** No data.
**Central Committee.** Nabih Rushaydat, Muhammad Khabbad, Issa Khuri, R. Kurdi, A.W. Rashwani; other names unknown
**Status.** Component of the ruling National Progressive Front (NPF)
**Last Congress.** Sixth, July 1986

**Last Election.**  February 1986; 8 out of 195 (presidential election; 1985)
**Auxiliary Organization.**  No data.
**Publications.**  *Nidal al-Sha'b*

The Party of the Lebanese People, founded in 1924, was one of several Marxist or quasi-Marxist groups that appeared in Syria and Lebanon during the early 1920s. It united with two other factions in 1925 to form the Communist Party of Syria and Lebanon (CPSL). The Syrian and Lebanese parties separated in 1944, soon after the two countries were officially declared independent, but they maintained close ties with each other. The CPSL and the subsequent SCP underwent alternate periods of toleration or legality and of suppression. The SCP often emphasized nationalism and reform and played down revolutionary ideology. It gained a considerable following and a membership that may have reached 10,000 by 1945. The party became quite influential between 1955 and 1958 but suffered a serious blow with the creation of the United Arab Republic and the subsequent suppression. Seemingly no longer a serious threat and following a foreign policy that often paralleled that of the Ba'thist regime, it gained a quasi-legal status after 1966 and finally joined the Ba'th-dominated NPF in 1972.

The Syrian communist movement has undergone several schisms in recent years. Riyad al-Turk, who was chosen general secretary of one breakaway group in 1974, has been imprisoned without trial since 1980, and has been subjected to beatings and torture. Three members of a proscribed group called the Communist Party Political Bureau—F. Tahhan, Mufid Mi'mari, and Umar Qasash (once director of the Syrian Printers' Union)—have been imprisoned without trial since 1981; Amnesty International adopted them as prisoners of conscience during 1986 (London, *Index on Censorship*, June). A writer, Wa'il Sawwah, has also been detained (Muhydin Lazikani, "Afraid of the Word," *Index on Censorship*, October 1985). According to one report, 340 communists and Ba'thists were arrested in Damascus, Homs, and Aleppo in August 1986 (Beirut, Voice of Lebanon, 13 August; *FBIS*, 13 August). The report did not indicate the name of any organization with which the detainees were associated. Yusuf Murad, a former member of the SCP Central Committee, formed another group, the Base Organization, in 1980. There is no recent information on this group.

**Leadership and Party Organization.**  Little is known about the dynamics of the SCP's leadership

except that General Secretary Bakhdash has long been the dominant figure. There have been some divisions among the top leadership; for example, Politburo member Daniel Ni'mah (now a representative of the SCP on the Central Command of the NPF) broke with the party temporarily during the early 1970s. In July 1986 there was a report of "a serious wave of dissent" within the party resulting from Bakhdash's insistence on convening the Sixth SCP Congress without regard to opposition to this move by most of the members of the Central Committee and the Politiburo and even despite attempts of other Arab communist parties to get him to reconsider his decision. Some members of the Politburo allegedly condemned the general secretary's arbitrary action. (Beirut, Voice of Lebanon, 23 July; *FBIS* 23 July.)

In any case, the congress met in Damascus in July. Moscow International Service (22 July; *FBIS*, 24 July) proclaimed it "an important event for Arab liberation movements, the international communist movement and the world proletarian movement." There is no information on meetings of the Politburo, Secretariat, or Central Committee during the year except for the fact that the Central Committee issued a statement on the eve of the general elections in February (*Pravda*, 10 February; *FBIS*, 11 February).

**Domestic Party Affairs.**  The SCP was described as upholding "the vital interests of the working class and broad masses of the working people" (TASS, 7 April; *FBIS*, 8 April). In a statement applauding the regime's foreign policy, Bakhdash added that his party continues to "struggle in the social sphere—in defense of the state sector of the national economy" and warned against the threat posed to "all those employed in physical and mental labor" by "international monopolies" and "the parasitic and bureaucratic bourgeoisie," whose robbery is causing "unrestrained" inflation and hurting "the living standards of the masses of the working people" (*Pravda*, 6 March; *FBIS*, 25 March).

With the Ba'th party getting 129 seats in the 195-member Parliament as a result of the February elections, other groups represented in the NPF won 31 seats, and 31 independents were elected (*NYT*, 13 February). The SCP won eight seats (*Pravda*, 6 March; *FBIS*, 25 March). There are two communists in the cabinet (*Pravda*, 6 March; *FBIS*, 25 March).

**Auxiliary and Front Organizations.** Little information on auxiliary organizations is available. The SCP probably participates in such groups as the Arab-Soviet Friendship Society, the Syrian Committee for Solidarity with Asian and African Countries, the National Council of Peace Partisans in Syria, and the Syrian-Bulgarian Friendship Society.

The present Syrian regime is officially based on the NPF, which includes the SCP, the Arab Socialist Party, the Socialist Union, and the Arab Socialist Union, in addition to the dominant Ba'th Party, which is non-Marxist. This does not mean that the SCP has any significant influence but rather that it has for the time being more or less abandoned revolutionism in favor of the comforts of a largely formal role. The quiet role as the regime's partner also conforms to the wishes of the USSR, whose foreign policy Syria tends to parallel in many respects. Exceptions are recent Syrian support for dissident elements of the Palestine Liberation Organization (PLO), Damascus's conflict with Iraq, and its support for Iran in the Iraqi-Iranian war. Syrian support for Iran is believed to have been a special source of unhappiness for the USSR during 1986 (*NYT*, 26 January), and this was paralleled by SCP criticism of Iran's occupation of the Fao peninsula in southern Iraq and its refusal to seek a negotiated peace (*CSM*, 28 May). Such criticism, however, came at a time when the Syrian regime's relationship with Iran was also under strain.

The importance of the NPF continued to be proclaimed. The SCP Central Committee called for its "consolidation," the enhancement of its role and the role of the parties belonging to it, increasing its "influence on the country's political, social, and economic life, and the expansion of cooperation within the framework at all levels and in various spheres" (*Pravda*, 10 February; *FBIS*, 11 February). Similarly, the Twenty-first conference of Syria's General Federation of Trade Unions called for "strengthening the various parties" belonging to the NPF (Damascus Domestic Service, 21 November; *FBIS*, 24 November). Moscow International Service (22 July; *FBIS*, 24 July) praised the SCP's "positive role" in the NPF, whose solidarity was said to provide "strength for the active policy of resistance to imperialism and zionism."

Soviet-Syrian cooperation continued on a large scale during 1986. Soviet arms—including advanced tanks and missiles—have been provided in such quantities since 1982 that Syria is said to be aiming at "strategic parity" with Israel (*NYT*, 9 May). About 2,500 Soviet military advisers remained with Syrian forces (*LAT*, 18 March). Karen Brutents, deputy chief of the CPSU Central Committee International Department reiterated his country's support for Syria against possible Israeli aggression (Damascus Domestic Service, 5 January; *FBIS*, 6 January). The Syrian press described relations with the USSR in glowing terms; the newspaper *al-Thawrah* called the "friendship and cooperation...a bright spot in the region's sky" (Damascus Domestic Service, 7 March; *FBIS*, 7 March). The two countries have been bound to each other by a treaty of friendship and cooperation since 1980.

During 1986, there were numerous exchanges of visits between delegations of Syrian state and Ba'th Party officials and delegations of state and communist party officials from the USSR, the German Democratic Republic (GDR), Czechoslovakia, Hungary, Cuba, North Korea, Poland, and China. This was the first time a Syrian Ba'th Party delegation had visited China (Beijing, Xinhua, 16 March; *FBIS*, 18 March). Abdullah al-Ahmar, deputy general secretary of the Ba'th Party of Syria participated in the Twenty-seventh CPSU Congress in March (*Pravda*, 5 March; *FBIS*, 25 March). Sulayman Kaddah, deputy regional secretary of the Ba'th Party, participated in the Eleventh Congress of the Socialist Unity Party of the GDR in April (East Berlin, *Neues Deutschland*, 23 April). Syrian premier Abd al-Ra'uf al-Qasim visited Czechoslovakia in August (primarily for medical treatment) (Prague, ČETEKA in English, 22 August; *FBIS*, 25 August). Vice President Abd al-Halim Khaddam led a delegation to Moscow in May (Damascus Television Service, 27 May; *FBIS*, 28 May). Delegations representing the French Communist Party and the Cypriot socialist party EDEK visited Damascus in July and September respectively for meetings with high-level Bathist officials. Rashid Akhtarini, a member of the regional (Syrian) leadership of the Ba'th Party, participated in a joint interview with leaders of the Maltese and Moroccan communist parties and with Hassan S. Grew of the Organisation of Progressive and Socialist Parties of Mediterranean Nations (*WMR*, October, p. 77).

Yet Syrian-Soviet cooperation is hardly the result of the official existence of the "national front" government in Damascus. Its basis is purely pragmatic, not ideological. Informed observers seem to be unanimous in rejecting the idea that Syria is a Soviet satellite. The Soviet ambassador to Damascus, Felix Fedotov, admitted that the USSR and Syria "have our differences" (*NYT*, 26 January).

**International Views, Positions, and Activities.** The Presidium of the USSR's Supreme Soviet awarded SCP deputy general secretary Faysal the Order of the Friendship of the Peoples in recognition of his "struggle for peace, democracy, and social progress," his contribution to Syrian-Soviet relations, and his sixtieth birthday (Moscow Domestic Service, 6 February; *FBIS*, 14 February). Bakhdash participated in the Twenty-seventh CPSU Congress in February and March (*Pravda*, 6 March; *FBIS*, 25 March). SCP Politburo member Hammami participated in the Eleventh Congress of the Socialist Unity Party of the GDR in April (Jerusalem, *The Soviet Union and the Middle East* 11, no. 6). Bakhdash led a delegation that included Faysal, four members of the SCP Politburo (Ni'mah, Hammami, Shaykhu, and Bahri), and two members of the Central Committee (Kurdi and Rashwani) to Moscow in April; the delegation met with Soviet party leaders (TASS, 7 April; *FBIS*, 8 April). The SCP joined seven other Arab communist and workers' parties in a statement calling for an end to repression and terror in Jordan on 17 May (*IB*, July). *Pravda* (26 June) published an interview with Bakhdash in Damascus. Hammami participated in a special meeting of the *World Marxist Review* Editorial Council in Prague (*WMR*, July).

Leaders of the SCP had only the highest praise for the USSR. Bakhdash told the Twenty-seventh CPSU Congress that "every congress of the CPSU . . . opens up new prospects not only for the Soviet people but also for all progressive mankind." The CPSU Central Committee Political Report delivered by General Secretary Mikhail Gorbachev was described as having "opened up extensive pros-

pects for solving all the political and social problems facing mankind." Bakhdash further lauded Gorbachev's program to eliminate nuclear arms and prevent the militarization of space. The new edition of the CPSU's program was called "the greatest document in mankind's history." (*Pravda*, 6 March; *FBIS*, 25 March.)

The SCP delegation to Moscow in April joined CPSU leaders in condemning the "imperialist concept of 'neoglobalism' assumed by the U.S. ruling circles, the concept that envisages interference in internal affairs of sovereign countries, the imposing of U.S. domination on them" (TASS, 7 April; *FBIS*, 8 April). The SCP Central Committee's pre-election statement described "U.S. imperialism [as doing] everything to establish undivided hegemony in the Middle East, to plunder its natural wealth, to undermine the economies of Arab countries and to deal a blow to the national liberation movement," with Israel serving as "an instrument for" plans to destroy the rights of the Palestinians, "putting through capitulatory versions of a solution to the Middle East problem, and drawing a number of Arab states into separate deals" (TASS, 9 February; *FBIS*, 10 February).

Bakhdash called for an international peace conference to settle the Middle East conflict, with the PLO as the sole representative of the Palestinian people (*The Soviet Union and the Middle East* 11, no. 3–4). The SCP "strongly condemned" Moroccan king Hassan's meeting with Prime Minister Shimon Peres of Israel as a "criminal and treacherous act" and as "a repetition . . . of [the late president Anwar] al-Sadat's ill-omened visit to Jerusalem" (Damascus, Saudi Arabia News Agency, 22 July; *FBIS*, 23 July).

Glenn E. Perry
*Indiana State University*

# Tunisia

**Population.** 7,424,000
**Party.** Tunisian Communist Party (Parti communiste tunisien; PCT)
**Date Founded.** 1934
**Membership.** 2,000 (estimated); PCT claims 4,000
**Composition.** Unknown
**General Secretary.** Muhammad Harmel
**Politburo.** 6 members: Muhammad Harmel, Muhammad al-Nafaʻa, ʻAbd al-Hamid ben Mustafa, Hisham
Sakik, ʻAbd al-Majid Tariki, Salah al-Hajji
**Secretariat.** 3 members: Muhammad Harmel, Muhammad al-Nafaʻa, ʻAbd al-Hamid ben Mustafa
**Central Committee.** 12 members
**Status.** Legal
**Last Congress.** Eighth, February 1981, in Tunis
**Last Election.** 2 November 1986 (*NYT*, 30 November); boycotted by PCT
**Auxiliary Organization.** Tunisian Communist Youth
**Publication.** *Al-Tariq al-Jadid* (New path), weekly

The Tunisian Communist Party was founded in 1920 as a branch of the French Communist Party and became independent in 1934. The banning of the PCT in 1963 formalized a single-party state under the direction of the Destourian Socialist Party (PSD). In July 1981, the government lifted the ban on the PCT, ending the party's eighteen-year period of clandestine existence. The PCT was the only opposition party allowed to operate openly from July 1981 to November 1983, when President Habib Bourguiba legalized two other opposition parties (see *YICA*, 1984).

**Leadership and Party Organization.** The PCT's Eighth Congress in February 1981 re-elected Muhammad Harmel as general secretary and elected a three-member Secretariat, a six-member Politburo, and a twelve-member Central Committee. Politburo and Secretariat member Muhammad al-Nafaʻa has occasionally contributed to the *World Marxist Review*.

**Domestic Party Affairs.** In the view of the PCT, Tunisia is in the midst of a prolonged and worsening economic and social crisis. The current situation is especially alarming because of the government crackdown on the opposition and the infringement of civil liberties. The salient features of this crackdown include: the repression of the major Tunisian labor union—the General Union of Tunisian Workers (UGTT)—in the fall of 1985, the imprisonment of union officials, the close surveillance of political parties, the harassment and occasional arrest of party leaders and militants, and the seizure and suspension of newspapers and indictment of their directors and editors. The PCT argues that the role of the opposition is to criticize, to propose solutions and even alternatives to problems, and finally, to create the conditions in which necessary changes can occur. Of special importance to the PCT was the arrest in May of Central Committee member Boujemaʻa Remili and his jail sentence of sixteen days. (Tunis, *Réalités*, 23 May.)

During 1986, the PCT continued to make a concerted effort to meet and coordinate with other Tunisian opposition groups. These other groups included not only the Movement of Democratic Socialists—the major opposition force in Tunisia—but also the less powerful Movement of Popular Unity and Movement of the Islamic Tendency (MTI). The PCT's stated objective in backing a unified opposition was to obtain a large consensus among its various elements and to end the passivity of the opposition and its marginal position in the Tunisian political system.

In an interview published in May, a member of the PCT Central Committee explained how a Marxist-Leninist party could form a working alliance with an Islamic fundamentalist group like the MTI. The party considers that Arab-Muslim culture is a foundation common to all Tunisians. As a general principle of policy, the PCT cannot refuse to collaborate on clear political points on the pretext of ideological differences. Although the party has repeatedly recognized the irreducible divergences with the Islamic fundamentalists, and it is out of the question for the PCT to lose its identity, common action with the MTI cannot contradict the party's principles. Perhaps, the party spokesperson suggests, this common action could contribute toward encouraging an evolution of the Islamic movement itself. Finally, the PCT argues that the critical split in Tunisia is not between secularists and Islamic fundamentalists but instead is over the question of democracy and social questions. (Ibid., 2 May.)

As for specific actions in the domestic field, the PCT organized meetings of party militants, which were held in January for the purpose of discussing the labor union situation. General Secretary Harmel made a presentation at these meetings. (Ibid., 26 January.) On 22 February, the PCT joined with four other Tunisian opposition groups to set up a "committee of solidarity with the UGTT" made up of the general secretaries of the five organizations (Le Monde, 25 February). A PCT spokesperson explained that the principal objectives of the committee were to counteract the Tunisian government's information about the UGTT, to organize an action of solidarity working with the labor union, and to oppose the government's campaign to liquidate the UGTT (Tunis, Réalités, 28 February). One of the main means of achieving these objectives was said to be an intensive press campaign (Tunis, al Batal, 24 February).

The PCT issued a communiqué announcing the party's decision on 22 September, following detailed consultation and a meeting of party representatives, to participate in the Tunisian parliamentary elections in November. The decision envisaged joint lists of candidates prepared in cooperation with other opposition parties. (Tunis, La Presse, 24 September.) Shortly before the elections, held on 2 November, the government closed some opposition newspapers and disqualified some opposition candidates. In response to these government measures, the PCT joined Tunisia's two other legal opposition parties (and several others that are tacitly permitted to operate) in a boycott of the elections. The ruling PSD won all 125 seats. (NYT, 30 November.)

**International Views, Positions, and Activities.** A member of the PCT Central Committee explained in an interview published in May that the party fully backs the Tunisian government's foreign policy of cooperation with other North African countries. The PCT believes in both the Greater Maghreb and Arab Unity but laments the slow progress toward those objectives. It is possible, in the PCT view, that Tunisia's current economic crisis could be resolved within the framework of the Greater Maghreb. Progress toward the construction of a North African union requires a clear and working solidarity with Libya, and the party supports any initiative in the direction of normalizing relations among North African countries. The party spokesperson argued further that North Africa is the target of aggressive American intervention, which endangers peace in the Mediterranean. The PCT has always focused attention on the sources of conflict, and it denounces any foreign intervention in North Africa. (Tunis, Réalités, 2 May.)

The PCT weekly newspaper, al-Tarik al-Jadid, criticized the absence of a reaction by the Tunisian government to the 15 April American bombing attacks against Libya. This issue, along with that of two other weekly newspapers, was seized by the government. (Le Monde, 22 April.) On 6 May, the government suspended al-Tarik al-Jadid for six months for "defamation and spreading false news." The PCT rejected these accusations as "unfounded" but was obliged to obey the suspension, which continued through the fall campaign for parliamentary elections. (Tunis, Les Temps Hebdomadaires, 19 May.)

At the end of July, PCT leader Harmel visited Bucharest at the invitation of the Romanian Communist Party (RCP) Central Committee. During his visit, he met on 30 July with Romanian president and RCP general secretary Nicolae Ceauşescu, who set forth to Harmel Romania's position on the need to halt the dangerous arms race and move on to disarmament, beginning with nuclear arms. On African issues, both parties expressed their solidarity with the struggle for independence of the Namibian people led by the South-West African People's Organization. Similarly, they expressed their solidarity with the struggle of all African people for the eradication of colonialism and the abolition of policies of racism and apartheid. On North-South issues, both sides welcomed the increased collaboration and unity of action among nonaligned states for a global settlement of issues such as high and burdensome foreign debts, and for the establishment of a new world economic order to help (especially) the least developed countries. (Bucharest, Agerpress, 30 July; *FBIS*, 31 July.)

In February, the PCT attended the congress of the Cuban Communist Party in Havana, where it was represented by Politburo member Sakik (Tunis, *Réalités*, 26 January).

John Damis
*Portland State University*

# Yemen: People's Democratic Republic of Yemen

**Population.** 2,275,000
**Party.** Yemeni Socialist Party (al-Hizb al-Ishtirakiya al-Yamaniya; YSP)
**Founded.** 1978
**Membership.** 26,000 (claimed before January civil war)
**President of the Presidium of the Supreme People's Council.** Haydar Abu Bakr al-'Attas
**Secretary-General.** 'Ali Salim al-Bayd (elected 7 February 1986)
**Assistant Secretary-General.** Salim Salih Muhammad (elected 7 February 1986)
**Politburo.** 15 members and 1 candidate; includes Salih Munassar al-Siyayli, Salim Salih Muhammad, 'Abd al-'Aziz al-Dali, Haydar Abu Bakr al-'Attas, 'Ali Salim al-Bayd, Yasin Sa'id Nu'man, Muhammad Sa'id 'Abdullah, Sa'id Salih Salim, and Fadl Muhsin 'Abdullah. 3 candidate members.
**Central Committee.** Membership unknown
**Status.** Ruling party
**Last Congress.** Third, 11–16 October 1985
**Last Election.** 1986: all candidates YSP approved

Since gaining its independence, the People's Democratic Republic of Yemen (PDRY)—also known as South Yemen, Southern Yemen, or (as is preferred by its government) Democratic Yemen—has pursued a path of "scientific socialism" in domestic policy and close alignment with the Soviet Union and other Eastern bloc countries in foreign affairs. The YSP, heir to the independence-winning National Liberation Front (NLF), remains the only legal party in the state and has had no significant opposition since independence in 1967. The party itself, however, has been riven with factionalism and infighting. Internal power struggles reached climaxes in 1969, 1971, 1978, 1980, and most recently, January 1986, and the list of leading personalities who have been imprisoned, exiled, or killed is long.

The constitution (adopted in 1970) specifies that the Supreme People's Council (SPC) is the highest authority. Elections to the council were first held in

1978, and members are elected for five-year terms. The SPC elects the president and eleven to seventeen members of the Presidium, to which the SPC's authority is delegated when the SPC is not in session. The SPC also elects the prime minister, the cabinet, and the members of the Supreme Court.

As in other socialist states, real power rests within the party. During the 1970s, several efforts were made to transform the ruling NLF into a true Marxist organization, and several other small legal parties were incorporated into it. Among these was the Popular Democratic Union, a local communist party, founded in Aden in 1961, which had never seriously challenged the NLF for power. The first general congress of the YSP was held in October 1972 after the moderates were defeated, and another was held in October 1980 following the ouster of the ultraradical faction. The third congress took place in October 1985 amidst considerable tension, and a fourth was postponed until June 1987 because of continuing fundamental differences.

The roots of the January 1986 civil war can be traced back at least to June 1978 when several days of pitched fighting in the PDRY capital of Aden left hard-line ideologue and party general secretary 'Abd al-Fattah Isma'il (al-Jawfi) the victor over the relatively more moderate head of state Salim Rubayyi' 'Ali, who was quickly tried and executed. Bitterness over the bloody results of this power struggle, 'Abd al-Fattah's extreme dependence on the Soviet bloc, his willingness to send South Yemeni troops to fight in the Horn of Africa, his strong-arm style of governing, and the dire economic straits in which the country found itself all combined to cause 'Abd al-Fattah's downfall, and within two years he had been forced into exile in Moscow.

Following 'Abd al-Fattah's exile 'Ali Nasir Muhammad (al-Hasani), who had been prime minister since 1971, assumed all three key positions: president of the state, head of the party, and prime minister. He resigned as prime minister in 1985. At the Second YSP Congress in 1980, a new Central Committee (the permanent authority of the party when the party congress is not in session) was elected, and the committee proceeded to select a new five-member Politburo that clearly reflected 'Ali Nasir's predominant position.

Although the new president instituted a number of welcome changes, he was still vulnerable to attack by the remaining members of the ultraradical or hard-line faction. A strong challenge was mounted during meetings of the SPC Presidium and the YSP Central Committee in May 1984, at which he was strongly criticized for ideological deviation and 'Abd al-Fattah's return was demanded. In addition, a prominent 'Abd al-Fattah supporter was named to the cabinet and four of his followers were added to the Politburo.

'Ali Nasir's attempts to strengthen his position by elevating former Ba'thists and Popular Democratic Union leaders further alienated the YSP old guard, as did his actions in having several prominent opponents killed. More changes occurred in February 1985, when the Central Committee elevated a candidate member of the Politburo to full member status, swelling the Politburo's ranks to eleven. At the same time, former president 'Abd al-Fattah, who had apparently returned to Aden from Moscow in early 1985, was given a minor party post. Albeit disturbing, these developments by themselves did not decisively indicate that 'Ali Nasir's position had been eroded.

However, the convening of the Third Congress of the YSP in October 1985 brought the underlying tensions into the open. 'Ali Nasir kept his titles as president and YSP general secretary and managed to retain control of the Central Committee, but the expansion of the more important Politburo to fifteen full members plus one candidate severely weakened his position. He could count on the support of five Politburo members: Abu Bakr and 'Abd al-Razzaq Ba Dhib (the two leaders of the Popular Democratic Union), Anis Hasan Yahya and 'Abd al-Ghani 'Abd al-Qadir (Arab Ba'th Socialist Party sympathizers), and Ahmad Musa'id Husayn ('Ali Nasir's security chief and protégé). Prime minister Haydar al-'Attas, foreign minister 'Abd al-'Aziz al-Dali, and Salih Munassar al-Siyayli could be considered neutral.

But the Politburo also contained six implacable hard-liners, who accused the president of betraying the revolution by going too far in liberalization and condoning corruption. 'Abd al-Fattah Isma'il was among this group, joining allies 'Ali 'Antar (a former defense minister) and Salih Muslih Qasim (the then-current defense minister). In addition, another key supporter of 'Abd al-Fattah from the past, the notorious Muhammad Sa'id 'Abdullah (also known as Muhsin al-Sharjabi, 'Abd al-Fattah's "enforcer" as head of state security from 1978 to 1980) had already been restored to the cabinet as minister of housing.

**The Civil War of January 1986.** By the beginning of 1986, it seemed only a matter of time before the tensions escalated into open violence. Few expected 'Ali Nasir, whose career and reputation had been built on compromise and even waffling, to strike first. But the deteriorating balance of power seemed to leave him with little choice and rumors abounded in the first weeks of January that his opponents were planning to assassinate him. The president appeared to be swayed in his decision to take the bloody initiative by the insistence of two key advisors, Muhammad 'Ali Ahmad, the powerful and nearly autonomous governor of Abyan Province and a fellow tribesman, and Ahmad Musa'id Husayn, his minister of state security (intelligence chief). In a subsequent interview, 'Ali Nasir claimed to have captured evidence that his opponents were planning to assassinate him and that, during the night of 12 January, they had set in motion a coup attempt to which he and his supporters had simply reacted (Abu Dhabi, *al-Ittihad*, 13 February).

It seems clear, however, that 'Ali Nasir indeed struck first, as his opponents have claimed; their accounts are given in the statement broadcast on the Aden Domestic Service on 20 January 1986 (*FBIS*, 21 January 1986; *al-Ittihad*, 26 January; *WP*, 3 February; *NYT*, 9 February; *LAT*, 13 February). According to their version, the six hard-liner members had already arrived at a scheduled Politburo meeting on the morning of 13 January and were awaiting the arrival of 'Ali Nasir and his allies. Without warning, 'Ali Nasir's bodyguards opened fire, killing Politburo members 'Ali 'Antar and 'Ali Shayi' Hadi and several aides. Defense minister Salih Muslih Qasim shot and killed one of the president's bodyguards before he himself was killed. A few hours later, Aden Radio broadcast a planted report (providing further evidence of 'Ali Nasir as the instigator) that a coup attempt by the four ringleaders of the hard-liners had failed and they had been arrested, tried, and executed—even though two of the four were still alive at that point.

The three survivors, 'Ali Salim al-Bayd, 'Abd al-Fattah Isma'il, and Salim Salih Muhammad, fled to an adjoining room, where torn curtains were used as ropes to raise Kalashnikovs passed up from comrades in the courtyard. They spent the next nine hours returning fire and telephoning for help as battles spread around the city. When the survivors reached Soviet ambassador Vladislav Zhukov on the telephone, he was said to be shocked and surprised at the attack. In the early evening, help arrived and the three hard-liners were driven away in separate vehicles.

The situation appeared stalemated for the first several days, as fighting intensified in Aden and spread throughout the countryside. The heaviest battles occurred near the airport at Khormaksar (an isthmus separating the city from the mainland) and around the port. The Italian and French embassies were heavily damaged, and several ships, caught in the crossfire between supporters of the hard-liners and the naval forces loyal to 'Ali Nasir, were hit and sunk in the harbor. Aden was completely cut off from the outside world, with the airport closed, telephone and telex links cut, and the border sealed. Information on the course of the fighting was confused, particularly because both sides began broadcasting in the name of Aden Radio.

By 15 and 16 January, however, 'Ali Nasir's opponents had gained the upper hand. Although the navy and much of the air force backed 'Ali Nasir, the army was split and the militia was divided on regional lines. A significant factor in the war's shift was the defection of the tank corps to the hard-liners (largely because of 'Ali 'Antar's role in organizing the corps during his tenure as defense minister). In addition, the security services tended to follow their old leader, 'Abd al-Fattah's henchman Muhammad Sa'id 'Abdullah. And the killing of 'Antar and indiscriminate massacres in officers' barracks pushed the mid-level military echelons over to the hard-liners' side.

'Ali Nasir's forces were soon driven back into the canyons of the Crater district of old Aden and the Steamer Point section of Tawahi, where the port, government offices, and fortified bunkers with anti-aircraft guns were situated. The president's indecisiveness struck again as he left the capital bound first for Abyan and then for Ethiopia on the eighteenth and then flying back to the Yemen Arab Republic (YAR or North Yemen) on the following day. The heaviest battles of the civil war were waged on the twenty-first and twenty-second as tribal backers of the hard-liners were reported to have joined the fighting at Khormaksar and the airport and to have occupied the workers' district of al-Shaykh 'Uthman and Little Aden, the site of the oil refinery.

By 24 January, 'Ali Nasir's forces had been defeated, and the hard-liners named a new interim government, with Prime Minister Haydar Abu Bakr al-'Attas as the titular head of state. Soviet-sponsored mediation got underway at the heavily damaged Soviet embassy as fighting died down in the capital. Despite radio broadcasts claiming that the cabinet had met under 'Ali Nasir's leadership in Abyan (at the same time as the new government announced its own cabinet meeting in Aden), and despite 'Ali Nasir's claims of a army of 40,000 to 50,000 supporters waiting to besiege Aden, the civil war was over. Telephone links to the outside were restored and television broadcasting resumed, a clean-up campaign for Aden was instituted, and al-Yemda (the national carrier) resumed flights, on 25, 26, and 27 January respectively. At the same time, the new regime sought to emphasize its control by publicizing huge rallies in Abyan province in support of the government.

The cost of the war was tremendous. Between 10,000 and 13,000 deaths were estimated, with the majority occurring in the chaotic first two days of combat. The government later announced that damage to public property alone totalled $115 million. Heroic efforts had been made to rescue the foreign community trapped in Aden. By the time the conflict ended, some 6,500 foreigners, about two-thirds of them Soviet bloc nationals, had been evacuated to nearby Djibouti by sundry Soviet, French, and British naval vessels and merchant ships. The royal British yacht Britannia was among them, pausing on its voyage to Australia to pluck more than a thousand people of 50 nationalities from Aden's beaches.

Unfortunately for the PDRY, the physical destruction paled beside other, more permanent, repercussions. One conspicuous result was a thinning of party ranks, with the new government contending that 4,230 YSP members had been killed. By the end of the latest round of fighting, almost all of the NLF/YSP founding fathers (most of whom had been born no earlier than the 1930s) were either dead or in exile. Only a few of the real "politicos" were left in Aden, and even these had been minor figures. The regrouped ranks of the Politburo and, even more, the ranks of the Central Committee consisted of obscure party hacks, a particularly unsavory fringe, and on the positive side, clusters of technocrats and bureaucrats.

In addition to ideology and personal ambition, ancient tribal antagonisms have played a part in provoking each new sequence in the unending struggle for power. Far from withering away, tribal affiliations have been carried over into the urban environment. Recruitment for the armed forces and militia still tends to rely on tribal ties. Smoldering tribal enmities intensify whenever the power struggle erupts into violence. The victory in January 1986 was in part a triumph of the tribes of al-Yafa' and al-Dali' (the home of Salih Muslih Qasim and of 'Ali 'Antar, who was credited with South Yemen's

revolution against the British in the early 1960s in the Radfan region of al-Dali').

The losers were the Dathina (the tribe of 'Ali Nasir Muhammad), the 'Awaliq (who provided many of the original British-trained army officers and who had also been losers before as backers of the late president Salim Rubayyi' 'Ali), and the tribes of Abyan. The impact on the small number of party officials of North Yemeni origin was mixed. The National Democratic Front (a North Yemen rebel group driven from the YAR in 1982) joined the fighting on the side of the hard-liners; this was in response to the backing given it by 'Abd al-Fattah Isma'il and 'Ali 'Antar and to 'Ali Nasir Muhammad's withdrawal of support due to his rapprochement with YAR.

The tribes of the eastern governorates of Hadramawt and Mahra essentially remained on the sidelines, although they leaned toward the government. Ironically, the decimation of the ranks allowed Hadramis to slip into a number of prominent positions. At least four Hadramis are now members of the Politburo where they fill the positions of president, prime minister, and YSP general secretary. Most members of these tribes, however, can be classified as relatively apolitical people or as technocrats.

Finally, to a certain extent, the ferocity of the fighting reflected the resentment of a tribal, rural peasantry at the perceived prosperity and corruption of the capital; the new French hotel was a particular if inexplicable target of destruction.

**The Exiled Opposition.** For perhaps the first time in the PDRY's history, an internal power struggle resulted in the mass defection of large numbers of the party and government elite. Most prominent of those going into exile was former president 'Ali Nasir Muhammad. Throughout 1986, he apparently shuttled between Addis Ababa, Damascus, and Sanaa. He was joined in exile by as many as 20,000 followers, some 10,000 to 15,000 of whom are in the YAR; there are also estimates of as many as 10,000 in Ethiopia. Among those in exile were fellow Politburo members Anis Hasan Yahya, 'Abd al-Ghani 'Abd al-Qadir, Ahmad Musa'id Husayn, Abu Bakr Ba Dhib, and 'Abd al-Razzaq Ba Dhib.

Other prominent officials who fled the country included the governor of Abyan and the ministers of health, agriculture, fisheries, and state security, as well as Central Committee members, party leaders in various governorates, court officials, and senior army and militia officers. The new regime subsequently arrested the former minister of the interior, the deputy minister of state security, and the commanders of the air force, navy, and militia. Most of the PDRY's naval personnel fled to Ethiopia with their gunboats. In October, 'Ali Nasir Muhammad's son Jamal, thought to have been killed in the fighting, emerged from the Ethiopian embassy with six compatriots where they had been sheltered secretly since January.

Not surprisingly, the two sides advanced diametrically opposing views of their respective status after January. Undoubtedly, there were elements of truth in both contentions. 'Ali Nasir Muhammad's supporters regularly released accounts of new defectors from Aden and alleged continuing unrest and plots against the government. In March, the exiles claimed that the new regime was holding over 10,000 people in various detention camps, that secret military trials had been carried out, and that there had been a demonstration of 1,500 women in Aden calling for the release of detained family members. (The government maintained that only 1,500 individuals had been arrested in the immediate aftermath of the fighting.) In June, the exiles alleged that 850 dissidents had been forcibly exiled to the island of Socotra and that PDRY aircraft had killed 8 people in aerial raids in Abyan governorate.

A former minister of fisheries, escaping across the Hadramawt desert in June, declared that there had been three attempts to assassinate the PDRY president and that an intense power struggle was continuing in Aden. In July, 'Ali Nasir Muhammad claimed Aden was still holding 17,000 prisoners and that more than 20,000 South Yemenis were refugees. Then in August, an aide made the claim that 14,500 people had been jailed following the fighting and that nearly 19,000 including 9,300 armed forces personnel, had fled the country. In September, it was reported that some 34 PDRY diplomatic personnel in at least 15 countries had resigned their posts and anounced their support for the former president.

For its part, the new government minimized the numbers and importance of exiles (claiming that they numbered somewhere between 4,000 and 6,000) and sought to sustain an impression of a return to normalcy. Nevertheless, clashes between the two sides continued throughout the year. Aden claimed to have arrested 500 'Ali Nasir supporters in February, alleging they had crossed the border from a military camp in Saudi Arabia. Fighting broke out around the border town of al-Bayhan in September, where the rebels reportedly shelled the

airport and a military camp, and other skirmishes were reported in the Hadramawt. At the same time, serious differences within the Central Committee were alleged to have forced a suspension of several hours in television and radio transmissions. Finally, the government announced at the end of the year that two networks of saboteurs, armed with automatic weapons and explosives and disguised as returning refugees, had been caught in Abyan and Shabwa governorates.

Despite recurrent rumors, there seems to be little chance of reconciliation between the two parties. The new government embarked on a policy of encouraging the return of exiles, particularly through the general amnesty declared on 29 March. By July, 3,300 prisoners had been released under the amnesty and the government had given wide publicity to the return of several prominent individuals.

Rumors of reconciliation efforts surfaced periodically throughout the year, with the Soviet Union, Libya, Syria, Algeria, the PLO, radical Palestinians, and the YAR all mentioned as having a try at mediating. The Aden government denied the report of talks held in Aden with the assistance of the Soviet Union in April. The exiles were apparently represented in these talks by the former interior minister and the commander of the People's Defense Committees (a cousin of the former president), both of whom were deported to Uzbekistan shortly afterward. Aden has also denied the rumors of talks in Sanaa in late June; in Aden, also in late June; and in Tripoli in July when President 'Attas met with his North Yemeni counterpart. There is little doubt that 'Attas and 'Ali Nasir Muhammad met while both were in Damascus in mid-November but the meeting seemed to have settled nothing. Indeed, even before 'Attas left Damascus, formal charges of treason, terrorism, and sabotage were lodged in Aden's Supreme Court against 'Ali Nasir and 141 of his supporters; of these, 'Ali Nasir and 47 others were to be tried in absentia.

**The Reconstituted Party and Government.** The civil war generated a number of obstacles that hampered the rebuilding process in Aden. First, the severe crippling of the hard-liner or radical faction that resulted from its losses during the fighting has meant that the new ruling condominium in Aden comprises an uneasy coalition of interests. The death or defection of so many top party leaders and government officials has forced elevation of many unlikely individuals. The armed forces, traditionally suspect because of their formation under the British and support for moderate factions in the past, are politically stronger than at any time in the past due to the thinning of ranks and to their role as guarantors of the January victory. Technocrats constitute another subgroup that has penetrated key decision making bodies, and Hadramis have come to the fore.

Among the latter is the new president, Haydar Abu Bakr al-'Attas, whose career was undistinguished until recently. A sayyid (descendant of the Prophet Muhammad), civil engineer, and former public works and construction minister, 'Attas was named to the Politburo and the position of prime minister only in 1985. He was traveling outside the country when the fighting broke out and made his way to Moscow. Soviet counsel to the remaining Adeni leadership that 'Attas was an ideal compromise candidate was quite likely behind his appointment as interim president on 24 January while he was still in Moscow. The rump Supreme People's Council (SPC) subsequently elected him president on 7 February, and he was reconfirmed along with the prime minister and cabinet by the newly elected SPC on 6 November.

The prime minister, Yasin Sa'id Nu'man, was similarly obscure until 1986. Also a Hadrami and a technocrat, Yasin received the positions of Central Committee member, deputy prime minister and minister of fisheries only when 'Attas became head of government in 1985. He did not become a Politburo member until after the civil war. The third most prominent member of the government, Foreign Minister 'Abd al-'Aziz al-Dali, is a dentist of North Yemeni origin. His northern roots precluded a power base in Aden and he entered the cabinet and Politburo only through the patronage of 'Ali Nasir Muhammad. Caught outside the country in January, he too went to Moscow and without hesitation deserted the president to join the new Adeni leaders. Despite their public prominence, these men are not the real leaders of the PDRY, but it is still not entirely clear where the locus of power lies.

Ever since the ouster of president Salim Rubayyi' 'Ali in 1978, the party has exercised dominance over the government, and the YSP's new leadership seems to enjoy the greatest strength in Aden. General Secretary 'Ali Salim al-Bayd, who is also a sayyid from the Hadramawt (although his mother is of Yafa'i origin), was a minor figure in the independence struggle. His career has been checkered, with appointments to cabinet and party posts followed by periods of disgrace. Bayd's record as guerrilla leader and public official undoubtedly contributed to his obtaining the post of general secretary but the Assistant General Secretary Salim Salih Muhammad may be more powerful. Although a former foreign minister, Politburo member (and cousin of another former foreign minister, Muhammad Salih Muti', who was executed by 'Ali Nasir in 1981), Salim has always remained in the background. His strength within party ranks, in combination with his Yafa'i background, makes him a formidable opponent in Aden.

Two other Politburo members cannot be ignored. Muhammad Sa'id 'Abdullah (also known as Muhsin or Muhsin al-Sharjabi) headed the state security apparatus for much of the 1970s and handled the dirty work for former president 'Abd al-Fattah Isma'il, a fellow North Yemeni. Muhammad followed 'Abd al-Fattah into exile in 1980 but returned to Aden as housing minister in 1984. His resuscitation was apparently engineered by 'Ali 'Antar and Salih Muslih Qasim as part of their efforts to displace 'Ali Nasir Muhammad. Muhammad Sa'id 'Abdullah is a force to be reckoned with, although his northern origins and notorious secret police reputation combine to make him an untrustworthy aspirant to top leadership. The new minister of state security, Sa'id Salih Salim, also bears watching because of the enormous powers associated with his postition and his reputation as a chief of the hardliner faction.

The immediate effects of the January conflagration have long since disappeared, and a perhaps deceptive state of normalcy has been restored to Aden. The present regime will not be dislodged easily. In the absence of any major support, either inside or outside the country, 'Ali Nasir's chances of returning are virtually nil. The Soviet Union has made its peace with the new regime, and North Yemen's president, 'Ali 'Abdullah Salih, is unwilling to risk hostilities. There is a tendency in Aden to play down any need for policy differences between the new regime and the previous one of 'Ali Nasir Muhammad, partly because the regime has found it necessary to maintain the same course and partly because 'Ali Nasir can be more easily discredited as simply a crazed individual.

But problems still remain. It would appear that no clique has yet amassed enough strength to take charge firmly. The existing state of uneasy balance has allowed the state to turn its attention to pressing matters of reconstruction, oil exploration, and the omnipresent search for foreign aid. The state managed to carry out the elections to the Supreme People's Council in late October and its pro forma confirmation of top government officials without any hitches. But the more significant, and thus more controversial, convening of the Fourth Congress of the YSP has been put off until at least June 1987 amid reports of divisions over the issues of reconciliation and ideological obduracy.

**The International Impact of the Fighting.** Aden's foreign relations illustrate something of the disarray the January civil war foisted on South Yemeni politics. Paradoxically, the PDRY regime remains on poor terms with its erstwhile radical allies in the Middle East and Africa, and relations are best with the conservative Gulf states.

Ties between South Yemen and Ethiopia, the two fellow Marxist regimes of the Red Sea, have always been close, particularly since South Yemeni troops fought alongside Ethiopian forces in the Ogaden and in Eritrea. The January fighting and Mengistu Haile Mariam's close personal ties to 'Ali Nasir, for whom he had publicly expressed his support during the fractious third YSP congress in 1985, severely strained the relationship between the countries. The large numbers of refugees and the presence of most of the PDRY navy in Ethiopia constituted another major stumbling block that was not redressed until announcement of the general amnesty and Aden's agreement to allow some naval personnel to return home. Relations have improved since then, and the two countries' deputy chiefs of staff met in June. In late October, YSP general secretary 'Ali al-Bayd made a three-day visit to Addis Ababa following the safe departure of the refugees sheltered in the Ethiopian embassy in Aden.

On the other hand, representatives of the new regime made goodwill visits to the Arab Gulf states even before the fighting had died down. The neutrality (at the least) of Saudi Arabia seemed assured with the visit of 'Attas to Riyadh in July and the subsequent provision of aid and soft loans exceeding $70 million. Aden has placed considerable emphasis on preserving the rapprochement with former archenemy Oman. At the beginning of February, a special envoy was dispatched to Muscat to dispel any fears of a radical change in PDRY policy. Oman's minister of state for foreign affairs made a four-day official visit to Aden in June; during that time, the decision was made to resume border negotiations and open embassies in each other's capital.

A major but brief, foreign relations problem developed in August when South Yemeni warplanes forced down an Air Djibouti airliner on its way from Sanaa to Djibouti, apparently acting on a tip that a key 'Ali Nasir aide was on board. The Ethiopian pilot refused to allow the aide to be taken from the plane and Djibouti cut off air and sea travel with Aden until the incident was resolved shortly afterward.

Ties between the two Yemens continue to be correct but tense. Yemen Arab Republic president 'Ali 'Abdullah Salih had been predisposed to support his southern counterpart because he had been the most moderate of the south's leaders, had allowed Sanaa to break the back of the Aden-supported National Democratic Front in 1982, and had struggled to keep the principal instigators of the 1979 Yemeni border war, 'Abd al-Fattah Isma'il and 'Ali 'Antar in check. The northern leader seemingly had been on the brink of either intervening himself during the January fighting or allowing PLO fighters based in North Yemen to head south. In the end, Soviet persuasion dissuaded him from taking any action. He might have changed his mind even without Soviet prodding, however, given 'Ali Nasir's negligence in sending an envoy to Sanaa until the fifth day of fighting. 'Ali Nasir's reputation as a waffler seemingly was confirmed by his failure to stay in Aden to lead the fighting or even make good on his threat to carry on the resistance in Abyan.

The presence of armed camps of refugees along the Yemens' border continues to poison relations. There is a long history of each country attempting to influence the other by supporting dissident movements on its soil; such activities led to border wars in 1972 and 1979 and could do so again. Although Sanaa officially supports reconciliation between the two sides and has balanced the presence of large numbers of refugees with its refusal to allow 'Ali Nasir to reside in North Yemen, it has reconciled itself to getting along with Aden. The popular, but intractable, issue of Yemeni unity has moved even farther away from reality.

Soviet confusion on the outbreak of the civil war was obvious. The chain of events over the year and a half prior to January 1986 exposed the Kremlin's inability to direct internal PDRY politics. The Soviets seem to have had a hand in 'Abd al-Fattah Isma'il's return to Aden, not to overthrow 'Ali Nasir, but to demonstrate that 'Ali Nasir indisputably was their man. This mistake was compounded by their failure to comprehend 'Ali Nasir's vulnerability, and so they stood idly by as tensions and quarrels built up.

Taken by surprise on 13 January, the Soviets initially announced over Radio Moscow that a "counterrevolutionary" coup attempt against 'Ali Nasir had failed and then omitted further mention until the defenders had gotten the upper hand. Once it became clear that 'Ali Nasir's cause was lost, the Soviet Union was quick to offer its support to the new government, a transparent opportunism that provoked the deliberate shelling of the Soviet embassy. Four thousand Soviet advisors and dependents were among the first evacuees and thirteen Russians, two of them women, were killed.

Moscow undoubtedly has exercised a constraining influence on the new Adeni leadership, having been burned by 'Abd al-Fattah Isma'il's pugnaciousness in the past; certainly it has no intention of jeopardizing its new links to Oman, the United Arab Emirates, and the Gulf Cooperation Council. Unwilling to hazard its foothold in Arabia and its strategic military sites, the Soviet Union was the first country to provide emergency aid. Although attempts were made to mediate between the two factions during the fighting and in subsequent months, Moscow has now clearly cast its lot in with the new leadership in Aden and abandoned 'Ali Nasir.

Its patronage is indicated by the frequency and nature of contacts between the two countries. 'Ali al-Bayd met Mikhail Gorbachev in Moscow on 4 March and again in Berlin on 21 April. A Soviet military delegation visited Aden a few days later. At a rally on 31 August, Soviet Fleet Admiral Nikolay I. Smirnov, the leader of a military delegation attending Aden's Armed Forces Day celebrations, praised "the glorious martyrs" killed on 13 January and hailed the armed forces' role in "foiling the lowly conspiracy conceived and implemented by the traitor 'Ali Nasir Muhammad and his gang against the party and against constitutional legality." CPSU Politburo member Geydar Aliyev visited Aden in late October.

In the economic realm, lengthy talks were held with the Soviets in Aden during April to consider cooperation in agriculture, fisheries, energy, oil and minerals, and geology. An economic protocol providing for assistance in reconstruction, trade development, and scientific cooperation was signed on 17 April, and further protocols were signed in early June. A number of trade agreements were signed in Aden on 21 July, including promises to export a number of specific items, the gift of 50,000 tons of gasoline from the oil being refined by the Soviet Union in Aden, and 5 million rubles worth of aid in kind. Further discussions in Moscow at the end of October led to an agreement for assistance in oil exploration, agricultural development, and training programs.

Economic and political ties were also maintained with other East European countries, and a number of visits to Aden by Palestinian and Lebanese Communist Party delegations were recorded. Politburo member Muhammad Sa'id 'Abdullah attended the twenty-fifth anniversary celebrations of Nicaragua's Sandinista Front in November.

J. E. Peterson
*Washington, D.C.*

# WESTERN EUROPE

# Introduction

The decade of the 1980s in Western Europe began with an electoral victory in France that many political observers described as a major challenge to the West. The resulting government coalition between the French Socialists and the French Communist Party (PCF) in 1981 gave the PCF four cabinet posts in one of the most important countries on the continent. Two years later the *World Marxist Review* drew the conclusion that "the ideas advanced by Europe's communists meet the innermost interests of the people" (November 1983); a reflection in part of the nationalization of French industry and the introduction of Socialist fiscal policies.

The apparent cohesion of Western Europe's communist parties began to deteriorate in 1984, however. The parties fared only moderately well at the polls, and the PCF resigned from the coalition. Emerging debates within many of the parties focused on differing views of the direction they should take in the future. In Italy, for example, party leadership changed hands in 1984 for the first time in twelve years, and by the end of 1985, the party had been unable to design a new program; indeed, in 1986 the party held its first extraordinary congress since 1945 to discuss its future. At the beginning of the same year, 1986, intense party factionalism in Spain resulted in three separate communist movements and a weak electoral coalition that consisted of seven different fragmented parties. The most dramatic, and in many ways the most ironic, development in 1986, however, occurred in France. The PCF polled 9.8 percent of the vote, its worst performance in 60 years of French parliamentary elections.

The French experience, although the most visible, mirrored developments within Western Europe's other communist parties. The hopes engendered by the PCF's electoral success in 1981 had turned to frustration by 1986 and contributed to increasingly acrimonious debates within communist party leaderships. What had represented a remarkable communist victory in 1981 had become an equally remarkable reversal just five years later. In 1985 two members of the British Communist Party, Andrew Rothstein and Robin Page Arnot, had argued that "the situation is crying out for the determined leadership which only a Communist Party united on the principles of Marxism-Leninism can give" ("The British Communist Party and Eurocommunism," *Political Affairs*, London, October 1985). But one year later, strong leadership in the West European communist movement was still absent, and the appeal of Marxism-Leninism had been given a resounding defeat in France.

The challenge to the West of 1981 had been replaced in 1986 with challenges to the very cohesion of the parties themselves. The validity of the conclusion drawn in 1984, that the communist parties enjoyed "little prospect of gaining the popular credibility and trust that they need to become more than minority forces" (Kevin Devlin, "The Decline of Eurocommunism: Downhill from the Summit," *RAD Background Report*, no. 60, 13 April 1984) was reinforced by events in 1985 and 1986. As 1986 began, each of Western Europe's communist parties faced an uncertain future; indeed, it seemed certain that the new year would see a continuation of party factionalism, internal strife, and ideological disarray.

This decline was already clearly evident in 1985. In each of the seven national elections held in Western

Europe, the communist parties received fewer votes than they had in the previous one, and in Belgium the Communist Party lost its parliamentary representation entirely. This trend continued in 1986, during which four national elections were held. In France the party received 9.8 percent of the vote (down from 16.2 percent in 1981). In the Netherlands the party dropped from 1.8 percent in 1982 to 0.6 percent. In Spain and Austria, electoral successes were achieved, but they amounted to negligible increases: Austria received 0.72 percent (up from 0.66 percent in 1983) and Spain 4.6 percent (up from 3.8 percent in 1982).

Internal party conflict was not the only reason the communist parties failed to achieve success at the polls. Common to them all was an absence of domestic programs designed to provide realistic solutions to such problems as unemployment, inflation, or the costs of social welfare programs. Their efforts to persuade the voters that their approaches for dealing with domestic and foreign policy issues represented viable alternatives were based primarily on negative criticism and not on constructive proposals. Confronted with relatively strong economies in Western Europe, the communist parties had little to offer voters who, for example, gave the conservative party of Jacques Chirac in France a resounding electoral victory in March and refused to elect to Parliament a single communist member from Paris, where Gisèle Moreau, the sole woman on the PCF Politburo and head of the PCF's Paris electoral list, was defeated. In 1986, as in 1984 and 1985, it was clear to Western Europe's voters that the promises of a better life through class struggle were hollow and that communist party assertions that the "cohesion of the working class" was necessary "to bar reaction, defend democratic achievements and open new prospects for social progress" were simply untrue (*WMR*, November 1982).

Western Europe's communist parties continued to find themselves in a dilemma very accurately described by Aleksandr Zinoviev, who was expelled from the USSR in 1978:

> If the Western Communists want to survive and to continue to have any influence over the masses they are doomed to repudiate Marxist ideology. Their future, if they are to have a future, is in any case bleak indeed. They must either follow the dictates of Moscow or break up. There is no other choice; they must be either pro-Soviet or anti-Soviet. (Kevin Devlin, "Zinoviev Sees Bleak Future for Western Communist Parties," *RAD Background Report*, no. 61, 2 July 1985.)

Zinoviev stressed that communist ideology "no longer reflects the interests of the working class," that "the defenders of communism in the West are no longer the workers but the intellectuals and state officials," and that "they must change their ideology and their slogans; otherwise they have no future" (ibid.). The point Zinoviev emphasized was valid not only for the continent's communist parties but also for parties of the left as a whole, as has been well illustrated by the conservative electoral victory in France in March.

In 1986, 12 of Western Europe's 23 parties were represented in their respective parliaments—those of Cyprus, Finland, France, Greece, Iceland, Italy, Luxembourg, Portugal, San Marino, Spain, Sweden, and Switzerland. With the exception of San Marino, party members held no cabinet posts for the third consecutive year. Four national elections were held during the year (seven elections were held in 1985, one in 1984, and ten in 1983). They took place in Austria, France, the Netherlands, and Spain. The Italian Communist Party remains the strongest in Western Europe, holding slightly less than one-third of the parliamentary seats (29.9 percent; 198 of 630 seats). Of the remaining parties with legislative representation, Cyprus held the highest percentage of seats based on votes received (27.4), followed by San Marino (24.3), Iceland (17.3), Portugal (15.5), Finland (14), Greece (9.9), France (9.8), Sweden (5.4), Luxembourg (4.9), and Switzerland (0.9). The 11 parties without legislative representation held between 0.03 (Great Britain) and 1.2 percent (Belgium) of their respective parliamentary seats based on votes received.

The views and positions of the French Communist Party (PCF) provide an excellent illustration of the problems confronting the communist parties of Western Europe. Following the 1981 election of François Mitterrand as president of France—the result of a coalition between the French Socialist (PS) and Communist parties—the CPSU endorsed this victory as "an historic event for France and all Western Europe" (London, *Guardian*, August/September 1981).

During 1983 the PCF shared major electoral losses with the PS in French municipal elections. At the same time, however, the party continued to maintain its own views on a variety of basic issues, even when these positions conflicted with official government policy. During 1984 and throughout 1985, the disastrous effects of socialist economic policies produced a major revision in Mitterrand's approach to solving the problems of the French economy and resulted in a policy of economic austerity with an emphasis on private enterprise and competition, this in an effort to counter the negative effects of domestic policies that had resulted in devaluation of the French franc, inflation, nationalization of major French banks and industries, and changes in tax policy that were aimed at a small minority and based on a rationale that was punitive by design and economically unsound in practice. In an effort to reverse these developments, Mitterrand appointed Laurent Fabius as the new prime minister in July 1984, and the PCF took this opportunity to withdraw from the cabinet, enter the opposition, and in effect terminate the "Union of the Left" of 1981. The socialist goal, according to Prime Minister Fabius, was "to forge a large party—some call it Social Democratic—able to obtain 30 to 40 percent of the vote" (Nicholas Bray, "French Socialists Losing Support, Edging Away from Marxist Roots," *WSJ*, 13 December 1985).

At the PCF's Twenty-fifth Congress, held in February 1985, the "Union of the Left" was formally abandoned, and party chairman Georges Marchais and his supporters moved to justify their retreat from leftist unity and to isolate dissent within the party. But results of an opinion poll taken the same month indicated that only 15 percent saw the PCF as a party "of the future," whereas a 60 percent majority considered it a party "of the past" (*News From France*, 15 February 1985).

During 1986 the leaders of the PCF spent virtually the entire year dealing with the domestic and international ramifications of the party's continued decline. Dissident leaders—increasingly isolated from positions of authority in the party—continued to press demands for internal reform. Unprecedented electoral losses in important legislative, regional, and by-elections prompted reformist demands for an extraordinary party congress (the Twenty-sixth Congress is scheduled for 1990), while changes to France's electoral system, enacted by the new conservative government, threatened to erode the PCF's electoral support even further. Marchais's decision not to stand as the PCF's candidate in the presidential elections (set for 1988) was, therefore, widely interpreted as a measure of compromise with both dissidents and others who blamed Marchais for much of the party's weakness.

The party's Central Committee, however, rejected demands for an extraordinary party congress and instead directed criticism at the Socialists for "doing everything possible to break" the PCF and for governing in such a way as to "give in to the economic crisis, unemployment, and austerity, and justify the existing capitalist order." The consequence was an open rift within the party. It included charges that Stalinism had returned to plague the PCF, public demands for the resignation of Marchais, and an analysis by former PCF spokesman, Pierre Juquin, which he entitled *Self-Criticism* and in which he argued that the party's decline was due to the leadership's refusal to make the appropriate analysis of, and adjust strategy to, fundamental changes in French society that, among other things, had altered the character of the working class. In addition, Juquin himself was accused by André Lajoinie, chairman of the PCF caucus in the French National Assembly, of "ultimately aiming to preserve capitalism" (*l'Humanité*, 7 April). As the year progressed, Lajoinie was rumored to be Marchais's successor as general secretary.

At the end of the year, few members had openly left the party, but its future direction would assure continuance of internal party debate concerning its proper and effective role in French society. It was equally clear that the stunning electoral defeat represented an erosion of half the PCF's strength in just five years and that the Socialist Party (PS), which fared better than expected with 30 percent of the vote, was still the largest party in France. Nonetheless, in elections to the French Senate in September, both communists and Socialists lost ground; the PS retained 64 of 69 seats, and the PCF emerged with only 15 of 24 seats previously held.

The Communist Party of Italy (PCI) was not fraught with the internal strife seen in the PCF but concentrated instead on an effort to cultivate the Euroleft. Thus, the party's parliamentary leader, Giorgio Napolitano, emphasized at the beginning of the year that "the communist parties can only go forward in the context of a European left. . . For many years I have been convinced that the old differences between the communists and the socialist movements are not sustainable" (James M. Markham, "Sharp Decline by Communists in West Europe," *NYT*, 3 February). Napolitano addressed a primary problem: Where are the struggling working classes that Western Europe's communist parties seek to represent? a question of fundamental significance for their future electoral success. As Annie Kriegel, a former member of the PCF, has explicitly stated, "The communists can do nothing if the working class disappears. . . The Communists lose their social base" (ibid.). The danger is a real one, but it does not mean that, in the case of the PCI, the party is incapable of making internal adjustments. According to Napolitano, "to avoid the danger of decline it is necessary to think in terms of the left and less in terms of communist politics . . . We cannot just be a party of preachers and oppositionists" (ibid.).

This analysis provided the background for the PCI's Seventeenth Party Congress held in April in Florence. At that meeting the PCI's task was defined as "first and foremost to import positive specificity to spontaneous condemnation and protest," a statement that reflected concern with the difficulty of controlling the people the PCI considers its most significant recent conquest, described as the "members who have participated, and still participate, in the movements characteristic of our time—movements for Women's Liberation, movements for the emancipation of oppressed peoples, and pacifist and environmental movements" (*l'Unita*, 10 April). In this connection the congress pointed to the historical decline of the PCF and the Spanish Communist Party and therefore deliberately chose to hold its party congress, originally planned for 1987, one year earlier in an effort to focus attention on "programmatic and organizational renewal." Thus, the congress described the party as a "party of modern reform" and as an "integral part of the European left." (*l'Unita*, 15 December 1985.)

The CPI's 1979 congress (the fifteenth) had eliminated from party statutes the obligation "to acquire and deepen the knowledge of Marxism-Leninism as well as to apply its teachings to the solution of concrete questions." But the congress also emphasized that the PCI was "anchored in the ideal and cultural tradition which has its roots and inspiration in the thought of Marx and Engels and which receives it impulse of historical significance from the . . . ideas and work of Lenin" (see Heinz Timmermann, "Italiens Kommunisten zwischen Stagnation und Wandel," *Berichte des Bundesinstituts für ostwissenschaftliche und internationale Studien* 35, 1986).

In April 1986, however, the party continued to stress the goal of "overcoming the capitalist system" but no longer referred to the teachings of Lenin. Party general secretary Alessandro Natta stressed instead that one must retain a sense of "utopia and grand values" and recognize the role of "political and cultural pluralism" in seeking a socialist society (ibid.). The ultimate aim of this strategy was to give the party, in the eyes of the Italian electorate, a credible voice in Italian politics. Although the party is represented in Parliament with 198 of 630 seats, it has not participated in an Italian government since 1979. This concern with political isolation was reflected in the point expressed during the congress that the PCI seeks dialogue with the Italian Socialists, and that, in the words of General Secretary Natta, "isolated is an unsuitable word for a party that enjoys the support of one-third of the electorate" (*l'Unita*, 10 April). It is difficult to assess how the PCI will proceed in 1987, but it is certain that the party seeks to avoid the difficulties plaguing the PCF. In this regard, therefore, its domestic and foreign policy positions will be aimed at the left, individually and as a whole, and not at achieving the "unity of the working class."

The Spanish Communist Party (PCE) has enjoyed legal status since 1977 and, under the leadership of Santiago Carrillo, was the leading proponent of Eurocommunism until 1981. Carrillo's successor in 1982, Gerardo Iglesias (then 37 years old), continues to serve as general secretary of the party. Between 1983 and 1986 Iglesias devoted a major effort toward healing internal party wounds and re-establishing the PCE as a prominent political party, an effort that met with mixed success.

The PCE is one of the most deeply divided parties in Europe; it is fragmented into three main parties in addition to several smaller ones. Pro-Soviet dissidents, calling themselves "Afghans," withdrew from the mainstream "Eurocommunist" PCE in 1983 to form the Communist Party of the Peoples of Spain (PCPE). Carrillo led his loyalists into opposition to the PCE leadership after he was displaced as general secretary in 1982, and he formally resigned from the PCE in early 1986. During the remainder of the year, he developed plans to form the Workers' Party–Communist Unity (PT-UC).

The principal cause of the dispute was the struggle between those members favoring close association with Moscow and those seeking to follow an independent, or Eurocommunist, path. A major issue in this rift centered on whether Spain should remain a member of NATO, membership in which the left asserted mortgaged Spain's sovereignty and strengthened dependence on the United States as well as undermined Spain's identification with Latin America. Spanish voters opted, 53 to 49 percent, to remain in NATO, and thus Prime Minister Felipe Gonzalez called elections, earlier than originally scheduled, for June in the expectation that he could capitalize on his victory in the NATO referendum before the left had an opportunity to organize effectively against him.

In preparation for the elections, the PCE formed a left-wing coalition with Ignacio Gallego's PCPE and also successfully persuaded Enrique Lister to merge his pro-Soviet Spanish Communist Workers' Party

(PCOE) back into the PCE after fifteen years of separation. Called the "United Left," the coalition was composed of seven parties, and in the election, it profited from a socialist loss of eighteen seats. The PCE itself received 4.6 percent of the vote (in 1982, it had received 3.8 percent) and won seven seats in the Spanish Cortes (in 1982, it had won four). Carrillo, failing in his efforts to persuade Iglesias and the PCPE's Gallego to join him in a communist unity ticket, campaigned alone under the banner of his own "Board for Communist Unity." Following the election Carrillo claimed that, had the three communist parties stood together, they would have obtained more than twenty deputies. But, indeed, he failed to win his own seat in Parliament, and his party drew only 1.12 percent of the vote.

At the end of the year the communist movement in Spain remained deeply divided. Carrillo's announcement in December that his Board of Communist Unity would hold a constituent congress in February 1987 to formally establish the Workers' Party–Communist Unity did not promise to resolve the division. The movement continued its march forward in disarray, and it may not be expected to exert a significant impact on Spanish politics in the new year.

The Portuguese Communist Party (PCP) has been under the leadership of Alvaro Cunhal since 1961. The party claims a membership in excess of 200,000, and in elections in 1985 won 38 of 250 parliamentary seats (15.5 percent of the vote). The communist movement remains controlled by one of the most Stalinist, pro-Soviet parties in Western Europe. Although the PCP's political influence continues to be significant, it is much reduced since an abortive 1976 coup attempt. An example was the support given by the PCP to socialist Mario Soares in his re-election as president in February (PCP endorsement was obtained only as a consequence of an extraordinary party congress convened for this purpose in early February, following failure to marshal sufficient support for its original candidate, Angelo Veloso, in January). Party backing for Soares was mocked by the press as a decision to "swallow the live toad" (*NYT*, 19 February), but Cunhal responded that the PCP's support was really a vote against the opposing candidate, Freitas do Amaral, rather than for Soares, whom he asserted—contrary to earlier statements—to be "the lesser of two major evils" (*LAT*, 27 January). For the remainder of the year, the PCP virtually ignored the new president and concentrated its energies on trying to negotiate "democratic convergence" in the national assembly to oppose the prime minister's minority government. By the end of the year, however, this effort had not proved successful, and the party focused its efforts on preparations for its Twelfth Congress, scheduled for 1987.

In Cyprus, Greece, Malta, San Marino, and Turkey, weakness prevented the communist parties from exerting significant influence on the conduct of domestic or foreign affairs. In San Marino the Communist Party (CPSM) is an extension of the Italian Communist Party, just as the country's other political parties are extensions of the Italian. Between 1978 and 1986 the CPSM formed part of a governing coalition that excluded only the Christian Democrats (DCS). In 1986, the party (which received 24.3 percent of the vote in 1983) and the DCS (42.1 percent in 1983) formed a coalition for the first time. Of the country's three executive secretaryships (finance, foreign affairs, and internal affairs), the CPSM received that of internal affairs.

In Malta the Communist Party (CPM) was founded in 1969 and is not represented in Parliament. The CPM has little impact on Maltese political life, but it does plan to participate in the next national elections, scheduled for April 1987. As in 1985, the CPM maintained extensive party contacts with representatives from communist parties throughout Europe, reflecting a major interest on behalf of the Soviet Union in Maltese affairs. Economic relations with the Soviet government are extensive, and the labor government of the island has significantly increased economic and cultural agreements with the countries of Eastern Europe during the past two years. The nature and extent of increased contact led the former deputy ambassador to the United Nations from the United States, Charles Lichenstein, to conclude in November that "the democracies in the West must view with growing concern Malta's drift towards the Soviet sphere. This compromises Malta's stability and the security of the Mediterranean region" (*The Times*, Malta, 7 December).

The Communist Party in Turkey (TCP) remains proscribed, the only communist party in this position in Western Europe.

The Communist Party of Cyprus (AKEL) draws its primary support from the Greek Cypriot majority, which comprises approximately 80 percent of the island's estimated population of 670,000. Party membership is claimed to be approximately 14,000, and it is proscribed in the northern sector of the island, the Turkish Republic of Northern Cyprus. In the most recent national elections, held in December 1985, the AKEL polled 27.4 percent of the vote and holds 15 of 56 parliamentary seats as the island's third strongest party. General Secretary Ezekias Papaioannou, 78 years of age in 1986, has led the party since 1949, and the average age of other senior party leaders is well over 65 years. Although the issue of gerontocracy was not an agenda item during the party's Sixteenth Congress, held in November, it unquestionably poses a major problem for the party's future direction and growth. Until the 1985 national elections, the party had consistently received approximately one-third of the vote. Thus, it must devote increased attention to generating new support, especially among younger voters, in the future. Whether the party will be successful will be evident during 1987 as it develops its campaign for the presidential elections scheduled for February 1988. If the timeworn admonitions to take the offensive on the ideological and political fronts are continued, the AKEL may lack the leadership necessary to capture the imagination and support of "other patriotic and democratic forces" on the island (Nicosia Domestic Service, 26 November).

In Greece the party remains split into the pro-Soviet and Eurocommunist factions into which it split during the period of military government in Greece (1967–1974). The pro-Soviet faction, the KKE, won 13 of 300 parliamentary seats in the 1985 national elections; its membership is estimated at 42,000. The Eurocommunist faction, known as KKE-Interior, has adopted an increasingly independent position and retains little of its Marxist-Leninist heritage. It is represented with one seat in the Greek Parliament, but announced at its Fourth Congress in May that it would dissolve itself in the spring of 1987 and re-emerge as a new party of the Greek noncommunist left, to be known as the New Greek Left (NEA). The objective of the new party will be to attract members of the leftist groups who are dissatisfied with the Panhellenic Socialist Movement (PASOK) led by Andreas Papandreou but are also unwilling to join the pro-Moscow KKE.

The domestic and foreign policy positions of the KKE have, in the past, normally paralleled those of Papandreou's governing PASOK. In 1985 the KKE received 9.9 percent of the vote and retained the number of parliamentary seats it had won in 1981 (13 of 300); the PASOK received 45.8 percent of the vote and 161 seats, ten more than the 151 required for a majority. In October 1985, however, the PASOK introduced austerity measures designed to improve the Greek economy, which in turn elicited significant KKE opposition to government economic policy; a situation reminiscent of the PCF's opposition to similar measures taken in France in 1984 and 1985.

The KKE faced the dilemma of whether to strongly criticize the PASOK economic policies and thereby force an early election that the PASOK might well lose to the conservative New Democracy Party (ND). If, on the other hand, the KKE were to ignore public discontent, it would incur the risk of losing credibility as the champion of the "downtrodden." The path chosen by the party was one of compromise. The KKE employed a middle-of-the-road policy that centered on continuing criticism of the austerity measures, on calls for closer cooperation between PASOK and other "progressive" forces (this, based on the assumption that PASOK cannot implement the policy of economic "change" alone), and on subtle efforts to attract to the party leftist supporters of the PASOK who were disillusioned by the government's policies.

The result was that, during municipal elections in October 1986, KKE-supported candidates fared much better than had parliamentary candidates in the June 1985 election. In the mayoral races in Athens, Piraeus, and Salonika, the party garnered 17.62, 16.42, and 23.27 percent of the vote, respectively. Although this outcome was insufficient to elect in the first electoral round, it nonetheless evinced sufficient support to allow the party to instruct its followers to refrain from supporting PASOK candidates in the second electoral round. The result was the election of members of the ND in all three cities (PASOK lost 20 mayorships, ND gained 14, and the KKE gained 9). It is unclear how the party will fare in 1987, but it is certain to address the nature and extent of future cooperation with the PASOK at its party congress scheduled for May 1987; a congress at which one may expect several older party leaders—possibly including General Secretary Kharilaos Florakis—to make room for younger members.

The Communist Party of Great Britain (CPGB) continued to experience declining influence. In Great Britain's last general election held in 1983, the party polled .03 percent of vote and has not been represented in the British Parliament since 1950; Lord Milford is the sole CPGB member of the House of Lords. Gordon McLennan continues as party chairman, and at a little over 15,000, membership is at its lowest point since World War II. The decline in electoral support was graphically illustrated during Britain's last general elections in 1983, when the party's 35 candidates polled only 11,598 votes. The poor showing of the

CPGB at the polls, however, belies the party's strength in the trade union movement and in influencing opinion. Although the party does not control any individual trade union, it is represented in most union executives and has played a major role in most government/union confrontations in recent years. The party continued to be plagued during the year, however, by the long-standing conflict between Eurocommunist leadership and the Stalinist hard left minority, conflict that is likely to continue in the new year as the next British election approaches; in turn, the CPGB is unlikely to increase its influence on British politics in the new year.

In Ireland the Communist Party (CPI) has never significantly affected political life. Although it does participate in local and national elections, it is not represented in Parliament. During the year, the CPI continued to give primary attention to advocacy of a single, united socialist Ireland, and the party thus supports unity among Protestants and Catholics, since this division allegedly divides the "working class."

The communist parties of Belgium, Denmark, the Netherlands, and Luxembourg exercised no significant influence in the political life of their respective countries during the year. In Luxembourg the Communist Party (CPL) continued to hold 2 of 64 parliamentary seats, no change from the national election of 1984. The party is strongly pro-Soviet, and party leadership remains in the hands of the Urbany family; Honorary Chairman Dominique Urbany, father of the current party chairman René Urbany, died in October. The party's domestic and foreign policy positions closely mirror those of the Soviet communist party and stress support of the peace movement and opposition to nuclear war.

The role played by the Communist Party of Denmark (DKP) during the year continued to be insignificant. Weaker than at any time since World War II, the DKP received a scant 0.8 percent of the vote in the last parliamentary elections in January 1984. It has not been represented in Parliament since 1979 when its vote fell below the 2 percent minimum required for proportional representation. The November 1985 municipal elections demonstrated continuing DKP weakness. Approximately 4,500 council seats were contested, and the party lost 14 of 22 seats previously held. Public opinion polls in 1986 gave the leftist bloc up to nearly 20 percent without any renewed support for the DKP. Writing in *Socialistisk Weekend* (15 August), former DKP Central Committee member and member of Parliament, Tove Jørgensen, painted a picture of the party as a closed Leninist clique that prohibits open debate and rejects any sustained efforts by the party rank and file to participate in the formulation of DKP policy. With the next DKP congress scheduled for April 1987, discussion at the end of the year focused on possible successors to party chairman Jørgen Jensen, who may resign at the age of 65 with a meagre record to show for his ten years of leadership. Without new membership and new leadership, the pattern of ineffectual political action is almost certain to continue.

In Belgium, the Communist Party (PCB) has an estimated membership of 5,000 in a country with a population of almost 10 million. In national elections held in 1985, the party received only 1.2 percent of the vote and lost its two parliamentary seats. For the first time since 1925, the party was without representation in the Belgian Parliament. In 1986, in an effort "to renew" the party, the PCB modified its structure and leadership. Announcements of the first changes in party organization came at the Twenty-fifth Congress held in April. In response to the marked decline in membership and electoral losses, as well as to the opportunities offered by growing public dissatisfaction with the economic austerity programs of the Belgian government, the party brought new members to its leadership. Although the chief spokesman for the party, Louis Van Geyt, retained his position as president, the two vice presidents for Wallonia and Flanders resigned to "leave a place for the young" (*Drapeau Rouge*, 17 June). In his address to the congress Van Geyt warned that the party would be passed by if it did not respond to the evolution of the working class reflected in the scientific and technological revolution and the "transnationalisation" of capital. Following the congress, the party moved in the direction of a federalized party structure and declared that regional economic differences would necessitate different strategies in Flanders, Brussels, and Wallonia so that each wing of the party would be able to modify its policy more easily to adapt to changing regional conditions. It is unlikely that these measures will generate a significant positive shift in party popularity in 1987 in the highly complex and divided political landscape of Belgium.

The Communist Party of the Netherlands (CPN) has an estimated party membership of 12,000. It exercises little influence on political life and, in fact, experienced major electoral setbacks during the year. In the March municipal elections, the CPN lost one-third of its seats on municipal councils and was reduced to a single council seat in the city of Groningen (down from its previous 6 seats). Two months later, in the

May parliamentary elections, the CPN plummeted from the 1.8 percent of the vote received in 1982 to 0.6 percent and lost all of the three seats it had held in the previous Parliament. The defeat left the CPN unrepresented in Parliament for the first time since 1918. Despite attempts to build electoral alliances, the CPN competed in the elections alone, since the Labor Party rejected all overtures for alliance with the smaller parties to its left, and the small leftist parties themselves were internally divided. The consequences of a prolonged electoral postmortem was the decision to advance the Thirtieth Congress, originally scheduled for the spring of 1987, to December 1986 in order to elect a new executive committee and determine party strategy for the elections to the provincial legislatures scheduled for mid-1987.

By the end of 1986, debate on the future of the CPN had not concluded. Although party leaders had expressed doubts about the CPN's previous emphasis on cooperation with other parties of the left, plans were underway to submit joint lists of candidates in ten of the Netherland's twelve provinces. But efforts to form an electoral coalition obscured the real issue, also common to other parties of Western Europe: on the one hand, the attempts to renew the party had alienated traditional working class supporters, while on the other hand, the traditional working class to which the CPN had always appealed was disappearing. To some observers, therefore, it seemed self-evident that the CPN must reform the party structure, develop new themes, and appeal to new groups; but to others, this did not seem necessary or obvious at all. How this dilemma would be resolved would determine the party's future in 1987 and beyond.

In the Nordic countries of Iceland, Norway, Sweden, and Finland, communist party activity did not significantly affect the conduct of domestic and foreign policy. The Communist Party of Iceland (AB) has remained in the political opposition since the dissolution of the coalition government in 1983 in which it held the cabinet posts of finance, industry, and social and health affairs. In 1986 it was the largest opposition party, with 10 of 60 parliamentary seats, while the governing coalition of the Progressive and Independence parties jointly held 37 seats. In a country in which economic affairs are dominant, 1986 was a remarkable economic year: GNP increased by 5 percent, inflation fell to 10 percent, and unemployment virtually disappeared. This outstanding performance was the result of strong demand for Icelandic fish products in Europe and the United States, the dramatic fall in the price of petroleum (which Iceland must import), and domestic economic restraint. The strength of the economy, however, could still prove a liability to the party in the national elections scheduled for the spring of 1987. Early forecasts predict a 2.7 percent growth in 1987, but by the end of the year, the party had not yet found a political profile that offered a realistic prospect of weakening the government's popularity. Thus, although it is the strongest of Iceland's leftist parties, the AB is unlikely to regain a major role in the country's political affairs in the new year.

In Norway the Communist Party (NKP) continues to be pro-Soviet. Its membership and popularity dwindled when Reidar Larsen (its chairman in 1975) and several other leaders abandoned the NKP and established the Socialist Left Party (SV). Although differences still exist between the NKP and the SV, NKP chairman Hans I. Kleven looked favorably on SV chairman Theo Koritzinsky's call for a broad, united front of left-wing parties in Norway. Kleven believed that it is especially important to establish "unity of action" in the labor movement, both in the unions themselves and in the political parties close to labor. In addition, he supported Koritzinsky's proposals for electoral cooperation between the NKP and the SV. The NKP remains, however, one of the weakest communist parties in Western Europe and polled just 0.2 percent of the vote in the general elections of September 1985. Internally the party continues to face a rift between those who strongly support the CPSU and those who advocate a more independent position. This debate has had a negative impact on the party's ability to attract new members, and has made it very difficult for the party to present a unified position on domestic and foreign policy issues comprehensible to the Norwegian electorate. As a consequence a new party program has been proposed for discussion at the NKP's next party congress scheduled for April 1987.

The Left Party Communists (VPK) in Sweden won 5.4 percent of the vote in national elections held in September 1985 and holds 19 of 349 parliamentary seats (in 1982, it had won 5.6 percent of the vote and held 20 of 349 seats). Its activity during the year, plus a public opinion poll taken in the spring, indicated that party's strength at 3.5 percent, a half-percentage fall from a poll taken earlier in the year. The significance of the 3.5 percent figure is that a political party must win at least 4 percent of the vote to be represented in the Swedish Parliament. Although no elections were scheduled for 1987, the party announced plans in May for development of a new party program at its next congress, scheduled for 1987. Reflecting concern evident in the positions taken by other West European communist parties during the year, Jörn Svensson, a VPK member of Parliament, emphasized that "the path to socialism in a developed capitalist country like Sweden must follow the democratic process and stay within the current Constitution." Thus, he stressed that the proposed party platform for the next congress would be less abstract than previous ones and that it would focus on two principal points: (1) the relative independence of the party in relation to other communist parties and (2) continued adherence to Marxism without "automatic interpretations of Marxist verbal symbolism" (*Dagens Nyheter*, 29 May). The crux of Svensson's comments seemed to indicate that the 1987 congress will be more pragmatic and less ideological than previous meetings.

The internal affairs of the Finnish Communist Party (SKP), as well as its relations with its electoral front, the Finnish People's Democratic League (SKDL), were characterized by factional strife throughout the year. In 1983 the SKP, which in 1958 had been represented by 50 seats in Parliament, suffered the sharpest electoral defeat in its history: its number of seats in Parliament was reduced from 35 to 27, and its percentage of the vote fell to 14 percent. During 1984 the divisiveness continued, with the moderate wing represented by new SKP chairman Arvo Aalto and the Stalinist wing by Taisto Sinisalo. The rift developed into a complete split in 1985. At an extraordinary party congress held in March, Aalto and his wing urged adoption of a party program of "Socialism with a Finnish Face," but the congress was boycotted by the Stalinist wing. In the autumn the SKP delivered an ultimatum to the Stalinist minority to dismantle its party organization or face expulsion. By the end of the year the wing led by Sinisalo had been expelled, but a new party had not yet been formally constituted.

In January 1986 Aalto made public a draft of the new program that would be presented to the 1987 party congress scheduled for June. The purpose of the new program was to put the past behind the party, to "examine Finland and the world in terms of the future," and to develop the SKP as a popular movement (*Kansan Uutiset*, 24 January). The entire draft program was written in general and vague terms, but the most striking feature was the absence of doctrinal and traditional phrases and professed allegiances to Marxism-Leninism. Aalto emphasized that the proposed program reflected a desire to expand "international activity, not Eurocommunism, [and] that the west European communist parties which operate in similar social circumstances [be] seen as natural and intimate collaborators with the SKP" (ibid.).

The draft endorses "proletarian internationalism," a point some observers believe was added to appease the CPSU (*Nordisk Kontakt*, no. 2), but it made clear the party's independence from the CPSU by defining the principles of communist party cooperation as respecting the equality and sovereign independence of each party. "Finland's path to Socialism" was replaced by the concept of "opportunity for democratic change." Despite Aalto's denials, Finnish observers concluded that the party had changed fundamentally. A commentator of the conservative *Uusi Suomi* concluded, indeed, the "the SKP is now backsliding in the direction of a reformist social democratic party of the masses" (28 January).

The response of the Stalinist wing of the party was a meeting in April, at which they elected a "shadow" SKP, a complete copy of SKP organs with Sinisalo as chairman. Sinisalo insisted that the newly elected officials were the true leaders of the SKP and legitimate heirs to the Twentieth SKP Congress (1984). As the year continued, Aalto estimated in June that the quarrel had, over the past two decades, alienated 150,000 supporters and 20,000 party members. The future of both parties was completely uncertain at the end of the year, but it seemed likely that the SKP and the shadow SKP would continue their feud with unabated vigor.

The communist parties of Austria (KPO) and Switzerland (PdAS) occupy minor roles in the political affairs of their respective countries. The KPO is without representation in the Austrian parliament and received 0.72 percent of the vote in the most recent national election (November). Throughout the year the party attacked the concept of a social partnership between capital and labor as exploitive and anticommunist. The party's failure to address concrete issues did not contribute to increased voter support. In Switzerland the activity of the PdAS was minimal. The PdAS holds one of 200 parliamentary seats (it garnered 0.9 percent of the vote in the 1983 national elections) and plays a minor role in Swiss political life. The party continued to incur losses in municipal elections, as it had in 1985, but it remains pro-Soviet in orientation. In 1987, it is unlikely that either party will gain increased support, since their authoritarian appeals for the support of the "working class" and for the "unity of the Left" have little in common with the interests of the broad spectrum of the electorate.

The Socialist Unity Party of West Berlin (SEW) was formally established in 1969. Since that time it has been without representation in the city's Parliament, and it exercises no significant influence in the city's political affairs. The SEW, whose membership remained unchanged at about 5,400 during 1986, is pro-

Soviet and depends financially on the East German Communist Party (SED). Its positions are virtually identical with the ideological and political views of the SED and the CPSU. In the last elections for the city's House of Representatives (March 1985), the SEW obtained 7,713 votes, or 0.6 percent, compared with 0.7 in 1981. Its future performance is unlikely to differ from that of the past. In a city divided by the Wall and surrounded by mine fields, communist appeals to the electorate generate little enthusiasm.

In the Federal Republic of Germany (FRG) the Communist Party (DKP) received 0.2 percent of the vote in the 1983 national elections and has never been represented in the West German Parliament (the next national elections are scheduled for late January 1987). Party headquarters are located in Düsseldorf, where the offices of the German Trade Unions Alliance (DKB) are also located; the party opened an office in the West German capital of Bonn in September 1985. Party membership is claimed to be in excess of 50,000.

The Eighth Congress of the DKP was held in Hamburg in May; its theme was "For a New Policy: A World Without Nuclear Weapons and Work For All." The congress confirmed as party chairman Herbert Mies, who in his executive report echoed the Soviet Union's opposition to "U.S. Imperialism," and "Star Wars" and its advocacy of disarmament and peace proposals. In municipal elections in Lower Saxony and Hamburg in June and November, the DKP suffered losses of approximately 50 percent (in Lower Saxony the party received 0.1 percent and in Hamburg 0.2 percent of the vote). The party did not participate in an election in Bavaria in October and did not plan to campaign as a party in the national elections scheduled for 1987 (although individual members planned to stand for election on a coalition ticket composed of various leftist political figures). The party continued to endorse "unity of action of the working class," which reflects the attempt to embrace collaboration with the left wing of the Social Democratic party within, for example, the peace movement. The party has never enjoyed widespread popularity, however, and as long as Germany remains divided, it is unlikely to be accorded respect in West German political affairs. Its role in 1987 will almost certainly continue unchanged in a country whose political and economic system is among the most stable in Western Europe.

Dennis L. Bark
*Hoover Institution*

# Austria

Population. 7,546,500
Party. Communist Party of Austria (Kommunistische Partei Österreichs; KPO)
Founded. 3 November 1918
Membership. 15,000 (estimated by Vienna, *Profil*, 14 July)
Party Chairman. Franz Muhri (b. 1924)
Politburo. 12 members: Michael Graber, Franz Hager, Anton Hofer, Hans Kalt (secretary of Central Committee), Gustav Loistl, Franz Muhri, Otto Podolsky (Vienna party secretary), Karl Reiter, Erwin Scharf, Irma Schwager, Walter Silbermayr, Ernst Wimmer
Secretariat. 3 members. Hans Kalt, Karl Reiter, Walter Silbermayr
Central Committee. 64 members
Status. Legal
Last Congress. Twenty-fifth, 13–15 January 1984, in Vienna
Last Election. Federal, 23 November 1986, 0.72 percent, no representation
Publications. *Volksstimme* (People's voice; Michael Graber, editor), KPO daily organ, Vienna; *Weg und Ziel* (Path and goal; Erwin Scharf, editor), KPO theoretical monthly, Vienna

Because of the breakdown of the governing coalition of the Socialist Party (SPO) and the Freedom Party (FPO), 1986 unexpectedly became a federal parliamentary election year. For the first time in more than three decades, the KPO managed to increase its vote share, by 0.06 percent. The most likely cause for the end to the long downward trend was the crisis of the nationalized industries, especially iron and steel.

Even when it looked as though the election would not be held until the spring of 1987, the KPO Central Committee began discussing election strategy early in the hope of making gains as a result of the nationalized industries crisis of December 1985 (*Volksstimme*, 30 January). The KPO fielded candidates in all of the nine provinces, which also serve as electoral districts. The percentage of preliminary election returns for the KPO, as compared with the 1983 election, were as follows:

Austria—0.72, up from 0.66
Burgenland—remained the same at 0.3
Carinthia—0.6, down from 0.7
Lower Austria—remained the same at 0.6

Salzburg—0.5, up from 0.4
Styria—0.9, up from 0.8
Tyrol—0.6, up from 0.4
Upper Austria—0.6, up from 0.5
Vienna—remained the same at 1.0
Vorarlberg—0.7, up from 0.5

The returns show modest gains in the west of Austria and in Styria and a slight loss in Carinthia.

It was also the year of the most notorious election in postwar Austria. After just missing being elected on 4 May, Kurt Waldheim, the former general secretary of the United Nations, was elected federal president on 8 June. The campaign was ugly, largely because of Waldheim's clumsiness in the face of allegations about his service as a Nazi intelligence officer during World War II, an activity he had denied as long as possible. Before there were any allegations against Waldheim, the KPO opposed both Waldheim (the candidate of the Austrian People's Party [OVP]) and Kurt Steyrer (the SPO candidate), urging its members and supporters to cast invalid ballots (*Volksstimme*, 21 February). Possibly because of the guarded pro-Waldheim stance of the USSR, the KPO's recommendation for the second election on 8 June, when only Waldheim and Steyrer were candidates, was "We leave it to our members and our voters to decide for themselves their stand on 8 June" (*Volksstimme*, 24 May).

The only provincial election of 1986 was held in Styria on 21 September. Styria was hardest hit by the nationalized industries crisis. A strong communist drive for the voters of Upper Styria, the seat of a number of nationalized steel plants, brought the party, as mentioned earlier, moderate gains in the November federal election. Overall, the KPO was less successful in the September provincial election, where its vote share of 1.18 percent was a loss of 0.16 percent when compared with the provincial election of 1981. However, it managed to increase its vote share in a few small Upper Styrian towns: in the industrial towns of Leoben (3.62 percent to 4.12 percent) and Zeltweg (3.03 percent to 4.07 percent) and the mining towns of Fohnsdorf (4.86 percent to 5.38 percent) and, especially, Eisenerz (2.76 percent to 7.65 percent).

**Party Organization.** In addition to the federal and Styrian campaigns, 1986 saw a few special organizational KPO events. Among the more regular ones were the Styrian provincial conference in January, devoted to the saving of workplaces and, as expected, campaigns for peace and against fascism (*Voksstimme*, 24 January); a session of Lower Austrian communal representatives, with emphasis on municipal finances (*Volksstimme*, 28 September); and a campaign of the Upper Austria Communist Youth for "work, equal rights, solidarity," with emphasis on girls' unemployment and discrimination against women at the workplace (*Volksstimme*, 9 September).

A New Year's celebration of the KPO Klagenfurt (capital of Carinthia) placed emphasis on the plight of nationalized industries (*Volksstimme*, 8 January). On the first of May, the party had its usual demonstration on the Ringstrasse in Vienna as well as eleven special district events. There were seven events in Lower Austria, four in Upper Austria, three each in Styria and Carinthia, and one each in Salzburg, Burgenland, Tyrol, and Vorarlberg. Among the Politburo members participating were Muhri, Silbermayr (main speaker in Vienna), Wimmer, Podolsky, Loistl, Graber, Hofer, Kalt, and Schwager (*Volksstimme*, 30 April).

On 30 and 31 August, *Volksstimme* organized a festival in the Prater, Vienna's major amusement and recreational park. The festival featured tours through the "red Vienna," combining the Social Democratic past of the 1920s with communist demands of the present (*Volksstimme*, 25 July). Guests from all East bloc countries and from Yugoslavia, West Germany, and Italy were in attendance (*Volksstimme*, 30 and 31 August). In a speech to the festival, Muhri stated that the crisis of capitalism had caught up with Austria and that the KPO was the only party fighting for social and democratic reforms (*Volksstimme*, 2 September).

One week later, 800 people attended a festival held in Villach, Carinthia's second city. Italians and Slovenes attended, Muhri spoke, and emphasis was placed on language rights of the Slovene minority in Carinthia (*Volksstimme*, 9 September). At the same time, Graz, the capital of Styria, had the first "truth" festival in more than twenty years. It had only 300 visitors and had more social than political events (*Volksstimme*, 9 September). On 5 October, Donaustadt, Vienna's 22d district, celebrated its 40th anniversary, which the KPO city council member from the district used to highlight communist activities and demands connected with that district (*Volksstimme*, 5 October).

On 14 July, *Profil*, Vienna's slightly right-of-center opinion magazine, reported a court victory of the KPO for the control of the oil company Turmoel and expressed surprise that neither Muhri nor *Volksstimme* would comment on the case (*Profil*, 14 July).

**Domestic Party Affairs.** Two largely domestic Austrian articles appeared in *World Marxist Review* in 1986. In the first, "Behind the Facade of 'Partnership,'" Muhri engaged in one of his periodic attacks on Austria's "social partnership" of capital and labor (*World Marxist Review*, May). "Social partnershp" is attacked as capital's means of suppressing the class struggle by conspiring with the Socialist Party and the Trade Union Congress to hold down the potentially revolutionary masses. This partnership has been able, thus far, to calm the masses at a time when the crisis of capitalism can no longer sustain Austrian properity. Muhri ends the article with a quotation from the KPO's 1982 progam calling for the destruction of the "social partnership." Erwin Scharf's article, "Ideological Principle and Political Reality" (*World Marxist Review*, August), deals with a similar theme but is much more erudite and scholastic.

In the last 1985 issue of *Weg und Ziel* (*IB*, March 1986), Silbermayr attacked the "social partnership" stance of the Austrian Trade Union Congress. Without going into specifics, he claims that there is a widening rift between the congress and its member unions. He points to a Workers' Chamber survey of the 1970s and reports: "About 20 percent of the polled jobholders declared for a trade union policy more closely linked with the enterprises, geared more to the interests of labor and showing greater military vis-à-vis capital. Those who belong to this current are the main object of our policy in factories and unions."

*Information Bulletin* (July) features a report by Hofer on the sixteenth plenary meeting of the KPO on 6 May 1986 in Vienna, two days after the first ballot of the presidential election. He reports on an effort to get 50,000 workers to demand tax reform, denies the continuation of prosperity claimed by the government, and quotes the Austrian Institute of Economic Studies to the effect that "the growth rate of property holders' incomes (leases, capital investment, rent) was 250 percent greater than that of wage and salary earners." Hofer warns that cutbacks in nationalized enterprises will increase foreign capital, which now controls 17 percent of the Austrian economy and employs 334,000 wage and salary earners, as compared with only 102,000 in the nationalized sector. He claims that, among the more than 200,000 unemployed Austrians, there are now 32,000 who are chronically unemployed. Hofer welcomes Waldheim's failure to capture the presidency on the first ballot but says that the KPO "should not urge the electorate to vote for Kurt Steyrer," the only alternative.

When the FPO replaced its liberal leader Steger with the young nationalist populist demagogue Haider and the SPO decided to end its coalition with the FPO and have an election on 23 November 1986, Muhri claimed that the SPO wanted the election before the consequences of the cutback in the nationalized industries and increasing unemployment could be felt (*Volksstimme*, 16 September). The same point was made by Silbermayr, when he reported on the 16 September meeting of the Central Committee (*Volksstimme*, 23 September). He also attacked Chancellor Franz Vranitzky and others as technocrats who were driving Austria to the right. In view of impending cutbacks, Silbermayr stated: "It is all the same for the working people whether SPO or OVP win the next election and furnish the chancellor. Things won't improve. On the contrary, both parties plan major tax burdens. The more votes the two parties receive in the election, the more they will feel justified in increasing the tax and dismissal pressure on the working popu-

lation." Silbermayr saw a move to the right in all parties, including the Greens. He urged a communist vote for peace, work, social security, democracy and equal rights, and a clean environment. It was clear that SPO and OVP were moving toward great coalition in order to increase the burden on the working population.

During the campaign, Podolsky urged a KPO vote rather than one for the Greens, who equate communism and fascism (*Volksstimme*, 12 October). Muhri, Hofer, and Susanne Sohn, in charge of women's issues on the Central Committee, held a major press conference (*Volksstimme*, 14 October). Muhri warned that a vote for Vranitzky was a vote for Alois Mock, the leader of the OVP.

Earlier in the year, when Lower Austria had a plebiscite on a provincial capital, the KPO urged abstention or an invalid vote (*Volksstimme*, 26 January).

Clearly the major domestic issue for the KPO in 1986 was the mostly projected, and to a small part realized, reduction in Austria's nationalized enterprises following the financial debacle of iron and steel's flagship, VOEST-Alpine, in late 1985—a process dubbed "shrinking process" (Schrumpfungsprozess) by the party. The issue was made the chief communist issue in the federal election and in the provincial election in Styria, along with Upper Austria, the main province affected. Muhri began the Styrian attack on OVP privatization plans at a conference in the Styrian steel city of Leoben (*Volksstimme*, 8 January). At the conference of the Vienna KPO, Podolsky warned of the possible consequences for employment in Vienna (*Volksstimme*, 18 January). The KPO was especially elated over the participation in general—not just communist—demonstrations against privatization in Linz (the capital of Upper Austria) and Leoben on 16 January, with 45,000 participants in Linz (*Volksstimme*, 19 January).

May Day demonstrations paid particular attention to the plight of the nationalized industries, and KPO speakers warned that any reduction would lead to increased imports of foreign products (*Volksstimme*, 3, 4, 7 May). After the first presidential ballot, Willi Gaisch, the Styrian party chairman, stated that the low Socialist vote, especially in nationalized industry areas, should cause the government to halt the "shrinking" policy (*Volksstimme*, 10 May). A few days later, Gaisch demanded that the government help nationalized industries instead of purchasing fighter planes from Sweden (*Volksstimme*, 16 May). In July, the KPO attacked the

Socialist executive of VOEST-Alpine for being unwilling to guarantee maintenance of all jobs into 1987 (*Volksstimme*, 3, 5 July).

On 21 August, demonstrating workers in the Styrian town of Zeltweg claimed, according to KPO assertions, that only communists were willing to defend their jobs (*Volksstimme*, 22, 23 August). Four days later, a delegation of the Styrian KPO and the GLB (Communist Trade Union Bloc) was received, with noncommittal results, by Josef Krainer, the OVP governor of Styria; Hans Gross, the SPO lieutenant-governor, refused to meet with them (*Volksstimme*, 26 August). The 3 September *Volksstimme* claimed that a job reduction (until 1990) of 9,480, mostly in Upper Austria and Styria, was already planned. One week later (10 September) *Volksstimme* dismissed the plan of the Styrian government to create 400 new jobs at VOEST-Alpine, as election propaganda. On 17 and 18 September, the KPO staged "antishrinking" demonstrations in Judenburg and Leoben (*Volksstimme*, 17 September). After the election, *Volksstimme* (7 October) reported that the board of VOEST-Alpine had accepted "shrinking" in principle and that a minor privatization in the mining town of Eisenerz, with losses of fringe benefits for workers, was already under way. According to the 10 October *Volksstimme*, 3,546 VOEST-Alpine jobs would be sacrificed in the foreseeable future.

The KPO's second domestic effort in 1986, a purely federal matter, was tax reform. Muhri attacked a statement by then minister of finance, Vranitzky, that a reduction in the wage tax would have to take budgetary necessities into consideration (*Volksstimme*, 9 April). Muhri added that, if the rich and the superrich paid, the tax reduction for wage earners could take place as early as 1 January 1987. Pointing to the finding of the Institute for Economic Studies that income from property had increased (between 1975 and 1984) three times as much as wages, Muhri claimed that KPO demands had been justified and legitimized (*Volksstimme*, 4 May). On 23 May, Muhri claimed 46,370 signatures for the wage tax reform of the KPO (*Volksstimme*, 24 May).

During the federal election campaign, Hofer demanded a reduction of the value-added tax (*Volksstimme*, 14 October). On 17 October, Muhri warned that all other parties would increase the tax load of the masses and that only the KPO favored workers and pensioners (*Volksstimme*, 18 October).

The KPO also attacked German nationalism in Austria during 1986. In their article "Shadows of the Past in the Political Scene" (*World Marxist Review*, April 1986), Walter Windischbauer and Rupert Herzog warned of neofascism in Austria. They pointed out that Hitler's vote in 1930 had been 110,000, less than the vote for neo-Nazi Burger in the presidential election of 1980. The authors blame the "social partnership" for having replaced antifascism with anticommunism. Although *Volksstimme* appears to have been silent during the Waldheim controversy, it referred to it later when it boasted that only the KPO had opposed a subsidy by the city of Linz for the OTB (Austrian Gymnastics Federation), which it claimed was a German nationalist organization (3 October). In August, the KPO of Carinthia demanded the maintenance, not the deterioration, of that province's bilingual (German-Slovene) school policy (*Volksstimme*, 17 August, 9 September).

At the Vienna conference of the KPO, Podolsky warned of the deindustrialization of the federal capital (*Volksstimme*, 18 January).

**International Views.** There was one contribution on an international topic by an Austrian to *World Marxist Review*, the self-explanatory "Economic Backwardness: A Global Problem," by Walter Baier (March).

At the Vienna KPO conference in January, Muhri came out for Gorbachev's disarmament proposals and against Reagan's "star wars" (*Volksstimme*, 19–20 January). In April, the Politburo condemned the American attack on Libya (*Volksstimme*, 16 April). On 1 May, Muhri and Silbermayr attacked U.S. nuclear and foreign policy (*Volksstimme*, 1, 3 May). Chernobyl was used to attack U.S. nuclear tests and nuclear armament in general (*Volksstimme*, 8, 24 May).

The KPO's position on Reykjavik was predictable: initial praise for the effort (*Volksstimme*, 10 October) and blame for the United States after the failure (*Volksstimme*, 15 October). Vladimir Lomeyko, the head of the USSR expert delegation to the Commission on Security and Cooperation in Europe (CSCE) conference in Vienna, gave *Volksstimme* a lengthy interview on Reykjavik (8 November).

The KPO attempted to prevent the 19 October showing of the Austrian television docudrama, "The Uprising," dealing with the Hungarian crisis of 1956. Despite a judge's reservations, the showing went forward (*Volksstimme*, 17, 18, 19 October; *Presse*, 21 October).

**International Activities.** The year began with a visit to Vienna by Harry Tisch, member of the SED Politburo and chairman of the FDGB, the GDR's trade union federations (*Volksstimme*, 23 January). Muhri attended the Twenty-seventh Congress of the CPSU and used the occasion to discuss Austro-Soviet trade relations with Alexej Manzhulo, the deputy minister of international trade of the USSR (*Volksstimme*, special edition, April). KPO member Matzinger attended the Communist Party of Italy's special congress in Florence, called to discuss 57 theses on democratic changes in Italy (*Volksstimme*, 9 April). The Soviet cosmonaut Popovich visited Muhri while on a lecture visit in Vienna (*Volksstimme*, 17 April).

Also in April, Scharf visited East Berlin (*Volksstimme*, 23 April), where he addressed the SED congress and stressed the improved cultural relations between Austria and the GDR as well as what he called the role of the GDR as a "decisive barrier against German militarism." In May, Muhri and Johann Steiner went to Poland. They first visited Radom, where they looked at the metal factory (Warsaw PAP, 8 May) and then Warsaw (*Trybuna Ludu*, 10–11 May), where they were received by Wojciech Jaruzelski. On 9 May, Jaruzelski decorated Muhri with the Grand Sash of the Order of Merit of the Polish People's Republic, the highest Polish decoration for foreigners.

In July, Vasil Bil'ak, secretary of the Central Committee of the Communist Party of the CSSR, visited Vienna (*Volksstimme*, 11 July). Although the main purpose of his visit was to see the federal government and the various party leaders, he held a special meeting with Muhri, Reiter, and Steiner. On 15 September, Muhri, Scharf, and Steiner received Szurov Matyas, the secretary of the Hungarian Socialist Workers Party (*Volksstimme*, 16 September). In October, Alvaro Cunhal, general secretary of the Communist Party of Portugal, visited Vienna and was received by Muhri (*Volksstimme*, 21 October). About the same time, Muhri received Boris Aristov, the USSR minister of foreign trade (*Volksstimme*, 22 October). Finally, when in Vienna for the CSCE meeting in November, Soviet foreign minister Eduard Shevardnadze had a meeting with Muhri and Steiner (*Volksstimme*, 5 November).

Frederick C. Engelmann
*University of Alberta*

# Belgium

**Population.** 9,868,000
**Party.** Belgian Communist Party (Parti communiste de Belgique; Kommunistische Partij van Belgie; PCB/KPB)
**Founded.** 1921
**Membership.** Under 5,000
**Leadership.** President: Louis Van Geyt; vice president: Claude Renard; Flemish president: Ludo Loose; Francophone president: Robert Dussart
**Politburo.** 14 members: Louis Van Geyt; Pierre Beauvois, Robert Dussart, Marcel Levaux, Jacques Moins, Jacques Nagels, Claude Renard, Jules Vercaigne (Francophone); Jan Debrouwere, Jos De Geyter, Miel Dullaert, Roel Jacobs, Ludo Loose, Jef Turf (Flemish)
**National Secretariat.** Marcel Couteau, Robert Dussart, Daniel Fedrigo (Francophone); Miel Dullaert, Roel Jacobs, Ludo Loose (Flemish)

**Francophone Bureau.** Didier Bajura, Pierre Beauvois, Marcel Bergen, Marcel Couteau, Robert Dussart, Daniel Fedrigo, Michel Godard, Marcel Levaux, Rosine Lewin, Maurice Magis (son), Jacques Moins, Jacques Nagels, Susa Nudelhole, Claude Renard, Jean-Marie Simon (Liège), Jules Vercaigne, Josiane Vrand

**Flemish Bureau.** Jos De Geyter, Filip Delmotte, Miel Dullaert, Roel Jacobs, Ludo Loose, Dirk Vonckx, Georges De Clercq, Claude De Smet, Hugo De Witte, Bernard Claeys, Tejo Cockx, Willy Minnebo

**Central Committee.** 72 members

**Status.** Legal

**Last Congress.** Twenty-fifth National, 18–20 April 1986. Second Francophone, 7–8 June 1986. Second Flemish, 7–8 June 1986

**Last Election.** 13 October 1985, 1.2 percent, no representation (*YICA*, 1986)

**Publications.** *Drapeau Rouge*, daily party organ in French, Pierre Beauvois, editor; *Rode Vaan*, Dutch-language weekly, Jef Turf, editor

The center-right government led by Flemish Christian Democrat Wilfried Martens was re-elected on 13 October 1985. In that election, the PCB/KPB lost its two parliamentary seats. Never a significant force in Belgian politics, the PCB/KPB has been forced to accept an even more marginal position. The much stronger Belgian Socialist Party (Parti Socialiste/Socialistische Partij; PS/SP) leads the opposition to the Martens VI government.

In an effort to cut the growing budget deficit, now 11 percent of the Belgian gross national product, the Martens VI government announced plans to reduce government spending by 4.5 billion dollars by the end of 1987. Prime Minister Martens explained that he was not surprised by the large strike movement in May opposing his programs, because 20 percent of the voting public is currently employed by the state. (*CSM*, 1 July.)

The Twenty-fifth Congress of the PCB/KPB launched an appeal to all sectors of the population to join with it in opposition to the government, declaring that the government's austerity program prepared at Val-Duchesse constituted a declaration of social war. To reduce the public debt, the government was jeopardizing the working conditions of the workers, condemning youth to public assistance and longer military or civil service, dismantling and privatizing public services, marginalizing the unemployed, reducing programs in public health, attacking the educational system, and liquidating the key industries of entire regions.

**Party Leadership and Organization.** In an effort "to renew" the party, the PCB/KPB has modified its structure and leadership in 1986. Announcements of the first changes in the party organization came at the Twenty-fifth Congress of the PCB/KPB held 18-20 April 1986. In response to the marked decline in membership and losses at the polls in

October 1985 as well as the opportunities offered by growing public dissatisfaction with the austerity programs of the Martens VI government, the PCB/KPB brought new members into its leadership and further regionalized its organization.

While the chief spokesman for the party, Van Geyt, retained his position as president, the two vice presidents, for Wallonia and Flanders, resigned to "leave a place for the young" (*Drapeau Rouge*, 17 June). Twenty-five percent of the members left the Politburo, and four new members were elected. These changes were echoed at the regional level. The leadership changes were most dramatic on the Flemish bureau. Half of the militants on the bureau will no longer be employees of the KPB.

Meeting under the banner "Adopter notre action aux exigences de notre temps/Onze aktie aanpassen aan de vereisten van dit tijdperk" (Adopt our action to the needs of our time), the leadership of the PCB/KPB emphasized the need to take account of societal change at the regional level. President Van Geyt, acknowledging that times were difficult for the left in general, warned that the party would be passed by if it did not respond quickly and dramatically.

In his address to the Twenty-fifth Congress, Van Geyt emphasized the evolution of the working class brought on by the scientific and technological revolution and by the "transnationalisation" of capital. The traditional working class that had always been the base of the communist movement, he suggested, had been severely affected by changes in working relations, leading to resignation and apathy rather than engagement in the struggle for a new society. Neither before nor immediately following the losses of 13 October 1985 had the party systematically re-evaluated its strategy or political programs. Instead, he explained, they had deplored their isolation. In conclusion, Van Geyt called for self-criticism and a re-evaluation of party positions to allow the party to appeal to the large sectors of the population alienated by the government's austerity programs.

In 1986, in addition to the change of leadership, the PCB/KPB also moved further in the direction of a federalized structure. The PCB/KPB was the last of the Belgian parties to abandon the unitary national organization. The leadership of the party has sought to maintain a strong national organization and to pursue national policies ever since the first acknowledgement of regional divisions in 1982 at the Twenty-fourth Party Congress. In 1986, at the Twenty-fifth Party Congress, Van Geyt declared that regional economic differences would necessitate different strategies in Flanders, Brussels, and Wallonia.

The Central Committee of the party, meeting in June, abolished the vice presidents for the Flemish and Walloon communities, thus eliminating the intermediary positions between the national president and the Flemish and Francophone presidents. Van Geyt described the change as, "another step in the direction of the growing federalism of the party" (*Drapeau Rouge*, 17 June). Each wing of the party would now be able to modify its policy more easily to adapt to changing regional conditions. A working group composed of members of the Politburo was established to further modify party organization along regional lines.

**Domestic Affairs.** The PCB/KPB has responded to its 1985 election losses and the new austerity measures of the Martens VI government by attempting to rally the "largest possible front to oppose the government." The focus of its activity in 1986 has been its attempt to lead an alliance of unions in the public and private sectors. It has called on "progressive forces" not only to oppose the budget cuts of the "neoliberal" government but also to support an alternative left program.

From January until April, the PCB/KPB mounted an escalating attack in the press against the government's proposed economic changes. Party leaders argued against the plans for increased privatization of the public sector as well as plans to cut social programs. Van Geyt referred frequently to the regression in social progress that had accompanied the scientific revolution and transnational capitalism (*Drapeau Rouge*, 1, 2 March). The PCB/KPB also questioned the ability of the Socialists, who controlled the opposition movement

throughout the spring and summer, to lead the masses.

At the April 1986 party congress, the call was issued for enlargement of the progressive opposition to the government's austerity programs. The traditional working class would lead the movement, but this constantly diversifying working class would be joined by its allies in the fight against "the aggressive right" (*Drapeau Rouge*, 19, 20 April). To combat effectively, Van Geyt explained, the "boundaries of the left would have to be passed"; new sectors of the population would have to be incorporated into the struggle. The fight for employment would have to be waged alongside the struggle for a human standard of living so that the employed, the unemployed, and consumers—all the sectors of society affected by the politics of economic crisis and armament could struggle together. Late in the spring, hoping to work with the Socialists and to win over the more progressive of the Christian Democratic unions, the party called for a united front of the left.

In early May, led by the Socialist unions, government workers went out on strike. Trains, post offices, schools, and most other government-run facilities were closed. Most Christian Democratic unions left it to their regional offices to decide whether to support the strike. The communists and Socialists called for extension of the massive strike to the private sector. Citing the "spectacular success" of the strikes—the joining together of educators, railroad personnel, and postal employees in a common front—the PCB/KPB urged the masses who had "risen spontaneously" for four 24-hour strikes to support their proposals for "a real alternative to neoliberalism." On 31 May, the date of the major organized national demonstration against the government plans, the PCB/KPB asked the Socialists to join in a common opposition to cuts in social services, excessive spending on nuclear plans and weapons, the extension of military service, and the wasting of human resources.

The Martens VI government survived the crisis of the summer. In the middle of October, a dispute over the French-speaking mayor of Voeren/Fourons in Flanders who refused to take the Dutch language exams as mandated by the courts, caused Martens to offer his resignation (*NYT*, 15, 18, 19 October; *WSJ*, 15 October). The king refused to allow the Christian Democratic–Liberal coalition government to fall over the linguistic quarrel. According to the PCB/KPB, the industrial leaders did not want their government to fall in the midst of such a crisis.

Although in the past, the PCB/KPB has not taken an active position on linguistic issues, preferring to emphasize economic struggles that transcend the language dispute, on October 15, the Walloon bureau of the party publicly announced its support of the mayor, Jose Happart, arguing that he represented the majority of the population of the French-speaking village. (*Drapeau Rouge*, 16 October.)

**International Positions and Activities.** The PCB/KPB has continued to argue against the deployment of NATO cruise missiles in Belgium and to urge the Belgian government to become more active in disarmament negotiations. In January, Van Geyt and Roger Broos participated prominently in a peace demonstration at Vilvoorde. Subsequently, *Le Drapeau Rouge* has featured letters from Van Geyt to Prime Minister Martens and Foreign Minister Tindemans demanding that Belgium take the initiative in promoting disarmament. In each of his letters and statements, Van Geyt has emphasized the importance of the participation of small countries in redirecting NATO policies.

The PCB/KPB, although recognizing the participation of a diverse range of groups in the peace movement, argues that disarmament must be seen in its larger perspective. Under the slogan "Economy of war/Economy of peace," leaders explain that the European subservience to the American military industrial complex and the escalating arms budgets are depressing the European standard of living and consigning the continent to underdevelopment.

The PCB/KPB, consistent with its Eurocommunist position, has persistently pointed to CPSU general secretary Mikhail Gorbachev's leadership in disarmament. The Russians are portrayed as working for peaceful coexistence while U.S. president Ronald Reagan pursues the policies of confrontation. Gorbachev has emphasized the interdependence of nations as opposed to the attitude of "Rambo-Reagan" (*Drapeau Rouge*, 18 February). Reagan's antiterrorism campaign has been seen as a flagrant attempt to remilitarize conflicts, and "star wars" is cited as the main obstacle to constructive negotiations between Moscow and Washington (*Drapeau Rouge*, 14 October).

In opposition to what the PCB/KPB explains is the growing European dependence on Washington, it has called for East-West cooperation: Europe need not be dependent on Russia or on the United States.

The theme of this year's May Day message was disarmament. As goals, the authors listed a global system of international security, renunciation of the use of nuclear weapons, prevention of the militarization of space, reduction of military budgets, national self-determination, and a new world economic order.

The PCB/KPB did criticize the Russian government over its failure to disclose immediately the details of the Chernobyl nuclear accident. Their criticism led to a wider appeal for humane use of technology and a re-evaluation of the safety of Belgian nuclear facilities.

On 7 July, Van Geyt met in Moscow with Anatolii Dobrynin, where they discussed the establishment of a broad front to work for international peace (*FBIS*, 11 July).

Janet L. Polasky
*University of New Hampshire*

# Cyprus

**Population.** 673,000 (80 percent Greek; 18 percent Turkish)
**Party.** Progressive Party of the Working People (Anorthotikon Komma Ergazomenou Laou; AKEL)
**Founded.** 1922 (AKEL, 1941)
**Membership.** 12,000 (estimated); 67 percent industrial workers and employees, 20 percent peasants and middle class, 24 percent women, 30 percent under 30 years old; 80 percent from Greek Cypriot community
**General Secretary.** Ezekias Papaioannou
**Politburo.** 13 members: Ezekias Papaioannou, Andreas Fandis, Dinos Konstantinou, G. Katsouridhis, Khambis Mikhailidhis, Andreas Ziartidhis, Khristos Petas, Kiriakos Khristou, Mikhail Poumbouris, G. Khristodoulidhis, A. Mikhailidhis. G. Sophokles, Dhonis Kristofinis
**Secretariat.** 3 members: Ezekias Papaoiannou, Andreas Fandis (deputy general secretary), Dinos Konstantinou (organizing secretary)
**Status.** Legal
**Last Congress.** Sixteenth, 26–30 November 1986
**Last Election.** 1985, 27.4 percent, 15 of 56 seats
**Auxiliary Organizations.** Pan-Cypriot Workers' Federation (PEO), 45,000 members, Andreas Ziartidhis, general secretary; United Democratic Youth Organization (EDON), 14,000 members; Confederation of Women's Organizations; Pan-Cyprian Peace Council; Pan-Cyprian Federation of Students and Young Professionals; Union of Greek Cypriots in England, 1,200 members (considered London branch of AKEL); Pan-Cypriot National Organization of Secondary Students; Cypriot Farmers' Union
**Publications.** *Kharavyi* (Dawn), AKEL daily and largest newspaper in Cyprus; *Demokratia*, AKEL weekly; *Neo Kairoi* (New times), AKEL magazine; *Ergatiko Vima* (Workers' stride), PEO weekly; *Neolaia* (Youth), EDON weekly

The AKEL, which since the establishment of the Republic of Cyprus in 1960 has enjoyed legal status and has consistently been the island's best organized grass roots party, claims to be "a peoples' party of Greek and Turkish working people" (*WMR,* September 1979). Although the AKEL is officially banned in the northern sector of the island, which has been named the Turkish Republic of Northern Cyprus (TRNC) since its declaration of independence in 1983, the communists have never stopped entreating the Turkish Cypriot minority population. One AKEL Politburo member recently claimed that "ours is the only party having hundreds of Turkish Cypriots in its ranks . . . [and] thousands of Turkish Cypriots belong to the Pan-Cypriot Workers' Federation (PEO)," the communist-controlled and largest national trade union in the country (ibid., October). One stated goal of the AKEL is to have "the patriotic front include, as is done in the 'free' territory, Turkish Cypriots (Marxists and members of progressive democratic groups living in the occupied areas)" (ibid., October 1982). Communist fronts do exist in the TRNC, and some of their representatives do attend the various communist-sponsored meetings outside of the island. There are two left-wing political parties in the TRNC, the Turkish Republican Party (CTP) and the Communal Liberation Party (TKP), and both operate legally. The CTP was founded in 1970 and publishes most of the AKEL propaganda in its party newspaper, *Yeni Duzen* (New order). In the TRNC elections of June 1985, the CTP gathered 21.3 percent of the popular vote and won 12 of the 50 seats in the new National Assembly. The TKP is smaller but did manage to win 15.9 percent of the vote and 10 seats in the same elections. During the year, delegations from both parties attended "world peace forums in Sofia and Prague, where they issued joint statements in favor of peace and an independent, sovereign, united, federal, non-aligned and fully demilitarised Cyprus" (ibid., October). Apparently, sympathetic Turkish Cypriots do not have to travel to such communist front meetings outside of the island in a clandestine manner. One newspaper in the TRNC, *Bozkurt* (Grey wolf), reported on 17 October that the delegations from the two left-wing parties also attended a World Peace Council meeting in Copenhagen and even showed a photograph identifying the attendees.

**Leadership and Organization.** The AKEL is reputed to be a tightly controlled apparatus, structured along the principle of democratic centralism. The highest body is the congress, which is convened once every four years. The Sixteenth Congress was held from 26–30 November, 1986 and coincided with the 60th anniversary of the first party congress of the founding Communist Party of Cyprus (CPC). A three-member secretariat runs its day-to-day business and a thirteen-member Politburo is AKEL's policymaking body. The highest continuing body is the 30-member Central Committee, while a three-member Central Control Commission oversees the Central Committee and other bodies in the party. All of the officials in the governing hierarchy are elected at the party congress. It was no surprise that the newly elected AKEL Central Committee unanimously re-elected Papaioannou as the general secretary. "Invited delegations from thirty fraternal parties, democratic organizations and liberation movements" were observers at the Sixteenth Congress (Nicosia Domestic Service, 26 November).

Replacement of the gerontocracy that now rules the AKEL will be a growing concern for the party as the current leaders grow older in their secure careerist positions. It is, nevertheless, this same leadership that has repeatedly delivered a third of the Cypriot electorate to the communist slates for the 25 years that preceded the December 1985 elections. How the AKEL has maintained its strength over the years may be explained by the fact that the party offers tangible rewards to its loyalists—for example, free higher education, medical care, and tourist trips in Eastern Europe. Still, the party lead-

ers are "grey men in grey suits, with grey hair and grey ideas" (*Economist*, 16 November 1985). General Secretary Papaioannou was born in 1908 and has held his present office since 1949; moreover, the average age of the other leaders is well over 65 years. Slavishly faithful to the Moscow line, the party has nonetheless "played the parliamentary game in Eurocommunistic style; but it has not joined the Eurocommunists in criticizing Soviet actions and policies" (ibid.). Perhaps that inertia may explain why the AKEL has never been able to increase its one-third voter share and why it may now be on the decline for future elections.

The AKEL attaches special importance to the recruiting and education of younger people and "sees to it that comrades receive proper Marxist-Leninist training" (*WMR*, October 1982). The important youth front, EDON, has a membership of "factory workers, peasants, white-collar workers and high school graduates between the ages of 14 and 30 . . . and it works in close cooperation with AKEL" (ibid., April 1984). At the Fifteenth Congress in May 1982, the leadership hailed its "great success in the organizational sector" and in recruitment of "new members from all strata of the people of Cyprus." Since the Fourteenth Congress, party membership had increased by 2,479 to "nearly 14,000 members" (*Kharavyi*, 30 May 1982), which remains its present strength. At the Fifteenth Congress, the AKEL also emphasized its propaganda work "among the masses" to take the offensive on the ideological and political fronts and expose imperialist and reactionary schemes more effectively (*WMR*, July 1985).

Normally during the fall months, the AKEL holds a "fundraising drive to provide money for the party's normal activities" and to demonstrate "a symbolic expression of mass support." Additional operating capital is generated "from activities under the indirect but tight control of the party in . . . branches of . . . production and distribution of goods (e.g. cooperatives, retail stores, financial enterprises, tourist agencies, export/import businesses)." As a consequence of these commercial endeavors, the AKEL has "probably become the major employer on the island" (*Andi*, Athens, 16 January 1981). The two best-known communist-controlled businesses are the Popular Distiller's Company of Limassol, which produces wines and brandies for the domestic market and export, and the People's Coffee Grinding Company in Nicosia. Moreover, the communist-controlled labor union, PEO, is the strongest in Cyprus, and its members work in virtually every phase of the island's economy. In the TRNC, the strong Confederation of Revolutionary Labor Unions (Dev-Is) is considered left wing, but its direct relationship with the PEO and the AKEL has not been clearly established.

**Domestic Party Affairs.** In his opening address at the Sixteenth Congress, General Secretary Papaioannou summarized the Cyprus domestic problems, noting that the Cypriot people are waging an "anti-occupation, anti-imperialist, and liberation struggle... to ensure the withdrawal of the Turkish troops and settlers, the dismantling of all foreign bases, and the complete demilitarization of the island" (Nicosia Domestic Service, 26 November). The immediate means to those ends should be "continued talks through the good offices of the U.N. secretary general to examine those topics on which agreement has not been reached, or which have yet to be discussed," such as troops, settlers, and international guarantees (ibid.). Concerning the external aspects of the problem—which are "linked and interdependent" with the internal aspects—an international conference should be "convened within the U.N. framework, as has been proposed by the Soviet Union" (ibid.). He almost gratuitously lamented that "the present domestic situation... is not what it should be" and then affirmed that his party "would seek cooperation with other patriotic and democratic forces, even those at the lowest levels," to prevent the "rightist, pro-NATO solution to the Cyprus issue" (ibid., 29 November).

Turning to the presidential elections due in February 1988, the AKEL leader stated that his party "is not in a position to announce its exact plans... bearing in mind our experience in the 1983 elections." Although he admitted that the cooperation between AKEL and President Spyros Kiprianou's Democratic Party (DIKO) at the time was "not a mistake," he did accuse Kiprianou "of seeing democratic cooperation as simply an opportunity to climb to authority." He vowed that DIKO would never "deceive AKEL again into supporting Kiprianou for the presidency." If it were not possible for AKEL to find a person from outside the party "who will inspire confidence by acting in accordance with principles... then we will most certainly be forced to nominate our own candidate." (Ibid.) Although the government of Cyprus had initially welcomed most of Papaioannou's remarks at the congress, the DIKO political arm denounced the AKEL's threat of being "better alone in the next presidential elections no matter what happens" as an effort to break up the democratic front and to create prior defections away from the incumbent president's re-election bid (ibid., 30 November).

On the subject of the domestic economy, Papaioannou averred that it seemed to be growing "on an ascending course," but he did express his party's concern over "industrial and commercial bankruptcies, rising unemployment, the imbalance in the balance of trade, foreign debts, and the planned EEC-Cyprus customs union (ibid., 29 November). Although the political resolutions issued at the close of the Sixteenth Party Congress were specific on certain issues—for example, the convening of an international conference to deal with the foreign aspects of the Cyprus issue—the AKEL's prescription for improving the domestic economy reverted back to its old slogans about nationalizing key industries and redistributing land to farmers.

**International Views, Positions, and Activities.** During its first meeting of the year, the AKEL Politburo discussed the U.S. military exercises in the Mediterranean. In what proved to be a partially prophetic statement, the Politburo claimed that such exercises "may develop into military aggression against Libya as part of the arrogant U.S. strategy that arbitrarily assumes the U.S. is a world gendarme" (*Kharavyi*, 26 January). After the U.S. attack on Libya in April, which was "assisted by their British flunkies," the AKEL Central Committee called on the Cyprus government "to unreservedly condemn this act of violence by the U.S." (ibid., 16 April). The British ambassador in Cyprus immediately denied that the British bases in Cyprus had been used in the U.S. raid on Libya, but this did nothing to ease the continual AKEL criticism of the two British bases on the island. In a later statement, the AKEL leadership insisted "that the presence of the bases is a deadly danger that must not be underestimated." They further demanded the abolition of all the British "rights of occupation that derive from the Treaty of Establishment," which was one of the basic documents that granted Cyprus its independence in 1960 (Nicosia Domestic Service, 8 August). Although the British bases on the island are not to be used for NATO maneuvers, the AKEL has long maintained "that U.S. imperialism wants to safeguard its military presence and to turn the island into a powerful strategic base in the Eastern Mediterranean and the Middle East" (*WMR*, October). At the Sixteenth Party Congress, the AKEL general secretary repeated his demand for "the dismantling of all foreign bases and the complete demilitarization of the island" (Nicosia Domestic Service, 26 November).

In what was termed a "dangerous deviation" in the course of President Kiprianou's foreign policy, an AKEL editorial denounced the expected removal of Foreign Minister Iakovou, who was "an advocate of a nonaligned policy," in favor of Education Minister Khristofidhis, "who believes in closer cooperation with the West" (*Kharavyi*, 10 November). The president was accused of beginning "to flirt with the Anglo-Americans and the West in general in the mistaken hope that he will win their favor and support on the Cyprus issue." The editorial charged that the president had "continued with the granting of facilities to NATO and permission to build a CIA spy station in Cyprus." Rather than "submission to imperialism," what Cyprus needs "is a consistent, militant and nonaligned policy of friendship and cooperation with countries, but especially with those that offer unselfish aid and support, namely the Soviet Union and the Eastern bloc countries (ibid.).

The AKEL even found an occasion to lash out at the socialist government of Andreas Papandreou in Greece. When the Greek prime minister congratulated President Kiprianou for his "great election victory" in the December 1985 parliamentary elections, an editorial in the AKEL newspaper claimed that such an "unfounded and arbitrary" remark constituted "unacceptable and harmful meddling in the political affairs of the Cyprus Republic" (*Kharavyi*, 12 February). What further irked the Cypriot communists was Papandreou's observation that the Kiprianou victory "stabilized the political structure and orientation of the Cyprus Republic." The AKEL, who opposed the president in the elections, saw Papandreou's statement as a "clear and unprecedented allegation" that communism in Cyprus "is a destabilizing factor." As such, the Greek prime minister's statement is "a provocative insult to the conscientious, patriotic, democratic forces which are fighting for a just solution to the Cyprus issue." (Ibid.)

After the two sides in the Cyprus issue arrived at a deadlock in the United Nations in late 1985, the Soviet Union made some proposals for a solution to the problem. Promoting these Soviet proposals became a major part of the AKEL's international activities throughout the year. Basically, these proposals call for all involved parties to work for the reunification of the island under conditions of peace and justice and without foreign troops and installations on the island. This is to be achieved through an international conference to be held under the auspices of the U.N. secretary general (ibid. 23 January). During the Twenty-seventh Congress of the CPSU, which met in February in Moscow, the leaders of the communist parties of Cyprus, Greece, and Turkey agreed in a joint communiqué that the Soviet initiative provided the "right international framework for a settlement and . . . proposed a concrete and realistic solution on the basis of the unity, sovereignty, and independence of the Cyprus state" (*Cyprus Mail*, 8 March). The three leaders took a stand against any kind of foreign interference in the internal affairs of Cyprus and declared that any solution "should safeguard the peaceful, democratic and mutually beneficial co-existence of the Greek and Turkish Cypriot communities." Although the governments of Cyprus and Greece have welcomed the Soviet initiative, the TRNC and the government have dismissed it as "having nothing new." (Ibid.) Disappointed with the latter response, the AKEL general secretary hammered away at the theme consistently and made it one of his key points at the Sixteenth Party Congress.

In April, a three-member AKEL delegation went to Moscow for "an exchange of views on how best to utilize the Soviet proposals on the Cyprus issue" (Nicosia Domestic Service, 25 April). This meeting paved the way for a visit to Moscow by Cypriot foreign minister Iakovou later the same month to discuss the same proposals. This meeting led to a visit by a three-member Soviet delegation to Cyprus in June, at which time assurances were given to the Cyprus government that the USSR would "exercise its influence in every direction to achieve the convening of an international conference on the Cyprus issue" (*Kharavyi*, 15 June). Possibly as a result of the good relations the government of Cyprus enjoyed with the Soviet Union over the year, a trade agreement was signed in Moscow "for the immediate export of 1,000 tons of black raisins from Cyprus to the Soviet Union at a satisfactory price" (Nicosia Domestic Service, 3 November). On the occasion of the Soviet national anniversary, the Cypriot ambassador to the Soviet Union, Mikhail Sierfis, expressed President Kiprianou's "gratitude for Soviet support" and then received General Secretary Mikhail Gorbachev's "full assurance that his country will continue actively to support Cyprus's struggle for vindication" (ibid., 10 November).

T. W. Adams
*Washington, D.C.*

# Denmark

**Population.** 5,097,000
**Party.** Communist Party of Denmark (Danmarks Kommunistiske Parti; DKP)
**Founded.** 1919
**Membership.** 10,000 (estimated, including youth and student fronts)
**Chairman.** Jørgen Jensen
**Party Secretary.** Poul Emanuel
**Executive Committee.** 16 members: Jørgen Jensen, Ib Nørlund (vice-chairman), Poul Emanuel, Jan Andersen, Villy Fulgsang, Margit Hansen, Bernard Jeune, Gunnar Kanstrup (coeditor of *Land og Folk*), Kurt Kristensen, Dan Lundstrup, Freddy Madsen, Jørgen Madsen, Anette Nielsen, Bo Rosschou, Ole Sohn, Ingmar Wagner
**Secretariat.** 7 members: Jørgen Jensen, Ib Nørlund, Poul Emanuel, Gunnar Kanstrup, Kurt Kristensen, Bo Rosschou, Anker Schjerning
**Central Committee.** 51 members, 15 candidate members
**Status.** Legal
**Last Congress.** Twenty-seventh, 12–15 May 1983; next congress scheduled for 1987
**Last Election.** 10 January 1984, 0.7 percent, no representation
**Auxiliary Organization.** Communist Youth of Denmark (Danmarks Kommunistiske Ungdom; DKU), Ole Jensen, chair; Communist Students of Denmark (Danmarks Kommunistiske Studenter; KOMM.S.), Mette Gjerløv, chair
**Publications.** *Land og Folk* (Nation and people), daily circulation 6,500 weekdays and 13,000 weekends; *Tiden-Verden Rund* (Times around the world), theoretical monthly; *Fremad* (Forward), DKU monthly

The year 1986 saw interesting developments among and within Denmark's several socialist parties, but the DKP remains a stagnant political backwater. Weaker than at any time since World War II, the DKP received a scant 23,085 votes (0.7 percent) at the last parliamentary elections in January 1984. The DKP has not been represented in Parliament since October 1979, when its vote fell below the 2 percent minimum required for proportional representation in the 179-seat unicameral Folketing (parliament). The November 1985 local elections demonstrated continuing DKP weakness. Approximately 4,500 council seats were contested, and the DKP lost 14 of the 22 seats previously held.

The Danish parliamentary balance remains precarious, but the coalition government of conservative Prime Minister Poul Schlüter navigated another year without elections. New elections must occur before January 1988, and an election in the spring or fall of 1987 is most likely. The 1984 elections had been the country's seventh in less than thirteen years. For a decade after the destabilizing elections of December 1973, parties of the extreme left and right held between a quarter and a third of the parliamentary seats, making it difficult for the more moderate parties to govern effectively. Schlüter's current four-party, center-right coalition, single-vote majority depends on the Radical Liberals (a center-left reformist party) and the nonsocialist representatives from the Faeroe Islands and Greenland. This complex coalition has kept the opposition led by the reformist Social Democratic Party (SDP) at bay on domestic issues.

On foreign and security policy issues, however, the SDP can count on the Radical Liberals and the two leftist parties to oppose and harass the government. This has forced the government, against its will, to challenge NATO decisions frequently since 1982. Thus far Schlüter has chosen not to make foreign and security policy issues matters of confidence.

For 25 years, the DKP has had to compete with other Marxist parties to the left of the SDP. During the past 15 years, these various leftist parties have typically attracted an eighth of the national vote. In 1984, they collectively polled 14.9 percent, but the DKP share continued to plummet. Public opinion polls in 1986 gave the leftist bloc up to nearly 20 percent without any renewed support for the DKP. Until recently, the SDP also was losing voters to the leftist parties, but during the past two years, this trend has ended. A May Gallup poll gave the three socialist parties a parliamentary majority, if they could agree on a coalition. The DKP still attracted less than 1 percent of the hypothetical vote (*Nordisk Kontakt*, no. 11). The independent Marxist Socialist People's Party (Socialistiske Folkeparti; SF) has advanced notably during the past eight years. It doubled its support in the 1981 parliamentary elections and held on to these gains in 1984. It advanced further in the 1985 local elections. During the summer, it gained two new members of Parliament as a result of the split in the Left Socialist Party (Venstresocialisterne; VS). The third leftist party with significant support, the VS is a contentious assembly of former student radicals (from the 1960s) that holds on to a base of support from students and public employees (as does the SF). The VS won five Folketing seats in 1984, but as mentioned, two of its members defected to the SF.

Less important are three small sects: the moribund Communist Workers' Party (Kommunistisk Arbejderparti; KAP), a "Maoist" relic that has unsuccessfully sought a closer relationship with the VS and did not run in the 1984 elections; the International Socialist Workers' Party (Internationalen Socialistisk Arbejderparti; SAP), the Danish branch of the Trotskyist Fourth International, which received 2,200 votes in 1984; and the latest leftist group, the Marxist-Leninist Party (Marxistisk-Leninistisk Parti; MLP), whose pro-Albania line attracted fewer than 1,000 votes in January 1984. Two new parties, the Greens (De Grønne) and the Humanist Party (Humanisterne) will be on the next parliamentary ballot, but only the Greens have registered any strength. Although the Greens and the Humanists may not be strictly Marxist parties, they are likely to appeal to some of the same voters.

**Leadership and Organization.** Through good times and bad, the DKP internal organization and leadership changes little. Despite the party's decline under his leadership, Jørgen Jensen was reconfirmed as chair at the DKP's Twenty-seventh Congress in May 1983. Jensen, a former activist and leader of a Metalworkers' Union local, succeeded to the party chair in 1977 and is a veteran of more than 30 years in the DKP. Ib Nørlund, the party's number-two man and chief theoretician, has been in his post for decades. The same is true for the party's secretary (administrative director) Poul Emanuel. There have been periodic challenges to the party leadership from within; these were quite vociferous in 1983 and somewhat less so in 1986. Such efforts at change are inevitably in vain, as the challengers are forced to leave the party by exclusion or resignation, usually accompanied by a barrage of calumny. Writing in the SF weekly, former DKP Central Committeemember and member of Parliament Tove Jørgensen painted a picture of a closed Leninist clique that prohibited open debate and rejected any sustained efforts by the party rank and file to influence matters (*Socialistisk Weekend*, 15 August). True to form, the DKP denied the charges and denounced the criticism as a plot to divide the leftist opposition to the Schlüter government (*Land og Folk*, 16–17 August). Efforts in 1985 by the boss of the Seamen's Union, Preben Møller Hansen, who was expelled from the DKP several years earlier, to increase communication between the DKP and his faction the Common Course Club (Fælles Kurs Klub; FKK) were repulsed by the communist leadership.

The party's highest authority is the triennial congress. The Central Committee is elected at the congress, and it in turn elects the party's Executive Committee (politburo), chair, secretary, and those who fill other posts. Despite the attendence of some 453 delegates at the 1983 congress, the DKP functions fully in the Leninist model of a self-perpetuating elite. In recent years, the Central Committee has met four to six times annually. During noncongress years, the party holds an annual meeting. Such meetings, typically held in early autumn, reaffirm the general party goals as set at the congress and are occasions for the party to use media coverage to make known views on domestic and foreign affairs. Despite the party's weak position, media coverage is surprisingly good.

The DKP does not encourage discussion of internal organization or leadership, but hints of changes occasionally appear in the noncommunist press.

With the next DKP congress (the 28th) due in April 1987, discussion focused on possible successors to Chair Jensen, who at 65 and with a meagre record for his ten years of leadership may resign. Speculation on his successor centered on communist trade union activist Ole Sohn, who is chair of the SID (Unskilled Workers' Union) local in Horsens, Jutland. Others likely to ascend the party leadership include Jens Peter Bonde, leader of the Popular Movement Against the EC (European Community) and Metalworker Union activist and Executive Committee member Jan Andersen (*Berlingske Tidende*, 23 May). Sohn has hinted that he would like to pursue a more offensive political line, including possibly cooperation with VS and other leftists not affiliated with specific parties (*Socialistisk Weekend*, 15 August).

Another source of internal DKP strife has been its daily paper *Land og Folk*. Although it remains Denmark's largest Marxist newspaper, its circulation has declined notably during the 1980s. Editor Gunnar Kanstrup was demoted into a collective editorial board, and former communist student leader Frank Aaen was assigned the important position of political editor.

The DKU is the DKP's largest affiliate; at the Twenty-seventh Congress in 1983, its leadership stressed two areas of activity: support for radical trade union factions appealing to apprentices and young workers and mobilization of and influence over young participants in the various peace organizations. The election of 23-year-old construction worker Ole Jensen as chair of the DKU at the annual Communist Youth Congress in March suggests a continuation of this thus-far unsuccessful line. Ole Jensen has been active in student politics and the DKU press.

The KOMM.S. overlaps with the DKU but concentrates its efforts on university students. Periodically, communists have held high posts in the Danish National Students' Council (Danske Studerendes Fællesrad; DSF), but the DSF's influence has declined in recent years. Nevertheless, the DSF took the lead in blocking the government's efforts to reduce the power of students and support personnel in making policy at the universities and other institutions of higher education (*Nordisk Kontakt*, no 1). The KOMM.S. maintains some organizational autonomy and has its own publications, *Røde Blade* (Red leaves) and *Spartikus*, and its own meetings (Sixth Congress, October 1982).

Although the DKP has policies regarding the self-governing territories of Greenland and the Faeroe Islands, it does not have organizations in either. Attempts to form an autonomous Faeroe communist party in 1975 and later years have apparently failed. Neither of the leftist parties active in Greenland has ties to the DKP.

**Domestic Affairs.** As usual, economic issues dominated the domestic political agenda. Expansion continued at a 2.7 percent annual rate, assisted by the fall in world petroleum prices. Inflation fell to practically zero, although tax increases propelled consumer prices ahead at 4.5 percent. Unemployment, another persistent problem during the past decade, declined to less than 8 percent. The nonsocialist government's recovery program was threatened primarily by a sharply deteriorating balance-of-trade deficit, which was expected to total 35 billion kroner in 1986 (approximately $4.7 billion), and by rising local government expenditure and taxes. Two economic restraint packages were passed in February and November. Both raised taxes, particularly on energy, and the autumn action sharply taxed and limited consumer credit.

Principally through its press, the DKP kept hammering away at its traditional themes in 1986: the Schlüter government was crushing the Danish wage earner, the disadvantaged have been seriously hurt by cuts in social assistance, and the rights' "class struggle" required response in kind rather than the failed "class cooperation" strategies of the Social Democrats and other leftist parties. Executive Committee member and DKP theorist Ib Nørlund announced a party slogan, "Unity Against the Right," with the aim of finding a common program for the period "after Schlüter" (*WMR*, March). Clearly the DKP was worried by the efforts by the SF leadership and some left-wing Social Democrats to prepare a new leftist alternative to the nonsocialist government. Although the DKP has traditionally avoided joint action that was not under its firm control, some DKP activists are anxious that the party prepare for a new "workers' government" should the Socialist party win the forthcoming parliamentary elections and agree to a common program or coalition (*Information*, 19 June). This topic dominated the DKP annual conference attended by 350 delegates in October. Chairman Jensen called for communist preparation for and leadership of massive strikes in connection with the coming round of wage talks in the spring of 1987. Such action would hasten the fall of the Schlüter government and its replacement with a workers' government (*Politiken Weekly*, 8 October).

The DKP's domestic program remains the manifesto adopted at the Twenty-seventh Congress, *The Denmark We Want* and the action program *Our Answer*. More recent statements adjust these provisions to current issues. Among the measures desired by the DKP are establishment of new public enterprises; nationalization of all banks and financial institutions; close state control of investment, including reductions in interest on public bonds; supervision of the cooperative movement, agriculture, and fisheries; and finally, the perennial DKP proposal to reduce the workweek to 35 hours, restrict overtime, extend various leaves, and implement other measures with no reduction in real wages. These last goals are common to all of the socialist parties, although the SDP sees them as the gradual fruits of free collective bargaining.

Although labor relations and trade union policy are major DKP concerns, the party has little formal influence over major trade unions, most of which are affiliated with the SDP. Communists are active in union locals, and compared with electoral politics, this is an area of some DKP strength. Communists have been especially visible in the metalworkers', typographers', and maritime unions. Although communist labor activist Andersen has periodically revived the radical Shop Stewards' Movement, especially in connection with collective bargaining confrontations, that group has normally been rejected by democratic unions. As mentioned, another labor activist, Ole Sohn, is touted as Jørgen Jensen's successor, and several new DKP parliamentary candidates are similarly active in the unions (*Information*, 19 June).

A bitter struggle in the Danish Nurses' Association saw DKP activist Inger Rasmussen seeking the vice-chair of the union in May. About a third of the delegates were committed to the communist candidate, a result blamed on low participation of the nurses in selecting congress delegates; DKP union activists typically thrive in unions with passive or alienated members. Press attention and intervention by long-time SDP chair of the Danish Nurses' Association, Kirsten Stallknecht, assisted in defeating the communist candidate (*Berlingske Tidende*, 9 April; *JPRS*, 16 May).

**Foreign Affairs.** Although it has little effect on Danish foreign policy, the international political situation has always had a direct impact on status of the DKP. Increased East-West tensions (such as the cold war of the late 1940s and the waning détente in the late 1970s), capped by the Soviet invasion of Afghanistan in 1979, spelled domestic disaster for the DKP. Few West European communist parties have been more steadfastly loyal to the foreign policy line of the Soviet Union than the DKP. On the other hand, the DKP has cleverly exploited international issues, such as the continuing unpopularity of Danish membership in the European Economic Community (EEC) and the strong revival of the European peace and antinuclear movements since 1980. Through front organizations, the DKP has been able to promote positions that would attract little attention under the DKP label. The DKP's foreign policy line follows the Soviet line not only in general but even in regard to specific details. Examples in 1986 included opposition to continued American nuclear weapons testing and development of the Strategic Defence Initiative.

Two traditional foreign policy issues dominated the agenda in 1986: Denmark's relationships with the EEC and NATO. Their prominence had little to do with the DKP; rather, they have become contentions between the governing nonsocialist parties and the SDP and within the latter party itself. Forty years of basic foreign policy consensus between the SDP and the main nonsocialist parties have been substantially undermined by the dominance of a resurgent revisionist group in the SDP headed by the party's principal foreign policy spokesperson, Lasse Budtz. Recurring parliamentary motions have required the government to reverse its position on NATO policies and actions. Although the SDP still supports NATO and EEC membership in principle and participated in the traditional Defense Act compromise of 1984 (setting defense program goals and financial limits for the four years), its left wing has denounced the installation of INF missiles in western Europe and U.S. foreign policy outside of Europe and advocated immediate establishment of a Nordic nonnuclear zone. These are long-term goals of the DKP and other leftist parties. The SDP believes that such "peace" issues have attracted many of its voters to the leftist parties, particularly the SF.

A package of EEC reforms, known as the European Act, proved divisive in January. Its provisions would reduce members' veto powers, strengthen the European Parliament, and increase EEC foreign policy cooperation. Lacking a parliamentary majority for ratification, the government scheduled a consultative referendum by whose results the SDP and most other parties were pledged to abide. On 27 February, Schlüter's gamble paid off; the EEC package was approved by a clear majority (56.2 percent in favor: mainly rural and suburban districts) (*Nordisk Kontakt*, no. 5).

Prominent in the campaign against the EEC package was the broadly based Popular Movement Against the EEC (Folkebevægelsen mod EF). Bonde is among its leadership and sits as one of the movement's four members in the European Parliament. Its expenses in the referendum campaign left the movement in some financial embarrassment, and Bonde's proposals to expand the scope of its activities and increase its national executive board were rejected at the annual meeting in November (ibid., no. 16).

The DKP's influence in the peace movement was apparent in the tumultuous "Copenhagen Peace Congress" arranged in October by the Soviet-controlled World Peace Council. The Danish delegation was nominally headed by the aged pacifist Hermod Lannung. A former Radical Liberal (a reformist center party), Lannung's idealistic pacifism has encouraged collaboration across the entire political spectrum including Bolsheviks in the 1920s and German occupation forces in the 1940s. The congress was boycotted by most Danish groups, including the SDP, and totally controlled by pro-Soviet elements (Foreign and Commonwealth Office, London, *Background Brief*, August). All threats to the peace were blamed on the United States. Fights and shouting matches broke out when people critical of Soviet foreign policy, especially in Afghanistan, sought to present their views (Danish Radio Shortwave Service, 20 October).

The DKP did criticize Soviet delays in providing complete information about the Chernobyl nuclear disaster in April (*Land og Folk*, 30 April). Human rights cases involving the USSR received no DKP support. DKP chair Jensen and Vice-Chair Nørlund reiterated their party's steadfast commitment to the USSR and "proletarian internationalism" (that is, the Soviet line) on all foreign policy issues (*WMR*, July).

**International Party Contacts.** The DKP leadership maintains close ties with other pro-Moscow communist parties, especially those in Eastern Europe. Delegations from all of the Warsaw Pact countries regularly attend DKP congresses, and DKP leaders are ardent travelers to foreign communist meetings and countries. A DKP delegation that included Nørlund participated in the Twenty-seventh Soviet Communist Party Congress in February.

Chair Jensen addressed the annual conference of the East German SED in April. His speech reiterated his party's analysis of the continuing crisis of Western capitalism and the need for continuing cooperation among communist parties and their allies (*Neues Deutschland*, 22 April).

In July, continuing a tradition of summer junkets, Jensen visited Bulgaria, where talks were held with Milko Balev, a member of the Bulgarian Communist Party Politburo (Sofia Domestic Radio Service, 16 July; *JPRS*, 13 August).

**Other Marxist/Leftist Groups.** The DKP is only one of several left-wing parties currently active in Danish politics. The SF, by far the most powerful of these groups, continued to gain strength in 1986. Originally a splinter from the DKP (in 1958), the SF has steadily gained ground despite a decade of internal splits and electoral setbacks between 1968 and 1977. Ever since it won its first parliamentary representation in 1960, the SF has sought to push the SDP leftward. In 1966–1967 and 1971–1973, SF votes kept the Social Democrats in power. The first experiment in formal SF-SDP collaboration (the so-called Red Cabinet) ended when the SF's left wing split off to form the VS. Such collaboration with the Marxist left has worried SDP moderates, and in 1973, several right-wing Social Democrats abandoned their party to form the Center Democrats. Following the SF's advance in December 1981, it appeared that another effort would be made at collaboration, but necessary support from the VS and centrist groups was absent. Because the SDP's traditional centrist ally, the Radical Liberals, has remained loyal to the nonsocialist coalition, a leftist alternative has again attracted a growing number of Social Democrats.

The SF program is decidedly socialist, pacifist, and Marxian, but it emphasizes Danish values and rejects foreign socialist models. The SF is explicitly non-Leninist, in both its internal party governance and its attitudes toward Danish parliamentary democracy. Its feuds and schisms now past, the SF thrives under the experienced leadership of its veteran chair, Gert Petersen, and is the natural alternative to dissatisfied SDP and other leftist voters. The SF's outstanding results in the November 1985 local elections, record high standing in public opinion polls, and absorption of two defecting VS members of Parliament (MPs) have given the party a sense that it is again time to share power.

The terms of SF-SDP cooperation dominated the SF's agenda in 1986. For such collaboration to succeed, agreement is required in two vital areas: economic policy and security policy. At the SF's summer party conference, the leadership stated that there were five basic conditions for coalition: adjustment of unemployment insurance and other social benefit payments to make up for inflation and cuts since 1982, reduction of the standard working day to seven hours (without wage cuts), compulsory employee profit-sharing and codetermination ("Economic Democracy"), fiscal and monetary policy free from EEC interference, and declaration of Denmark as an unconditionally nuclear weapons–free zone. Nevertheless, the SF stated that these goals and 279 detailed proposals for a future "workers' government" were open to negotiation. Finally, the SF expected to hold one of the important portfolios in such a coalition, such as Foreign Affairs or Finance. Petersen said that he personally was not interested in a seat in the cabinet. The party's EEC policy spokesperson, Steen Gade, was mentioned as a candidate for such a post (*Nordisk Kontakt*, nos. 8, 12–13).

Although discussion of a future coalition did not change the SF's formal program, there were signs of increased flexibility. The party was willing to live with the outcome of the February EEC referendum. Several party members discussed accepting NATO membership and a modification of Danish defense in the direction suggested by some SDP leaders. Social Democratic Party leader Anker Jørgensen said that an "opening to left" was possible provided that it did not exclude cooperation with the centrist forces, and SDP deputy leader Svend Auken warned that the SF's tradition of allowing the party's national executive to direct its MPs would not be compatible with a formal coalition (*Politiken Weekly*, 17 September).

Despite its "white collar/public employee" image, the SF continues to broaden its base of support, even within the labor unions. The SF has informal, but close, ties to analogous parties in Norway and Sweden and looser ties to the Italian Communist Party. With its membership approaching 10,000 (nearly doubling in ten years), the SF has become far more than a protest party, although dissatisfaction with the DKP, VS, and SDP have accounted for much of its renewed strength. It is a haven for activists and voters committed to a "soft" Danish Marxism and democratic-socialist solutions without reference to or apologies for less fortunate experiments elsewhere.

The VS is much weaker, and in 1986, the party replayed its internal factional struggles that have repeatedly plagued the party. For nearly a decade, the party has been divided into so-called "Red Realists"—moderates who favor cooperation with the SF and, possibly, parliamentary support for a broad leftist coalition—and the "Left Oppositionists"—whose dogmatic Marxism-Leninism precludes such tactical steps and rejects positive parliamentary action. Such internal debate exploded when a VS security policy expert, Klaus Birkholm, suggested that an isolated Danish withdrawal from NATO would accomplish nothing. He advocated considering proposals to reorient the Danish armed forces to a more limited defense role (*Nordisk Kontact*, no. 4).

Even before an extraordinary VS congress could be convened to determine the party's direction, two "Realist" MPs, Anne Grete Holmsgaard and Jørgen Lenger, announced that they would leave the party and reaffiliate with the SF. Other party leaders, including one of its founders and most effective leaders, Preben Wilhjelm, despaired of the viability of the VS. The October congress seemed to find a middle ground between the factions. It agreed that, following the next election, the VS could negotiate with other socialist parties for a common leftist program. Should the party succeed in returning to Parliament (1986 polls cast grave doubts that this will happen), its votes would be decisive for a leftist coalition (ibid., nos. 5, 9, 12–13; *Politiken Weekly*, 8 October).

There are at least three additional leftist groups participating in Danish elections. The SAP has only minimal support, but its newspaper, *Klassekampen* (Class struggle), is well-informed on Danish leftist politics and on the international Trotskyist movement. Efforts by Trotskyites to infiltrate other socialist parties (mainly the SDP following their British comrades' strategy in the British Labour Party) have been repulsed.

The Albanian perspective dominates the miniscule Marxist-Leninist Party (MLP) which was not allowed to appear on the ballot with its confusing full name: Communist Party of Denmark/Marxist-Leninist. The MLP publishes a newspaper, *Arbejderen* (Worker) and a theoretical journal, *Partiets Vej* (The party's way). Its program is similar to other extreme leftist groups.

The KAP, oldest of the extreme leftist sects, originated in the student uprisings of 1968. Under its veteran leader Copenhagen University historian Benito Scocozza, the KAP seeks to keep alive a "Maoist" tradition, even as China's own policies have changed dramatically in the past decade. The

KAP's overtures to other parties, such as the VS, have thus far been rejected (Ib Garodkin, *Håndbog i Dansk Politik*, 1985, 7th ed., Præstø: Mjølner, 1985).

Danish electoral laws make it possible to run nationally for Parliament with only about 20,000 signatures, and Danes willingly sign such petitions. A major incentive to undertake even a hopeless parliamentary campaign is the free and generous radio and television time allowed all parties. Most such media access is in the form of rigorous questioning by professional journalists, however, and inexperienced party spokesmen can find the procedure devastating. That is not likely to deter veteran Seaman's Union leader Hansen in his decision to have his FKK on the next parliamentary ballot. Hansen's party program, written by himself, is similar to DKP's without ties to Moscow. All of the sectarian Marxist groups are eclipsed by the possibility of an SDP-SF alternative government. They are all too small to have any political significance.

Eric S. Einhorn
*University of Massachusetts at Amherst*

# Finland

**Population.** 4,931,000
**Party.** Finnish Communist Party (Suomen Kommunistinen Puolue; SKP) runs as the Finnish People's Democratic League (Suomen Kansan Demokraattinen Liitto; SKDL) in parliamentary elections; "shadow" Finnish Communist Party (Suomen Kommunistinen Puolue; SKP) runs as the Democratic Alternative (Demokraattinen Vaihtoehto; DEVA) in parliamentary elections
**Founded.** SKP: 1918; shadow SKP: 1986
**Membership.** SKP: 20,000; shadow SKP: 16,663 (both claimed)
**Chairman.** SKP: Arvo Aalto; shadow SKP: Taisto Sinisalo
**General Secretary.** SKP: Esko Vainionpää; shadow SKP: Jouko Kajanoja
**Politburo.** SKP: Arvo Aalto, Esko Vainionpää, Aarno Aitamurto (vice-chair), Helja Tammisola (vice-chair), Erkki Kauppila, Arvo Kemppainen, Mirja Ylitalo, Timo Laaksonen, Olavi Hänninen; shadow SKP: Taisto Sinisalo, Yrjö Häkanen (vice-chair), Marita Virtanen (vice-chair), Jouko Kajanoja, Kalervo Ilmanen, Urho Jokinen, Eino Kaajakari, Markku Kangaspuro, Matti Kautto, Mikko Kuoppa, Ilmari Nieminen, Seppo Ruotsalainen, Pentti Salo, Cáy Seʹvon, Erkki Susi, Sten Söderström, Pirkko Turpeinen.
**Central Committee.** Both SKP and shadow SKP: 50 full and 15 alternate members
**Status.** Both parties: legal
**Last Congress.** SKP: twentieth, 24–26 May 1984, in Helsinki; an Extraordinary Congress was held on 23 March 1985; next congress, 12–14 June, 1987; shadow SKP: first, 5–7 June 1987
**Last Election.** 1983, 14 percent, 27 of 200 seats; present deputies: SKP 17 (14 moderate communists, 3 socialists), shadow SKP 10
**Auxiliary Organizations.** SKP: Finnish Democratic Youth League (SDNL); Finnish Women's Democratic League (SNDL); shadow SKP: Red Youth Council
**Publications.** SKP: *Kansan Uutiset* (daily); *Folktidningen* (Swedish-language weekly); shadow SKP: *Tiedonantaja* (daily); all published in Helsinki

From the time it was legalized at the end of World War II until 1983, the SKP, operating through its front party the SKDL, was a major political force that frequently participated in government coalitions. The principal exception was the period 1948 through 1966, after communist leaders came under suspicion of plotting a coup d'état in 1948. Differences between the more doctrinaire and the more nationalistic communists, which had existed since the party was formed on 29 August 1918, flared into its present factional framework when Arne Saarinen was elected party chair in 1966 and the party adopted a more reformist program in 1969. The hard-line Stalinists (sometimes referred to as "Taistoists" after their leader, Taisto Sinisalo, and more recently, simply the "minority" as opposed to the "majority" or "moderates") walked out in 1969 and formed separate organizational units. Pressure from the CPSU prevented a complete split between the two intransigent groups until 1986; from 1979 until 1985, the majority granted the Stalinists about one-third of leadership posts, and the Stalinist organizations operated as a party within a party, centering around the newspaper *Tiedonantaja*.

Popular support for the communists has declined as Finland has become more industrialized and the society has changed. The Stalinists, adhering to Marxist-Leninist principles, have opposed moderate efforts to adjust to these changes (*Helsingin Sanomat*, 25 October 1985; *JPRS-WER*-86-001, 2 January). The two factions came to swords' points when the 1984 congress swept the moderates into a dominating position and elected long-time party secretary, Aalto to the chair. The Stalinists refused to take any leadership positions and sought to overturn the 1984 congress by convoking, through petitions by district organizations they controlled, another special party congress. The Aalto forces bowed to CPSU pressure to hold the congress but, invoking loyalty regulations, created parallel district organizations alongside the Stalinist ones and empowered the new units to elect representatives to the congress. The Stalinists, now supported by the "third-line" group originally created by former SKP chair Kajanoja to bridge the two factions, boycotted the congress when it met in 1985, and it authorized the SKP Central Committee to expel party units for disloyalty. In 1985, despite CPSU opposition, the SKP starting purging the minority.

**Party Leadership and Party Organization.** The ouster of the Stalinists and third-liners was completed in 1986. The SKP Central Committee had expelled the eight Stalinist district organizations in October 1985 despite the CPSU warning that such action would have "negative consequences" for both the SKP and Finnish-Soviet relations. The committee announced on December 15 that new membership books would be issued to SKP members to assure that all members belonged to local units of loyal districts. It also revealed that the 1969 party program would be replaced.

On 23 January, Aalto made public a draft of the new program that would be presented to the 1987 party congress, telling the press that the purpose of adopting a new program was to put the past behind, "examine Finland and the world in terms of the future," and develop the SKP as a popular movement (*Kansan Uutiset*, 24 January; *JPRS-WER*-86-028, 24 March).

The entire program is written in general and vague terms, and its most striking feature is the absence of such doctrinal and traditional phrases as *proletarian dictatorship* and *Marxism-Leninism*. The SKP is defined as a "revolutionary Marxist party," and the term *workers* is replaced by *workers and employees*. Aalto explained that the use of everyday language in the draft did not mean a change in ideology and denied that the SKP had become Eurocommunist: "The SKP leadership considers it a sign of expanded international activity, not Eurocommunism, that the West European communist parties which operate in similar social circumstances are seen as natural and intimate collaborators with the SKP." On the other hand, he said there should be more democracy and debate on ideology in the party, ending its authoritarian tradition. (Ibid., *Nordisk Kontakt*, no. 2.)

More world-oriented in outlook, the program places great emphasis on the peace movement: "Communists believe the actions of peace movements in flashpoints of conflicts of imperialism is an important force for social change." The draft also endorses "a new, just international economic order, political and economic independence for less developed countries, an unconditional right to their own resources, a just price for their production, equal trade, development of education, and disinterested cooperation in all areas of social life." It declares that "the international solidarity of the working class is one of the SKP's most important principles." (*Kansan Uutiset*, 24 January; *JPRS-WER*-86-028, 24 March.)

The draft endorses "proletarian internationalism," a point some observers believed was added at the last minute to appease the CPSU (*Nordisk Kon-*

*takt*, no. 2) but makes clear the party's independence from the CPSU by defining the principles of intercommunist party cooperation as respecting the equality and sovereign independence of each party, noninterference in the internal affairs of another party, and respect for the individual path each party freely chooses. The SKP is no longer stated to be the leader of the democratic alliance that "will lead" in transforming the society to socialism. "Finland's path to socialism" is now replaced by a vague concept of "opportunity for democratic change." The draft calls for cooperation with the Social Democrats, as did the 1969 program, and also with the Greens. It states that there should be an alliance of "the working class, its different groups, and different kinds of political and trade organizations as well as national groups manifesting democratic and anticapitalist needs and endeavors." Finally, the draft devotes much space to addressing a need to seek solutions for problems affecting the environment. (*Kansan Uutiset*, 24 January; *JPRS-WER-86-028*, 24 March.)

Despite Aalto's denials, Finnish noncommunist observers as well as the Stalinists universally concluded that the party had changed fundamentally. A commentator of the conservative *Uusi Suomi* thought that the dropping of the Lenin theory of disciplined cadres was the most important change and that "the SKP is now backsliding in the direction of a reformist social democratic party of the masses" (28 January; *JPRS-WER-86-028*, 24 March). A commentary in the independent *Helsingin Sanomat* (24 January) headlined the provision allowing opposition parties, asserting that its application would lead to a multiparty state. Jokinen, long-time editor of Stalinist *Tiedonantaja*, termed the program a "declaration of war on Marxism-Leninism," and pointed out that it did not call for taking power through revolution. He claimed that internationalism was demoted to fifth priority and accused Aalto "along with the bourgeoisie" of following the path of historic compromise. (*Tiedonantaja*, 28 January.)

By mid-February moderate leaders concluded that their rank and file was accepting the radical organizational changes they had inaugurated (*Hufvudstadsbladet*, 18 February). The SKP Central Committee set a deadline of 1 March for Stalinists to recant, and on that date new membership books were issued (and immediately rejected by Stalinist and third-line leaders).

The minority responded vigorously to the moderate attacks. It had rallied its forces at a mass meeting of Stalinists and third-liners, the latter led by former SKP chair Kajanoja, at Lahti in October 1985 under the catchword of party unity. The eight expelled district organizations formed a Committee of SKP Organizations to direct minority activities. When the SKDL leaders refused minority appeals to allow minority representatives to run for office on SKDL lists (Helsinki Domestic Service, 12 January; *FBIS*, 13 January), the minority organized its own district and local electoral organizations in most SKDL districts (*Uusi Suomi*, 1 April). Within the nine original districts that had remained loyal to the moderates, "unity committees" that included Kajanoja followers were created to work with the Committee of SKP Organizations. In the latter part of February, the two groups proposed the establishment of a nationwide electoral organization (*Hufvudstadsbladet*, 19 February).

On April 12, representatives of "unity" forces, including both Stalinists and third-liners, met in Helsinki and founded the Democratic Alternative (Demokraattinen Vaihtoehto; DEVA). Like the SKDL, it consists of associations at the constituency level. A collective presidium of 11 members was created, with the septegenerian Leo Suonpää as its head. A 100-person "delegation," or Advisory Council, was also named. The only well-known leaders were Kajanoja (who took a place on the Presidium) and Sinisalo (who became a member of the Advisory Council). Speeches and resolutions warned of Finland's growing dependence on the West and urged greater cooperation with the USSR under the Treaty of Friendship, Commerce, and Mutual Assistance. (*Tiedonantaja*, 15 April; *JPRS-WER*-86-048, 16 May.)

Kajanoja and Sinisalo told the press that the object of forming the organization was merely to meet the requirement for registering under electoral laws so that their candidates could run in the 1987 parliamentary election and secure party subsidies and TV time for campaigning; participants regarded their membership in the SKP as still valid. The Finnish press reported that the CPSU approved the party formation as long as it was not another communist party (*Helsingin Sanomat*, 13 April). But observers generally considered the action as reflecting the stalemate facing the unity effort and as constituting a decisive step toward a definitive break in the communist movement (*Hufvudstadsbladet*, 18 April; *JPRS-WER-86-053*, 2 June; *Uusi Suomi*, 15 April; *JPRS-WER-86-048*, 16 May). It was noted that the organization would continue after the 1987 election and that it was attempting, like the

SKDL, to be a front and appeal to a wide variety of Finns. The Official Establishment Declaration, which said that assuring permanent peace in the world was the most important task, called for the support of "communists and people's democrats, socialists, and social democrats, Greens, progressive centrists and political independents... everyone who is honestly concerned about the Finnish nation" (*Tiedonantaja*, 15 April; *JPRS-WER*-86-048, 16 May). Noncommunist observers were quick to point out that it was absurd to think that DEVA would appeal more than the SKDL to left-socialist, centrist and environmentalist groups (*Hufvudstadsbladet*, 18 April; *JPRS-WER*-86-053, 2 June). On 13 May, Kajanoja presented DEVA's goals in a publication entitled "A New Trend for Finland—Peace for the World" and said it was an invitation for debate that would form a party platform. *Kansan Uutiset* (14 May) immediately labeled it just a compilation of populist clichés.

More dramatic was a constituent meeting of Stalinists and Kajanoja forces in Tampere on 26–27 April. Eight hundred two delegates, purporting to represent 765 party organizations (termed "SKP Organizations") and 16,633 SKP members (which, if true, would be a majority of all SKP members) elected what the press termed a "shadow SKP"—a complete copy of SKP organs (*Tiedonantaja*, 29 April; *JPRS-WER*-86-057, 12 June). Sinisalo was named chair; Kajanoja, general secretary (although the two vice-chairs Häkanen of Helsinki and Virtanen of Turku, outrank him). Four of the seventeen members of the Politburo and ten of the 50 Central Committee members are Kajanoja followers. Jokinen (*Tiedonantaja* now under the editorship of Susi was selected as the party's chief organ) was named chair of the Central Committee (called the "Central Committee of the SKP Organizations" to distinguish it from the SKP Central Committee). Sinisalo insisted that the newly elected officials were the true leaders of the SKP and legitimate heirs to the Twentieth SKP Congress, that the Aalto leadership had not been democratically elected and did not represent a majority of party members. He proclaimed SKP unity to be the chief goal of the party. The only discordant note came from the Uusimaa District, headed by Markus Kainulainen, which wanted to form a new Marxist-Leninist party, and it gave way after a mild protest. (*Hufvudstadsbladet*, 27, 28, 29 April; *JPRS-WER*-86-073, 22 July; *Nordisk Kontakt*, no. 8; AFP, 27 April; *FBIS*, 28 April.)

No new party program was announced, but a comprehensive policy document was adopted. It called for ending the low profile in foreign policy and strengthening Finland's cooperation with the USSR and other socialist countries, particularly by taking extensive measures to increase trade with the Soviet Union. It also called for increased nationalization of industries. (*Hufvudstadsbladet*, 28 April; *JPRS-WER*-86-073, 22 July.)

The counselor of the Soviet embassy attended the meeting, although not as an official representative of the CPSU, and *Pravda* (28 April) remarked approvingly that the shadow party was trying to strengthen Marxism-Leninism and return the SKP to democracy. The official SKP organ, *Kansan Uutiset* (24 April), had bitterly attacked the calling of the shadow party convention, claiming that the minority was abusing the name and tradition of the SKP and falsely asserting that it had the support of the bulk of local party organization members. Following the convention, the paper said the new party had no ideological platform but was merely trying to confuse the people by manipulating SKP symbols and traditions. It concluded that the minority could "cause considerable damage to the SKP and the SKDL, but it will not be able to destroy the party or the influential People's Democratic movement." (*Kansan Uutiset*, 29 April; *JPRS-WER*-86-057, 12 June.)

The party split was formalized on 5 June when the SKDL parliamentary group expelled 10 of its 27 deputies for adhering to DEVA. The 10 then formed their own caucus under the leadership of Ensio Laine (vice-leaders were Irma Rosnell and Kuoppa) and sat apart in the Eduskunta (*Nordisk Kontakt*, no. 11). On June 13, in what seemed an anticlimax, the SKP Central Committee completed the split by ousting 494 local party organizations and their 10,000 members for disloyalty. Aalto, who had earlier estimated that the twenty-year-old quarrel had alienated 150,000 supporters and 20,000 party members (*Helsingin Sanomat*, *Hufvudstadsbladet*, 2 March), said 805 local organizations with some 20,000 members remained loyal to the party (*Helsingin Sanomat*, *Hufvudstadsbladet*, 14 June). He later called for efforts to recruit working people and women (Helsinki Domestic Service, 15 August; *FBIS* 18 August). In early July, DEVA registered as a party (*Kansan Uutiset*, 8 July; *Hufvudstadsbladet*, 16 July).

The minority publicly continued to pursue its theme of communist unity (*Tiedonantaja*, 17 August; *JPRS-WER*-86-100, 8 October). In August the Central Committee of SKP Organizations sent a letter to the SKP Central Committee proposing that the SKP cancel its expulsions and that an SKDL-DEVA electoral alliance be formed (Helsinki Domestic Service, 14 August; *FBIS*, 15 August). A principal reason for that action was the devastating effect the split was having on communist political prospects. Opinion polls indicated that about 10 percent of the electorate supported the SKDL and between 1 and 3 percent DEVA, compared with the 14 percent the SKDL had received in the 1983 parliamentary elections. If those figures held in the next parliamentary election, communist parliamentary representation would drop from 27 to about 18 seats. (*Hufvudstadsbladet*, 7 August; *JPRS-WER*-86-095, 22 September.)

**Domestic Party Affairs.** A general trend to the right in the Finnish electorate further aroused communist concern. Polls indicated that support for the left as a whole—communists and the Social Democrats—had dropped some 4 percent since the 1983 elections and totaled only about 37 percent of the electorate. In comparison, the Center Party had risen slightly to some 18 percent and the tiny Greens had more than doubled their support, now receiving 4 to 5 percent, while the Conservatives (National Coalition Party) had stabilized at about 22 percent, second only to the approximately 25 percent held by the Social Democrats.

Moderate communists worried that, particularly because of the weakened position of the SKP, the leaders of the governing parties (Social Democrats, Center, Rural, and Swedish People's) might turn toward the Conservatives for future cooperation. Finnish leaders generally believed that the Conservatives could now be included in future coalitions without severe Soviet reaction. At the Center Party congress in the spring, party chair Paavo Väyrynen (who was also foreign minister under Prime Minister Kaleva Sorsa) severely criticized Sorsa and the Social Democrats on both domestic and foreign policy issues and suggested that the coalition might be widened to include the Conservatives. These statements were interpreted generally as a turn to the right and as the opening shot in the March 1987 parliamentary elections and the January 1988 presidential election; later (in June) Väyrynen was named the Center Party presidential candidate. Väyrynen's strategy for overturning highly popular President Mauno Koivisto (polls showed Koivisto's

popularity rating to be between 51 and 57 percent, while Väyrynen's was between 5 and 12 percent) was thought to be to try to head a center-right government as a stepping stone to the presidency, while maintaining the Kekkonen tradition of excellent relations with the USSR. (*Hufvudstadsbladet*, 29 April, 9 July; *JPRS-WER*-86-073, 22 July; *JPRS-WER*-86-095, 22 September.) Sorsa responded to Väyrynen's attacks by remarks friendly toward the Conservatives, in effect keeping Social Democratic options open, while the Conservative chair, Illka Suominen, who had earlier made a gesture toward the Finnish working class—a gesture perhaps intended to worry the Center Party— (*Kansan Uutiset*, 26 September), remained aloof from the Väyrynen-Sorsa exchanges.

In a speech in Kuopio on 13 April, Aalto warned of the danger of Social Democratic–Conservative cooperation; such a development would continue the shift to the right and strengthen economic ties to the West, weakening those with the USSR (*Helsingin Sanomat*, 14 April). On 19 April, Aalto told an audience in Kemi that the SKP would use the 1987 parliamentary election to create political conditions for its participation in government. Finland must strengthen its national independence, now threatened by the entry of international corporations and banks into Finland and by relations with the European Community. (*Nordisk Kontakt*, no. 8.)

At a meeting of the SKP Central Committee on 9 May, SKDL general secretary Reija Käkelä said that the SKP and SKDL must review their strategic thinking. Finnish politics no longer obeyed former president Kekkonen's injunction not to divide on a left-right axis. Käkelä addressed the Social Democratic problem sympathetically and did not believe the Social Democrats would cooperate with the Conservatives. After the next election, the parties on the right would try, probably not successfully, he thought, to form a government, driving the Social Democrats to the left; if the right did gain power, its rule should be made as short as possible. He concluded by saying that there is much "true" worker movement within the Social Democrats. Aalto publicly supported Käkelä and said the left should gather its forces. (*Nordisk Kontakt*, no. 9; *Kansan Uutiset*, 13 June.)

In his May Day speech, Sorsa reciprocated the SKP's kind words. He accused Väyrynen of trying to exploit the SKP's division, neglecting Kekkonen's legacy, and opting for a government of the right. In an interview in July, Sorsa said the Social Democrats had held talks with the SKDL, which was interested in government cooperation. Talks had also been held with Democratic Alternative representatives, and "correct ties" had been established with them. He noted that DEVA had a favorable attitude toward Koivisto (the shadow SKP constituent assembly had approved Koivisto's foreign policies—a slap at Väyrynen) and the Social Democrats. He expressed an unwillingness to cooperate with the Conservatives. (*Helsingin Sanomat*, 4 July.) These remarks were interpreted as an attempt to increase electoral support for Koivisto, who might need communist votes for an electoral college majority (*Hufvudstadsbladet*, 9 July; *JPRS-WER*-86-095).

Later in July, SKDL chair Esko Helle said that, although the SKDL would most probably name a candidate of its own, it could form an electoral alliance—an open hint that the SKDL might support Koivisto as it had in 1982 (*Helsingin Sanomat*, 19 July; *JPRS-WER*-86-088, 27 August). At its December meeting the SKDL Council deferred nomination of a candidate until after the parliamentary election but made clear that it would choose former SKDL chair Kaveli Kivistö (*Hufvudstadsbladet*, 10 December); DEVA did not choose a candidate either. Ele Alenius, former SKDL chair and head of the Socialist organization within the SKDL, told the press in late October that the SKDL and the Social Democrats should agree to support President Koivisto for re-election (all papers, 26 October). The idea of a coalition between the left, including the SKP, and the Conservatives was broached by Alenius and former SKP chair Saarinen (*Uusi Suomi*, 28 October; *Sosialdemokkraati*, 28 October).

Väyrynen's attacks on Sorsa grew sharper in the fall, and his tone aroused reaction in his own Center Party as well as in other parties. His charge that the government's budget proposal was too optimistic in outlook and that wages and salaries should be cut (*Helsingin Sanomat*, 12 October) caused Sorsa to call a cabinet committee meeting in mid-October and force coalition representatives to renew their support for the proposal. Väyrynen dropped his criticism (*Kansan Uutiset*, 15 October) but soon took strong exception to Sorsa's conduct of trade relations with the USSR (*Uusi Suomi*, 20 October). Sorsa hit back hard in a speech to a Social Democratic rally, and in a clear warning that the Center Party could not take coalition with the Social Demo-

crats for granted, said "the Social Democrats should be able to reach agreement on a government program with either of the two main bourgeois parties" (*Helsingin Sanomat*, 29 October). *Kansan Uutiset* (29 October) gloated: "The strike was natural and expected, given Väyrynen's unscrupulous and brazen behavior toward the prime minister." It commented hopefully that Väyrynen's courting of the Conservatives did not reflect the political will of Center Party supporters. Aalto, in an open letter to Sorsa as party chair, proposed that the SDP and the SKDL rally behind the stronger of their presidential candidates at the end of the presidential campaign and said that the fact that, in "many matters," the Center Party was now as far right as the Conservatives should not mean that the latter should be taken into the government (*Helsingin Sanomat*, 29 October; *Kansan Uutiset*, 29 October).

In early November, Väyrynen put out a peace feeler to the Social Democrats (*Uusi Suomi*, 7 November). The Conservatives also took a step back and said they could not contemplate entering a coalition with just the left, especially if the SKDL were included. By year's end the controversy had softened, but the communists could take little cheer from the situation. At an SKP Central Committee meeting in late November, Aalto sourly disagreed with the economic policy of the government (which he thought was increasing social problems) and criticized those Social Democrats who favored cooperating with the Conservatives (Helsinki Domestic Service, 23 November; *FBIS*, 24 November).

The Stalinists were also disturbed by the course of political developments, but their room to maneuver was even more limited. At a minority SKP Central Committee meeting in early October, Sinisalo said the committee had decided to extend to the Social Democrats, Center Party, Greens, and independents an invitation for cooperation to counter the trend to the right. The aim would be to promote cooperation with the USSR, lower unemployment, and promote peace and the defense of democracy. (*Hufvudstadsbladet*, 6 October; *FBIS*, 9 October.)

During the Chernobyl crisis, the SKDL came to the support of the government against a Conservative interpellation accusing the government of weak crisis readiness and of supplying insufficient information on the fallout in Finland. When the SKDL put forth a motion opposing the building of a fifth nuclear power plant in Finland, the minority SKDL deputies did not support it (*Kansan Uutiset*, 8 May; *JPRS-WER*-86-059, 19 June). In the summer, however, Swedish-Finnish members of DEVA opposed the fifth plant as not timely because current technology could not make it safe (*Hufvudstads-bladet*, 22 August).

The moderate-Stalinist political battle was mirrored in the trade union field. In late 1985 SAK secretary Lauri Ihalainen reported that communist strength in the Central Organization of Finnish Trade Unions (SAK) had dropped from 37 to somewhere between 15 and 20 percent since the last SAK federation meeting (*Helsingin Sanomat*, 7 September 1985; *JPRS-WER*-85-083, 8 October 1985). The communists now controlled only 5 of 27 SAK unions—the only important ones are the Construction Workers' Union (with nearly 100,000 members) and the Finnish Foodworkers' Union—in addition to retaining considerable influence in the powerful Metal Workers' and the Rubber and Leather Workers' unions. But the SAK remained the SKP's power base.

In February, the moderates dropped their demands for higher wages and supported the social democratic SAK leaders when the latter agreed to a modest wage increase after brief strikes. Because the government was concerned about the uncertain state of the economy, the fairly high unemployment rate, and the declining competitiveness of Finnish industry, it wanted a restrictive incomes policy and resisted higher wages. On 23 March, Sinisalo attacked the wage settlement, which he said aided "big business against the interests and rights of workers," and accused union leaders of betraying the wage earners (*Kansan Uutiset*, 26 March).

In an election in the important Rubber and Leather Workers' Union, the only union where the Stalinists were stronger than the moderates, the Social Democrats increased their lead from 51.7 to 54 percent over the communists' 46 percent. Although the Stalinists held their share of communist strength, the outcome was nevertheless considered a setback for them because there was considerable worker discontent in this declining industry. The chief Social Democratic organ, *Sosialdemokkraati* (12 May), asserted that the results showed that the union rank and file was not accepting Stalinist claims that moderates and the Social Democrats were betraying the workers.

In June, Olavi Hänninen, a moderate communist, was re-elected second chair at the SAK congress (though he later suffered a stroke), defeating his Stalinist opponent by 427 to 6 votes, and the moderates purged SAK's governing bodies of Sta-

linists almost completely. The latter now have no members on the executive board and only three on the 62-seat council. *Kansan Uutiset* (12 June) applauded the SAK congress's program of action, particularly its call for a 35-hour work week.

**Auxiliary and Front Organizations.** Under the strong domination of moderate communists, the SKDL virtually completed its ouster of the minority in 1986. At its 1985 convention, all but one minority member had been removed from the executive board and only four were left on the council. At the beginning of the year, Stalinists still controlled two district organizations, one in North Karelia (Pohjois-Karjola, around the city of Joensuu) and one in Kymi (*Helsingin Sanomat*, 24 March; *JPRS-WER*-86-042, 30 April). The moderates established their own organization in the first district and expanded their other districts to encompass the second, while the minority countered by setting up its own electoral organizations in most of the SKDL districts as constituent parts of DEVA. In mid-April, the SKDL leadership gave the Pohjois-Karjola and Kymi districts until 1 May to disassociate themselves from DEVA, and on 18 May they expelled them. (*Helsingin Sanomat*, 17 April; *Kansan Uutiset*, 20 May.)

After the SKDL parliamentary group ousted 10 of its 27 members on 5 June, its fortunes were further damaged by the fact that nearly half of the remaining deputies, including the better-known ones, would not run again in the 1987 election. Those retiring included Vekko Saarto, chair of the group, who was leaving Parliament to join the board of directors of the National Pension Fund; Kivistö, former SKDL chair; Ulla-Leena Alpi; Inger Hirvelä; and Terho Pursiainen. (*Hufvudstads-bladet*, 7 August; 10 December; *JPRS-WER*-96-095, 22 September.) Vice-Chair Lauha Männistö replaced Saarto as group chair; a Socialist, she was the first noncommunist to hold that position (*Kansan Uutiset*, 1 November).

The Center Party's shift toward the Conservatives caused SKDL leaders to search for new policies. In his speech to the SKP Central Committee on 8 May, General Secretary Käkelä said that the People's Democratic Movement should now return to its roots and emphasize its revolutionary character. In the main address he made to a meeting of SKDL-member organizations in mid-August, Käkelä sought to set the SKDL on a more radical course. He said it was time to turn away from Sorsa and Koivisto and create a new republic; issues should be examined from the perspective of the whole world. He considered a left-center coalition to be a tactical arrangement only, not a reform effort. In his view, the pressing need was to create economic equality and shift taxes from individuals to business; Finland's economic independence must be rebuilt. There should be a new foreign policy to preserve national and global life and abandon "slide rule" neutrality. Finland should actively promote an international conference of nuclear powers to prevent nuclear war by misinterpretation or technical error. (*Helsingin Sanomat*, 17 August; *JPRS-WER*-86-100, 8 October.)

Käkelä's most extreme proposal was to abolish the Finnish defense establishment (except for small specialized forces to guard borders), which he said was a ridiculous relic in the nuclear age. Civil resistance should defend national values. The money saved should be used to reduce the war threat. Käkelä also blasted security police, who in his opinion should not spy on citizens. (Ibid.) In the spring, Jorma Hentilä, the SKDL representative on the special Parliamentary Defense Commission, had dissented from the commission's recommendations that defense spending be increased, and in October, he opposed the call of the commander of the Finnish Defense Forces for more defense funds. Hentilä asserted that Finland did not have the resources for such expenditures and that the entire defense system should be reviewed. (*Helsingin Sanomat*, 13 April; *Hufvudstadsbladet*, 29 April; *Uusi Suomi*, 19 May; *JPRS-WER*-86-068, 11 July; *Kansan Uutiset*, 2 October.)

On the other hand, new SKDL chair, Helle, while criticizing the Center Party's turn to the right, said both that there should be rule by a center-left coalition of some sort and that the SKDL could not be expected to enter a coalition with the Conservatives.

Freed of the minority, the summer SKDL meeting quickly agreed on economic principles. A draft budget proposal (to counter that put forth by the government) was adopted. It did not seem very radical, seeking to (1) counter unemployment by increasing public works, housing, and road construction and by shortening working hours; (2) equalize income through tax changes; and (3) increase subsidies for families and small farmers. (*Hufvudstadsbladet*, 25 August.) At a council meeting in December, the SKDL adopted an electoral platform that repeated these themes. It stressed caring for the weak, instituting "society's responsibil-ity" for citizens' rights, protecting nature, carrying out a moralistic foreign policy, and promoting international solidarity. Käkelä, who again gave the main speech, said the SKDL should work for a coalition of Social Democrats, the SKDL, the Greens, and part of the Rural Party. (*Hufvudstadsbladet*, 1 December.)

In September, DEVA published its own budget proposal, which stressed increased social spending. It would finance its level of spending over the government's budget by abolishing tax relief granted big business firms, by reducing arms purchases, and by loans. The goals were more trade with the USSR, lower unemployment, and higher income for the lowest income groups. (*Helsingin Sanomat*, 23 September.) On defense policy, DEVA mirrored minority concerns. At a shadow SKP Central Committee meeting in May, Kajanoja declared that Finland was on a new, dangerous foreign and security policy course that departed from the former policy based on active peace efforts and the 1948 Treaty of Friendship, Commerce, and Mutual Assistance. (*Uusi Suomi*, 26 May.)

In a desperate attempt to improve its flagging fortunes—in December polls still indicated that it was supported by only 1.2 to 2.5 percent of the electorate—DEVA, at a special meeting on 6 and 7 December, elected a new leader and expanded its executive council to twenty members. Suonpää was replaced by a prominent actress, Kristiina Halkola, who was also an experienced politician on the local level. Among those added to the council were four DEVA parliamentarians, a member of the declining Social Labor Party (which had joined DEVA), and a Greens activist. The Stalinists took a lower profile. Although commentators believed Halkola would bring much-needed publicity to the movement, DEVA's prospects were not good, particularly since the CPSU had by the end of the year declared its neutrality between the two factions. The parliamentary election would then make or break the party. *Tiedonantaja* remarked that there were no illusions about any great victory for DEVA. (*Hufvudstadsbladet*, 10 December.)

The SDNL also suffered from the factional battle. In March, Stalinists were expelled from it (new membership books were issued) and founded their own organization, the Red Youth Council. At its first meeting, held in Helsinki on 26 and 27 March, Kangaspuro, ousted as deputy chair of the League, was elected to the chair. (*Helsingin Sanomat*, 26 March; *JPRS-WER*-86-042, 30 April.)

Slower to act was the SNDL. On 26 October it

elected new leaders and purged its leadership of DEVA supporters. The new chair was Outi Ojala, a nurse, who replaced the DEVA Eduskunta member Hirvelä. The new leadership took under advisement exclusion of all DEVA supporters from SNDL ranks. (*Hufvudstadsbladet*, 27 October.)

One communist student organization (Socialist Students, SOL) could not make up its mind. It joined DEVA to participate in electoral preparations but maintained its SKDL membership at the same time. (*Helsingin Sanomat*, 14 October.)

On the peace movement front, which both communist factions gave high priority, the Peace Defenders, an umbrella organization, was the main channel of activity. A member of the World Peace Council and close to Soviet organizations and officials, it counted among its constituent members all the major center and left parties, including the SKP and the SKDL, but its central board contained a dominant plurality, if not majority, of Stalinists. At its convention in Oulu on 5 and 6 April, Chair Matti Ruokola (a member of the Center Party) and General Secretary Johannes Pakaslahti (a Stalinist) were re-elected. The convention adopted resolutions demanding that the Finnish government condemn the U.S. strategic defense initiative (SDI) and technology embargo against the "socialist" countries. Ruokola created a storm in the Finnish press by saying that West German participation in the SDI raised the danger of war under the terms of the Finnish-Soviet Treaty of Friendship, Commerce, and Mutual Assistance. Foreign Minister Väyrynen rebuked Ruokola in a press interview (*Helsingin Sanomat*, 30 April), saying he disagreed and that there was more danger from cruise missiles. Pakaslahti was also named general secretary of the WPC, a post abolished in 1977 but now revived in an attempt to bolster the Secretariat's activities (*Kansan Uutiset*, 25 April).

On 3–6 July, the Defenders and the Artists for Peace group organized a "peace camp" at Turku as a part of the International Year of Peace. It concentrated on security policy issues, SDI, the U.S. air raid on Libya, and Third World and environment issues. (*Kansan Uutiset*, 7 July.)

**International Views, Positions, and Activities.** Hanging over moderate-Stalinist warfare was the question of what attitude and action the CPSU would take toward the old and new party units and their leaders. The CPSU's anger over the Aalto forces' determination to oust Stalinists from the SKP was given concrete expression in late 1985

when the CPSU transferred the contract for printing its magazine *Sputnik* from the SKP publishing firm, Yhteistyö Oy, to the Stalinist press, Kursiivi. This dealt the SKP a hard financial blow as a result of which *Kansan Uutiset* was reduced to five editions a week (*Helsingin Sanomat*, 13 October 1985; *JPRS-WER*-85-098, 27 November 1985).

Yet there was ambivalence in the CPSU attitude. Party leaders faced the dilemma of either continuing to support the Stalinists, a stump party likely not to survive, or turning away from their loyal followers and supporting the majority. If they were to seek reunification, they could not ignore Aalto, nor could they treat DEVA and the shadow SKP as parties (*Hufvudstadsbladet*, 7 August; *JPRS-WER*-86-095, 22 September; *Le Monde*, 20 February). In mid-December 1985, the CPSU sought to overcome the split by inviting representatives from the seventeen old party districts and the two factions to a "study" trip in Moscow and Kiev (*Tiedonantaja*, 17 December 1985; *JPRS-WER*-86-020, 21 February).

The issue became critical over the question of whether the CPSU should invite both or only one of the factions (and, if only one, which one) to the CPSU's Twenty-seventh Congress, which started February 25. Indecision delayed the invitation until 21 February, after the Social Democratic and Center parties had received theirs, and it was simply addressed to the SKP. Aalto quickly chose himself, two moderate colleagues (international affairs secretary Olavi Poikalainen and Central Committee official Vitali Lindberg), and Erkki Kivimäki, general secretary of the Finnish-Soviet Society, to make up the SKP delegation. Kivimäki's selection was meant to give the appearance of bipartisanship, since he was friendly to the Stalinists. (*Uusi Suomi*, 21, 22, 23 February; *Helsingin Sanomat*, 21, 22, 23 February.) Because Sinisalo and Kajanoja had not received invitations, as they had expected, Kivimäki decided not to attend.

Aalto was met at the lowest possible level in Moscow by Estonian party leader Karl Vaino and CPSU international division member Vitali Shaposhnikov. Aalto was not seated in the 100-member presidium composed of foreign guests, which had been the customary arrangement for the SKP leader, but made his address to a group of Moscovite activists on the evening of 1 March at the cinema "Oktyabr" in central Moscow. The Finnish press interpreted this reception as showing the low regard if not contempt in which the CPSU held Aalto. On returning to Helsinki, Aalto told the press that his talks with CPSU officials, especially with Vadim Zagladin, deputy head of the CPSU international division, were open, comradely, and focused on the future. He expected tensions to decline. (Helsinki Domestic Service, 7 March; *FBIS*, 11 March; *Helsingin Sanomat*, 8 March; *JPRS-WER*-86-045, 12 May.)

It took some time, but that expectation was borne out. In the spring, the CPSU recognized the new district organizations the moderates had set up to replace the expelled minority ones by authorizing a representative to tour them (*Uusi Suomi*, 2 April). In the summer, SKP journalists visited the USSR after receiving invitations sent through the SKP Central Committee. As a guest of *Pravda*, Heikki Korhonen, editor of *Kansan Uutiset*, interviewed Soviet deputy foreign trade minister A. N. Manzhulo on Soviet-Finnish trade problems, and the journalists also talked with officials in other ministries. (*Kansan Uutiset*, 8 July; *JPRS-WER*-86-086, 25 August.) Aalto vacationed in the USSR in August (*Hufvudstadsbladet*, 7 August; *JPRS-WER*-86-095, 22 September). In late September, an SKP delegation of economic experts headed by SKP vice-chair Aitamurto was received by Vice Foreign Trade Minister Vsevolod Vorontsov and Deputy Foreign Trade Minister Yuri Pikovov (*Kansan Uutiset*, 1 October).

In November, Aalto told a Finnish newspaper (*Helsingin Sanomat*, 4 November) that the period of tension between the SKP and the CPSU was over and said that plans were being made to exchange delegations led by high officials of the two parties in early 1987 at the latest. During his stay in Helsinki in mid-November, central committee secretary and Politburo member Yegor Ligachev, second only to Gorbachev in power, told a press conference that the CPSU maintained impartial relations with the two factions, although the situation was annoying and weakened democratic forces in Finland. He later received delegations headed by Aalto and Sinisalo separately and invited the two to send delegations to Moscow. (*Hufvudstadsbladet*, 14 November; *FBIS*, 17, 19 November; Helsinki Domestic Service, 15 November.)

Fear that the SKP split would harm Finnish-Soviet relations continued in 1986, despite Foreign Minister Väyrynen's effort in late 1985 to quiet such concerns (*Hufvudstadsbladet*, 14 October 1985). On 29 April the respected *Hufvudstadsbladet* remarked that "our relations with the Soviet Union are not dependent on the communists per se, but the two communist parties competing to score foreign pol-

icy points and gain favors are not exactly an asset." This fear was not borne out by events, since Soviet leaders apparently placed greater emphasis on state rather than on party relations (*Uusi Suomi*, 30 August; *JPRS-WER*-86-100, 18 October).

In February, CPSU Central Committee member Leonid Zamyatin, visiting Helsinki to speak before the Peace Defenders on Soviet nuclear disarmament initiatives, met with Foreign Minister Väyrynen and Prime Minister Sorsa, and the Social Democratic and Center parties received invitations to send representatives to the CPSU's Twenty-seventh Congress. At the height of the SKP feuding, Soviet premier Nikolai Ryzhkov accepted President Koivisto's invitation to meet at the Finnish embassy in Stockholm at the time of Prime Minister Olof Palme's funeral (*Helsingin Sanomat*, 16 March). The Chernobyl disaster temporarily marred the picture, when the Soviets charged that evacuation of foreign nationals (the Finnish government had Finnish nationals flown out of Kiev) was a "provocation" (Helsinki Domestic Service, 1 May; *FBIS*, 2 May).

The commander of the Finnish Defense Forces, General Jaakko Valtanen, made an official visit to the USSR at the invitation of Marshal S. F. Ahromeyev in April, and in July, Soviet defense minister Sergei Sokolov paid an official five-day visit to Finland, accompanied by a group of leading officials of the different services similar to Ustinov's entourage in 1978 (*Helsingin Sanomat*, 9 July; Moscow, *Krasnaya Zvezda*, 18, 19 July; *FBIS*, 30 July). The friendly nature of this exchange of top military officials created a strong impression on Finns; it was taken as proof that relations were "good, friendly, and trustful" (*Uusi Suomi*, cited by Helsinki Domestic Service, 19 July; *JPRS-WER*-86-086, 25 August). Also in the summer, the Soviet Ministry of Foreign Affairs Planning Department chief Lev Mendelovich and Foreign Trade Minister Boris Aristov visited Finland mainly to talk about Finnish-Soviet trade problems. In September, Deputy Chair of the USSR Supreme Soviet Presidium Piotr Demichev and Vice Foreign Minister Boris Chaplin led the Soviet delegation to former President Kekkonen's funeral, and Demichev publicly expressed satisfaction with "productive developments" in relations with Finland (*Helsingin Sanomat*, 9 September; *Hufvudstadsbladet*, 9 September).

The climax came in mid-November when Ligachev headed a CPSU delegation to Helsinki as the guest of the Finnish Social Democratic Party and held talks with Sorsa and President Koivisto. To the press, Ligachev said Finnish-Soviet relations were an example of cooperation between countries with different social systems that contributed to improvement of the international climate in northern Europe and the continent as a whole. (Helsinki International Service, 12 November; *FBIS*, 13 November.) He invited President Koivisto to visit Moscow. Ligachev's visit was interpreted as expressing both Soviet acceptance of the strong position the Social Democrats now have in Finnish politics and their recognition that the SKP was no longer a primary partner of the CPSU (*Hufvudstadsbladet*, 15 November; *FBIS*, 20 November).

Finally, Premier Ryzhkov accepted an invitation to make an official visit to Finland on 6–11 January (Helsinki Domestic Service, 17 December: *FBIS*, 18 December). In the eyes of Finnish observers, the fact that none of the prominent visitors sought to influence the upcoming Finnish parliamentary or presidential elections or affect Finnish political debates reflected the stable state of relations (*Uusi Suomi*, 13 October).

Traditional Soviet relations with the Center Party were also maintained. Yuri Deryabin, Soviet Foreign Ministry deputy department head (believed to be the author of articles on Finnish-Soviet relations written under the pseudonym "Yuri Komissarov"), attended a Center Party seminar honoring the 38th anniversary of the Treaty of Friendship, Commerce, and Mutual Assistance (*Sosialdemokkraati*, 7 April). Lev Tolkunov, chair of the Supreme Soviet Council of the Union, attended the Third Congress of European Center, Liberal, and Agrarian Parties on confidence-building measures (termed a mini-CSCE [Commission on Security and Cooperation in Europe]), held in Helsinki on 2–3 November and hosted by Väyrynen (*Helsingin Sanomat*, 28 October). In early December, Väyrynen led a Center Party delegation to Moscow in his capacity as party chair to take part in party-to-party talks (TASS, 1 December; *FBIS*, 4 December).

In mid-October President Koivisto, in a major foreign policy address to the Paasikivi Society, expressed the opinion that, despite significant escalation of military activity by the two superpowers in the Nordic region, particularly at sea, neither wanted to change the basic pattern in the area. After restating support for a Nordic nuclear-weapons-free zone, he launched the idea of creating confidence-building measures (CBMs) in the seas surrounding Scandinavia. The main object was to restrain great-power confrontation, particularly by

limiting the number of forces involved in the holding of naval and landing exercises and by attempting to control great-power competition over detection and interception of strategic nuclear submarines in the region. (*Helsingin Sanomat*, 16 October.) *Kansan Uutiset* (16 October) was effusive in its praise of the Koivisto "initiative," remarking that Koivisto was carrying on the "great legacy" left by Kekkonen, and an SKP Central Committee meeting in late November endorsed the initiative (*Hufvudstadsbladet*, 25 November; *FBIS*, 2 December). Yuri Komissarov wrote an article for *Helsingin Sanomat* (8 November) applauding the CBMs idea. On the other hand, Kajanoja did not agree with Koivisto's analysis of foreign policy; he believed Finland was losing ground as a "bridge-builder" between different political systems because of increasing commitments to cooperation with developed countries headed by NATO (*Helsingin Sanomat*, 19 October).

During his visit, Ligachev also applauded Koivisto's proposals but in effect shifted the focus by trying to launch a new initiative himself to encourage establishment of a Nordic nuclear-weapons-free zone. Although previous Soviet statements had left undefined the steps Moscow would be willing to take to further such a zone, Ligachev listed specific actions. He said Moscow had removed launching platforms for intermediate-range missiles in the Kola Peninsula and most such platforms in the Leningrad and Baltic military districts and had shifted "several" operative tactical missile divisions from the Leningrad and Baltic military districts to other Soviet areas—actions that seemed directed toward certain Norwegian objectives. He also said the USSR would remove Golf-class submarines from the Baltic if a weapons-free zone were achieved—an evident gesture toward Swedish demands that the Baltic be included in such a zone. Finally, Ligachev suggested restricting in the North, Norwegian, Barents, and Baltic seas naval maneuvers that concerned more than 25,000 men—an open response to Koivisto's Paasikivi Society initiative. (Helsinki International Service, 13 November; *FBIS*, 14 November.) The CPSU–Social Democratic Party joint communiqué endorsed Koivisto's CBMs initiative, Finland's proposal for a Nordic nuclear-weapons-free zone, and cooperation for peace, détente, and disarmament (Helsinki Domestic Service, 14 November; *FBIS*, 14 November).

Finnish commentators quickly pointed out that the Soviet actions taken had little military significance (*Helsingin Sanomat*, 14 November) and were intended to maintain the dynamics of Soviet initiatives at the Keflavik summit meeting (*Hufvudstadsbladet*, 14 November). Sorsa welcomed Ligachev's initiative but was cautious in supporting it. The Finnish (and other Nordic) communists of all factions had long held creation of a nuclear-weapons-free zone to be a major foreign policy objective. A two-day conference of the Nordic parties at Stockholm in early September had urged the Nordic governments to act urgently in this area. The Finnish communists seized on the Ligachev initiative, and on 23 and 24 November the SKP Central Committee urged the Nordic governments to start negotiations quickly (*Hufvudstadsbladet*, 25 November; *FBIS*, 2 December).

A growing imbalance in trade became an increasingly sensitive point in Finnish-Soviet relations during the year. The communists, and the Stalinists in particular, tried to exploit the issue, but Soviet leaders reduced the potential for friction by cooperating with the Finnish government in trying to resolve the problem. Because of the drop of oil prices by about one-half, and because of the fact that over two-thirds of Finnish imports from the USSR consisted of oil and oil products (by 1986, trade with the USSR amounted to some 25 percent of all Finnish foreign trade), the balance of trade shifted heavily in Finland's favor. According to Finnish-Soviet trade agreements, trade was to be kept in balance, and fear rose in Finland that Finnish exports might have to be cut as much as 50 percent (*Uusi Suomi*, 20 September). In August, the limit of 300 million rubles "temporary annual surplus" permitted by the agreements was exceeded. This came at a time when Finnish economic activity was slowing and unemployment was starting to rise. Demands that Finland increase its imports of Soviet goods became a constant theme in both Finnish communist camps (*Uusi Suomi*, 22 September; *Kansan Uutiset*, 2 October), and the issue was injected into the budding presidential election campaign when Väyrynen accused Sorsa, titular head of the Finnish trade commission that negotiated trade agreements with the USSR, of mismanaging the problem and worsening the situation.

The Soviets did not follow up a Stalinist attack on Finnish foreign trade minister Ensio Laine in January for having warned Finnish firms in late 1985 that they were making themselves vulnerable to recession by "one-sided" exports to the USSR. Finns were somewhat relieved when Soviet foreign trade minister Aristov, during his visit to Finland in

June, agreed to postpone seeking a balance in trade during 1986, and he and Laine signed a supplemental trade protocol providing for increased Soviet sales of coal, crude oil, natural gas, electricity, chemical raw materials, cars, and jewelry over the next four years. In September, Laine and Aristov signed an agreement in Moscow to neutralize the Finnish trade surplus gradually over several years; Finnish exports were allowed to remain at the planned level in 1986 (although they had decreased 14 percent by October) but were to decrease by one-fifth in 1987 (*Uusi Suomi*, 12 September). Finnish-Soviet meetings on trade stepped up in the late fall until they were almost constant. In November, Vice Foreign Trade Minister Vorontsov attended a CMEA-Finnish meeting intended to foster trade with Eastern Europe (Helsinki Domestic Service, 18 November; *FBIS*, 18 November). Aalto repeatedly warned that cuts in trade would harm political relations (*Nordisk Kontakt*, no. 8; *Helsingin Sanomat*, 22 September), and the shadow SKP Central Committee called for an all-out effort to correct the imbalance (*Hufvudstadsbladet*, 6 October).

Negotiations on the terms of the 1987 annual agreement were nearly completed in December and were to be signed by Premier Ryzhkov when he visited Finland in January. During his stay, Ligachev was optimistic about the outlook for trade and invited a group of Finnish businesspeople to Moscow to consider more joint Finnish-Soviet ventures. While in Moscow in early December, Laine signed a protocol authorizing Finnish participation in projects on the Kola Peninsula, and on 19 December, Sorsa met Premier Ryzhkov at Tallinn to open a new grain port constructed by a Finnish group (Helsinki Domestic Service, 11 December; *FBIS*, 12 December). But despite Soviet promises to make available more Soviet products desired by Finns, Finnish businesspeople still believed Finnish exports to the USSR would drop by 25 percent in 1987 and would especially harm metal, construction, textile, and shoe industries. The stickiest problem for the Finns was financing the Finnish surplus. The two sides agreed in October to open a special account for the surplus, and Finland wanted the Soviets to pay interest on it, relieving the Finnish burden of funding the surplus from European sources. This burden was causing monetary uncertainty, unemployment, and inflation problems. (Frankfurt am Main, *Financial Times*, 22 September; *Helsingin Sanomat*, 27 October.) At the end of the year, a rise in oil prices and an agreement to increase Soviet oil exports to the Finnish state-owned firm Neste Oy lightened the situation (Helsinki Domestic Service, 22 December; *FBIS*, 23 December).

Minority attempts to try to speak for the CPSU and use the threat of Soviet displeasure to affect Finnish events had little effect. Minority leaders' trips to Moscow and to other communist countries—as when Sinisalo received the order of Friendship of Peoples from Demichev in early August (Moscow Domestic Service, 8 August; *FBIS*, 11 August)—received little or no publicity. Sinisalo on returning from a trip to Moscow in September, for instance, said Moscow was disturbed over several Finnish developments and Finnish-Soviet relations in general. He especially mentioned trade issues and the "forms" Finland's westward orientation were taking. But these statements had little effect, and Ligachev's declaration that the CPSU was neutral toward the two communist groups further weakened the Stalinists. (*Hufvudstadsbladet*, 3 September.)

The foreign policy themes of both communist camps concentrated on disarmament and arms reduction, Nordic nuclear-weapons-free zone proposals, and condemnation of NATO and U.S. policies. Soviet disarmament proposals, particularly those put forth at the Reykjavik summit, were praised, while the United States' SDI proposal and deployment of missiles in Europe were severely criticized (*Kansan Uutiset*, 12 September). The U.S. raid on Libya received much attention; the SKP Politburo condemned the action, peace organizations held meetings, and protest rallies were formed (*Kansan Uutiset*, 16, 17 April; Helsinki Domestic Service, 16 April; *FBIS*, 17 April). The SAK organized "peace days" in Jykväskylä on 19 and 20 April to protest the Libyan action and developments in South Africa and Nicaragua (*Kansan Uutiset*, 22 April). The October visit of the USS *Thorn* and of Admiral Crowe, chief of the U.S. Joint Chiefs of Staff, aroused protests (*Tiedonantaja*, 2 October). *Tiedonantaja* (24 October) accused the United States of sending an increasing number of security experts and military leaders to secure Finland's military cooperation against countries bordering Finland. Both *Kansan Uutiset* and *Tiedonantaja* carried a report sourced to TASS (10 July) claiming that the United States had nuclear weapons on nineteen bases in seven West European

countries. Prime Minister Sorsa's initiatives as the vice chair of the Socialist International and head of its Disarmament Committee (SIDAC) were praised and supported. An example was Sorsa's pleading at the Lima SI conference on 5 June for continuation of SALT and the ABM treaty (*Kansan Uutiset*, 3 July).

Despite preoccupation with factional strife, the SKP and SKDL continued contacts with East European communists. In April, a member of the SKP Politburo, Timo Laaksonen, spoke to an East German party meeting in East Germany (*Neues Deutschland*, 24 April); on 18–24 May, an SKDL delegation led by Käkelä visited Hungary as the guest of the Hungarian Socialist Workers' Party Central Committee and conferred mainly on economic topics (Budapest, MTI, 19 May; *JPRS-EER*-86-101, 10 July); Kauppila, acting editor in chief of *Kansan Uutiset*, was to represent the SKP at the Polish United Workers Party congress in Warsaw from 29 June through 3 July (*Kansan Uutiset*, 27 June; *JPRS-WER*-86-086, 25 August); and in late August, an SKP delegation led by General Secretary Vainionpää went to Romania as the guest of the Romanian Communist Party and met with President Nicolae Ceauşescu (Bucharest, Agerpress, 29 August; *FBIS*, 4 September). In October the SKDL parliamentary group visited the GDR and paid a five-day visit to the Estonian Soviet Republic (*Kansan Uutiset*, 28 October). In November, a Cuban Communist Party delegation was the guest of the SKP (*Uusi Suomi*, 4 November; *Kansan Uutiset*, 8 November).

On 5–20 March, Käkelä led an SKDL delegation to China, and an invitation was extended through him for SKP leaders to visit China in early 1987 (Helsinki Domestic Service, 19 March; *FBIS*, 20 March; *Helsingin Sanomat*, 24 March; *JPRS-WER*-86-042, 30 April).

Noticeable was the lack of important contacts between the SKP and other West European communist parties, despite its declared intention of drawing closer to them. Probably concentration on the party division, improving relations with the CPSU, and maintaining links with the East European parties precluded or left little time for efforts in that direction.

F. Herbert Capps
*Bethesda, Maryland*

# France

**Population.** 55,239,000
**Party.** French Communist Party (Partie communists française; PCF)
**Founded.** 1920
**Membership.** 610,000 (*l'Humanité*, 2 November 1984)
**General Secretary.** Georges Marchais
**Politburo.** 22 members; Georges Marchais, Charles Fiterman (propaganda and communication), Jean-Claude Gayssot (party organization), Maxime Gremetz (foreign affairs), André Lajoinie (president of the communist group in the National Assembly), Paul Laurent (liaison with party federations), Gisèle Moreau (women's activities and family politics), Gaston Plissonnier (coordination of the work of the Politburo and Secretariat), Gustave Ansart (president of the Central Commission of Political Control), Mireille Bertrand (urbanism, environment, and consumption associations), Claude Billard (party activity in business and immigration), Pierre Boltin (education of communists), Guy Hermier (intellectual, cultural, educational, and university affairs), Philippe Herzog (economy), Francette Lazard (director of the Marxist Research Institute), René Le Guen (science, research, and technology), Roland Leroy (director of *l'Humanité*), René Piquet (president of the French communist group in the European Parliament), Claude Poperen (health and social security, retirement), Madelaine Vincent (local communities, elections), Henri Krasucki (secretary of the General Confederation of Labor), Louis Viannet (Mail Workers' Federation)
**Secretariat.** 7 members: Maxime Gremetz, Jean-Claude Gayssot, André Lajoinie, Paul Laurent, Gisèle Moreau, Gaston Plissonnier, Charles Fiterman
**Central Committee.** 145 members
**Status.** Legal
**Last Congress.** Twenty-fifth, 6–10 February 1985; next congress planned for 1990
**Last Election.** 1986, 9.8 percent, 35 of 577 seats
**Auxiliary Organizations.** General Confederation of Labor (CGT); World Peace Council; Movement of Communist Youth of France (MCJF); Committee for the Defense of Freedom in France and the World; Association of Communist and Republican Representatives
**Publications.** *L'Humanité* (Paris: Roland Leroy, director; daily national organ), *L'Echo du centre* (Limoges, daily), *Liberté* (Lille, daily), *La Marseillais* (Marseille, daily), *L'Humanité-Dimanche* (Paris, wekly), *Révolution* (Guy Hermier, director; weekly publication of the Central Committee), *La Terre* (weekly), *Cahiers du communisme* (monthly theoretical journal), *Europe* (literary journal), *Economie et politique* (economic journal), 5 journals published by the Marxist Research Institute; 4 monthly magazines; other periodicals on sports, children's themes, and the like, and books on political, economic, and social topics published by Editions sociales, the PCF publishing house in Paris.

Leaders of France's beleaguered Communist Party spent virtually all of 1986 grappling with the domestic and international ramifications of the PCF's continued decline. Dissident leaders—increasingly isolated from positions of authority in the party—continued to press embarrassing demands for internal reform, begging important questions about the extent to which factionalism has become institutionalized in the party. Unprecedented electoral losses in important legislative, regional, and by-elections prompted reformist demands for an extraordinary party congress, while changes to France's electoral system—enacted by the new conservative government—threatened to erode even further the PCF's electoral support. General Secretary Georges Marchais's decision not to stand as the PCF's candidate in the presidential elections (set for 1988) was widely interpreted as a measure of compromise both with dissidents and with others who blame Marchais for much of the party's marginalization. The announcement also raised questions about Marchais's continued leadership of the party and about the succession. The party's international initiatives remained both lackluster and unremarkable in their volume, and well-publicized frictions with Italian communists poured salt in wounds opened by the party's election defeats. By year's end, the leadership had characteristically hunkered down in an analysis that pictured the party as surrounded on all sides by class enemies—including Socialists—and beset internally by the machination of a handfull of misguided comrades.

**Leadership and Internal Affairs.** Party leaders faced the new year under grim predictions by pollsters and pundits that the pending vote in legislative elections set for March would see communist strength plummet below the historic low of 11.28 percent set in previous balloting for the European Parliament in June 1984. Clearly feeling the sting of such predictions, Marchais defined the challenge facing the party's election machine in a December speech in Toulon, admonishing each PCF member "to rally to the communist vote" (*Le Monde*, 3 December 1985). Early in the year, in keeping with the Twenty-fifth Congress line that the PCF's doldrums were partly due to ineffective education of the cadres on the party's strategy, *l'Humanité* proclaimed an educational campaign designed to fill gaps in "understanding" revealed at the Twenty-fifth Congress—an unambiguous reference to the unprecedented dissent that continued to flourish in the party, despite the leadership's (especially *l'Humanité* director Leroy's) efforts to isolate and punish outspoken critics (*WMR*, January).

Many of those who established themselves as leading "*renovateurs*" after the party's withdrawal from the Unity of the Left strategy (which had led it into junior partnership in Socialist governments be-

tween 1981 and 1984) continued to speak out. Former PCF spokesman Pierre Juquin maintained his edge as the party's most vocal dissident. The publication of Juquin's book *Self-Criticism*—in which he argued at length that the party's decline was due to the leadership's refusal to make the appropriate analysis of, and adjust strategy to, fundamental changes in French society that, among other things, had altered the character of the working class—triggered a new offensive against reformers in both the Central Committee and in some important regional federations. In Juquin's own Clermont-Ferrand organization, party members were publicly accused of siding with the "reformers," and local hard-liners ensured that Juquin's return to his hometown to launch his book was accomplished "without fanfare" (*Le Monde*, 28 February). Dissident leaders were already well on the way to isolation, according to *Le Monde*, having earned places on a "black list" being assembled by Leroy and other "conservatives." In the stormy, dissent-ridden federation of Seine-Saint-Denis, the once powerful Saint-Denis mayor, Marcelin Berthelot, found himself excluded from ceremonies in which President François Mitterrand dedicated a new school. Former communist minister Jack Ralite, was demoted from his place on the candidate list for the legislative elections and named to head the PCF list for the significantly less important regional elections, reportedly because he refused to take part in the offensive that sidelined Berthelot and ejected another prominent Paris-area dissident and former Seine-Saint-Denis first secretary François Asensi from the Central Committee. (Party leaders had not found it possible by that time to refuse Asensi eligibility for the National Assembly.) (*Le Monde*, 3 December 1985.) In Montpellier, majority conservatives in the Hérault federation failed to stop some elected officials and federation leaders who sympathize with reformers from inviting Juquin to speak in late November on the theme of peace and disarmament—still his primary function in the party. The Hérault federation secretariat boycotted the demonstration, however, and reportedly even intimated to the party bookstore manager in Montpellier that he should prohibit sales of *Self-Criticism* (*Le Monde*, 3 December 1985).

Although notable numbers of Hérault party officials bucked the secretariat and participated in demonstrations, Juquin clearly chafed under mounting indications that the leadership intended to isolate him in the forthcoming campaign for the National

Assembly. When he asked in one speech, "Am I a Central Committee member or not?" Juquin edged perilously close to breaking his self-imposed election truce with the leadership by voicing his disappointment at being offered only two official appearances during the campaign (*Le Monde*, 28 February). Although not attacking the leadership's stonewalling of reformist demands directly, Juquin used his podiums to warn of the consequences of the party's impending catastrophe at the polls. If the communist showing were worse than in June 1984, he predicted, "it would be a new and serious blow to its leadership." More important, perhaps, if the PCF merely equaled its previous disappointing performance, it would show that the party's decline was "not merely the result of cyclical causes." Previously, Juquin had set 15 percent as the mark below which the party would face yet another round of wide-ranging internal debate. (*Le Monde*, 28 February.)

It became clear as the campaign progressed that the leadership's strategy for staving off another humiliation and holding its militants was to attack Socialists as implicitly rightist and to warn that it was the failure of Socialist policies that was about to bring the right back to power. The resounding defeat that party lists suffered on March 16—in both the national legislative and simultaneous elections for regional councils—filled dissidents with new wind and gave them a platform from which to assail the leadership anew with demands for internal reform. Alain Amicabile, first secretary of the strife-torn Meurthe-et-Moselle federation (one of the key regional organizations that the leadership had failed to subdue completely before the Twenty-fifth Congress), resigned on March 19, vowing to "continue the struggle started by [his] federation to reform the PCF." Amicabile, one of the youngest members of the Central Committee, had been ousted from his national party post during the congress because he had promoted antileadership ferment in his federation; his resignation in the wake of the election fiasco came as part of a renewal of the same groundswell, which this time took the form of a campaign of petitions that aimed to "save the PCF."

Dissidents now called on Marchais to convene an extraordinary congress as quickly as possible to rechart a course that would take account of the party's third serious election failure. One dissident observed that the PCF was "now on the fringes and [running] the risk of being liquidated as a real political force in the next few years." As pundits across

the political spectrum speculated increasingly that a continuation of the same trend would see the party fall below 5 percent in the 1988 presidential contest, one local communist official demanded "a radical rethink" as the only way to save the PCF from being "doomed." Notably, some of the most strident dissidents to call for a congress were officials—like Michel Bertelle (Meurthe-et-Moselle) and Antoine Martinez (Hérault)—who had carried off substantial election victories in their own bailiwicks. The ferment among local representatives was reportedly excited in part by regulations from Paris that made it impossible for some to capitalize on electoral gains, especially a rule that forbade communists elected to regional councils to accept the vice-chairmanship of the executives when they were entitled to them—a command that one dissident representative in Limousin declared a "violation of universal suffrage and a distortion of party policy." (*Le Monde*, 21 March.)

Appeals for an extraordinary congress were especially rife in the Moselle, Puy-de-Dôme, and Paris regional organizations. One document, signed by several of the party's shrinking number of nationally reputed intellectuals, suggested that fundamental causes of the PCF's decline could be found in the "rigid functioning . . . inappropriate analyses and inconsistent actions of the party [leadership] itself" (*Le Monde*, 21 March). Finally—two days after the election disaster—Juquin appealed on national television for activists to "renovate" the party (Paris AFP, 21 March).

Newly invigorated dissidents called for resignations. Daniel Karlin, communist member of France's High Authority for Broadcasting, and psychiatrist Tony Lainé announced early in the ferment against the election results that "a discredited and irresponsible leadership group cannot be allowed to do what it wishes." Calls for resignations were apparently partly a reaction to self-serving analyses of the election results that emerged from a hastily convened, morning-after meeting of the Central Committee. Less than a week after the balloting, a group of about 100 communist political figures and intellectuals called publicly for the resignations of several PCF leaders, including that of General Secretary Marchais (AFP, 21 March).

By March 26, a two-day meeting of the Central Committee had rejected dissident demands for a special congress and instead—in an undisguised effort to redirect attention of the militants—issued a resolution that lambasted the Socialists for "doing everything possible to break" the PCF and for governing in such as way as to "give in to the economic crisis, unemployment, and austerity, and justify the existing capitalist order"—all familiar themes from the election campaign and earlier (AFP, 26 March). Politburo member Laurent reported the leadership's analysis, predicting that the Socialists would prove ineffective in opposition, would fail to attack the true causes of the economic crisis, and would thereby open opportunities for the PCF to "construct a new majority" (*l'Humanité*, 26 March). Most important, for the first time the Central Committee attacked Juquin by name, noting that it "regrets and disapproves of [his] behavior during this [election] campaign, which violates the party's democratic rules . . . and the efforts to mobilize people to vote Communist." Five well-known renovateurs abstained, but Juquin was the only member of the Central Committee to vote against the Laurent report. (Paris AFP, 26 March; *Le Monde*, 27 March.)

The Laurent report and subsequent resolution failed, however, to stem the tide of dissent that reemerged in the wake of the party's election defeat. Petitions and demands for a 26th congress multiplied, as did open criticism of the leadership's attempt to mobilize its strength through democratic centralism in order to silence protest. Some Central Committee members charged openly that Stalinism had returned to plague the PCF, only this time as "farce." Reformers—notably former ministers Ralite and Anicet Le Pors—who did not vote against the resolution (reportedly because they did not want to associate themselves with Juquin's methods) nonetheless made it known that they had criticized the leadership in Central Committee debate. (*Le Monde*, 27 March.) In early April *Le Monde* carried a full-page advertisement, placed by PCF dissidents, entitled "PCF: For the 26th Congress" and featuring six columns of signatures, including those of well-known reformers, many party journalists and intellectuals, and many of the party's growing number of disgruntled local officials (*Le Monde*, 2 April). High-profile defectors included Michel Lhomede—sole communist departmental councillor for the Loire-et-Cher—who announced his "discharge" from the party, 75 elected communist officials from the department of the Aisne who demanded an extraordinary congress (*Le Monde*, 27 March 86), and two leading editors of the PCF publications empire. (AFP, 2 April.) *L'Humanité*'s report of the Central Committee meeting lambasted

Juquin for sowing discord in communist ranks and emphasized that even the remarks of other reformers, notably those of former minister Marcel Rigout, were essentially critical of Juquin (*l'Humanité*, 27 March). National Assembly group leader Lajoinie joined the reviving chorus of abuse directed at Juquin, dismissing the 1,000 signatures on the congress petition as insignificant and denouncing Juquin as "ultimately aiming to preserve capitalism" (*l'Humanité*, 7 April).

Reformist momentum stimulated by the PCF's election fiasco appeared to fizzle in mid-April, however, when a group of some 300 ex-communists and renovateurs met and failed to map out strategy for a joint Marxist program in opposition to the current PCF line. The gathering was organized by independent communist National Assembly deputy Henri Fiszbin, who was booed loudly for having just won election as a Socialist candidate (AFP, 17 April). The Politburo tried to capitalize on the moment by issuing a communiqué on "Moving Ahead," which promised a number of initiatives in the remainder of the year on such controversial topics as the role of Marxism in society (the theme of a *l'Humanité* week of five special editions between 20 and 25 May), the party's relations with intellectuals, problems of local (especially regional) administration, and the party's objectives in the youth sphere (*l'Humanité*, 23 April), and an unattributed report, "Uniting to Overcome Problems," (ibid., 25 April). Efforts to short-circuit dissent peaked in early May, when Marchais unexpectedly announced that he would not lead the party in the next presidential contest. The decision, which Marchais characterized as "personal" and long-standing, sparked immediate speculation that he might also withdraw as party leader and that the leadership had forced Marchais to stand aside to project a more moderate image to reclaim wayward communist voters (*WSJ*, 13 May; *NYT*, 14 May). It also aroused some immediate speculation about who among the leading candidates would eventually succeed Marchais. The general secretary said that a decision would soon be made as to who would be the party's candidate in 1988 and reportedly made no secret of his preference for Gayssot, the Central Committee secretary responsible for organization. Lajoinie and former transportation minister Charles Fiterman were also mentioned early on as favorites to win the PCF candidacy and even to succeed Marchais as general secretary. No successor had been named by the end of the year, but as of late November, Lajoinie was reportedly acting very much the candidate. (Paris, AFP, 12 May; *WSJ*, 12 May; *Libération*, 26 November.)

Despite the leadership's efforts to divert attention from dissident demands through various initiatives and through its postelection line of "beating back the right-wing offensive," the reformist petition for a special congress continued to accumulate an embarrassingly large number of signatures. Lainé—who reportedly had become known as the dissidents' "mailbox"—claimed on May Day to have more than 5,000 letters of support; by mid-June *Le Monde* carried a new petition with the signatures of 3,000 PCF notables. (Paris Domestic Service, 16 June; *NYT*, 6 May.)

Throughout the summer and fall, Marchais and party leaders were confronted with questions about the persistence and scale of dissent in the formerly monolithic party, about Juquin's dissent, and about the disruption of such important federations as that of the Meurthe-et-Moselle (see, for example, Paris Domestic Service, 2 June, 3 July; TF1 TV, 13 September). By the annual "Fête de *l'Humanité*" in September, party leaders and publications were suggesting that renovateurs, and especially Juquin, had broken faith with the PCF; and at least one important federation (Hérault) went so far as to accuse Juquin of "factionalism"—almost certainly, according to knowledgeable observers, with the encouragement of the national leadership (*Le Monde*, 27 March). Yet, by the end of the year, few important dissidents had broken with the party.

**Domestic Affairs.** The legislative elections that had come to preoccupy the party even before the end of 1985 and that became the focal point of the PCF's entire year were another stunning defeat. After humiliating performances in biennial cantonal elections only one year earlier and in elections for the European Parliament the June before that, arguments of PCF leaders that the contests were not significant enough to mobilize the militants were beginning to wear thin. Nonetheless, Politburo stalwarts continued the chorus of predictions that a "real vote," such as the all-important legislatives, would bring the rank and file to the polls in numbers that would reverse dramatically the party's electoral slide.

More important, Marchais and other PCF leaders launched late in 1985, a campaign that focused almost exclusively on anti-Socialist themes, even connecting the widely expected return of the conservative coalition of neo-Gaullists and centrists to the failure of the Socialist Party (PS) to live up to the leftist program of 1980. In rebuttal to Socialist claims that the PCF's policy of attacking the PS amounted to objective aid to the right's reconquest of power, Marchais offered a formulation that defined the PCF's purpose as preventing "the Right from returning to power and entering into cooperation with the PS" (*l'Humanité*, 18 November 1985). Socialist slogans that urged communists to "vote usefully" and to cast a "sure vote for the left" by opting for PS lists riveted the PCF campaign on the developing struggle for domination of the left and on the already chronic difficulty of preventing Mitterrand from looting PCF ranks of disillusioned militants (*Le Monde*, 14 January). Marchais and the party press emphasized their twelve-point program (of which 8 million copies were distributed) that largely railed against deviations from leftist positions during the Socialists' five years in office. The PCF campaign fixed especially on claims that "3 million people [were] unemployed" because of PS lethargy, on diminished purchasing power of workers, and on long-standing PCF demands for job creation, especially in the public sector. Variously, Marchais and such communist firebrands as Moreau flailed Socialists for tampering with regulations governing the workplace and for reducing real incomes of workers by "7.8 percent." (*l'Humanité*, 13 January, 8 February; *Pravda*, 19 January.) Party spokesmen pounded away on the theme of "attacking the crisis" immediately by creating 1 million jobs, especially in the public sector where Marchais spoke of the need for thousands of new teachers and 400 lycées (*l'Humanité*, 22 February; *Le Monde*, 28 February). Moreover, neither Marchais nor Moreau nor other PCF candidates, would rule out eventually refashioning an alliance of the left (a prospect that PS secretary Lionel Jospin held out from time to time throughout 1986), but all made it clear that leftist unity would be possible only on the PCF's terms and that this would require the Socialists to abandon most of their policies in favor of what communist leaders characterized a return to leftist principles and the PCF catchphrase "resistance to the crisis" (Paris, AFP, 22 January; Paris Domestic Service, 6 March; Moscow, TASS, 31 January).

As the campaign came under full steam, opinion and preference polls indicated that the PCF would garner between 11 and 12.5 percent of the vote (Paris, AFP, 22 January; Paris Domestic Service, 30 January). Under intense questioning from journalists on numerous television and radio forum programs, Marchais predicted wildly that communists would elect deputies in every department—a feat that would have given the PCF over 100 seats in the National Assembly, when even the most optimistic simulations done at the time of the transition to proportional representation (April 1985) gave the communists only about 50 seats (*Le Point*, 2 September, 1985, 15 October 1985; *Economist*, 3 November 1984). Nonetheless, in midcampaign, communist militants professed in a reliable poll that Marchais continued to "symbolize best the Communist Party," and despite the virulence of PCF attacks on Socialists and the ritual spurning of suggestions from PS leaders that the unity of the left need not be dead, 46 percent of PCF activists also believed that "there would be a new alliance between the Socialist and Communist Parties" (*Le Point*, 24 February). Yet, despite this evidence of communist sentiment, PCF bludgeoning of the PS continued unabated throughout the campaign, opening Marchais to embarrassing questions about who the PCF's real adversary in the election was (Paris Television Service, "Hour of Truth," 22 January, and "Campaign Parties," 6 February; *l'Humanité*, 8, 11 February). Although criticisms of the Socialists clearly flew in the face of militants who continued to wax nostalgic about the unity of the left, Marchais did little to restrain the generally anti-Socialist thrust of the PCF campaign, except to punctuate diatribes against Mitterrand with aphorisms about the right being the real enemy and to note that, at the local level, Socialist and communist officials had sometimes continued to cooperate on the basis of the old unity (Paris Domestic Service, 6 March).

In the 16 March elections for all 577 seats in the newly enlarged National Assembly, communist lists polled 9.8 percent of the vote (2.7 million votes) and elected 35 deputies (Paris, AFP, 18 March). Most commentaries noted that this was the worst PCF performance in sixty years, was the first time in memory that the party had fallen below the symbolically significant 10 percent mark, and—most humiliating of all, perhaps—was virtually the same as the 9.7 percent garnered by the extreme-right National Front, which also collected 35 seats (*Le Monde*, 17 March; *LAT*, 17 March; *NYT*, 17 March; Kevin Devlin, "Election Disaster Seals Decline of the PCF," RFE, *RAD Background Report*, no. 58, 21 April; *WMR*, May; *IP*, 7 April). About the only saving feature of the PCF's achievement was that its 35 seats were sufficient to preserve the

party's official status as a parliamentary group—a position that brings with it access to television time and other perquisites. Party leaders glossed over the proportions of the defeat by noting that the party received several hundred thousand more popular votes in both the legislative and regional contests than it had in the two previous similar elections (*IP*, 7 April). Against this, however, it was clear to all that the stunning defeat represented an erosion of half the PCF's electoral strength in just five years and that the PS, which fared better than expected by a late surge of support that gave it 30 percent of the vote, was still the largest party in France (*Le Monde*, 17 March; RFE, *RAD Background Report*, no. 58, 21 April).

Some of the most dramatic declines in communist strength occurred in historic PCF strongholds, such as the Paris "Red Belt" Seine-Saint-Denis department. There, the vote plummeted from 36.3 percent in 1981 legislatives to 18.7 percent in 1986. In the same region, the National Front list polled 14.5 percent. (*IP*, 7 April.) As late as 1978, the PCF had won all nine of the National Assembly seats from the area; this time out communists won only 3 of 13, while Socialists claimed four and conservatives won six (Reuters, 17 March). In Paris itself, where the PCF had been the dominant leftist party as late as 1978, communists failed to elect a single deputy—a spectacular defeat for Moreau, the feminist darling of the Central Committee, sole woman on the Politburo, and head of the PCF's Paris list (*Le Monde*, 17 March; Reuters, 17 March). Communist candidates fared little better in the simultaneous elections for all newly reconstituted seats on France's 22 metropolitan regional councils: PCF lists polled 10.2 percent of the votes, compared with 29.9 percent for the PS (*Le Monde*, 18 March).

The leadership's response to its election failure was to blame the Socialists even more vehemently for the conservative victory, but the message was blurred by contradictions. At times, Marchais lashed out at the PS "blackmail" of communist voters—an admission that Socialists had been able to loot the PCF of straying militants who wanted their votes to count. (Paris Domestic Service, 16 March; *l'Humanité*, 17 March.) Commenting on the formation of the "cohabitation" government between Socialist president Mitterrand—whose term runs until 1988—and neo-Gaullist leader Jacques Chirac, *l'Humanité* lamented that "those men and women who voted Socialist thinking that they were making their votes count against the right have every right to be angry" (*l'Humanité*, 21 March). At other times, however, Marchais and party bosses denied that the crossover vote was a factor in the PCF's defeat, arguing that the party had fallen victim to abstentions rather than defections—dropouts who were disillusioned with leftist government as practiced by the Socialists (*IP*, 7 April).

The introduction of measures promised by the victorious conservative coalition in the election platform—notably a plan for privatization of 65 state-owned firms—evoked sharp criticism from PCF spokesmen, who characterized such moves as calculated to "give employers new opportunities for profit and the amassing of wealth" (Politburo statement issued 8 April; *l'Humanité*, 9 April). Party leaders were especially bitter about conservative initiatives to allow employers greater flexibility in hiring and firing without government interference, about wage freezes in the public sector (which struck at leftist-controlled unions), and the government's youth employment scheme, which Leroy labeled a smoke screen designed to disguise the actual loss of jobs due to conservative policies (*l'Humanité*, 17 March; 9, 15 April). Communist leaders also lambasted Chirac's proposals to liberalize rules governing ownership of print media and to sell off the flagship network of France's state-owned television system; the Central Committee's resolution of 12–13 May saw such measures as intended "to consolidate the dual rule of money and power in the areas of information" and media (ibid., 15 May). In tandem with point-by-point rejection of the right's panoply of reforms, the PCF continued to drive home the argument that "cohabitation" was a partnership between the triumphant right and Socialists who had sold out the interests of the left (ibid., 14 May). Such criticisms were both provoked and answered by well-publicized PS moves—often initiatives of Socialist Party secretary Jospin—to forge an alliance with dissident communists (*Le Monde*, 10 May).

The pitch of PCF opposition to the conservative program peaked in May, when Chirac introduced the right's long-promised plan to return France to a majority voting system for legislative elections. The reform, which featured a return to single-member districts, two-round voting, and redistricting (with the implicit threat of gerrymandering) prompted, successively, a joint walkout from the National Assembly by Socialists and communists, a censure motion that the government easily defeated, a series of presidential delays during which France's Constitutional Council issued grim strictures about excessive gerrymandering; in spite of all this the reform was finally passed into law (*NYT*, 21 May; Paris Domestic Service, 23 May). Opponents of the law argued that Chirac was merely attempting to rig forthcoming elections to favor the right (Marchais on Paris Domestic Service, 23 May). In fact, simulations based on the most recent voting indicated that the strength of the Gaullist-centrist coalition partners would increase significantly, that Socialist seats would be reduced somewhat, and that both the PCF and the National Front would be dispatched to legislative oblivion, retaining only a few seats in the National Assembly (Paris, AFP, 2 October).

Senate elections and National Assembly by-elections held in September demonstrated that PCF chest beating about the drift of France to the right and exuberant rhetoric about the need to unite behind communists to "break the back of the crisis" had fallen largely on deaf ears. In the Senate contests, where 120 of 319 seats were at stake, both communists and Socialists lost ground, but the PS retained 64 of 69 seats, while the PCF emerged with only 15 of 24 seats previously held. In by-elections for the National Assembly in Toulouse (Haute-Garonne) communists again failed, as they had the previous March, to elect a single deputy; but this time the PCF share of the vote fell to 6.3 percent from 8 percent in the previous outing, which was down from 13 percent in 1981, and down from 19 percent in March 1978 (UPI, 28 September; *L'Evénement du Jeudi*, 2–8 October). In a bitterly critical testimony published on the heels of the latest election losses and in response to the entire year of PCF reverses at the polls, Central Committee dissident Poperen lamented that "the presidential [elections] will take place in two years. On the politburo they have spoken of 5 or 6 percent and perhaps less" ("Le réquisitoire secret d'un dirigeant contre la direction du PC," ibid.).

In regard to other important domestic issues, the PCF condemned the unprecedented wave of terrorist violence that struck Paris in September in relation to demands for the release of jailed Lebanese terrorist leader Georges Abdallah (Paris Television Service, 8 October; Moscow, TASS, 15 September). Spokesmen for the PCF also supported the wave of violent student protests in early December against Chirac's plan to tighten access to the universities. Militants and members of the Communist Youth Movement (MJC) reportedly participated in (but did not lead) the demonstrations that eventually forced Chirac to withdraw the legislation. (*Economist*, 13 December.)

**Foreign Affairs and Security Issues.** Communist Party leaders continued through the year to support Soviet foreign policy initiatives, despite continued pressure from dissidents who demanded re-examination of the party's historic ties with Moscow and even called for distancing the PCF from the CPSU. Marchais was pressed (especially in the election campaign) on his views of the Soviet Union, on the PCF's relations with it, and on his opinions of General Secretary Mikhail Gorbachev's various initiatives. Party bosses uniformly continued to praise the advent of the Gorbachev era as a great departure in Soviet history, even looking forward to substantial improvements in the USSR's human rights record, the growth of political democracy, and developments in the Soviet economy that would satisfy the social needs of the Russian people. Marchais also backed Gorbachev's various arms control proposals on several occasions in the campaign, arguing that Gorbachev's daring had put the USSR "on a completely new path." Applauding the Soviet leader's vision of a nuclear-weapons-free world by the year 2000, he also sailed perilously close to reversing PCF policy from the unity era on the inclusion of French and British missiles in the current arms control negotiations when he told one journalist "just between us, I would like the French Government to participate actively in the negotiations that would enable progress on this road" (Paris Television Service, 22 January; Paris, AFP, 22 January).

Party spokesmen also continued to attack U.S. foreign and security policy as aggressive and hegemonic, and PCF leaders criticized both Chirac and Mitterrand regularly for alleged subservience to Washington. In April, shortly after the attack on Libya, a Politburo statement on U.S. foreign policy convicted the United States of aggression against the Arab world and argued that President Reagan was using terrorism as a pretext for imposing U.S. dominance over the Mediterranean (*l'Humanité*, 26 April). At the May summit in Tokyo, the exceptional degree of agreement of the seven industrialized countries touched off a barrage of PCF criticisms, directed at both Mitterrand and Chirac and consisting mostly of accusations that both surrendered French sovereignty and independence to Washington's efforts to bring "coordination of pol-

icy among all the most industrialized nations under US control" (Central Committee resolution, *l'Humanité*, 14, 15 May; 18 June). In the wake of the October Reykjavik summit, PCF bosses again parroted the Moscow line in blaming U.S. insistence on retaining the Strategic Defense Initiative for the "failure" (*l'Humanité*, 14 October).

"Tyrants Out" served as the slogan for a PCF drive to embarrass the Mitterrand/Fabius government for having given temporary "asylum" to ousted Haitian dictator Jean-Claude Duvalier, and for its own plans (eventually banned by the Chirac government) to stage street protests against the official visit of South Korean President Chun Doo Hwan in April (*Le Quotidien de Paris*, 14 April; Paris, AFP, 14 April; Moscow, TASS, 18 February). Party leaders also called on the Chirac government to refuse permission to Angolan rebel leader Jonas Savimbi to visit France on his way to address the European Parliament in Strasbourg (Paris, AFP, 15 October).

**International Activities.** Overt international activity on the part of the PCF appeared to slacken in 1986, although party delegations traveled to Moscow on several occasions, most notably to confer with CPSU counterparts on the Chernobyl disaster and to attend the Twenty-seventh Congress in March (*Pravda*, 1 March, 23 May). Meanwhile, Soviet delegations, including a parliamentary delegation headed by Lev Lolkunov, also visited France (Moscow, TASS, 24 January). Marchais met with numerous leaders of world communist parties; notable among them were Todor Zhivkov of Bulgaria and Hu Yaobang of the Peoples' Republic of China (*l'Humanité*, 3 January, 20 June, 19 August; Sofia, BTA, 17 August). Delegations from the PCF also visited several Eastern bloc countries, including well-publicized talks in Romania, East Germany, and Czechoslovakia (Bucharest Agerpress, 21 September; East Berlin, Allgemeiner Deutscher Nachrichtendienst International Service, 19 April; East Berlin *Neues Deutschland*, 17, 22, 25 September; Prague Domestic Service, 3 October).

The tone of PCF relations with other communist parties was marred by ugly exchanges with officials of the Italian Communist Party over differing analyses of the PCF election campaign and results of the French elections. On numerous occasions, PCI leaders insisted that the catastrophe was traceable to the PCF's "extremist positions and forms of sectarianism" and especially to the French party's miscalculation in making hostility to the Socialists the touchstone of its claim to legislative offices. French communists rejected such criticisms, both on their substance and as inadmissible meddling in the internal affairs of the French party. Officials of the PCI defended their assertions by pointing to both the policies and abysmal electoral record of the PCF over the past decade and by arguing that the Italian party was free to take an interest in something as important as the circumstances of the French left and the lessons that Italian communists could draw from the PCF's experiences. By year's end, the volleys from both camps had subsided, but the level of recrimination had clearly reached unprecedented proportions. (*l'Humanité*, 22 March, 1 October; RFE, *RAD Background Report*, no. 48, 8 April, and 145, 10 October.)

Edward A. Allen
*Washington, D.C.*

# Germany: Federal Republic of Germany

**Population.** 60,190,000, excl. West Berlin (1986)
**Party.** German Communist Party (Deutsche Kommunistische Partei; DKP)
**Founded.** 1968
**Membership.** 50,802 (claimed, 1986); 40,000 (Federal Security Service [Bundesverfassungsschutz; BVS])
**Chairman.** Herbert Mies
**Presidium.** 19 members: Herbert Mies, Ellen Weber (deputy chair), Jupp Angenfort, Kurt Bachmann, Irmgard Bobrzik, Martha Buschmann, Werner Cieslak, Heinz Czymek, Gerd Deumlich, Kurt Fritsch, Hermann Gautier, Wolfgang Gehrcke, Willi Gerns, Dieter Keller, Georg Polikeit, Rolf Priemer, Brigit Radow, Karl-Heinz Schröder, Werner Sturmann
**Secretariat.** 14 members: Herbert Mies, Ellen Weber, Vera Aschenbach, Werner Cieslak, Gerd Deumlich, Kurt Fritsch, Willi Gerns, Marianne Konze, Jofel Mayer, Fritz Noll, Rolf Priemer, Karl-Heinz Schröder, Wilhelm Spengler, Werner Sturmann
**Executive.** 94 members
**Status.** Legal
**Last Congress.** Eighth, 2–4 May 1986, in Hamburg
**Last Election.** 1983, 0.2 percent, no representation
**Auxiliary Organizations.** Socialist German Workers' Youth (Sozialistische Deutsche Arbeiter Jugend; SDAJ), ca. 15,000 members, Brigit Radow, chair; Marxist Student Union–Spartakus (Marxistischer Studentenbund–Spartakus; MSB-Spartakus), ca. 6,000 members (MSB-Spartakus claims 6,500), Thomas Harms, chair; Young Pioneers (Junge Pioniere; JP), ca. 4,000 members, Gerhard Hertel, chair
**Publications.** *Unsere Zeit* (Our time), Düsseldorf, DKP organ (editor: Georg Polikeit), daily circulation ca. 25,000, weekend edition ca. 48,000, Monday edition discontinued; *elan—Das Jugendmagazin*, SDAJ monthly organ, circulation ca. 25,000; *rote blätter* (Red pages), MSB-Spartakus monthly organ, circulation ca. 15,000; *pionier* (Pioneer), JP monthly organ

The Moscow-loyal DKP is the successor organization of the outlawed Communist Party of Germany (Kommunistische Partei Deutschlands; KPD), which was founded on 31 December 1918. In August 1956, when the Federal Constitutional Court outlawed the KPD for pursuing unconstitutional objectives, it went underground. It remained underground until September 1968, when the DKP was founded as result of a concession made by Chancellor Willy Brandt to Leonid Brezhnev. In 1971, the BVS declared that the DKP, which openly emphasizes that it is a party of the international communist movement and the only legitimate heir to the KPD, was the successor of the outlawed KPD. Thus a decree by the federal minister of interior could extend the outlawing of the KPD to the DKP, a move that for apparently political reasons, has not been taken so far. (For a more detailed history of the development of the DKP, see *YICA, 1986.*)

According to the annual report of the BVS, there were 2 orthodox communist organizations (membership 44,500) at the end of 1985, with 13 affiliated organizations (28,000) and 51 organizations influenced by communists (66,500). In addition there were 19 basic organizations of the dogmatic New Left (3,300) with 11 affiliated organizations (700) and 13 organizations in which these groups exerted some influence (2,000), as well as 58 groups of Social Revolutionaries (2,800). The statistics concerning the dogmatic New Left and the Social Revolutionaries cover only those groups and organizations that have organizational structures and were active over an extended period of time. The numerous loose groupings of the radical extreme left, with a membership of about 6,000, were not included. After deducting for membership in more than one organization and for children's groups, the BVS concluded that membership in these left-extremist organizations totaled 61,300 and membership in organizations influenced by these groups 51,500 (Bundesministerium des Innern, *Bundesverfassungsschutzbericht, 1985 [BVS-Bericht]*, Bonn, August).

The BVS estimated that the membership in left-extremist organizations of foreigners (mostly "guest workers") at the end of 1985 was 81,550 (orthodox communist groups: 59,450; organizations of the New Left: 22,100) (ibid.).

**Leadership and Organization.** The eighth Congress of the DKP (2–4 May) was held in Hamburg (Congress-Centrum) under the slogan "For a new policy: A world without nuclear weapons and work for all." The congress, located in Hamburg to honor the 100th anniversary of the birthday of former KPD chair Ernest Thälmann who was born in that city, was attended by 718 delegates and 165 guest delegates from affiliated and communist-influenced organizations and by representatives of 42 fraternal communist and workers' parties and 7 "anti-imperialist liberation movements." (On 3 and 4 May, *Neues Deutschland [ND]* reported on the attendance of 54 foreign delegations at the DKP congress.) The Soviet delegation was led by Boris N. Yeltsin, candidate member of the Communist Party of the Soviet Union Central Committee Politburo and first secretary of Moscow's City Committee (*Pravda*, 9 May; *FBIS*, 13 May), and Hermann Axen, member of the Politburo and Secretariat of the Central Committee of the Socialist Unity Party of Germany (SED) led the East German delegation (*Innere Sicherheit [IS]*, 4 July). The congress was also attended by members of thirteen embassies from socialist countries; among them were Yuri Kvizinski, Soviet ambassador to the Federal Republic of Germany (FRG); Ewald Moldt, East Germany's permanent representative in Bonn; and the first representative from the Embassy of the People's Republic of China to attend a DKP congress (*Deutscher Informationsdienst* [DID], May).

The congress confirmed Herbert Mies as DKP chair, elected Ellen Weber to replace Hermann Gautier as vice-chair, and elected the 94-member Executive, which in turn elected the 19-member Presidium and the 14-member Secretariat. Just over 93 percent of the 879 voting and guest delegates. were active members of trade unions (642 of them held offices in trade unions and in workers' representations in factories), and almost 43 percent of them were women (ibid.) The report of the DKP Executive claimed 10,282 new party members since the last party congress in 1984 for a total membership of 57,802 (*DID*, first June edition). (The German government estimates DKP membership at about 40,000 [*BVS-Bericht*, p. 36].)

Party chair Herbert Mies delivered the Executive report, which restated the party's political concepts, such as opposition to "U.S. imperialism" and "Star Wars" and support of the Soviet peace proposals. He demanded formation of a "worldwide alliance of reason," declared that the communists in the FRG belong to the forces of peace and progress, condemned the secret agreements between the FRG and the United States that have drawn the FRG into implementing the notorious U.S. Star Wars program, and demanded that the government of the

FRG publicly request the U.S. government to accept the constructive Soviet disarmament proposals and sign a nuclear test ban treaty. The West German government should further cancel participation in the Strategic Defense Initiative (SDI) program, request the removal of U.S. medium-range missiles from German soil, and support the establishment of a nuclear-free, chemical-weapons-free zone in Europe. Mies, like many SPD leaders, called for creation of a "security partnership" with the East.

Emphasizing that the most important work of the German communists is the support of the peace movement, Mies noted that the workers' and peace movements have joined forces. Of special significance are the peace groups of the various professions (such as teachers, physicians, artists, and—most important—natural scientists and technicians) and the peace movement's decisions, initiatives, and actions (especially with regard to the Easter Marches and the direction of its continuous struggle against the SDI and for withdrawal of U.S. medium-range missiles). Mies assured the congress that the party is a part of the world communist movement and is directed by class solidarity in the pursuance of the common objectives with the fraternal parties. In the forthcoming federal elections (25 January 1987), the DKP will support the candidates of the Peace List, comprised of DKP members, members of affiliated and communist-influenced organizations, and communist sympathizers (*ND*, 3,4 May).

The congress adopted a series of "theses" intended to supplement the 1978 party program. Presidium member Gerns pointed out that they, together with the report of the party Executive, provide the political-ideological orientation for every communist. The theses openly state the unconstitutional objective of the DKP and prescribe Marxism-Leninism as guide for its actions aimed at the creation of a socialist state in the FRG. The party's "basic principle of the communist alliance policy" was also reiterated. Communists are supposed to support the specific objectives of the various movements and "citizens' initiatives" and at the same time attempt to lead them in the direction of basic changes of the social system (*IS*, 4 July). The major topics of the theses, as proposed by the party presidium in June 1985, were adopted unanimously by the congress upon inclusion of a number of changes to the original draft. Topics included the worldwide controversy about war and peace, international power relations, foreign and security policy, the struggle against the change toward the right,

the struggle for work and democracy, new issues of the unity of action and alliance policy, the peace movement, democratic alliances, and the party itself (*DID*, first June edition).

The financial report stated the party's income for 1984 as 19,187,068.50 marks, not counting services party members rendered free of charge. Income from membership dues amounted to 8.5 million marks, and contributions accounted for 7.9 million marks. Income from the sale of publications amounted to 2.3 million marks, and the free services rendered by party members were estimated at 5.7 million marks. Total expenditures were reported as 17.4 million marks, an amount that could not cover salaries of the several hundred full-time party workers and staff members at party headquarters in Düsseldorf, the party office in Bonn, and the more than 200 local offices. And expenditures for the production and distribution of the voluminous propaganda material, for financing mass rallies and election campaigns, and finacial support for DKP-affiliated or communist-influenced organizations require many more millions of marks. To help cover these expenses, communist economic firms and communist-owned travel agencies directed by the Central Committee of the SED keep a number of DKP functionaries on their payrolls and, in addition, the SED provided more than 65 million marks, money that in most cases was brought from the GDR to the FRG via conspiratorial means. The GDR also provided many other services, such as use of training facilities, support for several hundred delegations, and provisions for holiday sick leave for DKP officials (*BVS-Bericht*, pp. 37–40). No other Western communist party is as dependent on and as strictly controlled by, a foreign party as the DKP is by the SED. The Department of International Politics and Economics of the SED Central Committee controls the DKP.

The ideological education program for its members remained a vital part of the party's internal activities, receiving substantial support from the GDR and the Soviet Union. Party members were able to attend cadre schools in these countries.

For purposes of idiological training and "socialism propaganda," the DKP operates a number of well-established institutions. The Institute for Marxist Studies and Research (IMSF) in Frankfurt was founded in 1968 and closely cooperates with the institutes for Marxism-Leninism of the central committees of the SED and the CPSU. The IMSF director is DKP Presidium member Dr. Heinz Jung. Almost all of the sixteen members of the "scientific advisory council" are communists, including DKP Presidium members Professor Josef Schleifstein and Dr. Robert Steigerwald (Hissischer Minister des Innern, *Verfassungsschutz in Hessen, Bericht 1985* [*VS-Hessen*], Wiesbaden, p. 26). The Marx-Engels Foundation in Wuppertal, which is headed by DKP official Dr. Richard Kumpf, serves as a meeting place for "scientific" seminars and conferences and has been visited by numerous groups from the workers' and peace movements as well as trade unions. The Marxist Workers' Education (MAB), directed by DKP Presidium member Hans Schneider, was founded in 1969 in Frankfurt for the purpose of organizing lectures and courses (frequently using instructors from the GDR) throughout the FRG for politically interested persons who do not belong to the DKP. Study groups of the MAB offered Marxist Evening Schools, consisting of evening courses lasting for several weeks (ibid.; *BVS-Bericht*, pp. 80–81). The DKP organizes about 8,000 "educational" lectures, seminars, and courses per year. The educational year 1986–1987 began in September and includes such topics as new security in the nuclear age, is the future going to be communist? what is an alternative economic policy? communists and the global problems, and communists and culture; special topics in view of the federal elections of 1987 'cover' communists, elections, and election alliances (*info-ch*, May, p. 7).

The DKP's publishing activities include the daily *Unsere Zeit* (*UZ*) (with occasional *Extra Blatter*—special editions with up to 300,000 copies), the *Deutsche Volkszeitung/die tat* (German people's newpaper/the deed; about 30,000 copies), and the quarterly *Illustrierte Volkszeitung* (Illustrated people's newspaper). Other DKP publications are *DKP-Pressedienst* (DKP–Press service); *infodienst* (Info service), which provides material for DKP factory, residential areas, and students' newspapers; and the *DKP-Landrevue* (DKP rural revue), all of which appear at irregular intervals. The DKP Presidium also publishes the bimonthly *praxis—Erfahrungen aus dem Leben und der Arbeit der Partei* (praxis—Experiences from the life and work of the party). The DKP produces some 360 factory newspapers and about 450 local newspapers, published by local party groups. Some of them, such as *Düsselpost, New Munich*, and *Frankfurt City Newspaper*, have as many as twelve editions per year with up to 120,000 copies. Important to DKP media work, the Progressive Press Agency (PPA), headquartered in Düsseldorf and with offices in Bonn,

Mannheim, Munich, and Kiel, has some fifteen editors and correspondents. Five times a week, the PPA publishes the PPA Daily Service, containing reports about party activities and selected reports from noncommunist newspapers. About one-third of the material used is taken from the GDR news agency, Allgemeiner Deutscher Nachrichtendienst (ADN) (*BVS-Bericht*, p. 40). The theoretical organ of the party is the bimonthly *Marxistische Blätter* (Marxist pages; 7,000 copies), which as of January 1987, will become a monthly magazine (*radical info*, July–September).

The SDAJ—largest of the DKP-affiliated organizations, with about 15,000 members organized in more than 900 local groups—refers to itself as the "revolutionary young workers' organization" dedicated to "the teaching of Marx, Engels, and Lenin" and to a fight for a "socialist Federal Republic" marked by power exercised by the workers and by a socialist, planned economy. Its chair is Brigit Radow, who is a member of the DKP Presidium and was elected in March to the party's Executive. Her deputy, Hans-Georg Eberhard, is also a member of the DKP. Of the twelve *Land* chair, ten belong to members of the corresponding DKP *Land* presidia (*BVS-Bericht*, p. 43).

The SDAJ's activities, which complemented those of the parent organization, were designed to influence students, apprentices, and soldiers (*IS*, 7 March). On 17 and 18 May, in cooperation with the MSB–Spartakus, the SDAJ held the Fifth Youth Festival in Dortmund. At the festival, attended by about 150,000 persons, 61 fraternal organizations represented 50 countries. One of the primary purposes of the festival was to attract new members. In addition, discussions concerning common actions against the political right were held with members of the Young Socialists (Jusos), the official youth organization of the SPD; the Greens; and Peace List (Friedensliste; FL) (*IS*, July, p. 5).

The SDAJ Presidium published several editions of an "educational" newspaper designed to support the educational work of the SDAJ groups, which includes educational evenings, district organizations' educational circles, *Land* organizations' schools for group-leaders, and week-long courses at the Youth Education Center Burg Wahrburg. Selected members attended the educational facilities of the DKP (*BVS-Bericht*, p. 44).

The official SDAJ organs are the monthly *elan—Das Jugendmagazin* (about 25,000 copies) and the *Jugendpolitische Blätter* (Youth political pages; about 2,500 copies) (*VS-Hessen*, p. 26). *Elan* also publishes a monthly *Artikeldienst für Betriebs-, Lehrlings-, Staddtteil- und Schülerzeitungen* (Article service for factory, apprentice, city area, and student newpapers) intended to assist in the preparation of hundreds of local papers. Two editions of the soldiers' newspaper *"Rührt Euch"* (At ease) were published by soldiers in cooperation with *elan* editors.

The SDAJ maintained numerous contacts with communist fraternal youth organizations in the GDR and other countries, and SDAJ members participated in the Solidarity Brigade in Nicaragua and in construction of an African National Congress school in Tanzania. For more than ten years, the SDAJ has provided the treasurer for the Soviet-controlled World Federation of Democratic Youth (*VSR-Bericht*, pp. 44–46).

The Young Pioneers—Socialist Children's Organization (JP)—has a membership of about 4,000 and is organized in 12 *Land* organizations. Its leaders are schooled at the Youth Education Center Burg Wahrburg. Its chair, Gerd Hertel, is a member of the SDAJ Executive; many JP functionaries also belong to the DKP and/or SDAJ. The JP Executive publishes the monthly *Pionierleiter Info* (Pioneer leader info), the children's newspaper *pionier*, and *Diskussionsmaterial fur Pionierleiter* (Discussion material for Pioneer leaders). The JP has maintained contact with children's organizations in the GDR and other socialist countries and belongs to the International Commission of Children's and Adolescents' Movements, CIMEA, a subsidiary of the Soviet-controlled World Federation of Democratic Youth (ibid., p. 46).

Another DKP-affiliated organization is the MSB-Spartakus with about 6,000 members (it claims 6,500), organized in groups in more than 100 postsecondary institutions. By far the largest and most influential left-extremist student organization, it advocates collaboration of all the forces of the political left. Its candidates occupy about 10 percent of the seats in student parliaments, and its permanent alliance partner, the Socialist University League (SHB) brings that figure to about 15 percent. Together they are represented in more than half of the student parliaments. Frequently, the Liberal Students' League and Juso-University groups collaborate with the MSB-Spartakus/SHB groups, refusing to work with the Christian democratic student organization (*Deutschland-Union-Dienst*, 18 September). The MSB-Spartakus uses the United German Students' Association (*Vereinigte Deutsche Studentenschaft*; VDS) for its activities and represents the VDS in the various coordinating committees of the peace and protest movements.

The MSB-Spartakus operates in close collaboration with the DKP. Chair Thomas Harms, his two deputies, all members of the Secretariat, and most members of the Presidium are members of the DKP. University groups comprised of all students and teaching and administrative personnel who belong to the DKP direct the MSB-Spartakus groups. The MSB-Spartakus declared the "struggle for peace" as part of the class struggle and thus a revolutionary task of highest priority. It was primarily responsible for the university campaigns for nuclear-free zones and, together with the "Initiative of Natural Scientists," organized discussions, seminars, and congresses against the American SDI project on more than 40 university campuses (*IS*, 7 March). *Rote blätter* is the MSB-Spartakus's central monthly organ. For special events, the *rote blätter Extra* was distributed (*BVS-Bericht*, 48).

To mobilize as many citizens as possible for such DKP objectives as the struggle against the militarization of space, the party has the support of about 50 organizations and initiatives (action groups) that outwardly appear to be independent but are, in fact, strongly influenced by communists. Although the majority of the members and functionaries of these organizations are not DKP members (the less the target groups recognize communist influence, the more effective the organization) key positions, especially those in the organizational sector (secretariats), are held by communist officials who are assigned to these posts by the party. Almost all of the larger of these organizations, which because they pursue objectives within the constitution and therefore can also be supported by democrats, belong to Soviet-directed front groups, such as the World Peace Council (WPC).

Among the more important organizations are the Association of Victims of the Nazi Regime/League of Antifascists (VVN/BdA; about 13,500 members), the German Peace Union (DFU; about 1,000 members; Secretary Heinz Dreibrodt was a member of the outlawed KPD), the Committee for Peace, Disarmament, and Cooperation (KFAZ), the German Peace Society/United War Resisters (DFG/VK; about 13,000 members), the Democratic Women's Initiative (DFI), the Association of Democratic Jurists (VDJ; about 1,000 members), and the Anti-imperialist Solidarity Committee for Africa, Asia, and Latin America (ASK) (*BVS-Bericht*, pp. 48–57; *radical info*, April–June).

The ASK provides the framework for "anti-imperialist alliances" of communists with democrats in solidarity actions on behalf of Chile and Nicaragua and for the "liberation movements" in the Third World. In 1986 it organized protests against the U.S. Strategic Defense Initiative (SDI) and accused the United States of trying to implement the "Final Solution [a reference to the Nazi extermination policy of the Jews] of the Communists." It publishes a monthly *Anti-imperialist Information Bulletin* (*AIB*; about 3,000 copies). The DFG/VK, which is the largest of the DKP-influenced organizations and has the largest number of noncommunists in its ranks, has within the past three years lost about 3,500 members and suffered a financial crisis marked by a monthly deficit of up to 20,000 marks and an accumulated debt of about 170,000 marks. On 15 March, in Wiesbaden, the organization held a special federal congress at which it was decided to reduce expenditures for its official publication *Civil Courage* by 50 percent and to lay off staff members (*radical info*, January–March; *DID*, February). One of the important newly founded DKP-influenced groups is the Patron Circle of the *Darmstädter Signal*, the latter a group of about 170 active duty soldiers and officers founded in September 1983 to influence the members of the Bundeswehr to reject participation in a nuclear war. Initiators of the Patron Circle include leading members of the peace movement, Greens, SPD, and numerous Protestant and Catholic ministers (*DID*, January, February). "Peace initiatives" of the various professions, such as physicians, scientists, and journalists, substantially increased their activities in support of DKP objectives (*DID*, first May edition).

**Domestic Attitudes and Activities.** In the *Land* elections held in Lower Saxony on 15 June, the DKP received 5,694 votes (0.1 percent) compared with 11,552 votes (0.3 percent) in March 1982 (*FAZ*, 18 June). In the elections in Hamburg on 9 November, they received 1,607 (0.2 percent) compared with 3,885 (0.4 percent) in December 1982 (*FAZ*, 11 November). The DKP did not participate in the Bavarian *Land* elections on 12 October; but in local elections in Schleswig-Holstein on 2 March, they received 3,971 votes (0.2 percent) (*FAZ*, 4 March), and in the local elections in Lower Saxony on 5 October between 0.2 and 0.3 percent (*FAZ*, 7 October).

The DKP decided not to run as DKP in the Bundestag elections to be held on 25 January 1987. Instead, following an almost unanimous decision of

a federal convention of the FL (8–9 March) to nominate direct candidates in all 248 Bundestag election districts, the DKP has chosen to run its candidate as part of the FL. According to FL spokesperson and executive member of the DKP Uwe Knickrehm, the objective of the FL is the attempt to unite all opposition forces left of the governing Christian Democrats (*FAZ*, 11 March; *Frankfurter Rundschau*, 11 March). To this end, the FL asked the Greens to join the FL and DKP effort to present a common front, a move that was rejected by the Greens' federal executive board (*FAZ*, 12 March).

In the middle of September, DKP chair Mies explained to a meeting of some 200 party officials and election candidates the decision of his party to ask communists to give their first vote to the direct candidates of the people's front alliance FL and their second vote to either the Social Democratic Party of Germany (SPD) or the Greens. (The German election law provides every voter with two votes: the first vote is for a direct candidate in the election district, to be elected by a plurality vote; the second is for a political party. The second vote determines the percentage and the number of elected candidates a party obtains, as long as the party has received at least 5 percent of the votes.) The DKP justified this decision on the basis that, on the one hand the main objectives of the FL and the DKP are the same and thus can be pursued more effectively in an alliance than by a small party. On the other hand, Mies declared that the Greens' position is close to that of the communists because the Greens are a consistent radical-democratic force that supports the extraparliamentary struggle. Votes in favor of the SPD are supposed to support those Social Democrats who favor the unity of action with communists and are for cooperation with the Greens (*DID*, September). The SPD, no longer considered an anticommunist party, has become eligible to receive communist votes as a noncommunist party.

At the beginning of the year, Mies declared that the party's alliance policy with Social Democrats, trade unionists, Greens, and members of the peace movement would continue, asserting that this policy will create the "alternative power" required to defeat the present government. According to Mies, the DKP played an essential and successful role during 1985 (*UZ*, 31 December 1985).

The DKP pursues two forms of alliances. The "unity of actions of the working class" refers to collaboration with Social Democrats, trade unionists, Christian workers, and workers not affiliated with any party. The "broad antimonopolistic alliance" (people's front) is directed against "monopoly capitalism." It builds on the "unity of actions" and includes collaboration with intellectuals and bourgeois elements. It operates with the slogan "coalition of reason" against the "militarization of space." The communists do not insist on leadership positions in alliances; however, according to them, their Marxist-Leninist ideology places them de facto in control, as has been observed in practically all cases. (*BVS-Bericht*, pp. 57–60.) Fritsch, member of the DKP Presidium and Secretariat, emphasized that the alliance policy required "political flexibility" of the party members and at the same time demands "ideological conviction." The setting aside of existing differences between communists and Social Democrats must be achieved through stressing the common interest without making any concessions to reformist positions. Members of the DKP must never surrender their ideological principles when asked to make compromises in the process of organizing common actions (*IS*, 12 May). According to DKP leadership, the wall between Social Democrats and communists has broken down, and collaboration was achieved within the peace movement and the antifascist movement, in factories, and in trade unions. Numerous alliances were organized at local, regional, and national levels, with Social Democrats and communists working as equals. Speakers from the SPD and DKP appeared at the same meetings and discussion sessions. The official DKP organ, *UZ*, published numerous interviews with high-ranking SPD officials on such issues as opposition to the SDI program or the stationing of U.S. medium-range missiles on the territory of the FRG. Members of the SPD hold leading positions in DKP-influenced organizations including the KFAZ, various friendship societies with socialist countries, and "citizens' initiatives," such as the one requesting removal of the ban on employing communists in the civil service (ibid.). The SHB, with about 2,000 members, mostly belonging to the SPD, has practiced "unity of actions" with the MSB-Spartakus for many years and strongly advocates an SPD-DKP alliance (ibid.).

Members of the DKP are ordered by their leaders to be active trade unionists and to strive to become influential trade union officials. The communists' objective is to convince the trade unions that the interests of the workers can only be served by means of class struggle. The DKP considers its "educational work" to be of great significance, especially for the trade union youth groups, and the majority of trade union instructors come from the student movement and advocate orthodox Marxism. The DKP observed that the concept of the class struggle has been widely accepted by the trade unions, which in turn have become more ready to collaborate with communists. Although they have captured only a few leading positions in the trade unions, the communists are exerting increasing influence in some of them, notably the trade unions of printers and journalists (ibid.). Various trade union congresses held in 1986 clearly revealed their move to the political left and their active opposition to the present government, referred to as reactionary and serving the entrepreneurs.

The DKP continues to demand that the government rescind its ban on the KPD, which was outlawed by the Federal Constitutional Court in 1956. Mies argued that repeal of the ban would be in the interest of peace and of the national and social interests of the German people (*Pravda*, 11 August; *FBIS*, 13 August; *ND*, 16, 17 August).

On 24 July the DKP published a "peace charter" that repeats its demands for removal of American nuclear missiles, an American nuclear test ban, prevention of the militarization of space, elimination of chemical weapons, and reduction of the armed forces and armament in Europe (TASS, 24 July; *FBIS*, 25 July). Copies were mailed to the federal chancellor's office and to all parties represented in the Bundestag. In many large enterprises and research centers, the DKP sponsor groups are articulate in their opposition to the U.S. Star Wars program and German cooperation with the SDI (TASS, 22 June; *FBIS*, 24 June).

Support of the peace movement remained a party priority and even though communists constituted a minority, the DKP and its affiliated and influenced organizations enjoyed a disproportionate degree of representation in the movement's operational coordinating committees; DKP representatives regularly attended meetings of the Coordinating Committee of the Peace Movement (KA) even though the party itself does not enjoy KA membership (*BVS-Bericht*, pp. 64–67). At the KA's "Seventh Action Conference" in Bonn-Beuel (1–2 February), attended by about 500 representatives of Christian, Social Democratic, Greens, and communist peace groups (*radical info*, January–March, reported 700 to 800), it was decided to organize a demonstration against the security policy of the FRG and NATO in Hasselbach (Hunsruck) on 11 October, just three months before the federal elections. The stationing of cruise missiles, scheduled for March, was given as the reason for the location. Although the KFAZ proposal that conformity of the Soviet peace offensive with the position of the KA be included in the conference's resolution was rejected by a representative of a Protestant action committee who also belongs to the SPD Presidium's Security Commission, the final resolution did contain practically all the communist propositions (*FAZ*, 3 February). The KA published in August a newsletter (*Rundbrief*), following serious internal strife, confirming the demonstration on 11 October (*radical info*, July–September).

In Cologne on 12 and 13 April, a Discussion Congress with the topic "Peace with NATO?" and organized by a coordinating committee comprised of independent peace groups, Democratic Socialists, Green-Alternatives, Trotskyites, and other left extremists concluded that peace is not possible because of NATO and demanded withdrawal from the Western Alliance and implementation of unilateral disarmament by the FRG (ibid., April–June). The Cologne Committee for Peace and Disarmament, together with the KFAZ, published a memorandum "Peace 2,000—Roads leading away from Disaster" (*Wege aus der Gefahr*). A conference dealing with the same topic was held in Cologne (21–22 June). The sixteen-member Cologne office of the KFAZ, which is primarily responsible for KFAZ operations, is comprised of representatives from the DKP, FL, VVN/BdA, DFG/VK, DFI, Christian Peace Conference, and Christians for Disarmament (ibid.).

The SDAJ and the Christian Association of Young Men organized a "Youth Peace Camp" in Hunsruck in connection with the anti–cruise missile demonstration on 11 October. At the camp, the communists and the Protestants planned to discuss the consequences of U.S. nuclear testing with American Indians from Nevada and meet with international brigadists from Nicaragua (*FAZ*, 2 October). To mobilize the youth, SDAJ members used such tactics as occupation of apprenticeship offices and workshops and chaining themselves to public buildings. The SDAJ was quite successful as witnessed by the willingness of democratic youth organizations, such as the Nature Friend Youth, and the Socialist Youth of Germany (the Falcans), to accept the communists as alliance partners. *Bundeswehr* soldiers were encouraged in leaflets and in the publication *Rührt Euch* (At ease) to join the communist-influenced Soldiers' Peace Initiatives and Working Groups of Democratic Soldiers, about twenty of which were known to exist. Although the SDAJ,

frequently joined by other left-extremist groups, carried out numerous actions against the German military, including distribution of leaflets and interruption of oath-taking ceremonies for new recruits, the SDAJ focused primarily on work in the factories where about 200 SDAJ factory groups were active (*BVS-Bericht*, pp. 74–77). At postsecondary institutions of learning, some 100 DKP university groups operated in addition to the MSB-Spartakus. The DKP considers the organized communist students as the essential contact between the working class and the intelligentsia (ibid., p. 77).

**International Views and Party Contacts.** The foreign policy statements of DKP officials are almost identical with those made by Moscow and East Berlin. The party supports every aspect of the Soviet peace policy and calls for withdrawal of U.S. nuclear weapons from Europe and termination of the American SDI program. The DKP strongly endorses the SPD's close contact with ruling communist parties in Eastern Europe and approved the SPD-SED appeal to make Europe a region free of chemical and nuclear warfare weapons.

Contacts were maintained with many fraternal communist parties, especially with those of the Soviet Union and the GDR. Their relations with the SED are determined by the strict supervision exercised over the activities of the DKP by the Department for International Politics and Economics (until 1984 known as "West Department") of the Central Committee of the SED, headed by Günter Rettner since November 1985. Leaders of the SED and the DKP agree on an annual plan for the German communists and the DKP reports regularly to the SED. The DKP personnel files are kept in East Berlin to ensure that the SED retains control over its "fraternal" party (*FAZ*, 11 June). A DKP delegation of the party's Control Commission, headed by Chair Ludwig Müller, visited the GDR in July on a study assignment (*ND*, 4 July).

Party chair Mies attended the Twenty-seventh CPSU Congress (25 February–6 March) at which he pledged his party's loyalty to the Soviet Union, assuring the congress that the German communists are fighting in the peace and workers' movements against the "arms race," against "total subjection under U.S. imperialism," and for a policy of peaceful coexistence and collaboration with the Soviet Union and all socialist states (*IS*, 12 May). Mies also was the head of the DKP delegation of the Eleventh SED Party Congress (17–21 April) in East Berlin.

DKP Presidium member Georg Kwiatowsky attended the Special Meeting of the World Marxist Review in Prague, where he asserted that the "antiwar demands should now be addressed to only one side, the USA, for the Soviet Union suggests and even unilaterally implements the measures whose adoption is sought by the peace movement itself" (*WMR*, July). Kwiatowsky represented the DKP at the meeting of the WMR Commission on the Exchange of Party Experience, held in Prague (*WMR*, October). Todor Zhivkov, general secretary of the Central Committee of the Bulgarian Communist Party received Mies on 18 July during the latter's vacation in Bulgaria (Sofia, BIA, 18 July).

Following Moscow's lead, the DKP actively supports liberation movements. At a 31 January–1 February conference of district organizations' delegates in Düsseldorf, Tony Seedat of the African National Congress in Bonn received a check for 10,365 marks, money collected at many solidarity actions and collections. Also in January, the SDAJ and its magazine *elan* began a solidarity campaign, "Action Nelson Mandela," and opened a bank account for contributions (*DID*, March).

The DKP's support for the Sandinista regime in Nicaragua included participation in the International Brigade; DKP member Berndt Koberstein was killed in Nicaragua while serving as a construction helper. The Jusos, who maintain a sixteen-person "Working Brigade" there, refused to withdraw after Koberstein's "murder," which they asserted could be traced directly to the White House because the "terrorist bands of the Contras are organized and financed by the U.S. security service" (*FAZ*, 31 July).

**Other Leftist Groups.** In addition to the Moscow-oriented orthodox communists, a number of left-extremist small parties and groups, initiatives, and revolutionary organizations of the New Left remained active during 1986. These organizations, all of which reject the pro-Soviet orthodox communist positions, are deeply divided among themselves along ideological lines. The New Left, comprised of Marxist-Leninists, Trotskyites, anarchists, autonomists, and antidogmatic revolutionaries, propagates the class struggle and considers the proletariat as the decisive revolutionary force leading the struggle for overthrow of the capitalist system and the bourgeois state. Most of them wish to establish a dictatorship of the proletariat leading to a socialist, and eventually communist, society. They are convinced that the bureaucratic failures of

the communist-ruled countries can be avoided. The autonomous anarchistic groups, who also aim at the destruction of the state, advocate its replacement by a "free" society. Most New Left groups openly endorse the use of violence in the pursuit of their objectives. Membership of the revolutionary Marxists and of anarchist groups remained about the same, and most Marxist-Leninist parties and associations managed to keep their organizational structure and membership. Efforts to form alliances continued among the anarchists, social revolutionary groups, and Trotskyist organizations. The autonomous groups, who regarded the many violent protest demonstrations—against the nuclear reprocessing plant (WAA) in Wackersdorf, for example—as signs of their increased influence, were responsible for the "organization of resistance," but they also warned against absorption by the "Green-Alternatives," the official organizers of the demonstrations (*BVS-Bericht*, pp. 92–94).

The membership of the Marxist-Leninist organizations (K-groups) and Trotskyist groups remained about constant, with some 3,300 members in their basic organizations and about 700 members in affiliated groups. Membership in the antidogmatic groups (about 58 were identified), including anarchists and social revolutionaries, continued to increase to about 8,800 (a figure that includes the membership of the loosely organized left-extremists [ibid., p. 20]). The autonomous and anarchist groups, which were mainly responsible for violence against the state, frequently formed the militant core of the protest movement directed against the United States, NATO, and nuclear power installations. Some of the autonomous groups came close to the position of the terrorists and were engaged in violent actions against fascism, the nuclear state, "computerization and surveillance," and imperialism (ibid., pp. 94, 105).

The groups of the New Left have a fairly extensive publication apparatus, with some 250 publications totaling more than 4.5 million copies per year. The alternative newspapers served the undogmatic New Left to exchange information; some of them printed appeals and statements that were used by the New Left for propaganda and information purposes (ibid., p. 92).

The dogmatic New Left included four K-groups, the Marxist-Leninist Party of Germany (Marxistische-Leninistische Partei Deutschlands; MLPD); the Communist Party of Germany, Marxist-Leninist (Kommunistische Partei Deutschlands, Marxistisch-Leninist; KPD; formerly known as

KPD-ML), which merged with the Group International Marxists (GIM) in October and adopted the name United Socialist Party (Vereinigte Sozialistische Partei; VSP); the League of West German Communists (Bund Westdeutscher Kommunisten; BWK); and the Communist League (Kommunistischer Bund; KB) (ibid., p. 95; *DID*, October). The "Group Z," which split in 1979 from the KB, joined the Green Party and former functionaries of this group occupy leadership positions in the Green Party at federal and *Land* levels.

The MLPD, presently the strongest of the K-groups, was able to increase its membership from 1,100 to 1,300. The party is organized in twelve districts with about 100 local groups. Its chair is Stefan Engel. Its official weekly organ *Rote Fahoe* (Red flag) has a circulation of about 10,000 copies. Its three affiliated organizations together have about 300 members and are considered ineffective by the party: the Marxist-Leninist Workers' Youth Association (AJV/ML), formerly called Revolutionary Youth Association of Germany, organ *Rebell*; the Marxist-Leninist Pupils' and Students' Association, organ *Roter Pfeil* (Red arrow); and the active Marxist-Leninist League of Intellectuals. The AJV/ML has initiated a children's organization, Red Foxes (*Rotfüchse*).

The KPD, the oldest of the K-groups had about 400 members left when it merged on 4 October with the approximately 250-member Trotskyist GIM to form the VSP following negotiations with the Trotskyists that caused a number of dissident KDP members to leave the party early in the year before culminating at the Merger Congress in Cologne (4–5 October). The VSP, under the leadership of Horst-Dieter Koch, is headquartered in Cologne. The former KPD organ *Roter Morgen* (Red morning) and the former GIM publication (Was tun) (What to do) were replaced in November by the biweekly Socialist Newspaper (*Sozialistische Zeitung*).

Calling themselves the "correct KPD," members of the KPD who had rejected the proposed merger with the Trotskyist GIM held its Sixth Party Congress in Bremen (25—26 January) and confirmed the old party program and statutes. Their headquarters is in West Berlin. Since May, they have published the *Roter Morgen*, the traditional name of the KPD organ. The KPD majority faction, which eventually merged with GIM, held its Sixth Party Congress in Dortmund (1–2 February), at which time it elected a new central committee and made the final decision concerning the merger (*IS*, July).

Contacts of the pro-Albanian KPD with the Albanian Communist Party became strained as a result of the merger with GIM (*BVS-Bericht*, p. 97).

At the same time as the Merger Congress (4–5 October), at a Revolutionary Youth Plenum North Germany held in Hamburg, the new youth organization of the VSP, the Autonomous Socialist Youth Group (ASJG), was formed—the result of the merger of the Communist Youth of Germany (KJV; about 200 members, formerly KPD-affiliated) and the Revolutionary Socialist Youth Red Mole (*Roter Maulwurf* [RSJ]; about 150 members, formerly GIM-affiliated). Other left-extremist youth organizations participating in the Plenum were the Socialist Pupils' League (the youth organization of the KB), the GJA/R (the youth organization of the Free Workers' Union/Council Communists [FAU/R Hamburg]), the BWK, the People's Front (an organization allied with the KPD), and a Women's AG HH. It appears that the revolutionary socialists are attempting to use their cooperating youth organizations to challenge the DKP-affiliated SDAJ. The Second Revolutionary Youth Plenum was planned for 20–21 December in Hamburg. The ASJC is run by a women's collective and for the present will keep the former KJV organ *Radikal* as its official publication (*DID*, September, October).

Prior to the merger of the respective youth organizations, the KJV held a special congress (15–16 February) in Cologne that was attended by about 30 delegates (*IS*, 12 May). The Revolutionary Trade Union Opposition has about 300 members left. Also other KPD-affiliated organizations, such as the Communist Students again lost influence (*BVS-Bericht*, pp. 97–98). Since November 1982, the People's Front against Reaction, Fascism, and War (*Volksfront*) is no longer affiliated with the KPD and is presently supported by the BWK, FAU/R, Anarchist Workers' Union (AAU Munich), and other splinter groups. Its membership dropped from some 1,000 to about 400. The organ of the AAU (Munich), *Freiraum* (Free area), declared that the People's Front is not connected with any K-group and is an organization of revolutionary antifascists left of the VVN/BdA and called on all anarchists/autonomists to join (*DID*, April).

The BWK, founded in 1980 as the result of a split of the now defunct KBW, has about 400 members, organized in groups in seven Länder. Its official biweekly, *Politische Berichte*, publishes about 1,300 copies, and its other publication, the *Nachrichtenhefte*, with special editions for the various industrial branches, about 1,000 copies. In an ongoing internal discussion, it is asserted that the program inherited from the KBW does not assist the communist forces in the party-building process of the Green-Alternatives because it fails to deal properly with the alliance policy. The People's Front offers an opportunity for an alliance of left-extremists. In the newly elected presidium (sixteen members), the BWK holds a majority, and the business office of the People's Front has been moved to the BWK central office in Cologne. The BWK is willing to cooperate with the DKP and its affiliated and influenced organizations. (*BVS-Bericht*, pp. 99–100.) The BKW participated in several Land elections but obtained very few votes.

The Hamburg-based KB has maintained its membership of about 400 (about 200 in Hamburg). Its monthly publication *Arbeiterkampf* has a circulation of about 4,500 copies. The KB exerts considerable influence over the Alternative List (AL) in Hamburg, known since November 1984 as Green–Alternative List (GAL). At the last elections in Hamburg (9 November), the GAL received 99,832 (10.4 percent) votes with an all-women list of candidates (*FAZ*, 11 November). The KB has encouraged its members to play an active part in the GAL. (Ibid., pp. 100–101.)

The Workers' League for the Reconstruction of the KPD maintained its membership of about 300. Its central organ *Kommunistische Arbeiterzeitung* (*KAZ*) published only two editions. The affiliated student organization, Communist University League, was active only in Bavaria (Ibid., p. 101.)

After the largest Trotskyist organization, GIM, merged with the KPD, the eleven remaining Trotskyist groups, some with only regional organizations, have a total membership of about 450. They advocate "permanent revolution" and "dictatorship of the proletariat" in the form of a council system. They regard the conditions of "real existing socialism" in the socialist countries, as the result of "bureaucratic" or "revisionist decadence." The League of Socialist Workers is the German section of the International Committee of the Fourth International in London. It has, together with its youth organization Socialist Youth League, fewer than 100 members. Its weekly *neue Arbeiterpresse* called for a general strike for overthrow of the government. It advocates support of the PLO and of the struggle against apartheid in South Africa and propagates solidarity with the liberation movements in Central America. The smaller Trotskyist groups and circles, such as the Trotskyist Liga of Germany, the International Socialist Workers' Organization,

the International Communist Movement, the Socialist Workers' Group, and the Posadistic Communist Party, agitate against the emerging animosity toward foreigners in the FRG and against apartheid policy in South Africa and support the "revolutionary struggle" in Central America. (Ibid., pp. 102–3.)

The Marxist Group (MG) is a Marxist-Leninist cadre party marked by a hierarchical structure, strict discipline, intense indoctrination, and secrecy. Its membership increased from 1,500 to 1,700 and consists mostly of students and academics. It has several thousand organized sympathizers. Its organizational main effort is in Bavaria. The MG believes that trained agitators must incite a class-conscious proletariat to carry on the class struggle. It publishes the monthly *MSZ-Marxistische Streit und Zeitschrift—Gegen die Kosten der Freiheit* (10,000 copies), the *Marxistische Arbeiterzeitung* (*MAZ*; appears at irregular intervals), the *Marxistische Hochschulzeitung* (14,000 copies), and the *Marxistische Schulzeitung*. The MG organized several hundred public discussion meetings, often well attended, and MG followers participated in numerous demonstrations and actions and interrupted meetings of other organizations. (Ibid., pp. 103–4.)

Various anarchist organizations and movements continued their activities in 1986. They all reject strict organizational structures, characteristic for most revolutionary Marxist organizations, but they are deeply divided about the methods (violent or nonviolent) to be pursued to change society as well as about concrete aims (ibid., p. 104).

The anarcho-syndicalist Free Workers' Union (FAU), with some 200 members organized in 22 local groups and contacts, is a member of the anarcho-syndicalist International Workers' Association (IAA). Its organ *direkte aktion* is published by the local FAU group in Dieburg. In June 1985, in Frankfurt, FAU members founded the Black Help (Schwarze Hilfe) to support imprisoned anarchists, anarcho-syndicalists, and autonomists. Contact with the international coordinating office of the anarchist Black Cross (London) is maintained. Anarcho-syndicalist principles are antistate, antiparliamentarism, and antimilitarism; FAU followers fight against Western capitalism as well as against the "state capitalism" of the socialist states. The most important task for FAU members is the revolutionary work in factories where the collective resistance against capitalism must be created. The aim is a society marked by self-administration and federalism. A number of independent oppositional FAU groups that have emerged do not wish to limit themselves to political work in factories. Four of these organizations (the anarcho-communist group), with a total membership of about 50, are the Free Workers'-Union/Council Communists (FAU/R); the Free Workers'-Union Heidelberg (Anarchist) (FAU HD [A]); the Anarchist Workers'-Union (AAU), Munich; and the Proletarian Action (PA). All of them participate in discussions aimed to bring together revolutionary socialists (*SI*, 7 March; *DID*, April; *BVS-Bericht*, p. 108).

The Violence-free Actions Groups—Grass-Roots Movement has about 800 members in some 70 groups and collectives. Their contact and coordinating organization is the Grass-Roots Revolution—Federation of Violence-free Action Groups (FoGA). The FoGA propagates a nonviolent revolution and the replacement of the power of the state with a decentralized society based on self-administration and anarchy. Antimilitarism, including the concept of "social defense" and "peace" activities continued to be the preference of the FoGA, although "ecological" issues, such as the resistance to the nuclear reprocessing plant at Wackersdorf, have been added to the repertoire of actions. Their monthly periodical, *grasswurzelrevolution*, prints about 4,000 copies (*SI*, 7 March; *DVS-Bericht*, pp. 107–8).

The autonomous anarchist groups of the undogmatic New Left follow various anarchistic, and even nihilistic, concepts. Their followers are mostly young people and number several thousand. Their outstanding characteristic is their readiness to use violence. Most groups are small, loosely organized, and short-lived. Their activities, which have increased, have included violence during anti-NATO, anti–United States, anti-nuclear power demonstrations; on many occasions they have resorted to terrorist actions, military sabotage, and arson. The great number of "solidarity actions" on behalf of "liberation movements" in Central America and South Africa indicate the international orientation of the New Left. However, lasting contacts with left-extremist organizations abroad remained the exception and were mostly limited to specific undertakings. The Trotskyists continue to maintain contacts with their international network (*BVS-Bericht*, p. 118).

The number of terrorist attacks has greatly increased in 1986. During the first half year, there were more than 2 terrorist incidents per day, and 203 of them were major attacks (*FAZ*, 9 Sep-

tember). During that period, 72 attacks were directed against nuclear installations (69 arson and 3 bombings). During the first six months of 1986, more than 750 police officials were injured, some of them seriously (*Deutschland Union Dienst*, 4 July). By the end of October, over 100 electric power poles had been destroyed, interrupting the power supply to industries (*FAZ*, 28 October).

An "International Congress: Anti-imperialism and Anti-capitalism Resistance in Western Europe," held at the postsecondary Vocational School in Frankfurt (31 January–4 February), was organized by supporters of terrorist organizations. Leaflets that were distributed carried symbols of the Red Army Faction (RAF), the Italian Red Brigades, and the French Action Direct. Preparatory meetings took place in several cities in the FRG. The personnel of the conference office, charged with preparation of the conference, included RAF sympathizers. One-third of about 1,000 participants, some wearing face masks, were "anti-imperialists" (supporters of the RAF). Two-thirds belonged to the "autonomists" (members of the "militant resistance"). Strict security measures were implemented by the organizers. Persons entering the meeting place had to pass metal detectors. Guards patrolled the area and the residences of the participants. Sentries, wearing black leather clothing and with faces painted black, stood guard at the entrance and on the roof. They listened to police radio communication and were to sound an alert in case of pending police action. Special escape routes were kept available for participants wearing face masks. Three working groups were formed: "Front sector of the international class war," "Formation of the imperialist world system," and "Sector Western Europe." The Frankfurt congress confirmed that the aims of the RAF had not changed. The targets remained the "military-industrial complex." A list of 49 endangered personalities, which included the name of Prof. Karl-Heinz Beckhurts (Siemens AG, Munich) who was assassinated by the RAF on 9 July, had been published in November 1985 in the *rote blätter*, the official organ of the DKP-affiliated MSB-Spartakus, under the heading "Our SDI Mafia" (*FAZ*, 15, 18 July).

The hard core, command level (*Kommandobereich*) of the RAF consists of about twenty terrorists who are responsible for the political assassinations and major bombings. A second level, the "RAF Militants" (about 200 persons recruited from the anti-imperialist resistance movement), provides most of the logistic support for the command level, including conspiratorial housing, weapons, explosives, vehicles, and documents. The RAF Militants carried out terrorist actions against material objectives, not persons. Finally, there are the "sympathizers of the RAF" (*Umfeld der RAF*), numbering about 2,000, who conduct public relations for the RAF, including propaganda concerning the terrorists' objectives. They also care for imprisoned RAF members (*DVS-Bericht*, pp. 119–26). The RAF maintained close relations with the French Action Direct, especially along ideological lines, both pursuing the unity of action of the revolutionaries of Western Europe (*FAZ*, 15 July).

Terrorist attacks were also committed by the Red Cells (RZ), by its autonomous women's group Rote Zora, and by the "autonomist" groups (*BVS-Bericht*, pp. 126–29). The RZ, whose terrorist attacks are primarily directed against businesses, research institutions, and nuclear military installations, is ideologically in agreement with the RAF's "socialist revolutionary and anti-imperialist" objectives. The "autonomists," responsible for 70 percent of all terrorist acts, select their targets along the same line as the RZ and use the same terminology and arguments as the RAF and RZ in their "letters taking responsibility" for their terrorist actions (*BVS-Bericht*, pp. 127–28). The anarchocommunist PA supports the armed struggle against "imperialism" and considers itself to be operating at the same front as the RAF (*DID*, April).

The Jusos and other youth, student, and women's organizations affiliated with the SPD and the Green Party are usually not perceived as left-radical organizations. However, they share many objectives with the extreme left and have increasingly participated in "unity of actions" with communists and other leftists. Their anti-NATO and anti-U.S. policies, support of Moscow's "peace plans," and agreements with East European ruling communist parties concerning establishment of nuclear-free, chemical-weapons-free zones, provide the basis for increased cooperation.

The Green Party's attitude toward left-extremists and their use of violence was well illustrated by the leader of the GAL women's group in Hamburg. She referred to their acts of violence as symbolically valuable (*FAZ*, 8 November). The Green Party's European Parliament deputy, Schwalba-Hoth, accused France of "state terrorism" and called the brutal terrorist attacks in Paris a "kind of balancing justice" (*CSU, Brief aus Bonn*, 16 July).

*Die Tageszeitung* (*taz*), a daily publication close to the alternative scene, increased the number of its subscribers from 27,000 to 33,000 (*FAZ*, 23 September). Following the assassinations of nuclear scientist Karl-Heinz Beckurts and his driver, *taz* printed "letters to the editor" that included such statements as "Bravo RAF!!! This was a spy! There is again one less of the imperialist swine" and "I have no pity with the liquidated manager of the nuclear industry of death" (*Deutschland-Union-Dienst*, 16 July).

## WEST BERLIN

**Population.** 1,861,000 (1986)
**Party.** Socialist Unity Party of West Berlin (Sozialistische Einheitspartei Westberlins: SEW)
**Membership.** 4,500
**Chairman.** Horst Schmitt
**Politburo.** 17 members: Dietmar Ahrens, Uwe Doering, Helga Dolinski, Detlef Fendt, Klaus Feske, Harry Flichtbeil, Margot Granowski, Heinz Grünberg, Klaus-Dieter Heiser, Volker June, Inge Kopp, Jörg Kuhle, Hans Mahle, Margot Mrozinski, Monika Sieveking, Erich Ziegler, Horst Schmitt
**Secretariat.** 7 members: Dietmar Ahrens, Klaus Feske, Harry Flichtbeil, Margot Granowski, Inge Kopp, Herwig Kurzendorfer, Horst Schmitt
**Executive.** 65 members
**Status.** Legal
**Last Congress.** Seventh, 25–27 May 1984, in West Berlin
**Last Election.** 1985, 0.6 percent, no representation
**Auxiliary Organizations.** Socialist Youth League Karl Liebknecht; (Sozialistischer Jugendverband Karl Liebknecht; SJ Karl Liebknecht), ca. 550 members; Young Pioneeres (Junge Pioniere; JP), ca. 250 members; SEW–University Groups, ca. 400 members
**Publications.** *Die Wahrheit* (The truth), SEW daily organ, circulation ca. 13,000.

West Berlin is still under Allied occupation by the forces of the United States, Britain, and France. The 1971 Quadripartite Agreement concerning Berlin confirmed its special status based on previous agreements in 1944 and 1945, declaring that the former German capital is not part of the FRG. Although the 1971 agreement was meant to cover the area of Greater Berlin, the Soviet-occupied eastern sector of the city has been declared the capital of the GDR. The Western allies have encouraged the FRG to maintain close ties with West Berlin, and West Berlin is represented in the federal Parliament by nonvoting deputies.

Berlin's special status made it possible for the SED to set up a subsidiary in West Berlin. In 1959, an "independent" organizational structure was introduced for the West Berlin section of the SED. In 1962, the party was renamed the Socialist Unity Party of Germany–West Berlin; in 1969, the present designation was introduced to make the party appear a genuine, indigenous political party.

The SEW, like the DKP, is a pro-Soviet party and depends financially on the SED. Its statements are identical with the ideological and political views of the East German and Soviet parties. Membership in the SEW remained unchanged at about 4,500. In the last elections for the city's House of Representatives (10 March 1985), the SEW obtained 7,713 votes, or 0.6 percent, compared with 0.7 percent in 1981.

Among the affiliated organizations of the SEW are the SJ Karl Liebknecht with about 800 members, 250 of them children in the JP. The SEW–University Groups have about 400 members, and the SEW-influenced Action Group of Democrats and Socialists about 500 members. Other SEW-led organizations include the Democratic Women's League Berlin (about 600 members), the Society for German-Soviet Friendship (about 500 mem-

bers), and the West Berlin organization of the Victims of the Nazi Regime/League of Antifascists (about 500 members) (*BSV-Bericht*, pp. 40–43).

During 1986, the SEW continued efforts to mobilize the masses for the extraparliamentary struggle and to establish a "mass basis" through alliance with noncommunist forces (ibid., pp. 57–58). The party considers the fight against the "militarization of space" to be the "priority peace issue," and its entire propaganda machinery was utilized to popularize the Soviet "peace policy" (ibid., p. 65). Chair Horst Schmidt endorsed the "Budapest Appeal" of the socialist states, which opposes the arms race, and proposed a "coalition of reason," embracing all segments of the population, including certain elements of "monopoly capitalism" (*ND*, 30 July).

The SEW maintained contacts with the international communist movement by means of mutual visits, especially with the SED. Schmidt, as head of the SEW delegation to the Twenty-first SED Party Congress in April, reported on his party's collaboration with trade unionists, Social Democrats, Liberals, and Christians on numerous peace initiatives in their fight for peace and disarmament (ibid., 22 April). An SEW delegation also attended the Twenty-seventh Congress of the CPSU in March.

Many New Left and left-extremist groups and organizations operate in West Berlin, where they turned many demonstrations, such as the protest against the U.S. bombing of Libya with more than 10,000 participants, into violent confrontations with the authorities. Terrorists, including those from foreign countries, were also active in West Berlin.

Eric Waldman
*University of Calgary*

# Great Britain

**Population.** 56,458,000
**Party.** Communist Party of Great Britain (CPGB)
**Founded.** 1920
**Membership.** 10,999 *Morning Star*, 29 August)
**General Secretary.** Gordon McLennan
**Political Committee.** 9 members: Ron Halverson (chairman), Gordon McLennon (general secretary), Ian McKay, Gary Pocock, Martin Jacques, Jack Ashton, Kerin Halpin, Vishnu Sharma, Nina Temple (*Morning Star*, 21 May 1985)
**Executive Committee.** 45 members
**Status.** Legal
**Last Congress.** Thirty-ninth Special, 18–20 May 1985
**Last Election.** June 1983, 0.03 percent, no representation
**Auxiliary Organizations.** Young Communist League (YCL); Liaison Committee for the Defense of Trade Unions (LCDTU)
**Publications.** *Morning Star*, *Marxism Today*, *Communist Focus*, *Challenge Spark*, *Our History Journal*, *Economic Bulletin*, *Medicine in Society*, *Education Today and Tomorrow*, *New Worker*, *Seven Days*.

The CPGB is a recognized political party and contests both local and national elections. It does not, however, operate in Northern Ireland, which it does not recognize as British territory. The party has had no members in the House of Commons since 1950 but has one member, Lord Milford, in the non-elected House of Lords.

**Leadership and Organization.** The CPGB is divided into four divisions: the National Congress, the Executive Committee and its departments, districts, and local and factory branches. Constitutionally, the biennial National Congress is the party's supreme authority, and except in unusual periods, such as the present, it rubber-stamps the decisions of the Political Committee. Responsibility for overseeing the party's activities rests with the 45-member Executive Committee, which is elected by the National Congress and meets every two months. The Executive Committee is comprised of members of special committees, fulltime departmental heads, and the sixteen members of the Political Committee, the party's innermost controlling conclave.

Party leaders remain deeply preoccupied with

the continuing decline in support for the party. Electorally, the party is so battered that it no longer contests as many seats as it once did. Membership, at a little over 15,000 (only some 50 percent of whom have actually paid their fees) is at its lowest point since World War II. The YCL, with only about 500 members, is close to collapse. The decline in electoral support was most graphically illustrated in Britain's last general elections (1983) when the party's 35 candidates polled a mere 11,598 votes.

However, the poor showing of the CPGB at the polls belies the party's strength in the trade union movement and in influencing opinion. Although it does not control any individual trade union, the party is represented on most union executive committees and has played a major role in most government-union confrontations of recent years. The CPGB's success is partly attributable to low turnouts in most union elections, to the fact that it is the only party seeking to control the outcome of these elections, and to its close interest in industrial affairs, which ensures support from workers who might not support other aspects of the party's program. There is one member of the CPGB on the

General Council of the Trades Union Congress: Ken Gill of the Technical and Supervisory Section of the Amalgamated Union of Engineering Workers. In addition, CPGB ideas exercise a considerable influence on other trade union executives and on several Labour Party members of Parliament.

**Domestic Affairs.** The long-standing conflict between the Eurocommunist leadership and the Stalinist hard left minority continued to intensify in 1986. The party remained in an obvious crisis that has been building for some years. It centers on the dispute between the party's Executive Committee and its chief theoretical journal, *Marxism Today*, on one hand, and the *Morning Star* on the other. The *Morning Star*, although nationally recognized as the party's daily newspaper, is technically owned by the communist, but separate, People's Press Printing Society (PPPS). Throughout 1986 the PPPS continued to be in the hands of Stalinist opponents of the Executive Committee's Eurocommunist policies. The *Morning Star* group was bitterly opposed to the leadership's criticisms (muted though they were) of the Soviet Union and to the transformation of *Marxism Today* into a popular, broad-based magazine.

The course of intraparty conflict during 1986 occurred in the context of, and in reaction to, a series of defeats for the wider political left in Britain. The miner's strike, the Liverpool debacle, the newspaper conflict, and the struggle with the Thatcher government on a whole range of issues all went badly. As a result, the already fractured communist movement drifted into an even sharper debate within itself. Who was to blame for these defeats? How should they proceed to bolster the party's position, along with the position of the left? Should the party adopt a more cooperative relationship with the Labour Party and even parties to the right? How should it deal with the British union movement? The Eurocommunist majority in control of the CPGB tended, during the year, to take stronger positions in favor of developing broad alliances with less ideological left parties and groupings. In reaction, the *Morning Star* and its Communist Campaign Group, as well as the breakaway New Communist Party, charged that it was just such soft-headed thinking that had caused the movement to lose its leadership of the working class.

During 1986, such tactical disagreements, together with the development of intraparty disputes about public policy, joined with the long-running and increasingly acrimonious arguments about abstract ideological matters. On all sides within the communist movement bitter feelings, which had been running high for months, were inflamed by the CPGB's aggressive moves not only to expel dissident members but also to make it clear that it would not tolerate internal dissention and sniping. Before 1986, intraparty disagreements about public policy issues had remained relatively minor—for example, the CPGB, the Communist Campaign Group, and the New Communists all supported Arthur Scargill and his National Union of Mineworkers throughout the long strike. They mostly agreed on a clear, consistent denunciation of almost everything the Tory government and Mrs. Thatcher did, especially changes in industrial relations law.

All of this changed in 1986 as the CPGB began to address the political future and rethink its policy positions. Reviewing the defeats the left had suffered during the previous couple of years, the CPGB appeared to reach the conclusion that a share of the blame for these reversals could be placed on uncompromising, confrontational positions and behavior. Special scorn was heaped, not on itself for instransigence, but on the Communist Campaign Group, the New Communist Party, and the Trotskyite Militant Tendency, which had controlled the Liverpool government. Whereas the CPGB, for example, had been supportive of Arthur Scargill and the miners' strike, its new analysis focused on the mineworkers' destructive behavior. Scargill's refusal to allow strike ballots was denounced as a major error leading to defeat. Contrasting these "mistakes," the CPGB pointed to one of its own members, Mick McGahey, retiring vice president of the miners, as an example of a leader who understood the need to build and hold wider public support to better hold out against the Thatcher intrasigence.

This kind of criticism was made part of formal CPGB policy during March when the CPGB industrial organizer, Peter Carter, offered a new industrial policy for the CPGB Executive Committee's approval. Carter clearly pointed the finger of blame for the decline in union strength and for the succession of defeats at what he characterized as an alliance of enemies on the left. In particular, Carter mocked the alliance for operating on four principles: no compromise, no retreats, no sacrifice, and socialism as the answer. His report went on to argue that in great measure, Thatcherism had succeeded because there was no alternative approach. He suggested that unions should reorganize in order to better cope with the new era in union power and that the party should not continue to press for a return to traditional legal protections for industrial action. In taking this position, Carter, and thus the Executive Committee, were clearly exacerbating disagreement with the *Morning Star* and the New Communist Party, both of which continue to argue vehemently for a complete restoration of the structure of industrial relations as it was before the Tories came to power in 1979—that is, traditional British trade union immunity from the law.

The Carter report and its subsequent approval by the CPGB stirred a great number of predictably ugly exchanges in the various publications of the CPGB and of its opposition. It also fueled a new round of CPGB expulsions, and spurred on dissolution of several branches that had become dominated by Campaign Group opponents. Further conflict is likely as the next British election approaches. The CPGB is increasingly concerned about the possibility that the election will result in a "hung Parliament"—that no major party will hold a majority and a coalition government may be necessary— although it does clearly see opportunity in this possibility if the coalition includes the Labour Party and wants to position itself to have some kind of influence if there is no majority. At the same time, its intraparty opposition senses a sellout. The Communist Campaign Group and the New Communists fear that for the CPGB the price of such influence will be far too high in terms of both policy and ideology.

The CPGB continued to support demonstrations against most aspects of government policy. The party was among the leaders in militant demands and protests concerning the increasingly conflictual issue of unemployment in Great Britain. It continued to be an active supporter of the Committee for Nucelar Disarmament and vigorously opposed the implanting of cruise missiles in Britain. The CPGB also supports unilateral nuclear disarmament by the United Kingdom, an issue it presses on the Labour Party and Neil Kinnock at every opportunity. In 1986, this issue was coupled with strong opposition to the U.S. eagerness to encourage "Star Wars," which was just as vigorously opposed by the Soviet Union.

**Auxiliary Organizations.** In industry, CPGB activity centers on its approximately 200 workplace branches. Its umbrella organization is the LCDTU. Although the CPGB is riven by internal disputes, its trade union structure can still command considerable support from prominent trade union leaders.

The YCL, the youth wing of the party, has only about 500 members.

The party retains a number of financial interests including Central Books, Lawrence and Wishart Publisher, Farleigh Press, London Caledonian Printers, Rodell Properties, the Labour Research Department, and the Marx Memorial Library.

**International Views and Activities.** Although the CPGB leadership is regarded as revisionist by its own dissident hard-line faction, there are in fact few areas in which the CPGB stints in its support of the Soviet Union. The party is still critical of the Soviet invasion of Afghanistan and Czechoslovakia. Otherwise, the CPGB favors arms reduction talks with the USSR and opposes the deployment of cruise and Pershing missiles in Europe and the development of U.S. space weapons. The party campaigns for British withdrawal from NATO and the European Economic Community. It is critical of Israel and seeks to promote recognition of the Palestine Liberation Organization. In 1986, Gordon McLennan represented the CPGB at the Twenty-seventh Congress of the CPSU in Moscow.

**Other Marxist Groups.** Besides the CPGB, several small, mainly Trotskyist groups are also active. Although some of these groups were growing swiftly in the 1970s, their memberships are now waning. This is probably partly attributable to Labour Party adoption of left policies, which has encouraged extremists to join the Labour Party itself rather than some of the fringe revolutionary groups.

The most important of the Trotskyist groups is Militant Tendency, which derives its name from its paper of the same name. Militant Tendency claims to be merely a loose tendency of opinion within the Labour Party, but there is no doubt that it possesses its own distinctive organization and for some years has been pursuing a policy of "entryism" (the tactic of penetrating the larger, more moderate Labour Party). Militant Tendency controls about 50 Labour Party constituencies. In 1986, there were continuing signs of a split within Militant Tendency over the role of Liverpool deputy leader, Derek Hatton, who is a leader in the fight with the Thatcher government.

The other significant Trotskyist organizations are the Socialist Workers' Party (SWP) and the Workers' Revolutionary Party (WRP). The SWP has been particularly active in single-issue campaigns, notably the antiunemployment campaign. It gave active support to striking miners' families but, in fact, enjoys little support in the coal mining industry. The WRP's activities are more secretive but are known to center in the engineering, mining, theater, and auto industries. It focuses its attention on the young and has set up six Youth Training Centres, which are primarily concerned with recruitment.

Gerald Dorfman
*Hoover Institution*

# Greece

**Population.** 9,954,000
**Party.** Communist Party of Greece (Kommunistikon Komma Ellados; KKE)
**Founded.** 1921
**Membership.** 42,000 (estimated)
**General Secretary.** Kharilaos Florakis
**Politburo.** 8 full members: Kharilaos Florakis, Nikos Kaloudhis, Grigoris Farakos, Kostas Tsolakis, Dimitris Gondikas, Andonis Ambatielos, Loula Logara, Roula Kourkoulou; 6 candidate members: T. Mamatsis, Orestis Kolozof, Mimis Androulakis, Sp. Khalvaatzes, M. Kostopoulos, and Aleka Papariga
**Status.** Legal
**Last Congress.** Eleventh, 15–18 December 1982, in Athens
**Last Election.** 2 June 1985, 9.9 percent, 13 of 300 seats
**Auxiliary Organization.** Communist Youth of Greece (KNE)
**Publications.** *Rizospastis*, daily; *Kommunistiki Epitheorisi* (*KOMEP*), monthly theoretical review

After the spring of 1987, Greece will no longer have two parties using the title "communist." During its Fourth Congress in May 1986, the KKE-Interior decided to dissolve itself next spring and re-emerge as a new party of the Greek noncommunist left.

The official pro-Moscow KKE received 9.9 percent of the popular vote in the parliamentary election of 2 June 1985. In the municipal elections of October 1986 it showed greater strength, mostly due to the decline in popularity of the governing PASOK and the appeal of local candidates. The KKE continues to have strong influence in the trade unions.

**Leadership and Organization.** The KKE is organized along traditional communist party pat-terns, with cells in factories, other places of work, and the universities and with local organizations in city neighborhoods and villages. Major cities, such as Athens, Piraeus, and Salonika, have city committees, and major sections of the country have regional secretaries. The party also has branch organizations that operate within the labor unions and the Workers' Centers.

Statutorily, the party congress convenes every four years, but this rule has not been observed consistently. The last congress (the eleventh) convened in December 1982; the next is scheduled for May 1987. A Central Committee elected by the congress normally meets in plenary session once every six months. The actual decisionmaking power, however, resides with the Politburo. In addition to General Secretary Florakis, the most influential members are Ambatielos, Kaloudhis, Farakos, and Tsolakis, all of whom belong to the older generation. Gondikas and Androulakis are two younger members, in their thirties, whose influence is on the rise. One may expect that, at the May 1987 congress, some of the older leaders, including Florakis, may leave their posts to make room for younger individuals. The party's youth organization, KNE, is very active and has considerable influence in the universities and among young workers.

The KKE-Interior came into being during the military dictatorship (1967–1974), when the communist party split into two factions. It has gradually adopted a much less militant and dogmatic line than that of the KKE, and is now preparing to drop such traditional marks of communist identity as the commitment to Marxism-Leninism, proletarian internationalism, the hammer-and-sickle symbol, and democratic centralism, as well as the appellation "communist." The tentative name for the new party, which will emerge from a wide convention scheduled for spring 1987, is New Greek Left (NEA). The new party will seek to attract most of the leftist groups that are dissatisfied with the Panhellenic Socialist Movement (PASOK) but unwilling to join the traditional, pro-Moscow KKE. Currently the KKE-Interior is dominated by Leonidas Kyrkos, its general secretary.

**Views and Positions.** Since the beginning of the year, the KKE has been wrestling with the question of how to react to the austerity measures introduced by the PASOK government in October 1985. A strong, militant attack on the PASOK government could play into the hands of the conservative New Democracy Party (ND) and force an early election the PASOK might well lose. The KKE strongly opposes a return of the conservative right to power. On the other hand, if the KKE ignores the public discontent, it may lose its credibility as the champion of the downtrodden. The KKE employed a middle-of-the-road policy that centers on continuing criticism of the austerity measures, calling for closer cooperation between the PASOK and the other "progressive" forces on the assumption that the PASOK cannot implement the policy of "Change" alone, and making subtle efforts to attract to the party the leftist PASOK supporters who have been disillusioned by the government's policies. Writing in the *World Marxist Review* in September

1986, Florakis expressed the view that "the Greek society is now acutely in need of radical economic, social, and political transformations and this, for its part, produces the need to unify all the progressive forces . . . The KKE programme requires our constant pressure in the forward positions of every front of the class struggle, and consistent efforts to unify the forces in the direction leading to the confluence of several streams into a single anti-imperialist, anti-monopoly tide." The KKE's efforts to unify the left will compete with the parallel campaign of the new NEA.

During the year, the KKE focused much of its effort on improving its vote-gathering potential for the October municipal elections. During the first round of the election, KKE-supported candidates fared much better than their parliamentary candidates in the June 1985 election: KKE-supported candidates for mayor received 17.62 percent in Athens, 16.42 percent in Piraeus, 23.27 percent in Salonika, 22.19 percent in Irakleion, Crete (KKE and KKE-Interior), 31.27 percent in Larisa, and 15.70 percent in Patras (KKE and KKE-Interior).

During the second round, KKE voters joined PASOK voters to defeat ND candidates who had received a plurality, but not a majority, during the first round (election in the first round requires more than 50 percent of the vote to be in favor of a candidate). In three major cities—Athens, Piraeus, and Salonika—the KKE instructed its followers to refrain from supporting the PASOK candidates. One reason for this move, which resulted in election of ND mayoral candidates in all three cities, was the refusal of PASOK leader Prime Minister Andreas Papandreou to commit himself to enactment of a simple proportional electoral system for the next parliamentary election. Another was Papandreou's refusal to agree to any revision of the austerity economic program. The KKE's action was a convincing demonstration that the communist party plays a major political role and its views cannot be easily ignored.

Improvement of relations with the United States and with the European Common Market is another point on which the KKE conflicts with the governing PASOK. The PASOK's foreign policy remains ambivalent. Although Papandreou continues to take initiatives that appear favorable to basic Soviet policies, the earlier strong anti-American, anti-NATO, anti-EEC posturing has given way to more businesslike, even friendlier, relations. The major issue concerning the fate of the American military bases Papandreou continues to say will have to leave

Greece in 1989 is likely to be resolved in favor of retention. The KKE is adamant against this, at least on the surface.

Whatever its disagreements with the PASOK government, the KKE has important reasons to be pleased with Papandreou's domestic initiatives in the area of "national reconciliation" and with the leftist tilt in the content of the radio and TV programs in the government-run facilities. The process of "national reconciliation," which started timidly in 1974 with legalization of the KKE and has proceeded at a greater pace since the PASOK attained power in 1981, reached its highest point in the fall of 1986 on the anniversary of the Gorgopotamos—the destruction of the Gorgopotamos bridge in 1942 by a group of British commandos and guerrilla forces of the nationalist EDES and the procommunist ELAS. The presence at that ceremony of ND leader Mitsotakis gave formal sanction to the policy of national reconciliation, which in effect did away with any final after effects of the civil war. This means that the three armed attempts of KKE to seize power during the 1940s have been completely forgiven and forgotten and that the KKE can be a fully acceptable partner, even in a government coalition. The significance of this may become more than theoretical in the event the PASOK fails to gain a clear majority in Parliament at the next election and can remain in office only by forming a coalition government with KKE or by accepting the support of KKE parliamentary deputies.

Relations between Florakis and Papandreou remain good. Papandreou met with the KKE general secretary twice during the year—in June and again in October. (There have been no similar meetings between Papandreou and the ND leader, Mitsotakis.)

The KKE remains hostile to any improvement in the relations between Greece and the United States. During the visit of U.S. secretary of state George Shultz in March, the KKE Central Committee issued a statement saying "using pressure and extortion, he will attempt to guarantee the presence of the U.S. bases and the imposition of U.S.-NATO solutions for the Cyprus issue and Greek-Turkish differences." The KKE denounced the American action in the Gulf of Sydra in very strong terms at the time it took place. The PASOK's International Relations Committee also attacked the action: "The people of the Mediterranean region will not accept the imposition of a new pax-Americana through the use of arms"; the PASOK government itself, however, showed much greater restraint, another display of Papandreou's ambivalent and confusing foreign policies.

**Domestic Activities.** During the year, the KKE focused its attention on three major areas: opposition to the government's austerity measures, expansion of the party's influence in the trade unions and among leftist voters dissatisfied with the PASOK, and the campaign to elect KKE-supported mayoral candidates in the October municipal elections.

In March the party rejected overtures by Papandreou for a "dialogue." A KKE Central Committee statement termed the proposal "a maneuver designed to conceal the conservative trend in government policy, mislead voters in the light of the upcoming municipal election, and halt the leftist undercurrent and changes which have been observed within PASOK and, generally, blunting the people's growing opposition to the government."

In September the KNE held its annual youth festival, which was well organized and was attended by several delegations from foreign communist parties. In November, the KNE participated actively in the annual commemoration of the "Polytekhnion uprising," a student uprising in November 1973 against the military dictatorship. The communist left dominated the activities and used the occasion to attack the PASOK for its economic policies and its efforts to improve relations with the United States and the EEC.

For the KKE-Interior, the major event was the Fourth Congress, which met in late May. The congress decided, by a narrow majority, to dissolve itself and to organize in the spring of 1987 a new party of the left with no communist connections. Kyrkos was elected secretary (45 votes in favor, 35 blank, 2 against, and one void). The new party hopes to attract the leftist voters who are leaving the PASOK because of its "rightist" policies but are unwilling to join a communist party. A similar effort may be undertaken by Gerasimos Arsenis, the erstwhile economic czar of the first PASOK government, who was expelled from the PASOK during the year. Efforts to bring Kyrkos and Arsenis together have failed because of conflicting ambitions and because Arsenis opposes Greece's membership in the EEC whereas Kyrkos is in favor.

**International Contacts.** Florakis made several trips abroad during the year. In late February, a KKE delegation including Dimitris Gondikas and Mimis Androulakis (both Politburo members) went to Moscow to attend the CPSU congress—and, it was rumored, so that the Soviet leaders could meet them in the light of a possible succession of Florakis in 1987. It may be noted that a PASOK delegation led by Akis Tzokhatzopoulos, a possible successor to Papandreou, also attended the congress. In late March a KKE delegation headed by Florakis went to Sofia, Bulgaria, to attend the Thirteenth Congress of the Bulgarian Communist Party. In the middle of April, a KKE delegation went to East Germany to attend the Eleventh Congress of the Socialist Unity Party of Germany (SED); the PASOK also sent a delegation. In early June, a CPSU delegation that included CPSU Central Committee members Karl G. Vanyo and Valentin K. Mesyats traveled to Athens for talks with Florakis. On 9 July Kaloudhis, Tsolakis, and Kolozof met with a delegation from East Germanys' SED under Joachim Bohm. (It may be noted that PASOK leader Papandreou met in August in Athens with Politburo member and secretary of the SED Central Committee Hermann Axen.) On 4 August, Florakis left for Sofia where he met Bulgarian leader Todor Zhivkov. On his return, Florakis met with SED Politburo member and Central Committee secretary Joachim Herrmann to discuss peace issues. On 31 October, Florakis went to Moscow to meet with Gorbachev. On the way back from Moscow, Florakis met with Bulgarian Communist Party Politburo member and Central Committee secretary Chudomir Aleksandrov.

In May, on the occasion of the fourth congress, KKE-Interior's Kyrkos received a warm message from Romanian party leader Nicolae Ceauşescu and another from the League of Communists of Yugoslavia. On 25 August, Kyrkos sent a message to Ceauşescu to mark the 42d anniversary of "Romania's antifascist victory."

During the year, the KKE faced a special problem in relation to the atomic accident in Chernobyl. A special plenum of the Central Committee issued a statement saying that "the main aim of the anti-Soviet campaign launched by the mass media of the West is to play down the importance of the peaceful Soviet proposals for peaceful cooperation. The accident should be regarded as a lesson indicating the vital need for struggle for disarmament, for an end to nuclear testing, for withdrawal of nuclear arms and dismantling of foreign bases on the Greek territory." (The results of the October municipal elections indicate that the Chernobyl accident had no serious effect on the communist standing in Greece.)

**Other Marxist-Leninist Organizations.** In November a new party was organized by the Greek Internationalist Union-Trotskyists. It supports "revolutionary internationalism, an international socialist revolution, the overthrow of the PASOK government and the establishing in Greece, too, of the dictatorship of the proleteriat." Its first congress elected Savvas Mikhail as general secretary. This is likely to be a marginal grouping with minimal political impact. Other groups with little political significance include the Revolutionary Communist Party of Greece, the Communist Internationalists of Greece, the Communist Marxist-Leninists, the Revolutionary Peoples' Struggle, and the "17 November," the latter two of which often engage in terrorist activities, mostly in the Athens area.

D. G. Kousoulas
*Howard University*

# Iceland

**Population.** 244,000
**Party.** People's Alliance (Althydubandalagid; PA)
**Founded.** 1968
**Membership.** 3,000 (estimated)
**Chairman.** Svavar Gestsson
**Executive Committee.** 14 members: Svavar Gestsson, Kristin Olafsdottir (deputy chair), Ludvik Josephsson, Helgi Gudmundsson (secretary), Margret Frimannsdottir (treasurer), Olafur Ragnar Grimsson (Executive Committee chair), Alfheidur Ingadottir, Asmundir Stefansson, Gudrun Agustdottir, Hansina Steffansdottir, Johannes Gunnarson, Sigrun Clausen, Sigurjon Petursson, Ossur Skarphedinsson (*Morgunbladid*, 12 November 1985)
**Central Committee.** 70 members, 20 deputies
**Status.** Legal
**Last Congress.** 7–10 November 1985
**Last Election.** 1983, 17.3 percent, 10 of 60 seats
**Auxiliary Organizations.** Organization of Base Opponents (OBO; organizer of peace demonstrations against U.S.-NATO bases)
**Publications.** *Thjodviljinn* (daily), Reykjavik; *Verkamadhurinn* (weekly), Akureyri; *Mjolnir* (weekly), Siglufjördhur

For the peaceful island republic of Iceland, 1986 was a dramatic political year. A major U.S.-Soviet summit conference (with only ten days advance notice) focused the global spotlight on the country to a degree unprecedented in its history. Record economic growth, subdued inflation, and spectacular sabotage by foreign environmental activists also made the year memorable. Iceland's half dozen political parties had no lack of opportunity to flex their political muscles. Local elections in the late spring were seen as a dress rehearsal for the general election that must be held by the spring of 1987.

The PA occupies the left flank of Icelandic politics. It is the successor to a line of leftist parties dating back to 1930, when the Icelandic Communist Party (Kommunistaflokkur Islands) was established by a left-wing splinter from the Labor Party. In 1938, the Social Democratic Party (SDP) splintered from the Labor Party and joined with the communists to create a new party, the United People's Party–Socialist Party (Sameiningar flokkur althydu–Sosialista flokkurinn; UPP-SP). Although its ideology was based on "scientific socialism–Marxism," the UPP-SP had no organizational ties to Moscow. Its first goal was support for complete Icelandic independence from Denmark. By the time this was achieved in 1944, the UPP-SP had participated in governing coalitions and was accepted as a responsible democratic leftist party. In 1956, the UPP-SP formed an electoral alliance with other small leftist and neutralist groups, and the coalition became known as the People's Alliance (PA). In 1968, the UPP-SP dissolved itself into the PA, which then became what is the current pragmatic Marxist party. It has participated regularly in coalition governments, most recently joining the Progressive Party (PP; agrarian liberal) in a coalition headed by the late maverick Gunnar Thoroddsen, formerly of the Independence (moderate-conservative) Party (IP). Several other IP members followed Thoroddsen. The Thoroddsen government resigned following the April 1983 parliamentary election, which had resulted in losses for all of the constituent parties. The PA held three cabinet posts: social and health affairs (Gestsson), finance (Ragnar Arnalds), and industry (Hjorleifur Guttormsson). It is now the largest opposition party.

The PA's 1983 electoral setback stemmed from the severe economic recession of 1981–1983 combined with hyperinflation, which had reached an unprecedented 159 percent annual rate at the time of the elections. In May 1983 Progressive Steingrimur Hermansson formed a new majority coalition government of the Progressive and Independence parties. That government enjoys a substantial parliamentary majority: 37 out of 60 seats.

Several years of severe austerity followed. The inflation rate declined throughout 1984, but so did real income. Suddenly labor unrest erupted, and the government's income policy collapsed. Trade imbalances and rising unemployment delayed recovery, but by late 1985 the economic picture began to brighten. Predictably the government's popularity has followed the sudden swings of the national economy. The PA has not gained greatly from the dissatisfaction, although it has regained some of the support lost since 1983. Of the four parties now comprising the opposition, the reformist SDP and the Women's Party (Samtok um kvennalista; WP) experienced notable gains. Jon Baldvin Hannibalsson, the dynamic new leader of the SDP, continues to attract broad public support. Local elections in May and June 1986, as well as incomplete public opinion polls, indicate that the SDP is ahead of where it was in 1983, but no longer as far ahead as it was in 1985. The governing IP and PP also lost ground, as did the small Social Democratic Alliance (Bandalag jafnadarmanna; SDA), which essentially collapsed as a viable party in 1986. The WP did reasonably well in the polls but less so in the local elections, both of which measures provide little certainty as Iceland enters an election year.

Iceland's economy is as changeable as its weather; in 1986 both were more pleasant than usual. It was a remarkable economic year: GNP increased by 5 percent (a historic high and second only to Turkey in the Organization for Economic Cooperation and Development); inflation fell to 10 percent; and unemployment, always remarkably low, disappeared. This outstanding performance was the result of strong demand for Icelandic fish products in Europe and the United States (as the Icelandic krona followed the U.S. dollar down in relation to most European currencies), the dramatic fall in the price of petroleum (Iceland must import

all it uses), and domestic economic restraint (wages, prices, and government fiscal policy (*Economist*, 10 January 1987; Central Bank of Iceland, *Economic Statistics Quarterly*, November). All was not roses, however. The bankruptcy of Hafskip Shipping threatened the solvency of the government-owned Fisheries Bank, which in turn affected the political status of both the cabinet and parliament, with their overlapping responsibilities for supervising banking. Disputes with the United States concerning economic, environmental, and foreign policy issues provided additional domestic political excitement.

**Leadership and Organization.** The PA's strong showing in the May local elections reduced some of the internal discontent that has plagued the party continuously since 1983. At the November 1985 PA annual conference, there was substantial criticism of Gestsson's leadership. Some blamed this on personality clashes between Gestsson and Asmundur Stefansson, chair of the powerful Icelandic Federation of Labor (ASI). These clashes continued in 1986, in particular over the composition of the party.

Not all of the PA's energies are directed toward personality struggles. The party has debated extensively both internal organization and external political strategy as leadership sought to respond to criticisms that the party is too introspective and dominated by an aging clique. The PA has never followed the Leninist organizational model, and leadership is divided among several independent and assertive personalities. Hence the public bickering is a sign of a relatively open, pluralistic, and lively party. Gestsson, who received 88 percent of the vote in his re-election as party chair, represents the party's "intellectual" faction. Composition of the Executive Committee, as well as the parliamentary group, reflects all of the significant party factions. It is notable that labor union activists increased their strength on the committee (*JPRS*, 12 November 1985, 7 January).

**Domestic Affairs.** Economic affairs dominate Icelandic politics. The PA generally speaks for the urban wage earner, but by no means does it dominate the labor union movement. Although PA groups are often the largest, Iceland's unions have strong factions that are loyal to the moderately conservative IP. There are signs that the revived SDP is making inroads in some unions. Periodic collective bargaining negotiations have a strong influence on the nation's economy and affect most employees. The government played an active role in leading these negotiations to a successful conclusion in February. Wages were scheduled to rise by a total of 13.6 percent in a series of steps throughout 1986, and the government promised tight fiscal policies aiming at lower inflation and interest rates and a stable currency. The timely, moderate agreement reflects the pragmatism of current labor leadership. The same forces and personalities within the PA are increasing their hold on the party leadership, but more ideological and radical groups around Chair Gestsson dominate the PA parliamentary group (*News from Iceland*, March). A major tax reform shifted the burden from income taxes and import duties to general sales taxes. The PA joined the broad parliamentary consensus favoring these reforms, but Gestsson used the labor agreements to fire a broadside at the government. The agreement between labor and management with the government as mere participant showed a lack of political leadership. Such "corporatist" tripartite agreements are not unprecedented in Iceland. When the government quickly ended a dairy strike in March, however, Gestsson criticized the intervention. In May the government ended a shipping strike to protect Icelandic trade and enforce the wage consensus (*Nordisk Kontakt*, nos. 3, 5, 6, and 9).

Success on the labor front, coupled with an accelerating economy, increased the center-right government's popularity as local elections approached. One poll indicated greater support for the government as a whole (63.7 percent) than for its constituent (Progressive and Independence) parties. The elections themselves produced few surprises. The IP maintained its stronghold in Reykjavik, while the PP lost ground generally. The SDP gained substantially, as compared with the elections of 1982 and 1983, but no longer seems to be riding the crest of a wave of popularity. The PA made gains but failed to recover what had been lost since 1983; their advance came in large part from the leftist WP (*Morgun-bladid*, 3 June; *JPRS*, 19 August).

The PA's long-term domestic program has stressed economic nationalism and Icelandic control of major industries and resources. The party has been especially suspicious of the large, Swiss-owned aluminum works that relies on cheap Icelandic hydroelectric power. The PA supports governmental regulation of the fishing industry including firm catch quotas, which were revised at the end of 1985. These quotas were instituted to stop overfish-

ing, which threatened this vital resource in the 1970s (*Nordisk Kontakt*, no. 16, 1985).

Other than calling for a "study leave" financed by a national fund and available to all employees, the PA announced no new domestic program goals in 1986. Continued criticism of the labor movement's moderation has not yet strengthened the party's standing. The nation's economy cannot maintain its 1986 pace, and the moderate wage settlements expire at the end of the year. Early forecasts predict a 2.7 percent growth in 1987, but the PA has not found a political profile that can deflate the rise of the SDP. Encouraged that its decline has at last stopped, the PA must pin its hopes on forthcoming parliamentary elections to maintain its position as the country's largest party on the left.

**Foreign Affairs.** Three issues consistently dominated Icelandic foreign policy discussions: the NATO bases at Keflavik and elsewhere on the island, trade relations with its principal export markets, and national economic control of resources on shore and in adjacent waters. The first issue has traditionally been the main source of controversy, but events in 1986 suggest that internal security and environmental policy will now be more closely scrutinized. Without the related issues of the Keflavik bases and NATO membership, it is unlikely that the PA would be the force it has been in Icelandic politics during the past 35 years. By participating in several governing coalitions over the decades, it has sought first to eliminate and later to modify the terms of Icelandic NATO membership. In 1978 it joined a coalition without making elimination of the bases a precondition and then later sought the right to veto any plans for changing their status. Gradually the Icelandic role in staffing and maintaining defense facilities has increased. To the chagrin of base opponents, the bases have significant economic importance to the country, both as communications infrastructure and as employers of more than 1,000 Icelanders. Polls on the defense question in 1983 indicated that 80 percent of the public supported NATO membership and 64 percent favored U.S.-Icelandic defense agreements (Bjorn Bjarnason, "General Consensus Emerges on Western Defense Interests," *News from Iceland*, May 1985).

Iceland maintains no armed forces as such (its coast guard is lightly armed), and 3,000 American troops at Keflavik and elsewhere provide the country's defense force (confusingly referred to as the Icelandic Defense Force). As a member of NATO, however, Iceland does participate in the alliance's political processes. In 1985 a new division of Defense Affairs was established within the Foreign Ministry to deal with security matters and sit on NATO's military committee.

Recognizing the depth of public support for current defense arrangements, the PA has recently tried to separate NATO membership from the bases issue. Even within the PA, some commentators have admitted that, given Soviet naval expansion, it is necessary to maintain a European balance of power, a need that increases the importance of the bases. The PA has turned more directly to issues popular among leftist forces in Europe and the Nordic countries: removal of nuclear weapons from Europe's NATO arsenal and the establishment of regional nuclear-free zones. The latter issue is attractive to the PA both substantively and because it has been a source of internal strife between the IP and the PP in the governing coalition. A new IP foreign minister, Matthias Mathiesen, replaced Geir Hallgrimsson in January, but no change was expected in the government's foreign or security policies. (*News from Iceland*, January.)

Progress was made in two areas of Iceland-U.S. antagonism that had provided the PA grist for its foreign policy mill. In 1984 Icelanders lost lucrative freight contracts to supply the U.S. forces, when a new American concern, Rainbow Navigation, invoked the obscure Cargo Preference Act of 1904, which gives American ships preference in carrying American defense goods. Aware that economic advantages smooth the way for the NATO bases, the U.S. Defense Department sought to return the business to Icelandic ships. In retaliation, Icelanders invoked their own protectionist legislation banning importation of fresh meat. A new treaty dividing the defense freight business between American and Icelandic carriers was signed in 1986 and quickly ratified by the U.S. Senate on the eve of the October summit meeting (*Nordisk Kontakt*, no. 15).

The other irritant involved threatened American sanctions against Icelandic fish imports (the U.S. is Iceland's largest export market) if Iceland continued to export whale meat. Under international agreements, Iceland is allowed to catch a small quota of whales for "scientific purposes" (mainly to determine whether continued whaling threatens certain species). Environmental activists seeking to end all whaling forced the U.S. government to threaten sanctions. All Icelandic parties supported the government's anger at what seemed a heavy-handed

move, but domestic legislation had forced the American government to act. A compromise was worked out, whereby at least half of the whale meat would be consumed in Iceland. The PA objected to the American tactics but supported the agreement. The SDP's Hannibalsson suggested that the new surplus of whale meat could be consumed at the Keflavik base, calling it healthier than hamburgers (ibid., no. 12–13).

Icelanders were again required to consider the whaling issue when in November an extremist foreign environmental group, Sea Shepard, sabotaged two whaling ships and a whale processing plant. The PA joined other parties in condemning the attacks but urged calm. The SDP stressed the need to find appropriate responses to international terrorism even in a small and previously isolated country like Iceland (ibid., no. 16).

Passions were also aroused in Iceland in the wake of the American air strikes against Libya in April. Although they condemned the provocations for the attack, Icelanders did not feel that the American response was justified or useful. The PA parliamentary spokesperson during the discussion, Steingrimur J. Sigfusson, used the occasion to make an intemperate attack on Iceland's association with the United States, urging isolation of the U.S. forces on the island as much as possible from the country's people and economy and denouncing the Americans as "vermin" (ibid. no. 9). Such extreme sentiments scarcely represent either Iceland in general or the PA in particular, but they do illustrate both the passion and xenophobia that often surfaces in foreign and security policy debates.

**International Party Contacts.** The PA and its predecessors have always remained aloof from the international communist movement. It has tended to identify more closely with democratic socialist parties, particularly those with strong leftist and pacifist positions. It interacts informally, but regularly, with the Socialist Left Party of Norway and the Socialist People's Party of Denmark. The annual sessions and regular meetings of its numerous committees of the interparliamentary Nordic Council provide such opportunities. In the past the PA has looked at such parties and the Italian Communist Party (PCI) as foreign allies. Recently SDP leader Hannibalsson contrasted the rigid and often xenophobic PA foreign and security policies with the growing pragmatism of other foreign left-socialist parties, such as the PCI and elements in the

Danish Left-Socialists (VS) (*Nordisk Kontakt*, no. 9).

**Other Marxist and Leftist Groups.** Icelandic communism has always been pluralistic, and the PA continues that tradition. Hence the country has had relatively few small Marxist sects which are common in most other Western countries. Nevertheless, there have been some, most notably a Maoist group—the Communist Union—formed in 1971. It peaked at 200 members and contained Trotskyist elements who had been active earlier. It went through numerous schisms and name changes and finally disbanded in 1985 (*News from Iceland*, May 1985).

The small SDA, a splinter from the SDP in the early 1980s, failed to capitalize on its parliamentary position (4 seats and 7.3 percent of the vote in 1983) following the untimely death of one of its leaders. The SDA's final party congress in December 1985 revised the party program, calling for direct election of the premier, equality between rural and urban parliamentary constituencies, and the use of referendums. In October SDA leaders and members of parliament (MPs) disbanded their party. Three MPs joined the SDP; one went to the IP. Several outside party activists denounced the desertion and urged that the SDA seats be made available to others remaining loyal to the party, a request rejected by the Althing president. The SDP would be the main beneficiary if, as seems likely, the SDA disappears and if former SDA voters follow their leaders (*Helgarposturinn*, 12 December 1985: *JPRS*, 23 April).

Iceland approaches its next parliamentary election with an unusual number of political uncertainties. Economic performance cannot be maintained at the 1986 pace; will a more "normal" rate frustrate wage earners seeking to make up for the living standard decline of the early 1980s? Iceland's brief, but dramatic, experience as summit conference host gave both the country and the government a genuine boost in prestige, but the actions of environmental extremists have disturbed the smug sense of isolation from the world's political problems that has traditionally shaped Icelandic foreign and security policy discussions. More important for the parliamentary elections is the volatility of nearly all political parties. The Independence Party remains the country's largest and stands to gain from electoral district reform (reducing the overrepresentation of rural districts). The Progressives have found their agricultural and fishing interests difficult to promote while holding government office and reforming national economic policies. Personality conflicts between the IP and PP, reflecting in part Iceland's intensely personalistic political culture, can reduce confidence in the coalition's future effectiveness.

The left's uncertainties are even greater. The dramatic surge of support for the SDP has come in large part at the expense of other parties of the left, especially the PA. The collapse of the SDA may sustain the SDP advance, but it could reintroduce factionalism into the SDP. The PA has checked its decline and restored some order to party internal affairs. It has not succeeded in shaping either a domestic or foreign policy profile that offers the voter a positive alternative—other than the opportunity to change governments. It gained nothing from the decline of the SDA. Its competition comes primarily from the WP, itself a phenomenon unique to Icelandic politics. The PA must clearly do more to win and hold support from political feminists if it is to undercut the WP alternative.

Eric S. Einhorn
*University of Massachusetts at Amherst*

# Ireland

**Population.** 3,624,000
**Party.** Communist Party of Ireland (CPI)
**Founded.** 1933 (date of record)
**Membership.** 500 (estimated)
**General Secretary.** James Stewart
**National Political Committee.** Includes Michael O'Riordan (chairman), Andrew Barr, Sean Nolan, Tom Redmond, Edwina Stewart, Eddie Glackin
**Status.** Legal
**Last Congress.** Nineteenth. 31 January–2 February 1986, in Dublin
**Last Election.** 1982, no representation
**Auxiliary Organizations.** Connelly Youth Movement
**Publications.** *Irish Socialist*, *Irish Workers' Voice*, *Unity*, *Irish Bulletin*

The CPI was founded in 1921, when the Socialist Party of Ireland expelled moderates and decided to join the Comintern. During the Civil War, the party became largely irrelevant and virtually disappeared, although very small communist cells remained intact. The CPI was refounded in June 1933, the date the communists now adopt as the founding date of their party.

The party organization was badly disrupted during World War II because of the neutrality of the South and the belligerent status of the North. In 1948, the communists in the South founded the Irish Workers' Party and those in the North the Communist Party of Northern Ireland. At a specially convened "unity congress" held in Belfast on 15 March 1970, the two groups reunited.

The CPI is a recognized political party on both sides of the border and contests both local and national elections. It has, however, no significant support and no elected representatives.

**Leadership and Organization.** The CPI is divided into two geographical branches, north and south, corresponding to the political division of the country. In theory, the Congress is the supreme constitutional authority of the party, but in practice it tends to serve as a rubber stamp for the national executive. The innermost controlling conclave is the National Political Committee. Such little support as the CPI enjoys tends to be based in Dublin and Belfast.

**Domestic Affairs.** The continuing political division of the country remained the main issue in 1986. The CPI views the United Kingdom as an imperialist power that gains economically from holding Ireland in a subordinate position. While continuing to advocate the creation of a single, united socialist Ireland, the party remains opposed to the use of violence and denounces the use of force by armed gangs on either side of the communal divide. For example, it was particularly vehement in its denunciation of the Provisional Irish Republican Army's bombing of the Grand Hotel in Brighton in 1984, which nearly killed several members of the British Cabinet including Prime Minister Margaret Thatcher.

The party believes Irish unification can be achieved only through bodies promoting working-class solidarity and thus overcoming the communal divide between Protestants and Catholics. Executive Committee member Morrissey put the CPI view succinctly: "As long as the working class is divided along religious or other lines, the exploiting classes will dominate the political stage and Ireland will remain subordinate to imperialism."

The Nineteenth Congress of the CPI, the first since 1982, met during late January and early February 1986. The delegates devoted the majority of their time to the problem of the North. They strongly denounced the recently concluded Anglo-Irish agreement, demanding that Britain immediately declare a fixed date by which it would withdraw its political, administrative, and military presence. Additionally, they declared their support for establishment of a devolved Assembly for the North during the transition to a united socialist Ireland. This assembly should have broad political and social powers, sufficient to radically restructure the state, and these powers should be accompanied by a strong Bill of Rights. Interestingly, the delegates also urged that, as a united socialist Ireland is established, it adopt the more liberal North Irish laws on divorce and abortion to replace what it described as the backward prohibitions existing in the South.

**International Views and Activities.** The CPI is quite untouched by the phenomenon of Eurocommunism and remains staunchly pro-Soviet. Indeed, in a country where there are several larger Marxist groups in operation, the distinctive feature of CPI attitudes is perhaps, simple pro-Sovietism. The party is strongly anti-American and denounces U.S. policy in Central America, the Middle East, and elsewhere. It favors arms-reduction talks in Europe and opposes the deployment of cruise and Pershing missiles and President Reagan's Strategic Defense Initiative.

The party also remains hostile to the European Economic Community, which it regards as a device for drawing Ireland into NATO planning.

Gerald Dorfman
*Hoover Institution*

# Italy

**Population.** 57,226,000
**Party.** Italian Communist Party (Partito Communista Italiano; PCI)
**Founded.** 1921
**Membership.** 1,595,739 (*Pravda*, 26 April)
**General Secretary.** Alessandro Natta. Heir apparent: Achille Occhetto
**Secretariat.** 9 members: Alessandro Natta, Alfredo Reichlin, Aldo Tortorella, Gavino Angius, Giuseppe A. Chiarante, Massima d'Alema, Giorgio Napolitano, Achille Ochetto, Livia Turco (*L'Unitá*, 24 April)
**Directorate.** 39 members
**Central Auditing Board.** 6 members
**Central Control Commission.** 61 members
**Central Committee.** 219 members
**Status.** Legal
**Last Congress.** Seventeenth (first special Congress since World War II); 9–13 April 1986, in Florence
**Last Election.** 1983, 29.9 percent, 198 seats in the 630-seat lower house and 107 of 315 seats in the Senate; election for regional and local offices, May 1985: regional offices, 30.2 percent (down from 31.5 percent in 1980) and local offices, 29.9 percent (down from 31.5 percent in 1980)

**Auxiliary Organizations.** Italian Communist Youth Federation (FGCI), Italian General Confederation of Labor (CGIL), National League of Cooperatives (INC), and the Gramsci Institute, a think-tank.

**Publications.** *L'Unità* (official daily), *Rinascita* (weekly), *Critica Marxista* (theoretical journal), *Politica ed Economia, Riforma della Scuola, Democrazia e Diritto, Donna e Politica, Studi Storici, Nuova Rivista Internazionale*; the party also runs a publishing house for books, Editori Riuniti.

In 1921, the Italian Socialist Party (PSI), which had recently lost a nationalist faction headed by Benito Mussolini, lost another faction headed by Antonio Growsci, Amedeo Bodriga, and Palmiro Togliatti. Mussolini's group became the Fascist Party that ruled Italy between 1922 and 1943, while the second group became the PCI and affiliated itself with the Third International. In the 1930s, Togliatti was a high official of the Comintern, whence he became general secretary of the PCI. Between 1924 and 1944, both the PSI and the PCI were cut off from sources of domestic support and lived in exile in France. Because the PCI was willing to share the support it received from the Comintern, the PSI became dependent on it and became a "brother Party" in the Third International. Thus, from 1944 until roughly 1979, the PCI was able in a variety of ways to direct not only its own militants, members of Parliament, union organizers, municipal officials, and the like but also many of those of the PSI. Between 1960 and 1979 the PSI helped the PCI to press one message upon Italy: "The people" will do whatever is necessary, including violence, to make the country ungovernable until the PCI is allowed to become a member of a national coalition government with a program of which it approves. Between 1975 and 1978, this strategy of forcing Italy's largest party, the Christian Democrats, to make a "historic compromise" with the PCI seemed to be working. But the 1978 murder of former prime minister Aldo Moro at the hands of the Red Brigades totally delegitimized threats of violence in Italian political life, and the PCI, distancing itself from such threats, lost its unique lever in interparty maneuvering. Meanwhile, under the leadership of Bettino Craxi the PSI, culminating a long process, suddenly ceased paying attention to that sector of its apparatus that remained tied to the PCI and ceased demanding the PCI's admission to the government coalition as part of the price for its own participation. The PSI also attacked the Soviet Union for its suppression of civil liberties and its aggression abroad and forced the PCI to choose between hurting itself defending such unpopular things and publicly castigating the source of communist legitimacy, the Soviet Union. At the same time, Socialists in the trade unions joined rank-and-file disaffection

with the communists' policy of industrial confrontation. Finally, in the mid-1980s, Socialists began to leave communist-dominated local government coalitions in large numbers. In 1985, despite its best attempts to change its image and its willingness to pay any price to lure the PSI back into the fold, the PCI found itself isolated, with its vote in local elections shrinking and with no prospects on the horizon for doing better. It thus called its first extraordinary congress, for April 1986.

**Leadership and Organization.** The PCI is organized into some 10,000 grass-roots sections, based on both municipality (or neighborhood) and workplaces. These send delegates to 94 provincial and 20 regional federations, which in turn send delegates to quadrennial congresses to elect a Central Committee, Directorate, and so forth, empowered to transact the party's business between congresses. Party headquarters also includes sixteen "working commissions" that are obviously shadow ministries headed by the party's leading personages. Like ministries, each of these working commissions tends to become part of its chief's power base within the party. This is especially true of the Regional and Local Government Commission, long held by Armando Cossutta and now by Gianni Pellicani, and of the Labor Commission currently held by Antonio Bassolino. In fact, the PCI's leadership is selected from the top down. This is most clearly evident in the organizations that are not nominally part of the party—a vast network of businesses, including radio and TV stations and organizations of lawyers, veterans, and the like, but chiefly the CGIL, the country's largest labor confederation.

To emphasize the "autonomy" of such organizations, and to argue that the communist militants within them are not mere agents of the Secretariat, their leaders no longer appear on the PCI's leadership masthead. Hence, in 1986 Luciano Lama, longtime secretary of the CGIL, finally received the party's permission to leave his post, following which he became a member of the PCI's Directorate. His replacement, Pizzinato, is the first man in his position to be nominally only a communist "militant" and not officially part of the party's leadership. Nevertheless, there is no doubt that Pizzinato was chosen for his post, not by the union's membership, but by the PCI leadership.

The essence of the party's approach to the control of leadership functions within the party and the "mass organizations" is to try to have its cake and eat it too. "Leadership functions must not overlap with the apparatus. . . Since we are in favor of transcending the rigid forms of incompatibility with the Party's leadership bodies, and pending the trade unions' and other mass organizations' autonomous definition of stances in this connection, forums should be identified within which it is possible to involve these comrades in the Party's life, with an invitation to attend leadership bodies' meetings and to be represented on standing committees" (Document on Party Organizational Reforms, *L'Unità*, 14 April).

The PCI is the very definition of a "mass party." Membership may be obtained without ideological tests or trials of obedience. Individual members may express whatever views they wish without fear of expulsion. The party advertises the diversity of opinion within its ranks. However, members are not free to join with others within the party to promote views, candidates, or actions at variance with the decisions of the Secretariat. The PCI's most recent statement on the subject was succinct. "Internal democratic life must be characterized by an expansion of dialogue and the rejection of monolithism and conformism, though without jeopardizing the Party's unitary nature. The rejection of currents [that is, the factions that exist in all other Italian parties] was therefore confirmed." (Ibid.) Maintaining iron unity and diversity at the same time requires, according to Natta, being "able continuously to invent new forms of organization" (ibid., 10 April). He stated clearly: "We reject Stalinist-type centralism, the conception of the Party as the supreme organization, but we also reject more modern and softer forms of absolute centralisms" (ibid.). On the other hand, he said just as clearly that the party must "more forcefully reassert the need for complete unity in the implementation of unanimous or majority decisions" (ibid.).

In practice, during 1986 this meant expressing concern for the difficulty of controlling the people the PCI considers its biggest conquest in recent years, people the party describes as the "members who have participated, and still participate, in the movements characteristic of our time—movements for Women's Liberation, movements for the emancipation of oppressed peoples, and pacifist and en-

vironmental movements" (ibid., 10 April). The party's task "is first and foremost to impart positive specificity to spontaneous condemnation and protest" (ibid.). This, rather than reining in any group embodying "conservative nostalgia," is the party's chief organizational worry.

Nevertheless, the major case of disciplining in 1986 involved Cossutta, precisely the man widely reputed to be the closest to the Soviet leadership. For the first time in the PCI's history, someone of Cossutta's rank brought a disagreement with the party to the floor of the party congress. He proposed that the congress thesis say "Communists work for the transcending of capitalism." The leadership answered that "the idea of the transcending of capitalism is made absolutely clear in the thesis, but that Cossutta's amendment embodied an element which exceeded the Party's immediate tasks and which conflicts with the view of socialism as a process." (Ibid., 9 December 1985.) Cossutta lost and was dropped from the Directorate, even though it was expanded from 33 to 39 members.

The published rules for the party congress (ibid. 12 January) are the best contemporary manual for how the PCI is supposed to work. The Central Committee and the Central Control Commission proposed a set of theses that the cells, sections, and federations in turn would debate and modify. The cells and sections would elect "for the organization and direction of their own work, a Presidium, policy committee, electoral committee, and credentials committee (the latter only for section congresses with delegates)." The federation congresses would elect a policy committee, electoral committee, and credentials committee. They would elect the federal leadership organs and the delegates to the national congress, as well as vote to amend the Central Committee thesis. Of those elected, "the majority. . . should be comrades involved in productive life." There had to be "proportional representation of young, middle-aged, and older comrades, and at least 25 percent had to be women. In addition, leadership organs throughout the party had to be increased in size by between 20 and 25 percent. (Ibid.)

On March 8, *L'Unità* published a letter by five members of the Central Committee in which they protested the procedures leading up to the congress because they claimed, although the party was proposing a domestic strategy it labeled "leftist alternative," which it said was different from the former strategy of "government by program," the distinction was so cloudy as to cause "widespread uncertainty, and, at times, disorientation." Second, the prevalence of fuzzy formulations was causing the precongress debate to swirl around unimportant points rather than focus on the party line. Finally, leaks about the preselection of the party central organs to be formally elected at the forthcoming congress were discrediting the process. The letter asked for a special meeting of the Central Committee to discuss the changes. On behalf of the Secretariat, Giorgio Napolitano rejected the request, stating in part that "rumors of future reshuffling of the leadership... are totally devoid of truth... This task falls within the jurisdiction of the Congress, and no one else's." (Ibid., 8 March.)

Whatever else the PCI's leadership sought to do via the Seventeenth Congress, it clearly meant to evoke a major media event. Indeed, the congress spawned stories concerning the party's future and gave an appearance of movement and vitality badly needed to counter precisely the opposite tendencies in the party. Another outcome of the thinking that brought about the congress was the reshaping of the party's flagship publications, the daily *L'Unità* and the weekly *Rinascita*, to look less like communist party organs and more like papers the general reader would want to pick up. In sum, the congress sought to give the impression that the PCI is "a modern reformist party" and "an integral part of the European left" (*Rinascita*, 3 May).

What, then, does it mean to be a communist in Italy? The leftist *La Repubblica* conducted a series of friendly interviews with PCI militants around the country and gathered the following images: "Produce, accumulate, and reinvest, also in services." "Good sentiments, good sense, moral commitment, production, accumulation, national redistribution, intelligent guidance of this world, and no longer the bulldozer of another era... Little matter what is its correct name, today this is the substance of Communism in Italy." "Effort toward mediation and correctness, more development and less ideology, more dialogue and fewer shutdowns. Yes, it is true: What we want, that is, more production within social justices, is also wanted by other social forces. One does not have to be a Communist. However, we Communists want to more strongly and better, that is the difference" (*La Repubblica*, 8 January.) That is precisely the tone set by Natta at the Seventeenth Party Congress: sweeping moderate generalities punctuated by pregnant references to a refusal of "interchangeability of values" and to "the values around which the struggle of the workers' movement has grown up and which are the outcome not

only of a spontaneous feeling, but of a lengthy cultural endeavor" (*L'Unità*, 10 April).

**Domestic Views and Activities.** "You are isolated, Mr. Natta," began an interview intended to explain why the PCI seems to be moving farther and farther away from power (*La Repubblica*, 6 September). Natta conceded that the fundamental reason for the PCI's continuing alienation is that people are afraid of the communists, although "nobody with any sense talks any longer about the PCI as it was talked about 20 or even 10 years ago." This fear will cease, as will the perception that the PCI is incompatible with "Italy's strongest ally," said Natta. Furthermore, "Isolated is an unsuitable word for a party that enjoys the support of one-third of the electorate." (Ibid.)

Trying to get out of isolation is what the PCI was about in 1986. Its primary and immediate problem—the focus of its strategy of "leftist alternative"—is the PSI. The PCI's line is that the PSI is coming around: "In fact, there has been a reappraisal within the Socialist Party's cultural area and within the ranks of its majority and minority... There have been some instances of direct dialogue between the two parties, significant joint cultural initiatives have been taken, and there have been convergences on important aspects of Italy's international stance and on a number of serious issues submitted to parliament as well as on assessments of matters outside the government's sphere of responsibility. The dialogue between Communists and Socialists has been, and still is, significant within the trade union movement and their cooperation in the local administrations where their alliance has been renewed." (*L'Unità*, 10 April.)

The PCI's "cultural" approach to the Socialists consists of reminding them at every possible turn that they are giving up any "moral" basis for their activities and turning into seekers of office for its own sake (ibid.). The silent premise of this is that only "scientific socialism" can provide such a basis. It is difficult to judge how successful this approach was in 1986. In foreign policy, the Socialists joined the PCI in condemning American actions in the Middle East. Also, the Socialist Party proved far less friendly to the U.S. government's abstract talk of antimissile defenses than it had to concrete U.S. proposals for stationing offensive missiles on Italian soil. Domestically, the PCI had fewer reasons to be happy with the Socialists. The major reason has been the historic turning of a significant portion of the PSI away from high technology and nuclear power toward attitudes similar to those of Germany's Greens. Thus, the PCI hopes for a convergence with the PSI on energy policy. (Ibid., 14 May.) But in the labor movement, the communists' hope of Socialist cooperation rests on hope alone. In the field of local government, the PCI can say at best that the disaster has not been absolute. Where ten years earlier all major Italian cities were ruled by coalitions containing the PCI, in 1986 Bologna remained the only major city with a communist mayor—and he ruled only by virtue of the PCI's plurality in the city council, with adhoc support, not from the Socialists, but from the Republicans and Social Democrats.

The PSI is an elusive target. Although in many ways it is susceptible to the PCI "call of the wild," it continues to draw from the well of anti-Soviet rhetoric to legitimize itself and to bash the PCI. Thus, Claudio Martelli, the PSI's deputy leader, and one of those on whom it pins its hopes, reacted in part to Gorbachev's speech to the Soviet Communist Party Congress: "I must say that one is somewhat shocked to hear that the Socialist world is the cradle of humanism when what we are talking about are regimes such as those of Jaruzelski, Husak, or Kadar, and Afghanistan" (*La Repubblica*, 27 February). Moreover, the PSI is openly flirting with the idea of scrapping Italy's electoral system of proportional representation, which the PCI considers a bulwark of such power as it has (*L'Unità*, 24 February). To underline the injury, as the PSI prepared for its 1987 congress, its leadership was proposing that all Marxist symbols be removed from the party's logo.

The PCI seems more sanguine about its other major problem, the Christian Democratic Party (DC). In a nutshell, the PCI believes that the divisions within the DC are so deep, and its relationship with certain DC elements so good, that were the PCI to re-establish a firm Socialist-communist axis, the establishment of a "truly progressive" coalition government would be no trouble, "but woe unto us if we forget that, in 40 years, not only the PCI has changed. There are more differences between the Catholic Church of Pope Pius XII—that of the excommunication of the Communists, of the "green berets," and of Luigi Gedda—and on the other hand, that of John XXIII, Paul VI, and Pope Wojtyla, than between the PCI of Togliatti and that of Natta. And the same can be said of the DC of DeGasperi and that of Moro." (Ibid., 26 January.)

Thus, the PCI is continuing its long-standing policy of offering its support to any Christian Democrat willing to use it against other forces in the DC.

Although the PCI recognizes that there is a growing similarity between the DC progressives' views and its own, it refers to this rapprochement as a political, rather than cultural, one: "We must aim to achieve a more direct and open relationship with them, and, at the same time, step up criticism and stimulation of those groups and individuals inside the DC who do not want to lose working-class support and working-class ideals, which are thwarted by the prevalence of more conservative factions" (ibid., 31 July). In 1986, as has been the case since Moro's death, the Communist Party's premier ally within the DC is Giulio Andreotti—whose rightist background is the very opposite of progressivism. In short, the PCI counts on seducing Socialists but counts on making political deals with Christian Democrats.

Yet, since the DC is under no pressure whatever to make any deal with the PCI so long as the PSI does not want such a deal, the PCI's frequent discussions about the conditions under which it would or would not agree to enter the government (ibid., 31 March) appear to be just so much whistling in the dark.

The PCI's substantive domestic pronouncements are vague and considerably less vehement than those of a decade earlier. When Prime Minister Craxi resigned on 27 June, the PCI privately favored Andreotti as his replacement. But Andreotti could not obtain the necessary support from the DC and the PSI, and Craxi was nominated to succeed himself. In the PCI's view, society is being run with criminal corruption and incompetence. As a result, the rich are "poisoning the water and the wine," and there is "destruction of so much of our artistic and cultural heritage, and of our countryside and environment" (ibid., 10 April). "There is a major need for a political and moral change of course—a program alternative in place of the program vaccuum and the erroneousness of the casual and contradictory options characteristic of the present majority" (ibid.). The PCI condemns corruption, "cronyism in politics and administration, to the extent of subversive conspiracies, the deviations within the services, and the unpublished massacres" (ibid.). This last is a charge that many of the terrorist acts in Italy are actually acts of provocation by the country's intelligence services. The PCI promises, among other things, "a system of local authorities that is not only an instrument of participation and an organ of the State, but also an agent of local government and planning; a judiciary whose independence is strengthened and made functional by modern laws and measures; and an administration selected on the basis of merit, instilled with a real sense of responsibility" (ibid.).

**International Views and Activities.** One of the PCI's major difficulties is that the Italian people think very well of the United States and intensely dislike the Soviet Union. Hence, much of what the PCI says is calculated to safeguard itself from the presumption that, if it could, it would make Italy less like the United States and more like the Soviet Union. On the other hand, the PCI is anything but pro-American and anti-Soviet. Clearly, the PCI wants to lead Italians to think better of the Soviets and worse of the United States. But this is a difficult, risky enterprise, which is why the PCI speaks on foreign affairs in terms that are often ambiguous and sometimes deliberately misleading. Adding to the confusion is the fact that the party encourages the expression of widely varying opinions.

This is so especially about the Soviet Union and Eastern Europe. Perhaps the most typical instance was the statement the PCI issued to the Western press in Moscow concerning Gorbachev's address to the Twenty-seventh Congress of the CPSU in February. This statement, which was supposed to reflect the speech the PCI representative had given to the congress, was widely interpreted as a criticism of the Soviet Union for abuses of human rights and for its invasion of Afghanistan. In fact, the PCI representative's speech contained no trace of criticism of the Soviet Union on human rights. Its "hottest" passage, split into two separate paragraphs, was

> Respect for the sovereignty of states and the independence of people is a matter of principle that allows no exceptions. Military intervention in other countries is not admissible. The spirit of negotiations must prevail...
>
> It is on the basis of these sample principles that we hope that political solutions will be negotiated as soon as possible in other areas of grave crisis, such as Central America, Southwest Asia, and South Africa...In the same way, we hope that a political solution of the grave question of Afghanistan will be reached as soon as possible. (Ibid., 27 February.)

Thus Natta and other PCI spokespeople typically and repeatedly make strong and emphatic, but vague, references to condemnations of the USSR that the PCI has supposedly made in the past but that, on examination, do not turn out to be condemnations at all: "We reasserted the PCI's stances, clearly stated in our Congress documents, the criticisms—including severe ones—of the USSR, its policy and its system. We do not change them. In fact, Gorbachev's report reassures us that the statements we made were true and real." (Ibid.)

By contrast, the PCI regularly expresses its support of Soviet positions and activities with great specificity. Thus Natta said to the congress: "The 27th CPSU Congress consolidated still more the process of new invigoration of Soviet foreign policy. It became apparent what a positive impetus the new Soviet peace initiatives can give and are giving, if they are consistently implemented, as it was also during the latest crisis in the Mediterranean, when the Soviet Union advanced the proposal for a simultaneous withdrawal of the fleets of the two great powers from the region." (Ibid., 10 April.) Natta and other spokespeople praised Gorbachev's conduct of the Geneva summit in November 1985, his arms control proposals of January 15, 1986, the Soviet proposal for a nuclear-test moratorium, and the declared unconditional opposition to any defense of the West against Soviet missiles. In sum, Natta said, "we consider our position with regard to the USSR in political and not in ideological terms." (Ibid.)

The PCI's opposition to U.S. foreign policy is total and vehement. The PCI, however, strives to give the impression that it is not anti-American: "The worst way to tackle the problem would be to draw no distinction between the people and the government...and to fail to perceive the differences among the various political forces in the United States and among the various forces that make up the Reagan administration itself" (ibid.). The divisions among Americans, says Natta, "extended as far as the assassination of a President and a Presidential candidate." Thus, "we do not confuse the struggle against the Reagan administration's policy with anti-Americanism...There are no friends of Reaganism in our Party." (Ibid.)

The PCI seeks to "establish relations with the U.S. democratic forces" (ibid., 5 January). It plans to increase the number of visits of left-wing Americans to PCI functions in Italy, and to increase the number of Italian communists who are received in the United States. The PCI expressed delight at the U.S. Democratic Party's recapture of a majority in the U.S. Senate on 5 November (ibid., 6 November).

The PCI mounted two principal foreign policy campaigns in 1986: against SDI and against U.S.

policy in the Middle East. On SDI, the principal tactic was to exploit the contradiction between the U.S. assertion that the West needs a defense against Soviet missiles and the U.S. government's expressed confidence that deep cuts in offensive weaponry are likely. Clearly the United States is insincere about something (ibid., 9 November). Concerning the Middle East, the PCI condemns U.S. actions against Libya as "aggressive" and U.S. resistance to Syria and support for Israel as "a threat to peace." The PCI urges the Italian government to prohibit the United States from using its bases on Italian soil to further its policy in the Mediterranean and to press for a Palestinian homeland led by the PLO, which would result from an international conference in which the Soviet Union would participate (ibid., 24 April, 24 July).

Although the PCI condemns terrorism, it refuses to link either Libya or Syria to terrorism other than by saying that they had not yet wholly removed their equivocation with regard to it (*La Repubblica*, 7–8 September). As for Arafat and the PLO, the PCI believes that their "resolute condemnation of the bloodthirsty acts must be emphasized" (*L'Unità*, 10 January).

The PCI had always contended that the charges of Bulgarian terrorism in Italy were trumped up by imperialism to cover itself and to besmirch the reputation of socialism. After an Italian court acquitted two Bulgarians for insufficient evidence on charges of masterminding the attempted murder of the Pope, PCI Central Committee member Luciano Barcu thus addressed the Congress of the Bulgarian Communist Party: "We opposed the purposeful campaign of those who were interested in creating tension between Bulgaria and Italy" (*JPRS-EER*-86065, 25 April).

The PCI presents itself as a party not essentially different from the German Social Democratic Party and the British Labour Party. To that end, PCI representatives have spent much time with Willy Brandt and Neil Kinnock and speak often of initiatives and positions on the part of the European left as a whole. In January, Natta proposed to the European Parliament in Strasbourg that it pass a resolution urging Moscow and Washington to reduce arms (*L'Unità*, 17 January). On 11 March, he delivered a major speech to the Federal Institute of International Studies in Cologne on the need for united action in foreign policy on the part of European leftist parties (ibid., 13 March). The PCI believes it would be dangerous to challenge the European countries' position within the Atlantic bloc, but that European leftist forces should use their influence to empty NATO of its aggressive content, to make sure U.S. policy in Europe will threaten peace less and less, and to make sure NATO is not used as a means of aggression beyond Europe's geographic area. Finally, on 20 March the PCI opened a "left wing for Europe center" in Rome. The center is meant to be "a political-cultural stimulating factor for the Left, but also for other forces and individual personalities not identified with the historic parties of the workers' movement, precisely with the objective of identifying fields for joint action in Italy and, naturally, beyond the national borders" (ibid., 21 March).

Perhaps most revealing of the PCI's thinking on foreign affairs in 1986 were two books by Italian communists on the Soviet Union's crushing of the Hungarian Revolution of 1956. The books by Adrianno Guerra and Armando Cossutta, and published by the Party publishing house, engage in their own versions of the standard communist inquiry into how much counterrevolutionary influence there was in Imre Nagy's government, and whether it came before or after the Soviet Union's decision to reinvade. Both books take the position that the Soviet action was regrettable, but they also give the impression that no one should forget that the future of socialism and progress lay in the balance. A book coauthored by Federico Argatieri and Lorenzo Giannatti, perhaps the most complete history of that revolution, is based on sympathy with a movement that aimed not at "a restoration of the past (although the risk was not altogether absent)" but at "pluralism and self-management, neutrality and national sovereignty." The book shows Nagy and others trying to be good communists, while Stalinist thugs, with support from the Soviet Union, overshadowed them and oppressed the people. When the people turned to the good communists, the Soviets crushed them all, and drove them into the unreceptive arms of the West. The authors called on the PCI to demonstrate the fact that "battles for democracy in the East—all of them—belong to the historic Patrimony of the European Left."

**International Party Contacts.** The PCI must consider contact with the Communist Party of the Soviet Union terribly important because it maintains it despite the fact that such contact is surely the factor that contributes most heavily to the Italian people's distrust of the PCI. Throughout its history, the PCI has accompanied its relationship with the CPSU with various kinds of declarations of independence. In 1981, after the imposition of martial law in Poland, the PCI had declared "that it no longer considers valid the idea of a Communist movement as something homogeneous and separate from the rest of the international workers' movement—that is, from the socialist, progressive and liberation movements" (*L'Unita*, 30 December 1981). Like other such statements, this triggered stories around the world that, once again, the PCI had finally broken with Moscow. Nevertheless, the contacts between the two parties, which both characterize as fraternal and which are obviously broad and deep, continue.

On 4 January *L'Unità* announced that Gianni Cervetti and Gerardo Chiaromonte of the PCI directorate had met with Egor Ligachev of the CPSU politburo while on vacation in the USSR and that they had arranged a meeting between Gorbachev and Natta for 20–28 January. The Italian delegation also included Giancarlo Pajetta (the principal chargé of relations with the CPSU) and Antonio Rubbi. On the Soviet side, in addition to Gorbachev, there were Geydar Aliyev, Vitali Vorotnikov, Andrei Gromyko, Ligachev, Mikhail Solomentsev, Viktor Chebrikov, Boris Ponomarev, and Vadim Zagladin (the number-two man in the CPSU Central Committee's International Department). The speeches both sides released (TASS, January; *L'Unità*, 29 January) showed a common commitment to advance the Soviet Union's arms control proposals, to fight all plans for defending the West against ballistic missiles, and to secure a Palestinian state, while discouraging "actions or words that damage the cause." The speeches mentioned the need to resolve the conflicts going on in various parts of the world and gave no hint of disagreement. Later, Natta reported that the PCI had interpreted these passages as "referring to Afghanistan and Nicaragua, but we cannot say what the Soviet interpretation was." The speeches on both sides repeatedly emphasized that the identity (or near identity) of views was reached in full autonomy and does not detract from the full autonomy of both sides.

Commenting on his meetings with Gorbachev, Natta stressed that he believed the press was wrong in saying there had ever been a "wrench" in relations between the two parties (*L'Unità*, 30 January) and that Gorbachev is intent on further democratizing the Soviet Union's government, society, and economy—including asking the labor unions to do their job of looking after the workers' interests (*Der Spiegel*, 26 May).

The PCI and the CPSU exchanged observers at their respective party congresses. The CPSU delegation to Florence was led by CPSU "number-three" man Lev Zaikov, who took the occasion of his visit to meet Prime Minister Craxi (ANSA, 9 April). The CPSU's message to the PCI congress stressed fraternal relations in full autonomy: "the communists' real unity is in their struggle for common goals" (*L'Unità*, 10 April).

In June, the PCI's Napolitano, member of the Secretariat and chair of the working commission on foreign affairs, traveled to Moscow for a meeting with the head of the CPSU International Affairs Department, Anatolii Dobrynin, and his deputy Zagladin. Neither side provided details (ibid., 9 June). A month later, Natta, again accompanied by Rubbi, went to Moscow to meet with Zagladin. In September, Zagladin went to Italy to meet with Napolitano and Rubbi, and later to address the party's annual festival, sponsored by *L'Unità*. In the spirit of the gathering, Zagladin said that the Soviet Union had changed, that it no longer believes it is necessary to prepare for war in order to avert it, that Marxism-Leninism is not a recipe—that in any given circumstance it can mean anything, and that the Soviet Union is engaging in "Westpolitik" (ibid., 15 September).

The PCI's Seventeenth Congress was attended not just by every major Moscow-line communist party (54) and movement (23) and by the aforementioned Socialist parties (29) but by the Chinese Communist Party as well. High-level Chinese delegations also visited Italy on other occasions during 1986. On June 21, in Rome, Vice-Premier Hu Yaobang addressed a group of Italian communists led by Natta. The main point of that meeting seemed to be to publicize the independence of communist parties. In August, Giovanni Chiarante visited Beijing, Hanzow, and Shanghai. Earlier in the year, the president of the FGCI had traveled to Beijing (Xinua, 28 February).

During 1986 Natta made a special effort to hasten the already good relations with the Yugoslav League of Communists (LCY) with a ceremonial visit and a speech touting the unity of the European left (*L'Unità*, 19 February). The PCI also sent a delegation to the congress of the LCY (ibid., 20 June). Natta also traveled to Hungary for meetings with János Kádár, Secretary of the Hungarian Social Workers' Party (ibid., 30 September). Napoleone Colajanni spent a working vacation in Hungary in August, and Hungarian television ran a long interview with Natta on 5 October. However, the PCI's delegation to the Congress of the German

Socialist Unity Party (SED) in East Berlin was headed by Adalberto Minucci, a member of the Directorate (ibid., 19 April). Whereas the PCI did not make much of its relationship with the SED, the latter's press made much of the excellent relations between the two great parties (*Neues Deutschland*, 9, 22 April, 12, 16 September).

The PCI's only quarrel in 1986 was with the French Communist Party, whose Pierre La Roche wrote in *Cahiers du Communisme* (July) that "the PCI no longer presents itself so much as a revolutionary party setting goals of transformation, as a modern reformist party." Chiaromonte replied in *Rinascita* (27 September) that the PCI's policy was dictated by Italian reality as it had developed since 1979 and that, if the PCI were to follow the PCF's advice, it would cease to exist. The PCI, for its part, judged the PCF's defeat in the 18 March parliamentary elections (the PCF got less than 10 percent of the vote) as a warning of what could happen to the PCI if it were to present itself with a more "sectarian" image (*L'Unità*, 18 March; *Corriene della Sera*, 18 March; *La Repubblica*, 18 March).

**Other Leftist Groups, and Terrorism.** The PCI has nearly achieved a monopoly of the far-left. Since the PCI's serious rapprochement with the Chinese Communist Party, the small pro-Chinese Italian Communist Party shifted its allegiance to Albania and then disappeared. In 1984 the Party for Proletarian Unity for Communism merged with the PCI. Only Proletarian Democracy, which received 1.5 percent of the vote in the parliamentary election of 1983, competes for votes on the PCI's left. In the 1986 Sicilian elections, DP was stagnant.

Between 1979 and 1982, the Italian government broke the major domestic organizations that had terrorized the country. The PCI, which had blocked vigorous antiterrorist action until 1978, enthusiastically backed the fight thereafter. In 1986 the minister of the interior reported that during the previous twelve months, 288 terrorist attacks had occurred (down from 384); 28 people were killed and 133 were injured. A total of 292 left-wing terrorists were wanted by police, but 210 of these were known to be in exile abroad, mostly in France (ANSA, 20 February). There had also been fewer apolitical, right-wing terrorist acts.

On 6 September, Giovanni Stefano, one of the founders of Prima Linea (Front line), one of the foremost terrorist groups of the late 1970s and early 1980s, was arrested by French police in the Basque country, where he had been hiding out for three years (ibid., 6 September). On 25 May, three members of the Red Brigades received life sentences for the murder of a prison guard, a move that brought the number of terrorists in Italian penitentiaries to 1,178.

The most clamorous act of domestic terrorism of 1986 was the 12 February murder of the former mayor of Florence, Lando Conti, claimed by the Red Brigades. On this occasion, the minister of defense, Giovanni Spadolini, as well as other Italian noncommunist politicians, publicly reiterated the ideological and logistical connections between the Red Brigades and "groups of Middle-Eastern origin" (ibid., 12 February). The police reported that Conti was killed with the same Czechoslovak Skorpion submachine gun that had been used in terrorist attacks the previous year (ibid., 15 February).

Angelo Codevilla
*Hoover Institution*

# Luxembourg

**Population.** 367,000
**Party.** Communist Party of Luxembourg (Parti communiste Luxembourgeois; CPL)
**Founded.** 1921
**Membership.** 600 (estimated)
**Chairman.** René Urbany
**Executive Committee.** 10 members: Aloyse Bisdorff, François Hoffmann, Fernand Hübsch, Marianne Passeri, Marcel Putz, René Urbany, Jean Wesquet, Serge Urbany, André Moes, Babette Ruckert
**Secretariat.** 1 member: René Urbany
**Central Committee.** 31 full and 7 candidate members
**Status.** Legal
**Last Congress.** Twenty-fourth, 4–5 February 1984
**Last Election.** 1984, 5.0 percent, 2 of 64 seats
**Auxiliary Organizations.** Jeunesse communiste Luxembourgeoise; Union des femmes Luxembourgeoises
**Publications.** *Zeitung vum Lëtzeburger Vollek* (Newspaper of the Luxembourgian people), official CPL organ, daily, 1,000–1,500 copies (CPL claims 15,000–20,000)

The pro-Soviet CPL played an insignificant political role in Luxembourg prior to World War II. After 1945 the CPL's position improved: communists were elected to serve in Parliament and in several communities. From 1945 to 1947, Luxembourg's cabinet included one communist minister. The best election results were achieved in 1968, but the communist vote declined steadily in 1974, 1979, and 1984. On 10 June 1979, in the first elections to the European Parliament, the CPL obtained 5.1 percent of the vote; in the second elections on 17 June 1984, the communist share declined to 4.1 percent. In municipal elections, too, the communist vote continued to decline.

The CPL leadership is dominated by the Urbany family. René Urbany succeeded his father, Dominique, as chair at the first meeting of the Central Committee after the Twenty-second Congress in 1977. Dominique Urbany remained in the CPL as honorary chair until his death in October 1986 (*Neues Deutschland*, 27 October). Members of the Urbany family hold many key positions in the party

and its auxiliaries, and René Urbany is also the director of the party press.

Party membership cards were exchanged in 1985. The Central Committee of the CPL claims that the number of party members and supporters has increased. It is further asserted that this improvement in turn strengthened the party's influence in Parliament and in municipal councils and enterprises. The Central Committee reported that the campaign for subscriptions to the party's official organ, *Zeitung vum Lëtzeburger Vollek*, was successful, although it continued to ask for financial contributions to the communist press fund. It appears that a front organization, the Society for the Development of the Press and Printing Industry, which was founded a few years ago by the Socialist Unity Party of Germany (the East German communist party), continues its financial support of communist publishing houses in non-communist-ruled countries in Europe.

The CPL's publishing company, COPE, prints the French edition of *The World Marxist Review*. Its new and modern technical equipment and production facilities, which exceed local requirements, serve communist parties and organizations in several other countries.

The CPL, like other communist parties in Western Europe, supported Soviet foreign policy objectives in its mass publications and its efforts to promote "unity of actions against the threat of war."

Contacts with fraternal parties were maintained during 1986. A delegation of the GDR's Peace Council, led by its vice president Dr. Georg Böhm, visited the Luxembourg Peace Committee on 19–20 April (*Neues Deutschland*, 23 April). René Urbany headed his party's delegation to the Eleventh SED Party Congress in April (Ibid., 24 April). Bisdorff, member of the Executive Committee of the CPL's Central Committee and one of the two communist members of the Luxembourg Parliament, wrote in the *World Marxist Review* about "Communists in Parliament" (*WMR*, February).

Luxembourg also witnessed violent activities committed by terrorists. Bombings were directed against public installations, such as airports and government buildings.

Eric Waldman
*University of Calgary*

# Malta

**Population.** 341,179 (Malta Central Office of Statistics: 1985 Census)
**Party.** Communist Party of Malta (Partit Komunista Malti: CPM)
**Founded.** 1969
**Membership.** 300 (estimated)
**General Secretary.** Anthony Vassallo (62)
**Central Committee.** 11 members: Anthony Baldacchino (president; 46), Lino Vella (vice president), Anthony Vassallo, Victor Degiovanni (second secretary, 34), Karmenu Gerada (international secretary, 45), Joseph Cachia (assistant international secretary), Mario Mifsud (propaganda secretary, 33), Michael Schembri (assistant propaganda secretary, 23), Dominic Zammit (financial secretary, 26), Francis X. Caruana (assistant financial secretary), Paul Agius (45)
**Status.** Legal
**Last Congress.** Extraordinary Congress, 18–25 May 1984
**Last Election.** 1981 (CPM did not contest)
**Auxiliary Organizations.** Peace and Solidarity Council of Malta, Malta-USSR Friendship and Cultural Society, Malta-Czechoslovakia Friendship Society, Malta-Cuba Friendship and Cultural Society, Communist Youth League (CYL), Malta-Korea Friendship and Cultural Society, Association of Progressive Journalists
**Publications.** *Zminijietna* (Our times), monthly tabloid, part in English and part in Maltese, Anthony Vassalo, editor; *International Political Review*, monthly, Malta edition of *World Marxist Review; Problemi ta Paci u Socjalizmu*, quarterly, Maltese-language abstract of *WMR; Bandiera Hamra* (Red flag), issued by CYL; *Bridge of Friendship and Culture Malta-USSR*, quarterly journal of the Malta-USSR Friendship and Cultural Society

As the next general elections loom on the horizon—these will take place by April 1987 at the latest—the ruling Malta Labor Party (MLP) accentuated its distance from the CPM. In turn, the CPM, which gave notice of contesting the next elections, increased its political visibility but did not conduct straightforward electoral work, at least not in the open. Its monthly publication gave front-page prominence to a proposal that its supporters maintain the unity of the left by voting first for CPM candidates and then to transfer their preferences to the MLP candidates under the Maltese proportional representation system (*Zminijietna*, February). In this way, the "unity of the left" would be safeguarded. The Soviet government and its agencies, as well as the Soviet satellite governments, maintained the intensity of their activity in the Maltese islands.

**Malta Government Policies.** As Malta edged toward the next general elections, its government found itself facing mounting problems, the most urgent of which is high unemployment. The year 1986 marked the launching of the island's sixth economic development plan, and its success depends on a substantial intake of overseas loan and grant aid. To this end, the Mifsud Bonnici government has been engaged in lengthy negotiations with the European Economic Community and Italy. Simultaneously, it has been hoping to benefit from Libyan help through the creation of job opportunities in Libya. Efforts to open up markets in the Soviet Union and other communist countries were marked with difficulty.

Negotiations with the EEC and Italy dragged along on a stop-and-go basis throughout the year. Malta's friendship with Libya became suspect as the United States and its European allies confronted Moammar Khadafy over the issue of terrorism. Rising tension in the Mediterranean, sparked initially by the *Achille Lauro* incident, affected the Malta tourist industry, discouraged Maltese workers from holding on to jobs in Libya, and was a disincentive to investment.

Evidence of increasing Soviet and other communist interest in Malta led to more curious questions by the international press, undoubtedly echoing feelings in Western chancelleries.

The CPM, as well as communist diplomats from various quarters, found plenty of scope for fishing in these troubled waters. On the one hand, they patted the Malta government on the back for keeping its lines open with Libya and extending moral support to the Khadafy government. The CPM general secretary parroted the Kremlin view on the subject in the April issue of *World Marxist Review*, under the heading "People's Protest Against Gunboat Diplomacy." His punchline read as follows: "the Communist Party of Malta has consistently criticised the Labour government on a number of domestic policy issues, but it supports the government's foreign policy and hails the course of nonalignment." On the other hand, the Soviets protracted their hard bargaining until year's end before concluding another four-year trade agreement. While the Malta government subsisted on hope throughout 1986, the Soviets obtained further concessions and consolidated their Malta foothold.

All along, the Mifsud Bonnici government insisted that it was undeterred by the tension and the turbulence sweeping across the Mediterranean. It claimed to be following a policy of neutrality, nonalignment, and equidistance from the superpowers. However, its treaty obligations to Libya and the Soviet Union and its membership in the Nonaligned Movement presented a number of anomalous situations. Vladimir P. Suslov, head of the Second European Department of the Ministry of Foreign Affairs in Moscow, had two occasions during the year to exploit these situations. In March, while in Malta to discuss bilateral relations (*Times*, 27 March) he confessed in an exclusive interview that he had held consultations related to Malta's initiative to call a United Nations Security Council meeting after the Gulf of Sidra incident (*Weekend Chronicle*, 29 March). He also took the opportunity to state that Mikhail Gorbachev's plans concerning the Mediterranean "included many points which coincide with Maltese ideas" (ibid.). Suslov returned to Malta in July without a previous announcement and without making any statement after his official talks (*Orizzont*, 22 July). Prime Minister Carmelo Mifsud Bonnici admits that his government's policy has been "misunderstood" by the United States and the West and that Malta's image has been "tarnished" as a result. He insists that "Malta wants neither the Soviet Union nor the United States to upset the political balance in the Mediterranean, and it views both countries with equal suspicion" adding that Malta sought a reduction of Soviet and American forces in the area (*NYT*, 6 August).

The ambiguous policy of the Mifsud Bonnici government has become the object of increasingly critical attention overseas, where questions are being asked about Malta's drift away from the West while professing to follow a policy of neutrality and nonalignment.

The New York–based International Security Council issued a declaration at the end of a roundtable on "Malta and Mediterranean Security" held in Milan on November 23–25 under the chairmanship of Ambassador Charles Lichenstein, former deputy American ambassador to the United Nations. The roundtable declaration stated that "the democracies in the West must view with growing concern Malta's drift towards the Soviet sphere. This compromises Malta's stability and the security of the Mediterranean region. Of equal concern are Malta's departures from its own traditions of parliamentary democracy and the safeguarding of human and civil rights." It calls on the government of Malta to reconsider the political and military provisions of its agreements with the Soviet Union, Libya, and North Korea, which place Malta in an anti-Western alignment, notwithstanding its formal declarations of neutrality and nonalignment. (*Times*, Malta, 7 December.)

In another article in the August issue of *Arab Asian Affairs*, which is a private international intelligence service provided by the London-based *International Currency Review*, Zbigniew Brzezinski, who had been President Carter's national security adviser, offered "an objective view of Malta's plight," in which he spoke of a "gradual drift away from the West" on the part of the Maltese government. He explained this by the cautious intent "not to unduly alarm the major Western powers which are conscious of the Island's strategic importance and of the inherently Western character of its people." Brzezinski claims that "The USSR realizes that the West would react vigorously to an eventual takeover of Malta by the Soviet bloc. The USSR has therefore followed a policy of gradual penetration and prefers to work through its surrogates."

These views do not seem to deter Mifsud Bonnici, who is quite candid in expressing his thoughts. In the very month the free world was commemorating the 30th anniversary of the Hungarian uprising, a group of Hungarian agricultural workers were visiting Malta where they called on the prime minister. Mifsud Bonnici was reported to have told them that "there are certain ideals which united Malta and Hungary and are common and dear to both of them . . . The two countries believed in the solidarity of socialism and both cherished the ideal of peace" (*Times*, Malta, 29 October).

Of equal interest was the refusal of the Mifsud Bonnici government to allow Soviet dissident, Vladimir Malinkovic, to visit Malta to speak at a university student meeting on "The Day-to-Day Defence of Human Rights: A Soviet Dissident's Experience." In this case, the Maltese immigration authorities asked the dissident to apply for a permit in terms of the Foreign Interference Act and to undertake in writing that he would not take part in the students' meeting. When Malinkovic refused to sign and said he would still travel to Malta, he was warned by the police that he would be sent back on the same aircraft. (Ibid., 3 November.)

**Domestic Party Affairs.** The CPM presence in the political scene was more noticeable in 1986 than in former years. Its objective was to establish an autonomous and independent left-wing profile capable of open dissent from the ruling MLP. In its New Year message, the CPM accused the MLP of letting down the working class all along the line (*Zminijietna*, January). A number of conferences, accessible to the public, were held at party quarters. Press statements in favor of divorce legislation were issued. The party staked a claim for airtime in the new series of party political broadcasts organized by the Broadcasting Authority, but that claim was denied on the grounds that the CPM was not represented in Parliament. Any airtime that will be granted for the pre-electoral broadcasts (which will be broadcast after the dissolution of Parliament) will be in proportion to the number of electoral candidates represented by each party.

The CPM did not display particular enthusiasm about conducting electioneering activities. The party went through the motions of opening an election fund (ibid., September) toward which thirteen contributors donated a total of $80 in September and October. It issued a statement to claim representation in any possible discussion to amend the rules of the electoral game in Malta and took the opportunity to incorporate in that statement the highlights of CPM foreign policy, namely: full sovereignty and political economic independence to advance the country's best interests; refusal to harbor foreign military bases; a nonaligned policy; detachment from imperialism, and solidarity with national liberation movements; a peace and disarmament policy; and a nuclear-free Mediterranean (ibid., June). In June, the party issued another press statement expressing solidarity with Libya (ibid.), and in August, another in which they condemned South Africa's apartheid policy and the Malta government for importing oranges and coal originating from South Africa (ibid., August).

Delegates from the CPM participated fully in the international congress circuit displaying the Malta flag. General Secretary Vassallo represented the CPM at the Twenty-seventh Congress of the CPSU in Moscow and at the congresses of the Bulgarian Communist Party and the Socialist Unity Party of Germany. Second Secretary Degiovanni attended the congresses of the Communist Party of Cuba and of the Italian Communist Party. David Mallia, Central Committee member, represented the CPM at the congress of the Communist Party of Czechoslovakia, and Francis X. Caruana, assistant finance secretary, attended the CPSU Congress and represented the CPM and the Peace and Solidarity Council of Malta at the Fourteenth General Council Meeting of the Afro-Asian People's Solidarity Organization (AAPSO) in Moscow. The MLP, which is a member of AAPSO, was conspicuous by its absence from their convention, but for the first time, it sent representatives to the congresses in Moscow, Prague, East Berlin, and Italy.

Thus, although the CPM continues to claim a stake in the 1987 electoral contest, its principal aim is to provide a voice, separate from that of the MLP and capable of supporting the policies of international communism as orchestrated by the Kremlin. Within the international communist community, the Kremlin thus has one more "national" vote in its favor. At the same time, it has its own reliable source of support in Malta.

With the approaching elections, the MLP indicated that it wanted to put some distance between it and the CPM. This was emphasized at a mass meeting by the general secretary designate of the General Workers Union (GWU), Angelo Fenech. The GWU is the largest trade union in Malta and is statutorily fused with the MLP. Fenech declared that "the GWU has never been and could never be a Communist Union" (*Orizzont*, 29 April). Nevertheless, the MLP and the GWU have been making determined attempts to expand Maltese trade with the USSR and have been claiming that they are prepared to go to the devil to create work for unemployed workers in Malta. The three-year trade protocol signed in Moscow in 1984 (the text of which has never been published) was not equal to the expectations of the two parties. Mifsud Bonnici told *Newsweek* (5 September 1984) that the protocol provided the assurance "of a new market of $260

million" and that Malta had to set up the productive capacity to cope with the ensuing demand. He then declared that the size of that agreement was dependent on the size of Malta's unemployment problem—which then amounted to 10,000 registered unemployed workers. Although Maltese exports had risen to a relatively small degree, and in spite of an order for the building of eight timber carriers in the Malta shipyard, the number of registered unemployed was still in the area of 9,000 as of October. Malta wanted a better trade protocol.

The Soviets, who have their own problems at home, have not been very forthcoming and openhanded. They are known to have had difficulties with the ship construction program in Malta and the commercial counselor at the Soviet Embassy pleaded for progress in the negotiations for another trade protocol so that the "momentum" would not be lost and no contracts would fall through as a result of the delay (*Lloyd*, 4 July). This notwithstanding, the negotiations dragged on until 24 November, when a four-year trade protocol was signed in Moscow by the Maltese minister of industry, Karmenu Vella. Like its predecessor, the text of the new trade protocol has been treated as a state secret and has not been published.

At an airport conference on his return to Malta, Minister Vella claimed that the protocol he signed with Soviet Foreign Trade Minister Boris Aristov would provide for Soviet purchases from Malta up to a value of $440 million and stated that $160 million would be allocated for the purchase of Maltese manufactured products, $140 million would go for the purchase of eight small ships, already being built in Malta on Soviet orders under the preceding trade protocol, and a further $140 million would be available for another eight ships. (*Orizzont*, 26 November.) The latter eight ships will be ordered only when the eight ships in hand have been completed, and work on these ships is behind schedule. The first two of these ships have yet to be launched, and work has not yet started on the third. A number of skilled Polish workers are to go to Malta to work on these ships. In view of the poor performance of the last trade protocol, a monitoring committee is to be set up to ensure that the new agreement reached will be implemented to the satisfaction of both sides. The request for this committee came from the Soviet side.

Bulgaria has negotiated a trade protocol involving a $10 million package. The new protocol was signed in Malta by Bulgarian Deputy Minister of

Foreign Trade Ivan Gospodinov with the aim of doubling the level of Maltese-Bulgarian trade (ibid., 7 November). The $10 million target overstates the level of existing trade between Malta and Bulgaria, which is well below $5 million per annum and, in any case, results in a favorable balance for Bulgaria.

In Malta government circles, these look like glittering, if hitherto elusive, prizes. Meanwhile, the Soviets and other satellite states have been consolidating their hold on Malta to a remarkable degree since 1981. The USSR has signed twelve such agreements: on merchant shipping, trade, air transport, and neutrality in 1981; on culture, education, and science in 1982; on economic and technical cooperation, trade and health in 1984; and on health, cultural and sports cooperation in 1986. Still another trade agreement was concluded in November. Bulgaria concluded eight other agreements covering health, tourism, trade, culture, air services, and banking. During 1986 alone, Malta also signed a trade protocol with Czechoslovakia, a health protocol with Hungary and another one with Poland, and an air services agreement with Romania.

The Revolutionary Trade Union Movement of Czechoslovakia renewed its two-year agreement with the GWU to enable relays of Maltese trade unionists to visit Czechoslovakia for trade union education courses (ibid., 4 March) and similar (but unpublished) arrangements have been made with the Hungarian National Council of Trade Unions to enable other Maltese trade unionists to visit Hungary (ibid., 17 July). As a result, a group of thirteen GWU activists, including three women, proceeded to Hungary on an "educational and cultural" visit (*Times*, 12 November). The deputy general secretary of the GWU, Harold Walls, and the secretary of the union's Metal Section, Ronnie Pellegrini, were subsequently invited by the Council of Bulgarian Trade Unions to visit Bulgaria, ostensibly to discuss "matters of common interest, particularly issues relating to the general situation of the working class throughout the world" (*Torca*, 7 December). A group of trade unionists from the Ukraine in the Soviet Union, said to be interested in the educational and science sectors, visited Malta, where they held talks with GWU officials. The Soviet workers, led by Viktor G. Koushnerov from the International Relations Department of the Council of Trade Unions of the Ukraine, also visited some trade schools and the island of Gozo. It was stated after their arrival that they were on the island on an exchange program between Malta and the USSR for "specialized tourists" (*Orizzont*, 5 November).

**Auxilliary and Front Organizations.** The Malta-USSR Friendship and Cultural Society had an active year with particular attention paid to furthering the Soviet peace initiative. To this end, a public forum held at society headquarters was addressed by the Soviet ambassador, Victor Smirnov, and after Reykjavik, the Soviet chargé d'affaires presented the USSR case at an open meeting. The society sent an official delegation to Moscow to sign a two-year cooperation agreement with the Union of Soviet Friendship Societies, which will allow Maltese citizens "to get acquainted with the 27th CPSU Congress and the guidelines of Soviet economic and social development as well as with the international activity of the USSR" (*Times*, 8 April). The society also established a youth section and appointed its first committee (*Orizzont*, 2 April).

The CYL took part in a peace march in Valletta organized by the MLP youth movement (*Zminijietna*, April) and hosted a two-member delegation from the Czechoslovakia Socialist Youth Union. The two delegates had meetings with other youth and government representatives and subsequently issued with the CYL a joint communiqué on international issues in which it was made known that a new communist nucleus at the university has come into the open under the name of Left Front of University Students (ibid.).

There was only negligible activity by the Malta-Cuba, Malta-Czechoslovakia, and Malta-Korea friendship and cultural societies, and the Peace and Solidarity Council of Malta was also quiet for most of the year, breaking its silence to issue a couple of press statements in support of Libya and to send its delegates to the AAPSO General Council meeting in Moscow. The Association of Progressive Journalists also issued a public statement to condemn U.S. aggression against Libya (*Weekend Chronicle*, 11 January).

**International Activities, Views, and Positions.** Communist interest and activities in Malta increased perceptibly during 1986 leading observers to question the significance of such a concentrated drive in an island of 100 square miles. Moscow sent two medical eye and heart specialists to discuss their own techniques and hold talks with the Maltese medical authorities. On the same circuit, the Soviets sent a high-powered economist, a team of academic journalists, and a Bolshoi Ballet troupe. There are plans to set up a ballet academy with Soviet help. Malta has become a point of departure for Mediterranean cruises by Soviet liners with Aeroflot flying cruise passengers to and from the island. There has been a program of photographic exhibitions and book presentations to schools and institutions. The broadcasting media have been increasing their intake of Soviet films and news clips. Scholarship offers and free trips to the USSR have become routine, with special attention paid to influential citizens, such as newspaper editors, artists, and even members of the judiciary. The Soviet embassy circulates, at strategic moments, rosy accounts of expanding Soviet trading relations.

In August a Komsomol delegation visited the island. Apart from meeting the prime minister and other representatives, this delegation signed a cooperation protocol with the Malta Labor Party Youth Movement (*Orizzont*, 11 August). The Supreme Soviet in Moscow invited a mixed five-member parliamentary delegation for a week's visit to Moscow and Leningrad (ibid., 23 October). The delegation was given red-carpet treatment and was engaged in several discussion meetings, some bearing on Soviet policy interests in the Mediterranean and others probing into Maltese-Soviet relations in case of a change of government in Malta. The Malta Chamber of Commerce also visited Moscow to sign a Cooperation Agreement with the Chamber of Commerce of the USSR (*Times*, 27 November). The agreement formalizes relations between the two chambers and is meant to facilitate two-way trade. The Malta Chamber delegation stated on its return home that it proposed a number of suggestions "which were well received" and that both sides "agreed to maintain close contact and to explore future possibilities" after the transition period that prevails in Moscow following structural changes in foreign trade policy authorized by the Supreme Soviet (ibid.).

Two curious news items disclosed that a Soviet Antonov 26 transport aircraft carrying military equipment made an overnight stop at Luga airport (*Democrat*, 7 June). No other information was made public. On August 16, the same newspaper, quoting from the Nineteenth Semi-Annual Report on the Implementation of the Helsinki Final Act by President Reagan to the Commission on Security and Cooperation in Europe (CSCE) and published by the U.S. Department of State, indicated that

Malta was among seven non–Warsaw Pact countries invited to observe the Kavkaz 85 maneuvers that took place in July in the Caucasus region (*Democrat*, 16 August). At the end of 1985, Malta's regular armed forces had a strength of only 1,100 men (Malta, *Annual Report of Department of Labour*, 1985).

The Soviets have discovered that their balance sheet is showing a small, if negligible, minus side as far as Malta is concerned. A Soviet citizen in Malta at the end of a Mediterranean cruise defected after escaping from his group. (*Orizzont*, 17 November.) This episode led to publication for the first time of the news that a number of Czech doctors working in the island had eloped and found refuge in various countries including the United States and South Africa (*Democrat*, 15 November).

The president of Hungary, Pál Losonczi, paid a brief visit to Malta, where he had talks with a Maltese delegatioin led by President Agatha Barbara and Prime Minister Mifsud Bonnici (*Times*, 25 April). Reportedly, matters of bilateral interest were discussed. Malta's minister of health, Vincent Moran, traveled to Budapest for talks about joint venture projects (*Orizzont*, 9 February). Groups of agricultural students and handicapped persons were invited to Hungary for educational and holiday visits respectively. Polish foreign minister Marian Orzechowski, visited Malta in May. After a series of official talks he said that "it was imperative that every possibility be explored to consolidate cooperation between the two countries" (*Weekend Chronicle*, 10 May). Concrete projects being considered included the possibility of Polish ships being repaired in Malta. Bulgaria promised to send more ships for repairs at Malta drydocks (*Times*, 5 March), gave a modest 125,000 dollar order to the new government-controlled foundry (ibid., 29 March), and started to negotiate a trade agreement with Malta in May (*Orizzont*, 27 May). Czechoslovakia held two exhibitions, invited its quota of Maltese guests to Prague and continued to buy the whole production of two engineering Maltese-Czechoslovak joint ventures. East Germany inaugurated a weekly air service from East Berlin to Tripoli in Libya using Malta as a transit point. Malta airport is now being used regularly by Aeroflot, Balkanair, and Interflug for the same purpose. Romania invited the speaker of the Malta Parliament for an official visit, and the GWU was asked to send a representative to the Congress of the Confederation of Romanian Trade Unions. A seven-man, high-level Malta delegation visited Cuba for talks on "political, economic and commercial matters" (*Torca*, 16 November). North Korea played host to the minister of works and sports, Lorry Sant, who was received by Kim il-Sung (*Orizzont*, 15 July). A team of North Korean experts visited Malta at the invitation of the government to examine the feasibility of a causeway between Malta and the sister island of Gozo (*Times*, 19 March).

Activity by the People's Republic of China slowed down as Malta used up its $21 million interest-free loan acquired from Chou En Lai in 1972. The last installment of $1.5 million was used to finance a Sino-Maltese joint venture for a factory that will produce silk garments (ibid., 16 October). The major part of the loan was used to build a drydock for supertankers, for a transshipment harbor project, and to start a number of factories. The factories were a failure and, with one exception, have closed down. The principal phases of the transshipment harbor have been completed and the small

workforce of Chinese technicians has returned home. Malta undertook to pay back the loan by exports of its "commodities" between 1984 and 1994. Four small ships have been built in Malta on orders from China. Following a visit to the island by the Chinese vice-minister of health, Gu Yingui, China and Malta announced another cooperation project—the opening of acupuncture and moxibustion units accessible to countries in the Mediterranean region. It is proposed that facilities also be provided for training in these specializations (ibid., 22 June). The Malta-China Friendship Society opened a film club, and the Hubei Province Council for the Promotion of International Fairs participated at the 28th International Fair of Malta (ibid., 1 July).

J. G. E. Hugh
*Valletta, Malta*

# The Netherlands

**Population.** 14,536,000
**Party.** Communist Party of the Netherlands (Communistische Partij van Nederland; CPN)
**Date Founded.** 1909
**Membership.** 12,000 (estimated)
**Chairman.** Elli Izeboud
**Party Executive.** (Partijbestuur). 55 members, including Elli Izeboud, Ina Brouwer, Marius Ernsting, Nico Scouten, Jan Berghuis, Leo Mollenaar, Boe Thio, Ton van Hoek, Geert Lameris
**Status.** Legal
**Last Congress.** Thirtieth, 29 November–2 December 1986, in Amsterdam
**Last Election.** 1986, 0.6 percent, no seats in the Second Chamber (lower house); 2 of 75 seats retained from previous elections to the upper house.
**Auxiliary Organizations.** General Netherlands Youth Organization (ANJV), CPN Women, Stop the Bomb/Stop the Nuclear Arms Race, CPN Youth Platform, Scholing en Onderwijs, Women Against Nuclear Weapons

**Publications.** *De Waarheid* (Truth), official daily; *CPN-Leden krant*, published ten times annually for CPN members; *Politiek en Cultuur*, theoretical journal published ten times yearly; *Komma*, quarterly issued by CPN's Institute for Political and Social Research. CPN owns Pegasus Publishers.

The year 1986 was a disastrous one for the Communist Party of the Netherlands. In the 19 March municipal elections, the CPN lost one-third of its seats on municipal councils and was reduced to a single council seat in the city of Groningen (previous representation: 6). Two months later, in the 21 May parliamentary elections, the CPN plummeted from its 1.8 percent of the national vote in 1982 to 0.6 percent and lost the three seats it had held in the previous Parliament. This left the CPN unrepresented in the Second Chamber (lower house) for the first time since 1918.

The electoral defeats of 1986 came at the end of a long period of crisis and internal conflict within the CPN. Through 1977, the CPN was a small but unreconstructed Marxist-Leninist party. Characterizing itself as a party of the working class, the CPN drew on long-established bases of support in older industries, such as shipbuilding and heavy metals, and could rely on support not only in working class neighborhoods in Amsterdam but also in urban and rural areas in the northeastern province of Groningen. Although Stalinist in its internal politics, the CPN was noted for the effectiveness of its representatives in municipal councils and the national Parliament. In the early 1970s, a period of realignment and change in Dutch politics, the CPN benefited from student protests and increased worker militancy, and the party's support increased to 3.9 percent (six seats) in the 1971 national elections and then to 4.5 percent (seven seats) in 1972. However, in the sharply polarized 1977 elections, the communists dropped to 1.7 percent, reducing their parliamentary representation from seven to two.

The 1977 elections triggered a series of changes within the party. Following electoral losses in the 1977 elections, the CPN ended its former isolation, tentatively adopted a Eurocommunist line, and began to consider alliances with other smaller parties on the left, such as the Pacifist Socialist Party (PSP) and the Radical Political Party (PPR), as well as possible coalitions with the Labor Party (PvdA), the principal representative of social democracy in the Netherlands. In the early 1980s, radical feminists and others gained influence within the party. Battles between the newer elements, who were committed to renewal of the party and its emergence as a radical party of the left, and diverse elements of

the old guard, who wanted the party to continue in its older role as a vanguard of the proletariat, resulted in the renewers narrowly gaining control of the party. From 1982 onward, the party, although divided, was increasingly committed to cooperation with the smaller left parties. The CPN assumed an active role within the peace movement and adopted advanced positions on feminist issues and the equality of homosexuals. These changing emphases resulted in increased internal division and, in 1984, the departure of part of the old guard and their formation of a rival party, the Association of Communists in the Netherlands (VCN). (*YICA*, 1985, 1986.)

Despite attempts to build electoral alliances, the CPN competed alone in the 1986 parliamentary elections. The PvdA, bent on increasing its strength vis à vis the ruling center-right coalition of Liberals and Christian Democrats, rejected any overtures for alliance with the smaller parties to its left, and the small left parties themselves were internally divided. In 1985, the PSP rejected the submission of a joint list of candidates for the 1986 parliamentary elections, leaving the communists and Radicals to compete on their own. In the 1986 election campaign, the communists stressed peace issues (particularly their opposition to the cruise missile deployment), unemployment, and feminist issues. One outcome of their 8 February election conference was a call for a binding referendum on the deployment of cruise missiles (*De Volkskrant*, 10 February; *FBIS*, 21 February). However, the communists' positions on these and other issues were barely distinguishable from those of other smaller parties on the left, or for that matter, the more moderate PvdA. Moreover, the 1986 parliamentary elections and the municipal elections that preceded them were defined by both the larger parties and the media as a vote on the continuation of Prime Minister Ruud Lubbers's center-right cabinet, which had been in office since 1982, and the austerity measures it had implemented. The PvdA, campaigning on its opposition to cruise missile deployment, the need for more effective measures against unemployment, and the necessity of bringing an alternate government into power, won 33.3 percent of the vote and gained five seats, gains that were largely at the expense of the smaller left parties. Because Christian Democratic increases (nine seats) offset

Liberal losses, the center-right coalition retained its narrow majority (81 of 150 seats). However, the three smaller left parties retained only three of the eight seats they had held since 1982. The only consolation for the CPN was that the rival VCN polled only 0.1 percent of the national vote. (*Keesings Historisch Archief*, 5 June.)

**Internal Party Affairs.** Election losses preoccupied the CPN in 1986. Following the 19 March municipal elections and the 1 May parliamentary elections, CPN parliamentary leader Ina Brouwer joined leaders of the PSP and the PPR in attributing their losses to the general climate of polarization and to the PvdA's "failed" election strategy, which had drawn support from the left rather than the right and ended up weakening the entire left (ibid.). The party newspaper, *De Waarheid* drew similar conclusions. Arguing that the PvdA's attempt to force the Christian Democrats into a center-left coalition had failed, and that the refusal of the PvdA to cooperate with parties to its left had succeeded only in weakening the left, *De Waarheid* maintained that cooperation among parties of the left both inside and outside of Parliament was essential if the PvdA or others were to retain any influence (ibid.).

The postmortems continued at a special party meeting of the party executive and district representatives, held on 25 May. According to *De Waarheid*, widely divergent views about the causes of the CPN's losses were expressed. Many argued that election defeats were less the result of "external factors" than "the course of action and character of the current CPN itself." However, relatively few direct attacks were directed against the party leadership. More traditional Marxist-Leninists within the party blamed the defeat on the CPN's "hodgepodge leftistist strategy," particularly its failure to direct itself, as it had in the past, to "the socioeconomic struggle of ordinary working people" and the failure of the party to assume a firm anticapitalist posture. Neglect of the party's former vanguard role in favor of broader alliances with other elements of the left deprived the CPN of its distinctive character and alienated longtime followers. However, a majority of those present rejected any attempt to take the party back to its more isolated past and argued instead that the only possible course was to continue working for cooperation among the communists, Pacifist Socialists, and Radicals. According to this view, voters had little interest in the CPN's past glories but were more interested in what it could do today. Divisions among the radical left deprived it not only of representation but also of the creative spark needed to establish a viable alternative to the left of the PvdA. Only cooperation and a joint parliamentary list could ensure a return to the Parliament. For their part, party leaders assumed a cautious stance. Parliamentary party chair Ina Brouwer argued that the CPN had neglected the maintenance and expansion of party organization in its quest for greater cooperation on the left and had given "too little thought to the question of what should be done if cooperation were to fail," while party chair Elli Izeboud stressed the importance of restoring either the CPN or communists to the Dutch Parliament. (*De Waarheid*, 26 May, cited in *JPRS*, 2 September.) According to Izeboud, this meant the CPN would have to profile itself more distinctively vis à vis the small left parties and that cooperation with them could no longer be a priority (*NRC Handelsblad*, 26 May). In doing so, Izeboud echoed sentiments that the CPN had placed too much emphasis on cooperation and that it had failed to bring its own views forward (*Volkskrant*, 26 May). Although no specific conclusions were reached on the future course of the party, it was decided that the Thirtieth Party Congress, which was to take place in late spring of 1987, should be advanced to elect a new executive and determine party strategy for the spring 1987 elections to provincial legislatures (*De Waarheid*, 26 May, cited in *JPRS*, 2 September).

The Thirtieth Party Congress opened in Amsterdam on 29 November. Originally scheduled to last only three days, the congress had to be extended for a fourth day to resolve disagreements over election of the party executive. Although a nominating committee had prepared a list of candidates representing different elements within the party, Marxist-Leninists, led by Geert Lameris, secretary of the CPN's Groningen district, submitted a competing list that omitted Brouwer and Evelien Eshuis, two of the three members of the parliamentary caucus defeated in the May elections. Lameris charged that the former executive lacked sufficient "analytical capabilities" and had been unable to bridge divisions within the party. After considerable debate, Lameris's list (consisting of members from his own district as well as North Holland North and Drente and members of the workgroup, *Marxism and Class Struggle*) was defeated, and the previous leadership group, including Brouwer, Eshuis, and party chair Izeboud, was re-elected. As in the past, the dissenters pledged to cooperate with the leadership despite their disagreements. (*NRC Handelsblad, Weekeditie voor Het Buitenland*, 16 December.)

Debate on the direction of the party continued outside of formal party meetings. At a special study day, organized on 7 June by the CPN's research bureau (the Institute for Social and Political Research; IPSO), a number of party members and ex–party members debated the future of the party. Although former member of Parliament Marius Ernsting was relatively optimistic and argued that the CPN could survive by maintaining its own identity and continuing to strive for cooperation on the left, others such as former *De Waarheid* editor André Roelofs and Marxist historian and former party member Ger Harmsen disagreed. Roelofs argued that the CPN had failed to de-Stalinize in the aftermath of the CPSU's revelations in 1956, while Harmsen traced the CPN's demise to mistakes made in the 1930s. Roelofs, in particular, argued that the party's attempts at renewal were both incomplete and too late. (*Trouw*, June 9.) Harry van den Berg, IPSO director, and a representative of the CPN's reformist wing, echoed similar themes, arguing that the CPN's problems reflected the insufficient and incomplete renewal of the party. The CPN had, in his view, failed to use its opening to new social movements to modify the party organization or develop a new party culture. Although room continued to exist for a consequential party to the left of the PvdA, the CPN came across as a small sectlike "witness party."

Elsewhere, Gijs Schreuder, a former *De Waarheid* editor who had left the party in 1983, argued that the CPN had little future. In Schreuder's view, the time for a party such as the CPN was largely past, and the party had little hope of regaining old support or emerging as a successful left alternative to the PvdA. Although the CPN's former positions were outdated, the incomplete party renewal and the party's embrace of feminism had made the party unrecognizable. Although there was, in Schreuders' view, still room for a party to the left of the PvdA, this role could not be filled by the small sectarian club the CPN had become. (*NRC Handelsblad*, 31 May.) In contrast Geert Lameris, an advocate of a return to the CPN's former role as a vanguard of the proletariat, argued that continuing problems, such as unemployment and the world situation meant that there was a role for a recognizable communist party (*Nieuwsblad van het Noorden*, 5 April).

By the end of 1986, debate on the future of the CPN remained unresolved. Although party leaders, such as Brouwer and Izeboud, had expressed doubts about the CPN's previous emphasis on cooperation with other parties to the left of the PvdA in preparation for the 1987 provincial elections, communists, Pacifist Socialists, and Radicals had agreed to submit joint lists of candidates in ten of the twelve provinces. Only in North Holland and Groningen, both strongholds of the orthodox Marxist-Leninists within the party, was the CPN planning to submit its list of candidates (*NRC Handelsblad Weekeditie voor het Buitenland*, 16 December). At the same time, however, in a recently published volume, *De Crisis van het Nederlandse Communisme* (D. Hellema, ed.), former parliamentary leader Brouwer, calling for flexibility, indicated that if necessary, communists might return to the Parliament by working through the PvdA (*NRC Handelsblad Weekeditie voor het Buitenland*, 2 December).

**Domestic Politics.** The CPN was largely preoccupied with municipal and parliamentary elections and their aftermath in 1986. In the 1986 election campaigns, the party played on both international and domestic issues. The CPN's opposition to the deployment of cruise missiles, the need to lower defense expenditures, and the need for relaxation of international tensions were prominent themes. On domestic issues, the CPN argued for closure of nuclear power plants, reducing income differences, increasing the buying power of middle and lower incomes, and combating unemployment through reducing the workweek to 32 and then 25 hours (while maintaining workers' incomes), and stimulating investment in sectors capable of providing employment. In addition, the CPN argued that emancipation of women must not be hindered by cutbacks in public spending. (*Keesings Historisch Archief*, 5 June.)

**International Contacts.** International contacts in 1986 included a visit to the German Democratic Republic by CPN party executive member Ton van Hoek. Themes touched on included disarmament, the CPN's opposition to the deployment of cruise missiles, the need for chemical-free zones in Europe, and the need for solidarity with African and Asian peoples. In addition, the use of technology, particularly microelectronics, to improve people's lives was dicussed. (*Neues Deutschland*, 24 April.)

Although relations with the Soviet Union remain cool, *Pravda* commented on both the May parliamentary elections and the CPN's Thirtieth Party Congress. Attributing the election results largely to economic issues, *Pravda* noted the persistence of antimissile sentiment among Dutch voters. However, the article made no mention of the CPN or its electoral losses. (*Pravda*, 23 May; *FBIS*, 30 May.) *Pravda*, which had virtually ignored the CPN's 1984 congress, devoted three columns to the Thirtieth Party Congress, paying particular attention to party chair Izeboud's speech and her criticisms of the United States for not joining with Soviet leaders at Reykjavik in ending the arms race (*Pravda*, 30 November). However, CPN positions were characterized as identical to those of the Soviet Union (which they are not), and the article made no reference to the deep divisions in the Dutch party (*NRC Handelsblad*, *Weekeditie van het Buitenland*, 9 December).

**Conclusion.** All in all, 1986 was anything but a banner year for the CPN. Electoral defeat exacerbated divisions within the party and raised serious questions about the future of the party. The issues involved not only strategy but also finances: loss of the CPN's seats in the Second Chamber deprived the party of subsidies used to finance its research bureau and forced the party to dismiss as many as ten salaried employees (*Volkskrant*, 26 May). Nor could strategic and ideological dilemmas be resolved easily. The claim by the party's orthodox Marxist-Leninist wing that the attempts to renew the party had alienated traditional working-class

supporters undoubtably contained an element of truth, but the traditional working class to which the CPN appealed and the older industries (textiles, shipbuilding, carton) in which they worked are rapidly disappearing. Even so, transforming the party, developing new themes, and appealing to new groups is at best uncertain. The smaller parties to the left of the PvdA appeal to similar electorates (typically elements of the new middle classes), and their terrain on the left of the political spectrum is, in polarized electoral contests such as those of 1977 and 1986, easily raided by the PvdA, which itself has become more open and interpenetrated by elements of the new middle classes. As several observers noted, Labor's continuing interest in governing and making itself available for coalitions allows room for at least one party to its left. However, the Dutch electoral law encourages the organization and success of smaller parties. Although in the past this has permitted several parties including the CPN to flourish, in a narrowing electoral market the smaller parties can readily defeat each other. Whether this will encourage greater cooperation and the formation of the new kind of party or alliance that reformers in the CPN have advocated remains to be seen.

Steven B. Wolinetz
*Memorial University of Newfoundland*

# Norway

**Population.** 4,165,000
**Parties.** Norwegian Communist Party (Norges Kommunistiske Parti; NKP); Socialist Left Party (Sosialistisk Venstreparti; SV); Workers' Communist Party (Arbeidernes Kommunistiske Parti; AKP), runs as Red Electoral Alliance (Rod Valgallians; RV) in elections
**Founded.** NKP: 1923, SV: 1976, AKP: 1973
**Membership.** NKP: 5,500, SV: 2,000, AKP: 10,000 (all estimated)
**Chairman.** NKP: Hans I. Kleven, SV: Theo Koritzinsky, AKP: Kjersti Ericsson
**Central Committee.** NKP. 14 full members: Hans I. Kleven, Ingrid Negard (deputy chair), Bjorn

Naustvik (organizational secretary), Arne Jorgensen, Trygve Horgen, Grete Trondsen, Asmund Langsether (trade-union affairs), Rolf Dahl, Gunnar Wahl, Kare Andre Nilsen, Arvid Borglund, Gunnar Sorbo, Kirsti Kristiansen, Ornulf Godager (*Friheten*, 20 September 1984); 6 alternate members: Martin Gunnar Knutsen (former party chair), L. Hammerstad, H. P. Hansen, Sturla Indregard, Fredrik Kristensen, Knut Johansen

**Status.** Legal

**Last Congress.** NKP: Eighteenth, 30 March–2 April 1984, in Oslo; SV March 1985, in Trondheim; AKP: December 1984, "somewhere in Norway" (*Arbeiderbladet*, 18 December 1984)

**Last Election.** 1985; NKP: 0.2 percent, no representation; SV: 5.5 percent, 6 of 157 seats; AKP: 0 percent, no representation

**Auxiliary Organization.** NKP: Norwegian Communist Youth League (NKU)

**Publications.** NKP: *Friheten* (Freedom), semiweekly, Arne Jorgensen, editor; *Vart Arbeid*, internal organ; AKP: *Klassekampen* (Class struggle), daily

Until 1979 the Norwegian Labor Party (Det Norske Arbeiderparti; DNA)—a moderate social-democratic reform movement—dominated postwar Norwegian politics. During this era, the DNA was the main governing party and all but monopolized the left in the country's politics. Three Marxist parties have stood to the left of the DNA: the pro-Soviet NKP and SV and Maoist AKP, which has campaigned in parliamentary elections as the RV. In the 1981 elections the DNA was ousted from power by a center-right coalition led by Conservative Party leader Kaare Willoch.

When Willoch's coalition was re-elected in the general election of 9 September 1985, he became the first conservative prime minister ever to win a second term in Norway. His coalition held only a one-seat majority in the Storting (parliament), however, and was forced to depend for support on the two representatives of the right-wing Progressive Party (which advocated the dismantling of the Norwegian welfare state).

In May 1986 Willoch resigned after losing a vote of confidence in the Storting over the austerity policies introduced by his government to cope with declining oil revenues. Gro Harlem Brundtland, head of the DNA, became the new prime minister. Her socialist alliance held only 77 parliamentary seats—two short of a majority and one less than the conservative coalition.

**The Norwegian Communist Party.** The NKP began as a small splinter group of radical trade unionists and politicians who left the DNA in 1923. It experienced many lean years until after World War II, when its support for the war effort against Nazi Germany and the Soviet liberation of northern Norway boosted the NKP's popularity at the polls (eleven seats in the first postwar Parliament). However, the party's fortunes fell with the onset of the Cold War.

The weakness of the NKP was due, in large part, to its decision in 1975 to remain a staunchly pro-Soviet, Stalinist party. Its membership and popularity dwindled when Reidar Larsen, then its chair, and several other leaders abandoned the NKP and established the SV.

Although differences still exist between the NKP and the SV, NKP chair Kleven looks favorably on SV chair Koritzinsky's call for a broad united front of left-wing parties in Norway. Kleven believes that it is especially important to establish unity of action in the labor movement, both in the unions themselves and in the political parties close to labor—the DNA, the SV, and the NKP.

In addition, Kleven supports Koritzinsky's proposals for electoral cooperation between the NKP and the SV. Kleven has suggested running SV and NKP candidates on joint election lists. He has also backed Koritzinsky's idea for the NKP and SV to cooperate on specific issues in order to reshape Norwegian society in a socialist direction.

The NKP continues to be one of the weakest communist parties in Western Europe. It received a mere 7,025 votes (0.3 percent) in the last parliamentary elections in 1981, far short of the number needed to win a seat in the Storting. In the local elections of 1983, the NKP captured only 0.4 percent of the vote, and in the general elections of September 1985, the party polled just 0.2 percent.

*The Nuclear Issue.* At its Seventeenth Congress in 1981, the NKP formally adopted a peace offensive. Its essence was the struggle against the deployment of new nuclear weapons in Europe and for a nuclear-free northern Europe. The party advocated a nuclear-free zone encompassing Norway,

Sweden, Denmark, and Finland that would be formalized by a treaty guaranteed by the great powers (*WMR*, April 1983). The NKP was active in preparations for Peace March 1983, a twenty-day affair that began on 10 July in Eidsvoll, in southern Norway, and finished in the northern city of Trondheim. The slogans were "No nuclear weapons in Norway" and "No to the deployment of new missiles in Europe." NKP-affiliated sponsors of the march included the Norwegian Peace Committee (a branch of the Soviet-controlled World Peace Council) and the Women's Committee for Peace.

In October 1982 the NKP supported the Labor Party's unsuccessful vote against NATO infrastructure appropriations needed to prepare sites for new U.S. missiles in Europe. The communists also praised the findings of the DNA commission, released in January 1983, that came out against the deployment of U.S. Pershing II and cruise missiles in Western Europe and in favor of a nuclear freeze and the creation of nuclear-free zones in northern Europe.

According to the NKP, the conservative-led coalition that came to power in 1981 increased Norway's subordination to the United States and exacerbated relations between Norway and the USSR, which share a border. The NKP accused the Willoch government of involvement in "U.S. militarist plans" and demanded that it pursue an "independent security and defense policy" (*WMR*, April 1983; *Aftenposten*, 9 March 1983; *JPRS*, 20 April 1983).

Differences emerged between the NKP and the DNA on the issue of Soviet responsibility for the growing nuclear threat in Europe. In particular, the NKP criticized the DNA's call for reductions in Soviet medium-range missiles on the continent. The NKP has also backed the ongoing Socialist bloc appeal to the United States to follow the Soviet example and pledge no first use of atomic weapons.

At the beginning of 1984, a subtle shift in the NKP's position on nuclear issues became apparent. On 8 January, *Aftenposten* printed a lengthy statement by Kleven, who had just chaired an NKP Politburo session on missiles and the peace movement in Europe. The bulk of Kleven's statement was strongly anti-American, as typified by the following passage: "The new U.S. missiles in Europe have brought us one step closer to disaster . . . The Norwegian Communist Party wants to stigmatize those who carry the main responsibility for this: the U.S. government and the arms industry . . . Moreover,

the U.S. NATO allies, among them the Willoch government, carry joint responsibility for the deterioration of the international situation." Kleven demanded withdrawal of the missiles and a return to the status quo that existed in Europe before their deployment. Nevertheless, he stipulated that, parallel to the withdrawal of the U.S. missiles, "counterefforts by the Warsaw Pact [to deploy its own missiles] must cease" and there must be a "halt to all testing, production and deployment of new nuclear weapons," presumably by the Soviets as well as the Americans.

The NKP has continued to promote in the trade unions an October 1982 directive from the Central Board of Communists to link the struggle for better working and living conditions with demands for cuts in military spending. The NKP advocates switching funds earmarked for military purposes to civilian needs.

In July 1985, the NKP issued a statement calling on the Norwegian government to bar nuclear-armed U.S. naval vessels from the country's ports. The statement was inspired by the example of New Zealand, which effectively barred all U.S. warships, inasmuch as the United States refuses to divulge which of its ships carry nuclear weapons.

*The Peace Issue and Norwegian Foreign Policy.* In a lengthy article entitled "National Interests and 'Atlantic Solidarity'" in the October 1986 issue of *World Marxist Review*, Kleven excoriated Norway's alleged subordination to U.S. global nuclear strategy and declared that Norwegian membership in NATO constituted a dilution of its national sovereignty. "Our country has been assigned the role of an unsinkable aircraft carrier on the bloc's northern flank," Kleven wrote. He placed most of the blame for this state of affairs on the Willoch government, "for it kept giving in to U.S. demands and pressures, behaving as one of its most loyal partners in NATO and disgracing the country by its submissively loyal and anti-national conduct." Kleven drew an analogy between NATO and the European Common Market (EEC), both of which he regarded as having "an imperialist character" and operating on the basis of "supranational organs" that forcibly integrate the policies of smaller and weaker countries with those of the larger and more powerful members.

The wide popular movement against Norway's entry into the Common Market, which involved the most diverse social and political forces, won the 1972 referendum, when a majority of the population clearly said "No" to the plans for integration. . . As earlier on, in the struggle against Norway's entry into NATO and the Common Market, so now, in the struggle against the country's integration with U.S. nuclear strategy, the issue is defense of the very foundations of the nation's life. . . There is a need for a truly national security policy within the framework of a Europe-wide system diametrically opposite to the U.S.-sponsored "Atlantic community." (Ibid.)

Basic elements of Kleven's proposed system included arms reductions throughout the continent and moves toward nuclear disarmament, beginning with the conclusion of a treaty transforming Nordic Europe into a nuclear-free zone. He evidently envisaged the Soviet Union as a member of his pan-European system, to be based on "the development of mutually advantageous ties between states, irrespective of their social system, on the basis of equality and respect for the national sovereignty of each country, whether big or small." The NKP chief called for the strengthening of "proletarian internationalism" (a favorite Soviet term that actually denotes international communist solidarity along lines dictated by the Kremlin). "There is no contradiction between Norway's national interests and the international interests of the working class," he wrote, "because the Communists are simultaneously patriots and internationalists." (Ibid.)

The NKP views the peace movement, which has taken deep root in Norway, as an important vehicle both for advancing communist positions on foreign policy and for expanding the party's influence among various sectors of Norwegian society. During an interview with *World Marxist Review* in August, NKP Central Committee member Jorgensen lavishly praised the work of the peace movement, especially its appeal "No to Nuclear Weapons—For a Nuclear-Free Zone in the North Formalized by a Treaty," which had garnered half a million signatures by the time it was formally presented to the Storting. Jorgensen said that "the Communists are calling on the peace forces to insist on an immediate ban on all nuclear tests [and] take a stand against Norway's further involvement in the USA's global strategy and in NATO's sinister activity on our continent." He also applauded Soviet leader Mikhail Gorbachev's 15 January proposal for the abolition of nuclear weapons by the year 2000 and Moscow's unilateral moratorium on nuclear testing. Jorgensen criticized certain noncommunist ele-

ments in the Norwegian peace movement for "implying that the USA and the Soviet Union are equally responsible for the rise and growth of tension. This weakens the peace movement because it confuses a section of the people in it." He noted, however, that the NKP's press was devoting a special effort to "countering inventions" about the equality of responsibility between the superpowers.

Wahl, another member of the NKP's Central Committee, discussed the Norwegian peace movement during a meeting in Prague in October. The gathering brought together delegates from various communist parties to participate in the *World Marxist Review's* Commission on the Exchange of Party Experience. Wahl called the peace movement an excellent political school for the Norwegian communists, who were particularly successful in steering trade unionists into peace activity and thereby making them more militant and receptive to communist influence.

*The Eighteenth NKP Congress and Its Aftermath.* Peace and jobs were the major themes at the NKP's Eighteenth Congress, held 30 March–2 April 1984. Kleven raised the familiar issues of U.S. nuclear missiles in Europe and the need for a Nordic nuclear-free zone. He proposed a conference of European communist parties to discuss concrete measures to ease world tension. At the same time, he urged the Norwegian government to initiate negotiations with the other Scandinavian countries to bring about a treaty for a nuclear-free zone in northern Europe. Kleven declared that NATO "does not give us protection; it means increased danger instead." Nevertheless, he conceded that the majority of Norwegian citizens favor continued participation in the NATO alliance. (Oslo, *Arbeiderbladt*, 31 March 1984.)

Kleven's speech expressed optimism that war could be averted in Europe. He cited the alleged shift in the "correlation of forces" away from "imperialism," the peace initiatives of the Socialist bloc, and the upsurge of the antiwar movement in Europe. Terminating the deployment of U.S. missiles on the continent and forcing the withdrawal of those already deployed would remain the key task of the peace movement, Kleven asserted (TASS, 30 March 1984).

On the issue of jobs, former NKP deputy chair Trygve Horgen reminded the congress of the party's ten-point program to fight unemployment and of its pressure on the government to uphold the right to work. He also reiterated the labor movement's responsibility to struggle against war and militarism. On 3 April, the day after the close of the congress, *Friheten* published an editorial headlined "To Work, Comrades!" In it, the NKP cited the need "to abolish the capitalist system and bring in a Socialist planned economy in which such crises will not take place."

On international issues, the NKP supported the Soviet stance not only on European issues but also on areas of crisis around the world. For example, the congress adopted a unanimous resolution of solidarity with Central America in its struggle against the allegedly aggressive actions of the United States (*Pravda*, 3 April 1984). A plenum of the NKP's Central Committee in May 1984 passed resolutions opposing the Pol Pot insurgents in Cambodia and the persecution of communists in Iran to cite examples of the party's international concerns (ibid., 9 May 1984).

Kleven was re-elected party chair at the congress, but elections for most of the NKP's other leading officials were postponed as a result of sharp personality conflicts. The post of deputy chair, for example, was the object of a contest between Langsether, an academic backed by Kleven, and Horgen, a worker supported by *Friheten* editor Jorgensen, among others. Another contentious issue was Kleven's reported proposal to exclude Knutsen, the former party chair, from the Central Committee (*Arbeiderbladet*, 1 June 1984).

In June 1984, former Central Committee member John Atle Krogstad sent Norwegian newspapers a remarkable letter that reflected disillusionment with the interparty struggles. "There is an atmosphere of distrust among leading party members," he wrote. "Personality conflicts in the [Central Committee] have convinced me to withdraw from the party . . . The party is permeated with personality conflicts, despite the unanimous agreements at the national congress . . . and despite the fact that the chairman was chosen unanimously." He went on to add, "The NKP is digging its own grave . . . [because of] the party's lack of ability to discuss and solve its differences" (ibid., 16 June 1984).

On 19 June 1984, Kleven published a "Letter to Members of the Norwegian Communist Party" in *Friheten*. It acknowledged the damage done to the NKP by "internal conflicts and disputes, which in most instances have generally been personal rather than political and ideological differences . . . It is most regrettable that we are losing members and officeholders who support the party's policies and ideology. We cannot afford this. We can only solve our differences in a productive manner . . . by means

of open, objective and thorough debate." Kleven appointed a temporary eight-member Central Committee, including Horgen, to serve until final selections could be made.

Magne Mortensen, the NKP's national director, sent *Friheten* a letter that summed up the leadership crisis as it evolved during 1984 and accused Kleven of divisive tactics and overweening personal ambition. Mortensen charged that the chair had transformed normal differences and conflicts among party members on various issues into a debilitating contest of personalities. (*Friheten*, 13 September 1984.)

In October 1984, the Central Committee passed a resolution that the party's infighting could no longer be aired on the pages of *Friheten*. The resolution was justified in the name of "democratic centralism," that is, adherence to the NKP's decisions once they were debated and adopted. The decision to gag *Friheten* reportedly was taken in the face of four nay votes in the Central Committee. Although Jorgensen was among the dissenters, he decided to remain as *Friheten's* editor, declaring that "the political debate will carry on in the paper's columns. But if it is decided that such a debate will not be permitted, well, then I will have to go." (*Aftenposten*, 16 October 1984.)

The NKP's Central Committee held a plenum in December 1984 at which a liveable compromise was reached to end the internecine disputes in the party (ibid., 18 December 1984). It was agreed that the quarrel over the composition of the Central Committee would cease but that interparty discussions would be more free in the future.

No sooner had the divisive debate over the composition of the NKP's Central Committee been relegated to history than a new crisis racked the party. This time, the focal point was international issues, particularly relations with the Soviet Union. According to an article in *Klassekampen* on 30 January 1985:

A new storm is brewing in the Norwegian Communist Party (NKP). Outwardly, there is an impression of calm, but internally the situation is extremely tense. The conflicts that led to an uncontrolled eruption last fall continue to tear the party apart. One group within the party wants it to reject the Soviet system. Another group is calling for closer relations with Eastern Europe and the Soviet Union . . . Many NKP members see support for "proletarian internationalism," i.e., Soviet foreign policy, as vital to the party's existence. On the other hand, strong forces within the party say that it will be destroyed unless it severs its ties with the Soviet Union.

The split within the NKP, which had previously seemed merely to pit the supporters of Kleven against those of former chair Knutsen, has acquired an extra dimension. Kleven, widely regarded as a political opportunist, heads the majority faction; Knutsen and Jorgensen lead a strongly pro-Soviet faction; and the party's youth group. The NKU represents a Eurocommunist-style faction. Kristiansen is the main supporter of the NKU faction on the party's Central Committee.

The continuing factional struggle in the NKP has severely affected the party's efforts not only to attract new members but also to remain a viable organization:

> The Norwegian Communist Party . . . has never been weaker in Norway than it is today. The party has some influence in the peace movement and in the labor movement, but that is all. Many members have left the party during the past year. Many others are making up their minds. Some members have gone over to the Labor Party. Others have gone into passivity. (Ibid.)

Party members and supporters emphasize that the factionalism can no longer be papered over, since it involves not only personalities but also major policy questions. As one interested observer pointed out:

> If the party leadership tries to avoid a battle with the Soviet faction, it will be a tragic mistake. The party leadership must realize how serious the situation is. We must discuss our relationship to the Soviet Communist Party and the Soviet Union. It is the party's national credibility that is at stake. (Ibid.)

The worsening of the internecine struggle in the NKP came at a peculiarly bad time, for the party was preparing to participate in the national elections. The electoral campaign was the primary topic under discussion at the NKP's national conference, which took place in Oslo in March 1985. Bolstering the unity of all "progressive" and democratic forces in the country was deemed the most important task facing the NKP (*Pravda*, 4 March 1985). The party issued an election manifesto that recommended the formation of election pacts among the NKP, the SV, and the Labor Party to contest the Storting elections scheduled for September. In addition, the party conference called for a cutback in the work week to 35 hours, flexible retirement ages for Norwegians over the age of 62, higher taxes on unearned income, the use of petrodollars to create up to 20,000 new jobs, and in the international arena, the establishment of a Nordic nuclear-free zone ratified by the major world powers (*Aftenposten*, 4–6 March 1985).

Naustvik, the NKP's organizational secretary, urged party members to seek contacts with Labor Party and SV representatives in each county of Norway, with the goal of forging electoral alliances; he also enlisted the help of the trade-union movement in this endeavor (ibid., 11 June 1985).

Kleven has conceded that the NKP must cooperate with other parties ("given the actual situation in the country, only the Norwegian Labor Party offers a real alternative to Conservative rule"), but must also carve out its own role, especially in the struggles for peace and improvement of conditions for the working class. He lamented that

> our party is small, it is not represented in the Storting and has virtually no access to the mass media. Still, advancing their election programs and delivering their speeches, Communists try to convince voters that there is a need for them to support the Communist Party.

A vote for the NKP, he declared,

> is not lost. It is a ballot cast for a policy of peace and détente, of fighting against unemployment, the crisis and inflation. Election of Communists to parliament will mean greater opportunities for . . . upholding working people's interests . . . The role of Communist parties in the trade union and antiwar movements . . . confirms that even a numerically small party can be a highly dynamic and elective social force. (*WMR*, March 1985.)

The NKP's next party congress is scheduled for April 1987. A Central Committee plenum held in October discussed preparations for the congress and approved the draft of a new party program. The draft was readied for circulation within primary party organizations and in the communist press prior to its formal presentation at the congress for final acceptance. The Soviet Union praised the draft for reinforcing the NKP's adherence to the principles of Marxism-Leninism and "proletarian internationalism" (*Pravda*, 3 October).

The NKP's international links revolve largely around meetings of the Nordic communist party and consultations with the Soviet and East European parties. During 1985, however, delegations from the NKP visited China (in January) and North Korea (in October). The wide-ranging issues discussed at Nordic communist gatherings were typified in a communiqué published after the parley on north European communist parties in Finland in November 1982. The document covered, inter alia, the inability of capitalism to solve unemployment problems in Scandinavia; the campaign for peace, disarmament, and a Nordic nuclear-free zone; and the right of the Palestinians to establish a state of their own (*IB*, February 1983).

In October 1984, Kleven led a party delegation to Sofia, where he held talks with Todor Zhivkov, general secretary of the Bulgarian Communist Party. They reportedly focused special attention on issues relating to peace and security in Europe (Sofia, BTA, 26 October 1984). In December of that year, in Czechoslovakia, the NKP participated in a meeting of world communist parties under the auspices of *World Marxist Review*. In February 1985, a delegation under Kleven's leadership visited Czechoslovakia for talks with General Secretary Gustav Husak. They condemned "U.S. imperialism," demanded an end to the arms race, and called for celebration of the 40th anniversary of the defeat of Nazi Germany by renewing the struggle for international peace and détente (*FBIS—Eastern Europe*, 22 February 1985). In May, the NKP organized a series of events commemorating the World War II victory. The Soviets sent a delegation headed by D.B. Golovko, secretary of the Kiev section of the Ukrainian Communist Party (*Pravda*, 8 May 1985). Representing the NKP at a *World Marxist Review*–sponsored meeting of communist party delegates in Prague, Wahl spoke in favor of more frequent international gatherings and more vigorous discussion of major issues facing the movement. He cited the concept of unity and diversity put forward at the Twenty-seventh Congress of the Communist Party of the Soviet Union to make the point that international communist gatherings need not result in the adoption of collective documents that would bind member parties. (*WMR*, October).

**The Socialist Left Party.** The SV is the strongest Marxist party to the left of the DNA. In the 1981 parliamentary elections, it received 4.9 percent of the vote and four seats in the Storting. The SV campaigned as a parliamentary ally of the DNA in the local elections of September 1983 (in which it received 5.2 percent of the vote) and in the general

election of September 1985 (in which it won 5.4 percent and 6 parliamentary seats).

**Leadership and Organization.** In January 1983 party leader Berge Furre was replaced by Koritzinsky, who had been chair of the Socialist Youth League. The SV congress in March of that year produced almost a completely new leadership. Koritzinsky was confirmed as chair, Tora Houg and Einar Nyheim were selected as the new deputy chairs, Erik Solheim continued to serve as party secretary, and a new Executive Committee was formed, including veteran Finn Gustavsen.

In the summer of 1984, a struggle broke out between Koritzinsky and Gustavsen (called by his detractors "a Social Democrat in a red coat") over who would be nominated to fill an upcoming vacancy in the Oslo delegation to the Storting (*Aftenposten*, 2 June 1984). The struggle revolved around personalities as well as policies. Women's groups within the SV, for example, announced their opposition to Gustavsen because he opposed SV participation in the campaign against pornography.

The main shift in leadership that occurred at the SV's congress in March 1985 was the replacement of Solheim—evidently at his own request—by Hilde Vogt. The congress also reaffirmed Nyheim's role as the individual in charge of trade union affairs and Kirsti Nost's position as head of women's issues (ibid., 7 March 1985).

**Views and Activities.** In January 1983, just before his replacement as party leader, Furre presented the SV Executive Committee's draft for a working program for the 1980s. The program called for stronger state power, increased government subsidies, and a further expansion of the public sector. It demanded higher taxes and wages, more housing, and nationalizations, as well as "self-sufficiency" and increased "power for the worker." (Ibid., 29 January 1983; *JPRS*, 23 February 1983.)

Shortly after he assumed the party chair, Koritzinsky came out in favor of broad case-by-case cooperation with the left, especially between the SV and the NKP. Koritzinsky has advocated cooperation among peace, environmental, women's, and labor-union groups. He has emphasized, however, that such cooperatioin must be under the control of local party groups and must not be aimed at party unifications (*Friheten*, 26 January 1983; *JPRS*, 3 March 1983). Hanna Kvanmo, the SV's parliamentary leader, has declared that she will not permit the impression to evolve that the SV is a "support party" for the DNA, with which it has an electoral pact (*Aftenposten*, 7 March 1985).

Unlike the NKP, the SV favors reforms rather than total rejection of current Norwegian institutions. Nevertheless, Koritzinsky stresses that reforms must be structural in nature, with a transfer of power to popularly elected delegates and organized labor. This program implies greater municipal and county authority and stronger company democracy. Koritzinsky says that the SV is considering the concept of wage-earner funds, which would give unions and elected delegates more control over capital.

The SV congress of 1983 focused on the struggle against growing unemployment in Norway and the struggle for women's equality (*FBIS—Western Europe*, 14 March 1983). It also passed a resolution urging party members to participate in local peace marches against several airports in Norway that the SV claims are a part of U.S. nuclear strategy, "so that the civilian population in the districts concerned understands the dangers it is exposed to" (*Aftenposten*, 14 March 1983; *JPRS*, 20 April 1983). On the international front, the congress issued a strongly worded statement condemning the Soviet war in Afghanistan (*Aftenposten*, 14 March 1983; *JPRS*, 20 April 1983).

At its 1985 congress, the SV declared that keeping Norway free of nuclear weapons, combatting unemployment, and bringing about a fairer distribution of the material goods of society constituted its top priorities, both in its day-to-day policy and in the national election campaign that was already underway. Probably the most controversial aspect of the party's proposals was the call for a six-hour workday, to be instituted before 1992. In addition, the party congress called for a lowering of the age for pension eligibility, the nationalizing of key industries and credit institutions, greater sympathy on the part of the government for women's rights, and a prohibition on visits to Norwegian ports by nuclear-armed ships (*Aftenposten*, 8, 11 March). Outgoing party secretary Solheim told the congress that "SV's influence cannot be measured in our number of election votes alone" and recalled the "countless issues that SV has pushed forth, and others have harvested the benefits" (ibid., 11 March).

**Current Developments.** As 1986 opened, the internal debate about the SV's future direction intensified. One SV official urged the party to "put less emphasis on the 'worker' profile. Most workers today do not identify at all with the traditional 'worker' image." (*Aftenposten*, 4 January.) Moreover, an article in the Norwegian press pointed out that only about 4 percent of people who cast votes for the SV work in industries or primary occupations. The party's main base of electoral support apparently lies among young, highly educated women and among Norwegians whose occupations are in the fields of culture, the media, research, education, health, and social services. None of these groups identify with a proletarian-oriented philosophy. Many of the SV's supporters are more interested in such issues as greater broadcasting activity—perhaps financed by advertising—and a more modern image in general for the party.

Houg, chair of the committee that drafted the SV's new party program, emphasized that it was built around the principle of a more modernized, albeit still Marxist, orientation. The draft is being circulated within the party and will be presented to the SV's next congress in 1987. The program proposal states that

Marxist traditions and ideas can be used to justify suppression. The "proletariat's dictatorship" theory has been used to justify suppression of political forces other than the Communist Party. The concept of "democratic centralism" has been used to justify suppression of opposition and debate within the party. The belief that Marxism is an infallible science and that history has but one outcome leads to intolerance and suppression and has been used to justify the liquidation of political opposition.

Terje Erikstad, deputy leader of Socialist Youth, stated in the SV's press organ *Ny Tid* that on several issues the party program took a more liberal stand than its predecessor (dating from 1977); for example, it displayed less blind adherence to the centralized power of the state, a clearer criticism of bureaucracy, a more positive view of local radio and TV, a more liberal attitude on closing laws and alcohol policy, and greater tolerance for private activities in such spheres as health and social services. Commenting on these changes, an article in the 4 January issue of the conservative newspaper *Aftenposten* said:

We can see the same sort of pattern in foreign policy . . . SV would naturally like to continue to love and hate America. Party people know better, but they pretend that the United States is nothing but "Dynasty," the CIA and United Fruit. It is more damaging that party criticism of the Soviet Union's brutal ways of assisting its neighbors is seldom more than a pale echo of the outraged cries about the less endearing aspects of the United States' superpower policies . . . And censure pours over [Ingolf Hakon] Teigene [editor of *Ny Tid*] every time he suggest that bombs in the East can be just as dangerous as bombs in the West, or when he sharpens his pen when he writes about the conduct of the Soviet dictatorship. There was a similar negative reaction when *Ny Tid* devoted its editorial page to some mild criticism of the state of emergency in Nicaragua.

Houg, interviewed in *Ny Tid*, noted that the SV party program committee's proposal refers to the USSR as a bureaucratic dictatorship and attributes equal responsibility to the Soviet Union and the United States for the arms race. Hostility toward NATO and Norway's bloc policy remains unmitigated, however, even though Houg noted that party members differ over how quickly, and in what manner, the country's membership in the alliance should be terminated. (*Ny Tid*, 8 February.)

During her interview, Houg declared that the SV could not point to any country as a model of the type of socialism it wished to achieve. The party's program committee referred to the Soviet Union and China as nations that "have broken with capitalism" but are not socialistic. She remarked that "there is great potential for democratic Socialism in Norway . . . but Socialism is both the means and the goal [for the SV]. Democracy alone—without Socialism's perspective on solidarity and fair distribution—is for me an inadequate goal." Houg added that "we have a . . . view of society in which the disparity between workers and capital interests is the key, but our basic view also takes into account knowledge of the Environmental Movement, the Peace Movement, the Women's Movement, and the leisure-time society." (Ibid.)

The debate between the more liberal or "progressive" elements of the SV and its more traditional or conservative adherents is expected to continue. Not even the most liberal members, however, appear willing to entertain a merger with the DNA, which some in the Labor Party have proposed. Houg (who regards herself as a traditionalist) has stated:

I consider the idea of a political rapprochement to a large degree as an illusion against the background of the Labor Party's conduct as an opposition party. The discussion climate has indeed become better . . . But the real political dividing lines continue to exist. (*Arbeiderbladet*, 8 January.)

Most SV members probably would agree that the main dividing lines involve security policy and the attitude toward NATO membership in foreign policy and continuation of a capitalist economic system at home. The SV believes that Norway's mixed economy, as presided over by the ruling DNA, does not represent a break with capitalism. However, the SV is vague about its economic goals. The party supports the present nationalization of banks and credit institutions in Norway but also claims to be in search of models of cooperative and community ownership of property and resources. (*Ny Tid*, 8 February.) Moreover, "we could meet the salary demand of 10 teachers today by dividing among them one top Norwegian industry executive's wage increase," declared Gustavsen, the recently selected editor of *Ny Tid* (*Aftenposten*, 3 March).

**The Workers' Communist Party.** The AKP was born in the late 1960s as an amalgam of various Maoist organizations that were disenchanted with the Soviet economic model and with Soviet foreign policy. The AKP was founded as a formal organization in 1973. Its electoral front, the RV, has not fared well, and the party has never garnered enough votes for even a single seat in the Storting.

A book by AKP member Dag Solstad provided a rare glimpse of life inside the party. Entitled *High School Teacher Pedersen's Account of the Big Political Revival in Our Country*, the book maintained that constant squabbling characterized the AKP during the early 1980s. A good deal of the squabbling may have involved the role of women in the organization, because at the party's congress in December 1984, women captured the leadership. Ericsson, a university instructor, succeeded Pal Steigan as the AKP's chair. Women also gained several other high-ranking posts, including that of political vice-chair, which went to a teacher named Jorun Gulbrandsen. Ericsson contends that "the women's struggle has been underestimated in the communist movement" and that Norwegian women will finally be able to exercise the role they deserve in the campaign for a communist revolution (Oslo, *Arbeiderbladet*, 18 December 1984). The 1984 congress, which was held in an undisclosed location to preclude intervention by security officials, passed a resolution stipulating that women must comprise half the membership of the AKP's Central Committee and half the delegates to party congresses (ibid.). With regard to the party's composition, it was also revealed that half the members come from the working classes—a term that was not further defined (*Klassekampen*, 5 January 1985).

According to the 5 January 1985 issue of *Klassekampen*, the "anti-Soviet AKP has taken the lead in making a six-hour workday the watchword from start to finish as a women's issue within the labor movement. The AKP also has had great and decisive significance for important campaigns in the battle to save jobs." At a press conference held shortly after its congress, the AKP emphasized that it continues to advocate armed revolution and a dictatorship of the proletariat (*Aftenposten*, 18 December 1984). On other issues, the party opposes Norway's membership in NATO; calls for a strong, independent defense posture; and asserts that the AKP has been too servile toward China (ibid., *Arbeiderbladet*, 18 December 1984).

**The Red Electoral Alliance.** The RV is no longer simply an offshoot of the AKP. It is a coalition of the AKP and independent Socialists. The RV has numerous representatives on municipal and county councils. The third annual RV congress was held in April 1983, at which time the independent Socialists in the RV and some AKP members pushed through a resolution guaranteeing "real, not just formal" democratic rights for working people after the revolution in Norway. The RV's electoral manifesto of that year stipulated that a postrevolutionary socialist government must allow "freedom of speech and organization, independent trade unions, the right to strike, legal protection, and control by the workers over state and production organs" (*Aftenposten*, 18 April 1983).

At the congress, a debate developed over Norway's membership in NATO. A motion on the country's withdrawal from the alliance was defeated by a vote of 54 to 35 (ibid.). As part of its manifesto, the RV agreed on a plank calling for strengthening the conventional defenses of Western Europe and building a strong independent defense system outside NATO. The RV argued that "the prospect of being rescued from across the Atlantic is doubtful. For this reason, the RV proposes that Norway must get out of NATO's integrated military cooperation" (ibid., 16 April 1983).

The RV discounts the Soviet "guarantee" not to use nuclear arms against the Nordic region. It also warns against relying on Soviet advocacy of arms reduction and argues for strong international pressure on the USSR to force it to destroy its SS-20 missiles under international supervision (ibid.). The RV's manifesto was critical of both superpowers, but according to the RV, the Soviet Union is the most aggressive power. Soviet power is regarded as ascendant and U.S. power as in decline. Thus, with no counterforce to Soviet combativeness, the threats of Soviet occupation of Europe and of a new world war are becoming greater (ibid.).

The RV manifesto maintained that real socialism could be introduced into Norway only through a socialist revolution in which the working class assumes state power after a prolonged struggle. The RV, therefore, is ultimately a revolutionary rather than a reform-minded party. Although it participates in elections, it contends that Norway "will never get socialism through the ballot box" (ibid., 13 April 1983).

Major points in the RV's platform for the general election of 1985 included demands for a six-hour workday, a campaign against pornography, a prohibition on shutting down state-owned enterprises, and the use of oil revenues to narrow the gap between the rich and poor in Norway (ibid., 1 July 1985). The RV placed great emphasis on winning votes among women and laborers but emphasized that a vote cast for the RV by any citizen would not be a lost vote. Stressing its own independent stance on a number of important issues, the RV has criticized the SV for entering into electoral pacts with the Labor Party without insisting on certain preconditions to ensure its separate identity (ibid.).

Marian Leighton
*Defense Intelligence Agency*

# Portugal

**Population.** 10,095,000 (July 1986)
**Party.** Portuguese Communist Party (Partido Communista Português; PCP)
**Founded.** 1921
**Membership.** Over 200,000 (claimed) (*Diário de Notícias*, 18 November; *JPRS*, 12 December)
**General Secretary.** Alvaro Cunhal (since 1961)
**Secretariat.** 8 full members: Alvaro Cunhal, Carlos Costa, Domingos Abrantes, Fernando Blanqui Teixeira, Joaquim Gomes, Jorge Araújo, Octávio Pato, Sérgio Vilarigues; 2 alternate members: Jaime Félix, Luísa Araújo
**Political Secretariat.** 5 members: Alvaro Cunhal, Carlos Brito, Carlos Costa, Domingos Abrantes, Octávio Pato
**Political Commission.** 18 full members: Alvaro Cunhal, Angelo Veloso, Dias Lourenço, António Gervásio, Carlos Brito, Carlos Costa, Diniz Miranda, Domingos Abrantes, Fernando Blanqui Teixeira, Jaime Serra, Joaquim Gomes, Jorge Araújo, José Soeiro, José Casanova, José Vitoriano, Octávio Pato, Raimundo Cabral, Sérgio Vilarigues; 7 alternate members: António Lopes, António Orcinha, Artur Vidal Pinto, Bernardina Sebastião, Carlos Ramildes, Edgar Correia, Zita Seabra
**Central Committee.** 91 full and 74 alternative members
**Status.** Legal
**Last Congress.** Eleventh (Extraordinary), February 2–6, 1986, in Lisbon
**Last Election.** 1985, Union for the Unity of the People (communist coalition), 15.49 percent, 38 of 250 seats
**Auxiliary Oranizations.** General Confederation of Portuguese Workers (Confederação Geral de Trabalhadores Portugueses—Intersindical Nacional; CGTP), which represents about half of Portugal's unionized labor force; Popular Democratic Movement/Democratic Electoral Commission (Movimento Democrático Popular/Comissão Eleitoral Democrático; MDP/CED), coalition partner of PCP in elections and reputed communist-front "satellite" party
**Publications.** *Avante!*, weekly newspaper; *O Militante*, theoretical journal; and *O Diário*, semiofficial daily newspaper (all published in Lisbon)

The communist movement and a powerful labor confederation are controlled in Portugal by the most Stalinist, Soviet-line party in Western Europe. The PCP's political influence continues to be significant although much reduced since an aborted 1976 coup attempt. It opposes the occasional terrorists acts of the Popular Forces of the 25th of April (Fôrças Populares do 25 de abril; FP-25), active since 1980, and of the Armed Revolutionary Orga-

nization, which emerged in 1986 to launch an "armed struggle" against the government.

**Organization and Leadership.** Reports of unrest among some party members surfaced during 1986 in a document critical of PCP leadership. Decried were the party's "poor capacity for mobilization," recent "political defeats," and "lack of internal democracy." Doubting the existence or reliability of such a document, Cunhal insisted that the party was "very strong, very united, and very active in national political life." (*Diário de Notícias*, 7 April; *FBIS*, 22 April.) As an example of the party's continuing prestige and influence, he cited the decisive effect of communist votes in securing victory for the socialist Mário Soares in a February runoff election for president. The PCP had previously vowed it would on no account endorse its arch rival. To get approval for the reluctant decision to reverse this categorical position, the Central Committee convened an extraordinary party congress in early February. Two of 944 militants were said to oppose the recommendation. (*Avante!*, 6, 27 February; *Diário de Lisboa*, 27 March; *FBIS*, 14 February; *JPRS*, 15 May, 3 April, 8 October.)

Cunhal indicated that the next congress would probably be held in 1987, four years following the last regular congress of 1983 (*Diário de Lisboa*, 27 March; *JPRS*, 15 March). Meanwhile, there were reports that Cunhal and Chair Mikhail Gorbachev of the Soviet Union had had consultations over possible "new theoretical concepts" for their respective parties (*Expresso*, Lisbon, 31 May; *JPRS*, 21 July).

**Domestic Affairs.** The PCP suffered a major disappointment in Portugal's presidential contest when the candidate it favored placed third. A runoff then pitted front-runner Diogo Freitas do Amaral against Mário Soares, both bitterly denounced by communists as "right-wing threats to democracy." (*LAT*, 27 January; *NYT*, 30 January.) The party wrenched "victory" from the jaws of defeat, not only by claiming credit for Soares's triumph in the second election, but also by making use of the change of leadership in the socialist party to resume "exploratory" dialogue with the latter (*Diário de Notícias*, 12 August; *JPRS*, 8 October).

Angelo Veloso was the official PCP candidate until he withdrew just before the January election, but he and his party campaigned for Francisco Salgado Zenha, a dissident Socialist. Although wary of the latter's previous anticommunist positions, the PCP regarded him as the best qualified "democrat"—despite his lackluster campaign—to defeat Soares and the conservative Freitas do Amaral of the Social Democratic Center (CDS). (EFE, Madrid, 5 January; *FBIS*, 8 January.) Cunhal attributed the subsequent victory of the "forces of the right" to the latter's "demagogic" campaign in all the media, "which are in their hands," and to a division of the leftist vote between Zenha and populist candidate Maria Lourdes Pintassilgo (Lisbon Domestic Service, 26 January; *FBIS*, 27, 29 January). The communists were indignant at charges that they sought, through their support of Zenha, to seize power and set up a dictatorship (*FBIS*, 29 January). The socialist and CDS candidates both campaigned vigorously for political reforms to curb "growing communist influence" (*CSM*, 24 January).

Communist party backing for Soares in the runoff was mocked by the Portuguese press as a decision to "swallow the live toad" (*NYT*, 19 February). Cunhal parried that his was really a vote against Freitas do Amaral rather than for Soares, whom he now perceived—contrary to his earlier statements—as "the lesser of two major evils" (*LAT*, 27 January; *Diário de Notícias*, 30 January; *FBIS*, 5 February). Controlling about 15 percent of the electorate, communists appeared to turn out solidly for Soares in the February runoff, pushing his vote share up to 51 percent (*NYT*, 17 February). The PCP saw this as a defeat not only for the CDS candidate but also for the government of Prime Minister Aníbal Cavaco Silva and the Social Democratic Party (PSD) that supported him. At the same time, it found worrisome the large number of "non-extreme-right" Portuguese "deceived" into voting for Freitas do Amaral. (*Avante!*, 27 February; *JPRS*, 3 April.)

Soares denied CDS charges that he would be beholden to the communists for their alleged negotiated support. He argued that he had promised nothing and that in his new position he would be able to keep the left and the unions in line while providing ideological balance to the centrist Cavaco Silva government. (*Diário de Notícias*, 30 January; *FBIS*, 31 January, 5 February; *NYT*, 17 February.) The communists henceforth virtually ignored the new president and concentrated their energies on trying to negotiate "democratic convergence" in the assembly to oppose the prime minister's minority government (*Avante!*, 10 April; *Diário de Notícias*, 12 August; *JPRS*, 23 May, 8 October). The PSD accused the socialists of forming a "popular front" with the communists, thereby revealing "despair at the successes of the government." Socialists called the charge unfounded and demagogic. Communists, on the other hand, were encouraged by the movement toward "strengthened democracy" through their discussions with Socialists, the Democratic Renewal Party (PRD), and the Portuguese Democratic Movement. (*Diário de Lisboa*, 15 March, *Diário de Notícias*, 17, 20 March; *FBIS*, 28

March; *JPRS*, 30 April.) They rejoiced that "creeping executive domination of all political power" had been halted with the transfer of real power to the assembly (*Diário de Notícias*, 12 August; *JPRS*, 8 October). By October, however, the PCP was regretting the "democratic parties' refusal" to consider the convergence essential for the dismissal of Cavaco Silva's government and the formation of a "democratic alternative" (*Avante!*, 9 october; *JPRS*, 17 October).

A popularity poll in May found Cunhal the least liked of present party leaders and the one who elicited the most negative opinions. Only 15 percent of those polled were undecided in their attitude toward the PCP leader; most had strong views for or against him. Among many communists, there was even a strong preference for ex-President António Ramalho Eanes over Cunhal. (*Expresso*, 17 May; *JPRS*, 21 July.) Eanes was later elected chair of the PRD (*Diário de Notícias*, 18 November; *JPRS*, 5 December).

**Auxiliary and Front Organizations.** The PCP disputed the government's claim that labor peace had been achieved through a "social pact" between government, management and the General Workers' Union (UGT) setting a ceiling for wage negotiations. The communist-controlled CGTP refused to agree to it. (*Diário de Notícias*, 12 August; *JPRS*, 8 October.) The UGT, organized by the Socialists and Social Democrats, represents somewhat less than half of unionized labor (*World Fact Book*, 1986).

The PCP was said to have vetoed the selection of a popular communist labor leader, José Luis Judas, as general secretary of the CGTP. Objections reportedly derived from his "disadvantage" of being a white-collar worker and from his "independent language" that smacked of unorthodoxy. (*O Jornal*, 23 May; *JPRS*, 8 July.) Meanwhile, a former CGTP leader, António Herculano Ferreira Jorge, was said to be the first PCP dissident to manage re-election to the National Labor Council. He explained that he had left the communists because he believed in labor union independence from political parties. (*O Jornal*, 6–12 June; *JPRS*, 22 July.)

The MDP/CED decided to abandon an "incompatible" ten-year electoral alliance with the communists on the national level. A "differing biorhythm" and "a change in events" now dictated a need for the party to seek its own identity "without being subjected to distorting stereotypes." (*Semanario*, Lisbon, 2 August; *Diário de Notícias*, 21 November, 1 December; *FBIS*, 8 October, 5, 10 December.) This was a euphemistic reference to frequent allegations that the MDP was merely an adjunct of the PCP (see *YICA*, 1986). Scorning the suggestion that the PCP had been the cause of the MDP's misfortunes, Cunhal remarked that this was regrettable talk in the face of a continuing need for "democratic unity." The MDP did agree to remain in the coalition for local elections provided terms more favorable to the MDP could be arranged. (*Diário de Notícias*, 18 November, 1 December; *Avante!*, 20 November; *FBIS*, 8, 10, 12 December.)

**International Views and Activities.** The Cavaco Silva government was assailed by communists for its capitulation to the European Economic Community and to United States authorities over the nation's industrial, agricultural, fisheries, and foreign policies (*Diário de Notícias*, 18 November; *JPRS*, 12 December). The PCP Central Committee cited "harsh blows" to the economy as confirmation of the party's warnings against Portugal's entry into the EEC (*Avante!*, 9 October; *JPRS*, 17 October). Communists objected to the idea of any "likely" attempt to use the Lajes Air Base for aggressive acts against Libya or any other country and denounced the government's expulsion of several members of Libya's diplomatic mission as an "unjustified act of hostility . . . clearly inspired" by U.S. pressure (Lisbon Domestic Service, 25 March; *FBIS*, 26 March; *Avante!*, 8 May; *JPRS*, 21 May).

Several times during 1986, PCP delegations visited countries of Eastern Europe, including the Soviet Union, Poland, Czechoslovakia, Hungary, Romania, and Bulgaria. Cunhal had extensive discussions in May with Gorbachev of the USSR (*Pravda*, 21 May; *FBIS*, 21 May). Austria, China, Vietnam, and North Korea also received PCP visits. The PCP in turn was host in Lisbon to communist groups from the Soviet Union, Poland, Romania, Czechoslovakia, and Vietnam as well as to members of the Palestine Liberation Organization.

**Other Far-Left Groups.** A bomb explosion in February in a car inside the U.S. Embassy compound was the third terrorist attack on the embassy committed by the extremist FP-25 (*NYT*, 20 February). The PCP fretted that such actions would provide a pretext for government repression and for the approval of antidemocratic security laws (*Avante!*,

27 February; *JPRS*, 3 April). In July, the previously unknown Armed Revolutionary Organization claimed responsibility for bombings in three Portuguese cities "to let the people know of the beginning" of their activities against the government. By then a total of 9 bombings by this group and by the FP-25 had been reported in Portugal during 1986; 30 since 1985. (*NYT*, 15 July.)

H. Leslie Robinson
*Stockton, California*

# San Marino

**Population.** 23,000
**Party.** Communist Party of San Marino (PCS)
**Founded.** 1921
**Membership.** 300
**General Secretary.** Gilberto Ghiotti
**Honorary Chairman.** Ermenegildo Gasparoni
**Status.** Legal
**Last Congress.** Eleventh, 27 January 1986

The PCS is an extension of the Italian Communist Party, just as the other political parties of San Marino, the Christian Democrats (DCS), Socialists (PSS), Social Democrats (PSUS), and Republicans (PRS) are extensions of their Italian counterparts. Between 1978 and 1986 the PCS was part of a governing coalition that excluded only the DCS. In 1986, the PCS (which received 24.4 percent of the vote in 1983) and the DCS (which received 42.1 percent) made a coalition among themselves, excluding the other parties. The DCS claimed two out of the three executive secretaryships (finance and foreign affairs) and three administrative departments, while the PCS took one executive secretaryship (internal affairs) and four administrative departments. As the negotiations for the deal proceeded, the PCS secretary was in constant contact with PCI headquarters in Rome (*La Repubblica*, 16 July). Gabriele Gatti, DCS secretary, received approval from Italy's foreign minister, Giulio An-

dreotti, who is also a leading Christian Democrat. Gatti traveled to the United States to soften the opposition of some 100 San Marinese–Americans who cast absentee ballots in San Marino, who habitually vote DCS, and who could have wrecked the coalition by voting for a party pledged not to ally with the communists (ibid.).

The PCS held its Eleventh Congress in January. The congress document stressed approval of the Soviet proposals for ridding the world of nuclear weapons by the year 2000 and the need for Europe to foster a policy of détente. Domestically, the congress pledged the party to cooperation with progressive forces (TASS, 27 January).

Prior to the congress, Ghiotti visited Moscow, where he met with Boris Ponomarev and Vadim Zagladin. The two parties informed each other of plans for their respective congresses, and "spoke in favor of preventing an arms race in space and ending it on earth" (ibid., 10 January). The Communist

Party of the Soviet Union sent a delegation to the PCS congress headed by R.G. Yanovskiy, rector of the Academy of Social Sciences at the CPSU Central Committee, and A.A. Krylov, "a senior official of the CPSU Central Committee International Department" (ibid., 23 January). The Communist Party of Vietnam also sent fraternal greetings to the congress.

Angelo Codevilla
*Hoover Institution*

# Spain

**Population.** 39,075,000
**Party.** Spanish Communist Party (Partido Comunista de España; PCE)
**Founded.** 1920
**Membership.** 60,000 (estimated)
**General Secretary.** Gerardo Iglesias
**President.** Dolores Ibárruri (legendary La Pasionaria of Civil War days)
**Secretariat.** 11 members: Andreu Claret Serra, José Maria Coronas, Enrique Curiel Alonso, Francisco Frutos, Gerardo Iglesias, Francisco Palero, Juan Francisco Pla, Pedro Antonio Rios, Francisco Romero Marin, Simón Sánchez Montero, Nicolás Sartorius
**Executive Committee.** 28 members
**Central Committee.** 102 members
**Status.** Legal
**Last Congress.** Eleventh, 14–18 December 1983, in Madrid
**Last Election.** 1986, United Left (coalition of 7 parties, dominated by the PCE), 4.6 percent, 7 of 350 seats
**Auxiliary Organization.** Workers' Commissions (Comisiones Obreras; CC 00), claimed membership of about 1 million, approximately one-third of Spain's unionized workers, Marcelino Camacho, chair
**Publications.** *Mundo Obrero* (Labor world), weekly; *Nuestra Bandera* (Our flag), bimonthly ideological journal; both published in Madrid.

An enfeebled Spanish communist movement has fragmented into three main parties plus several minor ones. Pro-Soviet dissidents called "Afghans" withdrew from the mainstream "Eurocommunist" PCE in 1983 to form the Communist Party of the Peoples of Spain (Partido Comunista de los Pueblos de España; PCPE). Santiago Carrillo, founder of Spanish Eurocommunism, led his loyalists into opposition to the PCE leadership after he was displaced as general secretary in 1983. After leaving the party in 1986, he made plans to convert his own group into the Workers Party—Communist Unity (Partido de los Trabajadores—Unidad Comunista; PT-UC).

The eighteen-year-old Marxist separatist organization called Basque Homeland and Liberty (Euzkadi ta Askatasuna; ETA) remains one of Europe's most elusive terrorist groups, although they have been less and less active in recent years. Membership is estimated to be between 200 and 500, although only a dozen are thought to be gunmen. The ETA is said to have forsaken most international links and is now almost entirely home-trained and home-financed. (*NYT*, 24 August.) A minor separatist guerrilla group in Catalonia is called Free Land (Terra Lliure).

**Organization and Leadership.** The PCE set rapprochement with all dissidents except Santiago Carrillo as a priority goal in 1986. Carrillo could apply for membership in the party whenever he liked, but there would be no negotiating with such a "disruptive element" that had left the party voluntarily after "literally destroying" it. (Barcelona, *La Vanguardia*, 20 May; Madrid, *Diário 16*, 3 July; *JPRS*, 12 June, 19 August.) Early in the year, Iglesias also refused to deal with Ignacio Gallego's PCPE, although he did join it and other leftist groups in an anti-NATO campaign (Madrid Domestic Service, 5, 6 February; *FBIS*, 7 February). In April, however, the PCE accepted the PCPE into a left-wing coalition for June parliamentary elections (Madrid Domestic Service, 24 April; *FBIS*, 25 April). By then Iglesias was elated over his success in persuading Enrique Lister to merge his Soviet-line Spanish Communist Workers' Party (PCOE) back into the fold after fifteen years of separation (Madrid Domestic Service, 21 March, 19 April; *FBIS*, 24 March, 21 April).

In July, the Central Committee decided to postpone the party's Twelfth Congress until after municipal elections in 1987 (Madrid Domestic Service, 8 July; *JPRS*, 9 July).

**Domestic Affairs.** Profiting from the momentum generated by a left-wing campaign against Spanish membership in NATO, the PCE and six other parties crafted an electoral coalition called United Left (Izquierda Unida; IU). The hope was, through unity, to displace more Socialists in June parliamentary balloting than would otherwise be possible. Prime Minister Felipe González had called elections earlier than originally scheduled in the expectation that he could capitalize on his victory in the March NATO referendum before the left had a chance to organize effectively against him. (*CSM*, 24 April; *NYT*, 2 June.) It was considered that a fragile alliance of quarreling communists plus pacifists, ecologists, humanists, and the monarchist Carlist Party was so uncongenial that it would be a miracle if they could quickly agree on an effective program on which to campaign (Madrid, *Ya*, 23 March; *JPRS*, 16 May; *CSM*, 19 June). In April

they did put together a platform that vaguely stressed social-democratic reformism along with pacifist and ecological concerns (*Radio Free Europe Research*, 20 June).

The coalition profited somewhat from a Socialist loss of 18 seats in the election, with the PCE professing to be reassured by its "moderately optimistic" gains. The IU, dominated by the PCE, won seven seats (4.6 percent of the vote), compared with the PCE's previous four seats (3.8 percent of the vote). (Madrid, *Diário 16*, 3 July; *JPRS*, 19 August.) Socialist losses, according to the communists, were the price of a four-year liberal-conservative policy that had brought unemployment to 3 million and had put Spain into NATO. Notwithstanding Socialist "dirty work" during the campaign, the IU had now demonstrated that it had "a present and a future." (*Mundo Obrero*, 26 June–27 July; *JPRS*, 8 July.) Carrillo, on the other hand, called the IU a failure since the constituent parties had separately won more total votes in 1982 elections (Barcelona, *La Vanguardia*, 1 July; *JPRS*, 15 July). Iglesias noted that the IU might be reorganized later to exclude the conservative Humanist and Carlist parties since their presence in the coalition had been "harmful" (Madrid Domestic Service, 8 July; *JPRS*, 9 July).

**Auxiliary Organization.** The communist and socialist labor confederations backed December marches by striking high school students protesting a tightening of college admissions policies. Workers' Commission leader Marcelino Camacho joined in the Madrid march. (*NYT*, 18 December.)

**International Views and Activities.** Polls indicated early in 1986 that Spanish membership in NATO was opposed by a majority of Spaniards, mostly non-Marxists from the center-left. An opposition campaign prior to a March referendum was organized, however—mainly by communists and far-left splinter groups. (ibid., 10 March.) Hundreds of thousands of demonstrators converged on Madrid in February, and a twelve-mile chain of protestors marched in Barcelona (ibid., 24 February; *FBIS*, 18 February).

The theme most emphasized throughout the campaign was that continued membership in NATO mortgaged Spain's sovereignty and strengthened dependence on the United States (Madrid Domestic Service, 15 February; *FBIS*, 18 February). An uncontrolled arms race would be "obligatory," and U.S. nuclear weapons would "inevitably" be installed in Spain. There was "no certainty," despite assurances to the contrary by the prime minister, that Spain would not be pulled into the entire NATO military structure or that the U.S military presence in Spain would be reduced. (Madrid Domestic Service, 8 January; *FBIS*, 13, 16 January.) Ties with NATO would undercut Spain's identification with Latin America, obliging it to side with its Atlantic allies in colonial disputes, the Central American conflict, or the problem of Latin America's foreign debt (*Mundo Obrero*, 23–29 January; *IB*, April). Finally, advances in Sweden and Switzerland, both outside NATO, were cited to argue that NATO membership was not needed to enhance Spain's technological and economic development (*NYT*, 12 March).

Spanish voters opted, 53 to 40 percent (with the remaining ballots blank or invalid), to remain in NATO, but communists spoke of "moral victory" for having come so close and for having waged a "responsible" campaign with limited means "without losing our political dignity" (ibid., 13 March; Madrid Domestic Service, 13 March; *FBIS*, 13 March). The government, on the other hand, had resorted to "pressure, blackmail, and intimidation" and the "partisan monopolization" of the public news media (*Mundo Obrero*, 20–26 March; *FBIS*, 31 March). Most important, "about 2 million Spaniards" changed their positions in the last five days of the campaign, "while holding their noses," because the prime minister hinted that, if defeated on this issue, he would resign and be replaced by a conservative government under Manuel Fraga Iribarne (Madrid, *El Pais*, 16 March; Madrid, *Tiempo*, 24 March; *JPRS*, 21 April, 1 May).

Iglesias said he would respect the referendum vote but promised to continue a public campaign of protests and marches that would aim at the dismantling of all American bases in Spain (*NYT*, 13 March). The following month, he condemned the presence at the Rota naval base of vessels of the U.S. Sixth Fleet that had taken part in the attack on Libya. He called this a "snub to the Spanish public" in the face of the recent referendum. (*Mundo Obrero*, 10–16 April; *FBIS*, 21 April.) In November, following a trip to Nicaragua and Cuba, he spoke of a "loss" of Spanish credibility and prestige in Latin America because of its entry into NATO and its lack of solidarity with Latin America against U.S. "trampling underfoot" of the whole continent (Madrid Domestic Service, 11 November; *JPRS*, 13 November). An Andalusian communist predicted that NATO would not help Spain in the event

of a Moroccan attack on the Spanish territories of Ceuta and Melilla (Madrid, *Diário 16*, 11 March; *JPRS*, 16 May).

Relations were restored between the Spanish and Czechoslovak communist parties during an October PCE visit to Prague (*Mundo Obrero*, 30 October–5 November; *FBIS*, 5 November). Also during 1986, party officials visited East Berlin, Hungary, and Bulgaria and received Romanian communists in Madrid. A Spanish communist youth group had visited Romania earlier in the year.

**Rival Communist Parties.** Carrillo, despairing of efforts to persuade Iglesias and the PCPE's Gallego to join him in a communist unity ticket for the June election, campaigned alone under the banner of his own "Board for Communist Unity" (Mesa Para la Unidad Comunista). He charged that, in forming a coalition with noncommunists in the IU, Iglesias had led the PCE to give up its communist identity. (*Radio Free Europe Research*, 20 June.) After the June election, he said he believed that, if the three communist families had stood together, they would have obtained more than twenty deputies (Madrid Domestic Service, 23 June; *FBIS*, 23 June). Actually, Carrillo failed to win back his own seat in Parliament; his "Communist Unity," which was dismissed by the PCE as a "shameless" instrument of the Socialist Party to reduce the IU's prospects, drew only 1.12 percent of the vote (*NYT*, 23 June; Madrid, *Spain '86, Information of the Diplomatic Information Office*, July; *Mundo Obrero*, 26 June–2 July; *JPRS*, 8 July).

Undaunted, Carrillo announced in December that his Board for Communist Unity was planning a constituent congress for February 1987 to launch the PT-UC. This was to be the anchor that one day would pull all communists back together; it would be too hard to rebuild around the "recently discredited" PCE. (Madrid Domestic Service, 4 December; *JPRS*, 5 December).

A rival communist party—in addition to the PCPE—that did participate in the IU electoral coalition was the Progressive Federation headed by Ramón Tamames, a top PCE official before he quit the party in 1981 (*Radio Free Europe Research*, 20 June).

**Left-Wing Terrorist Groups.** Just as ETA violence was thought to have been curbed, a fresh surge of bombings and assassinations followed French deportation of guerrilla suspects early in the summer, with 26 suspects handed over to Spanish authorities by year-end. There were 41 terrorist-caused deaths during the year (mostly from commando attacks in Madrid), compared with 50 in 1985 and a peak of 120 in 1980. (*Economist*, 4 January; *NYT*, 15 July, 24 August, 27 December; *CSM*, 15 August.) Prior to the French expulsions, ETA radicals were reportedly more amenable to compromise, dropping demands for full independence but still insisting on greater Basque autonomy. However, Madrid remained committed to forceful action, refusing to negotiate as long as violent acts continued. (*U.S. News & World Report*, 25 August.) The ETA's Domingo Iturbe ("Txomin") remarked that, as the authorities perceive they cannot bring Basques to their knees, "they will negotiate, like it or not." It was plain, he said, that the "worthless" autonomy statute was conceded only because of the pressure of violence. (Madrid, *ABC*, 27 November; *FBIS*, 10 December.)

Moderate Basque nationalists, encouraged by an April report of an international commission that urged negotiation, were dismayed by Madrid's position. They were said to be convinced that an influential ETA leader deported by France to Africa was willing to discuss terms with the government. (*CSM*, 15 August.) Polls showed that more than 75 percent of the Basques opposed both terrorism and the ETA demand for an independent Basque state, but they do favor more self-determination as the way to resolve the terrorist problem (ibid., 15 April).

Increased Basque radicalism and hostility to Madrid was reflected in elections. In March, Basques voted overwhelmingly against Spanish membership in NATO (ibid., 14 March). Herri Batasuna, ETA's political arm, won 17 percent of the Basque vote in June and increased its seats in the Spanish Parliament from two to five (ibid., 24 June; *NYT*, 24 August). In November regional elections, it won 13 of 75 seats in the Basque Parliament, compared with 11 in 1984. Socialists emerged as the leading party but this was because over 70 percent of the votes were divided among embittered regional parties, all united only in favoring more Basque autonomy and in opposing Madrid's tough antiterrorist laws. Having previously boycotted the Basque Parliament, Herri Batasuna said it was now prepared to take its seats to prevent the formation of a coalition government headed by the Socialists. (Madrid Domestic Service, 1 December; *JPRS*, 1 December; *WP*, 2 December; *CSM*, 8 December.)

A Catalan separatist organization, Free Land (Terra Lliure), claimed responsibility for two terrorist incidents, which it justified as a response to the rise in proindependence feeling in Catalonia and to opposition to plans for holding the Olympic Games in Barcelona (Madrid Domestic Service, 11 January, 14 September; *FBIS*, 13 January, 15 September).

H. Leslie Robinson
*Stockton, California*

# Sweden

**Population.** 8,357,000
**Party.** Left Party Communists (Vänsterpartiet Komunisterna; VPK)
**Founded.** 1921 (VPK, 1967)
**Membership.** 17,500, principally in the far north, Stockholm and Goteborg
**Chairman.** Lars Werner

**Executive Committee.** 9 members: Lars Werner, Viola Claesson, Bertil Mabrink (vice-chairman), Kenneth Kvist (secretary), Gudrun Schyman, Brit Rundberg, Lars-Ove Hagberg, Bror Engstrom, Lennart Beijer
**Party Board.** 35 members
**Status.** Legal
**Last Congress.** Twenty-seventh, 2–6 January 1985
**Last Election.** September 1985, 5.4 percent, 19 out of 349 seats
**Auxiliary Organization.** Communist Youth (KU)
**Publications.** *Ny Dag* (New day), semiweekly; *Socialistisk Debatt* (Socialist debate), monthly; both published in Stockholm.

The ancestor of the VPK, Sweden's Communist Party (Sveriges Kommunistiska Partiet) was established in 1921. Its greatest moment came right after World War II, when it obtained 11.2 percent of the vote in local elections, a result largely due to the popularity of the Soviet Union at the end of the war. Since that time the Communist Party (later the VKP) has usually garnered about 4 or 5 percent of the vote. The party, which has never made a truly major contribution to communist history, has had marginal influence in Swedish politics. Perhaps its most important role has been to allow the Social Democrats to govern during much of Sweden's recent history. During the last half-century, the Swedish Social Democrats have been Europe's most dominant social democratic party, and during many of their years in power they have relied on a combined majority with the communists in the Riksdag (parliament). The communists, however, have never been part of the government.

In Sweden, a party has to clear a 4 percent threshold to be represented in Parliament, and after the bitter reaction to the Soviet invasion of Czechoslovakia in 1968, the VPK went under the 4 percent mark and was not represented. In the 1970 and 1976 elections it received 4.8 percent, and in 1979 and 1982, 5.6 percent of the vote. The VPK dropped slightly to 5.4 percent in 1985.

The communists changed both the name and direction of the party congress in 1967. Blue-collar workers constituted the majority of the communist electorate in previous years, but increasingly the VPK is attracting white-collar workers and younger people. Voting studies indicated no significant age differentials among the voters of various parties except for the VPK. In the 1979 elections, approximately half of the VPK voters were under the age of 30. Most of the party's new white-collar supporters were in cultural, educational, and health-related occupations.

The VPK projects a Marxist image, even though it has disassociated itself from Moscow and is generally regarded as one of the more moderate West European communist parties. Its program states:

> The party's foundation is scientific socialism, the revolutionary theory of Marx and Lenin. It seeks to apply this theory, develop it, infuse it with the struggle of the Swedish working class. The party's goal is to have the struggle of the working class and of the people, guided by the ideas of revolutionary socialism, lead to victory over capitalism and to a classless society.

**Party Internal Affairs.** Jörn Svensson, a VPK member of Parliament and chair of the platform committee that is developing a new party program for the next Left Party Communists' congress in 1987, was quoted in *Dagens Nyheter* (29 May) as saying, "The path to socialism in a developed capitalist country like Sweden must follow the democratic process and stay within the current Constitution." Svensson suggested that communists don't "sit around in dark cafes devising plots for coups." Rather, he said, the VPK definition of revolution is "a fundamental change in the balance of social power within the framework of the Swedish Constitution."

Svensson said that the proposed party platform for the next congress will be less abstract than previous ones and that there will be two particularly important points: (1) the relative independence of the party in relation to other communist parties and, (2) continued adherence to Marxism without "automatic interpretations of Marxist verbal symbolism" (ibid.). The crux of Svensson's comments seemed to indicate that the 1987 Party Congress will be even more pragmatic and, ergo, less ideological than previous party programs.

*Domestic Affairs.* The dominant event in Sweden in 1986 was the assassination of Prime Minister Olof Palme on 28 February. He was shot and killed by a gunman as he and his wife, Elisabeth, were walking down a central Stockholm street without any bodyguards, returning home after seeing a movie. The assassination sent Sweden into a prolonged period of profound shock and deep mourning. Not only had Palme been at the center of the Swedish political stage for almost two decades, but he was also an international figure of considerable prominence. Swedes were especially numbed by the thought that such a violent act to the nation's leader could take place in a country so long characterized by a lack of violence. Representatives of 132 nations, including many heads of state, were in Stockholm for the funeral (Swedish Domestic Service, 14 March). Palme was succeeded as prime minister and head of the Social Democratic Party by Ingvar Carlsson, who had been deputy prime minister.

At the end of 1986, no one had yet been tried for the murder, although the police had arrested and then released a number of suspects over a period of months. There was speculation that the gunman was a professional killer, hired to carry out the assassination (AFP, in English, 9 December), and along with many other rumors, there was also considerable speculation that either Kurdish extremists or Swedes on the extreme right were responsible. The Soviet news agency, TASS, alluding to Palme's frequent criticism of the United States during the Vietnam war and its alleged persecution of peace activists, hinted that the CIA was responsible. TASS wrote "Unfortunately, the militarists are not abandoning their attempts to humiliate peace activists and punish those who do not give in to the scare campaign" (reported in *Svenska Dagbladet*, 2 March). Svensson picked up on the same theme in November. In a nineteen-page report to the Riksdag, he charged that the United States was implicated in the murder and spoke about the "political context" of the assassination. He said that Palme's deep commitment to disarmament "was a threat to the American administration." Svensson alleged that the killing was carefully planned and that the CIA "undoubtedly" played a role (Paris, AFP, in English, 7 November).

The VPK, in keeping with its parliamentary alliance with the Social Democrats (even though it is not part of the government) voted unanimously along with the Social Democrats to elect Carlsson prime minister. The combined Social Democrat–VPK vote was 178. There were no "no" votes, but there were 159 abstentions. The right-of-center parties abstained to signal that, although they did not

support the Social Democratic policies, they did think Carlsson's election was right in principle (Swedish Domestic Service, 12 March). In a number of statements made during the year, Carlsson pledged to carry forward Palme's policies. With Palme's death, Werner, who has been VPK chair since 1975, became the parliamentary party chair with the longest seniority.

Several times during the last year, there were indications of the continuing uneasy relationship between the Communist and Social Democratic parties. In *Dagens Nyheter*, an article by Aoke Ekdahl and headlined "No Rapprochement Between Social Democrats and VPK" said that there were "no signs of any rapprochement regarding economic policy between the administration and the VPK... Talks took place at the request of the Communists. The VPK refuses to be regarded as a spare wheel in Parliament, to which the government can resort when the nonsocialist parties form blocs" (*Dagens Nyheter*, 11 December 1985).

In January, Werner referred to the "Dala Uprising," in which 20,000 workers signed a petition for more equitable income distribution, and said that the VPK could win political advantage from the worker unrest. Speaking to his party board, he said, "The broad resistance struggle that we have wanted and tried to create against both the nonsocialist governments and the current government may become a reality, considering the way feelings are now growing. This opens up an opportunity to move politics to the left in a concrete way" (*Dagens Nyheter*, 31 January–1 February). In September, Werner made another attack on the Social Democrats at a meeting of the VPK executive committee, criticizing his parliamentary partners on a variety of economic issues, including scrapping the value-added tax on food, redistribution of income, and the plight of pensioners (*Dagens Nyheter*, 1 September). Over the years, the communists have voted in the Riksdag to form Social Democratic governments, even though no communists have been included in the government. To vote against the Social Democrats would mean aiding the so-called "bourgois parties," and that would be against their principle.

A public opinion poll released in late June showed that the VPK was losing support. The party won 5.4 percent of the vote in the 1985 election, and the *Dagens-Nyheter*-Institute for Market Research Poll, taken in May and June 1986, showed the Left Party Communists with 3.5 percent, which was a half-percentage fall from a poll taken in April and not enough to merit representation in Parliament. (*Dagens Nyheter*, 22 June.)

**Foreign Affairs.** Prime Minister Carlsson, who had not had much previous experience in foreign affairs, promised to follow Palme's foreign policy line. Palme, before his death, had been attempting to normalize relations with the Soviet Union, which had been decidedly cool since a Soviet submarine went aground near a naval base at Karlskrona in October 1981. Palme had accepted an invitation to visit Moscow, and that commitment was honored by Carlsson, who visited Moscow from 14 to 17 April. This was the first official visit by a Swedish prime minister to the Soviet Union in a decade. Because of repeated incursions of presumed Soviet submarines ever since 1981, Carlsson was under substantial domestic pressure to be firm in his meetings with Soviet officials and to insist that the territorial integrity of Sweden be respected. During a reception at the Kremlin, Soviet prime minister Nikolai Ryzhkov praised the Swedish government's readiness to establish "good and stable relations with the Soviet Union" (TASS, 15 April). At the end of his Moscow visit, Carlsson told reporters that his talks with the Soviet leaders had been constructive and had focused "on the future without forgetting the past" (Reuters, 16 April). He also said to the press that he told Soviet officials "that Sweden's borders are sacred: every violation will be met with military force" (Radio Stockholm, 17 April).

Soviet-Swedish relations continued to be uneasy during 1986. The Swedish Defense Staff reported fifteen observed submarine violations during July, August, and September; and throughout the year, Soviet officials used terms like "fantasy submarines" and "periscope sickness" (Moscow International Service in Swedish, 29 January). Not only were the alleged submarine incursions a point of friction, but it was also revealed in early November that the Swedish embassy building in Moscow had been bugged since it was opened in 1972. A Swedish Foreign Ministry statement said that "hidden electronic surveillance installations were discovered in connection with a rebuilding of the embassy" and that the equipment "could not have been installed without the knowledge of the Soviet authorities" (*NYT*, 3 November). The Swedish government made an official protest. Another continuing sore point was the question of how the border between the economic zones of the USSR and Sweden in the Baltic should be drawn. The Soviet Union wants the line drawn without any reference to the large Swed-ish island of Gotland, which is in the middle of the Baltic. Sweden's position is that an island as large as Gotland must be taken into account. Talks on the issue in 1986 yielded no concrete results, although there were some small hints of a shift in the Soviet position (Stockholm Domestic Service, 19 February). The VPK is not beholden to the Moscow line, yet at the same time, the VPK does have to operate within the context of Soviet-Swedish relations, and it can be argued that chilly relations between the two countries are not helpful to the VPK cause.

Other than the assassination of Palme, perhaps no events had as significant an impact on Sweden as the meltdown that occurred in the fourth reactor at Chernobyl in the Ukraine on 26 April. Sweden was the first country to reveal the unusual levels of radiation, although at first the source of the radiation was a mystery. High levels of radiation were reported in various parts of Sweden. Several thousand reindeer, upon whom many Lapps depend for their livelihood, had to be slaughtered several months later, because of radiation. A poll published shortly after Chernobyl showed 60 percent of the population to be against nuclear power (*Sweden Now*, no. 4). The VPK leadership met in late May and called for an earlier deadline for elimination of nuclear power than the one slated for 2010. The VPK and the Center Party, long opponents of nuclear power, communicated about a public campaign to speed up its elimination. The VPK leadership also demanded that the government stop export of nuclear power and that Sweden act for international elimination of nuclear power (*Dagens Nyheter*, 2 June).

**International Party Contacts.** In mid-March Werner met with Ryzhkov, Viktor Maltsev (first deputy USSR foreign affairs minister) and Boris Pankin (USSR ambassador to Sweden), all of whom were in Stockholm for the Palme funeral. The Soviet delegation met with Swedish leaders and members of the Sweden-USSR Friendship Society (TASS, 16 March). Erich Honecker, the state and party leader of the German Democratic Republic, made a three-day state visit to Sweden in late June. In addition to seeing King Carl Gustav, Prime Minister Carlsson, and members of the business community, Honecker had meetings with Werner and with Rolf Hagel, the leader of the Communist Workers' Party (APK) (Stockholm International Service, in Swedish, 25 June). At the invitation of the Hungarian Socialist Workers' Party (HSWP) Central Committee, Werner led a delegation of

VPK party leaders on a six-day visit to Hungary in early December. Janos Kadar, general secretary of the HSWP, held talks with Werner. According to the Hungarian news dispatch, "major issues of international life were reviewed." Perhaps of special interest was the fact that Kalman Abraham, the president of the National Office for Enviromental and Nature Protection, conducted talks with the Swedish delegation about environmental protection policy (Budapest, MTI, 5 December).

**Rival Communist Groups.** The pro-Soviet Communist Workers' Party (APK), founded in 1977, received only 5,877 votes (less than 0.1 percent) in the last election and therefore plays a minute role in Swedish politics. Nevertheless, the Soviets are attentive to the APK. At the party's Twenty-eighth Congress, held in November, one of the key speakers and head of a Soviet delegation to the

congress was Arkadiy Volski, head of the CPSU Central Committee's Department of Machine Building (TASS, 8 November). As mentioned earlier, APK chairman Hagel met with the GDR's Honecker when the latter made a state visit. During the party congress, Hagel was re-elected chair. Gustáv Husák, Czechoslovakia's communist party chief, sent Hagel a congratulatory message praising his "meritorious activity" (Prague Domestic Service, in Czech, 9 November). Hagel attended the meeting of the CPSU Congress in Moscow. The only note of discord, vis-à-vis Moscow, was an article in the 30 April issue of *Norreskenflamman*, the paper of the APK, criticizing as "indefensible" the fact that the Soviets kept the nuclear accident at Chernobyl a secret for more than a day.

Peter Grothe
*Monterey Institute of International Studies*

# Switzerland

**Population.** 6,466,000
**Party.** Swiss Labor Party (Partei der Arbeit der Schweiz/Parti suisse du travail/Partito Swizzero del Lavoro; PdAS)
**Founded.** 1921; outlawed 1940; re-established 1944
**Membership.** 3,000 (estimated)
**General Secretary.** Armand Magnin
**Honorary President.** Jean Vincent
**Politburo.** 14 members
**Secretariat.** 5 members
**Central Committee.** 50 members
**Status.** Legal
**Last Congress.** Twelfth, 21–22 May 1983; Thirteenth Congress scheduled for 27–28 February 1987
**Last Election.** 1983, 0.9 percent, 1 of 200 seats
**Auxiliary Organizations.** Communist Youth League of Switzerland (KVJS), Marxist Student League, Swiss Women's Organization for Peace and Progress, Swiss Peace Movement, Swiss-Soviet Union

Society, Swiss-Cuban Society, Central Sanitaire Swiss
**Publications.** *VO Realities*, formerly *Voix Ouvrière* (Geneva), weekly, circulation 5,000 copies; *Vorwärts* (Basel), weekly, circulation 4,000 copies; *Il Lavatore*, Italian-language edition; *Zunder*, KVJS organ.

Switzerland has three communist parties with some significance: PdAS, with most of its followers in the western part of the country; the Progressive Organizations Switzerland (POCH), which replaced its former Marxist-Leninist ideological concepts with those of the Greens; and the Trotskyist Socialist Workers' Party (SAP), which is active only in some urban centers. During 1986, these parties suffered further loss of influence, as demonstrated in their substantial losses of votes in local elections. The Social Democratic Party of Switzerland (SPS; chairman Helmuth Hubacher) also suffered significant election losses. Left-extremist SPS members gained greater influence within party leadership, causing a decline in the following of the traditionalist trade unions (*Schweizer Ostinstitut*, letter to author, September).

The pro-Soviet PdAS is the oldest of the communist parties in Switzerland. It was founded on 5 March 1921 as the Swiss Communist Party. The party was outlawed in 1940 and re-established on 15 October 1944 under its present name. The PdAS is in a deep crisis as a result of further election defeats in 1986 and was able to prevent even more serious losses only by joining coalition lists of candidates. At the March elections in the canton of Waadt, the PdAS lost three of its 6 seats (*FAZ*, 5 March).

There are several reasons for the decline of the party. The PdAS never openly rejected the Soviet interventions in East Germany, Hungary, Czechoslovakia, Poland, and Afghanistan. The party's close relations with the Italian Communist Party were gradually replaced by relations with the more orthodox French party. The PdAS was unable to replace its aging leadership: the leader of the canton of Waadt is 76-year-old André Muret; general secretary of the party, Armand Magnin, is 65. In 1969, about one hundred young intellectuals left the party and founded the Marxist League, thus depriving the PdAS of its future intellectual leadership. Probably the main reason for the crisis is the party's failure to adjust to the sociological revolution of the recent decades. The communists still address themselves with the old class-struggle vocabulary to the "working class" and the "proletariat," whereas Swiss employees, with an increasing number in the service industries, have aspired to be part of the middle class. It is doubtful party leadership has understood the problem because the text of a discussion paper in preparation for the Thirteenth Party Congress to be held on 27–28 February 1987, published in its official organ *Vorwärts*, fails to refer to these reasons for the party's crisis, explaining the party's severe election defeats as resulting from decreased interest in "these parliaments" by its followers, especially the youth. It is suggested that the best way to achieve recovery is to let the population participate in the party's social projects and in the political struggle. The gradual loss of the "workers' culture" is criticized, and the observation is made that striving for favorable election results made the party neglect the fight for its political and cultural alternatives (*Vorwärts*, 16 October; *info-ch*, 12 August). The KVJS advertised for the International Friendship Camp in the German Democratic Republic (16 July–1 August). Every year about 1,000 youths from six countries attend this camp (*info-ch*, 17 June).

The PdAS maintained its relations with fraternal parties. A PdAS delegation, headed by General Secretary Armand Magnin, visited Vietnam and Cambodia (13–23 January) (Hanoi Domestic Service, 16 January; Phom Penh, Sar-Pordamean Kampuchea, 20 January; *FBIS*, 22 January). Hansjörg Hofer, member of the Politburo of the Central Committee of the PdAS led the party's delegation at the Eleventh Socialist Unity Party of Germany Congress in East Berlin (April) (*Neues Deutschland*, 24 April). Armand Magnin was received in Moscow (18 November) by Anatoliy Dobrynin, secretary of the CPSU Central Committee, and Vadim Zagladin, first deputy head of the International Department of the CPSU Central Committee (TASS, 18 November; *FBIS*, 20 November).

The POCH was founded in 1972 by student dissidents from the PdAS who rejected the party's adherence to the world communist movement and the sterile policies of the old party. In spite of POCH's emphasis on its independence, it supports Soviet policies. During the founding phase, the Basel branch held the leadership position. Since 1973 the party's Secretariat has been in Zürich. Total membership is about 5,000, of which 65 percent are women. Its weekly publication,

*POCH-Zeitung*, with a circulation of about 6,000 copies, has financial difficulties and appeals for contributions.

The POCH's new policies along Green Party lines proved successful, at least in the short run. Its aggressive campaign style attracted support from the academic professions and from youth. In the 1983 federal elections, the POCH increased its representation from two to three seats (*Schweizer Ostinstitut*, September).

On 12 June, a conference of about 50 POCH delegates decided that women must hold 50 percent of the positions of the party's Secretariat and 60 percent of the 10-member Presidium and 40-member Executive. Eight seats of the Executive could not be filled in the immediately following party elections because of lack of candidates. The conference approved the request to change the party program and to make feminist issues a priority target. A resolution, unanimously adopted, requests the immediate shutdown of all nuclear power plants. Franz Cahannes, a POCH member, was elected secretary for the "wood" section of the Construction and Wood Trade Union (*info-ch*, 9 April).

The POCH supported by the Trotskyist SAP and PdAS, were the major promoters of the "spontaneous" anti-U.S. demonstrations in Zürich, Basel, and other cities in Switzerland. Its general secretary Georges Degen declared that the alleged terrorist activities of Libya are inventions of the secret service and are used as pretext for the U.S. policy aimed at world domination (*Neue Züricher Zeitung* [*NZZ*], 26–27 April). The POCH maintains relations with a number of "liberated" states and "liberation movements," such as the PLO and El Salvador's guerrillas. Official relations with the Communist Party of Cuba were established in 1981. Delegations were exchanged with Nicaragua, Algeria, Iraq, Angola, and North Korea. Since the late 1970s, close contacts have been developed with Libya. A POCH delegation attended the Second Mathaba Conference in Tripoli (1986) at which establishment of an "international armed front against imperialism" was discussed (ibid.). A POCH subsidiary, the Organization for Women's Affairs, is the most important women's group in Switzerland. The organization's magazine is the weekly *Emanzipation*. Other organizations affiliated with the POCH are the Solidarity Committee for Africa, Asia, and Latin America and the Swiss Society for Social Health. The organization Mouthpiece of the Liberation Movement and of the Progressive States of the Third World is dominated by POCH members (ibid.).

The SAP adopted its new name at the Fifth Congress of the Revolutionary Marxist League in 1980. The League was founded in 1969 by a group of young Trotskyists who left, or were expelled from, the PdAS. The SAP is the Swiss section of the Fourth International (Trotskyist), with headquarters in Brussels, and it advocates the revolutionary class struggle in production centers. It aims at eventual control of enterprises, a policy similar to former revolutionary syndicalism. Its leading theoretician is Fritz Osterwalder. Its membership of about 500 is supported by some 3,000 sympathizers. The SAP is a cadre party, organized according to the principle of democratic centralism and operates in eighteen sections, located in thirteen cantons. All members contribute 10 percent of their income to the party treasury. Even though the SAP is not directly connected with the CPSU, the party participates in the struggle for a communist world revolution. Because SAP members have attained influential positions in the educational system, church organizations, and trade unions, the party exercises a far greater influence than its small membership would seem to indicate (*info-ch*, Sondernummer, 1 September).

The youth organization of the SAP, Maulwurt (Mole), was dissolved in the late 1970s but reactivated in 1983 as the Revolutionary Socialist Youth Organization (RSJ). The SAP obtained 0.4 percent of the votes in the 1983 federal elections and has an insignificant number of elected representatives at local levels (*Schweizer Ostinstitut*, September). SAP publications include *Bresche* (German), *La Brèche* (French), *Rosso* (Italian), and *Roia* (Spanish).

The SAP is quite active in the anti–nuclear power plant movement. In 1982 the party was instrumental in organizing the Group for a Switzerland Without Military (*Gruppe Schweiz ohne Armee*, GSoA). On 21 March 1985 the GSoA started collecting signatures for a referendum calling for abolishment of the military. The goal was to obtain 100,000 signatures of eligible voters by September 1986 in order to force the government to place the referendum before the people. By September, 125,000 signatures had been obtained, one-fourth of which had been collected by the SAP (*Stars and Stripes*, 23 September; *NZZ*, 13–14 September). Although that referendum is supported by the SAP, RSJ, Swiss Peace Council, Soldiers' Committee, POCH, Greens, and Jusos (Young Socialists), it is inconceivable that it will succeed. The PdAS does not encourage the referendum because the party is in favor of supporting Swiss neutrality (*info-ch*, Sondernummer, 1 September).

The Autonomous Socialist Party (*Autonome Sozialistische Partei*/Parti socialiste autonome/Partito Socialista Autonomo; PSA) is the outcome of a split within the Social Democratic Party of Switzerland (SPS) of the canton of Tessin in 1960. Although the dissidents obtained majority support at the party congress in 1966, they were unable to assert themselves against the entrenched leadership and so founded the PSA in April 1969. Its membership is about 1,000 and its general secretary is Werner Carrobbio. The party considers itself an autonomous component of the world communist movement and rejects social democracy, Trotskyism, and spontaneity. In the federal elections in 1983, the PSA received 10 percent of the vote in Tessin, giving it one seat in the Nationalrat. This brought the strength of the PdAS/POCH/PSA parliamentary faction to five seats. The PSA is concerned that in the next federal elections it might lose its only seat, and it therefore indicated its readiness to merge with the SPS. However, the positive reaction of some SPS members to the proposed merger led to intraparty dissension and to the termination of further negotiations. The PSA publishes *Politika Nuova*.

The SDS is one of the Swiss governing parties, a fact that does not prevent the party from maintaining "very useful contacts" with the SED, the ruling communist party of the GDR. The SDS vice president, Peter Vollmer, represented his party at the Eleventh SED Party Congress (April), where he stated that the SDS-SED contacts were constructively intensified through exchange of delegations. He declared that in spite of being a governing party, the SDS stands in "very critical distance, even in clear opposition to our economic system and equally to the political hypocracy" in the Western democracies. He was impressed, according to his address to the congress, with the way the people in the GDR support peace and justice. (*Neues Deutschland*, 21 April.) The Jusos, the official youth organization of the SDS, strongly cooperated with GSoA.

The Green parties of Switzerland, having done well in recent local elections, have decided to run candidates in the next federal elections, scheduled for 1987. For this purpose, they adopted in the spring of 1986 the name Green Party Switzerland (*Grüne Partei Schweiz*; GPS). The GPS intends to distance itself from the left-alternative movements and present the party as an alternative for the moderate political spectrum. President of the GPS is Monica Zingg. (*info-ch*, 3 February.)

Other communist organizations, such as the Communist Party of Switzerland Marxist-Leninist (KPS/ML) and the Communist Organization—Labor Party, have shown no sign of activity during 1986. Anarchist groups showed some new life. The group in the canton of Zürich publishes a new magazine *Knastblatt* (Jail newspaper), which has announced that the Black Help (Schwarze Hilfe), an organization assisting imprisoned anarchists, will be reactivated (*info-ch*, 3 February).

The Swiss peace movement, including such groups as the *Schweizerische Friedensrat* (SFR) and the PdAS-controlled *Schweizerische Friendensbewegung* (SFB), was less active during 1986. However some protest groups, such as the International Physicians for the Prevention of Nuclear War, became the more aggressive agitators of the World Peace Council (WPC) (*Schweizerischer Ostinstitut*, September). The SFB maintained contacts with the GDR Peace Council, also a member of the WPC (Peace Council of the GDR, *information*, October). The Soldiers' Committee (SC) goes back to the soldiers' committees founded in 1973. Its organ, *Panzerknacker* (Tank breaker), a quarterly publication, has about 2,500 copies. The SC, which is engaged in antimilitary resistance within and outside the military establishment, maintains contacts with the Women for Peace Basel, GSoA, Violence-free Action against the Nuclear Power Plant at Kaiseraugust, and Working Group for Arms Control and Prohibition of Weapons Exports (*info-ch*, no. 82). The Service Civil International (SCI)—Switzerland was founded as early as 1920. It considers itself part of the international peace movement and aims at a basic change of the present social order. It supports all alternatives to the traditional security policy and approves "civil disobedience" as an appropriate instrument. The SCI is associated with the SFR and cooperates with the Christian Peace Service (CFD), Swiss League for Reconciliation, the International of War Resisters (IdK), and the Center Martin Luther King (*info-ch*, 3 February).

There was also occasional cooperation between members of the autonomous movement and terrorist groups and activists of communist parties and their youth organizations. The autonomous movement played a key role in the planning and support of terrorist activities. (Ibid.) The Central American Women's Committee organized "women's brigades," scheduled for July and August, each to last for four weeks, to do garden work at the hospital in Malagalpa, Nicaragua (*info-ch*, 6 March).

Additional left-extremist publications are the left-radical *Wochen-Zeitung* (circulation about 10,000 copies); the monthly or quarterly *plädoyer* (Democratic jurists), *Infrarot* (Jusos), and *Zeit-Dienst* (cadre paper of the left faction of the SPS).

Eric Waldman
*University of Calgary*

# Turkey

**Population.** 51,819,000
**Party.** Communist Party of Turkey (TCP)
**Founded.** 1920
**Membership.** Negligible
**General Secretary.** Haydar Kutlu
**Leading Bodies.** No data
**Status.** Illegal
**Last Congress.** Fifth, October or November 1983
**Last Election.** N/a
**Auxiliary Organizations.** Progressive Youth Societies of Turkey
**Publications.** *Atilim* (according to Voice of the Turkish Communist Party, this was a monthly publication slated to become weekly; no other information is available), *Ileri* (Forward), reportedly published by PYS; *Proleter Istanbul*, reportedly published by the Istanbul chapter of the TCP.

Although the TCP remained illegal during 1986, it appeared to be somewhat more active than in the past. This apparently higher level of activity was reflected in a reported Sixth Plenum of the party's Central Committee, and conferences of the party's domestic organizations (allegedly attended by General Secretary Kutlu and convened within Turkey) as well as its foreign branches (held in Denmark and also attended by Kutlu).

More general political affairs in the country were marked by an important series of parliamentary by-elections on 28 September, liberalization of some of the authoritarian measures imposed by the pre-1983 military regime, and continuation of detention and trial of leftist militants as well as Kurdish "separa-

tists." The southeastern sector of the country continued to be plagued by violent guerrilla activities on the part of Kurdish militants, punctuated by at least one major cross-border raid into Iraq (involving the use of ten jet fighters).

The by-elections resulted in significant new developments. The governing Motherland Party (MP) led by Prime Minister Turgut Ozal won six of the eleven seats at stake with 32 percent of the popular vote. Although this represented a majority of available seats and raised the party's parliamentary delegation to 237 (of a total of 400), the results were generally regarded as a defeat for the party; even Ozal himself confessed to being disappointed. The big gainer in the election was the True Path Party

(TPP), which garnered 23.5 percent of the vote and four of the seats at stake. The TPP, which is led from the political sidelines by former Justice Party leader and prime minister Suleyman Demirel, represents the greatest electoral threat to the governing MP, since the votes of the former were clearly diverted from the latter.

The only other party to gain any seats in the September election was the Social Democratic Populist Party (SDPP), which was formed by the merger of the former Social Democratic and Populist parties and whose leader, Professor Erdal Inonu, won the seat in the province of Izmir. The SDPP won somewhat less than 23 percent of the total votes cast, while another leftist party, the Democratic Left Party (DLP) won approximately 8.5 percent. Thus, the SDPP suffered the same fate as the MP, losing strength to a rival on its own side of the political spectrum. The DLP is led by Rahsan Ecevit, whose husband, former prime minister Bulent Ecevit, is active on the sidelines in a manner comparable to the role of Demirel in the TPP. Notably, the two moderate left parties together garnered just over 30 percent of the popular vote, approximating the level of support going to such parties in most elections since the mid-1960s. By contrast, center-right votes totaled approximately 55 percent, matching the highest level of support won by the now outlawed Justice Party in 1965. These results suggest the persistence of basic political cleavages in the national electorate, despite the military's determined efforts to reform party politics. There will undoubtedly be further attempts to sort out parties and leaders as the next general election approaches. Demirel was reported to feel he is now "not only irrepressible, but also unstoppable" (*Economist*, 4 October). Continuing economic difficulties, attributed at least in part to the Ozal government's economic reform program, were thought to have contributed to the MP's relative weakness (ibid.).

During 1986, there were also new efforts to improve relations between Turkey and the Soviet Union. Prime Minister Ozal paid an official visit to the Soviet Union in late July, but there were no major breakthroughs. Indeed, Soviet Secretary General Gorbachev was conspicuous by his absence from Moscow during the Ozal visit. Ozal afterward characterized the meetings as "not unsuccessful," but acknowledged that there had been no new page turned. He also suggested that he had changed some of his prejudices about the Soviet Union. Although he was initially reported as having asked for Soviet help in starting bilateral talks with Bulgaria regarding the pressures that government has exerted on its ethnic Turkish minority, Ozal later remarked that he was not asking for Soviet mediation, since this was a problem between Turkey and Bulgaria. Concretely, the visit was marked by agreements to encourage Soviet construction contracts for Turkish firms, as well as agreements on planning, tourism, and cultural relations. The Istanbul newspaper *Tercuman* later reported that the sale of more than 7 billion cubic feet of Soviet natural gas to Turkey over the next several years had been agreed on, with 65 percent of the payment to be made in Turkish goods; however, the two governments had failed to agree on the list of Turkish goods involved. (*FBIS*, 30 August.) The TCP commented on the Ozal visit by excoriating the prime minister for denigrating Turkish-Soviet relations. It predicted that the agreements reached would raise trade between the two countries to a level of $1 billion and characterized cooperation between them as "an objective necessity." It pointed out that whereas the Soviet Union offered natural gas to Turkey, the United States shut out Turkish textiles and tried to foist nuclear weapons on the country. In other words, the Soviet Union offered peace; the real threat to Turkey emanated from the United States. (*FBIS*, 17 August.)

The TCP's position on current political developments in Turkey, as reflected in clandestine radio broadcasts (The Voice of the TCP and Our Radio), did not change materially during 1986. The major themes were set early in the year, when the Central Committee reportedly called for cooperation among all opposition parties to "activate the masses." The Central Committee denied that the 1961 constitution was responsible for the conditions that brought about the 1980 military coup and denounced the clash between the SDPP and the DLP as sterile and as undermining cooperation among the "democratic opposition, the left, and the persistent democrats." (*FBIS*, 5 February.) The Central Committee also called for liberalization of constitutional amendments, which it regarded as necessary before the Evren/Ozal regime could be toppled; moreover, it warned that if the right wing parties were able unilaterally to determine the content of the amendments, they would maintain the legal ban on Marxism-Leninism (ibid.). Further, the Central Committee advocated early general elections, a general and unconditional amnesty (including those convicted of offenses under articles 141 and 142 of the Penal Code, which outlaw Marxism and associated ideologies), an end to massive arrests and torture at the hands of the police, an end to "state terrorism" in the southeastern (Kurdish) districts, the elimination of military influence in the government, bringing the perpetrators of the 1980 coup and the torturers who served them to justice, and supporting popular struggle against the economic policies of the Evren/Ozal regime—particularly high unemployment, layoffs, and the rising cost of living. The Central Committee declared itself in favor of democracy, jobs, bread, and national independence. It also supported cooperation among opposition parties, including not only the center-left SDPP and DLP but also the TPP. It especially favored the DLP's denunciation of articles 141 and 142 of the Penal Code, as well as the Turkish labor confederation's agitation for a new constitution and for mass action and a general strike. The latter points are perhaps significant, in view of the conservative character of the TPP as well as earlier denunciations of the labor confederation for its conservatism and cooperation with the regime.

The clandestine radio reported extensively on the proceedings of the sixth plenum of the TCP Central Committee (late May) as well as the domestic and foreign conferences held by the party (the former apparently in September, the latter in November). The report on the Central Committee plenum also touched on more general matters. It characterized the 1980 military coup as having "deep-rooted" effects on the state and the economy. Construction would be necessary in Turkey, although not yet socialist construction. The TCP rejected the option of creating a legal socialist party, because such a party would "lag behind its own social legitimacy." It would be better to push for reestablishment of the defunct Turkish Labor Party (TLP) and the Turkish Socialist Workers' Party (TSWP) instead. Further, the TCP was ready to support any democratic government that could implement its program. Its duty was "to create a united democratic front." The message the TCP wanted the Turkish masses to hear (and which they were hearing "through their parties") was "There is no democracy in Turkey; there is torture; the United States is interfering in our internal affairs; . . . militarism is continually undermining democracy; this government is oppressing the religious; Articles 141, 142, and 163 of the Penal Code must be abolished; the Constitution must be amended; this government must be toppled; this government, this parliament, and this president are not based on the will of the people." (*JPRS*, 25 June.)

The United States was further accused of want-

ing to use Turkey to broadcast anti-Soviet propaganda, to store new chemical and nuclear weapons, and to participate in the deployment of the Rapid Deployment Force. The American attack on Libya in April was denounced, as were alleged U.S. plans to attack Iran and Syria, Turkey's neighbors to the east and south. (Ibid.)

Liberalizing gestures by the Evren/Ozal regime (such as release of former officials of the now outlawed revolutionary labor federation known as DISK and of officials of the Peace Society, acquittal of a group of intellectuals who had signed an objectionable petition, lifting the ban on political expression by former politicians, conviction of police officials for torturing prisoners, and allowing a mass demonstration by the labor federation) were acknowledged, but it was pointed out that such gains were fragile and could be reversed at any time. The regime intended to confuse the masses by these measures and to gain the support of the imperialist West. The democratic opposition was warned not to expect conciliation from the regime or to expect that democracy could be achieved gradually. (Ibid.)

Communist radio broadcasts interpreted the September by-elections as transforming the Ozal government into a minority government that had lost all legitimacy. The victory had been achieved by "the TCP and Leftist Unity, the other leftist forces, and the intellectual movement." The TCP supported continuing unity among democratic parties and the Turkish labor confederation. It called for resignation of the Ozal government and for new elections. (*FBIS*, 1 October, 5 November.) Finally, the national conference held in Turkey, apparently during the run-up to the by-elections in September, was reported to have ratified the "national peace and democratic alternative program." General Secretary Kutlu was reported to have declared that "the fact that this conference could be held in a working class area in our country under difficult conditions is an indication of our party's development." (*FBIS*, 5 November.) At the conference in Denmark, Kutlu welcomed a delegation of members of the outlawed Turkish Labor Party (TLP) led by Behice Boran and looked forward to ultimate unification of the TLP with the TCP. (*FBIS*, 12 December.)

Whether the TCP has in fact gained credibility or strength, or whether the reported activities of the party perhaps reflected the greater energy of the relatively new leader Haydar Kutlu, is difficult if not impossible to judge. But there can be little doubt that the heavy-handed actions of the Evren regime have played into the hands of the TCP. An example is the treatment of some 30 members of the Turkish Peace Association, including the former mayor of Istanbul and his wife as well as a prominent theater director. Their case attracted the vocal protest of such international luminaries as Arthur Miller and Harold Pinter. Their purported offenses did not include violence or sedition, but rather "organizing support and promoting propaganda for Communism." Describing the trial as "Kafkaesque," one of the defendants reported that at one point the military trial judge "read at length from a document purporting to be the last will of Peter the Great . . . and proclaiming a Russian plan for world domination." It was not clear whether this document was genuine. The defendants in this bizarre trial were released after some of their sentences were voided on a legal technicality. Several of them had been imprisoned for as much as 37 months while the trial dragged on. (*NYT*, 10 August.) Given such developments, as well as the widely publicized charges of systematic torture in Turkish prisons, increased opposition to the Evren regime should not be surprising. Nor should it be surprising if the TCP attempted to capitalize on such resentment for its own purposes.

Frank Tachau
*University of Illinois at Chicago*

# Select Bibliography, 1985–1986

## GENERAL

Ailes, Catherine P., and Arthur E. Pardee, Jr. *Cooperation in Science and Technology: An Evaluation of the Soviet-U.S. Agreement*. Boulder, Colo.: Westview Press, 1986. 300 pp.

Berg, Hermann. *Marxismus-Leninismus: das Elend der halb-deutschen halb-russischen Ideologie*. Cologne: Bund Verlag, 1986. 335 pp.

Bobin, A. E., et al., eds. *Razvivaiushchiesia strany v sovremennom mire: puti revoliutsionnogo protsessa*. Moscow: Nauka, 1986. 406 pp.

Campeanu, Pavel. *The Origins of Stalinism*. Armonk, N.Y.: M. E. Sharpe, 1986. 184 pp.

Clawson, Robert W., ed. *East-West Rivalry in the Third World*. Wilmington, Del.: Scholarly Resources, 1986. 348 pp.

Dolgopolov, E. I. *Sotsial'no-politicheskaia rol' armii osvobodivshikhsia stran*. Moscow: Voenizdat, 1986. 143 pp.

Fedorowicz, Jan K., ed. *East-West Trade in the 1980s*. Boulder, Colo.: Westview Press, 1986. 250 pp.

Foner, Philip S. *May Day: A Short History of the International Workers' Holidays*. New York: International Publishers, 1986. 184 pp.

Furtak, Robert K. *The Political Systems of the Socialist States*. Brighton, Sussex: Harvester Press, 1986. 308 pp.

Gerner, Kristian. *The Soviet Union and Central Europe in the Post-War Era: A Study in Precarious Security*. Aldershot, England: Gower, 1985. 228 pp.

Gorman, Robert A., ed. *Biographical Dictionary of Marxism*. Westport, Conn.: Greenwood Press, 1986. 388 pp.

Hamilton, Geoffrey. *Red Multinationals or Red Herrings? The Activities of Enterprises from Socialist Countries in the West*. New York: St. Martin's Press, 1986. 214 pp.

Hobday, Charles. *Communist and Marxist Parties of the World*. Santa Barbara, Calif.: ABC-Clio, 1986. 529 pp.

Hough, Jerry F. *The Struggle for the Third World*. Washington, D.C.: Brookings Institution, 1986. 293 pp.

Irkhin, Iu. V. *Revoliutsionnyi protsess v stranakh sotsialisticheskoi orientatsii*. Moscow: Izdatel' stvo Universiteta druzhby narodov, 1985. 172 pp.

Jones, James R., ed. *East-West Agricultural Trade*. Boulder, Colo.: Westview Press, 1986. 256 pp.

Kapur, Harish. *China and the European Economic Community: The New Connection*. Dordrecht and Boston: Martinus Nijhoff, 1986. 351 pp.

Kim, G. F., ed. *Sovremennye problemy natsional'no-osvoboditel'nogo dvizhenia: referativnyi sbornik*. Moscow: Inion AN SSSR, 1985. 266 pp.

Kolkowicz, Roman. *Communism, Materialism, Imperialism: Soviet Military Politics after Stalin*. Boulder, Colo.: Westview Press, 1986. 230 pp.

Lider, Julian. *Correlation of Forces: An Analysis of Marxist-Leninist Concepts*. New York: St. Martin's Press, 196. 394 pp.

Marcou, Lilly. *Les Pieds d'argile: Le communisme mondial au présent 1970–1986*. Paris: Editions Ramsay, 1986. 491 pp.

Mastny, Vojtech. *Helsinki, Human Rights and European Security*. Durham, N.C.: Duke University Press, 1986. 389 pp.

McCauley, Martin, and Stephen Carter, eds. *Leadership and Succession in the Soviet Union, Eastern Europe and China*. Armonk, N.Y.: M. E. Sharpe, 1986. 256 pp.

Möttölä, Kari. *Ten Years After Helsinki: The Making of the European Security Regime*. Boulder, Colo.: Westview Press, 1986. 184 pp.

Obminskii, E. E. *Razvivaiushchiesia strany: teoriia i praktika mnogostoronnoi ekonomicheskoi diplomatii*. Moscow: Mezhdunarodnye otnosheniia, 196. 269 pp.

Pravda, Alex, and Blair A. Ruble, eds. *Trade Unions in Communist States*. Winchester, Mass.: Allen and Unwin, 1986. 153 pp.

Sejna, Jan, and Joseph D. Douglass, Jr. *Decision-Making in Communist Countries: An Inside View*. Washington, D.C.: Pergamon-Brassey's, 1986. 80 pp.

Shumeiko, A. V. *Vsemirnaia federatsiia profsoiuzov, 1945–1985 gg*. Moscow: Profizdat, 1985. 256 pp.

World Federation of Trade Unions. *World Federation of Trade Unions, 1945–1985*. Prague: Prace, 1985. 162 pp.

Zagladin, V. V., et al., eds. *Revoliutsionnyi protsess: natsional'noe i internatsional'noe*. Moscow: Mysl', 1985. 341 pp.

## AFRICA

African National Congress. National Consultative Conference (2d, 1985 Lusaka, Zambia) *Documents of the Second National Consultative Conference of the African National Congress: Zambia 16–23 June 1985*. Lusaka, Zambia: African National Congress, 1985. 64 pp.

Al-Shahi, Ahmed. *Themes from Northern Sudan*. Atlantic Highlands, N.J.: Ithaca Press, 1986, for British Society for Middle Eastern Studies. 152 pp.

Arnold, Millard W., et al. *Zimbabwe: Report on the 1986 General Elections*. Washington, D.C.: International Human Rights Law Group, 1986.

Bardill, John E. *Lesotho: Dilemmas of Dependence in Southern Africa*. Boulder, Colo.: Westview Press, 1985. 224 pp.

Baynham, Simon, ed. *Military Power and Politics in Black Africa*. London: Croom Helm, 1986. 333 pp.

Benson, Mary. *Nelson Mandela: The Man and the Movement*. New York: W. W. Norton & Co., 1986. 268 pp.

Carter, Gwendolen M. *Continuity and Change in Southern Africa*. Los Angeles: Crossroads Press, 1985. 117 pp.

Daly, M. W., ed. *Modernization in the Sudan*. New York: Barber Press, 1985. 177 pp.

Egero, Bertil. *Mozambique and the Southern Africa Struggle for Liberation*. Uppsala, Sweden: Scandinavian Institute for African Studies, 1985. 29 leaves

Erlich, Haggai. *Ethiopia and the Challenge of Independence*. Boulder, Colo.: Lynne Rienner Publishers, 1986. 265 pp.

Falola, Tony, and Julius Ihonvbere. *The Rise and Fall of Nigeria's Second Republic, 1979–84*. London: Zed Press, 1985. 290 pp.

Fatton, Robert. *Black Consciousness in South Africa: The Dialectics of Ideological Resistance to White Supremacy*. Albany: State University of New York Press, 1986. 189 pp.

Flint, Lane. *God's Miracles versus Marxist Terrorists*. Clocolan, South Africa: Meesterplan, 1985. 255 pp.

Gavrilov, N. I., et al., eds. *10 let Efiopskoi revoliutsii*. Moscow: Nauka, 1986. 140 pp.

———, chief ed. *Demokraticheskaia Respublika Madagaskar: Spravochnik*. Moscow: Nauka, 1985. 229 pp.

———, et al., eds. *Narodnaia Respublika Mozambik*. Moscow: Nauka, 1986. 240 pp.

Gill, Peter. *A Year in the Death of Africa: Politics, Bureaucracy, and the Famine*. London: Paladin, 1986. 191 pp.

Gromyko, A. A., chief ed. *Aktual'nye problemy otnoshenii SSSR so stranami Afriki*. Moscow: Mezhdunarodnye otnosheniia, 1985. 304 pp.

Grundy, Kenneth W. *The Militarization of South African Politics*. Bloomington: Indiana University Press, 1986. 133 pp.

Hancock, Graham. *Ethiopia: The Challenge of Hunger*. London: Gollancz, 1985. 127 pp.

Harrison, Nancy. *Winnie Mandela: Mother of a Nation*. London: Gollancz, 1985. 181 pp.

Hodd, Michael. *African Economic Handbook*. London: Euromonitor Publications, 1986. 335 pp.

Ikoku, Sam G. *Nigeria's Fourth Coup d'État: Options for Modern Statehood*. Enugu, Nigeria: Fourth Dimension Publishers, 1985. 182 pp.

Inanga, Eno L., ed. *Managing Nigeria's Economic System*. Ibadan, Nigeria: Heinemann Educational Books, 1985. 273 pp.

Jaffe, Hosea. *A History of Africa*. London: Zed Press, 1985. 172 pp.

Johnson, G. Wesley, ed. *Double Impact: France and Africa in the Age of Imperialism*. Westport, Conn.: Greenwood Press, 1985. 407 pp.

Katambo Wakano. *Coups d'État, Revolutions and Power Struggles in Post-Independence Africa*. Nairobi, Kenya: Afriscript, 1985. 329 pp.

Khazanov, A. M. *Agostin'o Neto*. Moscow: Nauka, 1985, 206 pp.

Korn, David A. *Ethiopia, The United States and the Soviet Union*. London: Croom Helm, 1986. 199 pp.

Leatt, James; Theo Kneifel; and Klaus Nürnberger, eds. *Contending Ideologies in South Africa*. Cape Town: David Philip Publishers, 1986. 318 pp.

Leeman, Bernard. *Lesotho and the Struggle for Azania*. London: University of Azania, PAC Education Office, 1985–1986. 3 vols.

Lipton, Merle. *Capitalism and Apartheid: South Africa, 1910–1984*. Aldershot, England: Gower, 1985. 448 pp.

Markakis, John, and Nega Ayele. *Class and Revolution in Ethiopia*. Trenton, N.J.: Red Sea Press, 1986. 191 pp.

Martin, Jane, ed. *Africa*. Guilford, Conn.: Dushkin Publishing Group, 1985. 244 pp.

Nzongola-Ntalaja, ed. *The Crisis in Zaire: Myths and Realities*. Trenton, N.J.: Africa World Press, Inc., 1986. 315 pp.

Ojo, J. D. *The Development of the Executive under the Nigerian Constitutions, 1960–81*. Ibadan, Nigeria: University Press, Ltd., 1985. 189 pp.

Ortlieb, Heinz-Dietrich, and Dieter Losch. *Was wird aus Südafrika: ein Subkontinent sucht den lenkbaren Wandel*. Zurich: Edition Interfrom, 1985. 133 pp.

Ottaway, Marina and David. *Afro-Communism*. 2d ed. New York: Holmes & Meier, 1986. 270 pp.

Ray, Donald I. *Ghana: Politics, Economics and Society*. Boulder, Colo.: Lynne Rienner Publishers, 1986. 160 pp.

Robertson, Claire, and Iris Berger, eds. *Women and Class in Africa*. New York: Africana Publishing Company, 1986. 310 pp.

Slipchenko, S. A. *Na Afrikanskom iuge* . . . Moscow: Nauka, 1986. 185 pp.

Somerville, Keith. *Angola: Politics, Economics and Society*. London: Frances Pinter, Ltd., 1986. 207 pp.

Spring, William. *The Long Fields: Zimbabwe since Independence*. Basingstoke, England: Pickering and Inglis, 1986. 194 pp.

*Sudan Today: Sudan Peoples Liberation Movement*. London: SPLM, 1985. 56 pp.

Verrier, Anthony. *The Road to Zimbabwe, 1890–1980*. London: J. Cape, 1986. 364 pp.

Ziegler, Jean. *Thomas Sankara: un nouveau pouvoir africain*. Lausanne, Switzerland: P. M. Favre, 1986. 176 pp.

## THE AMERICAS

Arévalo, Oscar, and Eugenia Cortés. *Ahora Contamos*. Buenos Aires: Ediciones 40. Anniversario, 1985. 128 pp.

Ashby, Timothy. *Bear in the Backyard: Moscow's Caribbean Strategy*. New York: D.C. Heath & Co., 1986. 256 pp.

Baber, Colin, and Henry B. Jeffrey. *Guyana: Politics, Economics and Society*. Boulder, Colo.: Lynne Rienner Publishers, 1986. 203 pp.

Bourne, Peter G. *Fidel: A Biography of Fidel Castro*. New York: Dodd, Mead & Co., 1986. 332 pp.

Child, Jack, ed. *Confict in Central America: Approaches to Peace and Security*. London: C. Hurst & Co., 1986. 222 pp.

Colburn, Forrest D. *Post-Revolutionary Nicaragua*. Berkeley: University of California Press, 1986. 145 pp.

Duflo, Marie, and Françoise Ruellan, eds. *Le Volcan nicaraguayen*. Paris: Editions La Découverte, 1985. 281 pp.

Falk, Pamela S. *Cuban Foreign Policy: Caribbean Tempest*. Lexington, Mass.: Lexington Books, 1986. 336 pp.

Knight, Alan. *The Mexican Revolution*. New York: Cambridge University Press, 1986. 2 vols.

Kruszewski, Zbigniew Anthony, and William Richardson. *Mexico and the Soviet Bloc: The Foreign Policy of A Middle Power*. Boulder, Colo.: Westview Press, 1986. 170 pp.

MacDonald, Theodore. *Making of New People: Education in Revolutionary Cuba*. Vancouver, B.C.: New Star Books, Ltd., 1985. 248 pp.

Maolain, Ciaran O., ed. *Latin American Political Movements*. New York: Facts on File Publications, 1986. 287 pp.

Miles, William E. S. *Elections and Ethnicity in French Martinique*. New York: Praeger, 1986. 284 pp.

Moore, John M. *The Secret War in Central America: Sandinista Assault on World Order*. Lanham, Md.: University Press of America, 1986. 195 pp.

Okuneva, M. A. *Rabochii klass v kubinskoi revoliutsi*. Moscow: Nauka, 1985. 153 pp.

Rudolph, James D., ed. *Argentina: A Country Study*. 3d ed. Washington, D.C.: American University Foreign Area Studies, 1985. 402 pp.

Sandford, Gregory. *The New Jewel Movement*. Washington, D.C.: U.S. Department of State, Foreign Service Institute, 1985. 215 pp.

Stanton, Fred, and Michael Faber, eds. *James P. Cannon: Writings and Speeches, 1932–1934: The Communist League of America, 1932–1934*. New York: Monad Press, 1985. 439 pp.

Stephens, Evelyn Huber and John D. *Democratic Socialism in Jamaica*. Princeton, N.J.: Princeton University Press, 1986. 423 pp.

Szulc, Tad. *Fidel: A Critical Portrait*. New York: William Morrow & Co., 1986. 703 pp.

United States. Central Intelligence Agency. Directorate of Intelligence. *Directory of the Republic of Nicaragua*. A Reference Aid. Washington, D.C.: National Technical Information Service, May 1986. 57 pp.

Valenta, Jiri, and Herbert J. Ellison, eds. *Grenada and the Soviet Cuban Policy: Internal Crisis and the U.S./ OECS Intervention*. Boulder, Colo.: Westview Press, 1986. 512 pp.

Valladares, Armando. *Against All Hope*. Translated by Andrew Hurley. New York: Knopf, 1986. 380 pp.

Vanderlaan, Mary B. *Revolution and Foreign Policy in Nicaragua*. Boulder, Colo.: Westview Press, 1986. 404 pp.

Varas, Augusto, ed. *Soviet-Latin American Relations in the 1980's*. Boulder, Colo.: Westview Press, 1986. 260 pp.

Vol'skii, V. V., ed. *Strany tsentral'noi Ameriki: tendentsii ekonomicheskogo i sotsial'no-politicheskogo razvitiia*. Moscow: Nauka, 1986. 336 pp.

Winn, Peter. *Weavers of the Revolution: The Yarur Workers and Chile's Road to Socialism*. New York: Oxford University Press, 1986. 328 pp.

Wynia, Gary W. *Argentina: Illusions and Reality*. New York: Holmes & Meier, 1986. 207 pp.

Zubritskii, Iu. A., ed. *Kolumbiia: tendentsii ekonomicheskogo i sotsial'no-politicheskogo razvitiia*. Moscow: Nauka, 1986. 304 pp.

## ASIA AND THE PACIFIC

Barme, Geremie, and John Minford, eds. *Seeds of Fire: Chinese Voices of Conscience*. Hong Kong: Far Eastern Economic Review, 1985. 143 pp.

Barnett, A. Doak, and Ralph N. Clough, eds., *Modernizing China: Post-Mao Reform and Development*. Boulder, Colo.: Westview Press, 1986. 136 pp.

Bauer, E. E. *China Takes Off: Technology Transfer and Modernization*. Seattle: University of Washington Press, 1986. 227 pp.

Becker, Elizabeth. *When the War Was Over: The Voices of Cambodia's Revolution and Its People*. New York: Simon & Schuster, 1986. 502 pp.

Blecher, Marc. *China: Politics, Economics and Society*. Boulder, Colo.: Lynne Rienner Publishers, 1986. 180 pp.

Brown, MacAlister, and Joseph Zasloff. *Apprentice Revolutionaries: The Communist Movement in Laos*. Stanford, Calif.: Hoover Institution Press, 1986. 463 pp.

Chanda, Nayan. *Brother Enemy: The War after the War*. San Diego: Harcourt Brace Jovanovich, 1986. 479 pp.

Chang, Pao-min. *The Sino-Vietnamese Territorial Dispute*. New York: Praeger, 1986. 119 pp.

Cheng, Nien. *Life and Death in Shanghai*. London: Grafton Books, 1986. 496 pp.

Doan Van Toai and David Chanoff. *The Vietnamese Gulag*. New York: Simon & Schuster, 1986. 351 pp.

Domes, Jürgen. *Peng Te-Huai: The Man and the Image*. Stanford, Calif.: Stanford University Press, 1985. 164 pp.

Dommen, Arthur J. *Laos: Keystone of Indochina*. Boulder, Colo.: Westview Press, 1985. 182 pp.

Edwards, R. Randle; Louis Henkin; and Andrew J. Nathan. *Human Rights in Contemporary China*. New York: Columbia University Press, 1986. 193 pp.

Glazunov, E. P., ed. *Sotsialisticheskaia Respublika V'etnam*. Moscow: Nauka, 1985. 288 pp.

Hung, Nguyen Tien, and Jerrold L. Schecter. *The Palace File*. New York: Harper & Row, 1986. 542 pp.

Isaev, M. P. *Sovremennyi revoliutsionnyi protsess v stranakh Indokitaia*. Moscow: Nauka, 1985. 240 pp.

Jung Chang with Jon Halliday. *Mme Sun Yat-sen*. London: Penguin, 1986. 143 pp.

Leng, Shao-chuan, and Hungdah Chiu. *Criminal Justice in Post-Mao China*. Albany: State University of New York Press, 1985. 330 pp.

Levtonova, Iu. O. *Evolutsiia politicheskoi sistemy sovremennykh Filippin*. Moscow: Nauka, 1985. 212 pp.

Leys, Simon. *The Burning Forest: Essays on Chinese Culture and Politics*. New York: Holt, Rinehart & Winston, 1986. 257 pp.

Liang Heng and Judith Shapiro. *After the Nightmare*. New York: Knopf, 1986. 240 pp.

Manila, Quijano de. *The Quartet of the Tiger Moon*. Manila: Book Stop, Inc., 1986. 138 pp.

Matveeva, L. V., ed. *Mongol'skaia narodnaia respublika: Spravochnik*. Moscow: Nauka, 1986. 440 pp.

May, Someth. *Cambodian Witness: The Autobiography of Someth May*. New London, Conn.: Faber & Faber, 1986. 287 pp.

McKnight, David, ed. *Moving Left: The Future of Socialism in Australia*. London: Pluto Press, 1986. 189 pp.

Medvedev, Roy. *China and the Superpowers*. Oxford: Basil Blackwell, 1986. 243 pp.

Mosiakov, D. V. *Kampuchiia: osobennosti revoliutsionnogo protsessa i polpotovskii "eksperiment."* Moscow: Nauka, 1986. 168 pp.

Moyer, Robin, ed. *Bayan Ko!* Text by Guy Sacerdoti and Lin Neuman. Hong Kong: Project 28 Days Ltd., 1986. 139 pp.

Nihal, Singh S. *The Yogi and the Bear: Story of Indo-Soviet Relations*. London: Mansell Publishing, 1986. 324 pp.

Nyrop, Richard F., ed. *India: A Country Study*. 4th ed. Washington, D.C.: American University Foreign Area Studies, 1985. 687 pp.

Perry, Elizabeth, and Christine Wong, eds. *The Political Economy of China*. Cambridge, Mass.: Harvard University Press, 1985. 331 pp.

Picq, Laurence. *Au-delà du ciel: une jeune Française, cinq ans chez les Khmer Rouges*. Paris: France-Loisiers, 1985. 211 pp.

Pike, Douglas E. *PAVN: People's Army of Vietnam*. Novato, Calif.: Presidio Press, 1986. 384 pp.

Pye, Lucien W. *Asian Power and Politics: The Cultural Dimension of Authority*. Cambridge, Mass.: Belknap Press, 1986. 414 pp.

Red'ko, I. B. *Politicheskaia istoriia Nepala*. Moscow: Nauka, 1986. 380 pp.

Scalapino, Robert A., and George T. Yu. *Modern China and Its Revolutionary Process: Recurrent Challenges to the Traditional Order, 1850–1920*. Berkeley: University of California Press, 1986. 814 pp.

Shapiro, Judith, and Liang Heng. *Cold Winds, Warm Winds: Intellectual Life in Post-Mao China*. Middletown, Conn.: Wesleyan University Press, 1986. 212 pp.

Stolper, Thomas E. *China, Taiwan and the Off-Shore Islands*. Armonk, N.Y.: M. E. Sharpe, 1985. 170 pp.

Sutter, Robert G. *Chinese Foreign Policy: Developments After Mao*. New York: Praeger, 1986. 240 pp.

Szymusiak, Molyda. *The Stones Cry Out: A Cambodian Childhood*. New York: Hill & Wang, 1986. 245 pp.

Tambiah, S. J. *Sri Lanka: Ethnic Fratricide and the Dismantling of Democracy*. Chicago: University of Chicago Press, 1986. 198 pp.

Thai Quang Trung. *An Essay on Ho Chi Minh's Legacy*. Singapore: Institute of Southeast Asian Studies, 1985. 131 pp.

Thurston, Anne F. *Enemies of the People*. New York: Knopf, 1986. 323 pp.

Trigubenko, M. E. *Koreiskaia Narodno-Demokraticheskaia Respublika*. Moscow: Nauka, 1985. 272 pp.

United States. Central Intelligence Agency. Directorate of Intelligence. *Central Government Organizations of the People's Republic of China*. A Reference Aid (chart). Washington, D.C.: National Technical Information Service, April 1986.

——. *Directory of Chinese Officials: Provincial Organizations*. A Reference Aid. Washington, D.C.: National Technical Information Service, March 1986. 235 pp.

Wakeman, Carolyn, and Yue Dayun. *To The Storm: The Odyssey of a Revolutionary Chinese Woman*. Berkeley: University of California Press, 1985. 405 pp.

World Bank. *China: Long-Term Development Issues and Options*. Baltimore, Md.: Johns Hopkins University Press, 1985. 183 pp.

Zagoria, Donald S. *China: Long-Term Development Issues and Options*. Baltimore, Md.: Johns Hopkins University Press, 1985. 182 pp.

## EASTERN EUROPE

Akademie für Staats-und Rechtswissenschaft der DDR. Institut für Internationale Beziehungen. *Zehn Jahre Freundschaftsvertrag DDR-UdSSR*. East Berlin: Staatsverlag der DDR, 1985. 112 pp.

Banc, C., and A. Dundes. *First Prize: Fifteen Years*. Cranbury, N.J.: Associated University Presses, 1986. 182 pp.

Biberaj, Elez. *Albania and China*. Boulder, Colo.: Westview Press, 1986. 180 pp.

Black, J. L., and J. W. Strong. *Sysyphus and Poland*. Winnipeg, Canada: Ronald P. Frye & Co., 1986. 191 pp.

Blumsztajn, Seweryn. *Je rentre au pays*. Paris: Calmann-Lévy, 1985. 206 pp.

Braginskii, M., chief ed. *Dogovornoe pravo stran-chlenov SEV i SFRIu*. Moscow: Sekretariat SEV, 1986. 612 pp.

Chukanov, O. A., ed. *Nauchno-tekhnicheskoe sotrudnichestvo stran SEV: Spravochnik*. Moscow: Ekonomika, 1986. 288 pp.

Ciechocinska, Maria K., and Lawrene S. Graham, eds. *The Polish Dilemma: Views from Within*. Boulder, Colo.: Westview Press, 1986. 300 pp.

Comas, José. *Polonia y Solidaridad*. Madrid: El Pais, 1985. 311 pp.

Chizmadia, A., et al. *Istoriia vengerskogo gosudarstva i prava*. Moscow: Iuridicheskaia literatura, 1986. 448 pp.

Czizmadia, Ernö, and Magda Székely. *Food Economy in Hungary*. Budapest: Akadémiai Kiadó, 1986. 217 pp.

Deletant, Andrea and Dennis, comps. *Romania*. Santa Barbara, Calif.: ABC-Clio Press, 1985. 236 pp.

Deutsch, Robert. *The Food Revolution in the Soviet Union and Eastern Europe*. Boulder, Colo.: Westview Press, 1986. 256 pp.

Deutsche Demokratische Republik. Ministerium für Auswärtige Angelegenheiten. *Die Organisation des Warschauer Vertrages: Dokumente und Materialen, 1955–1985*. East Berlin: Staatsverlag der DDR, 1985. 336 pp.

Flakierski, Henryk. *Economic Reform and Income Distribution: A Case Study of Hungary and Poland*. Armonk, N.Y.: M. E. Sharpe, 1986. 194 pp.

Galasi, Péter, and György Sziráczki. *Labour Market and Second Economy in Hungary*. Frankfurt am Main: Campus Verlag, 1985. 339 pp.

Gati, Charles. *Hungary and the Soviet Bloc*. Durham, N.C.: Duke University Press, 1986. 244 pp.

Havel, Václav, et. al. *The Power of the Powerless: Citizens against the State in Central-Eastern Europe*. Armonk, N.Y.: M. E. Sharpe, 1985. 228 pp.

Heinrich, Hans-Georg. *Hungary: Politics, Economics and Society*. London: Frances Pinter, Ltd., 1986. 198 pp.

Honecker, Erich. *Reden und Aufsätze* 10th vol. Berlin: Dietz Verlag, 1986. 730 pp.

Hoxha, Enver. *The Artful Albanian: Memoirs of Enver Hoxha*. Edited by Jon Halliday. London: Chatto & Windus, 1986. 394 pp.

Hungarian Socialist Workers Party. *The 13th Congress of the HSWP, 25–28 March 1985*. Budapest: Corvina, 1985. 291 pp.

Husák, Gustáv. *Speeches and Writings*. New York: Pergamon Press, 1986. 266 pp.

Husner, Gabriele. *Studenten und Studium in der DDR*. Cologne: Verlag Wissenschaft und Politik, 1985. 170 pp.

Jaeger, Joachim W. *Humor und Satire in der DDR—Ein Versuch zur Theorie*. Frankfurt am Main: Fischer, 1985. 143 pp.

Kaplan, Karel. *The Communist Party in Power: Profile of Party Politics in Czechoslovakia*. Translated and edited by Fred Eidlin. Boulder, Colo.: Westview Press, 1986. 175 pp.

Kardelj, Edvard. *Reminiscences: The Struggle for Recognition and Independence*. London: Blond & Briggs, Ltd., 1982. 279 pp.

Kavan, Rosemary. *Freedom at a Price: An Englishwoman's Life in Czechoslovakia*. London: Verso, 1985. 278 pp.

Kostunica, Vojislav, and Kosta Cavoski. *Party Pluralism or Monism: Social Movements and the Political System in Yugoslavia, 1944–1949*. New York: Columbia University Press, 1985. 257 pp.

Köves, András. *The CMEA Countries in the World Economy: Turning Inwards or Turnings Outwards*. Budapest: Akadémiai Kiadó, 1985. 247 pp.

Lammich, Siegfried. *Der "Popieluszko-Prozess": Sicherheitspolizei und katholische Kirche in Polen*. Cologne: Verlag Wissenschaft und Politik, 1985. 108 pp.

Lampe, John R. *The Bulgarian Economy in the Twentieth Century*. London: Croom Helm, 1986. 245 pp.

Lipski, Jan Józef. *KOR: History of the Workers' Defense Committee in Poland, 1976–1981*. Berkeley: University of California Press, 1985. 560 pp.

Mastny, Vojtech, ed. *Soviet/East European Survey, 1984–1985*. Durham, N.C.: Duke University Press, 1986. 440 pp.

Matejko, Alexander J. *Comparative Worksystems*. New York: Praeger, 1986. 237 pp.

McAdams, A. James. *East Germany and Détente: Building Authority after the Wall*. New York: Cambridge University Press, 1985. 233 pp.

Menge, Marlies. *Die Sachsen—Das Staatsvolk der DDR*. Munich: Piper, 1985. 118 pp.

Michnik, Adam. *Letters from Prison and Other Essays*. Berkeley: University of California Press, 1986. 354 pp.

Murashko, G. P. *Politicheskaia bor'ba v Chekhoslovakii v 1944–1948 gg. i natsionalizatsiia sredstv proiz-vodstva*. Moscow: Nauka, 1986. 328 pp.

Musatov, V. L., chief ed. *XIII s"ezd Vengerskoi Sotsialisticheskoi Rabochei Partii. Budapest, 25–28 marta 1985 g.* Moscow: Politizdat, 1986. 239 pp.

Narkiewicz, Olga A. *Eastern Europe, 1968–1984*. London: Croom Helm, 1986. 273 pp.

Nelson, Daniel N. *Alliance Behavior in the Warsaw Pact*. Boulder, Colo.: Westview Press, 1986. 134 pp.

Nikiforov, L. A., and Iu. P. Ostrovidov. *Sotsialisticheskaia Federativnaia Respublika Iugoslaviia: Spravochnik*. Moscow: Politizdat, 1985. 127 pp.

Pavlowitch, Stevan K. *Unconventional Perceptions of Yugoslavia, 1940–1945*. New York: Columbia University Press, 1985. 166 pp.

Prokop, Siegfried. *Übergang zum Sozialismus in der DDR*. East Berlin: Dietz Verlag, 1986. 420 pp.

Richet, Xavier. *Le Modèle hongrois; marché et plan en économie socialiste*. Lyons: Presses Universitaires de Lyons, 1985, 298 pp.

Riege, G. *Die Staatsbürgerschaft der DDR*. 2d expanded edition. East Berlin: Staatsverlag der DDR, 1986. 351 pp.

Sagajllo, Witold. *The Man in the Middle: A Story of the Polish Resistance, 1940–45*. New York: Hippocrene Books, 1985. 200 pp.

Sanford, George. *Military Rule in Poland: The Rebuilding of Communist Power, 1981–1983*. New York: St. Martin's Press, 1986. 298 pp.

Schmellentin, Karl. *Arbeiter, Schutzhäftling: Erinnerungen*. Berlin: Dietz Verlag, 1986. 324 pp.

Schönfeld, Roland, ed. *Reform und Wandel in Südosteuropa*. Munich: Oldenburg Verlag, 1985. 305 pp.

Schuette, Hans-Dieter. *Zeitgeschichte und Politik. Deutschland und blockpolitische Perspektiven der SED in den Konzeptionen Marxist-Leninistischer Zeitgeschichte*. Bonn: Verlag Neue Gesellschaft, 1985. 232 pp.

Sebastian, Tim. *Nice Promises*. London: Chatto & Windus, Hogarth Press, 1985. 225 pp.

Seroka, Jim, and Rados Smiljković. *Political Organizations in Socialist Yugoslavia*. Durham, N.C.: Duke University Press, 1986. 321 pp.

Short, K. R. M., ed. *Western Broadcasting over the Iron Curtain*. New York: St. Martin's Press, 1986. 276 pp.

Simon, Jeffrey, and Trond Gilberg. *Security Implications of Nationalism in Eastern Europe*. Boulder Colo.: Westview Press, 1986. 327 pp.

Slomczynski, Kazimierz, et al., eds. *Social Stratification of Poland: Eight Empirical Studies*. Armonk, N.Y.: M. E. Sharpe, 1986. 189 pp.

Spasowski, Romuald. *The Liberation of One*. San Diego: Harcourt Brace Jovanovich, 1986. 704 pp.

Szoboszlai, György. *Politics and Public Administration in Hungary*. Budapest: Akadémiai Kiadó, 1985. 485 pp.

Taras, Ray. *Poland: Socialist State, Rebellious Nation*. Boulder, Colo.: Westview Press, 1986. 200 pp.

Transylvanian World Federation and the Danubian Research Information Center. *Genocide in Transylvania: A Nation on Death Row*. Astor, Fla.: Danubian Press, 1985. 141 pp.

Turnock, David. *The Romanian Economy in the Twentieth Century*. London: Croom Helm, 1986. 296 pp.

United States. Central Intelligence Agency. Directorate of Intelligence. *Directory of Bulgarian Officials*. A Reference Aid. LDA 86 1–2408, October 1986. Springfield, Va.: National Technical Information Service, 1986. 138 pp.

Wedel, Janine. *The Private Poland*. New York: Facts on File Publications, 1986. 229 pp.

Woods, Roger. *Opposition in the GDR under Honecker, 1971–85*. London: Macmillan, 1986. 267 pp.

Zhivkov, Todor. *Peace and Security for the Peoples: The Helsinki Conference on Security and Cooperation in Europe—Ten Years After*. Sofia, Bulgaria: Sofia Press, 1985. 276 pp.

## USSR

Ambler, John; Denis J. B. Shaw; and Leslie Symons, eds. *Soviet and East European Transport Problems*. London: Croom Helm, 1985. 260 pp.

Baikova, V. G. *Spravochnik propagandista*. Moscow: Politizdat, 1985. 174 pp.

Bel'chuk, A. I., ed. *SSSR-razvivaiuschiesia strany: torgovo-ekonomicheskie otnosheniia.* Moscow: Mezhdunarodnye otnosheniia, 1985. 240 pp.

Benningsen, Alexandre, and S. Enders Wimbush. *Muslims of the Soviet Empire.* Bloomington: Indiana University Press, 1986. 296 pp.

Berg, Gerard Pieter van den. *The Soviet System of Justice: Figures and Policy.* The Hague: Martinus Nijhoff, 1985. 374 pp.

Bialer, Seweryn. *The Soviet Paradox: External Expansion, Internal Decline.* New York: Knopf, 1986. 391 pp.

Bondarenko, A. G. *Tsentral' naia zadacha desiatiletiia.* Moscow: Politizdat, 1985. 173 pp.

Borisov, Oleg B. *Sovetskii Soiuz i Man'chzhuriskaia revoliutsionnaia baza, 1945–1949.* 3d ed. Moscow: Mysl', 1985. 250 pp.

Brzezinski, Zbigniew K. *Game Plan: the Geostrategic Framework for the U.S.–Soviet Contest.* Boston: The Atlantic Monthly Press, 1986. 288 pp.

Bundesinstitut für ostwissenschaftliche und internationale Studien. *Sowjetunion 1984–85.* Munich: Carl Hansen Verlag, 1986. 386 pp.

Buszynski, Leszek. *Soviet Foreign Policy and Southeast Asia.* London: Croom Helm, 1986. 303 pp.

Campbell, Kurt M. *Soviet Policy towards South Africa.* New York: St. Martin's Press, 1986. 256 pp.

Cherniak, E. I., et al., comps. *Khrestomatiia po nauchnomu kommunizmu.* 4th rev. ed. Moscow: Politizdat, 1985. 576 pp.

Collins, Joseph J. *The Soviet Invasion of Afghanistan: A Study in the Use of Force in Soviet Foreign Policy.* Lexington, Mass.: Lexington Books, 1986. 195 pp.

Communist Party of the Soviet Union. *XXVII s"ezd Kommunisticheskoi Partii Sovetskogo Soiuza, 25 fevr.– 6 marta 1986 g. Stenograficheskii otchet.* Moscow: Politizdat, 1986. 3 vols.

Conquest, Robert. *The Harvest of Sorrow: Soviet Collectivization and the Terror-Famine.* New York: Oxford University Press, 1986. 412 pp.

Daniels, Robert Vincent. *Russia: The Roots of Confrontation.* Cambridge, Mass.: Harvard University Press, 1985. 411 pp.

De Jonge, Alex. *Stalin and the Shaping of the Soviet Union.* New York: William Morrow & Co., 1986. 542 pp.

Dellenbrant, Jan Åke. *The Soviet Regional Dilemma.* Armonk, N.Y.: M. E. Sharpe, 1986. 217 pp.

Dibb, Paul. *The Soviet Union: The Incomplete Superpower.* London: Macmillan, 1986. 293 pp.

Doder, Dusko. *Shadows and Whispers: Power Politics inside the Kremlin from Brezhnev to Gorbachev.* New York: Random House, 1986. 339 pp.

Durand, Christine. *Comprendre l'économie soviétique.* Paris: Syros, 1985. 136 pp.

Firsov, F. I. *Lenin, Komintern i stanovlenie kommunisticheskikh partii.* Moscow: Politizdat, 1985. 359 pp.

Fleischhauer, Ingeborg, and Benjamin Pinkus. *The Soviet Germans: Past and Present.* New York: St. Martin's Press, 1986. 197 pp.

Floridi, Alexis Ulysses, S.J. *Moscow and the Vatican.* Ann Arbor, Mich.: Ardis Publishers, 1986. 279 pp.

Gilbert, Martin. *Shcharansky: The Hero of Our Time.* New York: Viking, 1986. 467 pp.

Glazov, Yuri. *The Russian Mind since Stalin's Death.* Dordrecht and Boston: D. Reidel Publishers, 1985. 256 pp.

Gorbachev, Mikhail S. *Izbrannye rechi i stat'i.* Moscow: Politizdat, 1985. 383 pp.

Guerra, Adriano. *Il giorno che Chruscev parlo.* Rome: Editori Riuniti, 1986. 187 pp.

Hallas, Duncan. *The Comintern.* London: Bookmarks, 1985. 182 pp.

Hammer, Darrell P. *The USSR: The Politics of Oligarchy.* Boulder, Colo.: Westview Press, 1986. 275 pp.

Harrison, Mark. *Soviet Planning in Peace and War, 1938–1945.* New York: Cambridge University Press, 1985. 315 pp.

Hazan, Baruch A. *From Brezhnev to Gorbachev: Infighting in the Kremlin.* Boulder, Colo.: Westview Press, 1986. 250 pp.

Herrmann, Richard K. *Perceptions and Behavior in Soviet Foreign Policy.* Pittsburgh, Pa.: University of Pittsburgh Press, 1985. 266 pp.

Hill, Ronald J. *The Soviet Union: Politics, Economics and Society*. Boulder, Colo.: Lynne Rienner Publishers, 1985. 232 pp.

Höhmann, Hans-Hermann; Alec Nove; and Heinrich Vogel, eds. *Economics and Politics in the USSR: Problems of Independence*. Boulder, Colo.: Westview Press, 1986. 306 pp.

Hosking, Geoffrey. *The First Socialist Society: The History of the Soviet Union from Within*. Cambridge, Mass.: Harvard University Press, 1985. 526 pp.

Iakovlev, A. N., ed. *Ialtinskaia konferentsiia 1945: uroki istorii*. Moscow: Nauka, 1985. 191 pp.

Jones, Ellen. *Red Army and Society: A Sociology of the Soviet Military*. Winchester, Mass.: Allen and Unwin, 1986. 230 pp.

Karklins, Rasma. *Ethnic Relations in the USSR*. Boston: Allen and Unwin, 1986. 256 pp.

Kenez, Peter. *The Birth of the Propaganda State: Soviet Methods of Mass Mobilization, 1917–1929*. New York: Cambridge University Press, 1985. 308 pp.

Kharitonov, Iu. T., comp. *Vneshniaia politika Sovetskogo Soiuza i mezhdunarodnye otnosheniia, 1985 g.: Sbornik dokumentov*. Moscow: Mezhdunarodnye otnosheniia, 1986. 320 pp.

Kotelenetz, A. I., ed. *Materialy XXVII s"ezda Kommunisticheskoi Partii Sovetskogo Soiuza*. Moscow: Politizdat, 1986. 352 pp.

Krause, Joachim. *Sowjetische Militärhilfepolitik gegenüber Entwicklungsländern*. Baden-Baden: Nomos Verlag, 1985. 503 pp.

Laird, Roy D. *The Politburo: Demographic Trends, Gorbachev, and the Future*. Boulder, Colo.: Westview Press, 1986. 203 pp.

Lane, David, ed. *Labour and Employment in the USSR*. Brighton, Sussex: Harvester Press, 1986. 280 pp.

Lee, William T., and Richard F. Staar. *Soviet Military Policy Since World War II*. Stanford, Calif.: Hoover Institution Press, 1986. 263 pp.

Mahrad, Ahmad. *Zum Verhältnis zwischen Iran und der Sowjetunion*. Osnabrück: Biblio-verlag, 1985. 258 pp.

Medvedev, Zhores A. *Gorbachev*. New York: W. W. Norton & Co., 1986. 272 pp.

Petrenko, Fedor F. *Soviet Foreign Policy: Objectives and Principles*. Translated from the Russian by Joseph Shapiro. Moscow: Progress Publishers, 1985. 310 pp.

Reese, David. *The Soviet Seizure of the Kuriles*. New York: Praeger, 1985. 182 pp.

Schmidt-Häuer, Christian. *Gorbachev: The Path to Power*. Topsfield, Mass.: Salem House, 1986. 218 pp.

Schöpflin, George, ed. *The Soviet Union and Eastern Europe*. New York: Facts on File Publications, 1986. 637 pp.

Sherr, James G. *Soviet Power: The Continuing Challenge*. New York: St. Martin's Press, 1986. 260 pp.

Shvets, I. A., ed. *Kommunist 1986: Kalendar'-spravochnik*. Moscow: Politizdat, 1985. 318 pp.

Simon, Gerhard. *Nationalismus und Nationalitätenpolitik in der Sowjetunion*. Baden-Baden: Nomos Verlag, 1986. 486 pp.

Solovyov, Vladimir, and Elena Klepikova. *Behind the High Kremlin Walls*. New York: Dodd, Mead & Co., 1986. 248 pp.

Sorrento, Frank M., and Frances R. Curcio. *Soviet Politics and Education*. Lanham, Md.: University Press of America, 1986. 415 pp.

Spriano, Paolo. *Stalin and the European Communists*. New York: Schocken Books, 1985. 315 pp.

Stent, Angela E., ed. *Economic Relations with the Soviet Union: American and West German Perspectives*. Boulder, Colo.: Westview Press, 1985. 182 pp.

Streiff, Gerard. *Le dynamique Gorbachev*. Paris: Messidor/Editions Sociales, 1986. 246 pp.

Tomiak, J. J., ed. *Western Perspectives on Soviet Education in the 1980s*. New York: St. Martin's Press, 1986. 277 pp.

Tsygankov, V., ed. *Cooperation between the USSR and Developing Countries*. Moscow: Social Sciences Today, 1986. 197 pp.

United States Helsinki Watch Committee. *Violation of the Helsinki Accords: USSR*. New York: The U.S. Helsinki Watch Committee, 1986. 343 pp.

Van Goudoever, Albert P. *The Limits of Destalinization in the Soviet Union: Political Rehabilitation in the Soviet Union since Stalin*. New York: St. Martin's Press, 1986. 288 pp.

Vigor, Peter H. *The Soviet View of Disarmament*. London: Macmillan, 1986. 189 pp.

Vizulis, I. Joseph. *Nations Under Duress: The Baltic States*. Milkwood, N.Y.: Associated Faculty Press, 1985. 209 pp.

Voinovich, Vladimir. *The Anti-Soviet Soviet Union*. San Diego: Harcourt Brace Jovanovich, 1985. 325 pp.

Williams, E. S. *The Soviet Military: Political Education, Training and Morale*. New York: St. Martin's Press, 1986. 229 pp.

Yanowitch, Murray, ed. *The Social Structure of the USSR*. Armonk, N.Y.: M. E. Sharpe, 1986. 273 pp.

———. *Work in the Soviet Union: Attitudes and Issues*. Armonk, N.Y.: M. E. Sharpe, 1985. 196 pp.

Zemtsov, Ilya. *Soviet Sociology*. Fairfax, Va.: Hero Books, 1985. 103 pp.

## THE MIDDLE EAST

Afkhami, Gholam R. *The Iranian Revolution: Thanatos on a National Scale*. Washington, D.C.: Middle East Institute, 1985. 258 pp.

Anderson, Lisa. *The State and Social Transformation in Tunisia and Libya, 1830–1980*. Princeton, N.J.: Princeton University Press, 1986. 132 pp.

Committee against Repression and for Democratic Rights in Iraq (CADRI). *Saddam's Iraq: Revolution or Reaction*. London: Zed Press, 1986. 254 pp.

Dynin, I. M., ed. *Zvezdy podviga: na zemle Afganistana*. Moscow: Voen izdat, 1985. 205 pp.

Gataullin, M. F. *Agrarnaia reforma i klassovaia bor'ba v Egipte*. Moscow: Nauka, 1985. 204 pp.

Girardet, Edward. *Afghanistan: The Soviet War*. New York: St. Martin's Press, 1985. 258 pp.

Gusarov, V. I. *Trudovye resursy i sotsial'nye problemy Tunisa*. Moscow: Nauka, 1985. 90 pp.

Katz, Mark N. *Russia and Arabia: Soviet Foreign Policy toward the Arabian Peninsula*. Baltimore, Md.: Johns Hopkins University Press, 1986. 279 pp.

Keddie, Nikki R., and Eric Hooglund, eds. *The Iranian Revolution and the Islamic Republic*. Rev. ed. Syracuse, N.Y.: Syracuse University Press, 1986. 246 pp.

Khalidi, Rashid. *Under Siege: PLO Decisionmaking during the 1982 War*. New York: Columbia University Press, 1985. 241 pp.

Maoz, Moshe, and Avner Yaniv, eds. *Syria under Assad*. New York: St. Martin's Press, 1986. 273 pp.

Nelson, Harold D., ed. *Algeria: A Country Study*. 4th ed. Washington, D.C.: American University Foreign Area Studies, 1985. 414 pp.

———, ed. *Morocco: A Country Study*. 5th ed. Washington, D.C.: American University Foreign Area Studies, 1985. 448 pp.

Nyrop, Richard F., ed. *The Yemens: Country Studies*. Washington, D.C.: American University Foreign Area Studies, 1986. 378 pp.

——— and Donald M. Seekins. *Afghanistan: A Country Study*. 5th ed. Washington, D.C.: American University Foreign Area Studies, 1986. 408 pp.

Page, Stephen. *The Soviet Union and the Yemens*. New York: Praeger, 1985. 225 pp.

Ramazani, R. K. *Revolutionary Iran: Challenge and Response in the Middle East*. Baltimore, Md.: Johns Hopkins University Press, 1986. 311 pp.

Roy, Olivier. *L'Afghanistan: Islam et modernité politique*. Paris: Seuil, 1985. 324 pp.

Sen Gupta, Bhabani. *Afghanistan: Politics, Economics and Society*. Boulder, Colo.: Lynne Rienner Publishers, 1986. 206 pp.

Taheri, Amir. *The Spirit of Allah: Khomeini and the Islamic Revolution*. Washington, D.C.: Adler & Adler, 1986. 334 pp.

Zabih, Sepehr. *The Left in Contemporary Iran: Ideology, Organization and the Soviet Connection*. London: Croom Helm; Stanford, Calif.: Hoover Institution Press, 1986. 239 pp.

## WESTERN EUROPE

*The Austro-Marxists 1890–1918: A Psychobiographical Study.* Lexington: University of Kentucky Press, 1985. 245 pp.

*A Via do desenvolvimento para vencer a crise: documentos e intervençōes da Conferencia Nacional de Partito Comunista Português.* Lisbon: Avante, 1985. 2 vols.

Angius, Gavino. *I comunisti: dova si lavora e si studia.* Bari, Italy: Edizioni Dedalo, 1985. 111 pp.

Arfe, Gaetano, et al. *De Gaspari e Togliatti: Politiche a confronto.* Rimini: Maggiole Editore, 1985. 102 pp.

Aust, Stefan. *Der Baader Meinhof Komplex.* Hamburg: Hoffman und Campe, 1985, 599 pp.

Azema, Jean-Pierre. *Ouvrage collectif—Le Parti Communiste Française des années sombres, 1938–41.* Paris: Seuil, 1986. 317 pp.

Beaud, Michel. *La Politique économique de la gauche.* vol. 2. Paris: Syros, 1985, 236 pp.

Belleville, Jacques. *L'Avenir a changé.* Paris: Syros, 1985. 213 pp.

Briancon, Pierre. *A Droite en sortant de la gauche?* Paris: Grasset, 1986. 270 pp.

Bruneau, Thomas C., and Alex MacLeod. *Politics in Contemporary Portugal: Parties and the Consolidation of Democracy.* Boulder, Colo.: Lynne Rienner Publishers, 1986. 236 pp.

Buehl, Walter L. *Eine Zukunft für Deutschland: Grundlinien der technologischen, gesellschaftlichen und politischen Entwicklung.* Munich: Olzog Verlag, 1985. 252 pp.

Buschak, Willy. *Das Londoner: Büro: Europäischen Linkssozialisten in der Zwischenkriegszeit.* Amsterdam: Sichtung International Instituut voor Geschiedens, 1985. 359 pp.

Caminal I Badia, Miguel. *Joan Comorera: comunisme i nacionalisme, 1939–1958.* Barcelona: Universidad Empuries, 1985. 396 pp.

Carrillo, Santiago, and Adam Schaff. *Problemas de la Transición.* Madrid: Editorial Ahora, 1985. 150 pp.

Chevènement, Jean-Pierre. *Le Pari sur l'intelligence: entretiens avec Hervé Hamon et Patrick Rotman.* Paris: Flammarion, 1985. 300 pp.

Coates, David, and John Hillard, eds. *The Economic Decline of Modern Britain: The Debate Between the Left and the Right.* Brighton, Sussex: Harvester Press, 1986. 386 pp.

Converse, Philip E., and Roy Pierce. *Political Representation in France.* Cambridge, Mass.: Belknap Press, 1986. 996 pp.

Cossutta, Armando. *Dissenso e unità: il debattito politico nel PCI dal XV al XVII congresso.* Milan: Editori Nicola Teti, 1986. 124 pp.

Cunhal, Alvaro. *O partido com paredes de vidro.* Lisbon: Ediçoes Avante!, 1985. 271 pp.

Droit, Michel. *Lettre ouverte á ceux qui en ont plus qu'assez du socialisme.* Paris: Albin Michel, 1985. 183 pp.

Dutourd, Jean. *La Gauche la plus bête du monde.* Paris: Flammarion, 1985. 315 pp.

Edinger, Lewis J. *West German Politics.* New York: Columbia University Press, 1985. 342 pp.

Ferreira, Hugo Gil, and Michael W. Marshall. *Portugal's Revolution: Ten Years On.* New York: Cambridge University Press, 1986. 303 pp.

Findlay, A. M., and Paul White, eds. *West European Population Change.* London: Croom Helm, 1986. 256 pp.

Fonteneau, Alain. *La Gauche face á la crise.* Paris: Presses de Fondation National des Sciences Politiques, 1985. 389 pp.

Gaudin, Jean-Claude. *La Gauche á l'imparfait.* Paris: Editions France Empire, 1985. 215 pp.

Gilmour, David. *The Transformation of Spain: From Franco to the Constitutional Monarchy.* Salem, N.H.: Merrimack Publishing Corp., 1985. 322 pp.

Gramsci, Antonio. *Nouve lettere di Antonio Gramsci.* Rome: Editore Riuniti, 1986. 215 pp.

Gremion, Pierre. *Paris/Prague: La Gauche face au renouveau et a la regression tchechoslovaques, 1968–1978.* Paris: Juillard, 1985. 367 pp.

Gunther, Richard, et al. *Spain after Franco: The Making of A Competitive Party System.* Berkeley: University of California Press, 1986. 516 pp.

Hartmann, Jürgen. *Frankreichs Parteien.* Cologne: Verlag Wissenschaft and Politik, 1985. 120 pp.

Heath, Anthony. *How Britain Votes*. Elmsford, N.Y.: Pergamon Press, 1985. 260 pp.

Hyvärinen, Matti, and Jukka Pastela. *The Finnish Communist Party: The Failure of Attempts to Modernize a C.P.* Tampere, Finland: Tampereen Yliopisto, 1985. 42 pp.

Ibárruri, Delores. *Memorias de Delores Ibárruri—Pasionara; la lucha y la vida*. Barcelona: Planeta, 1985. 763 pp.

Kaltefleiter, Werner, and Robert L. Pfaltzgraff, eds. *The Peace Movements in Europe and the USA*. New York: St. Martin's Press, 1985. 212 pp.

Kisch, Richard. *The Days of the Good Soldiers: Communists in the Armed Forces World War II*. London: Journeyman Press, 1986. 200 pp.

Klein, Michael. *Antifaschistische Demokratie und nationaler Befreiungskampf: die nationale Politik der KPD, 1945-1953*. Berlin: Veronika Körner, 1986. 290 pp.

Labin, Suzanne. *Les Colombes rouges*. Boùere: D. M. Morin, 1985. 263 pp.

La Bortef, Guy. *Oú va la formation des cadres?* Paris: Editions d'Organisations, 1985. 106 pp.

Leduc, Victor. *Les Tribulations d'un ideologue*. Paris: Syros, 1985. 363 pp.

Lohberg, Lutz. *Friedensbewegung und blockübergreifende Strategien*. Frankfurt am Main: Marxistische Blätter, 1985. 192 pp.

Magaziner, Alfred. *Die Bahnbrecher: aus der Geschichte der Arbeiterbewegung*. Vienna: Europaverlag, 1985. 189 pp.

Matignon, A. *Au temps de l'union de la gauche*. Paris: Hachette, 1985. 365 pp.

Merson, Allan. *Communist Resistance in Nazi Germany*. London: Lawrence & Wishart, 1985. 350 pp.

Mitoyen, Jean. *C'est dur d'être gauche, surtout quand on n'est pas de droite*. Paris: Syros, 1985. 235 pp.

Morán, Gregorio. *Miseria y grandeza del Partido Comunista en España, 1939-45*. Barcelona: Planeta, 1986. 645 pp.

Naudy, Michel. *PCF, le suicide*. Paris: Albin, 1986. 209 pp.

Negri, Toni. *Italie: rouge et noir*. Paris: Hachette, 1985. 321 pp.

Olzog, Günter, and Hans J. Liese. *Die politischen Parteien in der BRD*. Munich: Olzog Verlag, 1986. 205 pp.

Partido Comunista de España. *Una alternativa a la crisis: las propuestas del PCE*. Barcelona: Planeta, 1985. 224 pp.

Partido Comunista Português. *Onzeno Congresso (Extraordinario) do Partido Comunista Português. 2 de fevreiro de 1986. Documentos politicos*. Lisbon: Avanti, 1986. 85 pp.

Partito Comunista Italiano. *Il PCI e la svolta del 1956*. Rome: L'Unitá, 1986. 141 pp.

———. *I Communisti—dove si lavora e si studia*. Atti del Convegno nazionale del PCI, Pisa, 4-6 Gennaio, 1985. Bari, Italy: Edizioni Dedalo, 1985. 111 pp.

Penniman, Howard R., and Eusebio M. Mujal-León, eds. *Spain at the Polls 1977, 1979 and 1982: A Study of National Elections*. Durham, N.C.: Duke University Press, 1985. 372 pp.

Sentis, Georges. *Les Communistes et la resistance dans les Pyrénées Orientales: 1939-47*. Lille: Institut des recherches marxistes, 1985. 175 pp.

Shinn, Rinn S., ed. *Greece: A Country Study*. 3d ed. Washington, D.C.: American University Foreign Area Studies, 1985. 408 pp.

Stich, Claudia, and Manfred Balder. *Derndruck—ein Sieg der Solidarität*. Frankfurt am Main: Nachrichten Verlagsgesellschaft, 1986. 112 pp.

Stössel, Frank Thomas. *Positionen und Strömungen in der KPD/SED 1945-1954*. Cologne: Verlag Wissenschaft und Politik, 1985. 2 vols. 966 pp.

Trans, Jean-François. *La Gauche bouge*. Paris: J. C. Lattès, 1985. 176 pp.

Urban, Joan Barth. *Moscow and the Italian Communist Party*. Ithaca, N.Y.: Cornell University Press, 1986. 370 pp.

Vilar, Sergio. *Por que se ha destruido el P.C.E.* Barcelona: Plaza y Janes, 1986. 281 pp.

Wolton, Thierry. *Le KGB en France*. Paris: Grasset, 1986. 310 pp.

# Cumulative Index of Biographies

# Index of Names

# Index of Subjects